If you're wondering why you should buy this new edition of *Government by the People*, here are 10 good reasons!

1. The **2008 presidential campaign and election** are explored throughout the book, including a look at the 2008 primary season, the party conventions, the role of the media, the historic election of Barack Obama and voter turnout. Figures and tables have also been completely updated with information on the 2008 election.

2. We have integrated the **latest examples and scholarship** on American politics and government, including recent Supreme Court decisions, the economic conditions at the end of 2008, and comparisons with countries around the world.

3. The new **Generation Next** feature presents information about 16-25 year olds, showing their issues, values, and challenges as they relate to specific questions such as partisan differences, the rise of small campaign donors, search and seizure in the age of terrorism, and levels of patriotism. Comparisons with older voters and demographic breakdowns help you understand where you fit and why government should matter to you.

4. Being part of a government by the people requires consideration of differing points of view. **You Will Decide/Thinking It Through** explores in-the-news questions like the impact of third-party candidates, the advantages and disadvantages of a national presidential primary, and the need for restrictions on civil liberties during the war on terror and then asks you to weigh options for resolving the issue.

5. Using a nationwide survey as a guide, we developed a master list of learning objectives to shape this edition. Learning Objectives appear at the beginning of each chapter, while individual Objectives and key coverage are called out in the text margins. A Summary and Self-Test at the end of each chapter provides you with a final check of your understanding.

6. The **growing importance of the Internet** and the declining importance of newspapers are discussed in detail, including the role of the Internet in the 2008 campaign and election (Chapter 10).

7. An updated chapter on **the presidency** (Chapter 12) includes information on George W. Bush's use of veto power, invocation of executive privilege, and use of signing statements. The section on the White House Staff now includes historic examples and explores the different leadership approaches of presidents.

8. An updated chapter on **civil liberties** (Chapter 15) combines two chapters and includes a new section distinguishing civil liberties from civil rights. New discussions include the *Morse* v. *Frederick* "Bong Hits 4 Jesus" case and a discussion of *habeas corpus* using the *Hamdan* and *Boumedienne* cases.

9. A new chapter on the **process of making public policy** (Chapter 17) provides a brief introduction to the topic to help you better understand the specific public policy chapters.

10. **MyPoliSciLab**, our Website that offers a wide array of multimedia activities—videos, simulations, exercises, and online newsfeeds—has been completely integrated with this edition to make learning more effective.

PEARSON

ELECTORAL COLLEGE VOTES IN THE 2008 ELECTION

THE UNITED STATES

A political map showing the number of electoral votes per state

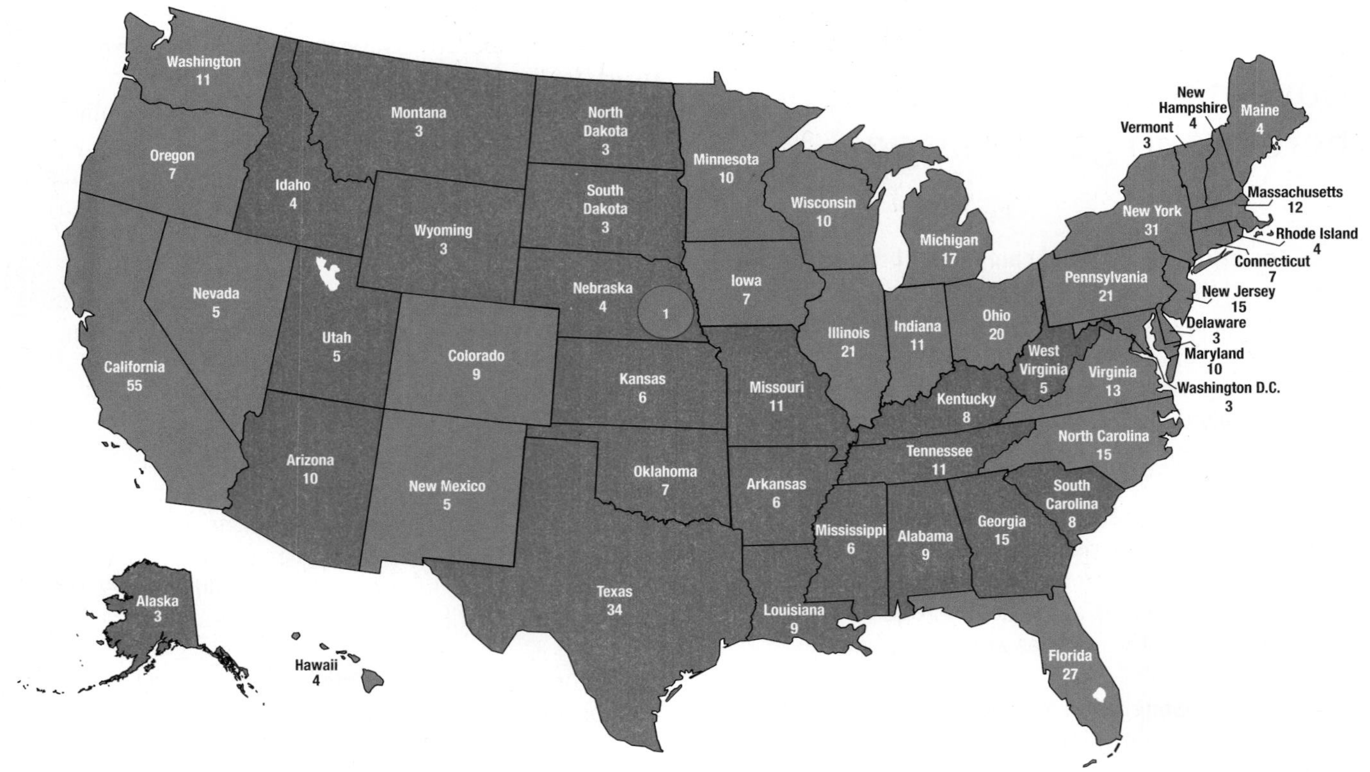

A political map with states drawn in proportion to the number of electoral votes

Washington 11
Oregon 7
California 55
Idaho 4
Nevada 5
Montana 3
Wyoming 3
Utah 5
Arizona 10
North Dakota 3
South Dakota 3
Nebraska 4
1
Colorado 9
New Mexico 5
Kansas 6
Oklahoma 7
Texas 34
Minnesota 10
Iowa 7
Missouri 11
Arkansas 6
Louisiana 9
Wisconsin 10
Illinois 21
Michigan 17
Indiana 11
Ohio 20
Kentucky 8
Tennessee 11
Mississippi 6
Alabama 9
Georgia 15
Florida 27
South Carolina 8
North Carolina 15
Virginia 13
West Virginia 5
Pennsylvania 21
Maryland 10
Delaware 3
New Jersey 15
New York 31
Vermont 3
New Hampshire 4
Maine 4
Massachusetts 12
Connecticut 7
Rhode Island 4
Washington D.C. 3
Alaska 3
Hawaii 4

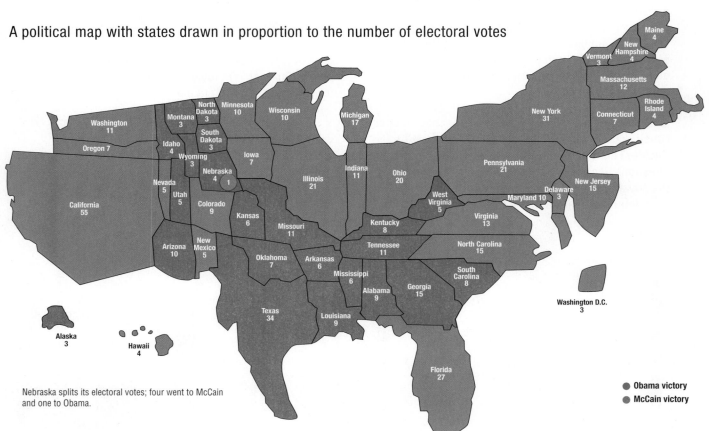

Nebraska splits its electoral votes; four went to McCain and one to Obama.

● Obama victory
● McCain victory

Government by the People

Government by the People

DAVID B. MAGLEBY
Brigham Young University

PAUL C. LIGHT
New York University

2009 National Edition

Longman
New York San Francisco Boston
London Toronto Sydney Tokyo Singapore Madrid
Mexico City Munich Paris Cape Town Hong Kong Montreal

Editor-in-Chief	Eric Stano
Assistant Development Manager	David Kear
Development Editor	Elisa Adams
Associate Development Editor	Donna Garnier
Senior Media Producer	Regina Vertiz
Marketing Manager	Lindsey Prudhomme
Production Manager	Bob Ginsberg
Project Coordination, Text Design, and Electronic Page Makeup	Elm Street Publishing Services
Cover Design Manager	John Callahan
Cover Designer	Maria Ilardi
Cover Photos	*(sailboat)* Gary John Norman/Taxi/Getty Images; *(flag)* Rich Vintage/iStockphoto
Pearson Image Resource Center/Photo Researcher	Teri Stratford
Image Permission Coordinator	Ang'John Ferreri
Senior Manufacturing Buyer	Dennis J. Para
Printer and Binder	Quebecor World/Dubuque
Cover Printer	Phoenix Color Corporation

Library of Congress Cataloging-in-Publication Data

Government by the people.—23rd ed.
p. cm.
Includes index.
ISBN 978-0-13-606242-4 (national, state, and local)—ISBN 978-0-13-606222-6 (national)—
ISBN 978-0-13-605040-7 (alternate)—ISBN 978-0-205-66637-9 (brief)
1. United States—Politics and government—Textbooks. I. Magleby, David B.

JK276.G68 2009i
320.473—dc22 2008024966

Longman
is an imprint of

www.pearsonhighered.com

12345678910—QWD—12 11 10 09

ISBN-13: 978-0-13-606222-6
ISBN-10: 0-13-606222-9

Brief Contents

Contents viii
Learning Objectives xii
Preface xvii
About the Authors xxviii

Part I Constitutional Principles

Chapter 1 Constitutional Democracy 2
Chapter 2 The Living Constitution 28
The Constitution of the United States 50
Chapter 3 American Federalism 62

Part II The Political Process

Chapter 4 Political Culture and Ideology 90
Chapter 5 The American Political Landscape 114
Chapter 6 Interest Groups 146
Chapter 7 Political Parties 178
Chapter 8 Public Opinion, Participation, and Voting 206
Chapter 9 Campaigns and Elections 238
Chapter 10 The Media and U.S. Politics 274

Part III Policy-Making Institutions

Chapter 11 Congress 298
Chapter 12 The Presidency 326
Chapter 13 The Federal Bureaucracy 356
Chapter 14 The Judiciary 382

Part IV Rights and Liberties

Chapter 15 Civil Liberties 408
Chapter 16 Civil Rights 438

Part V The Politics of National Policy

Chapter 17 Public Policy 468
Chapter 18 Making Economic Policy 488
Chapter 19 Making Social Policy 514
Chapter 20 Making Foreign and Defense Policy 538

Epilogue Sustaining Constitutional Democracy 564
Appendix The Declaration of Independence 572
The Federalist, No. 10 573
The Federalist, No. 51 576
The Federalist, No. 78 578
Presidential Election Results, 1789–2008 582

Glossary 584
Index 609

Contents

Learning Objectives xii
Preface xvii
About the Authors xxviii

Part I Constitutional Principles

1 Constitutional Democracy 2

U.S. Government and Politicians in Context 4
Defining Democracy 5
- YOU WILL DECIDE/THINKING IT THROUGH
  Should the United States Adopt a National Initiative Process? 6
- GENERATION NEXT
  For Better or Worse? 9

The Roots of the American Constitutional Experiment 13
The Constitutional Convention of 1787 15
- HISTORY MAKERS
  Alexander Hamilton and James Madison 16
- THE CHANGING FACE OF U.S. POLITICS
  The Constitutional Convention 17
- HOW OTHER NATIONS GOVERN
  Factors Contributing to Democratic Stability 22

To Adopt or Not to Adopt? 22
Summary 25 | Chapter Self-Test 26 | Key Terms 27 | Further Reading 27

2 The Living Constitution 28

Views of the Constitution 30
Checking Power with Power 31
- GENERATION NEXT
  Setting Aside the Constitution in an Age of Terror 35
- HOW OTHER NATIONS GOVERN
  Comparing Constitutional Governance 37

Judicial Review and the "Guardians of the Constitution" 38
- HISTORY MAKERS
  Thurgood Marshall's Living Constitution 39

The Constitution as an Instrument of Government 40
Changing the Letter of the Constitution 42
- THE CHANGING FACE OF U.S. POLITICS
  The United States' Racial Heritage 45
- YOU WILL DECIDE/THINKING IT THROUGH
  Should We Interpret the Constitution According to Original Intent or Today's Needs? 46

Summary 48 | Chapter Self-Test 48 | Key Terms 49 | Further Reading 49

The Constitution of the United States 50

3 American Federalism 62

Defining Federalism 64
- GENERATION NEXT
  A Preference for Local Government 66

The Constitutional Structure of American Federalism 68
- THE CHANGING FACE OF U.S. POLITICS
  Immigrants and Federal, State, and Local Responses 69
- HOW OTHER NATIONS GOVERN
  Different Visions of Federalism 75

The Federal Courts and Federalism 75
Regulatory Federalism 79
- HISTORY MAKERS
  Chief Justice William H. Rehnquist 80

The Politics of Federalism 83
- YOU WILL DECIDE/THINKING IT THROUGH
  Should the No Child Left Behind Act be Repealed? 84

The Future of Federalism 85
Summary 87 | Chapter Self-Test 87 | Key Terms 88 | Further Reading 89

Part II The Political Process

4 Political Culture and Ideology 90

Defining the American Political Culture 92
- THE CHANGING FACE OF U.S. POLITICS
  Immigrants and Assimilation into American Political Culture 94
- GENERATION NEXT
  Patriotism 97
- YOU WILL DECIDE/THINKING IT THROUGH
  Is the American Dream Still Alive and Important? 98
- HOW OTHER NATIONS GOVERN
  Government and Nation: Differing Public Perspectives 100

Political Ideology and Attitudes Toward Government 103
- HISTORY MAKERS
  Rachel Carson and the Environmental Movement 109

Political Ideology and the American People 109
Summary 111 | Chapter Self-Test 112 | Key Terms 113 | Further Reading 113

5 The American Political Landscape 114

A Land of Diversity 116
Where We Live 122
Who We Are 124
- THE CHANGING FACE OF U.S. POLITICS
  A More Diverse Population 125
- YOU WILL DECIDE/THINKING IT THROUGH
  Should We Sample? 128
- GENERATION NEXT
  Religion and Politics 130
- HISTORY MAKERS
  Lucretia Mott and Elizabeth Cady Stanton 134
- HOW OTHER NATIONS GOVERN
  Aging Populations 142

Unity in a Land of Diversity 142
Summary 143 | Chapter Self-Test 144 | Key Terms 144 | Further Reading 145

6 Interest Groups 146

Interest Groups Past and Present: The "Mischiefs of Faction" 148

Types of Interest Groups 150

■ HISTORY MAKERS
John Sherman and the Sherman Antitrust Act 151

■ HOW OTHER NATIONS GOVERN
Unions and the Minimum Wage 154

Characteristics and Power of Interest Groups 158

The Influence of Lobbyists 162

■ THE CHANGING FACE OF U.S POLITICS
Breaking into a Male-Dominated Profession 163

Money and Politics 164

■ YOU WILL DECIDE/THINKING IT THROUGH
Should Corporations and Unions Be Unlimited in Funding Parties and in Running Issue Ads? 168

How Much Do Interest Groups Influence Elections and Legislation? 172

■ GENERATION NEXT
Are Corporations Too Powerful? 173

Curing the Mischiefs of Faction—Two Centuries Later 173

Summary 175 | Chapter Self-Test 176 | Key Terms 176 | Further Reading 177

7 Political Parties 178

What Parties Do for Democracy 179

■ YOU WILL DECIDE/THINKING IT THROUGH
Is a Vote for a Third-Party Candidate with Little Chance of Winning a Wasted Vote? 184

A Brief History of American Political Parties 185

American Parties Today 188

■ HISTORY MAKERS
Franklin Delano Roosevelt and the Democratic Party 189

■ THE CHANGING FACE OF U.S. POLITICS
Portrait of the Electorate 195

■ GENERATION NEXT
Partisan Differences 196

How Parties Raise and Spend Money 199

Are the Political Parties Dying? 200

■ HOW OTHER NATIONS GOVERN
Campaign Finance Regulation 201

Summary 203 | Chapter Self-Test 204 | Key Terms 205 | Further Reading 205

8 Public Opinion, Participation, and Voting 206

Public Opinion 208

Participation: Translating Opinions into Action 218

■ HISTORY MAKERS
Lyndon Johnson and the Voting Rights Act of 1965 221

■ HOW OTHER NATIONS GOVERN
Electoral Institutions and Turnout 224

■ THE CHANGING FACE OF U.S. POLITICS
Voter Turnout by Demographic Factors 227

Voting Choices 229

■ GENERATION NEXT
Why Vote? 230

■ YOU WILL DECIDE/THINKING IT THROUGH
Should We Allow Voting by Mail and on the Internet? 232

Counting Votes 233

Summary 234 | Chapter Self-Test 235 | Key Terms 236 | Further Reading 236

9 Campaigns and Elections 238

Elections: The Rules of the Game 240

■ HOW OTHER NATIONS GOVERN
Two-Party vs. Multiparty Systems 241

Running for Congress 244

Running for President 248

■ GENERATION NEXT
Views on Large and Small Donors 250

■ THE CHANGING FACE OF U.S. POLITICS
More Diversity Among National Party Nomination Convention Delegates 253

■ HISTORY MAKERS
Henry George and the Secret Ballot 258

Money in U.S. Elections 259

Improving Elections 268

■ YOU WILL DECIDE/THINKING IT THROUGH
Should We Establish a National Presidential Primary? 270

Summary 271 | Chapter Self-Test 272 | Key Terms 273 | Further Reading 273

10 The Media and U.S. Politics 274

The Influence of the Media on Politics 276

■ HISTORY MAKERS
Walter Cronkite 278

■ THE CHANGING FACE OF U.S. POLITICS
Toward a More Representative Newsroom 279

The Changing Role of the U.S. News Media 280

Mediated Politics 283

■ GENERATION NEXT
Media Consumption 284

■ HOW OTHER NATIONS GOVERN
Freedom of the Press in Comparative Perspective 285

■ YOU WILL DECIDE/THINKING IT THROUGH
How Should the Media Report Sex Scandals? 288

The Media and Elections 290

The Media and Governance 294

Summary 296 | Chapter Self-Test 296 | Key Terms 297 | Further Reading 297

Part III Policy-Making Institutions

11 Congress 298

Congressional Elections 300

■ YOU WILL DECIDE/THINKING IT THROUGH
Should Congress Ban Earmarks? 302

The Structure and Powers of Congress 304

■ GENERATION NEXT
Support for Compromise 305

■ HOW OTHER NATIONS GOVERN
Strong and Weak Legislatures 308

Congressional Leadership and Committees 308

■ HISTORY MAKERS
Speaker Uncle Joe Cannon 310

■ THE CHANGING FACE OF U.S. POLITICS
Diversity in Congress 311

The Job of the Legislator 315

How a Bill Becomes a Law 320
An Assessment of Congress 322
Summary 323 | Chapter Self-Test 323 | Key Terms 324 | Further Reading 324

12 The Presidency 326
The Structure and Powers of the Presidency 328
Controversies in Presidential Power 335
The Evolution of Presidential Power 338
■ HOW OTHER NATIONS GOVERN Strong and Weak Chief Executives 339
Managing the Presidency 340
■ HISTORY MAKERS Condoleezza Rice 342
The President's Job 344
Congress and the Presidency 346
■ GENERATION NEXT The President's Approval Rating 347
■ THE CHANGING FACE OF U.S. POLITICS Presidential Appointees 349
■ YOU WILL DECIDE/THINKING IT THROUGH Should the Two-Term Limit Be Repealed? 350
Judging Presidents 351
Summary 353 | Chapter Self-Test 353 | Key Terms 354 | Further Reading 354

13 The Federal Bureaucracy 356
Understanding the Federal Bureaucracy 358
■ THE CHANGING FACE OF U.S. POLITICS A Representative Government 363
Leading the Federal Bureaucracy 367
■ HOW OTHER NATIONS GOVERN Bureaucracy Across the World 368
The Civil Service 369
■ GENERATION NEXT Trust in Government 371
The Job of the Federal Bureaucracy 373
■ YOU WILL DECIDE/THINKING IT THROUGH Who Wants a Federal Career? 374
Controlling the Federal Bureaucracy 375
■ HISTORY MAKERS Louis Brownlow 376
A History of Great Endeavors 378
Summary 379 | Chapter Self-Test 379 | Key Terms 381 | Further Reading 381

14 The Judiciary 382
Understanding the Federal Judiciary 384
The Three Types of Federal Courts 386
The Politics of Appointing Federal Judges 388
■ THE CHANGING FACE OF U.S. POLITICS Diversity in the Federal Courts 393
How the Supreme Court Decides 394
■ YOU WILL DECIDE/THINKING IT THROUGH Should the Federal Courts Be Active? 394
■ GENERATION NEXT Equal Rights 396
■ HISTORY MAKERS: Justice Sandra Day O'Connor 399
■ HOW OTHER NATIONS GOVERN Judicial Independence and Accountability 401
Limits on Judicial Action 402
Judicial Power in a Constitutional Democracy 404
Summary 405 | Chapter Self-Test 406 | Key Terms 406 | Further Reading 407

Part IV Rights and Liberties

15 Civil Liberties 408
Rights in the Original Constitution 410
The Bill of Rights and the States 411
First Amendment Freedoms 413
■ THE CHANGING FACE OF U.S. POLITICS The Continuing Importance of Religion and Personal Belief 415
■ YOU WILL DECIDE/THINKING IT THROUGH Should the Government Restrict Civil Liberties During the War on Terror? 418
Property Rights 422
Due Process Rights 423
Privacy Rights 424
■ HISTORY MAKERS Estelle Griswold 425
Rights of Criminal Suspects 427
■ GENERATION NEXT Searches and Seizures in an Age of Terrorism 429
The Death Penalty 432
■ HOW OTHER NATIONS GOVERN The Death Penalty Around the World 433
Protecting Our Civil Liberties: Whose Responsibility? 434
Summary 434 | Chapter Self-Test 435 | Key Terms 436 | Further Reading 436

16 Civil Rights 438
Equality and Equal Rights 440
Citizenship Rights 440
The Quest for Equal Justice 443
■ HISTORY MAKERS Martin Luther King Jr. 446
Equal Protection of the Laws: What Does It Mean? 451
■ HOW OTHER NATIONS GOVERN The Treatment of Homosexuality Across the World 453
■ YOU WILL DECIDE/THINKING IT THROUGH Should Marriage be Limited to Heterosexual Couples? 454
Voting Rights 454
Rights to Equal Access: Accommodations, Jobs, and Homes 456
Education Rights 458
■ THE CHANGING FACE OF U.S. POLITICS Racial and Ethnic Diversity in U.S. Public Elementary and Secondary Schools 459
The Affirmative Action Controversy 461
■ GENERATION NEXT Affirmative Action 462
Equal Rights Today 464
Summary 465 | Chapter Self-Test 466 | Key Terms 467 | Further Reading 467

Part V The Politics of National Policy

17 Public Policy 468
Defining Public Policy 470
■ YOU WILL DECIDE/THINKING IT THROUGH How Should We Fix Social Security? 472

The Eight Steps in Making Public Policy 472
- ■ HISTORY MAKERS Ralph Nader 474
- ■ THE CHANGING FACE OF U.S. POLITICS Think Tanks 476
- ■ HOW OTHER NATIONS GOVERN The Policy Process 479
- ■ GENERATION NEXT Government Control of Daily Life 480

Citizens and Public Policy 484

Summary 485 | Chapter Self-Test 485 | Key Terms 486 | Further Reading 486

18 Making Economic Policy 488

An Introduction to Economic Policy 490

Fiscal Policy 492
- ■ HOW OTHER NATIONS GOVERN Tax Rates Around the World 495
- ■ GENERATION NEXT Satisfaction with the Financial Situation 497

Monetary Policy 498
- ■ HISTORY MAKERS Alan Greenspan 499

Promoting the Economy 500
- ■ YOU WILL DECIDE/THINKING IT THROUGH Should the Federal Government Do More to Protect U.S. Jobs? 504

Regulating the Economy 504
- ■ THE CHANGING FACE OF U.S. POLITICS Female and Minority Board Members 506

The Deregulation Movement 509

A Continued Federal Role 511

Summary 511 | Chapter Self-Test 512 | Key Terms 513 | Further Reading 513

19 Making Social Policy 514

The Role of the Federal Government in Social Policy 516

Types of Social Policy 517
- ■ GENERATION NEXT Helping the Needy 518

The Expansion of Social Policy in the Twentieth Century 521
- ■ HISTORY MAKERS Marian Wright Edelman 523
- ■ YOU WILL DECIDE/THINKING IT THROUGH Should the Federal Government Promote Marriage? 526

Social Policy Challenges for the Future: Health, Education, and Crime 526
- ■ HOW OTHER NATIONS GOVERN Wealth and Health 530
- ■ THE CHANGING FACE OF U.S. POLITICS Access to College, 2000–2008 534

The Politics of Social Policy 535

Summary 535 | Chapter Self-Test 536 | Key Terms 537 | Further Reading 537

20 Making Foreign and Defense Policy 538

Understanding Foreign Policy and Defense 540

The Foreign Policy and Defense Agenda 542
- ■ GENERATION NEXT Hard Versus Soft Power 543
- ■ HISTORY MAKERS Woodrow Wilson 547

The Foreign Policy and Defense Bureaucracy 549
- ■ THE CHANGING FACE OF U.S. POLITICS Diversity in the Military 554

Foreign Policy and Defense Options 554
- ■ HOW OTHER NATIONS GOVERN Scandinavia's Foreign Aid 557
- ■ YOU WILL DECIDE/THINKING IT THROUGH Should Women Engage in Combat? 558

Prospects for the Future 559

Summary 560 | Chapter Self-Test 561 | Key Terms 562 | Further Reading 562

EPILOGUE Sustaining Constitutional Democracy 564

The Case for Government by the People 566

Participation and Representation 566

The Role of the Politician 569

Leadership in a Constitutional Democracy 569

The Importance of Active Citizenship 570

Further Reading 571

Appendix 572

The Declaration of Independence 572

The Federalist, No. 10 573

The Federalist, No. 51 576

The Federalist, No. 78 578

Presidential Election Results, 1789–2008 582

GLOSSARY 584

NOTES 590

PHOTO CREDITS 607

INDEX 609

LEARNING **OBJECTIVES**

Chapter 1

1 Define government, politics, politicians, political science, and constitutional democracy. 4
2 Differentiate democracy from other forms of government. 6
3 Identify the conditions that help democracy flourish and explain why they do so. 8
4 Explain the importance to successful democracy of values, political processes, and political structures. 10
5 Show how politics before 1787 shaped the Constitution. 13
6 Identify the most important compromises achieved by the delegates to the Constitutional Convention of 1787. 18
7 Assess the arguments for and against the ratification of the Constitution. 22

Chapter 2

1 Describe the basic structure of the Constitution and its Bill of Rights. 30
2 Summarize the basic principles of government established by the Constitution. 31
3 Compare and contrast the three main branches of the U.S. Government. 32
4 Show how the system of checks and balances operates among the three branches of the U.S. government. 32
5 Show how the use of judicial review strengthens the courts in a separation of powers system. 38
6 Analyze the effect of *Marbury v. Madison* on the role of the judiciary. 38
7 Explain how the meaning of the Constitution has evolved over time. 40
8 Outline the way we make formal changes to the Constitution. 41

Chapter 3

1 Compare and contrast the different interpretations of federalism. 64
2 Show how federalism protects citizens. 67
3 Differentiate between the types of national and state powers. 68
4 Describe and compare the constitutional pillars of national power. 70
5 Analyze the role of the national courts in regulating federalism. 76
6 Compare and contrast the arguments of decentralists and centralists. 77
7 Analyze the differences between grants and mandates. 79
8 Establish the link between the growth of the national government and federalism. 83

Chapter 4

1 Identify the most important elements of the American political culture and how we learn them. 92
2 Assess the importance of the "American dream" in the context of economic change. 99
3 Compare and contrast different ideological assumptions about government. 103
4 Assess the arguments for and against each ideology. 104
5 Analyze the importance of political ideology in light of competing ideas such as pragmatism, practicality, and the changing agenda of American politics. 111

Chapter 5

1 Describe the opportunities and challenges posed by the diversity of the American population. 116
2 Explain how geography affects politics. 117
3 Describe the political evolution of the South. 119
4 Evaluate the role of population density and where people live in American politics. 122
5 Assess the roles of race, ethnicity, religion, gender, and changing family demographics in American politics. 124
6 Evaluate the roles of education, income, class, and age in American politics. 136

Chapter 6

1 Evaluate the role of interest groups and social movements in American politics. 148
2 Identify the different types of interest groups in the United States. 150
3 Compare the sources of interest group power. 158

4 Describe lobbyists and how they influence policy. 159

5 Assess how some interest groups use money to pursue their agendas and evaluate the consequences for interest group pluralism of some groups having little money. 164

Chapter 7

1 Explain why parties arise in democracies and their primary functions. 180

2 Contrast the unique features of the American party system with those of other countries. 183

3 Understand the history of American political parties. 185

4 Distinguish parties' functions as institutions, in government, and in the electorate. 188

5 Discuss how parties and elections are financed. 199

6 Assess the long-term prospects for the current party system and, specifically, the Democratic and Republican Parties. 201

Chapter 8

1 Identify the key dimensions of public opinion and how we measure it. 208

2 Describe the forces that create and shape individuals' political attitudes. 212

3 Analyze the relationship between public opinion and public policy. 216

4 Assess non-voting participation and how it may change in the age of the Internet. 218

5 Describe the demographic, legal, and electioneering factors that affect voter turnout. 220

6 Explain why people vote the way they do in elections. 229

7 Identify the problems associated with administering elections and proposed solutions to those problems. 233

Chapter 9

1 Summarize election rules and assess their implications for elections in the United States. 240

2 Describe the electoral college, how it works, and its impact on presidential elections. 242

3 Identify the regularities of congressional elections and explain why they are generally not competitive. 244

4 Identify the stages in U.S. presidential elections and analyze the differences in campaigning at each stage. 248

5 Assess the influence of money in congressional and presidential elections and evaluate the main approaches to campaign finance reform. 259

6 Evaluate the need for improving presidential and congressional elections in the United States. 268

Chapter 10

1 Define the news media and show how their different forms connect the government and the people. 276

2 Describe the evolution of the media's interaction with politics from the Founding until today, including the changes brought by the Internet. 280

3 Evaluate the media's influence on public opinion and attention. 284

4 Identify the benefits and problems of the media's role in elections. 290

5 Assess the media's relationship to governance in the United States. 294

Chapter 11

1 Describe the congressional election process and demonstrate how it protects incumbents. 301

2 Differentiate the powers of Congress. 305

3 Compare and contrast the structure and powers of the House and Senate. 305

4 Compare the leadership systems used in the House and Senate. 308

5 Analyze the committee structure and show how members are assigned to committees. 312

6 Assess the effect of different forms of representation on citizen engagement. 316

7 Examine the influences on legislative decisions and how these influences may vary with issues. 317

8 Identify the key steps by which a bill becomes a law and the ways a bill can be stopped at each step. 320

Chapter 12

1 Describe the constitutional foundations of the presidency. 328

2 Compare and contrast the three types of presidential power. 331

3 Evaluate the controversies surrounding the president's assertion of additional executive powers and the evolution of presidential power. 335

4 Analyze the roles of the White House staff, Executive Office of the President, cabinet, and vice president. 340

5 Describe the president's job. 344

6 Identify the sources of presidential/congressional conflict and the tools presidents use to influence Congress. 347

7 Identify factors that make a great president. 352

Chapter 13

1 Understand why the federal bureaucracy is called the undefined branch. 358
2 Analyze the pros and cons of bureaucracy. 360
3 Compare and contrast the different types of federal organizations. 361
4 Describe the differences between the bureaucracy's two types of leaders. 367
5 Evaluate the differences between the spoils and merit systems. 369
6 Identify the key regulations that govern the civil service. 370
7 Analyze the tools of implementation and their effectiveness. 373
8 Compare and contrast efforts to control the federal bureaucracy. 376

Chapter 14

1 Analyze the implications of the adversarial process. 384
2 Explain the structure of the federal court system. 386
3 Evaluate factors important in appointing judicial nominees. 388
4 Compare and contrast arguments in favor of and against judicial activism. 392
5 Describe the process of reaching a decision in the U.S. Supreme Court. 394
6 Assess the influences on U.S. Supreme Court decision making. 399
7 Compare and contrast the limits on judicial action. 402
8 Assess the role of the judiciary in a constitutional democracy. 404

Chapter 15

1 Evaluate the arguments for amending a Bill of Rights to the original Constitution. 411
2 Identify protections under the establishment and free exercise clauses of the Constitution. 413
3 Contrast the categories of protected and unprotected speech. 417
4 Compare and contrast procedural and substantive due process. 423
5 Analyze the degree to which criminal suspects' rights are protected in our criminal justice system. 427

Chapter 16

1 Evaluate the importance of citizenship rights, particularly concerning immigration and the war on terror. 441
2 Compare and contrast different groups' efforts to obtain equal protection of the law. 443
3 Appraise the reasons for delay in the women's rights movement. 446
4 Assess the constitutional tests applied to discriminatory laws in the United States. 451
5 Analyze the protections provided by the 1965 Voting Rights Act. 454
6 Describe how Congress has legislated against discrimination in housing and accommodations. 456
7 Explain the difficulty of integration in a society largely segregated by housing patterns. 458
8 Evaluate the current state of affirmative action in the United States. 461

Chapter 17

1 Compare politics and public policy and show how each affects the other. 470
2 Analyze the three types of public policy. 471
3 Evaluate the eight steps in making public policy. 473
4 Compare and contrast the tools of public policy. 478
5 Identify how citizens can influence each step of the public policy process. 483

Chapter 18

1 Identify the two most important measures of economic performance and show how they interact. 490
2 Evaluate the role of fiscal policy in keeping the economy stable. 492
3 Outline the key steps in the federal budget process. 494
4 Evaluate the role of monetary policy in keeping the economy stable. 498
5 Analyze the federal government's role in promoting the economy. 500
6 Analyze the federal government's role in regulating the economy. 504
7 Contrast the advantages and disadvantages of the deregulation movement. 509

Chapter 19

1 Explain the difference between entitlements and means-tested entitlements. 517

2 Compare and contrast the two types of social policy. 519

3 Identify the major contributions of the New Deal and the Great Society to social policy. 521

4 Evaluate the impact of welfare reform. 525

5 Analyze the causes of and solutions for the lack of health coverage for all Americans. 529

6 Assess the tools of federal education and crime policy. 531

Chapter 20

1 Analyze the five questions that shape positions on U.S. foreign policy and defense. 540

2 Compare and contrast hard and soft power. 542

3 Evaluate the seven issues that currently dominate the foreign policy and defense agenda. 542

4 Identify the goals of the war in Iraq and evaluate the level of U.S. success. 546

5 Assess the components of the foreign policy and defense bureaucracy. 550

6 Examine the defense hierarchy. 552

7 Analyze the options for achieving foreign policy and defense goals. 554

Preface

Government and politics matter. Government matters in such areas as the economy, educational opportunity, and public health. One of the lessons from the government's poor response to Hurricane Katrina in 2005 is that in such times we all depend to a great degree on government to provide safety and security. Without that security, we face a world of anarchy. While government can fail, as it did in its response to Katrina, it can also succeed, as it did when the NASA space program placed astronauts on the moon, polio was largely eradicated, and the Cold War was peacefully resolved. We title this book *Government by the People* because we want to emphasize the important role people play in our constitutional democracy. Understanding American politics and government must include an appreciation of the people, their similarities and differences, their beliefs and attitudes, and their behaviors. A foundation of that understanding of the people is our chapter on the American political landscape in which we examine such aspects of our population as race, ethnicity, gender, age, religion, income, and region. Our country is diverse and that diversity is important politically.

The study of American government should be engaging, relevant, and rigorous. As authors of this book, we see politics and government as topics worthy of careful study. Constitutional democracy—the kind we have in the United States—is exceedingly hard to achieve, equally hard to sustain, and often hard to understand. Our political history has been an evolution toward an enlarged role for citizens and voters. Citizens have more rights and political opportunities in 2008 and 2009 than they had in 1800 or 1900. The framers of our Constitution warned that we must be vigilant in safeguarding our rights, liberties, and political institutions. But to do this, we must first understand these institutions and the forces that have shaped them.

We want you to come away from reading this book with a richer understanding of American politics, government, the job of politicians, and the important role you, as a citizen, play in this country's present and future. We hope you will participate actively in making this constitutional democracy more vital and responsive to the urgent problems of the twenty-first century.

What's New in This Edition

The new edition of *Government by the People* builds on the longstanding reputation of this book for strong coverage of the foundations of American government that is accurate, accessible, and current. We have integrated the latest in scholarship on American politics and government, the dramatic 2008 elections, recent Supreme Court decisions, and comparisons with countries around the world into a book that introduces you to the subject and the discipline of political science.

Also new to this edition are data on how young people see politics and government. Using data from studies of 18–24 and 18–29 year olds, we examine the attitudes, opinions, and values of this emerging generation of voters with "Generation Next" boxes. Each feature includes the actual question asked of others in the studies, allowing you to answer for yourself and compare your answers to others.

Building on the theme of the people in government, we examine the changing face of American politics in each chapter with current data on the importance of our diversity as a people. Each chapter also, as we suggest above, has a new approach to putting the U.S. government into comparative perspective.

Perhaps most strikingly, this edition introduces a new framework of learning pedagogy to help you navigate each chapter's discussion, focus on the most important concepts, and understand American politics and goverment. After surveying American government and politics courses taught around the country, we developed a list of "learning objectives"—the concepts professors teaching this course most often want their students to understand—to shape and guide the development of this edition. A master list of these objectives appears just before this Preface, providing a full inventory of the key concepts students must master to complete the course successfully. These objectives reappear at the beginning of each chapter, highlighting the learning goals for that chapter, while individual objectives are called out in the text margins as the key concepts are discussed. A summary and self-test at the end of each chapter provide students with a final check of their understanding, and the self-test includes both short and longer essay questions to promote critical thinking.

The 2009 Edition also includes the following changes:

Chapter 1 begins with a new introduction that uses the elections of 2000, 2004, and 2008 to frame the chapter.

Chapter 2 uses the issue of school prayer to establish the lack of specificity of the Constitution. The Democratic control of Congress in 2006 (continuing in 2008) has been added to the discussion of divided government. Methods for proposing amendments include examples to clarify the two methods.

Chapter 3 uses California's emissions-standard battle with the EPA to frame the chapter. The discussion of federalism providing training for national officials has been expanded. No Child Left Behind has been added to the discussion of federal mandates and unfunded mandates.

Chapter 4 looks at the struggle to establish Martin Luther King Jr. Day. The section on liberalism, conservatism, and criticisms of both has been updated to reflect recent issues, events and the 2008 campaign and election. "Socialism" has been expanded to "Socialism and Communism," with an expanded discussion of the Soviet Union.

Chapter 5 uses the 2008 primary season to explore identity politics and ethnocentrism. The demographic data in the discussions of different groups has been updated throughout the chapter. A discussion of the nomination and election of Barack Obama has been added to the section on African Americans. California's legalization and subsequent banning of same-sex marriage is explored.

Chapter 6 adds a discussion of the free rider problem. The Internet has been added to the discussion of techniques interest groups use to exert influence. The discussion of PACs notes the change in allegiance of PACs after the 2006 Democratic control of Congress.

Chapter 7 adds the Democratic control of Congress in 2006 to the discussion of party function in the government. The history of American political parties has been streamlined to focus on the major periods and events, and information on the impact of the 2008 election has been added. How parties raise and spend money has been streamlined, but the distinction between hard and soft money is covered.

Chapter 8 has been updated throughout to reflect the events and outcomes of the 2008 election. The role of the Internet and social networking sites in the 2008 campaign has been added. A section on absentee and early voting has been added to the discussion of voting.

Chapter 9 has been thoroughly updated to reflect the 2008 election, including new information in the introduction, a new figure on safe/competitive seats in the House, updated data for the rising campaign costs in general elections, the candidates and nomination process in the 2008 primaries and conventions, acceptance speeches at the conventions, the selection of Joe Biden and Sarah Palin as running mates, the party platforms, campaign finance, and the outcome of the election.

Chapter 10 discusses the role of the Internet in the 2008 campaigns and election. The declining importance of newspapers is discussed, as is the growing importance of the Internet.

Chapter 11 has been updated to reflect the 2008 Congressional elections. The discussion of senatorial consent has been moved to Chapter 14 on appointing federal judges.

Chapter 12 includes updated information on Bush's use of veto power, invocation of executive privilege, and use of signing statements.

Chapter 13 includes a new section on defining bureaucracy that includes Max Weber's work, describing the six characteristics of an effective bureaucracy, and identifying the major weaknesses of bureaucracy today. A new section at the end of the chapter discusses the great achievements of the bureaucracy.

Chapter 14 uses cases related to using race to assign students to individual public schools to show the importance of the membership of the Court. The section on Supreme Court decisions has been rewritten to more clearly guide the students through the entire process.

Chapter 15 has been combined with Chapter 16 from the last edition, bringing all the civil liberties topics together. The discussion of habeas corpus includes updates from the *Hamdan* and *Boumedienne* cases. A section distinguishing civil liberties from civil rights has been added. The discussion of property rights has been moved to this chapter from Chapter 16, including a new discussion of *Kelo* v. *City of New London*. Due process rights, privacy rights, including abortion and sexual orientation, the rights of the accused and the death penalty have been moved here from Chapter 16.

Chapter 16 (previously Chapter 17) adds Barack Obama's candidacy to the discussion of racial equality, and Hillary Clinton and Sarah Palin to the discussion of women's rights.

Chapter 17 is a new chapter that takes the brief introduction to public policy from Chapter 18 in the previous edition and expands it to provide a more thorough discussion of the process. It begins with a definition of public policy, including the various types of public policy. The chapter then explores the eight steps in making public policy, including more detail and examples.

Chapter 18 includes updated budget and expenditure data throughout the narrative and in figures and tables. The discussion of the Federal Reserve System includes a new section and figure on the prime interest rate and the Fed's recent activity. A new section on corporate responsibility has been added to the chapter.

Chapter 19 includes an expanded discussion of help for the unemployed, including a new section on low-income workers, the minimum wage, and the earned income tax credit. The section on education includes updated information on the impact of No Child Left Behind and Head Start.

Chapter 20 has been reorganized to focus on five approaches to foreign policy. The discussion of the war in Iraq has been updated to reflect events of the past two years. A new section on the role of contractors in Iraq and Afghanistan has been added.

A Focus on Foundations . . .

Read by over one million students, this new edition of the classic *Government by the People* has been substantially rewritten and redesigned to assist you in your study of American government and politics.

Each chapter begins with a **Chapter Outline** that breaks down larger subjects into important subparts and previews the topics to come.

CHAPTER **OUTLINE**

- What Parties Do for Democracy
- A Brief History of U.S. Political Parties
- U.S. Parties Today
- How Parties Raise and Spend Money
- Are the Political Parties Dying?

Local and judicial elections in most states are **nonpartisa** means no party affiliation is indicated. Such systems make it mor cal parties to operate—precisely why many jurisdictions have ad contending that party affiliation is not important to being a go board member. As in the community college board election at th chapter, many voters in nonpartisan elections rely more on how name of a candidate is, or whether he or she now holds office. In ad tend to turn out for nonpartisan elections than for standard partis

Unify the Electorate Parties are often accused of creating confli help unify the electorate and moderate conflict, at least within the strong incentive to fight out their internal differences but come tog

New! **Learning Objectives** help you identify the kinds of learning you will be expected to do with each chapter. We also integrate the **Learning Objectives** throughout the chapter and return to them at the end of the chapter in a short **Chapter Summary**. This closely knit pedagogical system helps you navigate through chapter discussions and demonstrate that you have mastered the concepts.

Political Parties

Essential to Democracy

Some years ago, a community college district in Los Angeles held a nonpartisan election for its trustees in which any registered voter could run if he or she paid the $50 filing fee and gathered 500 valid signatures on a petition. Each voter could cast up to seven votes. Political parties were not allowed to nominate candidates, and party labels did not appear on the ballot to help orient voters to the candidates.

A total of 133 candidates ran. They were listed alphabetically, and those whose names began with the letters A to F did better than those later in the alphabet. Being well known or having a Mexican American surname was also an advantage. Endorsements by the *Los Angeles Times* also influenced the outcome, as did campaigning by a conservative group. But how do people vote in an election without parties?

Parties are both a consequence of democracy and an instrument of it. They serve many functions, including narrowing the choices for voters[1] and making national and state elections work. American voters take for granted the peaceful transfer of power from one elected official to another and from one party to another, yet in new democracies where holding power may be more important than democratic principles, the transfer of power after an election is often problematic. Well-established parties help stabilize democracy.

This chapter begins by examining why parties are so vital to the functioning of democracy. We then examine the evolution of American political parties. Although U.S. political parties have changed over time, they remain important in three different settings: as institutions, in government, and in the electorate. We'll look at the way parties facilitate democracy in all three. Finally, we discuss the strength of parties today and the prospects for party reform and renewal.

What Parties Do for Democracy

American political parties serve a variety of political and social functions, some well and others not so well. The way they perform them differs from place to place and time to time.

Party Functions

Political parties are organizations that seek political power by electing people to office who will help party positions and philosophy become public policy.

Organize the Competition Parties exist primarily as an organizing mechanism to win elections and thus win control of government. For some races, parties recruit and nominate candidates for office; register and activate voters; and help candidates by training them, raising money for them, providing them with research and voter lists, and enlisting volunteers to work for them.[2]

LEARNING **OBJECTIVES**

1. Explain why parties arise in democracies and their primary functions.
2. Contrast the unique features of the American party system with those of other countries.
3. Understand the history of American political parties.
4. Distinguish parties' functions as institutions, in government, and in the electorate.
5. Discuss how parties and elections are financed.
6. Assess the long-term prospects for the current party system and, specifically, the Democratic and Republican Parties.

179

LEARNING **OBJECTIVE**

1 Explain why parties arise in democracies and their primary functions.

opposition. Moreover, to win elections, p party and gain their support. This action two large national political parties in the

Parties have great difficulty buildi abortion or gun control. Not surprisingl defining themselves or the election in si ers disagree with the party's stand on o agree on other issues. Deemphasizing s

CHAPTER **SUMMARY**

1. Explain why parties arise in democracies and their primary functions.

   Political parties are essential to democracy. They simplify voting choices, organize electoral competition, unify the electorate, help organize government by bridging the separation of powers and fostering cooperation among branches of government, translate public preferences into policy, and provide loyal opposition.

2. Contrast the unique features of the American party system with those of other countries.

. . . a Focus on Learning Objectives

YOU WILL **DECIDE**

Is a Vote for a Third-Party Candidate with Little Chance Winning a Wasted Vote?

In several close elections, including the 2000 presidential election, the v cast for one or another minor party, if cast for the likely second choice c those voters, would have changed the outcome of the election. In such situation, should voters care more about influencing who wins an electic more about casting a vote for a candidate whose views are closest to th own, even if that candidate has little chance of winning?

THINKING IT THROUGH

How you answer this question depends on what you want to accomplish with your vote. Those who see the vote as a largely symbolic exercise will likely vote for a minor party candidate with little chance of winning. The problem is that the more electable candidate who is clearly preferred over the other more competitive alternative may not win office at all if a voter does not consider electability. The winner-take-all system makes this trade-off more consequential. In a system in which proportional representation is possible, a voter is more likely to be able to translate policy preferences into a vote for representatives. But in our system, voters must often vote for their second choice in order to avoid letting their third choice win office. Interest groups, like environmental groups, often find themselves not endorsing a minor party candidate who may be closer to their views because they want to avoid helping to elect a competitive alternative candidate whose views they abhor.

One way to lessen the influence of these candidates is to require a run-off election of the top two vote-getters if no candidate gets a majority. Although this would force another election in some instances, it would also force people who vote to decide among the more viable options. A counterargument is that many people who support minor party candidates would opt out of an election without this chance to express their preferences, and so such a run-off is already accomplished with the plurality winner system we now have.

Questions

1. Was a vote for someone other than Bush or Gore in 2000 a wasted vote? Why or why not?
2. What are some issues a minor party might push that would affect the major parties, even if the minor party does not win an election?
3. What are the obstacles minor parties face that major parties do not?

New! The study of government and politics is not just about learning facts; it is about becoming good critical thinkers and, by extension, better citizens. This skill is enhanced with practice, and to assist you with this critical thinking we have provided a box in each chapter called **You Will Decide—Thinking It Through**. **You Will Decide** asks a question that you as a citizen will decide. **Thinking It Through** provides some ways to think through the question and discussion. There is no right or wrong answer—what is important is that you have considered multiple ways to answer the question and how you would go about approaching the issue.

Chapter Self-Test

1. Define the term *political party.* (p. 179)
2. Explain the five major functions of political parties, using one or two sentences for each one. (pp. 179–181)
3. In a short essay, describe the benefits and problems with each form of nominating candidates—caucus, open primary, closed primary, and blanket primary. Choose which method is best and defend your answer. (pp. 179–181)
4. Keeping in mind the five functions of political parties, discuss in a few sentences why partisan fighting is an inevitable part of the party system. (pp. 181–182)
5. From each pair, identify which feature is part of the U.S. party system and which is part of a typical parliamentary system. (pp. 179–183)
   a. winner-take-all/proportional representation
   b. multi-member districts/single-member districts
   c. party-centered campaigns/candidate-centered campaigns
   d. two dominant parties/many parties
   e. weak party organization/strong party organization
   f. ideological parties/centrist parties
6. In two or three sentences, explain why a vote for a third-party candidate in a U.S. election is typically considered a wasted vote. (pp. 183–185)
7. Place the following partisan realignments in chronological order and match them to the party that gained power as a result—Democratic, Republican or Federalist. (pp. 185–187)
   a. The Foun
   b. Jackson a
   c. The Civil War
   d. The progressive era
   e. The New Deal
8. Analyze the chart on page 195 and identify three or four changes in partisan identification in the last forty years. For example, far fewer men identify themselves as Democrats today.
9. Match each of the following activities with the aspect of a political party it best represents—(a) parties as institutions (b) in government, or (c) in the electorate. (pp. 188–194)
   i. A student registers to vote, stating-his party preference as Republican on the registration form before handing it to the county clerk
   ii. Howard Dean, Chair of the Democratic National Committee, decides whether the votes of Democrats in Michigan and Florida should count during the 2008 presidential primaries
   iii. The Senate splits 55–45 on a bill authorizing funds for the Iraq War, with Republicans voting 44–5 in favor and Democrats voting 50–1 against
10. A woman in Michigan learns about Barack Obama and begins campaigning enthusiastically for him, despite never caring much about politics before. This woman is most likely________. (p. 194)
    a. A party regular
    b. A candidate activist
    c. An issue activist

New! To assist you in preparing for exams and make your learning experience more effective, we have prepared a **Chapter Self-Test** which includes at least one essay question. A tip that will improve your performance in the class is to try and answer these questions soon after you read the chapter. Before you take an exam, practice on one or more of the essay questions.

Government...

Government by the people has become more and more a reality during the course of American history.

History Makers highlights the contributions people have made to our government and provides recognizable and tangible examples of the influence of the principles and theories discussed in the text.

HISTORY MAKERS

Chief Justice William H. Rehnquist

When asked his career plans by his elementary school teacher, William H. Rehnquist once recalled saying, I am going to change the government."* After serving in the army during World War II, Rehnquist majored in political science at Stanford University and later graduated first in his class from Stanford Law School. He then clerked for a Supreme Court justice and went into private legal practice while becoming active in Republican politics.

As an assistant attorney general in the administration of President Richard M. Nixon, Rehnquist was appointed associate justice of the Supreme Court in 1972. In his early years on the Court he emerged as a champion of federalism, limiting the power of the national government and returning power to the states. However, he could not persuade a majority to go along with his views and earned the nickname "Lone Ranger" for writing more dissenting opinions than any other justice at the time. In 1986, President Ronald Reagan elevated him to chief justice, and he presided over the Court until his death in 2005.

A major legacy of the Rehnquist Court is the way it curbed Congress in defense of the states. Besides resurrecting the rhetoric of states' rights and the Tenth Amendment, Chief Justice Rehnquist was central to a series of decisions that strengthened the states:

- Congress must make a "plain statement" of its intent to preempt state laws; otherwise the Court will defer to the states.†
- Congress's power over interstate commerce has inherent limits, and it may not compel states to enact laws in compliance with federal standards or compel them to enforce federal laws.‡
- Congress's power under the commerce clause permits it to regulate noneconomic activities, but only if they "substantially affect interstate commerce."§
- Congress's power to enforce the Fourteenth Amendment guarantee of equal protection of the law is limited to remedying violations that the Court recognizes; it does not extend to creating rights.‖
- States' immunity from lawsuits under the Eleventh Amendment bars lawsuits against them, without their consent, in federal and state courts, and by citizens of other states as well as of their own state who seek state compliance with federal laws forbidding, for example, discrimination on the basis of age or disability.¶

In short, Chief Justice Rehnquist presided over a Court that curbed the expansion of congressional powers and federal regulations in a renewed defense of the boundaries of federalism.

William H. Rehnquist

QUESTIONS

1. What do you think were Rehnquist's most important contributions in protecting states from the national government?
2. How can citizens influence Supreme Court decisions, and should they try?
3. How was Rehnquist able to influence the court even when he was in the minority?

*Quoted in Craig Bradley, "William H. Rehnquist," in Clare Cushman, ed., *The Supreme Court Justices* (CQ Press, 1993), p. 496.
†*Gregory v. Ashcroft,* 501 U.S. 452 (1991).
‡*New York v. United States,* 505 U.S. 144 (1992), and *Printz v. United States,* 521 U.S. 898 (1997).
§*United States v. Lopez,* 514 U.S. 549 (1995), and *United States v. Morrison,* 529 U.S. 598 (2000); but see *Nevada v. Hibbs,* 538 U.S. 721 (2003).
‖*City of Bourne v. Lopez,* 521 U.S. 507 (1997), and *United States v. Morrison,* 529 U.S. 598 (2000).

THE CHANGING FACE OF U.S. POLITICS

Immigrants and Federal, State, and Local Responses

For most of the twentieth century, the highest percentage of immigrants to the United States came from Europe. Today Latin Americans and Asians exceed Europeans as immigrants.

The number of immigrants arriving in the United States has been growing. Many enter the country illegally and join the workforce. According to the Pew Hispanic Center, in 2005 the United States had 35.7 million foreign-born residents, of whom 61 percent were legal permanent residents and 29 percent were undocumented migrants.*

The majority of undocumented aliens can be found in California, Texas, Florida, New York, Illinois, and New Jersey. However, almost two in five undocumented aliens now reside in other states, which makes the issue of immigration relevant in almost every election as the total number increases, including children who were born in the United States or crossed the border with a parent. Whereas 1.3 million illegal immigrants came to the United States in the 1980s, 5.8 million came in the 1990s, and 3.1 million arrived in 2000–2004.†

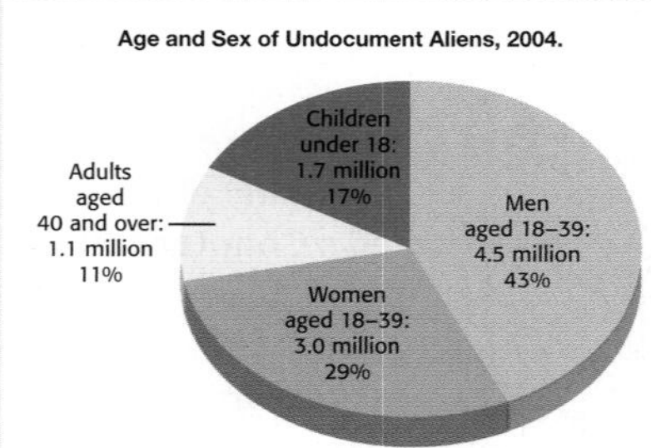

As a result of the substantial recent growth in illegal immigration, "broken borders" and the rising unemployment rate among U.S. citizens have become very controversial issues. Many object to undocumented workers taking jobs away from U.S. citizens, and the children of illegal immigrants often receive education and health benefits.

The controversy is complex, and there is no consensus about how to resolve it. More than 50 immigration bills have been introduced in Congress, and another 1,562 bills were introduced in state legislatures in 2007 alone. They address many solutions to immigration issues such as extending visas for highly educated workers in hard-to-recruit professions, establishing new procedures for legalizing undocumented workers, providing some form of amnesty for illegal immigrants who have been living in the United States for years, and increasing border security.

QUESTIONS

1. Why does the number of undocumented aliens provoke such controversy across the nation even though most immigrants live in California, Illinois, New York, Texas, and Florida?
2. Should the nation deny public benefits such as access to schools, health care, and housing to undocumented aliens who are children? Why or why not?

*Jeffrey S. Passel, "Estimates of the Size and Characteristics of the Undocumented Population," Pew Hispanic Center report, March 21, 2005, p. 7.
†National Conference of State Legislatures, "2007 Enacted State Legislation Related to Immigrants and Immigration," *Immigrant Policy Project,* November 29, 2007, p. 1.

The Changing Face of U.S. Politics. In important ways, the people of the United States today are much more diverse than at any previous time. This feature explores the impact of the ever-increasing level of diversity in the American political landscape, including how race and gender are changing the way the American government works. These unique boxes are designed to reflect the concerns and experiences of ethnic and minority groups in American politics.

. . . by the *People*

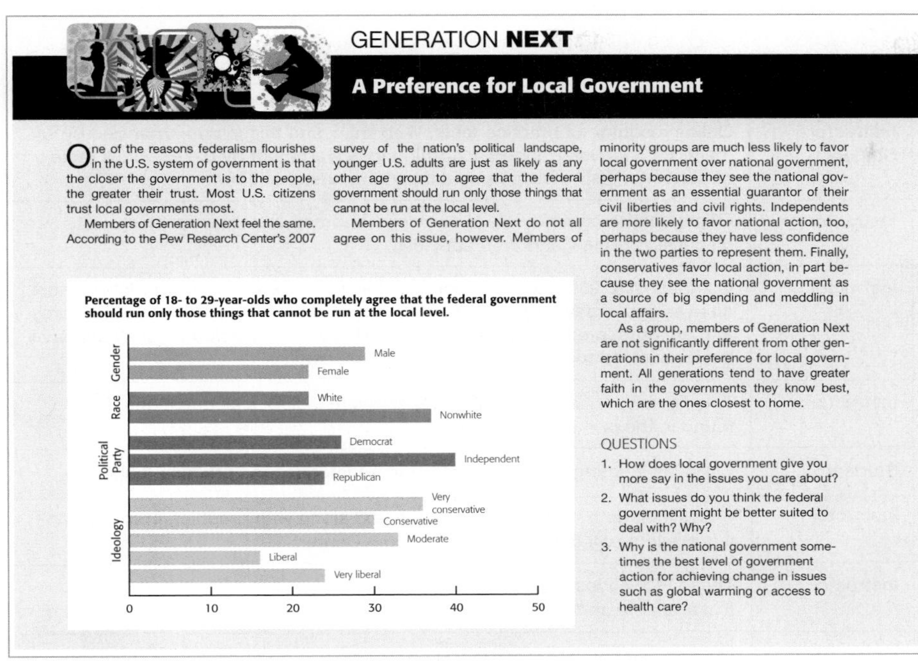

GENERATION **NEXT**

A Preference for Local Government

One of the reasons federalism flourishes in the U.S. system of government is that the closer the government is to the people, the greater their trust. Most U.S. citizens trust local governments most.

Members of Generation Next feel the same. According to the Pew Research Center's 2007 survey of the nation's political landscape, younger U.S. adults are just as likely as any other age group to agree that the federal government should run only those things that cannot be run at the local level.

Members of Generation Next do not all agree on this issue, however. Members of minority groups are much less likely to favor local government over national government, perhaps because they see the national government as an essential guarantor of their civil liberties and civil rights. Independents are more likely to favor national action, too, perhaps because they have less confidence in the two parties to represent them. Finally, conservatives favor local action, in part because they see the national government as a source of big spending and meddling in local affairs.

As a group, members of Generation Next are not significantly different from other generations in their preference for local government. All generations tend to have greater faith in the governments they know best, which are the ones closest to home.

Percentage of 18- to 29-year-olds who completely agree that the federal government should run only those things that cannot be run at the local level.

QUESTIONS

1. How does local government give you more say in the issues you care about?
2. What issues do you think the federal government might be better suited to deal with? Why?
3. Why is the national government sometimes the best level of government action for achieving change in issues such as global warming or access to health care?

New! Generation Next. Because you are the next generation to assume full citizenship responsibilities, we have identified key issues that persons under age 30 face now or will face in the future. Drawing from data gathered by the Pew study *How Young People View Their Lives: A Portrait of "Generation Next"* we have broken out the youngest cohort of persons, 18–25 or 18–29 depending on the survey, and contrasted the views and behaviors of this group with older citizens.

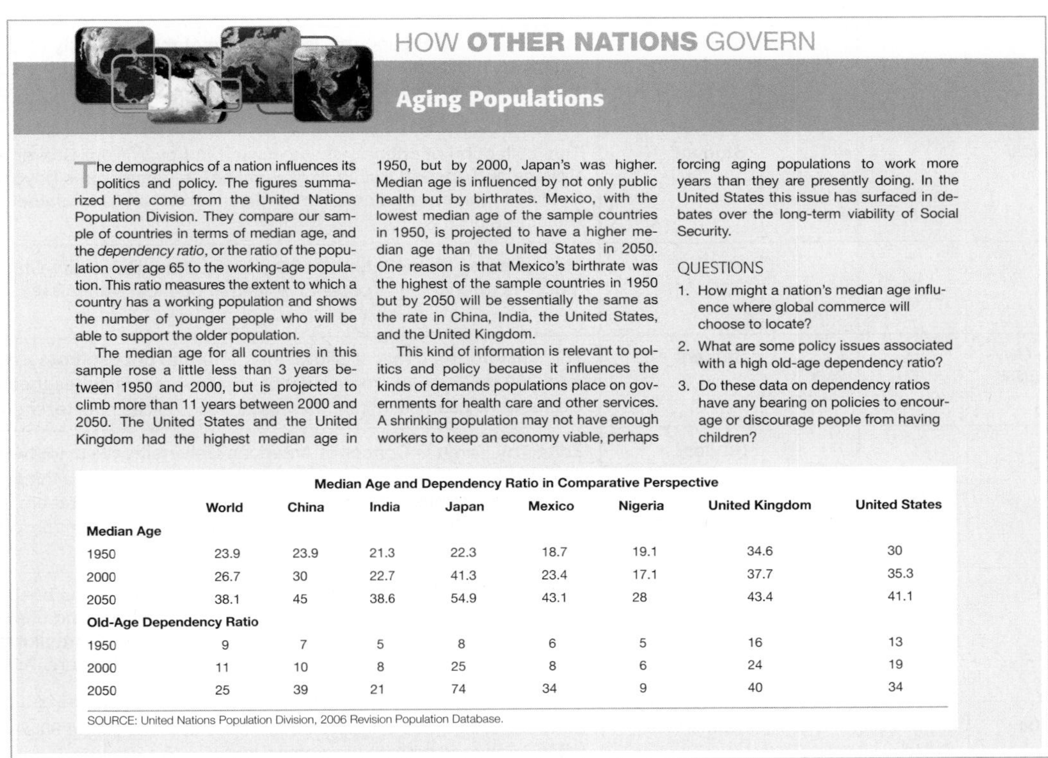

HOW **OTHER NATIONS** GOVERN

Aging Populations

The demographics of a nation influences its politics and policy. The figures summarized here come from the United Nations Population Division. They compare our sample of countries in terms of median age, and the *dependency ratio*, or the ratio of the population over age 65 to the working-age population. This ratio measures the extent to which a country has a working population and shows the number of younger people who will be able to support the older population.

The median age for all countries in this sample rose a little less than 3 years between 1950 and 2000, but is projected to climb more than 11 years between 2000 and 2050. The United States and the United Kingdom had the highest median age in 1950, but by 2000, Japan's was higher. Median age is influenced by not only public health but by birthrates. Mexico, with the lowest median age of the sample countries in 1950, is projected to have a higher median age than the United States in 2050. One reason is that Mexico's birthrate was the highest of the sample countries in 1950 but by 2050 will be essentially the same as the rate in China, India, the United States, and the United Kingdom.

This kind of information is relevant to politics and policy because it influences the kinds of demands populations place on governments for health care and other services. A shrinking population may not have enough workers to keep an economy viable, perhaps forcing aging populations to work more years than they are presently doing. In the United States this issue has surfaced in debates over the long-term viability of Social Security.

QUESTIONS

1. How might a nation's median age influence where global commerce will choose to locate?
2. What are some policy issues associated with a high old-age dependency ratio?
3. Do these data on dependency ratios have any bearing on policies to encourage or discourage people from having children?

Median Age and Dependency Ratio in Comparative Perspective

	World	China	India	Japan	Mexico	Nigeria	United Kingdom	United States
Median Age								
1950	23.9	23.9	21.3	22.3	18.7	19.1	34.6	30
2000	26.7	30	22.7	41.3	23.4	17.1	37.7	35.3
2050	38.1	45	38.6	54.9	43.1	28	43.4	41.1
Old-Age Dependency Ratio								
1950	9	7	5	8	6	5	16	13
2000	11	10	8	25	8	6	24	19
2050	25	39	21	74	34	9	40	34

SOURCE: United Nations Population Division, 2006 Revision Population Database.

How Other Nations Govern contrasts an important dimension of each chapter across the following countries: China, Great Britain, India, Japan, Mexico, Nigeria, and the United States. This feature highlights the experience of the people in other political systems and examines foreign political structures and processes, and how these similar and/or differing approaches can affect—and be affected by—American politics.

Resources in Print and Online

Name of Supplement	Print	Online	Available to	Description
American Government Study Site		✓	Instructor/ Student	Online resource of practice tests, Web links, and flashcards organized by major topics and arranged according to *Government by the People's* table of contents. Visit www.pearsonamericangovernment.com
Instructor's Manual 0-13-606243-1	✓	✓	Instructor	Offers chapter summaries, recent news and pop culture examples, discussion topics, and Web activities.
Test Bank 0-13-606253-9	✓	✓	Instructor	Contains over 200 questions per chapter in multiple-choice, true-false, short answer, and essay format. Questions address all levels of Bloom's taxonomy and are correlated to the Learning Objectives in the book. All questions have been reviewed for accuracy and effectiveness.
MyTest 0-13-606244-X		✓	Instructor	This flexible, online test generating software includes all questions found in the printed Test Bank.
Study Guide	✓	✓	Student	Contains learning objectives, chapter summaries, and practice tests.
PowerPoint Presentation		✓	Instructor	Slides include a lecture outline of the text along with graphics from the book. It is available on the Instructor Resource Center*.
Digital Transparency Masters		✓	Instructor	These PDF slides contain all maps, figures, and tables found in the text. It is available on the Instructor Resource Center*.
Longman Political Science Video Program	✓		Instructor	Qualified college adopters can peruse our list of videos for the American government classroom.
You Decide! Current Debates in American Politics, 2009 Edition 0-205-68405-X	✓		Student	This debate-style reader by John Rourke of the University of Connecticut examines provocative issues in American politics today by presenting various sides of key political topics.
Voices of Dissent: Critical Readings in American Politics, Eighth Edition 0-205-69797-6	✓		Student	This collection of critical essays assembled by William Grover of St. Michael's College and Joseph Peschek of Hamline University goes beyond the debate between mainstream liberalism and conservatism to fundamentally challenge the status quo.
Writing in Political Science, Third Edition 0-321-21735-7	✓		Student	This guide by Diane Schmidt of California State Univeristy-Chico takes students through all aspects of writing in political science step-by-step.
Choices: An American Gov-ernment Database Reader		✓	Student	This customizable reader allows instructors to choose from a database of over 300 readings to create a reader that exactly matches their course needs. Go to www.pearsoncustom.com/database/choices.html for more information.
Ten Things That Every American Government Student Should Read 0-205-28969-X	✓		Student	Edited by Karen O'Connor of American University. We asked American gov-ernment instructors across the country to vote for the 10 things beyond the text that they believe every student should read and put them in this brief and useful reader. Available at no additional charge when ordered packaged with the text.
American Government: Readings and Cases, Eighteenth Edition 0-205-69798-4	✓		Student	Edited by Peter Woll of Brandeis University, this longtime best-selling reader provides a strong, balanced blend of classic readings and cases that illustrate and amplify important concepts in American government, alongside extremely current selections drawn from today's issues and literature. Available at a discount when ordered packaged with this text.
Penguin-Longman Value Bundles	✓		Student	Longman offers 25 Penguin Putnam titles at more than a 60 percent discount when packaged with any Longman text. Go to www.pearsonhighered.com/penguin for more information.
Longman State Politics Series	✓		Student	These primers on state and local government and political issues are available at no extra cost when shrink-wrapped with the text. Available for Texas, California, and Georgia.

* Instructor Resource Center available at www.pearsonhighered.com/educator

Improve results with PEARSON mypoliscilab™

Designed to amplify a traditional course in numerous ways or to administer a course online, **MyPoliSciLab** combines pedagogy and assessment with an array of multimedia activities—videos, simulations, exercises, and online newsfeeds—to make learning more effective for all types of students. Now featuring the combined resources, assets, and activities of both Prentice Hall and Longman Publishers, this new release of **MyPoliSciLab** is visually richer and even more interactive than previous iterations—a quantum leap forward in design with more points of assessment and interconnectivity between concepts.

TEACHING AND LEARNING TOOLS

- ✓ **Assessment**: Comprehensive online diagnostic tools—learning objectives, study guides, flashcards, and pre- and post-tests—help students gauge and improve their understanding.
- ✓ **E-book:** Identical in content and design to the printed text, an e-book provides students access to their text wherever and whenever they need it.
- ✓ ***UPDATED!*** **PoliSci News Review:** A series of weekly articles and video clips—from traditional and non-traditional news sources—recaps the most important political news stories, followed by quizzes that test students' understanding.
- ✓ ***NEW!*** **ABC News RSS feed:** MyPoliSciLab provides an online feed from ABC News, updated hourly, to keep students current.
- ✓ **ABC News Video Clips**: Over 60 high-interest 2- to 4-minute clips provide historical snapshots in each chapter of key political issues and offer opportunities to launch discussions.
- ✓ ***UPDATED!*** **Roundtable and Debate Video Clips**: These video clips feature professors discussing key concepts from ideologically diverse perspectives and debating politically charged issues.
- ✓ **Student Polling:** Updated weekly with timely, provocative questions, the polling feature lets students voice their opinions in nationwide polls and view how their peers across the country see the same issue.
- ✓ **Political Podcasts:** Featuring some of Pearson's most respected authors, these video podcasts present short, instructive—and even entertaining—lectures on key topics that students can download and play at their convenience.
- ✓ ***NEW!*** **Student Podcasts:** The new MyPoliSciLab allows students to record and download their own videos for peer-to-peer learning.

INTERACTIVE ACTIVITIES

- ✓ **New and Updated Simulations:** Featuring an appealing new graphic interface, these role-playing simulations help students experience political decision-making in a way they never have before—including new "mini activities" within the simulations that prepare students to make the right decisions.

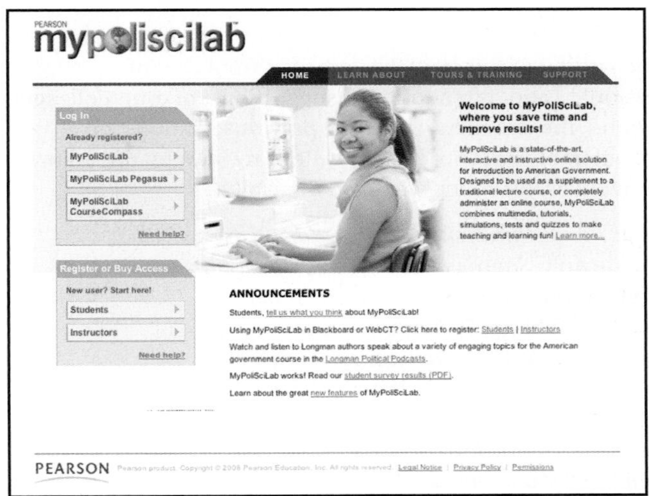

- ✓ ***NEW!*** **Debate Exercises:** These provocative new exercises present classic and contemporary views on core controversies, ask students to take a position, and then show them the potential consequences of taking that stand.
- ✓ **More Focused Comparative Exercises:** These exercises have been revised in scope to concentrate on a more specific issue when comparing the US to other political systems, giving students a more concrete foundation on which to analyze key similarities and differences.
- ✓ **More Interactive Timelines:** With redesigned media and graphics, these timelines let students step through the evolution of some aspect of politics and now include more interactive questions throughout.
- ✓ **More Dynamic Visual Literacy Exercises:** These revised exercises offer attractive new graphs, charts, and tables and more opportunities to manipulate and interpret political data.
- ✓ **Expanded Participation Activities:** Reflecting our country's growing political interest, these expanded activities give students ideas and instructions for getting involved in all aspects of politics.

Icons in the margins of this book direct students to the activities on MyPoliSciLab related to the topics they are studying.

ONLINE ADMINISTRATION

No matter what course management system you use—or if you do not use one at all, but still wish to easily capture your students' grades and track their performance—Pearson has a **MyPoliSciLab** option to suit your needs. Contact one of Pearson's Technology Specialists for more information or assistance.

A **MyPoliSciLab** access code is no additional cost when packaged with selected Pearson American Government texts. To get started, contact your local Pearson Publisher's Representative at **www.pearsonhighered.com/replocator.**

Acknowledgments

The writing of this book has profited from the informed, professional, and often critical suggestions of our colleagues around the country. This and previous editions have been considerably improved as a result of reviews by the following individuals, for which we thank them all:

Scott Adler, *University of Colorado*
Wayne Ault, *Southwestern Illinois College–Belleville*
Paul Babbitt, *Southern Arkansas University*
Thomas Baldino, *Wilkes University*
Barry Balleck, *Georgia Southern University*
Robert Ballinger, *South Texas College*
Jodi Balma, *Fullerton College*
Jeff Berry, *South Texas College*
Cynthia Carter, *Florida Community College–Jacksonville, North Campus*
Leonard Champney, *University of Scranton*
Mark Cichock, *University of Texas at Arlington*
Ann Clemmer, *University of Arkansas, Little Rock*
Alison Dagnes, *Shippensburg University*
Paul Davis, *Truckee Meadows Community College*
Ron Deaton, *Prince George's Community College*
Robert DeLuna, *St. Philips College*
Anthony Di Giacomo, *Wilmington College*
Richardson Dilworth, *Drexel University*
Rick Donohoe, *Napa Valley College*
Art English, *University of Arkansas, Little Rock*
Alan Fisher, *CSU–Dominguez Hills*
Bruce Franklin, *Cossatot Community College of the University of Arkansas*
Eileen Gage, *Central Florida Community College*
Richard Glenn, *Millersville University*
David Goldberg, *College of DuPage*
Nicholas Gonzalez, *Yuen DeAnza College*
Charles Grapski, *University of Florida*
Billy Hathorn, *Laredo Community College*
Max Hilaire, *Morgan State University*
James Hoefler, *Dickinson College*
Justin Hoggard, *Three Rivers Community College*
Gilbert Kahn, *Kean University*
Rogan Kersh, *Syracuse University*
Todd Kunioka, *CSU–Los Angeles*
La Della Levy, *Foothill College*
Jim Lennertz, *Lafayette College*
John Liscano, *Napa Valley College*
Amy Lovecraft, *University of Alaska–Fairbanks*
Howard Lubert, *James Madison University*
Michael McConachie, *Collin County Community College*
Lowell Markey, *Allegany College of Maryland*
Larry Martinez, *CSU–Long Beach*
Toni Marzotto, *Towson University*
Brian Newman, *Pepperdine University*
Adam Newmark, *Appalachian State University*
Randall Newnham, *Penn State University–Berks*
Keith Nicholls, *University of South Alabama*
Sean Nicholson-Crotty, *University of Missouri–Columbia*
Richard Pacelle, *Georgia Southern University*
William Parente, *University of Scranton*
Ryan Peterson, *College of the Redwoods*
Robert Rigney, *Valencia Community College–Osceola Campus*
Bren Romney, *Vernon College*
Jack Ruebensaal, *West Los Angeles College*
Bhim Sandhu, *West Chester University*
Gib Sansing, *Drexel University*
Colleen Shogan, *George Mason University*
Tom Simpson, *Missouri Southern*
Linda Simmons, *Northern Virginia Community College–Manassas Campus*
Dan Smith, *Northwest Missouri State University*
Jay Stevens, *CSU–Long Beach*
Lawrence Sullivan, *Adelphi University*
Halper Thomas, *CUNY–Baruch*
Jose Vadi, *CSU–Pomona*
Avery Ward, *Harford Community College*
Shirley Warshaw, *Gettysburg University*
Ife Williams, *Delaware County Community College*
Margie Williams, *James Madison University*
Christy Woodward-Kaupert, *San Antonio College*
Chris Wright, *University of Arkansas–Monticello*

This book builds on a long tradition of clear and accessible writing, good scholarship, and currency. James MacGregor Burns and Jack Peltason, the founding authors of the book, and Tom Cronin, who later joined them, set a high standard in these areas. We also express appreciation to David O'Brien for his work on the twenty-first and twenty-second editions of the book. As additional authors have joined the book we have worked hard to maintain this legacy while at the same time extensively revising each new edition. Joining us in writing four chapters of this edition has been Chris Nemacheck of the College of William and Mary. Professor Nemacheck is an expert in the courts and constitutional law and has substantially strengthened the book in those areas. We are grateful for her many contributions to the 2009 edition of the book. Writing the book requires teamwork—first among the coauthors who converse often about the broad themes, features, and focus of the book and who read and rewrite each other's drafts; then with our research assistants, who track down loose ends and give us the perspective of current students; and finally with the editors and other professionals at Pearson Longman. Important to each revision are the detailed reviews by teachers and researchers, who provide concrete suggestions on how to improve the book. We are grateful to all who helped with this edition.

Research assistants for the current edition of *Government by the People* are Aaron M. Anderson, E. Kyle Barnett, Bradley Jones, David Lassen, Tim Taylor, and Russell Thacker of Brigham Young University. Bryan Bradley, an expert in educational assessment, consulted with us on the chapter review questions found at the end of each chapter.

We gratefully acknowledge the professionalism, energy, and commitment of Political Science Editor-in-Chief Eric Stano. Our work with Eric and the Longman team was collegial and symbiotic.

Many skilled professionals were important to the publication of this book. They include Elisa Adams and David Kear for text development, Bob Ginsberg for production, Heather Johnson at Elm Street for page layout, Teri Stratford for photo research, and John Callahan for cover design.

We also want to thank you, the professors and students who use our book, and who send us letters and email messages with suggestions for improving *Government by the People.* Please write us in care of the Political Science Editor at Pearson Longman, 51 Madison Ave., New York, NY 10010, or contact us directly:

David B. Magleby Distinguished Professor of Political Science and Dean of FHSS, Brigham Young University, Provo, UT 84602 david_magleby@byu.edu

Paul C. Light Paulette Goddard Professor of Public Service at New York University and Douglas Dillon Senior Fellow at the Brookings Institution, pcl226@nyu.edu

About the Authors

David B. Magleby is nationally recognized for his expertise on direct democracy, voting behavior, and campaign finance. He received his B.A. from the University of Utah and his Ph.D. from the University of California, Berkeley. Currently Distinguished Professor of Political Science, Senior Research Fellow at the Center for the Study of Elections and Democracy, and Dean of the College of Family, Home and Social Science at Brigham Young University, Professor Magleby has also taught at the University of California, Santa Cruz, and the University of Virginia. He and his students have conducted statewide polls in Virginia and Utah. For the 1998–2008 elections he has directed national studies of campaign finance and campaign communications in competitive federal election environments involving a consortium of academics from nearly 80 universities and colleges in 38 states. This research is summarized in six edited books. In addition, he is co-editor of a longstanding series of books on financing federal elections. In partnership with colleagues, he has been studying the implementation of new voting technology, work funded in part by the National Science Foundation. He has been a Fulbright Scholar at Oxford University and a past president of Pi Sigma Alpha, the national political science honor society. Magleby is the recipient of many teaching awards including the 1990 Utah Professor of the Year award from the Council for the Advancement and Support of Education and the Carnegie Foundation, the 2001 Rowman & Littlefield Award for Innovative Teaching in Political Science, and several department and university awards. At BYU he served as Chair of the Political Science Department before being named dean. He is married to Linda Waters Magleby. They are the parents of four and grandparents of one.

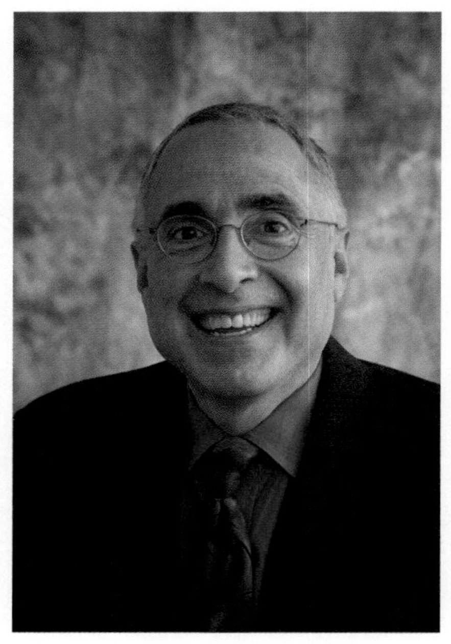

Paul C. Light is the Paulette Goddard Professor of Public Service at New York University's Wagner School of Public Service. He received his B.A. from Macalester College and his Ph.D from the University of Michigan. Professor Light has a wide-ranging career in both academia and government. He has worked on Capitol Hill as a senior committee staffer in the U.S. Senate and as an American Political Science Association Congressional Fellow in the U.S. House. He has taught at the University of Virginia, University of Pennsylvania, and Harvard University's John F. Kennedy School of Government. He has also served as a senior adviser to several national commissions on federal, state, and local public service. He is the author of 15 books on government, public service, and public policy. Light's current research focuses on government reform, Congress, the presidency, and social entrepreneurship. His latest books are *A Government Ill Executed* (Harvard University Press, 2008) and *The Search for Social Entrepreneurship* (Brookings Institution Press, 2008). He was the founding director of the Brookings Institution's Center for Public Service and continues his research on how to invite Americans to serve their communities through public service. His work has been funded by the Douglas Dillon Foundation, the Pew Charitable Trusts, the David and Lucille Packard Foundation, among many others. He is also an expert on preparing government, charitable organizations, and private corporations for natural and human-made disasters, and was a recognized leader in the response to Hurricane Katrina in 2005. He has testified before Congress more than a dozen times in the last five years.

A Special Acknowledgment

It is rare for a college textbook in any field to be a leader in its discipline for more than a generation. The competition between publishers is intense. Moreover, there is no shortage of leading scholars who are eager to share their ideas with students by publishing their own textbooks. With so many works to choose from, it is not surprising that some very good books cease publication after only two or three editions. James MacGregor Burns and Jack W. Peltason's book has more than stood the test of time, it has set a high standard for scholarship, clarity of writing, and currency. Their book, *Government by the People,* has been a leader among American government texts for *decades.*

Government by the People began when two young assistant professors, James MacGregor Burns of Williams College and Jack W. Peltason of Smith College, decided to partner and write an American government text sixty years ago, in 1948. Their first edition had a publication date of 1952. Although much has changed in college text book publishing since then, one constant has been the extraordinary commitment of the authors to producing a well-written, accessible, and balanced look at government and politics in the United States. Burns and Peltason were joined by Tom Cronin of Colorado College in the tenth edition of the book and by David O'Brien of the University of Virginia in the twenty-first and twenty-second editions of the book. As current authors of the book, we share the founding authors' passion for the subject of American government and their desire as teachers and authors to communicate the importance of government by the people. As the book now transitions to a new author team, we wish to acknowledge the important foundation provided by James MacGregor Burns, Jack W. Peltason, Thomas E. Cronin, and David M. O'Brien. We provide a brief personal acknowledgment below and we dedicate this edition to them.

James MacGregor Burns was the Woodrow Wilson Professor of Government at Williams College. He also taught at the University of Michigan and University of Richmond where he directed centers on leadership. A prolific writer, he won the Pulitzer Prize and National Book Award for his biographies of Franklin Roosevelt, *Roosevelt the Lion and the Fox* and *Roosevelt: The Soldier of Freedom.* His clarity of argument and willingness to challenge readers to think critically are his hallmarks. His book, *Deadlock of Democracy,* on how the separation of powers can result in deadlock, continues to foster healthy debate about the strengths and weaknesses of our constitutional system. More recently his focus has been on leadership, where he has published multiple books in the past several years. The University of Maryland has created the James MacGregor Burns Academy of Leadership, reflecting his contributions to that specialization. Burns was a leader in political science, having been elected president of the American Political Science Foundation.

Jack W. Peltason has shaped American higher education as well in his own discipline of political science. His teaching and writing is in the area of judicial process and public law. His book on the federal judges who implemented the Supreme Court's school integration decision in *Brown v. Board of Education of Topeka Kansas* is a classic which he titled, *Fifty-Eight Lonely Men: Southern Judges and School Desegregation.* Peltason was quickly seen as a leader and became the Chancellor of the University of Illinois, Chancellor of the University of California Irvine, and President of the University of California with leadership responsibility for all ten campuses of the University of California system. As President of the American Council on Education, he represented higher education before Congress and state legislatures. Peltason brought clarity of writing to *Government by the People* and a willingness to push himself and his coauthors to understand their audience and reach them. Peltason and Burns saw the entire book as their shared creation and pushed each other and the authors who later joined them to substantiate arguments, consider different points of view, fully document and support the text, and keep the book current and engaging.

Thomas E. Cronin joined the author team of *Government by the People* in the tenth edition. He fully subscribed to the approach of intense author interaction and as a skilled teacher at Colorado College and other institutions helped ensure that the book understood and spoke to college students. Cronin had been a White House Fellow and, like Burns, once ran for the U.S. Congress. He later became President of Whitman College. He is the McHugh Professor of American Institutions and Leadership at Colorado College.

David M. O'Brien participated in the twenty-first and twenty-second editions of the *Government by the People.* He is the Leone Reaves and George W. Spicer Professor at the University of Virginia. He was a Judicial Fellow and Research Associate at the Supreme Court of the United States, and a Fulbright Lecturer at Oxford University; he held the Fulbright Chair for Senior Scholars at the University of Bologna and was a Fulbright Researcher in Japan, as well as a Visiting Fellow at the Russell Sage Foundation. Among his publications are *Storm Center: The Supreme Court in American Politics,* 6th Ed.; a two volume casebook, *Constitutional Law and Politics,* 5th Ed.; an annual, *Supreme Court Watch;* and *Animal Sacrifice and Religious Freedom: Church of Lukumi Babablu Aye v. City of Hialeah.* He received the American Bar Association's Silver Gavel Award for contributing to the public's understanding of the law.

As the current authors of *Government by the People* we recognize the legacy we inherit and wish to express our appreciation to Jim Burns, Jack Peltason, Tom Cronin, and David O'Brien for their commitment to scholarship, teaching, and citizenship.

DAVID B. MAGLEBY
PAUL C. LIGHT

Government by the People

chapter 1

Constitutional Democracy

The peaceful transfer of power following elections is a process that U.S. citizens take for granted. Many people look on elections with disdain, saying things like, "Voting does not matter," "Nothing ever changes," or "It's just all politics." But in fact, U.S. elections are remarkable and consequential. They conclude with a rare event in human history: the peaceful transfer of political power. What is unusual is what is *not* happening. Most of the time in most nations, those in power got there because either they were born to the right family or they killed or jailed their opponents. During most of history, no one, especially not an opposition political party, could openly criticize the government, and a political opponent was an enemy.

Even in a highly contested election like the 2000 presidential election, Democrat Al Gore won the popular vote only to see George W. Bush declared the winner by the electoral college, after the Supreme Court effectively ruled 5 to 4 that Bush's slim Florida plurality should stand. Gore graciously conceded defeat: "I say to President-elect Bush that what remains of partisan rancor must now be put aside, and may God bless his stewardship of this country. Neither he nor I anticipated this long and difficult road. Certainly neither of us wanted it to happen. Yet it came, and now it has ended, resolved, as it must be resolved, through the honored institutions of our democracy."[1] The Democrats thus turned over the keys to the White House to George W. Bush and the Republicans. In many countries the irregularities of the voting process in Florida and other states would have been sufficient excuse for the party in power to declare that a new election needed to be held, and it would not be uncommon for that party to retain power until after the election or to pressure the high court to rule in its favor.

Eight years later, many Democrats still felt cheated by the process that occurred in 2000, and the close election in 2004 only reinforced their passion to win back the presidency. The Democratic standard-bearer, Illinois Senator Barack Obama, also had the advantage of negative public perceptions of President Bush's performance in office, especially in the war in Iraq. Republicans, who had built an effective political operation following the 2000 election only to see their party lose majorities in both houses of Congress in 2006, campaigned aggressively to retain power. Filling television screens, bookshelves, and blogs for months, both candidates and their allies did their utmost to demonstrate that they were most fit to lead the country.

After the 2008 election outcome appeared certain, John McCain graciously conceded defeat to Barack Obama and the process of organizing a new administration began. Obama's victory meant the eight year Republican control of the presidency shifted to the Democrats. Even though the day before the election John McCain, his running mate, Alaska Governor Sarah Palin, and their followers were insisting that if Barak Obama and his running mate, Delaware Senator Joe Biden, won the election there would be dire economic and national security consequences, once the votes were counted there was no serious consideration that anybody other than Barack Obama would become president. Outgoing President George Bush did not attempt to prolong his time in office by calling on the military to keep Obama from taking power. McCain's supporters did not take up arms or go underground to plan a revolution or leave the country. Instead, they almost immediately began planning how they could win the next election. Nor did Obama or his followers seriously think about punishing McCain and his supporters once they gained power.

LEARNING **OBJECTIVES**

1. Define government, politics, politicians, political science, and constitutional democracy.
2. Differentiate democracy from other forms of government.
3. Identify the conditions that help democracy flourish and explain why they do so.
4. Explain the importance to successful democracy of values, political processes, and political structures.
5. Show how politics before 1787 shaped the Constitution.
6. Identify the most important compromises achieved by the delegates to the Constitutional Convention of 1787.
7. Assess the arguments for and against the ratification of the Constitution.

CHAPTER **OUTLINE**

- U.S. Government and Politicians in Context
- Defining Democracy
- The Roots of the American Constitutional Experiment
- The Constitutional Convention of 1787
- To Adopt or Not to Adopt?

The Democrats wanted to throw the Republicans out of office, not in jail. In all these ways, the election of 2008 was a routine transfer—a constitutional democracy at work.

The peaceful transfer of power from one party and presidential administration to another is only one example of the successful functioning of our political system. There are many others, including, perhaps most important, George Washington relinquishing power after serving as our first president. In this chapter, we begin our exploration of the successful U.S. experiment with government by the people by taking a closer look at the meaning of democracy and the historical events that created the constitutional democracy of the United States.

U.S. Government and Politicians in Context

The oldest constitutional democracy in the world, the United States of America has survived for more than two centuries, yet it is still an experiment and a work in progress. We think of it as an enduring, strong government, but our constitutional political system is built on a fragile foundation. The U.S. Constitution and Bill of Rights survive not because we still have the parchment they were written on, but because each generation of U.S. citizens has respected, renewed, and worked to understand the principles and values found in these documents. Each generation has faced different challenges in preserving, protecting, and defending our way of government.

The U.S. constitutional democracy, founded on enduring values, has shown resilience and adaptability. We have held 111 presidential and midterm elections (including the 2008 election), and we have witnessed the peaceful transfer of power from one party to another on dozens of occasions. The United States has succeeded largely because its citizens love their country, revere the Constitution, and respect the free enterprise system. We also believe that debate, compromise, and free elections are the best ways to reconcile our differences. From an early age, we practice democracy in elementary school elections, for example, and even though we may be critical of elected leaders, we recognize the need for political leadership. We also know there are deep divisions and unsolved problems in the United States. Many people are concerned about the persistence of racism, about religious bigotry, about the gap in economic opportunities between rich and poor, and about the need to control the violence that disproportionately afflicts children and minorities. And we want our government, in addition to defending us against terrorism and foreign enemies, to provide us with basic health care and education, and to address other domestic problems.

But what is this government of which we expect so much? The reality is that "government by the people" is built on the foundation of hundreds of thousands of our fellow citizens: the people we elect and the people they appoint to promote the general welfare, provide for domestic tranquillity, and secure the blessings of liberty for us.

LEARNING **OBJECTIVE**

1 Define government, politics, politicians, political science, and constitutional democracy.

Before moving ahead, we need to define some of the basic terms we'll be using throughout this book. *Government* refers to the procedures and institutions (such as elections, courts, and legislatures) by which a people govern and rule themselves. *Politics*, at least in our system of government, is the process by which people decide who shall govern and what policies shall be adopted. Such processes invariably require discussions, debates, and compromises about tactics and goals. *Politicians* are the people who fulfill the tasks of overseeing and directing a government. Some politicians—legislators, mayors, and presidents—come to office through election. Nonelected politicians may be political party officials or aides, advisers, or consultants to elected officials. *Political science* is the study of the principles, procedures, and structures of government and the analysis of political ideas, institutions, behavior, and practices.

More than any other form of government, the kind of democracy that has emerged under the U.S. Constitution requires active participation and a balance between faith and skepticism. Government by the people does not, however, mean that *everyone* must be involved in politics and policy making. It requires people to run for office seeking to represent the voters, many of whom will always be too busy doing other things, and some of whom will always be apathetic about government and politics. But the public must be attentive, interested, involved, informed, and willing, when necessary, to criticize and change the direction of government.

Thomas Jefferson, author of the Declaration of Independence and one of our best-known champions of constitutional democracy, believed in the common sense of the people and in the possibilities of the human spirit. Jefferson warned that every government degenerates when it is left solely in the hands of the rulers. The people themselves, Jefferson wrote, are the only safe repositories of government. He believed in popular control, representative processes, and accountable leadership. But he was no believer in the simple participatory democracy of ancient Greece or revolutionary France. Even the power of the people must be restrained from time to time.

Government by the people requires faith in our common human enterprise, a belief that if the people are informed and care, they can be trusted with their own self-government, and an optimism that when things begin to go wrong, the people can be relied on to set them right. But we also need a healthy skepticism. Democracy requires us to question our leaders and never entrust a group or institution with too much power. And even though constitutional advocates prize majority rule, they must remain skeptical about whether the majority is always right.

Thomas Jefferson, author of the Declaration of Independence, third president of the United States, and founder of the University of Virginia.

Constitutional democracy requires constant attention to protecting the rights and opinions of others, to ensure that our democratic processes serve the principles of liberty, equality, and justice. Thus a peculiar blend of faith and skepticism is warranted when dealing with the will of the people.

Constitutional democracy means government by representative politicians. A central feature of democracy is that those who hold power do so only by winning a free election. In our political system, the fragmentation of powers requires elected officials to mediate among factions, build coalitions, and work out compromises among and within the branches of our government to produce policy and action. We expect our politicians to operate within the rules of democracy, and to be honest, humble, patriotic, compassionate, sensitive to the needs of others, well informed, competent, fair-minded, self-confident, and inspirational. We want politicians, in other words, to be perfect, to have all the answers, and to have all the "correct" values (as we perceive them). We want them to solve our problems, yet we also make them scapegoats for the things we dislike about government: taxes, regulations, hard times, and limits on our freedom. Many of these ideals are unrealistic, and no one could live up to all of them. Like all people, politicians live in a world in which perfection may be the goal, but compromise, ambition, fund raising, and self-promotion are necessary.

U.S. citizens will never be satisfied with their political candidates and politicians. The ideal politician is probably a myth, because no one could please everyone and make conflict disappear without asking us to make sacrifices. Politicians become "ideal" only when they are dead. Politicians and candidates, as well as the people they represent, all have different ideas about what is best for the nation. Indeed, liberty invites disagreements over ideology and values. That's why we have politics, candidates, opposition parties, heated political debates, and elections.

Defining Democracy

The word "democracy" is nowhere to be found in the Declaration of Independence or in the U.S. Constitution, nor was it a term the founders used. It is both an ancient term and a modern one. When this nation was founded, *democracy* was used to describe undesirable groups and conditions: mobs, lack of standards, and a system that encouraged leaders to gain power by appealing to the emotions and prejudices of the rabble.

The distinguishing feature of democracy is that government derives its authority from its citizens. In fact, the word comes from two Greek words: *demos,* "the people," and *kratos,* "authority" or "power." Thus **democracy** means *government by the people,* not government by one person (a monarch, dictator, or priest) or government by the few (an oligarchy or aristocracy).

democracy
Government by the people, both directly or indirectly, with free and frequent elections.

YOU WILL DECIDE

Should the United States Adopt a National Initiative Process?

Even though more than half the states have some form of initiative or popular referendum in which voters can petition to vote directly on policy issues, the national government does not provide for such a process. Voters in many other democracies directly ratify constitutional changes like our constitutional amendments in a national election.

Ancient Athens, a few other Greek city-states, and the Roman Republic had a **direct democracy** in which citizens assembled to discuss and pass laws and select their officials. Most of these Greek city-states and the Roman Republic degenerated into mob rule and then resorted to dictators or rule by aristocrats. When the word "democracy" came into use in English in the seventeenth century, it denoted power wielded by an unruly mob. It was a term of derision, a negative word.

LEARNING OBJECTIVE

2 Differentiate democracy from other forms of government.

In 1787, James Madison, in *The Federalist*, No. 10, reflected the view of many of the framers of the U.S. Constitution when he wrote, "Such democracies [as the Greek and Roman] . . . have ever been found incompatible with personal security, or the rights of property; and have in general been as short in their lives, as they have been violent in their deaths" (*The Federalist*, No. 10, is reprinted in the Appendix at the back of this book). Madison feared that empowering citizens to decide policy directly would be dangerous to freedom, minorities, and property, and would result in violence by one group against another.

direct democracy
Government in which citizens vote on laws and select officials directly.

Over time our democracy has increasingly combined representative and direct democracy. The most important examples of direct democracy were added roughly a century ago and include the direct primary, in which voters select who may run for office; the initiative and referendum, which allow citizens to vote on state laws or constitutional amendments; and the recall, which lets voters remove state and local elected officials from office between elections. Initiatives and referendums have been used frequently, and 2003 saw the first governor recalled in 82 years when California voters replaced Gray Davis with Arnold Schwarzenegger. Once in office, Governor Schwarzenegger attempted to govern by taking policy disputes directly to the voters. For example, he pressed for a special election in 2005 to decide four ballot initiatives. The voters roundly defeated all four measures, and Schwarzenegger later stated that thereafter he "would rely far less on campaigns and ballot fights as a governing strategy."[2] He also said, "If I were to do another *Terminator* movie, I would have the Terminator travel back in time to tell Arnold not to have a special election."[3]

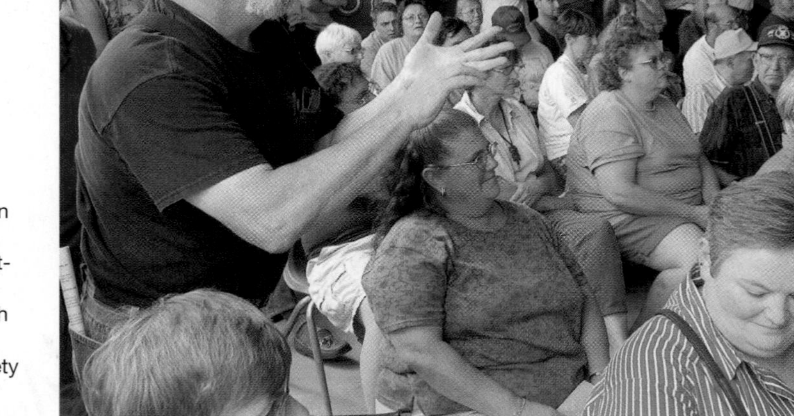

A New Hampshire man speaks at a local town meeting. Since Colonial times, many local governments in New England have held meetings in which all community members are invited to attend and discuss their opinions with public officials. In some cases, community members meet once a year to vote on a variety of issues that will affect their town over the following year.

Today it is no longer possible, even if it were desirable, to assemble the citizens of any but the smallest towns to make their laws or select their officials directly. Rather, we have invented a system of representation. Democracy today means **representative democracy,** or a *republic,* in which those who have governmental authority get and retain that power directly or indirectly by winning free elections in which all adult citizens are allowed to participate. The framers used the term "republic" to avoid any confusion between direct democracy, which they disliked, and representative democracy, which they liked and thought secured all the advantages of a direct democracy while curing its weaknesses.

Many of the ideas that came to be part of the Constitution can be traced to philosophers' writings—in some cases centuries before the American Revolution and the constitutional convention. Among those philosophers the framers would have read and been influenced by were Aristotle, Hobbes, Locke, and Montesquieu. Aristotle, a Greek philosopher writing in the fourth century BC, had provided important ideas on a political unit called a state, but also on the idea of a constitution, and on various forms of governing.[4] John Locke, an English philosopher, also profoundly influenced the authors of the Declaration of Independence and Constitution. Locke rejected the idea that kings had a divine right to rule, advocated a constitutional democracy, and provided a philosophic justification for revolution.[5] Locke, like his fellow Englishman Thomas Hobbes, asserted that there was a social contract whereby people formed governments for security and to avoid what he called the state of nature, where chaos existed and where "everyone was against everyone."[6]

In defining democracy, we need to clarify other terms. **Constitutional democracy** refers to a government in which individuals exercise governmental power as the result of winning free and relatively frequent elections. *It is a government in which there are recognized, enforced limits on the powers of all governmental officials.* It also generally includes a written set of governmental rules and procedures—a constitution. The idea that constitutional provisions can limit power by having another part of the government balance or check it is one more good example of how the founders applied ideas from earlier thinkers—in this case, the French philosopher Charles de Montesquieu.[7]

Constitutionalism is a term we apply to arrangements—checks and balances, federalism, separation of powers, rule of law, due process, a bill of rights—that require our leaders to listen, think, bargain, and explain before they make laws, in order to prevent them from abusing power. We then hold them politically and legally accountable for the way they exercise their powers.

Like most political concepts, democracy encompasses many ideas and has many meanings. It is a way of life, a form of government, a way of governing, a type of nation, a state of mind, and a variety of processes. We can divide these many meanings of democracy into three broad categories: a system of interacting values, a system of interrelated political processes, and a system of interdependent political structures.

THINKING IT THROUGH

Involving voters directly in the process of deciding public policy is appealing and consistent with the move toward direct democracy the United States has experienced over the past century. Such votes may help legitimate major constitutional changes by demonstrating voter approval of them, and if a petition process were permitted, citizens could directly put before their fellow voters whatever constitutional changes they wanted. Letting the voters decide legislation and constitutional changes instead of relying on Congress could engage more voters in politics and alleviate the low regard some have for Congress.

What might voters decide under such a reform? They could, for example, petition to change the Senate so that instead of two senators, each state have a minimum of one and the remainder be apportioned by population. Others might petition to institute mandatory school prayer, or to legalize medicinal marijuana as a guaranteed constitutional right. Do these possibilities affect your answer? Should some questions be out of bounds? If so, who decides? In most of the United States these kinds of issues are decided by courts, but that puts courts in a politically charged position. Is that a good idea?

Although letting voters decide policy questions is an extension of direct democracy, in practice the initiative and referendum may actually impede representative democracy. Congress and the president may evade tough issues by waiting for someone to put them to a vote of the people. An initiative also forces a "yes" or "no" vote and compromise is not possible. Who decides how the question will be worded? How many signatures would be required to place a measure on the ballot? How many initiatives or referendums can we put before the voters in any single election?

When it comes to implementing a successful initiative or referendum, does that vote supersede the Constitution itself? Could the Supreme Court declare a national initiative unconstitutional, or is the vote of the people the final word on a matter? How would Congress and the president allocate tax money for implementing an initiative? The authors of our Constitution clearly preferred a more representative and deliberative form of democracy to the initiative. What were their reservations about direct democracy, and were they correct?

Questions

1. Who should word the question put to voters in a referendum, and what effect does the way a question is worded have on the process?
2. Could a majority group vote to limit the rights of a minority in a referendum?
3. How is voters deciding a referendum different from legislators deciding legislation?

representative democracy
Government in which the people elect those who govern and pass laws; also called a *republic*.

constitutional democracy
Government that enforces recognized limits on those who govern and allows the voice of the people to be heard through free, fair, and relatively frequent elections.

constitutionalism
The set of arrangements, including checks and balances, federalism, separation of powers, rule of law, due process, and a bill of rights, that requires our leaders to listen, think, bargain, and explain before they act or make laws. We then hold them politically and legally accountable for how they exercise their powers.

Before we begin our discussion of these three categories, let's outline the conditions necessary to foster constitutional democracy.

Conditions Conducive to Constitutional Democracy

Although it is hard to specify the precise conditions essential for establishing and preserving a democracy, and it does not always flourish, we can identify some patterns that foster its growth.

LEARNING **OBJECTIVE**

3 Identify the conditions that help democracy flourish and explain why they do so.

Educational Conditions The exercise of voting privileges requires an educated citizenry. But a high level of education (measured by the number of high school diplomas and university degrees granted) does not guarantee democratic government, as the examples of Nazi Germany and the Soviet Union, where many had these credentials, illustrate. And in some democracies, such as India, many people are illiterate. Still, voting makes little sense unless many of the voters can read and write and express their interests and opinions. The poorly educated and illiterate often get left out in a democracy. Direct democracy puts a further premium on education. Better-educated persons are better able to understand and participate in policy making through initiatives and referendums.[8]

Economic Conditions A relatively prosperous nation, with an equitable distribution of wealth, provides the best context for democracy. Starving people are more interested in food than in voting. Where economic power is concentrated, political power is also likely to be concentrated; thus well-to-do nations have a better chance of sustaining democratic governments than do those with widespread poverty. As a result, the prospects for an enduring democracy are greater in Canada or France than in Zimbabwe or Egypt, for example.

Private ownership of property and a market economy are also related to the creation and maintenance of democratic institutions. Democracies can range from heavily regulated economies with public ownership of many enterprises, such as Sweden, to those in which there is little government regulation of the marketplace, such as the United States. But there are no democracies with a highly centralized, government-run economy and little private ownership of property, although many authoritarian nations like Oman or Saudi Arabia have a market economy. There are no truly democratic communist states, nor have there ever been any.

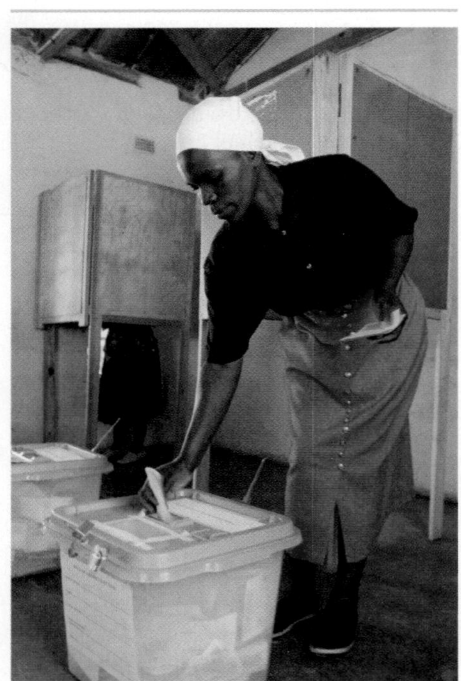

A woman casts her vote in Harare, Zimbabwe, where long lines formed at the polling stations hours before they opened.

Social Conditions Economic development generally makes democracy possible, yet proper social conditions are necessary to make it real.[9] In a society fragmented into warring groups that fiercely disagree on fundamental issues, government by discussion and compromise is difficult, as we have seen in Afghanistan and Iraq. When ideologically separated groups consider the issues at stake to be vital, they may prefer to fight rather than accept the verdict of the ballot box, as happened in the United States in 1861 with the outbreak of the Civil War.

In a society that consists of many overlapping associations and groupings, however, individuals are less likely to identify completely with a single group and give their allegiance to it. For example, Joe Smith is a Baptist, an African American, a southerner, a Democrat, an electrician, and a member of the National Rifle Association, and he makes $50,000 a year. On some issues, Joe thinks as a Baptist, on others as a southerner, and on still others as an African American. Sue Jones is a Catholic, a white Republican, a real estate agent, and a member of the National Organization for Women (NOW); she comes from a Polish background, and she makes $150,000 a year. Sometimes she acts as a Republican, sometimes as a real estate agent, and sometimes as a member of NOW. Jones and Smith differ on some issues and agree on others. In general, the differences between them are not likely to be greater than their common interest in maintaining a democracy.[10]

Ideological Conditions American adults have basic beliefs about power, government, and political practices—beliefs that arise from the educational, economic, and social conditions of their individual experience. From these conditions must also develop a

GENERATION **NEXT**

For Better or Worse?

Ask yourself the same question a national sample of young adults was asked in the 2006 Generation Next Survey (conducted by the Pew Research Center for the People and the Press): "In which of these areas do you think young adults in your age group (18–25) have it better and in which areas did young adults 20 years ago have it better?" Respondents were asked this question with specific reference to getting a job, living in an exciting time, having sexual freedom, enjoying financial security, bringing about social change, buying a house, and having opportunities to get a good education.

Most 18- to 26-year-olds see themselves as better off than the generation of 20 years ago in getting high-paying jobs, living in exciting times, having sexual freedom, and having opportunities to get a good education.

Generation Next is divided on whether today's 18- to 26-year-olds have it better in terms of financial security, with 48 percent saying today is better and 44 percent thinking it was better 20 years ago. For example, today's 18- to 26-year-olds see their generation as less able to buy a house than was the case for the same age group 20 years ago.

One item on which Generation Next disagrees along racial lines is whether today's generation has done more to bring about social change than yesterday's generation did. Almost as many of today's African Americans (45 percent) feel they have done more to bring about social change than those who feel yesterday's generation did (48 percent). Overall, 56 percent of Generation Next felt it was better at bringing about social change than the last generation.

The fact that today's generation sees educational opportunities as better for their generation suggests that this foundation of democracy remains strong. However, concerns about buying a house and achieving financial security raise questions about the economic confidence that helps sustain democracy. Although these may be short-term worries, they constitute a potential future challenge to democratic stability.

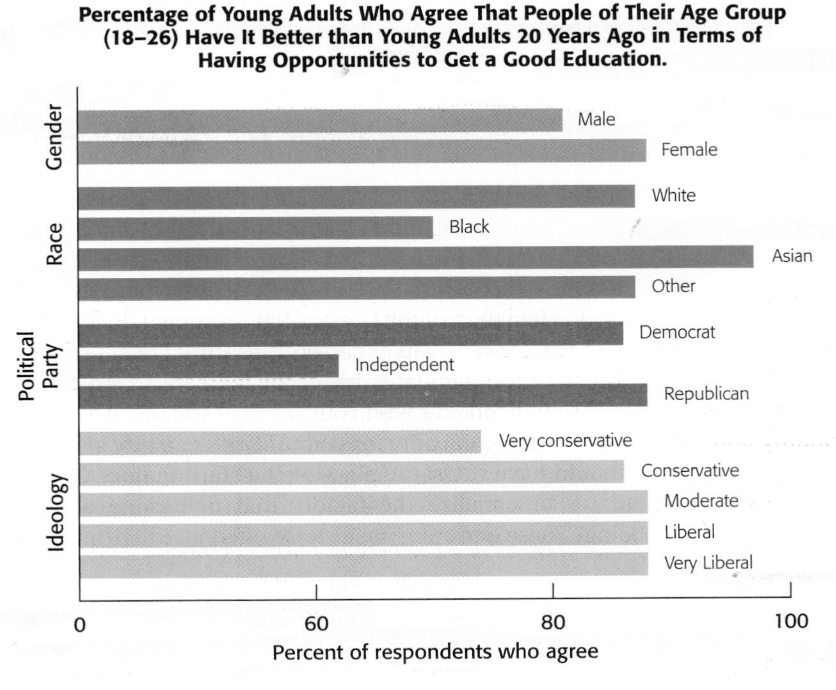

QUESTIONS

1. How does education enhance support for democracy? What are you learning while getting a college education that is relevant to active citizenship?
2. Why is economic opportunity important to sustaining democracy?

general acceptance of the ideals of democracy, and a willingness of a substantial number of people to agree to proceed democratically. This acceptance is sometimes called the *democratic consensus.* Widely accepted ideals of democracy include one person, one vote; majority rule; freedom of speech; and freedom of assembly.

Democracy as a System of Interacting Values

A constitutional democracy is strengthened by an educated and prosperous public that has confidence in its ability to work out differences in the political process. A set of interacting values, the first of the three ways we can look at a democracy, provides a foundation for that public confidence. Belief in representative democracy may be as near a universal faith as the world has today. Respect for human dignity, freedom, liberty, individual rights, and other democratic values are widespread. Personal liberty, respect for the individual, equality of opportunity, and popular consent are at the core of democratic values.

LEARNING **OBJECTIVE**

4 Explain the importance to successful democracy of values, political processes, and political structures.

Personal Liberty Liberty has been the single most important value in U.S. history. It was for "life, liberty, and the pursuit of happiness" that independence was declared; it was to "secure the Blessings of Liberty" that the Constitution was drawn up and adopted. Even our patriotic songs extol the "sweet land of liberty." The essence of liberty is *self-determination,* meaning that all individuals must have the opportunity to realize their own goals. Liberty is not simply the absence of external restraint on a person (freedom *from* something); it is also a person's freedom and capacity to reach his or her goals (freedom *to* do something). Moreover, both history and reason suggest that individual liberty is the key to social progress. The greater the people's freedom, the greater is the chance of discovering better ways of life.

Respect for the Individual Popular rule in a democracy flows from a belief that every person has the potential for common sense, rationality, and fairness. Individuals have important rights; collectively, those rights are the source of all legitimate governmental authority and power. These concepts pervade democratic thought. They are woven into the writings of Thomas Jefferson, especially in the Declaration of Independence: "All men . . . are endowed by their Creator with certain unalienable rights." (The Declaration of Independence is reprinted in the Appendix.) Constitutional democracies make the *person*—rich or poor, black or white, male or female—the central measure of value.

Not all political systems put the individual first. Some promote **statism,** a form of government based on centralized authority and control, especially over the economy. China, Vietnam, and Cuba, for example, take this approach. In a modern democracy, the nation, or even the community, is less important than the individuals who compose it.

Equality of Opportunity The democratic value of *equality* enhances the importance of the individual: "All men are created equal and from that equal creation they derive rights inherent and unalienable, among which are the preservation of liberty and the pursuit of happiness." So reads Jefferson's first draft of the Declaration of Independence, and the words indicate the primacy of the concept. The nineteenth-century French statesman Alexis de Tocqueville and other foreign students of American democracy were all struck by the strength of egalitarian thought and practice in our political and social lives.

But what does equality mean? And equality for whom? Does equality of opportunity mean that everyone should have the same place at the starting line? Or does it mean that society should try to equalize the factors that determine a person's economic or social well-being? These enduring issues arise often in American politics.

Popular Consent The animating principle of the American Revolution, the Declaration of Independence, and the resulting new nation was **popular consent,** the idea that a just government must derive its powers from the *consent of the people it governs.* A commitment to democracy thus means that a community must be willing to participate and make decisions in government. These principles sound unobjectionable, but in practice they mean that people must be willing to lose when more people vote the other way.

Democratic Values in Conflict The basic values of democracy do not always coexist happily. Individualism may conflict with the collective welfare or the public good. Self-determination may conflict with equal opportunity. A media outlet's freedom to publish classified documents about foreign or defense policy may conflict with the government's constitutional requirement to "provide for the common defense."

Much of our political combat revolves around how to strike a balance among democratic values. How, for example, do we protect the Declaration of Independence's unalienable rights of life, liberty, and the pursuit of happiness while trying to "form," as the Constitution announces, "a more perfect Union, establish Justice, insure domestic Tranquility, provide for the common defense, promote the general Welfare, and secure the Blessings of Liberty to ourselves and our Posterity"? (See the Preamble to the Constitution at the end of Chapter 2.) Over the years, despite occasional setbacks, the U.S. political system has moved toward greater freedom for individuals and more democracy.

statism
The idea that the rights of the nation are supreme over the rights of the individuals who make up the nation.

popular consent
The idea that a just government must derive its powers from the consent of the people it governs.

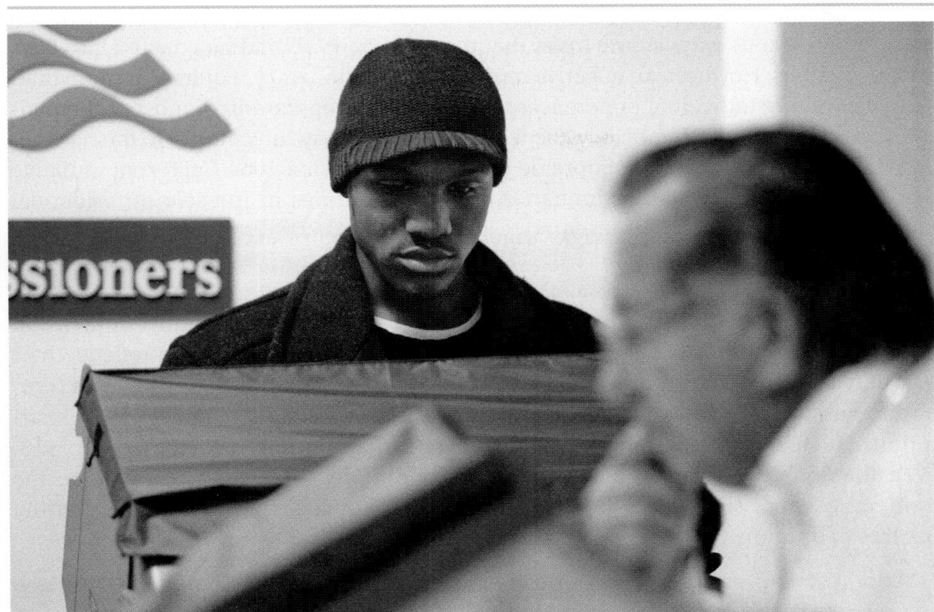

A student from Chicago casts an early vote in the 2008 Illinois presidential primary.

Democracy as a System of Interrelated Political Processes

In addition to meeting a few key conditions and having a consensus of core democratic values, a successful, democratic government requires a well-defined political process as well as a stable governmental structure. To make democratic values a reality, a nation must incorporate them into its political process, most importantly in the form of free and fair elections, majority rule, freedom of expression, and the right of its citizens to peaceably assemble and protest.

Free and Fair Elections Democratic government is based on free and fair elections held at intervals frequent enough to make them relevant to policy choices. Elections are one of the most important devices for keeping officials and representatives accountable to the voters.

Crucial to modern-day definitions of democracy is the idea that opposition political parties can exist, can run candidates in elections, and have a chance to replace those who currently hold public office. Thus *political competition and choice* are crucial to the existence of democracy. Although many agree that all citizens should have equal voting power, free and fair elections do not imply that everyone must or will have equal political influence. Some people, because of wealth, talent, or position, inevitably have more influence than others. How much they should be allowed to exercise it is frequently debated. But in an election, each citizen—president or plumber, corporate CEO or ditchdigger—casts only one vote.

Majority and Plurality Rule **Majority rule**—governance according to the expressed preferences of the majority—is a basic rule of democracy. The **majority** candidate or party is the one that receives *more than half* the votes and so wins the election and takes charge of the government until the next election. In practice, however, majority rule is often **plurality** rule, in which the candidate or party with the *most* votes wins the election, even though it may not have received more than half the votes because votes were divided among three or more candidates or parties. About a third of our presidents have won with pluralities in the popular vote rather than majorities.[11] Once elected, officials do not have a right to curtail the attempts of political minorities to use all peaceful means to become the new majority. Even as the winners take power, the losers are at work trying to get it back at the next election.[12]

majority rule
Governance according to the expressed preferences of the majority.

majority
The candidate or party that wins more than half the votes cast in an election.

plurality
The candidate or party with the most votes cast in an election, not necessarily more than half.

Should the side with the most votes always prevail? American citizens answer this question in various ways. Some insist that majority views should be enacted into laws and regulations. However, an effective representative democracy requires far more than simply counting individual preferences and implementing the will of most of the people. In a constitutional democracy, the will of a majority may run counter to the rights of individuals. For example, the Supreme Court struck down a 1964 California initiative that would have allowed discrimination against minorities in the sale of residential housing.[13] Legislating in a representative democracy is a complicated and often untidy process in which the people and their agents debate, compromise, and arrive at a decision only after thoughtful deliberation.

The framers of the U.S. Constitution wanted to guard society against oppression of any one faction of the people by any other faction. The Constitution reflects their fear of tyranny by majorities, especially momentary majorities that spring from temporary passions. They insulated certain rights (such as freedom of speech) and institutions (such as the Supreme Court and, until the Constitution was changed in 1913, even the Senate) from popular choice. Effective representation of the people, the framers insisted, should not be based solely on parochial interests or the shifting breezes of opinion.

Freedom of Expression Free and fair elections depend on voters having access to facts, competing ideas, and the views of candidates. This means that competing, nongovernment-owned newspapers, radio stations, and television stations must be allowed to flourish. If the government controls what is said and how it is said, elections cannot be free and fair and there is no democracy. We examine free expression in greater detail in Chapter 15.

The Right to Assemble and Protest Citizens must be free to organize for political purposes. Obviously, individuals can be more effective if they join with others in a party, a pressure group, a protest movement, or a demonstration. The right to oppose the government, to form opposition parties, and to have a chance to defeat incumbents is a defining characteristic of a democracy.

Democracy as a System of Interdependent Political Structures

Democracy is, of course, more than the values and processes we've discussed so far. Its third characteristic is political structures that safeguard these values and processes. The Constitution and its first ten amendments—the Bill of Rights—set up an ingenious structure that both grants and checks government power. A system of political parties, interest groups, media, and other institutions that intercede between the electorate and those who govern reinforces this constitutional structure and thus help maintain democratic stability.

The U.S. constitutional system has five distinctive elements: *federalism,* the division of powers between the national and state governments; *separation of powers* among the executive, judicial, and legislative branches; *bicameralism,* the division of legislative power between the House of Representatives and the Senate; *checks and balances* in which each branch is given the constitutional means, the political independence, and the motives to check the powers of the other branches so that a relative balance of power between the branches endures; and a judicially enforceable, written, explicit *Bill of Rights* that provides a guarantee of individual liberties and due process before the law.

We've now discussed the conditions conducive to viable constitutional democracy, as well as the values, political processes, and political structures that help foster it. These provide a foundation on which we can assess governments around the world, as well as the extraordinary story of the founding and enlargement of constitutional democracy in the United States, to which we turn next.

The Roots of the American Constitutional Experiment

Most of us probably consider the natural order of history democracy and a constitution. We take pride in our ability to make it work, yet we have essentially inherited a functioning system, the work of others, nine or ten generations ago. Yet our job is not just to keep it going, but to improve it and adapt it to the challenges of our times. To do so, however, we must first understand it by recalling our democratic and constitutional roots.

The Colonial Beginnings

Our democratic experiment might well have failed. The 13 original states (formerly colonies) were independent and could have gone their separate ways. Differences between them, based on social and economic conditions, especially the southern states' dependence on slavery, were an obvious challenge to unity. Religious, ethnic, and racial diversity, which frustrate so many governments around the world today, also existed in the early United States.

Given these potential problems, how did democracy survive? The framers of the Constitution had experience to guide them. For almost two centuries, Europeans had been sailing to the New World in search of liberty—especially religious liberty—as well as land and work. In 1620, while still aboard the *Mayflower,* the Pilgrims had drawn up a compact to protect their religious freedom and to make possible "just and equal laws." The experience of settling a new land, overcoming obstacles, and enjoying the fruits of their labors was also important to the spirit of independence in the colonies.[14]

LEARNING **OBJECTIVE**

5 Show how politics before 1787 shaped the Constitution.

But freedom in the colonies was limited. The Puritans in Massachusetts established a **theocracy,** a system of government in which religious leaders claimed divine guidance and in which other sects were denied religious liberty. Later, as that system was challenged, the Puritans continued to worry "about what would maintain order in a society lacking an established church, an attachment to place, and the uncontested leadership of men of merit."[15] Nine of the 13 colonies eventually set up a state church. Throughout the 1700s, Puritans in Massachusetts barred certain men from voting on the basis of church membership. Women, slaves, and Native Americans could not vote at all.

By the 1700s, editors in the colonies found they could speak freely in their newspapers, dissenters could distribute leaflets, and agitators could protest in taverns or in the streets. And yet dissenters were occasionally exiled, imprisoned, and even executed, and some printers were beaten and had their shops closed. In short, the colonists struggled with the balance between unity and diversity, stability and dissent, order and liberty.

The Rise of Revolutionary Fervor

As resentment against British rule mounted during the 1770s and revolutionary fervor rose, the colonists became determined to fight the British to win their rights and liberties. In 1776, a year after the fighting broke out in Massachusetts, the Declaration of Independence proclaimed in ringing tones that all men are created equal, endowed by their Creator with certain unalienable rights; that among them are "life, liberty, and the pursuit of happiness"; that to secure those rights, governments are instituted among men; and that whenever a government becomes destructive of those ends, it is the right of the people to alter or abolish it. (Read the full text of the Declaration of Independence in the Appendix.)

We have heard these great ideals so often that we take them for granted. Revolutionary leaders did not. They were deadly serious about these rights and willing to fight and pledge their lives, fortunes, and sacred honor for them. Indeed, by signing

theocracy
Government by religious leaders, who claim divine guidance.

The American Revolutionary War was waged by militias and volunteers who overcame many challenges to prevail.

the Declaration of Independence they were effectively signing their own death warrants if the Revolution failed.[16] In most cases, state constitutions guaranteed free speech, freedom of religion, and the natural rights to life, liberty, and property. All their constitutions spelled out the rights of persons accused of crime, such as knowing the nature of the accusation, confronting their accusers, and receiving a timely and public trial by jury.[17] Moreover, these guarantees were set out *in writing,* in sharp contrast to the unwritten British constitution.

Toward Unity and Order

As the war against the British widened to include all 13 colonies, the need arose for a stronger central government to unite them. In 1777 Congress established a new national government, the Confederation, under a written document called the **Articles of Confederation**.[18] Though they were established in 1777, the Articles were not approved by all the state legislatures until 1781, after Washington's troops had been fighting for six years.

The Confederation was more like a fragile league of friendship than a national government. There was no national executive, judiciary, or coinage. Congress had to work through the states and had no direct authority over citizens. It could not levy taxes, regulate trade between the states or with other nations, or prevent the states from taxing each other's goods or issuing their own currencies. The lack of a judicial system meant that the national government had to rely on state courts to enforce national laws and settle disputes between the states. In practice, state courts could overturn national laws. Moreover, with the end of the Revolutionary War in 1783, the sense of urgency that had produced unity among the states began to fade. Conflicts between states and between creditors and debtors within the various states grew intense. Foreign threats continued; territories ruled by England and Spain surrounded the weak new nation. As pressures on the Confederation mounted, many leaders became convinced that a more powerful central government was needed to create a union strong enough to deal with internal diversity and factionalism and to resist external threats.

Articles of Confederation
The first governing document of the confederated states, drafted in 1777, ratified in 1781, and replaced by the present Constitution in 1789.

Annapolis Convention
A convention held in September 1786 to consider problems of trade and navigation, attended by five states and important because it issued the call to Congress and the states for what became the Constitutional Convention.

In September 1786, under the leadership of Alexander Hamilton, supporters of a truly national government took advantage of the **Annapolis Convention**—a meeting in Annapolis, Maryland, on problems of trade and navigation attended by delegates from five states—to issue a call for a convention to consider basic amendments to the Articles of Confederation. The delegates were to meet in Philadelphia on the second Monday of May 1787, "to devise such further provisions as shall appear to them necessary to render the Constitution of the Federal Government adequate to the exigencies of the Union."[19] This meeting became the **Constitutional Convention.**

For a short time, all was quiet. Then, late in 1786, messengers rode into George Washington's plantation at Mount Vernon in Virginia with the kind of news he and other leaders had dreaded. Farmers in western Massachusetts, crushed by debts and taxes, were rebelling against foreclosures, forcing judges out of their courtrooms, and freeing debtors from jails. As a patriot and a wealthy landowner, Washington was appalled. "What, gracious God, is man?" he exclaimed.

Not all reacted as Washington did to what became known as **Shays' Rebellion** (named for Daniel Shays, its leader). When Abigail Adams, the politically knowledgeable wife of John Adams, the Revolutionary statesman from Massachusetts, sent news of the rebellion to Thomas Jefferson, the Virginian replied, "I like a little rebellion now and then," noting also that the "tree of liberty must be refreshed from time to time with the blood of patriots and tyrants. It is its natural manure."[20] But the rebellion highlighted the lack of a mechanism to enforce contractual obligations in the absence of a strong central government. Some, like historian Charles A. Beard, have argued that the primary motive of the authors of the U.S. Constitution was the protection of their economic interests more than a concern for other values.[21] Beard's views have been challenged.[22] Most agree that while the early leaders of the United States were protecting their own economic interests, that was not their only motive.

Shays' Rebellion petered out after the farmers attacked an arsenal and were cut down by cannon fire. The uprising had threatened prosperity, the established order, and the rule of law, and reinforced the view that a stronger national government was needed. Congress issued a cautiously worded call to all the state legislatures to appoint delegates for the "sole and express purpose of revising the Articles of Confederation."[23] The call for a convention specified that no recommendation would be effective unless approved by Congress and confirmed by all the state legislatures, as provided by the Articles.

The Constitutional Convention of 1787

The delegates who assembled in Philadelphia in May 1787 had to establish a national government powerful enough to prevent the young nation from dissolving but not so powerful that it would crush individual liberty. What these men did continues to have a major impact on how we are governed. It also provides an outstanding lesson in political science for the world.

The Delegates

The various states appointed 74 delegates, but only 55 arrived in Philadelphia. Of these, approximately 40 actually took part in the work of the convention. It was a distinguished gathering. Many of the most important men of the nation were there: successful merchants, planters, bankers, lawyers, and former and present governors and congressional representatives (39 of the delegates had served in Congress). Most had read the classics of political thought. Most had experience constructing local and state governments. Many had also worked hard to create and direct the national confederation of the states. And the Constitutional Convention also included eight of the 56 signers of the Declaration of Independence.

The convention was as representative as most political gatherings were at the time: The participants were all white male landowners. These well-read, well-fed,

Constitutional Convention
The convention in Philadelphia, from May 25 to September 17, 1787, that debated and agreed on the Constitution of the United States.

Shays' Rebellion
A rebellion led by Daniel Shays of farmers in western Massachusetts in 1786–1787 protesting mortgage foreclosures. It highlighted the need for a strong national government just as the call for the Constitutional Convention went out.

HISTORY MAKERS

Alexander Hamilton and James Madison

In the Constitution of the United States, the framers offered perhaps the most brilliant example of collective intellectual genius combining theory and practice in the history of the Western world. How could a country so sparsely populated by today's standards produce several dozen men of genius who met in Philadelphia, not to mention another hundred or so equally talented political thinkers who did not attend? The lives of two prominent delegates, Alexander Hamilton and James Madison, help explain the origins of this collective genius.

Alexander Hamilton (1757–1804) came to the United States from the West Indies and while still a college student won national attention for his brilliant pamphlets in defense of the Revolutionary cause. During the war, he served as General Washington's aide, and his experiences confirmed his distaste for a Congress so weak it could not even supply the Revolution's troops with enough food or arms. He was the engineer of the Annapolis Convention, and as early as 1778, he had been urging that the national government be made stronger.

James Madison (1751–1836) helped frame Virginia's first constitution in 1780 and served both in the Virginia Assembly and in the Continental Congress. Madison was also a leader of those who favored a stronger national government.

Like most of the other framers, Hamilton and Madison were superbly educated. Both had extensive private tutoring—a one-to-one teacher–student ratio. Like scores of other thinkers of the day, both also had wide practical experience in religion, politics, and government.

Both men were also "moral philosophers." They had strong views on the supreme value of liberty as well as on current issues. Instead of simply sermonizing about liberty, they analyzed it; they debated what liberty meant, how to protect it, and how to expand it.

Alexander Hamilton.

James Madison.

QUESTIONS

1. Do we have exceptional leaders like Hamilton and Madison today? How were the framers of the Constitution different from today's politicians?
2. How did Hamilton and Madison's education and experience help them be more creative and combine theory with practice in their role as political inventors?

well-bred, and often well-wed delegates were mainly state or national leaders, for in the 1780s, ordinary people were not likely to participate in politics. (Even today, farm laborers, factory workers, and truck drivers are seldom found in Congress, although a haberdasher, a peanut farmer, and a movie actor have made their way to the White House.)

Although active in the movement to revise the Articles of Confederation, George Washington had been reluctant to attend the convention and accepted only when persuaded that his prestige was needed for its success. He was selected unanimously to preside over the meetings. According to the records, he spoke only twice during the deliberations, yet his influence was felt in the informal gatherings as well as during the sessions. Everyone understood that Washington favored a more powerful central government led by a president. In fact, the general expectation that he would be the first president played a crucial role in the creation of the presidency. "No one feared that he would misuse power.... His genuine hesitancy, his reluctance to assume the position, only served to reinforce the almost universal desire that he do so."[24]

To encourage everyone to speak freely and allow delegates to change their minds after debate and discussion, the proceedings of the convention were kept secret and delegates were forbidden to discuss them with outsiders. The delegates also knew that if word of the inevitable disagreements got out, it would provide ammunition for the many enemies of the convention.

THE CHANGING FACE OF U.S. POLITICS

The Constitutional Convention

If the Constitutional Convention were convened today, how would the delegates compare to the all-white, all-male, property-owning delegates who drafted the Constitution in Philadelphia in 1787? One likely similarity is that they would be successful and generally well-educated individuals willing to engage in public service.

Many of those who drafted the Constitution had served in state legislatures. If the Constitutional Convention were held today and included state legislators, it would be much more diverse. Almost 25 percent of state legislators are now female on average, including at least a third in Maryland, Delaware, Arizona, Colorado, Kansas, Nevada, and Vermont. At the same time, state legislatures remain almost entirely white—only 9 percent were African American in 2007, and just 3 percent were Hispanic.

Many of those who drafted the Constitution were also lawyers and successful business managers. If the Constitutional Convention were held today and included these professions, the proportion of women participating would be between 35 and 40 percent, and 15 percent of the delegates would not be white.* Although these proportions show a growing diversity among the delegates who might be called to Philadelphia today, they do not yet reflect the diversity of the population at large.

QUESTIONS

1. How would the recent changes in U.S. demographics translate into changes in the content of any constitution produced by a Constitutional Convention held today?
2. Why are lawyers disproportionately represented in politics, both today and at the Constitutional Convention? What difference does having so many lawyers as constitution makers have on the process and on the document they produce?

*U.S. Equal Employment Opportunity Commission, "Diversity in Law Firms," www.eeoc.gov/stats/reports/diversitylaw/index.html.

Consensus

The Constitutional Convention is usually discussed in terms of its three famous compromises: the compromise between large and small states over representation in Congress, the compromise between North and South over the regulation and taxation of foreign commerce, and the compromise between North and South over the counting of slaves for the purposes of taxation and representation. There were other important compromises. Yet on many significant issues, most of the delegates were in agreement.

All the delegates publicly supported a republican form of government based on elected representatives of the people. This was the only form the convention seriously

Representing different constituencies and different ideologies, the Constitutional Convention devised a totally new form of government that provided for a central government strong enough to rule but still responsible to its citizens and to the member states.

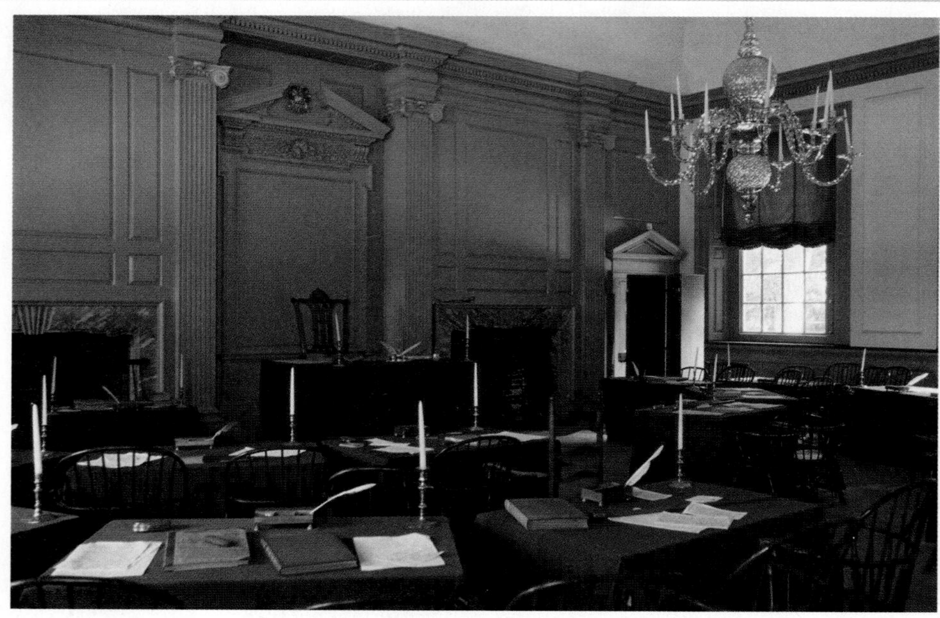

The Assembly Room of Independence Hall in Philadelphia, Pennsylvania.

considered and the only form acceptable to the nation. Equally important, all the delegates opposed arbitrary and unrestrained government.

Most of the delegates were in favor of *balanced government* in which no single interest would dominate, and in which the national government would be strong enough to protect property and business from outbreaks like Shays' Rebellion.

Benjamin Franklin, the 81-year-old delegate from Pennsylvania, favored extending the right to vote to all white males, but most of the delegates believed landowners were the best guardians of liberty. James Madison feared that those without property, if given the right to vote, might combine to deprive property owners of their rights. Delegates agreed in principle on limited voting rights but differed over the kind and amount of property owned as a prerequisite to vote. The framers recognized that they would jeopardize approval of the Constitution if they made the qualifications to vote in federal elections more restrictive than those of the states. As a result, each state was left to determine its own qualifications for electing members of the House of Representatives, the only branch of the national government that was to be elected directly by the voters.

Within five days of its opening, the convention voted—with only the Connecticut delegates dissenting—that "a national government ought to be established consisting of a supreme legislative, executive, and judiciary." This decision profoundly changed the nature of the union, from a loose confederation of states to a true nation.

Few dissented from proposals to give the new Congress all the powers of the old Congress, plus all other powers necessary to ensure that state legislation would not challenge the integrity of the United States. After the delegates agreed on the extensive powers of the legislative branch and the close connection between its lower house and the people, they also agreed that a strong executive, which the Articles of Confederation had lacked, was necessary to provide energy, direction, and a check on the legislature. They also accepted an independent judiciary without much debate. Other issues, however, sparked conflict.

LEARNING **OBJECTIVE**

6 Identify the most important compromises achieved by the delegates to the Constitutional Convention of 1787.

Conflict and Compromise

Serious differences among the various delegates, especially between those from the large and small states, predated the Constitutional Convention. With the success of the War of Independence, the United States gained the formerly British land west of the colonial borders. States with large western borders such as Virginia claimed that their borders

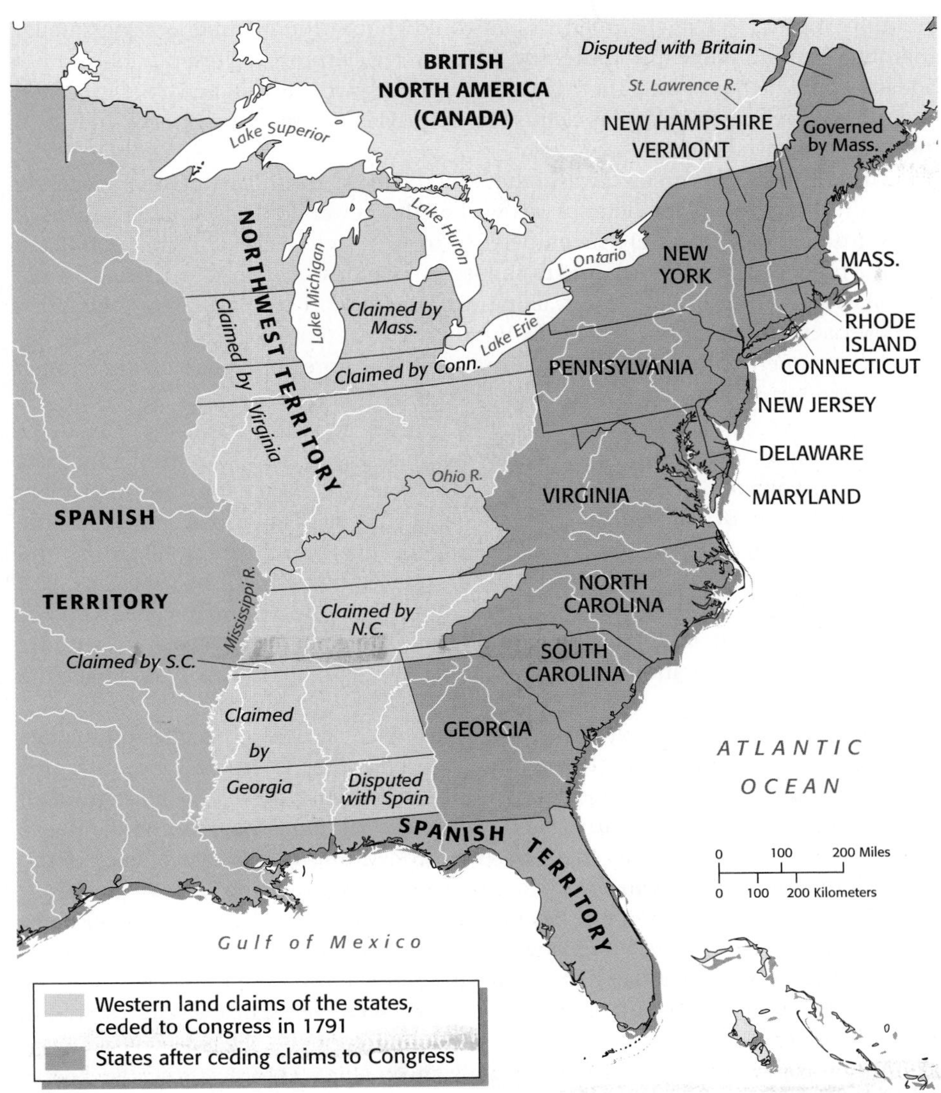

FIGURE 1–1
Western expansion, 1791.

should simply be extended, as depicted in Figure 1–1. Colonies without open Western borders such as New Jersey and Connecticut took exception to these claims, reinforcing the tension between the colonies. The matter was resolved in the Land Ordinance of 1785 and the Northwest Ordinance of 1787, when all states agreed to cede the western lands to the national government and permit them to eventually become part of new states rather than expand the borders of existing states. But the rivalries between the former colonies remained sharp at the convention in Philadelphia in 1787. For example, the large states also favored a strong national government (which they expected to dominate), while delegates from small states were anxious to avoid being dominated.

This tension surfaced in the first discussions of representation in Congress. Franklin favored a single-house national legislature, but most states had had two-chamber legislatures since colonial times, and the delegates were used to this system. **Bicameralism**—the principle of the two-house legislature—reflected delegates' belief in the need for balanced government. The Senate, the smaller chamber, would represent the states and to some extent the wealthier classes, and it would offset the larger, more democratic House of Representatives.

bicameralism
The principle of a two-house legislature.

The Virginia Plan The Virginia delegation took the initiative. They presented 15 resolutions known as the **Virginia Plan.** This called for a strong central government with a legislature composed of two chambers. The voters were to elect the members of

Virginia Plan
The initial proposal at the Constitutional Convention made by the Virginia delegation for a strong central government with a bicameral legislature dominated by the big states.

the more representative chamber, which would choose the members of the smaller chamber from nominees submitted by the state legislatures. Representation in both houses would be based on either wealth or numbers, which would give the wealthier and more populous states—Massachusetts, Pennsylvania, and Virginia—a majority in the national legislature.

The Congress thus created was to have all the legislative power of its predecessor under the Articles of Confederation, as well as the power "to legislate in all cases in which the separate States are incompetent," to veto state legislation that conflicted with the proposed constitution, and to choose a national executive with extensive jurisdiction. A national Supreme Court, along with the executive, would have a qualified veto over acts of Congress. In sum, the Virginia Plan would have created a strong national government with disproportionate power to the more populous states and much less powerful smaller states.

The New Jersey Plan The Virginia Plan dominated the discussion for the first few weeks. That changed when delegates from the small states put forward their plan. William Paterson of New Jersey presented a series of resolutions known as the **New Jersey Plan.** Paterson did not question the need for a strengthened central government, but he was concerned about how this strength might be used. The New Jersey Plan would give Congress the right to tax and regulate commerce and to coerce states, and it would retain the single-house or unicameral legislature (as under the Articles of Confederation) in which each state, regardless of size, would have the same vote.

The New Jersey Plan contained the germ of what eventually came to be a key provision of our Constitution: the *supremacy clause.* The national Supreme Court was to hear appeals from state judges, and the supremacy clause would require all judges—state and national—to treat laws of the national government and the treaties of the United States as superior to the constitutions and laws of each of the states. (Table 1–1 outlines the key features of the Virginia and New Jersey Plans.)

For a time the convention was deadlocked. The small states believed that all states should be represented equally in Congress, especially in the smaller "upper house" if there were to be two chambers. The large states insisted that representation in both houses be based on population or wealth, and that voters, not state legislatures, should elect national legislators. Finally, the so-called Committee of Eleven was elected to devise a compromise. On July 5, it presented its proposals, including what came to be known as the great or Connecticut Compromise.

New Jersey Plan
The proposal at the Constitutional Convention made by William Paterson of New Jersey for a central government with a single-house legislature in which each state would be represented equally.

Connecticut Compromise
The compromise agreement by states at the Constitutional Convention for a bicameral legislature with a lower house in which representation would be based on population and an upper house in which each state would have two senators.

The Connecticut Compromise The **Connecticut Compromise** (so labeled because of the prominent role the Connecticut delegation played in constructing it) called for one house in which each state would have an equal vote, and a second house in which representation would be based on population, and in which all bills for

TABLE 1–1 The Virginia and New Jersey Plans

Virginia Plan	New Jersey Plan
Legitimacy derived from citizens, based on popular representation	Derived from states, based on equal votes for each state
Bicameral legislature	Unicameral legislature
Executive size undetermined, elected and removable by Congress	More than one person, removable by state majority
Judicial life tenure, able to veto state legislation	No power over states
Legislature can override state laws	Government can compel obedience to national laws
Ratification by citizens	Ratification by states

raising or appropriating money—a key function of government—would originate. This proposal was a setback for the large states, which agreed to it only when the smaller states made it clear this was their price for union. After the delegates accepted equality of state representation in the Senate, most objections to a strong national government dissolved.

President Bill Clinton addresses a joint session of Congress in the House chamber during his 1999 State of the Union Address (top), and the Senate allows for a rare photograph of proceedings inside the Senate chamber (bottom).

North–South Compromises Other issues split the delegates from the North and South. Southerners were afraid that a northern majority in Congress might discriminate against southern trade. They had some basis for this concern. John Jay, a New Yorker who was secretary of foreign affairs for the Confederation, had proposed a treaty with Great Britain that would have given advantages to northern merchants at the expense of southern exporters of agricultural products such as tobacco and cotton. To protect themselves, the southern delegates insisted that a two-thirds majority in the Senate be required to ratify a treaty.

One subject that appears not to have been open for resolution was slavery. The view widely shared among historians is that the states with a greater reliance on slaves would have left the convention if the document had reduced or eliminated the practice. The issue did arise over whether to count slaves for the purpose of apportioning seats in the House of Representatives. To gain more representatives, the South wanted to count slaves; the North resisted. After heated debate, the delegates agreed on the **three-fifths compromise.** Each slave would be counted as three-fifths of a free person for the purposes of apportionment in the House and of direct taxation. This fraction was chosen because it maintained a balance of power between North and South The compromise also included a provision to eliminate the importation of slaves within 20 years, and Congress did so in 1808. The issue of balance between North and South would recur in the early history of our nation as territorial governments were established and territories that applied for statehood decided whether to permit or ban slavery.

Other Issues Delegates also argued about other issues. Should the national government have lower courts, or would one federal Supreme Court be enough? This issue was left to Congress to resolve. The Constitution states that there shall be one Supreme Court and that Congress may establish lower courts.

How should the president be selected? For a long time, the convention favored allowing Congress to pick the president, but some delegates feared that Congress would then dominate the president, or vice versa. The convention also rejected election by the state legislatures because the delegates distrusted the state legislatures. The delegates finally settled on election of the president by the electoral college, a group of individuals equal in number to the U.S. senators and representatives. Originally it was thought electors would exercise their own judgment in selecting the president. But the college quickly came to reflect partisanship, and today for most states, electors cast ballots for the candidate who wins the popular vote of that state. (We discuss the electoral college in greater detail in Chapter 9.) This was perhaps the delegates' most novel contribution as well as the most contrived, and it has long been one of the most criticized provisions in the Constitution.[25] (See Article II, Section 1 of the Constitution, which is reprinted between Chapters 2 and 3.)

After three months, the delegates stopped debating. On September 17, 1787, all but three of those still present signed the document they were recommending to the nation. Others who opposed the general drift of the convention had already left. Their work well done, the delegates adjourned to the nearby City Tavern to celebrate.

three-fifths compromise
The compromise between northern and southern states at the Constitutional Convention that three-fifths of the slave population would be counted for determining direct taxation and representation in the House of Representatives.

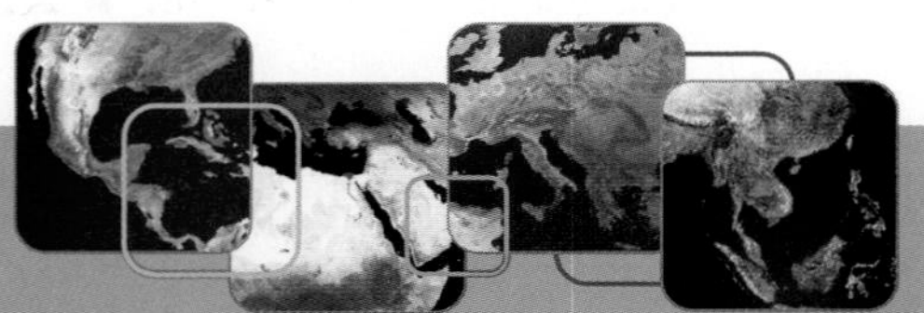

HOW **OTHER NATIONS** GOVERN

Factors Contributing to Democratic Stability

Political scientists have long tried to determine what factors contribute to stability in a democracy. Comparative studies have often linked national prosperity to democratic success. Other factors, such as education and literacy, are important as well. The following table lists several different dimensions for the countries that we will be comparing to the United States throughout the book.

These countries vary dramatically in some aspects. For example, note the extremely young population of Nigeria compared to the generally older population of Japan. The problems facing Japan in the future—namely, how to deal with an increasingly older society—are much different than in AIDS-ravaged Nigeria. Their respective governments will necessarily approach these problems differently. There are also similarities between countries; for example, China and India both must cope with the challenges presented by populations of more than one billion people.

QUESTIONS

1. What surprises you as you compare the United States to the other countries in this table?
2. Notice that the U.S. population is less than one-fourth that of China. What are the implications of that difference?
3. What do you think accounts for the difference in literacy between men and women in India, Nigeria, and to a lesser extent China?
4. Japan has the longest life expectancy (82 years) and Nigeria the shortest (47.4 years). What are the implications of this difference for both governments?

	World	Britain	China	India	Japan	Mexico	Nigeria	United States
Population (millions; July 2007 est.)	6,602.22	60.78	1,321.85	1,129.87	127.43	108.7	135.03	301.14
Median Age	28.1	39.9	33.6	25.1	43.8	26	18.7	36.7
Life Expectancy	65.8	78.7	72.9	68.6	82	75.6	47.4	78
Literacy								
Male	87	99	95.1	73.4	99	92.4	75.7	99
Female	77	99	86.5	47.8	99	89.6	60.6	99
Government Type		Constitutional monarchy	Communist state	Federal republic	Constitutional monarchy	Federal republic	Federal republic	Federal republic
GDP[1]	46.77	2.35	2.53	0.81	4.88	0.74	0.08	13.16
Freedom House[2]		Free	Not Free	Free	Free	Free	Partly free	Free

SOURCES: Central Intelligence Agency, *The 2008 World Factbook,* at www.cia.gov/library/publications/the-world-factbook, and Freedom House, *Freedom in the World 2007: The Annual Survey of Political Rights and Civil Liberties,* at www.freedomhouse.org/template.cfm?page=363&year=2007.

NOTES: 1) Calculated based on the country's official exchange rate in trillions of USD; 2) For more on Freedom House's Freedom Index, see www.freedomhouse.org/template.cfm?page=351&ana_page=333&year=2007.

According to an old story, a woman confronted Benjamin Franklin as he left the last session of the convention.

"What kind of government have you given us, Dr. Franklin?" she asked. "A republic or a monarchy?"

"A republic, Madam," he answered, "if you can keep it."

LEARNING **OBJECTIVE**

7 Assess the arguments for and against the ratification of the Constitution.

To Adopt or Not to Adopt?

The delegates had gone far. Indeed, they had disregarded Congress's instruction to do no more than revise the Articles of Confederation. In particular, they had ignored Article XIII, which declared the Union to be perpetual and prohibited any alteration of the Articles unless Congress and *every one of the state legislatures* agreed—a provision that had made it impossible to amend the Articles. The convention delegates, however, boldly declared that their newly proposed Constitution should go into effect when ratified by popularly elected conventions in nine states.

They turned to this method of ratification for practical considerations as well as to secure legitimacy for their proposed government. Not only were the delegates aware that there was little chance of winning approval of the new Constitution in all state legislatures, but many also believed that a constitution approved *by the people* would have higher legal and moral status than one approved only by a legislature. The Articles of Confederation had been a compact of state governments, but the Constitution was based on the will of the people (recall its opening words: "We the People..."). Still, even this method of ratification would not be easy. The nation was not ready to adopt the Constitution without a thorough debate.

Federalists Versus Antifederalists

Supporters of the new government, by cleverly appropriating the name **Federalists,** forced their opponents to be known as the **Antifederalists** and pointed up the negative character of the arguments opposing ratification. While advocating a strong national government but also retaining state prerogatives, the Federalists took some of the sting out of charges that they were trying to destroy the states and establish an all-powerful central government.

The split was in part geographic. Seaboard and city regions tended to be Federalist strongholds; backcountry regions from Maine (then part of Massachusetts) through Georgia, inhabited by farmers and other relatively poor people, were generally Antifederalist. But as in most political contests, no single factor completely accounted for the division between Federalists and Antifederalists. Thus in Virginia, the leaders of both sides came from the same general social and economic class. New York City and Philadelphia strongly supported the Constitution, yet so did predominantly rural New Jersey and Connecticut.

You Are James Madison

The great debate was conducted through pamphlets, newspapers, letters to editors, and speeches. It provides an outstanding example of a free people publicly discussing the nature of their fundamental laws. Out of the debate came a series of essays known as ***The Federalist***, written under the pseudonym Publius by Alexander Hamilton, James Madison, and John Jay to persuade the voters of New York to ratify the Constitution. *The Federalist* is still "widely regarded as the most profound single treatise on the Constitution ever written and as among the few masterly works in political science produced in all the centuries of history."[26] (Three of the most important *Federalist* essays, Nos. 10, 51, and 78, are reprinted in the Appendix of this book.)

The Antifederalists' most telling criticism of the proposed Constitution was its failure to include a bill of rights.[27] Antifederalists opposed the creation of a strong central government because they believed state and local governments would remain more responsive to local needs and concerns. They worried that under the Constitution, Congress would "impose barriers against commerce," and they were concerned that the Constitution did not do enough to ensure "frequent rotation of office," meaning elected officials could not be recalled through elections and over time would become less concerned with their constituents.[28] The Federalists believed a bill of rights was unnecessary because the proposed national government had *only* the specific powers that the states and the people delegated to it. Thus there was no need to specify that Congress could not, for example, abridge freedom of the press, because the states and the people had not given the national government power to regulate the press in the first place. Moreover, the Federalists argued, to guarantee some rights might be dangerous, because rights not listed could be assumed to be denied. The Constitution itself already protected some important rights—the requirement of trial by jury in federal criminal cases, provided for in Article III, for example. Hamilton and others also insisted that paper guarantees were feeble protection against governmental tyranny.

The Antifederalists were unconvinced. If some rights were protected, what could be the objection to providing constitutional protection for others? Without a bill of rights,

Federalists
Supporters of ratification of the Constitution and of a strong central government.

Antifederalists
Opponents of ratification of the Constitution and of a strong central government generally.

The Federalist
Essays promoting ratification of the Constitution, published anonymously by Alexander Hamilton, John Jay, and James Madison in 1787 and 1788.

Patrick Henry's famous cry of "Give me liberty or give me death!" helped rally support for the revolution against Britain. Later he was an outspoken opponent of ratification of the Constitution and was instrumental in forcing adoption of the Bill of Rights.

what was to prevent Congress from using one of its delegated powers to abridge free speech? If bills of rights were needed in state constitutions to limit state governments, why did the national constitution not include a bill of rights to limit the national government? This was a government further from the people, they contended, with a greater tendency to subvert natural rights than was true of state governments.

COMPARATIVE

Comparing Political Landscapes

TABLE 1–2 Ratification of the U.S. Constitution

State	Date
Delaware	December 7, 1787
Pennsylvania	December 12, 1787
New Jersey	December 18, 1787
Georgia	January 2, 1788
Connecticut	January 9, 1788
Massachusetts	February 6, 1788
Maryland	April 28, 1788
South Carolina	May 23, 1788
New Hampshire	June 21, 1788
Virginia	June 25, 1788
New York	July 26, 1788
North Carolina	November 21, 1789
Rhode Island	May 29, 1790

The Politics of Ratification

The absence of a bill of rights in the proposed Constitution dominated the struggle over its adoption. In taverns, churches, and newspaper offices, people were muttering, "No bill of rights—no Constitution!" This feeling was so strong that some Antifederalists, though they were far more concerned with states' rights than individual rights, joined forces with those wanting a bill of rights in order to defeat the proposed Constitution.

The Federalists began the debate over the Constitution as soon as the delegates left Philadelphia in mid-September 1787. Their tactic was to secure ratification in as many states as possible before the opposition had time to organize. The Antifederalists were handicapped because most newspapers supported ratification. Moreover, Antifederalist strength was concentrated in rural areas, which were underrepresented in some state legislatures and in which it was more difficult to arouse the people to political action. The Antifederalists needed time to organize, while the Federalists moved in a hurry.

Most of the small states, now satisfied by getting equal Senate representation, ratified the Constitution without difficulty. Delaware was the first, and by early 1788, Pennsylvania, New Jersey, Georgia, and Connecticut had also ratified (see Table 1–2). In Massachusetts, however, opposition was growing. Key leaders, such as John Hancock and Samuel Adams, were doubtful or opposed. The debate in Boston raged for most of January 1788 and into February. But in the end, the Massachusetts Convention narrowly ratified the Constitution in that state, 187 to 168.

By June 21, 1788, Maryland, South Carolina, and New Hampshire had also ratified, giving the Constitution the nine states required for it to go into effect. But two big hurdles remained: Virginia and New York. It would be impossible to begin the new government without the consent of these two major states. Virginia was crucial. As the most populous state and the home of Washington, Jefferson, and Madison, Virginia was a link between North and South. The Virginia ratifying convention rivaled the Constitutional Convention in the caliber of its delegates. Madison, who had only recently switched to favoring a bill of rights after saying earlier that it was unnecessary, captained the Federalist forces. The fiery Patrick Henry led the opposition. In an epic debate, Henry cried that liberty was the issue: "Liberty, the greatest of earthly possessions...that precious jewel!" But Madison promised that a bill of rights embracing the freedoms of religion, speech, and assembly would be added to the Constitution as soon as the new government was established. Washington tipped the balance with a letter urging ratification. News of the Virginia vote, 89 for the Constitution and 79 opposed, was rushed to New York.[29]

What Are American Civic Values?

The great landowners along New York's Hudson River, unlike the southern planters, opposed the Constitution. They feared federal taxation of their holdings, and they did not want to abolish the profitable tax New York had been levying on trade and commerce with other states. When the convention assembled, the Federalists were greatly outnumbered, but they were aided by Alexander Hamilton's strategy and skill, and by word of Virginia's ratification. New York approved by a margin of three votes. Although North Carolina and Rhode Island still remained outside the Union (the former ratified in November 1789, the latter six months later), the new nation was created. In New York, a few members of the old Congress assembled to issue the call for elections under the new Constitution. Then they adjourned without setting a date for reconvening.

CHAPTER **SUMMARY**

1 Define government, politics, politicians, political science, and constitutional democracy.

The United States operates under a constitutional democracy. Within our system, the Constitution lays out the basic rules of the game under which politicians act to accomplish their different agendas. "Politics" is a broad term that can be used to describe what happens between these politicians in pursuit of their goals. "Government" is another broad term that encompasses the many different institutions enumerated by the Constitution in which the politicians function. Political science studies the interaction between politics, politicians, the government, and, within the American context, our constitutional democracy.

2 Differentiate democracy from other forms of government.

In the United States, we often use the term "democracy" to describe our form of government. This is true to an extent, but a more accurate term would be "representative democracy" or "republic." The politicians in our system are elected representatives meant to stand up for the interests of their constituents. Many other forms of government have been tried throughout the world's history. Representative democracy differs from direct democracy in the level of citizen participation. Citizens of the United States take for granted the peaceful transfer of power as happened after the 2008 presidential election.

3 Identify the conditions that help democracy flourish and explain why they do so.

In recent years, political scientists have directed much attention to the question of what conditions are conducive to democratic governments. Scholars have identified several factors that may help democratic governments form and consolidate. Among these, educational, economic, social, and ideological conditions are the most important.

4 Explain the importance to successful democracy of values, political processes, and political structures.

The essential democratic values are a belief in personal liberty, respect for the individual, equality of opportunity, and popular consent. Essential elements of the democratic process are free and fair elections, majority rule, freedom of expression, and the right to assemble and protest. Political structures include courts, legislatures, the executive, and administrative agencies. In the United States the political structure also includes federalism and the principle of limited government.

5 Show how politics before 1787 shaped the Constitution.

In the formative years of American democracy, several competing factions worked, sometimes at cross purposes, to develop the Constitution. Some of the most divisive issues that the framers had to address were the challenges presented by a federal system. Small states had real concerns about their role in a democratic system. There were also issues that had more to do with geography and economics. The divide between the North and the South on slavery was also important at the convention.

6 Identify the most important compromises achieved by the delegates to the Constitutional Convention of 1787.

The framers came up with some brilliant compromises to address these issues, such as the Connecticut Compromise that led to our current bicameral legislative branch. Other issues were put on hold. For example, the framers postponed dealing with slavery and compromised on counting slaves as three-fifths of a person for purposes of apportionment.

7 Assess the arguments for and against the ratification of the Constitution.

Some of the same themes that dominated the debate over ratification can still be heard today. Federalists argued for a central government that would be strong enough to make the newly united states capable of standing up to the great powers of the time. Antifederalists worried about what might come of a strong central government and were particularly concerned about the lack of any bill of rights in the document.

Chapter Self-Test

1. Write a short essay discussing the intersection between government and politics. In what ways are they similar? How are they different? (pp. 4–5)
2. In a few sentences, define political science and discuss why it is a useful field of study. (p. 4)
3. Explain the differences and similarities between direct democracy and representative democracy in a short paragraph. (pp. 5–7)
4. The framers of the Constitution had concerns about unlimited direct democracy. List some of those concerns. (pp. 5–7)
5. Russia has a well-educated population and a fairly strong economy. However, its people do not have much experience with democracy and many are suspicious of it. Given these facts, assess the prospects for democracy in Russia using the criteria listed in the chapter. (pp. 8–9)
6. Write a short essay explaining how democratic values are important to a successful democracy. (pp. 9–10)
7. Write a short essay explaining how specific values have contributed to the relative longevity of democracy in the United States. Which values seem most important to U.S. citizens? (pp. 9–10)
8. Identify three or four issues the United States faces today that the founders could not have foreseen. Discuss briefly how the Constitution is relevant to these issues. (pp. 7–12)
9. Put the following events in chronological order: (pp. 13–25)

   a. Drafting of the Articles of Confederation
   b. Revolutionary War
   c. Declaration of Independence
   d. Constitutional Convention
   e. Shay's Rebellion
   f. Ratification of the Constitution

10. Identify three or four historical tensions that impeded ratification of the constitution that have persisted into present-day politics. (pp. 18–25)
11. Which state was the compromise that led to a bicameral legislature named after? (p. 20)

    a. Rhode Island
    b. Connecticut
    c. New Hampshire
    d. Maine

12. The critical compromise reached to accommodate concerns over how to count slaves for apportionment purposes was known as the __________ compromise: (p. 21)

    a. 3/4
    b. 3/5
    c. 2/3
    d. 5/7

13. Write a brief persuasive essay adopting the Antifederalist position against ratification of the constitution. In your essay list two or three arguments that you feel Federalists would put forward and then counter those with your persuasive arguments. (pp. 23–25)
14. Match the following articles with their appropriate subject (see Appendix):

a. Art. I	i. Interstate Relations
b. Art. II	ii. Ratification
c. Art. III	iii. Congressional
d. Art. IV	iv. Amending Power
e. Art. V	v. Executive
f. Art. VI	vi. Supremacy Act
g. Art. VII	vii. Judiciary

15. Assess the arguments for and against the ratification of the Constitution. Write one paragraph for each, being sure to explain the best arguments and the criticisms against them.

Key Terms

democracy, p. 5
direct democracy, p. 6
representative democracy, p. 7
constitutional democracy, p. 7
constitutionalism, p. 7
statism, p. 10
popular consent, p. 10
majority rule, p. 11
majority, p. 11
plurality, p. 11
theocracy, p. 13
Articles of Confederation, p. 14
Annapolis Convention, p. 14
Constitutional Convention, p. 15
Shays' Rebellion, p. 15
bicameralism, p. 19
Virginia Plan, p. 19
New Jersey Plan, p. 20
Connecticut Compromise, p. 20
three-fifths compromise, p. 21
Federalists, p. 23
Antifederalists, p. 23
***The Federalist*,** p. 23

Further Reading

BERNARD BAILYN, ED., *The Debate on the Constitution: Federalist and Antifederalist Speeches, Articles, and Letters During the Struggle over Ratification*, 2 vols. (Library of America, 1993).

LANCE BANNING, *The Sacred Fire of Liberty: James Madison and the Founding of the Federal Republic* (Cornell University Press, 1995).

ROBERT A. DAHL, *How Democratic Is the American Constitution*, 2d ed. (Yale University Press, 2003).

ROBERT A. DAHL, *On Democracy* (Yale University Press, 1998).

STANLEY ELKINS AND **ERIC MCKITRICK,** *The Age of Federalism: The Early American Republic, 1788–1800* (Oxford University Press, 1994).

DAVID HACKETT FISCHER, *Washington's Crossing* (Oxford University Press, 2004).

ALAN GIBSON, *Understanding the Founding: Crucial Questions* (University Press of Kansas, 2007).

ALEXANDER HAMILTON, JAMES MADISON, AND **JOHN JAY,** *The Federalist Papers*, ed. Clinton Rossiter (New American Library, 1961). Also in several other editions.

MATTHEW S. HOLLAND, *Bonds of Affection: Civic Charity and the Making of America–Winthrop, Jefferson and Lincoln* (Georgetown University Press, 2007).

PHILIP B. KURLAND AND **RALPH LERNER,** *The Founders' Constitution*, 5 vols. (University of Chicago Press, 1987).

SANFORD LEVINSON, *Our Undemocratic Constitution* (Oxford University Press, 2006).

AREND LIJPHART, *Patterns of Democracy: Government Forms and Performance in Thirty-Six Countries* (Yale University Press, 1999).

PAULINE MAIER, *American Scripture: Making the Declaration of Independence* (Vintage Books, 1997).

STEPHEN MACEDO ET AL., *Democracy at Risk: How Political Choices Undermine Citizen Participation, and What We Can Do About It* (Brookings Institution Press, 2005).

RICHARD B. MORRIS, *Witnesses at the Creation: Hamilton, Madison, and Jay and the Constitution* (Holt, Rinehart & Winston, 1985).

PIPPA NORRIS, ED., *Critical Citizens: Global Support for Democratic Institutions* (Oxford University Press, 1999).

ROBERT PUTNAM, *Making Democracy Work* (Princeton University Press, 1993).

JACK N. RAKOVE, *Original Meanings: Politics and Ideas in the Making of the Constitution* (Vintage Books, 1997).

GARY ROSEN, *American Compact: James Madison and the Problem of Founding* (University Press of Kansas, 1999).

MICHAEL J. SANDEL, *Democracy's Discontent: America in Search of a Public Philosophy* (Belknap Press, 1996).

MICHAEL SCHUDSON, *The Good Citizen: A History of American Civic Life* (Harvard University Press, 1998).

CASS R. SUNSTEIN, *Designing Democracy: What Constitutions Do* (Oxford University Press, 2001).

ALEXIS DE TOCQUEVILLE, *Democracy in America*, 2 vols. (1835).

SEAN WILENTZ, *The Rise of American Democracy* (Norton, 2005).

GARRY WILLS, *A Necessary Evil: A History of American Distrust of Government* (Simon & Schuster, 1999).

GORDON S. WOOD, *The Radicalism of the American Revolution* (Knopf, 1992).

See also the *Journal of Democracy* (Johns Hopkins University Press).

chapter 2

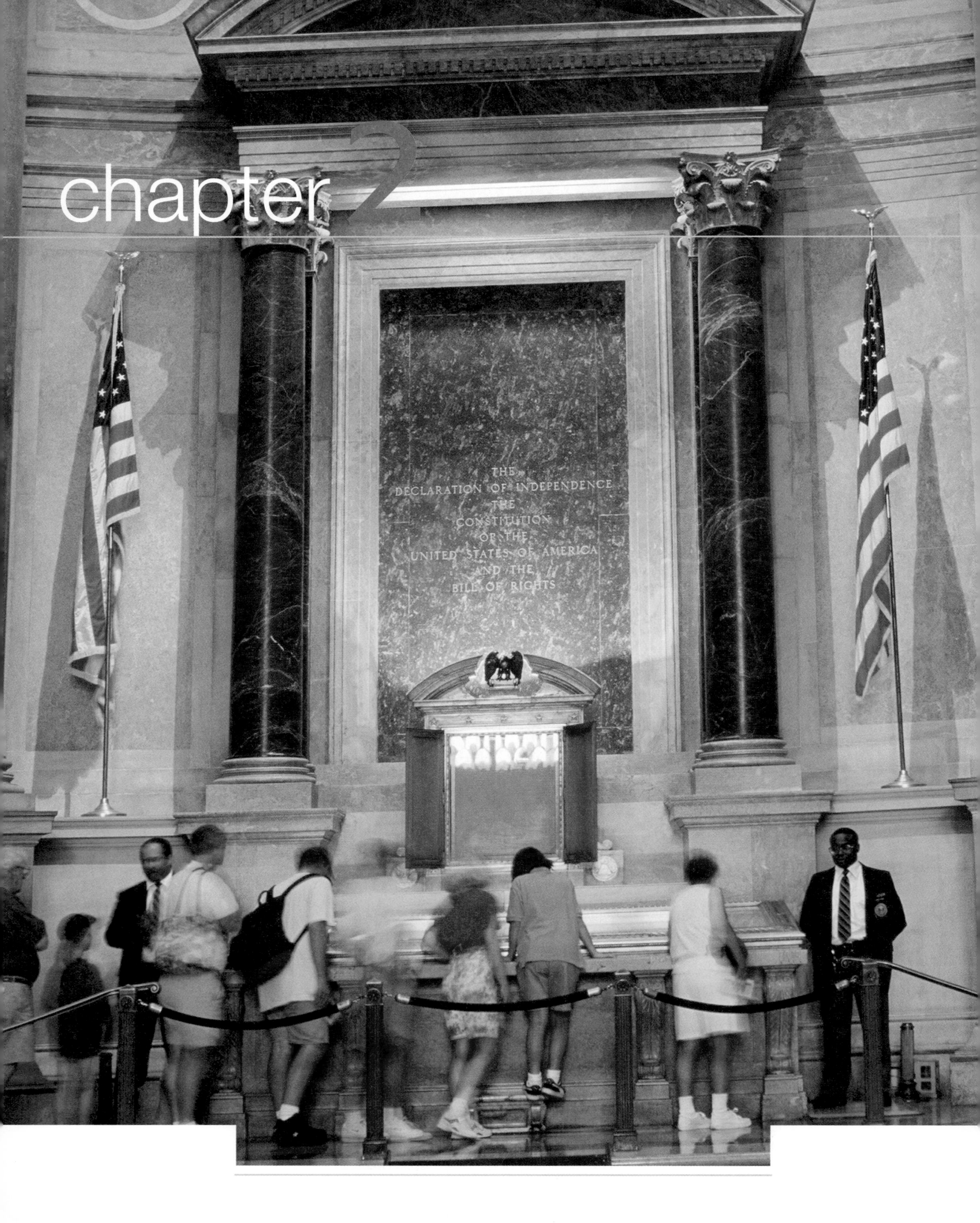
THE
DECLARATION OF INDEPENDENCE
THE
CONSTITUTION
OF THE
UNITED STATES OF AMERICA
AND THE
BILL OF RIGHTS

The Living Constitution

The Constitution of the United States is the world's oldest written constitution. Some 224 other countries have written constitutions, but more than half (122) have been adopted or significantly revised since 1990, with 17 new ones ratified since 2000. Nine countries have no written constitution, including Oman, New Zealand, and the United Kingdom.[1]

Debate was critical in getting the signers' agreement to the initial document of the U.S. Constitution in 1787. Since then, the ambiguity and brevity of many constitutional provisions have spurred a great deal of additional debate, although there has not been a serious effort to alter our basic constitutional system of government since the Constitution went into effect in 1789. Indeed, the potential to alter the Constitution through the amendment process has created a remarkable democratic system of government capable of withstanding a civil war, two world wars, and internal and external security threats, all the while providing individual protections for an increasingly heterogeneous population.

One recent constitutional debate concerned students' efforts to pray before their high school football game. Written more than 200 years before this dispute, the First Amendment provided the framework to determine whether such an effort was constitutional. In September 1999, high school senior Marian Ward led a prayer before the football game between the Santa Fe Indians and the Crosby Cougars. In it, she said "God, thank you for this evening. . . . I pray that you'll bless each and every person here tonight."[2] She ended her message by saying "In Jesus' name, amen."[3]

A little over a year later, the U.S. Supreme Court considered whether the pre-game prayer at a public high school football game violated the First Amendment's restriction on establishing religion. In a 6-to-3 decision in *Santa Fe Independent School District v. Doe,* the Court said that it did. The justices' decision was based on a number of factors, including the coercive pressure exerted on students, particularly nonbelievers.[4]

The continuing debate regarding prayer in the public schools highlights both the genius and a flaw in the Constitution—its lack of specificity. In composing the Constitution, the framers were conscious that they were writing a document that needed to withstand the test of time. By not specifying how the government should administer the separation of church and state, they designed a document that others could apply to changing circumstances. However, this generality also results in continuing debates, which have included the appropriate authority of the governing branches and the extent of national government authority over the states. The power of the courts to determine what exactly the Constitution means has also led many to scrutinize the ways by which it reaches those decisions.

Understanding the Constitution and considering its strengths and weaknesses is a necessary step in studying and participating in U.S. government. After such study, one student turned his college research paper at the University of Texas into a successful drive to ratify the Twenty-Seventh Amendment (concerning congressional salaries) in 1992. We won't all achieve such a result through our participation, but by being more knowledgeable about our system, we can better protect our own individual liberties, evaluate the appropriate authority of various elected and appointed governmental officials, and understand what it means to have a government with powers that are separated, shared, and checked.

LEARNING **OBJECTIVES**

1. Describe the basic structure of the Constitution and its Bill of Rights.
2. Summarize the basic principles of government established by the Constitution.
3. Compare and contrast the three main branches of the U.S. government.
4. Show how the system of checks and balances operates among the three branches of the U.S. government.
5. Show how the use of judicial review strengthens the courts in a separation of powers system.
6. Analyze the effect of *Marbury v. Madison* on the role of the judiciary.
7. Explain how the meaning of the Constitution has evolved over time.
8. Outline the way we make formal changes to the Constitution.

CHAPTER OUTLINE

- Views of the Constitution
- Checking Power with Power
- Judicial Review and the "Guardians of the Constitution"
- The Constitution as an Instrument of Government
- Changing the Letter of the Constitution

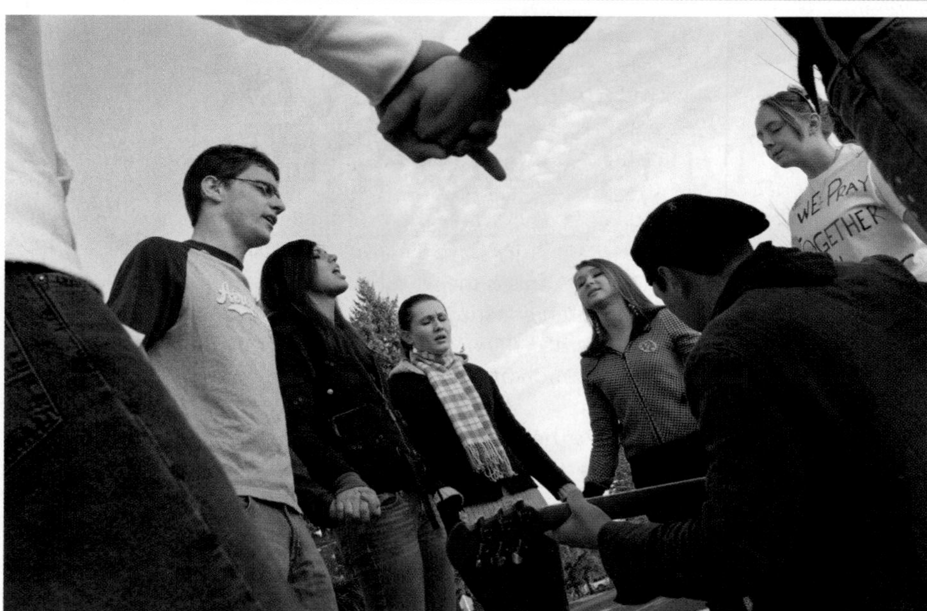

High school students pray outside their school before classes begin for the day. Although this type of prayer has been upheld by the courts, the Supreme Court struck down student-led prayer broadcasted over a stadium loudspeaker before a high school football game.

In this chapter we'll discuss our constitutionally arranged system of separation of powers and checks and balances, as well as how special-interest groups and political parties try to circumvent these protections. We'll see how the judiciary came to be widely accepted as the final interpreter of constitutional meaning, and the way both the executive and the legislature have used the Constitution to pursue their own ends. Finally, we will examine the difficult process through which citizens can amend the Constitution. As the framers intended, that is no small feat, and one that is an important factor in the stability of our Constitution.

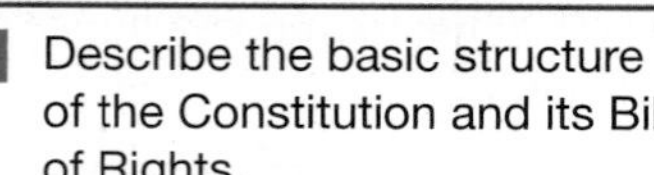

LEARNING **OBJECTIVE**

1 Describe the basic structure of the Constitution and its Bill of Rights.

Views of the Constitution

In addition to being the oldest written Constitution in the world, the U.S. Constitution is also one of the shortest. The original Constitution, excluding the Bill of Rights, contains just 4,543 words. Its basic structure is straightforward. Article I establishes a bicameral Congress, with a House of Representatives and a Senate, and empowers it to enact legislation; for example, governing foreign and interstate commerce (as discussed further in Chapter 11). Article II vests the executive power in the president (as discussed in Chapter 12), and Article III vests the judicial power in the Supreme Court and other federal courts that Congress may establish (as discussed in Chapter 14). Article IV guarantees the privileges and immunities of citizens and specifies the conditions for admitting new states. Article V provides for the methods of amending the Constitution, and Article VI specifies that the Constitution and all laws made under it are the supreme law of the land. Finally, Article VII provides that the Constitution had to be ratified by nine of the original 13 states to go into effect. In 1791 the first ten amendments, the Bill of Rights, were added, and another 17 amendments have been added since. The entire Constitution and its amendments appear at the end of this chapter.

Comparing Constitutions

Despite its brevity, the Constitution firmly established the framers' experiment in free-government-in-the-making that each generation reinterprets and renews. That is why after more than 220 years we have not had another written Constitution—let alone two, three, or more, like other countries around the world. Part of the reason is the widespread acceptance of the Constitution across our population. But the

Constitution has also endured because it is a brilliant structure for limited government and one that the framers designed to be adaptable and flexible.

As the Constitution won the support of citizens in the early years of the Republic, it took on the aura of **natural law**—law that defines right from wrong, which is higher than human law. The framers "grew ever larger in stature as they receded from view; the era in which they lived and fought became a Golden Age; in that age there had been a fresh dawn for the world, and its men were giants against the sky."[5] Like the crown in Great Britain, the Constitution became a symbol of national unity and loyalty, evoking both emotional and intellectual support from Americans, regardless of their differences. The framers' work became part of the U.S. creed and culture.[6] The Constitution stands for liberty, equality before the law, limited or expanded government—indeed, for just about anything anyone wants to read into it.

James Madison was the fourth president of the United States (1809–1817) and an author of *The Federalist.* Madison's view on a separated system of government in which each branch checks the power of other branches shapes our governmental structure.

Even today, U.S. citizens generally revere the Constitution, though many do not know what is in it. A poll by the National Constitution Center found that nine of ten U.S. adults are proud of the Constitution and feel it is important to them. However, a third mistakenly believe the Constitution establishes English as the country's official language. One in six believes it establishes the United States as a Christian nation. Only one of four could name a single First Amendment right. Although two in three knew the Constitution created three branches of the national government, only one of those could name all three branches.[7]

The Constitution is more than a symbol, however. It is the supreme and binding law that both grants and limits powers. "In framing a government which is to be administered by men over men," wrote James Madison in *The Federalist,* No. 51, "the great difficulty lies in this: you must first enable the government to control the governed; and in the next place oblige it to control itself." (See *The Federalist,* No. 51, in the Appendix of this book.) The Constitution is both a positive instrument of government, which enables the governors to control the governed, and a restraint on government, which enables the ruled to check the rulers. How does the Constitution limit the power of the government? How does it create governmental power? How has it managed to serve as a great symbol of national unity and at the same time as an adaptable instrument of government? The secret is an ingenious separation of powers and a system of checks and balances that limits power with power.

Checking Power with Power

LEARNING **OBJECTIVE**

2 Summarize the basic principles of government established by the Constitution.

"If men were angels," James Madison argued in *The Federalist,* No. 51, "no government would be necessary. If angels were to govern men, neither external nor internal controls on government would be necessary."[8] But the framers knew well that men were not angels, and thus to create a successful government, they would need to create a government of *limited* authority. How? Within the government, competing interests would check each other, and externally the governed would check the government through elections, petitions, protests, and amendments. The framers wanted a stronger and more effective national government than they had under the Articles of Confederation. But they were keenly aware that the people would not accept too much central control. Efficiency and order were important concerns, but liberty was more important. The framers wanted to ensure domestic tranquillty and prevent future rebellions, but they also wanted to forestall the emergence of a homegrown King George III. Accordingly, they allotted certain powers to the national government and reserved the rest for the states, thus establishing a system of *federalism* (whose nature and problems we discuss in Chapter 3). Even this was not enough. The framers believed additional restraints were needed to limit the national government.

The most important means they devised to make public officials observe the constitutional limits on their powers was *free and fair elections,* through which voters could throw those who abuse power out of office. Yet the framers were not willing to depend solely on political controls, because they did not fully trust the people's judgment. "Free government is founded on jealousy, and not in confidence," said Thomas Jefferson. "In questions of power, then, let no more be heard of confidence in man, but bind him down from mischief by the chains of the Constitution."[9]

natural law
God's or nature's law that defines right from wrong and is higher than human law.

No less important, the framers feared a majority might deprive minorities of their rights. This risk was certainly real at the time of the framing, as it is today. In the *Santa Fe* case, for example, students voted both on who would be their "Student Chaplain" and on whether that person should deliver a pregame prayer over the football stadium's loudspeaker. However, the majority vote of Santa Fe's student body did nothing to protect the rights of religious minorities. "A dependence on the people is, no doubt, the primary control on the government," Madison contended in *The Federalist,* No. 51, "but experience has taught mankind the necessity of auxiliary precautions."[10] What were these "auxiliary precautions" against popular tyranny?

LEARNING **OBJECTIVE**

3 Compare and contrast the three main branches of the U.S. government.

Separation of Powers

The first step was the **separation of powers**, the distribution of constitutional authority among the three branches of the national government. In *The Federalist,* No. 47, Madison wrote, "No political truth is certainly of greater intrinsic value, or is stamped with the authority of more enlightened patrons of liberty, than that...the accumulation of all powers, legislative, executive, and judiciary, in the same hands...may justly be pronounced the very definition of tyranny."[11] Chief among the "enlightened patrons of liberty" to whose authority Madison was appealing were the eighteenth-century philosophers John Locke and Montesquieu, whose works most educated citizens knew well.

The intrinsic value of the dispersion of power, however, is not the only reason the framers included it in the Constitution. It had already been the general practice in the colonies for more than 100 years. Only during the Revolutionary period did some of the states concentrate authority in the hands of the legislature, and that unhappy experience as well as that under the Articles of Confederation confirmed the framers' belief in the merits of the separation of powers. Many attributed the evils of state government and the lack of energy in the central government under the Articles of Confederation to the lack of a strong executive to check legislative abuses and to give energy and direction to administration.

The American System of Checks and Balances

Still, separating power by itself was not enough. It might not prevent the branches of the government and officials from pooling their authority and acting together, or from responding alike to the same pressures—from the demand of an overwhelming majority of the student body to allow student prayer over the loudspeaker at public high school football games, for example, or to impose confiscatory taxes on the rich. If separating power was not enough, what else could be done?

LEARNING **OBJECTIVE**

4 Show how the system of checks and balances operates among the three branches of the U.S. government.

Checks and Balances: Ambition to Counteract Ambition

The framers' answer was a system of **checks and balances** (see Table 2–1). "The great security against a gradual concentration of the several powers in the same department," wrote Madison in *The Federalist,* No. 51, "consists in giving to those who administer each department the necessary constitutional means and personal motives to resist encroachments of the others:...Ambition must be made to counteract ambition."[12] Each branch therefore has a role in the actions of the others (see Figure 2–1).

Congress enacts legislation, which the president must sign into law or veto. The Supreme Court can declare laws passed by Congress and signed by the president unconstitutional, but the president appoints the justices and all the other federal judges, with the Senate's approval. The president administers the laws, but Congress provides the money to run the government. Moreover, the Senate and the House of Representatives have absolute veto power over each other, because both houses must approve bills before they can become law.

Not only does each branch have some authority over the others, but each is politically independent of the others. Voters in each local district choose members of the House; voters in each state choose senators; the president is elected by the voters in all the states. With the consent of the Senate, the president appoints federal judges, who remain in office until they retire or are impeached.

separation of powers
Constitutional division of powers among the legislative, executive, and judicial branches, with the legislative branch making law, the executive applying and enforcing the law, and the judiciary interpreting the law.

checks and balances
A constitutional grant of powers that enables each of the three branches of government to check some acts of the others and therefore ensure that no branch can dominate.

TABLE 2–1 The Exercise of Checks and Balances, 1789–2009

Vetoes Presidents have vetoed more than 2,500 acts of Congress. Congress has overridden presidential vetoes more than 100 times.

Judicial review The Supreme Court has ruled some 176 congressional acts or parts thereof unconstitutional.

Impeachment The House of Representatives has impeached two presidents, one senator, one secretary of war, and 13 federal judges; the Senate has convicted seven of the judges but neither president.

Confirmation The Senate has refused to confirm nine cabinet nominations. Many other cabinet and subcabinet appointments were withdrawn because the Senate seemed likely to reject them.

For additional resources on the Constitution, go to www.archives.gov/exhibits/charters/constitution.html

How does the Legislative check Executive?
list 2 ways

Passes laws

CONGRESS
THE LEGISLATIVE BRANCH

- Approves federal budget
- Can override presidential veto by two-thirds vote of both houses and can propose constitutional amendments to counter Supreme Court rulings
- House can impeach president, other federal officials including federal judges
- Senate approves treaties
- Senate tries all impeachments
- Determines number, location, and jurisdiction of federal courts
- Senate confirms senior federal appointments, including federal judges

Enforces laws

PRESIDENT
THE EXECUTIVE BRANCH

- Can propose laws
- Can veto laws
- Can call special sessions of Congress
- Can appeal directly to public
- Can pardon people convicted of federal crimes (excludes impeachments)
- Nominates officers of the U. S. government and federal judges

SUPREME COURT AND LOWER COURTS
THE JUDICIAL BRANCH

Can declare executive actions and laws unconstitutional

Interprets laws

FIGURE 2–1
The Separation of Powers and Checks and Balances.

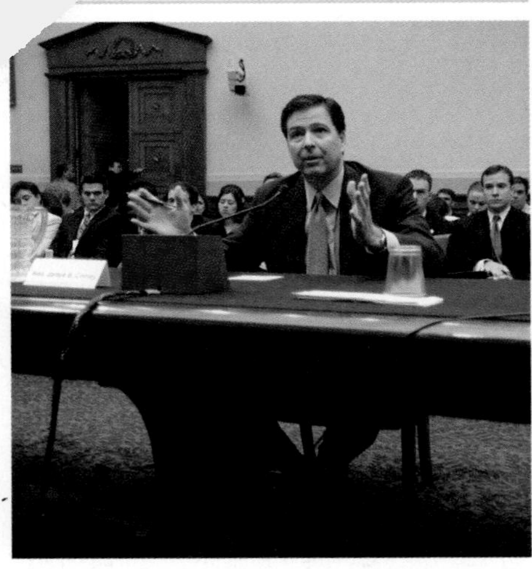

James Comey, former Deputy Attorney General of the United States, testifies about the firing of eight U.S. Attorneys. Congress investigated whether the terminations were made for political reasons.

The framers also ensured that a majority of the voters could win control over only part of the government at one time. Although in an off-year (nonpresidential) election a new majority might take control of the House of Representatives, the president still has at least two more years, and senators hold office for six years. Finally, there are independent federal courts, which exercise their own powerful checks.

Distrustful of both the elites and the masses, the framers deliberately built into our political system mechanisms to make changing the system difficult. They designed the decision-making process so that the national government can act decisively only when there is a consensus among most groups and after all sides have had their say. "The doctrine of separation of powers was adopted by the convention of 1787," in the words of Justice Louis D. Brandeis, "not to promote efficiency but to preclude the exercise of arbitrary power. The purpose was not to avoid friction, but, by means of the inevitable friction incident to the distribution of the governmental powers among three departments, to save the people from autocracy."[13] Still, even though the fragmentation of political power written into the Constitution remains, constitutional silences, or topics the Constitution does not address, and subsequent developments have modified the way the system of checks and balances works.

The Rise of National Political Parties and Interest Groups

Political parties—the Republican and Democratic parties being the largest—can serve as unifying factors, at times drawing the president, senators, representatives, and sometimes even judges together behind common programs. When parties do this, they help bridge the separation of powers. Yet they can be splintered and weakened by having to work through a system of fragmented governmental power, and by the increasing influence of special-interest groups (discussed further in Chapter 6), so they never become too strong or cohesive. When one party controls Congress or one of its chambers and the other party controls the White House, in a situation called **divided government**, **partisanship** is intensified, and Congress is inclined to more closely monitor the executive branch. Because his party controlled Congress during much of his presidency, President Bush was remarkably free from congressional investigations of his administration. However, when Democrats regained control in both the Senate and the House of Representatives in 2006, they quickly began congressional investigations into the use of intelligence leading up to the war in Iraq and the firing of U.S. Attorneys by the U.S. Justice Department. More conflict is certainly to be expected during divided government, but even when one party controls both branches, the pressures of competing interest groups may make cooperation among legislators difficult.

divided government
Governance divided between the parties, especially when one holds the presidency and the other controls one or both houses of Congress.

partisanship
Strong allegiance to one's own political party, often leading to unwillingness to compromise with members of the opposing party.

Because of this institutional competition between the legislative and executive branches, we find "each institution protecting and promoting itself through a broad interpretation of its constitutional and political status, even usurping the other's power when the opportunity presents itself."[14] Thus we have had battles over the budget and angry confirmation hearings for the appointment of justices of the Supreme Court, and even of lower federal courts and members of the executive branch. The division of powers also makes it difficult for the voters to hold anyone or any party accountable. "Presidents blame Congress... while members of Congress attack the president.... Citizens genuinely cannot tell who is to blame."[15]

Yet when all the shouting dies down, political scientist David Mayhew concludes, there have been just as many congressional investigations and just as much important legislation passed when one party controls Congress and another controls the presidency as when the same party controls both branches.[16] And Charles Jones, a noted authority on Congress and the presidency, adds that divided government is precisely what the voters appear to have wanted through much of our history.[17]

GENERATION **NEXT**

Setting Aside the Constitution in an Age of Terror

One of the difficulties in dealing with the threat of terrorism in an open society is the need to protect individual liberties at the same time. The Constitution provides for such protections, but they are not absolute. Moreover, the U.S. Supreme Court has made it clear that the government may infringe on individual rights and liberties in times of crisis.*

Many members of Generation Next disagree. According to the Pew Research Center's 2007 survey of the nation's political landscape, only a minority of young people think the average person will need to give up some civil liberties to fight terrorism.

Although members of Generation Next don't differ much on this question based on race or gender, Republicans and those who consider themselves very conservative are more likely to think it will be necessary to restrict civil liberties to deal with the threat of terrorism. Conversely, 18- to 29-year-olds who consider themselves liberal or very liberal are least likely to believe there is a need to restrict civil liberties in order to curb terrorism, perhaps because of their concern for protecting individual liberties more generally.

There are even greater differences between Generation Next and older U.S. adults. For example, 47 percent of adults between ages 40 and 49 believe it will be necessary to restrict civil liberties to fight terrorism.

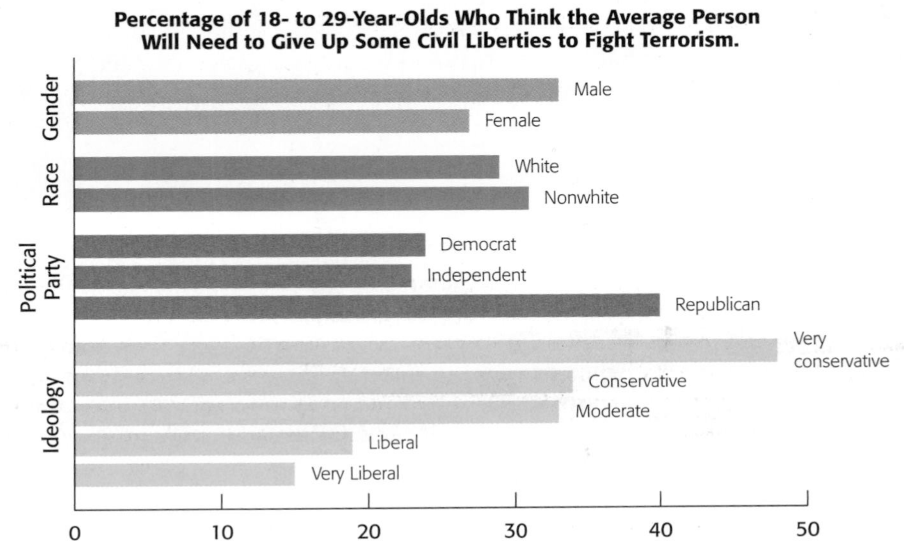

QUESTIONS

1. Why doesn't the Constitution protect our civil liberties absolutely?
2. Should you be concerned with restrictions in civil liberties that are only temporary?
3. Why might other people feel differently about this polling question than you do?

*See, for example, *Schenck v. United States*, 249 U.S. 47 (1919).

Expansion of the Electorate and the Move Toward More Direct Democracy

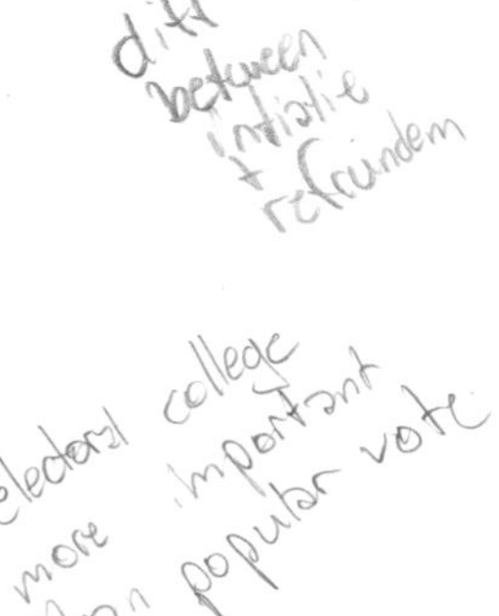

The framers wanted the electoral college—wise, independent citizens free of popular passions and hero worship—to choose the president rather than leave the job to ordinary citizens. Almost from the beginning, though, the electoral college did not work this way.[18] Rather, voters actually do select the president, because the presidential electors the voters choose pledge in advance to cast their electoral votes for their party's candidates for president and vice president. Nevertheless, presidential candidates may occasionally win the national popular vote but lose the vote in the electoral college, as happened when Al Gore won the popular vote in the 2000 presidential election but lost the electoral college with 266 votes to George W. Bush's 271.

The kind of people allowed to vote has expanded from free, white, property-owning males to include all citizens over age 18. In addition, during the past century, U.S. states have expanded the role of the electorate by adopting **direct primaries**, in which the voters elect party nominees for the House and Senate and even for president; by permitting the voters in about half the states to propose and vote on

direct primary
An election in which voters choose party nominees.

Voter turnout in the 2008 Democratic primary race was high across the United States. In many states additional ballots had to be printed to meet the demand of high numbers of voters.

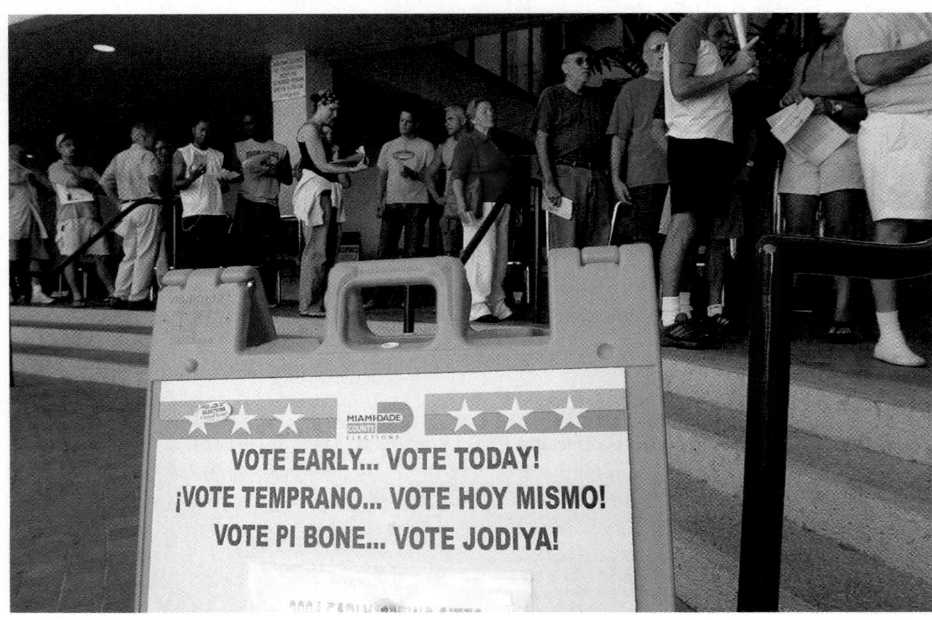

laws through **initiatives**; by allowing voters to reconsider actions of the legislature through **referendums**; and even by allowing voters to remove elected state and local officials from office in a **recall**. And since the ratification of the Seventeenth Amendment in 1913, senators are no longer elected by state legislatures but are chosen directly by the people.

Establishment of Agencies Designed to Exercise Legislative, Executive, and Judicial Functions

When the national government began to regulate the economy in the late nineteenth and twentieth centuries, it found that it was impossible to legislate precise and detailed rules on complex matters such as railroad safety, mass communications, the health and safety of working conditions, and environmental protection. Congress has thus provided administrative agencies with the power to make and apply rules and to decide disputes. Beginning in 1887, Congress created *independent regulatory commissions*, for example in 1934 it established the Federal Communications Commission. More recently, it has established *independent executive agencies*, which typically have broader authority and are more responsive to the administration than are commissions. One example is the Environmental Protection Agency.

TIMELINE

Major Technological Innovations that Have Changed the Political Landscape

initiative
A procedure whereby a certain number of voters may, by petition, propose a law or constitutional amendment and have it submitted to the voters.

referendum
A procedure for submitting to popular vote measures passed by the legislature or proposed amendments to a state constitution.

recall
A procedure for submitting to popular vote the removal of officials from office before the end of their term.

Changes in Technology

The system of checks and balances operates differently today from the way it did in 1789. Back then, there were no televised congressional committee hearings; no electronic communications; no *Larry King Live* talk shows; no *New York Times*, *USA Today*, CNN, Fox News, or C-SPAN; no Internet; no nightly news programs with national audiences; no presidential press conferences; and no live coverage of wars and of U.S. soldiers fighting in foreign lands. Nuclear bombs, television, computers, cellular telephones, and the Internet—these and other innovations

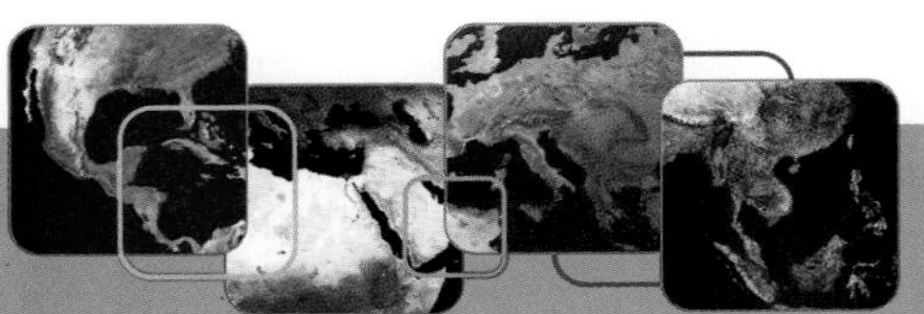

HOW OTHER NATIONS GOVERN

Comparing Constitutional Governance

The U.S. Constitution is unusual in several ways. One distinguishing factor is its brevity. Compare its seven articles and 27 amendments to India's constitution, the longest in the world at 395 articles and 8 schedules. Another unique characteristic of the U.S. Constitution is its age; it is the world's oldest written constitution. It was ratified in 1789, compared to India's, which was passed in 1949.

A hallmark of the U.S. Constitution is its protection of individual liberties, provided for in the Bill of Rights. In comparison, some countries such as China might promise a rule of law and equality under it but fall short of meeting this goal. Some type of dictatorship has been the basis of the constitutional structure under all of China's several constitutions since 1949, and government officials have routinely been shielded from the law. In contrast, India used the U.S. Constitution as the basis for several aspects of its constitution, including the protection of individual rights and a system of federalism.

Not all countries even have constitutions. Great Britain, for example, has an uncodified constitution, not a written one. Instead, its government has developed over many years through custom, history, and a series of laws enacted to provide for the legal structure that exists.

Informal powers and politics can be more important than constitutional provisions granting power. According to Articles 76–81 of Japan's 1947 constitution, the judiciary is independent, as it is in the U.S. system. However, because of the Liberal Democratic Party's long dominance in Japan, it controls court appointments, ensuring that the court reaches decisions it favors.

Of course, as our own Civil War reminds us, the existence of a constitution does not ensure stability. Nigeria, which has undergone four major constitutional changes since 1960, interspersed with military coups and dictatorships, is certainly a case in point. Nigeria's current constitution providing for democratic governance has been in place since 1999. However, allegations of government corruption are widespread, and the government's adherence to the constitution continues to seem tenuous.

QUESTIONS

1. Why might it be an advantage to have a written constitution?
2. What factors might contribute to a successful and stable constitution?

create conditions today that are unimaginably different from those of two centuries ago. We also live in a time of instant communication and polls that tell us what people are thinking about public issues almost from one day to the next.

In some ways, these new technologies have added to the powers of presidents by permitting them to appeal directly to millions of people and giving them immediate access to public opinion. And in turn they have enabled interest groups to target thousands of letters and calls at members of Congress, to orchestrate campaigns to write letters to editors, and to organize and mobilize on the Internet. New technologies have also given greater independence and influence to nongovernmental institutions such as special-interest groups and the press. They have made it possible for rich people to bypass political parties and carry their message directly to the electorate, as former U.S. senator and now New Jersey governor Jon Corzine and religious leaders such as Pat Robertson have done.

The Growth of Presidential Power

Today, problems elsewhere in the world—Afghanistan, Israel, Pakistan, Iran, North Korea, Iraq—often create crises for the United States. The need to deal with perpetual emergencies has concentrated power in the hands of the chief executive and the presidential staff. The president of the United States has emerged as the most significant player on the world stage, and media coverage of summit conferences with foreign leaders enhances his status. Headline-generating events give the president a visibility no congressional leader can achieve. The office of the president has on occasion modified the system of checks and balances, especially between the executive branch and Congress, and provided a measure of national unity. Drawing on constitutional, political, and emergency powers, the president can sometimes overcome the restraints the Constitution imposes on the exercise of governmental power—to the applause of some and the alarm of others.

LEARNING **OBJECTIVE**

5 Show how the use of judicial review strengthens the courts in a separation of powers system.

Judicial Review and the "Guardians of the Constitution"

The judiciary has become so important in our system of checks and balances that it deserves special attention. Judges did not claim the power of **judicial review**—the power to strike down a law or a government regulation that judges believe conflicts with the Constitution—until some years after the Constitution had been adopted. From the beginning, however, judges were expected to check the legislature. "The independence of judges," wrote Alexander Hamilton in *The Federalist*, No. 78 (which appears in the Appendix), "may be an essential safeguard against the effects of occasional ill humors in the society."[19]

Judicial review is a major contribution of the United States to the art of government, one that many other nations have adopted. In Canada, Germany, France, Italy, and Spain, constitutional courts review laws referred to them to ensure that the laws comply with their constitutions, including with the charter of rights that is now part of those constitutions.[20]

LEARNING **OBJECTIVE**

6 Analyze the effect of *Marbury v. Madison* on the role of the judiciary.

judicial review
The power of a court to refuse to enforce a law or a government regulation that in the opinion of the judges conflicts with the U.S. Constitution or, in a state court, the state constitution.

Origins of Judicial Review

The Constitution says nothing about who should have the final word in disputes that may arise over its meaning. Scholars have long debated whether the delegates to the Constitutional Convention of 1787 intended to give the courts the power of judicial review. The framers clearly intended that the Supreme Court have the power to declare state legislation unconstitutional, but whether they meant to give it the same power over *congressional* legislation and the president is not clear. Why didn't the framers specifically provide for judicial review? Probably because they believed justices could infer they had the power, from certain general provisions and the necessity of interpreting and applying a written constitution.

The Federalists—who urged ratification of the Constitution and controlled the national government until 1801—generally supported a strong role for federal courts and thus favored judicial review. Their opponents, the Jeffersonian Republicans (called *Democrats* after 1832), were less enthusiastic. In the Kentucky and Virginia Resolutions of 1798 and 1799, respectively, Jefferson and Madison (who by this time had left the Federalist camp) came close to arguing that state legislatures—and not the Supreme Court—had the ultimate power to interpret the Constitution. These resolutions seemed to question whether the Supreme Court even had final authority to review *state* legislation, a point about which there had been little doubt.

When the Jeffersonians defeated the Federalists in the election of 1800, the question of whether the Supreme Court would actually exercise the power of judicial review was still undecided. Then in 1803 came *Marbury v. Madison,* the most pathbreaking Supreme Court decision of all time.[21]

Chief Justice John Marshall (1755–1835), our most influential Supreme Court justice. Appointed in 1801, Marshall served until 1835. Earlier he had been a staunch defender of the U.S. Constitution at the Virginia ratifying convention, a member of Congress, and a secretary of state. He was one of those rare people who served in all three branches of government.

Marbury v. Madison

President John Adams and fellow Federalists did not take their 1800 defeat by Thomas Jefferson easily. Not only did they lose control of the executive office, they also lost both houses of Congress. That left the judiciary as the last remaining Federalist stronghold.

To further shore up the federal judiciary, the outgoing Federalist Congress consequently created dozens of new judgeships. By March 3, 1801, the day before Jefferson was due to become president, Adams had appointed, and the Senate had confirmed, loyal Federalists to all of these new positions. Although the commissions were signed and sealed, a few, for the newly appointed justices of the peace for the District of Columbia, were not delivered. John Marshall, the outgoing secretary of state and newly confirmed chief justice of

HISTORY MAKERS

Thurgood Marshall's Living Constitution

As a leader in the civil rights movement in the 1940s and 1950s, Thurgood Marshall was a crusading lawyer for the Legal Defense and Educational Fund of the National Association for the Advancement of Colored People (NAACP). He argued before the Supreme Court and won a companion case with the landmark ruling in *Brown v. Board of Education of Topeka* (1954), which held that segregated public schools were unconstitutional. President John Kennedy appointed him to the federal appellate bench in 1961. President Lyndon Johnson then persuaded Marshall to become solicitor general of the United States (the solicitor general argues the government's cases before the Supreme Court), and appointed him to the Supreme Court in 1967. As the first African American on the Supreme Court, Justice Marshall served until 1991 and continued to champion the cause of civil rights throughout his career.

On the Bicentennial of the Constitution in 1987, he spoke out in dissent and defended his view of our "living Constitution":

> I do not believe that the meaning of the Constitution was forever "fixed" at the Philadelphia Convention. Nor do I find the wisdom, foresight, and sense of justice exhibited by the framers particularly profound. To the contrary, the government they devised was defective from the start, requiring several amendments, a civil war, and momentous social transformation to attain the system of constitutional government, and its respect for the individual freedoms and human rights, that we hold as fundamental today. When contemporary Americans cite "The Constitution," they invoke a concept that is vastly different from what the framers barely began to construct two centuries ago.
>
> For a sense of the evolving nature of the Constitution we need look no further than the first three words of the document's preamble: "We the People." When the Founding Fathers used this phrase in 1787, they did not have in mind the majority of America's citizens. "We the People" included, in the words of the framers, "the whole Number of free Persons." On a matter so basic as the right to vote, for example, Negro slaves were excluded, although they were counted for representational purposes—at three-fifths each. Women did not gain the right to vote for over a hundred and thirty years...
>
> And so we must be careful, when focusing on the events which took place in Philadelphia two centuries ago, that we not overlook the momentous events which followed, and thereby lose our proper sense of perspective.... If we seek, instead, a sensitive understanding of the Constitution's inherent defects, and its promising evolution through 200 years of history, the celebration of the "Miracle at Philadelphia" will, in my view, be a far more meaningful and humbling experience. We will see that the true miracle was not the birth of the Constitution, but its life, a life nurtured through two turbulent centuries of our own making, and a life embodying much good fortune that was not.*

Justice Thurgood Marshall.

QUESTIONS

1. How do you think Justice Marshall's experiences with the NAACP Legal and Educational Defense Fund affected his view of the Constitution?
2. Building on the ideas of Justice Marshall, how is our conception of the Constitution today different from citizens' understanding in 1787?

*Remarks at the annual seminar of the San Francisco Patent and Trademark Law Association, Maui, Hawaii, May 16, 1987. Quoted in David M. O'Brien, ed., *Judges on Judging*, 2d ed. (CQ Press, 2004).

the Supreme Court, left the delivery of these commissions for his successor as secretary of state, James Madison.

This "packing" of the judiciary angered Jefferson, now inaugurated as president. When he discovered that some of the commissions were still lying on a table in the Department of State, he instructed a clerk not to deliver them. Jefferson could see no reason why the District needed so many justices of the peace, especially Federalist justices.[22]

William Marbury never received his commission and decided to seek action from the courts. Section 13 of the Judiciary Act of 1789 authorized the Supreme Court "to issue **writs of mandamus**," orders directing an official, such as the secretary of state, to perform a duty, such as delivering a commission. Marbury went directly to the Supreme Court and, citing Section 13, made his request.

writ of mandamus
A court order directing an official to perform an official duty.

Marbury's request presented Chief Justice John Marshall and the Supreme Court with a difficult dilemma. On the one hand, if the Court issued the writ, Jefferson and

Madison would probably ignore it. The Court would be powerless, and its prestige, already low, might suffer a fatal blow. On the other hand, by refusing to issue the writ, the judges would appear to support the Jeffersonian Republicans' claim that the Court had no authority to interfere with the executive. Would Marshall issue the writ? Most people thought he would; angry Republicans even threatened impeachment if he did so.

On February 24, 1803, the Supreme Court delivered what is still considered a brilliantly written and politically savvy decision. First, Marshall, writing for a unanimous Court, took Jefferson and Madison to task. Marbury was entitled to his commission, and Madison should have delivered it to him. Moreover, the proper court could issue a writ of mandamus, even against so high an officer as the secretary of state.

However, Marshall concluded that Section 13 of the Judiciary Act, giving the Supreme Court original jurisdiction to issue writs of mandamus, was in error. It impermissibly expanded the Court's original jurisdiction, which is detailed in Article III of the Constitution. Marshall concluded that the grant of original jurisdiction in Article III was meant to be limited to those cases explicitly mentioned: when an ambassador, foreign minister, or a state is a party. Because none of these was at issue in Marbury's request for the writ of mandamus, the Court deemed Section 13 of the Judiciary Act contrary to the Constitution. Given that Article VI provided that the Constitution is the "supreme Law of the Land," and judges took an oath to uphold the Constitution, any law in conflict with it could not withstand the Court's review.

Although the Federalists suffered a political loss in not seating all their "midnight judges" on the bench, Marshall and the Court gained a much more important power to declare laws passed by Congress unconstitutional. Subsequent generations might have interpreted *Marbury v. Madison* in a limited way, such as that the Supreme Court had the right to determine the scope of its own powers under Article III, but Congress and the president had the authority to interpret their powers under Articles I and II. But over the decades, building on Marshall's precedent, the Court has taken the commanding position as the authoritative interpreter of the Constitution.

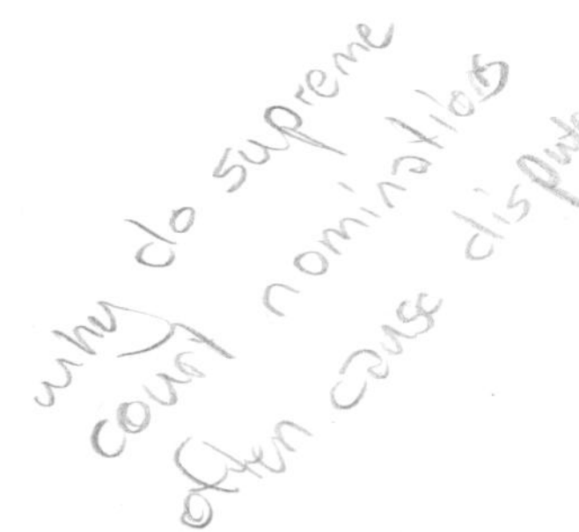

Once we accept Marshall's argument that judges are the official interpreters of the Constitution, several important consequences follow. The most important is that people can challenge laws enacted by Congress and approved by the president. Simply by bringing a lawsuit, those who lack the clout to get a bill through Congress can often secure a judicial hearing. And organized interest groups often find they can achieve goals through litigation that they could not attain through legislation. Litigation thus supplements, and at times even takes precedence over, legislation as a way to make public policy.[23]

LEARNING **OBJECTIVE**

7 Explain how the meaning of the Constitution has evolved over time.

The Constitution as an Instrument of Government

As careful as the Constitution's framers were to limit the powers they gave the national government, the main reason they assembled in Philadelphia was to create a stronger national government. Having learned that a weak central government was a danger to liberty, they wished to establish a national government within the framework of a federal system with enough authority to meet the needs of all time. They made general grants of power, leaving it to succeeding generations to fill in the details and organize the structure of government in accordance with experience.

Hence our formal, written Constitution is only the skeleton of our system. It is filled out in numerous ways that we must consider part of our constitutional system in a larger sense. In fact, our system is kept up to date primarily through changes in the informal, unwritten Constitution. These changes exist in certain basic statutes and historical practices of Congress, presidential actions, and, as we discuss in the "You Will Decide" feature, Supreme Court decisions.

The Unwritten Constitution

Congressional Elaboration Because the framers gave Congress authority to provide for the structural details of the national government, it is not necessary to amend the Constitution every time a change is needed. Rather, Congress can create legislation to meet the need, with what we refer to as **congressional elaboration.** The Judiciary Act of 1789, for example, laid the foundations for our national judicial system, just as other laws established the organization and functions of all federal executive officials subordinate to the president and enacted the rules of procedure, internal organization, and practices of Congress.

A dramatic example of this congressional elaboration of our constitutional system is the use of the impeachment and removal power. An **impeachment** is a formal accusation against a public official and the first step in removing him or her from office. Constitutional language defining the grounds for impeachment is sparse. Look at the Constitution and note that Article II, the Executive Article, calls for removal of the president, vice president, and all civil officers of the United States on impeachment for, and conviction of, "Treason, Bribery, or other High Crimes and Misdemeanors." Still, Congress has to give meaning to that language.

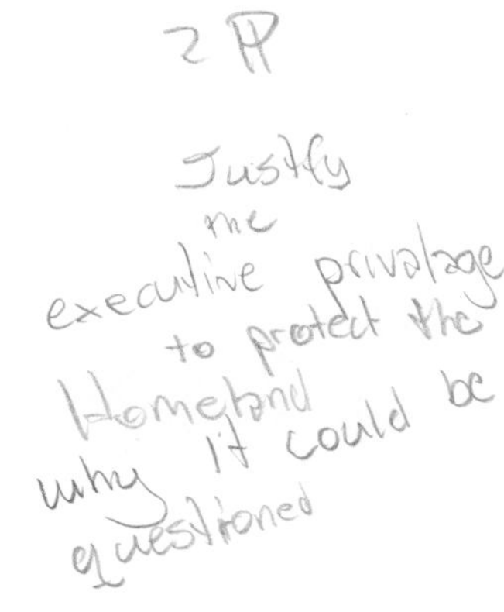

Article I, the Legislative Article, gives the House of Representatives the sole power to initiate impeachments and the Senate the sole power to try them. If the president is tried, the chief justice of the United States presides, as Chief Justice William H. Rehnquist did in the impeachment of President Bill Clinton in 1999. Article I also requires conviction on impeachment charges to have the agreement of two-thirds of the senators present. Judgments shall extend no further than removal from office and disqualification from holding any office under the United States, but a person convicted by the Senate may also be liable to indictment, trial, judgment, and punishment according to the law. Article I also exempts cases of impeachment from the president's pardoning power. Article III (the Judicial Article) exempts cases of impeachment from the jury trial requirement. That is all the relevant constitutional language about impeachment. We must look to history to answer most questions about the proper exercise of these and other powers.[24]

Fortunately, there is little history to go on. The House of Representatives has investigated 67 individuals for possible impeachment and has impeached 17 (including two presidents—Andrew Johnson in 1868 and Bill Clinton in 1999).

LEARNING **OBJECTIVE**

8 Outline the way we make formal changes to the Constitution.

Presidential Practices

Although the formal constitutional powers of the president have not changed, the office is dramatically more important and more central today than it was in 1789. Vigorous presidents—George Washington, Thomas Jefferson, Andrew Jackson, Abraham Lincoln, Theodore Roosevelt, Woodrow Wilson, Franklin Roosevelt, Harry Truman, Lyndon Johnson, Bill Clinton, and George W. Bush—have boldly exercised their political and constitutional powers, especially during times of national crisis such as the current war against international terrorism. Their presidential practices have established important precedents, building the power and influence of the office.

A major practice is the use of **executive orders**, which carry the full force of law. They may make major policy changes, such as withholding federal contracts from businesses engaging in racial discrimination, or they may simply be formalities, such as the presidential proclamation of Earth Day.

Other practices include **executive privilege**, the right to confidentiality of executive communications, especially those that relate to national security; **impoundment** by a president of funds previously appropriated by Congress; the power to send armed forces into hostilities; and the authority to propose legislation and work actively to secure its passage by Congress.

Foreign and economic crises as well as nuclear-age realities and the war against international terrorism have expanded the president's role: "When it comes to action risking nuclear war, technology has modified the Constitution: the President, perforce, becomes the only such man in the system capable of exercising judgment under the

congressional elaboration
Congressional legislation that gives further meaning to the Constitution based on sometimes vague constitutional authority, such as the necessary and proper clause.

impeachment
A formal accusation by the lower house of a legislature against a public official, the first step in removal from office.

executive order
A directive issued by a president or governor that has the force of law.

executive privilege
The power to keep executive communications confidential, especially if they relate to national security.

impoundment
Presidential refusal to allow an agency to spend funds that Congress authorized and appropriated.

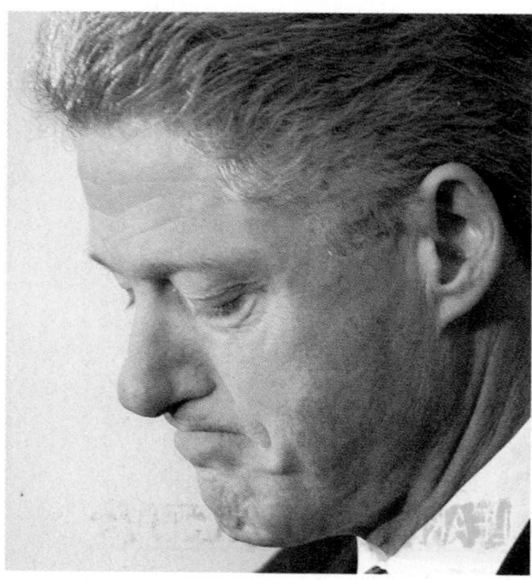

Two U.S. presidents, Andrew Johnson and Bill Clinton, have been impeached by the U.S. House of Representatives. In both cases the U.S. Senate did not muster a two-thirds majority vote, which would have been needed to convict these two presidents. President Richard Nixon almost surely would also have been impeached by the House of Representatives in 1974, but he resigned and left the presidency, a decision that preempted the House's action.

extraordinary limits now imposed by secrecy, complexity, and time."[25] The presidency has also become the pivotal office for regulating the economy and promoting the general welfare through an expanded federal bureaucracy (as we discuss in Chapter 13). In addition, the president has become a leader in sponsoring legislation as well as the nation's chief executive.

Custom and Usage

Custom and usage also play a role in our governmental system. The development of structures outside the formal Constitution—such as national political parties, interest groups, and expanded suffrage—has democratized our Constitution. Other examples of custom and usage are in televised press conferences and presidential and vice presidential debates. Through such developments, the president has become responsive to the people and has a political base different from that of Congress. Consequently, the constitutional relationship between the branches today is considerably different from what the framers envisioned.

Changing the Letter of the Constitution

The idea of a constantly changing system disturbs many people. How, they contend, can you have a constitutional government when the Constitution is constantly being twisted by interpretation and changed by informal methods? This view fails to distinguish between two aspects of the Constitution. As an expression of *basic and timeless personal liberties*, the Constitution does not, and should not, change. For example, a government cannot destroy free speech and still remain a constitutional government. In this sense, the Constitution is unchanging. But when we consider the Constitution as an *instrument of government* and a positive grant of power, we realize that if it did not grow with the nation it serves, it would soon be irrelevant and ignored.

The framers could never have conceived of the problems facing the government of a large, powerful, and wealthy nation of about 300 million people at the beginning of the twenty-first century. Although the general purposes of government remain the same—to establish liberty, promote justice, ensure domestic tranquillity, and provide for the common defense—the powers of government that were adequate to accomplish these purposes in 1787 are simply insufficient more than 220 years later. The framers knew that future experiences would call for changes in the text of the Constitution and that it would need to be formally amended. In Article V, they gave responsibility for amending the Constitution to Congress and to the states. The president has no formal authority over constitutional amendments; presidential veto power does not extend to them, although presidential influence is often crucial in getting amendments proposed and ratified.

Proposing Amendments

The first method for proposing amendments—and the only one used so far—is by *a two-thirds vote of both houses of Congress*. Dozens of resolutions proposing amendments are introduced in every session, but Congress has proposed only 31 amendments, of which 27 have been ratified (see Figure 2–2).

Why is introducing amendments to the Constitution so popular? In part because groups frustrated by their inability to get things done in Congress hope to bypass it. In part because Congress, the president, interest groups, or the public may want to overturn unpopular Supreme Court decisions. In part because the nation needs to make government more responsive to changing times. Although amendments are debated rather frequently, very few have made it through Congress to begin the ratification process.

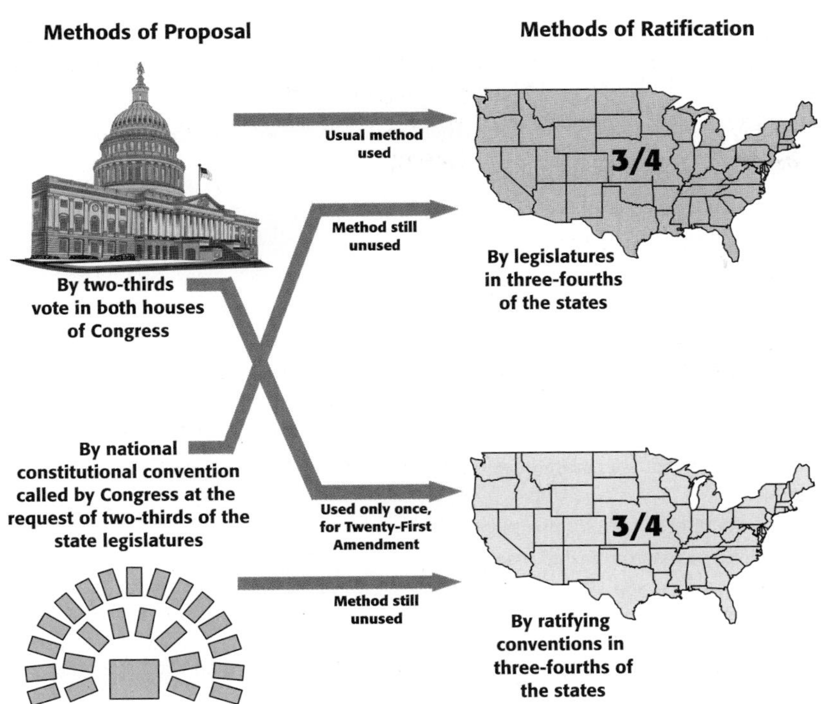

FIGURE 2–2
Four Methods of Amending the Constitution.

Congress, the president, interest groups, and the public were all involved in an effort to overturn the Supreme Court's decision to strike down a Texas law barring flag burning (*Texas v. Johnson* [1989]).[26] Though Congress attempted to bypass the decision with the Federal Flag Protection Act of 1989, which prohibited intentionally burning or defiling the flag, the Court struck down that law as well (*United States v. Eichman* [1990]).[27] In doing so, the Court ruled that the First Amendment protects burning the flag as a form of political speech.

You Are Proposing a Constitutional Amendment

Following its failure to overturn the decision through new laws, Congress has made repeated efforts to send a constitutional amendment banning flag burning to the states.[28] The House of Representatives has voted seven times since the early 1990s on an amendment prohibiting the "physical desecration of the flag of the United States," but the Senate has been unable to garner the necessary two-thirds vote. It came close to succeeding in June 2006, but the vote fell one short of the number required to send the amendment to the states for ratification.[29] See Table 2–2 on how the amending power has been used.

Outside the 1984 Republican National Convention, Gregory Johnson burned an American flag to protest the Reagan administration's policies. The U.S. Supreme Court upheld his right to do so as a protected form of expression under the First Amendment.

The second method for proposing amendments—*a convention called by Congress at the request of the legislatures in two-thirds of the states*—has never been used. Under Article V of the Constitution, Congress could call for such a convention without the concurrence of the president. This method presents difficult questions.[30] First, can state legislatures apply for a convention to propose specific amendments on one topic, or must they request a convention with full powers to revise the entire Constitution? How long do state petitions remain alive? How should delegates to a convention be chosen? How should such a convention be run? Congress has considered bills to answer some of these questions but has not passed any, in part because most members do not wish to encourage a constitutional convention for fear that once in session it might propose amendments on any and all topics.

Under most proposals, each state would have as many delegates to the convention as it has representatives and senators in Congress. Finally, and crucially, a constitutional convention would be limited to considering only the subject specified in the state legislative petitions and described in the congressional call

TABLE 2–2 The Amending Power and How It Has Been Used

Leaving aside the first ten amendments (the Bill of Rights), the power of constitutional amendment has served a number of purposes:

To Increase or Decrease the Power of the National Government

The Eleventh took some jurisdiction away from the national courts.
The Thirteenth abolished slavery and authorized Congress to legislate against it.
The Sixteenth enabled Congress to levy an income tax.
The Eighteenth authorized Congress to prohibit the manufacture, sale, or transportation of liquor.
The Twenty-First repealed the Eighteenth and gave states the authority to regulate liquor sales.
The Twenty-Seventh limited the power of Congress to set members' salaries.

To Expand the Electorate and Its Power

The Fifteenth extended suffrage to all male African Americans over age 21.
The Seventeenth took the right to elect U.S. senators away from state legislatures and gave it to the voters in each state.
The Nineteenth extended suffrage to women over age 21.
The Twenty-Third gave voters of the District of Columbia the right to vote for president and vice president.
The Twenty-Fourth outlawed the poll tax, thereby prohibiting states from taxing the right to vote.
The Twenty-Sixth extended suffrage to otherwise qualified persons age 18 or older.

To Reduce the Electorate's Power

The Twenty-Second took away from the electorate the right to elect a person to the office of president for more than two full terms.

To Limit State Government Power

The Thirteenth abolished slavery.
The Fourteenth granted national citizenship and prohibited states from abridging privileges of national citizenship; from denying persons life, liberty, and property without due process; and from denying persons equal protection of the laws. This amendment has come to be interpreted as imposing restraints on state powers in every area of public life.

To Make Structural Changes in Government

The Twelfth corrected deficiencies in the operation of the electoral college that the development of a two-party national system had revealed.
The Twentieth altered the calendar for congressional sessions and shortened the time between the election of presidents and their assumption of office.
The Twenty-Fifth provided procedures for filling vacancies in the vice presidency and for determining whether presidents are unable to perform their duties.

The History of Constitutional Amendments

for the convention. Scholars are divided, however, on whether Congress has the authority to limit what a constitutional convention might propose.[31]

Ratifying Amendments

After Congress has proposed an amendment, the states must ratify it before it takes effect. Again, the Constitution provides two methods, and Congress may choose: approval by the legislatures in three-fourths of the states, or approval by special ratifying conventions in three-fourths of the states. Congress has submitted all amendments except one—the Twenty-First (to repeal the Eighteenth, the Prohibition Amendment)—to the state legislatures for ratification.

Seven state constitutions specify that their state legislatures must ratify a proposed amendment to the U.S. Constitution by majorities of three-fifths or two-thirds of each chamber. Although a state legislature may change its mind and ratify an amendment after it has voted against ratification, the weight of opinion is that once a state has ratified an amendment, it cannot "unratify" it.[32]

The Supreme Court has said that ratification must take place within a "reasonable time," so that it is "sufficiently contemporaneous to reflect the will of the people."[33] However, Congress approved ratification of the Twenty-Seventh Amendment, which had been before the nation for almost 203 years, so there seems to be no limit on what it considers a "reasonable time." In fact, ratification ordinarily takes place rather quickly (see Figure 2–3), and Congress will probably

THE **CHANGING FACE** OF U.S. POLITICS

The United States' Racial Heritage

During his rise as one of golf's greatest players, Tiger Woods has repeatedly refused to identify himself as a member of any one race, be it white, African American, Asian American, or Hispanic. Instead, Woods says that he decided as a child that he was a "Cablinasian," a reference to being *Cau*casian (white), *Bl*ack, American *In*dian, and *Asian*. However, before the 2000 census (the census is conducted every ten years as mandated by the Constitution), he would not have been allowed to declare himself as a member of more than one race. He could have checked only one of the following boxes for race—Caucasian, African American, Asian, or Native American. Hispanics and Latinos were identified separately.

Tiger Woods is one of an increasing number of Americans of mixed racial heritage.

Starting in 2000, Woods and millions of other multiracial citizens were able to identify themselves more accurately in the census. Under federal rules adopted in 1998, they were allowed to check off one or all of seven boxes, including new categories for Native Hawaiian and other Pacific Islanders, which used to be included in "Asian." Once Woods identified himself as any race other than white, he was also free to identify with one or more of the following races, or with another race entirely:

- American Indian or Alaska Native
- Asian Indian
- Chinese
- Filipino
- Japanese
- Korean
- Vietnamese
- Native Hawaiian
- Guamanian or Chamorro
- Samoan
- Other Pacific Islander

The new rules reflect the reality that the United States is becoming more diverse and now includes more people of mixed racial heritage. The census, which is used to divide the states into congressional districts, is working to keep up with the changing face of the United States, which means that citizens like Tiger Woods will be able to find a home in the portraits of the citizenry. Although the percentage of multiracial citizens is low, it still represents more than seven million of the nation's 281 million people.

QUESTIONS

1. How would you identify yourself?
2. What kind of changes in survey participation might we see with more options for self-identification?

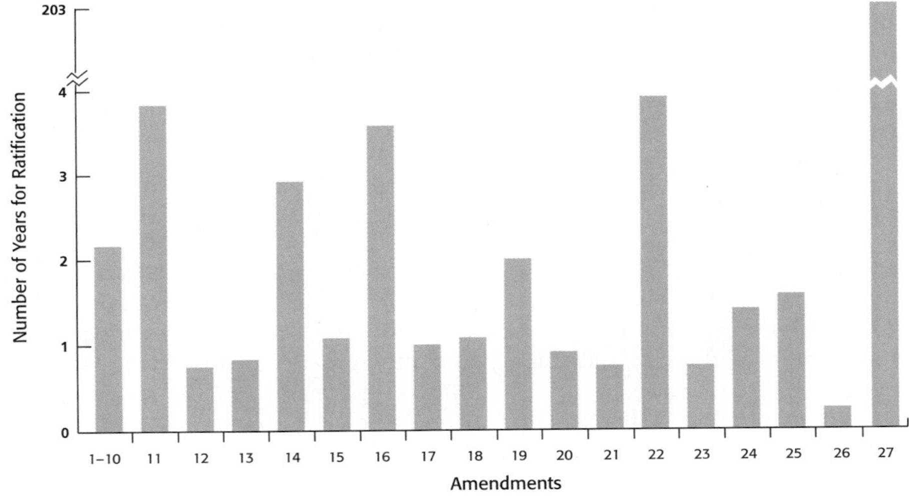

FIGURE 2–3
The Time for Ratification of the 27 Amendments to the Constitution.

YOU WILL **DECIDE** Should We Interpret the Constitution According to Original Intent or Today's Needs?

Debate about how to interpret the Constitution began almost immediately, and as we've seen, it continues to this day, with very important practical implications for citizens.

One kind of constitutional interpretation is the *originalist* approach. Originalists believe that the Constitution should be understood according to the framers' intent. Others believe that whenever possible, a strict reading of the text should guide decision making. But if the exact wording of the document does not provide a conclusive answer, originalists consider the context of the times in which it was written and interpret it in light of the history and writings of the time. Especially important are writings or speeches by the founders themselves or by proponents of subsequent amendments.

A second approach to interpreting the Constitution sees it as a changing and evolving document that provides a basic framework for government but that allows, and even encourages, new generations to interpret ideas such as "equal justice" and "due process" in light of the needs of their time. This *adaptive* approach may mean that subsequent generations will interpret the same document differently from prior generations.

The adaptive approach makes the court a more powerful institution in U.S. government. The originalist approach forces people and institutions to adopt amendments if they want constitutional change.

continue to stipulate that it must occur within seven years of the date it submits an amendment to the states.

Ratification Politics

The failure of the Equal Rights Amendment (ERA) to be ratified provides a vivid example of the pitfalls of ratification. First introduced in 1923, the ERA did not get much support until the 1960s. An influential book by Betty Friedan, *The Feminine Mystique* (1963), challenged stereotypes about the role of women. The National Organization for Women (NOW), formed in 1966, made passage of the ERA its central mission. By the 1970s, the ERA had overwhelming support in both houses of Congress and in both national party platforms. Every president from Harry Truman to Ronald Reagan, and many of their wives, endorsed the amendment. More than 450 organizations with a total membership of more than 50 million were on record in support of the ERA.[34] The ERA provided for the following:

Section 1. Equality of rights under the law shall not be denied or abridged by the United States or by any State on account of sex.

People came from every state in the union to march in support of the passage of the Equal Rights Amendment.

Section 2. The Congress shall have power to enforce, by appropriate legislation, the provisions of this article.

Section 3. This amendment shall take effect two years after the date of ratification.[35]

Soon after Congress passed the amendment and submitted it to the states in 1972, many legislatures ratified it—sometimes without hearings—and by overwhelming majorities. By the end of that year, 22 states had ratified the amendment, and it appeared that the ERA would soon become part of the Constitution. But because of opposition organized under the leadership of Phyllis Schlafly, a prominent spokesperson for conservative causes, the ERA became controversial.

Opponents argued that "women would not only be subject to the military draft but also assigned to combat duty. Full-time housewives and mothers would be forced to join the labor force. Further, women would no longer enjoy existing advantages under state domestic relations codes and under labor law."[36] The ERA also became embroiled in the controversy over abortion. Many opponents contended that its ratification would jeopardize the power of states and Congress to regulate abortion and would compel public funding of abortions.[37]

State legislatures held lengthy hearings, and floor debates became heated. Legislators hid behind parliamentary procedures and avoided making a decision for as long as possible. Opposition to ratification arose chiefly in the same cluster of southern states that had opposed ratification of the Nineteenth Amendment, which gave women the right to vote. As the opposition grew more active, proponents redoubled their efforts.

In the autumn of 1978, it appeared that the ERA would fall three short of the necessary number of ratifying states before the expiration of the seven-year limit on March 22, 1979. After an extended debate, and after voting down provisions that would have authorized state legislatures to change their minds and rescind ratification, Congress, by a simple majority vote, extended the time limit until June 30, 1982. Nonetheless, by the final deadline, the amendment was still three states short of the 38 needed for ratification.

The framers intended that amending the Constitution should be difficult, and the ERA ratification battle demonstrates how well they planned. Through interpretation, practices, usages, and judicial decisions, the Constitution has proved a remarkably enduring and adaptable governing document and one that is frequently used as a model for emerging democracies. But it is essential for citizens, individually and together, to keep watch that constitutional provisions are enforced and that change comes when necessary. Not all efforts for constitutional change are successful, but even failed drives for constitutional amendments can achieve a degree of success through the legislative process, influence on the executive, or calls for action by the judiciary, as the students from the Santa Fe Independent School District learned firsthand.

THINKING IT THROUGH

Differences between the adaptive and the originalist views do not necessarily align with political labels such as *conservative* or *liberal*, though they may in particular cases. For example, Justice Antonin Scalia, who tends to be originalist in his approach, voted in *Santa Fe Independent School District v. Doe* (the case discussed at the beginning of the chapter) to allow pregame prayer at public high school football games because according to his reading of the First Amendment, the activity does not amount to an establishment of religion. An originalist interpretation of the First Amendment requires only that Congress refrains from establishing a national religion and does not interfere with already established state churches, many of which existed at the time the Constitution was ratified.

Justice Stephen Breyer typically favors a more adaptive approach. He interpreted the same clause as aiming to lessen religious strife and avoid the "social conflict, potentially created when government becomes involved in religious education."* He therefore ruled that the school district's policy violated the First Amendment and joined the Court's majority opinion striking it down.

If the Constitution is indeed open to changing interpretations, are any constitutional principles absolute and *not* open to new interpretation? Or are the law and the courts largely ideological institutions? This danger in the adaptive approach worries some because the selection of judges is only indirectly democratic, and with lifetime appointments judges could lose the people's confidence yet retain their power.

There are problems with the originalist approach as well. A global economy, electronic and mass media, and the need to respond immediately to national security threats are only some examples of circumstances the founders could not consider or address in the Constitution. In other instances, such as with privacy, for example, the original wording of the Constitution implies an interpretation but does not explicitly say it.

Questions

1. How do you think we should interpret the Constitution? What are the best arguments of both sides of this question?
2. Why does it matter whether we take an originalist or an adaptive approach to interpreting the Constitution?

*Stephen Breyer, *Active Liberty: Interpreting Our Democratic Constitution* (Knopf, 2005), pp. 120–121.

CHAPTER **SUMMARY**

1 Describe the basic structure of the Constitution and its Bill of Rights.

The U.S. Constitution's first three articles establish the legislature, the executive, and the judiciary. The Bill of Rights, the first ten amendments to the Constitution, was added in 1791 and provides protections from federal government infringement on individual liberties.

2 Summarize the basic principles of government established by the Constitution.

The U.S. Constitution, adopted in 1789, is the world's oldest. It both grants and limits governmental power. The Constitution's separation of powers distributes authority among three branches of government: the legislative, executive, and judicial. Checks and balances limit the power of each branch.

3 Compare and contrast the three main branches of the U.S. government.

The Constitution separates power vested in the legislature, which has the power to create law; the executive, with the power to enforce the law; and the judiciary, which interprets the law. None of the branches depends on the others for its authority, and each branch has the power to limit the others.

4 Show how the system of checks and balances operates among the three branches of the U.S. government.

Competing interests within our governmental structure check and balance one another. Political parties may sometimes overcome the separation of powers, especially if the same party controls both houses of Congress and the presidency. Typically, this is not the case, however, and a divided government intensifies checks and balances. Presidential power, which has increased over time, has sometimes overcome restraints the Constitution imposes on it.

5 Show how the use of judicial review strengthens the courts in a separation of powers system.

Judicial review is the power of the courts to strike down acts of Congress, the executive branch, and the states as unconstitutional. This authority provides the judiciary a powerful check on the other branches of government.

6 Analyze the effect of *Marbury v. Madison* on the role of the judiciary.

In deciding that it lacked the jurisdiction to order a judicial commission be delivered, the Supreme Court established its authority to rule an act of the federal legislature unconstitutional. The Court's decision was politically savvy and greatly enhanced the role of the judiciary in a separation-of-powers system.

7 Explain how the meaning of the Constitution has evolved over time.

The Constitution is the framework of our governmental system. The constitutional system has been modified over time, adapting to new conditions through congressional elaboration, presidential practices, custom and usage, and judicial interpretation, as was the case in *Santa Fe Independent School District v. Doe* (2000). The First Amendment's brevity allows courts to interpret it in light of changing circumstances, but also engenders continuing debate about its meaning.

8 Outline the way we make formal changes to the Constitution.

Although adaptable, the Constitution itself needs to be altered from time to time, and the framers provided a formal procedure for its amendment. An amendment must be both proposed and ratified: proposed by either a two-thirds vote in each chamber of Congress or by a national convention called by Congress on petition of the legislatures in two-thirds of the states; ratified either by the legislatures in three-fourths of the states or by special ratifying conventions in three-fourths of the states.

Chapter Self-Test

1. How many amendments does the U.S. Constitution have? (p. 30) Does this number seem high or low to you? Why?

2. Write two or three paragraphs to explain the ways the writers of the constitution attempted to limit the power of the branches in the federal government. (pp. 31–32)

3. The Constitution reflects the Founders' respect for _______ law, which implies a universal sense of right and wrong. (p. 31)

   a. Natural
   b. Formal
   c. Federal
   d. Corporal

4. Write a persuasive essay (2–3 paragraphs) justifying the use of executive privilege (p. 41) to protect the homeland. Be sure to address why this privilege might be questioned.

5. How does the legislative branch check the authority of the executive branch? List and briefly explain at least two ways. (pp. 32–33)

6. Draw a diagram that shows how the different branches of government check one another. (Table 2–1 can provide useful examples.)

7. Describe the difference between an initiative and a referendum. (pp. 35–36)
8. Many people are uncomfortable with what they term "activist judges." Explain the Constitutional grounds for and against judicial activism in 4 sentences or less. (p. 38)
9. Describe the details of *Marbury v. Madison* and who the major actors were. Explain why the case was heard in the first place. Describe the impact of the decision. (pp. 38–40)
10. Explain why nominations to the Supreme Court are often so contentious. (p. 40)
11. Describe a writ of mandamus. Give an example of an occasion when it might be appropriate for the court to issue such a writ. (p. 39)
12. What are some of the advantages of having a written constitution? List 4 or 5. Can you think of any disadvantages? (p. 37)
13. The chapter lists two ways to propose amendments. Name these two ways and describe how they are different. How is an amendment ratified? (pp. 42–43)
14. Write a brief essay detailing the difficulties that politicians would face in holding a new constitutional convention. Which individuals or groups might be opposed to a new convention? What are some of the procedural hurdles supporters would have to overcome? (pp. 43–44)
15. How many states would need to agree to hold a new constitutional convention? (p. 43)

Key Terms

natural law, p. 31
separation of powers, p. 32
checks and balances, p. 32
divided government, p. 34
partisanship, p. 34
direct primary, p. 35
initiative, p. 36
referendum, p. 36
recall, p. 36
judicial review, p. 38
writ of mandamus, p. 39
congressional elaboration, p. 41
impeachment, p. 41
executive order, p. 41
executive privilege, p. 41
impoundment, p. 41

Further Reading

AKHILL REED AMAR, *America's Constitution: A Biography* (Random House, 2005).

LANCE BANNING, *The Sacred Fire of Liberty: James Madison and the Founding of the Federal Republic* (Cornell University Press, 1995).

CAROL BERKIN, *A Brilliant Solution: Inventing the American Constitution* (Harcourt, 2002).

STEPHEN BREYER, *Active Liberty: Interpreting Our Democratic Constitution* (Knopf, 2005).

JAMES MACGREGOR BURNS, *The Vineyard of Liberty* (Knopf, 1982).

NEIL H. COGAN, *The Complete Bill of Rights: The Drafts, Debates, Sources, and Origins* (Oxford University Press, 1997).

MICHAEL KAMMEN, *A Machine That Would Go of Itself: The Constitution in American Culture* (Knopf, 1986).

KEN I. KERSCH, *Constructing Civil Liberties: Discontinuities in the Development of American Constitutional Law* (Cambridge University Press, 2004).

PHILIP B. KURLAND AND **RALPH LERNER,** *The Founders' Constitution*, 5 vols. (*University of Chicago Press*, 1987).

LIBRARY OF CONGRESS, CONGRESSIONAL RESEARCH SERVICE, JONNY KILLIAN, ED., *The Constitution of the United States of America: Analysis and Interpretation* (U.S. Government Printing Office, 2006).

ANTONIN SCALIA, *A Matter of Interpretation: Federal Courts and the Law* (Princeton University Press, 1997).

CASS SUNSTEIN, *Designing Democracy: What Constitutions Do* (Oxford University Press, 2001).

JOHN R. VILE, ED., *Encyclopedia of Constitutional Amendments, Proposed Amendments, and Amending Issues, 1789–2002* (ABC-Clio, 2003).

KEITH E. WHITTINGTON, *Political Foundations of Judicial Supremacy: The Presidency, the Supreme Court, and Constitutional Leadership in U.S. History* (Princeton University Press, 2007).

On Reading the Constitution

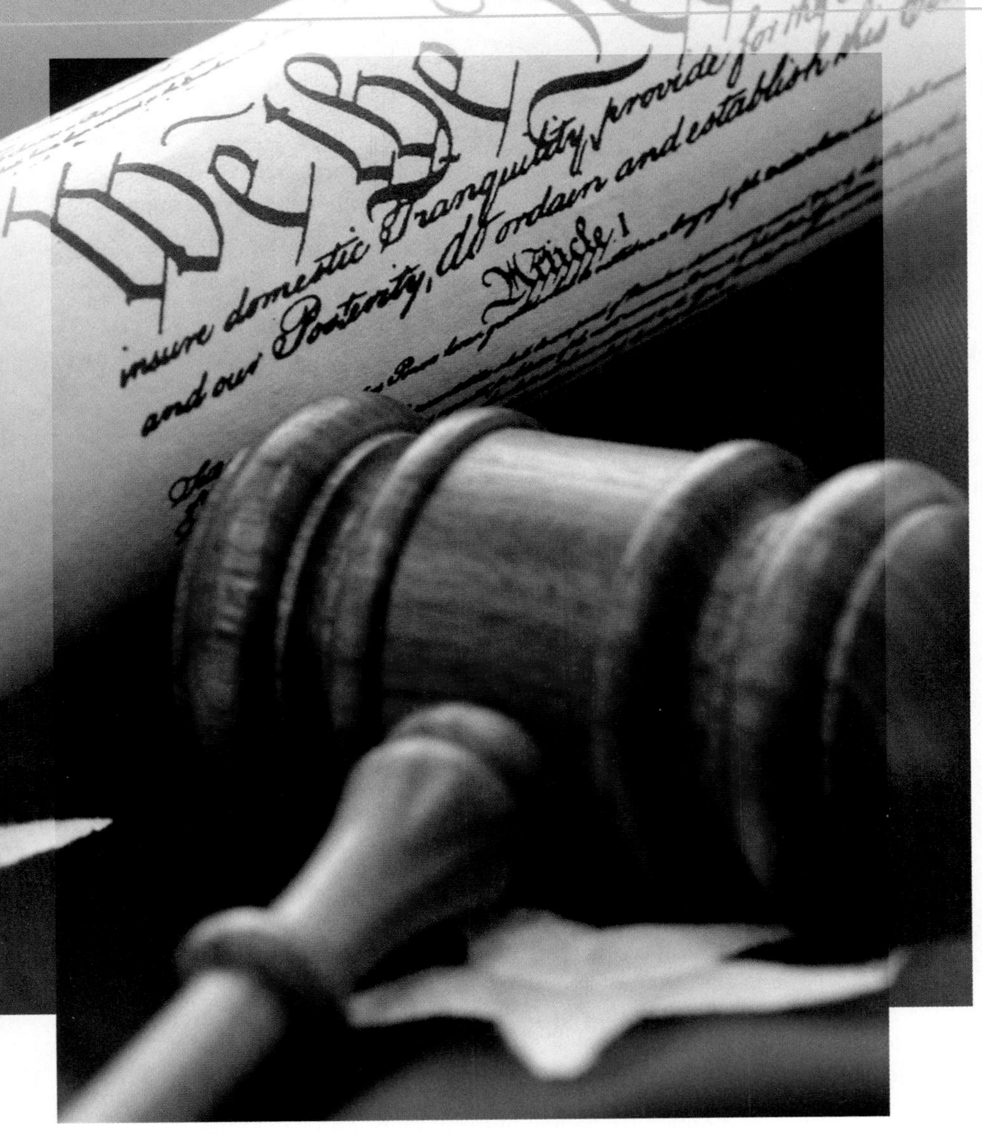

More than 218 years after its ratification, our Constitution remains the operating charter of our republic. It is neither self-explanatory nor a comprehensive description of our constitiutional rules. Still, it remains the starting point. Many Americans who swear by the Constitution have never read it seriously, although copies can be found in most American government and American history textbooks.

Justice Hugo Black, who served on the Supreme Court for 34 years, kept a copy of the Constitution with him at all times. He read it often. Reading the Constitution would be a good way for you to begin (and then reread again to end) your study of the government of the United States. We have therefore included a copy of it at this point in the book. Please read it carefully.

The Constitution of the United States

The Preamble

We the People of the United States, in Order to form a more perfect Union, establish Justice, insure domestic Tranquility, provide for the common defense, promote the general Welfare, and secure the Blessings of Liberty to ourselves and our Posterity, do ordain and establish this Constitution for the United States of America.

Article I—The Legislative Article

Legislative Power

SECTION 1 All legislative Powers herein granted shall be vested in a Congress of the United States, which shall consist of a Senate and House of Representatives.

House of Representatives: Composition; Qualifications; Apportionment; Impeachment Power

SECTION 2

Clause 1 The House of Representatives shall be composed of Members chosen every second Year by the People of the several States, and the Electors in each State shall have the Qualifications requisite for Electors of the most numerous Branch of the State Legislature.

Clause 2 No Person shall be a Representative who shall not have attained to the Age of twenty five Years, and been seven Years a Citizen of the United States, and who shall not, when elected, be an inhabitant of that State in which he shall be chosen.

Clause 3 Representatives and direct Taxes[1] shall be apportioned among the several States which may be included within this Union, according to their respective Numbers, which shall be determined by adding to the whole Number of free Persons, including those bound to Service for a Term of Years, and excluding Indians not taxed, three fifths of all other Persons.[2] The actual Enumeration shall be made within three Years after the first Meeting of the Congress of the United States, and within every subsequent Term of ten Years, in such Manner as they shall by Law direct. The Number of Representatives shall not exceed one for every thirty Thousand, but each State shall have at Least one Representative; and until such enumeration shall be made, the State of New Hampshire shall be entitled to chuse three, Massachusetts eight, Rhode-Island and Providence Plantations one, Connecticut five, New-York six, New Jersey four, Pennsylvania eight, Delaware one, Maryland six, Virginia ten, North Carolina five, South Carolina five, and Georgia three.

Clause 4 When vacancies happen in the Representation from any State, the Executive Authority thereof shall issue Writs of Election to fill such Vacancies.

Clause 5 The House of Representatives shall chuse their Speaker and other Officers; and shall have the sole Power of Impeachment.

Senate Composition: Qualifications, Impeachment Trials

SECTION 3

Clause 1 The Senate of the United States shall be composed of two Senators from each State, chosen by the Legislature thereof,[3] for six Years; and each Senator shall have one Vote.

Clause 2 Immediately after they shall be assembled in Consequence of the first Election, they shall be divided as equally as may be into three Classes. The Seats of the Senators of the first Class shall be vacated at the Expiration of the second Year, of the second Class at the Expiration of the fourth Year, and of the third Class at the Expiration of the sixth Year, so that one third may be chosen every second Year; and if Vacancies happen by Resignation, or otherwise, during the Recess of the Legislature of any State, the Executive thereof may make temporary Appointments until the next Meeting of the Legislature, which shall then fill such Vacancies.[4]

Clause 3 No person shall be a Senator who shall not have attained to the Age of thirty Years, and been nine Years a Citizen of the United States, and who shall not, when elected, be an Inhabitant of that State for which he shall be chosen.

Clause 4 The Vice President of the United States shall be President of the Senate, but shall have no Vote, unless they be equally divided.

Clause 5 The Senate shall chuse their other Officers, and also a President pro tempore, in the Absence of the Vice President, or when he shall exercise the Office of President of the United States.

[1]Modified by the 16th Amendment
[2]Replaced by Section 2, 14th Amendment
[3]Repealed by the 17th Amendment
[4]Modified by the 17th Amendment

Clause 6 The Senate shall have the sole Power to try all Impeachments. When sitting for that Purpose, they shall be on Oath or Affirmation. When the President of the United States is tried, the Chief Justice shall preside: And no Person shall be convicted without the Concurrence of two thirds of the Members present.

Judgment in Cases of Impeachment shall not extend further than to removal from Office, and disqualification to hold and enjoy any Office of honor, Trust or Profit under the United States; but the Party convicted shall nevertheless be liable and subject to Indictment, Trial, Judgment and Punishment, according to Law.

Congressional Elections: Times, Places, Manner

SECTION 4 The Times, Places and Manner of holding Elections for Senators and Representatives, shall be prescribed in each State by the Legislature thereof; but the Congress may at any time by Law make or alter such Regulations, except as to the Places of chusing Senators.

The Congress shall assemble at least once in every Year, and such Meeting shall be on the first Monday in December, unless they shall by Law appoint a different Day.[5]

Powers and Duties of the Houses

SECTION 5

Clause 1 Each House shall be the Judge of the Elections, Returns and Qualifications of its own Members, and a Majority of each shall constitute a Quorum to do Business; but a smaller Number may adjourn from day to day, and may be authorized to compel the Attendance of absent Members, in such Manner, and under the Penalties as each House may provide.

Clause 2 Each House may determine the Rules of its Proceedings, punish its Members for disorderly Behaviour, and, with the Concurrence of two thirds, expel a Member.

Clause 3 Each House shall keep a Journal of its Proceedings, and from time to time publish the same, excepting such Parts as may in their Judgment require Secrecy; and the Yeas and Nays of the Members of either House on any question shall, at the Desire of one fifth of those Present, be entered on the Journal.

Clause 4 Neither House, during the Session of Congress, shall, without the Consent of the other, adjourn for more than three days, nor to any other place than that in which the two Houses shall be sitting.

Rights of Members

SECTION 6

Clause I The Senators and Representatives shall receive a Compensation for their Services, to be ascertained by Law, and paid out of the Treasury of the United States. They shall in all Cases, except Treason, Felony and Breach of the Peace, be privileged from Arrest during their Attendance at the Session of their respective Houses, and in going to and returning from the same; and for any Speech or Debate in either House, they shall not be questioned in any other Place.

Clause 2 No Senator or Representative, shall, during the time for which he was elected, be appointed to any civil Office under the Authority of the United States, which shall have been created, or the Emoluments whereof shall have been increased during such time; and no Person holding any Office under the United States, shall be a Member of either House during his Continuance in Office.

Legislative Powers: Bills and Resolutions

SECTION 7

Clause 1 All Bills for raising Revenue shall originate in the House of Representatives; but the Senate may propose or concur with Amendments as on other Bills.

Clause 2 Every Bill which shall have passed the House of Representatives and the Senate, shall, before it becomes a Law, be presented to the President of the United States; if he approve he shall sign it, but if not he shall return it, with his Objections to that House in which it shall have originated, who shall enter the Objections at large on their Journal, and proceed to reconsider it. If after such Reconsideration two thirds of that House shall agree to pass the Bill, it shall be sent, together with the Objections, to the other House, by which it shall likewise be reconsidered, and if approved by two thirds of that House, it shall become a Law. But in all such Cases the Votes of both Houses shall be determined by yeas and Nays, and the Names of the Persons voting for and against the Bill shall be entered on the Journal of each House respectively. If any Bill shall not be returned by the President within ten Days (Sundays excepted) after it shall have been presented to him, the Same shall be a Law, in like Manner as if he had signed it, unless the Congress by their Adjournment prevent its Return, in which Case it shall not be a Law.

Clause 3 Every Order, Resolution, or Vote to which the Concurrence of the Senate and House of Representatives may be necessary (except on a question of Adjournment) shall be presented to the President of the United States; and before the Same shall take Effect, shall be approved by him, or being disapproved by him, shall be repassed by two thirds of the Senate and House of Representatives, according to the Rules and Limitations prescribed in the Case of a Bill.

Powers of Congress

SECTION 8

Clause 1 The Congress shall have Power To lay and collect Taxes, Duties, Imposts and Excises, to pay the Debts and provide for the common Defence and general Welfare of the United

[5]Changed by the 20th Amendment

States; but all Duties, Imposts and Excises shall be uniform throughout the United States.

To borrow Money on the credit of the United States;

To regulate Commerce with foreign Nations, and among the several States, and with the Indian Tribes;

To establish an uniform Rule of Naturalization, and uniform Laws on the subject of Bankruptcies throughout the United States;

To coin Money, regulate the Value thereof, and of foreign Coin, and fix the Standard of Weights and Measures;

To provide for the Punishment of counterfeiting the Securities and current Coin of the United States;

To establish Post Offices and post Roads;

To promote the Progress of Science and useful Arts, by securing for limited Times to Authors and Inventors the exclusive Right to their respective Writings and Discoveries;

To constitute Tribunals inferior to the supreme Court;

To define and punish Piracies and Felonies committed on the high Seas, and Offences against the Law of Nations;

To declare War, grant Letters of Marque and Reprisal, and make Rules concerning Captures on Land and Water;

To raise and support Armies, but no Appropriation of Money to that Use shall be for a longer Term than two Years;

To provide and maintain a Navy;

To make Rules for the Government and Regulation of the land and naval Forces;

To provide for calling for the Militia to execute the Laws of the Union, suppress Insurrections and repel Invasions;

To provide for organizing, arming, and disciplining the Militia, and for governing such Part of them as may be employed in the Service of the United States, reserving to the States respectively, the Appointment of the Officers, and the Authority of training the Militia according to the discipline prescribed by Congress;

Clause 2 To exercise exclusive Legislation in all Cases whatsoever, over such District (not exceeding ten Miles square) as may, by Cession of particular States, and the Acceptance of Congress, become the Seat of the Government of the United States, and to exercise like Authority over all Places purchased by the Consent of the Legislature of the State in which the Same shall be, for the Erection of Forts, Magazines, Arsenals, dock-Yards; and other needful Buildings;—And

Clause 3 To make all Laws which shall be necessary and proper for carrying into Execution the foregoing Powers, and all other Powers vested by this Constitution in the Government of the United States, or in any Department or Officer thereof.

Powers Denied to Congress

Section 9

Clause 1 The Migration or Importation of such Persons as any of the States now existing shall think proper to admit, shall not be prohibited by the Congress prior to the Year one thousand eight hundred and eight, but a Tax or duty may be imposed on such Importation, not exceeding ten dollars for each Person.

Clause 2 The privilege of the Writ of Habeas Corpus shall not be suspended, unless when in Cases of Rebellion or Invasion the public Safety may require it.

Clause 3 No Bill of Attainder or ex post facto Laws shall be passed.

Clause 4 No Capitation, or other direct, Tax shall be laid, unless in Proportion to the Census or Enumeration herein before directed to be taken.[6]

Clause 5 No Tax or Duty shall be laid on Articles exported from any State.

Clause 6 No Preference shall be given by any Regulation of Commerce or Revenue to the Ports of one State over those of another; nor shall Vessels bound to, or from, one State, be obliged to enter, clear, or pay Duties in another.

Clause 7 No Money shall be drawn from the Treasury, but in Consequence of Appropriations made by Law; and a regular Statement and Account of the Receipts and Expenditures of all public Money shall be published from time to time.

Clause 8 No Title of Nobility shall be granted by the United States; And no Person holding any Office of Profit or Trust under them, shall, without the Consent of Congress, accept of any present, Emolument, Office, or Title, of any kind whatever, from any King, Prince, or foreign State.

Powers Denied to the States

Section 10

Clause 1 No State shall enter into any Treaty, Alliance, or Confederation; grant Letters of Marque and Reprisal; coin Money; emit Bills of Credit; make any Thing but gold and silver Coin a Tender in Payment of Debts; pass any Bill of Attainder, ex post facto Law, or Law impairing the Obligation of Contracts of grant any Title of Nobility.

Clause 2 No State shall, without the Consent of the Congress, lay any Imposts or Duties on Imports or Exports, except what may be absolutely necessary for executing its inspection Laws: and the net Produce of all Duties and Imposts, laid by any State on Imports or Exports, shall be for the Use of the Treasury of the United States; and all such Laws shall be subject to the Revision and Controul of the Congress.

Clause 3 No State shall, without the Consent of Congress, lay any Duty of Tonnage, keep Troops, or Ships of War in time of Peace, enter into any Agreement or Compact with another State, or with a foreign Power, or engage in War, unless actually invaded, or in such imminent Danger as will not admit of Delay.

[6]Modified by the 16th Amendment

Article II—The Executive Article

Nature and Scope of Presidential Power

SECTION 1

Clause 1 The executive Power shall be vested in a President of the United States of America. He shall hold his Office during the Term of four Years and, together with the Vice President, chosen for the same Term, be elected as follows:

Clause 2 Each State shall appoint, in such Manner as the Legislature thereof may direct, a Number of Electors, equal to the whole Number of Senators and Representatives to which the State may be entitled in the Congress: but no Senator or Representative, or Person holding an Office of Trust or Profit under the United States, shall be appointed an Elector.

Clause 3 The Electors shall meet in their respective States, and vote by Ballot for two Persons, of whom one at least shall not be an Inhabitant of the same State with themselves. And they shall make a List of all the Persons voted for, and of the Number of Votes for each; which List they shall sign and certify, and transmit sealed to the Seat of the Government of the United States, directed to the President of the Senate. The President of the Senate shall, in the Presence of the Senate and House of Representatives, open all the Certificates, and the Votes shall then be counted. The Person having the greatest Number of Votes shall be the President, if such Number be a Majority of the whole Number of Electors appointed; and if there be more than one who have such Majority and have an equal Number of Votes, then the House of Representatives shall immediately chuse by Ballot one of them for President; and if no Person have a Majority, then from the five highest on the List the said House shall in like Manner chuse the President. But in chusing the President, the Votes shall be taken by States, the Representation from each State having one Vote; A quorum for this Purpose shall consist of a Member or Members from two thirds of the States, and a Majority of all the States shall be necessary to a Choice. In every Case, after the Choice of the President, the person having the greatest Number of Votes of the Electors shall be the Vice President. But if there should remain two or more who have equal Vote, the Senate shall chuse from them by Ballot the Vice President.[7]

Clause 4 The Congress may determine the Time of chusing the Electors, and the Day on which they shall give their Votes; which Day shall be the same throughout the United States.

Clause 5 No Person except a natural born Citizen, or a Citizen of the United States, at the time of the Adoption of this Constitution, shall be eligible to the Office of President; neither shall any Person be eligible to that Office who shall not have attained to the Age of thirty five Years, and been fourteen Years a Resident within the United States.

Clause 6 In Case of the Removal of the President from Office, or of his Death, Resignation, or Inability to discharge the Powers and Duties of the said Office, the same shall devolve on the Vice President, and the Congress may by Law provide for the Case of Removal, Death, Resignation, or Inability, both of the President and Vice President, declaring what Officer shall then act as President, and such Officer shall act accordingly, until the Disability be removed, or a President shall be elected.[8]

Clause 7 The President shall, at stated Times, receive for his Services, a Compensation, which shall neither be increased nor diminished during the Period of which he shall have been elected, and he shall not receive within that Period any other Emolument from the United States, or any of them.

Clause 8 Before he enter on the Execution of his Office, he shall take the following Oath or Affirmation:—"I do solemnly swear (or affirm) that I will faithfully execute the Office of President of the United States, and will to the best of my Ability, preserve, protect and defend the Constitution of the United States."

Powers and Duties of the President

SECTION 2

Clause 1 The President shall be the Commander in Chief of the Army and Navy of the United States, and of the Militia of the several States, when called into the actual Service of the United States, he may require the Opinion, in writing, of the principal Officer in each of the executive Departments, upon any Subject relating to the Duties of their respective Offices, and he shall have the Power to grant Reprieves and Pardons for Offences against the United States, except in Cases of Impeachment.

Clause 2 He shall have Power, by and with the Advice and Consent of the Senate to make Treaties, provided two thirds of the Senators present concur; and he shall nominate, and by and with the Advice and Consent of the Senate, shall appoint Ambassadors, other public Ministers and Consuls, Judges of the supreme Court, and all other Officers of the United States, whose Appointments are not herein otherwise provided for, and which shall be established by Law: but the Congress may by Law vest the Appointment of such inferior Officers, as they think proper in the President alone, in the Courts of Law, or in the Heads of Departments.

Clause 3 The President shall have Power to fill up all Vacancies that may happen during the Recess of the Senate, by granting Commissions which shall expire at the End of their next Session.

SECTION 3 He shall from time to time give to the Congress Information of the State of the Union, and recommend to their Consideration such Measures as he shall judge necessary and expedient; he may, on extraordinary Occasions, convene both Houses, or either of them and in Case of Disagreement between them, with Respect to the Time of Adjournment, he may adjourn them to such Time as he shall think proper; he shall receive Ambassadors and other public Ministers; he shall

[7]Changed by the 12th and 20th Amendments

[8]Modified by the 25th Amendment

take Care that the Laws be faithfully executed, and shall Commission all the Officers of the United States.

SECTION 4 The President, Vice President and all civil Officers of the United States, shall be removed from Office on Impeachment for, and Conviction of, Treason, Bribery, or other High Crimes and Misdemeanors.

Article III—The Judicial Article

Judicial Power, Courts, Judges

SECTION 1 The judicial Power of the United States, shall be vested in one supreme Court, and in such inferior Courts as the Congress may from time to time ordain and establish. The Judges, both the supreme and inferior Courts, shall hold their Offices during good Behaviour, and shall, at stated Times, receive for their Services, a Compensation, which shall not be diminished during their Continuance in Office.

Jurisdiction

SECTION 2 The judicial Power shall extend to all Cases, in Law and Equity, arising under this Constitution, the Laws of the United States, and Treaties made, or which shall be made, under their Authority;—to all Cases affecting Ambassadors, other public Ministers and Consuls;—to all Cases of admiralty and maritime Jurisdiction;—to Controversies to which the United States shall be a Party;—to Controversies between two or more States; between a State and Citizens of another State;[9]—between Citizens of different States;—between Citizens of the same State claiming Lands under Grants of different States, and between a State, or the Citizens thereof, and foreign States, Citizens, or Subjects.

In all Cases affecting Ambassadors, other public Ministers and Consuls, and those in which a State shall be Party, the supreme Court shall have original Jurisdiction. In all the other Cases before mentioned, the supreme Court shall have appellate Jurisdiction, both as to Law and Fact, with such Exceptions, and under such Regulations as Congress shall make.

The Trial of all Crimes, except in Cases of Impeachment, shall be by Jury; and such Trial shall be held in the State where the said Crimes shall have been committed; but when not committed within any State, the Trial shall be at such Place or Places as the Congress may by Law have directed.

Treason

SECTION 3 Treason against the United States, shall consist only in levying War against them, or in adhering to their Enemies, giving them Aid and Comfort. No Person shall be convicted of Treason unless on the Testimony of two Witnesses to the same overt Act, or on Confession in open Court.

The Congress shall have Power to declare the Punishment of Treason, but no Attainder of Treason shall work Corruption of Blood, or Forfeiture except during the Life of the Person attainted.

[9]Modified by the 11th Amendment

Article IV—Interstate Relations

Full Faith and Credit Clause

SECTION 1 Full Faith and Credit shall be given in each State to the public Acts, Records, and judicial Proceedings of every other State. And the Congress may by general Laws prescribe the Manner in which such Acts, Records and Proceedings shall be proved, and the Effect thereof.

Privileges and Immunities; Interstate Extradition

SECTION 2

Clause 1 The Citizens of each State shall be entitled to all Privileges and Immunities of Citizens in the several States.

Clause 2 A person charged in any State with Treason, Felony or other Crime, who shall flee from Justice, and be found in another State, shall on Demand of the executive Authority of the State from which he fled, be delivered up, to be removed to the State having Jurisdiction of the Crime.

Clause 3 No person held to Service or Labour in one State, under the Laws thereof, escaping into another, shall, in Consequence of any Law or Regulation therein, be discharged from such Service or Labour, but shall be delivered up on Claim of the Party to whom such Service or Labour may be due.[10]

Admission of States

SECTION 3 New States may be admitted by the Congress into this Union; but no new State shall be formed or erected within the Jurisdiction of any other State; nor any State to be formed by the Junction of two or more States, or Parts of States, without the Consent of the Legislatures of the States concerned as well as of the Congress.

The Congress shall have Power to dispose of and make all needful Rules and Regulations respecting the Territory or other Property belonging to the United States; and nothing in this Constitution shall be so construed as to Prejudice any Claims of the United States, or of any particular State.

Republican Form of Government

SECTION 4 The United States shall guarantee to every State in this Union a Republican Form of Government, and shall protect each of them against Invasion; and on Application of the Legislature, or of the Executive (when the Legislature cannot be convened) against domestic Violence.

Article V—The Amending Power

The Congress, whenever two thirds of both Houses shall deem it necessary, shall propose Amendments to this Constitution, or, on the Application of the Legislatures of two thirds of several States, shall call a Convention for proposing Amendments,

[10]Repealed by the 13th Amendment

which, in either Case, shall be valid to all Intents and Purposes, as Part of this Constitution, when ratified by the Legislatures of three fourths of the several States, or by Conventions in three fourths thereof, as the one or the other Mode of Ratification may be proposed by the Congress; Provided that no Amendment which may be made prior to the Year One thousand eight hundred and eight shall in any Manner affect the first and fourth Clauses in the Ninth Section of the first Article; and that no State, without its Consent, shall be deprived of its equal Suffrage in the Senate.

Article VI—The Supremacy Act

Clause 1

All Debts contracted and Engagements entered into, before the Adoption of this Constitution, shall be as valid against the United States under the Constitution, as under the Confederation.

Clause 2

This Constitution, and the Laws of the United States which shall be made in Pursuance thereof; and all Treaties made, or which shall be made, under the Authority of the United States, shall be the supreme Law of the Land; and the Judges in every State shall be bound thereby, any Thing in the Constitution or Laws of any State to the Contrary notwithstanding.

Clause 3

The Senators and Representatives before mentioned, and the Members of the several State Legislatures, and all executive and judicial Officers, both of the United States and of the several States, shall be bound by Oath or Affirmation, to support this Constitution; but no religious Test shall ever be required as a Qualification to any Office or public Trust under the United States.

Article VII—Ratification

The Ratification of the Conventions of nine States, shall be sufficient for the Establishment of this Constitution between the States so ratifying the Same.

Done in Convention by the Unanimous Consent of the States present the Seventeenth Day of September in the Year of our Lord one thousand seven hundred and Eighty seven and of the Independence of the United States of America the Twelfth In Witness whereof We have hereunto subscribed our Names.

Amendments

The Bill of Rights

[The first ten amendments were ratified on December 15, 1791, and form what is known as the "Bill of Rights."]

Amendment 1—
Religion, Speech, Assembly, and Politics

Congress shall make no law respecting an establishment of religion, or prohibiting the free exercise thereof; or abridging the freedom of speech, or of the press; or the right of the people peaceably to assemble, and to petition the government for a redress of grievances.

Amendment 2—
Militia and the Right to Bear Arms

A well-regulated Militia, being necessary to the security of a free State, the right of the people to keep and bear Arms, shall not be infringed.

Amendment 3—Quartering of Soldiers

No Soldier shall, in time of peace be quartered in any house, without the consent of the Owner, nor in time of war, but in manner to be prescribed by law.

Amendment 4—Searches and Seizures

The right of the people to be secure in their persons, houses, papers, and effects, against unreasonable searches and seizures, shall not be violated, and no Warrants shall issue, but upon probable cause, supported by Oath or affirmation, and particularly describing the place to be searched, and the persons or things to be seized.

Amendment 5—Grand Juries,
Self-Incrimination, Double Jeopardy, Due Process,
and Eminent Domain

No person shall be held to answer for a capital, or otherwise infamous crime, unless on a presentment or indictment of a Grand jury, except in cases arising in the land or naval forces, or in the Militia, when in actual service in time of War or public danger; nor shall any person be subject for the same offence to be twice put in jeopardy of life or limb; nor shall be compelled in any criminal case to be a witness against himself, nor be deprived of life, liberty, or property, without due process of law; nor shall private property be taken for public use, without just compensation.

Amendment 6—
Criminal Court Procedures

In all criminal prosecutions, the accused shall enjoy the right to a speedy and public trial, by an impartial jury of the State and district wherein the crime shall have been committed, which district shall have been previously ascertained by law, and to be informed of the nature and cause of the accusation; to be confronted with the witnesses against him; to have compulsory process for obtaining Witnesses in his favor, and to have the Assistance of Counsel for his defence.

Amendment 7—Trial by Jury in Common Law Cases

In Suits at common law, where the value in controversy shall exceed twenty dollars, the right of trial by jury shall be preserved, and no fact tried by a jury shall be otherwise re-examined in any Court of the United States, than according to the rules of the common law.

Amendment 8—Bail, Cruel and Unusual Punishment

Excessive bail shall not be required, nor excessive fines imposed, nor cruel and unusual punishments inflicted.

Amendment 9—Rights Retained by the People

The enumeration in the Constitution, of certain rights, shall not be construed to deny or disparage others retained by the people.

Amendment 10—Reserved Powers of the States

The powers not delegated to the United States by the Constitution, nor prohibited by it to the States, are reserved to the States respectively, or to the people.

Amendment 11—Suits Against the States

[Ratified February 7, 1795]

The Judicial power of the United States shall not be construed to extend to any suit in law or equity, commenced or prosecuted against one of the United States by Citizens of another State, or by Citizens or Subjects of any Foreign State.

Amendment 12—Election of the President

[Ratified June 15, 1804]

The Electors shall meet in their respective states, and vote by ballot for President and Vice-President, one of whom, at least, shall not be an inhabitant of the same state with themselves; they shall name in their ballots the person voted for as President, and in distinct ballots the person voted for as Vice-President, and they shall make distinct lists of all persons voted for as President, and of all persons voted for as Vice-President, and of the number of votes for each, which lists they shall sign and certify, and transmit sealed to the seat of the government of the United States, directed to the President of the Senate;—The President of the Senate shall, in presence of the Senate and House of Representatives, open all the certificates and the votes shall then be counted;—The person having the greatest number of votes for President, shall be the President, if such number be a majority of the whole number of Electors appointed; and if no person have such majority, then from the persons having the highest numbers not exceeding three on the list of those voted for as President, the House of Representatives shall choose immediately, by ballot, the President. But in choosing the President, the votes shall be taken by states, the representation from each state having one vote; a quorum for this purpose shall consist of a member or members from two-thirds of the states, and a majority of all states shall be necessary to a choice. And if the House of Representatives shall not choose a President whenever the right of choice shall devolve upon them, before the fourth day of March next following, then the Vice-President shall act as President, as in the case of the death or other constitutional disability of the President.[11] The person having the greatest number of votes as Vice-President, shall be the Vice-President, if such a number be a majority of the whole numbers of Electors appointed, and if no person have a majority, then from the two highest numbers on the list, the Senate shall choose the Vice-President; a quorum for the purpose shall consist of two-thirds of the whole number of Senators, and a majority of the whole number shall be necessary to a choice. But no person constitutionally ineligible to the office of President shall be eligible to that of Vice-President of the United States.

Amendment 13—Prohibition of Slavery

[Ratified December 6, 1865]

SECTION 1 Neither slavery nor involuntary servitude, except as a punishment for crime whereof the party shall have been duly convicted, shall exist within the United States, or any place subject to their jurisdiction.

SECTION 2 Congress shall have power to enforce this article by appropriate legislation.

Amendment 14—Citizenship, Due Process, and Equal Protection of the Laws

[Ratified July 9, 1868]

SECTION 1 All persons born or naturalized in the United States, and subject to the jurisdiction thereof, are citizens of the United States and of the State wherein they reside. No State shall make or enforce any law which shall abridge the privileges or immunities of citizens of the United States; nor shall any State deprive any person of life, liberty, or property, without due process of law; nor deny to any person within its jurisdiction the equal protection of the laws.

SECTION 2 Representatives shall be apportioned among the several States according to their respective numbers, counting the whole number of persons in each State, excluding Indians not taxed. But when the right to vote at any election for the choice of electors for President and Vice President of the United States, Representatives in Congress, the Executive and Judicial officers of a State, or the members of the Legislature thereof, is denied to any of the male inhabitants of such State, being twenty-one[12] years of age, and citizens of the United States, or in any way abridged, except for participation in rebellion, or other crime, the basis of representation therein shall be reduced in the proportion which the number of such

[11]Changed by the 20th Amendment
[12]Changed by the 26th Amendment

male citizens shall bear to the whole number of male citizens twenty-one years of age in such State.

SECTION 3 No person shall be a Senator or Representative in Congress, or elector of President and Vice President, or hold any office, civil or military, under the United States, or under any State, who, having previously taken an oath, as a member of Congress, or as an officer of the United States, or as a member of any State legislature, or as an executive or judicial officer of any State, to support the Constitution of the United States, shall have engaged in insurrection or rebellion against the same, or given aid or comfort to the enemies thereof. But Congress may by a vote of two-thirds of each House, remove such disability.

SECTION 4 The validity of the public debt of the United States, authorized by law, including debts incurred for payment of pensions and bounties for services in suppressing insurrection or rebellion, shall not be questioned. But neither the United States nor any State shall assume or pay any debt or obligation incurred in aid of insurrection or rebellion against the United States, or any claim for the loss or emancipation of any slave; but all such debts, obligations and claims shall be held illegal and void.

SECTION 5 The Congress shall have power to enforce, by appropriate legislation, the provisions of this article.

Amendment 15—The Right to Vote

[Ratified February 3, 1870]

SECTION 1 The right of citizens of the United States to vote shall not be denied or abridged by the United States or by any State on account of race, color, or previous condition of servitude.

SECTION 2 The Congress shall have power to enforce this article by appropriate legislation.

Amendment 16—Income Taxes

[Ratified February 3, 1913]

The Congress shall have power to lay and collect taxes on incomes, from whatever source derived, without apportionment among the several States, and without regard to any census or enumeration.

Amendment 17—Direct Election of Senators

[Ratified April 8, 1913]

The Senate of the United States shall be composed of two Senators from each State, elected by the people thereof, for six years; and each Senator shall have one vote. The electors in each State shall have the qualifications requisite for electors of the most numerous branch of the State legislatures.

When vacancies happen in the representation of any State in the Senate, the executive authority of such State shall issue writs of election to fill such vacancies: Provided, That the legislature of any State may empower the executive thereof to make temporary appointment until the people fill the vacancies by election as the legislature may direct. This amendment shall not be so construed as to affect the election or term of any Senator chosen before it becomes valid as part of the Constitution.

Amendment 18—Prohibition

[Ratified January 16, 1919. Repealed December 5, 1933 by Amendment 21]

SECTION 1 After one year from the ratification of this article the manufacture, sale, or transportation of intoxicating liquors within, the importation thereof into, or the exportation thereof from the United States and all territory subject to the jurisdiction thereof for beverage purposes is hereby prohibited.

SECTION 2 The Congress and the several states shall have concurrent power to enforce this article by appropriate legislation.

SECTION 3 This article shall be inoperative unless it shall have been ratified as an amendment to the Constitution by the legislatures of the several states, as provided in the Constitution, within seven years from the date of the submission hereof to the States by the Congress.[13]

Amendment 19—For Women's Suffrage

[Ratified August 18, 1920]

The right of the citizens of the United States to vote shall not be denied or abridged by the United States or by any State on account of sex.

Congress shall have power, by appropriate legislation, to enforce the provision of this article.

Amendment 20—The Lame Duck Amendment

[Ratified January 23, 1933]

SECTION 1 The terms of the President and Vice President shall end at noon on the 20th day of January, and the terms of the Senators and Representatives at noon on the 3rd day of January, of the years in which such terms would have ended if this article had not been ratified, and the terms of their successors shall then begin.

SECTION 2 The Congress shall assemble at least once in every year, and such meeting shall begin at noon on the 3rd day of January, unless they shall by law appoint a different day.

SECTION 3 If, at the time fixed for the beginning of the term of the President, the President elect shall have died, the Vice President elect shall become President. If a President shall not have been chosen before the time fixed for the beginning of his term, or if the President elect shall have failed to qualify, then the Vice President elect shall act as President until a President shall have qualified; and the Congress may by law provide for the case wherein neither a President elect nor a Vice President elect shall have qualified, declaring who shall then act as President, or the manner in which one who is to act shall be selected, and such person shall act accordingly until a President or Vice President shall have qualified.

[13]Repealed by the 21st Amendment

SECTION 4 The Congress may by law provide for the case of the death of any of the persons from whom the House of Representatives may choose a President whenever the right of choice shall have devolved upon them, and for the case of the death of any of the persons from whom the Senate may choose a Vice President whenever the right of choice shall have devolved upon them.

SECTION 5 Sections 1 and 2 shall take effect on the 15th day of October following the ratification of this article.

SECTION 6 This article shall be inoperative unless it shall have been ratified as an amendment to the Constitution by the legislatures of three-fourths of the several States within seven years from the date of its submission.

Amendment 21—Repeal of Prohibition

[Ratified December 5, 1933]

SECTION 1 The eighteenth article of amendment to the Constitution of the United States is hereby repealed.

SECTION 2 The transportation or importation into any State, Territory, or Possession of the United States for delivery or use therein of intoxicating liquors, in violation of the laws thereof, is hereby prohibited.

SECTION 3 This article shall be inoperative unless it shall have been ratified as an amendment to the Constitution by conventions in the several States, as provided in the Constitution, within seven years from the date of the submission hereof to the States by the Congress.

Amendment 22—Number of Presidential Terms

[Ratified February 27, 1951]

SECTION 1 No person shall be elected to the office of the President more than twice, and no person who has held the office of President, or acted as President, for more than two years of a term to which some other person was elected President shall be elected to the office of the President more than once. But this Article shall not apply to any person holding the office of President when this article was proposed by the Congress, and shall not prevent any person who may be holding the office of President, or acting as President, during the term within which this Article becomes operative from holding the office of President or acting as President during the remainder of such term.

SECTION 2 This Article shall be inoperative unless it shall have been ratified as an amendment to the Constitution by the legislatures of three-fourths of the several states within seven years from the date of its submission to the States by the Congress.

Amendment 23—Presidential Electors for the District of Columbia

[Ratified March 29, 1961]

SECTION 1 The District constituting the seat of government of the United States shall appoint in such manner as the Congress may direct:

A number of electors of President and Vice President equal to the whole number of Senators and Representatives in Congress to which the District would be entitled if it were a State, but in no event more than the least populous State; they shall be in addition to those appointed by the States, but they shall be considered for the purposes of the election of President and Vice President, to be electors appointed by a State; and they shall meet in the District and perform such duties as provided by the twelfth article of amendment.

SECTION 2 The Congress shall have power to enforce this article by appropriate legislation

Amendment 24—The Anti-Poll Tax Amendment

[Ratified January 23, 1964]

SECTION 1 The right of citizens of the United States to vote in any primary or other election for President or Vice President, for electors for President or Vice President, or for Senator or Representative in Congress, shall not be denied or abridged by the United States or any state by reason of failure to pay any poll tax or other tax.

SECTION 2 The Congress shall have power to enforce this article by appropriate legislation.

Amendment 25—Presidential Disability, Vice Presidential Vacancies

[Ratified February 10, 1967]

SECTION 1 In case of the removal of the President from office or his death or resignation, the Vice President shall become President.

SECTION 2 Whenever there is a vacancy in the office of the Vice President, the President shall nominate a Vice President who shall take the office upon confirmation by a majority vote of both Houses of Congress.

SECTION 3 Whenever the President transmits to the President pro tempore of the Senate and the Speaker of the House of Representatives his written declaration that he is unable to discharge the powers and duties of his office, and until he transmits to them a written declaration to the contrary, such powers and duties shall be discharged by the Vice President as Acting President.

SECTION 4 Whenever the Vice President and a majority of either the principal officers of the executive departments, or of such other body as Congress may by law provide, transmit to the President pro tempore of the Senate and the Speaker of the House of Representatives their written declaration that the President is unable to discharge the powers and duties of his office, the Vice President shall immediately assume the powers and duties of the office as Acting President.

Thereafter, when the President transmits to the President pro tempore of the Senate and the Speaker of the House of Representatives his written declaration that no inability exists, he shall resume the powers and duties of his office unless the Vice President and a majority of either the principal officers of the executive departments, or of such other body as Congress may by law provide, transmit within four days to the President pro tempore of the Senate and the Speaker of the House of Representatives their written declaration that the President is unable to discharge the powers and duties of his office. Thereupon Congress shall decide the issue, assembling within forty-eight hours for that purpose if not in session. If the Congress, within twenty-one days after receipt of the latter written declaration, or, if Congress is not in session, within twenty-one days after Congress is required to assemble, determines by two-thirds vote of both houses that the President is unable to discharge the powers and duties of his office, the Vice President shall continue to discharge the same as Acting President; otherwise, the President shall resume the powers and duties of his office.

Amendment 26—Eighteen-Year-Old Vote

[Ratified July 1, 1971]

SECTION 1 The right of citizens of the United States, who are 18 years of age, or older, to vote shall not be denied or abridged by the United States or by any state on account of age.

SECTION 2 The Congress shall have power to enforce this article by appropriate legislation.

Amendment 27—Congressional Salaries

[Ratified May 7, 1992]

No law, varying the compensation for the services of the Senators and Representatives, shall take effect, until an election of Representatives shall be intervened.

chapter 3

American Federalism

Since the founding of the Republic, American citizens have debated the relationship of the national government to the states.[1] In 1787, members of what would become the Federalist Party defended the creation of a strong national government, whereas the Antifederalists warned that a strong national government would overshadow the states. The great debate over which level of government best represents the people continues to rage.

State governments have often complained that the national government is either taking over their responsibilities or controlling too much of what they do. At the same time, in policy areas such as civil rights, educational opportunities for people with disabilities, and handgun control, the states have been slow to respond to citizens, and the national government has taken steps.

In recent years, the national government has given states more freedom to act on issues such as health care and global warming, and removed some restrictions on states' management of national programs such as welfare.[2] At the same time, states have been pushing hard to be what Supreme Court justice Louis Brandeis called "laboratories of democracy."[3]

Impatient with the lack of action in Washington, D.C., for example, California acted to set emissions standards on cars and trucks in 2002. Under the new law, the first in the nation designed to curtail greenhouse gases, automobile manufacturers have to cut car and light truck emissions of carbon dioxide by 30 percent starting in 2009.

The automobile industry argues that the California law will add $3,000 to the average cost of a car or truck.[4] It also claims that the law illegally assumes responsibilities of the national government and its Environmental Protection Agency (EPA), which sets emission standards for the entire nation. The Alliance of Automobile Manufacturers immediately sued to stop the law, threatening to take the issue all the way to the U.S. Supreme Court. In turn, California has sued the EPA for permission to set a higher standard than the national law permits. In 2003, for example, the agency ruled that carbon dioxide was not a pollutant and could not be regulated. However, California includes carbon dioxide among its regulated gases.

California is not alone in the fight to end global warming. As of 2007, 28 states had developed action plans to reduce greenhouse gases; 12 had taken steps to lower emissions of carbon dioxide by power plants, cars, and/or state governments; and 12 had joined California in fighting the EPA for permission to set higher standards.

However, California has long been a leader in enacting environmental laws because of its large size—when California raises emission standards, automobile manufacturers raise their standards for all states. Otherwise, they would have to make two different models of every car and light truck, which would be enormously expensive.

California's ongoing effort to improve the environment shows just how important the people can be in shaping the future, not only at the national level, but within their states as well. Environmental groups have concentrated on state legislatures and even local governments for new laws. In doing so, they have taken advantage of the Constitution's protections of state rights, even if it means a dispute with the national government that will be decided by the highest court in the nation.

LEARNING **OBJECTIVES**

1. Compare and contrast the different interpretations of federalism.
2. Show how federalism protects citizens.
3. Differentiate between the types of national and state powers.
4. Describe and compare the constitutional pillars of national power.
5. Analyze the role of the national courts in regulating federalism.
6. Compare and contrast the arguments of decentralists and centralists.
7. Analyze the differences between grants and mandates.
8. Establish the link between the growth of the national government and federalism.

CHAPTER **OUTLINE**

- Defining Federalism
- The Constitutional Structure of American Federalism
- The Federal Courts and Federalism
- Regulatory Federalism
- The Politics of Federalism
- The Future of Federalism

California and other states sued the national government in 2008 to impose higher gas milleage standards on automobiles and light trucks. The Hummer is considered a light truck.

In this chapter, we first define federalism and its advantages. We then look at the constitutional basis for our federal system and how court decisions and political developments have shaped, and continue to shape, federalism in the United States. Throughout, you should think hard about how you influence the issues you care about, even in your local city council or mayor's office. The Constitution clearly encourages, indeed depends on you to express your view at all levels of government, which is why action in a single state can start a process of change that spreads to other states or the national government.

Defining Federalism

LEARNING **OBJECTIVE**

1 Compare and contrast the different interpretations of federalism.

Scholars have argued and wars have been fought over what federalism means. One scholar recently counted 267 definitions of the term.[5]

Federalism, as we define it, is a form of government in which a constitution distributes authority and powers between a central government and smaller regional governments—usually called states, provinces, or republics—giving to both the national and the regional governments substantial responsibilities and powers, including the power to collect taxes and to pass and enforce laws regulating the conduct of individuals. When we use the term "federalism" or "federal system," we are referring to this system of national and state governments; when we use the term "federal government," we are referring to the national government headquartered in Washington, D.C.

The mere existence of both national and state governments does not make a system federal. What is important is that a *constitution divides governmental powers between the national government and smaller regional governments,* giving clearly defined functions to each. Neither the central nor the regional government receives its powers from the other; both derive them from a common source—the Constitution. No ordinary act of legislation at either the national or the state level can change this constitutional distribution of powers. Both levels of government operate through their own agents and exercise power directly over individuals.

federalism
A constitutional arrangement in which power is distributed between a central government and subdivisional governments, called states in the United States. The national and the subdivisional governments both exercise direct authority over individuals.

Our definition of federalism is broad enough to include competing ideas of it as well as the range of federal systems around the world. Here are some of the leading interpretations of federalism.

- *Dual federalism* views the Constitution as giving a limited list of powers—primarily foreign policy and national defense—to the national government, leaving the rest to sovereign states. Each level of government is dominant within its own sphere. The Supreme Court serves as the umpire between the national government and the states in disputes over which level of government has responsibility for a particular activity. During our first hundred years, dual federalism was the favored interpretation given by the Supreme Court.
- *Cooperative federalism* stresses federalism as a system of intergovernmental relationships in delivering governmental goods and services to the people and calls for cooperation among various levels of government.
- *Marble cake federalism,* a term coined by political scientist Morton Grodzins, conceives of federalism as a mixed set of responsibilities in which all levels of government are engaged in a variety of issues and programs, rather than a layer cake, or dual federalism, with fixed divisions between layers or levels of government.[6]
- *Competitive federalism,* a term first used by political scientist Thomas R. Dye, views the national government, the 50 states, and the thousands of local governments as competing with each other over ways to put together packages of services and taxes. Applying the analogy of the marketplace, Dye emphasizes that at the state and local levels, we have some choice about which state and city we want to "use," just as we have choices about what kind of telephone service we use.[7]
- *Permissive federalism* implies that although federalism provides "a sharing of power and authority between the national and state government, the states' share rests upon the permission and permissiveness of the national government."[8]
- *The new federalism,* championed by Ronald Reagan, Justices Antonin Scalia and Clarence Thomas, former chief justice William Rehnquist, and former justice Sandra Day O'Connor, presumes that the power of the federal government is limited in favor of the broad powers reserved to the states. Strict federalism presumes that every power not delegated to the national government is reserved for the states. Reagan was particularly important to supporting what he called this "new federalism."

President Ronald Reagan was deeply committed to returning responsibilities to the states, but he was unable to achieve much of his new federalism agenda.

Constitutionally, the federal system of the United States consists of only the national government and the 50 states. "Cities are not," the Supreme Court reminded us, "sovereign entities." But in a practical sense, we are a nation of almost 88,000 governmental units, from the national government to the school board district.[9] This does not make for a tidy, efficient, easy-to-understand system; yet as we shall see, it has its virtues.

Alternatives to Federalism

Among the alternatives to federalism are **unitary systems** of government, in which a constitution vests all governmental power in the central government. The central government, if it so chooses, may delegate authority to constituent units, but what it delegates, it may take away. China, France, the Scandinavian countries, and Israel have unitary governments. In the United States, state constitutions usually create this kind of relationship between the state and its local governments.

Comparing Federal and Unitary Systems

unitary system
A constitutional arrangement that concentrates power in a central government.

GENERATION **NEXT**

A Preference for Local Government

One of the reasons federalism flourishes in the U.S. system of government is that the closer the government is to the people, the greater their trust. Most U.S. citizens trust local governments most.

Members of Generation Next feel the same. According to the Pew Research Center's 2007 survey of the nation's political landscape, younger U.S. adults are just as likely as any other age group to agree that the federal government should run only those things that cannot be run at the local level.

Members of Generation Next do not all agree on this issue, however. Members of minority groups are much less likely to favor local government over national government, perhaps because they see the national government as an essential guarantor of their civil liberties and civil rights. Independents are more likely to favor national action, too, perhaps because they have less confidence in the two parties to represent them. Finally, conservatives favor local action, in part because they see the national government as a source of big spending and meddling in local affairs.

As a group, members of Generation Next are not significantly different from other generations in their preference for local government. All generations tend to have greater faith in the governments they know best, which are the ones closest to home.

Percentage of 18- to 29-Year-Olds Who Completely Agree That the Federal Government Should Run Only Those Things That Cannot Be Run at the Local Level.

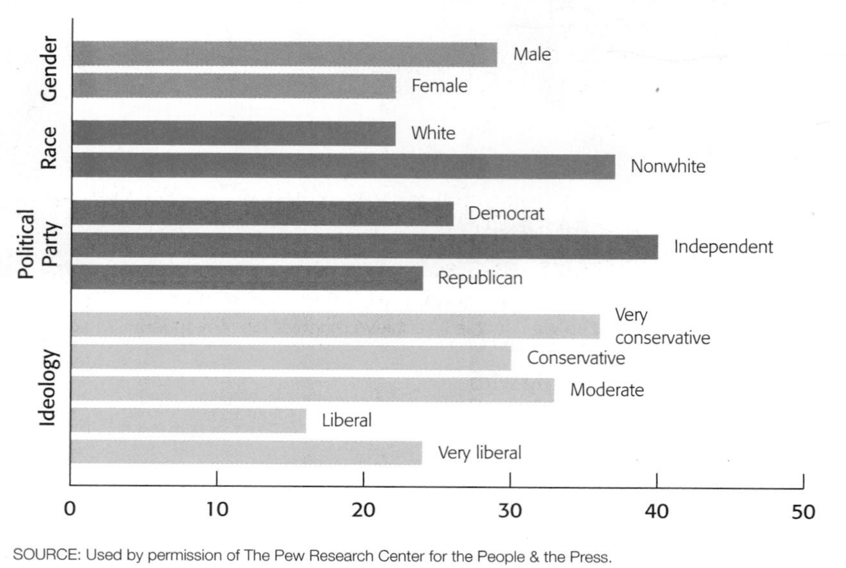

SOURCE: Used by permission of The Pew Research Center for the People & the Press.

QUESTIONS

1. How does local government give you more say in the issues you care about?
2. What issues do you think the federal government might be better suited to deal with? Why?
3. Why is the national government sometimes the best level of government action for achieving change in issues such as global warming or access to health care?

At the other extreme from unitary governments are **confederations,** in which sovereign nations, through a constitutional compact, create a central government but carefully limit its authority and do not give it the power to regulate the conduct of individuals directly. The central government makes regulations for the constituent governments, but it exists and operates only at their direction. The 13 states under the Articles of Confederation operated in this manner, as did the southern Confederacy during the Civil War. The European Union is another example, though debates over its integration continue.[10]

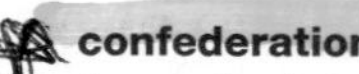

confederation
A constitutional arrangement in which sovereign nations or states, by compact, create a central government but carefully limit its power and do not give it direct authority over individuals.

Why Federalism?

In 1787, federalism was a compromise between centrists, who supported a strong national government, and those who favored decentralization. Confederation had proved unsuccessful. A unitary system was out of the question because most people were too deeply attached to their state governments to permit subordination to central rule. Many scholars think that federalism is ideally suited to the needs of a diverse people spread over a large continent, suspicious of concentrated power, and desiring unity but not uniformity. Federalism offered, and still offers, many advantages for such a people.

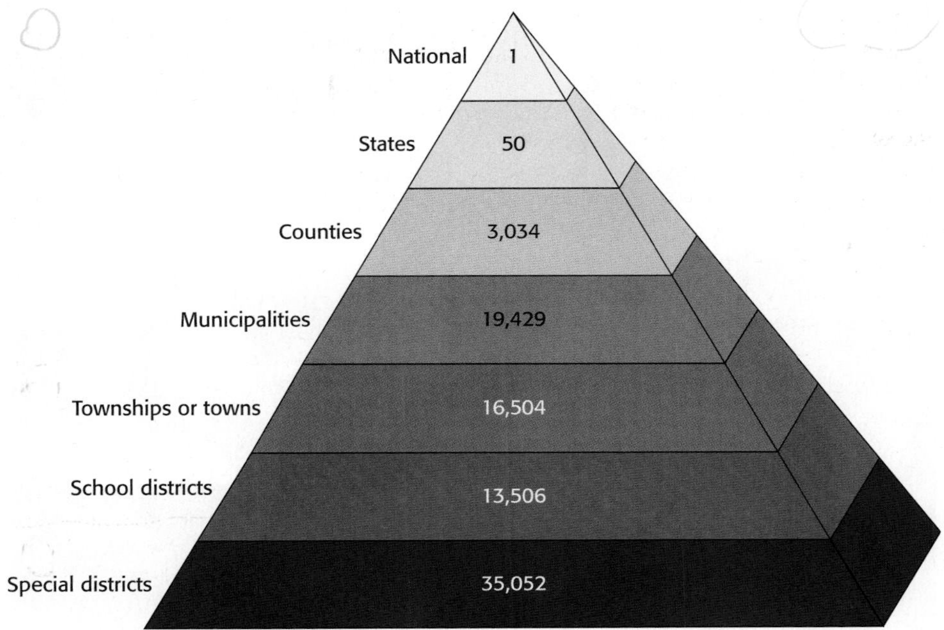

FIGURE 3–1
Number of Governments in the United States, 2007.

SOURCE: U.S. Bureau of the Census, *Statistical Abstract of the United States*, www.census.gov/prod/2006pubs/07statab/stlocgov.pdf.

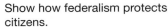

LEARNING **OBJECTIVE**

2 Show how federalism protects citizens.

Federalism Checks the Growth of Tyranny Although in the rest of the world, federal forms have not always prevented tyranny (Germany's federal constitution did not, for example, prevent Hitler from seizing power in the 1930s), U.S. citizens tend to associate federalism with freedom.[11] When one political party loses control of the national government, it is still likely to hold office in a number of states and can continue to challenge the party in power at the national level. See Figure 3–1 for the number of governments in the United States.

Such diffusion of power creates its own problems. It makes it difficult for a national majority to carry out a program of action, and it permits those who control state governments to frustrate the policies enacted by Congress and administered by federal agencies. To the framers, these obstacles were an advantage. They feared that a single interest group might capture the national government and suppress the interests of others.

Federalism Allows Unity Without Uniformity National politicians and parties do not have to iron out every difference on every issue that divides us, whether it be abortion, same-sex marriage, gun control, capital punishment, welfare financing, or assisted suicide. Instead, these issues are debated in state legislatures, county courthouses, and city halls. But this advantage of federalism is becoming less significant today as many local issues quickly move to the national level. Information about state action spreads quickly from government to government, especially during periods when the national government is relatively slow to respond to pressing issues such as global warming.

Federalism Encourages Experimentation As Justice Louis Brandeis once argued, states are "laboratories of democracy." If they adopt programs that fail, the negative effects are limited; if programs succeed, they can be adopted by other states and by the national government. Georgia, for example, was the first state to permit 18-year-olds to vote; Wisconsin was a leader in requiring welfare recipients to work; California moved first on global warming; Massachusetts created one of the first state programs to provide health insurance to all its citizens. Not all innovations, even those considered successful, become widely adopted.

Federalism Provides Training for National Officials While encouraging experiments in public policy, federalism also provides a training ground for state and local politicians to gain experience before moving to the national stage. Before becoming president, Jimmy Carter, Ronald Reagan, Bill Clinton, and George W. Bush served as governors of

States such as Wisconsin were leaders in helping welfare recipients find work long before the federal government became involved. Here a recipient receives training for her move off the welfare rolls.

Georgia, California, Arkansas, and Texas respectively. Three governors and one mayor ran for the presidential nomination in 2008, but all were defeated.

Federalism Creates Opportunities for Future National Candidates While encouraging experiments in public policy, federalism also provides a training ground for state and local politicians to gain experience before moving to the national stage. Presidents Jimmy Carter, Ronald Reagan, Bill Clinton, and George W. Bush previously served as governor of the respective states of Georgia, California, Arkansas, and Texas. In addition, three governors and one mayor ran for the Republican Party nomination for president in 2008, and another governor, Alaska's Sarah Palin, was selected as the Republican vice presidential candidate. Although all were defeated, they are already front-runners to challenge President Barack Obama in 2012.

Federalism Keeps Government Closer to the People By providing numerous arenas for decision making, federalism engages many people in the process of government and helps keep government closer to the people. Every day, thousands of U.S. adults serve on city councils, school boards, neighborhood associations, and planning commissions.

The Constitutional Structure of American Federalism

LEARNING **OBJECTIVE**

3 Differentiate between the types of national and state powers.

The division of powers and responsibilities between the national and state governments has resulted in thousands of court decisions, as well as hundreds of books and endless speeches to explain them—and even then the division lacks precise definition. Nonetheless, it's helpful to have a basic understanding of how the Constitution divides these powers and responsibilities and what obligations it imposes on each level of government.

THE **CHANGING FACE** OF U.S. POLITICS

Immigrants and Federal, State, and Local Responses

For most of the twentieth century, the highest percentage of immigrants to the United States came from Europe. Today Latin Americans and Asians exceed Europeans as immigrants.

The number of immigrants arriving in the United States has been growing. Many enter the country illegally and join the workforce. According to the Pew Hispanic Center, in 2005 the United States had 35.7 million foreign-born residents, of whom 61 percent were legal permanent residents and 29 percent were undocumented migrants.*

The majority of undocumented aliens can be found in California, Texas, Florida, New York, Illinois, and New Jersey. However, almost two in five undocumented aliens now reside in other states, which makes the issue of immigration relevant in almost every election as the total number increases, including children who were born in the United States or crossed the border with a parent. Whereas 1.3 million illegal immigrants came to the United States in the 1980s, 5.8 million came in the 1990s, and 3.1 million arrived in 2000–2004.†

Age and Sex of Undocument Aliens, 2004.

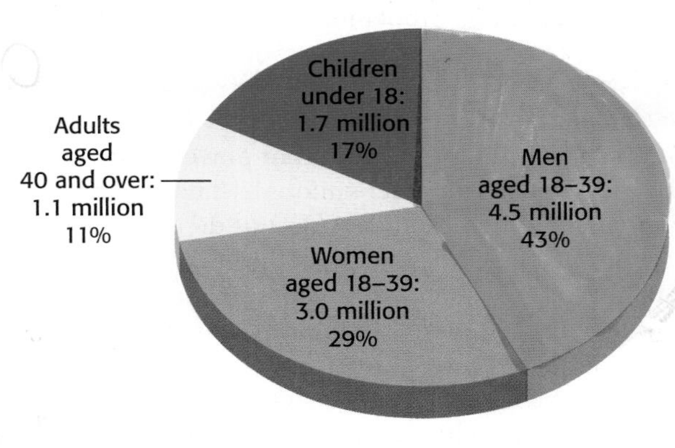

As a result of the substantial recent growth in illegal immigration, "broken borders" and the rising unemployment rate among U.S. citizens have become very controversial issues. Many object to undocumented workers taking jobs away from U.S. citizens, and the children of illegal immigrants often receive education and health benefits.

The controversy is complex, and there is no consensus about how to resolve it. More than 50 immigration bills have been introduced in Congress, and another 1,562 bills were introduced in state legislatures in 2007 alone. They address many solutions to immigration issues such as extending visas for highly educated workers in hard-to-recruit professions, establishing new procedures for legalizing undocumented workers, providing some form of amnesty for illegal immigrants who have been living in the United States for years, and increasing border security.

QUESTIONS

1. Why does the number of undocumented aliens provoke such controversy across the nation even though most immigrants live in California, Illinois, New York, Texas, and Florida?
2. Should the nation deny public benefits such as access to schools, health care, and housing to undocumented aliens who are children? Why or why not?

*Jeffrey S. Passel, "Estimates of the Size and Characteristics of the Undocumented Population," Pew Hispanic Center report, March 21, 2005, p. 7.

†National Conference of State Legislatures, "2007 Enacted State Legislation Related to Immigrants and Immigration," *Immigrant Policy Project*, November 29, 2007, p. 1.

The constitutional framework of our federal system is relatively simple:

1. The national government has only those powers delegated to it by the Constitution (with the important exception of the inherent power over foreign affairs).
2. Within the scope of its operations, the national government is supreme.
3. The state governments have the powers not delegated to the central government, except those denied to them by the Constitution and their state constitutions.
4. Some powers are specifically denied to both the national and state governments; others are specifically denied only to the states or to the national government.

delegated powers
Powers given explicitly to the national government and listed in the Constitution.

implied powers
Powers inferred from the express powers that allow Congress to carry out its functions.

necessary and proper clause
The clause in the Constitution (Article I, Section 8, Clause 3) setting forth the implied powers of Congress. It states that Congress, in addition to its express powers, has the right to make all laws necessary and proper to carry out all powers the Constitution vests in the national government.

Powers of the National Government

The Constitution delegates legislative, executive, and judicial powers to the national government. In addition to these **delegated powers,** such as the power to regulate interstate commerce and to appropriate funds, Congress has assumed constitutionally **implied powers,** such as the power to create banks, which are inferred from delegated powers. The constitutional basis for the implied powers of Congress is the **necessary and proper clause** (Article I, Section 8, Clause 3). This clause gives Congress the right

TABLE 3–1 The Federal Division of Powers

Examples of Powers Delegated to the National Government	Examples of Powers Reserved for State Governments	Examples of Concurrent Powers Shared by the National and State Governments
Regulate trade and interstate commerce	Charter local governments	Impose and collect taxes and fees
Declare war	Police citizens	Borrow and spend money
Create post offices	Oversee primary and elementary education	Establish courts
Coin money	Take land for public use	Enact and enforce laws
Establish national courts		Protect civil rights
		Conduct elections
		Protect health and welfare

"to make all Laws which shall be necessary and proper for carrying into Execution the foregoing Powers, and all other Powers vested . . . in the Government of the United States." These delegated powers are sometimes labeled **express powers,** which means they are expressly noted in the Constitution.

In foreign affairs, the national government has **inherent powers.** The national government has the same authority to deal with other nations as if it were the central government in a unitary system. Such inherent powers do not depend on specific constitutional provisions. For example, the government of the United States may acquire territory by purchase or by discovery and occupation, though no specific clause in the Constitution allows such acquisition. See Table 3–1 for examples of federal and state powers.

LEARNING **OBJECTIVE**

4 Describe and compare the constitutional pillars of national power.

Together, these express, implied, and inherent powers create a flexible system that allows the Supreme Court, Congress, the president, and the people to expand the central government's powers to meet the needs of a modern nation in a global economy and confront threats of international terrorism. This expansion of central government functions rests on four constitutional pillars.

These constitutional pillars—the *national supremacy article,* the *war power,* the *commerce clause,* and especially the *power to tax and spend* for the general welfare—have permitted a tremendous expansion of the functions of the national government. Despite the Supreme Court's recent declaration that some national laws exceed Congress's constitutional powers, the national government has, in effect, almost full power to enact any legislation that Congress deems necessary, so long as it does not conflict with the provisions of the Constitution designed to protect individual rights and the powers of the states. In addition, Section 5 of the Fourteenth Amendment, ratified in 1868, gives Congress the power to enact legislation to remedy constitutional violations and the denial of due process and the equal protection of the laws.

The National Supremacy Article One of the most important constitutional pillars is found in Article VI: "This Constitution, and the Laws of the United States which shall be made in Pursuance thereof; and all Treaties made . . . under the Authority of the United States, shall be the supreme Law of the Land; and the Judges in every State shall be bound thereby; any Thing in the Constitution or Laws of any State to the Contrary notwithstanding." All officials, state as well as national, swear an oath to support the Constitution of the United States. States may not override national policies; this restriction also applies to local units of government, because they are agents of the states. National laws and regulations of federal agencies *preempt* the field, so that conflicting state and local regulations are unenforceable.

The War Power The national government is responsible for protecting the nation from external aggression, whether from other nations or from international terrorism.

express powers
Powers that the Constitution specifically grants to one of the branches of the national government.

inherent powers
The powers of the national government in foreign affairs that the Supreme Court has declared do not depend on constitutional grants but rather grow out of the very existence of the national government.

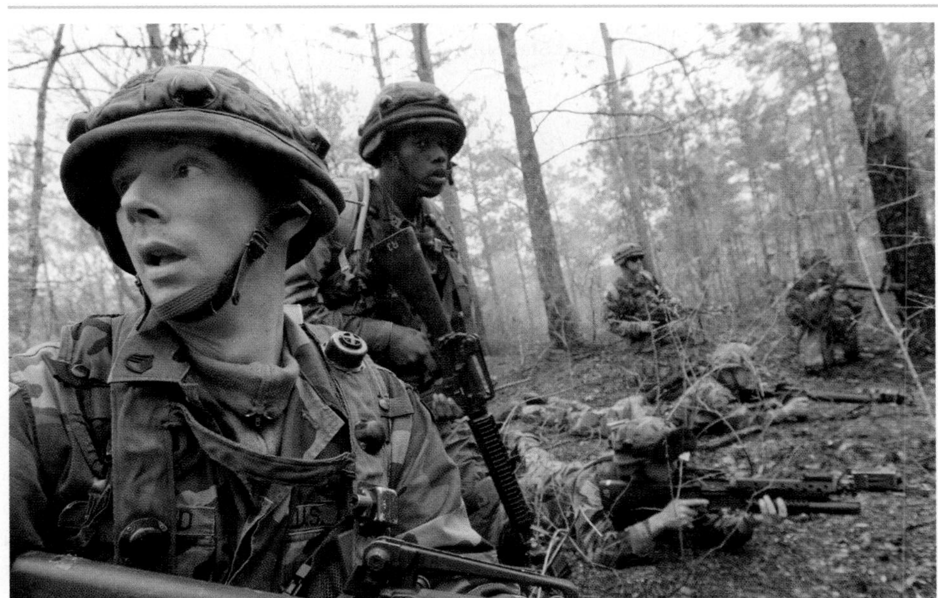

Each state is responsible for maintaining its own militia called a National Guard. However, the national government provides all the funds for maintaining each state's National Guard unit. A state's National Guard can be mobilized by either the state or national government.

The government's power to protect national security includes the power to wage war. In today's world, military strength depends not only on the presence of troops in the field, but also on the ability to mobilize the nation's industrial might and apply scientific and technological knowledge to the tasks of defense. As Charles Evans Hughes, who became chief justice in 1930, observed: "The power to wage war is the power to wage war successfully."[12] In short, the national government has the power to do almost anything not in direct conflict with constitutional guarantees.

The Power to Regulate Interstate and Foreign Commerce Congressional authority extends to all commerce that affects more than one state. Commerce includes the production, buying, selling, renting, and transporting of goods, services, and properties. The **commerce clause** (Article I, Section 8, Clause 1) packs a tremendous constitutional punch; it gives Congress the power "to regulate Commerce with foreign Nations, and among the several States, and with the Indian Tribes." In these few words, the national government has found constitutional justification for regulating a wide range of human activity, because few aspects of our economy today affect commerce in only one state and are thus outside the scope of the national government's constitutional authority.

The landmark ruling of *Gibbons v. Ogden* in 1824 affirmed the broad authority of Congress over interstate commerce. There, in interpreting the commerce clause, Chief Justice John Marshall asserted national interests over those of the states and laid the basis for the subsequent growth in congressional power over commerce and over activities that affect interstate commerce as the nation steadily expanded. See Figure 3–2 for a map showing the major events in this growth.

Gibbons v. Ogden arose from a dispute over a monopoly to operate steamboats in New York waters that the state of New York had granted to Robert Livingston and Robert Fulton. Livingston and Fulton in turn licensed to Aaron Ogden the exclusive right to operate steamboats between New York and New Jersey. Ogden sued to stop Thomas Gibbons from running a competing ferry. Gibbons countered that his boats were licensed under a 1793 act of Congress governing vessels "in the coasting trade and fisheries." New York courts sided with Ogden in holding that both Congress and the states may regulate commerce, just as each has the power to tax. Congress, therefore, had not preempted New York from granting the monopoly. Gibbons appealed to the Supreme Court.

The stakes were high in *Gibbons v. Ogden,* for at issue was the very concept of "interstate commerce." May both Congress and the states regulate interstate commerce? And when conflicts arise between national and state regulations, which prevails?

commerce clause
The clause in the Constitution (Article I, Section 8, Clause 1) that gives Congress the power to regulate all business activities that cross state lines or affect more than one state or other nations.

FIGURE 3-2
An Expanding Nation. The dates indicate when each area became part of the United States.

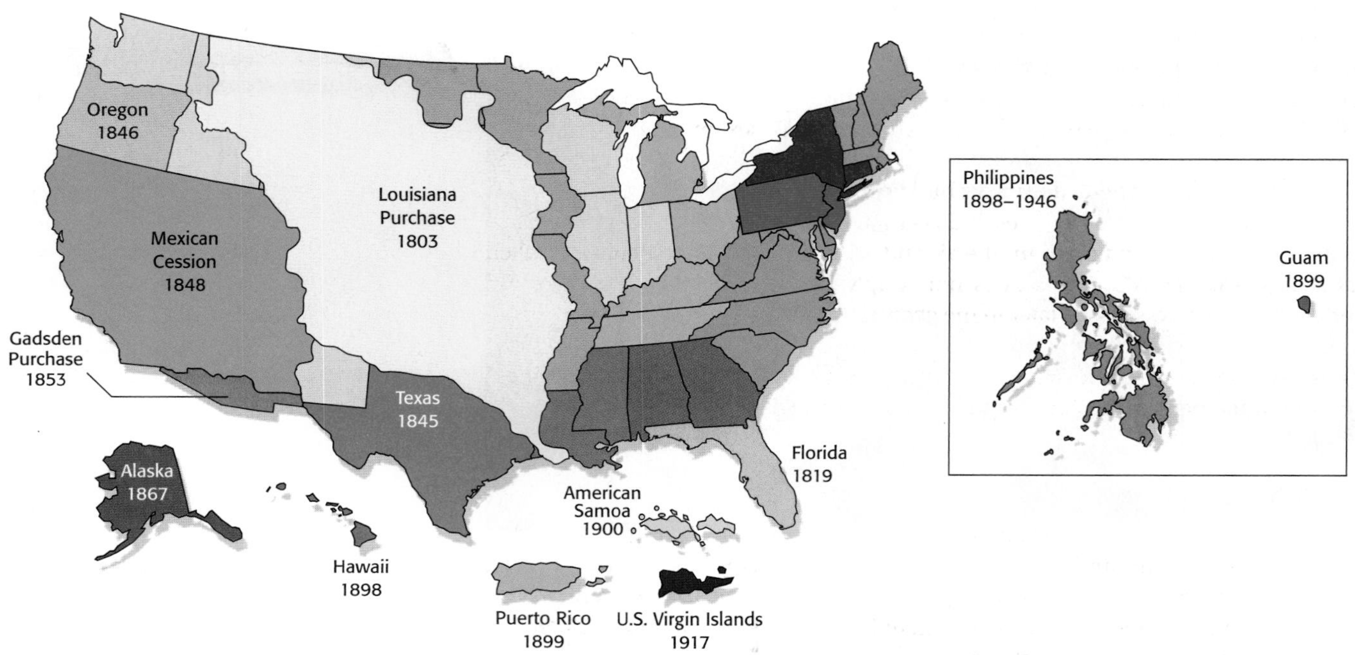

Chief Justice Marshall asserted that national interests prevail and astutely defined "interstate commerce" as "intercourse that affects more states than one." Unlike the power of taxation, Congress's power over interstate commerce is complete and overrides conflicting state laws.[13]

Gibbons v. Ogden was immediately heralded for promoting a national economic common market, in holding that states may not discriminate against interstate transportation and out-of-state commerce. Marshall's brilliant definition of "commerce" as *intercourse among the states* provided the basis clause for national regulation of "things in commerce"[14] and an expanding range of economic activities, including the sale of lottery tickets,[15] prostitution,[16] radio and television broadcasts,[17] and telecommunications and the Internet.

More recently, the Court has limited congressional power to address similar harms when it did not find a substantial connection with interstate commerce. In *United States v. Lopez*,[18] for example, the Supreme Court struck down the Gun-Free School Zones Act, which made it a federal crime to possess a firearm within 1,000 feet of a school, because the justices did not find a substantial connection between violence in schools and the national economy. However, in *Gonzales v. Raich* (2005), the Court upheld Congress's power to criminalize the use of marijuana, even for medicinal purposes by seriously ill people, as ten states had permitted.[19] The Court ruled that the aggregative impact of such individual marijuana usage had a substantial connection to, and would undercut the regulation of, marijuana in interstate commerce.

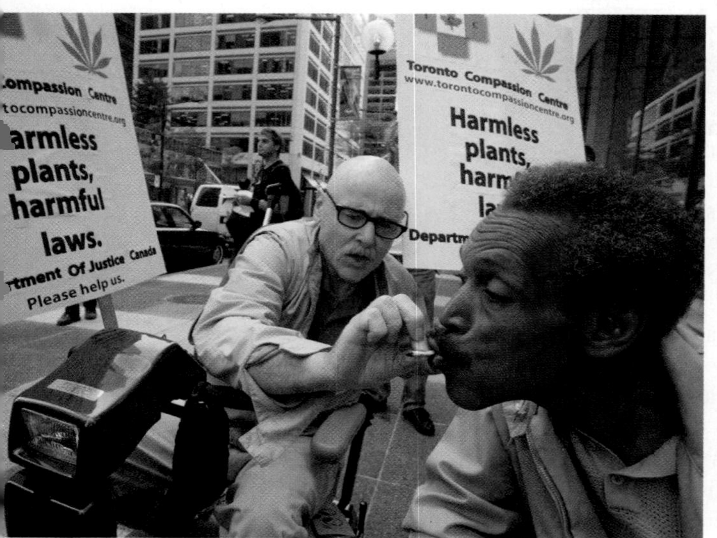

Some states such as California legalized the use of marijuana to help people with cancer endure chemotherapy. The Supreme Court ruled in 2005 that the federal law prohibiting the use of medical marijuana was an appropriate application of the commerce clause.

The Power to Tax and Spend Congress lacks constitutional authority to pass laws solely on the grounds that they will promote the general welfare, but it may raise taxes and spend money for this purpose. For example, Congress lacks the power to regulate education or agriculture directly, yet it does have the power to appropriate money to support education or to pay farm subsidies. By attaching conditions to its grants of money, Congress may thus regulate what it cannot directly control by law.

When Congress provides the money, it determines how the money will be spent. By withholding or threatening to withhold funds, the national government can influence or control state operations and regulate individual conduct. For example, Congress has stipulated that federal funds should be withdrawn from any program in which any person is denied benefits because of race, color, national origin, sex, or physical handicap. Congress also used its power of the purse to force states to raise the drinking age to 21 by tying such a condition to federal dollars for building and maintaining highways.

Congress frequently requires states to do certain things—for example, provide services to indigent mothers and clean up the air and water. These requirements are called **federal mandates.** Often Congress does not supply the funds required to carry out "unfunded mandates" (discussed later in the chapter). Its failure to do so has become an important issue as states face growing expenditures with limited resources. The Supreme Court has also ruled that Congress may not compel states through "unfunded mandates" to enforce or implement particular laws such as handgun registration.[20]

Powers of the States

The Constitution *reserves for the states all powers not granted to the national government,* subject only to the limitations of the Constitution. Only the states have the **reserve powers** to create schools and local governments, for example. Both are powers not given exclusively to the national government by the Constitution or judicial interpretation, as long as the exercise of those powers does not conflict with national law.

The national and state governments also share powers. These **concurrent powers** with the national government include the power to levy taxes and regulate commerce internal to each state.

In general, states may levy taxes on the same items the national government taxes, such as incomes, alcohol, and gasoline, but a state cannot, by a tax, "unduly burden" commerce among the states, interfere with a function of the national government, complicate the operation of a national law, or abridge the terms of a treaty of the United States. Where Congress has not preempted the field, states may regulate interstate businesses, provided these regulations do not cover matters requiring uniform national treatment or unduly burden interstate commerce.

Who decides which matters require "uniform national treatment" or what actions might place an "undue burden" on interstate commerce? Congress does, subject to final review by the Supreme Court. When Congress is silent or does not clearly state its intent, the courts—ultimately, the Supreme Court—decide whether there is a conflict with the national Constitution or whether a state law or regulation has preempted federal authority.

Constitutional Limits and Obligations

To ensure that federalism works, the Constitution imposes restraints on both the national and the state governments. States are prohibited from doing the following:

1. Making treaties with foreign governments
2. Authorizing private persons to prey on the shipping and commerce of other nations
3. Coining money, issuing bills of credit, or making anything but gold and silver coin legal tender in payment of debts
4. Taxing imports or exports
5. Taxing foreign ships
6. Keeping troops or ships of war in time of peace (except the state militia, now called the National Guard)
7. Engaging in war, unless invaded or in such imminent danger as will not admit of delay

federal mandate
A requirement the federal government imposes as a condition for receiving federal funds.

reserve powers
All powers not specifically delegated to the national government by the Constitution. The reserve power can be found in the Tenth Amendment to the Constitution.

concurrent powers
Powers that the Constitution gives to both the national and state governments, such as the power to levy taxes.

The U.S. Supreme Court ruled that the national government cannot demand that states enforce the federal law requiring handgun dealers to run background checks on potential buyers. States are free, however, to use a national registry of criminals in doing background checks, which almost all do.

In turn, the Constitution requires the national government to refrain from exercising its powers, especially its powers to tax and to regulate interstate commerce, in such a way as to interfere substantially with the states' abilities to perform their responsibilities. But politicians, judges, and scholars disagree about whether the national political process—specifically in Congress and the presidency—or the courts should ultimately define the boundaries between the powers of the national government and the states. Some argue that the states' protection from intrusions by the national government comes primarily from the political process, because senators and representatives elected from the states participate in the decisions of Congress.[21] Others maintain that the Supreme Court should limit the national government and defend the states.[22]

The Court has held that Congress may not command states to enact laws to comply with or order state employees to enforce unfunded federal mandates; for example, as we noted earlier, *Printz v. United States* held that Congress may not require local law enforcement officials to make background checks prior to handgun sales.[23] It has also ruled that the Eleventh Amendment's guarantee of states' sovereign immunity from lawsuits forbids state employees from suing states in federal and state courts to force state compliance with federal employment laws.[24] Although Congress may not use those sticks, it may still offer the carrot of federal funding if states comply with national policies, such as lowering the minimum drinking age.

The Constitution also obliges the national government to protect states against *domestic insurrection.* Congress has delegated to the president the authority to dispatch troops to put down such insurrections when the proper state authorities request them.

Interstate Relationships

Three clauses in the Constitution, taken from the Articles of Confederation, require states to give full faith and credit to each other's public acts, records, and judicial proceedings; to extend to each other's citizens the privileges and immunities of their own citizens; and to return persons who are fleeing from justice.

full faith and credit clause
The clause in the Constitution (Article IV, Section 1) requiring each state to recognize the civil judgments rendered by the courts of the other states and to accept their public records and acts as valid.

extradition
The legal process whereby an alleged criminal offender is surrendered by the officials of one state to officials of the state in which the crime is alleged to have been committed.

Full Faith and Credit

The **full faith and credit clause** (Article IV, Section 1), one of the more technical provisions of the Constitution, requires state courts to enforce the civil judgments of the courts of other states and accept their public records and acts as valid.[25] It does not require states to enforce the criminal laws or legislation and administrative acts of other states; in most cases, for one state to enforce the criminal laws of another would raise constitutional issues. The clause applies primarily to enforcing judicial settlements and court awards.

Interstate Privileges and Immunities

Under Article IV, Section 2, states must extend to citizens of other states the privileges and immunities they grant to their own citizens, including the protection of the laws, the right to engage in peaceful occupations, access to the courts, and freedom from discriminatory taxes. Because of this clause, states may not impose unreasonable residency requirements; that is, withhold rights to American citizens who have recently moved to the state and thereby have become citizens of that state.

Extradition

In Article IV, Section 2, the Constitution asserts that when individuals charged with crimes have fled from one state to another, the state to which they have fled is to deliver them to the proper officials on demand of the executive authority of the state from which they fled. This process is called **extradition.** "The obvious objective of

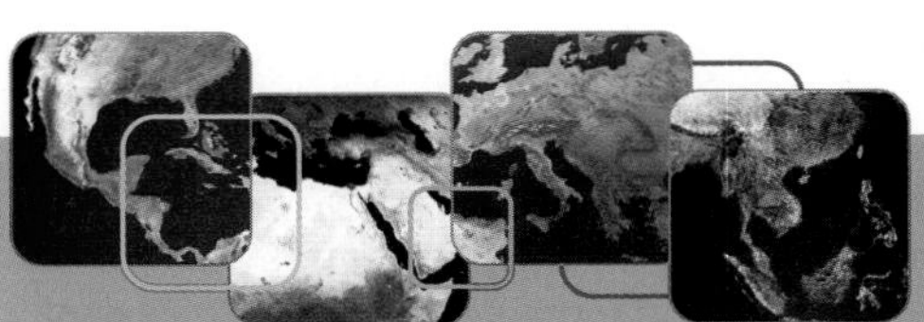

HOW **OTHER NATIONS** GOVERN

Different Visions of Federalism

There is no single model for dividing authority between the national and smaller regional governments of the other nations covered in this book. Some have no federal system at all, while others have different variations of power sharing between the national and smaller regional governments.

Britain's government is divided into three tiers: national, county, and district governments. County and district governments deliver roughly one-fifth of all government services, including education, housing, and police and fire protection. As a rule, most power is reserved for the central government on the theory that there should be "territorial justice," which means that all citizens should be governed by the same laws and standards. In recent years, however, Great Britain has devolved substantial authority to Scotland, Wales, and Northern Ireland.

China actually has two governments. One is built around traditional institutions of government, while the other is built around the Communist Party. China's traditional government extends to the local level through provincial governments, municipal governments, county governments, township governments, and villages, all of which have councils or legislatures. Despite more than 600,000 villages that exist at the very bottom of this complex system, there is no delegation of authority downward. The Communist Party is the real government and makes all policy decisions for the country.

India follows the same three-tiered pattern of most governments in the world: national, regional, and local. Unlike the United States, however, the Indian national government retains almost all authority to make decisions—its 36 states and seven territories do not have their own constitutions, for example, and its local governments rarely act without delegation of authority from the top of the system. More recently, however, state governments have become more powerful as India has become divided between ethnic groups.

Japan's government is also divided into three tiers, also without federalism. Local government receives all its authority through national government decisions. And what the national government grants through delegation can be easily taken away. Nevertheless, local governments account for about two-thirds of all government spending, but raise only one-third of taxes.

Mexico has the same three-tiered structure, again with very little federalism. Instead, power is concentrated at the top of government through centralization. This centralization contributes stability in the face of continued tensions between Mexico's 36 states. Although the Mexican constitution promises *municipio libre*, meaning that local governments should be free to act, local governments rely on the national government for their revenue and therefore their authority.

In contrast to most other nations, Nigeria is highly decentralized, and its 36 states have considerable power under Nigeria's most recent constitution. The national government is not powerless, however. It controls all revenues from Nigeria's substantial oil industry and thereby it has considerable influence over how much its regions can deliver.

QUESTIONS

1. What seems to be the primary reason for the lack of federalism in most countries?
2. Why do nations with histories of violence tend to avoid federalism?
3. Where should the people put their energies in changing the basic policies of each nation discussed here? Why?

the Extradition Clause," the courts have claimed, "is that no State should become a safe haven for the fugitives from a sister State's criminal justice system."[26] Congress has supplemented this constitutional provision by making the governor of the state to which fugitives have fled responsible for returning them.

Interstate Compacts The Constitution also requires states to settle disputes with one another without the use of force. States may carry their legal disputes to the Supreme Court, or they may negotiate **interstate compacts.** Interstate compacts often establish interstate agencies to handle problems affecting an entire region. Before most interstate compacts become effective, Congress has to approve them. Then the compact becomes binding on all signatory states, and the federal judiciary can enforce its terms. A typical state may belong to 20 compacts dealing with such subjects as environmental protection, crime control, water rights, and higher education exchanges.[27]

The Federal Courts and Federalism

Although the political process ultimately decides how power will be divided between the national and the state governments, the federal courts—especially the Supreme Court—are often called on to umpire the ongoing debate about which level of government should do what, for whom, and to whom. The courts claimed this role in the celebrated case of *McCulloch v. Maryland.*

You Are a Federal Judge

interstate compact
An agreement among two or more states. Congress must approve most such agreements.

McCulloch v. Maryland

LEARNING **OBJECTIVE**

5 Analyze the role of the national courts in regulating federalism.

TIMELINE

Federalism and the Supreme Court

In *McCulloch v. Maryland* (1819), the Supreme Court had the first of many chances to define the division of power between the national and state governments.[28] Congress had established the Bank of the United States, but Maryland opposed any national bank and levied a $10,000 tax on any bank not incorporated within the state. James William McCulloch, the cashier of the bank, refused to pay on the grounds that a state could not tax an instrument of the national government.

Maryland was represented before the Court by some of the country's most distinguished lawyers, including Luther Martin, who had been a delegate to the Constitutional Convention. Martin said the Constitution did not expressly delegate to the national government the power to incorporate a bank. He maintained that the necessary and proper clause gives Congress only the power to choose those means and to pass those laws absolutely essential to the execution of its expressly granted powers. Because a bank is not absolutely necessary to the exercise of its delegated powers, he argued, Congress had no authority to establish it. As for Maryland's right to tax the bank, the power to tax is one of the powers reserved to the states; they may use it as they see fit.

Equally distinguished counsel, including Daniel Webster, represented the national government. Webster conceded that the power to create a bank is not one of the express powers of the national government. However, the power to pass laws necessary and proper to carry out Congress's express powers is specifically delegated to Congress. Although the power to tax is reserved to the states, Webster argued that states cannot interfere with the operations of the national government. The Constitution leaves no room for doubt; when the national and state governments have conflicts, the national government is supreme.

Speaking for a unanimous Court, Chief Justice John Marshall rejected every one of Maryland's contentions. He summarized his views on the powers of the national government in these now-famous words: "Let the end be legitimate, let it be within the scope of the Constitution, and all means which are appropriate, which are plainly adapted to that end, which are not prohibited, but consist with the letter and spirit of the constitution, are constitutional." Having thus established the doctrine of *implied national powers,* Marshall set forth the doctrine of **national supremacy.** No state, he said, can use its taxing powers to tax a national instrument. "The power to tax involves the power to destroy. . . . If the right of the States to tax the means employed by the

national supremacy
A constitutional doctrine that whenever conflict occurs between the constitutionally authorized actions of the national government and those of a state or local government, the actions of the federal government prevail.

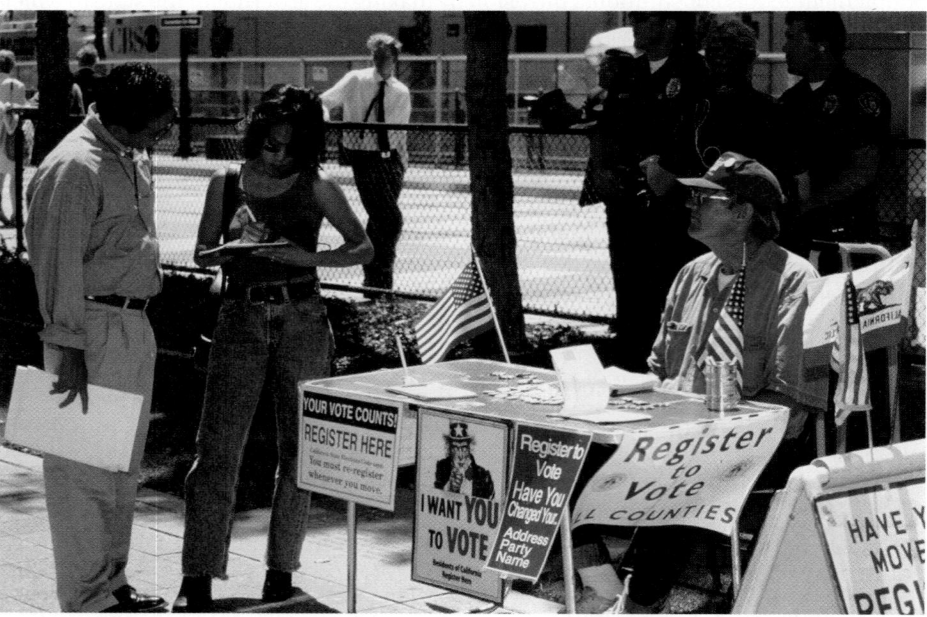

Under the Voting Rights Act of 1965, the federal government ordered southern states to remove the barriers to registration. The act still guarantees voting rights today

general government be conceded, the declaration that the Constitution, and the laws made in pursuance thereof, shall be the supreme law of the land, is empty and unmeaning declamation."

It's difficult to overstate the long-range significance of *McCulloch v. Maryland* in providing support for the developing forces of nationalism and a unified economy. If the contrary arguments in favor of the states had been accepted, they would have strapped the national government in a constitutional straitjacket and denied it powers needed to deal with the problems of an expanding nation.

Federal Courts and the Role of the States

The authority of federal judges to review the activities of state and local governments has expanded dramatically in recent decades because of modern judicial interpretations of the Fourteenth Amendment, which forbids states to deprive any person of life, liberty, or property without *due process of the law.* States may not deny any person the *equal protection of the laws,* including congressional legislation enacted to implement the Fourteenth Amendment. Almost every action by state and local officials is now subject to challenge before a federal judge as a violation of the Constitution or of federal law.

Preemption occurs when a federal law or regulation takes precedence over a state or local law or regulation. State and local laws are preempted not only when they conflict directly with federal laws and regulations, but also when they touch on a field in which the "federal interest is so dominant that the federal system will be assumed to preclude enforcement of state laws on the same subject."[29] Examples of federal preemption include laws regulating hazardous substances, water quality, clean air standards, and many civil rights acts, especially the Civil Rights Act of 1964 and the Voting Rights Act of 1965.

Over the years, federal judges, under the leadership of the Supreme Court, have generally favored the powers of the federal government over those of the states. Despite the Supreme Court's recent bias in favor of state over national authority, few would deny the Supreme Court the power to review and set aside state actions. As Justice Oliver Wendell Holmes of the Supreme Court once remarked: "I do not think the United States would come to an end if we lost our power to declare an Act of Congress void. I do think the Union would be imperiled if we could not make that declaration as to the laws of the several States."[30]

The Great Debate: Centralists Versus Decentralists

LEARNING **OBJECTIVE**

6 Compare and contrast the arguments of decentralists and centralists.

From the beginning of the Republic, there has been an ongoing debate about the "proper" distribution of powers, functions, and responsibilities between the national government and the states. Did the national government have the authority to outlaw slavery in the territories? Did the states have the authority to operate racially segregated schools? Could Congress regulate labor relations? Does Congress have the power to regulate the sale and use of firearms? Does Congress have the right to tell states how to clean up air and water pollution?

During the Great Depression of the 1930s, the nation debated whether Congress had the constitutional authority to enact legislation on agriculture, labor, education, housing, and welfare. Only 40 years ago, legislators and public officials—as well as scholars—questioned the constitutional authority of Congress to legislate against racial discrimination. The debate continues between **centralists,** who favor national action, and **decentralists,** who defend the powers of the states and favor action at the state and local levels.

preemption
The right of a federal law or regulation to preclude enforcement of a state or local law or regulation.

centralists
People who favor national action over action at the state and local levels.

decentralists
People who favor state or local action rather than national action.

states' rights
Powers expressly or implicitly reserved to the states.

The Decentralist Position

Among those favoring the decentralist or **states' rights** interpretation were the Antifederalists, Thomas Jefferson, the pre–Civil War statesman from South Carolina John C. Calhoun, the Supreme Court from the 1920s to 1937, and more recently, Presidents Ronald Reagan and George H. W. Bush, the Republican leaders of Congress, former chief justice William H. Rehnquist, and current justices Antonin Scalia and Clarence Thomas.

Most decentralists contend that the Constitution is basically a compact among sovereign states that created the central government and gave it limited authority. Thus the national government is little more than an agent of the states, and every one of its powers should be narrowly defined. Any question about whether the states have given a particular function to the central government or have reserved it for themselves should be resolved in favor of the states.

Decentralists hold that the national government should not interfere with activities reserved for the states. The Tenth Amendment, they claim, makes this clear. It states: "The powers not delegated to the United States by the Constitution, nor prohibited by it to the States, are reserved to the States respectively, or to the people." Decentralists insist that state governments are closer to the people and reflect the people's wishes more accurately than the national government does. The national government, they add, is inherently heavy-handed and bureaucratic; to preserve our federal system and our liberties, we must keep central authority under control.

The Centralist Position The centralist position has been supported by presidents, Congress, and the Supreme Court. Presidents Abraham Lincoln, Theodore Roosevelt, Franklin Roosevelt, and Lyndon Johnson were particularly strong supporters, while the Supreme Court has generally ruled in favor of the centralist position.

Centralists reject the whole idea of the Constitution as an interstate compact. They view it as a supreme law established by the people. The national government is an agent of the people, not of the states, because it was the people who drew up the Constitution and created the national government. They intended that the national political process should define the central government's powers, and that the national government be denied authority only when the Constitution clearly prohibits it from acting.

Centralists argue that the national government is a government of all the people, whereas each state speaks for only some of the people. Although the Tenth Amendment clearly reserves powers for the states, it does not deny the national government the authority to exercise all of its powers to the fullest extent. Moreover, the supremacy of the national government restricts the states, because governments representing part of the people cannot be allowed to interfere with a government representing all of them.

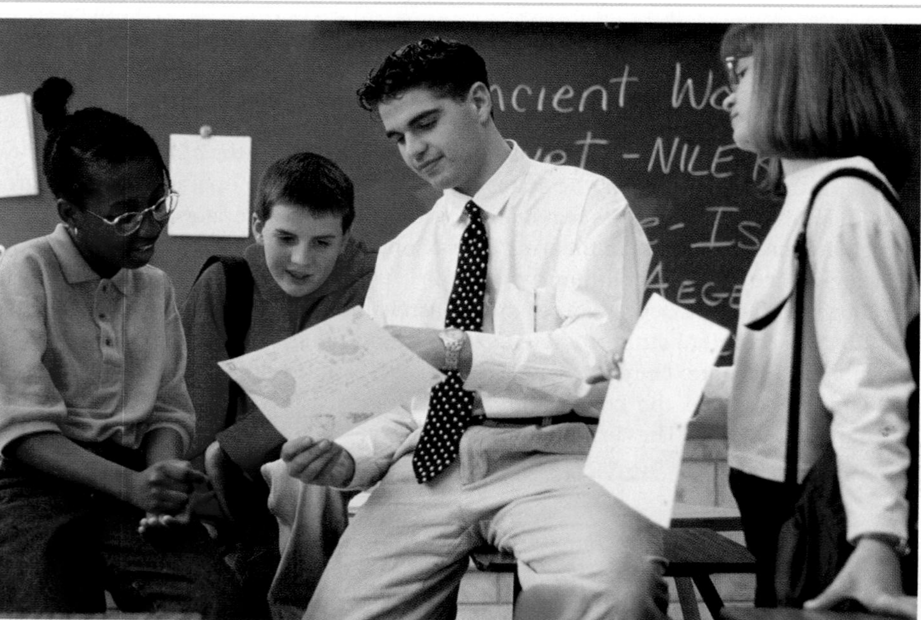

Decentralists believe that education should be a state responsibility. However, because the national government provides money to the states, it has the power to impose strings on how the money is spent.

The Supreme Court and the Role of Congress

From 1937 until the 1990s, the Supreme Court essentially removed federal courts from what had been their role of protecting states from acts of Congress. The Supreme Court broadly interpreted the commerce clause to allow Congress to do whatever Congress thought necessary and proper to promote the common good, even if federal laws and regulations infringed on the activities of state and local governments.

In the past decade, however, the Supreme Court has signaled that federal courts should be more active in resolving federalism issues.[31] The Court declared that a state could not impose term limits on its members of Congress, but it did so by only a 5-to-4 vote. Justice John Paul Stevens, writing for the majority, built his argument on the concept of the federal union as espoused by the great chief justice John Marshall, as a compact among the people, with the national government serving as the people's agent.

The Court also declared that the clause in the Constitution empowering Congress to regulate commerce with the Indian tribes did not give Congress the power to authorize federal courts to hear suits against a state brought by Indian tribes.[32] Unless states consent to such suits, they enjoy "sovereign immunity" under the Eleventh Amendment. The effect of this decision goes beyond Indian tribes. As a result—except to enforce rights stemming from the Fourteenth Amendment, which the Court explicitly acknowledged to be within Congress's power—Congress may no longer authorize individuals to bring legal actions against states to force their compliance with federal law in either federal or state courts.[33]

Building on those rulings, the Court continues to press ahead with its "constitutional counterrevolution"[34] and returning to an older vision of federalism from the 1930s. Among other recent rulings, in *United States v. Morrison* the Court struck down the Violence Against Women Act, which had given women who are victims of violence the right to sue their attackers for damages.[35] Congress had found that violence against women annually costs the national economy $3 billion, but a bare majority of the Court held that gender-motivated crimes did not have a substantial impact on interstate commerce and therefore that Congress had exceeded its powers in enacting the law and intruded on the powers of the states.

These Supreme Court decisions—most of which split the Court 5 to 4 along ideological lines, with the conservative justices favoring states' rights—have signaled a shift in the Court's interpretation of the constitutional nature of our federal system. It is a shift that has become somewhat more pronounced, however, with the arrival of President George W. Bush's two appointees, Chief Justice John Roberts and Justice Samuel A. Alito Jr., joined by Justices Scalia and Thomas and frequently Justice Anthony M. Kennedy.

Federalism

Regulatory Federalism

Congress authorizes programs, establishes general rules for how the programs will operate, and decides whether room should be left for state or local discretion and how much. Most important, Congress appropriates the funds for these programs and generally has deeper pockets than even the richest states. Federal grants are one of Congress's most potent tools for influencing policy at the state and local levels.

Federal grants serve four purposes, the most important of which is the fourth:

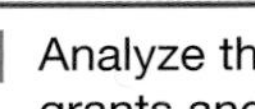

7 Analyze the differences between grants and mandates.

1. To supply state and local governments with revenue
2. To establish minimum national standards for such things as highways and clean air
3. To equalize resources among the states by taking money from people with high incomes through federal taxes and spending it, through grants, in states where the poor live
4. To attack national problems yet minimize the growth of federal agencies

HISTORY MAKERS

Chief Justice William H. Rehnquist

When asked his career plans by his elementary school teacher, William H. Rehnquist once recalled saying, "I am going to change the government."* After serving in the army during World War II, Rehnquist majored in political science at Stanford University and later graduated first in his class from Stanford Law School. He then clerked for a Supreme Court justice and went into private legal practice while becoming active in Republican politics.

As an assistant attorney general in the administration of President Richard M. Nixon, Rehnquist was appointed associate justice of the Supreme Court in 1972. In his early years on the Court he emerged as a champion of federalism, limiting the power of the national government and returning power to the states. However, he could not persuade a majority to go along with his views and earned the nickname "Lone Ranger" for writing more dissenting opinions than any other justice at the time. In 1986, President Ronald Reagan elevated him to chief justice, and he presided over the Court until his death in 2005.

A major legacy of the Rehnquist Court is the way it curbed Congress in defense of the states. Besides resurrecting the rhetoric of states' rights and the Tenth Amendment, Chief Justice Rehnquist was central to a series of decisions that strengthened the states:

- Congress must make a "plain statement" of its intent to preempt state laws; otherwise the Court will defer to the states.†
- Congress's power over interstate commerce has inherent limits, and it may not compel states to enact laws in compliance with federal standards or compel them to enforce federal laws.‡
- Congress's power under the commerce clause permits it to regulate noneconomic activities, but only if they "substantially affect interstate commerce."§
- Congress's power to enforce the Fourteenth Amendment guarantee of equal protection of the law is limited to remedying violations that the Court recognizes; it does not extend to creating rights.‖
- States' immunity from lawsuits under the Eleventh Amendment bars lawsuits against them, without their consent, in federal and state courts, and by citizens of other states as well as of their own state who seek state compliance with federal laws forbidding, for example, discrimination on the basis of age or disability.¶

In short, Chief Justice Rehnquist presided over a Court that curbed the expansion of congressional powers and federal regulations in a renewed defense of the boundaries of federalism.

William H. Rehnquist.

QUESTIONS

1. What do you think were Rehnquist's most important contributions in protecting states from the national government?
2. How can citizens influence Supreme Court decisions, and should they try?
3. How was Rehnquist able to influence the court even when he was in the minority?

*Quoted in Craig Bradley, "William H. Rehnquist," in Clare Cushman, ed., *The Supreme Court Justices* (CQ Press, 1993), p. 496.
†*Gregory v. Ashcroft,* 501 U.S. 452 (1991).
‡*New York v. United States,* 505 U.S. 144 (1992), and *Printz v. United States,* 521 U.S. 898 (1997).
§*United States v. Lopez,* 514 U.S. 549 (1995), and *United States v. Morrison,* 529 U.S. 598 (2000); but see *Nevada v. Hibbs,* 538 U.S. 721 (2003).
‖*City of Bourne v. Lopez,* 521 U.S. 507 (1997), and *United States v. Morrison,* 529 U.S. 598 (2000).
¶See, for example, *Alden v. Maine,* 527 U.S. 706 (1998).

Types of Federal Grants

The federal government currently administers three types of federal grants: *categorical-formula grants, project grants,* and *block grants* (sometimes called *flexible grants*). From 1972 to 1987, there was also *revenue sharing*—federal grants to state and local governments to be used at their discretion and subject only to general conditions. But when budget deficits soared in the second Reagan administration (1985–1989) and there was no revenue to share, revenue sharing was terminated—to the states in 1986 and to local governments in 1987.

Categorical-Formula Grants Congress appropriates funds for specific purposes, such as providing school lunches or building airports and highways. These funds are allocated by formula and are subject to detailed federal conditions, often on a matching basis; that is, the local government receiving the federal funds must put up some of its own dollars.

Categorical grants also provide federal supervision to ensure that the money is spent as Congress wants. There are hundreds of grant programs, but two dozen, including Medicaid, account for more than half of total categorical-formula spending.

Project Grants Congress appropriates a certain sum in project grants, allocated to state and local units and sometimes to nongovernmental agencies, based on applications from those who wish to participate. Examples are grants by the National Science Foundation to universities and research institutes to support the work of scientists, and grants to state and local governments to support training and employment programs.

Block Grants Block grants are broad grants to states for prescribed activities—welfare, child care, education, social services, preventive health care, and health services—with only a few strings attached. States have great flexibility in deciding how to spend block grant dollars, but when the federal funds for any fiscal year are gone, there are no more matching federal dollars.

The Politics of Federal Grants

Republicans "have consistently favored fewer strings, less federal supervision, and the delegation of spending discretion to the state and local governments."[36] Democrats have generally been less supportive of broad discretionary block grants, instead favoring more detailed, federally supervised spending. The Republican-controlled Congress in the 1990s gave high priority to creating block grants, but it ran into trouble when it tried to lump together welfare, school lunch and breakfast programs, prenatal nutrition programs, and child protection programs in one block grant.

Republicans, however, with President Clinton's support, did make a major change in federal–state relations—a transfer of responsibility for welfare from the national government to the states. The Personal Responsibility and Work Opportunity Reconciliation Act of 1996 put an end to the 61-year-old program of Aid to Families with Dependent Children (AFDC), a federal guarantee of welfare checks for all eligible mothers and children. The 1996 act substituted for AFDC a welfare block grant to each state, with caps on the amount of federal dollars that the state will receive. It also put another big federal child care program into another block grant—the Child Care and Development Block Grant (CCDBG).

The Americans with Disabilities Act of 1990 required state and local governments to improve access to buildings and public transportation for people with disabilities.

Welfare block grants offer states flexibility in providing for welfare, but states cannot give federal funds to recipients who do not go to work within two years, and no one can receive federally supported benefits for more than five years. To slow down the "race to the bottom," in which states may try to make themselves "the least attractive state in which to be poor,"[37] Congress also stipulated that to receive their full share of federal dollars, states must continue to spend at least 75 percent of what they had been spending on welfare before 1996.

The battle over which is the appropriate level of government to control funding and to exercise principal responsibility for social programs tends to be cyclical. As one scholar of federalism explains, "Complaints about excessive federal control tend to be followed by proposals to shift more power to state and local governments. Then, when problems arise in state and local administration—and problems inevitably arise when any organization tries to administer anything—demands for closer federal supervision and tighter federal controls follow."[38]

Federal Mandates

Fewer federal dollars do not necessarily mean fewer federal controls. On the contrary, the federal government has imposed mandates on states and local governments, often without providing federal funds. State and local officials complained about this, and their protests were effective. The Unfunded Mandates Reform Act of 1995 was championed by then House Republican Speaker Newt Gingrich as part of the GOP's Contract with America.

The law requires Congress to evaluate the impact of unfunded mandates and imposes mild constraints on Congress itself. A congressional committee that approves any legislation containing a federal mandate must draw attention to the mandate in its report and describe its cost to state and local governments. If the committee intends any mandate to be partially unfunded, it must explain why it is appropriate for state and local governments to pay for it.

At least during its first fifteen years, the Unfunded Mandates Reform Act has been mostly unsuccessful in restraining mandates. The No Child Left Behind Act of 2002 placed enormous new burdens on public schools with very little increase in funding, for example. Still, state officials praise the Unfunded Mandates Reform Act for increasing congressional awareness of unfunded mandates. It has forced members of Congress to take into account how a bill would affect state and local governments.[39]

New Techniques of Federal Control

In recent decades, Congress has used other techniques to establish federal regulations, including *direct orders, cross-cutting requirements, crossover sanctions,* and *total and partial preemption.*

Direct Orders In a few instances, federal regulation takes the form of direct orders that states must comply with under threat of criminal or civil sanction. An example is the Equal Employment Opportunity Act of 1972, barring job discrimination by state and local governments on the basis of race, color, religion, sex, and national origin.

Cross-Cutting Requirements Federal grants may establish certain conditions that extend to all activities supported by federal funds, regardless of their source. The first and most famous of these is Title VI of the 1964 Civil Rights Act, which holds that in the use of federal funds, no person may be discriminated against on the basis of race, color, or national origin. Other laws extend these protections to persons because of gender or disability status.

Crossover Sanctions Crossover sanctions permit the use of federal money in one program to influence state and local policy in another. For example, a 1984 act reduced federal highway aid by up to 15 percent for any state that failed to adopt a minimum drinking age of 21.

Total and Partial Preemption Total preemption rests on the national government's power under the supremacy and commerce clauses to preempt conflicting state and local activities. Building on this constitutional authority, federal law in certain areas entirely preempts state and local governments from the field.[40] Sometimes federal law provides for partial preemption in establishing basic policies but requires states to administer them. Some programs give states an option not to participate, but if a state so chooses, the national government steps in and runs the program. Homeland security legislation is another example of a mostly unfunded requirement to the states. States were given great responsibility in 2007 for acting as the first responders to national emergencies such as Hurricane Katrina, but only received a fraction of the funds needed to do so.

The Politics of Federalism

LEARNING **OBJECTIVE**

8 Establish the link between the growth of the national government and federalism.

The formal structures of our federal system have not changed much since 1787, but the political realities, especially during the past half-century, have greatly altered the way federalism works. To understand these changes, we need to look at some of the trends that continue to fuel the debate about the meaning of federalism.

The Growth of National Government

Federalism and Regulations

Over the past two centuries, power has accrued to the national government. As the Advisory Commission on Intergovernmental Relations observed in a 1981 report, "No one planned the growth, but everyone played a part in it."[41] This shift occurred for a variety of reasons. One is that many of our problems have become national in scope. Much that was local in 1789, in 1860, or in 1930 is now national, even global. State governments could supervise the relationships between small merchants and their few employees, for instance, but only the national government can supervise relationships between multinational corporations and their thousands of worldwide employees, many of whom are organized in national unions.

As industrialization proceeded in the early nineteenth century, powerful interests made demands on the national government. Business groups called on the government for aid in the form of tariffs, a national banking system, subsidies to railroads and the merchant marine, and uniform rules on the environment. Farmers learned that the national government could give more aid than the states, and they too began to demand help. By the beginning of the twentieth century, urban groups in general and organized labor in particular were pressing their claims. Big business, big agriculture, and big labor all added up to big government.

The growth of the national economy and the creation of national transportation and communications networks altered people's attitudes toward the national government. Before the Civil War, citizens saw the national government as a distant, even foreign, entity. Today, in part because of television and the Internet, most people know more about Washington than they know about their state capitals, and more about the president and their national legislators than about their governor, their state legislators, or even the local officials who run their cities and schools.

The Great Depression of the 1930s stimulated extensive national action on welfare, unemployment, and farm surpluses. World War II brought federal regulation of wages, prices, and employment, as well as national efforts to allocate resources, train personnel, and support engineering and inventions. After the war, the national government helped veterans obtain college degrees and inaugurated a vast system of support for university research. The United States became the most powerful leader of the free world, maintaining substantial military forces even in times of peace. The

YOU WILL DECIDE

Should the No Child Left Behind Act Be Repealed?

Early in 2002, President George W. Bush signed the No Child Left Behind Act into law, thereby creating one of the most significant mandates ever imposed on the states. Although primary and secondary education has long been considered an almost exclusive responsibility of state and local governments, the No Child Left Behind Act required states to create a new system of standardized testing for every public school. States could either implement the new mandate or lose their federal funding, which amounts to about 10 percent of all school budgets.

Under the No Child Left Behind Act, schools were required to adopt a number of separate reforms for improving student achievement. Students in grades three through eight were to be tested each year in reading and math, while students in high school were to be tested at least once in reading, math, and science. Based on the test results, schools were also required to show academic progress or risk the possibility of losing federal money. If a school failed two years in a row, parents were to be given the option to move their children to another school, while schools that failed three years in a row were required to establish special programs to help their students advance. Finally, the act required states to give parents report cards on the performance of their schools, rating them as "failing," "in need of improvement," or "making adequate yearly progress."

Like many national laws, however, the No Child Left Behind Act is not permanent. It must be renewed every five years, which means that it can be changed. As they gain more experience with the act, parents and teachers will have more influence over the future of the tests and report cards that now govern their schools.

Great Society programs of the 1960s poured out grants-in-aid to states and local governments.

Although economic and social conditions created many of the pressures for expanding the national government, so did political claims. Until federal budget deficits became a hot issue in the 1980s and early 1990s, members of Congress, presidents, federal judges, and federal administrators actively promoted federal initiatives. Even with the return of deficit spending in the 2000s, Congress appears willing to actively promote some federal programs, at least in homeland security and prescription drug coverage. True, when there is widespread conflict about what to do—how to reduce the federal deficit, adopt a national energy policy, reform Social Security, provide health care for the indigent—Congress waits for a national consensus. But when an organized constituency wants something and there is no counterpressure, Congress "responds often to everyone, and with great vigor."[42] Once established, federal programs generate groups with vested interests in promoting, defending, and expanding them. Associations are formed and alliances are made. "In a word, the growth of government has created a constituency of, by, and for government."[43]

The politics of federalism are changing, however, and Congress is being pressured to reduce the size and scope of national programs, but at the same time to deal with the demands for homeland security.

Fears of terrorism have led state and local governments to take action to protect their citizens. Much of this activity is mandated by the federal government with limited funds. In this photo, New York City police patrol the subway looking for suspicious behavior.

Meanwhile, the cost of entitlement programs such as Social Security and Medicare are rising because there are more older people and they are living longer. These programs have widespread public support, and to cut them is politically risky. "With all other options disappearing, it is politically tempting to finance tax cuts by turning over to the states many of the social programs...that have become the responsibility of the national government."[44]

The Devolution Revolution

Recent Congresses, like their predecessors, have increased the authority of the national government in many areas, an increase often called the **devolution revolution**.[45] Despite its dramatic name, the revolution has fallen short of the hoped-for return of state responsibilities. To be sure, the Republican-controlled Congress in the 1990s returned some functions, especially welfare, to the states. President Clinton also proclaimed, "The era of big government is over," though he tempered his comments by saying, "But we cannot go back to the time when our citizens were left to fend for themselves."

Indeed, the national government's role has actually grown stronger over the past decade, especially in dealing with the continued threat of terrorism; the role of the federal government in defending homeland security has expanded; and some states, such as New York, have objected to inadequate federal funding and to the increased cost of using state agencies as "first responders." Congress also established national criteria for state-issued drivers' licenses, forbade states to sell drivers' personal information, ended state regulation of mutual funds, nullified state laws restricting telecommunications competition, and made a host of offenses federal crimes, including carjacking and acts of terrorism. Appropriation bills pressured states to keep criminals behind bars by threatening to take grants away from states that fail to meet federal standards for prison security.

The Future of Federalism

Despite new mandates and continued national oversight, states are stronger than ever. During recent decades, state governments have undergone a major transformation. Most have improved their governmental structures, taken on greater roles in funding education and welfare, launched programs to help distressed cities, expanded their tax bases by allowing citizens to deduct their state and local taxes from the national income tax, and assumed greater roles in maintaining homeland security and fighting corporate corruption.

THINKING IT THROUGH

Parents and teachers already seem to agree that the No Child Left Behind Act created three significant problems that must be fixed if the overall effort is to succeed.

First, they complain that instead of inspiring schools to focus on reading, math, and science, the act may encourage them to "teach to the test"—to prep students on how to take tests in reading, math, and science. There is no question, for example, that primary school students now spend enormous amounts of time practicing for the annual reading and math tests, or that teachers are being encouraged to produce the highest scores possible, even if that occasionally means giving students extra practice on the test instead of instruction on basic skills. There have also been several highly publicized scandals in which schools cheated on the tests.

Second, parents and teachers worry that the federal government has not provided enough funding to make the law work. Failing public schools cannot be improved simply by giving parents the right to remove their children, if only because they may not be able to find a better school. Moreover, new programs such as mentoring, after-school tutoring, and summer school cost money that is often in short supply in large, urban school districts. These districts may also have much higher proportions of students who speak English as a second language, which can lead to lower test scores.

Teach for America helps public schools by training young college graduates to spend two years teaching low-income students. These volunteers are sometimes the only source of new teachers for poor school districts.

Third, many of the most troubled schools have severe problems recruiting talented teachers and maintaining their facilities. Hard as they try, parents and teachers may be unable to raise scores if school buildings continue to crumble. Nor can they succeed unless school districts provide proper equipment such as computers and recruit talented teachers. Having already absorbed deep cutbacks as wealthier families move to suburban districts, inner-city schools may be destined to fail, and parents unable to find another option for their children.

Despite these concerns, the act is almost certain to be renewed. Even though some say it focuses on testing, not learning, No Child Left Behind has created significant pressure for higher performance. The question is how its provisions might be changed to increase success.[46]

Questions

1. What changes do you recommend when Congress and the president renew the No Child Left Behind Act?
2. Why does the support of teachers and parents matter to renewal of the No Child Left Behind Act?
3. Does the act ask too much of state and local governments given that the federal government supplies only 10 percent of all school funding?
4. Should the national government become more involved in other issues such as health insurance to make sure all states act the same way?

After the civil rights revolution of the 1960s, segregationists feared that national officials would work for racial integration. Thus they praised local government, emphasized the dangers of centralization, and argued that the protection of civil rights was not a proper function of the national government. As one political scientist observed, "Federalism has a dark history to overcome. For nearly two hundred years, states' rights have been asserted to protect slavery, segregation, and discrimination."[47]

Today the politics of federalism, even with respect to civil rights, is more complicated than in the past. The national government is not necessarily more sympathetic to the claims of minorities than state or city governments are. Rulings on same-sex marriages and "civil unions" by state courts interpreting their state constitutions have extended more protection for these rights than has the Supreme Court's interpretation of the Constitution. Other states, however, are passing legislation that would eliminate such protections, and opponents are pressing for a constitutional amendment to bar same-sex marriages.

States are also increasingly aggressive in addressing economic and environmental matters. State attorneys general are prosecuting anticompetitive business practices, as they did in joining the suit against Microsoft and more recently, as New York's then attorney general Eliot Spitzer did in suing the mutual fund industry and spammers. After the Bush administration abandoned 50 investigations into violations of the Clean Air Act and changed its policy on regulating power plants, Spitzer and other state attorneys general sued the Bush administration and power plant companies to force them to improve pollution controls.[48] Business interests have argued that conflicting state regulations unduly burden interstate commerce; they have sought broader preemptive federal regulation to save them not only from stringent state regulations but also from the uncertainties of complying with 50 different state laws. As a lawyer representing trade groups in the food and medical devices industries observed: "One national dumb rule is better than 50 inconsistent rules of any kind."[49]

The national government is not likely to retreat to a pre-1930 or even a pre-1960 posture. Indeed, international terrorism, the wars in Afghanistan and Iraq, and rising deficits have substantially altered the underlying economic and social conditions that generated the demand for federal action. In addition to such traditional challenges as helping people find jobs and preventing inflation and depressions—which still require national action—combating terrorism and surviving in a global economy based on the information explosion, e-commerce, and advancing technologies have added countless new issues to the national agenda.

Most American citizens have strong attachments to our federal system—in the abstract. They remain loyal to their states and show a growing skepticism about the national government. Yet evidence suggests the anti-Washington sentiment "is 3,000 miles wide but only a few miles deep."[50] The fact is that we are pragmatists: we appear to prefer federal–state–local power sharing and are prepared to use whatever levels of government are necessary to meet our needs and new challenges.[51]

Federalism can be a source of great reward for the people, especially when it allows states to lead the nation in creating new programs to address problems such as global warming and health care access. If the people cannot move the national government toward action, they can always push their state and local governments. By giving them different leverage points to make a difference, the Constitution guarantees that government *is* by the people.

Federalism can also be a source of enormous frustration, especially when national and state governments disagree on basic issues such as civil rights and liberties. This is when the people need to step forward not as citizens of their states, but as citizens of the nation as a whole. Even as they influence their state and local governments, the people must understand they have a national voice that often needs to be heard. California cannot solve global warming unless the nation and world acts.

devolution revolution
The effort to slow the growth of the federal government by returning many functions to the states.

CHAPTER SUMMARY

1 Compare and contrast the different interpretations of federalism.

A federal system is one in which the constitution divides powers between the central government and subdivisional governments—states or provinces. Alternatives to federalism are unitary systems, in which all constitutional power is vested in the central government, and confederations, which are loose compacts among sovereign states.

2 Show how federalism protects citizens.

Federal systems can check the growth of tyranny, allow unity without uniformity, encourage state experimentation, permit power sharing between the national government and the states, and keep government closer to the people.

3 Differentiate between the types of national and state powers.

The Constitution provides three types of powers to the national and state governments: delegated powers to the national government, reserve powers for the states, and concurrent powers that the national and state governments share. Beyond delegated powers, the national government also has implied powers under the necessary and proper clause and inherent powers during periods of war and national crisis.

4 Describe and compare the constitutional pillars of national power.

The national government's power over the states stems primarily from the national supremacy clause; the war powers; its powers to regulate commerce among the states to tax and spend; and to do what Congress thinks is necessary and proper to promote the general welfare and to provide for the common defense. These constitutional pillars have permitted tremendous expansion of the functions of the federal government.

5 Analyze the role of the national courts in regulating federalism.

The federal courts umpire the division of power between the national and state governments. The Marshall Court, in decisions such as *Gibbons v. Ogden* and *McCulloch v. Maryland,* asserted the power of the national government over the states and promoted a national economic common market. These decisions also reinforced the supremacy of the national government over the states.

6 Compare and contrast the arguments of decentralists and centralists.

Today, debates about federalism are less often about its constitutional structure than about whether action should come from the national or the state and local levels. Recent Supreme Court decisions favor a decentralist position and signal shifts in the Court's interpretation of the constitutional nature of our federal system.

7 Analyze the differences between grants and mandates.

The major instruments of federal intervention in state programs have been various kinds of financial grants-in-aid, of which the most prominent are categorical-formula grants, project grants, and block grants. The national government also imposes federal mandates and controls activities of state and local governments by other means.

8 Establish the link between the growth of the national government and federalism.

Over the past three decades, the national government has become more powerful, especially when compared to the states. Recently, however, Congress has been pressured to reduce the size and scope of national programs and to shift some existing programs back to the states. Although responsibility for welfare has been turned over to the states, the authority of the national government has increased in many other areas.

Chapter Self-Test

1. Match each term with its appropriate definition: (pp. 64–65)

a. Dual federalism
b. Cooperative federalism
c. Marble cake federalism
d. Competitive federalism
e. Permissive federalism
f. The new federalism

i. The power of the federal government is limited in favor of the broad powers reserved to the states
ii. All levels of government are engaged in a variety of policy areas,without rigid divisions between governmental jurisdictions
iii. Local governments, state governments, and the federal government offer various "packages" of taxes and services, and citizens can choose which package they like best
iv. A system that requires intergovernmental support to deliver goods and services to the people
v. Limited powers are given to the national government, while the rest are retained by the states; the Supreme Court resolves disputes between the two
vi. Power is shared between the state and national governments, but the national government determines what powers are given to the states

2. Canada has a central government in Ottawa, the nation's capital, along with ten provinces and three territories, each of which has its own government. According to Canada's constitution, both the provinces and the central government have powers to tax and regulate individual citizens. Which type of government best describes Canada? (pp. 64–66)
   a. A unitary state
   b. A federalist state
   c. A confederation
   d. A territorial union
3. Federalism affords five benefits to its citizens. List each benefit along with a sentence or two that describes it. (pp. 66–68)
4. Analyze the table on p. 54 and write a few sentences about the differences among groups of people and possible reasons for those differences.
5. Determine whether the following powers are delegated to the national government, reserved for the states, or shared by both: (pp. 66–70)
   a. Power to establish courts
   b. Power to tax citizens and businesses
   c. Express powers stated in the Constitution
   d. Power to oversee primary and elementary education
   e. Inherent powers to present a united front to foreign powers
6. Create a diagram showing the relationships among *express, implied, inherent, reserved,* and *concurrent* powers. (pp. 69–73)
7. In one paragraph, describe which of the four constitutional pillars of national power you believe is the most powerful and why. (pp. 70–73)
8. In one paragraph, explain the national supremacy article and provide an analysis of its consequences for state and local governments. (pp. 68–72; 75–77)
9. Write a persuasive essay showing why the balance of governmental power should tip more towards either the federal government or the states. Note the main arguments of both centralists and decentralists, then refute the arguments of the side you disagree with. (pp. 77–79)
10. In a few sentences, discuss the "constitutional counterrevolution" instigated by Chief Justice William Rehnquist and continued by Chief Justice John Roberts. (pp. 77–80)
11. Give an example of a program funded by (1) a *categorical-formula grant,* (2) a *project grant,* and (3) a *block grant.* (pp. 80–81)
12. Explain why unfunded mandates can cause problems. (p. 82)
13. Identify which of the following is an example of a *federal mandate*: (p. 82)
   a. The New York state legislature passes a law requiring all New York school teachers to spend ten hours a year learning new teaching techniques
   b. Congress passes a law requiring all coal plants in the United States to reduce their carbon emissions by 30 percent by 2015
   c. The Supreme Court upholds a law requiring teenage women to get parental permission before having an abortion
   d. The Federal Emergency Management Agency sends funds from the federal government to help clean up after a tornado
14. Write an essay that explains the reasons for the growth of the federal government since the Founding and outlines the pressures that exist today that encourage further expansion of the federal government. (pp. 83–86)
15. Do you think the national government should increase its power or retreat? Write a short essay addressing the benefits and problems of both strong state governments and a strong central government, especially given the unique challenges we face today. (pp. 83–86)

Key Terms

federalism, p. 64
unitary system, p. 65
confederation, p. 66
delegated powers, p. 69
implied powers, p. 69
necessary and proper clause, p. 69
express powers, p. 70
inherent powers, p. 70
commerce clause, p. 71
federal mandate, p. 73
reserve powers, p. 73
concurrent powers, p. 73
full faith and credit clause, p. 74
extradition, p. 74
interstate compact, p. 75
national supremacy, p. 76
preemption, p. 77
centralists, p. 77
decentralists, p. 77
states' rights, p. 77
devolution revolution, p. 86

Further Reading

SAMUEL H. BEER, *To Make a Nation: The Rediscovery of American Federalism* (Harvard University Press, 1993).

MICHAEL BURGESS, *Comparative Federalism Theory and Practice* (Routledge, 2006).

CENTER FOR THE STUDY OF FEDERALISM, *The Federalism Report* (published quarterly by Temple University; this publication notes research, books and articles, and scholarly conferences).

CENTER FOR THE STUDY OF FEDERALISM, *Publius: The Journal of Federalism* (published quarterly by Temple University; one issue each year is an "Annual Review of the State of American Federalism"; Web site is at www.lafayette.edu/~publius).

TIMOTHY J. CONLAN, *From New Federalism to Devolution: Twenty-Five Years of Intergovernmental Reforms* (Brookings Institution Press, 1998).

DANIEL J. ELAZAR AND **JOHN KINCAID,** EDS., *The Covenant Connection: From Federal Theology to Modern Federalism* (Lexington Books, 2000).

JOHN FEREJOHN AND **BARRY WEINGAST,** EDS., *The New Federalism: Can the States Be Trusted?* (Hoover Institute Press, 1998).

LARRY N. GERSTON, *American Federalism: A Concise Introduction* (Sharp, 2007).

JOHN KINCAID AND **G. ALLEN TARR,** EDS., *Constitutional Origins, Structure, and Change in Federal Countries* (McGill-Queens University Press, 2005).

NEIL C. MCCABE, ED., *Comparative Federalism in the Devolution Era* (Rowman & Littlefield, 2002).

FORREST MCDONALD, *States' Rights and the Union: Imperium in Imperio, 1776–1876* (University Press of Kansas, 2000).

KALYPSO NICOLAIDIS AND **ROBERT HOWSE,** EDS., *The Federal Vision: Legitimacy and Levels of Governance in the United States and the European Union* (Oxford University Press, 2001).

PIETRO NIVOLA, *Tense Commandments: Federal Prescriptions and City Problems* (Brookings Institution Press, 2002).

JOHN T. NOONAN, *Narrowing the Nation's Power: The Supreme Court Sides with the States* (University of California Press, 2002).

WILLIAM H. RIKER, *The Development of American Federalism* (Academic Press, 1987).

DENISE SCHEBERLE, *Federalism and Environmental Policy: Trust and the Politics of Implementation* (Georgetown University Press, 2004).

KEVIN SMITH, ED., *State and Local Government, 2008–2009* (CQ Press, 2008).

CARL VAN HORN, ED., *The State of the States, 4e* (CQ Press, 2008).

chapter 4

Political Culture and Ideology

On the third Monday of January, the United States commemorates the birth of Dr. Martin Luther King Jr. as a federal holiday. Designated as a day of service, the holiday has come to celebrate the civil rights movement and progress toward Dr. King's dream of racial equality and social justice. Many have long forgotten the controversy surrounding its creation, however. Legislation to create Martin Luther King Jr. Day was first introduced in Congress just days after Dr. King's assassination in 1968, but fifteen years elapsed before Congress passed it and President Reagan signed the holiday into law.

Early support for the idea of the holiday came from labor unions, who pressed for the holiday in contract negotiations and at all levels of U.S. government. The entertainer Stevie Wonder helped advance the campaign with his single "Happy Birthday." A petition for the holiday with six million signatures was presented to Congress in 1982.[1]

Opposition centered on the costs of giving workers the day off, concerns about creating national holidays for persons other than U.S. presidents, the view that the importance of Dr. King's accomplishments would fade with time, and even attacks on Dr. King's reputation that linked him to communists.[2] When Arizona voters defeated a referendum to establish the holiday in 1990, the National Football League moved the 1993 Super Bowl from Arizona to Pasadena, California.[3] Some states adopted the holiday but at first named it "Human Rights Day" (Utah) or "Lee-Jackson-King Day" (oddly, Virginia combined the two confederate generals and Dr. King). In 2000, South Carolina became the last state to adopt the holiday.

During the 2008 presidential election, though racial tensions were never far from the headlines, candidates from both parties celebrated the accomplishments of Dr. King. Republican candidate Mike Huckabee attended an event at the Atlanta church where Dr. King served as pastor, and Democratic candidates Clinton, Edwards, and Obama honored Dr. King in South Carolina before their debate cohosted by the Congressional Black Caucus.

Although substantial progress has been made in achieving Dr. King's dream of equal opportunity for all races, challenges remain. As we discuss in Chapter 5, substantial differences persist between the races in the rate of poverty, educational attainment, and income. Racial minorities and women continue to be underrepresented in Congress, on corporate boards, and as partners in law firms. Racial tensions persist in some neighborhoods and schools. Our society has not become free of racism, but we have seen substantial changes in voting rights, access to public accommodations, and educational opportunity as a result of the civil rights movement, one leader of which was Dr. King.

These changing attitudes toward civil rights and toward a holiday honoring one of the movement's central figures exemplify a shift in political culture in the United States. Dr. King's famous "I have a dream" speech expressed the idea that the American dream of freedom, opportunity, and tolerance for others should be open to everyone. The story of how Martin Luther King Jr. Day came about is not only a story of political persistence, but also an example of how political attitudes can change over time. Political culture can also be understood in terms of attitudes and values, which when they are coherent and consistent are known as *ideology.* In this chapter we look at political culture and ideology.

LEARNING **OBJECTIVES**

1. Identify the most important elements of the American political culture and how we learn them.
2. Assess the importance of the "American dream" in the context of economic change.
3. Compare and contrast different ideological assumptions about government.
4. Assess the arguments for and against each ideology.
5. Analyze the importance of political ideology in light of competing ideas such as pragmatism, practicality, and the changing agenda of American politics.

CHAPTER OUTLINE

- Defining the American Political Culture
- Political Ideology and Attitudes Toward Government
- Political Ideology and the American People

Defining the American Political Culture

Many American citizens' first experience with democracy is a school election, sometimes as early as in elementary school. What are the expectations of these young voters, and what do their expectations teach us about our political culture? Were we to observe such an election, we would see recurrent patterns. For example, it would be considered unfair if some students' votes counted for more than others, or if some students were not allowed to vote at all. The candidates would probably be asked to speak, and might even make campaign promises. When the votes are counted, the young participants expect the person with the most votes to be elected.

Other elements of our political culture are learned in the family or from peers. Many important elements of our political culture are widely shared by Americans, others are evolving, and some are no longer widely shared. This chapter examines our assumptions, beliefs, and values about politics, government, participation, freedom, and liberty.

Political scientists use the term **political culture** to refer to the widely shared beliefs, values, and norms citizens hold about their relationship to government and to one another. We can discover the specifics of a nation's political culture not only by studying what its people believe and say, but also by observing how they behave. That behavior includes such fundamental decisions as who may participate in political decisions, what rights and liberties citizens have, how political decisions are made, and what people think about politicians and government generally.

Some elements of our political culture—such as our fear of concentrated power and our reverence for individual liberty—have remained constant over time. Our ideas about **suffrage,** the right to vote, however, have changed from a belief that only property-owning white men should be allowed to vote to a conviction that all adults, excluding felons in some states, should have the right. Thus, citizens now vote in party primaries to select nominees for office, whereas for much of our history party leaders determined who would run for office. The surge in political activity on the Internet in the 2004 and 2008 elections may be a harbinger of a new political culture in which citizens interact more with candidates, contribute money to campaigns, and mobilize each other.

Like many 2008 presidential candidates, Ron Paul used the Internet extensively to allow more people to participate in the election process and thereby build social capital.

The idea of people coming together, listening to each other, exchanging ideas, learning to appreciate each other's differences, and defending their opinions is sometimes called "deliberation" and builds what has been called **social capital.** Such interaction is thought to foster and strengthen community and relationships in ways that do not happen when citizens only cast ballots. Political scientist Robert Putnam has defined social capital as "features of social organization such as networks, norms, and social trust that facilitate coordination and cooperation for mutual benefit."[4] In at least some respects the Barack Obama campaign, through its extensive use of the Internet to network volunteers and donors, is an application of the social capital idea to political campaigning.

LEARNING OBJECTIVE

Identify the most important elements of the American political culture and how we learn them.

American political culture centers on democratic values such as liberty, equality, individualism, justice, the rule of law, patriotism, optimism, and idealism. There is no "official" list of American political values; however, and as we noted in Chapter 1, these widely shared democratic values overlap and sometimes conflict with each other.

political culture
The widely shared beliefs, values, and norms about how citizens relate to government and to one another.

suffrage
The right to vote.

social capital
Democratic and civic habits of discussion, compromise, and respect for differences, which grow out of participation in voluntary organizations.

Shared Values

Before the American and French Revolutions of the late eighteenth century, discussions about individual liberty, freedom, equality, private property, limited government, and popular consent were rare. Europe had been dominated by aristocracies, had experienced centuries of political and social inequality, and had been ruled by governments that often exercised power arbitrarily. Political philosophers rebelled against these traditions and proclaimed the principles of classical liberalism.

The founders of our nation claimed that individuals have certain **natural rights**—the rights of all people to dignity and worth—and that government must be limited and controlled because it was a threat to those rights. During this same period, the economic system was changing from a *mercantile system,* under which countries sought to strengthen the role of the state, establish colonies, and develop industry by encouraging exports and discouraging imports, to a *free market system* with the government taking a more "hands off" approach to the economy and setting up fewer trade barriers.[5] People began to think they could improve their lot in life and enhance their political and social status. Radical new ideas such as these influenced the thinking of the founders and shaped the values essential to the United States' political culture today.

Liberty No value in the American political culture is more revered than liberty. "We have always been a nation obsessed with liberty. Liberty over authority, freedom over responsibility, rights over duties—these are our historic preferences," wrote the late Clinton Rossiter, a noted political scientist. "Not the good man but the free man has been the measure of all things in this sweet 'land of liberty'; not national glory but individual liberty has been the object of political authority and the test of its worth."[6] Not all students of U.S. thought accept this emphasis on freedom and individualism over virtue and the public good, and in reality both sets of values are important.[7]

Equality Thomas Jefferson's famous words in the Declaration of Independence express the strength of our views of equality: "We hold these truths to be self-evident, that all men are created equal, that they are endowed by their Creator with certain unalienable rights, that among these are life, liberty, and the pursuit of happiness." In contrast to Europeans, our nation shunned aristocracy, and our Constitution explicitly prohibits governments from granting titles of nobility. Although our rhetoric about equality was not always matched by our policy—slavery, racial segregation in schools—the value of social equality is now deeply rooted.

American citizens also believe in *political equality,* the idea that every individual has a right to equal protection under the law and equal voting power. Although political equality has always been a goal, it has not always been a reality. In the past, African Americans, Native Americans, Asian Americans, and women were denied the right to vote and otherwise participate in the nation's political life.

Equality encompasses the idea of *equal opportunity,* especially with regard to improving our economic status. American adults believe social background should not

natural rights
The rights of all people to dignity and worth; also called *human rights.*

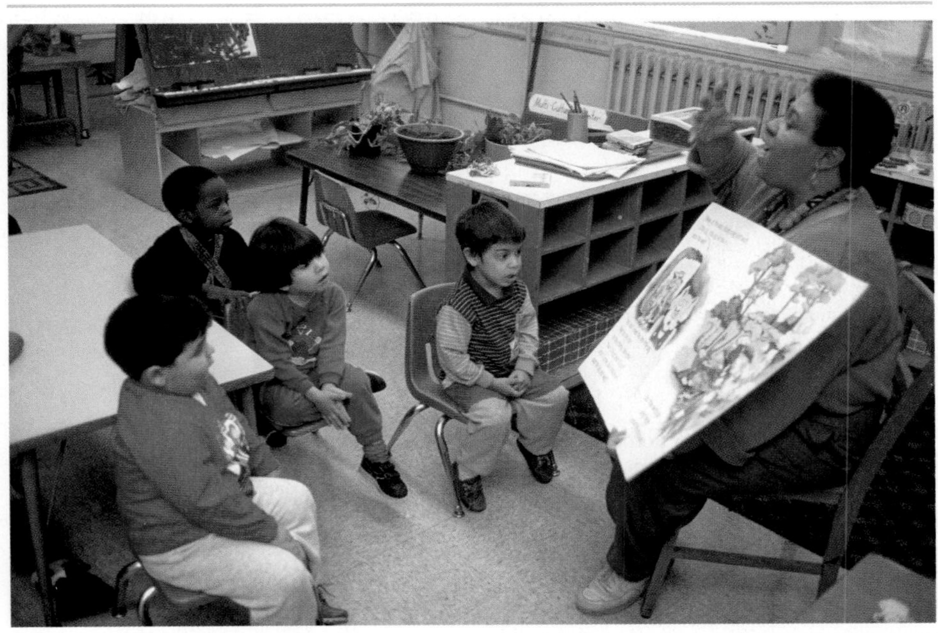

A teacher reads a book to a multi-ethnic class as part of the Head Start program in Washington, D.C.

THE **CHANGING FACE** OF U.S. POLITICS

Immigrants and Assimilation into American Political Culture

As a nation of immigrants, the United States has assimilated individuals from many countries. This process takes time as new immigrants learn the language, pursue education, and begin to understand the institutions and process of government, including elections. The scholar Samuel Huntington has argued that over time, immigrants from Mexico are less likely to support core American values and learn English than are immigrants from other Latin American countries. Huntington quotes others who have also found that Mexican immigrants have "a strong resistance to acculturation...[and] persistence of their communal bonds."*

Huntington's findings have been challenged. One study found that "nearly all Hispanic adults born in the United States of immigrant parents report they are fluent in English," suggesting assimilation after the first generation. Others have come to similar conclusions.† The data presented in the figure is from a survey of Latinos in the United States. Latinos who are not American citizens are more likely to identify themselves with their country of birth and less likely to ever describe themselves as "American." But for both groups the political focus is on the United States.

The immigration/assimilation debate inspires strong emotions on both sides. Some, like Huntington, fear that the influx of immigration will challenge "American" ideals. These groups and individuals are fearful that the immigration trends will mean the end of something—although they rarely specify what that will be. Fox News commentator John Gibson called on his presumably white viewers to "make more babies," otherwise, in "twenty-five years...the majority of the population [will be] Hispanic."‡ The United States has been down this road before. In the 1850s, following a devastating period of famine due to a potato mold, Irish émigrés began arriving in the Americas in droves. In the United States, the Irish settled mainly in the population centers of the Northeast, and today more than 34 million Americans claim Irish ancestry—that number is more than nine times the population of Ireland today.§ However, in the 1850s, these immigrants were held in contempt. They were predominantly Catholic and generally poor. In short, they represented—at least in the minds of their contemporaries—a threat to American culture.

QUESTIONS

1. What factors may make it more or less difficult to assimilate new waves of immigrants into U.S. society today?
2. How does the racial composition of the United States affect the country's political culture?
3. Is the comparison between the Irish immigration of the 1850s and our current situation valid?

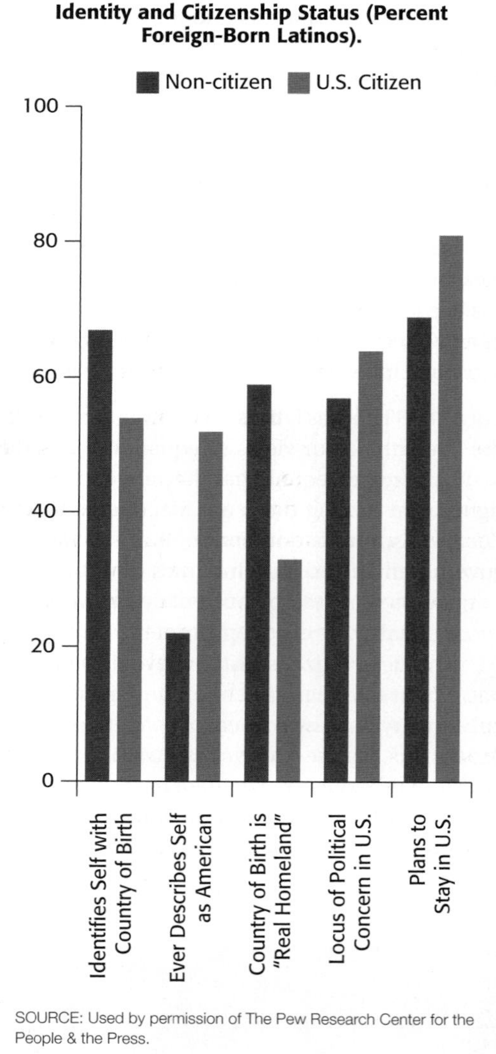

SOURCE: Used by permission of The Pew Research Center for the People & the Press.

*Samuel P. Huntington, *Who Are We? The Challenges to America's National Identity* (Simon & Schuster, 2004), pp. 189–190.

†Shirin Hakimzadeh and D'Vera Cohn, "English Usage Among Hispanics in the United States," *Pew Hispanic Center*, November 29, 2007; see also Mary C. Water and Tomas R. Jimenez, "Assessing Immigrant Assimilation: Empirical and Theoretical Challenges," *Annual Review of Sociology* (2005), pp. 105–125; and Jack Citrin, Amy Lerman, Michael Murakami, and Kathryn Pearson, "Testing Huntington: Is Hispanic Immigration a Threat to American Identity?" *Perspectives on Politics*, March 2007.

‡John Gibson, "My Word," *Fox News*, May 11, 2006.

§U.S. Census Bureau, "Facts for Features: Irish-American Heritage Month," March 10, 2006, www.census.gov/Press-Release/www/releases/archives/facts_for_features_special_editions/006328.html.

limit our opportunity to achieve to the best of our ability, nor should race, gender, or religion. The nation's commitment to public education programs such as Head Start for disadvantaged preschool children, state support for public colleges and universities, and federal financial aid for higher education reflects this belief in equal opportunity.

Individualism The United States is characterized by a persistent commitment to the individual, who has both rights and responsibilities. Policies that limit individual choice generate intense political conflict. The debates over legalized abortion and universal health care are often framed in terms of our ability to exercise choices. A single-payer system of health care, which generally means the government as payer, would ensure universal coverage but limit choice and run counter to the norm of individualism. The counterargument says that all persons in the United States have a right to health care and that is more important than individualism. Although American citizens support individual rights and freedoms, they also understand that their rights can conflict with another person's or with the government's need to maintain order or promote the general welfare.

Respect for the Common Person Most American adults prefer action to reflection. We are often anti-expert and sometimes anti-intellectual, and an emphasis on practicality and common sense has become part of our national image. Poets such as Walt Whitman and Carl Sandburg and storytellers such as Mark Twain, Will Rogers, Eudora Welty, and Garrison Keillor helped shape this tradition. Reverence for the common people helps explain our ambivalence toward power, politics, and government authority. In the 2008 presidential primaries, for example, Democrat John Edwards made frequent reference to his father's work in textile mills, and Republican Mike Huckabee frequently mentioned that he was the first male in his family to graduate from high school.

Democratic Consensus We are a people from many different cultural and ethnic backgrounds, histories, and religions. Despite these differences, our political culture includes a **democratic consensus,** a set of widely shared attitudes and beliefs about government and its values, procedures, documents, and institutions. We have strong opinions about fundamental "rules of the game" such as who has power to do what, how people acquire power, and how they are removed from power. But this shared commitment does not necessarily mean that people vote, keep up with public affairs, or believe government is always fair or just.

We believe in **majority rule**—governance according to the preferences of the majority as expressed through regular elections. Yet we also believe that people in the minority should be free to try to win majority support for their opinions. Even though many lack strong party attachments, we favor a two-party system and the idea of competition between the parties. Our institutions are based on the principles of representation and consent of the governed. We believe in **popular sovereignty**—the idea that ultimate power resides in the people. Government exists to serve the people

You Are a Polling Consultant

democratic consensus
Widespread agreement on fundamental principles of democratic governance and the values that undergird them.

majority rule
Governance according to the expressed preferences of the majority.

popular sovereignty
A belief that ultimate power resides in the people.

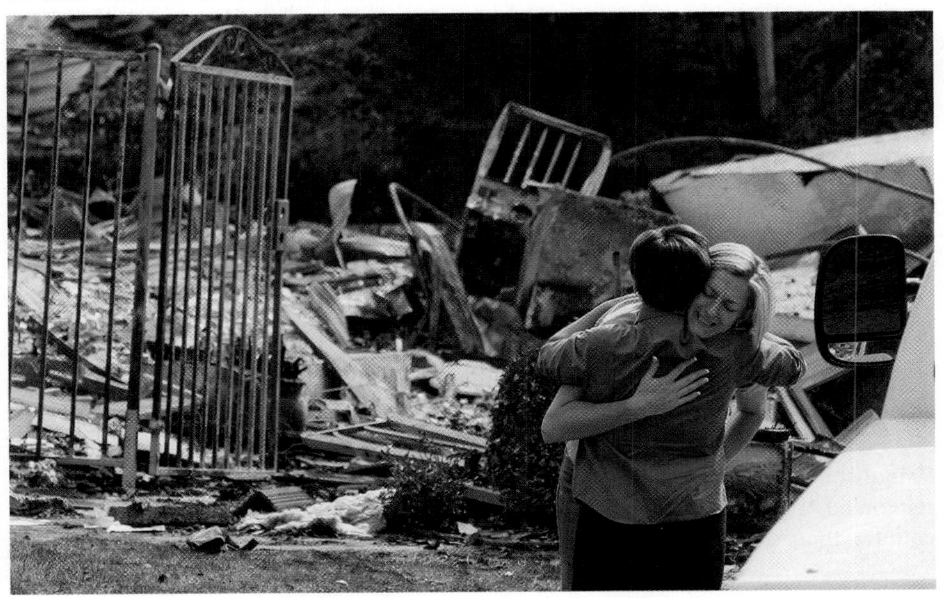

A woman reacts as a passerby offers her a hug of consolation in front of her home destroyed by fire. The October 2007 fire in San Diego County, California, burned nearly 200,000 acres, destroyed more than 1,000 homes, and resulted in two deaths.

TABLE 4–1 What Do You Mean by Rights and Freedoms? It Depends...

	Agree	Disagree	Don't Know
Freedom of speech should apply to groups that are sympathetic to terrorists.	45%	50%	5%
There has been real improvement in the position of African Americans.	49	41	10
Books that contain dangerous ideas should be banned from public school libraries.	46	50	4
Abortions should be more difficult to obtain.	35	56	9
The police should be allowed to search the houses of known terrorist sympathizers without a court order.	37	61	2
School boards ought to have the right to fire teachers who are known homosexuals.	28	66	6

SOURCE: Used by permission of The Pew Research Center for the People & the Press.

rather than the other way around. The government learns the will of the people through *elections,* the most important expression of popular consent, and to an extent through public opinion polls (see Chapter 8). But sometimes other fundamental rights limit popular sovereignty and majority rule.[8] Examples include California's vote in a 1964 referendum that permitted race discrimination in the sale of residential housing; the courts later overturned it.

The Constitution, especially the first ten amendments (the Bill of Rights) and the Thirteenth, Fourteenth, Fifteenth, and Nineteenth amendments, spells out many of the limits on what governments can do. The Constitution is revered as a national symbol, yet we often differ about what it means, and we honor many constitutional rights more in the abstract than in the particular. About half of us, for instance, think books with dangerous ideas should be banned from public school libraries (see Table 4–1). Intolerance of dissenting or offensive views is amply demonstrated in public opinion polls and on college and university campuses. Still, most of us support democratic and constitutional values.

Justice and the Rule of Law Inscribed over the entrance to the U.S. Supreme Court are the words "Equal Justice Under Law." The *rule of law* means government is based on a body of law applied equally and by just procedures, as opposed to arbitrary rule by an elite whose whims decide policy or resolve disputes. In 1803, Chief Justice John Marshall summarized this principle: "The government of the United States has been emphatically termed a government of laws, not of men."[9] American adults believe strongly in fairness: Everyone is entitled to the same legal rights and protections.

To adhere to the rule of law, government should follow these five rules:

1. *Generality:* Laws should be stated generally and not single out any group or individual.
2. *Prospectivity:* Laws should apply to the present and the future, not punish something someone did in the past.
3. *Publicity:* Laws cannot be kept secret and then enforced.
4. *Authority:* Valid laws are made by those with legitimate power, and the people legitimate that power through some form of popular consent.
5. *Due process:* Laws must be enforced impartially with fair processes.

War, Peace, and Public Opinion

nationalism
An enduring sense of national identity or consciousness that derives from cultural, historic, linguistic, or political forces.

Patriotism, Optimism, and Idealism The terrorist attacks of 2001 united the nation and reinforced American **nationalism.** As President George W. Bush said, "We are a different country than we were on September 10th: sadder and less innocent; stronger and

GENERATION **NEXT**

Patriotism

The horrors of September 11, 2001, rekindled among many a greater sense of patriotism. The nation was drawn together across party lines and ideological divides. American citizens have generally been more patriotic than people from other countries (see the results from the World Values Survey in the "How Other Nations Govern" feature in this chapter). Indeed, we have what some social scientists have termed a "civil religion" in the United States, and this common bond is one of the strongest cross-cutting cleavages in the United States.* But are there differences in the level of patriotism among those in Generation Next and older persons? Respondents were asked, "Do you agree with the statement 'I am very patriotic'?" The figure plots the percentage of respondents who reported that they completely or mostly agreed with the statement.

Patriotism seems to generally increase with age, but 18- to 25-year-olds today are less patriotic than this same age group was 20 years ago. With one notable exception, patriotism seems to be trending downward among this age group. However, one event stands out immediately when we first look at these charts: the jump in patriotism across all age groups and political persuasions between 1999 and 2002. Another interesting difference is how much lower Independents are in self-reported patriotism than Democrats or Republicans. Among those older than 25, patriotism fluctuates mostly between 90 and 95 percent, while younger voters vary widely between a low of 50 percent and a high of 94 percent.

Percentage of Respondents Who Completely Agreed or Mostly Agreed with the Statement, "I Am Very Patriotic."

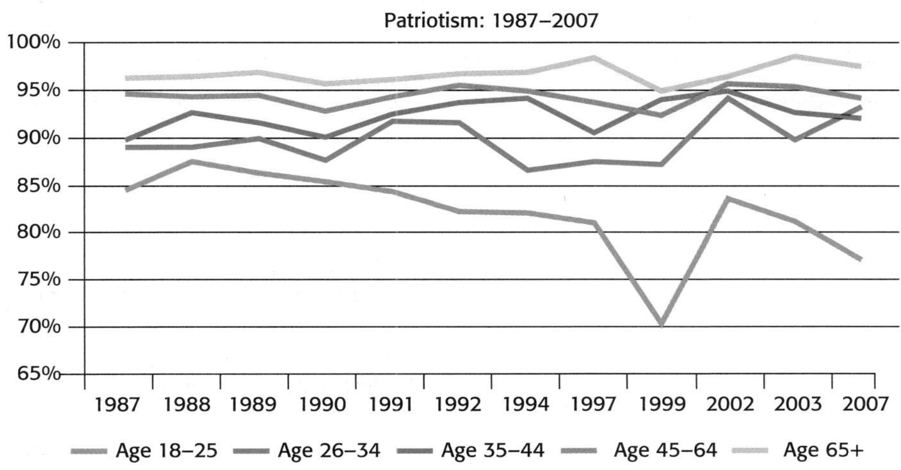

SOURCE: Used by permission of The Pew Research Center for the People & the Press.

Percentage of 18- to 25-Year Old Respondents Who Completely Agreed or Mostly Agreed with the Statement, "I Am Very Patriotic."

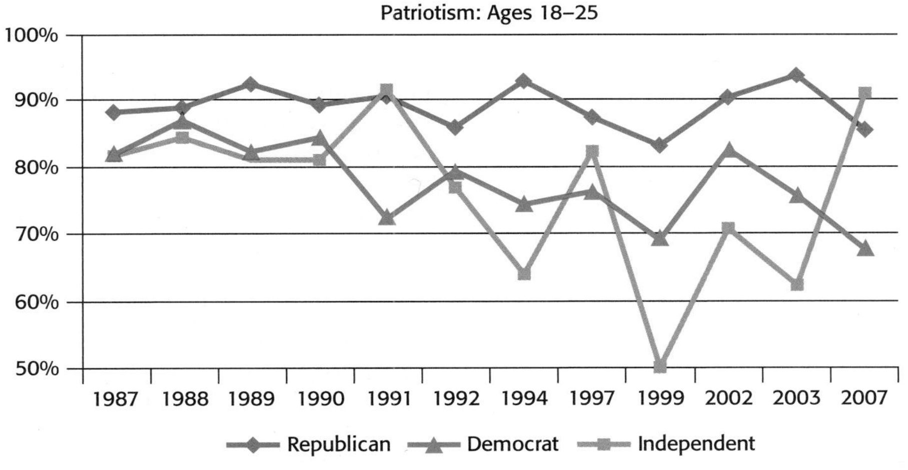

SOURCE: Used by permission of The Pew Research Center for the People & the Press.

QUESTIONS

1. Why does Generation Next report being less patriotic than older citizens?
2. What factors might account for the gradual decline in patriotism between 1988 and 1999? Do you think this trend would have continued if September 11 had never happened?
3. Why might there be partisan differences in patriotism? Why might these differences be more pronounced in younger people?

*Robert N. Bellah, "Civil Religion in America," *Daedalus* 96 (Winter 1967), pp. 1–21.

YOU WILL **DECIDE** Is the American Dream Still Alive and Important?

Is the American dream alive? Is it important to people? Some argue that the wealth and prosperity so many have achieved in the United States means that for most the dream has been achieved and is no longer important as a motivating force or a way to explain behavior. Others contend that for people in poverty, the hopelessness of their situation makes the American dream seem far-fetched and unattainable. The American dream also includes the idea of the United States as a land of opportunity, beyond economic opportunities. What do you think? Is the American dream still an important element of the political culture of the United States?

more united; and in the face of ongoing threats, determined and courageous."[10] However, as the wars in Afghanistan and Iraq became less popular, the country became sharply divided on how best to confront the terrorism threat.

We believe in opportunity, choice, individualism, and most of all, in the freedom to improve ourselves and to achieve success with as little interference as possible from others or from government. U.S. citizens are more satisfied with their democratic government than are the citizens of many other countries.[11]

We know that our system is imperfect, yet we still believe in government by the people. We often grumble that elected officials have lost touch with us, we are disgusted by scandals, and we are impatient with how long the system takes to solve problems such as high gas taxes, crime, drug abuse, and terrorism. Despite the dissatisfactions, we believe that America is better, stronger, and more virtuous than other nations. Like every country, the United States has interests and motives that are selfish as well as generous, cynical as well as idealistic. Still, our support of human needs and rights throughout the world is evidence of an enduring idealism.

Where We Learn the American Political Culture

One important source of political culture in the United States, as in other nations, is the family. Young children are taught what it means to be an American. They are curious about why people vote, what the president does, and whether Grandpa fought in Korea or Vietnam. The questions may vary from family to family, yet the themes of authority, freedom, equality, liberty, and partisanship are common. Families are the most important reference group, with parents and siblings orienting each other to politics, the media, and the community more generally. Compared to families in other cultures, American families are much more egalitarian, with children having more input in family decisions than in other cultures.[12]

Public schools are another source of the American political culture. Children and teachers often begin the school day by saluting the flag, reciting the Pledge of Allegiance, or singing the national anthem. Political and economic values are part of the curriculum. Not only are values taught in American history classes, but they are put into practice in school elections and newspapers and in everyday economic activities such as work and saving.[13]

Colleges and universities also help foster the American political culture. Students who attend college are often more confident than others in dealing with bureaucracy and politics generally and are more likely to participate in politics, vote, and know more about government.[14] Many states require students at state colleges and universities to take courses in American or state government, in part to instill a sense of civic duty.

American churches, synagogues, and mosques have long fostered a common understanding of right and wrong and of freedom—including freedom of religion, individualism, pluralism, and civic duty. Churches do not all take the same positions on political issues, but they have played important roles in such major social and political movements as the abolition of slavery, the expansion of civil rights, and opposition to war.

In modern times, the mass media have taken over some functions the family used to perform. By the time children leave high school, they will have spent more time watching television than talking to their parents. They may have learned more about politics from Comedy Central and Jon Stewart than from their parents, schools, or other media.[15] Finally, American adults educate each other about political values at work, at PTA meetings, and in more expressly political activities.

The American Dream

Many of our political values come together in the **American dream,** a complex set of ideas that holds that the United States is a land of opportunity where individual initiative and hard work can bring economic success. Whether fulfilled or not, this dream speaks to our most deeply held hopes and goals. Its essence is expressed in our enthusiasm for **capitalism,** an economic system based on private property, competitive markets, economic incentives, and limited government involvement in the production, pricing, and distribution of goods and services.[16]

The concept of *private property* enjoys extraordinary popularity in the United States. Most cherish the dream of acquiring property and believe that the owners of property have the right to decide how to use it. In many European democracies, the state owns and operates transportation systems and other businesses that are privately owned and operated in the United States. Even in Europe, though, some privatization has occurred in communications systems such as telephone companies and broadcast media.

The right to private property is just one of the economic incentives that cement our support for capitalism and fuel the American dream. Although it is difficult to compare social mobility across countries, especially because of differences in rates of immigration, the American dream is more attainable for middle-income persons in the United States than in Europe. But the bottom fifth of the economic distribution in the United States appears to be less upwardly mobile than in Europe.[17]

What explains these differences? We assume that people who have more ability or who work hard will get ahead, earn more, and enjoy economic rewards. We also believe that people should be able to pass most of the wealth they have accumulated along to their children and relatives. Even the poorest generally oppose high inheritance taxes or limits on how much someone can earn. American adults believe that the free market system gives almost everyone a fair chance, that capitalism is necessary, and that freedom depends on it. We reject communism and socialism—a rejection fortified in recent decades as most communist nations shifted toward capitalism. In the United States, individuals and corporations have acquired wealth and, at the same time, exercised political clout. Their power has in turn been widely criticized. Wealthy individuals have used their assets to fund their campaigns for public office (Jon Corzine spent $60 million on his successful New Jersey Senate race in 2000 and another $43 million on his successful gubernatorial race in 2005,[18] and Mitt Romney spent $44.6 million of his own money on his 2008 presidential campaign), or to influence elections or public policy (George Soros gave $27 million to organizations such as America Coming Together, the Media Fund, MoveOn.org, Joint Victory Campaign, Young Democrats of America, and a few other groups working to defeat George W. Bush in 2004).[19] In 2008 there was less activity by wealthy individuals funding outside groups. This decline may have been due to the requests from both presidential candidates that supporters not fund these kinds of groups. Some individuals like T. Boone Pickens, who had given millions to groups in 2004 that promoted President Bush and attacked John Kerry, spent millions in 2008 on advertising supporting his "Pickens Plan" to develop wind energy as a way to reduce our dependence on foreign oil.

THINKING IT THROUGH

The persistence of poverty in a land of plenty is perplexing, but it does not change the reality that some are able to escape it. Examples of individuals who have achieved at least a portion of the American dream arise often enough to reinforce acceptance that the dream can come true. Although some achieve the dream because they win the lottery, more do so because of opportunities such as education.

The American dream does not have to be achieved by everyone to be an important motivator. New immigrant groups have long been an incubator of the American dream, and they continue to be so today. Parents working multiple low-paying jobs while stressing education for their children provide an example of both the work and the dream components of this aspiration. At the same time, it is also clear that the American dream is less available to some than to others and that access to it can be limited by larger forces such as recessions, unemployment, and illness. Some problems that many middle-class individuals can take in stride can derail the hopes and aspirations of those without a safety net.

The American dream also includes the idea that people in this country have more opportunity to pursue an education, to express themselves, and to associate with others as they see fit. In short, part of the dream is that the United States is a more open society. The extent to which the American dream persists in our political culture, despite its limitations, is evidence of its power and importance.

Questions

1. What examples can you identify of people who have achieved the American dream, and what difference has that success made to others having the dream?
2. Is the American dream more attainable for some than others? If so, why is that the case?
3. Does the American dream encompass more than economic wealth? How important is religious or political freedom to the idea that the American dream is about opportunity?

LEARNING OBJECTIVE

2 Assess the importance of the "American dream" in the context of economic change.

Coming from humble beginnings, Oprah Winfrey—television host, movie actress, and one of the highest-paid people in the country—epitomizes the American dream.

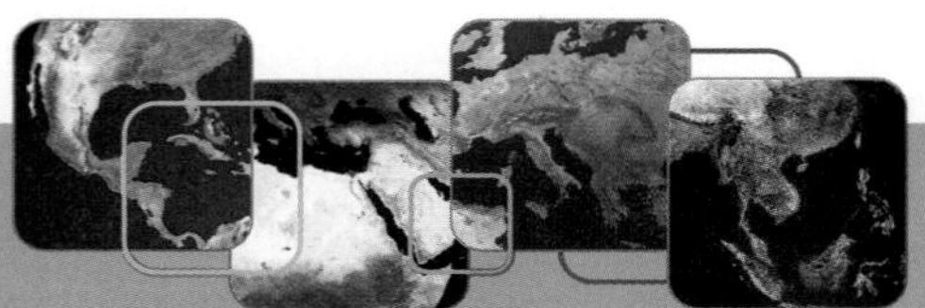

HOW **OTHER NATIONS** GOVERN

Government and Nation: Differing Public Perspectives

To understand the politics and government of a country, we must understand its political culture in terms of how people view the political system or government, how involved they feel in the political process, the extent to which they have become assimilated, and how well diversity is tolerated. Scholars have gathered these and other dimensions of public opinion in more than 80 societies. To learn more about their work, go to www.worldvaluessurvey.org. In the table following we compare our sample of seven countries on a set of questions related to political culture and ideology.

There are some surprises here. People in China, for example, say they are more confident in their government than are people in Japan or the United States. This may reflect differences in what people mean by a term like "confidence." For the Chinese it may mean predictability, while in the United States or Japan it may mean efficiency.

On other items, such as the frequency with which people discuss political matters with friends, there is greater similarity, with no more than 24 percent in any country reporting that they do so frequently. In all but Japan, roughly three-quarters of people report being willing to fight for their country, while in Japan only 25 percent so reporting. Japanese respondents are also least likely to report that they are proud of their country.

QUESTIONS

1. Do any other numbers in this table surprise you? Why or why not?
2. What methodology problems do you think pollsters face when trying to collect data across countries? How might those problems have affected World Values Survey data?
3. What factors do you think may explain why Japan is so different from the other countries in nationalism and willingness to fight for the country?

World Values Survey.

	Total	China (2001)	Great Britain (1999)	India (2001)	Japan (2000)	Mexico (2000)	Nigeria (2000)	United States (1999)
Confidence in the government (% "A great deal" or "Quite a lot")	50%	97%	n/a	56%	27%	37%	48%	38%
Political involvement (% "Frequently" discuss political matters with friends)	15	24	10%	17	7	13	17	17
War (% Yes, "Willing to fight for country")	73	97	n/a	82	25	74	n/a	73
Proud of nationality (% "Very proud" or "Quite proud")	84	82	90	93	59	95	91	96
Language at home (% who report speaking the national language at home)	n/a	n/a	n/a	35	100	96	14	95

SOURCE: World Values Survey, "World Values Survey 2005," downloaded data files, www.worldvaluessurvey.org.

The conflict in values between a *competitive economy,* in which individuals reap large rewards for their initiative and hard work, and an *egalitarian society,* in which everyone earns a decent living, carries over into politics. How the public resolves this tension changes over time and from issue to issue.

As important as the American dream is to the national consciousness, it remains unfulfilled. The gap between rich and poor has grown in recent years, and a sharp income difference between whites and blacks remains tenacious.[20]

For more people than we want to admit, chances for success still depend on the family they were born into, the neighborhood they grew up in, or the college they attended. An underclass persists in the form of impoverished families, malnourished and poorly educated children, and the homeless.[21] Many cities are actually two cities, where some residents live in luxury, others in squalor. This reality was starkly reinforced in the aftermath of Hurricane Katrina in 2005 as the world observed that poor people were much more likely to lack the transportation or resources to flee the hurricane-stricken city. National public opinion polls showed stark differences along racial lines in perceptions of whether the government's response would have been different if most of the victims had been white and not black. Two-thirds of African Americans held this view, compared to fewer than one in five whites.[22]

American dream
The widespread belief that the United States is a land of opportunity and that individual initiative and hard work can bring economic success.

capitalism
An economic system characterized by private property, competitive markets, economic incentives, and limited government involvement in the production, distribution, and pricing of goods and services.

Three years after Hurricane Katrina, many people still live in large trailer parks set up by FEMA as temporary housing after the strom.

Political and Economic Change

Historical developments and economic and technological growth affect political values. The Declaration of Independence and the Constitution identified such important political values as individual liberty, property rights, and limited government.[23] These values have been shaped by events and political movements as have others such as political equality and more democratic forms of participation.

The Industrial Transformation By 1900, industrial capitalism and the growth of giant corporations had largely replaced the agrarian society of small farmers and plantations that the framers had known. These changes irreversibly transformed our political and social ideology. Large privately owned corporations changed not only the economic order, but the role of government and the way people viewed each other. No one captures the implications of this shift better than political scientist Robert A. Dahl:

> One of the consequences of the new order has been a high degree of inequality in the distribution of wealth and income, and far greater inequality than had ever been thought likely or desirable under an agrarian order by Democratic Republicans like Jefferson and Madison, or had ever been thought consistent with democratic or republican government in the historic writings on the subject from Aristotle to Locke, Montesquieu, and Rousseau. Previous theorists and advocates had, like many of the framers of our own Constitution, insisted that a republic could exist only if the citizen body continued neither rich nor poor. Citizens, it was argued, must enjoy a rough equality of conditions.[24]

The success of the American economy led to the concentration of great wealth in the hands of a few—the "robber barons" or tycoons. Many had taken great risks or earned their fortunes through inventions and efficient production practices. But as disparities of income grew, so did disparities in political resources. People with more economic resources can invest time, energy, and money in political campaigns, parties, and candidates, which in turn enhance their power and influence.[25]

Plumes of black smoke rise from steel mills in Homestead, Pennsylvania, behind a group of children on their way to school in the early 1900s. The rapid industrialization of the United States around the beginning of the 20th century resulted in an increased disparity between the richest and the poorest Americans.

The Great Depression and the New Deal The Great Depression of the 1930s and the near collapse of the capitalistic system that followed it shaped much of our thinking about the role of government in a capitalistic system. The Depression was largely blamed on unrestrained capitalism and an unregulated market. The collapse of the stock market, massive unemployment, and a failed banking system caused widespread

Bread lines like this provided handouts of food to thousands of unemployed and destitute people during the Great Depression.

suffering. Workers had no unemployment compensation, no guarantee for the money they put in banks, no federal regulation of the stock market, and no Social Security. People turned to the government to improve the lot of millions of jobless and homeless citizens. Beginning with President Franklin D. Roosevelt's New Deal in the 1930s, most people came to accept that governments, at both the national and state levels, should use their powers and resources to ensure some measure of equal opportunity and social justice.

Building on Roosevelt's policies, Presidents John F. Kennedy and Lyndon B. Johnson worked with the civil rights movement in the 1960s to pass civil rights and voting rights legislation and launch a "war on poverty." Modern-day liberalism and conservatism turn, in large measure, on how much we believe that governments should help minorities, women, and others who have suffered discrimination or been left behind by the industrial or technological revolutions of the twentieth century.

Today, free enterprise is no longer unbridled. Government regulations, antitrust laws, job safety regulations, environmental standards, and minimum wage laws try to balance freedom of enterprise against the rights of individuals. Most people today support a semiregulated or mixed free enterprise system that checks the worst tendencies of capitalism, but they reject excessive government intervention (see Table 4–2). Much of American politics centers on how to achieve this balance. Currently, most liberals and conservatives agree that some governmental intervention is necessary to assist those who fall short in the competition for education and economic prosperity. This was brought sharply into focus in 2008 when banks and other financial institutions faced a crisis leading to a $700 billion bailout.

TABLE 4–2 Attitudes About Business and Labor

	Percentage Agreeing
The strength of this country is mostly based on the success of American business.	72%
Government regulation of business usually does more harm than good.	57
Business corporations generally strike a fair balance between making profits and serving the public interest.	38
There is too much power concentrated in the hands of a few big companies.	76
Labor unions are necessary to protect the working person.	68

SOURCE: Used by permission of The Pew Research Center for the People & the Press.

Political Ideology and Attitudes Toward Government

Are You a Liberal or a Conservative?

LEARNING **OBJECTIVE**

Compare and contrast different ideological assumptions about government.

Political ideology refers to a consistent pattern of ideas or beliefs about political values and the role of government, including how it should work and how it actually does work.

Two major schools of political ideology dominate American politics: *liberalism* and *conservatism.* Two less popular schools of thought—*socialism* and *libertarianism*—also help define the spectrum of ideology. (See Table 4–3.)

political ideology
A consistent pattern of beliefs about political values and the role of government.

liberalism
A belief that government can and should achieve justice and equality of opportunity.

Liberalism

In the eighteenth and nineteenth centuries, classical liberals favored *limited government* and sought to protect people from governmental harassment in their political and economic lives. Over time, the liberal emphasis on individualism has remained constant, but the perception of the need for government changed.

Contemporary Liberals In its current U.S. usage, **liberalism** refers to a belief that government can bring about justice and equality of opportunity. Modern-day liberals

TABLE 4–3 Differences in Political Ideology

	Conservative	Moderate	Liberal	Don't Know/Haven't Thought About It
Sex				
Male	36%	26%	21%	17%
Female	24	27	24	25
Race				
White	35	26	24	15
Black	14	31	12	43
Asian	27	26	26	21
Hispanic	20	25	30	25
Age				
18–34	23	30	30	18
35–45	34	26	17	23
46–55	34	24	26	16
56–64	36	23	22	19
Religion				
Protestant	41	24	15	20
Catholic	31	27	25	17
Jewish	13	23	64	0
Education				
Less than high school	16	18	16	50
High school diploma	26	34	13	27
Some college	34	27	24	15
Bachelor's degree	42	23	32	3
Advanced degree	33	17	47	3
Party				
Democrat	9	28	40	23
Independent	16	31	10	43
Republican	59	23	5	13

SOURCE: Center for Political Studies, University of Michigan, *2004 American National Election Study Guide to Public Opinion and Electoral Behavior.*

Patrick Leahy (D-Vermont) has promoted liberal programs and legislation for many years.

wish to preserve the rights of the individual and the right to own private property, yet they believe that some government intervention in the economy is necessary to remedy the defects of capitalism. Liberals advocate equal access to health care, housing, and education for all citizens. They generally believe in affirmative action programs, protections for workers' health and safety, tax rates that rise with a person's income, and unions' rights to organize and strike. Liberals are generally more inclined to favor greater environmental protection and individual choice in such matters as same-sex marriage and abortion.

Liberals generally believe that the future will be better than the past or the present—that obstacles can be overcome and the government can be trusted to, and should, play a role in that progress. They contend that modern technology and industrialization cry out for government programs to offset the loss of liberties that the poor and the weak suffer. Liberals such as Senators Edward Kennedy, Barack Obama, and Hillary Rodham Clinton frequently stress the need for an involved and affirmative government.

Liberals led in expanding civil rights in the 1960s and 1970s and favor affirmative action today. Some liberals favor reducing the great inequalities of wealth that make equality of opportunity impossible. Most favor a certain minimum level of income for all. Rather than placing a cap on wealth, they want to build a floor beneath the poor. In short, liberals seek to extend opportunities to all, regardless of how poor they may be. If necessary, they favor raising taxes to achieve these goals.

LEARNING **OBJECTIVE**

 Assess the arguments for and against each ideology.

Who Are Liberals and Conservatives? What's the Difference?

Criticisms of Liberalism Critics say liberals rely too much on government, higher taxes, and bureaucracy to solve the nation's problems. They argue that liberals have forgotten that government has to be limited if it is to serve our best interests. Power tends to corrupt, and too much dependence on government can corrupt the spirit, undermine self-reliance, and make people forget those cherished personal freedoms and property rights our Republic was founded to secure and protect. In short, critics of modern liberalism contend that the welfare and regulatory state liberals advocate will ultimately destroy individual initiative, the entrepreneurial spirit, and the very engine of economic growth that might lead to true equality of economic opportunity.

In recent elections, Republicans have made liberalism a villain while claiming that their own presidential candidates represent the mainstream. Bill Clinton was careful not to label his programs liberal, focusing on the need for economic growth, jobs, and a balanced budget. He insisted he was a "New Democrat." In 2000, Al Gore also positioned himself as a centrist, not a liberal, but George W. Bush claimed that Gore was an advocate of "tax and spend" big government. Their Republican opponents and their allies often level the same charge against Democratic congressional candidates.

The movement to the center by some Democrats and the conventional wisdom that liberal or progressive approaches are in decline are disputed. The three major Democratic candidates for the presidency in 2008 (Clinton, Obama, and Edwards) rarely used the word "liberal" but aggressively campaigned for change and an agenda in health care, the environment, and the economy that stood in stark contrast to the Bush administration and conservatism.

The popularity of particular issues changes with world events. For a time, we were preoccupied with budget deficits. With the end of the Cold War we became more concerned about domestic than foreign policy. Policy concerns changed again with the terrorist attacks of September 11, 2001, and the war on terrorism that followed. National security became a central focus of the 2002 and 2004 elections. Budget deficits replaced projected surpluses, and in 2008 we focused attention on the economy, environment, and places such as Iraq, Afghanistan, Iran, and North Korea.

Conservatives for decades have emphasized differences with liberals on social and moral matters. For example, in 2004 referendums in 13 states defining marriage as between a man and a woman forced moral values questions into the presidential election.

Efforts by liberals to define the same-sex marriage issue as primarily about rights failed, and all the referendums passed, providing Republicans with an issue that helped motivate conservatives to vote in key states such as Ohio.[26]

With the collapse of some large investment banks, a large drop in the value of stocks, a rise in home foreclosures, and growing unemployment, the 2008 election focused largely on the economy and on which candidate was better able to manage these problems. While John McCain's campaign tried to shift the focus to Obama as a "tax and spend liberal" or paint him as "among the most liberal U.S. Senators," these arguments did not carry much sway with voters who were not already committed to McCain. Obama's campaign countered by linking John McCain to Bush's deficits and to deregulation which Obama claimed was a major factor in the economic problems the country faced. Unlike 2000 and 2004 when social issues or national security fears were used to the benefit of Republicans, the primacy of the economy and the need for change worked to the advantage of Obama and the Democrats.

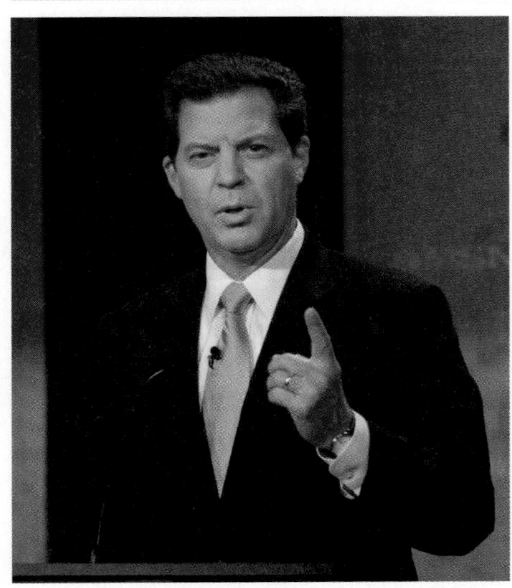

Sam Brownback (R-Kansas) has been a leader of conservative causes in the Senate.

Conservatism

Belief in private property rights and free enterprise are cardinal attributes of contemporary **conservatism.** In contrast to liberals, conservatives want to enhance individual liberty by keeping government small, especially the national government, although they support a strong national defense. Conservatives take a more pessimistic view of human nature than liberals do. They maintain that people need strong leadership, firm laws, and strict moral codes. The primary task of government is to ensure order. Conservatives also believe that people are the architects of their own fortune and must solve their own problems and create their own successes.

Traditional Conservatives Conservatives are emphatically pro-business. They favor tax cuts and resist all but the minimum antitrust, trade, and environmental regulations on corporations. They believe that the sole functions of government should be to protect the nation from foreign enemies, preserve law and order, enforce private contracts, encourage economic growth by fostering competitive markets and free and fair trade, and promote family values. Traditional conservatives favor dispersing power throughout the political and social systems to avoid an overly powerful national government; they believe that the market, not the government, should provide services. These views were tested by the Bush Administration's advocacy of a massive government bailout of financial institutions in 2008 leading GOP candidate John McCain to call for new regulation.

Conservatives opposed the New Deal programs of the 1930s, the War on Poverty in the 1960s, and many civil rights and affirmative action programs. Families and private charities, they say, can and should take care of human needs and social and economic problems. Conservatives are more inclined to trust the private sector and dislike turning to governments, especially the national government, to solve social problems. Government social activism, they say, has been expensive and counterproductive. State and local government should address those social problems that do need a government response. For example, conservatives have long held abortion to be a matter for state and local governments to decide, as well as education. President Bush's education reform created under the No Child Left Behind Act of 2002 encountered opposition from some of the most conservative and Republican states, because they saw the policy as interfering with the ability of states and local school districts to manage education.

Conservatives, especially those in office, do, however, selectively advocate government activism, often expressing a desire for a more effective and efficient government. Early in the 2000 presidential campaign, George W. Bush said, "Too often, my party has confused the need for a limited government with a disdain for government itself." Love of country, he said, "is undermined by sprawling, arrogant, aimless government. It is restored by focused and effective and energetic government."[27]

conservatism
A belief that limited government ensures order, competitive markets, and personal opportunity.

Social Conservatives Some conservatives focus less on economics and more on morality and lifestyle. Social conservatives favor strong governmental action to protect children from pornography and drugs. They want to overturn or repeal judicial rulings and laws that permit abortion, same-sex marriage, and affirmative action programs. This brand of conservatism—sometimes called the New Right—emerged in the 1980s. The New Right shares traditional conservatism's love of freedom and backs an aggressive effort to defend American interests abroad. It favors the return of organized prayer in public schools and opposes policies such as job quotas, busing, and tolerance of homosexuality.

Accordingly, a defining characteristic of the New Right is a strong desire to impose *social controls.* Christian conservatives, who are disproportionately evangelical, want to preserve traditional values and protect the institution of the family. Groups like Focus on the Family, which along with its leader Dr. James Dobson promotes traditional marriage and committed parenting, wax and wane in importance. In the 1980s and early 1990s, the Christian Coalition, founded by Reverend Pat Robertson, was an important political force that has become much less prominent in recent years.[28] Evidence of the decline of the coalition is the fact that the Republican Party created its own large-scale effort to mobilize conservative religious voters in the 2000 election and since.[29] In 2008, the connection between Christian conservatives and the GOP was further reinforced by the candidacy of former Arkansas governor and ordained Baptist minister Mike Huckabee, who emphasized his being a conservative Christian in his 2008 campaign.[30] In the 2008 Iowa caucuses, 60 percent of all Republican caucusgoers were evangelicals who backed Huckabee 46 percent to Mitt Romney's 19 percent.[31]

Criticisms of Conservatism Not everyone agreed with Ronald Reagan's statement that "government is the problem." Indeed, critics point out that conservatives themselves urge more government when it serves their needs—to regulate pornography and abortion, for example—but are opposed to government when it serves somebody else's. Conservatives may also have fewer objections to big government when individuals have a choice in determining how government will affect them. Vouchers for schools, choices in prescription drug benefit plans, and options to manage Social Security savings are examples of such choices.[32]

Their great faith in the market economy often puts conservatives at odds with labor unions and consumer activists and in close alliance with businesspeople, particularly large corporations. Hostility to regulation and a belief in competition lead conservatives to push for deregulation. This approach has not always had positive results, as the collapse of many savings and loan companies in the 1980s[33] and the energy crisis in California in the early 2000s demonstrated.[34] Conservatives counter that overall it is still best to rely on the free market.

The policy of lowering taxes is consistent with the conservative hostility to big government. Many conservatives embrace the idea that if the rich pay fewer taxes, they will spend and invest more, and the benefits of this increased economic activity will "trickle down" to the poor. But Democrats argue that most of the growth in income and wealth that followed the Bush tax cuts was largely concentrated among the well-to-do and that reduced taxes and increased government spending, especially for defense, tripled the deficit during the 1980s, when conservatives were in control.[35] President George W. Bush pushed through tax cuts during his first term and pressed to make them permanent after his reelection in 2004. Republican nominee John McCain, who had initially opposed the Bush tax cuts, campaigned in 2008 on a platform to make them permanent. Democrats criticized Bush for lowering taxes at the same time the budget deficit was growing, and Barack Obama proposed expanding social welfare programs with the revenue from allowing the Bush tax cuts to lapse. They also proposed redirecting the tax cuts to lower- and middle-class Americans. McCain and other Republicans charged that this would be tantamount to a tax increase. Obama and McCain voted for the government bailout of financial institutions in part because both agreed regulations had been too lax.

Liberals charge that some conservatives repeatedly fail to acknowledge and endorse policies that deal with racism and sexism. They cite conservative opposition to civil rights laws in the 1960s and more recently to affirmative action. They also blame conservatives for trying to weaken the enforcement of these laws by the executive branch and the courts.

Socialism and Communism

Socialism is an economic and governmental system based on public ownership of the means of production and exchange. The nineteenth-century German philosopher Karl Marx once described socialism as a transitional stage of society between capitalism and communism. In a capitalist system, the means of production and most property are privately owned; in a communist system, the state owns property in common for all the people, and a single political party that represents the working classes controls the government.

In communist countries such as Cuba and China, the Communist Party allows no opposition. Some countries, such as Sweden, have combined limited government ownership and operation of business with democracy. Most western European countries and Canada have various forms of socialized or government-run medical systems and sometimes telecommunications networks, while keeping most economic sectors private.

In one of the most dramatic transformations in recent times, Russia, its sister republics, and its former eastern European satellites abandoned communism in the early 1990s and have been attempting to establish free markets. These countries previously had a system of rigid state ownership and centralized government planning of the economy. The government arbitrarily set prices and production levels, which ultimately led to a very unstable economic system. But political and economic failure in the Soviet Union demoralized its communist leadership and weakened its hold over its satellite states. With the collapse of the Soviet Union in 1989, a tide of political and economic reform left communism intact in only a few countries, such as Cuba and North Korea. In addition, China and Vietnam, once also communist, now have growing private sectors and are thus not fully communist.

American socialists—of whom there are only a few prominent examples, including one United States senator, Vermont's Bernie Sanders—favor a greatly expanded role for the government but argue that such a system is compatible with democracy. They would nationalize certain industries, institute a public jobs program so that all who want to work could work, tax the wealthy much more heavily, and drastically cut defense spending.[36] Canada and most of the democracies of western Europe are more influenced by socialist ideas than we are in the United States, but they remain, like the United States, largely market economies. Debate will continue about the proper role of government and what the market can do better than government can.[37]

Bernie Sanders, a self-described socialist, represents Vermont in the U.S. Senate as an Independent.

Libertarianism

Libertarianism is a political ideology that cherishes individual liberty and insists on sharply limited government. It carries some overtones of anarchism, of the classical English liberalism of the nineteenth century (defined earlier in this chapter), and of a 1930s-style conservatism. The Libertarian Party has gained a small following among people who believe that both liberals and conservatives are inconsistent in their attitude toward the power of the national government.

Libertarians oppose almost all government programs. They favor massive cuts in government spending and an end to the Federal Bureau of Investigation (FBI), the Central Intelligence Agency (CIA), the Internal Revenue Service (IRS), and most regulatory commissions. They oppose American participation in the United Nations and favor armed forces that would defend the United States only if directly attacked. They oppose *all* government regulation, including, for example, mandatory seat-belt and helmet laws, in part because they believe individuals will all benefit more from an undistorted free market, and more generally because they embrace the attitude "live and let live." Unlike conservatives, libertarians would repeal laws that regulate personal morality, including abortion, pornography, prostitution, and illicit drugs.

A Libertarian Party candidate for president has been on the ballot in all 50 states in recent presidential elections, although the party has never obtained more than 1 percent of the vote, and in 2008 received less than one-half of one percent of the vote. The 2000

socialism
An economic and governmental system based on public ownership of the means of production and exchange.

libertarianism
An ideology that cherishes individual liberty and insists on minimal government, promoting a free market economy, a noninterventionist foreign policy, and an absence of regulation in moral, economic, and social life.

Former Republican Congressman Bob Barr accepts the 2008 Libertarian Party nomination with his wife, Jeri Barr, looking on.

Libertarian platform called for immediate and complete removal of the federal government from education, energy, regulation, crime control, welfare, housing, transportation, health care, and agriculture; repeal of the income tax and all other direct taxes; decriminalization of drugs and pardons for prisoners convicted of nonviolent drug offenses; and withdrawal of overseas military forces. Libertarian positions are rarely timid; at the least, they prompt intriguing political debate.[38] In 2008, the Libertarian Party endorsed same-sex marriage, legalizing drugs, repealing the Patriot Act, withdrawing from Iraq, eliminating all gun control laws, repealing business regulations, and eliminating the Food and Drug Administration. Texas representative Ron Paul, an unsuccessful candidate for the 2008 Republican presidential nomination, had run as the Libertarian nominee for president in 1988, getting only 0.4 percent of the popular vote. His positions on several issues in 2008 embraced Libertarian ideals.[40] The competitive nature of the presidential campaign and the historic nature of the Obama candidacy meant minor parties were given even less attention in 2008 than in prior campaigns. Moreover, the centrality of the economic crisis pushed voters to find a candidate who could provide solutions and get things done. In such times voters turn to established parties.

A Word of Caution

Political labels have different meanings across national boundaries as well as over time. To be a liberal in most European nations and Australia is to be on the right; to be a liberal in the United States and Canada is to be on the left. In recent elections, the term "liberal"—which while Franklin Roosevelt was president in the 1930s and 1940s had been popular—became "the L-word," a label most politicians sought to avoid. But liberalism is more than a label. On big questions—such as the role of government in the economy, in promoting equality of opportunity, and in regulating the behavior of individuals or businesses—real differences separate conservative and liberal groups. This does not mean, however, that people who are conservative in one area are necessarily conservative in another, or that all liberals always agree with each other.

Ideology both causes events and is affected by them. For example, World War II, which showed how government can work to defend freedom, increased support for the role of the national government. The Vietnam War probably had the opposite effect, producing disillusionment with government. The antigovernment sentiment in recent presidential elections is undoubtedly related to Vietnam, the Watergate scandal of the early 1970s, allegations of sexual and financial misconduct by political leaders, and the inadequate response to Hurricane Katrina in 2005. The surge in patriotism and sense of national unity in the war against terrorism after the September 11 terrorist attacks stands in sharp contrast to the national mood during the mid-1970s, the final years of the Vietnam War. It reflected a view that government has an important role to play in responding to a crisis. But by the 2006 and 2008 elections, the country was increasingly opposed to the wars in Iraq and Afghanistan and looking for new leaders and different policies.

Unlike in 2000 and 2004, the 2008 election produced a winner with a large enough majority in the popular vote and electoral college to claim a mandate. Moreover the Democrats began 2009 with expanded majorities in both houses of congress. The extent to which the mandate was an ideological one will be debated. The major theme of the Obama campaign was change and while he and his party provided some specifics as to what they wanted to change—for example ending the war in Iraq, expanding health care coverage, and increasing educational opportunity—it was also the case that much of the rhetoric was couched in terms like "ending the failed Bush administration policies." Obama made clear that accomplishing the changes he proposes will require greater cooperation and bipartisanship. Obama also cautioned his supporters that the costs of dealing with the economic challenges the country faces will mean slowing the pace of change in other areas. Whether Obama can hold his coalition together when he must compromise will be a measure of his skill as a leader.

HISTORY MAKERS

Rachel Carson and the Environmental Movement

"There was once a town in the heart of America where all life seemed to live in harmony with its surroundings.... Then a strange blight crept over the area and everything began to change.... There was a strange stillness.... The few birds seen anywhere were moribund; they trembled violently and could not fly. It was a spring without voices."* These words of Rachel Carson, from the beginning of her most famous book, *Silent Spring*, published in 1962, elicited a response that was anything but silent.

Rachel Carson.

A gifted marine biologist and writer, Carson had been one of only two women employed on a professional level by the U.S. Bureau of Fisheries (later the U.S. Fish and Wildlife Service). Her first book, *Under the Sea Wind*, demonstrated her ability to describe the natural world. During her years in government service, from 1936 to 1949, she became alarmed by the harmful effects of pesticides on the environment. She contacted *Reader's Digest* to write an article on the subject, but was met with a lack of concern.† Eventually, the alarming death rates among wildlife in areas sprayed by pesticides drove her to write and publish *Silent Spring* despite the deaths of a niece and her mother and her own diagnosis of terminal cancer.‡ In response to attacks by the chemical industry, the Department of Agriculture, and many in the media, Carson said, "I have felt bound by a solemn obligation to do what I could."§ Carson's book had an enormous popular impact abroad and in the United States, where it virtually created the modern environmental movement. It led to legislation banning the use of DDT and to the establishment of the Environmental Protection Agency.‖

QUESTIONS

1. To what extent is Al Gore's book *An Inconvenient Truth* like Carson's *Silent Spring*?
2. What elements of global warming are similar to scenes described by Carson in *Silent Spring*?
3. How do you think an idea such as protecting the environment becomes part of the political culture?

*Peter Matthiessen, "Rachel Carson," *Time*, March 29, 1999, www.time.com/time/time100/scientist/profile/carson02.html.
†www.pbs.org/wgbh/aso/databank/entries/btcars.html.
‡Matthiessen, www.time.com/time/time100/scientist/profile/carson03.html.
§For a more detailed biography of Rachel Carson, see www.fws.gov/northeast/rachelcarson/carsonbio.html.
‖Rachel Carson, *Silent Spring* (Houghton Mifflin, 1962), pp. 1, 2.

Political Ideology and the American People

For some people, ideological controversy today centers on the role of the government in improving schools, encouraging a stronger work ethic, and stopping the flow of drugs into the country. For others, ideology focuses on whether to permit openly gay people into the military or sanction same-sex marriages, and on the best ways to instill moral values, build character, and encourage cohesive and lasting families. Ideology has economic, social/lifestyle, environmental, civil rights/civil liberties and foreign/defense policy dimensions. It is not surprising that some individuals are liberal or conservative in one dimension but not another.

Despite the twists and turns of American politics, the distribution of ideology in the nation has been remarkably consistent (see Figure 4–1). Conservatives outnumber liberals, but the proportion of conservatives did not increase substantially with the decisive Republican presidential victories of the 1980s or the congressional victories of the 1990s.

Moreover, in the United States most people are moderates or report not knowing whether they are liberal or conservative. In recent years, only 2 percent of the population saw themselves as extreme liberals, while extreme conservatives ranged from 2 to 4 percent (see Figure 4–2). These percentages have changed little over time. Despite claims by ideological extremes in both parties of a move to the right or to the left, there are simply more voters in the middle who are moderate or do not have a preferred ideology.[41]

Both major parties target moderate or centrist voters, as reflected in the stands of the candidates on key issues, including their efforts to minimize ideological

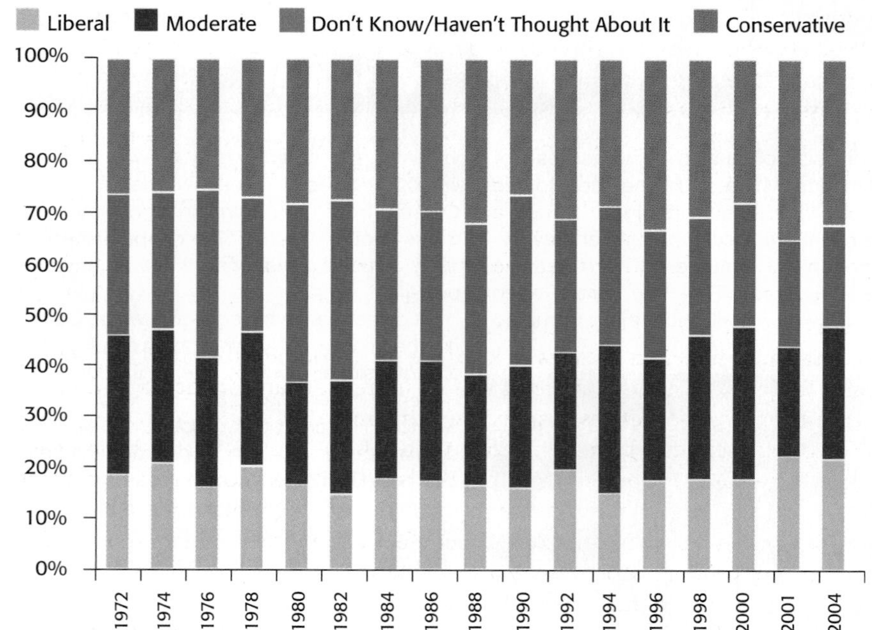

FIGURE 4–1
Ideology over Time.

SOURCE: Center for Political Studies, University of Michigan, *2004 American National Election Study.*

battles at the conventions. In 2008, John McCain won the GOP nomination despite opposition from some visible conservative leaders. At the same time, candidates from both parties also work hard to activate more ideological voters, sometimes called the "base" vote.

For those with a liberal or conservative preference, ideology provides a lens through which to view candidates and public policies. It helps simplify the complexities of politics, policies, personalities, and programs. However, most voters are selective or even inconsistent in their political views. A voter may support increased spending for defense but vote for the party that is for reducing defense spending because he or she has always voted for that party or prefers its stand on the environment. Or a person may favor tax cuts and a balanced budget while opposing substantial reductions in government programs.

The degree to which people have ideologically consistent attitudes and opinions varies but is often relatively low. Much of the time, people look at political issues individually and do not evaluate parties or candidates systematically or according to an ideological litmus test. Indeed, many citizens favor specific policies at variance with their broader political philosophy. This problem becomes more complex as

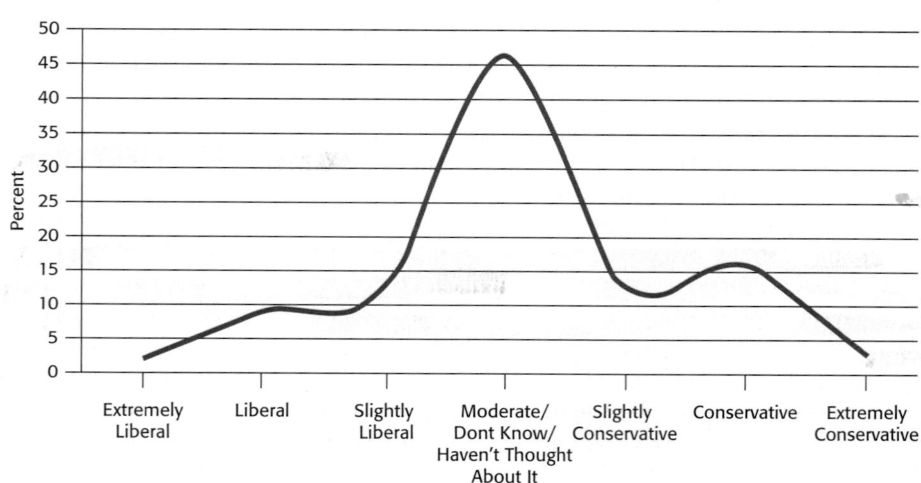

FIGURE 4–2
Distribution of Ideology in the U.S.

SOURCE: Center for Political Studies, University of Michigan, *2004 American National Election Study.*

government gets involved in more and more policy areas. Hence many people, not surprisingly, have difficulty finding candidates who reflect their ideological preferences across a wide range of issues.

The absence of widespread and solidified liberal and conservative positions in the United States makes for politics and policy-making processes that are markedly different from those in most nations. Policy making in this country is characterized more by ad hoc coalitions than by fixed alignments that pit one set of ideologies against another. Our politics are marked more by moderation, pragmatism, and accommodation than by a prolonged battle between competing philosophies of government. Elsewhere, especially in countries such as Sweden or Germany, where a strong Socialist, Green, or Christian Democratic Party exists, things are different.

LEARNING **OBJECTIVE**

5 Analyze the importance of political ideology in light of competing ideas such as pragmatism, practicality, and the changing agenda of American politics.

This does not mean that policies or ideas are not important in American politics. Since 1995, for instance, there has been a shift to more partisan and ideological voting in the House of Representatives. Part of the explanation is that Republicans have become more conservative and Democrats more liberal. Conservative Republicans have made large gains in the South, while the remaining Democrats have become more liberal;[42] in other parts of the country, such as New England and parts of the Midwest, liberal Democrats have replaced moderate Republicans. Perhaps even more important, congressional districts are now being drawn to make more of them safe for one party or the other, so Republican members of Congress tend to appeal to the more conservative wing of their party, while Democratic members of Congress tend to appeal to the more liberal wing of their party.

Ideologies have consequences. These sharp cleavages in political thinking stir opposing interest groups into action. A wide variety of groups promote their views of what is politically desirable. It is also these differences in ideological perspectives that reinforce party loyalties and divide us at election time. Policy fights in Congress, between Congress and the White House, and during judicial confirmation hearings also have their roots in our uneasily coexisting ideological values.

Our hard-earned rights and liberties are never entirely safeguarded; they are fragile and shaped by the political, economic, and social climate of the day. In later chapters, we examine the interest groups and political parties that are battling to advance their values and compete in the American political culture. But before turning to those topics, we examine the social and economic diversity of the American political landscape in Chapter 5 and see why agreement on shared democratic values is all the more remarkable.

CHAPTER **SUMMARY**

1 Identify the most important elements of the American political culture and how we learn them.

The American political culture consists of a widely held set of fundamental political values and accepted processes and institutions that help us manage conflict and resolve problems. American adults share a widespread commitment to classical liberalism, which embraces the importance of individual liberty, equality, individualism, power to the people, private property, limited government, nationalism, optimism, idealism, the democratic consensus, and justice and the rule of law. People respect the Constitution, the Bill of Rights, the two-party system, and the right to elect officials on the basis of majority rule. We learn American political culture in the family, schools, religious and civic organizations, and through the mass media and political activities.

2 Assess the importance of the "American dream" in the context of economic change.

Even with the dramatic changes experienced in the United States, the American dream persists as an ideal. Reasons for this persistence include highly visible examples of people achieving the American dream, and more broadly, as a nation of immigrants, American residents perceive this to be a land of opportunity and upward mobility.

3 Compare and contrast different ideological assumptions about government.

The two most important ideologies in American politics are liberalism, a belief that government can and should help achieve justice and equality of opportunity, and conservatism, a belief in limited government to ensure order, competitive markets, and personal opportunity while relying on free markets and individual initiative to solve social and economic problems. Socialism, which favors public ownership of the means of production, and libertarianism, which puts a premium on individual liberty and limited government, attract only modest followings in the United States.

4 Assess the arguments for and against each ideology.

Liberals hold the view that government can and should bring about justice, equality, and opportunity. Conservatives are less optimistic about what government can accomplish and fear that government solutions will limit liberty and stifle individual initiative. Critics of liberalism contend that liberals, by favoring government solutions to problems, limit the capacity of markets to function well and create large and unmanageable bureaucracies. Critics of conservatism contend that some problems require government to become part of the solution and that too much faith in the market to solve problems is misplaced.

5 Analyze the importance of political ideology in light of competing ideas such as pragmatism, practicality, and the changing agenda of American politics.

Few in the United States are extremists. There are more conservatives than liberals, and ideology has come to be more important in the nomination battles in both parties and Congress. Because a large fraction of the public is moderate or has not thought much about ideology, politicians can expand their coalition of voters and supporters by being pragmatic. Because nonideological persons are less likely to vote, they are not as important in elections as the more committed ideologues. However, in close elections these pragmatic centrist voters can be critical.

Chapter Self-Test

1. Identify and define four of the shared political values listed on (pp. 92–98).
2. Which has been defined as "features of social organization such as networks, norms, and social trust that facilitate coordination and cooperation for mutual benefit"? (p. 92)
   a. Pragmatism
   b. Social capital
   c. Political parties
   d. Political ideology
3. Which of the following "has taken over some functions the family used to perform"? (p. 98)
   a. Schools
   b. Churches
   c. The internet
   d. The mass media
4. What role do educational opportunity, economic wealth, and religious freedom play in achieving the American Dream? (pp. 99–100)
5. Which view was the result of a major shift in public perception after the Great Depression and New Deal? (pp. 101–102)
   a. Government should focus on defense issues
   b. Government should only regulate moral issues
   c. Government should work to ensure social justice
   d. Government should not become involved in the private lives of its citizens
6. Identify each belief as either conservative or liberal: (pp. 103–107)
   a. Belief that government can bring about equality of opportunity
   b. Belief that some government intervention in the economy is necessary to remedy the defects of capitalism
   c. Pessimistic view of human nature
   d. Preference for greater environmental protection
   e. Belief in keeping government small, especially the national government
   f. Preference for business
   g. Preference for individual choice in moral issues such as same-gender marriage and abortion
   h. Belief that the primary task of government is to ensure order
7. In a short essay, compare and contrast the major beliefs of liberalism and conservatism. Consider each ideology's approach to moral, economic, and national defense issues. How are they alike? How are they different? Which do you think is more effective in today's world? (pp. 103–107)
8. In a short essay define three major criticisms of both conservatism and liberalism. Which criticism do you find more persuasive? (pp. 103–107)
9. Identify which of the following is a major tenet of Libertarianism: (pp. 107–108)
   a. Public ownership of business
   b. Opposition to all government regulation
   c. Government provision of universal health care
   d. Use of government regulation only for moral issues such as abortion

10. In recent years, about how many people in the United States have identified themselves as "extreme" conservatives or liberals? (p. 109)
    a. 6%
    b. 23%
    c. 65%
    d. 80%
11. How widespread and how solid are political parties in the United States? With this in mind, how important are values like moderation, pragmatism, and accommodation in policy making? (pp. 109–111)
12. During which of the following administrations was the term "liberal" popular among politicians in general? (p. 108)
    a. Bill Clinton
    b. John F. Kennedy
    c. Lyndon B. Johnson
    d. Franklin D. Roosevelt

Key Terms

political culture, p. 92
suffrage, p. 92
social capital, p. 92
natural rights, p. 93
democratic consensus, p. 95
majority rule, p. 95
popular sovereignty, p. 95
nationalism, p. 96
American dream, p. 99
capitalism, p. 99
political ideology, p. 103
liberalism, p. 103
conservatism, p. 105
socialism, p. 107
libertarianism, p. 107

Further Reading

H. W. BRANDS, *The Strange Death of American Liberalism* (Yale University Press, 2001).

JIMMY CARTER, *Our Endangered Values: America's Moral Crisis* (Simon & Schuster, 2005).

JAMES W. CEASER, *Reconstructing America: The Symbol of America in Modern Thought* (Yale University Press, 1997).

E. J. DIONNE JR., *They Only Look Dead: Why Progressives Will Dominate the Next Political Era* (Simon & Schuster, 1996).

JEAN BETHKE ELSHTAIN, *Democracy on Trial* (Basic Books, 1995).

E.H.H. GREEN, *Ideologies of Conservatism: Conservative Political Ideas in the Twentieth Century* (Oxford University Press, 2004).

AMY GUTMANN AND **DENNIS THOMPSON,** *Democracy and Disagreement: Why Moral Conflict Cannot Be Avoided in Politics, and What Should Be Done About It* (Harvard University Press, 1996).

SAMUEL P. HUNTINGTON, *Who Are We? The Challenge to America's National Identity* (Simon & Schuster, 2004).

LOUIS HARTZ, *The Liberal Tradition in America* (Harcourt, 1955).

CAROL A. HORTON, *Race and the Making of American Liberalism* (Oxford University Press, 2005).

GEORGE KLOSKO, *Democratic Procedures and Liberal Consensus* (Oxford University Press, 2000).

IRVING KRISTOL, *Neoconservatism: The Autobiography of an Idea* (Free Press, 1995).

DAVID C. LEEGE, KENNETH D. WALD, BRIAN S. KRUEGER, AND **PAUL D. MUELLER,** *The Politics of Cultural Differences* (Princeton University Press, 2002).

HERBERT MCCLOSKY AND **JOHN ZALLER,** *The American Ethos: Public Attitudes Toward Capitalism and Democracy* (Harvard University Press, 1984).

LISA MCGIRR, *Suburban Warriors: The Origins of the New American Right* (Princeton University Press, 2001).

CHARLES MURRAY, *What It Means to Be a Libertarian: A Personal Interpretation* (Broadway Books, 1997).

MICHAEL NEWMA, *Socialism: A Very Short Introduction* (Oxford University Press, 2005).

MARCUS G. RASKIN, *Liberalism: The Genius of American Ideals* (Rowman & Littlefield, 2004).

JOHN RENSENBRINK, *Against All Odds: The Green Transformation of American Politics* (Leopold Press, 1999).

ALEXIS DE TOCQUEVILLE, *Democracy in America*, 2 vols. (1835).

GARRY WILLS, *A Necessary Evil: A History of American Distrust of Government* (Simon & Schuster, 1999).

chapter 5

The American Political Landscape

The 2008 presidential election provided voters with a wide array of possible "firsts": including the first woman president, the first African American president, the first Hispanic-American president, and the first Mormon president. Hillary Clinton, though not the first woman to run for the White House, was the early front runner, and no previous female candidate was as strong a contender. The same was true for Barack Obama as a black candidate. Other blacks had run for president, including the Reverend Jesse Jackson, but Obama was the most serious black contender for the presidency in U.S. history. Mitt Romney was not the first of his Latter-day Saints (LDS) faith to seek the White House, but like Obama and Clinton he was the first to get serious and sustained attention. New Mexico governor Bill Richardson did not generate the votes of Clinton, Obama, or Romney, but none of the early-primary states had substantial Hispanic populations. This meant that the impact of his being Hispanic was not tested. Senator John McCain rounded out this cast of firsts as the oldest nominee of a major party running for a first term as president.

In 2008's crowded primary field race, gender, age, and religious affiliations proved important. African Americans gave Senator Obama overwhelming support. For example, he got more than three-quarters of the black vote in South Carolina and Tennessee; more than 80 percent in Alabama, Georgia, Illinois, Maryland, and Louisiana; and more than 90 percent in Virginia, Mississippi, and North Carolina.[1] Senator Clinton targeted women, especially those over age 50. She got large majorities of these voters in Pennsylvania, Ohio, and California.[2] Both Obama and Clinton clearly had strong support from other voter segments. Clinton did especially well among Hispanics,[3] and Obama generated strong support among younger voters and upper-income voters and professionals.[4]

Senator John McCain's selection of Alaska Governor Sarah Palin to be his running mate provided another "first" in the 2008 election. Palin was the first female to be nominated for Vice President by the Republican party. The first female nominated for the office was Democratic Congresswoman Geraldine Ferraro who ran with Walter Mondale in 1984. Palin presented herself as a small-town parent of five, "hockey mom," from the middle class who worked hard, later became mayor of her town and governor of her state. Her mode of speech was folksy. She frequently characterized herself as a maverick and outsider. She generated controversy over her uninformed answers to some media interviews, claiming for example, foreign policy expertise because of Alaska's proximity to Russia. But in her acceptance speech at the GOP convention and in the vice presidential debate with Democrat Joe Biden she energized important parts of the Republican base.

The nomination phase of the 2008 presidential election had more than the normal amount of "identity politics," in which voters identify with a particular candidate because of personal attributes such as gender, race, or religion. Do these still matter in American politics? The answer is clearly yes. In the United States we celebrate our diversity and our immigrant past and proudly recite the words of Emma Lazarus, inscribed at the base of the Statue of Liberty: "Give me your tired, your poor, your huddled masses yearning to breathe free." Albert Einstein, who himself immigrated to the United States from Germany in the 1930s, once said that most people are incapable of expressing opinions that differ

LEARNING **OBJECTIVES**

1. Describe the opportunities and challenges posed by the diversity of the American population.
2. Explain how geography affects politics.
3. Describe the political evolution of the South.
4. Evaluate the role of population density and where people live in American politics.
5. Assess the roles of race, ethnicity, religion, gender, and changing family demographics in American politics.
6. Evaluate the roles of education, income, class, and age in American politics.

CHAPTER **OUTLINE**

- A Land of Diversity
- Where We Live
- Who We Are
- Unity in a Land of Diversity

much from the prejudices of their social upbringing.[6] This **ethnocentrism**—selective perception based on our background, attitudes, and biases—is not uncommon. People often assume that others share their economic opportunities, social attitudes, sense of civic responsibility, and self-confidence. In this chapter, we consider how our social environment explains, or at least shapes, our opinions and prejudices. We also look at our diversity and at how geographic, social, and economic divisions can affect politics and government.

Specifically, this chapter explores the effects of regional or state identity on political perspectives; how differences in race, ethnicity, gender, family structure, religion, wealth and income, occupation, and social class influence opinions and voting choices; and the relationship between age, education, and political participation. Because people's personal characteristics or attributes are important to political interest groups (Chapter 6), we examine attitudes and behavior before discussing political parties (Chapter 7); public opinion, participation, and voting (Chapter 8); and campaigns and elections (Chapter 9). This chapter lays the foundation of how different aspects of who we are as people influence how we behave politically.

LEARNING **OBJECTIVE**

1 Describe the opportunities and challenges posed by the diversity of the American population.

Using the Census to Understand Who Americans Are

A Land of Diversity

Most nations consist of groups of people who have lived together for centuries and who speak the same language, embrace the same religious beliefs, and share a common history. Most Japanese citizens are Japanese in the fullest sense of the word, and this sense of shared identity is generally as strong in Sweden, Saudi Arabia, and China. The United States is different. We have attracted the poor and oppressed, the adventurous, and the talented from all over the world, and we have been more open to accepting strangers than many other nations.

Many people want to come to the United States because it holds a promise of religious, political, and economic freedom. It is also a place of opportunity for the enterprising. Our economic system has provided widespread (but not universal) opportunity for individuals to improve their economic standing. The American dream—that anyone through hard work can find success in the United States—is widely shared. Perceptions about the American way of life gleaned from popular culture—movies, music videos, TV shows—also attract some to our shores.

In the pages that follow, we examine a variety of factors that shape individuals' political orientation and views on such issues as health care and economic policy. What becomes clear through this discussion is that in a nation as geographically large and ethnically diverse as the United States, many characteristics differentiate us from each other. They can also unite us. In the late 1990s, for example, Senators Ted Kennedy (D-Mass.) and Orrin Hatch (R-Utah), ideologically opposed on many policy issues, worked together to expand spending on health care for children.

Several elements of our diversity have political significance. Many retain an identity with the land of their ancestors, even after three or four generations. Families, churches, and other close-knit ethnic groups foster these ties. **Political socialization** is the process by which parents and others teach children about political values, beliefs, and attitudes. This teaching occurs in the home, in school, on the playground, and in the neighborhood. In addition to fostering group identities, political socialization also strongly influences how individuals see politics and which political party they prefer. Where we live and who we are in terms of age, education, religion, and occupation affect how we vote. Social scientists use the term **demography** to describe the study of such population characteristics. Persons in certain demographic categories tend to vote alike and to share certain **political predispositions** that can predict political behavior, despite individual differences within socioeconomic and demographic categories.

When social and economic differences reinforce each other, social scientists call them **reinforcing cleavages;** they can make political conflict more intense and society more polarized. In Italy, for example, the tendency of parts of the industrialized north to lean toward the Socialist or Communist Party, and of the poorer and more agrarian south

ethnocentrism
Belief in the superiority of one's nation or ethnic group.

political socialization
The process by which we develop our political attitudes, values, and beliefs.

demography
The study of the characteristics of populations.

political predisposition
A characteristic of individuals that is predictive of political behavior.

reinforcing cleavages
Divisions within society that reinforce one another, making groups more homogeneous or similar.

to be politically conservative and Catholic, reinforces the divide between north and south that has existed for centuries.

Nations can also have **cross-cutting cleavages,** when, instead of reinforcing each other, differences pull people in different directions. To illustrate, if all the rich people in a nation belong to one religion and the poor to another, the nation would have reinforcing cleavages that would intensify political conflict between the groups. But if there are both rich and poor in all religions, and if people sometimes vote on the basis of their religion and sometimes on the basis of their wealth, the divisions would be cross-cutting. American diversity has generally been more of the cross-cutting than the reinforcing type. As a result, people have multiple allegiances that lessen political conflict. Winning in the American electoral system requires building a broad coalition that reinforces cross-cutting cleavages.

Even though ours has been and remains a nation of immigrants from around the world, we often prefer to associate only with people "like us" and are suspicious of people "like them." From hostility toward different religions in the early colonies to the "nativist" and anti-Asian movements of the 1800s, to the anti-immigration and anti-civil rights ballot initiatives of the last two decades, people in the United States have exhibited ethnocentrism. Indeed, for much of our history, minorities have been excluded from full participation in American political and economic life. That is changing. In 2008 the Spanish-speaking network Univision sponsored the first presidential debate in Spanish. Hispanic turnout was seen as critical in some presidential primaries,[7] and both parties aggressively courted Hispanic voters in the general election.

Slavery epitomizes the dark side of this country's national identity. During Reconstruction, some former slaves were able to purchase and work their own land; others moved north to take part in the industrial revolution of the late nineteenth century.

Geography and National Identity

The United States is a geographically large and historically isolated country. In the 1830s, French commentator Alexis de Tocqueville studied its early development and observed that the country had no major political or economic powers on its borders "and consequently no great wars, financial crises, invasions, or conquests to fear."[8] Geographic isolation from the major powers of the world during our government's formative period helps explain American politics.[9] The Atlantic Ocean served as a barrier to foreign meddling, giving us time to establish our political tradition and develop our economy. The western frontier provided room to grow and avoid some of the social and political tensions Europe experienced. American reluctance to become involved in foreign wars and controversies still emerges in debates over foreign policy.

LEARNING **OBJECTIVE**

2 Explain how geography affects politics.

Remarkably few foreign enemies have successfully struck within U.S. continental borders: most notably, England in the War of 1812 and terrorists in the World Trade Center bombing in 1993 and the attacks of September 11, 2001.[10] By contrast, Poland has been invaded repeatedly and was partitioned by Austria, Prussia, and Russia in the eighteenth century and by Nazi Germany and the Soviet Union in 1939. The difference is explained largely by location: Poland was surrounded by great powers. Had the United States been closer to Europe and not isolated by two oceans, it might have been overrun and its Constitution and institutions repeatedly changed or eliminated to suit the invaders. The presence of powerful and aggressive neighbors can impede the development of democracy in relatively weak nations.

Though geographic location may have previously provided a substantial buffer from foreign attack, technological advances make that less the case today. The ability of terrorists to harm the United States and other countries, especially if they are willing to die along with their victims, means that national defense and homeland security need to be rethought. The two oceans that protected the United States for so long cannot deter a small band of determined terrorists. Our newly recognized vulnerability to terrorist attacks on our own soil has changed the context in which we debate the balance between liberty and security and has led some to advocate the idea of preemptive war.

cross-cutting cleavages
Divisions within society that cut across demographic categories to produce groups that are more heterogeneous or different.

Size also confers an advantage. The landmass of the United States exceeds that of all but Russia and Canada. In contrast, India has a population more than three and a

The diversity of its natural resources, including farmland, forests, waterways, and coal mines, is one of the advantages of the United States' large landmass.

half times that of the United States on a landmass one-third the size. Geographic space gave the expanding population of the United States room to spread out. This defused some of the political conflicts arising from religion, social class, and national origin because groups could isolate themselves from one another. Moreover, plentiful and accessible land helped foster the perspective that the United States had a **manifest destiny** to be a continental nation reaching from the Atlantic to the Pacific Ocean. Early settlers used this notion to justify taking land from Native Americans, Canadians, and Mexicans, especially the huge territory acquired after victory in the Mexican-American War.

The United States is also a land of abundant natural resources. We have rich farmland, which not only feeds our population but also makes us the largest exporter of food in the world.[11] We are rich in such natural resources as coal, iron, uranium, oil, and precious metals. All of these resources enhance economic growth, provide jobs, and stabilize government. As de Tocqueville observed, "Yet what takes place in the United States is much less attributable to the institutions of the country than to the country itself."[12]

manifest destiny
A notion held by nineteenth-century Americans that the United States was destined to rule the continent, from the Atlantic to the Pacific.

Our isolation, relative wealth, prosperity, and sense of destiny have fostered a view that the United States is different from the world. This *American exceptionalism*, a term first used by de Tocqueville in 1831, has historically been defined as "the perception that the United States differs qualitatively from other developed nations, because of its unique origins, national credo, historical evolution, and distinctive political and religious institutions."[13] The term has long been used to describe not only the distinctive elements of the United States, but the sense that the United States is a just and moral country. Exceptionalism can thus convey a sense of moral superiority or power that is not well received outside the United States, especially when the United States is seen to be acting in ways that other nations find objectionable or hypocritical. For some, at least, the Bush doctrine of preventive war—the idea that American power can and should be used preemptively against other nations that pose a danger, immediate or potential, to the United States—is an extension of exceptionalism.

Geography also helps explain our diversity. Parts of the United States are wonderfully suited to agriculture, others to mining or ranching, and still others to shipping and manufacturing. These differences produce diverse regional economic concerns, which in turn influence politics. For instance, a person from the agricultural heartland may see foreign trade differently from the way an automobile worker in Detroit sees it.

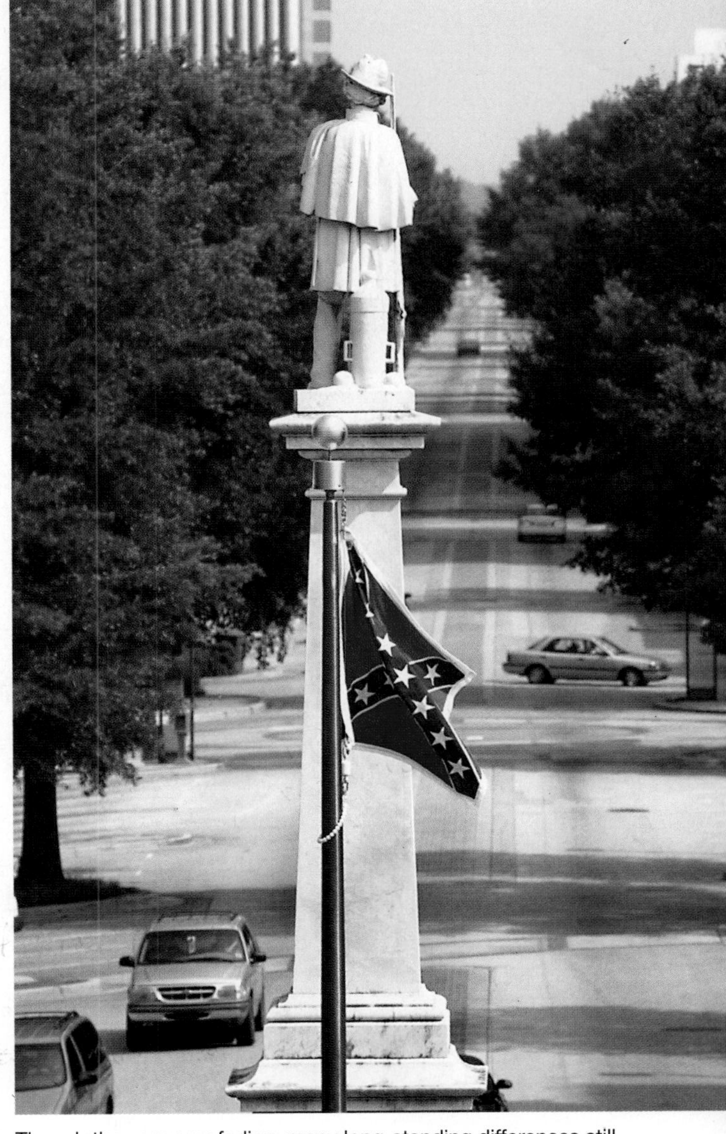

Though they are now fading, many long-standing differences still distinguish the U.S. South from other parts of the country, as the Confederate flag flying outside South Carolina's memorial for confederate soldiers demonstrates.

Regional Differences

Unlike the case in many other countries, geography in the United States does *not* define an ethnic or religious division. All the Serbs in the United States do not live in one place, nor do all French-speaking Catholics and Hispanic immigrants reside in others. Sectional, or regional, differences in the United States are primarily geographic, not ethnic or religious.

The most distinct section of the United States remains the South, although its differences from other parts of the country are diminishing. From the beginning of the Republic, the agricultural South differed from the North, where commerce and later manufacturing were more significant. But the most important difference between the regions was the institution of slavery. Northern opposition to slavery, which grew increasingly intense by the 1850s, reinforced sectional economic interests. The eleven Confederate states, by deciding to secede from the Union, reinforced a common political identity. After the Civil War, Reconstruction and the problems of race relations reinforced regional differences.

LEARNING **OBJECTIVE**

3 Describe the political evolution of the South.

The South is becoming less distinct from the rest of the United States. In addition to undergoing tremendous economic change, a large in-migration has diminished the sense of regional identity. The civil rights revolution of the 1960s eliminated legal and social barriers that prevented African Americans from voting, ended legal segregation, opened up new educational opportunities, and helped integrate the South into the national economy. African Americans still lag behind Southern white people in voter registration, but the gap is now no wider in the South than elsewhere and is explained more by differences in education than by race.[14] In economic terms, the South still falls below the rest of the country in per capita income and education, but much less so than 50 years ago. The traditional religious and moral conservatism of the South, however, remains notable.

Until the 1970s, political observers spoke of the "solid South"—a region that voted for Democrats at all levels. "The Civil War made the Democratic party the party of the South, and the Republican party, the party of the North."[15] The Democratic "solid South" remained a fixture of American politics for more than a century. Since 1968 that has changed dramatically, first at the presidential level and increasingly at the state and local levels. As two respected observers of the region comment, "The fall of the South as an assured stronghold of the Democratic Party in presidential elections is one

TABLE 5–1 Voting Patterns in the 11 Former Confederate States

Republican Vote for President			
1960	46%	1988	59%
1964	49	1992	43
1968	35	1996	46
1972	70	2000	54
1976	45	2004	57
1980	50	2008	54
1984	62		
Republican Vote for U.S. Representatives			
1960	22%	1990	43%
1964	37	1992	48
1968	35	1994	58
1972	42	1996	53*
1976	36	1998	58
1980	40	2000	53
1982	39	2002	56
1984	42	2004	55
1986	41	2006	53
1988	42	2008	52
Republican Share of State Legislators		**House**	**Senate**
1960		5%	4%
1964		7	11
1968		13	13
1972		17	15
1976		12	10
1980		18	17
1982		22	14
1984		23	17
1986		24	20
1988		27	24
1990		28	26
1992		31	31
1994		37	37
1996		44	44
1998		42	40
2000		44	42
2002		47	46
2004		50	49
2006		48	49
2008		48	50

*The 1996 Texas runoff elections are not included.

SOURCE: CQ Voting and Election Database; Todd Edwards, Council of State Governments, Southern Office, personal communication, December 22, 2000; and Doris Smith, Council of State Governments, Southern Office, personal communication, November 10, 2004. National Conference of State Legislatures. State Vote 2008. At http://www.ncsl.org/statevote/StateVote2008.htm, accessed November 10, 2008.

of the most significant developments in modern American politics."[16] "The decline of the South in the Democratic party would fundamentally reorder the American party system and realign the electorate."[17]

The political alignment has shifted as African Americans have been enfranchised and become overwhelmingly Democrats, and many white Southerners have become Republicans. In 1992 and 1996, even with two southerners—Bill Clinton and Al Gore—on the ticket, Democrats won only four of the eleven former Confederate states. In 2000 and 2004, George W. Bush carried all eleven southern states, including Al Gore's home state of Tennessee in 2000 and vice presidential candidate John Edwards's home state of North Carolina in 2004. In 2008, Barack Obama won in Florida, Virginia, and North Carolina. In both North Carolina and Florida the margins were close.

Republican success at the presidential level was slow to affect contests for Congress and state legislatures. More recently, Republicans have had more than half of southern votes for the U.S. House of Representatives (see Table 5–1), GOP share of U.S. House vote was 52 percent and in 2009 they controlled four of the eleven governorships in the former Confederate states. Democrat Beverly Perdue won in North Carolina, the only southern Governorship up for election in 2008. In the state legislatures, remnants of the old Democratic "solid South" remain, but Republicans have made major inroads, and politics in the region is now predictably Republican, at least at the presidential level.

Another sectional division is the Sun Belt—the eleven former Confederate states plus New Mexico, Arizona, Nevada, and the southern half of California. Sun Belt states are growing much more rapidly than the rest of the country. Arizona, California, Florida, Georgia, Nevada, North Carolina, and Texas gained twelve seats in the House of Representatives after the 2000 census.[18] Moreover, population growth in the South and West is occurring in different age groups. In the South, growth is largest among those over age 65; in the West, younger persons provide the growth. Sun Belt states have also experienced greater economic growth as industries have headed south and southwest, where land and labor are cheaper and more abundant (see Figure 5–1). The shift of seats to the Sun Belt has helped Republicans, as the states picking up additional seats have tended to be more Republican.

State and Local Identity

States have distinctive political cultures that affect public opinion and policies. Individuals often have a sense of identification with their state.[19] Part of the reason for enduring state identities is that we elect members of Congress and the president at the

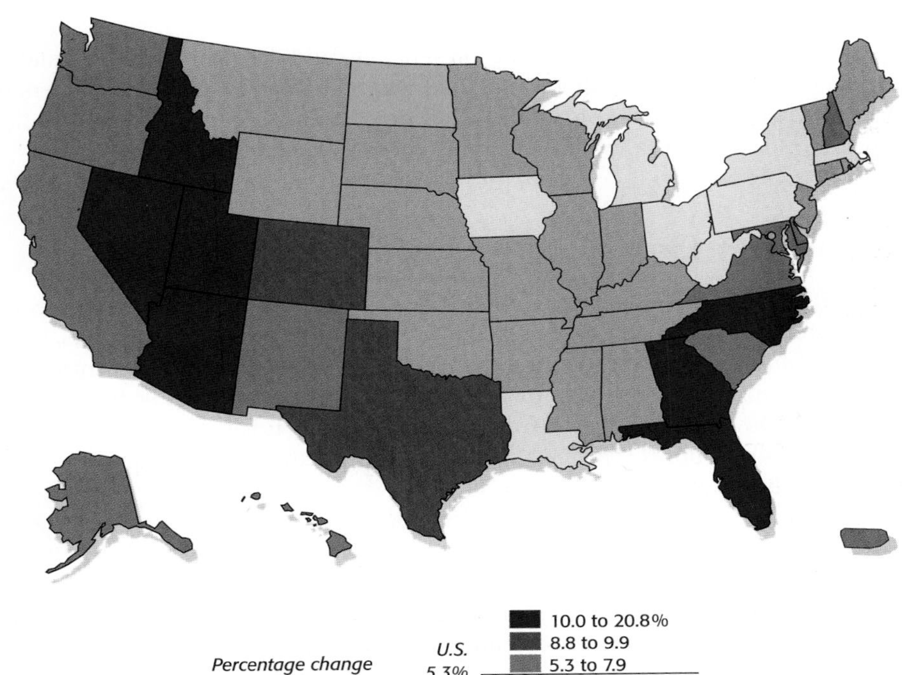

FIGURE 5–1
Percentage Change in Resident Population, 2000–2007.

SOURCE: U.S. Bureau of the Census, www.census.gov/popest/gallery/maps/st-perchg-map2007.pdf.

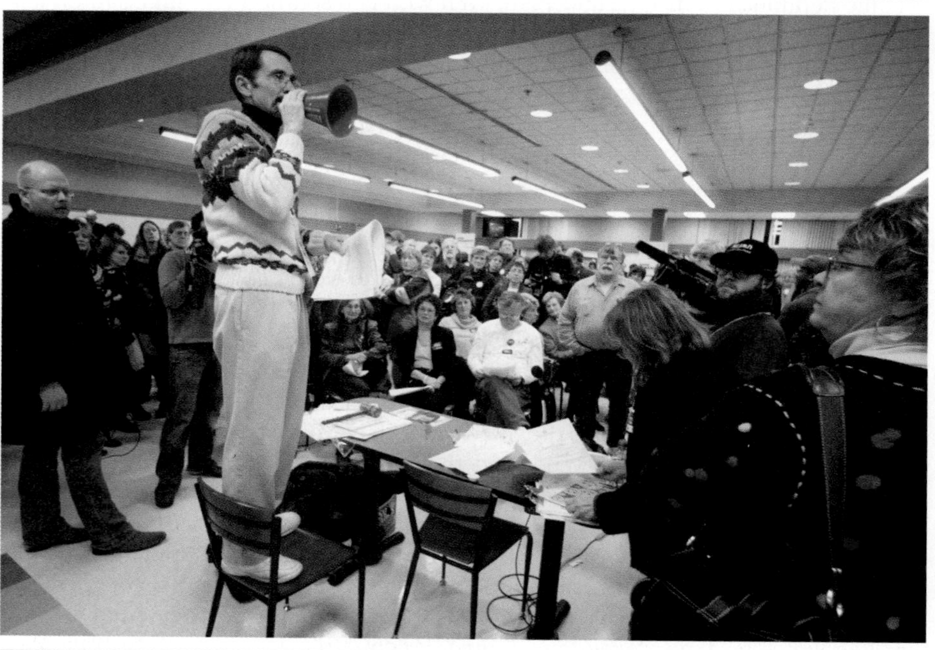

The influential Iowa caucus represents one reason why citizens can develop a strong sense of identification with their state and help it develop a distinctive political culture.

state level. States such as Iowa and New Hampshire play important roles in narrowing the field of presidential candidates seeking their party's nomination. Differences in state laws relating to driving, drinking, gambling, and taxes reinforce the relevance of state identity. Colleges and universities may have the same effect while reinforcing competition between different states.

California also stands out in American politics today, if only because nearly one of eight U.S. citizens lives in the state.[20] In economic and political importance, California is in a league by itself; its 53 members of the House of Representatives exceed the number of representatives from the smallest 20 states combined. California's 55 electoral votes provide a large advantage for any presidential candidate who carries the state.[21] The state's reputation for distinctive politics was reinforced in 2003 when voters replaced Governor Gray Davis with movie star Arnold Schwarzenegger in the first recall of a governor since North Dakota voters recalled Governor Lynn G. Frazier in 1921.[22]

Where We Live

LEARNING **OBJECTIVE**

4 Evaluate the role of population density and where people live in American politics.

Four of five people in the United States now live in urban areas.[23] During the early twentieth century, the movement of population was from rural areas to central cities, which we call *urbanization*, but the movement since the 1950s has been from the central cities to their suburbs. Today the most urban state is California (more than 94 percent of its population lives in cities or suburbs). Vermont is the least urban, with only 38 percent living in cities or suburbs.[24] Regionally, the West and Northeast are the most urban, the South and Midwest the most rural.

People move from cities to the suburbs for many reasons—better housing, new transportation systems that make it easier to get to work, a lower cost of living, the desire for cleaner air and safer streets. Another reason is "white flight," the movement of white people away from the central cities so children can avoid being bused for racial balance and attend generally better schools. White, middle-class migration to the suburbs has made American cities increasingly poor, African American, and Democratic. More than half of all African Americans now live in central cities, as opposed to only about one-quarter of white people, and the poverty level among black people living in central cities is higher than among whites living in the same cities.[25]

Although four of five citizens live in urban areas, since about the 1950s there has been a steady flow outward to the suburbs, particularly among the middle and upper classes.

These proportions are nearly reversed for the suburbs, where more than half of all white American citizens reside. Slightly less than 40 percent of African Americans live in the suburbs, up from one-fifth in 1980.[26] In large cities such as Washington, D.C.; Detroit; Baltimore, and Atlanta, the city population is now well over 50 percent African American (see Table 5–2). Noteworthy in Table 5–2 is the more than 50 percent decline in population in New Orleans between 2000 and 2006, a change largely attributed to Hurricane Katrina. Other cities in Table 5–2 also lost population in the same time period with, Atlanta and Washington, D.C., the exceptions. Hispanics constitute roughly three-fourths of the population of El Paso, Texas, and Santa Ana, California, and nearly two-thirds the population of Miami, Florida.[27]

TABLE 5–2 Cities with Populations of 100,000 or More That Are at Least 50 Percent African American, 2006

City	Population 2006	Percent African American 2006
Detroit, Mich.	834,116	83.1
Memphis, Tenn.	643,122	63.5
Baltimore, Md.	631,366	64.4
Washington, D.C.	581,530	55.4
Atlanta, Ga.	442,887	55.7%
Newark, N.J.	266,736	53.9
New Orleans, La.	223,388	58.8
Birmingham, Ala.	217,131	74.6
Richmond, Va.	192,913	54.3
Jackson, Miss.	176,227	75.8
Savannah, Ga.	128,418	57.1

SOURCE: U.S. Bureau of the Census, American Community Survey, 2006.

As the economically better-off have left many of the cities, the cities' challenges have become more acute, and their tax base has not increased in proportion to the problems they must solve. Older suburban areas now face the same problems as the inner cities, as they too suffer from out-migration to newer cities and towns, the so-called exurbs. High-tech and professional service companies frequently relocate to the suburbs to avoid traffic congestion and to be closer to the "bedroom communities" where their workers live. Political boundaries, which define local governments and delineate responsibility for services, create understandable tensions among cities, suburbs, and rural areas. Determining these boundaries has crucial implications for tax revenues, legislative representation, zoning laws, and governmental priorities.

Who We Are

Sectional distinctions, which separate populations by geography and regions, less prominently distinguish us from one another in the United States today than they did a century or even a half-century ago. Today we are more likely to define ourselves by a number of other characteristics, each of which may influence how we vote or think about candidates, issues, or policies.

Race and Ethnicity

Racial and ethnic differences have always had political significance. **Race** groups human beings with distinctive physical characteristics determined by genetic inheritance. Some scholars define it as more culturally determined than genetic.[28] **Ethnicity** is a social division based on national origin, religion, and language, often within the same race, and includes a sense of attachment to that group. Examples of ethnic groups with enduring relevance to American politics include Italian Americans, Irish Americans, Polish Americans, and Korean Americans, though most race and ethnicity issues in the United States today focus primarily on African Americans, Asian Americans, Native Americans, and Hispanics.

LEARNING **OBJECTIVE**

5 Assess the roles of race, ethnicity, religion, gender, and changing family demographics in American politics.

There are more than 38 million African Americans in the United States, nearly 13 percent of the population. Asian Americans constitute 4.4 percent of the population, and Native Americans, 1 percent.[29] Most American Hispanics classify themselves as white, although Hispanics can be of any race. At 41 million, Hispanics are the fastest-growing U.S. ethnic group, constituting nearly 15 percent of the population.[30] Because of differences in immigration and birthrates, non-Hispanic whites will increase to about 50 percent of the population by 2050.[31]

Native Americans The original inhabitants of what became the United States have played an important role in its history and continue to be important to the politics of states like South Dakota, New Mexico, and Oklahoma. More than half the names of states and hundreds of the names of cities, rivers, and mountains in the United States are Native American. During much of our history, the policy of the U.S. government was to remove Native Americans from their tribal lands and relocate them to reservations, where they were isolated and their poverty and related social problems were reinforced for decades. More recently, with the advent of tribe-owned casinos, some Native Americans have achieved wealth and political influence but also experienced increases in violent crime.[32] In recent United States Senate elections in South Dakota, the Native American vote has been important.[33] Ben Nighthorse Campbell from Colorado, who served in the U.S. Senate from 1993 to 2005, is a Native American.

race
A grouping of human beings with distinctive characteristics determined by genetic inheritance.

ethnicity
A social division based on national origin, religion, language, and often race.

One of the overlooked groups, Native Americans and Alaskan Natives have averaged poverty rates of 26 percent in recent years, slightly higher than for African Americans and Hispanics.[34] The relative poverty of many Native Americans and Alaskan Natives has been a persistent problem that illustrates that these racial and ethnic distinctions have political consequences.

THE CHANGING FACE OF U.S. POLITICS

A More Diverse Population

The United States has become much more diverse over the past 50 years and will become even more so over the next half-century. In 1950, nearly nine of every ten persons in the United States was white, and Hispanics were not a category the U.S. Census Bureau reported. By 2006, just over four in five persons in the United States were white, but that fraction included Hispanic whites. Today, non-Hispanic whites are about two-thirds of the U.S. population. Groups projected to have the most growth between 1990 and 2025 are Asians, Pacific Islanders, and Hispanics. In the aggregate, about one in every four persons in the United States in 2025 will be Asian, Pacific Islander, or Hispanic. Although regional differences matter less to American politics than they once did, the emergence of "majority minority" communities and legislative districts, in which a majority of the population are from racial minorities, ensures that race will have a greater influence in some areas of the country than others.

The changing face of U.S. politics is increasingly diverse. Despite the surge in Hispanic population, there has not been a similar surge in political participation or representation. Researchers cite many reasons for this, including redistricting, low rates of citizenship and motivations for voting, and a lack of common party commitment.

Changing Racial Composition of the U.S. Polity, 1950–2050.

	1950	1990	2006	2025	2050
White	89.4%	83.9%	80.1%	76.8%	72.1%
Non-Hispanic White	—	75.7	66.4	59.5	50.1
African American	10.0	12.2	12.8	13.7	14.6
Native American, Inuit, Aleut	0.2	0.8	1.0	1.0	1.1
Asian and Pacific Islander	0.2	3.0	4.6	6.5	9.3
Hispanic	—	8.9	14.8	18.9	24.4

NOTE: Percentages do not equal 100 because Hispanics can be of any race. Figures for 2025 and 2050 are projections. Categories from the 1950 census are different from those used in the last several decades. For example, the 1950 census did not provide a classification for Hispanic, Native Americans were classified as "Indian," and Asians were separated into Japanese and Chinese.

SOURCE: 1950 figures from U.S. Bureau of the Census, *Census of Population: 1950, Volume II Part I* (U.S. Government Printing Office, 1950), p. 106. 1990 figures from U.S. Bureau of the Census, *Statistical Abstract of the United States, 2001* (U.S. Government Printing Office, 2001), pp. 16–17. 2006 figures from U.S. Bureau of the Census, *Statistical Abstract of the United States, 2008* (U.S. Government Printing Office, 2008), p. 11. All other figures from U.S. Bureau of the Census, *Statistical Abstract of the United States, 2003* (U.S. Government Printing Office, 2003), pp. 15, 18.

African Americans Most immigrants chose to come to this country in search of freedom and opportunity. In contrast, most African Americans came against their will, as slaves. Although the Emancipation Proclamation and Thirteenth Amendment ended slavery in the 1860s, racial divisions still affect American politics. Until 1900, more than 90 percent of all African Americans lived in the South; a century later, that figure was 55 percent.[35] Many African Americans left the South hoping to improve their lives by settling in the large cities of the Northeast, Midwest, and West. But what many of them found was urban poverty. More recently, African Americans have been returning to the South, especially its urban areas.

Most African Americans are more vulnerable economically than most whites. African American median family income is around $35,000, compared to about $59,000 for whites.[36] About 22 percent of African American families live below the poverty level, compared to about 8 percent of white families.[37] However, African Americans have been doing better in recent years; 35 percent of African American households earned more than $50,000 in 2008 (compared to 58 percent of white households).[38] Some African Americans, like Boston Celtics basketball player Kevin Garnett and syndicated talk show host and corporate chief executive Oprah Winfrey, have risen to the top of their professions in terms of earnings.

Another way to measure economic well-being is in terms of assets or wealth. *Wealth* is the economic value of the things you own (savings, stocks, property), compared to *income,* which is how much money you make from your job or investments.

Basketball star Kevin Garnett of the Boston Celtics is one of the highest-earning African Americans today. In 2008 David A. Paterson became New York's first African American governor.

One way to measure wealth is called *net worth,* which is the sum of assets a person has in savings, property, and stocks. The median net worth of African Americans as a group is less than one-tenth that of whites, and the median net worth of Hispanics is only slightly more than that of African Americans (see Figure 5–2).[39]

Wealth is intimately related to education. Most African Americans and Hispanics have fewer resources to fall back on in hard times, and they are less likely to have the savings to help a child pay for college. The growing numbers of middle-class African Americans are role models for the young of all races, yet their still comparatively small number is a reminder that most African Americans remain behind in an economy that relies more and more on education and job skills. Among recent high school graduates, 66 percent of white Americans go on to college, but only 58 percent of African Americans do.[40] About 28 percent of whites graduate from college, whereas only about 18 percent of African Americans do.[41]

Finally, the African American population is much younger than the white population; the median age for whites in 2006 was 37.8 years, compared to 31 for African Americans.[42] The combination of a younger African American population, a lower level of education, and their concentration in economically depressed urban areas has resulted in a much higher unemployment rate for young African Americans. Unemployment can in turn contribute to social problems such as crime, drug and alcohol abuse, and family dissolution.

African Americans had little political power until after World War II. Owing their freedom from slavery to the "party of Lincoln," most African Americans initially identified with the Republicans, but this loyalty started to change in the 1930s and 1940s under President Franklin D. Roosevelt, who insisted on equal treatment for African Americans in his New Deal programs.[43] After World War II, African Americans came to see the Democrats as the party of civil rights. The 1964 Republican platform position on civil rights espoused *states' rights*—at the time, the creed of southern segregationists—in what appeared to be an effort to win the support of southern white voters. Virtually all African Americans voted for Lyndon Johnson in 1964, and in presidential elections between 1984 and 2008, their Democratic vote averaged more than 86 percent.[44] In 2008, with an African American running for President, 95 percent of blacks voted for Obama and their share of total votes rose from 11 percent in 2004 to 13 percent in 2008.[45]

African Americans have become much more important politically as their voting turnout increases, particularly in certain regions. African Americans constitute only 0.3 percent of the population in Montana and 0.6 percent in Idaho, but 37 percent in Mississippi, 30 percent in Georgia, and 29 percent in South Carolina.[46] Southern senators and representatives can no longer afford to ignore the African American vote.[47] Evidence of growing African American political power is the dramatic increase in the number of African American state legislators, which rose from 168 in 1970 to 599 in 2004.[48] Georgia

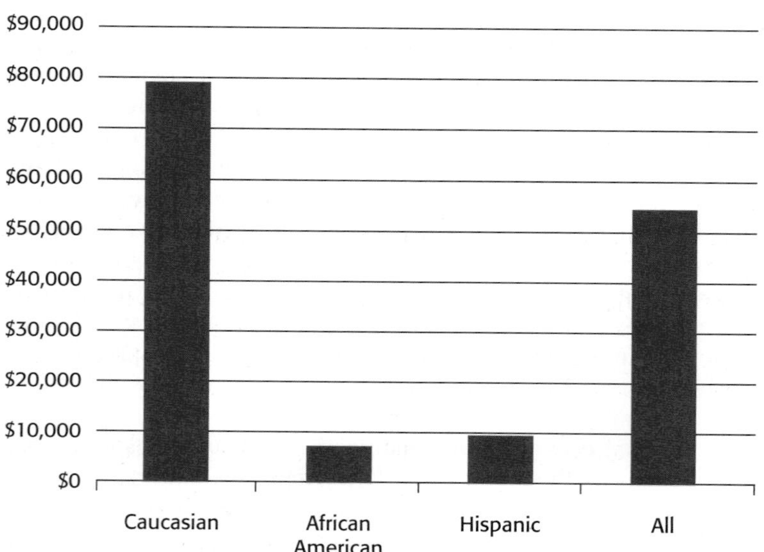

FIGURE 5–2
Median Net Worth of Households in the United States by Race, 2000.

SOURCE: U.S. Bureau of the Census, www.census.gov/prod/2003pubs/p70-88.pdf.

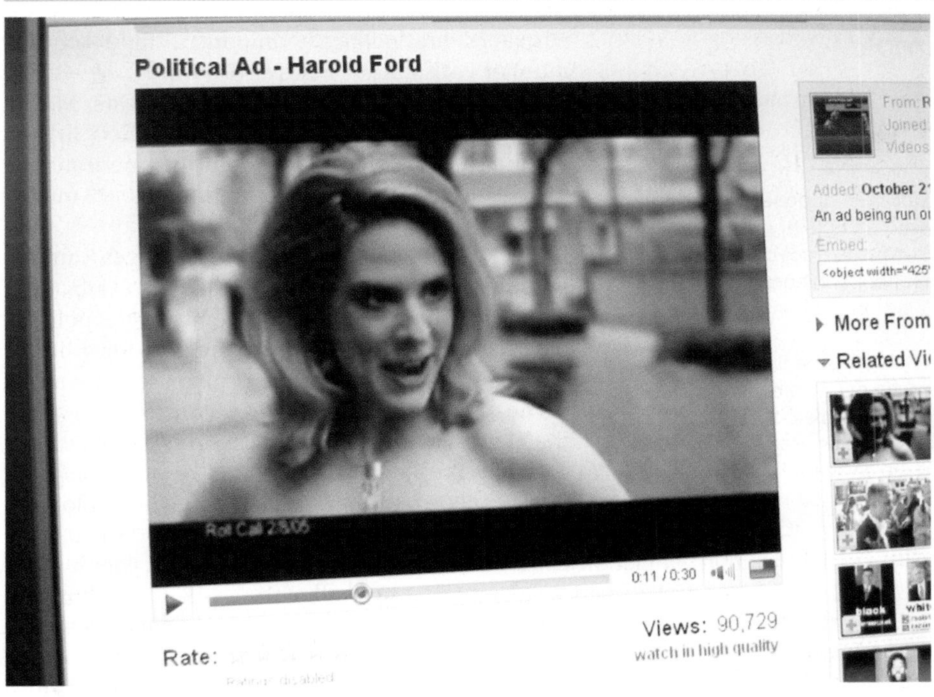

The Republican Party ad opposing Tennessee Democrat Harold Ford, who is black, took advantage of lingering racist fears of black men having relationships with white women, among other issues.

has 49 African American state legislators, the most of any state. Alabama, Louisiana, Maryland, Mississippi, New York, and South Carolina all have more than 30.[49]

The dramatic success of Illinois Democratic senator Barack Obama in several presidential primaries and caucuses in 2008 was due in part to his ability to secure large majorities of African American voters. Race was raised indirectly in the South Carolina primary by former president Bill Clinton,[50] and later by Clinton supporter Geraldine Ferraro, who said, "If Obama was a white man, he would not be in this position." Obama rejoined by denouncing the "slice and dice politics that's about race and gender and about this and that, and that's what Americans are tired of because they recognize that when we divide ourselves in that way we can't solve problems."[51] Obama also confronted the issue of racism directly in a major speech after media reports of his pastor Reverend Jeremiah Wright's inflammatory statements generated widespread attention. While Obama had very high levels of support among black voters, he also carried states with few black voters such as Iowa, Utah, Wyoming, Idaho, Alaska, Colorado, Kansas, Minnesota, North Dakota, Nebraska, Washington, Maine, Wisconsin, and Vermont. Barack Obama launched his general election campaign from Invesco Field, the large stadium where the Denver Broncos play football. The speech occurred on the forty-fifth anniversary of Martin Luther King's famous "I Have a Dream" speech. While Obama and his campaign did not make race a major theme of the speech or their campaign, pollsters and pundits speculated about what effect his race would have on voters. Exit polls found Obama did better among white voters than John Kerry had done in 2004 and substantially better among Latinos and African Americans. Among white voters age 18-29, Obama received 54 percent of the vote.[52] Obama got two-thirds of the Latino vote nationwide and 95 percent of the African-American vote. In his victory speech on election night delivered to over 200,000 people in Chicago's Grant Park, Obama recalled the events of the last century through the eyes of a 106 year old voter, Ann Nixon Cooper, who "was there for the buses in Montgomery, the hoses in Birmingham, a bridge in Selma and a preacher from Atlanta who told a people that We Shall Overcome."

Ken Salazar, elected to the U.S. Senate from Colorado in 2004, is the fourth U.S. senator of Latino descent in American history. Salazar replaced Ben Nighthorse Campbell, a Native American and Republican, who did not seek reelection. Salazar previously served two terms as Colorado attorney general.

Hispanics Hispanic Americans are not a monolithic group, and although they share a common linguistic heritage in Spanish, they often differ from one another depending on which country they or their forebears emigrated from. Cuban Americans, for instance, tend to be Republicans, while Mexican Americans and Puerto Ricans living on the

YOU WILL DECIDE

Should We Sample?

The Census Bureau, which conducts the once-a-decade count of all persons in the United States, proposed using random sampling rather than attempting to count all households in the 2000 census. Republicans opposed sampling because they considered it unreliable. The proposed sample approach would have contacted 90 percent of the households in a census tract consisting of roughly 1,700 individuals. The bureau would then check the accuracy of the sample by surveying 750,000 households throughout the nation and adjusting the final total accordingly.

The sampling approach responded to complaints about the flawed 1990 census, which cost $2.6 billion (a 400 percent increase over the cost of the 1980 census) and failed to account for 10 million people while double-counting 6 million others, according to a study by the National Academy of Sciences.

As we look to the next census in 2010, should we sample?

mainland are disproportionately Democrats.[53] Hispanics are politically important in a growing number of states. Nearly two-thirds of Cuban Americans live in Florida, especially in greater Miami. Mainland Puerto Ricans are concentrated in and around New York City; many Mexican Americans live in the Southwest and California. More than 13 million Hispanics live in California.[54]

A recent study found differences among Hispanics of Mexican, Puerto Rican, and Cuban descent in partisanship, ideology, and rates of political participation, but widespread support for a liberal domestic agenda, including increased spending on health care, crime and drug control, education, the environment, child services, and bilingual education.[55] But because Hispanics are not politically homogeneous, they are not a united voting bloc.

The many noncitizen Hispanics and the relative youth of the Hispanic population also diminish the group's political power. For example, 13.2 million foreign-born Hispanics are not citizens,[56] and of the estimated 11.6 million unauthorized immigrants, more than half—57 percent—are from Mexico.[57] This group cannot vote, nor can those under age 18, who make up a greater percentage of the Hispanic population than in other ethnic groups. Language problems also reduce Hispanic citizens' voter registration and turnout. The redrawing of legislative district boundaries after the 2000 census, despite their huge increase in population, disappointed Hispanic groups.[58] This has spurred lawsuits as Hispanic activists seek to eliminate gerrymandering (the drawing of district boundaries to benefit a group or party).

The Mexican-American Civil Rights Movement

Both major parties are aggressively cultivating Hispanic candidates. Several Hispanics have been cabinet members. Mel Martinez resigned as secretary of the Department of Housing and Urban Development (HUD) to run successfully for the U.S. Senate from

New Mexico governor Bill Richardson (D), himself a 2008 presidential candidate, seen here endorsing Barack Obama.

Florida in 2004. His endorsement of fellow U.S. senator John McCain was helpful to McCain's carrying the critical Florida presidential primary in 2008.[59] Ken Salazar, a Hispanic Democrat, was also elected to the Senate in 2004 from Colorado. Bob Mendez, a Democrat, was appointed to the Senate from New Jersey and then elected in a contested race in 2006. The 2008 presidential primaries and caucuses exposed a long-standing divide in the Democratic party between African Americans and Hispanics. Barack Obama did very well among African Americans, but Hispanics voted for Clinton in substantial proportions. In turn, Clinton won 67 percent of the Hispanic vote in California, 55 percent in Arizona, and 66 percent in Texas.[60] In the general election two-thirds of Latinos voted for Obama. Hispanic voters were important to his victories in New Mexico, Nevada, Colorado, and Florida.

THINKING IT THROUGH

The battle over sampling is not so much about *how* to count as *whom* to count. The proposed sampling method would have produced a more accurate count of inner-city Hispanics and African Americans—the most difficult to count. This would likely have resulted in a greater representation for Hispanics and African Americans in state legislatures and the U.S. House of Representatives. A more complete count of minorities could also mean that the Republican Party would lose a few seats in the House to Democrats, which is one reason Republicans generally opposed the sampling approach while Democrats favored it.

The constitutionality of sampling is also disputed, as the Constitution calls for an "actual enumeration" of the people. Democrats are quick to point out that under three presidents—Jimmy Carter, George Bush, and Bill Clinton—the Justice Department concluded that sampling is legal. Sampling as a method of determining population for congressional apportionment is not allowed under current law,* while methods similar to sampling in order to fill in data missing from the "actual enumeration" has been upheld in the Supreme Court.†

Questions

1. Why do you think sampling may result in higher counts of minorities?
2. Do you think it is possible to decide questions about representation without considering partisan politics?

**Department of Commerce et al. v. U.S. House of Representatives et al.*, 119 S.Ct. 765 (1999).
†*Utah v. Evans*, 122 S.Ct. 2191 (2002).

Asian Americans The Census Bureau classifies Asian Americans together for statistical purposes, but like Hispanics they show significant differences in culture, language, and political experience in the United States. Asian Americans include, among others, persons of Chinese, Japanese, Indian, Korean, Vietnamese, Filipino, and Thai origin, as well as persons from the Pacific Islands. As with Hispanics, there are differences among these subgroups.[61] For example, Japanese Americans were more likely to register as Democrats than Korean Americans or other Asian Americans. Japanese Americans also were somewhat more likely to vote than other Asian ethnic groups.[62]

Many Asian Americans have done well economically and educationally. Their income is well above the national median, and 49 percent have graduated from college, compared to 28 percent of whites and 18 percent of African Americans.[63] Asian Americans are becoming more politically important and more visible in politics. Gary Locke, the first Chinese American governor of a state in the continental United States, served two terms in Washington. Elaine Chao, who emigrated from China at age 8, served as secretary of labor in the Bush administration.

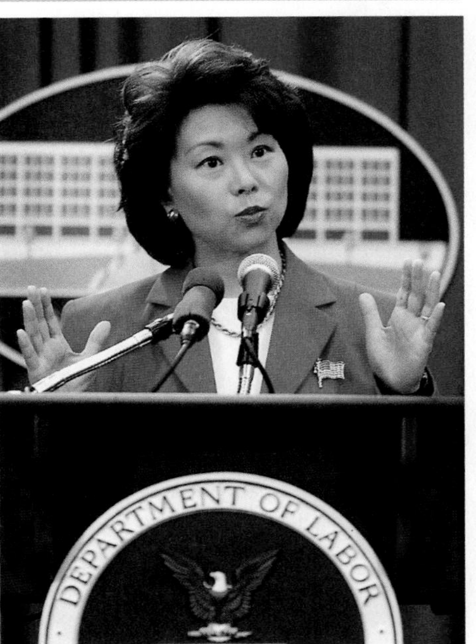

Elaine Chao, secretary of labor for all 8 years of the Bush administration, was the first Asian American to head this department.

The Ties of Ethnicity Except for Native Americans and the descendants of slaves, all U.S. citizens have immigrant ancestors who chose to come to the American continent. There have been two large waves of new immigrants to the United States. The first, 17.3 million people, came between 1900 and 1924. The second large wave is now underway. From 1991 to 2004, the United States has seen nearly 15.5 million immigrants, primarily from the Caribbean, Mexico, and Asian countries such as the Philippines, Vietnam, and China. Of this group, an estimated 10.5 million came into the country illegally.[64]

The foreign-born population in the United States increased from 14 million in 1980 to more than 35.6 million in 2005. Today there are more foreign-born people in the United States than ever before,[65] although at 10 percent, they represent a smaller proportion of the population than the 14.8 percent that was foreign born in 1890.[66]

Large numbers of immigrants can pose challenges to any political and social system. Immigrants are often a source of social conflict as they compete with more established groups for jobs, rights, political power, and influence.

Religion In many parts of the world, religious differences, especially when combined with disputes over territory or sovereignty, are a source of violence. The conflict between Israelis and Palestinians has motivated suicide bombers who kill Israeli civilians along with themselves, and Israelis have attacked Palestinian settlements and leaders. The war

GENERATION **NEXT**

Religion and Politics

It is interesting to analyze Generation Next not only in terms of attitudes and behaviors but also in light of important demographic variables such as religion. How does Generation Next compare to older age cohorts in religious affiliation, and what relationship, if any, existed for Generation Next between religion and partisanship and ideology?

Questions: "What is your religious preference—Protestant, Roman Catholic, Jewish, Muslim, Mormon, or an orthodox church such as the Greek or Russian Orthodox Church?" (Respondents were classified as "Other" if they answered Jewish, Muslim, Mormon, Orthodox, or any other religion.)

"Aside from weddings and funerals, how often do you attend religious services... more than once a week, once a week, once or twice a month, a few times a year, seldom, or never?" (Respondents who reported attending religious services "more than once a week," "once a week," or "once or twice a month" were classified as "Regular Attenders." Individuals who reported attending "a few times a year," "seldom," or "never" were classified as "Non-Attenders.")

Generation Next is the most likely of any age cohort to not claim a religious preference, with more than one in five people in this category. This was more than double the proportion of persons over age 45 with no preferred religious denomination. The proportion of Catholics showed much less variance between Generation Next and age cohorts over age 45. In contrast, for persons over age 60, the proportion seeing themselves as Protestants was larger. Consistent with these data is the finding that the age group that attends church the least is Generation Next, with 55 percent saying they are "non-attenders." Four of five members of Generation Next identify with a religious tradition.

When we look at party identification for the different categories of age and religion, we find generally little difference between Generation Next and other age cohorts. Catholics under age 45 are somewhat less likely to be Democrats than Catholics over age 45, but the real difference is that Catholics in Generation Next are less likely to be Independent (13%) and more likely to be Republicans (43%), while a plurality (45%) are Democrats.

Generation Next across all denomination types is consistently most likely to say they are moderate (42–46%), even more so than older cohorts. Those in Generation Next who are Protestant are more likely to see themselves as conservative, Catholics are more evenly divided between conservative and liberal, and all others in Generation Next are more likely to be liberal than conservative.

QUESTIONS

1. Why is Generation Next less affiliated with a particular religion than older age cohorts?
2. Does the lower level of regular church attendance among those in Generation Next have implications for churches as sources of information relevant to politics?

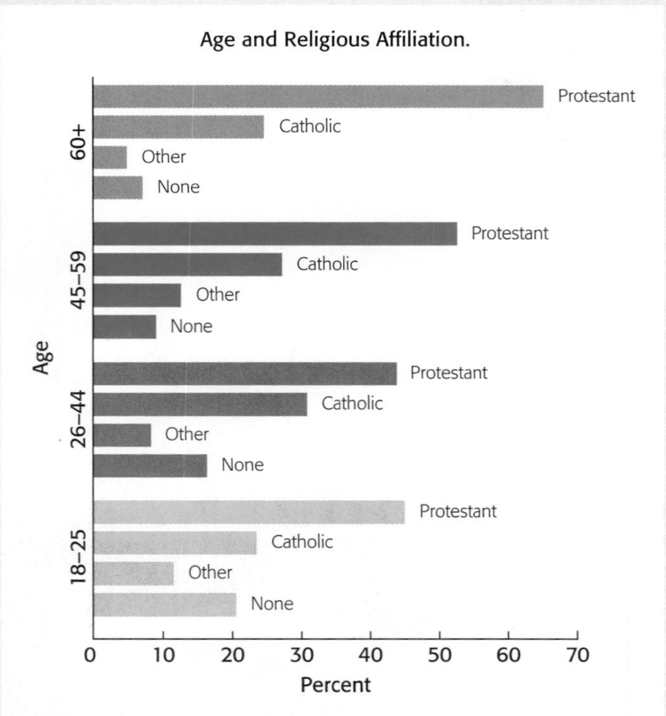

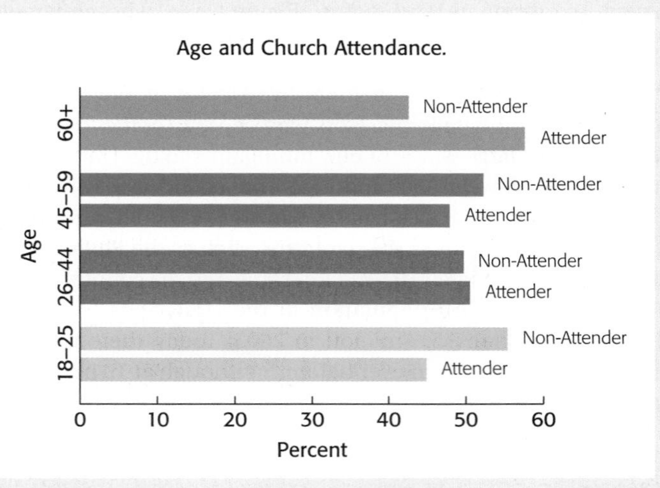

between India and Pakistan over Kashmir is largely a religious battle between Muslims and Hindus, as are the conflicts between Muslims and Christians in Indonesia and Nigeria. Afghanistan, Lebanon, Northern Ireland, Sri Lanka, and Sudan have also experienced intense religious conflicts in recent years. The Shi'ite–Sunni conflict among different branches of Islam threatens the stability of the new government in Iraq.

Jews have often been the target of religious discrimination and persecution (anti-Semitism), which reached its greatest intensity in the Holocaust of the 1940s, during which the Nazis murdered an estimated 6 million Jews.[67] The United States has not been immune from such hatred, despite its principle of religious freedom. In 1838, Governor Lilburn W. Boggs of Missouri issued an extermination order that made legal the killing of any Mormons in the state.[68]

Our government is founded on the premise that religious liberty flourishes when there is no predominant or official faith, which is why the framers of the Constitution did not sanction a national church. In fact, James Madison wrote in *The Federalist*, No. 51, "In a free government the security for civil rights must be the same as that for religious rights. It consists in the one case in the multiplicity of interests, and in the other in the multiplicity of sects" (see the Appendix).

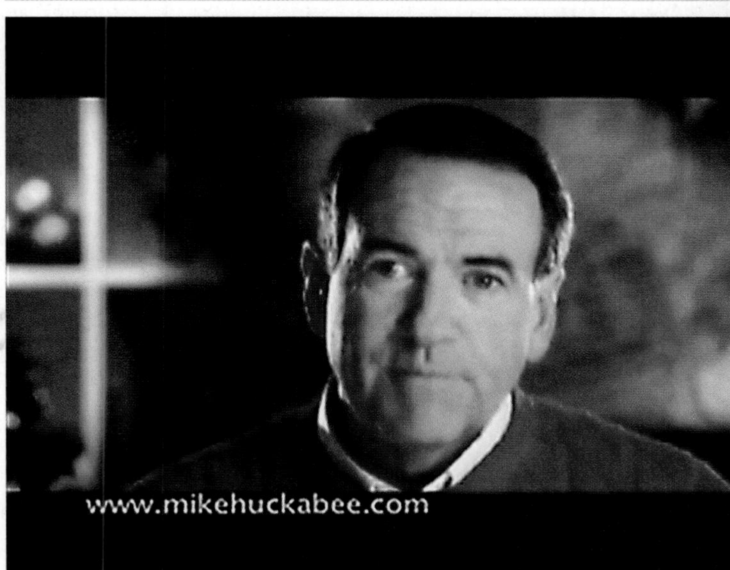

Republican presidential primary candidate Mike Huckabee, an ordained minister, often invoked his Christianity during his campaign. This advertisement ran during the Christmas season and some saw a symbolic cross over Huckabee's right shoulder.

The absence of an official church does not mean that religion is unimportant in American politics; indeed, there were established churches in individual states in this country until the 1830s. Some observers contend that "the root of American political and social values . . . is the distinctive Puritanism of the early New England settlers."[69] Politicians frequently refer to God in their speeches or demonstrate their piety in other ways.

At one time, people thought voters' religious preferences could prevent a Catholic from being elected president. John F. Kennedy's election in 1960 resolved the issue of whether a Catholic would put aside religious teachings if they conflicted with constitutional obligations. He said, "I am not the Catholic candidate for President. I am the Democratic party's candidate for President who happens also to be Catholic. I do not speak for my church on public matters, and the church does not speak for me."[70] Nevertheless, a candidate's religion may still become an issue today if the candidate's religious convictions on sensitive issues such as abortion threaten to conflict with public obligations. In 2008, Barack Obama distanced himself from his minister, Jeremiah Wright, after Wright's heated statements generated widespread negative media attention. In an earlier speech on race, Obama condemned the controversial and divisive statements while pointing to positive attributes of Reverend Wright. Obama said, "He strengthened my faith, officiated my wedding, and baptized my children . . . I can no more disown him than I can disown the black community. I can no more disown him than I can my white grandmother—a woman who helped raise me."[71] Later in the primary season, Reverend Wright again garnered widespread media attention after discussing his controversial views in interviews and media events. Obama responded by saying "I am outraged by the comments that were made and saddened by the spectacle that we saw . . . comments were divisive and destructive and I believe they end up giving comfort to those that prey on hate . . . and they certainly do not portray accurately my values and beliefs."[72]

Religion has also been an important catalyst for political change. The Catholic church helped overthrow communism in parts of eastern Europe. Black churches provided many of the leaders in the American civil rights movement. As Taylor Branch explains in his history of the civil rights movement, the black church "served not only as a place of worship but also as a bulletin board to a people who owned no organs of communication, a credit union to those without banks, and even a kind of people's court."[73] African American ministers, such as the Reverend Martin Luther King, Jr., became leaders of the civil rights movement; others, such as Jesse Jackson and more recently Al Sharpton, have run for national office. Hence, religion can be not only a source of personal values but also a foundation for political activity.

More recently, political activity among fundamentalist Christians has increased. Led by ministers such as Pat Robertson and Focus on the Family leader James Dobson, evangelicals, sometimes called **fundamentalists,** are an important force in the Republican

fundamentalists
Conservative Christians who as a group have become more active in politics in the last two decades and were especially influential in the 2000 and 2004 presidential elections.

FIGURE 5–3
Religious Groups in the United States.

SOURCE: U.S. Religous Landscape Survey, Pew Forum on Religion & Public Life, http://religions.pewforum.org. Copyright 2008 Pew Research Center.

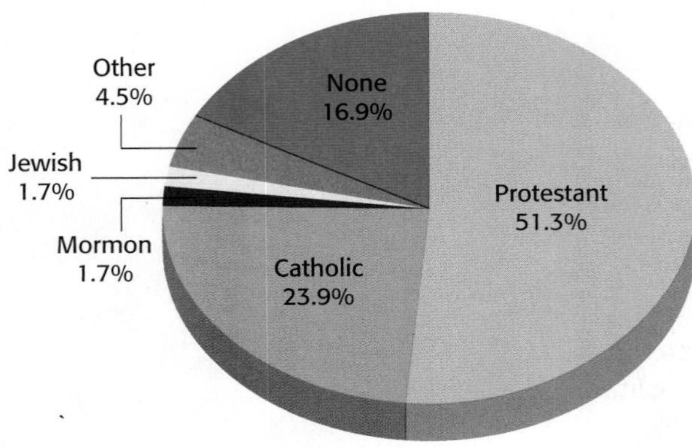

party and in some local governments.[74] Their agenda includes the return of school prayer, the outlawing of abortion, restrictions on homosexuals, opposition to gun control, and opposition to the teaching of evolution and sex education in public schools.

Many American adults take their religious beliefs seriously, more than do citizens of other democracies.[75] About 32 percent attend houses of worship at least once a week, 12 percent almost every week, and 12 percent more at least once a month.[76] Religion, like ethnicity, is a *shared identity.* People identify themselves as Baptist, Catholic, Jewish, or Buddhist. Sometimes religious attendance or nonattendance rather than belonging to a particular religion or denomination determines attitudes toward issues. "Among both Catholics and Protestants, opposition to abortion increases with frequency of church attendance, but the percentages expressing pro-choice and pro-life sentiments are quite similar for the Catholic and Protestant groups."[77]

The United States houses a tremendous variety of religious denominations. About half the people in the United States describe themselves as Protestant (see Figure 5–3). The largest Protestant denomination is Baptist, followed by Methodists, Lutherans, Presbyterians, Pentecostals, and Episcopalians. Because Protestants are divided among so many different churches, Catholics have the largest single membership in the United States, constituting nearly a quarter of the population.[78] Jews represent about 2 percent of the population.[79] Muslims number more than 1,100,000, which is less than one-half of one percent of the U.S. population.[80]

Religion is important in American politics in part because people of particular religions are concentrated in a few states. Catholics number over half the population of Rhode Island.[81] Baptists represent 16 percent of the American population, yet they account for roughly a third of the population of Mississippi and Alabama.[82] Mormons represent less than 2 percent of the American population but two-thirds of the population of Utah.[83] The state of New York has the highest percentage of Jews with 9 percent; the New York City metro area is 11 percent Jewish.[84]

In recent presidential elections, most Protestants voted Republican, while most Catholics and Jews voted Democratic.[85] However, in 2004, Bush received a majority of the Catholic vote and increased his majority among Protestants to 59 percent. Kerry received 75 percent of the Jewish vote. In 2008, McCain got 54 percent of the all Protestants, but Obama did better among Protestants than either Gore or Kerry in 2000 and 2004. Obama received a majority of the Catholic vote.[88] The perception among many Catholics and Jews that the Democratic party is more open to them helps explain the strength of their Democratic identification. For at least several decades, Democrats won the loyalty of many Catholics by their willingness to nominate Al Smith for the presidency in 1928 and John Kennedy in 1960. Jewish voters' long-standing identification with the Democratic Party may have been reinforced by Al Gore's selection of Joseph Lieberman to be his running mate in 2000.

Religious groups vary in their rates of political participation. In recent elections Jews have the highest rate of reported voter turnout, more than 90 percent in 2000 and 2004, while those who claim no religious affiliation have the lowest, an average of 60 percent in 2000 and 2004.[87] In 2008, even with strong efforts by the McCain campaign to court Jewish voters, Obama received 78 percent of the Jewish vote.[86]

Religion can be related to other politically important characteristics. For instance, Jews are the most prosperous and best educated of any ethnic or religious group. Nearly 59 percent of Jewish adults are college graduates, compared to 34 percent of mainline Protestants and 26 percent of Catholics,[89] and 35 percent of Jews in the United States have a postgraduate education.[90] Religion is a cross-cutting cleavage in American politics; differences do not reinforce one another. On the basis of income and education, we might expect Jews to be Republicans, but 79 percent of American Jews voted for Al Gore in 2000.[91] Catholics had cross-pressures in 2004 because John

and family services. They also identify work and family issues such as day care, maternity leave, and equal treatment in the workplace as important.[103] Other gender issues, some of them focal points in recent elections, include reproductive rights and restrictions on pornography, gun control, and sexual harassment.[104]

There are serious income inequalities between men and women. Nearly twice as many women than men have an annual income of less than $15,000, and nearly three times as many men as women make more than $75,000 a year.[105] Because an increasing number of women today are the sole breadwinners for their families, the implications of this low income level are significant. Women earn on average less than men for the same work. Even among college graduates aged 25 to 34, women earn an average of 84 cents for every dollar earned by men of the same age and education level.[106] After controlling for characteristics such as job experience, education, occupation, and other measures of productivity, a U.S. Census Bureau study shows that wage discrimination between the genders is 77 cents on every dollar.[107] As age increases, the earnings gap widens. Women have reached parity with men in attending law schools, but only about 17 percent of partners in law firms are women.[108] In business schools women constitute less than a third of entering classes,[109] and among the largest 100 companies in the United States, women make up only 17 percent of the boards of directors.[110]

Sexual Orientation

Civil Rights and Gay Adoption

The modern movement for expanded rights for gays and lesbians traces its roots to 1969, when New York City police raided the Stonewall Inn, a bar in Greenwich Village, and a riot ensued.[111]

The precise number of homosexuals in the United States is unclear. The gay and lesbian communities offer a figure of 10 percent; other estimates are much lower.[112] One source estimates that 2.5 percent of men and 1.8 percent of women are gay or bisexual.[113] Whatever its overall size, the gay and lesbian community has become important politically in several cities, notably San Francisco. Its lobbying power has increased noticeably in many states as well, and being gay or lesbian is no longer a barrier to election in many places.

The political agenda for gay and lesbian advocacy groups includes fighting discrimination, such as the military's "don't ask, don't tell" policy. On some fronts, the groups have been successful. Many local governments and private employers now grant health care and other benefits for same-sex domestic partners. Cities, counties, and states have passed antidiscrimination statutes protecting people from discrimination in housing and employment on the basis of sexual orientation. Groups like the Human Rights Campaign advocate eliminating restrictions based on sexual orientation. Hate crimes against gays and lesbians have led some to propose including sexual orientation in federal hate crimes legislation.[114]

Some states have passed legislation granting gay and lesbian couples "civil union" status, conferring many of the legal benefits of marriage. State supreme courts in Vermont and Massachusetts have ruled that not allowing gay couples to marry is discriminatory and unconstitutional.[115] In 2008, California's supreme court struck down the state's ban on gay marriage.[116] This lead to legal same-gender marriages in California in addition to some local governments in other states which have also issued marriage licenses to gay couples.[117] An intensely fought ballot initiative to reverse the California court decision and constitutionally ban same-gender marriages was narrowly passed by California voters in the 2008 general election. Proponents of gay marriage once again quickly brought legal challenges to the successful proposition and vow to continue their fight for legal gay marriage.

Rosie O'Donnell, a gay parent, is a vocal advocate for gays who want to adopt children.

These efforts have also produced some backlash. Congress passed the Defense of Marriage Act in 1996, which excludes same-sex spouses from federal benefits. Conservative groups with support from conservative Protestants, Catholics, and Mormons enacted initiatives in 20 states in 2004 and 2006 defining marriage as a union between a man and a woman. Only in Arizona was such an amendment defeated.

The courts have also been drawn into the battle over sexual orientation. In 2000, the Supreme Court ruled 5 to 4 that requiring the Boy Scouts of America to allow gays to occupy local leadership positions violated Scouts' First Amendment right to freedom of association.[118] However, just three years later, the Supreme Court's decision in *Lawrence v. Texas* overturned state laws against sodomy on privacy grounds.[119] Both critics and supporters of the Court's decision contended that it could provide a basis for a more expansive set of court decisions on same-sex marriage.

Family Structure

Over the past half-century, the typical American family (mother and father married, with children in the home) has become anything but typical. The traditional family had several key characteristics: it married early, had children, and stayed together through thick and thin.

Marriage itself used to be essential to be a family at all. From 1996 to 2002, however, the number of American adults who live with someone of the opposite sex without being married increased by 50 percent.[120] In 2006, 5.3 percent of households had unmarried partners. Living together raises public policy questions, such as whether the live-in partner is eligible for employment benefits and welfare payments.

Marriage also used to occur earlier in life, but people now marry later: The average age for first marriage for men is 27; for women it is 26.[121] Yet marrying later has not reduced the divorce rates.

Children were also essential to the traditional families, but birthrates have been falling for decades. Birthrates in the United States dropped in the late 1960s and 1970s. In the early 1960s, a woman statistically averaged about 3.5 children. By 2001, that number dropped to 2.1 children, barely meeting the 2.1 needed to replace the population. In other words, if the current trend continues, the native-born population will actually decrease over time.[122] Some other countries have even lower average fertility rates per woman: Japan 1.3, Italy 1.3, Spain 1.3, and Sweden 1.6.[123]

LEARNING **OBJECTIVE**

6 Evaluate the roles of education, income, class, and age in American politics.

Finally, the traditional family stayed together, but the divorce rate has nearly doubled since 1950.[124] Today it is estimated that about half of all marriages will end in divorce.[125] Divorce is one reason why the number of households headed by women has risen. Attitudes about the role of women in marriage and the family have also changed. In 1972, one-third of American adults thought a woman belonged in the home and should not work outside it, but in 1998, only one-sixth felt this way.[126]

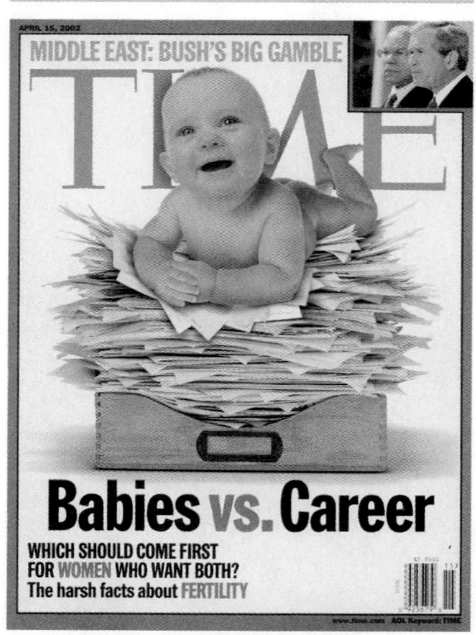

The risk of having children later in life has recently been the subject of cover stories in news magazines.

Education

Differences in education affect not only economic well-being but political participation and involvement as well. Thomas Jefferson wrote of education, "Enlighten the people generally, and tyranny and oppressions of body and mind will vanish like evil spirits at the dawn of day."[127] Most American students are educated in public schools. Nine of every ten students in kindergarten through high school attend public schools, and more than three of four college students are in public institutions.[128]

In 1992, for the first time the number of American college graduates surpassed the number of persons who did not graduate from high school.[129] Just over half of all U.S. adults have not gone to college, though many college students assume that almost everyone goes to college. Around 28 percent of whites are college graduates, compared to 17 percent of African Americans and 12 percent of Hispanics; roughly 19 percent of African Americans and 41 percent of all Hispanics left school before completing high school (see Figure 5–5).[130]

FIGURE 5–5
Educational Attainment in the United States.

SOURCE: U.S. Census Bureau, *Educational Attainment in the United States: 2007*, www.census.gov/population/www/socdemo/education/cps2007.html.

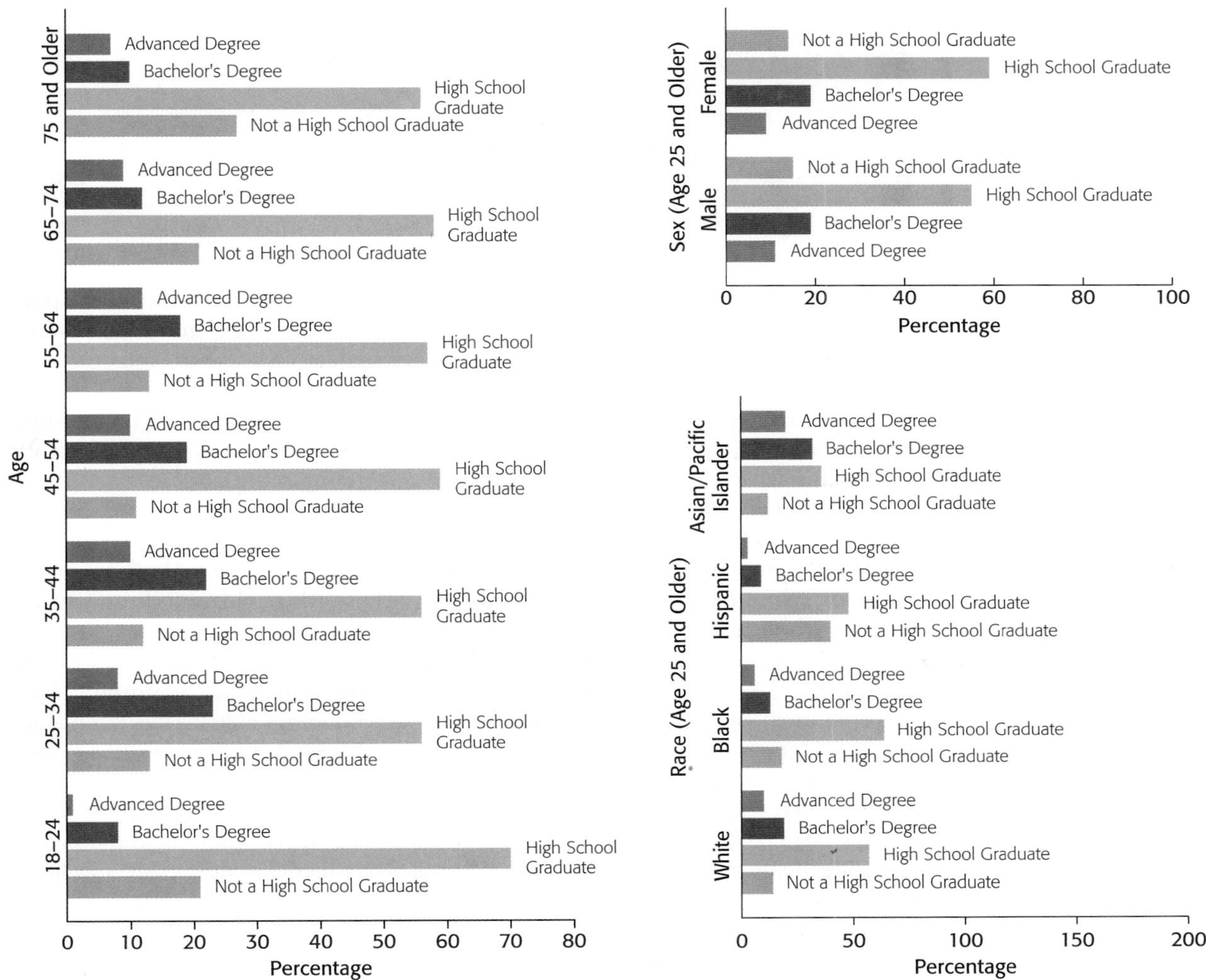

Education is one of the most important variables in predicting political participation, confidence in dealing with government, and awareness of issues. Education is also related to the acquisition of democratic values. People who have failed to learn the prevailing norms of American society are far more likely to express opposition to democratic and capitalist ideals than those who are well educated and politically knowledgeable.[131]

Wealth and Income

The United States is a wealthy nation. Indeed, to some knowledgeable observers, "the most striking thing about the United States has been its phenomenal wealth."[132] Most American citizens lead comfortable lives. They eat and live well and have first-class medical care. But the unequal distribution of wealth and income results in political divisions and conflicts.

Wealth, which we defined earlier as the total value of someone's possessions, is more concentrated than income (annual earnings). The wealthiest families hold most of the property and other forms of wealth such as stocks and savings. Historically,

FIGURE 5–6
Inflation Adapted Change in Median Family Income, 1980–2005.

SOURCE: Harold W. Stanley and Richard G. Niemi, *Vital Statistics on American Politics, 2007–2008* (CQ Press, 2008), pp. 374–375.

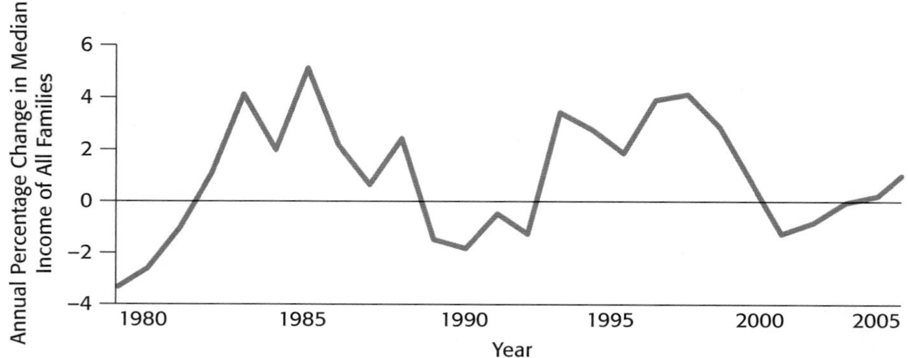

concentrated wealth fosters an aristocracy. Thomas Jefferson sought to break up the "aristocracy of wealth" by changing from laws based on *primogeniture* (which give the eldest son exclusive right to inherit his father's estate) to laws that encouraged or compelled people to divide their estates equally among all their children. Jefferson wanted to encourage an "aristocracy of virtue and talent" through a public school system open to all for the primary grades and for the best students through the university level.[133]

The framers of the Constitution recognized the dangers of an unequal concentration of wealth. "The most common and durable source of factions has been the various and unequal distribution of property," wrote James Madison in *The Federalist,* No. 10 (reprinted in the Appendix). "Those who hold, and those who are without property, have ever formed distinct interests in society." Madison was right. Economic differences often lead to conflict, and we remain divided politically along economic lines. Aside from race, income may be the single most important factor in explaining views on issues, partisanship, and ideology. Most rich people are Republicans, most poor people are Democrats, and this has been true since at least the Great Depression of the 1930s.

Between the 1950s and the 1970s, inflation-adjusted income doubled. More recently, as Figure 5–6 shows, inflation-adjusted income has gone up and down.[134] Why has the pattern changed? Some economists cite higher energy costs, low levels of personal savings, and the worldwide slowdown in productivity.[135] Others point to the reduction of graduated income tax rates, the weakening of unions, and the shift from low-skill to high-skill jobs.[136]

As of 2007, 12.6 percent of the population fell below the poverty line and had the lowest per capita incomes, after factoring in family size.[137] In 2007, the official poverty level for a family of four with two children was an income below $21,027.[138] Families headed by a single female are more than two times as likely to fall below the poverty line than families headed by a single male, with 29 percent of all households headed by females falling below the poverty line.[139] Almost 35 percent of the poor are children under age 18, and many appear to be trapped in a cycle of poverty (see Figure 5–7).[140] African American and Hispanic children are more than twice as likely to be poor as white children.[141]

The definition of poverty is itself political, and a change in the definition of poverty can make it appear that there are more or fewer poor people than before. Whether we define poverty at a lower or higher level of income also determines who becomes eligible for some government programs. The poverty classification is intended to identify persons who cannot meet a minimum standard in such basics as housing, food, and medical care. Regardless of how we define poverty, however, the poor are a minority who lack political power. They vote less than wealthier people and are less confident and organized in dealing with politics and government. The gap between rich and poor is increasing.[142] Income is related to participation in politics. People who need the most help from government are the least likely to participate. They are also the most likely to favor social welfare programs.

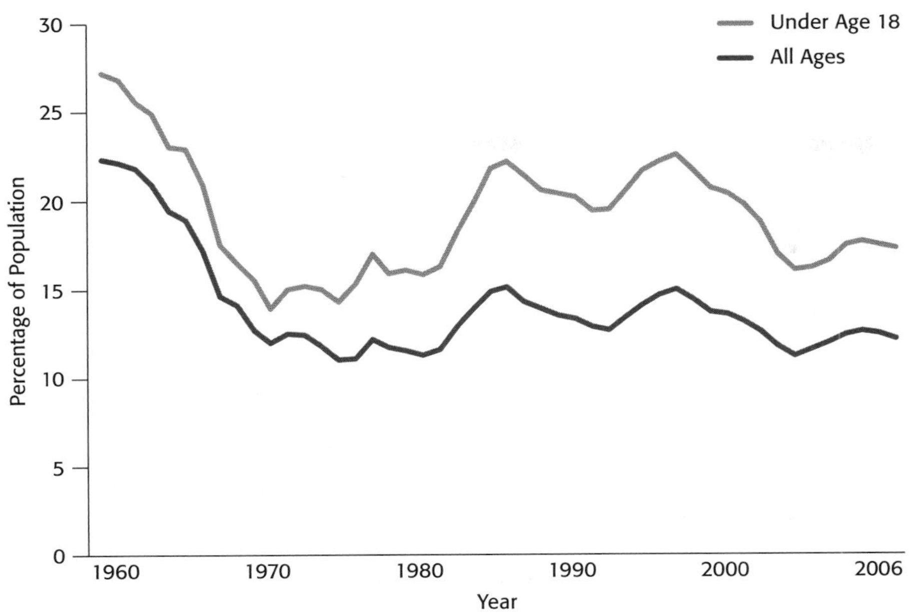

FIGURE 5–7
Percentage of Americans Living in Poverty, by Age, 1959–2006.

SOURCE: http://www.census.gov/hhes/www/poverty/histpov/hstpov2.html. Reports, P60–226, *Income, Poverty, and Health Insurance in the United States 2003* (U.S. Government Printing Office, 2004).

The distribution of income in a society can have important consequences for democratic stability. If enough people believe that only the few at the top of the economic ladder can hope to earn enough for an adequate standard of living, domestic unrest and even revolution may follow.

In the United States, greater wealth and higher income is correlated with being Republican and favoring low taxes. There are, of course, wealthy Democrats. In 2008, higher-income Democrats and Independents favored Obama in the presidential nomination campaign. Wealth and affluence is also correlated to self-confidence in dealing with bureaucracy and government. Another characteristic associated with confidence in dealing with government is education.

gross domestic product (GDP)
The total output of all economic activity in the nation, including goods and services.

Occupation

In Jefferson's day and for several generations after, most people in the United States worked primarily on farms, but by 1900, the United States had become the world's leading industrial nation. As workers moved from farms to cities to find better-paying jobs, the cities rapidly grew. Labor conditions, including child labor, the length of the workweek, and safety conditions in mines and factories, became important political issues. New technology, combined with abundant natural and human resources, meant that the American **gross domestic product (GDP)** rose, after adjusting for inflation, by more than 460 percent from 1960 to 2007.[143] Gross domestic product is one measure of the size of a country's economy. It is the total market value of goods and services produced in that country in a specified period of time.

Women continue to be less frequently employed as managers or supervisors and more often as clerical or service workers. They are also still paid less than men doing the same kind of work.

The United States has entered what Daniel Bell, a noted sociologist, labeled the "postindustrial" phase of its development. "A postindustrial society, being primarily a technical society, awards less on the basis of inheritance or property...than on education and skill."[144] *Knowledge* is the organizing device of the postindustrial era. Postindustrial societies have greater affluence and a class structure less defined along traditional labor-versus-management lines. Figure 5–8,

FIGURE 5–8
Occupational Groups, 2002.

SOURCE: U.S. Bureau of the Census, *Statistical Abstract of the United States, 2008* (U.S. Government Printing Office, 2008), p. 388.

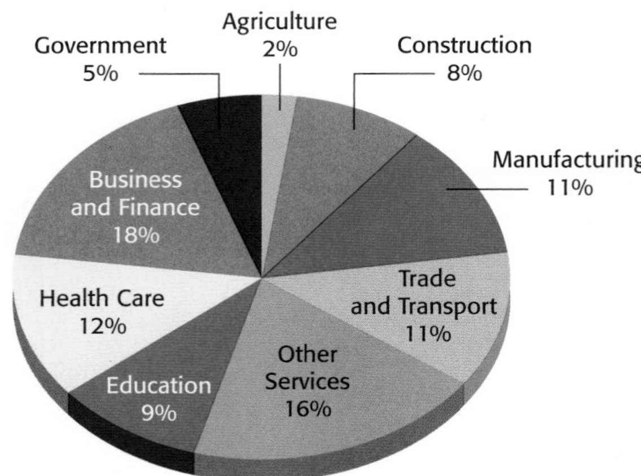

which shows the percentage of American workers in various occupations, demonstrates the changing dynamics of the country's labor force.

The white-collar sector of our economy has grown tremendously over the past 50 years. This sector includes managers, accountants, and lawyers, as well as professionals and technicians in such rapid-growth areas as computers, communications, finance, insurance, and research. A dramatic decline in the number of people engaged in agriculture and a more modest decline in the number of people in manufacturing (which together make up the blue-collar sector) has accompanied this shift. Today agriculture employs less than 1 percent of working adults, and manufacturing employs only 6.5 percent.[145] Governments are among the biggest employers, with federal, state, and local governments accounting for more than 19 percent of our gross domestic product.[146]

Men hold most blue-collar jobs.[147] We have noted already that women generally earn less than men of the same age and education. Occupations in which women predominate, such as teaching and clerical work, are generally lower-paying than industrial or management jobs. And as women try to advance in their careers, especially in management, they encounter a barrier that has been referred to as the "glass ceiling."

Social Class

Why do U.S. citizens not divide themselves into social classes as Europeans do? American workers have not formed their own political party, nor does class seem to dominate our political life. Karl Marx's categories of *proletariat* (those who sell their labor) and *bourgeoisie* (those who own or control the means of production) are far less important here than they have been in Europe. Still, we do have social classes and what social scientists call **socioeconomic status (SES)**—a division of the population based on occupation, income, and education.

Most American adults say they are "middle class." Few admit to seeing themselves as lower class or upper class. In many other industrial democracies, large proportions of the population think of themselves as "working class" rather than middle class.[148]

What constitutes the "middle class" in the United States is highly subjective. For instance, some individuals perform working-class tasks (such as plumbing), but their income places them in the middle class or even the upper-middle class. A schoolteacher's income is below that of many working-class jobs, but in terms of status, teaching ranks among middle-class jobs.

People may define themselves as middle class because the American dream promises upward mobility. Or their responses may reflect the hostility many feel toward organized labor. In any case, compared to many countries, class divisions in the United States are less defined and less important to politics. As political scientist Seymour Martin Lipset has written, "The American social structure and values foster an emphasis on competitive individualism, an orientation that is not congruent with class consciousness, support for socialist or social democratic parties, or a strong union movement."[149]

socioeconomic status (SES)
A division of population based on occupation, income, and education.

Age

We are living longer, a phenomenon that has been dubbed the "graying of America" (Figure 5–9). This demographic change has increased the proportion of the population over age 65 and increased the demand for medical care, retirement benefits, and a host of other age-related services. Persons over age 65 constitute less than 13 percent of the population yet account for more than 26 percent of the total medical expenditures.[150] With the decreasing birthrate discussed earlier, the graying of America has given rise to concern about maintaining an adequate workforce in the future. Other industrialized countries are also experiencing this demographic shift.[151]

Older adults are more politically aware and vote more often than younger ones, making them a potent political force. Their vote is especially important in western

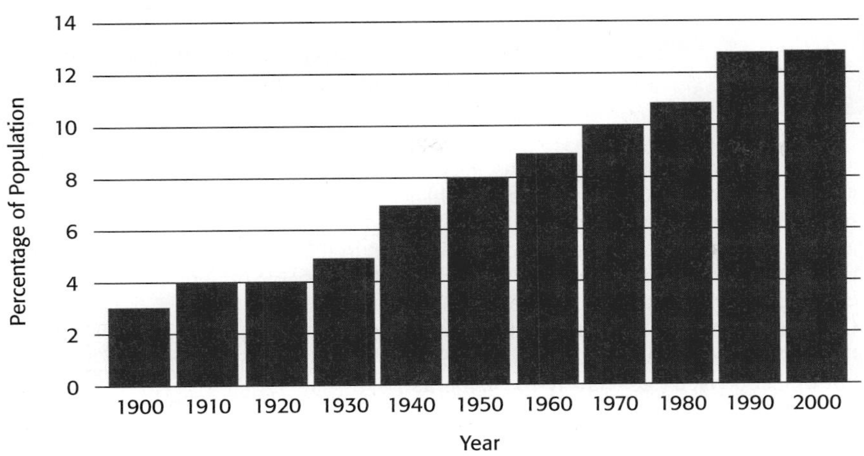

FIGURE 5–9
Percentage of Population over Age 65, 1900–2000.

SOURCE: U.S. Bureau of the Census, www.census.gov/statab/hist/HS-03.pdf.

states and in Florida, the state with the largest proportion of people over age 65. The "gray lobby" not only votes in large numbers but also has four political assets not found in other age groups that make it politically powerful: disposable income, discretionary time, a clear focus on issues, and effective organization. When older voters compete for their share of the budget pie, the young, minorities, and the poor often lose out.[152]

Age is important to politics in two additional ways: lifecycle and generational effects. *Lifecycle effects* have shown that as people become middle-aged, they become more politically conservative, less mobile, and more likely to participate in politics. As they age further and rely more on the government for services, they tend to grow more liberal.[153] Young people, in contrast, are more mobile and less concerned about the delivery of government services.

Several groups made registering younger voters and getting them to the polls a high priority in 2004. Exit polls from the 2004 election found that turnout among 18–29 year olds rose from 42 percent in 2000 to 51 percent in 2004. An estimated 4.6 million more 18–29 year olds voted in 2004. But because overall turnout was also higher in 2004, the proportion of the voters aged 18 to 29 remained constant at 17 percent.[154]

Generational effects in politics arise when a particular generation has had experiences that make it politically distinct. For example, for those who lived through it, the Great Depression of the 1930s shaped their lifelong views of political

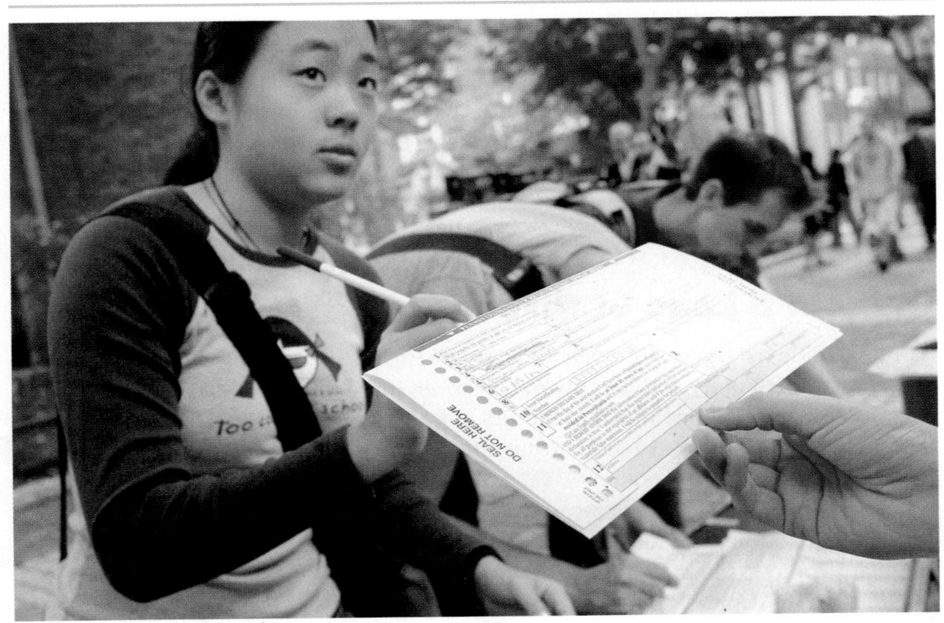

As was the case in 2004, the 2008 election cycle saw an increase in the number of young persons registering to vote.

HOW OTHER NATIONS GOVERN

Aging Populations

The demographics of a nation influences its politics and policy. The figures summarized here come from the United Nations Population Division. They compare our sample of countries in terms of median age, and *the dependency ratio*, or the ratio of the population over age 65 to the working-age population. This ratio measures the extent to which a country has a working population and shows the number of younger people who will be able to support the older population.

The median age for all countries in this sample rose a little less than 3 years between 1950 and 2000, but is projected to climb more than 11 years between 2000 and 2050. The United States and the United Kingdom had the highest median age in 1950, but by 2000, Japan's was higher. Median age is influenced by not only public health but by birthrates. Mexico, with the lowest median age of the sample countries in 1950, is projected to have a higher median age than the United States in 2050. One reason is that Mexico's birthrate was the highest of the sample countries in 1950 but by 2050 will be essentially the same as the rate in China, India, the United States, and the United Kingdom.

This kind of information is relevant to politics and policy because it influences the kinds of demands people place on governments for health care and other services. A shrinking population may not have enough workers to keep an economy viable, perhaps forcing older people to work more years than they had planned on doing. In the United States this issue has surfaced in debates over the long-term viability of Social Security.

QUESTIONS

1. How might a nation's median age influence where global commerce will choose to locate?
2. What are some policy issues associated with a high old-age dependency ratio?
3. Do these data on dependency ratios have any bearing on policies to encourage or discourage people from having children?

Median Age and Dependency Ratio in Comparative Perspective.

	World	China	India	Japan	Mexico	Nigeria	United Kingdom	United States
Median Age								
1950	23.9	23.9	21.3	22.3	18.7	19.1	34.6	30
2000	26.7	30	22.7	41.3	23.4	17.1	37.7	35.3
2050	38.1	45	38.6	54.9	43.1	28	43.4	41.1
Old-Age Dependency Ratio								
1950	9	7	5	8	6	5	16	13
2000	11	10	8	25	8	6	24	19
2050	25	39	21	74	34	9	40	34

SOURCE: United Nations Population Division, 2006 Revision Population Database.

parties, issues, and political leaders. Some members of this generation saw Franklin D. Roosevelt as the leader who saved the country by pulling it out of the Depression; others felt he sold the country down the river by launching too many government programs. More recently and to a lesser extent, the baby boomers shared a common and distinctive political experience. These Americans came of age politically in the 1960s and 1970s during the civil rights movement and the Vietnam War.

Unity in a Land of Diversity

As remarkable as American diversity is, the existence of a strong and widely shared sense of national unity and identity may be even more remarkable. Economic and social mobility have unified much of the U.S. population. Education has been an important part of this, as was the nationalizing influence of World War II. We are united by our shared commitment to democratic values, economic opportunity, work ethic, and the American dream. Social scientists used to speak of the "melting pot," meaning that as various ethnic groups associate with other groups, they are assimilated into U.S. society and come to share democratic values such as majority rule, individualism, and the ideal of the United States as a land of opportunity. Critics have argued that the melting pot idea assumes there is something wrong with differences between groups, and that these distinctions should be discouraged. In its place, they propose the concept of the "salad bowl," in which "though the salad is an entity, the lettuce can still be distinguished from the chicory, the tomatoes from the cabbage."[155]

As this chapter has demonstrated, regional, social, and economic differences have important political consequences. They influence public opinion, participation, voting, interest groups, and political parties. At the same time, our country has achieved a sense of unity despite our remarkable diversity.

More broadly, education and age are especially important predictors of citizen engagement and participation. As we have shown, education is also associated with having confidence in dealing with government and asserting rights and liberties. As people move through the lifecycle, they become more involved in their communities and are more likely to vote. The 2008 election was noteworthy for the rise in proportions of young people who voted and sought to influence how others voted. Voters under thirty years of age were more than twice as likely to vote Obama as McCain. Obama's vote share of these voters was the highest share of any candidate since exit polls reported the vote by age in 1976.[156]

CHAPTER **SUMMARY**

1 Describe the opportunities and challenges posed by the diversity of the American population.

The character of a political society and its social environment are important to understanding its politics and government. Because the United States is a large continental nation with abundant natural resources and political freedom, immigrants from many nations have come here. The widely shared perceptions of economic opportunity have also fostered a diverse polity. Social and economic differences can also foster conflict and in some countries violence. The continuing controversy over illegal immigration in the United States is an example of such a conflict. The laws of the country have fostered religious diversity, and residential and settlement patterns have reinforced ethnic identify for some groups.

2 Explain how geography affects politics.

Geography, room to grow, abundant natural resources, wealth, and relative isolation from foreign entanglements help explain American politics and traditions, including the notions of manifest destiny, ethnocentrism, and isolationism.

3 Describe the political evolution of the South.

Until recently, the South was a distinct region in the United States, in large part because of its agricultural base and its history of slavery and troubled race relations. With migration from other parts of the country and the impact of the civil rights movement, it is becoming more Republican.

4 Evaluate the role of population density and where people live in American politics.

Recently, the most significant migration in the United States has been from cities to suburbs. Today many large U.S. cities are increasingly poor, African American, and Democratic, surrounded by suburbs that are primarily middle class, white, and Republican. Social class is less important in America than in other industrialized democracies.

5 Assess the roles of race, ethnicity, religion, gender, and changing family dynamics in American politics.

Race has been and remains among the most important of the differences in our political landscape. Although we fought a civil war over freedom for African Americans, racial equality was largely postponed until the latter half of the twentieth century. Ethnicity, including the rising numbers of Hispanics, continues to be a factor in politics. The United States has many religious denominations, and these differences help explain public opinion and political behavior. Important differences also exist between those who are religious and those who are not. Gender is important in American politics. Women now play important roles in our government, and they differ from men in their attitudes on some issues. Sexual orientation policies, especially relating to same-sex marriage, are among the most contentious in our society. Since World War II, attitudes toward sexuality, marriage, and family have changed in important ways. More people cohabit, and those who marry are older. Divorce has also become much more commonplace. Changing family structures and attitudes affect our tax policies, child care, parental leave, and gender equality. They are also important political issues.

6 Evaluate the roles of education, income, class, and age in American politics.

Although the United States is a land of wealth with a large middle class, not everyone has an adequate share in the American economic success. Poverty has grown over the past two decades, and it is most concentrated among African Americans, Native Americans, Hispanics, and single-parent households. Women as a group continue to earn less than men, even in the same occupations. Differences in income and wealth remain important. Age and education are important to understanding American politics. Older citizens participate more than young voters and are a potent political force. Education not only opens up economic opportunities in the United States but also explains many important aspects of political participation.

Chapter Self-Test

1. List four dimensions of diversity in the American population. (pp. 116–117)

2. Compared to other countries in the world, the United States does not have many deep cleavages. Why do you think this is? (hint: think about the differences between **cross-cutting cleavages** and **reinforcing cleavages**). Explain your opinion in a short paragraph. (pp. 116–117)

3. In a short essay, explain how the concept of manifest destiny relates to the current political geography of the United States. (pp. 117–119)

4. Imagine you were a campaign consultant hired to advise a presidential candidate. List and describe three ways geography would affect your recommendations and decisions. (pp. 118–124)

5. Below is a blank timeline. Fill in the important turning points for Southern politics. (pp. 119–121)

   <--->
   1787 2008

6. In a short essay, describe two or three ways in which urbanization has affected American politics. (pp. 122–124)

7. Population growth patterns include all the following *except* (pp. 118–124)
   a. In the West population growth is occurring among younger persons.
   b. Growth in the South is occurring primarily in the population over age 65.
   c. There has been a resurgence of industrial growth in the New England states.
   d. Sun Belt states have experienced greater economic growth than most other areas.

8. In a short paragraph, define ethnocentrism. Is it different from racism? Why or why not? (pp. 115–116)

9. How can religion be both a **cross-cutting cleavage** and a **reinforcing cleavage** in American politics? Give two ways for each type of cleavage. (pp. 116–117)

10. During the 2008 presidential election and nomination contest, much was made of "identity politics" in which individuals vote for the candidate most like them demographically. From what you know about the 2008 campaigns, how important was identity politics to the outcome? (pp. 117–142)

11. Remembering that they are correlated explain in a short essay whether you think regional or demographic distinctions are more important. (pp. 117–142)

12. List and describe 7 demographic categories. (pp. 124–142)

13. A study of the causes of diversity in the United States include an analysis of the implications of all *except*: (pp. 124–142)
    a. geography or demographics.
    b. social and ethnic background.
    c. economic or class divisions.
    d. politics and ideology.

14. Studies show that, after we control for **socioeconomic status,** many apparent racial divisions disappear. In a short essay, explain how race and socioeconomic status are related. (pp. 124–131; 137–139)

15. How might Figure 5.5 on page 137 look if we were to add a section showing the relationship between income and education? Fill in the table below with some feasible numbers representing the percent of population in each category. Write 2–3 sentences justifying your table.

Income	Not a High School Graduate	High School Graduate	Bachelor's Degree	Advanced Degree
Less than $15,000				
$15,000–$34,999				
$35,000–$49,999				
$50,000–$99,999				
Over $100,000				

Key Terms

ethnocentrism, p. 116

political socialization, p. 116

demography, p. 116

political predisposition, p. 116

reinforcing cleavages, p. 116

cross-cutting cleavages, p. 117

manifest destiny, p. 118

race, p. 124

ethnicity, p. 124

fundamentalists, p. 131

gender gap, p. 134

gross domestic product (GDP), p. 139

socioeconomic status (SES), p. 140

Further Reading

EARL BLACK AND **MERLE BLACK,** *The Rise of Southern Republicans* (Belknap Press, 2002).

DAVID T. CANON, *Race, Redistricting, and Representation: The Unintended Consequences of Black Majority Districts* (University of Chicago Press, 1999).

MAUREEN DEZELL, *Irish America: Coming into Clover* (Anchor Books, 2000).

JULIE ANNE DOLAN, MELISSA M. DECKMAN, AND **MICHELLE L. SWERS,** *Women in Politics: Paths to Power and Political Influence* (Prentice Hall, 2006).

LOIS LOVELACE DUKE, ED., *Women in Politics: Outsiders or Insiders?* 4th ed. (Prentice Hall, 2005).

SARAH H. EVANS, *Born for Liberty: A History of Women in America* (Free Press, 1989).

RODOLFO O. DE LA GARZA, LOUIS DE SIPIO, F. CHRIS GARCIA, JOHN GARCIA, AND **ANGELO FALCON,** *Latino Voices: Mexican, Puerto Rican, and Cuban Perspectives on American Politics* (Westview Press, 1992).

JOHN C. GREEN, MARK J. ROZELL, AND **CLYDE WILCOX,** EDS., *The Christian Right in American Politics: Marching to the Millennium* (Georgetown University Press, 2003).

DONALD R. KINDER AND **LYNN M. SANDERS,** *Divided by Color: Racial Politics and Democratic Ideals* (University of Chicago Press, 1996).

MATTHEW D. LASSITER, *The Silent Majority: Suburban Politics in the Sunbelt South* (Princeton University Press, 2005).

TAEKU LEE, S. KARTHICK RAMAKRISHNAN, AND **RICARDO RAMIREZ,** *Transforming Politics, Transforming America: The Political and Civic Incorporation of Immigrants in the United States (Race, Ethnicity, and Politics)* (University Press of Virginia, 2006).

JAN E. LEIGHLEY, *Strength in Numbers? The Political Mobilization of Racial and Ethnic Minorities* (Princeton University Press, 2001).

PEI-TE LIEN, M. MARGARET CONWAY, AND **JANELLE WONG,** *The Politics of Asian Americans* (Routledge, 2004).

JEREMY D. MAYER, *Running on Race: Racial Politics in Presidential Campaigns, 1960–2000* (Random House, 2002).

NANCY E. McGLEN, KAREN O'CONNOR, LAURA VAN ASSENDELFT, AND **WENDY GUNTHER-CANADA,** *Women, Politics, and American Society*, 4th ed. (Longman, 2004).

S. KARTHICK RAMAKRISHNAN, *Democracy in Immigrant America: Changing Demographics and Political Participation* (Stanford University Press, 2005).

MARK ROBERT RANK, *One Nation, Underprivileged: Why American Poverty Affects Us All* (Oxford University Press, 2004).

STANLEY A. RENSHON, ED., *One America? Political Leadership, National Identity, and the Dilemmas of Diversity* (Georgetown University Press, 2001).

RUBEN G. RUMBAUT AND **ALEJANDRO PORTES,** *Ethnicities: Children of Immigrants in America* (University of California Press, 2001).

ARTHUR M. SCHLESINGER, JR., *The Disuniting of America* (Norton, 1992).

PETER H. SCHUCK, *Diversity in America* (Belknap Press, 2003).

JEFFREY M. STONECASH, *Class and Party in American Politics* (Westview Press, 2000).

MARCELO M. SUAREZ-OROZCO AND **MARIELA PAEZ,** *Latinos: Remaking America* (University of California Press, 2002).

ALEXIS DE TOCQUEVILLE, *Democracy in America*, ed. J. P. Mayer, trans. George Lawrence (Doubleday, 1969). Originally published 1835.

KENNETH D. WALD, *Religion and Politics in the United States*, 5th ed. (Rowman & Littlefield, 2006).

JANELLE WONG, *Democracy's Promise: Immigrants and American Civic Institutions (The Politics of Race and Ethnicity)* (University of Michigan Press, 2006).

chapter 6

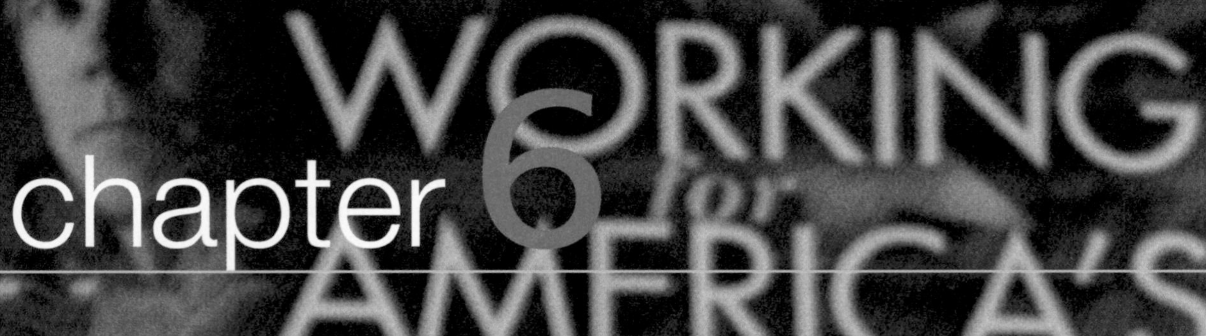

Interest Groups

The Politics of Influence

While most of the country was focused on the 2008 presidential election, voters in ten states also had highly contested U.S. senate races. Most of these contests were in Republican seats going into the election. Outside interest groups clashed heavily in the 2008 Senatorial elections. Many conservatives worried that the Democrats would also gain the Presidency and a filibuster-proof, sixty member majority in the Senate, meaning it would be harder for Republicans to block legislation they opposed in 2009 and 2010. In response, the U.S. Chamber of Commerce spent heavily in contested Senate elections like the ones in New Hampshire, North Carolina, and Colorado fearing that a filibuster-proof majority would lead to greater unionization, higher taxes, and more trade restrictions. They consequently supported "pro-business" candidates which were almost exclusively Republican. The Chamber's ads were specifically targeted to the contest and often negative in tone. For example the Chambers' ad in New Hampshire labeled Democratic U.S. Senate candidate Jean Shaheen a "taxing machine."[1] The Chamber of Commerce spent approximately $35 million in 2008.[2] Democratic candidates in these contests had interest group allies as well. For example, the Service Employees International Union (SEIU) spent approximately $17 million in independent expenditures aimed at electing mostly Democrats to the White House and U.S. Senate.[3] Groups like the Chamber of Commerce and SEIU can raise and spend unlimited amounts of money a long as the expenditures are independent of the candidates or parties.

Interest groups running their own ads attacking candidates was not new to 2008. Negative personal attacks have come to be called "swift boating," a term linked to the ads run by a group in the 2004 presidential election. During the Democratic convention that year, John Kerry emphasized his preparation to be Commander-in-Chief and his Vietnam War heroism. Shortly after the convention, a group called Swift Boat Veterans for Truth started running ads questioning Kerry's heroism and patriotism. The Swift Boat ads damaged Kerry's credibility and played a role in his eventual defeat, in part because he did not aggressively counter the charges. John McCain had also been the target of a similar attack. In the 2000 South Carolina primary anonymous "push polling" calls were made that insinuated that McCain had fathered an illegitimate black child. The child was actually McCain's adopted Bangladeshi daughter. McCain lost South Carolina and ultimately the nomination.

Interest groups like these have long been important in electing and defeating candidates, in providing information to officeholders, and in setting the agenda of American politics. U.S. citizens have long been concerned about the power of "special interest" and the tendency of groups to pursue their self-interest at the expense of less-organized groups or the general public. Restraining the negative tendencies of these interest groups while protecting their liberty is not easy. In this chapter we examine the full range of interest group activities as well as efforts to limit thier potentially negative influences, including reforming campaign finance.

LEARNING **OBJECTIVES**

1. Evaluate the role of interest groups and social movements in American politics.
2. Identify the different types of interest groups in the United States.
3. Compare the sources of interest group power.
4. Describe lobbyists and how they influence policy.
5. Assess how some interest groups use money to pursue their agendas and evaluate the consequences for interest group pluralism of some groups having little money.

CHAPTER **OUTLINE**

- Interest Groups Past and Present: The "Mischiefs of Faction"
- Types of Interest Groups
- Characteristics and Power of Interest Groups
- The Influence of Lobbyists
- Money and Politics
- How Much Do Interest Groups Influence Elections and Legislation?
- Curing the Mischiefs of Faction—Two Centuries Later

LEARNING **OBJECTIVE**

1 Evaluate the role of interest groups and social movements in American politics.

faction
A term the founders used to refer to political parties and special interests or interest groups.

pluralism
A theory of government that holds that open, multiple, and competing groups can check the asserted power by any one group.

Interest Groups Past and Present: The "Mischiefs of Faction"

The founders of the Republic were very worried about groups with common interests, which they called **factions.** (They also thought of political parties as factions.) For the framers of the Constitution, the daunting problem was how to establish a stable and orderly constitutional system that would both respect the liberty of free citizens and prevent the tyranny of the majority or of a single dominant interest.

As a talented practical politician and a brilliant theorist, James Madison offered both a diagnosis and a solution in *The Federalist*, No. 10 (reprinted in the Appendix). He began with a basic proposition: "The latent causes of faction are...sown in the nature of man." All individuals pursue their self-interest, seeking advantage or power over others. Acknowledging that we live in a maze of group interests, Madison argued that the "most common and durable source of factions has been the various and unequal distribution of property." Madison called a faction "a number of citizens, whether amounting to a majority or minority of the whole, who are united and actuated by some common impulse of passion, or of interest, adverse to the rights of other citizens, or to the permanent and aggregate interests of the community." For Madison, "the *causes* of faction cannot be removed, and...relief is only to be sought in the means of controlling its *effects*."[4]

James Madison played a critical role in drafting and enacting the Constitution, and many of its provisions are aimed at limiting the "mischiefs of faction." Separation of powers and checks and balances make it hard for a faction to dominate government. Staggered terms of office make it necessary for a faction to endure to prevail. But rather than trying to encourage one or another faction, the Constitution encourages competition between them. Indeed, checks and balances arguably function best when factions within the branches work to counter one another. The Constitution envisions a plurality of groups competing with each other, an idea that has been called **pluralism.**

How well pluralism has worked in practice is debated.[5] We'll see that over time government has sought to regulate factions as a response to the power some groups such as corporations, unions, and wealthy individuals have had in American government. The debate about how to check their power without damaging their liberty is an enduring one.

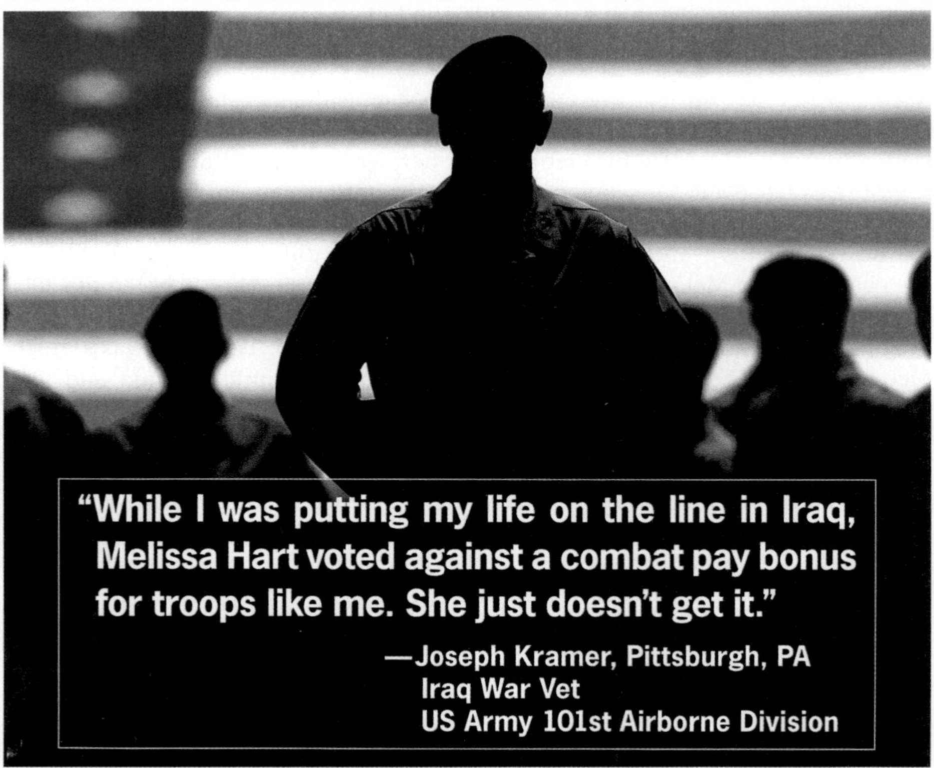

"While I was putting my life on the line in Iraq, Melissa Hart voted against a combat pay bonus for troops like me. She just doesn't get it."
—Joseph Kramer, Pittsburgh, PA
Iraq War Vet
US Army 101st Airborne Division

This mailer against House candidate Melissa Hart was sent by the interest group Vote Vets, or what James Madison would call a "faction."

A Nation of Interests

Some U.S. citizens identify with groups distinguished by race, gender, ethnic background, age, occupation, religion or sexual orientation. Others form voluntary groups based on their opinions about issues such as gun control or tax reduction. When such associations seek to influence government, they are called **interest groups.**

Comparing Interest Groups

Interest groups are also sometimes called "special interests." Politicians and the media often use this term in a pejorative way. What makes an interest group a "special" one? The answer is highly subjective. One person's *special* interest is another's *public* interest. Yet so-called public interest groups such as Common Cause or the League of Women Voters support policies that not everyone agrees with. Politics is best seen as a clash among interests, with differing concepts of what is in the public interest, rather than as a battle between the special interests on one side and "the people" or the public interest on the other.

In fact, the term "special interest" conveys a selfish or narrow view, one that may lack credibility. For this reason, we use the neutral term "interest groups." An interest group simply speaks for some, but not all, of us. A democracy includes many interests and many organized interest groups. The democratic process exists to decide among them. Part of the politics of interest groups is thus to persuade the general public that their interest is more important.

Social Movements

Interest groups sometimes begin as social movements. A social **movement** consists of many people interested in a significant issue, idea, or concern who are willing to take action to support or oppose it. Examples include the civil rights, environmental, anti-tax, animal rights, women's rights, Christian Right, gay rights, anti-immigration, and anti-war movements. Each represents a group that has felt unrepresented by government.

interest group
A collection of people who share a common interest or attitude and seek to influence government for specific ends. Interest groups usually work within the framework of government and try to achieve their goals through tactics such as lobbying.

movement
A large body of people interested in a common issue, idea, or concern that is of continuing significance and who are willing to take action. Movements seek to change attitudes or institutions, not just policies.

Social movements often arise at the grassroots level and spread across the nation. They tend to see their causes as morally right and their opponents as morally wrong. As movements mature they develop interest groups that pursue public policies, as we'll see later.

The Bill of Rights protects movements, popular or unpopular, by supporting free assembly, free speech, and due process. Consequently, those who disagree with government policies do not have to engage in violence or other extreme activities in the United States,

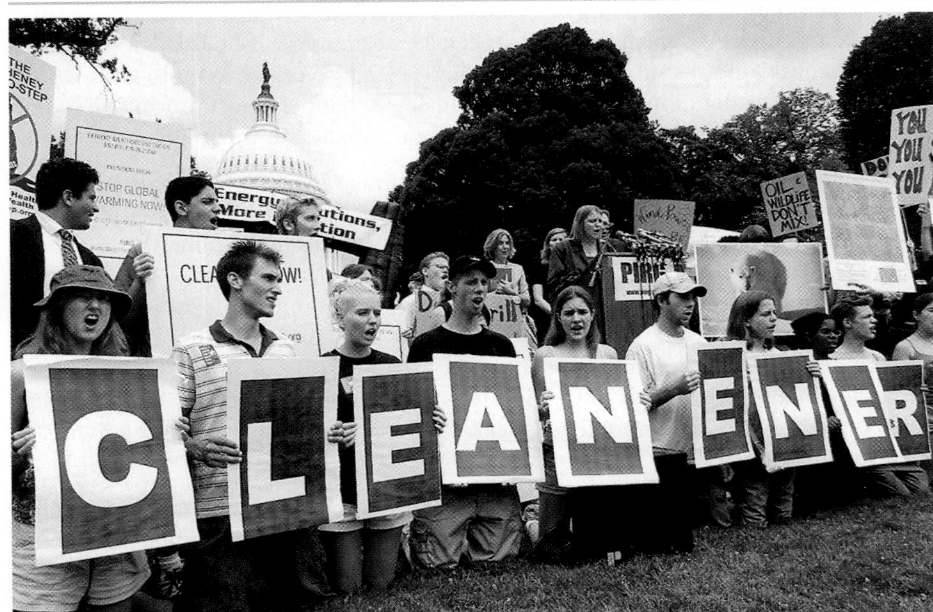

A group of supporters from the U.S. Public Interest Research Group (U.S. PIRG) protest drilling for oil in the Artic National Wildlife Refuge on Capitol Hill in 2001.

as they do in some countries, and they need not fear persecution for demonstrating peacefully. In a democratic system that restricts the power of government, movements have considerable room to operate *within* the constitutional system.

Types of Interest Groups

Interest groups vary widely. Some are formal associations or organizations like the National Rifle Association (NRA); others have no formal organization. Some are organized primarily to persuade public officials on issues of concern to the group such as reducing greenhouse gases; others conduct research, or influence public opinion with published reports and mass mailings.

LEARNING **OBJECTIVE**

2 Identify the different types of interest groups in the United States.

We can categorize interest groups into several broad types: (1) economic, including both business and labor; (2) ideological or single-issue; (3) public interest; (4) foreign policy; and (5) government itself. Obviously, these categories are not mutually exclusive. Most American adults are represented by a number of interest groups, even if they don't know it. For instance, people age 50 and older may not be aware that AARP (which began as the American Association of Retired Persons) claims to represent *all* older citizens, not just those who are actually members. Similarly, the American Automobile Association (AAA) claims to represent all motorists, not just those who join. The varied and overlapping nature of interest groups in the United States has been described as *interest group pluralism*, meaning that competition among open, responsive, and diverse groups helps preserve democratic values and limits the concentration of power in any single group. We look at each category of interest group next.

Economic Interest Groups

There are thousands of economic interests: agriculture, consumers, plumbers, the airplane industry, landlords, truckers, bondholders, property owners, and more. Economic interests pursue what benefits them both financially and politically.

Business The most familiar business institution is the large corporation. Corporations range from one-person enterprises to vast multinational entities. General Motors, AT&T, Microsoft, Coca-Cola, McDonald's, Wal-Mart, and other large companies exercise considerable political influence, as do hundreds of smaller corporations. For example, as Microsoft and Wal-Mart came under heightened government and public scrutiny, their political contributions expanded.[6] Corporate power and a changing domestic and global economy make business practices important political issues.

Cooperation between groups can increase their effectiveness, giving even small business an important voice in public policy. The Commerce Department includes a Small Business Administration. Small businesses are also organized into groups such as the National Federation of Independent Business that help elect pro-business candidates and persuade the national government on behalf of its members.

Trade and Other Associations Businesses with similar interests join together as *trade associations*, as diverse as the products and services they provide. Businesses of all types are also organized into large nationwide associations such as the National Association of Realtors and smaller ones like the American Wind Energy Association.

The broadest business trade association is the Chamber of Commerce of the United States. Organized in 1912, the Chamber is a federation of thousands of local Chambers of Commerce representing tens of thousands of firms. Loosely allied with the Chamber on most issues is the National Association of Manufacturers, which, since 1893, has tended to speak for the more conservative elements of American business.

Labor Workers' associations have a range of interests, including professional standards and wages and working conditions. Labor unions are one of the most important groups representing workers, yet the American workforce is the least unionized of almost any

HISTORY MAKERS

John Sherman and the Sherman Antitrust Act

The Sherman Antitrust Act was the first legislation enacted by Congress to prohibit trusts or monopolies. In the 1880s some corporations formed "trusts" to gain greater control of the market. They assigned shares of stock to a single set of trustees, thus forming a monopoly that could control prices and deter competition. The Sherman Act permitted the government to take action against these trusts and break them up.*

The act is named for Senator John Sherman of Ohio, who served in the U.S. Senate for 16 years. He was a candidate for president in 1880 and also served as secretary of the treasury and secretary of state. Beginning in 1888, Sherman began to take an active interest in antitrust legislation. Because he was one of the most senior Republicans in the Senate and a ranking member of the Senate Finance Committee, Sherman was uniquely positioned to take on the problem of corporate monopolies. He was the primary author of the Sherman Act, his most lasting legacy.†

Only five years after the Sherman Act was enacted, the Supreme Court refused to apply it in a case involving the American Sugar Refining Company, which controlled 98 percent of all sugar refining in the United States. But with the election of Theodore Roosevelt as president in 1904 and his "trust-busting" agenda, the government began to use the Sherman Act with considerable success. The act remains relevant today, and in the late 1990s the federal government used it against Microsoft.‡ John Sherman's leadership in fostering economic competition lives on through the legislation that bears his name.

QUESTIONS

1. Besides Microsoft, what examples exist today of businesses whose size and share of the market raise concerns about unfair competition in the marketplace?
2. In an increasingly global economy, is the domestic size and market share of a U.S. corporation still a concern? Why or why not?
3. What does the Supreme Court's reversing itself in applying the Sherman Act suggest to us about American politics?

*George Bittlingmayer, "Antitrust and Business Activity: The First Quarter Century," *Business History Review* 70 (Autumn 1996), p. 377.
†William Letwin, *Law and Economic Policy in America* (Random House, 1965), pp. 87–88.
‡*Commonwealth of Massachusetts v. Microsoft Corporation*, www.usdoj.gov/atr/cases/f204400/204468.htm.

industrial democracy (see Figure 6–1). Disagreements among unions about tactics and leadership have grown more public and more intense in recent years.

Probably the oldest unions in the United States are farm organizations. The largest, the American Farm Bureau Federation, is especially strong in the Corn Belt, states such as Iowa, Nebraska, and Illinois that produce large quantities of corn. Originally organized around government agents who helped farmers in rural counties,

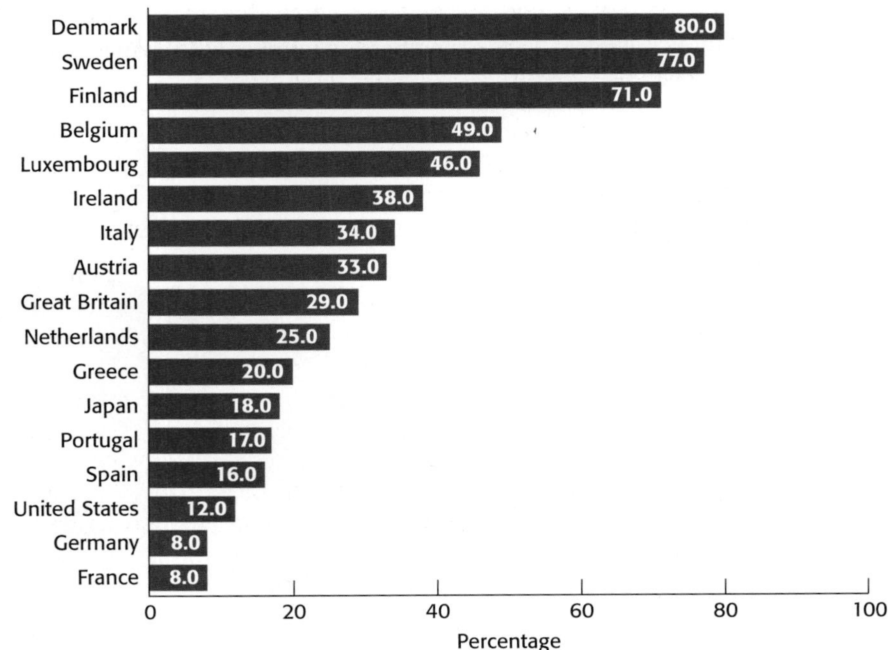

FIGURE 6–1
Union Membership in the United States Compared to Other Countries (Estimated Percentage of the Workforce).

SOURCE: European Foundation for the Improvement of Living and Working Conditions, 2008, Wyattville Road, Lough linstown, Dublin 18, Ireland.

the federation today is almost a semigovernmental agency, but it fights for such goals as price supports and expanded credit. As farms grow bigger and farm workers are less likely to be members of the farmer's family, activists have tried to organize farm workers into unions. The late César Chávez and others have worked to organize migrant farm workers.

Throughout the nineteenth century, workers organized political parties and local unions. Their most ambitious effort at national organization, the Knights of Labor, registered 700,000 members in the 1890s. But by about 1900, the American Federation of Labor (AFL), a confederation of strong and independent-minded national unions mainly representing craft workers, was the dominant organization. During the 1930s, unions more responsive to industrial workers broke away from the AFL and formed a rival national organization organized by industry, the Congress of Industrial Organizations (CIO). In 1955, the AFL and CIO reunited. Recently more than a third of AFL-CIO members (4.5 of 13 million members), affiliated with the Service Employees International Union (SEIU), the International Brotherhood of Teamsters, and two other unions, split off from the AFL-CIO, forming a new group named the Change to Win Federation.[7] Unions today are thus less unified, but by 2007, dues payments to the AFL-CIO exceeded levels before the division.[8]

Union membership is optional in states whose laws permit the **open shop,** in which workers cannot be required to join a union as a condition of employment. In states with the **closed shop,** workers may be required to join a union to be hired at a particular company if most employees at that company vote to unionize. In both cases, the unions negotiate with management, and all workers share the benefits the unions gain. In open-shop states, many workers may choose not to affiliate with a union because they can secure the same benefits that unionized workers enjoy without incurring the costs of joining the union. When a person benefits from the work or service of an organization like a union (or even a public TV or radio station) without joining or contributing to it, this condition is referred to as the **free rider** problem. We discuss how groups and government deal with the free rider challenge later in the chapter.

open shop
A company with a labor agreement under which union membership cannot be required as a condition of employment.

closed shop
A company with a labor agreement under which union membership can be a condition of employment.

free rider
An individual who does not join a group representing his or her interests yet receives the benefit of the group's influence.

The AFL-CIO speaks for about two thirds of unionized labor,[9] but unions represent just over 12 percent of the nation's workforce (see Figure 6–2).[10] The proportion of the U.S. workforce belonging to all unions has fallen, in part because of the shift from an industrial to a service and information economy. Dwindling membership limits organized labor's influence. Recently, however, some service and public sector unions have begun to expand, and even some doctors have unionized. Membership in SEIU rose from 1.58 million in 2006, a membership number little changed from 2003, to 1.9 million in 2008.[11]

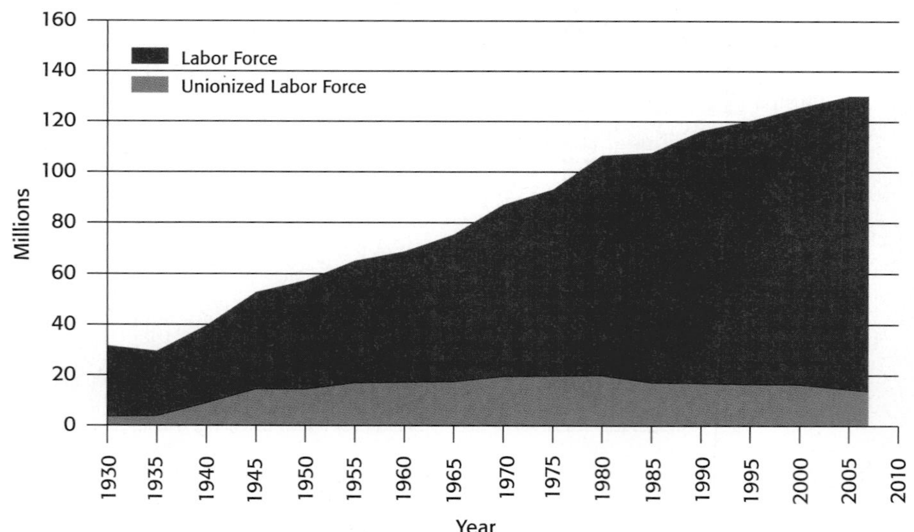

FIGURE 6–2
Labor Force and Union Membership, 1930–2007.

SOURCE: *The World Almanac and Book of Facts, 2000.* Copyright © 1999 Primedia Reference, Inc. Reprinted with permission; all rights reserved. 1973–2007, Barry Hirsch, Georgia State University, and David Macpherson, Florida State University, "Union Membership, Coverage, Density, and Employment Among All Wage and Salary Workers, 1973–2007," http://www.unionstats.com.

For some years, the Committee on Political Education (COPE) of the AFL-CIO was one of the most respected—and feared—political organizations in the country. In the Kennedy and Johnson years (1961–1969), it encouraged and supervised grassroots political activity, and at the national level, it adopted a detailed platform that spelled out labor's position on issues. Labor contributed money to candidates and ran voter registration and get-out-the-vote campaigns. Recently, COPE has had a fairly successful record of wins for its endorsed House and Senate candidates.[12]

Since 1998, unions have emphasized direct contact with members and their families through mail, through e-mail, on the phone, and in person. They have organized get-out-the-vote drives and paid for television advertising. Unlike the case in 2000, when unions were important to securing Al Gore's nomination,[13] in the 2004 and 2008 Democratic presidential primaries they were divided. In 2008 some unions such as SEIU and the Change to Win Federation supported Senator Barack Obama, while the United Steel Workers supported John Edwards, and the American Federation of State, County, and Municipal Employees supported Senator Hillary Clinton. In the 2008 general election unions were unified in backing Barack Obama for president and campaigned aggressively for pro-labor congressional, gubernatorial, and state legislative candidates. In the general election all unions endorsed Senator Barack Obama.

Traditionally identified with the Democratic Party, unions have not enjoyed a close relationship with Republican administrations. Given labor's limited resources, one option for unions is to form temporary coalitions with consumer, public interest, liberal, and sometimes even industry groups, especially on issues related to foreign imports. Labor has been unsuccessful in blocking free trade agreements like the North American Free Trade Agreement (NAFTA).[14]

Professional Associations Professional people join **professional associations** such as the American Medical Association (AMA) and the American Bar Association (ABA), which serve some of the same functions as unions. Other professions are divided into many subgroups. Teachers and professors, for example, belong to the National Education Association, the American Federation of Teachers, and the American Association of University Professors, and also to subgroups based on specialties, such as the Modern Language Association and the American Political Science Association.

professional associations
Groups of individuals who share a common profession and are often organized for common political purposes related to that profession.

Democratic presidential candidate Illinois Senator Barack Obama meets with labor union members over breakfast in 2008. Labor unions have traditionally identified themselves with the Democratic party.

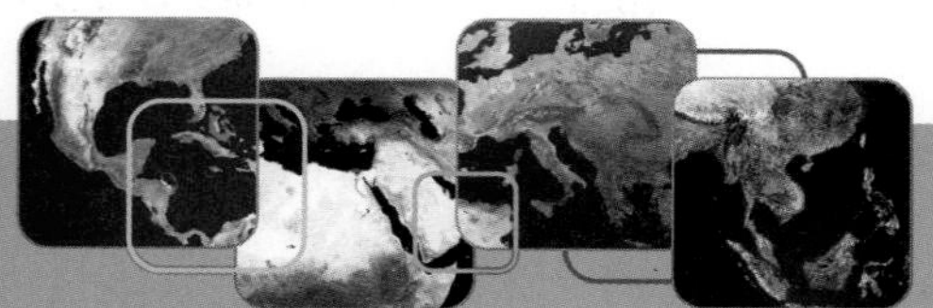

HOW OTHER NATIONS GOVERN

Unions and the Minimum Wage

Several factors contribute to the size and power of unions in different countries. The following table compares our sample of nations in union density, the extent to which they are unionized, and in one measure of the impact of unions, the level the country has set for the minimum wage.

Mexico and China are heavily unionized, while India and Nigeria are not. Why? As political scientists Alan Draper and Ansil Ramsay point out, highly diverse populations struggle to organize labor unions because their workers are so different from one another.* For example, in Nigeria there are different religions and in India different languages. Great Britain, which is relatively homogenous, is more strongly unionized than the more diverse United States.

A nation's minimum wage rates increase with unionization. The United States' minimum wage was $6.55 an hour in September 2006, increasing to $7.25 per hour by July 2009. In contrast, the United Kingdom's minimum wage is $10.84 per hour thanks to labor's relationship with political parties and degree of engagement in the political process. Labor is a strong part of the United Kingdom's Labour Party coalition, and a high minimum wage is a priority of the party.

QUESTIONS

1. What factors make it easier or more difficult for workers to form labor unions?
2. What are the consequences of a heavily unionized workforce in a nation?
3. Why are there so few unionized workers in the United States? Is this a good thing or a bad thing?

	China	Great Britain	India	Japan	Mexico	Nigeria	U.S.A.
Union density	70%	32%	22%	24%	72%	18%	12%
Minimum wage	$0.24–$0.66	$10.84	$0.11–$0.58	$5.75–$6.63	$0.54–$0.58	$0.29	$5.15

SOURCE: Minimum wage data compiled from International Labour Organization, Working Time Database, Minimum Wages Database, www.ilo.org/travaildatabase/servlet/minimumwages, minimum wage rates converted to American dollars per hour based on a 40-hour workweek; union density from Gabriel A. Almond, G. Bingham Powell, Jr., Russell J. Dalton, and Kaare Strøm, *Comparative Politics Today*, 9th ed. (Pearson Longman, 2008), p. 70.

*Alan Draper and Ansil Ramsay, *The Good Society: An Introduction to Comparative Politics* (Pearson Longman, 2008), p. 260.

Government, especially at the state level, regulates many professions. Lawyers are licensed by states, which, often as a result of pressure from lawyers themselves, set standards of admission to the state bar. Professional associations also use the courts to pursue their agendas. In the area of medical malpractice, for example, doctors lobby hard for limited-liability laws, while trial lawyers resist them. Teachers, hairstylists, and marriage therapists work for legislation that concerns them. It is not surprising, then, that groups representing professional associations such as the AMA and the National Association of Home Builders are among the largest donors to political campaigns.

Ideological or Single-Issue Interest Groups

Ideological groups focus on issues—often a single issue. Members generally share a common view and a desire for government to pursue policies consistent with it. Such *single-issue* groups are often unwilling to compromise. Right-to-life and pro-choice groups on abortion fit this description, as do the National Rifle Association (NRA) and anti-immigration groups.

Countless groups have organized around other specific issues, such as civil liberties, environmental protection, nuclear energy, and nuclear disarmament.[15] Such associations are not new. The Anti-Saloon League of the 1890s was devoted solely to barring the sale and manufacture of alcoholic beverages, and it did not care whether legislators were drunk or sober as long as they voted dry. One of the best-known single-issue groups today is the NRA, with more than four million members committed to protecting the right to bear arms.[16] Other single-issue groups include the Club for Growth, a generally libertarian and antitax group. Partly as a reaction to

The Woman's Christian Temperance Union, a movement dedicated to the prohibition of drinking liquor, succeeded in passing the Eighteenth Amendment, which outlawed the manufacture and sale of alcoholic beverages. It was later repealed by the Twenty-First Amendment.

the tendency of single-issue groups to be strongly liberal or conservative, some centrist or moderate groups have formed. The Concord Coalition is concerned about government deficits and what it calls "responsible fiscal policy."[17]

Public Interest Groups

Out of the political ferment of the 1960s came groups that claim to promote "the public interest." For example, Common Cause campaigns for electoral reform, for making the political process more open and participatory, and to stem media consolidation. Its Washington staff raises money through direct-mail campaigns, oversees state chapters of the group, publishes research reports and press releases on current issues, and lobbies Congress and government departments.

Ralph Nader started a conglomerate of consumer organizations that investigate and report on governmental and corporate action—or inaction—relating to consumer interests. Public interest research groups (PIRGs) today seek to influence policy on Capitol Hill and in several state legislatures on environmental issues, safe energy, and consumer protection. Nader ran for president in 2000 as the nominee of the Green Party and in 2004 and 2008 as an Independent. He received only 3 percent of the popular vote in 2000, less than a half percent in 2004, and in 2008 Nader again received only one-half of one percent of the popular vote.

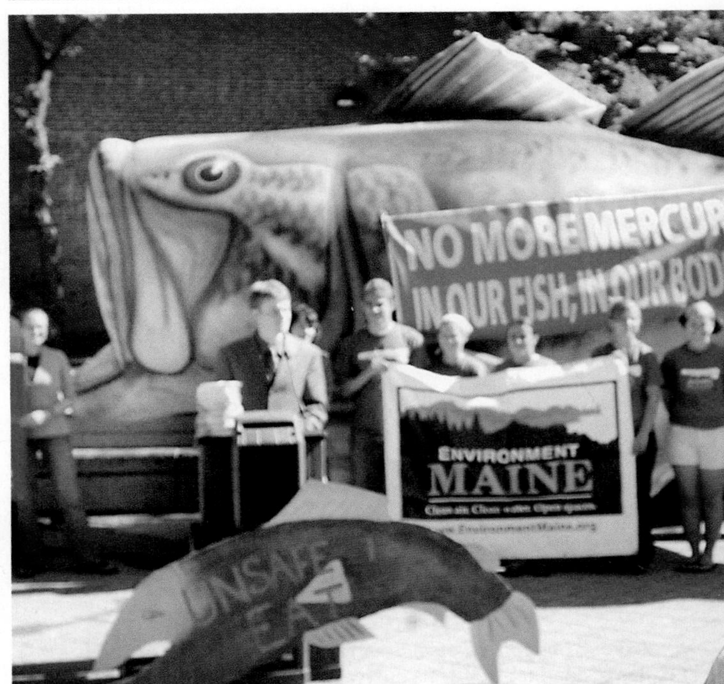

A speaker at a Public Interest Research Group (PIRG) news conference on mercury-contaminated fish.

Foreign Policy Interest Groups

Interest groups also organize to promote or oppose foreign policies. Among the most prestigious is the Council on Foreign Relations in New York City. Other groups pressure Congress and the president to enact specific policies. For example, interest groups have been trying to influence American policy on China's refusal to grant independence for Tibet. Other groups support or oppose free trade. Foreign policy groups should not be confused with foreign groups, which are banned from making campaign contributions but often seek to influence policy through lobbying firms.

Interest groups such as Greenpeace stage demonstrations to call attention to environmental issues.

One of the most influential foreign policy groups is the American Israel Political Action Committee (AIPAC), with more than 50,000 members. Because AIPAC's primary focus is influencing government directly, not distributing campaign funds, it is not required to disclose where its money comes from or goes. Included in the long list of AIPAC successes are enactment of aid packages to Israel, passage of the 1985 United States–Israel Free Trade Agreement, and emergency assistance to Israel in the wake of the 1992 Gulf War. Its counterpart, the Arab American Institute, lobbies to support Arab causes. Efforts to secure a negotiated settlement between the Palestinians and Israel have kept U.S. interest groups on both sides visible and important.

Nongovernmental organizations (NGOs), nonprofit groups that operate outside the institutions of government but often pursue public policy objectives and lobby governments are another type of foreign policy interest group. The most common are social, cultural, or environmental groups such as Greenpeace, Amnesty International, and the Humane Society of the United States (Chapter 17 discusses nonprofit groups in greater detail).

Public Sector Interest Groups

Governments are themselves important interest groups. Many cities and most states retain Washington lobbyists, and cities also attempt to influence Congress and the executive branch of the federal government. Governors are organized through the National Governors Association, cities through the National League of Cities, and counties through the National Association of Counties. Other officials—lieutenant governors, secretaries of state, mayors—have their own national associations.

nongovernmental organization (NGO) A nonprofit association or group operating outside government that advocates and pursues policy objectives.

Government employees form a large and well-organized group. The National Education Association (NEA), for example, has 3.2 million members.[18] The NEA

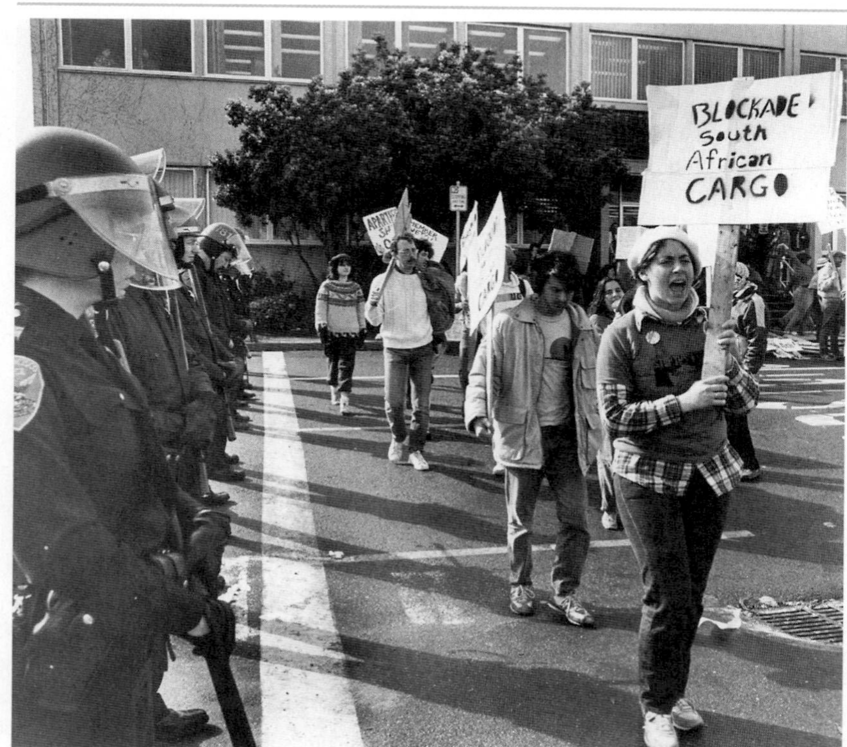

A group of people protest South Africa's practice of apartheid. Protests such as the one pictured here became increasingly common until South African apartheid was eliminated in 1991.

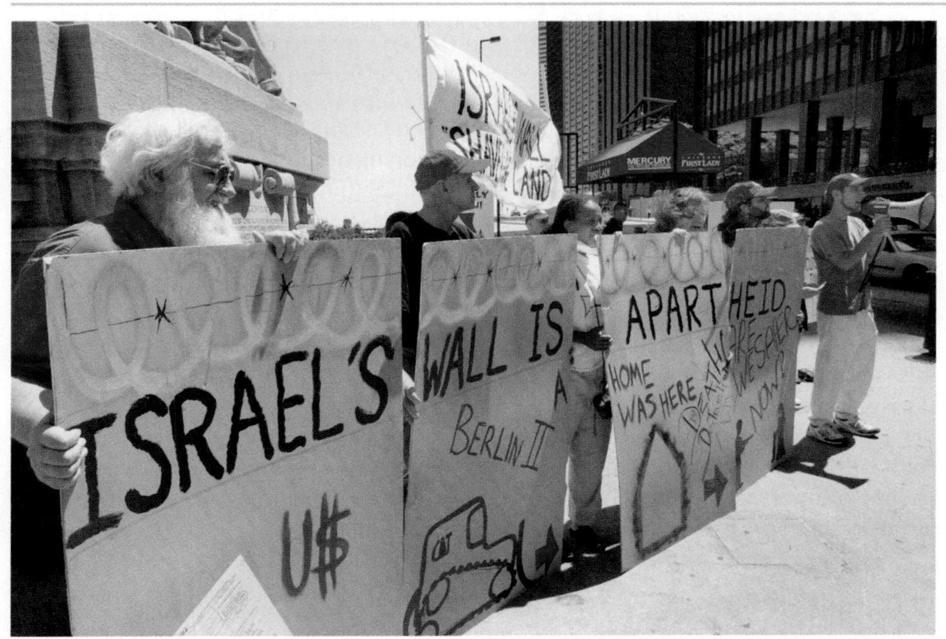

Some interest groups focus on foreign policy issues, such as U.S. aid to Israel in light of Israel's construction of a separation wall along the West Bank. Opponents argue that the wall is tantamount to apartheid, and the Israeli government argues that it is a necessary security measure.

endorses politicians from both parties but more typically supports Democrats. In 2008, the NEA endorsed Barack Obama for the presidency. The NEA fits the definition of a professional association, labor union, and public sector interest group. Bush administration secretary of education Rod Paige had to apologize after he labeled the NEA a terrorist organization in 2004.[19] At the time, Paige was at odds with teachers' unions because they disagreed with his agenda. Public employees are increasingly important to organized labor, because they constitute the fastest-growing unions.

Other Interest Groups

American adults are often emotionally and financially engaged by a variety of groups: veterans' groups, nationality groups, and religious organizations. An area of increasing activity is environmental groups (see Table 6–1).

TABLE 6–1 Environmental Groups' Resources and Strategies

Group	Membership	Issues	Activities
Greenpeace USA	250,000	Forests, global warming, genetically engineered foods, oceans, persistent organic pollutants, nuclear weapons	Media events; mass mailings; grassroots activity; does not lobby government
Natural Resources Defense Council	1,200,000	Resources, energy, global warming, pollution, nuclear weapons	Lobbying; litigation; watchdog; its scientists compete with experts from agencies and industry
Sierra Club	1,300,000	Wilderness, pollution, global warming, human rights, population, suburban sprawl	Grassroots action; litigation; news releases
Wilderness Society	300,000	Wilderness areas, public lands, energy development	Scientific studies; analysis; advocacy group

SOURCE: Greenpeace USA, www.greenpeaceusa.org; Natural Resources Defense Council, www.nrdc.org; Sierra Club, www.sierraclub.org; Wilderness Society, www.wilderness.org.

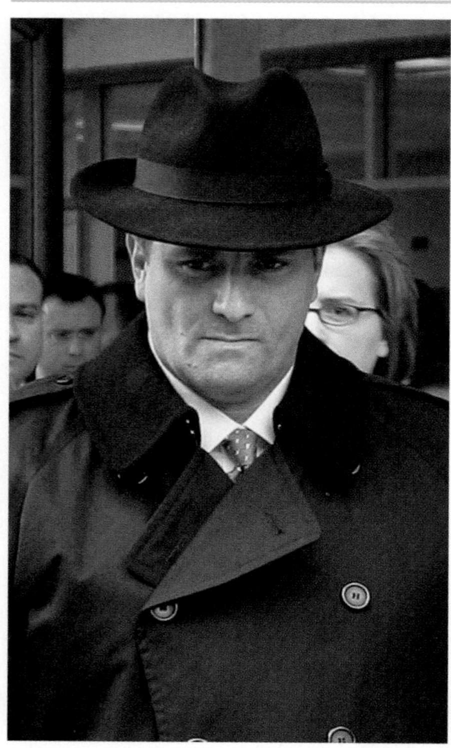

Jack Abramoff leaves federal court after pleading guilty to three counts of fraud, tax evasion, and conspiracy to bribe political officials. The plea bargain required the once-powerful lobbyist to provide evidence about members of Congress.

LEARNING **OBJECTIVE**

Compare the sources of interest group power.

Characteristics and Power of Interest Groups

Political scientists, sociologists, and economists have described the differing ways groups form and organize to pursue their goals or objectives. Securing the participation of individuals in groups—what economist Mancur Olson labeled **collective action,**[20] and others describe as **public choice**[21]—is challenging because often the benefits from the group efforts are shared with everyone, including those who do not participate in the work of securing the benefit. This creates what is called the *free rider* problem. For example, unions that achieve wage concessions from management do so for all workers in and out of the union. This results in little incentive to join the union or support it financially. Groups sometimes attempt to sanction or punish free riders, which is why unions prefer that only union workers be employed in a given firm or industry. When this is not possible, group leaders try to reduce the free rider problem through persuasion or group pressure.

Groups vary in their goals, methods, and power. Among their most important characteristics are size, incentives to participate, resources, cohesiveness, leadership, and techniques. As we will demonstrate, these different resources and objectives help us understand the power and resources of interest groups.

Size and Resources

Obviously, size is important to political power; an organization representing five million voters has more influence than one speaking for 5,000. Perhaps even more important is the number of members who are active and willing to fight for policy objectives. Interest groups often provide tangible incentives to join, such as exclusive magazines, travel benefits, professional meetings and job opportunities, and discounts on insurance, merchandise, and admission to cultural institutions. Some are compelling enough to attract the potential free rider.[22]

Many government programs provide services that benefit everyone such as clean air, national defense, and public fireworks on July 4. One solution to the free rider problem is to pay for these widely shared benefits through taxes. Nongovernment service providers can require a number of people to pay for the service before providing it. It is then in everyone's interest to pay for the service or face the prospect that no one will have it. Groups rarely overcome the risk of free riders, but unless we offer some compensation for providing easily shared goods and services, they are not likely to be produced.

Although the size of an interest group is important to its success, so is its *spread*—the extent to which membership is concentrated or dispersed. Because automobile manufacturing is concentrated in Michigan and a few other states, the auto industry's influence does not have the same spread as the AMA, which has an active chapter in virtually every congressional district. Concentration of membership in a key battleground state, however, such as Cuban Americans in Florida or ethanol producers in Iowa, enhances that group's influence. Interest groups also differ in the extent to which they preempt or share a policy area. Doctors and the AMA have effectively preempted the health care policy area because they play such an important role in health care, have substantial spread, and only recently had to compete with other health care interests with similar size and influence. But in transportation policy, for example, railroads must compete with interstate trucking and even air freight companies.

Finally, groups differ in the extent of their *resources*—money, volunteers, expertise, and reputation. Some groups can influence many centers of power—both houses of Congress, the White House, federal agencies, the courts, and state and local governments—while others cannot.

collective action
How groups form and organize to pursue their goals or objectives, including how to get individuals and groups to participate and cooperate. The term has many applications in the various social sciences such as political science, sociology, and economics.

public choice
Synonymous with "collective action", specifically studies how government officials, politicians, and voters respond to positive and negative incentives.

Cohesiveness

Most mass-membership organizations include three types of members: (1) a relatively small number of formal leaders who may hold full-time, paid positions or devote much time, effort, and money to the group's activities; (2) a few hundred people intensely involved in the group who identify with its aims, attend meetings, pay dues, and do much of the legwork; and (3) thousands of people who are members in name only and cannot be depended on to vote in elections or act as the leadership wants.[23] When these groups share common views on the aims of the organization, the group is more cohesive.

Another factor in group cohesiveness is *organizational structure*. Some associations have a strong formal organization; others are local organizations joined into a loose state or national federation in which they retain a measure of separate power and independence. Separation of powers may also exist within groups. Often a national assembly or board of an organization establishes policy; an executive committee meets more frequently; a president or director is elected to head and speak for the group; and permanent paid officials form the organization's bureaucracy. Power may be further divided between the organization's main headquarters and its Washington office. An organization of this sort tends to be far less cohesive than a centralized, disciplined group such as some trade unions and associations for trial lawyers and real estate agents.

Leadership

In a group that embraces many attitudes and interests, leaders may either weld the various elements together or sharpen their disunity. The leader of a national business association, for example, must tread cautiously between big business and small business, between exporters and importers, between chain stores and corner grocery stores, and between the producers and the sellers of competing products. The group leader is in the same position as a president or a member of Congress; he or she must know when to lead and when to follow.

Techniques for Exerting Influence

Our separation-of-powers system provides many access points for any group attempting to influence government. They can present their case to Congress, the White House staff, state and local governments, and federal agencies and departments. Efforts by individuals or groups to inform and influence public officials is called **lobbying.** Groups also become involved in litigation, protests, and election activities and even establish their own political parties.

LEARNING **OBJECTIVE**

4 Describe lobbyists and how they influence policy.

Publicity, Mass Media, and the Internet One way to attempt to influence policy makers is through the public. Interest groups use the media—television, radio, the Internet including Web sites, newspapers, leaflets, signs, direct mail, and word of mouth—to influence voters during elections and motivate them to contact their representatives between elections. Businesses enjoy a special advantage because, as large-scale advertisers, they know how to deliver their message effectively or can find an advertising agency to do it for them. But organized labor is also effective in communicating with its membership through shop stewards, mail, phone calls, and personal contact.

Mobilization increasingly occurs through the Internet. Business organizations like the Business and Industrial Political Action Committee (BIPAC) have used the Internet to communicate with members and employees of affiliated businesses. BIPAC's Web site provides downloadable forms to request absentee ballots and the roll call votes of legislators on issues of interest to their businesses.[24] Some groups, such as MoveOn.org, operate almost exclusively online, while massive forums such as DailyKos.com and Townhall.com act as a clearinghouse for left- and right-wing causes. As one scholar noted, much of what modern interest groups do "could not work without the Internet."[25]

lobbying
Engaging in activities aimed at influencing public officials, especially legislators, and the policies they enact.

The Internet helps interest groups in two ways. First, it allows citizens to easily organize themselves for rallies, marches, letter-writing drives, and other kinds of civic participation. Second, the Internet opens new, exclusively online forms of political action, such as sending mass e-mails, posting videos, joining Facebook groups, donating money online, commenting on articles, and blogging. We discuss these developments in greater detail in Chapter 10.

Mass Mailing One means of communication that has increased the reach and effectiveness of interest groups is computerized and targeted mass mailing.[26] Before computers, interest groups could either cull lists of people to contact from telephone directories and other sources or send mailings indiscriminately. Today's computerized mailing-list technology can target personalized letters to specific groups. Environmental groups make extensive use of targeted mail and e-mail.[27]

SIMULATION
You Are a Lobbyist

Direct Contact with Government Organized groups have ready access to the executive and regulatory agencies that write the rules implementing laws passed by Congress. Government agencies publish proposed regulations in the ***Federal Register*** and invite responses from all interested persons before the rules are finalized—in the "notice and comments period."[28] Well-staffed associations and corporations use the *Register* to obtain the specific language and deadlines for pending regulations. Lobbyists prepare written responses to the proposed rules, draft alternative rules, and make their case at the hearings. These lobbyists seek to be on good terms with the staff of the agency so that they can learn what rules are being considered long before they are released publicly and thus have early input. Administrative rules are defined over time through legal cases and agency modifications, so even if an interest group fails to get what it wants, it can go to court or press for a reinterpretation when the agency changes leadership.

Federal Register
An official document, published every weekday, that lists the new and proposed regulations of executive departments and regulatory agencies.

***amicus curiae* brief**
Literally, a "friend of the court" brief, filed by an individual or organization to present arguments in addition to those presented by the immediate parties to a case.

Finally, an interest group can seek to modify rules it does not like by pressuring Congress to change the legal mandate for the governing agency or reduce its budget, making it difficult to enforce rules. In short, interest groups and lobbyists never really quit fighting for their point of view.

Will America's Wildlife
Survive the Next Congress?
DEFENDERS OF WILDLIFE ACTION FUND
Defenders of Wildlife, a wildlife conservation group, tries to elect its allies to Congress. While non-partisan, the group usually backs Democrats, as Democrats tend to be more sympathetic to its interests.

Litigation When groups find the political channels closed to them, they may turn to the courts.[29] The Legal Defense and Educational Fund of the National Association for the Advancement of Colored People (NAACP), for example, initiated and won numerous court cases in its efforts to end racial segregation and protect the right to vote for African Americans. Urban interests, feeling underrepresented in state and national legislatures, turned to the courts to press for one-person, one-vote rulings to overcome the disproportionate power rural interests had in legislatures and to otherwise influence the political process.[30] Women's groups, such as the National Organization for Women (NOW) and the ACLU's Women's Rights Project, also used the courts to pursue their objectives.[31] In the aftermath of liberal groups' success before the courts, many conservative groups such as the Washington Legal Foundation and the American Center for Law and Justice are now litigating and winning their own cases before the courts.[32] Another conservative group is the James Madison Center for Free Speech. This group and its general counsel, James Bopp, have taken the lead in challenging many campaign finance laws and hope to overturn the 2002 McCain-Feingold law that banned party soft money and restored the prior ban on corporations and unions using their general funds for candidate electioneering purposes.[33]

In addition to initiating lawsuits, associations can gain a forum for their views in the courts by filing ***amicus curiae* briefs** (literally, "friend of the court" briefs) presenting arguments in cases in which they are not direct parties. It is not unusual for courts to cite such briefs in their opinions. Despite the general impression that associations achieve great success in the courts, groups are no more likely than individuals to win at the district court level.[34]

Protest To generate interest and broaden support for their cause, movements and groups often use protest demonstrations. For example, after the House of Representatives passed new laws on illegal immigration in 2006, pro-immigrant groups mounted protests in cities such as Phoenix and Washington, D.C., with more than one million participants.[35] Two months later, in a protest called "A Day Without Immigrants," more than 600,000 protesters gathered in Los Angeles to focus greater media attention on the important role immigrants play in the economy; similar rallies in Chicago drew more than 400,000 people.[36] (The legislation died when differences between the Senate and House versions of the bill could not be reconciled.) Other movements or groups that have used protest include the civil rights movement and antiwar, environmental, and antiglobalization groups.[37]

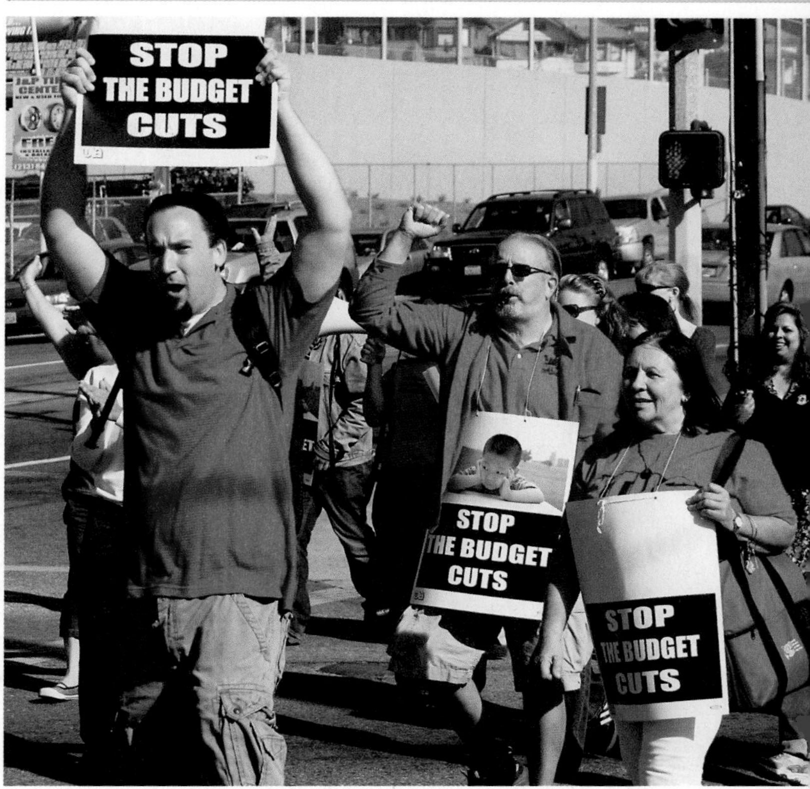

Teachers in downtown Los Angeles protest proposed state budget cuts for education. Groups often use protest as a way of generating interest and increasing support for their causes.

Support of Candidates Most large organizations are politically engaged in some way, though they may be, or try to be, *nonpartisan.* Most organized interest groups try to work through *both* parties and want to be friendly with the winners, which often means they contribute to incumbents. But as competition for control of both houses of Congress has intensified and with presidential contests also up for grabs, many interest groups invest mostly in one party or the other.

Many interest groups publicly endorse candidates for office, either directly by issuing a statement or hosting an event, or indirectly by publishing scorecards of how candidates responded to roll call votes or questionnaires administered by the group. Some groups give candidates letter grades from A to F. The League of Conservation Voters names candidates it opposes to its "environmental dirty dozen," while praising others as "environmental champions."[38]

Labor usually favors Democrats. The AFL-CIO has supported every Democratic candidate for president since the New Deal in the 1930s. Although the Teamsters Union has often endorsed Republicans, in 2004, it joined most other unions in backing John Kerry and it endorsed Barack Obama for president in the 2008 general election. Business groups generally favor Republicans. The differing views of their members prevent some organizations from taking a firm position.

Ideological groups target certain candidates, seeking to change their positions or influence voters against them. Americans for Democratic Action and the American Conservative Union publish ratings of the voting records of members of congress on liberal and conservative issues; so do the U.S. Chamber of Commerce, the AFL-CIO, and other groups on issues important to them.

Contributions to Campaigns Interest groups also form political action committees (PACs), which are the legal mechanism for them to contribute money to candidates, political party committees, and other political committees. One of the oldest PACs is the Committee on Political Education (COPE) of the AFL-CIO, but business groups and others have long existed to direct money to favored candidates. PACs also encourage other PACs to contribute to favored candidates, occasionally hosting joint fund-raisers for candidates.We discuss PACs in greater detail later in the chapter.

Federal Election Rules, PACs, and the Money Trail

Individuals clearly associated with an interest group also contribute to campaigns as individuals in ways that make clear to the candidate the interest of the donor. Often one party gathers contributions from several individuals and then gives the checks made out to the candidate's campaign in a bundle, a process called **bundling.** This can also be done via computer.

bundling
A tactic in which PACs collect contributions from like-minded individuals (each limited to $2,000) and present them to a candidate or political party as a "bundle," thus increasing the PAC's influence.

A group of people protest the Supreme Court nomination of Robert Bork in 1987. Due in part to the pressure of such protests, Bork's nomination was not confirmed.

New Political Parties Another interest group strategy is to form a political party, not so much to win elections as to publicize a cause. Success in such cases may occur when a major party co-opts the interest group's issue. The Free Soil Party was formed in the mid-1840s to work against the spread of slavery into the territories, and the Prohibition Party was organized two decades later to ban the sale of liquor. Farmers have formed a variety of such parties. More often, however, interest groups prefer to work through existing parties.

Today, environmental groups and voters for whom the environment is a central issue must choose between supporting the Green Party, which has yet to elect a candidate to federal office, an Independent candidate such as Ralph Nader in 2008, or one of the two major parties. Sometimes minor-party candidates can spoil the chances of a major-party candidate. In a New Mexico congressional special election in 1997, the Green Party candidate won 17 percent of the vote, taking some votes from the Democrat and thereby helping to elect a Republican to what had been a Democratic seat. In the 1998 election, environmental groups campaigned aggressively for the Democrat in the same district, who obtained 53 percent of the vote, while all minor parties combined got only 4 percent.[39] In South Dakota's 2002 Senate race between Tim Johnson (D) and John Thune (R), the Libertarian candidate got more than 3,000 votes. Johnson defeated Thune by just over 500 votes. After the 2000 presidential election, many Democrats blamed Green Party candidate Ralph Nader for diverting votes from Gore in such battlegrounds as Florida and New Hampshire, costing him the election. Explicit appeals from the party and from interest groups may have helped reduce Nader's impact in 2004.[40] In 2008, the closeness of the race and the scope of the issue agenda meant that Nader was largely overlooked by the major party presidential candidates, parties, interest groups and the media.

SIMULATION

You Are the Leader of Concerned Citizens for World Justice

Cooperative Lobbying Like-minded groups often form cooperative groups. In 1987, the Leadership Conference on Civil Rights and People for the American Way brought together many groups to defeat the nomination of outspoken federal judge Robert Bork to the U.S. Supreme Court.[41] Different types of environmentalists work together, as do consumer and ideological groups on the right and on the left. For example, although a large variety of groups that reflect diverse interests represent women, the larger the coalition, the greater the chance that members may divide over such issues as abortion. Another example of a cooperative group is the Business Roundtable, an association of chief executive officers of the 200 largest American corporations, which promotes policies that help large businesses, such as free trade and less government regulation.

The Influence of Lobbyists

Individuals who try to influence policy decisions and positions, often representing groups, are called **lobbyists.** The term "lobbying" was not generally used until around the midnineteenth century in the United States. These words refer to the lobby or hallway outside the House and Senate chambers in the U.S. Capitol and to those who hung around the lobby of the old Willard Hotel in Washington, D.C., when presidents dined there. The noun "lobby" is now used as a verb.

lobbyist
A person who is employed by and acts for an organized interest group or corporation to try to influence policy decisions and positions in the executive and legislative branches.

Despite their negative public image, lobbyists perform useful functions for government. They provide information for decision makers in all three branches of government, help educate and mobilize public opinion, help prepare legislation and testify before legislative hearings, and contribute a large share of the costs of campaigns. Yet many people

THE CHANGING FACE OF U.S. POLITICS

Breaking into a Male-Dominated Profession

Relatively few women and minorities are lobbyists. The first woman to own a lobbying firm was Anne Wexler, who started her own firm after leaving the Carter administration in 1981. Wexler observes that when she started, "there were very few women in lobbying. It was completely male dominated."* That remains the case today. In a 2001 study, nearly four-fifths of lobbyists were male† and more than 99 percent were white.‡

Women have begun to make inroads into the lobbying profession, especially in areas such as health care, reproductive rights, and education. Because the number of women serving in senior congressional and White House staffs has grown, the pool of women that may become senior lobbyists has similarly grown.§ Lewis was the senior advisor for Hillary Clinton for President and served as the director of communications for HillPAC and Friends of Hillary 2005–2007. She was also the director of communications and then counselor to Bill Clinton. She was the head of the political division of the DNC from 1981–1985. She was the VP for public policy at Planned Parenthood from 1994–1995.

*Jeffrey H. Birnbaum, "Women, Minorities Make Up New Generation of Lobbyists," *Washington Post,* May 1, 2006, p. D1.
†Paul C. Light and Virginia Thomas, "Posts of Honor: How America's Corporate and Civic Leaders View Presidential Appointments," *Presidential Appointee Initiative Paper* (Brookings Institution, 2001).
‡Jeffrey H. Birnbaum, "Number of Black Lobbyists Remains Shockingly Low," *Washington Post,* August 7, 2006, p. D01.
§Birnbaum, "Women, Minorities Make Up New Generation of Lobbyists."

fear that lobbyists have too much influence on government and add to legislative gridlock by stopping action on pressing problems.

Who Are the Lobbyists?

The typical image of policy making is of powerful, hard-nosed lobbyists who use a combination of knowledge, persuasiveness, personal influence, charm, and money to influence legislators and bureaucrats. Often former public servants themselves, lobbyists are experienced in government and often go to work for one of the interests they dealt with while in government, or for a lobbying firm.

Moving from a government job to a job with an interest group—or vice versa—is so common that this career path is called the **revolving door.** Although it is illegal for former national government employees to directly lobby the agency from which they came, their contacts made during government service are helpful to interest groups. Many former members of Congress use their congressional experience as full-time lobbyists. In 2007, Congress passed the Honest Leadership and Open Government Act, which requires more disclosure of employment history of lobbyists, sets stricter limits on lobbyist activities, requires senators to wait two years before lobbying, and requires staff to wait one year before lobbying any Senate office. Although this may slow the revolving door, it will not likely stop it.

The revolving door creates **issue networks** or relationships among interest groups, congressional committees and subcommittees, and government agencies that share a common policy concern. Sometimes these networks become so strong and mutually beneficial that they form a sort of subgovernment. A former senior staff person from a House or Senate agriculture committee now working as a lobbyist for an agricultural corporation who has ongoing friendships with his former staff colleagues, including some who now work at the Department of Agriculture, is an example of how personal relationships work within an issue network.

Legal and political skills, along with specialized knowledge, are so crucial in executive and legislative policy making that they have become a form of power in themselves. Elected representatives increasingly depend on their staffs for guidance, and these issue specialists know more about "Section 504" or "Title IX" or "the 2002 amendments"—and who wrote them and why—than most political and administrative leaders, who are usually generalists.[42] New laws often need specific rules and applications spelled out in detail by the agencies charged to administer them. In this rule-making activity, interest groups and issue networks assume even more significance.

revolving door
An employment cycle in which individuals who work for government agencies that regulate interests eventually end up working for interest groups or businesses with the same policy concern.

issue network
Relationships among interest groups, congressional committees and subcommittees, and the government agencies that share a common policy concern.

What Do Lobbyists Do?

Thousands of lobbyists are active in Washington, but few are as glamorous or as unscrupulous as the media suggest, nor are they necessarily influential. One limit on their power is the competition among interest groups. As we've seen, rarely does any one group have a policy area all to itself.

To members of Congress, the single most important thing lobbyists provide is money for their next reelection campaign. "Reelection underlies everything else," writes political scientist David Mayhew.[43] Money from interest groups is the most important source funding this driving need among incumbents. Interest groups also provide volunteers for campaign activity. In addition, their failure to support the opposition can enhance an incumbent's chances of being reelected.

Beyond their central role in campaigns and elections, interest groups provide information of two important types, political and substantive. *Political information* includes such matters as who supports or opposes legislation, including the executive branch, and how strongly they feel about it.[44] *Substantive information*, such as the impact of proposed laws, may not be available from any other source. Lobbyists often provide technical assistance for drafting bills and amendments, identifying persons to testify at legislative hearings, and formulating questions to ask administration officials at oversight hearings.

Money and Politics

Interest groups also seek to influence politics and public policy by spending money on elections. They can do this in several ways. One way is by contributing money to candidates for their election campaigns; another is by contributing to political parties that assist candidates seeking office, especially in contested races. They can also contribute money to other interest groups; communicate to the members of their group, including employees; and spend money independently of the parties and candidates.

LEARNING **OBJECTIVE**

5 Assess how some interest groups use money to pursue their agendas and evaluate the consequences for interest group pluralism of some groups having little money.

Helping to elect candidates creates a relationship between the interest group and the elected official that a group may exploit in the policy process. At a minimum, substantial involvement in the election process helps provide access to policy makers.[45] We discuss the dynamics of campaign finance and efforts to reform or regulate it in Chapter 9. Here we discuss the most important ways interest groups organize and participate in funding campaigns and elections.

Political Action Committees (PACs)

A **political action committee (PAC)** is the political arm of an interest group legally entitled to raise limited and disclosed funds on a voluntary basis from members, stockholders, or employees in order to contribute funds to favored candidates or political parties. PACs link two vital techniques of influence—giving money and other political aid to politicians and persuading officeholders to act or vote "the right way" on issues. Thus PACs are one important means by which interest groups seek to influence which legislators are elected and what they do once they take office.[46] We categorize PACs according to the type of interest they represent: corporations, trade and health organizations, labor unions, ideological organizations, and so on.

political action committee (PAC)
The political arm of an interest group that is legally entitled to raise funds on a voluntary basis from members, stockholders, or employees to contribute funds to candidates or political parties.

PACs grew in number and importance in the 1970s, in part because of campaign finance reform legislation enacted in that decade. The number of PACs registered rose from 608 in 1974 to 4,234 today.[47] Corporations and trade associations contributed most to this growth; today their PACs constitute the majority of all PACs. Labor PACs, by contrast, represent less than 7 percent of all PACs.[48] But the increase in the number of PACs is less important than the intensity of PAC participation in elections and lobbying (see Figure 6–3).

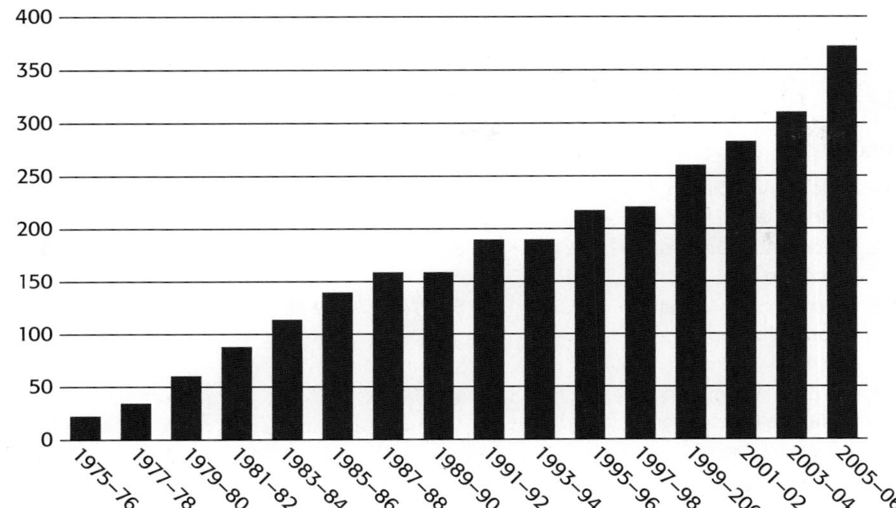

FIGURE 6–3
Total PAC Contributions to Federal Candidates, 1975–2006 (in Millions).

SOURCE: Harold W. Stanley and Richard G. Niemi, *Vital Statistics on American Politics 2005–2006* (CQ Press), p. 103; Federal Election Commission, "PAC Activity Continues to Climb in 2006," press release, October 5, 2007, www.fec.gov/press/press2007/20071009pac/20071009pac.shtml.

Surprisingly, considering that the growth in numbers of PACs has occurred mainly in the business world, organized labor invented this device. In the 1930s, John L. Lewis, president of the United Mine Workers, set up the Non-Partisan Political League as the political arm of the newly formed Congress of Industrial Organizations (CIO). When the CIO merged with the American Federation of Labor (AFL), the new labor group established the Committee on Political Education (COPE), whose activities we have already described. This unit came to be the model for most political action committees: "From the outset, national, state, and local units of COPE have not only raised and distributed funds, but have also served as the mechanism for union activity in the electoral process, including voter registration, political education, and get-out-the-vote drives."[49] Some years later, manufacturers formed the Business and Industry Political Action Committee (BIPAC), but the most active business PAC today is the one affiliated with the National Federation of Independent Business.[50] Table 6–2 lists the most active PACs in elections since 2000.

More recently, elected officials have begun to form their own PACs to collect contributions from individuals and other PACs and then make contributions to candidates and political parties.[51] These committees, called **leadership PACs,** were initially a tool of aspiring congressional leaders to curry favor with candidates in their political party. For example, House Speaker Nancy Pelosi has a leadership PAC that raised and spent more than $1 million dollars in the 2000, 2002, and 2004 election cycles each, and more than $800,000 in 2006.[52] She, in turn, contributed to other Democratic House candidates which helped her win support when she campaigned to be Speaker of the House in 2007.

How PACs Invest Their Money

PACs take part in the entire election process, but their main influence lies in their capacity to contribute money to candidates. Candidates today need a lot of money to wage their campaigns. And as PACs contribute more, their influence grows. What counts is not only how much they give, but who gets it. PACs give to the most influential incumbents, to committee chairs, to party leaders and whips, and to the Speaker of the House. More pragmatic PACs give not only to the majority party, but also to key incumbents in the minority party, because today's minority could be tomorrow's majority. One scholar of congressional elections states that although PACs' "avowed intention is 'to keep our friends in office and elect those

leadership PAC
A PAC formed by an officeholder that collects contributions from individuals and other PACs and then makes contributions to other candidates and political parties.

TABLE 6–2 PACs That Gave the Most to Federal Candidates, Cumulatively, 2000–2006 (Millions of Dollars)

PAC	2000	2002	2004	2006	Total
1. National Association of Realtors	$3,423	$3,649	$3,787	$3,752	$14,611
2. National Auto Dealers Association	$2,499	$2,579	$2,603	$2,822	$10,502
3. Laborers International Union of North America	$2,246	$2,814	$2,684	$2,687	$10,432
4. American Association for Justice (Association of Trial Lawyers of America)	$2,661	$2,814	$2,181	$2,558	$10,214
5. International Brotherhood of Electrical Workers	$2,635	$2,249	$2,370	$2,797	$10,051
6. National Beer Wholesalers Association	$1,872	$2,065	$2,314	$2,947	$9,197
7. Teamsters Union	$2,555	$2,390	$1,917	$2,085	$8,948
8. National Association of Home Builders	$1,846	$1,925	$2,202	$2,900	$8,872
9. United Auto Workers	$2,150	$2,339	$2,076	$2,220	$8,785
10. American Federation of State, County, and Municipal Employees	$2,586	$2,424	$1,639	$2,049	$8,698

SOURCE: Center for Responsive Politics, "Political Action Committees," www.opensecrets.org/pacs/index.asp.

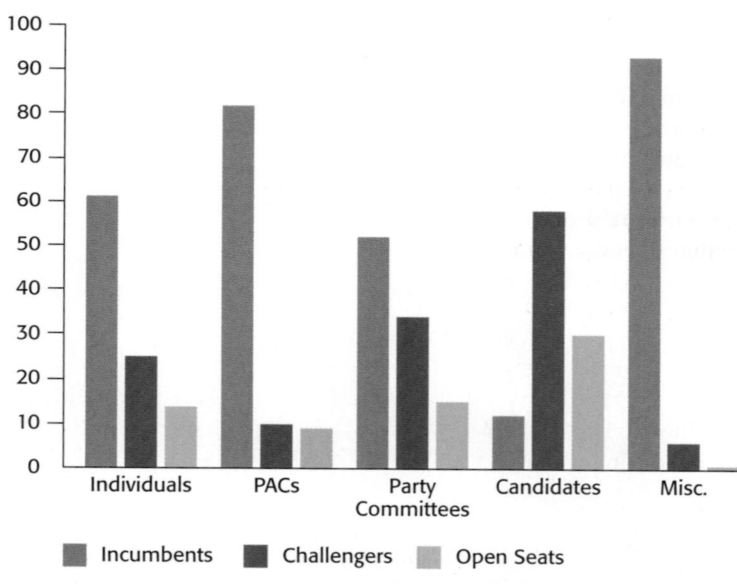

FIGURE 6–4
How PACs and Others Allocated Campaign Contributions to House Candidates, 2005–2006.

SOURCE: Compiled from Federal Election Commission data, "Candidate Financial Summaries," www.fec.gov/finance/disclosure/ftpsum.shtml.

who are our friends,' it is perhaps more accurate to say that they aim to ensure that those in office remain their friends."[53]

PACs are important not only because they contribute such a large share of the money congressional candidates raise for their campaigns, but also because they contribute so disproportionately to incumbents. In the most recent election cycle, House incumbents seeking reelection raised 46 percent of the funds for their campaigns from PACs, compared to only 17 percent for the challengers opposing them. In total, House incumbents raised almost ten PAC dollars for every one PAC dollar going to a challenger. Senate incumbents raise proportionately more from individuals, but also enjoy a fundraising advantage among PACs compared to Senate challengers (see Figure 6–4). One reason members of Congress become entrenched in their seats is that PACs fund them. Many members of Congress thrive on the present arrangements, and the leaders and members of both parties actively compete for PAC dollars.

The law limits the amount of money that PACs, like individuals, can contribute to any single candidate in an election cycle. But raising money from PACs is more efficient for a candidate than raising it from individuals. Since the

1970s, PAC contributions to any federal candidate have been limited to $10,000 per election cycle (primary and general elections), while individuals are limited to $4,600 per candidate per election cycle. The **Bipartisan Campaign Reform Act (BCRA)** doubled individual contribution limits and mandated that they increase with inflation while leaving PAC contribution limits unchanged. This probably reflected the view of the legislators that actual corruption or the appearance of it is more likely to come from organized interests such as unions, trade associations, and businesses than from individuals.

PACs have found creative ways around this limit. They can host fund-raisers attended by other PACs to boost their reputation with the candidate, or they can collect money from several individual contributors and give it to the candidate as a bundle, a process called *bundling*. Two of the most important groups doing bundling in recent elections were EMILY's List and the Club for Growth. EMILY's List, which stands for "Early Money Is Like Yeast," raises money from individuals committed to electing Democratic women who are pro-choice on abortion. It identifies candidates who fit its criteria and then solicits checks for them at an early stage in a campaign. The Club for Growth, a libertarian, anti-tax group, sees itself as applying the same bundling techniques as EMILY's List but for pro-growth and antitax candidates who are mainly Republicans.

PAC contributions are especially made to committee chairs and party leaders. To reinforce this relationship, the Republicans developed a strategy, the "K Street Project," to do even better in getting PAC contributions. (K Street in Washington, D.C., houses many of the lobbying and law firms that represent trade associations and corporations that make contributions.) Former House Republican leader Tom DeLay, a prime mover in the K Street Project, once said, "If you want to play in our revolution you have to live by our rules," meaning contribute to our candidates.[54] DeLay, under indictment in Texas for money laundering, resigned his seat in 2006.

Since the Democratic party took control of Congress in 2007, some PACs have changed loyalties. In the House, approximately 60 percent of PAC money goes to Democrats and 40 percent to Republicans. Before Congress changed hands, just the opposite was true—about 60 percent of PAC money went to Republicans. In the Senate, Republicans still receive more PAC money than Democrats, but the gap is decreasing.

Mobilizing Employees and Members

Another way interest groups can influence the outcome of elections is by persuading their employees, members, or stockholders to vote in a way consistent with the interests of the group. They accomplish this mobilization through targeted communications at the workplace, through the mail, on the telephone, or on the Internet. As we discuss elsewhere in this chapter, labor unions have been especially effective in member communications. Corporations and business associations have been following labor's lead. Membership organizations such as the NRA have also been able to mobilize their members and allied individuals and groups.[55]

Other Modes of Electioneering

Until the 2004 election cycle, interest groups and individuals could avoid the contribution limitation to political parties by contributing so-called **soft money** to political parties. Originally justified as an exception to contribution limits to help the political parties by funding get-out-the-vote drives or party appeals that are not specific, soft money came to be used for candidate-specific electioneering.[56] Corporations and unions, long banned from giving directly to candidates and parties from their general funds for election-specific purposes, were permitted to give soft money, and they did so in large amounts. By the 2000 and 2002 election cycles, soft money had climbed to around $500 million. BCRA banned soft money

Bipartisan Campaign Reform Act (BCRA)
Largely banned party soft money, restored long-standing prohibition on corporations and labor unions for using general treasury funds for electoral purposes, and narrowed the definition of issue advocacy.

soft money
Money raised in unlimited amounts by political parties for party-building purposes. Now largely illegal except for limited contributions to state or local parties for voter registration and get-out-the-vote efforts.

YOU WILL DECIDE Should Corporations and Unions Be Unlimited in Funding Parties and in Running Issue Ads?

Does limiting the ability of corporations or unions to use their general or "treasury" funds for election-related expenditures violate the constitutional guarantee of freedom of speech? Corporations and unions, like other groups, are free to form political action committees to make contributions to candidates and parties. What has been at dispute is whether they could take their profits or general funds and spend those on electing or defeating candidates or in support of party efforts. For more than a century, federal law had banned unions and corporations from spending general or treasury funds on electoral politics. That changed with 1979 legislation allowing unions and corporations to give unlimited general treasury funds or profits to help political parties generally. This was called soft money. In 1996 unions and later corporations began spending unlimited and undisclosed amounts of money on "issue ads," which were really campaign commercials. The Bipartisan Campaign Reform Act banned soft money contributions to parties and more clearly defined what unions and corporations could spend general treasury money on before an election. BCRA expanded the definition of an election communication to include television or radio ads that refer to or show the image of a clearly identified federal candidate targeted to that Candidate's Constituency and air within 30 days of the primary or 60 days of the general election. The Supreme Court initially upheld both bans but later reversed itself on election communications. Given this reversal, opponents of the soft money ban are likely to again challenge this provision in court.

after the 2002 elections. We discuss party soft money in greater detail in Chapter 7 and BCRA in Chapter 9.

Between 1996 and 2002, interest groups could also help fund so-called issue ads supporting or opposing candidates as long as the ads did not use certain words. The Supreme Court in 2007 declared parts of BCRA relating to these kinds of ads unconstitutional, allowing corporations and unions to again spend their general funds on ads that advocate a point of view on political issues, which may affect elections.[57] Groups ran ads in 2008 that would have been banned by BCRA. Interest groups can avoid disclosure if they communicate with voters through the mail, in newspaper ads, on billboards, on the phone, and by e-mail.

Interest groups typically make the presidential campaign their highest priority. Some groups, such as the League of Conservation Voters (LCV), in the past had invested some of their resources in presidential races but made House and Senate races higher priorities. LCV did just the opposite in 2004.

Independent Expenditures

The Supreme Court in 1976 declared that limits on independent expenditures were unconstitutional when the contributions or expenditures were truly independent of a party or candidate. Hence, groups, like individuals, can campaign for or against a candidate, independent of a party or

Sen. John McCain, second left, and Sen. Russell Feingold smile during a news conference after the McCain-Feingold bill, also known as the Bipartisan Campaign Reform Act (BCRA), was passed in Congress. BCRA was created primarily to address the strong influence of soft money, and the increasing use of issue-advocacy advertisements in federal elections.

candidate committee and in addition to making contributions to candidates and party committees from their PAC. These **independent expenditures** are unlimited but must be disclosed to the Federal Election Commission (FEC). Interest-group independent expenditures fall well below PAC contributions to candidates and parties. Groups that have made heavy use of independent expenditures include MoveOn PAC, NRA, EMILY's List, several unions, National Right to Life PAC, the Club for Growth, and the National Association of Realtors. (See Table 6–3.) Independent expenditures enable groups to direct more money to a particular race than they can through PAC contributions, while still getting credit with their members for their activity because the source of independent expenditures is clearly communicated.

THINKING IT THROUGH

The Supreme Court in *McConnell v. FEC* cited a long list of precedents in upholding the limitation on unions and corporations using their general funds to influence elections. The economic power of corporations such as Microsoft or major unions could, if unconstrained, drown out the voices of other participants and corrupt the electoral process. The opinion of the majority quoted corporate executives who made illegal donations in the late 1960s and early 1970s, saying that "they were motivated by the perception that this was a 'calling card, something that would get us in the door and make our point of view heard.'"*

But unions and corporations have a point in arguing that constraints on them are unfair when compared with the ability of wealthy individuals to spend unlimited amounts of their own money on politics via independent expenditures, which the Court allowed in its prior landmark decision, *Buckley v. Valeo.*† Corporations and unions would also contend that soft money contributions were not bribes nor were they corrupting. Finally, they would agree with Justice Scalia's dissent in *McConnell v. FEC* that restricting how much a group "can spend to broadcast [its] political views is a direct restriction on speech."‡

With respect to electioneering or issue ads, in 2007 the reconstituted Supreme Court in *FEC v. Wisconsin Right to Life, Inc.* said the BCRA language was too broad in defining electioneering and that unions and corporations had a right to communicate with voters about political topics in the days and weeks before primary and general elections. Chief Justice Roberts substituted a new definition of electioneering communication. He defined an electioneering ad as one that "is susceptible of no other reasonable interpretation other than as an appeal to vote for or against a specific candidate."§ In the past, language like that used by Chief Justice Roberts provided media consultants with enough latitude to craft election communications, arguing that they were about issues and not candidates. This means that future elections could have substantial electioneering by unions and corporations on the eve of elections that is not subject to the other limitations of the law.

McConnell v. FEC, 124 S. Ct. 533 (2003).
†*Buckley v. Valeo*, 96 S. Ct. 760 (1976).
‡Justice Antonin Scalia, dissenting in *McConnell v. FEC*, 124 S. Ct. 618 (2003).
§*Federal Election Commission v. Wisconsin Right to Life Inc.*, 466 F. Supp. 2d 195 (2007).

Campaigning Through Other Groups

For more than a century, reformers had sought disclosure of money in politics. In campaigns and elections, disclosure was often incomplete, and groups quickly found ways to avoid it. Then the disclosure provisions of the Federal Election Campaign Act of 1971, amended in 1974, defined electioneering ads as communications that used words such as "vote for" or "vote against" and made them subject to disclosure and spending limits.

For a time, citizens, journalists, and scholars had a complete picture of who was giving what to whom, and who was spending money and in what ways, to influence elections. That changed in 1996, when interest groups found a way to circumvent disclosure and contribution limits through **issue advocacy.** They simply made election ads without the words "vote for" or "vote against," and then spent millions attacking or promoting particular candidates.

Labor unions were the first to exploit this tactic in a major way, spending an estimated $35 million in 1996, mostly against Republican candidates.[58] Corporations and ideological groups quickly followed labor's lead, spending millions on issue ads in 1996–2002. Not only did they avoid contribution limits, but they masked their identity by creating new names behind which to campaign. Citizens for Better Medicare was largely funded by the pharmaceutical industry, and the Coalition to Make Our Voices Heard was funded in part by labor unions.[59] Republicans for Clean Air, which attacked John McCain's environmental record in the 2000 presidential primaries, was really two Texas business executives, Sam and Charles Wyly.[60]

In the post–campaign reform elections of 2004, 2006, and 2008, interest groups continued to mount their own campaigns against or for candidates in ways similar to the old issue advocacy. For example, a group of Vietnam War veterans formed a group they named Swift Boat Veterans for Truth and ran ads attacking Senator John Kerry's Vietnam War record.[61] Groups like Swift Boat Veterans for Truth are called **527 organizations** because they are tax-exempt groups organized under section 527 of the Internal Revenue Service Code. They can run ads against or for candidates, but under somewhat more restrictive conditions than existed before 2004.

independent expenditures
The Supreme Court has ruled that individuals, groups, and parties can spend unlimited amounts in campaigns for or against candidates as long as they operate independently from the candidates. When an individual, group, or party does so, they are making an independent expenditure.

issue advocacy
Unlimited and undisclosed spending by an individual or group on communications that do not use words like "vote for" or "vote against," although much of this activity is actually about electing or defeating candidates.

TABLE 6–3 Independent Expenditures by Top Interest Groups, 2006

Interest Group	Expenditure
AFSCME–PEOPLE, Qualified	$4,537,070
National Association of Realtors PAC	3,739,173
EMILY's List	3,535,113
MoveOn.org PAC	2,857,643
Club for Growth, Inc. PAC	2,754,109
National Right to Life PAC	2,695,527
Service Employees International Union COPE	2,404,427
National Rifle Association of America Political Victory Fund	2,141,015
NEA Fund for Children and Public Education	1,977,435
American Medical Association PAC	1,434,453
VoteVets	842,096
League of Conservation Voters Action Fund	831,042
Sierra Club PAC	819,053

NOTE: Expenditures for all national affiliates of an organization are combined, but expenditures for state affiliates are excluded.

SOURCE: Federal Election Commission, ftp://ftp.fec.gov/FEC.

527 organization
A political group organized under section 527 of the IRS Code that may accept and spend unlimited amounts of money on election activities so long as they are not spent on broadcast ads run in the last 30 days before a primary or 60 days before a general election in which a clearly identified candidate is referred to and a relevant electorate is targeted.

During the 2004 election cycle, 527 groups were much more active on the liberal or Democratic side than on the conservative or Republican side. Democratic activists and allied interest groups understood that the Bipartisan Campaign Reform Act ban on soft money would leave the party and its presidential candidate at a disadvantage against the fund-raising prowess of President Bush and the Republicans. As we discuss in Chapter 7, the Democrats were more dependent on soft money than the Republicans before BCRA. Thus after BCRA they started early and invested

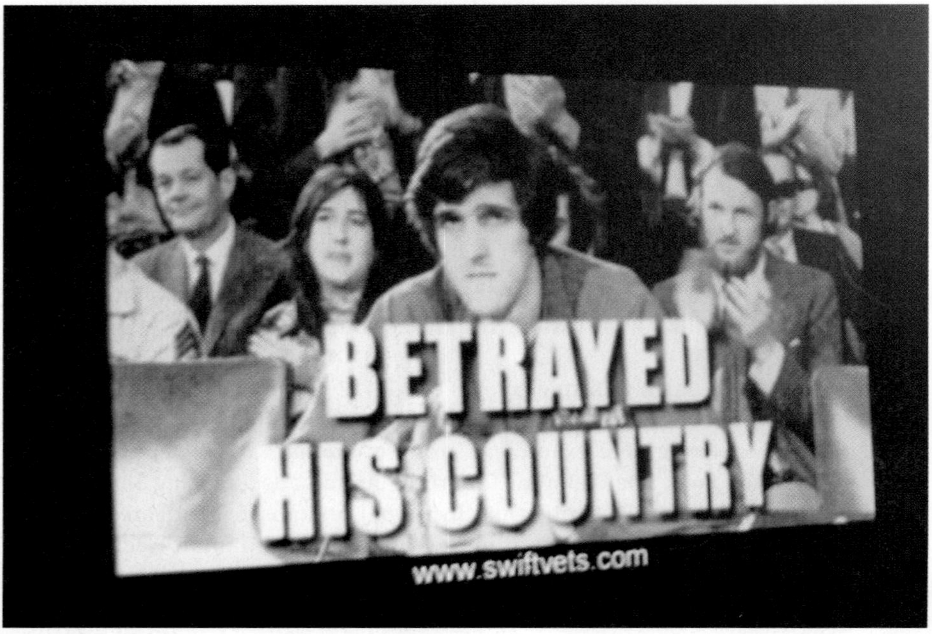

In this image from one of Swift Boat Veterans for Truth's television advertisements, then presidential nominee John Kerry's patriotism and Vietnam War record are called into question. Issues groups such as the Swift Boat Veteran's for Truth avoid many of the regulations that individual campaigns face, and can play an important role in elections.

TABLE 6–4 Top Twenty 527 Committees by Expenditures, Cumulative, 2003–2004 and 2005–2006

Rank	Committee	2004	2006	Total
1	America Coming Together	$78,040,480	$ 6,998,238	$85,038,718
2	Service Employees International Union	47,695,646	28,212,510	75,908,156
3	Joint Victory Campaign 2004	72,588,053	123,337	72,711,390
4	Media Fund	57,694,580	1,985,044	59,679,624
5	Progress for America	35,631,378	13,000,574	48,631,952
6	College Republican National Committee	17,260,655	10,260,343	27,520,998
7	Swift Vets & POWs for Truth	22,565,360	1,092,373	23,657,733
8	MoveOn.org	21,565,803	261,733	21,827,536
9	Club for Growth	11,943,415	8,157,383	20,100,798
10	EMILY's List	8,100,752	11,128,005	19,228,757
11	America Votes	2,769,752	14,108,355	16,878,107
12	New Democrat Network	12,524,063	1,256,434	13,780,497
13	International Brotherhood of Electrical Workers	7,368,841	5,529,067	12,897,908
14	GOPAC	2,367,852	8,394,833	10,762,685
15	Citizens for a Strong Senate	10,228,515	329,334	10,557,849
16	Voices for Working Families	7,202,695	809,999	8,012,694
17	National Education Association	3,906,333	3,576,428	7,482,761
18	Sierra Club	6,261,811	1,121,016	7,382,827
19	Citizens United	0	7,256,082	7,256,082
20	Laborers Union	3,294,785	3,762,110	7,056,895

SOURCE: Center for Responsive Politics, "527 Committee Activity," www.opensecrets.org/527s/527cmtes.asp.

heavily in their 527 groups. Interest groups allied to Democrats, including 527 groups, were again more active in 2006 than Republican-allied groups. Labor unions, teachers' unions, trial lawyers, and 527 organizations such as America Votes all were active in competitive federal races. Corporations have been less likely to fund 527 groups

Interest groups also used other sections of the tax code to involve themselves in the election. Section 501(c) of the tax code permits some groups to organize, and for some purposes such as nonpartisan voter registration drives, donations to the group are tax deductible. Contributions to partisan groups such as the NRA and MoveOn are tax deductible. Nor are contributions to labor unions and business groups such not tax deductible. Nor are contributions to labor unions and business groups such as the Chamber of Commerce.[62] In 2004, Republicans found more allies in 501(c) organizations.[63] In 2006 and 2008, 501(c) organizations were involved in activities that helped register and inform voters, often with an indirect benefit to one party. In 2008 groups on both sides of the partisan divide made use of 501(c) groups. Among those most active were Planned Parenthood, the League of Conservation Voters, and Defenders of Wildlife who mostly supported Democrats, and the Chamber of Commerce which largely supported Republicans.[64]

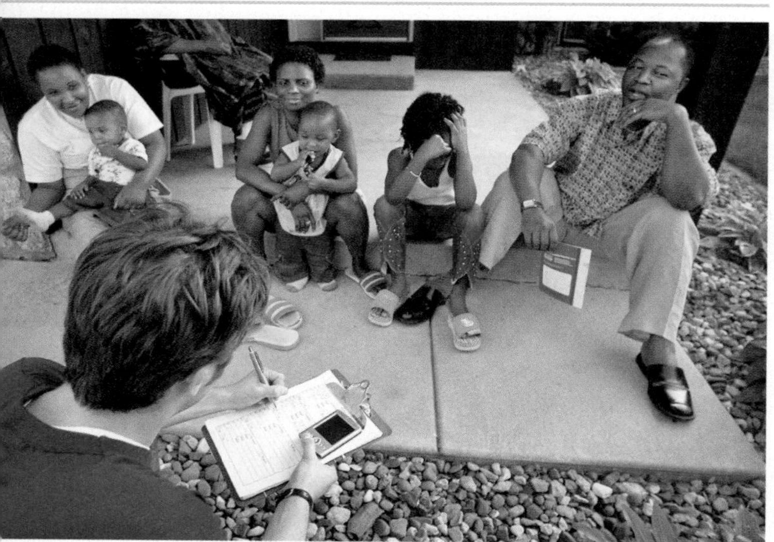

An important part of campaigns is registering new voters and canvassing them about their views on issues. In this photo Tim Schumann uses a palm pilot to record survey responses from a Minnesota family. Tim worked with America Coming Together, an interest group active in the 2004 election.

How Much Do Interest Groups Influence Elections and Legislation?

We've said that because PACs give more money to incumbents, challengers have difficulty funding their campaigns and have to rely more on individual contributors. Even with the larger individual contribution limits allowed in 2004 and since, most challengers still had less money than their incumbent opponents.

How much does interest group money influence election outcomes, legislation, and representation? Former U.S. senator Alan Simpson (R-Wyo.) said that "too often, members' first thought is not what is right or what they believe, but how it will affect fundraising. Who, after all, can seriously contend that a $100,000 donation does not alter the way one thinks about—and quite possibly votes on—an issue?"[65] Another former senator, Warren Rudman (R-N.H.), says, "you can't swim in the ocean without getting wet; you can't be part of this system without getting dirty."[66] In this area, as in others, money obviously talks. But it is easy to exaggerate its influence. Although a candidate may receive a great amount of interest group money, only a fraction of that total comes from any single group. It is also debatable how much campaign contributions affect elections, and there is no guarantee that money produces a payoff in legislation.

Much depends, however, on the context in which money is given and received. Many campaigns—especially state and local campaigns—are small-scale undertakings in which a big contribution makes a difference. Amid all the murk of campaigning, a candidate may feel grateful for so tangible and useful a contribution as money. Studies demonstrate a significant relationship between the frequency of lobbying contacts and favorable treatment in the House Ways and Means and Agriculture Committees. Campaign contributions are correlated with lobbying patterns, meaning that contributions to representatives and senators are more likely to result in committee action, "formulating amendments, negotiating specific provisions or report language behind the scenes, developing legislative strategy, and in other activities that require substantial time, information, and energy on the part of member and staff."[67]

Communicating with Voters and Members

How effective is electioneering by interest groups? In general, mass-membership organizations fail to mobilize their full membership in elections, although they can effectively mobilize when their interests are directly attacked.[68] More typically, too many cross-pressures operate in the pluralistic politics of the United States for any one group to assume a commanding role. Some groups reach their maximum influence only by allying themselves closely with one of the two major parties. They may place their members on local, state, and national party committees and help send them to party conventions as delegates, but forming such alliances means losing some independence.

Numerous groups sought to mobilize their membership in recent elections. They created Web sites for members to obtain information about their view of candidates and provided voter registration materials and absentee ballot request forms. They also solicited contributions to help fund these efforts. Organized labor, long perceived to be the leader in voter mobilization, has been especially active. The Republican Party and allied groups, having learned from labor's techniques, have

GENERATION NEXT

Are Corporations Too Powerful?

Corporations possess substantial wealth and have on occasion been major players in the political process. As noted in this chapter, government regulation of the political activity of corporations has been in place for more than a century. Even with those regulations in place, the question remains, are corporations too powerful? The data summarized here look at a general question on corporate power and then compare attitudes of persons from households that are professional or business-class and those from working-class households.

Age does not make much difference in how people view corporations. Between 75 and 81 percent of the different categories of age say corporations are too powerful. Among 18–29 year olds only, women, Democrats, and moderates were more likely to agree that corporations are too powerful.

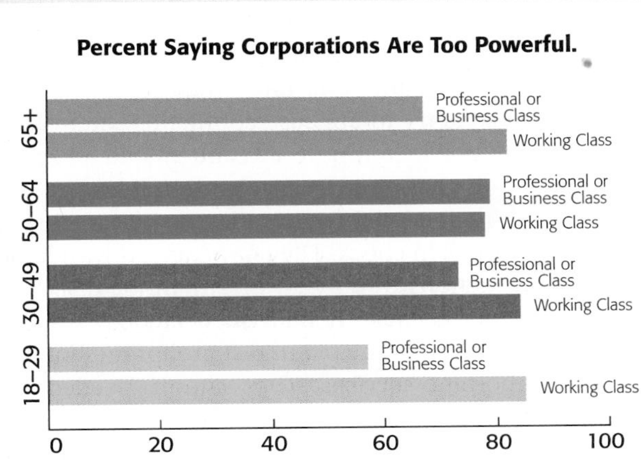

In the accompanying figure, we look at whether it makes a difference if a person comes from a household that is working class or professional/business class. The answer is that it makes a substantial difference, especially for 18–29 year olds. In this age cohort, persons from working-class households were far more likely to see corporations as too powerful (85 percent) than persons from professional or business-class households (57 percent). Moreover, compared to all age groups from business/professional households, the 18–29 year olds were the least likely of any age group to think corporations are too powerful.

QUESTIONS

1. What are some of the arguments for and against the idea that corporations have too much power?
2. Why do you think corporations continue to spend millions of dollars on campaign contributions?
3. The average congressional incumbent in 2006 received more than 50 percent of his or her funds from individual donors. Does this suggest that corporate campaign contributors exert too much influence over candidates?

mounted successful party-based voter mobilization efforts.[69] Business groups like the Chamber of Commerce have come to use the Internet as a way to help members and supporters register to vote, request absentee ballots, and remind them to vote on election day. But most voter mobilization on the Republican side is done by the party. Democrats rely much more on allied groups such as unions, environmental and pro-choice groups, and 527 organizations.

Curing the Mischiefs of Faction—Two Centuries Later

If James Madison were to return today, neither the existence of interest groups nor their variety would surprise him. However, the varied weapons of group influence, the deep investment of interest groups in the electoral process, and the vast number of lobbyists in Washington and the state capitals might come as a surprise. And doubtless Madison would still be concerned about the power of faction, especially its tendency to foster instability and injustice.

Concern about the evils of interest groups has been a recurrent theme throughout U.S. history. President Ronald Reagan in his Farewell Address warned of the power of "special interests,"[70] and President Dwight Eisenhower used his Farewell Address to warn against the "military-industrial complex," the alliance of defense industries and the U.S. military formed to pursue more spending on weapons.

Single-issue interest groups organized for or against particular policies—abortion, handgun control, tobacco subsidies, animal rights—have aroused increasing concern in recent years. "It is said that citizen groups organizing in ever greater numbers to push single issues ruin the careers of otherwise fine politicians who disagree with them on one emotional issue, paralyze the traditional process of governmental compromise, and ignore the common good in their selfish insistence on getting their own way."[71] But which single issues reflect narrow interests? Women's rights—even a specific issue such as sexual harassment—are hardly "narrow," women's rights leaders contend, because women represent more than half the population. Peace groups, too, claim that they represent the whole population, as do those who support prayer in schools. These issues may seem different from those related to subsidies for dairy farmers, for example.

One of the main arguments against interest groups is that they do not represent people equally. For example, fewer interest groups represent young or low-income people than represent senior citizens or corporations. Further, some groups are better organized and better financed, allowing them a decided advantage over more general groups. And the existence of a multiplicity of interests often leads to incoherent policies, inefficiency, and delay as lawmakers try to appease conflicting interests. In addition, the propensity of interest groups to support incumbents in elections increases the advantages of incumbency, which is often seen as undesirable.

What—if anything—should we do about factions? For decades, American citizens have tried to find ways to keep interest groups in check. They have agreed with James Madison that the "remedy" of outlawing factions would be worse than the disease. It would be absurd to abolish liberty simply because it nourished faction. And the Constitution solidly protects the existence and activity of interest groups and lobbies. Moreover, interest groups provide important services. They supply needed and accurate information to government officials. But by safeguarding the value of liberty, have we allowed interest groups to threaten equality, the second great value in our national heritage? The question remains: How can we regulate interest groups in a way that does not threaten our constitutional liberties?

The United States has generally responded to this question by seeking to regulate lobbying in general and political money in particular. Concern over the use of money—especially corporate funds—to influence politicians goes back well over a century, to the administration of Ulysses S. Grant in the 1870s, when members of Congress promoted the Crédit Mobilier construction company in exchange for the right to make huge profits by buying its stock below market value. In the Progressive Era during the first two decades of the twentieth century, Congress legislated against corporate contributions in federal elections and required disclosure of the use of the money.

In 1921, President Warren G. Harding's administration allowed private companies to secretly lease public land in order to extract oil that had been reserved for the navy. In response to this "Teapot Dome scandal," Congress passed the Federal Corrupt Practices Act of 1925. It required disclosure reports, both before and after elections, of receipts and expenditures by Senate and House candidates and by political committees that sought to influence federal elections in more than one state. Note that these were *federal* laws applying to *federal* elections; the states were left to regulate their own lobbying and elections.

But federal legislation was not very effective and was loosely enforced. Many candidates filed incomplete reports or none at all. The reform mood of the 1960s and the Watergate scandal of 1972 brought basic changes. The outcome was the Federal Election Campaign Act of 1971 (FECA), amended in 1974. We discuss FECA and the more recent Bipartisan Campaign Reform Act in greater detail in Chapter 9.

During President Bill Clinton's first term, and after the Republicans won control of Congress in 1994, Congress passed the first major overhaul of lobbying laws since 1946. Under the Lobbying Disclosure Act of 1995, the definition of a lobbyist was expanded to include part-time lobbyists, those who deal with congressional staff or executive branch agencies, and those who represent foreign-owned companies and foreign entities. This act was expected to increase the number of registered lobbyists to as much as ten times its then current level.[72] In fact, the number of registered "clients" nearly doubled eight years after enactment of the act,[73] and more recent estimates show additional growth in numbers. The act also included specific disclosure and information requirements.

As we have seen, groups are an important part of how democracy functions. But they can pose challenges and dangers to democracy, which Madison called the "mischiefs of faction." Limiting the negative impact of corruption, the appearance of corruption, and undue influence by some groups to the detriment of others or the country as a whole is a formidable challenge. Fostering competition among groups is one important response; government regulation including full disclosure of group activity is another. At the same time, government must be careful not to stifle or limit the positive role groups play in the functioning of a constitutional democracy.

Interest groups provide important opportunities for individuals to work together to pursue common objectives. Sometimes this means that individuals join existing groups, other times they form new ones. Groups not only foster healthy competition in our politics, but also teach important lessons about self-government.

CHAPTER **SUMMARY**

1 Evaluate the role of interest groups and social movements in American politics.

Interest groups form when a collection of people share similar political goals and organize to achieve them. Sometimes these groups are based on a shared group identity, such as race, ethnicity, gender, or sexual orientation. Others are based on specific policy issues, such as reducing taxes or combating global warming. Still others claim to operate in the public interest on broad issues, such as educating voters or reducing the federal deficit, but often many people do not agree with these groups actual positions on issues. Interest groups sometimes begin as social movements, which consist of many people at the grassroots level who are interested in a significant issue, idea, or concern and take action to support or oppose it.

2 Identify the different types of interest groups in the United States.

Interest groups can be categorized as economic, ideological or single-issue, public interest, foreign policy, and government itself. Economic groups include corporations, labor unions, and professional and trade associations; they lobby officials and campaign for candidates whose trade, tax, and regulation policies favor their financial situation. Ideological groups typically pursue a single policy goal through many means; for example, National Right to Life seeks to elect like-minded representatives, the ACLU litigates on behalf of clients whose civil liberties have been violated, and antiwar groups stage protests. Public interest groups claim to work on behalf of all citizens and include watchdog groups and charities. Foreign policy groups work to influence some area of the United States' international affairs and include organized lobbies such as AIPAC and grassroots movements such as Greenpeace. Finally, government groups include public sector unions such as the National Education Association and organizations that lobby on behalf of cities, states, and other government entities.

3 Compare the sources of interest group power.

Size, resources, cohesiveness, leadership, and techniques, especially the ability to contribute to candidates and political parties and to fund lobbyists, affect interest group power. But the actual power of an interest group stems from how these elements relate to the political and governmental environment in which the interest group operates. Interest groups typically include people with many other cross-cutting interests, which both reduces and stabilizes their influence.

4 Describe lobbyists and how they influence policy.

Lobbyists represent organized interests before government. Lobbying involves communicating with legislators and executive-branch officials, making campaign contributions, and assisting in election activity especially through political action committees (PACs). Interest groups also take their message directly to the public through mass mailings, advertising, and online media.

5 Assess how some interest groups use money to pursue their agendas and evaluate the consequences for interest group pluralism of some groups having little money.

Interest groups spend money to lobby government officials and to involve themselves in elections, especially through the expanded use of PACs. Groups that lack money typically struggle to get their message out to the public and fail to influence public officials.

Congress has enacted laws to regulate and reform excesses of interest groups in electoral democracy. The Federal Election Campaign Act (FECA) was passed in the 1970s in response to the Watergate scandal, and the Bipartisan Campaign Reform Act (BCRA) was passed in 2002 in response to soft money and other abuses by political parties and interest groups. In *WRTL v. FEC*, the Supreme Court ruled to remove some of the restrictions on interest group activities during elections.

Chapter Self-Test

1. In two or three sentences, analyze how the idea of pluralism explains the founders' method for protecting against overwhelming factions. (p. 148)
2. Briefly explain the differences between *special interests* and *public interests.* (p. 149)
3. Describe what a social movement is and explain how it differs from an interest group or public interest. (p. 149)
4. List five different types of interest groups. (pp. 150–157)
5. Match each interest group with the category it most closely fits. (pp. 150–157)

a. American Gaming Association	i. Public
b. National Right to Life	ii. Government
c. Project Vote Smart	iii. Economic
d. American-Israel Political Action Committee	iv. Ideological
e. The State Department	v. Foreign policy

6. A ________ PAC is a group formed by an office holder that collects contribution from individuals and other PACs and then makes contributions to other candidates and political parties. (p. 165)
7. In a short essay, compare and contrast the three sources of interest group power: size, cohesiveness, and leadership. In your answer provide an example of at least one group that exhibits each of the three sources and assess how it uses that power to influence national policy, and why. (pp. 158–159)
8. In a few sentences, explain the free rider problem as it applies to labor unions. (p. 152)
9. This Act permitted the government to take action against those trusts and banks that form a monopoly. (p. 151)
   a. Princeton
   b. Greenspan
   c. Wall Street
   d. Sherman
10. List three or four arguments against allowing interest groups to donate money to political campaigns. Responding to those arguments, write a brief, persuasive essay explaining why interest groups should be allowed to donate money to political campaigns. (pp. 164–171)
11. Describe five ways in which lobbyists attempt to influence policy (pp. 159–162).
12. Associations can gain a forum for their views by filing ________ briefs with courts. (p. 160)
13. PACs that collect contributions from a number of individuals and present them as a single package to a candidate engage in the practice of ________. (p. 161)
    a. targeting
    b. bundling
    c. giving soft money
    d. influence peddling
14. Describe what a PAC is and its characteristics. (pp. 164–165)
15. Write a short, persuasive essay that explains why it is important to allow well-funded groups to function at the expense of less well-funded groups. (pp. 164–171)

Key Terms

faction, p. 148
pluralism, p. 148
interest group, p. 149
movement, p. 149
open shop, p. 152
closed shop, p. 152
free rider, p. 152
professional associations, p. 153
nongovernmental organization (NGO), p. 156
collective action, p. 158
public choice, p. 158
lobbying, p. 159
***Federal Register*,** p. 160
***amicus curiae* brief,** p. 160
bundling, p. 161
lobbyist, p. 162
revolving door, p. 163
issue network, p. 163
political action committee (PAC), p. 164
leadership PAC, p. 165
Bipartisan Campaign Reform Act (BCRA), p. 167
soft money, p. 167
independent expenditures, p. 169
issue advocacy, p. 169
527 organization, p. 169

Further Reading

SCOTT H. AINSWORTH, *Analyzing Interest Groups: Group Influence on People and Policies* (Norton, 2002).

JEFFREY M. BERRY, *New Liberalism: The Rising Power of Citizen Groups* (Brookings Institution Press, 1999).

JEFFREY H. BIRNBAUM, *The Money Men: The Real Story of Fund-Raising's Influence on Political Power in America* (Crown, 2000).

WILLIAM P. BROWNE, *Groups, Interests, and Public Policy* (Georgetown University Press, 1998).

ALLAN J. CIGLER AND **BURDETT A. LOOMIS,** EDS., *Interest Group Politics,* 7th ed. (CQ Press, 2006).

MARTHA A. DERTHICK, *Up in Smoke,* 2d ed. (CQ Press, 2004).

KENNETH M. GOLDSTEIN, *Interest Groups, Lobbying, and Participation in America* (Cambridge University Press, 1999).

GENE GROSSMAN AND **ELHANAN HELPMAN,** *Special Interest Politics* (MIT Press, 2001).

PAUL S. HERRNSON, RONALD G. SHAIKO, AND **CLYDE WILCOX,** *The Interest Group Connection: Electioneering, Lobbying, and Policymaking in Washington,* 2d ed. (CQ Press, 2004).

ALLEN D. HERTZKE, *Representing God in Washington: The Role of Religious Lobbies in the American Polity* (University of Tennessee Press, 1988).

KEVIN W. HULA, *Lobbying Together: Interest Group Coalitions in Legislative Politics* (Georgetown University Press, 1999).

DAVID B. MAGLEBY, ANTHONY D. CORRADO, AND **KELLY D. PATTERSON,** EDS., *Financing the 2004 Election* (Brookings Institution Press, 2006).

DAVID B. MAGLEBY, J. QUIN MONSON, AND **KELLY D. PATTERSON,** EDS., *Electing Congress: New Rules for an Old Game* (Prentice Hall, 2006).

DAVID B. MAGLEBY AND **KELLY D. PATTERSON,** EDS., *The Battle for Congress: Iraq, Scandal, and Campaign Finance in the 2006 Election* (Paradigm, 2008).

MICHAEL J. MALBIN, ED., *The Election After Reform: Money, Politics, and the Bipartisan Campaign Reform Act* (Rowman & Littlefield, 2006).

ANTHONY J. NOWNES, *Total Lobbying: What Lobbyists Want (and How They Try to Get It)* (Cambridge University Press, 2006).

MANCUR OLSON, *The Logic of Collective Action* (Harvard University Press, 1965).

MARK J. ROZELL, CLYDE WILCOX, AND **DAVID MADLAND,** EDS., *Interest Groups in American Campaigns,* 2d ed. (CQ Press, 2005).

DAVID VOGEL, *Kindred Strangers: The Uneasy Relationship Between Politics and Business in America* (Princeton University Press, 1996).

JACK L. WALKER, JR., *Mobilizing Interest Groups in America: Patrons, Professions, and Social Movements* (University of Michigan Press, 1991).

chapter 7

Political Parties

Essential to Democracy

Some years ago, a community college district in Los Angeles held a nonpartisan election for its trustees in which any registered voter could run if he or she paid the $50 filing fee and gathered 500 valid signatures on a petition. Each voter could cast up to seven votes. Political parties were not allowed to nominate candidates, and party labels did not appear on the ballot to help orient voters to the candidates.

A total of 133 candidates ran. They were listed alphabetically, and those whose names began with the letters A to F did better than those later in the alphabet. Being well known or having a Mexican American surname was also an advantage. Endorsements by the *Los Angeles Times* also influenced the outcome, as did campaigning by a conservative group. But how do people vote in an election without parties?

Parties are both a consequence of democracy and an instrument of it. They serve many functions, including narrowing the choices for voters[1] and making national and state elections work. American voters take for granted the peaceful transfer of power from one elected official to another and from one party to another, yet in new democracies where holding power may be more important than democratic principles, the transfer of power after an election is often problematic. Well-established parties help stabilize democracy.

This chapter begins by examining why parties are so vital to the functioning of democracy. We then examine the evolution of American political parties. Although U.S. political parties have changed over time, they remain important in three different settings: as institutions, in government, and in the electorate. We'll look at the way parties facilitate democracy in all three. Finally, we discuss the strength of parties today and the prospects for party reform and renewal.

LEARNING **OBJECTIVES**

1. Explain why parties arise in democracies and their primary functions.
2. Contrast the unique features of the American party system with those of other countries.
3. Understand the history of American political parties.
4. Distinguish parties' functions as institutions, in government, and in the electorate.
5. Discuss how parties and elections are financed.
6. Assess the long-term prospects for the current party system and, specifically, the Democratic and Republican Parties.

What Parties Do for Democracy

American political parties serve a variety of political and social functions, some well and others not so well. The way they perform them differs from place to place and time to time.

Party Functions

Political parties are organizations that seek political power by electing people to office who will help party positions and philosophy become public policy.

Organize the Competition Parties exist primarily as an organizing mechanism to win elections and thus win control of government. For some races, parties recruit and nominate candidates for office; register and activate voters; and help candidates by training them, raising money for them, providing them with research and voter lists, and enlisting volunteers to work for them.[2]

CHAPTER OUTLINE

- What Parties Do for Democracy
- A Brief History of American Political Parties
- U.S. Parties Today
- How Parties Raise and Spend Money
- Are the Political Parties Dying?

LEARNING OBJECTIVE

Explain why parties arise in democracies and their primary functions.

COMPARATIVE

Comparing Political Parties

Local and judicial elections in most states are **nonpartisan elections,** which means no party affiliation is indicated. Such systems make it more difficult for political parties to operate—precisely why many jurisdictions have adopted this reform, contending that party affiliation is not important to being a good judge or school board member. As in the community college board election at the beginning of this chapter, many voters in nonpartisan elections rely more on how recognizable the name of a candidate is, or whether he or she now holds office. In addition, fewer voters tend to turn out for nonpartisan elections than for standard partisan elections.[3]

Unify the Electorate Parties are often accused of creating conflict, but they actually help unify the electorate and moderate conflict, at least within the party. Parties have a strong incentive to fight out their internal differences but come together to take on the opposition. Moreover, to win elections, parties need to reach out to voters outside their party and gain their support. This action also helps unify the electorate, at least into the two large national political parties in the American system.

Parties have great difficulty building coalitions on controversial issues such as abortion or gun control. Not surprisingly, candidates and parties generally try to avoid defining themselves or the election in single-issue terms. Rather, they hope that if voters disagree with the party's stand on one issue, they will still support it because they agree on other issues. Deemphasizing single issues in this way helps defuse conflict and unify the electorate.

Help Organize Government Although political parties in the United States are not as cohesive as in some other democracies, they are important when it comes to organizing our state and national governments. Congress is organized along party lines. The political party with the most votes in each chamber elects the officers of that chamber, selects the chair of each committee, and has a majority on all the committees. State legislatures, with the notable exception of Nebraska, are also organized along party lines. The 2006 election gave the Democrats winning majorities in both houses of Congress, and as a result Democrats took over all the committee chairs.

The party that controls the White House, the governor's mansion, or city hall gets **patronage,** which means it can select party members as public officials or judges. Such appointments are limited only by civil service regulations that restrict patronage typically to the top posts, but these posts, which number about 3,000 in the federal government (not including ambassadors, U.S. Marshals, and U.S. Attorneys), are also numerous at the state and local levels. Patronage provides an incentive for people to become engaged in politics and gives party leaders and elected politicians loyal partisans in key positions to help them achieve their policy objectives. Patronage, sometimes called the *spoils system*, has declined dramatically in importance.

Translate Preferences Into Policy One of the great strengths of our democracy is that even the party that wins an election usually has to moderate what it does to win reelection. Thus, public policy seldom changes dramatically after elections. Nonetheless, the party that wins the election has a chance to enact its policies and campaign promises.

American parties have had only limited success in setting the course of national policy, especially compared to countries with strong parties. The European model of party government, which has been called a *responsible party system*, assumes that parties discipline their members through their control over nominations and campaigns. Officeholders in such party-centered systems are expected to act according to party wishes and vote along party lines—or they will not be allowed to run again under the party label, generally preventing their reelection. Candidates also run on fairly specific party platforms and are expected to implement them if they win control in the election.

Because American parties do not control nominations, they are less able to discipline members who express views contrary to those of the party.[4] The American system is largely *candidate-centered*; politicians are nominated largely on the basis of their qualifications and personal appeal, not party loyalty. In fact, it is more correct to

political party
An organization that seeks political power by electing people to office so that its positions and philosophy become public policy.

nonpartisan election
An election in which candidates are not selected or endorsed by political parties and party affiliation is not listed on ballots.

patronage
The dispensing of government jobs to persons who belong to the winning political party.

say that in most contests, we have *candidate* politics rather than *party* politics. As a consequence, party leaders cannot guarantee passage of their program, even if they are in the majority.

Provide Loyal Opposition The party out of power closely monitors and comments on the actions of the party in power, providing accountability. When national security is at issue or the country is under attack, parties restrain their criticism, as the Democrats in Congress did for some time after September 11, 2001. There is usually a polite interval following an election—known as the **honeymoon**—after which the opposition party begins to criticize the party that controls the White House, especially when the opposition controls one or both houses of Congress.[5] The length of the honeymoon depends in part on how close the vote was in the election, on how contentious the agenda of the new administration is, and on the leadership skills of the new president. Early success in enacting policy can prolong the honeymoon; mistakes or controversies can shorten it.

The Nomination of Candidates

From the beginning, parties have been the mechanism by which candidates for public office are chosen. The **caucus** played an important part in pre-Revolutionary politics and continued to be important in our early history as elected officials organized themselves into groups or parties and together selected candidates to run for higher office, including the presidency. This method of nomination operated for several decades after the United States was established.

As early as the 1820s, however, critics were making charges of "secret deals." Moreover, the caucus was not representative of people from areas where a party was in a minority or nonexistent, because only officeholders took part in it. Efforts were made to make the caucus more representative of rank-and-file party members. The *mixed caucus* brought in delegates from districts in which the party had no elected legislators.

Then, during the 1830s and 1840s, a system of **party conventions** was instituted. Delegates, usually chosen directly by party members in towns and cities, selected the party candidates, debated and adopted a platform, and built party spirit by celebrating noisily. But the convention method soon came under criticism that it was subject to control by the party bosses and their machines.

To draw more voters and reduce the power of the bosses to pick party nominees, states adopted the **direct primary,** in which people could vote for the party's nominees for office. Primaries spread rapidly after Wisconsin adopted them in 1905—in the North as a Progressive Era reform and in the South as a way to bring democracy to a region that had seen no meaningful general elections since the end of Reconstruction in the 1870s, because of one-party rule by the Democrats. By 1920, direct primaries were the norm for some offices in almost all states.

Today the direct primary is the typical method of picking party candidates. Primaries vary significantly from state to state. They differ in terms of (1) who may run in a primary and how he or she qualifies for the ballot; (2) whether the party organization can or does endorse candidates before the primary; (3) who may vote in a party's primary—that is, whether a voter must register with a party to vote; and (4) how many votes are needed for nomination—the most votes (a plurality), more than 50 percent (a majority), or some other number determined by party rule or state law. The differences among primaries are not trivial; they have an important impact on the role played by party organizations and on the strategy used by candidates.

In states with **open primaries,** any voter, regardless of party, can participate in the primary of whichever party he or she chooses. This kind of primary permits **crossover voting**—Republicans and Independents helping to determine who the Democratic nominee will be, and vice versa. Other states use **closed primaries,** in which only persons already registered in that party may participate. Some

honeymoon
The period at the beginning of a new president's term during which the president enjoys generally positive relations with the press and Congress, usually lasting about six months.

caucus
A meeting of local party members to choose party officials or candidates for public office and to decide the platform.

party convention
A meeting of party delegates to vote on matters of policy and in some cases to select party candidates for public office.

direct primary
An election in which voters choose party nominees.

open primary
A primary election in which any voter, regardless of party, may vote.

crossover voting
Voting by a member of one party for a candidate of another party.

closed primary
A primary election in which only persons registered in the party holding the primary may vote.

states, such as Washington and California, experimented with *blanket primaries*, in which all voters could vote for any candidate, regardless of party. Blanket primaries permitted voters to vote for a candidate of one party for one office and for a candidate from another party for another office, something that is not permitted under either closed or open primaries. In 2000, the Supreme Court held that California's blanket primary violated the free association rights of political parties, in part because blanket primaries permit people who have "expressly affiliated with a rival" party to have a vote in the selection of a nominee from a different party.[6] In a detailed study of California's blanket primary, political scientists found that fewer than 5 percent of voters associated with one party actually voted for nominees from another party.

Along with modern communications and fund-raising techniques, direct primaries have diminished the influence of leaders of political parties. Many critics believe this change has had more undesirable than desirable consequences. Party leaders now have less influence over who gets to be the party's candidate, and candidates are less accountable to the party both during and after the election.

Nominating Process

Direct primaries nominate most party candidates for most offices. Yet in some states, local caucuses choose delegates to attend regional meetings, which in turn select delegates to state and national conventions, where they nominate party candidates for offices. The Iowa presidential caucuses, in which a record-setting 347,000 Iowans participated in 2008,[7] are highly publicized as the first important test of potential presidential nominees.[8]

In a few states, conventions still play a role in the nominating process for state and federal candidates. In Connecticut, for example, convention choices become the party nominees unless they are challenged. Candidates who attain at least 15 percent of the vote in the convention have an automatic right to challenge the winner at the convention, but they do not always exercise this right.[9] In Utah, if a candidate gets 60 percent of the delegate vote at the convention, there is no primary election for that office. If no candidate gets 60 percent, the top two candidates in delegate votes at the convention are listed on the primary ballot. In other states, convention nominees are designated as such on the primary ballot; they may or may not receive help from the party organization. Conventions also invigorate the party faithful by enabling them to meet with their leaders.

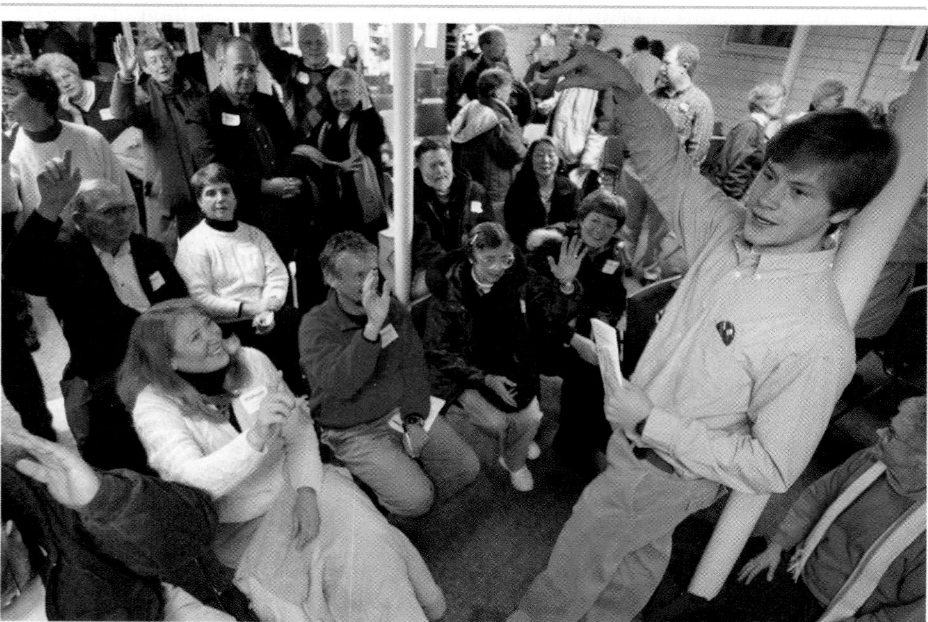

Iowa's Democratic caucus is an unwieldy and complex process. Here, a precinct captain takes a head count to determine support for various candidates.

Party Systems

Ours is a two-party system; most other democracies have a multiparty system. Although the United States has many **minor parties,** only the two major parties have much of a chance to win elections. Multiparty systems are almost always found in countries that have a parliamentary government, in contrast to our presidential system.

LEARNING **OBJECTIVE**

2 Contrast the unique features of the American party system with those of other countries.

Parliamentary systems usually have a *head of state,* often called the president, but they also have a *head of the government,* often called the prime minister or chancellor, who is the leader of one of the large parties in the legislature. In Germany, the chancellor, currently Angela Merkel, is elected by parliament and holds the greatest share of executive power. Typically, the chancellor comes from the largest party of a coalition of two or more parties and maintains power throughout a four-year term. In Germany, the president's responsibilities are mostly ceremonial, and he or she is expected to function in a politically neutral way. In democracies with multiparty systems, such as Israel and Italy, because no one party has a majority of the votes, *coalition* governments are necessary. Minor parties can gain concessions—positions in a cabinet or support of policies they want implemented—in return for joining a coalition. Major parties need the minor parties and are therefore willing to bargain.

Thus the multiparty system favors the existence of minor parties by giving them incentives to persevere and disproportionate power if they will help form a government. In some multiparty parliamentary systems, parties run slates of candidates for legislative positions, and winners are determined by **proportional representation,** in which the parties receive a proportion of the legislators corresponding to their proportion of the vote. In our single-member district, **winner-take-all system,** only the candidate with the most votes in a district or state takes office.[10] Because a party does not gain anything by finishing second, minor parties in a two-party system can rarely overcome the assumption that a vote for them is a wasted vote.[11] For this reason an election system in which the winner is the candidate in a single-member district with the plurality deciding the winner, there is tendency to have two parties. This regularity is called *Duverger's law.*[12]

In multiparty systems, parties at the extremes are likely to have more influence than in our two-party system, and in nations with a multiparty system, legislatures more accurately reflect the full range of the views of the electorate. Political parties in multiparty systems can be more doctrinaire than ours because they do not have to appeal to masses of people. Even though parties that do not become part of the governing coalition may have little to say in setting government policy, they survive because they appeal to some voters. Under such a system, third, fourth, or additional parties have an incentive to run because they may win some seats. In contrast, our two-party system tends to create *centrist* parties that appeal to moderate elements and suppress the views of extremists in the electorate. Moreover, once elected, our parties do not form as cohesive a voting bloc as ideological parties do in multiparty systems.

Multiparty parliamentary systems often make governments unstable as coalitions form and collapse. In addition, swings in policy when party control changes can be dramatic. In contrast, two-party systems produce governments that tend to be stable and centrist, and as a result, policy changes occur incrementally.

minor party
A small political party that persists over time, is often composed of ideologies on the right or left, or that is centered on a charismatic candidate. Such a party is also called a *third party*.

proportional representation
An election system in which each party running receives the proportion of legislative seats corresponding to its proportion of the vote.

winner-take-all system
An election system in which the candidate with the most votes wins.

Minor Parties: Persistence and Frustration

Although we have a primarily two-party system in the United States, we also have minor parties, sometimes called *third parties.* Candidate-based parties that arise around a candidate usually disappear when the charismatic personality does. In most states, candidates can get their names on the ballot as an Independent or minor party candidate by securing the required number of signatures on a nomination petition. This is hard to do. In 1992, Ross Perot spent his own money to build an

YOU WILL **DECIDE** Is a Vote for a Third-Party Candidate with Little Chance of Winning a Wasted Vote?

In several close elections, including the 2000 presidential election, the vote cast for one or another minor party, if cast for the likely second choice of those voters, would have changed the outcome of the election. In such a situation, should voters care more about influencing who wins an election or more about casting a vote for a candidate whose views are closest to their own, even if that candidate has little chance of winning?

organization of volunteers who put his name on the ballot in all 50 states. Minor party candidates such as Ralph Nader in 2000 secured their nominations as candidates of existing minor parties.

Minor parties that are organized around an ideology usually persist over a longer time than those built around a particular leader. Communist, Prohibition, Libertarian, Right to Life, and Green parties are of the ideological type. Minor parties of both types come and go, and several minor parties usually run in any given election. Some parties arise around a single issue, like the Right to Life party active in states like New York. The Green Party is another example of an ideological third party.

TIMELINE
Third Parties in American History

Major parties have criticized minor parties as "spoilers," diverting votes away from the major party candidate and costing that candidate the election. Nader was accused of doing this to Al Gore in 2000, just as Perot was accused of costing George Bush reelection in 1992. Minor parties have had an indirect influence in our country by drawing attention to controversial issues and by organizing such groups as the antislavery and civil rights movements.[13] Ross Perot, for example, elevated the importance of balanced budgets in 1992 and made it more difficult for George Bush to attack Bill Clinton on character issues.[14] However, minor parties have never won the presidency (see Table 7–1) or more than a handful of congressional seats.[15] They have done only somewhat better in gubernatorial elections.[16] They have never shaped national policy from *inside* the government, and their influence on national policy and on the platforms of the two major parties has been limited.[17] Minor parties operating in recent elections include the Libertarian, Green, and Reform Parties.

TABLE 7–1 Minor Parties in the United States

Year	Party	Presidential Candidate	Percentage of Popular Vote Received	Electoral Votes
1832	Anti-Masonic	William Wirt	8	7
1856	American (Know-Nothing)	Millard Fillmore	22	8
1860	Democratic (Secessionist)	John C. Breckinridge	18	72
1860	Constitutional Union	John Bell	13	39
1892	People's (Populist)	James B. Weaver	9	22
1912	Bull Moose	Theodore Roosevelt	27	88
1912	Socialist	Eugene V. Debs	6	0
1924	Progressive	Robert M. La Follette	17	13
1948	States' Rights (Dixiecrat)	Strom Thurmond	2	39
1948	Progressive	Henry A. Wallace	2	0
1968	American Independent	George C. Wallace	14	46
1980	National Unity	John Anderson	7	0
1992	Independent	Ross Perot	19	0
1996	Reform	Ross Perot	8	0
2000	Reform	Pat Buchanan	0	0
2000	Green	Ralph Nader	3	0
2004	Reform	Ralph Nader	0	0
2008	Independent	Ralph Nader	0	0

A Brief History of American Political Parties

To the founders of the young Republic, parties meant bigger, better-organized, and fiercer factions, which they did not want. Benjamin Franklin worried about the "infinite mutual abuse of parties, tearing to pieces the best of characters." In his Farewell Address, George Washington warned against the "baneful effects of the Spirit of Party." And Thomas Jefferson said, "If I could not go to heaven but with a party, I would not go there at all."[18]

How, then, did parties start?

THINKING IT THROUGH

How you answer this question depends on what you want to accomplish with your vote. Those who see the vote as a largely symbolic exercise will likely vote for a minor party candidate with little chance of winning. The problem is that the more electable candidate who is clearly preferred over the other more competitive alternative may not win office at all if a voter does not consider electability. The winner-take-all system makes this trade-off more consequential. In a system in which proportional representation is possible, a voter is more likely to be able to translate policy preferences into a vote for representatives. But in our system, voters must often vote for their second choice in order to avoid letting their third choice win office. Interest groups, like environmental groups, often find themselves not endorsing a minor party candidate who may be closer to their views because they want to avoid helping to elect a competitive alternative candidate whose views they abhor.

One way to lessen the influence of these candidates is to require a run-off election of the top two vote-getters if no candidate gets a majority. Although this would force another election in some instances, it would also force people who vote to decide among the more viable options. A counterargument is that many people who support minor party candidates would opt out of an election without this chance to express their preferences, and so such a run-off is already accomplished with the plurality winner system we now have.

Questions

1. Was a vote for someone other than Bush or Gore in 2000 a wasted vote? Why or why not?
2. What are some issues a minor party might push that would affect the major parties, even if the minor party does not win an election?
3. What are the obstacles minor parties face that major parties do not?

Our First Parties

Political parties emerged largely out of practical necessity. The same early leaders who so frequently stated their opposition to them also recognized the need to organize officeholders who shared their views so that government could act. In 1787, parties began to form as citizens debated over ratifying the U.S. Constitution. To get Congress to pass its measures, the Washington administration had to fashion a coalition among factions. This job fell to Treasury secretary Alexander Hamilton, who built an informal Federalist party, while Washington stayed "above politics."

Secretary of state Jefferson and other officials, many of whom despised Hamilton and his aristocratic ways as much as they opposed the policies he favored, were uncertain about how to deal with these political differences. Their overriding concern was the success of the new government; personal loyalty to Washington was a close second. Thus Jefferson stayed in the cabinet, despite his opposition to administration policies, during most of Washington's first term. When he left the cabinet at the end of 1793, many who joined him in opposition to the administration's economic policies remained in Congress, forming a group of legislators opposed to Federalist fiscal policies and eventually to Federalist foreign policy, which appeared "soft on Britain." This party was later known as Republicans, then as Democratic-Republicans, and finally as Democrats.[19]

LEARNING **OBJECTIVE**

Understand the history of American political parties.

The Evolution of Political Parties in the United States

Realigning Elections

American political parties have evolved and changed over time, but some underlying characteristics have been constant. Historically, we have had a two-party system with minor parties. This differentiates us from most nations, which have one-party or multiparty systems. Our parties are moderate and accommodative, meaning they are open to people with diverse outlooks. Political scientist V. O. Key and others have argued that our party system has been shaped in large part by **realigning elections.** Also called *critical elections,* these are turning points that define the agenda of politics and the alignment of voters within parties during periods of historic change in the economy and society.

Realigning elections are characterized by intense voter involvement, disruptions of traditional voting patterns, changes in the relationships of power within the broader political community, and the formation of new and durable electoral groupings. They have occurred cyclically, roughly every 32 years, and tend to coincide with expansions of suffrage or changes in the rate of voting.[20] Political scientists generally agree that there have been four realigning elections in American party history: 1824, 1860, 1896,

realigning election
An election during periods of expanded suffrage and change in the economy and society that proves to be a turning point, redefining the agenda of politics and the alignment of voters within parties.

and 1932. Although some argued that the United States was due for another in the 1970s and 1980s, there is little evidence that such an election occurred or is likely in the immediate future.

1824: Andrew Jackson and the Democrats Party politics was invigorated following the election of 1824, in which the leader in the popular vote—the hero of the battle of New Orleans, Democrat Andrew Jackson—failed to achieve the necessary majority of the electoral college and was defeated by John Quincy Adams in the runoff election in the House of Representatives. Jackson, brilliantly aided by Martin Van Buren, a veteran party builder in New York State, later knitted together a winning combination of regions, interest groups, and political doctrines to win the presidency in 1828. The Whigs succeeded the Federalists as the opposition party. By the time Van Buren, another Democrat, followed Jackson in the White House in 1837, the Democrats had become a large, nationwide movement with national and state leadership, a clear party doctrine, and a grassroots organization. The Whigs were almost as strong; in 1840, they put their own man, General William Henry Harrison ("Old Tippecanoe"), into the White House. A two-party system had been born.

1860: The Civil War and the Rise of the Republicans Out of the crisis over slavery evolved the second Republican party—the first being the National Republican Party that existed for barely a decade in the 1820s. The second Republican Party ultimately adopted the nickname "Grand Old Party" (GOP).[21] Abraham Lincoln was elected in 1860 with the support not only of financiers, industrialists, and merchants but also of many workers and farmers. For 50 years after 1860, the Republican coalition won every presidential race except for Grover Cleveland's victories in 1884 and 1892. The Democratic party survived with its durable white male base in the South.

1896: A Party in Transition Economic changes, including industrialization and hard times for farmers, led to changes in the Republican Party in the late 1800s.[22] Some Republicans insisted on maintaining their party's Reconstruction policies into the 1890s until it became obvious it would jeopardize their electoral base.[23] A combination of western and southern farmers and mining interests sought an alliance with workers in the East and Midwest to "recapture America from the foreign moneyed interests responsible for industrialization. The crisis of industrialization squarely placed an agrarian-fundamentalist view of life against an industrial-progressive view."[24] The two parties also differed over whether American currency should be tied to a silver or gold

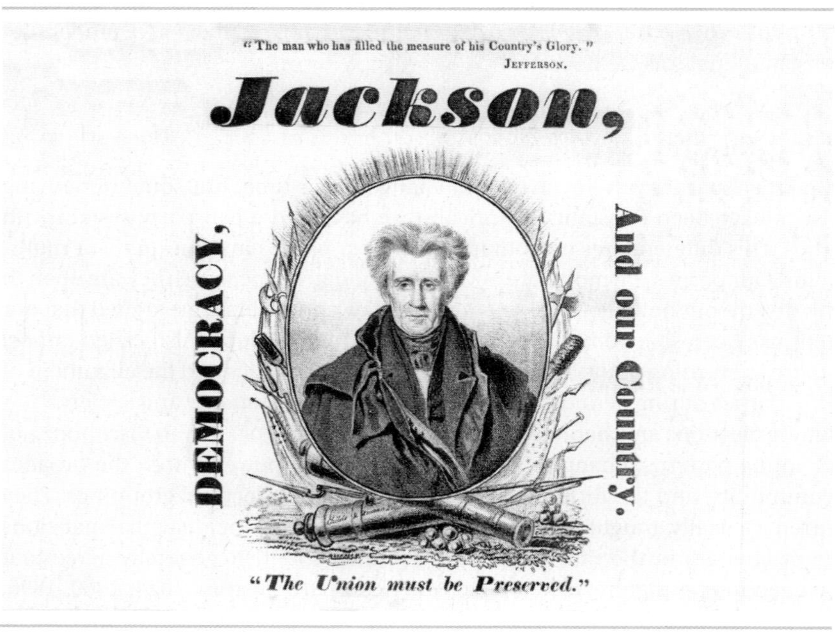

Campaigns are nothing new, dating back to the earliest days of the United States.

standard, with Republicans favoring gold and Democrats silver. William Jennings Bryan, the Democratic candidate for president in 1896, was a talented orator but lost the race to William McKinley.[25] The 1896 realignment differs from the others, however, in that the party in power did not change hands. In that sense it was a *converting realignment* because it reinforced the Republican majority status that had been in place since 1860.[26]

The Progressive Era, the first two decades of the twentieth century, was a period of political reform led by the Progressive wing of the Republican Party. Much of the agenda of the Progressives focused on the corrupt political parties. Civil service reforms shifted some of the patronage out of the hands of party officials. The direct primary election took control of nominations from party leaders and gave it to the rank-and-file. And a number of cities instituted nonpartisan governments, totally eliminating the role of a party. With the ratification of the Seventeenth Amendment to the Constitution in 1913, U.S. senators came to be popularly elected. Women obtained the right to vote when the Nineteenth Amendment was ratified in 1920. Thus within a short time, the electorate changed, the rules changed, and even the stakes of the game changed. Democrats were unable to build a durable winning coalition during this time and remained the minority party until the early 1930s, when the Great Depression overwhelmed the Hoover administration.

1932: Franklin Roosevelt and the New Deal Alignment The 1932 election was a turning point in U.S. politics. In the 1930s, the United States faced a devastating economic collapse. Between 1929 and 1932, the gross national product fell more than 10 percent per year, and unemployment rose from 1.5 million to more than 15 million, with millions more working only part-time.

With the economic crisis deepening, Franklin D. Roosevelt and the Democrats were swept into office in 1932 on a tide of anti-Hoover and anti-Republican sentiment. Roosevelt promised that his response to the Depression would be a "New Deal for America." After a century of sporadic government action, the New Dealers fundamentally altered the relationship between government and society by providing government jobs for the unemployed and using government expenditures to stimulate economic growth (see Chapter 18).

The dividing line between Republicans and Democrats was the role of government in the economy. Roosevelt Democrats argued that the government had to act to pull the country out of the Depression, but Republicans objected to enlarging the scope of government and intruding it into the economy. This basic disagreement about whether the national government should play an active role in regulating and promoting our economy remains one of the most important divisions between the Democratic and Republican Parties today, although, with time, the country and both parties accepted many of the New Deal programs.

Divided Government

Major shifts in party demographics have occurred in recent decades. The once "Solid South" that the Democrats could count on to bolster their legislative majorities and help win the White House has now become the "Solid Republican South" in presidential elections, and increasingly in congressional elections as well. Republican congressional leaders have often been from southern states that once rarely elected Republicans. This shift is explained by the movement of large numbers of white people out of the Democratic Party, in part because of the party's position on civil rights but also because of national Democrats' stand on abortion and other lifestyle issues. The rise of the Republican South reinforced the shift to conservatism in the GOP. This shift, combined with the diminished ranks of conservative southern Democrats, made the Democratic party, especially the congressional Democrats, more unified and more liberal than in the days when more of its congressional members had "safe" southern seats.[27]

Since 1953, **divided government,** with one party controlling Congress and the other the White House, has been in effect twice as long as united government in which one party controls both legislative and executive branches, and at other times Congress has had divided control with one party having a majority in the House and the other in the Senate. Until the 1992 and 1994 elections, the Republicans' strength had been

divided government
Governance divided between the parties, as when one holds the presidency and the other controls one or both houses of Congress.

in presidential elections, which they often won with landslide margins. Part of the explanation was their ability to attract popular candidates like Dwight Eisenhower and Ronald Reagan, but Republicans also reaped the rewards of Democratic Party divisiveness and generally weaker Democratic presidential candidates.

Evidence that voters are inclined to favor divided government came in the 1990s, when voters elected a Republican congressional majority in 1994 and then retained it in 1996 and 1998. Building on the Republicans' securing unified party control of government in 2002, the GOP in 2004 expanded its congressional majorities. This was especially the case in 2005 when the Republican majority in the U.S. Senate climbed to 55 Republicans versus 44 Democrats, and 1 Independent. However, in 2006 the Republicans lost control of both houses of Congress. The Democrats gained six Senate seats in the 2006 election, and in the 110th Congress held a majority in the Senate with 51 seats to the Republicans' 49 seats. In 2008, the Democrats had a 57–40 advantage over Republicans with three races undecided; in the House, the Democrats strengthened their hold with a 256–175 advantage with four races still undecided.

Could 2008 have been the long-awaited realigning election? A possible indicator is the expanding electorate. Over the course of the 2008 election twenty states saw record-setting levels of voter registration.[28] Another sign that 2008 may have been a realigning election is the surge in turnout in the 2008 presidential primaries. The rate of participation was at historic highs in many states. Exit polls also found that more than one-in-ten voters in 2008 were first time voters.

Young and new voters cast their ballots in large majorities for Obama. This was true regardless of race. For example, among white voters under thirty years of age, 54 percent voted for Obama. This was the only age group of white voters that gave Obama a majority of its votes and it may portend a shift in allegiance for the future. Young Latinos were also even more drawn to Obama than other Latinos. More than three-quarters of Latinos under age 30 voted for Obama, while Latinos as a whole gave Obama two-thirds of their vote. This may reflect disappointment among Latinos with some of the anti-Immigration rhetoric from the Republican party in recent years. As the civil rights laws of the 1960s reinforced the allegiance of African Americans with the Democrats so too do the Democrats now have an opportunity to garner increased loyalty from Latinos.

It is too soon to know if the attraction of Obama to new, young and Latino voters will strengthen over time. It is also not clear if the enthusiasm evident in the 2008 contest is sustainable. But the 2008 election presents the Democrats with an opportunity to expand their share of the electorate.

Republican victories in presidential elections between 1952 and 1992 were achieved with the support of some elements of Roosevelt's New Deal coalition. New Deal programs that benefited these voters had expanded the middle class and made possible the conservative "hold on to what we've got" thinking of voters in the 1980s, 1990s, and 2000 elections.

The terrorist attacks on September 11, 2001, provided President Bush and the Republican Party with an opportunity to assert strong leadership against terrorism. The "war on terror," as President Bush labeled it, was an important issue in the 2002 and 2004 elections. The Democrats have not had a unified response to the terrorism challenge. By 2006 and 2008 the mood of the country had changed to concern with the war in Iraq, and other issues like the economy were even more important. The Democrats could also campaign on the need for change, given the public's low approval of the Bush administration.

American Parties Today

LEARNING **OBJECTIVE**

4 Distinguish parties' functions as institutions, in government, and in the electorate.

American adults typically take political parties for granted.[29] If anything, most people are critical or distrustful of them. Some see parties as corrupt institutions, interested only in the spoils of politics. Critics charge that parties evade the issues, fail to deliver on their promises, have no new ideas, follow public opinion rather than lead it, or are just one more special interest.

Still, most people understand that parties are necessary. They want party labels kept on the ballot, at least for congressional, presidential, and statewide elections.

HISTORY MAKERS

Franklin Delano Roosevelt and the Democratic Party

From the critical election of 1860 until the election of 1932 in the midst of the Great Depression, the Republicans were the majority party. The economic and social challenges the country faced going into the 1932 presidential election, however, gave the Democratic Party the opportunity to emerge as the majority party under the leadership of Franklin D. Roosevelt. Roosevelt—sometimes known by his initials, FDR—and the Democrats gained widespread acceptance of their response to unemployment and the other challenges facing the nation, which they called the New Deal.

The new Democratic coalition expanded on the party's long-standing base of southern voters to include strong support from labor union members, farmers, urban ethnic voters, academics, and African Americans who, since emancipation, had been more predictably Republican. The Democrats' inroads among black Americans were noteworthy because of the Democrats' strong support among southern white people. FDR and his party not only included black people in the design and benefits of New Deal programs but also formed a new party organization, the National Colored Committee of the Good Neighbor League. This group turned out 16,000 black voters for a Roosevelt rally at New York's Madison Square Garden.* As one author put it, "the struggle to survive took precedence over the struggle for equality."†

Roosevelt's leadership and style held the party coalition together and even expanded party membership. Part of the strength of the attachment to Roosevelt was personal. For Democrats and "New Dealers," it was a positive attachment; for Republicans and those who felt he had "sold the country down the river," it was negative. Later—as the country faced the challenge of World War II, followed closely by the cold war—Roosevelt and his successor, Harry S. Truman, demonstrated leadership in defense and foreign policy as well.

QUESTIONS

1. How did African Americans' shift in allegiance during the Roosevelt years change the U.S. political landscape?
2. Roosevelt's views that government has a role in providing economic growth and social security are still a key difference between the parties more than 75 years later. Why has there not been a major realignment since 1932?
3. Does the idea that views of presidents are personal—with some seeing the incumbent in very positive terms while others hold the opposite view—extend to President George W. Bush? What are the implications of people personalizing politics?

*Jules Witcover, *Party of the People: A History of the Democrats* (Random House, 2003), pp. 372–376.
†John F. Bibby, *Politics, Parties, and Elections in America* (Nelson-Hall, 1992), pp. 32–33.

Most voters think of themselves as Democrats or Republicans and typically vote for candidates from their party. They collectively contribute millions of dollars to the two major parties.[30] Thus they appreciate, at least vaguely, that you cannot run a big democracy without parties.

Both the Democratic and Republican national parties and most state parties are moderate in their policies and leadership.[31] Successful party leaders must be diplomatic; to win presidential elections and congressional majorities, they must find a middle ground among competing and sometimes hostile groups. Members of the House of Representatives, to be elected and reelected, have to appeal to a majority of the voters from their own district. As more districts have become "safe" for incumbents, the House has had fewer moderates and is prone to more partisan ideological clashes than the Senate.

Although each party usually takes its extremist supporters more or less for granted and seeks out the voters in the middle, both parties retain some ideological diversity. The Democratic coalition includes the conservative New Democrat Coalition, the moderate Democratic Leadership Council, and the liberal Americans for Democratic Action. The Democratic coalition embraces activists in the civil rights and other liberal-left movements. Republicans, though more homogeneous, have their contentious factions as well. On the more conservative side are the Religious Right, staunch supporters of the right to bear arms, and antitax activists, but also young professionals who are conservative economically but moderate or liberal on social issues such as abortion and gay marriage.

Parties as Institutions

Like other institutions of government—Congress, the presidency, and the courts—political parties have rules, procedures, and organizational structure. What are the institutional characteristics of political parties?

State Control and National Platforms

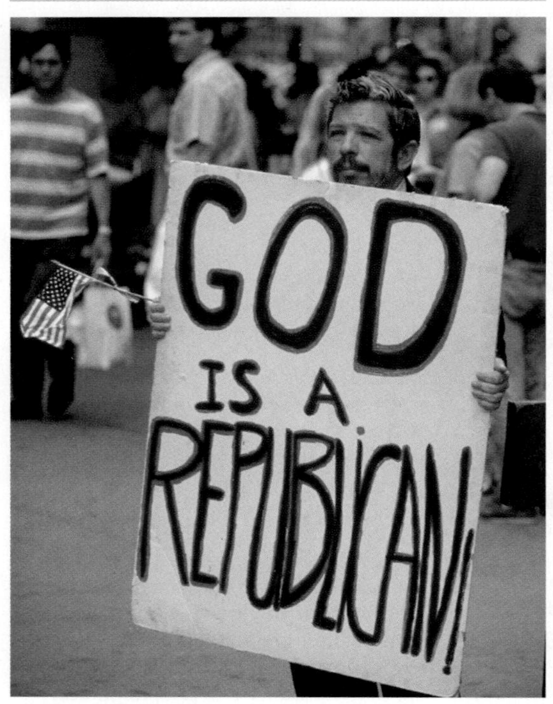

Religion is sometimes linked to partisanship. In reality, devoutly religious people are found in both major parties.

National Party Leadership The supreme authority in both major parties is the **national party convention,** which meets every four years for four days to nominate candidates for president and vice president, to ratify the party platform, and to adopt rules.

In charge of the national party when it is not assembled in convention is the *national committee.* In recent years, both parties have strengthened the role of the national committee and enhanced the influence of individual committee members. The committees are now more representative of the party rank-and-file. But in neither party is the national committee the center of party leadership.

Each major party has a *national chair* as its top official. The national committee formally elects the chair, but in reality this official is the choice of the presidential nominee. For the party that controls the White House, the chair actually serves at the pleasure of the president and does the president's bidding. Party chairs often change after elections. During the 2008 election cycle, the Republican National Committee (RNC) chair was Mike Duncan, a veteran political strategist and campaign manager.

Howard Dean, the Democratic National Committee (DNC) chair, was elected after his Democratic presidential election defeat in 2004. Dean served in the Vermont legislature before running successfully for lieutenant governor and was elected Vermont's governor eight times. Dean made party organizing in all 50 states a priority, even in strongly Republican states. This approach was criticized by some fellow partisans as missing chances for more victories in 2006 and 2008 by spending money in staunchly Republican states like Utah rather than in competitive contests elsewhere. During the 2008 primary campaign, Dean had to resolve a dispute over the scheduling of the Florida and Michigan primaries. Both states had scheduled primaries earlier than DNC rules permitted.

national party convention
A national meeting of delegates elected in primaries, caucuses, or state conventions who assemble once every four years to nominate candidates for president and vice president, ratify the party platform, elect officers, and adopt rules.

The chair of the party without an incumbent president has considerable independence yet works closely with the party's congressional leadership. The national committee often elects a new head after an electoral defeat. Although chairs are the heads of their national party apparatus, they remain largely unknown to the voters. The chair may play a major role in running the national campaign; after the election, the power of the national chair of the victorious party tends to dwindle.

Mike Duncan, Republican National Committee chair, seen applauding President Bush. (Duncan is to the right of Bush in the photo.)

National party organizations are often agents of an incumbent president in securing his renomination. When there is no incumbent president seeking reelection, the national party committee is generally neutral until the nominee has been selected. Although heated primary contests often preclude a united party in the general election, national and state parties can attempt to dissuade candidates but in the end cannot prevent them from running.[32]

In addition to the national party committees there are national congressional and senatorial campaign committees. These committees work to recruit candidates, train them, make limited contributions to them and spend independently in some of the most competitive contests.[33] The National Republican Senatorial Committee (NRSC) and Democratic Senatorial Campaign Committee (DSCC) are led by senators elected to two-year terms by their fellow party members in the Senate. The National Republican Campaign Committee (NRCC) and Democratic Congressional Campaign Committee (DCCC) have leaders chosen in the same manner by fellow partisans in the House. Chairs of campaign committees are nominated by their party leadership and typically ratified by their party caucus.

Howard Dean, chair of the Democratic National Committee, attends the DNC's Rules and By-laws Committee meeting on May 31, 2008, which determined the fate of Michigan's and Florida's contested presidential primary votes.

Party Platforms Although national party committees exist primarily to win elections and gain control of government, policy goals are also important. Every four years each party adopts a platform at the national nominating convention. The typical party *platform*—the official statement of party policy, that hardly anyone reads—is often a vague and ponderous document, the result of many meetings and compromises between groups and individuals. Platforms are ambiguous by design, giving voters few obvious reasons to vote against the party. This generalization about party platforms does not mean that political parties do not stand for anything. Most business and professional people believe that the Republican Party best serves their interests, while working people tend to look to the Democrats to speak for them. The proportion of voters discerning important differences between the parties has increased sharply as the parties have become more polarized (see Figure 7–1).[34]

Many politicians contend that platforms rarely help elect anyone, but platform positions can hurt a presidential candidate. Because the nominee does not always control the platform-writing process, presidential candidates can disagree with their own party platform. But the platform-drafting process gives partisans, and generally the nominee through people he or she appoints, an opportunity to express their views, and it spells out the most important values and principles on which the parties are based. Once elected, politicians are rarely reminded what their platform position was on a given issue. In reality, the winning party actually seeks to enact much of its party platform.[35] One major exception was former president George H. W. Bush's memorable promise not to raise taxes if elected in 1988, "Read my lips—no new taxes." He was forced to eat those words when taxes were raised in 1990.[36]

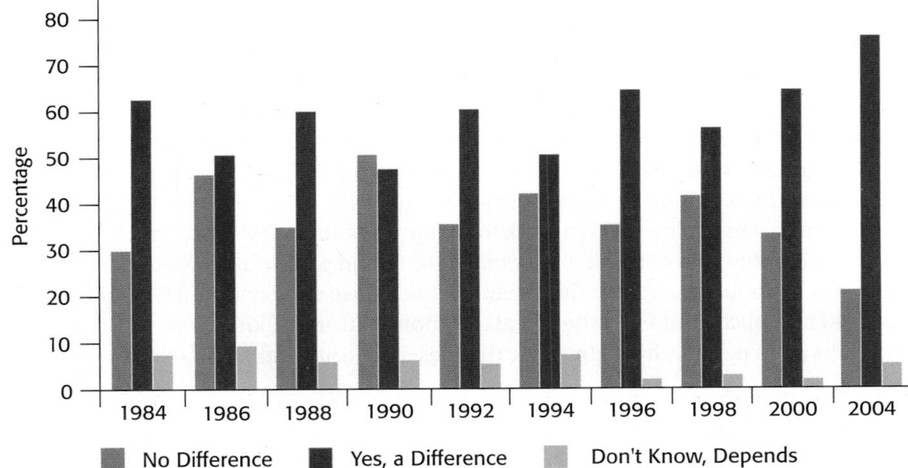

FIGURE 7–1
Important Difference in Perception of What Democratic and Republican Parties Stand For, 1984–2004.

SOURCE: *2004 National Election Study,* "Important Difference in What Democratic and Republican Parties Stand For, 1952–2004" (Center for Political Studies, University of Michigan, 2004).

Neither of the party platforms in 2008 generated much attention or controversy. Both parties sought to reinforce the basic positions of their presidential standard bearers. Ideological groups in both parties did not use the platform in 2008 as a way to score points or generate media attention. Rather the focus of the convention was on the nominees and those endorsing them. In the Democratic convention the speeches by Senator Hillary Clinton and former President Bill Clinton helped signal to Clinton supporters the need for unity. The Republican convention, which was shortened by one day due to hurricane conditions in the Gulf Coast region, had as its primary focus the speeches by John McCain and his running mate, Sarah Palin.

Parties at the State and Local Levels The two major parties are decentralized, organized around elections in states, cities, or congressional districts. They have organizations for each level of government: national, state, and local. The state and local levels are structured much like the national level. Each state has a *state committee* headed by a *state chair.* State law determines the composition of the state committees and regulates them. Members of state committees are usually elected from local areas.

Powerful state parties have developed in recent years. Despite much state-to-state variation, the trend is toward stronger state organizations, with Republicans typically being much better funded.[37] Some states have significant third and fourth parties. New York, for instance, has a Conservative Party in addition to the Democratic and Republican Parties. The role that minor parties play in statewide elections can be important, even though they rarely win office themselves.

Below the state committees are *county committees,* which vary widely in function and power. These committees recruit candidates for such offices as county commissioner, sheriff, and treasurer. Often this means finding a candidate for the office, not deciding among competing contenders. For a party that rarely wins an election, the county committee has to struggle to find someone willing to run. When the chance of winning is greater, primaries, not the party leaders, usually decide the winner.[38] Many county organizations are active, distributing campaign literature, organizing telephone campaigns, putting up posters and lawn signs, and canvassing door-to-door. Other county committees do not function at all, and many party leaders are just figureheads.

Parties in Government

Political parties are central to the operation of our government. They help bridge the separation of powers and facilitate coordination between levels of government in a federal system.

In the Legislative Branch Members of Congress take their partisanship seriously, at least while in Washington. Their power and influence are determined by whether their party is in control of the House or Senate; they also have a stake in which party controls the White House. The chairs of all standing committees in Congress come from the majority party, as do the presiding officials of both chambers. Members of both houses sit together with fellow partisans on the floor and in committee. (We discuss the role of parties in Congress in greater detail in Chapter 11.) Political parties help bridge the separation of powers between the legislative and executive branches by creating partisan incentives to cooperate. Partisanship can also help unify the two houses of Congress.

Congressional staffs are also partisan. Members of Congress expect their staff—from the volunteer intern to the senior staffer—to be loyal, first to them and then to their party. Should you decide to go to work for a representative or senator, you would be expected to identify yourself with that person's party, and you would have difficulty finding a job with the other party later. Employees of the House and Senate—elevator operators, Capitol Hill police, and even the chaplain—hold patronage jobs. With few exceptions, such jobs go to persons from the party that has a majority in the House or the Senate.

In the Executive Branch Presidents select almost all senior White House staff and cabinet members from their own party. Presidents, however, typically surround themselves with advisers who have campaigned with them and proved their party loyalty.

Members of Congress sit together by party during the annual State of the Union address. Here, President Bush gives the 2008 address.

Partisanship is also important in presidential appointments to the highest levels of the federal workforce. Party commitment, including making campaign contributions, is expected of those who seek these positions.

In the Judicial Branch The judicial branch of the national government, with its life time tenure and political independence, is designed to operate in an expressly nonpartisan manner. Judges, unlike Congress, do not sit together by political party. But the appointment process for judges has been partisan from the beginning. The landmark case establishing the principle of judicial review, *Marbury v. Madison* (1803), concerned the efforts of one party to stack the judiciary with fellow partisans before leaving office.[39] (See Chapter 2.) Today, party identification remains an important consideration when nominating federal judges.

At the State and Local Levels The importance of party in the operation of local government varies among states and localities. In some states, such as New York and Illinois, local parties play an even stronger role than they do at the national level. In others, such as Nebraska, parties play almost no role. In Nebraska, the state legislature is expressly nonpartisan, though factions perform like parties and still play a role. Parties are likewise unimportant in the government of most city councils. But in most states and many cities, parties are important to the operation of the legislature, governorship, or mayoralty. Judicial selection in most states is also a partisan matter. Much was made by the 2000 Bush campaign of the fact that six of the seven Florida Supreme Court justices deciding the 2000 ballot-counting case in favor of Gore were Democrats. Democrats noted that the five U.S. Supreme Court justices who decided the election in favor of Bush were nominated by Republican presidents.

Parties in the Electorate

Political parties would be of little significance if they did not have meaning to the electorate. Adherents of the two parties are drawn to them by a combination of factors, including their stand on the issues; personal or party history; religious, racial, or social peer grouping; and the appeal of their candidates. The emphases among these factors change over time, but they are remarkably consistent with those that political scientists identified more than 40 years ago.[40]

party registration
The act of declaring party affiliation; required by some states when one registers to vote.

Party Registration For citizens in most states, "party" has a particular legal meaning—**party registration.** When voters register to vote in these states, they are asked to state

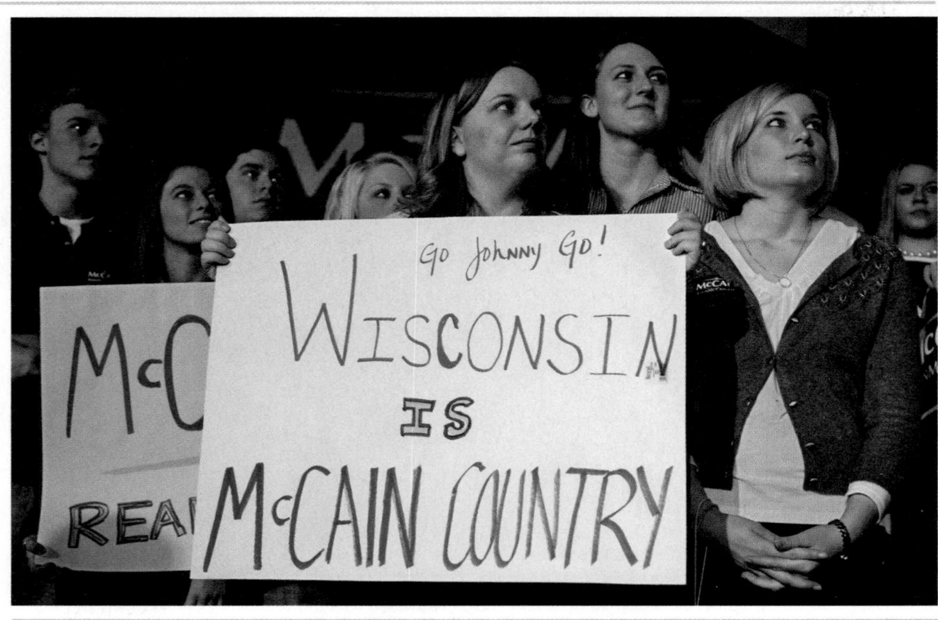

Young people are valued by political candidates for their enthusiasm and creativity.

their party preference. They then become registered members of one of the two major parties or a third party, although they can change their party registration. The purpose of party registration is to limit the participants in primary elections to members of that party and to make it easier for parties to contact people who might vote for their party.

Party Activists Activists tend to fall into three broad categories: party regulars, candidate activists, and issue activists. *Party regulars* place the party first. They value winning elections and understand that compromise and moderation may be necessary to reach that objective. They also realize that it is important to keep the party together, because a fractured party only helps the opposition.

Candidate activists are followers of a particular candidate who see the party as the means to elect their candidate. Candidate activists are often not concerned with the other operations of the party—with nominees for other offices or with raising money for the party. For example, people who supported Ron Paul in his unsuccessful run for the presidency as a Republican were candidate activists. Paul, a libertarian Republican congressman from Texas, had previously run for the presidency as a Libertarian.

Issue activists wish to push the parties in a particular direction on a single issue or a narrow range of issues: the war in Iraq, abortion, taxes, school prayer, the environment, or civil rights, among others. To issue activists, the party platform is an important battleground because they want the party to endorse their position. Issue activists are also often candidate activists if they can find a candidate willing to embrace their position.

Both issue activists and candidate activists insist on making their "statement" regardless of the electoral consequences. They would rather lose the election than compromise. Party activists thus include a diverse group of people who come to the political party with different objectives. It is not surprising, then, that some of the most interesting politics are over candidate selection and issue positions within the political parties. Fights over strategy and party position are conducted in open meetings and under democratic procedures. Political parties foster democracy not only by competition *between* the parties but *within* the parties as well.

Party Identification

Party registration and party activists are important, but many voters are not registered with a political party. Most American adults are mere spectators of party activity. They lack the partisan commitment and interest needed for active involvement. This is not

THE **CHANGING FACE** OF U.S. POLITICS

Portrait of the Electorate

Over a 40-year period, the demographic composition of the two major political parties has undergone some changes while at the same time retaining some important similarities. Consistent with the Republican Party's having become stronger, we find near equal numbers of Republicans and Democrats among men in 2004. In 1964, men were twice as likely to be Democrats as Republicans. Women continued to be disproportionately Democratic in 2004, as they were in 1964. Lower-income voters have consistently been more Democratic, and higher-income voters more Republican. Younger voters in both 1964 and 2004 were more likely to be Democrats; in 2004, Republicans were at near-parity with Democrats for those ages 35–64, something that was not the case in 1964. In 1964, Democrats enjoyed strong support from Protestants, Catholics, and Jews. By 2004, Protestants were evenly divided and the Democratic margin among Catholics had dropped significantly. Jewish voters remained heavily Democratic. In 1964, 59 percent of whites were Democrats; by 2004, the white population was more Republican than Democratic. Blacks were heavily Democratic in both 1964 and 2004. The changing face of party composition has implications for electoral competition and campaign strategy.

QUESTIONS

1. Why have more white men become Republicans while white women have remained Democratic?
2. What might explain the shift to the GOP among Protestants and Catholics but not Jews?
3. How does the changing demographics of the two parties affect campaigns?

	1964				2004			
	Republican	**Democrat**	**Independent**	**Other**	**Republican**	**Democrat**	**Independent**	**Other**
Sex								
Male	30%	61%	8%	1%	44%	45%	10%	1%
Female	30	61	7	1	37	53	9	2
Race								
White	33	59	8	1	49	41	9	2
Black	8	82	6	4	8	81	12	0
Hispanic	—	—	—	—	23	60	14	2
Age								
18–34	26	64	9	1	34	56	8	2
35–45	32	59	8	1	43	44	11	2
46–55	26	65	8	1	44	45	9	1
56–64	28	66	6	0	46	45	8	1
65+	43	49	6	2	37	50	11	2
Income*								
Less than $14,999	24	65	9	3	27	56	16	1
$15,000–$34,999	24	66	9	0	34	55	11	0
$35,000–$64,999	25	66	8	1	43	50	7	1
$50,000–$124,999	38	55	6	0	47	47	6	0
$125,000+	48	44	8	1	51	45	4	0
Religion								
Protestant	34	58	7	1	44	46	9	1
Catholic	22	70	9	0	37	48	13	1
Jewish	11	76	13	0	29	71	0	0
Other	28	55	16	1	33	55	9	2
Region								
Northeast	36	54	10	0	37	51	12	0
North-Central	36	55	8	0	42	43	13	3
South	20	71	7	2	41	50	7	2
West	30	63	7	0	40	51	8	1
Total	30	61	8	1	40	49	10	2

*Income is given in 2000 dollars.

NOTE: Numbers may not add to 100 because of rounding. Independents who lean toward a party are classified with the party toward which they lean. Race is defined by the first race with which a respondent identifies. Income is classified as the respondent's household income.

SOURCE: *1964 National Election Study* (Center for Political Studies, University of Michigan, 1964); and *2004 National Election Study* (Center for Political Studies, University of Michigan, 2004).

GENERATION **NEXT**

Partisan Differences

Generation Next has distinct political views and party affiliations. A recent survey asked 18- to 25-year-olds, "In politics today, do you consider yourself a Republican, a Democrat, or Independent?" Here are the results:

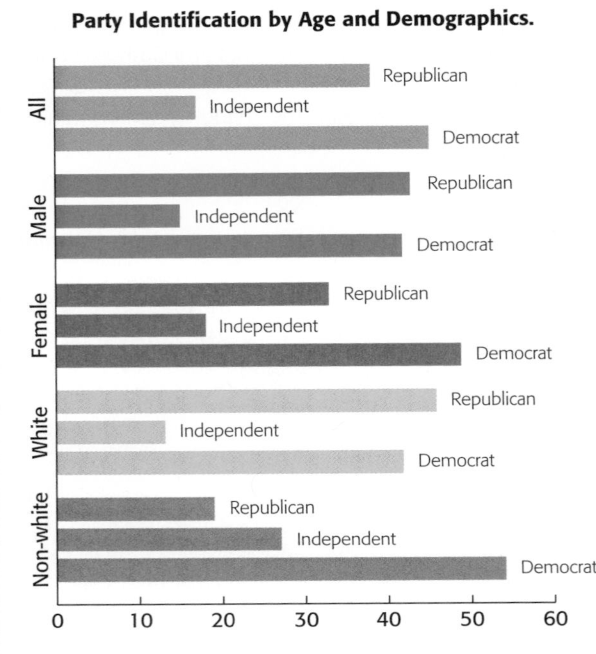

As the figure shows, partisan identification varies among young people depending on their characteristics. Although Generation Next is more Democratic than Republican or Independent, roughly equal numbers of men between ages 18 and 25 are Republicans and Democrats. In contrast, in Generation Next women are more likely to be Democrats (49 percent) than Republicans (33 percent). An even larger difference exists in Generation Next between nonwhites, who are much more likely to be Democrats than Republicans, and whites, who are slightly more likely to be Republicans than Democrats.

These differences are also found in persons older than age 26. The similarity between Generation Next and older persons who share their gender or race is striking. This reinforces the sense that party identification is a stable attachment. The proportion of persons who are Independents without leanings toward either party is also quite consistent within demographic categories. Among all nonwhites in the sample, there were more pure Independents than Republicans, a finding that underscores the challenges the GOP faces with racial minorities.

The Generation Next survey was conducted in September 2006, well before the Obama campaign generated widespread attention among young voters. More recent research shows that Obama clearly struck a responsive chord with younger voters,* and so subsequent surveys may find some growth in the proportions classifying themselves as Democrats.

QUESTIONS

1. What accounts for the differences in partisanship between men and women and among different racial and ethnic groups?
2. Generation Next is, on balance, less Republican than older generations. Why do you suppose this is true, and what implications does it have for future policy?
3. What impact, if any, did Barack Obama have on party identification among voters aged 18–25 and why?

*Scott Keeter, Juliana Horowitz, and Alec Tyson, "Gen Dems: The Party's Advantage Among Young Voters Widens," Pew Research Center for the People and the Press, April 28, 2008.

to say that they find parties irrelevant or unimportant. For them, partisanship is what political scientists call **party identification**—a psychological attachment to a political party that most people acquire in childhood from their parents.[41] This type of voter may sometimes vote for a candidate from the other party, but without a compelling reason to do otherwise, most will vote according to their party identification. Peers and early political experiences reinforce party identification as part of the political socialization process described in Chapter 4.

Political scientists and pollsters use the answers to the following questions to measure party identification: "Generally speaking, in politics do you usually think of yourself as a Republican, a Democrat, an Independent, or what?"

Persons who answer Republican or Democrat are then asked: "Would you call yourself a strong or a not very strong Republican/Democrat?"

Persons who answer Independent are asked: "Do you think of yourself as closer to the Republican or the Democratic Party?"

Persons who do not indicate Democrat, Republican, or Independent to the first question rarely exceed 2 percent of the electorate and include those who are apolitical or who identify with one of the minor political parties.

party identification
An affiliation with a political party that most people acquire in childhood.

Party identification is the single best predictor of how people will vote.[42] Unlike candidates and issues, which come and go, party identification is a long-term element in voting choice. The strength of party identification is also important in predicting participation and political interest. Strong Republicans and strong Democrats participate more actively in politics than any other groups and are generally better informed about political issues. Pure Independents are just the opposite; they vote at the lowest rates and have the lowest levels of interest and awareness of any of the categories of party identification. This evidence runs counter to the notions that persons who are strong partisans are unthinking party adherents and that independents are informed and ideal citizens.[43]

Partisan Realignment and Dealignment

As discussed earlier in this chapter, with the exception of the shift of southern white people to the Republican Party[44] and the enfranchisement of black voters who remain Democrats, the current system of party identification is built on a foundation of the New Deal and the critical election of 1932, events that took place three-quarters of a century ago. How can events so removed from the present still shape our party system? When will there be another realignment—an election that dramatically changes the voters' partisan identification? Or has such a realignment already occurred? The question is frequently debated. Most scholars believe that we have not experienced a major realignment since 1932.[45] Partisan identification has been stable for more than four decades, and even though new voters have been added to the electorate—minorities and 18- to 21-year-olds—the basic nature of the party system has not changed dramatically but trended slightly Republican. Table 7–2 presents the party identification breakdown from the 1950s to the 2000s.

Evidence of a possible voting realignment came in the early 1980s, when Republicans won several close Senate elections and gained a majority in that body.[46] Democrats, however, won back the Senate in 1986, and until 1994 they appeared to have a permanent majority in the House. All that changed with the 1994 election, as Republicans were swept into office on a tidal wave of victories. Republicans made major inroads in the South and strengthened their share of the vote among white males.

As Figure 7–2 suggests, American voters have shown no consistent preference for one party over the other. In a time of electoral volatility, the basics of politics determine the winners and losers: who attracts positive voter attention, who strikes themes that motivate voters to participate, and who communicates better with voters.

Some experts argue that independents are increasing in number, suggesting that the party system may be in a period of **dealignment.** However, two-thirds of all self-identified Independents are really partisans in their voting behavior and attitudes.

dealignment
Weakening of partisan preferences that points to a rejection of both major parties and a rise in the number of Independents.

TABLE 7–2 Party Identification, 1950s–2000s

Decade	Strong Democrat	Weak Democrat	Independent-Leaning Democrat	Independent	Independent-Leaning Republican	Weak Republican	Strong Republican	Other
1950*	23%	23%	8%	7%	7%	15%	13%	4%
1960	22	25	8	10	7	15	12	2
1970	17	24	12	14	10	14	9	2
1980	18	26	11	12	11	14	11	2
1990	18	19	13	10	12	15	13	1
2000†	17	17	16	11	11	12	13	1

*1950s percentages based on years 1952, 1956, and 1958.
†2000s percentages based on years 2000, 2002, and 2004.

NOTE: Data may not sum to 100 percent because of averaging.

SOURCE: *National Election Study* (Center for Political Studies, University of Michigan, 2004).

FIGURE 7–2
Presidential Vote by Party.

SOURCE: Data obtained from CQ Voting and Elections Collections, library.cqpress.com/elections/.

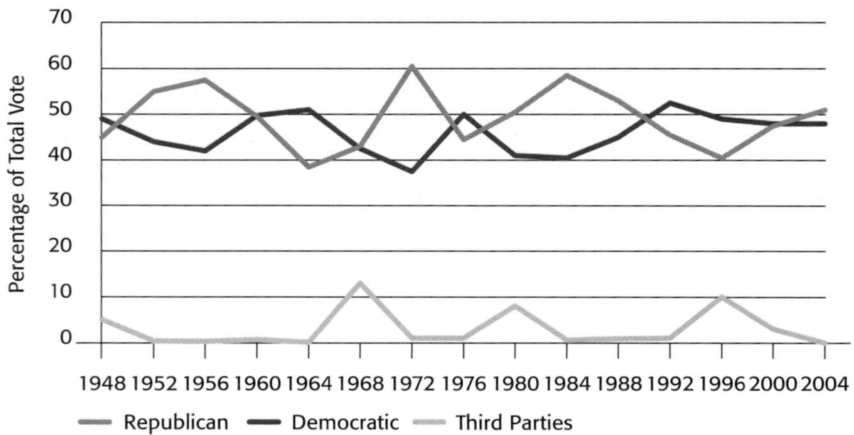

One-third of those who claim to be Independents lean toward the Democratic Party and vote Democratic in election after election. Another third lean toward Republicans and just as predictably vote Republican. The remaining third, who appear to be genuine Independents and who do not vote predictably for one party, turn out to be people with little interest in politics. Despite the reported growth in numbers, there are proportionately about the same number of pure Independents now as in 1956.[47] There are, in short, at least three types of Independents, most of them predictably partisan. Table 7–3 summarizes voting behavior in recent contests for president and the House of Representatives.

There are seven categories of partisan identification: strong Democrats, weak Democrats, Independent-leaning Democrats, pure Independents, Independent-leaning Republicans, weak Republicans, and strong Republicans. Over the more than 50-year period during which political scientists have been conducting such surveys, partisan preferences of the public have remained remarkably stable.

TABLE 7–3 Voting Behavior of Partisans and Independents, 1992–2004

Percent Voting for Democratic Presidential Candidate

	1992	1996	2000	2004
Strong Democrats	93%	96%	97%	96%
Weak Democrats	68	82	89	84
Independent-Leaning Democrats	70	76	72	83
Pure Independents	41	35	44	51
Independent-Leaning Republicans	11	20	13	14
Weak Republicans	14	20	14	10
Strong Republicans	3	5	2	3

Percent Voting for Democratic House Candidate

	1994	1996	1998	2000	2002	2004
Strong Democrats	88%	87%	77%	90%	89%	90%
Weak Democrats	73	70	57	73	71	85
Independent-Leaning Democrats	68	69	63	73	67	80
Pure Independents	55	41	41	50	35	54
Independent-Leaning Republicans	25	21	24	26	27	33
Weak Republicans	21	21	25	18	25	17
Strong Republicans	7	3	7	12	8	10

SOURCE: *2004 National Election Study* (Center for Political Studies, University of Michigan, 2004).

How Parties Raise and Spend Money

Though parties cannot exert tight control over candidates, their ability to raise and spend money has had a significant influence. Political parties, like candidates, rely on contributions from individuals and interest groups to fund their activities. Because of the close connection political parties have with officeholders, the courts have long permitted regulation of the source and amount of money people and groups can contribute to parties, as well as the amount parties can spend with or contribute to candidates.

LEARNING **OBJECTIVE**

5 Discuss how parties and elections are financed.

Under the post-Watergate reforms (Federal Election Campaign Act or FECA, as amended in 1974), contributions to the parties from individuals were limited to $20,000, while the limit for PACs was $15,000.[48] As we discuss in Chapter 6, PACs are more inclined to give to candidates than party committees.

After the 1976 election, both parties pressed for further amendments to FECA, claiming that campaign finance reforms resulted in insufficient money for generic party activities such as billboard advertising and get-out-the-vote drives. The 1979 amendments to FECA and the interpretations of this legislation by the Federal Election Commission (FEC) permitted unlimited **soft money** contributions to the parties by individuals and PACs for these party-building purposes. Unions and corporations were also allowed to give parties unlimited amounts of soft money. This unregulated money was thus easier to raise and could be spent in unlimited amounts as long as the parties could claim a party-building purpose.

soft money
Money raised in unlimited amounts by political parties for party-building purposes. Now largely illegal except for limited contributions to state or local parties for voter registration and get-out-the-vote efforts.

hard money
Political contributions given to a party, candidate, or interest group that are limited in amount and fully disclosed. Raising such limited funds was harder than raising unlimited soft money, hence the term "hard money."

In the 1996 election cycle, both parties found ways to spend this soft money to promote the election or defeat of specific candidates, effectively circumventing party spending limits.[49] In the 1998, 2000, and 2002 elections, congressional campaign committees, following the lead of the national party committees in the 1996 presidential election, raised unprecedented amounts of soft money. In 2000, all party committees combined raised $500 million in soft money. This money was spent in large amounts in the most competitive races. In many instances this soft money paid for broadcast advertisements that did not even mention the party.[50]

After repeated defeats in one or both houses of Congress over 15 years, Congress regulated this unrestricted soft money under the Bipartisan Campaign Reform Act (BCRA) in 2002. As we will see in Chapter 9, soft money was almost entirely banned under the act, while the limits on individual contributions to candidates and party committees were roughly doubled and indexed to inflation and a more realistic definition of what constituted election communications by groups was enacted.

The new laws raised serious questions about how the parties would cope without this once-unregulated money in 2004 and thereafter. In 2004, individual giving to both parties set new records, and the DNC and RNC raised as much in **hard money** from individuals and PACs as they had raised in both hard and soft money combined in 2000 or 2002. Much of this money is coming from individuals, including many small contributions.

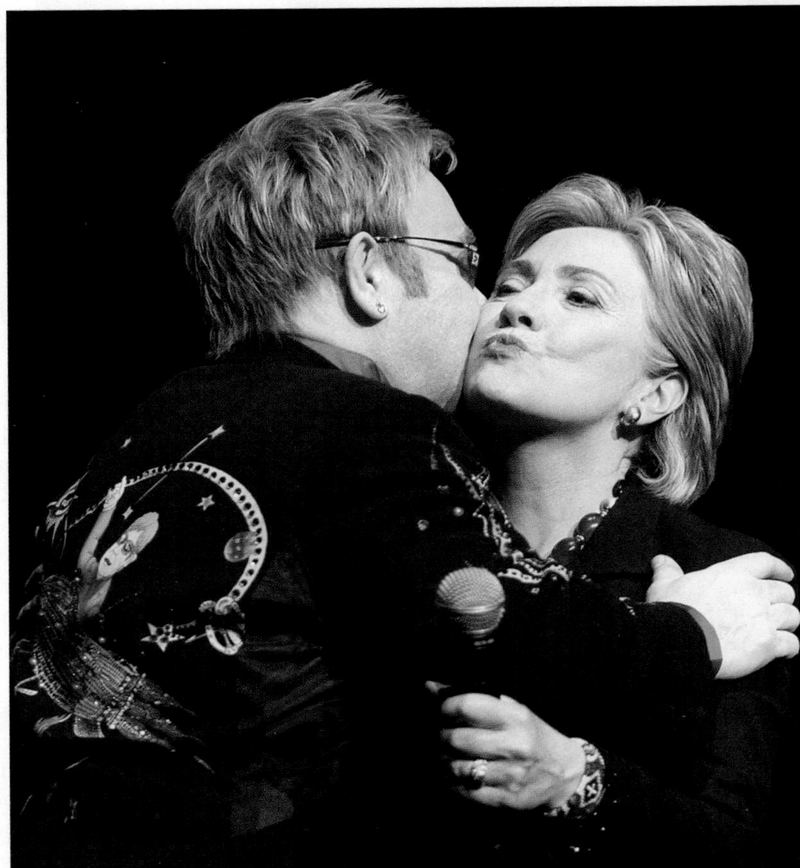

Elton John raised millions of dollars for Hillary Clinton at a high-priced concert. Candidates for office often hold elaborate events to attract fundraisers.

Party Expenditures

Party committees are permitted to make contributions to candidates and can also spend a limited amount of money in what are called "coordinated expenditures." In the last several election cycles the party committees have concentrated their contributions and coordinated expenditures in the most competitive contests. (See Table 7–4.)

Parties, like individuals and groups, can now also spend unlimited amounts for and against candidates as long as the expenditures were independent of the candidate or a party

TABLE 7–4 Independent Expenditures by Party Committee, 1994–2004

	1994	1996	1998	2000	2002	2004	2006
DNC	$0	$0	$0	$0	$0	$120,333,466	−$23,104
DSCC	0	1,386,022	1,359,000	133,000	0	18,725,520	41,990,526
DCCC	0	0	0	1,916,489	1,106,113	36,923,726	63,399,473
RNC	0	0	0	0	500,000	18,268,870	14,022,675
NRSC	0	9,875,130	194,573	267,600	0	19,383,692	19,159,901
NRCC	0	0	0	548,800	1,203,854	47,254,064	81,827,610

SOURCE: Federal Election Commission, "Party Financial Activity Summarized for the 2004 Election Cycle," press release, March 2, 2005, www.fec.gov/press/press2005/20050302party/Party2004final.html; and David B. Magleby and Kelly D. Patterson, eds., *War Games: Issues and Resources in the Battle for Control of Congress*, monograph (Center for the Study of Elections and Democracy, 2007), p. 47.

This ad, sponsored by the Republican National Committee, questions Barack Obama's experience and judgment. The law requires that political advertisements reveal who paid for them.

committee.[51] Unlike soft money, party-independent expenditures had to use money raised with normal hard money contribution limits. As long as the party committees could use soft money, independent expenditures were of lesser importance, but with the BCRA ban on soft money, there has been a surge in party independent expenditure activity.

As noted, in addition to the national party committees, there are national congressional and senatorial campaign committees. Former Federal Election Commission commissioner Michael Toner noted that party committees are attempting "to replace the old soft money issue advertising with hard money independent expenditures."[52] Aside from the Democratic National Committee, all other party committees in Table 7–4 continued to spend heavily in independent expenditures in 2008. The House and Senate Democratic committees spent more independently in 2008 than their GOP counterparts. This money in 2008 was again spent in only a few competitive races. But where parties invest, they do so in substantial amounts. A party committee could spend well over $1 million independently in a targeted House race and over $9 million in a competitive Senate race. Spending in such large amounts makes party committees important in the overall campaign.

During the debate over BCRA, and in the court case on its constitutionality, some such as political scientist Sidney Milkes speculated that BCRA's soft money ban would weaken political parties.[53] The surge in individual contributions has demonstrated the opposite; the DNC and RNC could and did find an alternative to unregulated money. It remains unclear whether the four congressional party committees can make up for the loss of soft money, but the surge in individual contributions to them is promising. The independent expenditure option allows parties to continue to direct money well in excess of the normal limits to races they thought were more competitive.

Are the Political Parties Dying?

Critics of the U.S. party system make three allegations against it: (1) parties do not take meaningful and contrasting positions on most issues, (2) party membership is essentially meaningless, and (3) parties are so concerned with accommodating the middle of the ideological spectrum that they are incapable of serving as an avenue for social progress. Are these statements accurate? And if they are accurate, are they important?

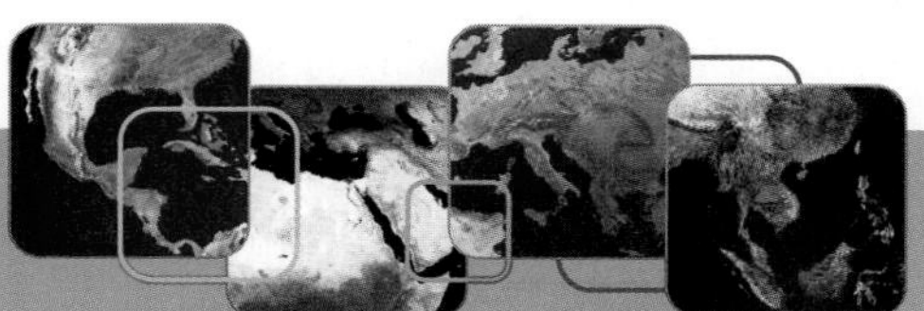

HOW OTHER NATIONS GOVERN

Campaign Finance Regulation

For political parties to function they need resources, and one of those resources is money. There are important differences in the ways countries regulate how political parties can raise and spend money. The following table compares our sample of countries along several dimensions: whether there is direct public funding of political parties, whether there are limits on how much individuals or groups can contribute to parties, whether there are limits on party spending, whether there is disclosure of individuals who contribute to parties (all of these countries, with the exception of China, require some party finance disclosure), whether the government provides access to free television time, and finally whether paid television ads are allowed.

China is clearly different from all of the other countries in this table in not having a functioning party system, and therefore many of these regulations are not relevant. China's village election system, though in only rudimentary stages, promotes some wealthy self-financed candidates who have an unfair advantage.* Each of the other countries has taken a different approach to regulating campaign finance. In general, the wealthier countries (by GDP per capita) have broader regulations than do the less-wealthy countries. Britain and Japan both have regulations in seven of the eight categories, while Mexico has regulations in six and the United States in five. Nigeria only has regulations on disclosure of donors, which could account for the overwhelming role that money plays in Nigerian elections.† Interestingly, India is the only country to offer free TV time without also offering some form of public financing or limits on sources, amount, or spending. The U.S. electoral system has weaker parties and is more candidate centered. In many countries the parties are more in control of election finance than they are in the United States.

QUESTIONS

1. What are some reasons one nation might impose more restrictions on campaign finance than another?
2. What effects could relaxing campaign finance laws have in the United States?
3. Why might a nation such as the United States offer public funding and regulate campaign finance, but not offer free TV time as do most of the countries in the table?

Party Finance Regulation in Comparative Perspective.

	Direct Public Funding for Parties	Limits on Contribution Amount to Parties	Limits on Sources of Contributions	Limits on Spending by Parties	Any Disclosure of Individual Donors	Free TV Time	Banned Paid TV Ads
Britain	Yes	No	Yes	Yes	Yes	Yes	Yes
India	No	No	No	No	No	Yes	No
Japan	Yes	Yes	Yes	No	Yes	Yes	Yes
Mexico	Yes	Yes	Yes	Yes	No	Yes	No
Nigeria	No	No	No	No	Yes	No	No
United States	No	Yes	Yes	No	Yes	No	No

SOURCE: Reproduced by permission of International IDEA from Political Finance Database © International Institute for Democracy and Electoral Assistance.

*Tan Qingshan, "Building Institutional Rules and Procedures: Village Election in China," *Policy Sciences* 37 (2004), pp. 1–22.
†Ndubisi Obiorah, *Political Finance and Democracy in Nigeria* (Center for Law and Social Action, 2004).

LEARNING OBJECTIVE

6 Assess the long-term prospects for the current party system and, specifically, the Democratic and Republican Parties.

Some analysts fear that parties are in severe decline or even mortally ill. They point first to the long-run adverse impact on political parties of the Progressive movement reforms early in this century, reforms that robbed party organizations of their control of the nomination process by allowing masses of independent and "uninformed" voters to enter the primaries and nominate candidates who might not be acceptable to party leaders. They also point to the spread of nonpartisan elections in cities and towns and to the staggering of national, state, and local elections that made it harder for parties to influence the election process.

Legislation limiting the viability and functions of parties was bad enough, say the party pessimists, but parties suffer from additional ills. The rise of television and electronic technology and the parallel increase in the number of campaign, media, and direct-mail consultants have made parties less relevant in educating, mobilizing, and organizing the electorate. Television, radio, the Internet, and telephones have strengthened the role of candidates and lessened the importance of parties. (See Chapter 10 for more on the media in this role.)

Advocates of strong parties concede that parts of this diagnosis may be correct, including the demise of political machines at the local level, the decline in strong partisan affiliations, and the weakness of grassroots party membership, but they also see signs of party revival, or at least the persistence of party. The national party organizations—the national committees and the congressional and senatorial campaign committees—are significantly better funded than they were in earlier days; they even own permanent, modern headquarters buildings in Washington, D.C., located a few blocks from the U.S. Capitol. Moreover, the parties remain capable of providing assistance to candidates in competitive races and to state and local party organizations because of their financial base. Until 2004, they did this with soft money, and since then they have done it with independent expenditures.[54]

Reform among the Democrats

In Chicago in 1968, the Democratic National Convention saw disputes inside the hall and riots outside, largely because of protests against the country's policy in Vietnam. Responding to the disarray and to disputes about the fairness of delegate selection procedures, members of the party agreed to a number of reforms. They established a process that led to greater use of direct primaries for the selection of delegates to the national convention and greater representation of younger voters, women, and minorities as elected delegates. Another reform was the abolition of the winner-take-all-rule (the *unit rule*) that gave all delegates to the primary or convention winner. This rule was replaced by a system of *proportionality* in which candidates won delegates in rough proportion to the votes they received in the primary election or convention in each state. These rule changes became important in 2008 as proportionality rules meant that neither Hillary Clinton nor Barack Obama could benefit from the "winner-take-all" rules that helped propel John McCain to his party's nomination.

The reforms following 1968 achieved greater diversity of representation among delegates and, as noted, meant that more states adopted primaries. But the new process also meant that elected officials who wanted a voice in determining presidential candidates had to run for delegate to the national convention. Some elected officials feared losing in their own party process, and others wanted to delay endorsing a candidate. Responding to this criticism, the party created "superdelegate" positions for elected officials and party leaders who were not required to run for election as delegates. In 2008 it was the superdelegates who early on favored Clinton, but by late May 2008, a majority of them supported Obama. In the Democratic party in 2008 it was the super delegates who were decisive in determining the nominee, as neither Hilary Clinton nor Barack Obama had enough delegates selected in primaries or caucuses to win the nomination. Clinton, who at one time had a large lead among superdelegates, saw that margin erode as Obama made the case that he had more elected delegates.

Reform Among the Republicans

Republicans have not been immune to criticism that their conventions and procedures were keeping out the rank-and-file. They did not make changes as drastic as those made by the Democrats, but they did give the national committee more control over presidential campaigns, and state parties were urged to encourage broader participation by all groups, including women, minorities, youth, and the poor.

The Republican Party has long been better organized than the Democrats. In the 1970s, the GOP emphasized grassroots organization and membership recruitment. Seminars taught Republican candidates how to make speeches and hold press conferences, and weekend conferences were organized for training young party professionals. The Democrats have become better organized and more professional.[55] Until 2004 Republicans had cultivated a larger donor base and were less reliant on the large-donor soft money contributions that became so controversial in recent elections. In 2006, however, the Democratic committees closed the donor gap, with 45 percent of their money raised from small donors, compared to 46 percent from small donors among the Republican committees. The trend toward small donors continued in 2008,

Republican nominee John McCain's selection of Alaska Governor Sarah Palin (seen here with McCain at the convention) helped McCain with the base of his party and helped energize volunteers.

especially in the Obama campaign which set new records not only for total contributions but also for the number of individuals contributing to the campaign. Many of these donors were new donors making contributions that did not exceed $200.

As we have demonstrated in this chapter, political parties are vital to the functioning of democracy. They organize electoral competition, unify large portions of the electorate, simplify democracy for voters, help transform individual preferences into policy, and provide a mechanism for opposition.

Parties are just as important in organizing the government. They help straddle the separation of powers as fellow partisans cooperate between the executive and legislative branches, or between the House and Senate. Senior government appointees get their jobs in part because of their party loyalty.

Parties also provide an important way for citizens to influence government. As a well-known political scientist wrote many years ago, "The political parties created democracy, and modern democracy is unthinkable save in terms of the parties."[56] Because they are the means by which politicians secure office, participation in the parties can help determine the course of American government. Parties also provide opportunities to learn about how other people see issues and to learn to compromise. Rather than being an impediment to democracy, they make government by the people possible.

CHAPTER **SUMMARY**

1 Explain why parties arise in democracies and their primary functions.

Political parties are essential to democracy. They simplify voting choices, organize electoral competition, unify the electorate, help organize government by bridging the separation of powers and fostering cooperation among branches of government, translate public preferences into policy, and provide loyal opposition.

2 Contrast the unique features of the American party system with those of other countries.

American elections are based on single-member-district, winner-take-all election rules. In systems with proportional representation or multimember districts, there is a greater tendency for more parties to form and consequently a need to assemble governing coalitions of several parties. Compared to some European parties, American parties remain organizationally weak.

Another unique feature is the candidate nomination process. With rules determined by each state, voters determine party nominees for office through primaries, caucuses, or mixed systems.

3 Understand the history of American political parties.

American parties have experienced critical elections and realignments. Most political scientists agree that the last realignment occurred in 1932. In recent years, there has been divided government and an increase in the number of persons who call themselves Independents. This trend is sometimes called dealignment, but most Independents are closet partisans who vote fairly consistently for the party toward which they lean.

For half a century, it has been routine to have divided government, with one party in control of the presidency and the other in control of one or both houses of Congress. Successful presidents have found ways to cope with divided government and enact important parts of their agenda. The 2002 election gave Republicans unified government with control of both houses of Congress and the White House. Democrats took control of Congress in 2006 and the 2008 election gave Democrats unified control of government with enlarged majorities in the House and Senate.

4 Distinguish parties' functions as institutions, in government, and in the electorate.

Parties play many different roles. As institutions, they are governed by their national and state committees, and the focal points of party organization are the national and state party chairs, which use permanent party staff to recruit and elect candidates, promote their party's principles, and keep the party organized. In government, Congress is organized around parties, and judicial and many executive branch appointments are based in large part on partisanship. In the electorate, parties actively seek to organize elections, simplify voting choices, and strengthen individuals' party identification.

5 Discuss how parties and elections are financed.

With the rise of soft money in recent elections, parties had more resources to spend on politics. In 2002, Congress passed the Bipartisan Campaign Reform Act (BCRA), which banned soft money except for some narrowly defined and limited activities. The parties adapted to BCRA by building a larger individual donor base. Donors wanting to spend more than the BCRA limits did so in 2008 through a range of interest groups, many of which were allied 527 groups that ran parallel campaigns with the candidates and parties.

6 Assess the long-term prospects for the current party system and, specifically, the Democratic and Republican Parties.

Frequent efforts have been made to reform our parties. The Progressive movement saw parties, as then organized, as an impediment to democracy and pushed direct primaries as a means to reform them. Following the 1968 election, the Democratic Party took the lead in pushing primaries and stressing greater diversity among the individuals elected as delegates. Republicans have also encouraged broader participation, and they have improved their party structure and finances. There has been some party renewal in recent years as party competition has grown in the South and the parties themselves have initiated reforms.

Chapter Self-Test

1. Define the term *political party.* (p. 179)
2. Explain the five major functions of political parties, using one or two sentences for each one. (pp. 179–181)
3. In a short essay, describe the benefits and problems with each form of nominating candidates—caucus, open primary, closed primary, and blanket primary. Choose which method is best and defend your answer. (pp. 179–181)
4. Keeping in mind the five functions of political parties, discuss in a few sentences why partisan fighting is an inevitable part of the party system. (pp. 181–182)
5. From each pair, identify which feature is part of the U.S. party system and which is part of a typical parliamentary system. (pp. 179–183)
   a. winner-take-all/proportional representation
   b. multi-member districts/single-member districts
   c. party-centered campaigns/candidate-centered campaigns
   d. two dominant parties/many parties
   e. weak party organization/strong party organization
   f. ideological parties/centrist parties
6. In two or three sentences, explain why a vote for a third-party candidate in a U.S. election is typically considered a wasted vote. (pp. 183–185)
7. Place the following partisan realignments in chronological order and match them to the party that gained power as a result—Democratic, Republican or Federalist. (pp. 185–187)
   a. The Founding
   b. Jackson and grassroots democracy
   c. The Civil War
   d. The progressive era
   e. The New Deal
8. Analyze the chart on page 195 and identify three or four changes in partisan identification in the last forty years. For example, far fewer men identify themselves as Democrats today.
9. Match each of the following activities with the aspect of a political party it best represents—(a) parties as institutions, (b) in government, or (c) in the electorate. (pp. 188–194)
   i. A student registers to vote, stating his party preference as Republican on the registration form before handing it to the county clerk
   ii. Howard Dean, Chair of the Democratic National Committee, decides whether the votes of Democrats in Michigan and Florida should count during the 2008 presidential primaries
   iii. The Senate splits 55–45 on a bill authorizing funds for the Iraq War, with Republicans voting 44–5 in favor and Democrats voting 50–1 against

10. A woman in Michigan learns about Barack Obama and begins campaigning enthusiastically for him, despite never caring much about politics before. This woman is most likely________. (p. 194)
    a. A party regular
    b. A candidate activist
    c. An issue activist

11. Many positions in the executive, legislative, and judicial branches of government are likely to be filled by loyal, active members of the political party in power. In one paragraph, discuss what problems may arise from this system. (pp. 192–193)

12. Describe why soft money was banned by the Bipartisan Campaign Reform Act. (p. 199)

13. From where do the national party committees get most of their money today? (pp. 199–200)
    a. Soft money
    b. Individual donors
    c. The general funds of unions and corporations
    d. Their parties' candidates

14. Examine Tables 7-2, 7-3, and 7-4 on page 197, 198, and 200. In a paragraph, discuss which party, if either, you think will have the advantage in the coming years. Use specific numbers from the tables to support your argument. (pp. 197, 198, 200)

15. In a short essay, describe two or three benefits and two or three problems of parties, then argue for keeping or doing away with our current party system. (pp. 179–194)

Key Terms

political party, p. 179
nonpartisan election, p. 180
patronage, p. 180
honeymoon, p. 181
caucus, p. 181
party convention, p. 181
direct primary, p. 181
open primary, p. 181
crossover voting, p. 181
closed primary, p. 181
minor party, p. 183
proportional representation, p. 183
winner-take-all system, p. 183
realigning election, p. 185
divided government, p. 187
national party convention, p. 190
party registration, p. 193
party identification, p. 196
dealignment, p. 197
soft money, p. 199
hard money, p. 199

Further Reading

JOHN H. ALDRICH, *Why Parties? The Origin and Transformation of Party Politics in America* (University of Chicago Press, 1995).

JOHN F. BIBBY AND **BRIAN F. SCHAFFNER,** *Politics, Parties, and Elections in America,* 6th ed. (Wadsworth, 2007).

SIDNEY BLUMENTHAL, *The Strange Death of Republican America: Chronicles of a Collapsing Party* (Union Square Press, 2008).

DAVID BOAZ, *Libertarianism: A Primer* (Free Press, 1998).

BRUCE E. CAIN AND **ELISABETH R. GERBER,** EDS., *Voting at the Political Fault Line: California's Experiment with the Blanket Primary* (University of California Press, 2002).

DONALD T. CRITCHLOW, *The Conservative Ascendancy: How the GOP Right Made Political History* (Harvard University Press, 2007).

LEON EPSTEIN, *Political Parties in the American Mold* (University of Wisconsin Press, 1986).

JOHN C. GREEN AND **DANIEL J. COFFEY,** EDS., *The State of the Parties: The Changing Role of Contemporary American Parties,* 5th ed. (Rowman & Littlefield, 2006).

JOHN C. GREEN AND **PAUL S. HERRNSON,** EDS., *Responsible Partisanship? The Evolution of American Political Parties Since 1950* (University Press of Kansas, 2002).

MARJORIE RANDON HERSHEY, *Party Politics in America,* 13th ed. (Longman, 2008).

WILLIAM J. KEEFE AND **MARC J. HETHERINGTON,** *Parties, Politics, and Public Policy in America,* 10th ed. (CQ Press, 2006).

BRUCE E. KEITH, DAVID B. MAGLEBY, CANDICE J. NELSON, ELIZABETH ORR, MARK C. WESTLYE, AND **RAYMOND E. WOLFINGER,** *The Myth of the Independent Voter* (University of California Press, 1992).

MICHAEL S. LEWIS-BECK, HELMUT NORPOTH, WILLIAM G. JACOBY, AND **HERBERT F. WEISBERG,** *The American Voter Revisited* (University of Michigan Press, 2008).

DAVID B. MAGLEBY, ANTHONY D. CORRADO, AND **KELLY D. PATTERSON,** EDS., *Financing the 2004 Election* (Brookings Institution Press, 2006).

DAVID B. MAGLEBY AND **KELLY D. PATTERSON,** EDS., *The Battle for Congress: Iraq, Scandal, and Campaign Finance in the 2006 Election* (Paradigm, 2008).

L. SANDY MAISEL AND **KARA Z. BUCKLEY,** *The Electoral Process,* 4th ed. (Rowman & Littlefield, 2005).

KELLY D. PATTERSON, *Political Parties and the Maintenance of Liberal Democracy* (Columbia University Press, 1996).

STEVEN J. ROSENSTONE, ROY L. BEHR, AND **EDWARD H. LAZARUS,** *Third Parties in America: Citizen Response to Major Party Failure,* 2d ed. (Princeton University Press, 1996).

JAMES SUNDQUIST, *Dynamics of the Party System: Alignment and Realignment of Political Parties in the United States,* rev. ed. (Brookings Institution Press, 1983).

chapter 8

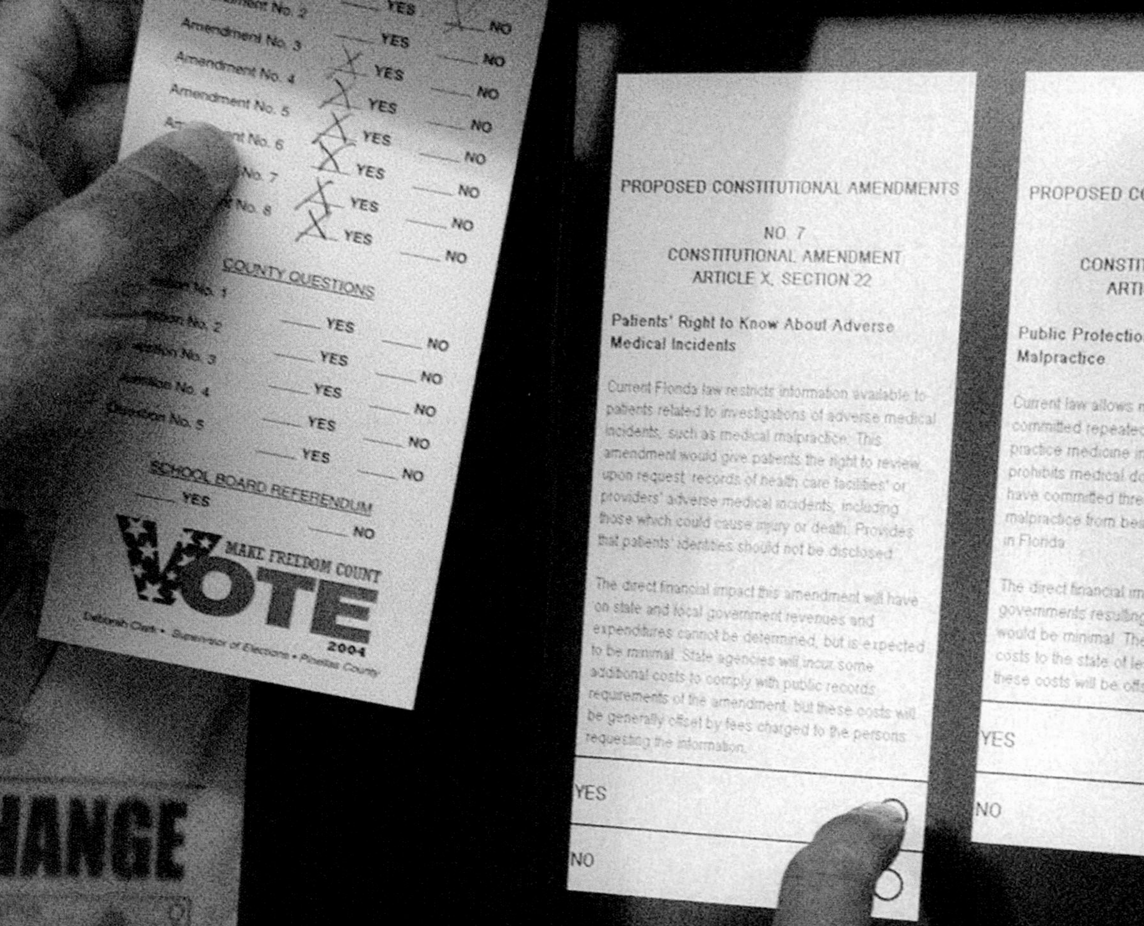

General Election – November 2, 2004
COUNTY QUESTIONS
SCHOOL BOARD REFERENDUM
MAKE FREEDOM COUNT
VOTE
2004
PROPOSED CONSTITUTIONAL AMENDMENTS
NO. 7
CONSTITUTIONAL AMENDMENT
ARTICLE X, SECTION 22
Patients' Right to Know About Adverse Medical Incidents
YES
NO

Public Opinion, Participation, and Voting

In both 2000 and 2004, concerns about the voting process lingered long after the election. The center of attention in 2000 was Florida, where contested ballots and outdated voting machines added to the drama of a close election and determined the outcome of the presidential election. Some of the problems that became front-page stories included the handling of absentee ballots and, in some Florida counties, punch-card ballots with punches that did not completely perforate the card, leaving "hanging chads." (A chad is the part of a punch-card ballot that the machine should remove as part of the voting process.) Other counties in Florida had "butterfly ballots," on which the candidates' names are staggered on opposite sides of the ballot with the punch holes in a straight line in the middle. Because the names were not listed in a straight line, many people claimed that they were confused while voting about which hole corresponded with which candidate.

Lingering perceptions of partisanship in the Florida outcome include the way the Florida secretary of state, Republican Katherine Harris, handled the recounts and other aspects of the election under her control. To many foreign observers, the fact that partisan officials, including secretaries of state and county clerks, administer U.S. elections raises concerns about objectivity and fairness. Such observers often ask whether neutral, nonpartisan—or at least bipartisan—commissions should administer elections instead.

The 2000 election in Florida demonstrated the acute need to modernize the way we vote in the United States. Many states and the federal government responded by authorizing money to provide new voting equipment. Some of that new equipment was used for the first time in the 2004 election. But in Ohio, the new machines and the way they were administrated generated added controversy. Indeed, if the Ohio outcome had been as close as Florida was in 2000, the country would have faced another set of legal challenges to the presidential election. In 2004, the Ohio secretary of state, Republican Kenneth Blackwell, was criticized as Harris had been in Florida four years before for his decisions about voter eligibility, requiring voter registration to be on cardstock of a certain weight, and restricting the use of provisional ballots in ways Democrats claimed reduced the pool of votes cast.

Following the controversy of the 2000 election, Florida enacted legislation modernizing its election process, establishing minimum standards for polling places and voting machines, and purchasing more than $30 million worth of new touchscreen machines. Even with these changes, some machines did not work and some poll workers were not adequately prepared to help voters with the new voting technology.

At the national level, in 2002 Congress passed the Help America Vote Act (HAVA), providing $3.9 billion in federal funds to modernize voting procedures and mandating that states maintain accurate statewide voter registration lists.[1] The legislation allows voters to cast provisional ballots if there is uncertainty about their registration. Advocates of the new voting technology hoped it would improve accuracy and make voting more accessible for persons who have disabilities or do not speak English.[2] Opponents saw the funding as inadequate to meet the need and worried about the accuracy and security of the new systems.[3] Some of these concerns were validated in the 2006 elections when states such as Ohio had problems with machines not working or

LEARNING **OBJECTIVES**

1. Identify the key dimensions of public opinion and how we measure it.
2. Describe the forces that create and shape individuals' political attitudes.
3. Analyze the relationship between public opinion and public policy.
4. Assess non–voting participation and how it may change in the age of the Internet.
5. Describe the demographic, legal, and electioneering factors that affect voter turnout.
6. Explain why people vote the way they do in elections.
7. Identify the problems associated with administering elections and proposed solutions to those problems.

CHAPTER OUTLINE

- Public Opinion
- Participation: Translating Opinions into Action
- Voting Choices
- Counting Votes

missing electronic voting cards. Some states, such as Ohio, Florida, and California, have abandoned voting machines for optical scan paper ballots.

Despite the high turnout in the 2008 general election, there were only isolated problems with voting machines. Problems were more prevalent in battleground states, but they seemed to result more from mistakes or random breakdowns rather than any systematic effort at slowing down the voting process as some had feared. The new technology did not work perfectly. Several precincts in Florida had optical scan machines break down, preventing officials from scanning thousands of ballots until sometime later. Voters in some states with touch-screen machines reported problems with malfunctioning machines. The larger problem was how long people had to stand in line to vote. While estimates varied, many voters waited an hour or more to vote and some much longer. Anticipating the possibility of long lines, many jurisdictions allowed early voting or encouraged people to vote by mail.[4]

As recent elections demonstrate, our country has a lot of work to do to make voting fair and transparent to all voters. In this chapter, we explore issues such as those that affected voting processes in 2000 and since. We also look at the nature and level of political participation in the United States, and why people vote the way they do. We begin by exploring public opinion, how to measure it, and what factors affect the formation of opinions.

Comparing Governments and Public Opinion

Public Opinion

LEARNING OBJECTIVE

Identify the key dimensions of public opinion and how we measure it.

All governments in all nations must be concerned with public opinion. Even in nondemocratic nations, unrest and protest can topple those in power. And in a constitutional democracy, citizens can express opinions in a variety of ways, including through demonstrations, in conversations, by writing to their elected representatives and to newspapers, and by voting in free and regularly scheduled elections. In short, democracy and public opinion go hand in hand.

public opinion
The distribution of individual preferences for or evaluations of a given issue, candidate, or institution within a specific population.

random sample
In this type of sample, every individual has a known and equal chance of being selected.

What Is Public Opinion?

Politicians frequently talk about what "the people" think or want. But social scientists use the term "public opinion" more precisely: **public opinion** is the distribution of individual preferences for or evaluations of a given issue, candidate, or institution within a specific population. *Distribution* means the proportion of the population that holds a particular opinion, compared to people who have opposing opinions or no opinion at all. The most accurate way to study public opinion is through systematic measurement in polls or surveys. For instance, final preelection polls in 2004 by the Gallup Poll found that among potential voters, 49 percent reported that they would vote for George W. Bush, 49 percent for John Kerry, and 1 percent for Ralph Nader. The actual vote was Bush 51 percent, Kerry 48 percent, and Nader 0.35 percent. For instance, final preelection polls in 2008 by the Gallup Poll found that among likely voters and removing those with no opinion, 54 percent said they were voting for Barack Obama, 44 percent said they were voting for John McCain and 2 percent said they were voting for someone else.[5] The actual vote was Obama 52 percent, McCain 46 percent, and 1 percent voted for all others.

In addition to polls conducted by Gallup, Pew, and other such organizations, newspapers and TV networks conduct polls on election preferences and numerous other subjects.

Taking the Pulse of the People In a public opinion poll, a relatively small number of people can accurately represent the opinions of a larger population if the researchers use random *sampling.* In a **random sample,** every individual in the group has a known and equal chance of being selected. For instance, a survey of 18- to 24-year-olds should not consist solely of college students, because nearly half of this age group do not attend college.[6] If only college students are selected, everyone in this age group does not have an equal chance of being included.

One classic example of a flawed poll was the 1936 *Literary Digest* poll, which predicted that Republican Alf Landon would defeat Democrat Franklin D. Roosevelt. However, *Literary Digest*'s Depression-era sample was drawn from subscribers to the magazine who owned cars and had telephones. In fact, Roosevelt decisively defeated Landon in the actual election, carrying every state except Vermont and Maine. Problems with the *Literary Digest* poll were not limited to its flawed sample but also included bias in the response rate.[7] A much more reliable way to draw a sample today is with random-digit dialing, in which a computer generates phone numbers at random, allowing the researcher to reach unlisted numbers and cell phones as well as home phones. Exit polls, when properly administered, interview voters at random as they leave the polls at a randomly selected set of precincts.

Even with proper sampling, surveys have a *margin of error,* meaning the sample accurately reflects the population within a certain range—usually plus or minus 3 percent for a sample of at least 1,000 individuals. If, for example, a preelection poll had one candidate getting 50 percent of the vote and another 48 percent, and the margin of error was plus or minus 3 percent, the first candidate's share could be as high as 53 percent or as low as 47 percent, and the second candidate's could be as high as 51 percent or as low as 45 percent. In such a race the result would be within the margin of error and too close to say who was ahead. If the sample is sufficiently large and randomly selected, these margins of error would apply in about 95 of 100 cases. The final preelection survey results in 2004 were within this margin of error for the actual vote.

The *art of asking questions* is also important to scientific polling. Questions can measure respondents' factual knowledge, their opinions, the intensity of their opinions, or their views on hypothetical situations. The way questions are worded and the order in which they are asked can influence respondents' answers. Researchers should pretest their questions to be sure they are as clear and as specific as possible. Professional interviewers, who read the questions exactly as written and without any bias in their voices, should ask them.

Open-ended questions permit respondents to answer in their own words rather than by choosing responses from set categories. These questions are harder to record and compare, but they allow respondents to express their views more clearly and may provide deeper insight into their thinking. (See Table 8–1.)

TABLE 8–1 The Way You Ask the Question Matters

The way you ask a polling question makes a lot of difference in the way people answer it, as demonstrated by the way three different polls asked about partial-birth or late-term abortion. All polls were conducted in April 2007.

1. "Which of the following best represents your views about abortion? The choice on abortion should be left up to the woman and her doctor. Abortion should be legal only in cases in which pregnancy results from rape or incest or when the life of the woman is at risk. Or, abortion should be illegal in all circumstances."*

   Woman and doctor—55% | Rape, Incest, Life of Woman—30% | Always illegal—13% | Unsure — 2%

2. "As you may know, the Supreme Court recently upheld a law that makes the procedure commonly known as a partial birth abortion illegal. Do you favor or oppose this ruling by the Supreme court?"

   Favor—53% | Oppose—34% | Unsure—13%

3. "As you may know, the Supreme Court recently upheld a law that makes the procedure commonly known as a partial-birth abortion illegal. A partial-birth abortion is a procedure performed in the late term of pregnancy, when in some cases the baby is old enough to survive on its own outside the womb. The court's ruling outlaws using this procedure, and does not make an exception for the health of the mother. Do you favor or oppose this ruling by the Supreme Court?"

   Favor—47% | Oppose—43% | Unsure—10%

4. "Do you agree or disagree with the recent Supreme Court decision on partial-birth abortion?"

   Agree—41% | Disagree—41% | Unsure—19%†

* NBC News/Wall Street Journal Poll conducted by the polling organizations of Peter Hart (D) and Neil Newhouse (R). April 20–23, 2007. N=1,004 adults nationwide. MoE ± 3.1 (for all adults).

† Quinnipiac University Poll, April 25–May 1, 2007.

In addition to random sampling, clearly worded questions, and the absence of bias in the way questions are asked, scientific polls also require thorough *analysis and reporting of the results.* Scientific polls must specify the sample size, the margin of error, and when and where the poll was conducted. Moreover, because public opinion can change from day to day and even from hour to hour, polls are really only snapshots of opinion at a particular point in time. One way to track opinion *change* is to interview the same sample more than once. Such surveys are called *panel surveys.* Although they can be informative, it can also be difficult and expensive to contact respondents for a second or third set of interviews, and those in the sample may know they will be interviewed again, which may influence their responses.

Defining public opinion as the distribution of *individual preference* emphasizes that the unit of measurement is *individuals*—not groups. The *universe* or *population* is the group of people of whom we asked the question. The universe of subscribers to *Literary Digest* was not representative of the universe of all voters in 1936, for instance, a major reason the poll incorrectly predicted the election.[8] When a substantial percentage of a sample agrees on an issue—say, that we should honor the U.S. flag—there is a *consensus.* But on most issues, opinions are divided. When two opposing sides feel intensely about an issue and the difference between the major alternatives is wide, the public is said to be *polarized.* On such issues it can be difficult to compromise or find a middle ground. The Vietnam War in the 1960s and 1970s was a polarizing issue. A more recent example is gay marriage. Neither those who favor legalizing gay marriage nor those who unequivocally oppose it see much room for compromise. Somewhere in the middle are those who oppose gay marriage but favor giving gay couples legal rights through "civil unions." (See Table 8–2.)

Intensity *Intensity*—the degree to which people feel strongly about their opinions—produces the brightest and deepest hues in the fabric of public opinion. For example, some individuals mildly favor gun control legislation, others mildly oppose it; some people are emphatically for or against it; and some have no interest in gun control at all. Others may not have even heard of it. People who lost their jobs or retirement savings because of corporate scandals are likely to feel more intensely about enhanced regulation of corporations and accounting firms than those not directly affected. We typically measure intensity by asking people how strongly they feel about an issue or about a politician. Such a question is sometimes called a *scale.*

Latency *Latency* describes the political opinions people may hold but have not fully expressed. These opinions may not have crystallized, yet they are still important, because they can be aroused by leaders or events and thereby motivate people to support them. Latent opinions set rough boundaries for leaders, who know that if they take certain actions, they will trigger either opposition or support from millions of people. If leaders understand people's unexpressed wants, needs, and hopes, they will know how to mobilize people and draw them to the polls on election day. A recent example of a latent opinion is the concern for security from foreign enemies, which had not been an issue in the United States before the terrorist attacks of September 11, 2001. The need for homeland security has now become a **manifest opinion,** a widely shared and consciously held view.

Salience *Salience* measures the extent to which people believe issues are relevant to them. Most people are more concerned about personal issues such as paying their bills and keeping their jobs than about national issues, but if national issues somehow threaten their security or safety, their salience rises sharply. Salience and intensity, though different, are often correlated on the same issue.

The salience of issues may change over time. During the Great Depression of the 1930s, people were concerned mainly about jobs, wages, and economic security. By the 1940s, with the onset of World War II, foreign affairs came to the forefront. In the 1960s, problems of race and poverty were important to many. In the 1970s, Vietnam and then the Watergate scandals became the focus of attention. In 2008, rising gas and food prices

manifest opinion
A widely shared and consciously held view, such as support for abortion rights or for homeland security.

TABLE 8–2 Differing Opinions on Gay Marriage

	Gay Marriage Should Not Be Allowed	Gay Marriage Should Not Be Allowed, But Civil Unions Should Be Allowed (volunteered response)	Gay Marriage Should Be Allowed
Total	**63%**	**3%**	**34%**
Gender			
Men	64	3	32
Women	61	3	36
Region			
Northeast	55	3	42
Midwest	71	3	25
South	70	2	28
West	47	5	48
Age			
18–29	49	2	49
30–44	59	4	37
45–64	64	4	32
65+	85	2	13
Church Attendance			
Every week	84	2	14
Almost every week	78	5	17
Once or twice a month	66	5	29
A few times a year	51	4	45
Never	44	0	56
Race			
White	63	3	34
African American	69	3	29
Hispanic	53	5	42
Other	56	8	36
Party			
Republican	80	4	17
Democrat	54	3	43
Independent	57	3	41
Other	60	5	35
Political Philosophy			
Conservative	82	4	14
Moderate	57	4	39
Liberal	32	2	66
Don't know/Haven't thought about it	66	2	32
Marital Status			
Married	68	3	29
Widowed	81	2	17
Divorced	57	8	35
Separated	74	0	26
Single, never married	49	1	50
Partnered, not married	37	5	59
Education			
High school or less	72	2	25
Some college	60	5	35
College degree or more	49	3	48

NOTE: Numbers may not add to 100 because of rounding. Independents who lean toward a party are classified with the party toward which they lean. Race is defined by the first race with which a respondent identifies.

SOURCE: *2004 National Election Study* (Center for Political Studies, University of Michigan, 2004).

raised the salience of energy policy. The economy took center stage in 2008 as Wall Street investment banks went under. Congress enacted a $700 billion infusion of federal dollars into the banking system and the stock market fluctuated wildly from day to day.

How Do We Get Our Political Opinions and Values?

LEARNING **OBJECTIVE**

2 Describe the forces that create and shape individuals' political attitudes.

No one is born with political views. We develop our political attitudes from many mentors and teachers through a process called **political socialization.** As we discussed in Chapter 4, this process starts in childhood, and families and schools are usually our two most important political teachers. As children we learn about our culture in childhood and adolescence but reshape it as we mature.[9] Socialization—the way in which we come to see ourselves and society and learn to interact with other individuals and groups—lays the foundation for political beliefs, values, ideology, and partisanship. A common element of political socialization in most cultures is *nationalism,* a consciousness of the nation-state and of belonging to it.

The pluralistic political culture of the United States makes the sources of our views immensely varied. Political attitudes may stem from religious, racial, gender, or ethnic backgrounds, or economic beliefs and values. But we can safely make at least one generalization: We form our attitudes through participation in *groups* (see Chapters 4 and 6). This includes families, schools, social organizations, and more political groups such as the National Rifle Association (NRA) or Planned Parenthood. Close-knit groups such as the family are especially influential. When we identify closely with the attitudes and interests of a particular group, these attitudes color how we see things.[10] Group affiliation does not necessarily mean that individual members do not think for themselves. Each member brings his or her own emotions, memories, and resistance to groups.

Children in the United States tend at an early age to adopt common values that provide continuity with the past and that legitimate the U.S. political system. Young children know what country they live in, and their loyalty to the nation develops early. Although the details of our political system may elude them, most young citizens acquire a respect for the Constitution and for the concept of participatory democracy, as well as an initially positive view of the most visible figure in our democracy, the president.[11]

political socialization
The process—most notably in families and schools—by which we develop our political attitudes, values, and beliefs.

Family Most social psychologists agree that family is the most powerful socializing agent.[12] What we first learn in the family is not so much specific political opinions as

Most U.S. children have ample opportunity to learn the importance of participatory democracy.

basic *attitudes,* broad or general, that shape our opinions about our neighbors, political parties, other classes or types of people, particular leaders (especially presidents), and society in general.

American children typically show political interest by age 10, and by the early teens their awareness may be fairly high. Studies of high school students indicate a strong correlation between their partisan identification and their parents' political party that continues throughout life. In other words, people tend to belong to the same political party as their parents did. Does the direct influence of parents create the correspondence? Or does living in the same social environment—neighborhood, church, socioeconomic group—influence parents and children? The answer is *both.* One influence often strengthens the other.

Schools Schools also mold young citizens' political attitudes. U.S. schools see part of their purpose as preparing students to be citizens and active participants in governing their communities and the nation. Especially important in fostering later political involvement are extracurricular activities such as student government and debate.[13]

From kindergarten through college, students generally develop political values consistent with the democratic process and supportive of the U.S. political system. In their study of U.S. history, they are introduced to our nation's heroes and heroines, important events, and the ideals of U.S. society. Other aspects of their experience, such as the daily Pledge of Allegiance and school programs or assemblies, seek to reinforce respect for country. Children also gain practical experience in the way democracy works through elections for student government. In many states, high school and even college students are required by law to take courses in U.S. history or government to graduate.

Do school courses and activities give young people the skills needed to participate in elections and democratic institutions? A study of 18- to 24-year-olds commissioned by the National Association of Secretaries of State found that young people "lack any real understanding of citizenship . . . information and understanding about the democratic process . . . and information about candidates and political parties."[14] Furthermore, the Secretaries of State report noted that "most young people do not seek out political information and that they are not very likely to do so in the future."[15] You and your classmates are not a representative sample, in

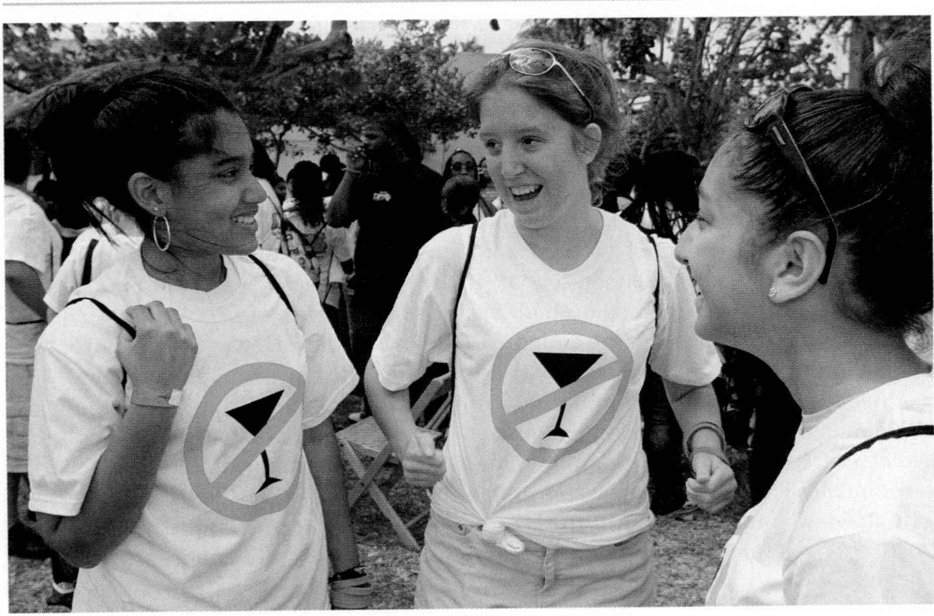

This SADD (Students Against Destructive Decisions), originally formed as a student group against drunk driving, is an example of how students are socialized at school.

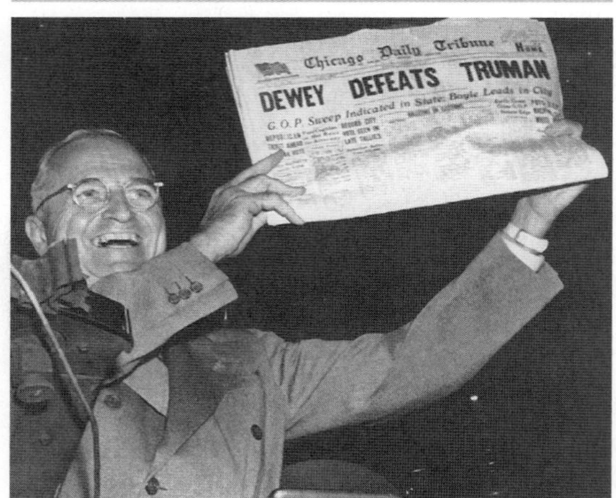

Chicago *Daily Tribune* was so sure of its polling data in the 1948 election that it predicted a win for Republican Thomas Dewey before the results were final. A victorious Harry Truman displays the mistaken headline.

part because you are taking this course and therefore have more interest and knowledge than most people.

The debate about whether there is peer pressure on college campuses to conform to certain acceptable ideas or to use particular language highlights how higher education can shape attitudes and values. How does college influence political opinion? One study suggests that college students are more likely than non–college students of the same age to be knowledgeable about politics, more in favor of free speech, and more likely to talk and read about politics.[16]

Mass Media Like everyone else, young people are exposed to a wide range of media—school newspapers, national and local newspapers, the Internet, movies, radio, television—all of which influence what they think, and like everyone else they often pick and choose the media with which they agree, a process called **selective exposure.** The mass media also serve as agents of political socialization by exposing individuals to the values and behavior of others. Media influence is greater on attitudes about issues and individual politicians than on underlying values.[17]

Other Influences Religious, ethnic, and racial backgrounds as well as the workplace can also shape opinions, both within and outside the family. Some scholars have found, for example, that the religious composition of a community has a direct impact on knowledge, discussion, and self-confidence among students in dealing with politics.[18] But although generalizations about how people vote are useful, we have to be careful about stereotyping. For example, not all African Americans vote Democratic, and many Catholics disagree with their church's opposition to abortion. It is a mistake to assume that because we know a person's religious affiliation or racial background, we know his or her political opinions.

Stability and Change in Public Opinion

Adults are not simply the sum of their early experiences, but adults' opinions do tend to remain stable. Even if the world around us changes rapidly, we are slow to shift our loyalties or to change our minds about things that matter to us. In general, people who remain in the same place, in the same occupation, and in the same income group throughout their lives tend to have stable opinions. People often carry their attitudes with them, and families who move from cities to suburbs often retain their big-city attitudes after they have moved, at least for a time. Political analysts are becoming more interested in how adults modify their views. A harsh experience—a war, an economic depression, or the loss of a job—may be a catalyst that changes attitudes and opinions.

The September 11, 2001, terrorist attacks had at least a short-term impact on public trust and confidence in government. Political scientist Robert D. Putnam studied the public's views of political institutions and community interaction following the terrorist attacks (see Table 8–3). More than half of his sample expressed greater confidence in government after the attacks than before. Interest in public affairs grew by 27 percent among people age 35 and under, and by 8 percent among older respondents. Putnam's subsequent research found that trust in community leaders, neighbors, other races, and so on had declined by the spring of 2002. Confidence in community cooperation also "tended to fade over time." However, for those aged 18–25, Putnam finds that the post-2001 increase in civic engagement continues.[19]

Because they are part of our core values, views on abortion, the death penalty, and doctor-assisted suicide, for example, tend to remain stable over time. On issues less central to our values, such as how a president is performing, opinions can change substantially. Figure 8–1 contrasts the public's opinion toward President George W. Bush with its views on abortion over time. Although the electorate's opinion of President Bush changed noticeably over time, opinions on abortion remained remarkably

selective exposure
Individuals choosing to access media with which they agree or avoiding media with which they disagree.

TABLE 8–3 Changes in Public Perception After Terrorist Attacks of September 11, 2001

	Increased	Decreased	Net Change
Trust national government	51%	7%	44%
Trust local government	32	13	19
Hours watching TV	40	24	16
Interest in politics	29	15	14
Trust local police	26	12	14
Inter racial trust	31	20	11
Trust shop clerks	28	17	11
Support for unpopular book in library	28	18	10
Trust neighbors	23	13	10
Contributions to religious charity	29	20	9
Expect crisis support from friends	22	14	8
Trust "people running my community"	32	24	8
Worked with neighbors	15	8	7
Trust local news media	30	23	7
Gave blood	11	4	7
Volunteered	36	29	7
Expect local cooperation in crisis	23	17	6
Worked on community project	17	11	6
Attend political meeting	11	6	5
Newspaper readership	27	24	3
Visit with relatives	43	40	3
Attended club meeting	29	26	3
Attended public meeting	27	26	3
Contributions to secular charity	28	27	1
Attend church	20	19	1
Organizational memberships (number)	39	39	0
Had friends visit your home	39	45	−6
Support for immigrants' rights	21	32	−11

SOURCE: *The Saguaro Seminar: Civic Engagement in America,* January 15, 2002, www.hks.harvard.edu/saguaro/press/press.htm.

stable. On many issues, opinion can change once the public learns more about the issue or perceives another side to the question. These are the issues politicians can help shape by calling attention to them and leading the debate.

Public Opinion and Public Policy

For much of human history, public opinion has been difficult to measure. "What I want," Abraham Lincoln once said, "is to get done what the people desire to be done, and the question for me is how to find that out exactly."[20] Politicians today do not face such uncertainty about public opinion—far from it.[21] Polling informs them about public opinion on all major policy issues. Politicians can commission polls themselves, or they can turn to public or media polls. All national and most local newspapers and television stations conduct or commission their own polls.[22]

Many examples from history show how public opinion can shape policy and, in turn, of how policies shape opinion. On May 3, 2003, the day after President Bush announced "Mission Accomplished" in the Iraq War, 72 percent of American adults approved of the

LEARNING **OBJECTIVE**

 Analyze the relationship between public opinion and public policy.

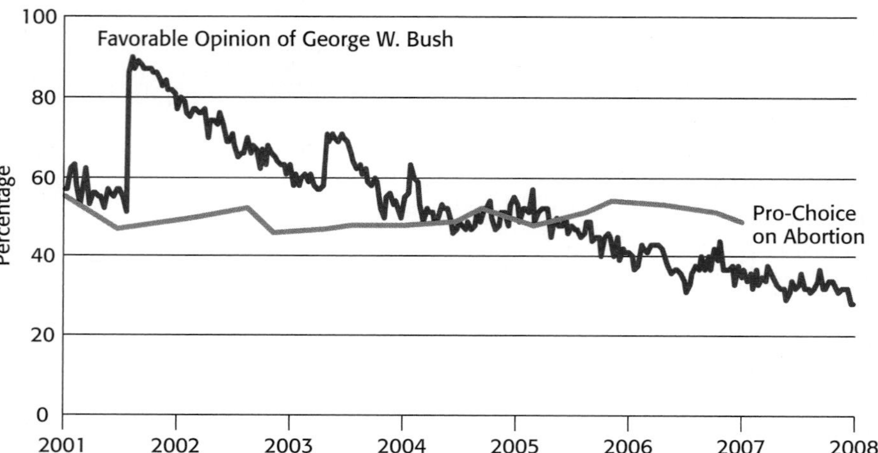

FIGURE 8–1
Comparison of Opinion of President George W. Bush and Attitude on Abortion Over Time.

SOURCE: Gallup and Gallup/USA Today polls, compiled by Polling Report, www.pollingreport.com/abortion and www.pollingreport.com/BushJob1.htm.

way he had handled the situation in Iraq. About a year later, after revelations of torture by U.S. soldiers in the Abu Ghraib prison and repeated attacks on U.S. forces in Iraq, Bush's approval rating had fallen to 34 percent,[23] and in 2008 it fell to less than 30 percent.[24]

Typically, elected officials focus on issues of importance to the public.[25] In a sense they follow public opinion, by using polls to learn how to talk about issues in ways that resonate with the public. Members of Congress want to win reelection by showing greater attention to public opinion as election day looms.[26] Candidates use polls to determine where, how, and even whether to campaign. The decision in 2008 about which states John McCain and Barack Obama campaigned in most aggressively was driven by the polls. Both campaigns lavished time and attention on Florida, Ohio, Pennsylvania, Virginia, North Carolina and Missouri. The map of competitive states was larger in 2008 than in 2000 or 2004.[27] Even smaller states such as New Hampshire and New Mexico received substantial attention. Larger states such as New York, California, Illinois, and Texas were taken for granted because one side or the other was so far ahead in them, and gaining a plurality in the national popular vote was a secondary objective to securing 270 electoral votes.

When properly conducted, polls provide valuable data on public opinion and voting behavior. When they have poorly worded questions or rely on flawed samples such as the self-selected participants in many Internet polls, they are inaccurate and give scientific polling a bad name. Before taking the results of a poll seriously, we need to know the nature of the sample, the timing of the survey—events may have occurred since the survey that make its results questionable—and the wording and order of the questions.

Polls are no substitute for elections. With a choice between candidates before them, voters must now translate their opinions into concrete decisions and decide what is important and what is not. Democracy is more than the expression of views, a simple mirror of opinion. It is the thoughtful participation of people in the political process. Elections are the critical link between the many opinions "We the People" hold and how we select our leaders.

Awareness and Interest

Many people find politics complicated and difficult to understand. And they should, because democracy *is* complicated and difficult to understand. The mechanics and structures of our government, such as how the government operates, how the electoral college works, how Congress is set up, and the length of terms for the president and for members of the Senate and House of Representatives are examples of such complexity that are important to our constitutional democracy.

Younger adults who remember learning the details in school typically know most about how the government works. In general, however, adults fare poorly when quizzed about their elected officials.[28] Just over 15 percent know the names of the congressional

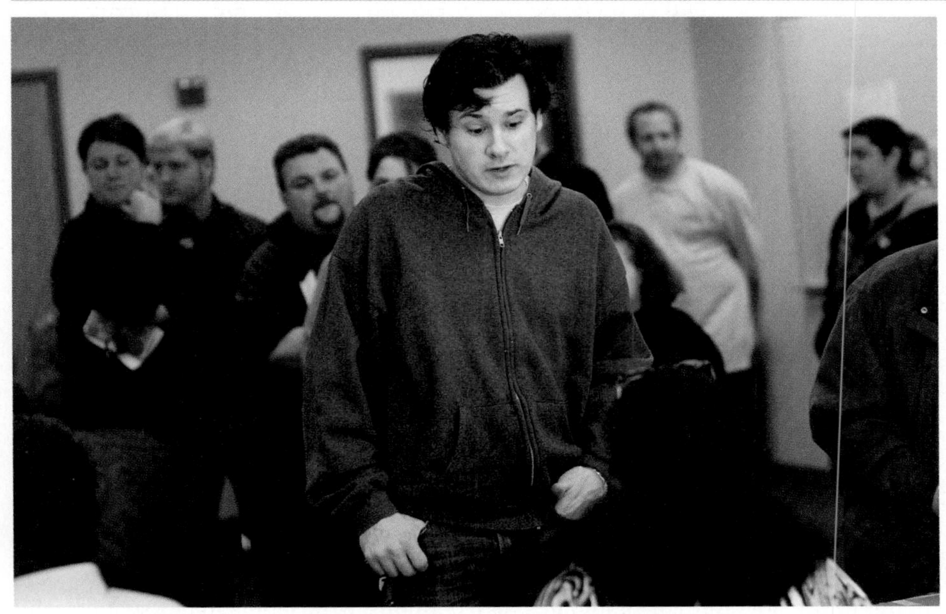

These college students took the initiative to line up on a campus to fill out absentee ballot requests so they could vote in their home states.

candidates from their district.[29] With so few voters knowing the candidates, it is not surprising that "on even hotly debated issues before congress, few people know where their Congress member stands."[30]

The public knows even less about important public policy issues (see Figure 8–2). In 2004, only 28 percent could identify William Rehnquist as the then chief justice of the U.S. Supreme Court. Fortunately, not everyone is uninformed or uninterested. About 25 percent of the public is interested in politics most of the time. This is the **attentive public,** people who know and understand how the government works. They vote in most elections, read a daily newspaper, and "talk politics" with their families and friends. They tend to be better educated and more committed to democratic values than other adults.

attentive public
Citizens who follow public affairs carefully.

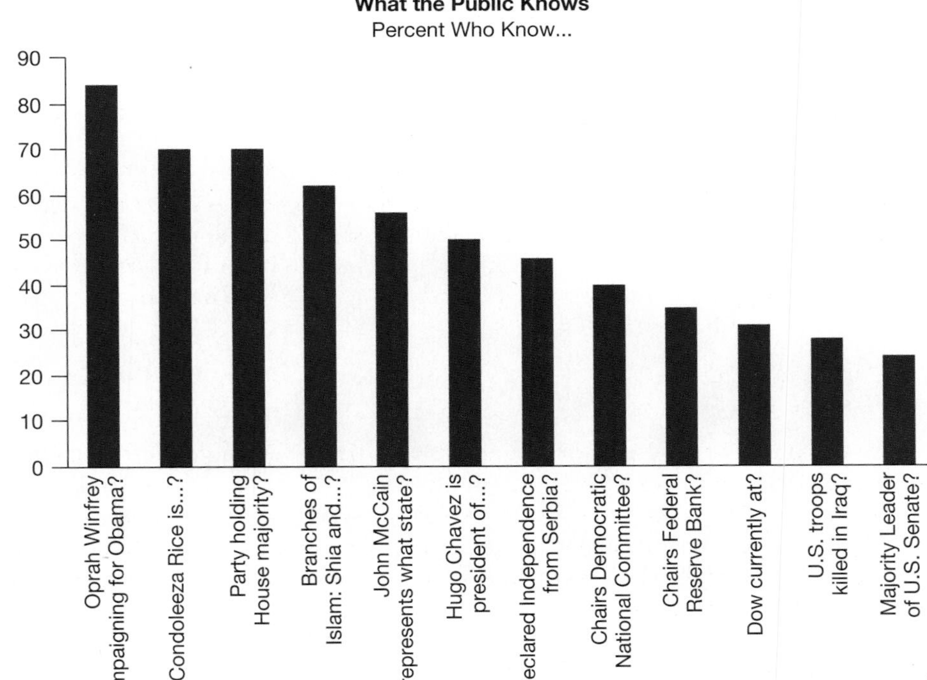

FIGURE 8–2
What the Public Knows.

SOURCE: Scott Keeter and Robert Suls, "Awareness of Iraq War Fatalities Plummets," Pew Research Center for the People and the Press, March 12, 2008, pewresearch.org/pubs/762/political-knowledge-update.

At the opposite end of the spectrum are political know-nothings, people who are rarely interested in politics or public affairs and seldom vote. About one third of American adults have indicated that they are interested in politics "only now and then" or "hardly at all."[31]

Between the attentive public and the political know-nothings are the *part-time citizens,* roughly 40 percent of the U.S. public. These individuals participate selectively in elections, voting in presidential elections but usually not in others. Politics and government do not greatly interest them, they pay only minimal attention to the news, and they rarely discuss candidates or elections with others.

Democracy can survive even when some citizens are passive and uninformed, as long as many others serve as opinion leaders and are interested and informed about public affairs. Obviously, these activists will have much greater influence than their less-active fellow citizens.

Participation: Translating Opinions into Action

LEARNING **OBJECTIVE**

4 Assess non–voting participation and how it may change in the age of the Internet.

U.S. citizens influence their government's actions in several ways, many of which the Constitution protects. In addition to voting in elections, they participate in Internet political blogs, join interest groups, go to political party meetings, ring doorbells, urge friends to vote for issues or candidates, sign petitions, write letters to newspapers, and call radio talk shows. This kind of "citizen-to-citizen" participation can be important and may become more so as more people use the Internet and its social capital–building applications, such as social networking sites.[32]

Protest is also a form of political participation. Our political system is remarkably tolerant of protest that is not destructive or violent. Boycotts, picketing, sit-ins, and marches are all legally protected. Rosa Parks and Martin Luther King, Jr., used nonviolent protest to call attention to unfair laws (see Chapter 16). Few people participate in protests, but the actions of those who do can substantially shape public opinion.

Even in an established democracy, people may feel so strongly about an issue that they would rather fight than accept the verdict of an election. The classic example is the American Civil War. Following the election of 1860, in which Abraham Lincoln—an antislavery candidate who did not receive a single electoral vote from a slave state—won the presidency, most of the South tried to secede from the Union. The ensuing war marked the failure of democracy to resolve sectional conflict. Examples in our own time include antiabortion and animal rights groups that use violence to press

When the student pro-democracy protest was stopped by the Chinese government tanks in Tiananmen Square on June 5, 1989, one man stood up in defiance until he was pulled to safety by bystanders.

their political agenda, and militia groups that arm themselves for battle against government regulations.

For most people, politics is a private activity. Some still consider it impolite to discuss politics at dinner parties. To say that politics is private doesn't mean that people don't have opinions or won't discuss them when asked by others, including pollsters. But many people avoid discussing politics with neighbors, co-workers, or even friends and family because it is too divisive or upsetting. Typically, fewer than one person in four attempts to influence how another person votes in an election.[33] But in 2004 the proportion reporting that they tried to influence another person's vote rose to nearly 50 percent. Even fewer actually work for a candidate or party. Only about 13 percent contribute financially to a candidate,[34] and only 11 percent of taxpayers designate $3 of their taxes to the presidential public financing fund that provides matching funds for participating primary candidates and a grant to participating general election candidates.[35] Few individuals attempt to influence others by writing letters to elected officials or to newspapers for publication. Fewer still participate in protest groups or activities. Despite the small number of persons who engage in these activities, small numbers of people can make a difference in politics and government. An individual or small group can generate media interest in an issue and thereby expand the issue's impact.

Levels of political participation rose during the 2008 presidential election, in part because of increased use of the Internet (see Figure 8–3). Candidates' Web sites allowed individuals to register with the campaign and be connected with other politically active individuals in their area. They also provided calling lists for volunteers to call from their own phones. Local campaign leaders in turn used the Internet to contact individuals in the area who had expressed an interest in working with the campaign. For example, before Barack Obama started his primary and caucus campaign in Texas, more than 125,000 individuals had already used his Web page to sign up to volunteer.[36] The Internet helped campaigns organize more effectively and made it easier for interested people to participate. Supporters of several candidates in 2008 went so far as to create their own music videos and political advertisements, which they uploaded to YouTube and other video hosting websites.

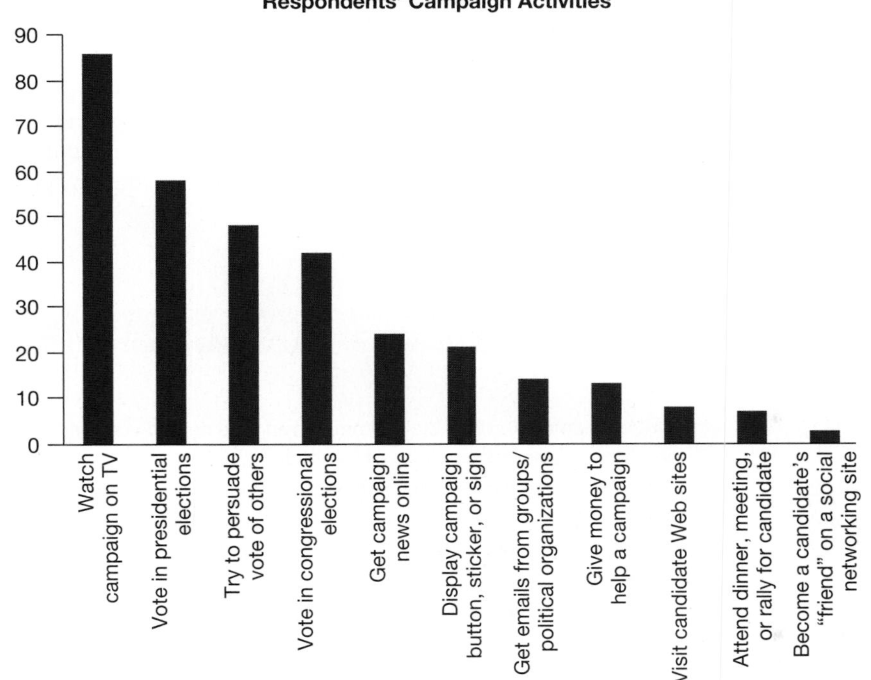

FIGURE 8–3
Political Participation and Awareness in the United States.

SOURCE: U.S. Bureau of the Census, *Statistical Abstract of the United States: 2006* (U.S. Government Printing Office, 2006), p. 263; *2004 National Election Study*, Center for Political Studies, University of Michigan; NES Guide to Public Opinion and Electoral Behavior, www.umich.edu/~nes/nesguide/gd-index.htm#6; and Pew Research Center, "Social Networking and Online Videos Take Off," January 11, 2008, www.pewinternet.org/pdfs/Pew_Media.

"I Got a Crush...On Obama" By Obama Girl

Actress/model Amber Lee Ettinger, popularly known as "Obama Girl," created a media stir with her sexually charged Internet video, "I've Got a Crush on Obama." The video had been viewed nearly nine million times by mid-2008, while several of her other pro-Obama videos also broke one million views.

More candidates and interest groups also used the Internet for fund raising in the 2008 campaign. Candidates' Web sites made it easy for individuals to donate and to invite their friends to donate through e-mail, Facebook, MySpace, and other social-networking Web sites. The Obama campaign was especially innovative in its use of the Internet. When people went to the Obama web site they were asked to provide an email address; the same was true of those who came to campaign events. Later these individuals would get an email from Barack Obama, Michelle Obama, Joe Biden or the campaign staff asking for a contribution of money or time contacting others. ActBlue, a liberal political action committee (see Chapter 6), has used the Internet to make it much easier for people to donate to the Democratic candidates of their choice, while Slatecard has tried to achieve the same for Republicans. Supporters of the Republican candidate Ron Paul independently organized Internet fund-raisers that netted him more than $10 million over two 24-hour periods.[37]

Voting

Voting is our most typical political activity. The United States is a constitutional democracy with more than 200 years of free and frequent elections and a tradition of the peaceful transfer of power between competing groups and parties.

Originally, the Constitution left it to the individual states to determine who could vote, and qualifications for voting differed considerably from state to state. All states except New Jersey barred women from voting, most did not permit African Americans or Native Americans to vote, and until the 1830s, property ownership was often a requirement. By the time of the Civil War (1861–1865), however, every state had extended the franchise to all white male citizens. Since that time, eligibility standards for voting have been expanded seven times by congressional legislation and constitutional amendments (see Table 8–4).

The civil rights movement in the 1960s made voting rights a central issue. As the "History Makers" feature summarizes, the Twenty-Fourth Amendment and 1965 Voting Rights Act were noteworthy pieces of legislation. Anticipating that some state or local governments would change election rules to foster discrimination, the act also required that any changes to

LEARNING **OBJECTIVE**

5 Describe the demographic, legal, and electioneering factors that affect voter turnout.

TABLE 8–4 Changes in Voting Eligibility Standards Since 1870

Timeline	Change
1870	Fifteenth Amendment forbade states from denying the right to vote because of "race, color, or previous condition of servitude."
1920	Nineteenth Amendment gave women the right to vote.
1924	Congress granted Native Americans citizenship and voting rights.
1961	Twenty-Third Amendment permitted District of Columbia residents to vote in federal elections.
1964	Twenty-Fourth Amendment prohibited the use of poll taxes in federal elections.
1965	Voting Rights Act removed restrictions that kept African Americans from voting.
1971	Twenty-Sixth Amendment extended the vote to citizens age 18 and older.

HISTORY MAKERS

Lyndon Johnson and the Voting Rights Act of 1965

Even though the Fifteenth Amendment granted African Americans the right to vote in 1870, it took another 95 years for Congress to enact laws that made this right an actuality. Through a variety of means, including literacy tests, poll taxes, and physical violence, for many years black persons were effectively denied the right to vote.

An important leader in extending the right to vote to all was a son of the segregated South, Lyndon Johnson. As president, Johnson pushed for passage of the Twenty-Fourth Amendment banning poll taxes and, in 1965, for passage of the National Voting Rights Act. This act outlawed the use of literacy tests as a requirement for voting, provided federal registrars for voter registration, and required the Department of Justice or U.S. District Court for the District of Columbia to approve in advance any change in voting laws in districts where black people made up at least 5 percent of the population.*

Johnson made passage of the Voting Rights Act a major priority and used his considerable talents of persuasion to defeat a Senate filibuster against this legislation. In a nationwide broadcast, he signed the act in a ceremony at the U.S. Capitol Rotunda. On that occasion he said the act would "strike away the last major shackle of the Negro's 'ancient bonds.'"† The impact of the act was immediate and continues today. For example, Mississippi saw voting registration for black people climb from less than 7 percent in 1965 to more than 74 percent in 1988.‡ The act was extended in 1970, 1975, 1982 (with amendments), and most recently in 2006 by President George W. Bush.

*National Voting Rights Act of 1965, 89th Cong., 1st sess., H.R. 1564.
†*Congress and the Nation, 1965–68: A Review of Government and Politics During the Johnson Years*, vol. 11 (CQ Press, 1969), p. 362.
‡U.S. Department of Justice, Civil Rights Division Voting Section, "Introduction to General Voting Rights Law," www.usdoj.gov/crt/voting/intro/intro_c.htm.

voting practices, requirements, or procedures must be cleared in advance with the Department of Justice or the U.S. District Court for the District of Columbia. The ban on the poll tax and the provisions of the Voting Rights Act resulted in a dramatic expansion of registration and voting by black Americans (See Figure 8–4). Once African Americans were permitted to register to vote, "the focus of voting discrimination shifted . . . to preventing them from winning elections."[38] In southern legislative districts where black people are in the majority, however, there has been a "dramatic increase in the proportion of African American legislators elected".[39]

Comparing Voting and Elections

Registration One legal requirement—**voter registration**—arose as a response to concerns about voting abuses, but it also discourages voting. Most other democracies have automatic voter registration. Average turnout in the United States, where voters must register before voting, is more than 30 percentage points lower than in countries such as Austria, Denmark, Germany, and Israel.[40] This was not always the case. In fact, in the 1800s, turnout in the United States was much like that of these

voter registration
A system designed to reduce voter fraud by limiting voting to those who have established eligibility to vote by submitting the proper documents including proof of residency.

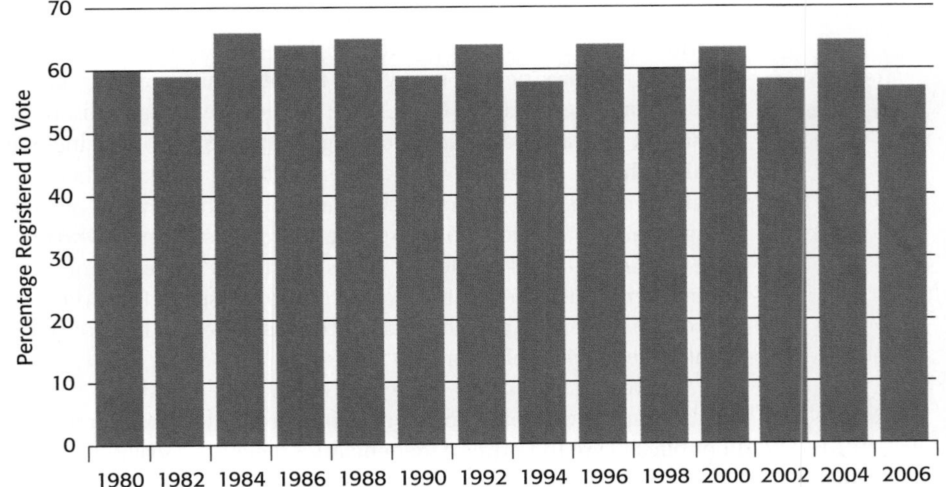

FIGURE 8–4
Percentage of African Americans Registered to Vote, 1980–2006.

SOURCE: U.S. Bureau of the Census, *Statistical Abstract of the United States, 1993* (U.S. Government Printing Office, 1993), p. 283; *Statistical Abstract, 2001*, p. 251; *Statistical Abstract, 2008*, p. 256.

FIGURE 8–5
Voter Turnout in Presidential Elections, 1789–2008.

SOURCE: Curtis Gans, Howard W. Stanley and Richard G. Niemi, *Vital Statistics on American Politics, 2007–2008* (CQ Press, 2008), pp. 13–14. See also "Much-hyped Turnout Record Fails to Materialize: Convenience Voting Fails to Boost Balloting," at http://www.american.edu/media/electionexperts/election_turnout_08.pdf, accessed November 12, 2008.

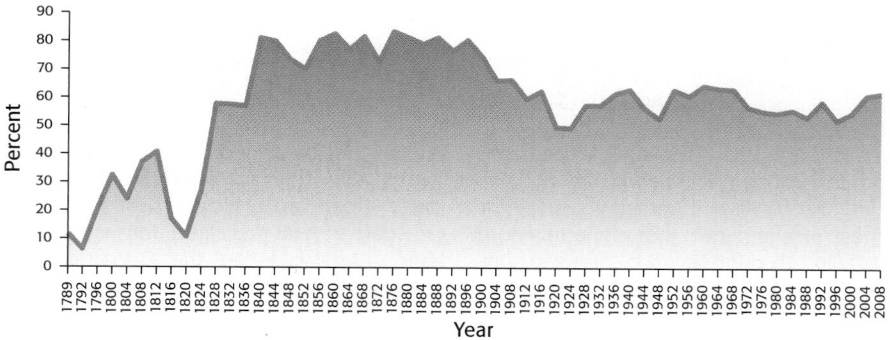

countries today. It began to drop significantly around 1900, in part as a result of election reforms (see Figure 8–5). Voter registration requirements substantially affect rates of voting.[41]

Voters wait to cast their ballots in a primary election. Voting reforms have led to more early voting, helping cut congestion on election day.

U.S elections in the 1800s were different from those of today. The parties printed the ballots, often using different-colored paper for each party, and ballots were cast in public, so party officials could monitor how people had voted. In some areas, charges that people voted more than once generated a reform movement that replaced the party-printed ballots with the Australian ballot, which the government prints and which is cast in secret (see Chapter 9). The same reformers also pressed for voter registration to prevent multiple voting and to limit voting to those who had previously established their eligibility.

Laws vary by state, but every state except North Dakota requires registration, usually in advance. Idaho, Maine, Minnesota, New Hampshire, Wisconsin, and Wyoming permit election-day registration. The most important provision regarding voter registration may be the closing date. Until the early 1970s, closing dates in many states were six months before the election. Now, federal law prevents a state from closing registration more than 30 days before a federal election.[42] Voter registration requires voters to take an extra step—usually filling out a form at the county courthouse, when renewing a driver's license, or with a roving registrar—days or weeks before the election and every time they move to a new address. Other important provisions include places and hours of registration and in some states, a requirement that voters show a photo identification before voting.[43]

Motor Voter In 1993, the burdens of voter registration were eased a bit with the National Voter Registration Act—called the "Motor Voter" bill—which allows people to register to vote while applying for or renewing a driver's license. Offices that provide welfare and disability assistance can also facilitate voter registration. States may include public schools, libraries, and city and county clerks' offices as registration sites. The law requires states to allow registration by mail using a standardized form. To purge the voting rolls of voters who may have died or changed residence, states must mail a questionnaire to voters every four years. But Motor Voter forbids states from purging the rolls for any other reasons, such as because a person has not voted in multiple previous elections.

As a result of this law, more new voters have registered.[44] Data on the impact of Motor Voter suggest that neither Democrats nor Republicans are the primary beneficiaries, because most new voters who have registered claim to be Independent.[45] Yet Motor Voter does not appear to have increased turnout.

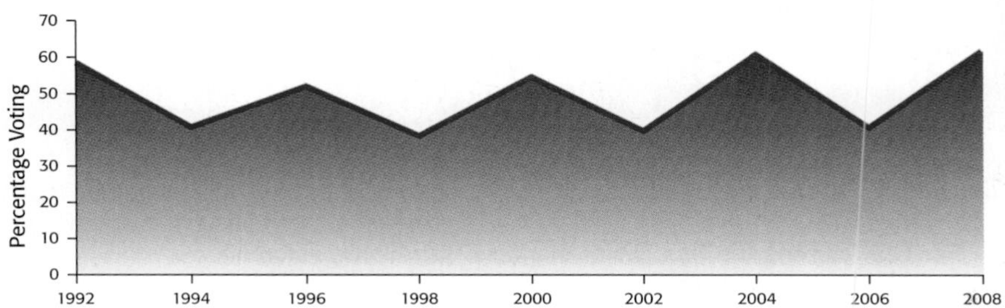

FIGURE 8–6
Voter Turnout in Presidential and Midterm Elections, 1990–2008.

SOURCE: Curtis Gans, Howard W. Stanley and Richard G. Niemi, *Vital Statistics on American Politics, 2007–2008* (CQ Press, 2008), pp. 13–14. See also "Much-hyped Turnout Record Fails to Materialize: Convenience Voting Fails to Boost Balloting," at http://www.american.edu/media/electionexperts/election_turnout_08.pdf, accessed November 12, 2008.

Absentee and Early Voting Today many people choose not to vote in person at their local voting places on election day. Instead they use *absentee voting* to vote early by mail. (Absentee votes must be postmarked no later than election day.) The oldest form of nontraditional voting, absentee voting has been used since the Civil War[46] and has recently become more popular. More than one in five voters in 2004 cast their vote away from a traditional, election-day polling location, the most in the history of the United States.[47]

Another innovation designed to make voting easier is allowing people to vote early but at a polling location. This change was in part the result of concerns about having insufficient voting machines for election day. By 2008, 31 states allowed early voting without needing to claim travel, work, or other reasons to vote early.[48] Partly because of these policy changes, a steadily larger number of people now vote before election day.

Turnout

The United States holds more elections for more offices than any other democracy. That may be why U.S. voters tend to be selective about which elections they vote in. We elect officeholders in **general elections,** determine party nominees in **primary elections,** and replace members of the House of Representatives who have died or left office in *special elections.*

Elections held in years when the president is on the ballot are called **presidential elections;** elections held midway between presidential elections are called **midterm elections,** and elections held in odd-numbered calendar years are called *off-year elections.* Midterm elections (such as the ones in 2002 and 2006) elect one-third of the U.S. Senate; all members of the House of Representatives; and many governors, other statewide officeholders, and state legislators. Many local elections for city council members and mayors are held in the spring of odd-numbered years.

Critical Congressional (Mid-Term) Elections

Turnout—the proportion of the voting-age public that votes—is higher in general elections than in primary elections, and higher in primary elections than in special elections. It is also higher in presidential general elections than in midterm general elections, and higher in presidential primary elections than in midterm primary elections (see Figure 8–6).[49] Presidential elections attract greater interest and awareness. Turnout is also higher in elections in which candidates for federal office are on the ballot (U.S. senator, member of the House of Representatives, president) than in state elections in years when there are no federal contests. Some states—for example, New Jersey, Virginia, and Kentucky—elect their governor and other state officials in odd-numbered years to separate state from national politics. The result is generally lower turnout. Finally, local or municipal elections have lower turnout than state elections, and municipal primaries generally have the lowest rates of participation.

Turnout reached more than 65 percent of those eligible to vote in the presidential election of 1960, but it has since declined to just over 60 percent in 2004, and rose again in 2008.[50] In midterm elections, turnout was 40 percent nationally in 2006, up about 1 percent from 2002 and up more than 2 percent since 1998. More competitive elections generate more interest among the public and more spending by the candidates, which in turn stimulate participation. However, more

general election
Elections in which voters elect officeholders.

primary election
Elections in which voters determine party nominees.

presidential election
Elections held in years when the president is on the ballot.

midterm election
Elections held midway between presidential elections.

turnout
The proportion of the voting-age public that votes, sometimes defined as the number of registered voters that vote.

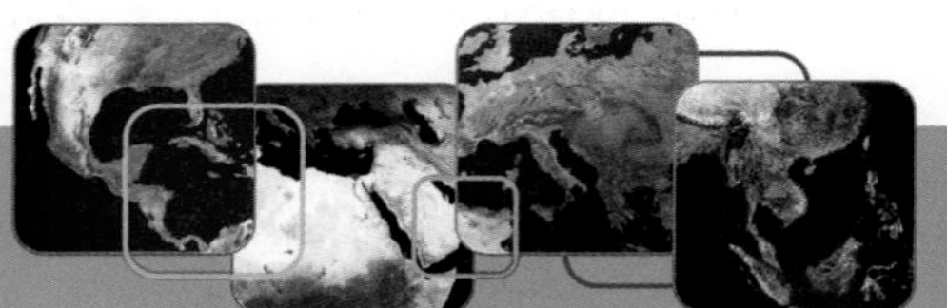

HOW **OTHER NATIONS** GOVERN

Electoral Institutions and Turnout

Studying voter turnout across different countries faces considerable challenges. For example, China technically holds elections every three years at the village level, but there is some doubt about the statistics that come out of Chinese local governments and it is uncertain how free or fair these elections are. India also has reporting problems. India's large rural population poses logistical challenges for the Indian election commission responsible for maintaining voter registration rolls. The accompanying table compares our sample of countries in how they regulate and manage voting.

For U.S. citizens the thought of mandatory voting is foreign. Mexico is not the only country with mandatory voting laws, and as evidenced by the Mexican turnout rates it is unenforced. Election frequency varies. The United States votes more frequently than any of these sample countries, and much more frequently than some like Nigeria, which votes only every four years. Another major difference between the United States and other countries is that the United States is the only country with voluntary voter registration. In all other countries in the sample, voter registration is automatic.

QUESTIONS

1. How do you think U.S. citizens would respond if voting were made mandatory?
2. How does voluntary voter registration impact participation?
3. If U.S. elections were held only every four years as in Nigeria, how do you think that would change participation?

Electoral Institutions and Turnout.

	Eligible Voters	Voter Registration	Mandatory Voting	Election Frequency	Year and Type of Elections	Turnout
Britain	All citizens 18 and over	Automatic	No	At least every 5 years for parliament	2005, General Parliamentary	61.7
China	All villagers 18 and over	Varies across provinces and counties		Every 3 years	Varies	n/a
India	All citizens who are 18 as of the 1st of January of the election year	Automatic	No	At least every 5 years for parliament	2004, Lok Sabah	61.8
Japan	All citizens 20 and over	Automatic	No	At least every 4 years for local elections and the lower house; every 3 years for the upper house	2007, House of Councilors	67.5
Mexico	All citizens 18 and over	Automatic	Yes*	Every 3 years	2006, General Presidential	59
Nigeria	All citizens 18 and over	Automatic	No	Every 4 years	2007, General Presidential	57.5†
United States	All citizens 18 and over	Voluntary	No	Every 2 years	2008, General Presidential	55.3‡

* Unenforced.
† The 2007 Nigerian presidential election was largely thought to be a sham.
‡ As a percentage of the voting-age population.

than 80 million eligible citizens failed to vote in the 2004 presidential election, and even more did not vote in midterm, state, and local elections.[51] Turnout in 2008 was up only slightly over 2004.[52]

Voting Turnout: Who Votes in the United States

Who Votes?

The extent of voting varies widely among different groups. Level of education especially helps predict whether people will vote; as education increases, so does the propensity to vote. "Education increases one's capacity for understanding complex and intangible subjects such as politics," according to one study, "as well as encouraging the ethic of civic responsibility. Moreover, schools provide experience dealing with a variety of bureaucratic problems, such as coping with requirements, filling out forms, and meeting deadlines."[53]

Race and ethnic background are linked with different levels of voting, largely because they correlate with education. In other words, racial and ethnic minorities with college degrees vote at about the same rate as white people with college degrees. As a group, black people vote at lower rates than white people, although this is beginning to change.[54] In 2008, Blacks were 13 percent of the vote, a 2 percent increase over 2004.[55]

In 2004, both parties mounted major efforts to register and mobilize Hispanic voters, as Hispanics have become the largest minority group in the United States. Despite these efforts, the proportion of Hispanics voting in 2004 was no higher than in 1992 and the same as in 2000. As the illegal immigrant issue took center stage in 2006, Democrats, Republicans, and allied groups again sought to expand the number of Hispanic voters. Exit polls found that 9 percent of voters in 2008 were Latinos, with two-thirds of them voting for Obama.[56]

Women, another historically underrepresented group, have voted in greater numbers than men since 1984.[57] That was true again in 2008.[58] Women's higher turnout is generally attributed to increasing levels of education and employment. Interest groups including prominent pro-choice groups have sought to mobilize female supporters of their agenda in recent elections.

Age is also highly correlated with the propensity to vote. As age increases, so does the proportion of persons voting. Older people, unless they are very old and infirm, are more likely to vote than younger people. The greater propensity of older persons to vote will amplify the importance of this group as baby boomers age and retire.

In 2004, parties and groups under took a major initiative to register and encourage young persons to vote. For example, the cable station MTV had a "Rock the Vote" effort. The mobilization effort appeared to work: 4.6 million more young voters between ages 18 and 29 voted in 2004 than in 2000. In absolute numbers this was an impressive gain, but because more people voted in 2004, young voters as a percentage of all voters did not increase. Young voters saw the 2004 election as more consequential than the 2000 election. Studies found that 57 percent of young adults said the election would have a "great deal" or "quite a bit" of impact on the country's future. Only 33 percent of young adults responded this way during the 2000 election.[59]

Young voters volunteered in large numbers for candidates in 2008, especially for the Obama campaign. Based on exit polls their share of the vote also rose slightly. In 2004, 17 percent of all voters were 18-29 years of age. In 2008 they were 18 prcent of all voters.[60]

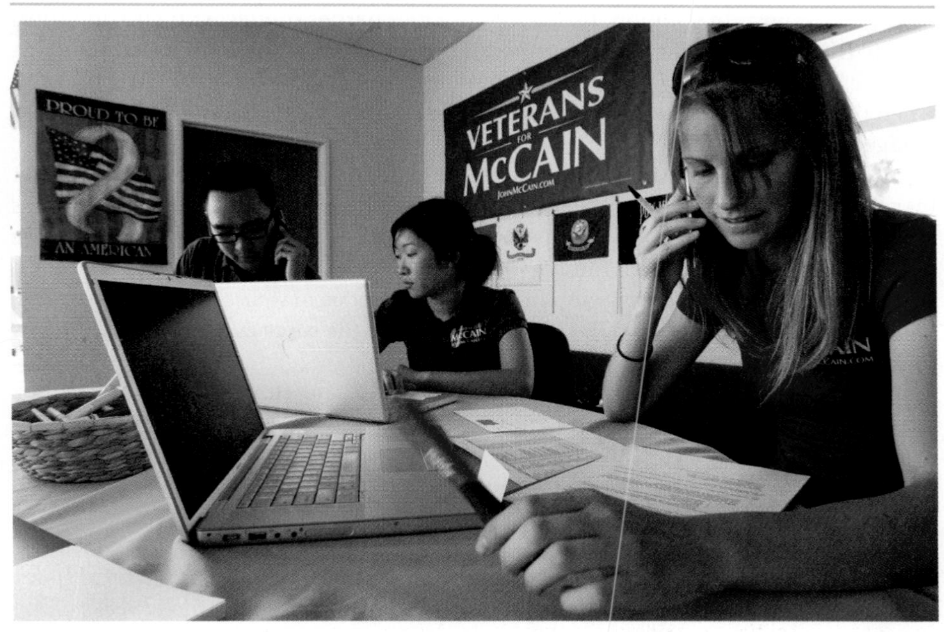

Volunteers for the John McCain campaign call likely supporters, reminding them to vote. Many groups conduct get-out-the-vote operations in hopes of turning out people likely to vote for their favored candidate.

Young people have become increasingly engaged in political campaigns over the last decade. Ron Paul's supporters in the Republican primary were especially enthusiastic.

Mobilization

You Are a Campaign Manager: Voter Mobilization and Supression—Political Dirty Tricks or Fair Games?

In a nation as evenly divided politically as the United States is now, candidates must also mobilize their most loyal supporters, or their "base." To do this, they reaffirm their support for issues or groups that matter to the base. In 2008 John McCain did this by calling for domestic offshore drilling, supporting continuing the Bush tax cuts, and by selecting Sarah Palin as his running mate. On the Democratic side, Barack Obama argued for greater investment in wind and solar energy and held to his position on a set timetable to end the war in Iraq.

In the 2008 "battleground" states where the vote seemed highly competitive, postcards urging residents to vote and phone calls reminding them it was election day bombarded voters who were already likely to vote and had already decided which candidate to support. In addition, the candidates and parties mobilized their supporters to vote early in states where that was possible. This effort, sometimes called "banking the vote," reduced the list of people the campaigns needed to mobilize on election day, when poll watchers would track those who had not yet voted and urge those who had pledged support to vote.

Campaigners learn which issues matter to potential voters and which candidates these voters prefer by conducting interviews on the telephone or in person, a process called a *canvass.* Individuals who are undecided and probable voters in competitive races are likely to receive communications designed to persuade them to vote for a particular candidate. Interest groups and political parties may also conduct a canvass, followed by mail and phone calls that often reinforce the same themes the candidates themselves express.

Undecided or "swing voters" are a major focus of mobilization efforts, and they received a lot of attention in competitive states in recent elections. Both sides intensely courted these voters through numerous person-to-person contacts, mailings, telephone calls, and efforts to register new voters. Candidates, groups, and parties are all part of this "ground war."

You Are a Campaign Manager: McCain and the Swingers—Help McCain Win Swing States and Swing Voters

The volume of communication in competitive contests and battleground states in recent elections has been extraordinary. In 2004, voters in competitive presidential states received on average more than ten different pieces of mail in the last three weeks of the

THE CHANGING FACE OF U.S. POLITICS

Voter Turnout by Demographic Factors

Over the course of U.S. history, the right to vote has been extended and protected for women and racial minorities. Groups that did not have the franchise, or that had been effectively barred or discouraged from using it, have become as active in their rates of voting as white men.

In the following data, note that women have voted in higher percentages than men in each election since 1992. It took decades for women to reach this milestone and dismiss the old adage that "politics is men's business." The rate of voting among black persons was about ten percentage points below white persons in 1992 and 1994 but more recently has lagged by only about four percentage points. Hispanics are not yet participating at rates similar to those of women and black persons. History suggests that over time this will change.

Percentage of People in Different Groups Who Voted.

	1992	1994	1996	1998	2000	2002	2004	2006
Sex								
Men	60%	44%	53%	41%	53%	41%	56%	42%
Women	62	45	56	42	56	43	60	45
Race								
White	64	47	56	43	56	44	60	46
Black	54	37	51	40	54	40	56	39
Hispanic	29	19	27	20	28	19	28	19

SOURCE: U.S. Census Bureau, *Statistical Abstract of the United States, 2008* (U.S. Government Printing Office, 2008), p. 256.

election about the presidential race, compared to only two pieces in noncompetitive states. One voter in Florida received 44 pieces of mail about the presidential race in the last three weeks. In the same year, voters in competitive U.S. Senate races received more than three pieces of mail in the last three weeks compared to an average of less than one piece in noncompetitive states. One voter in South Dakota, a very competitive Senate race in 2004, received 55 pieces of mail about the race in the last three weeks.[61]

How Serious Is Nonvoting?

Although voters can hardly avoid reading or hearing about political campaigns, especially during an election as intensely fought as recent presidential elections, about 40 percent of all eligible citizens fail to vote. This amounts to about 80 million people.[62] Who are they? Why don't they vote? Is the fact that so many people choose not to vote a cause for alarm? If so, what can we do about it?

There is considerable disagreement about how to interpret low voter turnout. The simplest explanation is that people are lazy and voting takes effort, but there is more to it than that. Of course, some people are apathetic, but most are not. Paradoxically, we compare favorably with other nations in political interest and awareness, but for a variety of institutional and political reasons, we fail to convert this interest in politics into voting (see Table 8–5).

In the United States, voting is more difficult and takes more time and effort than in other democracies. In our system, as we have seen, people must first register to vote and then decide how to vote, not only for many different offices but also often for referendums on public policy or constitutional amendments. The United States also holds elections on weekdays, when people are at work, rather than on holidays or weekends as other countries often do. Another factor in the percentage decline of voter turnout since the 1960s is, paradoxically, the Twenty-Sixth Amendment, which increased the number of eligible voters by lowering the voting age to 18. But young people are the least likely to vote. After the amendment was ratified in 1971, turnout in the presidential election fell from 62 percent in 1968 to 57 percent in 1972.[63]

This poster, published by the League of Women Voters, urged women to use the vote the Nineteenth Amendment had given them.

TABLE 8–5 Why People Don't Vote

Reason	Percent
Too busy, conflicting schedule	19.9%
Illness or disability	15.4
Other reason	10.9
Not interested	10.7
Did not like candidates or campaign issues	9.9
Out of town	9.0
Don't know or refused	8.5
Registration problems	6.8
Forgot to vote	3.4
Inconvenient polling place	3.0
Transportation problems	2.1
Bad weather conditions	0.5

SOURCE: U.S. Bureau of the Census, "Reasons for Not Voting, by Sex, Age, Race and Hispanic Origin, and Educational Attainment: November 2004," www.census.gov/population/www/socdemo/voting/cps2004.html.

Some political scientists argue that nonvoting does not change the outcome, as nonvoters closely resemble voters in policy views.[64] "Nonvoting is not a social disease," wrote Austin Ranney, a noted political scientist. He pointed out that legal and extralegal denial of the vote to African Americans, women, Hispanics, persons over age 18, and other groups has been outlawed, so nonvoting is voluntary. The late Senator Sam Ervin of North Carolina provided a rationale for registration when he said "I don't believe in making it easy for apathetic, lazy people to vote."[65] Some may even contend that nonvoting is a sign of voter satisfaction.

Those who argue that nonvoting *is* a serious problem cite the "class bias" of those who do vote. The social makeup and attitudes of nonvoters differ significantly from those of voters and hence distort the representative system. "The very poor...have about two-thirds the representation among voters than their numbers would suggest." Thus the people who need the most help from the government lack their share of electoral power to obtain it.[66] Some may contend that younger voters, the poor, and minority citizens do not vote because politicians pay less attention to them. But politicians understandably cater to people who vote more than to people who don't.

Declining participation in voting and other political acts has puzzled some political scientists because voting rates have continued to drop even as the overall level of education, a strong predictor of voting, has increased. Part of the reason may be that political parties and other groups have done less voter mobilization over time. In other words, some people don't vote because no one asks them to. Furthermore, advances in technology allow parties and campaigns to target their appeals narrowly to people who are already likely to turn out.[67]

Low levels of voting, according to those who see a class bias in voting, reflect "the underdevelopment of political attitudes resulting from the historic exclusion of low-income groups from active electoral participation."[68] In short, part of the problem of nonvoting among low-income, less-educated people is their failure to be aware of their own interests. Dynamic leadership or strong party organization, or both, would not only attract the poor to the polls but also make clear their "class grievances and aspirations."[69] Others reject the class bias argument. They admit that nonvoters are demographically different but cite polls showing that nonvoters' attitudes are not much different from those of voters. One study, comparing the party identification of voters with that of all citizens, found that the proportion of Democrats was nearly identical (51.4 percent of all citizens and 51.3 percent of voters), while Republicans as voters were slightly overrepresented (36 percent of citizens and 39.7 percent of voters). All other political differences were much smaller than this 3.7 percent gap in terms of party identification. Further, voters are not "disproportionately hostile" to social welfare policies compared to citizens generally.[70]

How might increased voter turnout affect national elections? It might make a difference, because there are partisan differences between different demographic groups and poorer persons are more likely to be Democrats. Candidates would have to adjust to the demands of this expanded electorate. A noted political scientist, while acknowledging that no political system could achieve 100 percent participation, pointed out that if the large nonvoter population decided to vote, it could overturn the balance of power in the political system.[71] However, others contend that the difference may not be that pronounced, because on many issues nonvoters have much the same attitudes as voters. For example, nonvoters do not favor government ownership or regulation of industry more than voters do. Nor are nonvoters more egalitarian. They are, however, more inclined to favor additional spending on welfare programs.[72]

Finally, for better or worse, low voter turnout may indicate approval of the status quo, whereas high voter turnout may signify disapproval and widespread desire for change.

Voting Choices

LEARNING **OBJECTIVE**

6 Explain why people vote the way they do in elections.

Why do people vote the way they do? Political scientists have identified three main elements of the voting choice: party identification, candidate appeal, and issues. These elements often overlap.

Voting on the Basis of Party

Party identification is our sense of identification or affiliation with a political party (see Chapter 7). It often predicts a person's stand on issues. It is part of our national mythology that we vote for the person and not the party. But in fact we vote most often for a person *from the party we prefer.*

The number of self-declared Independents since the mid-1970s has increased dramatically, and today Independents outnumber Republicans. But two-thirds of all Independents are, in fact, partisans in their voting behavior. There are three distinct types of Independents: Independent-leaning Democrats, Independent-leaning Republicans, and Pure Independents. Independent-leaning Democrats are predictably Democratic in their voting behavior, and Independent-leaning Republicans vote heavily Republican. Independent "leaners" are thus different from each other and from Pure Independents. Pure Independents have the lowest rate of turnout, but most of them generally side with the winner in presidential elections. Independent leaners vote at about the same rate as partisans and more than Pure Independents. Independent leaners vote for the party toward which they lean at about the same rate, or even more so, than weak partisans do. This data on Independents only reinforces the importance of partisanship in explaining voting choice. When we consider Independent-leaning Democrats and Independent-leaning Republicans as Democrats and Republicans respectively, only 10 percent of the population were Pure Independents in 2004.[73] In early 2008 that number was even smaller.[74] This proportion is consistent with earlier election years. In short, there are few genuinely independent voters.

Although party identification has fluctuated in the past 40 years, it remains more stable than attitudes about issues or political ideology. Fluctuations in party identification appear to come in response to economic conditions and political performance, especially of the president. The more information voters have about their choices, the more likely they are to defect from their party and vote for a candidate from the other party.

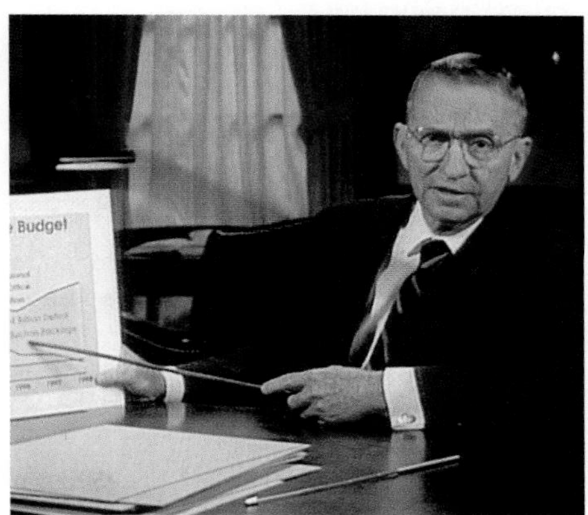

Because they do not have the benefits of a well-known party, third-party candidates must rely on their personal appeal to voters. Independent Ross Perot's fiery style and sense of humor helped him garner 19.8 percent of the vote in 1992, the best showing for a third-party presidential candidate since 1912.

Voting on the Basis of Candidates

Although long-term party identification is important, it is clearly not the only factor in voting choices. Otherwise, the Democrats would have won every presidential election since the last major realignment in partisanship, which occurred during the Great Depression in the election of Franklin Roosevelt in 1932. In fact, since 1952, there have been five Democratic presidents elected and the same number of Republicans.[75] The reason is largely found in a second major explanation of voting choice—**candidate appeal.**

Candidate-centered politics means that rather than rely on parties or groups to build a coalition of supporters for a candidate, the candidates make their case directly to the voters. In many races, the parties and groups also make the candidate the major focus of attention, minimizing partisanship or group identification.[76] The fact that we vote for officials separately—president/vice president, senator, governor, state attorney general, and so on—means voters are asked repeatedly to choose from among competing candidates. Although the party of the candidates is an important clue to voters, in most contested races voters also look to candidate-specific information.

Candidate appeal often includes an assessment of a candidate's character. Is the candidate honest? Consistent? Dedicated to "family values"? Does the candidate have religious or spiritual commitments? In recent elections the press has sometimes played the role of "character cop," asking questions about candidates' private lives and lifestyles. The press asks these questions because voters are interested in a political leader's background—perhaps even more interested in personal character than in a candidate's political position on hard-to-understand health care or regulatory policy issues.

party identification
An informal and subjective affiliation with a political party that most people acquire in childhood.

candidate appeal
How voters feel about a candidate's background, personality, leadership ability, and other personal qualities.

GENERATION **NEXT**

Why Vote?

One reason frequently given for why people vote or not is whether they feel they have a say in what the government does, or more broadly can have an effect in what happens in their lives. This concept is called efficacy. The combined 1987–2007 Political Landscape Survey allows us to look at rates of voting for different age groups and also examine different levels of efficacy by these same age groups.

The data from the Political Landscape Survey shows the relationship between age and turnout. Eighteen- to 24-year-olds were 6 percent less likely to report always voting than persons 25–34 and less than half as likely to always vote as persons over age 34.

Are the 18– to 24-year-olds less confident in dealing with government? The answer is no. In contrast to the wide variance in reported rates of voting, 18- to 24-year-olds are about in the middle of the age groups in confidence in dealing with government. Thus the low rates of turnout among Generation Next are not explained by efficacy.

QUESTIONS

1. Why do you think 18- to 24-year-olds vote less frequently than all others?
2. Why do you think there are no significant differences between Generation Next and older generations in their confidence in dealing with government?
3. Why do older people vote more often?

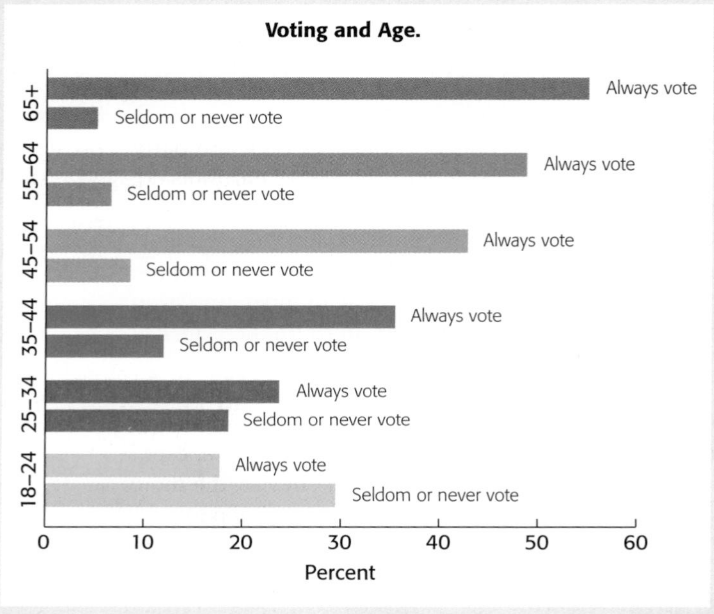

Candidate appeal, or the lack of it—in terms of leadership, experience, good judgment, integrity, competence, strength, and energy—is sometimes more important than party or issues. Many voters saw Bill Clinton in 1992 and 1996 as a regular working-class person who had risen against the odds. Dwight Eisenhower, who was elected president in 1952 and reelected in 1956, had great candidate appeal. He was a five-star general, a legendary hero of the Allied effort in World War II. His unmilitary manner, his moderation, his personal charm, and his appearance of seeming to rise above partisanship appealed across the ideological spectrum. In the 2004 presidential primaries, Howard Dean was initially perceived in positive terms, but that changed with his speech following the Iowa caucus. “The Scream,” as the media labeled it, called into question his self-control.[77] In 2008, Republicans attempted to define Barack Obama as arrogant, aloof, and a celebrity. Democrats, while praising Mc Cain as a war hero, tried to define him as out of touch and “more of the same [Bush].” John McCain, his running mate Sarah Palin, the Republican party, and outside groups all repeatedly called attention to Barack Obama's associations with William Ayres, now a college professor in Chicago. During the 1960s and 1970s, Ayers, helped lead a radical group that bombed public buildings as a form of protest. Obama was also criticized for not objecting more strongly to the rhetoric of his former pastor, Reverend Jeremiah Wright. Obama denounced Wright's rhetoric and said his association with Ayres had been limited and came years after his radical activities. Neither association seemed to hold much sway with voters.

Increasingly, campaigns today focus on the negative elements of candidates' history and personality. Opponents and the media are quick to point out a candidate's limitations or problems. George W. Bush's record in the National Guard during the Vietnam War became the subject of a CBS *60 Minutes* segment, only to have CBS admit that it could not authenticate the documents it used in this critical story. A group called Swift Boat Veterans for Truth also attacked John Kerry for his war record in Vietnam. (See Chapter 6.) This attack put the Kerry campaign on the defensive for days.[78] While the tone of the 2008 presidential campaign was often negative, the attacks came largely from the candidates and their political parties and not from otside groups.

Voting on the Basis of Issues

prospective issue voting
Voting based on what a candidate pledges to do in the future about an issue if elected.

retrospective issue voting
Holding incumbents, usually the president's party, responsible for their records on issues, such as the economy or foreign policy.

Most political scientists agree that issues, though important, have less influence on how people vote than party identification and candidate appeal do.[79] This occurs partly because candidates often intentionally obscure their positions on issues—an understandable strategy.[80] When he was running for president in 1968, Richard Nixon said he had a plan to end the Vietnam War, which was clearly the most important issue that year, but he would not reveal the specifics. By not detailing his plan, he stood to gain votes both from those who wanted a more aggressive war effort and those who wanted a cease-fire.

For issue voting to become important, a substantial number of voters must find the issue itself important, opposing candidates must take opposite stands on the issues, and voters must know these positions and vote accordingly. Rarely do candidates focus on only one issue. Voters often agree with one candidate on one issue and with the opposing candidate on another. In such cases, issues will probably not determine how people vote. But voters' lack of interest in issues does not mean candidates can take any position they please.[81]

Political parties and candidates often look for issues that motivate particular segments of the electorate to vote, and on which the opposing candidate or party has a less popular position. These issues are sometimes called *wedge issues.* In recent elections wedge issues have been gay marriage, the minimum wage, and abortion. One way to exploit a wedge issue is to place on the ballot an initiative to decide a proposed law or amendment on the issue. Both parties and allied groups are expanding their use of ballot initiatives in this way.

More likely than **prospective issue voting,** or voting based on what a candidate pledges to do about an issue if elected, is **retrospective issue voting,** or holding incumbents, usually the president's party, responsible for past performance on issues, such as the economy or foreign policy.[82] In times of peace and prosperity, voters will reward the incumbent. If the nation falls short on either, voters are more likely to elect the opposition.

But good economic times do not always guarantee that an incumbent party will be reelected, as Vice President Al Gore learned in 2000 when he was the Democratic candidate for president. Part of Gore's problem in that election was that only half the public felt that their family's financial situation improved during the Clinton administration. Sixty-one percent of these voters voted for Gore.[83] But his inability to effectively claim credit for the good economic times hurt him, especially when Republicans contended that the American people, not the government under President Bill Clinton, had produced the strong economy. A similar debate arose in 2004 over the state of the economy and the extent to which President

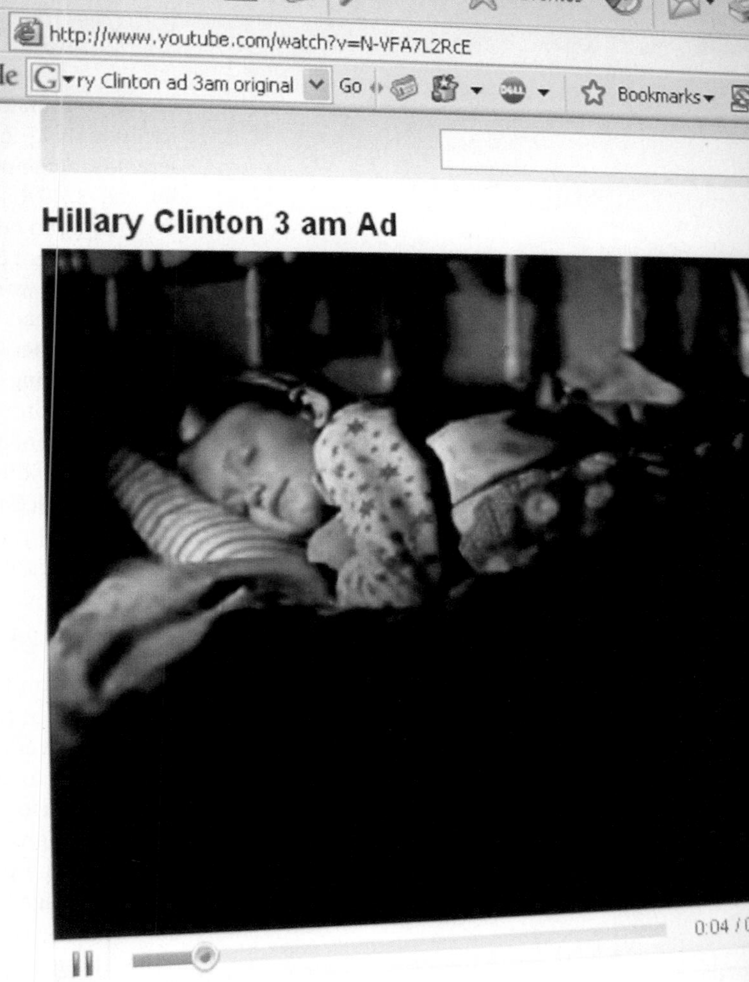

This advertisement from the Hillary Clinton campaign used a hypothetical national-emergency phone call at 3 a.m. to highlight her relative wealth of experience when compared to Barack Obama.

YOU WILL **DECIDE** Should We Allow Voting by Mail and on the Internet?

During the past two centuries of constitutional government, this nation has gradually adopted a more expansive view of popular participation. Not only has the right to vote been extended to more people, but the decisions made in the voting booth have been expanded as well to include primary elections to nominate party candidates and ballot referendums in which state constitutional amendments and state laws are adopted.

It seems logical that the next step in our democratic progress is permitting voters to cast ballots through the mail or via the Internet. Not only would such a reform make voting easier, but it would permit us to have more elections. For example, when a city council wants voters to decide whether to build a new football stadium or when there is need for a special election to fill the term of a member of Congress who has died or resigned, election officials could mail out the ballots and then in two or three weeks count up those that have been returned. The state of Oregon has already conducted several general elections by mail, and other states have considered adopting the Oregon system.

What do you think? Should we move toward replacing the ballot box with the mailbox or the computer? What arguments would you make for and against such an idea?

George W. Bush's policies or the terrorist attacks of September 11, 2001, had resulted in lost jobs and other economic problems. Democrats argued that the tax cuts Bush sponsored were irresponsible, especially when the country was at war. The Republicans countered that the tax cuts helped stimulate the economy.

The state of the economy is often the central issue in both midterm and presidential elections. Studies have found that the better the economy seems to be doing, the more congressional seats the "in" party retains or gains. The reverse is also true. The worse the economy seems to be doing, the more seats the "out" party gains.[84] Political scientists have been able to locate the sources of this effect in the way individual voters decide to vote. Voters tend to vote against the party in power if they perceive that their personal financial situations have declined or stagnated.[85]

The most important issue in the 2008 elections was the economy. Three-fifths of voters reported that issues were more important to their vote than candidate personal qualities. According to nearly two-thirds of voters, the economy was the most important issue. As the campaign unfolded, the economy became more and more important with the collapse of investment banks, a dramatic drop in the value of stocks, and restricted availability of money for banks to make loan to individuals and businesses. The two candidates demonstrated different leadership styles in their approach to the crisis even though both ended up voting for the $700 billion bailout package originally proposed by Bush and his Treasury Secretary, and later modified by Congress. Of voters who thought the economy was the most important issue, 53 percent voted for Obama, and for voters whose family economic situation was worse than it had been previously, Obama received 71 percent of their vote.

The Primacy of the economy as the central issue in the 2008 election also lessened the impact of other issues like McCain's age and Obama's race. Obama's ability to win the votes of working class white voters had been in doubt after his primary election battle with Hillary Clinton who had won many of those votes in states like Pennsylvania. But in Pennsylvania nearly 90 percent said they were worried about the country's economic conditions and of this group 58 percent voted for Obama. The remaining ten percent voted 60 percent for McCain. Unions, an important reference group for these working class voters, were important to persuading these voters to vote for Obama. More than three-fifths of Pennsylvania voters form households with a union member voted for Obama.[86]

The Impact of Campaigns

Candidates and campaigns are important to the voting choice. Given the frequency of elections in the United States and the number of offices people vote for, it is not surprising that voters look for simplifying devices such as partisanship to help them decide how to vote. Effective campaigns give them reasons to vote for their candidate and reasons to vote against the opposition.

Campaigns are a team sport, with the political parties and interest groups also important to the process of persuading and motivating voters. Groups and parties are heavily engaged in all aspects of campaigns, and their efforts are often indistinguishable from the candidates' campaigns.

Although adequate money is needed to run a competitive campaign, spending more money does not guarantee that a candidate will win. Effective campaigners find ways to communicate with voters that are memorable and persuasive.

Campaigns are not for the faint of heart. Electoral politics is intensely competitive, and campaigns are often negative and personal. Campaigns give voters a sense of how politicians react to adversity, because most competitive races involve adversity. Skills learned in the campaign environment, in some respects at least, carry over into the skill set needed to govern.

Counting Votes

Until the 2000 election, most people took the counting of ballots for granted. But with the closeness of that election and the controversy surrounding how the election was administered in Florida, the public became aware that counting votes is not a simple matter.

Votes are counted in the United States according to state law as administered by local officials. The technology used in voting varies greatly from state to state and in different parts of the same state. In Florida in 2000, some counties used paper ballots, others voting machines, and others punch-card ballots, and at least one county used ballots that a computer could scan. More recently, states have moved from touchscreen computerized voting systems to paper ballots that can be optically scanned.

The recent changes in how we vote are part of a broader effort to modernize democracy. State legislatures and Congress will eventually debate permitting voting via the Internet. If people can make purchases online, why not let them vote electronically as well? Some states experimented with "e-voting" on a small scale in presidential primaries in 2000, and some counties in California have also tried it. A shift to e-voting is in some respects an extension of the Oregon system of vote-by-mail adopted statewide in 1996. Oregon now conducts elections by mailed ballots, a process that reduces costs and has increased participation. Yet critics worry that important elements of community and democracy are lost when people do not vote collectively at the local schoolhouse or fire station. Another concern is that mail or electronic voting may encourage more elections and referendums. If we can vote from home, why not vote on more things more often?

Another lesson the recent ballot-counting controversies have reinforced is that in every election, in every jurisdiction, and with every technology, voting is imperfect. Touchscreen software can be manipulated; people can miscount paper ballots; punch cards may not always be completely perforated, and so on. The goal in election administration is to minimize errors and eliminate as much bias and outright fraud as possible.

But counting votes is more complicated than the means by which we vote. Election officials have to make judgment calls about incomplete or flawed ballots. Decisions about which ballots to count and which ones not to count matter in an election decided by only 537 votes, as Florida's presidential election was in 2000. With the growth in absentee voting, and with military personnel and civilians living abroad voting by mail, a close election may not be decided until days after the polls officially close.

The process of voting in person is administered by people from the neighborhood who serve as poll workers and arrive at the polls hours before voting starts to set up equipment and ensure that the voter lists, ballots, and physical facilities are in order. Recent research has found that poll workers can greatly influence the security, efficiency, and overall environment of polling locations. Those who receive high-quality training and are confident in both their expertise and the accuracy of the polling location create an overall environment that makes voters feel more confident.[87]

Who is and who is not allowed to vote on election day is also a source of controversy. As discussed, in most states persons must be registered voters in order to vote.

THINKING IT THROUGH

One of the problems with making elections more frequent is that voters will tire. Americans already vote more frequently and for more offices than citizens of any other democracy. Asking them to make voting choices even more frequently could result in lower turnout and less rational consideration. Many voters may be unaware that an election is going on. Yet the advantage of the vote-by-mail system employed by Oregon and some cities and counties is that it increases turnout, at least initially. What political scientists dispute is whether such increases in participation will continue when the novelty wears off.

Some critics of voting by mail or electronic democracy worry about fraud. Even when voters are required to sign their mailed-in ballots, the possibility of forgery still exists. Also, voting by mail or computer has the possibility of allowing people to pressure or harass voters. Another concern is late returns. Concerns about electronic voting have been reinforced by claims that the computer software is not secure and that some electronic voting fails to count all the votes.*

Another criticism is that mail and electronic voting could be skewed toward participation by better-educated and higher-income voters, who routinely pay their bills by mail, make purchases on their computer, and own a personal computer with Internet access. Advocates of these new voting procedures contend that voters who do not own computers can drop off their ballots in some public building and that eventually computers will be available widely enough that access will not be a problem.†

However, if voting can be made easier and more convenient, why not do it? If the integrity of the vote can be protected and the new ways of voting become widely accessible, such changes are probably inevitable.

*E. J. Dionne, Jr., "Election Dangers to be Avoided," *Washington Post*, May 25, 2004.
†Adam J. Berinsky, Nancy Burns, and Michael W. Traugott, "Who Votes By Mail? A Dynamic Model of the Individual-Level Consequences of Voting-by-Mail Systems," *Public Opinion Quarterly* 65 (Summer 2001), pp. 178–197.

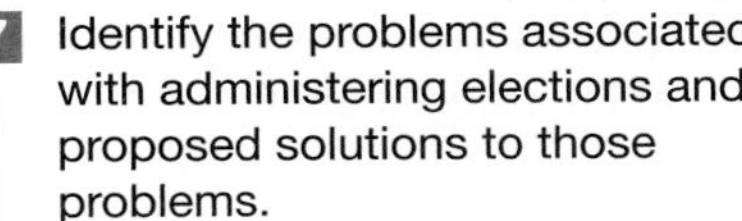

LEARNING **OBJECTIVE**

7 Identify the problems associated with administering elections and proposed solutions to those problems.

Voters are expected to vote in designated voting places. In 2004, as a result of the 2002 redistricting, some voting places and precincts in parts of the country had changed, which confused some voters who voted only in presidential elections and had not voted since 2000. The law permits voters who think they should be allowed to vote but who are not on the rolls to cast what are called provisional ballots. These ballots are counted only if the voter is, in fact, registered to vote.

In the wake of the 2000 and 2004 elections, federal and state governments have invested billions of dollars in new voting technology, established new rules on provisional ballots, and modernized voting methods. Interest groups, political parties, and candidates have made the integrity of the voting process a high priority. In 2004 and 2008 thousands of people worked as poll watchers. Groups established toll-free hotlines for voters to call if they felt they were not being treated fairly, and in key jurisdictions, lawyers were on call to file immediate challenges when a person's right to vote was contested.

Who votes and how have changed dramatically over the course of U.S. history. Our process has become more democratic, and citizens today have a wider array of candidates and ballot referendums than ever before. Although progress has been made in making the process of voting more problem free, important challenges remain. It is important to the confidence of the polity that every vote be counted and counted accurately. That goal has not yet been achieved.

Government by the people is most frequently exercised by voting. This is why when younger persons do not vote, they leave to others decisions about important parts of their lives. Government, directly or indirectly, has a direct bearing on educational opportunity, taxes, and the environment, to name only a few examples. Elected officials are most attuned to the will of those who vote, and so when young persons fail to vote, they lessen their impact and enlarge the voice of those who do register and vote.

CHAPTER **SUMMARY**

1 Identify the key dimensions of public opinion and how we measure it.

Public opinion is the distribution across the population of a complex combination of views and attitudes that individuals hold, and we measure it through careful, unbiased, random-selection surveys. Public opinion takes on qualities of intensity, latency, consensus, and polarization—each of which is affected by people's feelings about the salience of issues.

2 Describe the forces that create and shape individuals' political attitudes.

People's political attitudes form early in life, mainly through the influence of family. Schools, the media, social groups, and changing personal and national circumstances can cause attitudes to change, though most of our political opinions remain constant throughout life. Most people do not follow politics and government closely and have little knowledge of political issues.

3 Analyze the relationship between public opinion and public policy.

Sometimes politicians follow prevailing public opinion on policy questions; in other cases they attempt to lead public opinion toward a different policy option. Citizens who wish to affect opinion, policy, or both, can take action by voting, joining interest groups and political parties, working on campaigns, writing letters to newspaper editors or elected officials, blogging, donating money to political causes, or even protesting. Major events, such as economic crises and wars affect both public opinion and government policy.

4 Assess non–voting participation and how it may change in the age of the Internet.

One of the hallmarks of democracy is that citizens can participate in politics in a variety of ways. Citizens who are dissatisfied with government can protest. Protests vary greatly in size, intensity, and rate of success. Individual citizens participate by writing letters to elected officials, calling radio talk shows, serving as jurors, voting, or donating time and money to political campaigns. The Internet has allowed individuals to volunteer for campaigns in a wider variety of ways, to donate money more easily, and to produce content that can be uploaded onto the Internet and viewed by any interested people. Although exactly how the Internet will be adapted for future political participation isn't clear, it will certainly continue to expand its role in the U.S. political process.

5 Describe the demographic, legal, and electioneering factors that affect voter turnout.

Better-educated, more affluent, and older people and those who are involved with parties and interest groups tend to vote more. The young vote the least. Voter turnout is usually higher in national elections than in state and local elections, higher in presidential elections than in midterm elections, and higher in general elections than in primary elections. Close elections generate interest and efforts to mobilize voters and thus have higher turnout than uncompetitive elections.

6 Explain why people vote the way they do in elections.

Party identification remains the most important element in determining how most people vote. It represents a long-term attachment and is a "lens" through which voters view candidates and issues as they make their voting choices. Candidate appeal, including character and record, is another key factor in voter choice. Less frequently, voters decide on the basis of issues.

7 Identify the problems associated with administering elections and proposed solutions to those problems.

Ballot-counting irregularities, equipment shortages and problems, and voter registration challenges have been problems with recent elections. After the voting controversy in Florida in 2000, Congress passed the Help America Vote Act (HAVA). Standardizing election administration, replacing old voting machines with computers, Internet and mail-only elections, and reforming registration procedures are all potential solutions to election problems.

Chapter Self-Test

1. Which of the following was a major flaw in the 1936 *Literary Digest* poll? (pp. 208–209)
   a. Biased questions
   b. A flawed sample
   c. Incorrectly counted results
   d. Poorly trained interviewers
2. What word describes opinions people may hold but have not fully expressed (p. 210)
   a. Interest
   b. Salience
   c. Latency
   d. Intensity
3. In a short essay, identify and describe two major groups that influence the formation of individuals' political opinions and values. Which has had a greater influence in your life? (pp. 212–214)
4. Which of the following statements is true? (p. 214)
   a. Most people never change their political opinions.
   b. Most people change their political opinions quite often.
   c. Many people change their political opinions only when they meet new people.
   d. Many people change their political opinions after major experiences such as a war.
5. In a short essay, explain why many politicians pay attention to public opinion and the public policy implications of their interest. (pp. 214–216)
6. In a short essay, explain what the "attentive public" is. How are they different from part-time citizens and political know-nothings? Which group has greater influence on public policy? (pp. 216–218)
7. According to the U.S. Census Bureau, which of the following was the second most common non-voting form of political participation in 2006? (p. 219)
   a. Visiting candidate websites
   b. Getting campaign news online
   c. Giving money to help a campaign
   d. Trying to influence the votes of others
8. Which of the following is *not* a way individuals have used the internet to participate in recent campaigns? (p. 220)
   a. Use candidate websites to participate in local caucuses
   b. Create campaign-centered music videos to upload to YouTube
   c. Call other individuals using calling lists provided on a candidate's website
   d. Invite other individuals to donate to campaigns through Facebook and MySpace
9. Which of the following was a major goal of the Voting Rights Act of 1965? (p. 221)
   a. Increase turnout of Native Americans
   b. Ease registration requirements for the poor
   c. Ensure widespread use of the Australian ballot
   d. Eliminate literacy tests as a requirement for voting
10. In a short essay, analyze the impact voter registration laws have on turnout. Consider state specific laws, Motor Voter, and automatic registration. What changes, if any, do you think should be made to increase registration? (pp. 220–224)
11. In a short essay, identify whether more women or more men have voted in recent elections.

Has this always been the case? Why is it this way now? (p. 225)

12. In a short essay, explain which is more common, prospective issue voting or retrospective issue voting, and why. (p. 231)
13. Think of the three main elements of vote choice—party identification, candidate appeal, and issues. In a short essay, evaluate which best explains the results of the 2008 presidential election. (pp. 229–232)
14. In a short essay, describe HAVA and how it has changed the way elections are run in the United States. (pp. 207–208, 233–234)
15. In a short essay, describe how Oregon has changed the way it administers elections since 1996. What two concerns have been raised about voting in this method? (pp. 232–234)

Key Terms

public opinion, p. 208

random sample, p. 208

manifest opinion, p. 210

political socialization, p. 212

selective exposure, p. 214

attentive public, p. 217

voter registration, p. 221

general election, p. 223

primary election, p. 223

presidential election, p. 223

midterm election, p. 223

turnout, p. 223

party identification, p. 229

candidate appeal, p. 229

prospective issue voting, p. 231

retrospective issue voting, p. 231

Further Reading

R. MICHAEL ALVAREZ AND **JOHN BREHM,** *Hard Choices, Easy Answers: Values, Information, and American Public Opinion* (Princeton University Press, 2002).

R. MICHAEL ALVAREZ AND **THAD E. HALL,** *Electronic Elections: The Perils and Promises of Digital Democracy* (Princeton University Press, 2008).

HERBERT ASHER, *Polling and the Public: What Every Citizen Should Know,* 7th ed. (CQ Press, 2007).

BARBARA A. BARDES AND **ROBERT W. OLDENDICK,** *Public Opinion: Measuring the American Mind* (Wadsworth, 2006).

M. MARGARET CONWAY, *Political Participation in the United States,* 4th ed. (CQ Press, 2000).

ROBERT M. EISINGER, *The Evolution of Presidential Polling* (Cambridge University Press, 2002).

ROBERT S. ERIKSON AND **KENT L. TEDIN,** *American Public Opinion: Its Origins, Content and Impact,* updated 7th ed. (Longman, 2006).

WILLIAM H. FLANIGAN AND **NANCY H. ZINGALE,** *Political Behavior of the American Electorate,* updated 11th ed. (CQ Press, 2007).

DONALD P. GREEN AND **ALAN S. GERBER,** *Get Out the Vote!: How to Increase Voter Turnout,* 2d ed. (Brookings Institution Press, 2008).

ROBERT HUCKFELDT AND **JOHN SPRAGUE,** *Citizens, Politics, and Social Communication: Information and Influence in an Election Campaign* (Cambridge University Press, 1995).

LAWRENCE R. JACOBS AND **ROBERT Y. SHAPIRO,** *Politicians Don't Pander: Political Manipulation and the Loss of Democratic Responsiveness* (University of Chicago Press, 2000).

BRUCE E. KEITH, DAVID B. MAGLEBY, CANDICE J. NELSON, ELIZABETH ORR, MARK C. WESTLYE, AND **RAYMOND E. WOLFINGER,** *The Myth of the Independent Voter* (University of California Press, 1992).

V. O. KEY, JR., *Public Opinion and American Democracy* (Knopf, 1961).

JAN E. LEIGHLEY, *Strength in Numbers? The Political Mobilization of Racial and Ethnic Minorities* (Princeton University Press, 2001).

MICHAEL B. MACKUEN AND **GEORGE RABINOWITZ,** EDS., *Electoral Democracy* (University of Michigan Press, 2004).

RICHARD G. NIEMI AND **HERBERT F. WEISBERG,** *Classics in Voting Behavior* (CQ Press, 1993).

RICHARD G. NIEMI AND **HERBERT F. WEISBERG,** *Controversies in*

Voting Behavior, 4th ed. (CQ Press, 2001).

FRANK R. PARKER, *Black Votes Count: Political Empowerment in Mississippi After 1965* (University of North Carolina Press, 1990).

THOMAS E. PATTERSON, *The Vanishing Voter: Public Involvement in the Age of Uncertainty* (Vintage Books, 2003).

JAMES A. THURBER AND **CANDICE J. NELSON,** EDS., *Campaigns and Elections American Style*, 2d ed. (Westview Press, 2004).

MICHAEL W. TRAUGOTT AND **PAUL J. LAVRAKAS,** *The Voter's Guide to Election Polls,* 3d ed. (Rowman & Littlefield, 2004).

MARTIN P. WATTENBERG, *Is Voting For Young People?* (Longman, 2007).

MARTIN P. WATTENBERG, *Where Have All the Voters Gone?* (Harvard University Press, 2002).

JOHN ZALLER, *The Nature and Origins of Mass Opinion* (Cambridge University Press, 1992).

See also *Public Opinion Quarterly, The American Journal of Political Science,* and *American Political Science Review.*

chapter 9

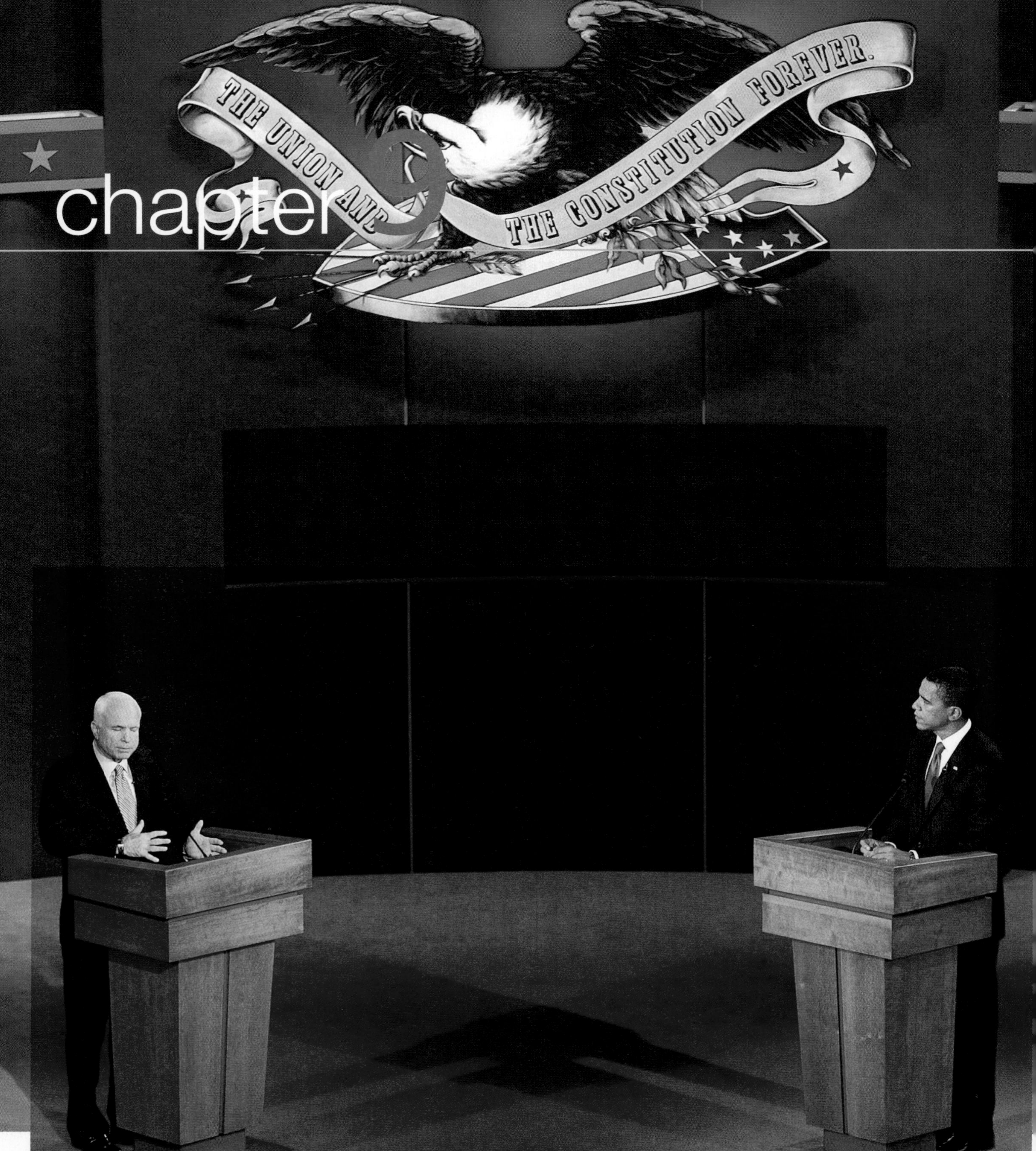

Campaigns and Elections

Democracy in Action

Some cynics contend that elections do not matter and there is little point in voting. The 2000 presidential elections proved them wrong, when Al Gore won the national popular vote by 539,947 votes, or only slightly more than 180 votes per county! The contest was especially close in Florida, which Bush carried by 537 votes, and New Mexico, which Gore won by 366 votes. In these and other close elections, including congressional races, a few more people staying home or turning out could have changed the outcome. For example, the 2006 Connecticut 2nd congressional race was decided by 91 votes. At the state and local levels, races are often decided by only a few votes.

The 2008 presidential race did not have the drama of 2000 and 2004 when a single state would have had the ability to change the outcome of the election if it had voted in a different way and when some potential "game changer" states were decided by razor thin margins. But some U.S. Senate and U.S. House contests in 2008 were again very close. The Minnesota and Alaska Senate races were in this category, and no candidate in the Georgia Senate race got a majority so the race by state law had to go to a run-off. Other U.S. House, state and local races were again decided by close margins.

Another reason voting is important is that elections matter. For example, the outcome of the 2000 presidential election has had important policy consequences. Presidents elected by the slimmest of margins still get to appoint Supreme Court justices and other federal judges, select their entire cabinet and other executive branch officials, and exercise all the other powers of the office. Had Al Gore won in the electoral college in 2000, he would not have chosen John Roberts or Samuel Alito for the Supreme Court. By selecting these relatively young Supreme Court nominees, Bush demonstrated that he clearly understood the president's role in nominating justices who can influence public policy for generations. A Gore presidency would have differed from the Bush presidency in other respects, including environmental policy, economic policy, social policy, and in how the U.S. would have approached international alliances and treaties.

In the United States, citizens vote more often and for more offices than citizens of any other democracy. We hold thousands of elections for everything from community college directors to county sheriffs. About half a million persons hold elected state and local offices.[1] In 2006, we elected 33 U.S. senators,[2] all 435 members of the U.S. House of Representatives, 36 state governors, about a dozen state treasurers, nine secretaries of state, and, in many states, judges.

In addition to electing people, voters in 27 states are allowed to vote on laws or constitutional amendments proposed by initiative petitions or on popular referendums put on the ballot by petition. In every state except Delaware, voters must approve all changes to the state constitution.

In this chapter, we explore our election rules. We note four important problems: the lack of competition for some offices, the complexities of nominating presidential candidates, the distortions of the electoral college, and the influence of money. We also discuss proposed reforms in each of these areas.

LEARNING **OBJECTIVES**

1. Summarize election rules and assess their implications for elections in the United States.
2. Describe the electoral college, how it works, and its impact on presidential elections.
3. Identify the regularities of congressional elections and explain why they are generally not competitive.
4. Identify the stages in U.S. presidential elections and analyze the differences in campaigning at each stage.
5. Assess the influence of money in congressional and presidential elections and evaluate the main approaches to campaign finance reform.
6. Evaluate the need for improving presidential and congressional elections in the United States.

CHAPTER OUTLINE

- Elections: The Rules of the Game
- Running for Congress
- Running for President
- Money in U.S. Elections
- Improving Elections
- Elections in the Internet Age

LEARNING OBJECTIVE

1 Summarize election rules and assess their implications for elections in the United States.

Elections: The Rules of the Game

The rules of the game—the electoral game—make a difference. Although the Constitution sets certain conditions and requirements, state law determines most electoral rules. Our focus in this chapter is on presidential and congressional elections, although much of the discussion is also relevant to state and local elections.

Regularly Scheduled Elections

In our system, elections are held at fixed intervals that the party in power cannot change. It does not make any difference if the nation is at war, as we were during the Civil War, or in the midst of a crisis, as in the Great Depression; when the calendar calls for an election, the election is held. Elections for members of Congress occur on the first Tuesday after the first Monday in November of even-numbered years. Although there are exceptions (for special elections or peculiar state provisions), participants know *in advance* just when the next election will be. In most parliamentary democracies, such as Great Britain and Canada, the party in power can call elections at a time of its choosing. The predetermined timing of elections is one of the defining characteristics of democracy in the United States.

Fixed, Staggered, and Sometimes Limited Terms

Our electoral system is based on *fixed terms,* meaning the length of a term in office is specified, not indefinite. The Constitution sets the term of office for the U.S. House of Representatives at two years, the Senate at six years, and the presidency at four years.

Our system also has *staggered terms* for some offices; not all offices are up for election at the same time. All House members are up for election every two years, but only one-third of senators are up for election at the same time. Because presidential elections can occur two or four years into a senator's six-year term, senators can often run for the presidency without fear of losing their seat, as John Kerry did in 2004 and John McCain, Barack Obama, Hillary Clinton, and Joe Biden did in 2008. But if their Senate term expires the same year as the presidential election, the laws of many states require them to give up their Senate seat to run for president, vice president, or any other position. An example of a state that permits a candidate to run for election to two offices is Connecticut, where Joseph Lieberman was reelected to the U.S. Senate in 2000 while being narrowly defeated in his race for vice president. Had he been victorious in both campaigns, he would have resigned his Senate seat.

Term Limits

The Twenty-Second Amendment to the Constitution, adopted in 1951, limits presidents to two terms. Knowing that a president cannot run again changes the way members of Congress, the voters, and the press regard the chief executive. A politician who cannot, or has announced he or she will not, run again is called a *lame duck*. Lame ducks are often seen as less influential because other politicians know that these officials' ability to bestow or withhold favors is coming to an end. Efforts to limit the terms of other offices have become a major issue in several states. The most frequent targets have been state legislators. One consequence of term limits is more lame ducks.

Term limits are popular. Currently 15 states have term limits for state legislatures. Six states have rescinded term limits. South Dakota voters were given the option of repealing term limits and they overwhelmingly voted to keep them.[3] Despite their popularity at the state level, proposals for term limits on federal legislators have repeatedly been defeated when they have come to a vote in Congress. The Supreme Court, by a vote of 5 to 4, declared that a state does not have the constitutional power to impose limits on the number of terms for which its members of the U.S. Congress are eligible, either by amendment to its own constitution or by state law.[4] Congress has refused to propose a constitutional amendment to impose a limit on congressional terms.

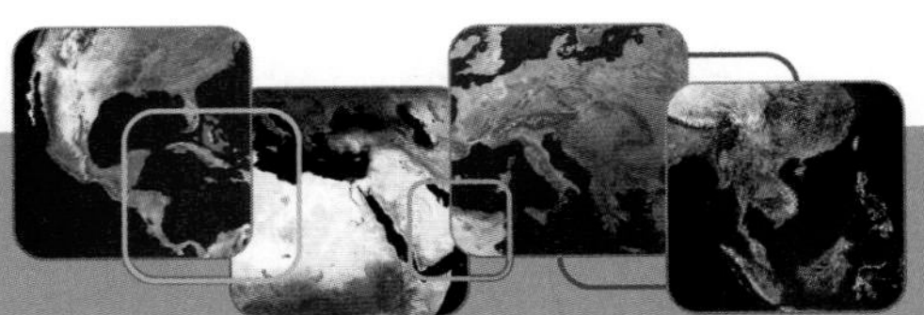

HOW OTHER NATIONS GOVERN

Two-Party vs. Multiparty Systems

Most democracies have more than two parties, whereas authoritarian countries generally have only one real party. The United States is unusual in that, despite occasional challenges from third parties, the Democrats and the Republicans have thrived as the only major parties for almost 150 years. How does this compare to other countries? The following table compares seven countries in terms of their electoral systems. It is drawn from the work of well-known scholars of comparative politics. The electoral system for representatives in the national legislature is typically single-member district (SMD); the representative is the person winning the plurality. Scholars have computed a measure of the number of parties operating through a complex formula based on number of parties and relative vote shares.

Most other countries have three or more parties that regularly receive at least some of the electorate's vote. Our sample countries range from one party in China to 7.5 in India. The case of India illustrates the fact that party dynamics do not depend on election rules alone. In India, several regional parties exist, whereas in other countries, parties are based on class, religion, economic interests, or individual politicians. The United States' strong two-party system is a rare case.

Countries that use proportional representation, such as Japan and Mexico, tend to field more parties than countries that use single member districts. Political scientist Maurice Duverger first identified this phenomenon. Duverger's law,* as it is known, holds that the simple majority single-ballot system of election fosters a two-party system because a minor party cannot elect representatives. A vote for a minor party is generally a wasted vote in this system.

QUESTIONS

1. Why do other countries have more parties than the United States?
2. Should the United States change its election rules to encourage more parties?
3. What are the advantages of a stable two-party system?

	China	India	Great Britain	Japan	Mexico	Nigeria	U.S.A.
Electoral system	No contested elections	SMD plurality	SMD plurality	SMD plurality and PR	SMD plurality and PR	SMD plurality	SMD plurality
Effective number of parties by vote share	No contested elections	7.50	3.56	3.72	3.60	2.62	2.17
Competitive parties	No party competition	Moderate	High	High	Moderate	Moderate	High

SMD = single-member district.
PR = proportional representation.
Effective number of parties by vote share is calculated by finding the inverse of the sum of the squared values of each party's vote share.
SOURCE: Gabriel A. Almond, G. Bingham Powell, Jr., Russell J. Dalton, and Kaare Strøm, *Comparative Politics Today: A World View*, 9th ed. (Pearson Longman, 2008), pp. 81, 89.

*Maurice Duverger, "Factors in a Two-Party and Multiparty System," in *Party Politics and Pressure Groups*, trans. David Wagoner (Crowell, 1972), pp. 23–32.

Winner Take All

An important feature of our electoral system is the **winner-take-all system,** sometimes referred to as "first past the post" in other countries.[5] In most U.S. electoral settings, the candidate with the most votes wins. The winner does not need to have a *majority* (more than half the votes cast); in a multicandidate race, the winner may have only a *plurality* (the largest number of votes). An example is the 1992 presidential election—Bill Clinton (D) got 43 percent of the vote, George H. W. Bush (R) got 37 percent, and Ross Perot, an independent candidate, got 19 percent. Clinton's margin in the electoral college was greater—370 electoral votes compared to 168 for Bush and none for Perot.[6] Winner-take-all electoral systems tend to reinforce moderate and centrist candidates because they are more likely to secure a plurality or a majority. Candidates in a winner-take-all system often stress that a vote for a minor party candidate is a "wasted vote" that may actually help elect the voter's least desired candidate.

winner-take-all system
An election system in which the candidate with the most votes wins.

Most U.S. electoral districts are **single-member districts,** meaning that in any district for any given election—senator, governor, U.S. House, state legislative seat—the voters choose *one* representative or official.[7] When the single-member-district and

single-member district
An electoral district in which voters choose one representative or official.

winner-take-all systems are combined, minor parties find it especially hard to win. For example, even if a third party gets 25 percent of the vote in several districts, it still gets no seats.

The combination of single-member districts and winner-take-all is different from a **proportional representation** system, in which political parties secure legislative seats and power in proportion to the number of votes they receive in the election. Let us assume a state has three representatives up for election. In each of the three contests, the Republican defeats the Democrat, but in one district by only a narrow margin. If you add up the statewide vote, the Republicans get 67 percent and the Democrats 33 percent. Under our single-member-district and winner-take-all system, the Republicans get all three seats. But under a system of proportional representation, in which the three seats represent the whole state, the Democrats would receive one seat because they got roughly one-third of the vote in the entire state. Proportional representation thus rewards minority parties and permits them to participate in government. Countries that practice some form of proportional representation include Germany, Israel, Italy, and Japan.

Proportional representation more accurately reveals the division of voter preferences and gives those who do not vote with the plurality some influence as a result of their vote. For this reason, proportional representation may encourage greater turnout for people who identify with parties that rarely win elections, such as Democrats in Utah or Republicans in Massachusetts. Proportional representation may also encourage issue-oriented campaigns and enhance the representation of women and minorities.

But proportional representation can cause problems. It may make it harder to have a clear winner, especially if minor parties are likely to win seats. As a result, it may encourage the proliferation of minor parties. Opponents of proportional representation worry that it can contribute to political instability and ideological extremism.

DEBATE

Electoral College

The Electoral College

We elect our president and vice president not by a national vote but by an indirect device known as the **electoral college.** The framers of the U.S. Constitution devised this system because they did not trust the choice of president to a direct vote of the people. Under this system, each state has as many electors as it has representatives and senators. California therefore has 55 electoral votes (53 House seats and two Senate seats), whereas seven states and the District of Columbia have three electoral votes each.

LEARNING **OBJECTIVE**

2 Describe the electoral college, how it works, and its impact on presidential elections.

Each state legislature is free to determine how it selects its electors. Each party nominates a slate of electors, usually longtime party workers. They are expected to cast their electoral votes for the party's candidates for president and vice president if their party's candidates get a plurality of the vote in their state. In our entire history, no "faithless elector"—an elector who does not vote for his or her state's popular vote winner—has ever cast the deciding vote, and the incidence of a faithless elector is rare.[8]

Candidates who win a plurality of the popular vote in a state secure all of that state's electoral votes, except in Nebraska and Maine, which allocate electoral votes to the winner in each congressional district plus two electoral votes for the winner of the state as a whole. Winning electors go to their state capital on the first Monday after the second Wednesday in December to cast their ballots. These ballots are then sent to Congress, and early in January, Congress formally counts the ballots and declares who won the election for president and vice president.

It takes a majority of the electoral votes to win. If no candidate gets a majority of the electoral votes for president, the House chooses among the top three candidates, with each state delegation having one vote. If no candidate gets a majority of the electoral votes for vice president, the Senate chooses among the top two candidates, with each senator casting one vote.

When there are only two major candidates for the presidency, the chances of an election being thrown into the House are remote. But twice in our history, the House

proportional representation
An election system in which each party running receives the proportion of legislative seats corresponding to its proportion of the vote.

electoral college
The electoral system used in electing the president and vice president, in which voters vote for electors pledged to cast their ballots for a particular party's candidates.

has had to act: In 1800, before the Twelfth Amendment was written, the House had to choose in a tie vote between Thomas Jefferson and Aaron Burr; and in 1824, the House picked John Quincy Adams over Andrew Jackson, who had won the popular vote, and William Crawford.

As we were reminded in 2000, our electoral college system makes it possible for a presidential candidate to receive the most popular votes, as Al Gore did, and yet not get enough electoral votes to be elected president. Gore lost the electoral college vote 271 to 266, and George Bush became president.[9] This also happened in 1824, when Andrew Jackson won 12 percent more of the vote than John Quincy Adams; in 1876, when Samuel Tilden received more popular votes than Rutherford B. Hayes; and in 1888, when Benjamin Harrison won in the electoral college despite receiving fewer popular votes than Grover Cleveland. It almost happened in 1916, 1960, and 1976, when the shift of a few votes in a few key states could have resulted in the election of a president without a popular majority. Some believe this was also the case with the Nader vote in 2000 (see Chapter 7).

In two of the four elections in which winners of the popular vote did not become president, the electoral college did not decide the winner. The 1824 election was decided by the U.S. House of Representatives. In 1876, the electoral vote in three southern states and Oregon was disputed, resulting in the appointment of an electoral commission to decide how those votes should be counted. In 1888 and 2000, the candidate with fewer popular votes was elected by the electoral college.

Questions about the electoral college arise every time a serious third-party candidate runs for president. If no candidate receives a majority in the electoral college and the decision is left to Congress, which Congress casts the vote, the one serving during the election, or the newly elected one? The answer is the newly elected one, the one elected in November and taking office the first week in January. Because each state has one vote in the House, what happens if a state's delegation is tied, 2 to 2 or 3 to 3? The answer is, its vote does not count. Would it be possible to have a president of one party and a vice president of another? Yes, if the election were thrown into the House and Senate, and a different party controlled each chamber.

The electoral college sharply influences presidential politics. To win a presidential election, a candidate must appeal successfully to voters in populous states such as California, Texas, Ohio, Illinois, Florida, and New York. California's electoral vote of 55 in 2008 exceeded the combined electoral votes of the 14 least populous states plus the District of Columbia. Sparsely populated states such as Wyoming and Vermont also have disproportionate representation in the electoral college because each has one

The Electoral Commission of 1877 met in secret session to decide the controversial presidential election between Rutherford B. Hayes and Samuel Tilden. After many contested votes Hayes was elected.

TABLE 9–1 2004 and 2008 Battleground States

State	Electoral Votes in 2004	% Difference in 2000 Popular Vote	% Difference in 2004 Popular Vote	How the Battlefield Changed in 2008
Wisconsin	10	0.22 Gore	0.39 Kerry	14.08 Obama
New Mexico	5	0.06 Gore	0.80 Bush	14.95 Obama
Iowa	7	0.32 Gore	0.91 Bush	9.41 Obama
New Hampshire	4	1.27 Bush	1.36 Kerry	9.64 Obama
Pennsylvania	21	4.17 Gore	2.27 Kerry	10.48 Obama
Ohio	20	3.51 Gore	2.49 Bush	3.97 Obama
Nevada	5	3.54 Gore	2.62 Bush	12.70 Obama
Michigan	17	5.13 Gore	3.40 Kerry	16.76 Obama
Oregon	7	0.48 Gore	3.90 Kerry	16.62 Obama
Florida	27	0.01 Gore	5.02 Bush	2.53 Obama
Missouri	11	3.34 Gore	7.31 Bush	0.20 McCain

SOURCE: www.cbsnews.com/htdocs/politics/campaign2004/03%20battleground.pdf; and "2004 Battleground," usinfo.state.gov/dhr/democracy/elections/battleground_states.html.

representative, regardless of population. When the contest is close, as it was in recent elections, every state's electoral votes are crucial to the outcome, and so greater emphasis is given to states in which the contest is close, even less populated states[10] (see Table 9–1).

Running for Congress

How candidates run for Congress differs depending on the nature of their district or state, on whether candidates are incumbents or challengers, on the strength of their personal organization, on how well known they are, and on how much money they have to spend on their campaign. There are both similarities and differences between House and Senate elections.

LEARNING **OBJECTIVE**

3 Identify the regularities of congressional elections and explain why they are generally not competitive.

First, most congressional elections are not close (see Figure 9–1). In districts where most people belong to one party or where incumbents are popular and enjoy fund-raising and other campaign advantages, there is often little competition.[11] Districts are typically drawn in ways that enhance the reelection prospects of incumbents or one party, a process called *partisan gerrymandering*. We explore this process in greater detail in Chapter 11, which deals with Congress. Those who believe that competition is essential to constitutional democracy are concerned that so many officeholders have **safe seats.** When officeholders do not have to fight to retain their seat, elections are not performing their proper role.[12]

safe seat
An elected office that is predictably won by one party or the other, so the success of that party's candidate is almost taken for granted.

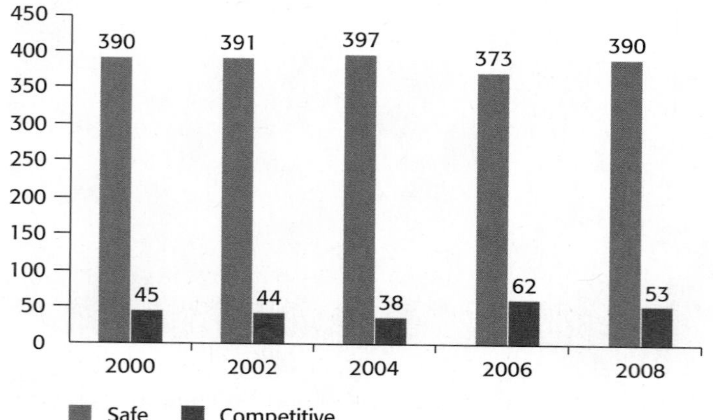

FIGURE 9–1
Safe and Competitive House Seats, 2000–2008.

SOURCE: Charlie Cook, "National Overview," *Cook Political Report*, October 16, 2008, p. 6; and Charlie Cook, "Competitive House Race Chart," *Cook Political Report*, http://cookpolitical.com/charts/house/competitive_2008-10-16_09-21-12.php.

Competition is more likely when both candidates have adequate funding, which is not often the case in U.S. House elections (see Chapters 7 and 11). Elections for governor and for the U.S. Senate are more seriously contested and more adequately financed than those for the U.S. House.

Presidential popularity affects both House and Senate races both during presidential election years and in midterm elections. The boost candidates get from running along with a popular presidential candidate from their party is known as the **coattail effect.** But winning presidential candidates do not always provide such a boost. The Republicans suffered a net loss of six House seats in 1988, even though George H. W. Bush won the presidency, and the Democrats suffered a net loss of ten House seats in 1992 when Bill Clinton won the presidential election. Democrats fared better in 1996, registering a net gain of nine House seats. On the coattails of Barack Obama's convincing presidential win in 2008, the Democrats saw a net gain of 20 House seats and 6 Senate Seats (with 4 House and 3 Senate races still undecided). Overall, "measurable coattail effects continue to appear," according to congressional elections scholar Gary Jacobson, but their impact is "erratic and usually modest."[13]

In midterm elections, presidential popularity and economic conditions have long been associated with the number of House seats a president's party loses.[14] These same factors are associated with how well the president's party does in Senate races, but the association is less strong.[15] Figure 9–2 shows the number of seats in the House of Representatives and U.S. Senate gained or lost by the party controlling the White House in midterm elections since 1942. Republicans did better in 1994 than in any midterm election since 1946, picking up 53 seats. The Republican tide also produced a net gain of 9 Senate seats.[16] In all of the midterm elections between 1934 and 1998, the party controlling the White House lost seats in the House. But in 2002, as in 1998, the long-standing pattern of the president's party losing seats in a midterm election did not hold. Republicans picked up a net gain of 2 seats in the Senate and 6 seats in the House. In 2006, however, the long-standing pattern reemerged, with the Republicans losing 30 House seats and 6 Senate seats. Exit polls and other surveys show that the Bush administration's handling of the war in Iraq, relief efforts after Hurricane Katrina in 2005, and scandals involving Republicans troubled voters.[17]

FIGURE 9–2
Seats Lost by the President's Party in Midterm Elections for the House of Representatives and the Senate, 1954–2006.

SOURCE: Harold W. Stanley and Richard G. Niemi, *Vital Statistics on American Politics 2007–2008* (CQ Press, 2008), p. 54.

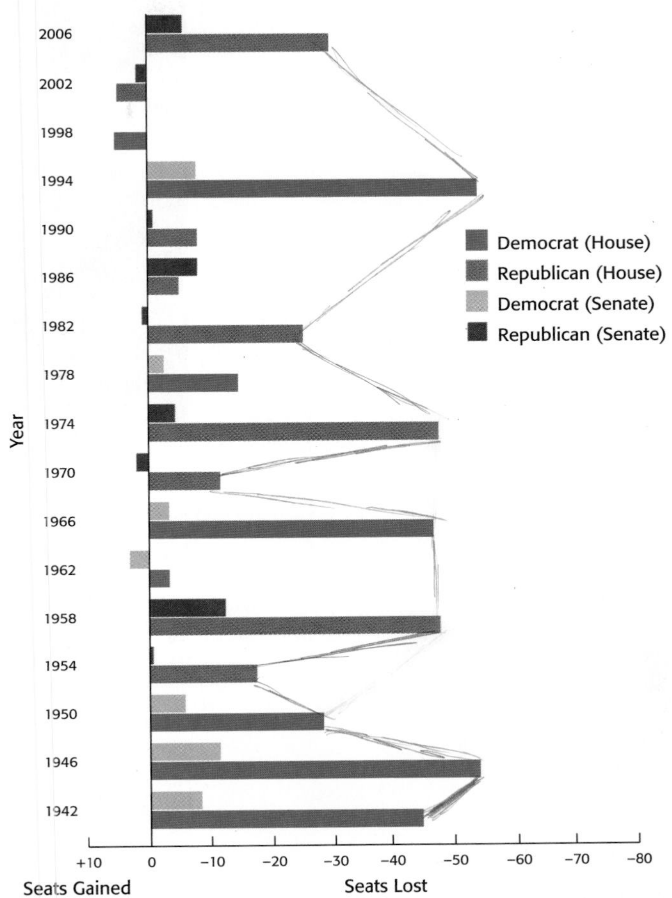

The House of Representatives

Every two years, as many as 1,000 candidates—including approximately 400 incumbents—campaign for Congress. Incumbents are rarely challenged for renomination from within their own party, and when they are, the challenges are seldom serious. In the 1990s, for example, on average only two House incumbents were denied renomination in each election. In 2006, 81 percent of all U.S. Representatives[18] and 54 percent of all U.S. Senators had no opponent in the primaries.[19] In 2008, three House incumbents were denied renomination and one Senator ran unopposed.[20] Fifty-five U.S. House candidates and one U.S. Senate candidate ran unopposed in the 2008 election. Challengers from other parties running against incumbents rarely encounter opposition in their own party.[21]

Mounting a Primary Campaign The first step for would-be challengers is to raise hundreds of thousands of dollars (or even more) to mount a serious campaign. This requires asking friends and acquaintances as well as interest groups for money. Candidates need money to hire campaign managers and technicians, buy television and other advertising, conduct polls, and pay for a variety of activities. Parties can sometimes help, but they shy away from giving money in primary contests. The party organization usually stays neutral until the nomination is decided.

coattail effect
The boost that candidates may get in an election because of the popularity of candidates above them on the ballot, especially the president.

Democrat Tom Udall won election to the U.S. Senate from New Mexico in 2008. Like Barack Obama, Udall benefitted from strong support from New Mexico's Hispanic voters.

SIMULATION

You Are a Media Consultant to a Political Candidate

COMPARATIVE

Comparing Political Campaigns

candidate appeal
The tendency in elections to focus on the personal attributes of a candidate, such as his or her strengths, weaknesses, background, experience, and visibility.

national tide
The inclination to focus on national issues, rather than local issues, in an election campaign. The impact of a national tide can be reduced by the nature of the candidates on the ballot who may have differentiated themselves from their party or its leader if the tide is negative, as well as competition in the election.

Another early step is to build a *personal organization.* A congressional candidate can build an organization while holding another office, such as a seat in the state legislature, by serving in civic causes, helping other candidates, and being conspicuous without being controversial.

A candidate's main hurdle is gaining visibility. Candidates work hard to be mentioned by the media. In large cities with many simultaneous campaigns, congressional candidates are frequently overlooked, and in all areas, television is devoting less time to political news.[22] Candidates rely on personal contacts, on hand shaking and door-to-door campaigning, and on identifying likely supporters and courting their favor—the same techniques used in campaigns for lesser offices. Despite these efforts, the turnout in primaries tends to be low, except in campaigns in which large sums of money are spent on advertising.

Campaigning for the General Election The electorate in a general election is different from that in a primary election. Many more voters turn out in general elections, especially the less-committed partisans and Independents. Partisanship is more important in a general election, as many voters use party as a simplifying device to select from among candidates in the many races they decide. Not surprisingly, candidates in districts where their party is strong make their partisanship clear, and candidates from a minority party deemphasize it. General elections also focus on the strengths and weaknesses of the candidates and their background, experience, and visibility. Political scientists describe this dimension as **candidate appeal.** Issues can also be important in general elections, but they are often more local than national issues. Occasionally a major national issue arises that can help or hurt one party. Candidates who have differentiated themselves from their party or its leader can reduce the impact of such a **national tide** if it is negative. Some elections for Congress or the state legislature are in part referendums on the president or governor, but public opinion concerning the president or governor is rarely the only factor at play in these elections.

As we have mentioned, most incumbent members of Congress win reelection.[23] In 2006, 94 percent of House incumbents won reelection.[24] Since 1970, just over 95 percent of incumbent House members seeking reelection have won, and since 2000, more than 98 percent of incumbent House members running for reelection have been successful (see Figure 9–3).[25] This lends credibility to the charge that we have a "permanent Congress."

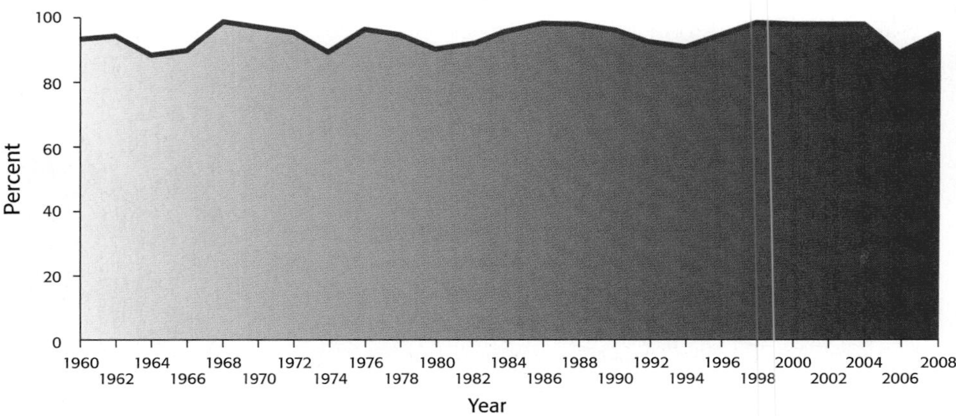

FIGURE 9–3
U.S. House Incumbents Reelected, 1960–2008.

SOURCE: Harold W. Stanley and Richard G. Niemi, *Vital Statistics on American Politics 2007–2008* (CQ Press, 2008), pp. 57–59; Center for Responsive Politics. *Congressional Races 2008,* at http://www.opensecrets.org/races/index.php, accessed November 12, 2008.

Why is reelection to a House seat so much easier than defeating an incumbent or winning an open seat? As we discuss in Chapter 11, incumbents have a host of advantages that help them win reelection. These include free mailings (the *franking privilege*) and telephone calls to constituents; the free use of broadcast studios to record radio and television tapes to be sent to local media outlets; and perhaps most important, a large staff to perform countless favors for constituents and send a stream of press reports and mail back to the district.[26] Representatives also try to win committee posts, even on minor committees, that relate to the needs of their districts and build connections with constituents.[27] Incumbents are generally better known than challengers, something called **name recognition,** and benefit from years of media coverage of their generally positive efforts on behalf of the district.

Incumbents also win so often because they are able to outspend challengers in campaigns by roughly 3 to 1 in the House and about 1.75 to 1 in the Senate.[28] Most challengers run campaigns that are much less visible than incumbents, contact few voters, and lose badly. Many potential challengers are scared away by the prospect of having to raise more than $1 million in campaign funds, and some do not want to face the media scrutiny that comes with a serious race for Congress. Nonetheless, in each election, a few challengers mount serious campaigns because of the incumbent's perceived vulnerability, the challengers' own wealth, party or political action committee efforts, or other factors.

In addition, incumbents generally win because their district boundaries have been drawn to be made up of voters who favor their party. Retirements and redistricting create *open seats,* which can result in more competitive elections. If, however, the district is heavily partisan, the predominant party is likely to retain the seat, and once elected the incumbent then reaps the other incumbency advantages as well. In these cases the contest for the nomination in the predominant party effectively determines who will be the new representative.

The Senate

Running for the Senate is generally more high-profile than running for the House. The six-year term, the fact that there are only two senators per state, and the national exposure many senators enjoy make a Senate seat a glittering prize, leading to more intense competition. Senate campaigns cost more than House races and are more likely to be seriously contested (see Figure 9–4).[29] The essential tactics are to raise large amounts of money, hire a professional and experienced campaign staff, make as many personal contacts as possible (especially in states with smaller populations), avoid giving the opposition any positive publicity, and have a clear and consistent campaign theme. Incumbency is an advantage for senators, although not as much as it is for representatives.[30] Incumbent senators are widely known, but often so are their opponents, who generally raise and spend significant amounts of money.[31]

name recognition
Incumbents have an advantage over challengers in election campaigns because voters are more familiar with them, and incumbents are more recognizable.

FIGURE 9–4
Rising Campaign Costs in Congressional General Elections.

SOURCE: 1976–2004, Harold W. Stanley and Richard G. Niemi, *Vital Statistics on American Politics 2007–2008* (CQ Press, 2008), p. 101; 2006, Center for Responsive Politics, "Price of Admission: Winners," www.opensecrets.org/bigpicture/stats.php?cycle=2006. Amounts are in 2006 dollars.

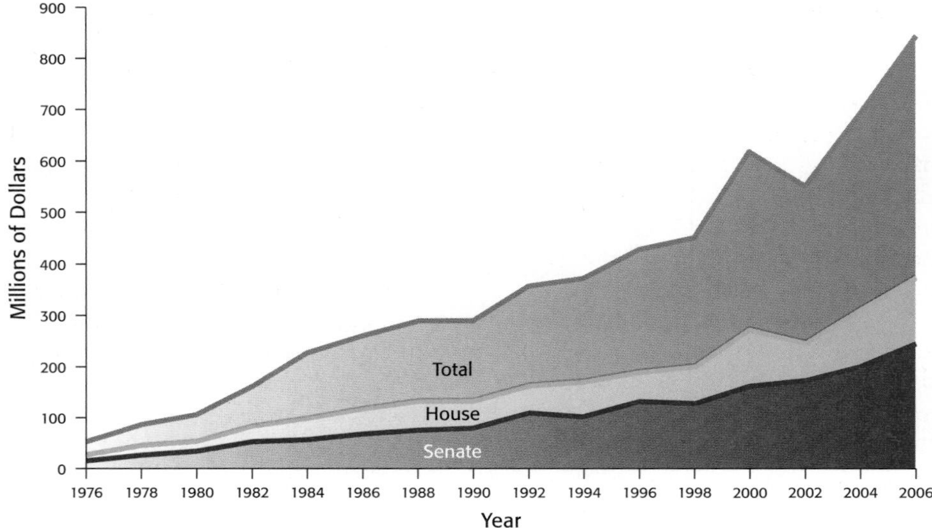

When one party controls the Senate by only a few seats, as has been the case in recent years, both parties and the White House become more involved in recruiting competitive candidates. Sometimes the party leadership attempts to "clear the field" for a preferred candidate by discouraging other candidates from running while endorsing a candidate it considers to be more competitive. The Bush White House was especially active in clearing the field and candidate recruitment in 2002 and to a lesser extent in 2004 and 2006.[32]

The cost of Senate campaigns can vary greatly. California has nearly 70 times the number of potential voters as Wyoming; not surprisingly, running for a seat from Wyoming is much cheaper than running for a seat from California. As a result, interest groups and parties direct more money to competitive races in small states where their campaign dollars have a greater potential impact.[33]

Television and Presidential Campaigns

Running for President

Presidential elections are major media events, with candidates seeking as much positive television coverage as possible and trying to avoid negative coverage. The formal campaign has three stages: winning the nomination, campaigning at the convention, and mobilizing support in the general election.

LEARNING **OBJECTIVE**

 Identify the stages in U.S. presidential elections and analyze the differences in campaigning at each stage.

Stage 1: The Nomination

Presidential hopefuls must make a series of critical tactical decisions. The first is when to start campaigning. For the presidential election of 2008, some candidates began soon after the 2004 presidential election.[34] Some candidates formally announced in December 2006 and most had announced by the end of February 2007. Republican Fred Thompson delayed his entry until September 6, 2007, a decision that meant he was less competitive in recruiting staff, fund raising, and visibility.[35] Early decisions are increasingly necessary for candidates to raise money and assemble an organization. Campaigning begins well before any actual declaration of candidacy, as candidates try to line up supporters to win caucuses or primaries in key states and to raise money for their nomination effort. This period in the campaign has been called the "invisible primary."[36]

You Are a Campaign Manager: Countdown to 270! Choose Your Candidate and Lead Him or Her to Electoral College Victory

One of the hardest jobs for candidates and their strategists is calculating how to deal with the complex maze of presidential primaries and caucuses that constitutes the delegate selection system. The system for electing delegates to the national party convention varies from state to state and often from one party to the other in the same state. In some parties in some states, for example, candidates must provide lists of delegates who support them months before the primary.

Another decision candidates must make is whether to participate in partial public financing of their campaigns. The presidential campaign finance system provides funds to match small individual contributions during the nomination phase of the campaign for candidates who agree to remain within spending limitations. George W. Bush declined federal funds in the 2000 and 2004 nomination phase, as did Democrats John Kerry and Howard Dean in 2004. In 2008, Barack Obama, Hillary Clinton, Mitt Romney, Rudy Giuliani, Ron Paul, Mike Huckabee, and Fred Thompson all turned down matching funds. John McCain at one point said he would accept them and then later declined them. Forgoing the public matching funds allows greater flexibility in spending campaign money and removes the overall limit for this phase of the process.

Presidential Primaries State presidential primaries, unknown before 1900, have become the main method of choosing delegates to the national convention. A delegate is a person chosen by local partisans to represent them in selecting nominees, party leaders, and party positions. Today, more than three-fourths of the states use presidential primaries. In 2008, 67 percent of the Democratic delegates and 77 percent of the Republican delegates were chosen in the primaries.[37] The rest of the delegates were chosen by state party caucuses or conventions, or were party leaders who serve as "superdelegates."

Republican presidential primaries may have two features: a so-called *beauty contest,* or popularity vote, in which voters indicate which candidate they prefer but do not actually elect delegates to the convention, and *actual voting* for delegates pledged to a candidate. States that use this beauty contest system include Montana, Nebraska, Illinois, and Pennsylvania.[38] Since 1996, the Democrats require delegates to be allocated proportionately to the vote in the primary.

Senator Barack Obama's campaign was characterized by his appeal to younger voters. In Oregon he reportedly drew a crowd of 70,000–80,000.

Candidates may win the beauty contest but gain fewer delegates than their opponents because they failed to put a full slate of delegates on the ballot or because local notables were listed on the ballot as delegates pledged to another candidate. Different combinations of the popularity vote and the actual vote for delegates have produced the following systems:[39]

- *Proportional representation:* Delegates to the national convention are allocated on the basis of the percentage of votes candidates win in the primary. This system has been used in most of the states, including several of the largest ones. The Democrats mandate proportional representation for all their primaries, with three-quarters elected in primaries determined by the proportional vote in congressional districts.[40] In some states, Republicans use this same system, but Republicans are much more varied in how they select their delegates.[41]
- *Winner take all:* Whoever gets the most votes wins all that state's delegates or the share of delegates from each congressional district. Republicans still use the winner-take-all system at the state level, and in 2008, most states used this rule at either the state or congressional district levels.[42] To win all the delegates of a big state such as California is an enormous bonus to a candidate, as it was to John McCain in 2008.

GENERATION **NEXT**

Views on Large and Small Donors

Would you be more willing to vote for a candidate who raises more of his or her money from donors who give large donations, or from donors who give small donations? Why? One of the interesting developments of the 2008 presidential election was the increase in the number of people making contributions to a presidential candidate, many of them less than $200. The number of individuals contributing more than $2,000 also grew. Does the profile of contributors—more small or more large donors—make a difference in the way you see the candidate? That question was asked in a survey organized by one of the authors of this book, which included a large enough sample for us to examine the views of 18- to 29-year-olds compared to older voters.

Most respondents aged 18–29 were indifferent between candidates who rely more on small donors and those who rely more on large donors. For all but liberals, the most common response was "neutral," but that was not always the majority view.

When the level of contribution matters, it positively affects views of candidates who raise more than half their money from small donors. For example, 45 percent of women and whites, 47 percent of Democrats, and 53 percent of liberals are more positive toward such a candidate. In all cases those who reported that relying on small donors was a positive attribute outnumbered those who said it was a negative.

Candidates who raised more than half of their money in amounts of $2,000 or more in 2008 again largely evoked a neutral response. But if respondents had a position on this mode of fund raising, they were far more likely to say it was a negative attribute. Twenty-nine percent of men in this age range saw fund raising in larger amounts negatively, as did 28 percent of Independents and 25 percent of Democrats. Republicans were divided, with 17 percent saying it made their view of the candidate more negative and the same proportion saying it made their view more positive.

This distinction between candidates reflected the fund raising of Barack Obama and Hillary Clinton through much of the nomination contest in 2008. Obama relied on both large and small contributions but set new records in the numbers of small donors, whereas Clinton's campaign was more traditional in relying heavily on large donors.

QUESTIONS

1. Why may some members of Generation Next prefer candidates who secure a larger number of small donations?
2. What electoral advantages may candidates have who are able to attract small donors?
3. Would you be more or less willing to contribute to a candidate who relies heavily on small contributions? Why?

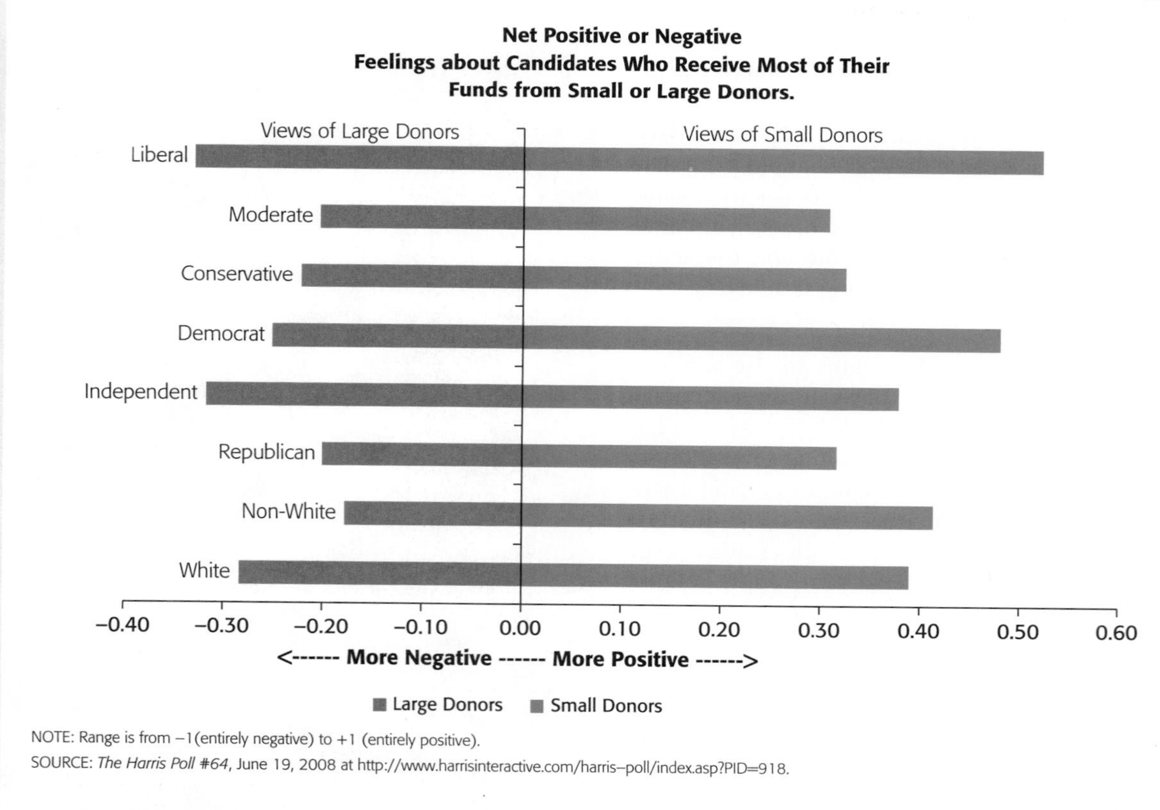

NOTE: Range is from –1 (entirely negative) to +1 (entirely positive).

SOURCE: *The Harris Poll #64*, June 19, 2008 at http://www.harrisinteractive.com/harris–poll/index.asp?PID=918.

- *Delegate selection without a commitment to a candidate:* New York Republicans allow the state committee to select 12 at-large delegates who are officially unpledged, as are the party chair and national committee representatives.[43] In 2008 a lot of attention was paid to Democratic superdelegates, who included party leaders, elected officials, and others who were selected for reasons other than which candidate they ended up backing. These superdelegates cast the deciding vote for Obama because no candidate secured a majority of all delegates through the primary and caucus process.
- *Delegate selection and separate presidential poll:* In several states, voters decide twice: once to indicate their choice for president and again to choose delegates pledged, or at least favorable, to a presidential candidate. In 2008 this was the process Democrats used in Texas, with a primary during the day to elect 126 delegates and a caucus that night electing 67 delegates.

Voters in states such as Iowa and New Hampshire, which are the first states to pick delegates, bask in media attention for weeks and even months before they cast the first ballots in the presidential sweepstakes. Because these early contests have had the effect of limiting the choices of voters in states that come later in the process, states have tended to move their primaries up in a process called "front loading." California, which traditionally held its primary in June, moved it to March in 2000, so its voters would play a more important role in selecting the nominee. Other states did the same thing. Front loading was even more prominent in 2004 and 2008.[44] The parties have sought to prevent too much front loading. In 2008 when Florida and Michigan moved their primaries up to January 29 and January 15 (respectively), ahead of what party rules allowed, the Democratic National Committee (DNC) voted that delegates so selected would not be seated.[45] The controversy was resolved by each Florida and Michigan delegate receiving a half vote, but at the convention each delegate was given a full vote.

In 2000 and 2004, both the Democratic and Republican nominations were decided by March. This had the effect of compressing the nomination battle into several weeks of intense activity in the spring, followed by months of much less activity before the fall general election campaign. Some saw this as an advantage because it meant the winner could pursue party unity and focus on fund raising.[46]

In 2008, the Republican nomination again reached an early resolution, with John McCain effectively winning it after his victories in Ohio and Texas on March 4.[47] The Republican rules, which clearly advantage candidates who win states, even by narrow margins, helped McCain. The Democrats had a highly contested and protracted race until June 2008.

Caucuses and Conventions A meeting of party members and supporters of various candidates who may elect state or national convention delegates, who in turn vote for the presidential nominee, is called a **caucus.** In about a dozen states, one or both parties use a caucus or convention system (or both) to choose delegates.[48] Each state's parties and legislature regulate the methods used.[49] The caucus or convention is the oldest method of choosing delegates and, unlike the primary system, it centers on staffing local party positions such as voting district chair and often includes party discussions of issues and candidates in addition to a vote on candidates or policies.

In caucus or convention states, delegates who will attend the national party conventions are chosen by delegates to state or district conventions, who themselves are chosen earlier in county, precinct, or town caucuses. The process starts at local meetings

caucus
A meeting of local party members to choose party officials or candidates for public office and to decide the platform.

open to all party members, who discuss and take positions on candidates and issues and elect delegates to represent their views at the next level. This process is repeated until conventions of delegates from a district or state choose delegates to the national nominating convention.

The best-known example of a caucus is in Iowa, because Iowa has held the earliest caucuses in the most recent presidential nominating contests. Every January or February in a presidential election year, Iowans have the opportunity to attend Republican and Democratic precinct meetings.[50] In 2008, all Democratic caucus states except Nevada went heavily to Obama. Highlighting the distinction between the primary and caucus systems, Senator Clinton said that her campaign had "been less successful in caucuses because it brings out the activist base of the Democratic Party." Of these activists she said, "I don't agree with them. They know I don't agree with them. So they flood into these caucuses and dominate them and really intimidate people who actually show up to support me."[51]

Strategies Presidential hopefuls face a dilemma: To get the Republican nomination, a candidate has to appeal to the more intensely conservative Republican partisans, those who vote in caucuses and primaries and actively support campaigns. Democratic hopefuls have to appeal to the liberal wing of their party as well as to minorities, union members, and environmental activists. But to win the general election, candidates have to win support from moderates and pragmatic voters, many of whom do not vote in the primaries. If candidates position themselves too far from the moderates in their nomination campaign, they risk being labeled extreme in the general election and losing these votes to their opponent.

Strategies for securing the nomination have changed over the years. Some candidates think it wise to skip some of the earlier contests and enter first in states where their strength lies. John McCain pursued such a strategy in 2000 and again in 2008, ignoring Iowa and concentrating on New Hampshire. In 2008 former New York City mayor Rudy Giuliani also bypassed Iowa, but unlike McCain he did not win in New Hampshire and dropped out of the race after losing in Florida to McCain a few weeks later. Most candidates choose to run hard in Iowa and New Hampshire, hoping that early showings in these states, which receive a great deal of media attention, will move them into the spotlight for later efforts.

During this early phase, the ability of candidates to generate momentum by managing the media's expectations of their performance is especially important. Winning in the primaries thus centers on a game of expectations, and candidates may intentionally seek to lower expectations so that "doing better than expected" will generate momentum for their campaign. The media and pollsters generally set these expectations in its coverage of candidates. In 2008 polls consistently had Clinton in the lead in New Hampshire until the Iowa caucus the week before New Hampshire. With Obama's win in Iowa, however, Clinton's ability to win in New Hampshire was in doubt, and when she won her victory was interpreted as a "stunner" by MSNBC.[52]

Stage 2: The National Party Convention

The delegates elected in primaries, caucuses, or state conventions assemble at their **national party convention** in the summer before the election to pick the party's presidential and vice presidential candidates. Conventions follow standard rules, routines, and rituals. Usually, the first day is devoted to a keynote address and other speeches touting the party and denouncing the opposition; the second day, to committee reports, including party and convention rules and the party platform; the third day, to presidential and vice presidential balloting; and the fourth day, to the presidential candidate's acceptance speech.

national party convention
A national meeting of delegates elected in primaries, caucuses, or state conventions who assemble once every four years to nominate candidates for president and vice president, ratify the party platform, elect officers, and adopt rules.

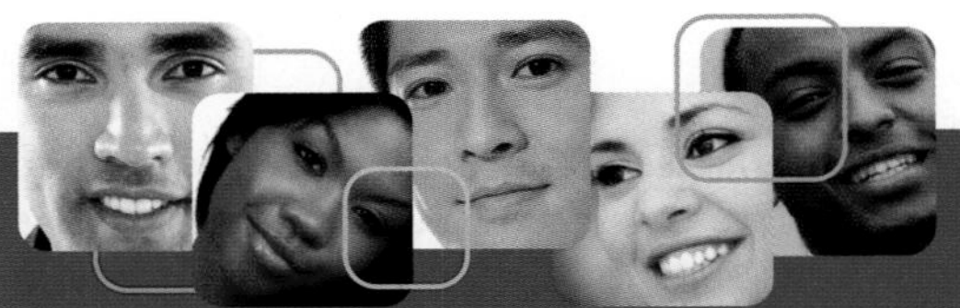

THE CHANGING FACE OF U.S. POLITICS

More Diversity Among National Party Nomination Convention Delegates

One of the criticisms of the Democratic and Republican Parties in the contentious 1968 election was that the delegates to the national party nominating conventions were not representative of their parties as a whole. A commission was formed in the Democratic Party to reform the process of delegate selection. One result was a rise in the number of states holding presidential primaries rather than caucuses. Another consequence was a much more diverse group of delegates in nominating conventions.

In 1968 delegates were mostly older white males. By 1972, in response to the recommendations of the Democratic Party reform commission, the proportion of males had dropped from nearly 90 percent to 60 percent. In that same four-year period the proportion of black delegates tripled and the proportion of younger delegates rose from 4 percent to 21 percent. In all cases except young delegates, the 2008 Democratic delegates approximated the composition of the 1972 Democratic delegates.

Republicans have not become as diverse in their delegate composition. In 2008 one-third of GOP delegates were women, compared to 49 percent for Democrats. There were fewer minority and young delegates at the 2008 Republican convention than at the 2008 Democratic convention. Only 2 percent of GOP delegates were black compared to 23 percent for Democrats. Ninety-three percent of Republican delegates were white compared to 65 percent of Democratic delegates. In 2008, only 3 percent of Republican delegates were under 30 years of age compared to 7 percent for Democrats. But both parties are sensitive to the symbolism of diversity and showcase delegates and others who can help the party connect to different demographic groups.

Demographic Makeup of Democratic National Delegates.

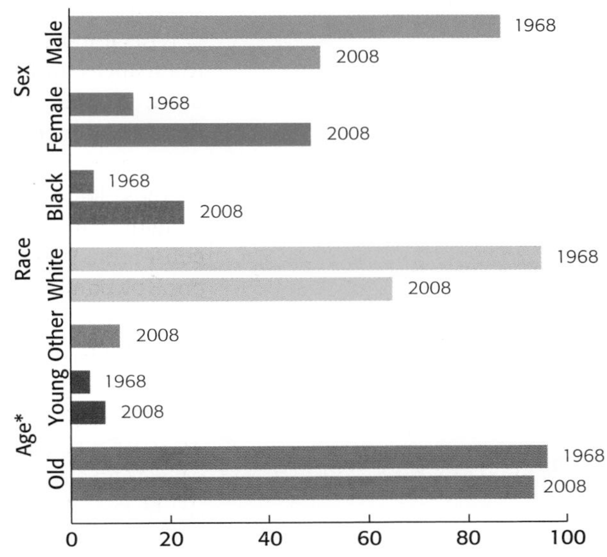

*Note that the 2008 source lists "young" as 18 to 29 years old, whereas the 1968 source lists "young" as 30 years old and under.

SOURCE: 1968 data from Austin Ranney, *Curing the Mischiefs of Faction: Party Reform in America* (University of California Press, 1975), p. 155. 2008 data for Republicans from the *New York Times*/CBS Poll, "2008 Republican National Delegate Survey," July 23 – August 26, 2008. Available at http://graphics8.nytimes.com/packages/pdf/politics/20080901-poll.pdf Data for the Democrats from the *New York Times*/CBS Poll, "2008 Democratic National Delegate Survey," July 16 – August 17, 2008. Available at http://graphics8.nytimes.com/packages/pdf/politics/demdel20080901-poll.pdf from the *New York Times*/CBS News Poll, "2004 Republican National Delegate Survey," August 29, 2004, and "2004 Democratic National Delegate Survey," July 23, 2004, www.nytimes.com/packages/html/politics/20040829_gop_poll/2004_gop_results.pdf

National party conventions used to be events of high excitement because there was no clear nominee before the convention. In the past, delegates also arrived at national nominating conventions with differing degrees of commitment to presidential candidates; some delegates were pledged to no candidate at all, others to a specific candidate for one or two ballots, and others firmly to one candidate only. Because of reforms encouraging delegates to stick with the person to whom they are pledged, there has been less room to maneuver at conventions. For a half century, conventions have ratified a candidate who has already been selected in the primaries and caucuses.

Despite the lack of suspense about who the nominee will be, conventions continue to be major media events. As recently as 1988, the major networks gave the Democratic and Republican national conventions gavel-to-gavel coverage, meaning that television covered the conventions from the beginning of the first night to the end of the fourth night. Now the major networks leave comprehensive coverage to C-SPAN. The long-term decline in viewership and the reduced hours of coverage have altered the parties' strategies. The parties feature their most important speakers and highlight their most important messages in the limited time the networks give them. In 2008, coverage and viewership of the conventions increased, this was especially the case for the Obama, Palin, and McCain acceptance speeches. An estimated 40 million people viewed the McCain speech, slightly higher than the number who saw Obama's acceptance speech.[53]

Acceptance speeches provide the nominees with an opportunity to define themselves and their candidacy. An example of an acceptance speech that worked more to the benefit of the opposition was Barry Goldwater's speech to the Republican convention in 1964 when he said "extremism in the defense of liberty is no vice."[54] This only helped to define Goldwater as "dangerous" and "extreme," themes his opponent, Lyndon Johnson, exploited. Democrats hoped Ronald Reagan would also self-destruct in 1980. Instead, Reagan came off as warm and confident. At two places in his acceptance speech, he quoted Franklin D. Roosevelt, once by name. Candidates of one party rarely quote a president of the other party in favorable terms as Reagan did.[55] This was clearly an effort to reach out to Democrats.

The Party Platform Delegates to the national party conventions decide on the *platform*, a statement of party perspectives on public policy. Why does anyone care what is in the party platform? Critics have long pointed out that the party platform is binding on no one and is more likely to hurt than to help a candidate, by advocating positions unpopular to moderate or Independent voters, whose support the candidate may need to win in the general election. But presidential candidates, as well as delegates, take the platform seriously because it defines the direction a party wants to take. Also, despite the charge that the platform is ignored, most presidents try to implement much of it.[56] Neither party had a platform fight in 2008 and press reporting on the party platforms was very limited.

The Vice Presidential Nominee The choice of the vice presidential nominee garners widespread attention. Rarely does a person actually "run" for the vice presidential nomination, because only the presidential nominee's vote counts. But there is a good deal of maneuvering to capture that one vote. Sometimes the choice of a running mate is made at the convention—not a time conducive to careful and deliberate thought. But usually it is made before, and the announcement is timed to enhance media coverage and momentum going into the convention. The last time a presidential candidate left the choice of vice president to the delegates was the Democratic convention in 1956.

In 2008 Barack Obama selected Delaware Senator Joe Biden to be his running mate. Biden, Who himself had twice been a candidate for the presidency including a bid in 2008, was seen as adding extensive foreign policy experience to the ticket because of his long service on the Senate Foreign Relations Committee. Biden was also expected to assist in winning working class and Catholic support in his native Pennsylvania and other battleground states. John McCain's selection of Alaska Governor Sarah Palin surprised many but quickly helped energize the Republican party base. Later in the campaign Palin became a liability to the campaign as her media interviews were seen as showing a lack of knowledge and experience. Exit polls found that three-in-five voters thought Palin was not qualified to be president if necessary compared to 32 percent having that view of Biden.

The Value of Conventions Why do the parties continue to have conventions if the nominee is known in advance and the vice presidential nominee is the choice of one person? What role do conventions play in our system? For the parties, they are a time of "coming together" to endorse a party program and to build unity and enthusiasm for the fall campaign. For candidates, as well as other party leaders, conventions are a chance to capture the national spotlight and further their political ambitions. For nominees, they are an opportunity to define themselves in positive ways. The potential exists to heal wounds festering from the primary campaign and move into the general election united, but it is not always achieved. Conventions can be potentially divisive, as the Republicans learned in 1964 when conservative Goldwater delegates loudly booed New York governor Nelson Rockefeller and as the Democrats learned in 1968 in Chicago when the convention spotlighted divisions within the party over Vietnam, as well as ugly battles between police and protesters near the convention hotels.

Nomination by Petition There is a way to run for president of the United States that avoids the grueling process of primary elections and conventions—if you are rich enough or well-known enough to use it. Third-party and Independent candidates can qualify for the ballot by meeting each state's ballot access requirements. This takes time, organization, and money (see Chapter 7). In 2008, the petition process was as simple as submitting the signatures of 1,000 registered voters in Washington State,[57] or by paying $500 in Colorado or Louisiana,[58] or as difficult as getting the signatures of currently registered voters equal to 2 percent of total votes cast in the last election in North Carolina (69,734 signatures).[59] Nader is on "*45*" state ballots plus DC. He is excluded from "five" states including Georgia, Indiana, North Carolina, Oklahoma, and Texas.

Stage 3: The General Election

The national party convention adjourns immediately after the presidential and vice presidential candidates deliver their acceptance speeches to the delegates and the national television audience. Traditionally, the weeks between the conventions and Labor Day were a time for resting, for binding up wounds from the fight for the nomination, for gearing up for action, and for planning campaign strategy. In recent elections, however, the candidates have not paused after the convention but launched directly into all-out campaigning. In 2008, the Democratic race became a marathon with Senators Obama and Clinton campaigning in nearly every state and

Democratic presidential nominee Barack Obama campaigned unceasingly throughout the summer and fall of 2008 in hopes of winning the election.

territory. McCain had already secured the nomination by March. This gave Obama some advantages in the general election as he was able to capitalize on late primaries and caucuses by easily carrying over his campaign organization into the general election. At the same time the long nomination fight generated some hard feeling among Hillary Clinton supporters and gave Obama little time to refresh himself before the general election contest.

Presidential Debates Televised presidential debates are a major feature of presidential elections. Presidential debates have come to be more of a joint appearance with opening and closing statements than a debate in which the candidates interact much with each other.

Since 1988, the nonpartisan Commission on Presidential Debates has sponsored and produced the presidential and vice presidential debates. The commission includes representatives from such neutral groups as the League of Women Voters. Before the commission became involved, there was often a protracted discussion about the format, the timing, and even whether to have debates. No detail seemed too small to the candidates' managers—whether the candidates would sit or stand, whether they would be able to ask each other questions, whether they would be allowed to bring notes, and whether a single journalist, a panel of reporters, or a group of citizens would ask the questions. By negotiating in advance many of the contentious details and arranging for debate locations, the commission now facilitates the presidential and vice presidential debates. The format of the 2008 presidential debates had one "town hall meeting" where the questions came from a group of citizens, which was preferred by McCain. The first and third debates had a journalist ask the questions, but with some encouragement of an exchange between the candidates. The Vice Presidential debate allowed for shorter answers without exchanges between candidates. Given the interest in Republican running mate Sarah Palin, the Vice Presidential debate had a large audience. Neither candidate made any major mistakes.

The 2008 presidential debates were widely watched and largely reinforced the candidate preferences of the viewers. Obama was seen as the "winner" by polls taken soon after all three debates. Neither nominee made a major mistake, and both candidates were able to state their positions and draw contrasts with their opponent. Obama in all three debates maintained a calm demeanor, even when it

Republican presidential nominee John McCain worked seemingly endless hours to attract voters during the 2008 campaign season.

The 2008 debate between the vice presidential candidates had a large audience. Prior to the debate, Republican nominee Sarah Palin had been criticized for her lack of knowledge in media interviews which added to the voter interest. Both Democrat Joe Biden and Palin made no major mistakes in the debate.

appeared McCain was trying to provoke him. McCain came out as more aggressive, especially in the third debate. But for voters who had not made up their minds, Obama made headway, denying McCain the chance to change the dynamic of the race. A recurrent theme in the debates was the economic crisis the country faced with home foreclosure, the collapse of large investment banks, and a looming recession. The economy became so central that in the last debate the war in Iraq was not mentioned by either candidate.

Minor party candidates often charge that those organizing debates are biased in favor of the two major parties. To be included in presidential debates, such candidates must have an average of 15 percent or higher in the five major polls the commission uses for this purpose. Candidates must also be legally eligible and on the ballot in enough states to be able to win at least 270 electoral votes.[60] In 2004 and 2008 Ralph Nader failed to meet these criteria for inclusion, as did both he and Patrick Buchanan in 2000. Neither Nader nor Libertarian Bob Barr was invited to participate in the 2008 presidential debates.[61] Including or excluding minor party candidates remains a contentious issue. Including them takes time away from the major party candidates, especially if two or more minor party candidates are invited. It may also reduce the likelihood of both major parties' candidates' participating. But excluding them raises issues of fairness and free speech.

Although some critics are quick to express their dissatisfaction with presidential candidates for being so concerned with makeup and rehearsed answers, and although the debates have not significantly affected the outcomes of elections, they have provided important opportunities for candidates to distinguish themselves and for the public to weigh their qualifications. Candidates who do well in these debates are at a great advantage. They have to be quick on their feet, seem knowledgeable but not overly rehearsed, and project a positive image. Most presidential candidates are adept at these skills.

You Are a Campaign Manager: Lead Obama to Battleground State Victory

Television and Radio Advertising Presidential candidates communicate with voters in a general election and in many primary elections through the media: broadcast television, radio and cable television, and satellite radio. 630,000 commercials were run across the country during the 2004 presidential election.[62] Radio and television ads are also widely used. 1.6 billion was spent on radio ads in 2004.[63] Compared to an estimated $623 million in 2000.[64]

HISTORY MAKERS

Henry George and the Secret Ballot

One of the elements of democracy we take for granted is the secrecy of the ballot, but for much of the nineteenth century, voters in the United States cast ballots printed and distributed by the political parties. They were on different-colored paper, and poll monitors could easily determine which party a voter supported by the color of the ballot he cast. Party machines often rewarded loyal supporters with jobs and other compensation. Parties could also stuff ballot boxes because the government did not know how many ballots had been printed.* Party-printed ballots also made it hard for people to vote for candidates from more than one party for different offices, what we call split-ticket voting.†

The person most responsible for the introduction of a "public" ballot (sometimes called the Australian ballot), which is printed by the government and provided to voters at the polls, was an economist and author named Henry George. The secret ballot made the following changes:

- Ballots were printed and distributed at government expense.
- Ballots contained the names of all legally nominated candidates.
- Ballots were distributed only by election officials at the polling place.
- Provisions were made for privacy and secrecy in casting ballots.

Kentucky was first to adopt the secret ballot in 1888. Massachusetts followed one year later. By 1910, nearly all states had adopted the secret ballot. Although it had many positive benefits, the secret ballot led to a decline in turnout. Political scientists attribute this decline to the diminished role of party bosses and the reduction in voting fraud.‡

George's efforts to secure the secret ballot started with a December 1871 article in *Overland Monthly.* In another article in the *North American Review*, George contended that the secret ballot would "be the greatest single reform possible."§ The author of the law establishing the secret ballot in Kentucky credited George's article in the *North American Review* with influencing him and his state. George and his supporters formed the United Labor Party, which encouraged adoption of the secret ballot, as did other groups. As we shift to new voting technologies in future elections, we should remember that an even more fundamental change was the introduction of secret ballots more than a century ago.‖

QUESTIONS

1. What core principles of fair elections do secret ballots foster?
2. What reforms could we adopt today that would make elections better?
3. How would you feel about voting if you voted as people did before the secret ballot?

*John C. Fortier and Norman J. Ornstein, "The Absentee Ballot and the Secret Ballot: Challenges for Election Reform," *University of Michigan Journal of Law Reform* 36 (Spring 2003), pp. 483–517.

†Jerrold G. Rusk, "The Effect of the Australian Ballot Reform on Split Ticket Voting: 1876–1908," *American Political Science Review* 64 (December 1970), pp. 1220–1238.

‡Fortier and Ornstein, "The Absentee Ballot and the Secret Ballot."

§Ibid.

‖L. E. Fredman, "The Introduction of the Australian Ballot in the United States," *Australian Journal of Politics and History* 13 (June 1967), pp. 204–220.

You Are a Campaign Manager: Seven Days to Victory —Obama's Last Minute Choices in the Election's Final Week

Close Calls in Presidential Elections

As with campaign activity generally—candidate visits, mail or phone calls about the candidates—the competitive or battleground states see much more activity. Candidates and their consultants believe that advertising on television and radio helps motivate people to vote and persuade voters to vote for them—or against their opponent. With the growth in cable television, candidates can target ads to particular audiences—people who watch the Golf Channel or Fox News, for instance. Political party committees and interest groups also run television and radio ads for and against candidates.

The Outcome Though each election is unique, politicians, pollsters, and political scientists have collected enough information to agree broadly on a number of basic factors they believe affect election outcomes. Whether the nation is prospering probably has the most to do with who wins a presidential election, but as we have noted, most voters vote on the basis of party and candidate appeal.[65] Who wins thus also depends on voter turnout, and here the strength of party organization and allied groups is important. The Democrats' long-standing advantage in the sheer number of people who identify themselves as Democrats has declined in recent years and is mitigated by higher voter turnout among Republicans. Republican candidates also usually have better access to money, which means they can run more television ads in more places and more often.

In 2008 the tables were turned and the Democratic nominee had a large advantage because he had raised so much more money than his Republican opponent. Obama outspent McCain in television advertising, campaign staffing, and get-out-the vote efforts. Obama had such a money advantage that he was able to purchase a primetime half-hour commerical slot on NBC, CBS and FOX six days before the election, at the cost of $1 million per slot.

ıs. The elec...
...nine whether state and federal la...
...der from one individual or party to another,
...ulminating event in electoral democracy.

critical in cl... had deployed th... launch legal challeng... machines and long lines for p... challenges many had anticipated... spread challenges to voters because of... issued photo identification. As we were rem... sarily the deciding vote in presidential elections... role to play, and the courts may have to de... been fairly applied. The peaceful transfe... especially after such contested electi...

Money in U.S. ...

Election campaigns... been controversi... parties, intere... a variety... interest... par...

...thods of obtaining the money have long ...ne from a candidate's own wealth, political ...ps. Money is contributed to candidates for ...oup identification and support and self-...ems from the possibility that candidates or ...vill decide it is more important to represent ... the voters. The potential corruption from ... concerns many observers of U.S. politics.

...ney on policy are not new. In 1925, respond-... cabinet member was convicted of accepting ... federal land in Wyoming and California for ...d the Corrupt Practices Act, which required ...tten in such a way as to exempt virtually all ...67

...ch persons associated with the Nixon cam-...headquarters to steal campaign documents ...dia scrutiny and congressional investigations ...r money from corporations and individuals had ...ccounts outside the country for political and cam-...tcry from these discoveries prompted Congress to enact ...ull largely regulate the financing of federal elections.

...n other campaign ex-... voter, ...f reformers in recent ...BCRA) in 2002. ...of both parties for ...ending that were ...nding limits by ...nation phase ...p to $250. ...spending ...t for the ...didates ...s that ...ged, ...m,

LEARNING **OBJECTIVE**

Assess the influence of money in congressional and presidential elections and evaluate the main approaches to campaign finance reform.

...eform

...have tried three basic strategies to prevent abuse in political contributions: ...posing limits on giving, receiving, and spending political money; (2) requiring public ...closure of the sources and uses of political money; and (3) giving governmental subsidies to presidential candidates, campaigns, and parties to reduce their reliance on campaign contributors. Recent campaign finance laws have tended to use all three strategies.

You Are a Campaign Manager: McCain Navigates Campaign Financing—Rules and Trends Regarding the "Mother's Milk" of Politics

The Federal Election Campaign Act In 1971, Congress passed the Federal Election Campaign Act (FECA), which limited amounts that candidates for federal office could spend on advertising, required disclosure of the sources of campaign funds and how they are spent, and required political action committees to register with the government and report all major contributions and expenditures.

In 1974, Watergate helped push Congress to amend the FECA in what was the most sweeping campaign reform measure in U.S. history. These amendments established more realistic limits on contributions and spending by candidates and party committees, strengthened disclosure laws, created the **Federal Election Commission (FEC)** to administer the new laws, and provided for partial public funding for presidential primaries and a grant to major party presidential candidates in the general election.

Federal Election Commission (FEC)
A commission created by the 1974 amendments to the Federal Election Campaign Act to administer election reform laws. It consists of six commissioners appointed by the president and confirmed by the Senate. Its duties include overseeing disclosure of campaign finance information, public funding of presidential elections, and enforcing contribution limits.

...ne, and to sp...
...ongressional investigation...
...inance in the 1996 election cycle reinfor...
...made raising and spending soft money a major pri...
the money in targeted contests or battleground states. From the ...
the advertising purchased by soft money was indistinguishable fro...
penditures.[74] Banning soft money became the primary objective o...
years and led to the passage of the **Bipartisan Campaign Reform Act (**...

One of the success stories of FECA was that presidential candidates ...
20 years chose to accept the limitations on fund raising and campaign sp...
part of the public financing provisions. Candidates could have had no spe...
bypassing the public subsidizing and matching funds. During the nomi...
candidates receive federal matching funds for campaign contributions ...
Accepting the federal matching funds means candidates accept state-by-state ...
limits for the caucuses and the primaries. Major party candidates receive a gra...
general election but also stop their own fund raising. Until 2000, presidential can...
(except a few wealthy, self-financed candidates) accepted the voluntary limitation...
come with partial public financing of presidential nomination campaigns. That chan...
however, when George W. Bush, who raised more than $125 million for his campai...
declined federal matching funds in the 2000 primaries but accepted the public fundin...
grant of $67.5 million for the general election. In 2004, having raised more than $366 million, he again turned down the matching funds in the primaries, as did two of the Democrats, Howard Dean and John Kerry (Kerry raised more than $322 million and Dean raised $60 million).[75] In 2004, both Bush and Kerry accepted the federal general election grant of roughly $75 million, along with the general election spending limit.

As noted, in 2008 the number of candidates in both parties turning down the matching funds in the primaries increased, while some candidates such as John Edwards accepted them. In the primary election phase of 2008, neither Hilary Clinton nor Barack Obama accepted matching funds (see Figure 9–5). McCain at one point said he would accept public matching funds in the nomination phase but later reversed himself. In the general election phase, McCain accepted the $84 million public financing grant. Clinton raised $229.4 million before dropping out of the race with $22.5 million in debt.[76] Obama who originally indicated he would accept public funding in the general election, abandoned that position and ended up raised $639 million.[77] Obama was the first major-party candidate since the system was created to reject taxpayers' money for the general election and ultimately had access to much higher funds for use in his campaign.

soft money
Money raised in unlimited amounts by political parties for party-building purposes. Now largely illegal except for limited contributions to state or local parties for voter registration and get-out-the-vote efforts

hard money
Political contributions given to a party, candidate, or interest group that are limited in amount and fully disclosed. Raising such limited funds is harder than raising unlimited funds, hence the term "hard money."

Bipartisan Campaign Reform Act (BCRA)
Largely banned party soft money, restored a long-standing prohibition on corporations and labor unions for using general treasury funds for electoral purposes, and narrowed the definition of issue advocacy.

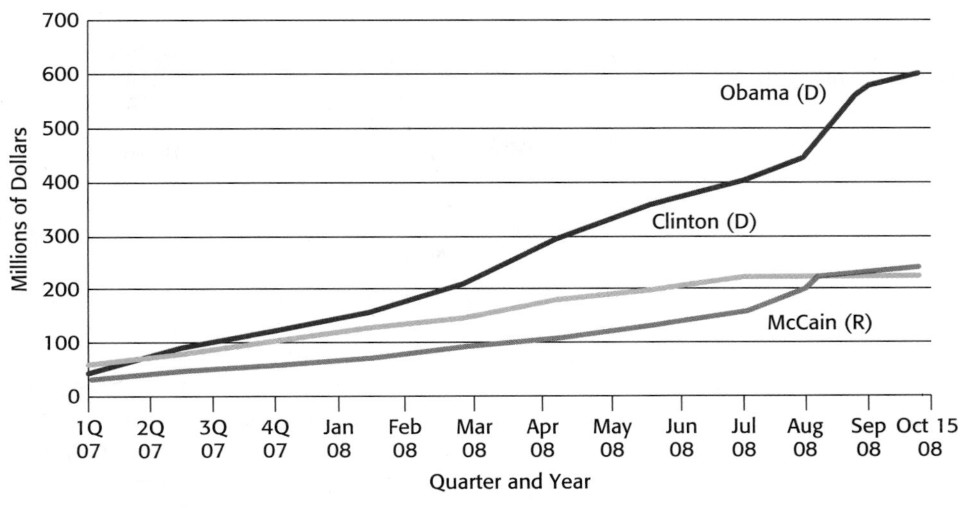

FIGURE 9–5
Presidential Primary Cumulative Receipts, 2007–2008 (millions of dollars).

SOURCE: Center for Responsive Politics, "Banking on Becoming President," www.opensecrets.org/pres08/index.php?cycle=2008; and Campaign Finance Institute, "Releases and Analysis," 2007 and 2008 press releases, www.cfinst.org/pr.

The Bipartisan Campaign Reform Act (BCRA) After years of legislative debate, Senate filibusters, and even a presidential veto, Congress passed and President Bush signed into law in 2002 the Bipartisan Campaign Reform Act (BCRA). This legislation, often known as the McCain–Feingold bill after its two chief sponsors in the Senate, was written with the understanding that it would immediately be challenged in court—and it was. The Supreme Court upheld most of the provisions of BCRA in *McConnell v. FEC*.[78] BCRA is best understood as incremental change. It kept the FEC with its six commissioners appointed by the president with the consent of the Senate, and continued the public financing of presidential campaigns with funds from the income tax checkoff. It left unchanged the limits on spending by candidates for presidential nominations (on a state-by-state basis and in total) and in the presidential general elections for those candidates who accept public funding. It also continued public subsidies for the two national parties' convention expenses and allowed subsidies for minor parties that had polled 5 percent of the total vote in the previous election. While recognizing that individuals are free to spend unlimited amounts on their own campaigns, BCRA provided increased contribution limits for candidates running against an opponent who was spending substantial amounts of his or her own money, a provision later declared unconstitutional in the Supreme Court. Finally, it left unchanged the limits on the amounts the national parties can spend on presidential campaigns and on individual congressional and senatorial campaigns.[79]

The hard money limits in BCRA for 2007–2008 for individuals giving to candidates are $2,300 for each primary, general, or runoff election. Runoffs are rare in the United States, so for most individuals the contribution limit to a candidate in 2007–2008 was $4,600. Individuals can give $10,000 per cycle to a PAC or federal or state party committee. Contribution limits under BCRA are indexed to inflation. Individuals also have an aggregate two-year election cycle limit. In 2007–2008 they could give up to $42,700 to federal candidates, and up to $65,500 to national party committees, federal PACs, and state party federal accounts. Of the $65,500, only $42,700 can be given to federal PACs and state party federal accounts. Individuals who want to give the maximum total of $108,200 allowable in hard money in the 2007–2008 election cycle must thus allocate money to candidates, party committees, and PACs under the constraints noted.[80] BCRA thus gave party committees an opportunity to thus appeal to "max out" donors, something both parties pursued.

Soft Money The most frequently given justification for BCRA was the need to ban soft money. Soft money, as noted, had been allowed initially to help parties with such party-building activities as voter registration drives, mailings, and generic party advertising. The parties came to use it to influence the election of federal candidates by transferring funds to state parties, which then ran ads for and against local federal candidates. Both parties made raising soft money a high priority, and soft money spending rose dramatically. All national party committees combined raised more than $509 million of soft money in the 1999–2000 election cycle, up from $110 million adjusted for inflation in 1991–1992.[81] In 2001–2002, the party committees raised more than $495 million combined in soft money.[82]

Until 1998, soft money had been more important in presidential contests than in congressional contests. The most dramatic growth in 2000 and 2002 came among Senate Democrats. Figure 9–6 plots the surge in soft money funds for the

FIGURE 9–6
Congressional Campaign Committee Soft Money Spending, 1994–2002.

SOURCE: Federal Election Commission, "Party Committees Raise More Than $1 Billion in 2002–2003," press release, March 20, 2002, www.fec.gov, April 29, 2003. Adjusted by CPI, ftp://ftp.bls.gov/pub/special.requests/cpi/cpiai.txt, January 15, 2003.

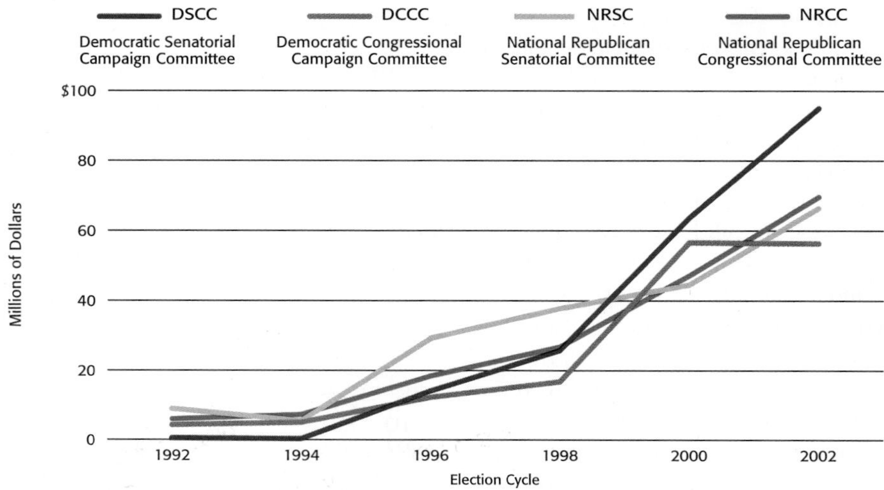

NOTE: The totals for each party do not equal the sum of the party committee receipts because the numbers provided by the FEC have been adjusted to account for transfers between party committees so as not to double-count money in the total receipts.

four congressional campaign committees. The 2002 election cycle also saw extraordinary soft money activity by all party committees. Overall, the parties raised nearly as much soft money in 2001–2002 as they raised in 1999–2000, which was a presidential election cycle. When we compare 2002 with the previous midterm year, 1998, we see soft money more than doubling.

Soft money enabled large donors to be major players in campaign finance. It also strengthened the power of the national party committees, which allocated the money to state parties and indirectly to candidates. To the Supreme Court, which upheld the BCRA soft money ban, one of the major problems with soft money was that it purchased access to elected officials, and with that access came influence and the possibility or appearance of corruption.[83]

BCRA banned most forms of soft money. All soft money contributions to national party committees were banned, as was soft money spending by state parties for or against federal candidates. However, BCRA permits state and local party committees to raise and spend limited amounts of soft money for voter registration and get-out-the-vote efforts. Such activities may be funded with soft money contributions of no more than $10,000 per individual or group to a state or local party committee. The funds raised under this provision of BCRA are called "Levin Funds," after Michigan senator Carl Levin, who sponsored this as an amendment. Compared to other kinds of spending, this activity by state and local parties has been relatively small.[84]

Issue Advocacy Advertising Another way the post-Watergate election reforms were undermined was with the upsurge of interest groups running election ads. These ads typically attack a candidate, but the sponsor can avoid disclosure and contribution limitations because the ads do not use electioneering language, such as "vote for" or "vote against" a specific candidate. The Supreme Court in its 1976 *Buckley v. Valeo* decision on FECA defined election communication as "communications containing express words of advocacy of election or defeat, such as 'vote for,' 'elect,' 'support,' 'cast your ballot for,' 'Smith for Congress,' 'vote against,' 'defeat,' 'reject.'"[85] Communications that did not use these "magic words" were defined as issue ads, not subject to disclosure required by FECA restrictions. Not surprisingly, interest groups and media consultants found a way to communicate an electioneering message without using the magic words.

issue advocacy
Promoting a particular position or an issue paid for by interest groups or individuals but not candidates. Much issue advocacy is often electioneering for or against a candidate, avoiding words like "vote for," and until 2004 had not been subject to any regulation.

The 1996 election saw a surge in **issue advocacy.** Money spent on issue advocacy ads is unlimited and undisclosed because it presumably deals with issues, not candidates. Issue ad spending in some U.S. House races exceeded $1 million in some elections. A prominent example of issue advocacy against a candidate was two Texans who formed a group named Republicans for Clean Air and ran ads in some 2000 presidential primaries attacking John McCain.[86] In the 1998, 2000, and 2002 elections, businesses, labor unions, health maintenance organizations, environmental groups, the Business Roundtable, pro- and antigun groups, pro- and antiabortion groups, and the pharmaceutical industry ran issue ads.

Campaign issue advertisements sponsored by interest groups are largely indistinguishable from candidate-run ads.[87] The same was also true for party ads paid for with soft money. In some competitive contests, interest groups and parties spent more money than the candidates did themselves. Typically these party and group ads are even more negative than the ads run by candidates. Often the group identified as paying for the ad gave itself a nondescript name like "Citizens for . . ." or "Coalition Against. . . ." Many candidates have disavowed ads intended to help them and hurt their opponent. One of the problems with noncandidate ads in an election context is determining who is accountable for the content of the ads.

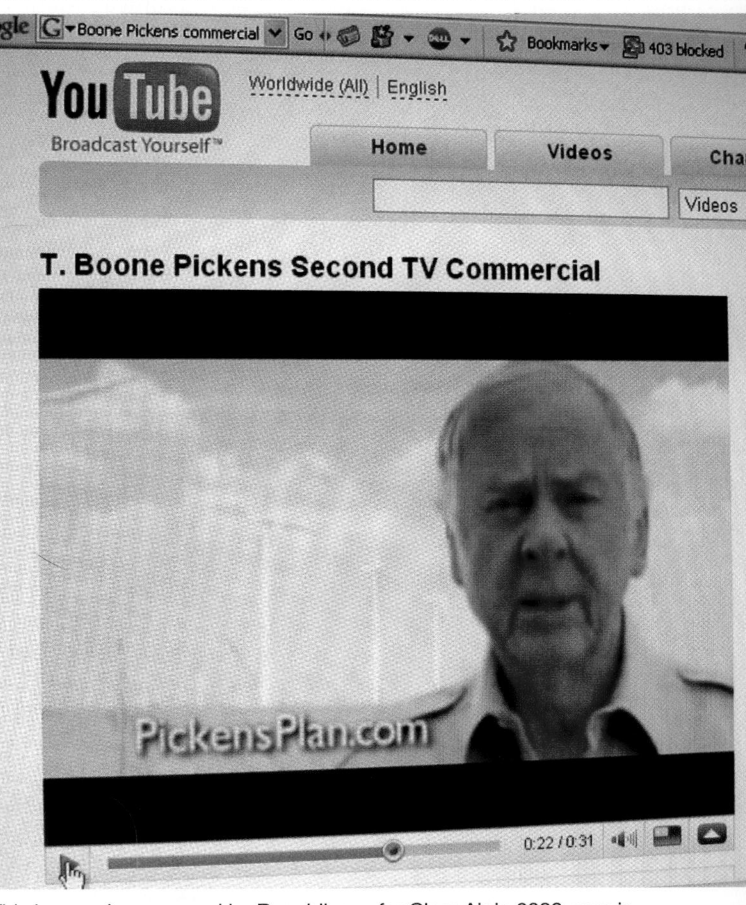

This issue ad, sponsored by Republicans for Clear Air in 2000, was intended to hurt John McCain's election chances rather than advocate a particular environmental policy.

BCRA only partially addressed the issue ads loophole of 1996–2002. It redefined "electioneering communications" to include much of what claimed to be issue ads. Under BCRA an electioneering communication is "any broadcast, cable, or satellite communication which refers to a clearly identified candidate for Federal office [and in the case of House and Senate candidates is targeted to their state or district], is made within 60 days before a general, special, or runoff election for the office sought by the candidate; or 30 days before a primary or preference election."[88] BCRA prohibited unions and corporations from using treasury funds to pay for broadcast ads that fit this definition.

In a 2007 decision the Supreme Court in a 5-to-4 decision declared the BCRA "electioneering communication" definition too broad and substituted a new definition that an ad is considered "express advocacy" only if there is no reasonable way to interpret it except "as an appeal to vote for or against a certain candidate."[89] The court also struck the BCRA ban on unions and corporations using their general funds on ads that are "genuine issue ads." In 2008, unions made greater use of this new interpretation than did corporations. Unions like the Service Employees International Union (SEIU) were active in several battleground states. Corporations were less inclined than unions to exploit the 2007 court ruling but did contribute substantially to the Chamber of Commerce's large scale effort to counteract the unions.

BCRA does not extend to other forms of interest group campaigning such as mail, phone calls, e-mail, and get-out-the-vote efforts. Groups can spend substantial amounts on these activities.[90]

Interest Groups and Campaign Finance

Section 527 and 501(c) Organizations One predictable consequence of BCRA's ban on soft money, while leaving open the possibility of some electioneering communications, was increased interest-group electioneering through what are called 527 or 501(c) groups. These groups get their names from the section of the Internal Revenue Service code under which they are organized. Section **527 organizations** existed long before BCRA, but after BCRA these groups had an incentive to expand their efforts. Section 527 groups are formed to influence elections. Section 501(c) groups include nonprofit groups whose purpose is not

527 organizations
Interest groups organized under Section 527 of the Internal Revenue Code may advertise for or against candidates. If their source of funding is corporations or unions, they have some restrictions on broadcast advertising.

political. Money given to (Section 501(c)3 groups) is tax deductible, and they can engage in nonpartisan voter registration and turnout efforts but cannot endorse candidates. Other 501(c) groups can and are expressly political, and money contributed to them is not tax deductible. Disclosure of contributions to these groups and spending by them are less frequent than for Section 527 groups, political parties, or PACs.[91]

BCRA restricted the way 527 groups communicate with voters. Any 527 organization wishing to broadcast an electioneering communication within one month of a primary or two months of a general election must not use corporate or union treasury funds; it must report the expenditures associated with the broadcast; and it must disclose the sources of all funds it has received since January 1 of the preceding calendar year. Although contribution sources are restricted in this case, contribution amounts are not. Nor are people spending their own money individually, and not as part of a group. The Supreme Court permitted this exemption on free speech grounds.

In 2004, the first post-BCRA election, the best funded 527 organization was America Coming Together (ACT), which raised and spent an estimated $76 million in presidential battleground states in 2004. Much of the early money for ACT came from wealthy investor George Soros. ACT helped organize many other interest groups to register and mobilize voters. A related group, the Media Fund, spent $54 million in ads against President Bush up until 60 days before the election.[92] The advent of groups such as ACT and the Media Fund, while benefiting John Kerry and the Democrats, constitutes a shift in power toward groups and away from candidates and parties. Republicans, in part because they were in power and had the fund-raising abilities of President Bush, did not see as many allied 527 groups as did the Democrats. Some examples of Republican 527 groups in 2004 included Progress for America, Leadership Forum, and the Republican Governors Association. The 527 group that may have had the greatest impact on the 2004 campaign was Swift Boat Veterans for Truth, which attacked Senator Kerry's war record. The modest initial budget for this group's ads generated widespread news coverage, especially on cable news stations. The message of the ads cut to the core of the persona that Kerry had presented at the Democratic National Convention. President Bush was not drawn into the controversy, but former senator Bob Dole's assertion that there might be something to the Swift Boat Veterans charges added to the attention the group received.

You Are a Campaign Manager: Navigating Negativity—Help Obama Handle Negative Attacks

The attack by the Swift Boat Veterans was effective in part because of the lack of a strong response and rebuttal from Kerry, his campaign, or his party. Nearly two years later, Kerry himself acknowledged his mistake by saying he should have responded and "we should have put more money behind it. . . . I take responsibility for it; it was my mistake. They spent something like $30 million, and we didn't. That's just a terrible imbalance when somebody's lying about you."[93] Given the effectiveness of this attack on Kerry, similar attacks can be expected in the future, and candidates will likely respond much more aggressively to these attacks than Kerry did. In the 2008 campaign there was speculation about how different candidates could be attacked in the same fashion as Kerry was. These attacks led to a term, being "swift-boated."[94]

Without a presidential election in 2006, some 527 organizations shifted their focus and funds from federal races to state and local issues, where many groups felt they could be more effective. At the federal level, groups selected key battleground areas and often communicated with voters in targeted ways. Unions, the Chamber of Commerce, environmental groups, and pro-choice groups were all very active in this election.

Given the important role outside groups played in 2004 in attacking John Kerry and promoting George Bush as well in voter registration and mobilization many anticipated they would play an even larger role in 2008. While some groups ran ads for and against the presidential candidates, no group had the impact that Swift Boat Veterans for Truth or Progress for America had in 2004. Donors and groups that would have run independent ads supporting Obama and opposing McCain took Obama seriously when he said publicly he did not want groups running ads. The presence of such groups and ads in 2004 was one reason Obama gave for turning down public financing and spending limits saying he would need to have the extra funds to counter any claims by outside groups. McCain, a champion of campaign finance reform had also long opposed outside groups spending unlimited amounts of money for and against candidates and that may have deterred these groups from playing a major role on his side. In terms of voter mobilization, outside groups remained important in 2008. On the Democratic side a group called America Votes coordinated the voter mobilization efforts. On the Republican side business, pro-life, and gun rights groups were active. Some groups like the Chamber of Commerce invested heavily in supporting Senate candidates; in the case of the Chamber these were mostly Republicans. In competitive House and Senate races groups like the League of Conservation Voters, Defenders of Wildlife and Planned Parenthood were active, often for Democrats.

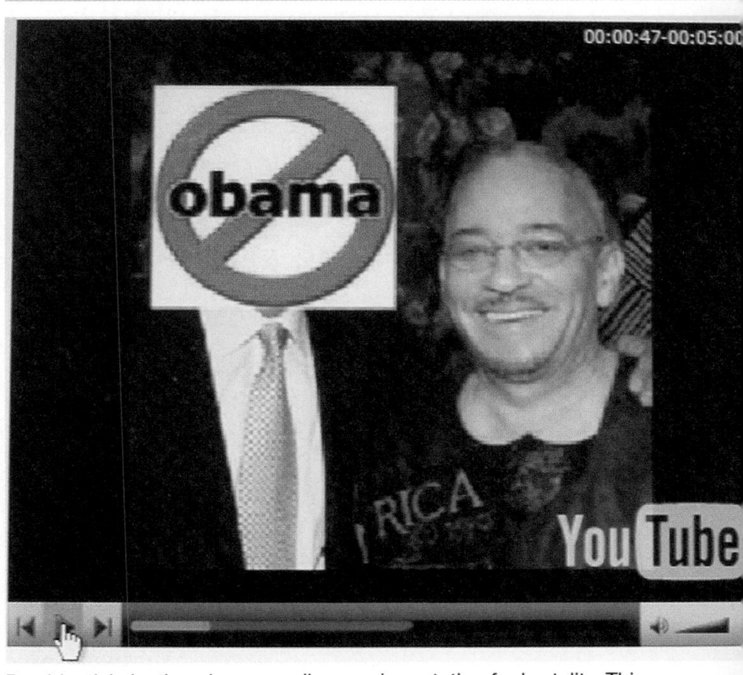

Presidential elections have a well-earned reputation for brutality. This advertisement exploits the relationship between Barack Obama and his former pastor Jeremiah Wright in order to raise fears of "Obama" being too extreme for most voters.

Independent Expenditures The Supreme Court made clear in its ruling on FECA in 1976 that individuals and groups have the right to spend as much money as they wish for or against candidates as long as they are truly independent of the candidate and as long as the money is not corporate or union treasury money. Some groups such as the American Medical Association, the National Education Association, and the National Rifle Association have long tried to influence elections independently rather than through a party committee or a candidate's campaign (see Chapter 6). As discussed in Chapter 7, the Supreme Court extended to political parties the same rights to make independent expenditures afforded to groups and individuals.[95]

Individuals have made large independent expenditures, such as Michael Goland, a California entrepreneur who spent $1.1 million against Senator Charles Percy (R-Ill.) in the 1984 election because he considered Percy unfriendly to Israel. In the 2000 presidential election, Stephen Adams, owner of an outdoor advertising firm, spent $2 million to support George W. Bush.[96] In 2004, billionaire George Soros, who gave millions to 527 organizations opposing the reelection of Bush, also spent $2.3 million in independent expenditures against the president. In 2008 groups did not have individual donors giving very large amounts to them as was the case in 2004.

BCRA does not constrain **independent expenditures** by groups, political parties, or individuals, as long as the expenditures by those individuals, parties, or groups are independent of the candidate and fully disclosed to the FEC.

Continuing Problems with Campaign Finance

The continuing problems with federal election fund raising are easy to identify: dramatically escalating costs, a growing dependence on PAC money for congressional candidates, decreasing visibility and competitiveness of challengers (especially for the House), and the advantage wealthy individuals have in funding their own campaigns. BCRA reduced the danger of large contributions influencing lawmakers directly or indirectly through political parties. But large contributions can still influence the outcome of elections, as 527 and other groups have demonstrated.

Rising Costs of Campaigns The U.S. ideal that anyone—even a person of modest or little wealth—can run for public office and hope to win has become more of a myth than a reality.[97] And rising costs also mean that incumbents spend more time raising funds and therefore less time legislating and representing their districts. Since the FECA became law in 1972, total expenditures by candidates for the House of Representatives have more than doubled after controlling for inflation, and they have risen even more in Senate elections (see Table 9–2). One reason for escalating costs is television. Organizing and running a campaign is expensive, limiting the field of challengers to those who have their own resources or are willing to spend more than a year raising money from interest groups and individuals.

Declining Competition Unless something is done to help finance challengers, incumbents will continue to have the advantage in seeking reelection. Nothing in BCRA addresses this problem. Challengers in both parties are typically underfunded.

independent expenditures
Money spent by individuals or groups not associated with candidates to elect or defeat candidates for office.

TABLE 9–2 Average Campaign Expenditures of Candidates for the House of Representatives, 1988–2006 General Election (in Thousands of 2008 Dollars)

	Incumbent	Challenger	Open Seat
Republican			
1988	425.6	104.4	504.0
1990	414.0	115.2	471.6
1992	571.1	196.3	379.0
1994	478.8	252.9	666.9
1996	767.7	219.8	654.2
1998	725.4	270.7	843.4
2000	911.5	261.7	1289.9
2002	922.4	201.1	1234.9
2004	1129.5	259.3	1311.1
2006	1574.1	268.5	1422.4
Democrat			
1988	372.6	148.5	464.9
1990	418.0	114.9	556.9
1992	629.0	167.2	501.4
1994	630.4	168.4	605.0
1996	594.4	308.2	653.2
1998	584.8	253.3	778.2
2000	765.1	372.8	1090.4
2002	844.7	336.9	1079.6
2004	963.4	299.5	993.6
2006	1010.4	574.5	1465.6

SOURCE: Federal Election Commission, "FEC Reports on Congressional Financial Activity for 2000," press release, May 15, 2001; and Federal Election Commission, "Congressional Candidates Spend $1.16 Billion During 2003–2004," press release, June 9, 2005.

House Democratic challengers averaged $147,300 in spending in 2004,[98] while incumbents in both parties spent an average of about $1 million each in 2004.[99] In today's expensive campaigns, candidates are generally invisible if they have less than $200,000 to spend.

The high cost of campaigns dampens competition by discouraging individuals from running for office. Potential challengers look at the fund-raising advantages incumbents enjoy—at incumbents' campaign war chests carried over from previous campaigns that can reach $1 million or more and at the time it will take them to raise enough money to launch a minimal campaign—and they decide not to run. Moreover, unlike incumbents, whose salaries are being paid while they are campaigning and raising money, most challengers have to support themselves and their families throughout the campaign, which for a seat in Congress lasts roughly two years.

Increasing Dependence on PACs for Congressional Incumbents Where does the money come from to finance these expensive election campaigns? For most House incumbents, it comes from political action committees (PACs), which we discussed in Chapter 6. In recent years, nearly two out of five incumbents seeking reelection raised more money from PACs than from individuals (see Figure 9–7).[100] Senators get a smaller percentage of their campaign funds from PACs, but because they spend so much more, they need to raise even more money from PACs than House incumbents do. PACs are pragmatic, giving largely to incumbents. Challengers receive little because PACs do not want to offend politicians in power. BCRA raised the individual contribution limit to a candidate in the two-year campaign cycle to $4,600, but did not raise PAC contribution limits above the pre-BCRA levels of $10,000 for the primary and

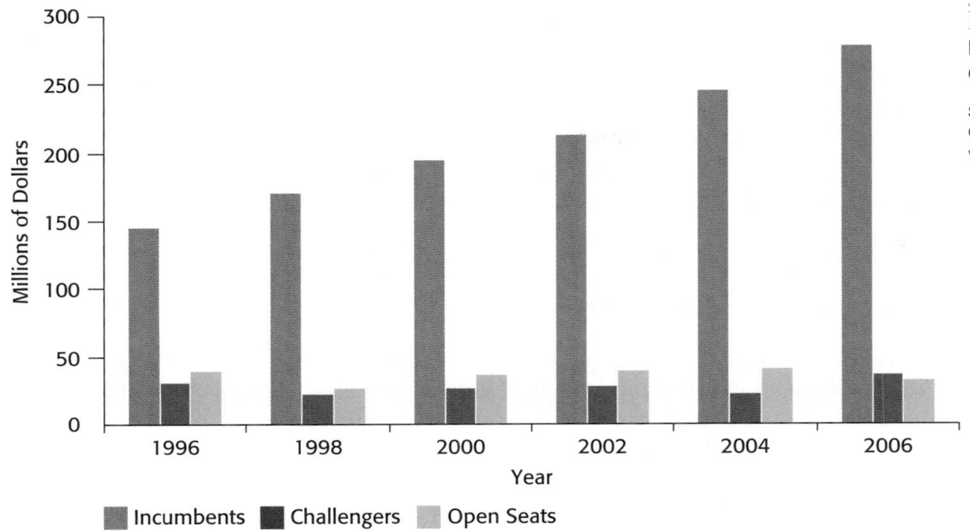

FIGURE 9–7
PAC Contributions to Congressional Candidates, 1996–2006.

SOURCE: Federal Election Commission, "PAC Activity Continues Climb in 2006," press release, October 5, 2007, www.fec.gov/press/press.shtml.

general election combined. Incumbents will continue to rely on PACs because relatively few individuals have the means to give $4,600 to a campaign. It also often takes less time to raise money from PACs than from individuals.

To be sure, PACs and individuals spend money on campaigns for many reasons. Most of them want certain laws to be passed or repealed, certain funds to be appropriated, or certain administrative decisions to be rendered. At a minimum, they want access to officeholders and a chance to talk with members before key votes.

Defenders of PACs point out that there is no demonstrable relationship between contributions and legislators' votes. But influence in the legislative process depends on access to staff and members of Congress, and most analysts agree that campaign contributions give donors extraordinary access. PACs influence the legislative process in other ways as well. Their access helps them structure the legislative agenda with friendly legislators and influence the drafting of legislation or amendments to existing bills. These are all advantages that people outside PACs do not have.

Democracy and the Internet

Candidates' Personal Wealth Campaign finance legislation cannot constitutionally restrict rich candidates—the Rockefellers, the Kennedys, the Perots, the Clintons, the Romneys—from spending heavily on their own campaigns. Big money can make a big difference, and wealthy candidates can afford to spend big money. In presidential politics, this advantage can be most meaningful before the primaries begin. The personal wealth advantage also applies to congressional races. The 2000 New Jersey U.S. Senate race, for example, set new records for a candidate's personal spending in an election. Wall Street investment banker Jon Corzine, a newcomer to elections, spent a total of $60 million, $35 million of it on the primary alone.[101] Corzine was elected to the U.S. Senate and later spent another $45 million of his own money on his successful 2005 gubernatorial election in New Jersey.[102] BCRA includes a millionaire's provision that the Supreme Court upheld in *McConnell v. FEC.* The provision allows candidates running against self-financed opponents to have higher contribution limits from individuals or parties contributing to their campaigns.

After successfully running a self-financed campaign for the Senate, John Corzine spent millions of his own money on a successful bid for the governship of New Jersey.

Growth in Individual Contributions and Use of the Internet to Fund Campaigns BCRA made individuals more important as sources of money to candidates because it increased the amount they could give and indexed those limits to inflation. In the election cycles since BCRA took effect, there has been substantial growth in individual contributions, especially to the Democrats, who once were more reliant on soft money. As we've noted in this chapter, the growth in individual contributions to both parties has been pronounced at the large and small donor levels.

Another development that has made individual donors more important is the Internet. Starting in 2000 with the McCain presidential campaign and then expanding with the Howard Dean candidacy for presidency in 2004, individuals started giving to candidates via the Internet. But it was the Obama campaign in 2008 that demonstrated the extraordinary power of the Internet as a means to reach donors and a way for people to contribute to a candidate. As former senator Tom Daschle said, the Internet "is an evolution away from Washington's control, away from the power that big money and big donors used to have a monopoly on."[103] It is clear that the Internet has the potential to change the way campaigns are funded.

Improving Elections

A combination of party rules and state laws determines how we choose nominees for president. Reformers agree that the current process is flawed but disagree over which aspects should be changed. Concern over how we choose presidents now centers on three issues:[104] How we fund presidential elections; the number, timing, and representativeness of presidential primaries and caucuses; and the role of the electoral college, including the possibility that a presidential election may be thrown into the House of Representatives.

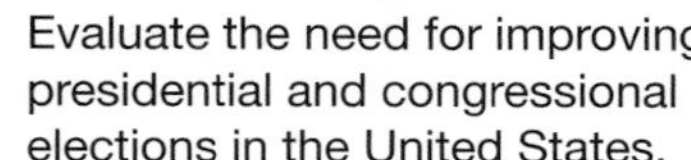

6 Evaluate the need for improving presidential and congressional elections in the United States.

Reforming Campaign Finance

The incremental reforms of BCRA and the subsequent Supreme Court decisions have not resolved the issues of campaign finance. Among the unresolved issues are how presidential campaigns will be financed, the role of Section 527 and 501(c) groups, the adequacy of disclosure, and the long-term strength and viability of the political parties. More broadly, the FEC's inability to reach decisions because of its partisan deadlock, as demonstrated by its inaction on Section 527 groups, has helped generate growing pressure to reform the agency.

Campaign Finance Regulations

The 2004 election cycle, with its substantial interest group activity through Section 527 and 501(c) organizations, was seen by those who favor deregulation of campaign finance as another example of the impossibility of limiting money in elections. This school of thought will continue to push for disclosure as the regulatory aim of government in this area.

Another group of reformers will press for more aggressive reforms than those found in BCRA. Included in this agenda will be reining in the 527 and 501(c) groups, restructuring the public financing of presidential elections to sustain this element of FECA, and possibly extending public financing of congressional elections. Both sides are likely to agree that the FEC needs change but will not agree on how to change it.

Reforming the Nominating Process

Iowa Caucuses

In 2008, the importance of voters in early primary or caucus states such as Iowa and New Hampshire 2008 again generated controversy. Moreover, these early states are not broadly representative of the country or of their respective parties. Voters in primaries and caucuses also tend to be more ideological than voters generally, a further bias in the current nominating process. As noted, the relative representation of primaries and caucuses was debated by Barack Obama and the Clintons and will likely be an enduring topic for discussion by party reformers. The 2008 contest pushed to the forefront controversy over whether the Democrats' proportionality rule made it more difficult to have a winner emerge from the process. Finally, the role of superdelegates in determining the 2008 nominee raised concerns about their role compared to delegates selected through a democratic process.

Only some of these concerns are new. What would the critics substitute for state presidential primaries (see Figure 9–8)? Some argue in favor of a *national presidential primary* that would take the form of a single nationwide election, probably held in May or September, or separate state primaries held in all the states on the same day.[105] Supporters contend that a one-shot national presidential primary (though a runoff might be necessary) would be simple, direct, and representative. It would cut down the wear-and-tear on

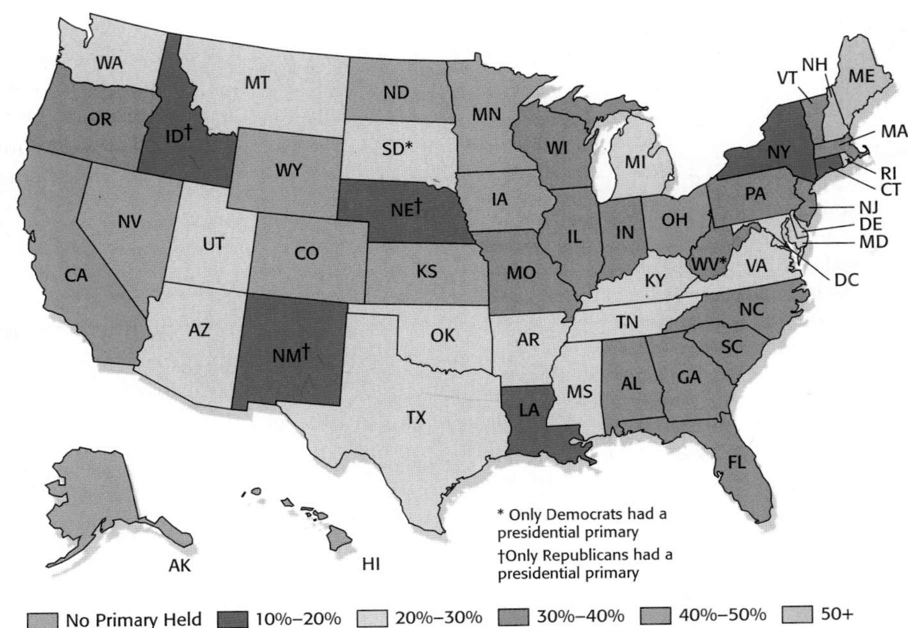

FIGURE 9–8
Voter Turnout in the 2008 Presidential Primaries.

SOURCE: Michael McDonald, "2008 Presidential Primary Turnout Rates," United States Election Project at George Mason University, at elections.gmu.edu/Voter_Turnout_2008_primaries.htm.

candidates, and the media coverage would attract a large turnout. Opponents argue that such a reform would make the present system even worse. It would enhance the role of showmanship and gamesmanship, and because it would be enormously expensive, it would hurt the chances of candidates who lack strong financial backing.

A more modest proposal is to hold *regional primaries*, possibly at two- or three-week intervals across the country. Regional primaries might bring more coherence to the process and encourage more emphasis on issues of regional concern. But such primaries would retain most of the disadvantages of the present system—especially the emphasis on money and media. Clearly, they would give an advantage to candidates from whatever region held the first primary, and this advantage would encourage regional candidates and might increase polarization among sections of the country. In recent years, many states have sought to move their primaries to the week(s) soon after the New Hampshire primary.

You Are an Informed Voter Helping Your Classmates Decide How to Vote

A different proposal is to drastically reduce the number of presidential primaries and make more use of the caucus system. The turnout of voters in Democratic caucuses in 2008 shows that participation can be high, and the time participants spent discussing candidates and issues shows that such participation can be thoughtful and informed. However, 2008 was unusual in its highly competitive prolonged competition. If more states adopted caucuses, their turnout would not likely be as high as in 2008 because they would lack the media and candidate attention that came that year. In caucus states, candidates are more dependent on convincing political activists, who will show up for a political meeting. By relying on party meetings to select delegates, the caucus system would also, some say, enhance the role of the party.[106]

Given the problems with the current nomination process, why has it not been reformed? Part of the answer is strong resistance from the states that benefit from the current system. In our federal system, imposing a national or regional primary means those states would lose power.

Does the present nominating process help or hurt candidates and parties? News coverage of candidates in nomination contests allows them to evaluate the candidates' political qualities and their abilities to organize campaigns; communicate through the media; stand up under pressure; avoid making mistakes (or recover if they do make them); adjust their appeals to shifting events and to different regions of the country; control their staffs as well as make good use of them; and be decisive, articulate, resilient, humorous, informed, and ultimately successful in winning votes. In short,

YOU WILL DECIDE Should We Establish a National Presidential Primary?

States that have their caucuses or conventions early in the presidential selection process get more attention and have generally had a greater say in selecting the presidential candidates. For several election cycles prior to 2008, many states held presidential primaries after the nominee had effectively been selected. Continuing a trend from past election cycles, several states moved up their primary or caucus dates in 2008. The ordering of the states, with Iowa and New Hampshire first, has been disputed by other states that have proposed either a national primary or a set of regional primaries.

Another criticism of the current system is that the states asserting a claim to going first are not representative of their party or the country. Yet another problem is the threat of one party's voters participating in another's primary in hopes of nominating a weak candidate or prolonging the primary contest, such as when Rush Limbaugh urged Republicans, through his "Operation Chaos," to vote for Hillary Clinton to draw out the 2008 Democratic race for as long as possible. A national primary would give all U.S. voters an equal say in who their party nominee would be. Should we establish a national presidential primary?

supporters of the current system claim, primaries test candidates on the very qualities they must exhibit in the presidency.[107] The protracted 2008 Democratic nomination also meant that both Obama and Clinton registered and activated votes in most states and built a network of volunteers ready to go to work for them in the general election.

Reforming the Electoral College

The Florida ballot counting and recounting after the 2000 election and the fact that the winner of the popular vote did not become president prompted a national debate on the electoral college. The most frequently proposed reform is *direct popular election* of the president. Presidents would be elected directly by the voters, just as governors are, and the electoral college and individual electors would be abolished. Such proposals usually provide that if no candidate receives at least 40 percent of the total popular vote, a *runoff election* would be held between the two contenders with the most votes. Supporters argue that direct election would give every voter the same weight in the presidential balloting in accordance with the one-person, one-vote doctrine. Plus, each voter would feel that his or her vote counts, even Republican voters in Massachusetts and Democratic voters in Utah. Winners would take on more legitimacy because their victories would reflect the will of the voters.

The Electoral College: Campaign Consequences and Mapping the Results

Opponents contend that the plan would further undermine federalism, encourage unrestrained majority rule and hence political extremism, and hurt the most populous and competitive states, which would lose some of their present influence. Others fear that the plan would make presidential campaigns more remote from the voters; candidates might stress television and give up their forays into shopping centers and city malls.[108]

From time to time, Congress considers proposals for a constitutional amendment to elect presidents directly.[109] Such proposals seldom get far, however, because of strong opposition from those who believe they may be disadvantaged by such a change, especially small states and minority groups whose role is enlarged by the electoral college. Groups such as African Americans and farmers, for example, fear they might lose their swing vote power—their ability to make a difference in key states that may tip the electoral college balance.

Another alternative to the electoral college is sometimes called the National Bonus Plan. This plan would add another 102 electoral members to the current 538. These 102 members would be awarded on a winner-take-all basis to the candidate with the most votes, so long as that candidate received more than 40 percent of the popular vote. This system would avoid elections' being thrown into the House of Representatives and would help ensure that the candidate who won the popular vote became president. The most serious liabilities of the plan are that it is complicated and that it requires a runoff election if there is no winner.

Finally, two states, Maine and Nebraska, have already adopted a district system in which the candidate who carries each congressional district gets that electoral vote and the candidate who carries the state gets the state's two additional electoral votes. This quasi-proportional representation system has the advantage of not shutting out a candidate who is strong in some areas of a state but not others, but otherwise it does not address the larger concerns with the electoral college.

Republican Presidential candidate John McCain, seen here campaigning with his wife Cindy, was tireless in his pursuit of votes. Both McCain and Obama focused on what are called battleground states.

The failure of attempts to change the system of elections points to an important conclusion about procedural reform: U.S. voters normally do not focus on procedures. Even after the intense controversy on the outcome of the 2000 election, including the role of the electoral college, reform was not seriously considered.

Elections in the Internet Age

We've seen that elections matter in a constitutional democracy. They determine who holds office and what policies the government adopts. Elections are complex, and the rules of the game affect how it is played. Our winner-take-all system is an example of a rule that has influenced the nature of our party system, the strategy of candidates, and the stability of our institutions. Over time the rules of the electoral game have been changed. Today party nominees are largely selected by voters in primaries, whereas early in our nation's history candidates were selected by party caucuses. Over time our system has expanded the role of citizens and voters, as illustrated by the predominance of primaries.

Central to the functioning of a constitutional democracy like that in the United States is a system of fair elections that is well administered, so the outcome has legitimacy. Voter trust and confidence in elections centers on the kinds of issues we have examined in this chapter. Over time we have learned ways to make elections better, including the secret ballot, disclosure and limitation of campaign contributions, and expansion of the role of citizens through primaries. As important as these structural and institutional changes are, without the participation of people in politics the system will not function well.

Individual citizens can make a difference in elections in many ways. They do this through voting, being active in selecting candidates, working for political parties, and organizing groups around common interests. Because candidates, parties, and groups need money and volunteers to operate, donating money and time are also important ways in which people invest in elections. People also influence the votes of friends and neighbors, as voters are more likely to respond positively to a personal request to vote for a candidate or ballot proposition than they are to requests from other sources. As the 2008 election demonstrated, the Internet is a way for large numbers of individuals to donate money, volunteer time, and mobilize their friends.

THINKING IT THROUGH

Our current system of state primaries or caucuses grows out of federalism and the rights of the states to govern elections. Mandating a national primary, though likely constitutional, would be a departure from federalism, and some may object to it as a step toward the federal government's controlling voter registration, voting technology, and other aspects of election administration that were long the province of the states. A national primary could force states that prefer the caucus system to adopt primaries. Because states sometimes combine the presidential primary with their primary for other offices, it may mean adding another election to the calendar.

A national primary would have the advantage of giving every voter an equal say in determining the nominee. It would also take away the kind of dispute that clouded the 2008 Democratic contest, in which Florida and Michigan voted earlier than the national party rules allowed, resulting in a disputed election.

A national primary would substantially change the nature of the campaign. Our current system means candidates with less money can spend more time meeting the voters of Iowa and New Hampshire and prove themselves so as to move on in the process. A national primary would help candidates with more money and greater name recognition because there would be little person-to-person campaigning.

Questions

1. Do you think it is fair that Iowa and New Hampshire are always first in the nominating process?
2. What are the strengths and weaknesses of the current system?
3. When should a national primary be held, and why?

CHAPTER SUMMARY

1 Summarize election rules and assess their implications for elections in the United States.

The U.S. electoral system is based on winner-take-all rules, typically with single-member districts or single officeholders. These rules encourage a moderate, two-party system. Fixed and staggered terms of office add predictability to our electoral system. Although term limits have been popular with the public, Congress has not introduced any term limits to its members.

2 Describe the electoral college, how it works, and its impact on presidential elections.

The electoral college is the means by which presidents are actually elected. To win a state's electoral votes, a candidate must have a plurality of votes in that state. Except in two states, the winner takes all. Thus candidates cannot afford to lose the popular vote in the most populous states. The electoral college also gives disproportionate power to the largest and smallest states, especially if they are competitive. It has the potential to defeat the national popular vote winner.

3 **Identify the regularities of congressional elections and explain why they are generally not competitive.**

Candidates for Congress must raise money, develop a personal organization, and increase visibility in order to be nominated for the election. Incumbents have significant advantages over their challengers, with House incumbents having stronger advantages than their Senate counterparts, whose challengers often have strong name recognition and more easily raise money. The cost of elections and incumbency advantages make congressional elections widely noncompetitive.

4 **Identify the stages in U.S. presidential elections and analyze the differences in campaigning at each stage.**

The three stages in a presidential election are winning enough delegate support in presidential primaries and caucuses to secure the nomination, campaigning at the national party convention, and mobilizing voters in enough states to with the most votes in the electoral college.

5 **Assess the influence of money in congressional and presidential elections and evaluate the main approaches to campaign finance reform.**

The rising costs of campaigns have led to declining competition for congressional seats and increasing dependence on PACs and wealthy donors. Because large campaign contributors are suspected of improperly influencing public officials, Congress has long sought to regulate political contributions. The main approaches to reform have been (1) imposing limitations on giving, receiving, and spending political money; (2) requiring public disclosure of the sources and uses of political money; and (3) giving governmental subsidies to presidential candidates, campaigns, and parties, including incentive arrangements. Present regulation includes all three approaches.

6 **Evaluate the need for improving presidential and congressional elections in the United States.**

The present presidential selection system is under criticism because of its length and expense, because of uncertainties and biases in the electoral college, and because it seems to test candidates for media skills less needed in the White House than the ability to govern, including the capacity to form coalitions and make hard decisions. Reform efforts center on presidential primaries, the electoral college, and campaign finance.

Chapter Self-Test

1. Write two to three paragraphs detailing what would likely happen to the major and minor parties in the United States if we adopted proportional representation. (pp. 241–242)
2. Which system allows political parties to secure legislative seats and power in proportion to the number of votes they receive in the election? (p. 242)
   a. cumulative voting
   b. winner-take-all system
   c. single-member districts
   d. proportional representation
3. Describe the original intention of the Electoral College. (pp. 242–244)
4. Examine the map on page 269. Analyze what John McCain should have done differently to win the election. In a short essay, justify your answer (make a believable case that he could actually have taken the states in question).
5. List four reasons why congressional elections are generally not very competitive. (pp. 244–248)
6. Many think it would be better for the country if congressional elections were more competitive. Write a short persuasive essay defending the current system. (pp. 244–248)
7. Most U.S. electoral districts are (competitive/uncompetitive) districts. (p. 244)
8. Choose from the following to complete the paragraph below: *strong partisans, moderates, win the nomination, win the election*

   During the primary stage of the presidential campaign, candidates need to appeal to ________ in order to ________. During the general election, however, they need to appeal to ________ in order to ________ (pp. 248–253)
9. List 3 important elements of the party convention.
10. Name and explain 3 ramifications of BCRA on political candidates and groups or individuals who contribute to their campaigns. (pp. 253–255)
11. Describe how the FEC influences congressional and presidential fund raising. (pp. 260–265)
12. The boost candidates from the president's party get from running along with a popular presidential candidate is known as the ________. (p. 245)
    a. safe effect
    b. wave effect
    c. coattail effect
    d. proportional effect

14. In a paragraph, list and discuss two or three aspects of the 2008 presidential campaign that suggested potential reforms to the current electoral process. (pp. 268–271)

15. Choose one potential reform to the current electoral process, and write a brief persuasive essay about why it should or should not be adopted. Be sure to address the issue from multiple perspectives. (pp. 268–271)

Key Terms

winner-take-all system, p. 241

single-member district, p. 241

proportional representation, p. 242

electoral college, p. 242

safe seat, p. 244

coattail effect, p. 245

candidate appeal, p. 246

national tide, p. 246

name recognition, p. 247

caucus, p. 251

national party convention, p. 252

Federal Election Commission (FEC), p. 259

soft money, p. 260

hard money, p. 260

Bipartisan Campaign Reform Act (BCRA), p. 260

issue advocacy, p. 262

527 organizations, p. 263

independent expenditures, p. 265

Further Reading

R. MICHAEL ALVAREZ, *Information and Elections* (University of Michigan Press, 1998).

LARRY M. BARTELS, *Presidential Primaries and the Dynamics of Public Choice* (Princeton University Press, 1988).

EARL BLACK AND **MERLE BLACK,** *The Vital South: How Presidents Are Elected* (Harvard University Press, 1992).

DAVID W. BRADY, JOHN F. COGAN, AND **MORRIS P. FIORINA,** EDS., *Continuity and Change in House Elections* (Stanford University Press, 2000).

BRUCE BUCHANAN, *Presidential Campaign Quality: Incentives and Reform* (Pearson, 2004).

ANN N. CRIGLER, MARION R. JUST, AND **EDWARD J. MCCAFFERY,** EDS., *Rethinking the Vote: The Politics and Prospects of American Election Reform* (Oxford University Press, 2004).

RONALD KEITH GADDIE, *Born to Run: Origins of the Political Career* (Rowman & Littlefield, 2004).

PAUL GRONKE, *The Electorate, the Campaign, and the Office: A Unified Approach to Senate and House Elections* (University of Michigan Press, 2000).

RODERICK P. HART, *Campaign Talk* (Princeton University Press, 2000).

PAUL S. HERRNSON, *Congressional Elections: Campaigning at Home and in Washington*, 5th ed. (CQ Press, 2007).

GARY C. JACOBSON, *The Politics of Congressional Elections*, 7th ed. (Longman, 2008).

KIM F. KAHN AND **PATRICK J. KENNEY,** *The Spectacle of U.S. Senate Campaigns* (Princeton University Press, 1999).

DAVID B. MAGLEBY, ANTHONY CORRADO, AND **KELLY D. PATTERSON,** EDS., *Financing the 2004 Election* (Brookings Institution Press, 2006).

DAVID B. MAGLEBY, J. QUIN MONSON, AND **KELLY D. PATTERSON,** EDS., *Dancing Without Partners: How Candidates, Parties and Interest Groups Interact in the Presidential Campaign* (Rowman & Littlefield, 2007).

DAVID B. MAGLEBY AND **KELLY D. PATTERSON,** EDS., *The Battle for Congress: Iraq, Scandal, and Campaign Finance in the 2006 Election* (Paradigm, 2008).

L. SANDY MAISEL AND **MARK D. BREWER,** *Parties and Elections in America: The Electoral Process*, 5th ed. (Rowman & Littlefield, 2007).

MICHAEL J. MALBIN, ED., *The Election After Reform: Money, Politics, and the Bipartisan Campaign Reform Act* (Rowman & Littlefield, 2006).

JEREMY D. MAYER, *Running on Race: Racial Politics in Presidential Campaigns, 1960–2000* (Random House, 2002).

WILLIAM G. MAYER, ED., *The Making of the Presidential Candidates 2008* (Rowman & Littlefield, 2008).

WILLIAM G. MAYER AND **ANDREW E. BUSCH,** *The Front-Loading Problem in Presidential Nominations* (Brookings Institution Press, 2004).

STEPHEN K. MEDVIC, *Political Consultants in U.S. Congressional Elections* (Ohio State University Press, 2001).

SAMUEL L. POPKIN, *The Reasoning Voter: Communication and Persuasion in Presidential Campaigns*, 2d ed. (University of Chicago Press, 1994).

STEPHEN J. WAYNE, *The Road to the White House 2008* (Wadsworth, 2008).

See also *Public Opinion Quarterly, The American Journal of Politics,* and *American Political Science Review.*

chapter 10

The Media and U.S. Politics

No candidate in the 2008 presidential campaign better understood the way the delivery of news is changing than Barack Obama. Having learned from past campaigns like those of Republican John McCain in 2000 and Democrat Howard Dean in 2004, Obama not only recognized the Internet's potential for fund raising, but he also effectively used it for recruiting and organizing volunteers, for getting his message directly to voters, and for generating enthusiasm for his campaign.

The impact of the Internet cut across demographic groups but was most concentrated among younger voters. A study by the Pew Research Center for the People and the Press done in late 2006 found that less than a quarter of people under age 30 watch local news regularly for campaign coverage, compared with half of those over age 50 and 39 percent of those between ages 30 and 49. Part of this difference may be due to the fact that younger people are generally less interested in politics and elections, but in 2008 the level of interest among younger persons grew dramatically, and many turned to the Internet to access and share news. For example, "4 out of 10 young people have watched candidate speeches, interviews, commercials, or debates online."[1]

The young are much more likely to use social networking sites like MySpace and Facebook. By March 2008 the Obama campaign had about 1.7 million "friends" compared to about 330,000 for Hilary Clinton and 140,000 for McCain. As a "friend" of a candidate you are likely to receive invitations to campaign events, links to speeches, and requests for campaign contributions. The campaign also encouraged friends to forward messages to others, thereby widening its circle of influence. This strategy worked well for the Obama campaign. For example, far more viewers watched his speech on race and his pastor, Reverend Jeremiah Wright, on YouTube than on CNN. By late March 2008 it had been viewed almost 3.4 million times and was being frequently shared on Facebook.[2] Six months later, Obama's campaign had 1.7 million friends.[3]

Even more widely viewed was a music video supporting Obama called "Yes We Can" with a lead performance by will.i.am of the Black Eyed Peas and including Scarlett Johansson, Kareem Abdul-Jabbar, John Legend, and other stars. The video was released on YouTube shortly before the "Super Tuesday" primaries on February 5 and had soon been viewed more than 17 million times.[4] Other candidates also used the Internet to push their message and define themselves. John Edwards cultivated a strong following in the liberal blogosphere, John McCain bought thousands of keywords on Google and other search engines, and Hillary Clinton used coordinated lists of voters online as targets for an army of cell phone callers.[5] As we discussed in Chapter 9, the Internet was an important part of fund raising for several candidates in 2008, including Republican Ron Paul, who raised $32 million on the Internet out of a total of $35 million raised through February 2008. In that same period Obama raised $112 million via the Internet out of a total of $193 million.[6]

Some of the Obama campaign's success on the Internet seemed to happen spontaneously, but the campaign also advertised on Web sites. If you went to the *Dallas Morning News* Web site in the weeks before the Texas presidential primary, you saw an Obama ad. The campaign also attached ads to such terms as "Ohio primary" on search engines such as Yahoo, Google, and Microsoft Live.[7] Howard Dean's campaign manager in 2004, Joe Trippi, is credited with effectively using the Internet. He said, "The beauty and also the curse of the Web… [is that] like it or not, an army of people are working for you or against you."[8]

LEARNING **OBJECTIVES**

1. Define the news media and show how their different forms connect the government and the people.
2. Describe the evolution of the media's interaction with politics from the Founding until today, including the changes brought by the Internet.
3. Evaluate the media's influence on public opinion and attention.
4. Identify the benefits and problems of the media's role in elections.
5. Assess the media's relationship to governance in the United States.

CHAPTER OUTLINE

- The Influence of the Media on Politics
- The Changing Role of the U.S. News Media
- Mediated Politics
- The Media and Elections
- The Media and Governance

LEARNING OBJECTIVE

Define the news media and show how their different forms connect the government and the people.

Comparing News Media

Use of Media by the American Public

The Influence of the Media on Politics

The media, in particular the print media, have been called the "fourth estate" and the "fourth branch of government."[9] Evidence that the media influence our culture and politics is plentiful. In one form or another, the **mass media**—newspapers and magazines, radio, television (broadcast, cable, and satellite), the Internet, films, recordings, books, and electronic communication—reach almost everyone in the United States.[10] The **news media** are the parts of the mass media that tell the public what is going on in the country and the world, although the distinctions between entertainment and news have become increasingly blurred. News programs often have entertainment value, and entertainment programs often convey news. Programs in this latter category include TV newsmagazines such as *60 Minutes* and *Dateline*; talk shows with hosts such as Larry King, Oprah Winfrey, Sean Hannity, and Alan Colmes; Jon Stewart's parody of the news, *The Daily Show;* and *The Colbert Report.*

By definition, and to make money, the mass media disseminate messages to a large and often heterogeneous audience. Because they must have broad appeal, their messages are often simplified, stereotyped, and predictable. But how much political clout do the media have? Two factors are important in answering this question: the media's pervasiveness, and their role as a link between politicians and government officials and the public.

The Internet has become a more important source of news in the United States, taking its place alongside print, radio, and television. The number of people who go online for news has grown dramatically and promises to become even more politically important as organizations like MoveOn increasingly use the Internet to reach the public.[11] The Internet enables people to obtain information on any subject and from multiple sources—some of which may be unreliable—at any time of the day or night. The Internet also allows people to communicate and organize rapidly in response to political events.

The Pervasiveness of Television

Television has changed U.S. politics more than any other invention. With its visual imagery and drama, television has an emotional impact that print media can rarely match.[12] It cuts across age groups, educational levels, social classes, and races. In contrast, newspapers provide more detail about the news and often contain contrasting points of view, at least on the editorial pages, that help inform the public.

Most people in the United States watch some kind of television news every day. The average viewer watches more than four and one-half hours of television a day, and most homes have more than two television sets.[13] Television provides instant access to news from around the country and the globe, permitting citizens and leaders alike to observe events firsthand.

The growth of around-the-clock cable news and information shows is one of the most important developments in recent years. Until the late 1980s, the network news programs on CBS, NBC, and ABC captured more than 90 percent of the audience for television news in the morning and early evening. Although the "big three" networks have seen their audiences decline by about a million viewers a year since then, they still hold the majority of viewers. In 2007, the networks attracted on average 23.1 million evening news viewers and 12.7 million daytime news viewers.[14] The cable news networks CNN, Fox News, and MSNBC had average audiences of 2.7 million evening viewers and 1.6 million daytime viewers.[15]

Satellites, cable television, Internet search engines such as Google, and podcasts make vast amounts of political information available 24 hours a day. These technologies eliminate the obstacles of time and distance and increase the volume of information that viewers can store, retrieve, and watch. They have also reduced the impact of single sources of broadcast or cable news. Competition from cable stations has put pressure on broadcast networks to remain profitable, which has both reduced budgets for broadcast news coverage and created the need to boost its entertainment value. For example, more viewers watched Barack Obama's acceptance speech at the Democratic Convention on cable stations than on ABC, CBS, and NBC. CNN had the most viewers.[16]

mass media
Means of communication that reach the public, including newspapers and magazines, radio, television (broadcast, cable, and satellite), films, recordings, books, and electronic communication.

news media
Media that emphasize the news.

For more than 40 years, Americans have been getting their news primarily from television. Whenever there is a crisis, most people turn first to television for information. No event in recent history has done more to underscore the importance of television as the primary source of news in contemporary U.S. society than the terrorist attacks that took place on September 11, 2001.

One of the biggest changes in U.S. electoral politics of the last half-century is that most voters now rely more on television commercials for information about candidates and issues, and less on news coverage.[17] Although debates and speeches by candidates generate coverage, the more pervasive battleground for votes is radio and TV ads. As a result, electoral campaigns now focus on image and slogans rather than substance. Successful candidates must be able to communicate with voters through this medium, attempting to define their opponent as well as themselves. To get their message across to TV audiences, politicians rely on media advisers.

The amount of local television news devoted to politics has been declining, however, and now constitutes less than one minute per half-hour broadcast.[18] A major effort to get local television stations to devote a few minutes to candidate debate in their nightly local news ended up with stations averaging 45 seconds a night, or as one observer put it, just enough time to "let candidates clear their throats."[19]

In large urban areas, viewers rarely see stories about their member of Congress, in part because those media markets usually contain several congressional districts. Newspapers do a better job of covering politics and devote more attention to it than television stations do. The decline in news coverage of elections and voting, especially on television, has only increased the impact of political advertising on television, through the mail, and over the telephone.

In most contested referendums, advertising is the most important source of information for voters.[20] The campaign finance reforms enacted in 2002 will over time likely increase the amount of *issue advocacy* (see Chapter 6), especially through the mail and over the telephone. The Bipartisan Campaign Reform Act (BCRA) bans issue advocacy on television or radio that mentions a candidate by name in the two months before a general election or one month before a primary election (see Chapters 6 and 9). But it does not limit what interest groups can do through the mail, over the phone, or in person, and in the last several elections, a wide range of groups communicated directly with voters in these ways. This "ground war" had been growing in importance before passage of BCRA, but the reforms intensified it. In battleground states or districts, interest groups often canvassed voters and then sent mail and phone calls to reinforce the message. Even more effective are face-to-face conversations, especially with people the voter knows.

HISTORY MAKERS

Walter Cronkite

For nearly 20 years (from 1962 to 1981), Walter Cronkite anchored *The CBS Evening News.* Throughout his long tenure, the public saw him as authoritative and fair—the "most trusted figure" in U.S. life.*

Walter Cronkite.

His reporting of such events as the assassination of President Kennedy and the NASA space flights, especially the *Apollo 11* flight to the moon, made him not only an observer of history but also a part of it.

Cronkite began his career by working for small public relations firms, newspapers, and radio stations in the Midwest. In 1939, he went to work for United Press (UP), a wire service that provided news stories to many newspapers. Cronkite reported extensively on World War II and the Nuremberg trials for UP and helped open its Moscow bureau.† Cronkite joined CBS television in 1950, doing both news and entertainment programming. He hosted a documentary series named *Twentieth Century* (1957–1967) and later *21st Century* (1967–1970).

It was Cronkite's hosting of *The CBS Evening News,* however, that linked him to the rise of television news and the visual imagery that reinforced its impact. His voice and manner made him seem mainstream and believable. He rarely showed emotion, which made the tears he shed during his reporting of the Kennedy assassination all the more exceptional.‡ He ended each nightly news program with the words, "And that's the way it is." Chet Huntley and David Brinkley of NBC led in the ratings until 1967, but from then until his retirement, Cronkite was the ratings leader. Early news anchors such as Cronkite, Huntley and Brinkley, and Edward R. Murrow not only reported the news but helped make television the most influential source of news for most U.S. citizens.

*"Cronkite: Trust Is 'Individual Thing,'" *USA Today,* July 16, 2002, p. 1A.
†Smithsonian Associates, "Walter Cronkite: A Lifetime Reporting the News," smithsonianassociates.org/programs/cronkite/cronkite.asp.
‡Charles Wheeler, "Kennedy: The Enduring Allure," BBC, November 19, 2003, news.bbc.co.uk/1/hi/world/americas/3265185.stm.

The Persistence of Radio

Television and the newer media have not displaced radio. On the contrary, radio continues to reach more U.S. households than television does. Only 1 household in 100 does not have a radio, compared with 2 in 100 without a TV.[21] More than 8 in 10 people listen to the radio every week,[22] and nearly 7 in 10 do so every day.[23] Many consider the radio an essential companion when driving. Certainly American adults get more than "the facts" from radio; they also get analysis and opinion from commentators and talk show hosts.

Political campaigns continue to use radio to communicate with particular types of voters. Because radio audiences are distinctive, campaigns can target younger or older voters, women, Hispanics, and so on. Many candidates in 2008 used radio to "microtarget" particular audiences in this way.[24] One particularly important source of news on the radio is National Public Radio (NPR). An estimated audience of 26 million listens to programs such as *Morning Edition.*[25] NPR even rivals conservative radio commentator Rush Limbaugh for size of audience.[26]

The Declining Importance of Newspapers

You Are the News Editor

Despite vigorous competition from radio and television, newspapers remain important. Daily newspaper circulation has been declining for the past 30 years to less than 53 million nationwide—or less than one copy for every five people.[27] The circulation figures for newspapers reflect a troubling decline in readership among younger persons: the percentage of young people who read newspapers on a regular basis declined by more than half between 1967 and 2007.[28]

In addition to metropolitan and local newspapers, we now have national newspapers. Created in 1982 by the Gannett Company, *USA Today,* with a circulation of nearly 2.3 million, recently replaced the *Wall Street Journal* as the top-circulating U.S.

THE **CHANGING FACE** OF U.S. POLITICS

Toward a More Representative Newsroom

The newspaper industry has worked hard to achieve greater diversity in the newsroom. The American Society of Newspaper Editors has stated that diverse newsrooms cover U.S. communities more effectively. Because many stories require contacts with a diverse public, the industry adopted a goal to make all newsrooms representative of the nation as a whole by 2025. Although the largest U.S. newspapers, such as the *New York Times* and *Washington Post,* have made progress toward a more representative newsroom, smaller papers have had much more difficulty attracting and retaining minority reporters. Thus, less than 30 percent of smaller newspapers with circulations of less than 10,000 readers employ at least some minority reporters, compared to 100 percent of large newspapers with circulations of more than 500,000 readers. Moreover, the percentage of minority journalists varies greatly from one region of the country to another. Newspapers in the Midwest and New England have the smallest percentage of minority reporters, while newspapers in the western states have the highest percentage.

Diversity at U.S. Newspapers.

	Women		Minority*	
	1999	**2007**	**1999**	**2007**
Position				
Supervisors	34%	35%	9%	11%
Copy-Layout Editors	40	42	11	12
Reporters	40	40	13	15
Photographers	26	27	15	17

*African American, Asian American, Native American, Hispanic.

SOURCE: American Society of Newspaper Editors, "Newsroom Employment Census," www.asne.org/index.cfm?id=1138.

newspaper. The *Wall Street Journal,* with a circulation of more than 2 million, has long acted as a national newspaper specializing in business and finance. The *New York Times* publishes a national edition read by more than 1.1 million people.

Some major newspapers such as the *Washington Post* have experienced sharp declines in readership.[29] Newspapers have become less profitable because of declining circulation, in part because the Internet provides instantly available information for free.[30] Some newspapers, most notably the *Wall Street Journal,* experimented with charging readers for online access; the *Journal* still retains some premium content for subscribers only, but it has not become a widely used strategy.[31] The Internet has hurt newspapers' bottom line most by providing an alternative medium for retail advertisers, and particularly for classified ads via sites such as Craigslist. Newspapers once earned about 40 percent of their revenue from classifieds; today, they receive only 20 percent.[32]

The Growing Popularity of the Internet

From its humble beginnings as a Pentagon research project in the 1960s,[33] the Internet has blossomed into a global phenomenon. There are now more than 12 billion publicly accessible documents on the Web,[34] and more than 153 million unique domains have been registered worldwide.[35]

The Internet opens up resources in dramatic ways. One study found that nearly half of Internet users go online to search for news on a particular topic; somewhat smaller proportions go online for updates on stock quotes and sports scores. For about 37 percent of people, the Internet is a primary source of news.[36] Internet users can also interact with other people or politicians about politics through e-mail, social

People can now access news and other information through their cell phones. They are also frequently invited by news organizations to upload photos and video from their cell phones to help cover news events.

networking sites, and blogs. Younger people, including teenagers, use the Internet extensively for schoolwork, and nearly three in four of them prefer it to the library.[37] A remarkable 77 percent of teens get news online, and 61 percent of teens use the Internet every day.[38]

We've noted that candidates are using the Internet for fundraising more effectively than ever before. Once a candidate gains recognition, as Howard Dean did in his campaign to win the Democratic nomination for president in 2004, he or she can raise money quickly and inexpensively via the Web. The success of parties and candidates in Internet fund raising has significantly changed the way politics is financed. As people have gained confidence in making credit card transactions via the Internet, they have become more willing to support parties and candidates in this way.

The Internet provides an inexpensive way to communicate with volunteers, contributors, and voters and promises to become an even larger component of future campaigns. Candidates' Web sites offer not only extensive information about the candidates themselves and their stands on issues, but also tools for meeting fellow supporters, for receiving news and materials from the campaign, for volunteering, and for setting up personalized home pages, such as at my.barackobama.com and McCainSpace.com. This is in addition to candidates' YouTube channels, social networking profiles, and affiliated blogs. Although much is still unknown about the impact of the Internet, it has at least the potential to fragment the influence of other media.[39]

The Changing Role of the U.S. News Media

LEARNING **OBJECTIVE**

2 Describe the evolution of the media's interaction with politics from the Founding until today, including the changes brought by the Internet.

American adults spend on average 67 minutes per day consuming news, and the older they are, the more time they spend.[40] Yet media bashing has become a national pastime. We blame the media for phenomena as varied as increased tension between the races, biased attacks on public officials, sleaze and sensationalism, increased violence in our society, and the elevation of the profit motive over the job of conveying information. Many in the media agree with these charges and think the media are headed in the wrong direction.[41] But complaints may simply be a case of criticizing the messenger to avoid dealing with the message.

A Political Tool

The news media have changed dramatically over the course of U.S. history. When the Constitution was being ratified, newspapers consisted of a single sheet, often published irregularly by merchants to hawk their services or goods. Delinquent subscribers and high costs meant that newspapers rarely stayed in business more than a year.[42] But the framers understood the importance of the press as a watchdog of politicians and government, and the Bill of Rights guaranteed freedom of the press.

There are occasional examples of fabrication or plagiarism by reporters. Jayson Blair of the *New York Times* made up some stories and plagiarized others, including one from a Texas newspaper about the family of Iraqi prisoner of war Jessica Lynch.

The new nation's political leaders, including Alexander Hamilton and Thomas Jefferson, recognized the need to keep voters informed. Political parties as we know them did not exist, but the support the press had given to the Revolution had fostered a growing awareness of the political potential of newspapers. Hamilton recruited staunch Federalist John Fenno to edit and publish a newspaper in the new national capital of Philadelphia. Jefferson responded by attracting Philip Freneau, a talented writer and editor and a loyal Republican, to do the same for the Republicans. (Jefferson's Republicans later became the Democratic Party.)

The two papers became the nucleus of a network of competing partisan newspapers throughout the nation. Although they competed in Philadelphia for only a few years, they became a model for future partisan papers. The early U.S. press served as a mouthpiece for political leaders. Its close connection with politicians and political parties offered the opportunity for financial stability—but at the cost of journalistic independence.

Financial Independence

During the Jacksonian era of the late 1820s and 1830s, the right to vote was extended to all free white adult males through the elimination of property qualifications. The press began to shift its appeal away from elite readers and toward the mass of less-educated and less politically interested readers. Thus increased political participation by the common people—along with the rise of literacy—began to alter the relationship between politicians and the press.

Some newspaper publishers began to experiment with a new way to finance their newspapers. They charged a penny a paper, paid on delivery, instead of the traditional annual subscription fee of $8 to $10, which most readers could not afford. The "penny press," as it was called, expanded circulation and increased advertising, enabling newspapers to become financially independent of the political parties.

The changing finances of newspapers also affected the definition of news. Before the penny press, all news was political—speeches, documents, editorials—directed at politically interested readers.[43] The penny press reshaped the definition of news as it sought to appeal to less politically aware readers with human interest stories and reports on sports, crime, trials, fashion, and social activities.

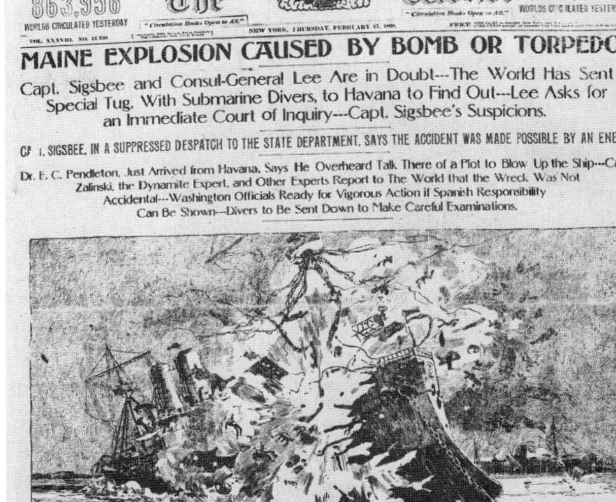
863,956 WORLDS CIRCULATED YESTERDAY — The World. — "Circulation Books Open to All." — NEW YORK, THURSDAY, FEBRUARY 17, 1898.

MAINE EXPLOSION CAUSED BY BOMB OR TORPEDO

Capt. Sigsbee and Consul-General Lee Are in Doubt---The World Has Sent Special Tug, With Submarine Divers, to Havana to Find Out---Lee Asks for an Immediate Court of Inquiry---Capt. Sigsbee's Suspicions.

CAPT. SIGSBEE, IN A SUPPRESSED DESPATCH TO THE STATE DEPARTMENT, SAYS THE ACCIDENT WAS MADE POSSIBLE BY AN ENEMY

Dr. E. C. Pendleton, Just Arrived from Havana, Says He Overheard Talk There of a Plot to Blow Up the Ship---Capt. Zalinski, the Dynamite Expert, and Other Experts Report to The World that the Wreck Was Not Accidental---Washington Officials Ready for Vigorous Action if Spanish Responsibility Can Be Shown---Divers to Be Sent Down to Make Careful Examinations.

The New York World a day after

As the nineteenth century progressed, literacy grew among the U.S. masses and more people began to get their news from newspapers. The popularization of the print media forced politicians and public officials to devote growing attention to their relationship with the press.

"Objective Journalism"

By the early twentieth century, many journalists began to argue that the press should be independent of the political parties. *New York Tribune* editor Whitelaw Reid eloquently expressed this sentiment: "Independent journalism! That is the watchword of the future in the profession. An end of concealments because it would hurt the party; an end of one-sided expositions . . . ; an end of assaults that are not believed fully just but must be made because the exigency of party warfare demands them."[44] Objective journalism was also a reaction to exaggeration and sensationalism in the news media, something called *yellow journalism* at the time.

Journalists began to view their work as a profession, and they established professional associations with journals and codes of ethics. This professionalization reinforced the notion that journalists should be independent of partisan politics. Further strengthening the trend toward objectivity was the rise of the wire services, such as the Associated Press and Reuters, which remained politically neutral to attract more customers.

Three Hundred Years of American Mass Media

The Impact of Broadcasting

Radio and television nationalized and personalized the news. People could now follow events as they were happening and not have to wait for the publication of a newspaper. From the 1920s, when radio networks were formed, radio carried political speeches, campaign advertising, and coverage of political events such as national party conventions.[45] Politicians could now speak directly to listeners, bypassing the screening of editors and reporters. Radio also increased interest in national and international news because it enabled its audience to follow faraway events as if they were actually there.

Beginning in 1933, President Franklin Roosevelt used radio with remarkable effectiveness. Before then, most radio speeches were formal orations, but Roosevelt spoke to his audience on a personal level, seemingly in one-on-one conversations. These "fireside chats," as he called them, established a standard that politicians still follow today. When Roosevelt began speaking over the microphone, he would visualize a tiny group of average citizens in front of him. He "would smile and light up," observers said, "as though he were actually sitting on the front porch or in the parlor with them."[46]

Franklin D. Roosevelt was the first president to recognize the effectiveness of radio to reach the public. His fireside chats were the model for later presidents.

Television added a dramatic visual dimension, which increased audience interest in national events and allowed viewers to witness lunar landings and the aftermath of political assassinations, as well as more mundane events. By 1963, the two largest networks at the time, CBS and NBC, had expanded their evening news programs from 15 to 30 minutes. Today news broadcasting has expanded to the point that many local

In 2004 an investigative team at CBS News uncovered and aired this and other photos of prisoner abuse in Abu Ghraib. Although the military had been privately investigating the situation for several months, the actions of the CBS reporters brought the tragedy into the national spotlight.

stations provide 90 minutes of local news every evening as well as a half-hour in the morning and at noon. Programs such as *20/20* and other newsmagazine shows are among the most popular in the prime-time evening hours.

Cable television brought round-the-clock news coverage. During the Clinton impeachment hearings in 1998, the 2000 Florida ballot-counting controversy, and the "shock and awe" bombing of Iraq in March 2003, audiences around the world watched U.S. cable news for its instantaneous coverage. C-SPAN now provides uninterrupted coverage of congressional deliberations, trials, and state and local governments.

Investigatory Journalism

News reporters today do more than convey the news; they investigate it, and their investigations often have political consequences. An investigative team at *60 Minutes* of CBS News broke the story of torture of Iraqi prisoners held by U.S. soldiers at Abu Ghraib in 2004,[47] and Dana Priest of the *Washington Post* revealed the existence of secret CIA prisons in 2005 that were being used to hold and interrogate suspected terrorists.[48]

In many ways the best example of the power of investigatory journalism is in the role the media played in the Watergate scandal.[49] Without persistent reporting by columnist Jack Anderson and two young *Washington Post* reporters, Robert Woodward and Carl Bernstein, the story would probably have been limited to a report of a failed burglary of the headquarters of the Democratic National Committee at the Watergate building.[50] The news reporting, coupled with congressional investigations, put a spotlight on the inner workings of the Nixon White House and the Nixon reelection committee, which had funded the attempted burglary and other political dirty tricks. Critical to the reporting on the broadening scandal, which ultimately brought down the president, was a confidential source, nicknamed Deep Throat by Woodward and Bernstein.[51] In 2005, more than 30 years after these events, the former deputy director of the FBI, W. Mark Felt, identified himself as Deep Throat.

Media Consolidation

Local firms used to own the regional newspapers, radio, and television stations. As in other sectors of the economy, media companies have merged and created large conglomerates of many newspapers and broadcasting stations. Some of these conglomerates are multinational. Rupert Murdoch, an Australian-born U.S. citizen and founder of the FOX network, owns 35 television stations in the United States, DirecTV, 20th Century Fox, HarperCollins Publishers, MySpace.com, and *TV Guide,* which has the largest magazine circulation in the United States. His most recent acquisition is the *Wall Street Journal,* giving him one of the few national newspapers in the United States.[52] Murdoch also owns nine newspapers abroad and two TV networks—one in Asia and one in Europe.[53]

Nina Totenberg of National Public Radio, whose reporting on sexual harassment charges against Clarence Thomas helped force the Senate Judiciary Committee to extend the hearings on his confirmation to the U.S. Supreme Court.

When television was in its infancy, radio networks and newspapers were among the first to purchase television stations. These mergers established cross-ownership patterns that persist today. The Gannett Company, for example, owns 102 daily newspapers in the United States and United Kingdom and 23 television stations and cable television systems—assets that provide news coverage to more than 20 million households in the United States.[54] The Tribune Company, parent of the *Chicago Tribune,* purchased Times-Mirror, publisher of the *Los Angeles Times,* in 2000, resulting in combined assets of 11 newspapers, 23 TV stations, one radio station, superstation WGN, and a growing online business.[55] In such acquisitions some newspapers are subsequently sold to other conglomerates. At the same time, on the national level, the cable networks—CNN, Fox News, and others such as TruTV and C-SPAN—have expanded the number of news sources available to the 86 percent of households with TV cable or satellite service.[56]

The courts and the Federal Communications Commission (FCC)—an independent regulatory commission charged with licensing stations—are reinforcing the trend toward media conglomeration by relaxing and striking down regulations that limit cable and television network ownership by the same company.[57] In response to congressional

Rupert Murdoch, third from left, and his daughter Elisabeth have created a vast network of media outlets. Rupert's holdings include Twentieth Century Fox, Fox News, the *Wall Street Journal,* and Harper Collins Publishers. Elisabeth Murdoch is the CEO of the Shine Group and has developed such TV shows as the U.K. versions of *Project Catwalk, The Biggest Loser,* and *Gladiators.*

opposition, the FCC had lowered the maximum population a conglomerate could reach.[58] An appeals court called the FCC limits on media ownership "arbitrary and capricious" and overturned them,[59] a decision the Supreme Court let stand.[60] More recently, the FCC approved the merger of satellite radio corporation XM and Sirius, suggesting the commission is still friendly to media consolidation.[61]

Will greater concentration of media ownership limit or restrict the free flow of information to the public? This concern is most evident in cities that once had two or more competing daily papers and now have only one newspaper. Although the number of local broadcast stations has not declined to the same extent, conglomerates without ties to the community now own more of these stations.

Regulation of the Media

The government has regulated the broadcast media in some form since their inception. Because of the limited number of television and radio frequencies, the national government oversees their licensing, financing, and even content through the FCC. The FCC continues to regulate licensing issues and occasionally fines or penalizes broadcasters that violate decency standards. For example, the FCC fined CBS for broadcasting as part of its 2004 Super Bowl halftime show an incident in which Justin Timberlake removed part of Janet Jackson's costume, exposing her right breast.[62] A federal appeals court later overruled the FCC fine.[63]

Osama bin Laden is seen at an undisclosed location in this television image, broadcast Sunday, October 7, 2001. Bin Laden praised God for the September 11 terrorist attacks and swore America "will never dream of security" until "the infidel's armies leave the land of Muhammad." The recorded video was broadcast on Al-Jazeera television and was seen throughout the world.

Mediated Politics

When dramatic events such as the terrorist attacks on September 11, 2001, occur, we realize television's power to bring world events into our lives. Osama bin Laden, the purported mastermind behind those attacks, also understands the power of the media both inside and outside the United States, as evidenced by his release of videotapes of himself since the attacks.

The pervasiveness of newspapers, magazines, radio, and television confers enormous influence on the individuals who

GENERATION **NEXT**

Media Consumption

Generation Next has witnessed phenomenal changes in the way people receive information about the world around them. Further, this generation is the first to grow up in the wired (and wireless) era of live-blogging, podcasts, satellite radio, and HD television. With so many tools at their disposal, it's no wonder that most young people are keeping up with the news some or a lot of the time. Only 19% report they do not keep up with the news.

Among Generation Next there are not major differences by gender, party, or race for which type of media they rely on most for news about national and international issues. With the exceptions of Asians, the model response for all categories was television. Asians rely, about equally, on newspapers and television, and they use the Internet more than others. There are ideological differences as well. Conservatives are more apt to turn to television and less likely to use the Internet for news. Liberals rely more than conservatives and moderates on newspapers.

Conservative 18–25 year olds are especially fond of the television and the radio while liberals of the same age make more use of newspapers and the Internet. Moderates fall between the two. Yet, while liberal adults are more likely to use the Internet for news than moderates or conservatives, three groups of youth use the Web more often than older voters. When a survey by the Pew Research Center asked people what their main source of news about the 2008 election was, 26 percent of people in general gave the Internet as their first or second mention. That number increased to 46 percent for those aged 18 to 29.*

QUESTIONS

1. Do you believe young people follow the news closely or are mostly disengaged?
2. Why do liberal, moderate, and conservative youth differ in their preferred sources of media? Think about the personalities, programs, and viewpoints most prominent in each source.

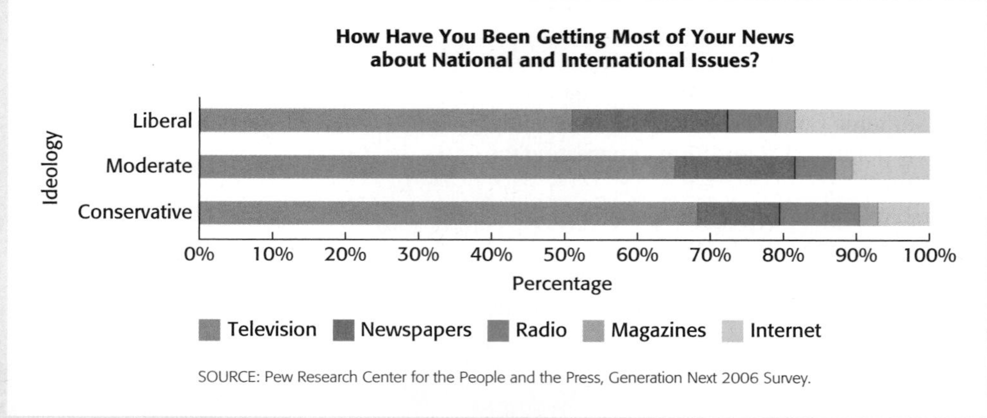

SOURCE: Pew Research Center for the People and the Press, Generation Next 2006 Survey.

*Pew Research Center for the People and the Press, "Social Networking and Online Videos Take Off: Internet's Broader Role in Campaign 2008," January 11, 2008, http://www.pewinternet.org/PPF/r/234/report_display.asp.

LEARNING **OBJECTIVE**

 Evaluate the media's influence on public opinion and attention.

determine what we read, hear, and see because they can reach so many people so quickly. While the majority of people still get their news from television and newspapers, the internet is quickly becoming a popular source of information for many. In a survey conducted late in 2008, 58 percent of respondents reported television news as the source of most of their political information. This is down from 68 percent in 2004. Newspaper readership is down about a third from 2004, with internet rising about a third.[64]

Political parties and interest groups have long been political mediators that help organize the world of politics for the average citizen. Their role is less important today, because the media now mediate what news is covered and because political parties have largely lost control over the nominating process (see Chapters 7 and 9). As a result, the candidates' perceived character and competence matter more than their party affiliations or platforms. The press, not the parties, evaluates these qualities.

The news media have also assumed the role of speaking for the people. Journalists report what "the people" want and think, and then they tell the people what politicians and

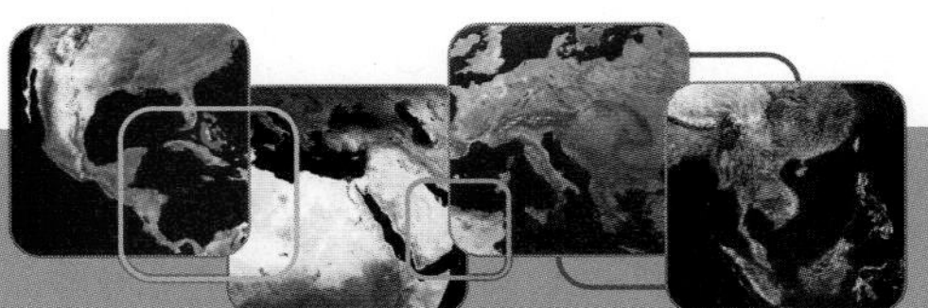

HOW **OTHER NATIONS** GOVERN

Freedom of the Press in Comparative Perspective

The First Amendment of the Bill of Rights lays out one of the United States' most fundamental liberties: freedom of the press. But just how free, actually, are journalists in the United States and across the world? Freedom House's annual *Freedom of the Press* report evaluates the legal, political, and economic freedom of print, broadcast, and electronic media in every country of the world. Are journalists allowed to criticize the government, or do they face retribution for doing so? Are major media outlets independent, or sounding boards for the state? Is starting a radio station or blog expensive and difficult, or hassle-free?

Answers to questions like these are scored on a scale of 0 (most free) to 100 (least free) and a country's overall score results in a rating of "free" (score of 0–30), "partly free" (31–60), or "not free" (61–100). Overall in 2007 the best rating went to Finland and Iceland, which had scores of 0.9. The table below shows the results for our sample countries.

As the table shows, the most-developed countries have the greatest freedom of the press. Partly free countries such as India, Mexico, and Nigeria have less press freedom, while China's press remains one of the least free in the world. As Freedom House's 2006 report notes, "The year 2006 was marked by an increased crackdown on press freedom in China. President Hu Jintao's administration effectively silenced the press by introducing new media regulations, jailing outspoken journalists, and restricting coverage of breaking news."* China also heavily restricts its citizens' Internet use. The "Great Firewall of China" comprises an estimated 30,000 Internet police who monitor Chinese Web sites and e-mail, keyword blocking on the Chinese versions of search engines such as Google, filters on the five gateways that connect China to the global Internet,† and, until November 2006, a complete block of Chinese-language articles on Wikipedia.‡

QUESTIONS

1. What legal, political, and economic conditions encourage or discourage a free press?
2. How do you think technological and economic advances in China may affect the government's efforts to restrict the press?
3. Did the Chinese Olympic Games foster greater freedom of the press in China? Why or why not?

	China	Great Britain	India	Japan	Mexico	Nigeria	United States
Overall Score	Not Free	Free	Partly Free	Free	Partly Free	Partly Free	Free
2007 Press Freedom Rank*	84	19	35	21	48	55	16

*Among 195 countries.

*Freedom House, "China," in *Freedom of the Press 2007,* www.freedomhouse.org/template.cfm?page=251&year=2007.
†Gabriel A. Almond, G. Bingham Powell, Jr., Russell J. Dalton, and Kaare Strøm, *Comparative Politics Today: A World View,* 9th ed. (Pearson Longman, 2008), p. 56.
‡Freedom House, "China."

policy makers are doing about it. Politicians know they depend on the media to reach voters, and they are well aware that a hostile press can hurt or even destroy them. That explains why today's politicians spend so much time developing good relationships with the press.

The Media and Public Opinion

Television's ability to present images and communicate events has influenced U.S. public opinion. Footage of the violence done to black and white protesters during the civil rights revolution of the 1950s and 1960s made the issue more real and immediate. News coverage of the war in Vietnam galvanized the antiwar movement in the United States because of the horrible images news shows brought into people's homes. The testimony of White House staff before the Senate about Watergate and later House Judiciary committees further weakened confidence in the Nixon administration. Television coverage of the terrorist attacks on the World Trade Center and the Pentagon and the devastation left by Hurricane Katrina made indelible impressions on all who watched.

For a long time, analysts argued that political leaders wielded more influence in U.S. politics than the media did. FDR's fireside chats symbolized the power of the politician over that of the news editor. Roosevelt spoke directly to his listeners over the radio in a way and at a time of his own choosing, and no network official could block or influence that direct connection. President John Kennedy's use of the televised press conference established similar direct contact with the public. President Ronald Reagan was nicknamed "the Great Communicator" because of his ability to talk with the people persuasively and often passionately about public policy issues through television. Now the media is more

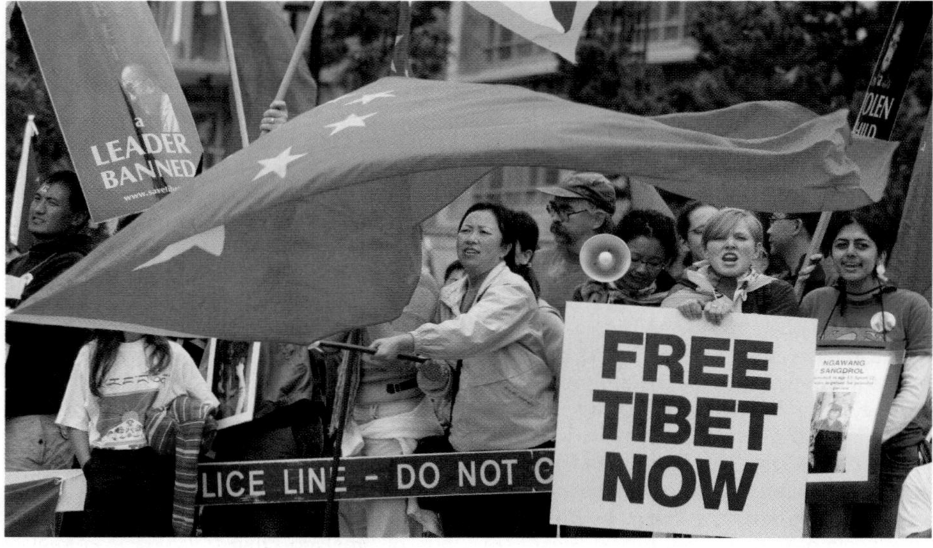

Media coverage of protests such as the one pictured here increased public scrutiny of China's treatment of Tibet. In 2008, similar protests led to a swell in criticism of China's policy as it prepared to host the Beijing Summer Olympics.

aggressive in news gathering. Today's media would have reported on FDR's declining health and John F. Kennedy's private life. Controversy in the press over the justification for going to war with Iraq became a major focus of the media in George W. Bush's second term and helped explain the declining public assessment of his performance.

Factors That Limit Media Influence on Public Opinion

People are not just empty vessels into which politicians and journalists pour information and ideas. The way we interpret political messages depends on a variety of factors: political socialization, selectivity, needs, and our ability to recall and comprehend the message.

Political Socialization We develop our political attitudes, values, and beliefs through an education process social scientists call **political socialization.**[65] (See Chapters 4 and 8 for more detail on this process.) Although they are not as important as family in influencing our values and attitudes,[66] the media are a socializing force and help shape public perceptions and knowledge. Face-to-face contacts with friends and business associates (*peer pressure*) often have far more impact than the information or views we get from an impersonal television program or newspaper article. Strong identification with a party also acts as a powerful filter.[67] A conservative Republican from Arizona may watch the "liberal eastern networks" and complain about their biased news coverage while sticking to her own opinions. A liberal from New York will often complain about right-wing talk radio, even if he listens to it occasionally (see Figures 10–1 and 10–2).

Selectivity We all practice **selective exposure**—screening out messages that don't conform to our own biases. We subscribe to newspapers or magazines or turn to television and cable news outlets that support our views.[68] We also practice **selective perception**—perceiving what we want to in media messages.[69] One dramatic example was the differing reactions of Democrats and Republicans to reports of President Clinton's sexual misconduct with Monica Lewinsky, a former White House intern, and the possibility that he encouraged her to lie under oath. In the first weeks after the story broke, Republicans were four times as likely as Democrats to believe that Clinton had been sexually involved with Lewinsky.[70] More than two-thirds of Republicans and Democrats agreed that Clinton committed perjury before the grand jury, but they had dramatically different opinions on whether Clinton should remain in office. Nearly two-thirds of Republicans wanted Clinton removed from office, while 63 percent of Independents and 87 percent of Democrats felt that Clinton should remain president.[71]

Needs People read newspapers, listen to the radio, or watch television for different reasons.[72] Media affect people differently depending on whether they are seeking

political socialization
The process by which we develop our political attitudes, values, and beliefs.

selective exposure
The process by which individuals screen out messages that do not conform to their own biases.

selective perception
The process by which individuals perceive what they want in media messages.

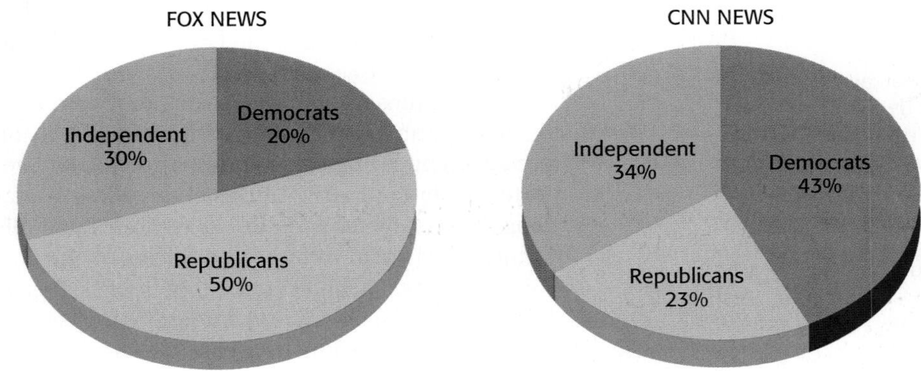

FIGURE 10–1
Partisanship and Preferred News Source.

SOURCE: Pew Research Center for the People and the Press, July 2007 Political Survey dataset, people-press.org/dataarchive; compiled by Tim Taylor.

information about politics or want to be entertained. For those seeking entertainment, gossip about politicians' sex lives is more important than what those politicians think about issues or how they vote. Members of the broader audience are also more likely to pay attention to news that directly affects their lives, such as interest rate changes or the price of gasoline.[73]

Audience Fragmentation The growth of cable television and new media such as the Internet have reduced the dominance of broadcast media and newspapers in transmitting information. Because people are scattered across more press outlets and these outlets cover politics in varied ways, the impact of the press has become more diffuse. People can now tailor their news to their preferred point of view. Fragmentation of the media audience has tended to counteract the impact of media conglomeration. But as media giants acquire both cable and broadcast stations and outlets and promote their own online sites, the importance of media conglomerates such as NBC, CNBC, and MSNBC will increase.

Are the Media Biased?

Media Bias

We tend to blame the media for being either too conservative or too liberal. Conservatives often complain that the media are too liberal. For example, radio talk show host Rush Limbaugh even once said, "They all just happen to believe the same way.... They are part

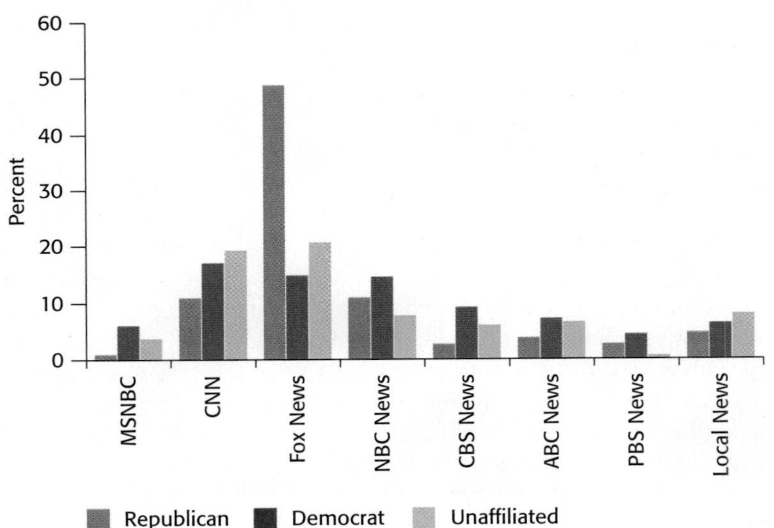

FIGURE 10–2
Partisanship and News Source Credibility.

SOURCE: Sacred Heart University Poll on media and politics, November 2007; data compiled by Jerry Lindsay, April 30, 2008.

YOU WILL DECIDE — How Should the Media Report Sex Scandals?

Sex scandals involving politicians have always been an inviting media target. Most notably, President Bill Clinton was dogged by a series of accusations of unwanted sexual advances toward Paula Jones and Kathleen Willey and of a consensual affair with Monica Lewinsky. Ultimately, President Clinton was impeached for perjury connected to the Lewinsky scandal. Media scrutiny of this scandal faded, however, and President Clinton still plays an active role in U.S. politics. New York governor Eliot Spitzer resigned his office in March 2008 for his involvement in a high-priced prostitution ring. Photos of Spitzer littered the front pages of the *New York Times* for several days, the Web site of the prostitution ring registered 6 million page views the day after the scandal broke,* and the MySpace page of Spitzer's prostitute, Ashley Alexander Dupré, had received more than 10.5 million hits by late April.†

Sex scandals can have electoral consequences. Congressman Mark Foley (R-Fla.) resigned from Congress after allegations arose that he had sent sexually explicit e-mails and text messages to teenage boys serving as congressional pages. Foley had been known previously as a staunch fighter against child exploitation and abuse. Many feel the Foley scandal cost the Republicans the House and Senate in 2006. The cover of an October 2006 *Time* magazine read, "What a Mess.... Why a tawdry Washington sex scandal may spell the end of the Republican revolution." Similarly, Republican senator Larry Craig was accused of lewd conduct in a men's bathroom of the Minneapolis–St. Paul International Airport, where an undercover police officer claimed Craig had made sexual advances toward him in the adjoining stall. Despite a media firestorm, Craig refused to resign his Senate seat, although he announced he would not run for reelection in 2008.

*Data from Alexa Internet Inc., www.alexa.com.
†Data from MySpace, www.myspace.com.

of the same culture as Bill Clinton."[74] Some liberal critics contend that the media reflect a conservative bias not only in what they report but also in what they choose to ignore. They point to Fox News as an example of conservative cable TV.

In fact, most U.S. news media are committed to being unbiased. Newspapers and television management go to some lengths to insulate reporters from their advertising and business operations, in part to reduce criticism about favorable editorial treatment of large advertisers or the corporate owners. The management of the *Los Angeles Times* was criticized in 2007 for attempting to foster closer relationships between the business and news divisions out of a concern that advertisers would influence news coverage.[75] News coverage requires many reporters and a host of editors, all of whom have input into what is covered and how it is presented. This can provide another internal check on media bias.

Some commentators have suggested that a possible bias flows from the fact that reporters and editors become too friendly with the people and organizations they write about. According to David Broder of the *Washington Post,* many members of the print and television media have crossed the line that should divide objective journalism from partisan politics. Broder opposes the idea of journalists becoming government officials and vice versa.[76] Others argue that journalists with previous government service have close working relationships with politicians and can give us a valuable perspective on government without losing their professional neutrality.

Bill O'Reilly, conservative TV and radio pundit, seen here as a guest on Comedy Central's show, "The Colbert Report."

THINKING IT THROUGH

Some people dismiss reporting on sex scandals as sensationalist and unrelated to governing. Others, like Larry Sabato, a political scientist who has written on the media, disagree. Sabato criticized the press for not reporting "what most of them [the press] knew then about Clinton and all the other women. If the press had done its job in '92, the country would not be facing this horrible dilemma in '98."*

The question of how to report sexual misbehavior by political candidates is unresolved. It is debatable whether such matters ought to be reported at all. Some people, including some reporters, think sex scandals are not important. The public wants to know whether candidates meet high standards of personal conduct, but they react negatively to coverage that is too aggressive. Public reaction to the explicit details of the Starr report about President Clinton's improper relationships is instructive: 84 percent of the public wanted to know the conclusions of the investigation, but 70 percent felt that Congress should have omitted the details of the sexual encounters.†

Questions

1. What is the relevance to politics and elections of sex scandals like the one involving Governor Spitzer?
2. Why does the media give attention to the private lives of politicians?
3. Should politicians be held to a higher standard than other people in their private lives? Why or why not?

*Larry J. Sabato, quoted in William Power, "News at Warp Speed," *National Journal*, January 31, 1998, p. 220.

†Frank Newport, "Initial Reaction Mixed on Delivery of Starr Report to Congress," *Gallup News Service*, September 12, 1998, http://www.gallup.com/poll/4168/Initial-Reaction-Mixed-Delivery-Starr-Report-Congress.aspx.

The media's alleged political bias is a frequent target of criticism (see Table 10–1). Journalists are usually more liberal than the population as a whole; editors tend to be a bit more conservative than their reporters; and media owners are more conservative still. Elite journalists—those who work for national news media organizations—tend to share a similar culture: cosmopolitan, urban, upper-class, and often liberal. Their common worldview, some contend, may govern their choice of issues to cover and the way they cover them.[77] Critics counter that the idea of a liberal media bias is a myth. They point to conservative forces in the media such as corporate ownership, which leads to a bias against unions, and the disproportionate time and influence given to conservative radio, TV, and print pundits such as Bill O'Reilly, Sean Hannity, and Rush Limbaugh.[78] The question of whether there is an ideological bias in the media has not been authoritatively answered. A further question is whether bias, if it exists and whatever its direction, seeps into the content of the news. The answer remains unclear.

One bias that does not have a partisan or ideological slant is the bias toward sensationalism. Scandals happen to liberals and conservatives, Republicans and Democrats. Once the province of tabloids like the *National Enquirer,* stories about these scandals involving celebrities, sex, or both have become commonplace in the mainstream media.

Public Opinion

Two important influences that print and broadcast media exert on public opinion are *agenda setting* and *issue framing.*

Agenda Setting By calling public attention to certain issues, the media help determine what topics will become subjects of public debate and legislation.[79] However, the media

TABLE 10–1 Partisanship and Ideology of Journalists, Policy Makers, and the Public

	Journalists	Policy Makers	Public
Party Identification			
Democrat	27%	43%	34%
Republican	4	24	28
Independent	55	26	21
Other	5	5	12
Don't Know/Refused	9	2	4
Self-Described Ideology			
Liberal	25%	25%	21%
Moderate	59	52	37
Conservative	6	18	35
Don't Know/Refused	11	5	7

SOURCE: The Kaiser Foundation, *The Role of Polls in Policy Making,* Combined Topline Results, June 2001, p. 27. www.kff.org/kaiserpolls/loader.cfm?url=/commonspot/security/getfile.cfm&PageID=13842.

do not have absolute power to set the public agenda. The audience and the nature of any particular issue limit it.[80] According to former vice president Walter Mondale, "If I had to give up . . . the opportunity to get on the evening news or the veto power, . . . I'd throw the veto power away. [Television news] is the President's most indispensable power."[81] Ronald Reagan, more than any president before him, effectively used the media to set the nation's agenda. Reagan and his advisers carefully crafted the images and scenes of his presidency to fit television. Thus television became an "electronic throne."

Communicating through the media works, especially when the communication is—or at least appears to be—natural and unscripted. When President Bush first visited the scene of the destruction of the World Trade Center in New York City in September 2001, he took a bullhorn and said, "I can hear you. The rest of the world hears you, and the people who knocked these buildings down will hear all of us soon."[82] This action projected presidential leadership and empathy to a nation that was still shocked by the attacks.

Issue Framing Politicians, like everyone else, try to frame issues to win support, and they try to influence the "spin" the media will give to their actions or issues. The media provide the means. Opponents of U.S. intervention in Bosnia in the 1990s tried to portray it as another Vietnam. Objectors to normal trade relations with communist China frame that relationship as a human rights travesty. People who favor the right to have an abortion define the issue as one of freedom of choice; those who oppose it define it as murder. In referendum campaigns, the side that wins the battle of defining what the referendum is about, wins.[83]

The Media and Elections

LEARNING **OBJECTIVE**

4 Identify the benefits and problems of the media's role in elections.

News coverage of campaigns and elections is greatest in presidential contests, less in statewide races for governor and U.S. senator, and least for other state and local races. Generally, the more news attention given the campaign, the less likely voters are to be swayed by any one source. Hence news coverage is likely to be more influential in a city council contest than in an election for president or the Senate. For most city elections, there are only one or two sources of information about what candidates say and stand for; for statewide and national contests, there are multiple sources.

Diversification of the news media lessens the ability of any one medium to influence the outcome of elections. Newspaper publishers who were once seen as key figures in state and local politics are now less important because politicians and their media advisers are no longer so dependent on newspapers and other news media to communicate their messages. Candidates can use ads on radio and television, direct mail, phone, the Web, and cable television to reach voters. In local contests, or even in larger settings such as the Iowa caucuses or the New Hampshire primary, personal contact can also be important.

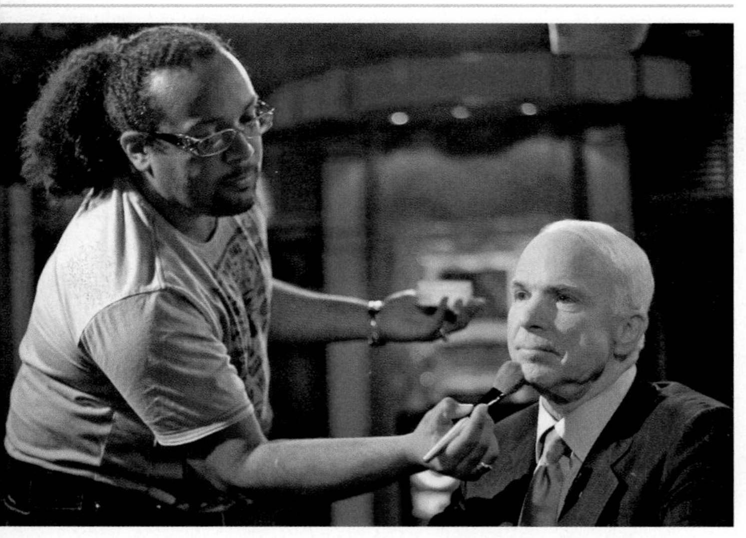

Senator John McCain sits as makeup is applied in preparation for an interview on Fox News Channel's "The O'Reilly Factor." A candidate's appearance on television can strongly impact the public's opinion of that candidate.

Choice of Candidates

The extensive use of television has made looking and sounding good on television much more important. It has also led to the growth of the political consulting industry and made *visibility* the watchword in politics. Television strongly influences the public's idea of what traits are important in a candidate. A century ago, successful candidates needed a strong pair of lungs; today they need a telegenic appearance, a pleasing voice, and no obvious physical impairments.

Consistent with the media's focus on personality is its highlighting of mistakes and gaffes by candidates and officeholders. Long before Jon Stewart and *The Daily Show,* print and broadcast media devoted considerable attention to such things as Gerald Ford mistakenly classifying Poland as a free country in the 1976 presidential debates.[84] Some mistakes can be more than silly; George Romney's statement in 1968 that he had been brainwashed while on a tour of Vietnam by U.S. government officials helped end his campaign for the Republican presidential nomination when it was mostly mistaken phrasing.[85] More recently, Hillary Clinton's exaggeration about snipers shooting at her on a visit to Bosnia became the subject of ridicule by comedians and meant she had to repeatedly apologize for the mistaken statements.[86] During the Pennsylvania primary, Barack Obama characterized residents of small, economically depressed towns as "bitter," stating, "They cling to guns or religion or antipathy to people who aren't like them... as a way to explain their frustrations."[87] Although neither of these mistakes ended the Clinton or Obama campaign, the candidates were put on the defensive for several days. For Clinton, polls showed that voters increasingly saw her as dishonest and untrustworthy.[88] Obama received little support from rural and working-class voters in the Pennsylvania primary, which he lost by ten points.

In the general election phase of the campaign, Obama ran a series of ads targeted at the rural and working class voters. He also benefitted from the endorsement of unions and their independent efforts on his behalf. Finally, as the focus of the campaign became the economy, Obama became the candidate more that voters were more likely to say "cares about people like me".[89]

Although the media insist that they pay attention to all candidates who have a chance to win, they also influence who gets such a chance. Consequently, candidates have to come up with creative ways to attract media attention. The late Paul Wellstone, in his 1996 campaign for the Senate in Minnesota, said in his advertisements that he did not have much money to pay for ads, so he would have to talk fast to cram what he had to say into fewer commercials. His witty commercial became a news event itself—it got Wellstone additional coverage. Sometimes a limited ad buy can generate funding for a much larger one. This was the case with the group that attacked the credibility and heroism of John Kerry in the 2004 presidential election; the Swift Boat Veterans for Truth turned a $550,000 ad buy[90] into millions of dollars in contributions, which funded the airing of additional ads. Critical to this expanded campaign was the widespread news coverage generated by the controversy the first ad set off.[91]

These photos from the Obama and Clinton election night speeches following the Iowa caucuses contrast two different ways to stage such a speech. The Clinton staging included former secretary of state Madeleine Albright, union leaders, and other notables. Obama, on the other hand, is surrounded by a sea of ordinary people, many of them more diverse and younger than in the Clinton staging. As the campaign progressed, Clinton adopted what later became the Obama staging.

Campaign Events

Candidates schedule events—press conferences, interviews, and "photo ops"—in settings that reinforce their verbal messages and public image. Barack Obama skillfully used a backdrop of young and diverse voters for his rallies and postprimary speeches. In contrast, other candidates were often surrounded by older and less diverse political leaders from the state or community. Many campaign events fail to receive attention from reporters because others are more newsworthy stories or the media may sense that they have been staged to generate news coverage.

The parties' national conventions used to capture national attention. However, because party primaries now select candidates, the conventions no longer provide much suspense or make news, except perhaps over who will be the vice presidential nominee. This is one reason the networks have cut back their coverage of presidential nominating conventions. In 1952, the average television set was tuned to the political conventions for 26 hours, or an average of more than three hours a night for the eight nights of convention coverage.[92] During the 2000 presidential conventions, by contrast, the major networks provided only one or two hours of prime-time coverage each evening. But cable channels now carry extensive coverage of the proceedings. The 2008 conventions had increased viewership in part because of excitement around the Obama and Palin candidacies. When Obama delivered his acceptance speech to a crowd of 80,000 at the Denver Bronco's football stadium, over 38 million households tuned in. One week later, John McCain and Sarah Palin delivered speeches to audiences of similar sizes.[93] Political parties have sought, in vain, to regain audience interest by relying on "movie stars, entertainment routines, and professionally produced documentaries to spice up their conventions."[94]

Technology

Although the expense associated with television advertising has contributed to the skyrocketing costs of campaigning, it has also made politics more accessible to more people. Thanks to satellites, candidates can conduct local television interviews without having to travel to local studios. They can target specific voter groups through cable television or low-power television stations that reach homogeneous neighborhoods and small towns. DVDs and CDs with messages from the candidates further extend the campaign's reach.[95] All serious candidates for Congress and governor since 2000 have made themselves and their positions available through a web page on the Internet.

Campaigns have primarily used the Internet and e-mail to reinforce voter preferences or help answer questions, more than to reach and persuade more passive citizens. But citizens can now interact with each other online on a wide range of political topics. In this sense, the Internet is like a town meeting, but one that people can attend without leaving their homes or offices. In recent elections people have made greater use of blogs as sources of information, and campaigns have often created their own blogs. Of growing importance are political communications posted on YouTube or Facebook, as illustrated by the examples cited at the beginning of this chapter.

Image Making and Media Consultants

A candidate's image often takes precedence over that candidate's message in the mass media. This was as true in the mid-nineteenth century as it is today. This is why image makers and media consultants have been in such high demand for so long. In the painting above, we see a portrait of Abraham Lincoln as "Abe the Rail Splitter."

Candidates recognize that their messages about issues are often ignored. The press tends to emphasize goofs and gossip, or tension among party leaders. Candidates in turn try to spin the news. Attempts to shape the news and portray candidates in the best possible light are not new. Presidential campaign sloganeering such as "Tippecanoe and Tyler Too" in 1840, "Honest Abe the Rail Splitter" in 1860, and "I Like Ike" in 1952 tried to convey the candidate's image. Radio, television, and the Internet have expanded the ability to project images, and that expansion has in turn affected candidates' vote-getting strategies and their manner of communicating messages. Television is especially important because of the power of the visual image and because it reaches so many people.

Television has contributed to the rise of new players in campaign politics, most notably *media consultants,* campaign professionals who provide candidates with advice and services on media relations, advertising strategy, and opinion polling.[96] For example, candidates regularly receive consultants' advice on what colors work best for them, especially on television. Male U.S. senators often appear in light blue shirts with red ties, sometimes called "power ties." A primary responsibility of a campaign media consultant is to present a positive image of the candidate and to reinforce negative images of the opponent. Both parties have scores of media consultants who have handled congressional, gubernatorial, and referendum campaigns. These consultants have also been blamed for the negative tone and tactics of recent campaigns.

Media consultants have taken over the role party politicians formerly played. Before World War II, party professionals groomed candidates for office at all levels. Such leaders selected candidates they thought could win. They watched how potential candidates behaved under fire and judged their decisiveness, conviction, political skill, and other leadership qualities. Party professionals advised candidates which party and interest group leaders to placate, which issues to stress, and which topics to avoid.

Today, consultants coach candidates about how to act and behave on TV and what to discuss on the air. Consultants report the results of *focus groups* (small sample groups of people who are asked questions about candidates and issues in a discussion setting) and *public opinion polls,* which in turn determine what the candidate says and does. Some critics allege that political consultants have become a new "political elite" that can virtually choose candidates by determining in advance which men and women have the right images, or at least images that the consultants can restyle for the widest popularity.[97] But political consultants who specialize in media advertising and image making know their own limitations in packaging candidates. As one media consultant put it, "It is a very hard job to turn a turkey into a movie star; you try instead to make people like the turkey."[98]

The Media and Voter Choice

As television has become increasingly important to politics—and reforms such as primary elections have weakened the political parties and made news coverage of candidates more important—the question arises, what difference does the media make?

Personality Over Substance Some critics think reporters pay too much attention to candidates' personality and background, and not enough attention to issues and policy. Others say character and personality are among the most important characteristics for readers and viewers to know about. The public appetite for stories on candidates' personal strengths and weaknesses is not new and is likely to continue. Making our campaigns more substantive and fostering election news coverage that reflect substance are challenging tasks, in part because of the many contests in each media market. Some groups have called for television stations to include brief three-to-five-minute live candidate debates in their evening news programs.[99] To date, only a few stations have implemented the idea.

The influence of the media on the public varies by level of sophistication of the voters. Better-informed and more-educated voters are more sophisticated and therefore less swayed by new information from the media.[100] But for the public generally, other scholars contend that "television news is news that matters."[101]

The Horse Race A common tendency in the media is to comment less on a candidate's position on issues than on a candidate's position in the polls compared with other candidates—what is sometimes called the **horse race.**[102] "Many stories focus on who is ahead, who is behind, who is going to win, and who is going to lose, rather than examining how and why the race is as it is."[103] Reporters focus on the tactics and strategy of campaigns because they think such coverage interests the public.[104] The media's propensity to focus on the "game" of campaigns displaces coverage of issues.

Negative Advertising Paid political advertising, much of it negative in tone, is another source of information for voters. Political advertising has always attacked opponents, but recent campaigns have taken on an increasingly negative tone. A rule of thumb in the old politics was to ignore the opposition's charges and thus avoid giving them, or the opposition, importance or standing. Today candidates trade charges and countercharges.

Voters say the attack style of politics turns them off, but most campaign consultants believe that negative campaigning works. This seeming inconsistency may be explained by evidence suggesting that negative advertising may discourage some voters who would be inclined to support a candidate (a phenomenon known as *vote suppression*) while making supporters more likely to vote.[105] Other research suggests that negative advertising is more informative than positive advertising and does not discourage voter turnout, but it does alienate people from government.[106]

Information About Issues In recent elections, the media have experimented with a more issues-centered focus, what has been called *civic journalism.* With funding from charitable foundations, some newspapers have been identifying the concerns of community leaders and talking to ordinary voters and then writing campaign stories from their point of view.[107] Some newspaper editors and reporters disagree with this approach; they believe the media should stick to responding to newsworthy events. Advocates of civic journalism counter that news events such as murders and violence often overshadow coverage of issues that concern the community.

horse race
A close contest; by extension, any contest in which the focus is on who is ahead and by how much rather than on substantive differences between the candidates.

Making a Decision Newspapers and television seem to have more influence in determining the outcome of primaries than of general elections,[108] probably because voters in a primary are less likely to know about the candidates and have fewer clues about how they stand. By the time of the November general election, however, party affiliation, incumbency, and other factors diminish the impact of media messages. The mass media are more likely to influence undecided voters, who, in a close election, can determine who wins and who loses.

Election Night Reporting Does TV coverage on election night affect the outcome of elections? Election returns from the east come in three hours before the polls close on the West Coast. Because major networks often project the presidential winner well before polls close in western states, some western voters have been discouraged from voting. This has dampened voter turnout in congressional and local elections. In a close presidential election, however, such early reporting may stimulate turnout because voters know their vote could determine the outcome. In short, television reporting may make voters believe their vote is meaningless when one candidate appears to be winning by a large margin.[109]

At 7:50 pm (EST) on election night, November 7, 2000, television networks projected that Al Gore had won Florida, but they soon had second thoughts and revoked their announcement. Hours later Fox News projected Bush winning Florida. The truth was that the vote in Florida was by every measure too close to judge and no network should have called the race. In 2004 the exit polls again generated controversy because leaks of early exit polls in the media showed John Kerry winning Ohio.[110] In 2008 the networks had few reported leaks of exit polling and were careful to not overstate the predictive power of the polls. Exit polls provided the public with important information about who voted any why people voted the way they did.

The Media and Governance

LEARNING **OBJECTIVE**

5 Assess the media's relationship to governance in the United States.

When policies are being formulated and implemented, decision makers are at their most impressionable.[111] Yet by that time, the press has moved on to another issue.

Lack of press attention to the way policies are implemented explains in part why we know less about how government officials go about their business than we do about heated legislative debates or presidential scandals. Only in the case of a policy scandal, such as the lax security surrounding nuclear secrets at Los Alamos National Laboratory, does the press take notice.

Some critics contend that the media's pressuring policy makers to provide immediate answers forces them to make hasty decisions, a particular danger in foreign policy:

> If an ominous foreign event is featured on TV news, the president and his advisers feel bound to make a response in time for the next evening news broadcast.... If he does not have a response ready by the late afternoon deadline, the evening news may report that the president's advisers are divided, that the president cannot make up his mind, or that while the president hesitates, his political opponents know exactly what to do.[112]

Political Institutions and the News Media

Presidents have become the stars of the media, particularly television, and have made the media their forum for setting the public agenda and achieving their legislative aims. Presidential news conferences command attention (see Table 10–2). Every public activity a president engages in, both professional and personal, is potentially newsworthy; a presidential illness can become front-page news, as can the president's vacations and pets.

A president attempts to manipulate news coverage to his benefit, as in the Bush administration's decision to embed reporters with U.S. forces during the early stages of the Iraq War. Presidents or their staff also selectively leak news to reporters. Presidents use speeches to set the national agenda or spur congressional action. Presidential travel to foreign countries usually boosts popular support at home, thanks to largely favorable news coverage. Better yet for the president, most coverage of the president—either at home or abroad—is favorable to neutral.[113]

TABLE 10–2 Presidential Press Conferences: Joint* and Solo Sessions, 1913–April 20, 2006

President	Total	Solo	Joint	Joint as Percentage of Total	Months in Office
Wilson	159	159	0	0	96
Harding	No Transcripts Available				29
Coolidge	521	521	0	0	67
Hoover	268	267	1	0.4	48
Roosevelt	1020	984	33	3.2	145.5
Truman	324	311	13	4.0	94.5
Eisenhower	193	192	1	0.5	96
Kennedy	65	65	0	0	34
Johnson	135	118	16	11.9	62
Nixon	39	39	0	0	66
Ford	40	39	1	2.5	30
Carter	59	59	0	0	48
Reagan	46	46	0	0	96
G. H. W. Bush	143	84	59	41.3	48
Clinton	193	62	131	67.9	96
G. W. Bush†	204	49	155	76	90

*In a joint press conference the president answers questions along with someone else, most often a foreign leader. In a solo session, only the president answers questions. There are three missing transcripts for Roosevelt and one for Johnson, which makes it impossible to determine whether those sessions were solo or joint ones.
†Bush through July 2008.

SOURCE: Adapted from Martha Joynt Kumar, "Presidential Press Conferences: The Evolution of an Enduring Forum," *Presidential Studies Quarterly,* 35, no. 1 (March 2005); and Kumar 2006, 2007 and 2008 updates.

Members of Congress have long sought to cultivate positive relationships with news reporters in their states and districts. They typically have a press relations staffer who informs local media of newsworthy events, produces press releases, and generally tries to promote the senator or representative.[114] Congress also provides recording studios for taping of news segments, and both parties have recording studios near the Capitol explicitly for electoral ads. Finally, politicians often appear on talk radio, which they can readily do from their offices in Washington. But the focus of this media cultivation is on the individual member and not on the institution of Congress as a whole.

Congress is a fragmented body that is usually unable to act quickly, made up as it is of 435 representatives, 100 senators, and scores of committees and subcommittees, all governed by complex rules. It is also more likely to get negative coverage than either the White House or the Supreme Court. Unlike the executive branch, it lacks an ultimate spokesperson, a single person who can speak for the whole institution.[115] Congress does not make it easy for the press to cover it. Whereas the White House attentively cares for and feeds the press corps, Congress does not arrange its schedule to accommodate the media; floor debates, for example, often compete with committee hearings and press conferences.[116] Singularly dramatic actions rarely occur in Congress; the press therefore turns to the president to describe the activity of the federal government on a day-to-day basis and treats Congress largely as a foil to the president. Most coverage of Congress is about how it reacts to the president's initiatives.[117]

The federal judiciary is least dependent on the press. The Supreme Court does not rely on public communication for political support. Rather, it depends indirectly on public opinion for continued deference to or compliance with its decisions.[118] The Court does not allow television cameras to cover oral arguments, rarely allows audiotaping, and bars reporters when it votes. It has strong incentives to avoid being seen as manipulating the press, so it retains an image of aloofness from politics and public opinion. The justices' manipulation of press coverage is far more subtle and complex than that of the other two institutions.[119] For example, the complexity of the Supreme Court's decision in the 2000 Florida presidential vote recount case, with multiple dissents and concurrences and no press release or executive summary, made broadcast reporting on the decision difficult.

The news media may be most influential at the local level.[120] Most of us have multiple sources for finding out what is happening in Washington that act as a check on the biases and limitations of reporters who cover national government and policy. But when it comes to finding out about the city council, the school board, or the local water district, most of us depend on the work of a single reporter. Consequently, the media's influence is much greater because there are fewer news sources.

Not all who think the media are powerful agree that power is harmful. After all, they argue, the media perform a vital educational function. Almost 70 percent of the public thinks the press is a watchdog that keeps government leaders from doing bad things.[121] At the least, the media have the power to mold the public agenda; at most, in the words of the late Theodore White, they have the power to "determine what people will talk and think about—an authority that in other nations is reserved for tyrants, priests, parties, and mandarins."[122]

CHAPTER **SUMMARY**

1 Define the news media and show how their different forms connect the government and the people.

The news media include newspapers, magazines, radio, television, films, recordings, books, and electronic communications in all their forms. These means of communication have been called the "fourth branch of government," for they are a pervasive feature of U.S. politics. The media provide and carry information among political actors, the government, and the public.

2 Describe the evolution of the media's interaction with politics from the Founding until today, including the changes brought by the Internet.

Our modern news media emerged from a more partisan and less professional past. Journalists today strive for objectivity and also engage in investigatory journalism. Corporate ownership and consolidation of media outlets raise questions about media competition and orientation. Radio and television broadcasting have changed the news media, and these are the sources from which most people get their news. The Internet has recently emerged as a new source of both information and political participation.

3 Evaluate the media's influence on public opinion and attention.

The mass media's influence over public opinion is significant but not overwhelming. People may not pay much attention to the media or may not believe everything they read or see or hear. They may be critical or suspicious of the media and hence resistant to it. People tend to filter the news through their political socialization, selectivity, needs, and ability to recall or comprehend the news. Although conservatives charge that the media are too liberal and liberals charge that the media are captive to business interests, little evidence exists of actual, deliberate bias in news reporting. The media's influence is most strongly felt in their ability to determine what problems and events will come to the public's attention and how those issues are framed.

4 Explain the benefits and problems of the media's role in elections.

Media coverage dominates presidential campaigns, and candidates depend on media exposure to build name recognition, a positive image, and thereby votes. Because of the way the media cover elections, most people seem more interested in the contest as a game or "horse race" than as a serious discussion of issues and candidates. Another effect of media influence has been the rise of image making and the media consultant.

5 Assess the media's relationship to governance in the United States.

The press serves as both observer and participant in politics, and as a watchdog, agenda setter, and check on the abuse of power, but it rarely gives much attention to the implementation or administration phases of the policy process. Exceptions include major mistakes such as the government's response to Hurricane Katrina.

Chapter Self-Test

1. Briefly explain the distinction between the **mass media** and the **news media.** (p. 276)
2. The media has been referred to as: (p. 276)
   a. a bully pulpit
   b. the great mediator
   c. the voice of the people
   d. the fourth branch of government
3. In a short essay, discuss how presidential campaigns would differ without television. Would they be better or worse? Why? (pp. 276–277; 290–294)

4. In one or two paragraphs, define the "penny press" and discuss why its development was significant in the history of U.S. media. (pp. 280–281)

5. True or False: The FCC has been relaxing regulations that limit cable and television network ownership by the same company. (pp. 282–283)

6. The process by which individuals perceive what they want to in media messages is (p. 286)
   a. selective exposure.
   b. political alienation.
   c. selective perception.
   d. political socialization.

7. List four factors that limit the influence media has on public opinion (pp. 286–287), and explain each in a few sentences.

8. If a media outlet decides to report on a recent housing crisis but not on a corn shortage, it is engaging in (p. 290)
   a. issue framing
   b. agenda setting
   c. partisan politics
   d. value construction

9. Explain how *issue framing* is different from *agenda setting.* In a few sentences, tell which of these two possible approaches by the media you think has a greater influence on national policy and why. (pp. 289–290)

10. Write a brief persuasive essay showing the media's role in elections is a problem that calls for significant changes. Use the examples from the chapter as well as any personal experiences you have had. (pp. 290–294)

11. In a few sentences, explain how television and the media in general affect the choice of candidates for presidential elections. (pp. 290–294)

12. In a short essay, discuss why the federal judiciary is the branch that is least dependent on the press. (pp. 295–296)

13. In a short essay, describe how the President manipulates news coverage. In your opinion, is the president's ability to manipulate news coverage a positive or negative power? (pp. 294–296)

Key Terms

mass media, p. 276

news media, p. 276

political socialization, p. 286

selective exposure, p. 286

selective perception, p. 286

horse race, p. 293

Further Reading

ERIC ALTMAN, *What Liberal Media? The Truth About Bias and the News* (Basic Books, 2004).

STEPHEN ANSOLABEHERE AND **SHANTO IYENGAR,** *Going Negative: How Attack Ads Shrink and Polarize the Electorate* (Free Press, 1996).

BRUCE BIMBER AND **RICHARD DAVIS,** *Campaigning Online: The Internet in U.S. Elections* (Oxford University Press, 2003).

KEITH BYBEE, *Bench Press: The Collision of Courts, Politics, and the Media* (Stanford Law and Politics Press, 2007).

JEFFREY E. COHEN, *The Presidency in the Era of 24-Hour News* (Princeton University Press, 2008).

TIMOTHY E. COOK, *Making Laws and Making News: Press Strategies in the U.S. House of Representatives* (Brookings Institution Press, 1990).

STEPHEN J. FARNSWORTH AND **S. ROBERT LICHTER,** *Mediated Presidency: Television News and Presidential Governance* (Rowman & Littlefield, 2005).

JOHN G. GEER, *In Defense of Negativity: Attack Ads in Presidential Campaigns* (University of Chicago Press, 2006).

JAMES G. GIMPEL, J. CELESTE LAY, AND **JASON E. SCHUKNECHT,** *Cultivating Democracy: Civic Environments and Political Socialization in America* (Brookings Institution Press, 2003).

KENNETH M. GOLDSTEIN AND **PATRICIA STRACH,** *The Medium and the Message: Television Advertising and American Elections* (Prentice Hall, 2004).

DORIS A. GRABER, *Mass Media and American Politics,* 7th ed. (CQ Press, 2005).

RODERICK P. HART, *Campaign Talk: Why Elections Are Good for Us* (Princeton University Press, 2002).

KATHLEEN H. JAMISON, *The Press Effect: Politicians, Journalists, and the Stories That Shape the Political World* (Oxford University Press, 2003).

PHYLLIS KANISS, *Making Local News* (University of Chicago Press, 1997).

DAVID D. PERLMUTTER, *Blog Wars: The New Political Battleground* (Oxford University Press, 2008).

DONALD A. RITCHIE, *Reporting from Washington: The History of the Washington Press Corps* (Oxford University Press, 2006).

CASS SUNSTEIN, *Republic.com 2.0* (Princeton University Press, 2007).

DARRELL M. WEST, *Air Wars: Television Advertising in Election Campaigns, 1952–2004,* 5th ed. (CQ Press, 2008).

chapter 11

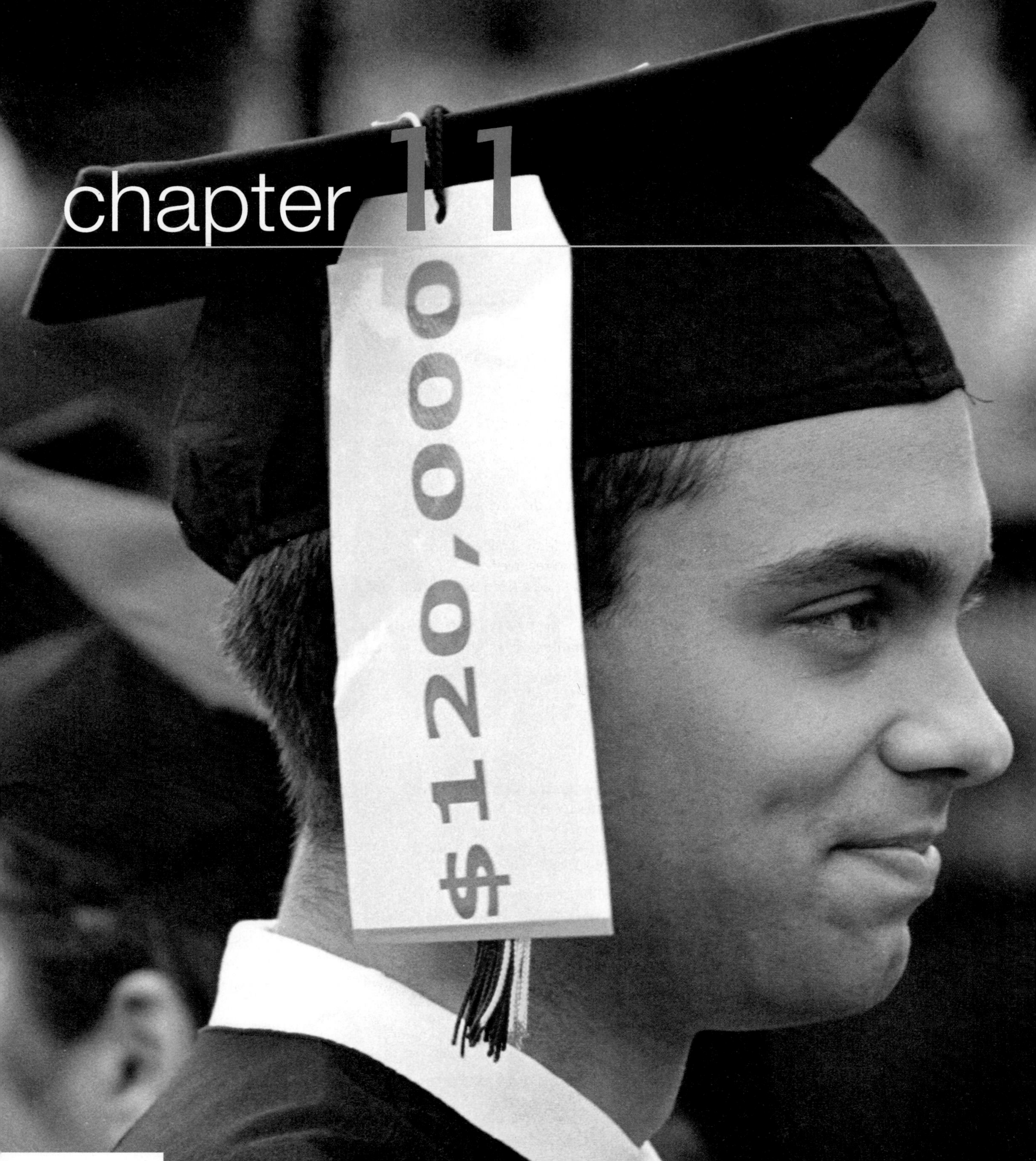

Congress

The People's Branch

For most of U.S. history, the federal government left higher education to individuals and the states. Although Congress, the president, and the judiciary understood that an educated public was essential to economic growth, the federal government did not become involved in providing access to college until Congress passed the Servicemen's Readjustment Act of 1944, popularly known as the "G.I. Bill." The G.I. Bill provided grants to send veterans to college and supported the construction of thousands of libraries, classrooms, and dormitories.

Over the next 50 years, Congress and the president expanded the loan system to make a college or university education almost universally available to anyone who wanted to go. Roughly a quarter of all loans come from the federal government directly, while the other three-quarters come from private lenders who receive federal dollars to make the loans profitable. As of July 1, 2006, private loans carried a fixed interest rate of 6.8 percent, with origination fees of up to 2 percent.

By 2008, however, federal guarantees to encourage private lenders to make loans had reached $8 billion a year on more than $90 billion in loans.[1] Under increasing pressure from parents and students, Congress began investigating the private loan industry, which often imposed exorbitant loan origination fees and high interest rates on borrowers. Congress soon discovered that loan companies were giving free travel, gifts, and money to some college and university officials to steer borrowers their way.

Congress drafted a bill to reform the system. As Senator Ted Kennedy (D-Mass.) said, "The reality is that our bill restores the balance to this grossly unfair student loan system by directing funds to the students, not to the banks."[2] Under the proposal, the federal government would cut its subsidies to private lenders in half, lower interest rates to a maximum of just 3.4 percent, and put most of the savings into Pell Grants.

Although the bill had many supporters, the loan industry opposed it and created a group called America's Student Loan Providers to lobby against the cuts. One lobbyist said the bill would punish the industry, while another predicted that banks would simply stop lending money, thereby denying education to millions of students. Some Republicans also argued that the bill would do nothing to reduce tuition, which is what drives the need for college loans in the first place.

After months of debate, Kennedy was finally able to pull together a coalition of Democrats and Republicans to bring the bill to a vote, arguing for "bold new commitment to enable the current generation of Americans to rise to the global challenges we face." The proposal passed 79 to 12 in the Senate and 292 to 97 in the House, and only days later President George W. Bush signed the bill into law.

U.S. citizens expect Congress to act on important issues such as student loan reform, and sometimes it does. However, Congress was not designed to be an efficient lawmaking machine. The founders wanted it to represent the people, the states, and the nation, and created a variety of checks and balances within Congress to keep it from moving too fast on controversial issues.

LEARNING **OBJECTIVES**

1. Describe the congressional election process and demonstrate how it protects incumbents.
2. Differentiate the powers of Congress.
3. Compare and contrast the structure and powers of the House and Senate.
4. Compare the leadership systems used in the House and Senate.
5. Analyze the committee structure and show how members are assigned to committees.
6. Assess the effect of different forms of representation on citizen engagement.
7. Examine the influences on legislative decisions and how these influences may vary with issues.
8. Identify the key steps by which a bill becomes a law and the ways a bill can be stopped at each step.

CHAPTER **OUTLINE**

- Congressional Elections
- The Structure and Powers of Congress
- Congressional Leadership and Committees
- The Job of the Legislator
- How a Bill Becomes a Law
- An Assessment of Congress

Citizens have significant influence on congressional action, although interest groups may have even more. Citizens can lobby Congress by joining those interest groups, of course, but they can also make their voices heard through phone calls, e-mails, and letters. Because members of Congress care so much about reelection, they pay close attention to the citizens back home. If enough citizens participate, they can have substantial influence on legislation.

In this chapter, we examine how the framers designed the legislative branch and how it actually works today. We will also explore the role of interest groups, colleagues, congressional staff, the two parties, and the president in shaping decisions; explore the ethics issue in more detail; and discuss how a bill becomes a law.

Before turning to these questions, however, we'll look at how members of Congress reach office in the first place. The way we elect members of the House and Senate has a great deal to do with how they behave once in office, and it influences everything from committee assignments to legislative interests. We will also ask why individual members of Congress win reelection so easily.

Comparing Legislatures

Congressional Elections

There is only one Congress in the Constitution, but the 435 House members and 100 senators serve in bodies that are significantly different. One important distinction is the different election calendars. Because all House members serve two-year terms, while senators serve six-year terms, House members start worrying about the next election almost as soon as they have won the last one. And because all House seats are up for election every two years, versus only a third of Senate seats, the House as a whole is more sensitive about issues that may affect elections than is the Senate as a whole. The framers believed these rules would make the House and its members much more sensitive than senators to the opinions of their **constituents,** meaning residents of their districts or states.

constituents
The residents of a congressional district or state.

House members and senators also run for their first elections under slightly different entry rules. House members must be 25 years old at the time they take office and must have been citizens for seven years, while senators must be 30 years old and have been citizens for nine years. House and Senate candidates must be residents of the states from which they are elected. The framers hoped that by setting the Senate's requirements higher and giving its members a six-year term, they would shape the Senate as a check against what they saw as the less predictable House. Concerned about the "fickleness and passion" of the House of Representatives, James Madison in particular saw the Senate as "a necessary fence against this

Amy Klobuchar (Democrat from Minnesota) campaigns for the U.S. Senate in 2006.

danger."[3] This is why the founders decided that senators would be selected by their state legislatures—the Constitution was amended in 1913 to require the direct election of all senators.

Senators are not free to ignore their constituents, however. Because the framers did not limit the number of terms House members or senators can serve, they must defend their records at some point if they want to stay in office.

Drawing District Lines

The framers of the Constitution set the Senate and the House apart in terms of the populations they serve. Every state has two senators, each of whom represents the entire state. Members of the House of Representatives, on the other hand, serve districts within their states. A state's population determines the number of districts—hence, states with more citizens have more districts, and big states clearly have more influence in the House.

The exact number of districts in each state is determined by a national census of the population taken every ten years, which is also specified in the Constitution. When the population changes, so does the potential number of districts, or seats in each state. This process of changing the number of seats allotted to each state is called **reapportionment.** Each seat in the House represents roughly 650,000 citizens. House members from small states often represent even fewer—Wyoming has just 580,000 citizens, for example, but each state is guaranteed one House member. The House limited the total number of districts to 435 after the 1910 census.

Although states have the power to determine what areas each district covers, they cannot change the number of districts they have. States control the **redistricting** process needed to assign voters to districts.[4] Under the Constitution, states, not the federal government, are responsible for determining the time, place, and manner of elections, which includes district lines.

District lines can be drawn several ways to favor one party—a district can be "packed" with a large number of party voters, thereby diluting that party's strength in the districts next door, or a party stronghold can be dispersed into several districts, thereby possibly weakening that party's strength in several districts. In extreme cases, this process is known as **gerrymandering,** a term dating to the early 1800s when Massachusetts governor Elbridge Gerry won passage of a redistricting plan that created a salamander-shaped district drawn to help his party win another seat.

LEARNING **OBJECTIVE**

1 Describe the congressional election process and demonstrate how it protects incumbents.

Congressional Redistricting

You Are Redrawing the Districts in Your State

Why Is It So Hard to Defeat an Incumbent?

Advantages of Incumbency

It only takes one defeat to end a House or Senate career, which is why so many House members and senators work so hard to create safe seats. A **safe seat** is almost certain to be won by the current officeholder, or **incumbent.** It usually occurs in a district where one party has a clear majority of voters, virtually ensuring the election of the candidate from the dominant party.

Although there are still competitive seats in the House, most are considered invulnerable to challenge. Of 435 seats up for election in 2008, only a handful, perhaps no more than 100, were considered competitive. In contrast, Senate seats are considered more vulnerable. Opponents are often well financed, in part because Senate elections are so visible nationally. With just a third of the Senate up for reelection at any one time, the public can pay closer attention to campaign issues and advertisements, and the two parties can invest more money in their candidates.[5]

Incumbents benefit from several advantages.

- Under the *franking privilege,* incumbents do not have to pay postage on their mail to their district, except during the last 90 days before an election.
- Incumbents are allowed to send bulk e-mails any time.[6]

reapportionment
The assigning by Congress of congressional seats after each census. State legislatures reapportion state legislative districts.

redistricting
The redrawing of congressional and other legislative district lines following the census, to accommodate population shifts and keep districts as equal as possible in population.

gerrymandering
The drawing of legislative district boundaries to benefit a party, group, or incumbent.

safe seat
An elected office that is predictably won by one party or the other, so the success of that party's candidate is almost taken for granted.

incumbent
The current holder of elected office.

YOU WILL DECIDE Should Congress Ban Earmarks?

Earmarks, or pork, are viewed as one of the greatest abuses of power in Congress. Under standard practices, the earmarks are hidden in last-minute legislation and are doled out to members on the basis of friendships with more powerful members and with almost no public or media attention. Everyone knows the earmarks are coming, but they come so late and are buried so deep they cannot be stopped.

Congress acted in 2007 to reduce the number of earmarks. Under new rules adopted after the breakdown in congressional ethics discussed previously, the House and Senate were required to disclose all earmarks to the public. "We are blowing away the fog of anonymity," said Rep. David Dreier (R-Calif.), chairman of the House Rules Committee. "The goal is to pull back the curtain on earmarks to the public."

- Incumbents have greater access to the media, especially on local or state issues, and have very high name recognition in their districts.
- Incumbents have a natural advantage in raising campaign contributions over their challengers, in part because they have such high odds of victory.
- Incumbents are usually better candidates than their challengers, in part because they have more experience.
- Incumbents have great influence in helping their constituents solve problems with government, and they often take credit for federal spending in their districts or state.

Incumbents also control federal spending for pet projects through **earmarks,** which are usually slipped into large legislative packages at the last minute. These earmarks instruct the executive branch to spend money on specific items such as new highways or research centers.[7] Earmarks give incumbents the opportunity to "bring home the pork," which is another term for helping their constituents back home.

earmarks
Special spending projects that are set aside on behalf of individual members of Congress for their constituents.

The 2008 Congressional Elections

The 2008 congressional elections took place at one of the worst moments for Republicans in recent history. Unemployment was rising rapidly, Americans were losing their homes at record rates, banks and the automobile industry were failing, Iran was promising to build its first nuclear weapon, and the war in Afghanistan was getting worse.

Framed as a referendum on George W. Bush, Democrats had a clear advantage as the campaign began and never lost it. On Election Day, Democrats won at least five Senate seats and 19 House seats, increasing their majorities in both chambers.

Members of Congress often appear to ribbon-cuttings for important public projects. It is one way they help their districts and maintain their visibility.

Assuming that Democrats would win the two too-close-to-call elections in Alaska and Minnesota, as well as the run-off election for Senate in Georgia, their working majority in the Senate could rise to 59 if the two Senate independents vote with them. Similarly, if all six of the too-close-to-call House elections turned in their favor, their majority in the House would rise by 25.

The Democratic gains involved more than a sour economy and an overwhelming sense among voters that the nation was headed in the wrong direction. It also involved Barack Obama's huge advantage in spending, which helped increase voting turnout among Democrats, and at least three other factors.

First, a large number of Republicans retired from Congress rather than seek reelection, creating open seats that pitted new candidates against each other. Because incumbents have such high reelection rates, these open seats allowed Democrats to mount successful challenges and raise extra money. Suddenly, they were running in states and districts where they might have lost despite the national tide toward Obama. They were also able to exploit voter anger toward Bush, in part because the president and vice president removed themselves from the campaign trail because they were so unpopular.

Second, Democrats had very high quality candidates in most of the races where Republicans were most vulnerable. Candidate quality does matter in elections, and Democrats worked hard to recruit candidates who had significant campaign

THINKING IT THROUGH

Earmarks often cover special projects that have little discernible general public benefit but may help one member's district. In 2007, for example, Congress provided more than $2 billion to buy fighter jets that had already been replaced by better, cheaper models and $3 million for a program called "First Tee" that seeks to help young people improve their lives through golf.*

But many earmarks are perhaps more useful to the nation, including dollars for body armor for the troops in Iraq, funds for cancer research, support for homeland security planning, and aid to schools that have high enrollments of children from military families. In 2007, for example, Congress provided more than $18 million in an earmark to help mathematics and technology teachers keep up with their field. The problem with both good and bad earmarks is that neither is subject to competition.

One way to stop these practices is to ban earmarks altogether. But that kind of absolute ban would give more power to Appropriations Committees to create earmarks of a different sort. Instead of "airdropping" them into bills at the last minute, the Appropriations Committees could build them into their huge bills, thereby hiding them from the disclosure process that has helped cut the number of earmarks already.

Questions

1. Would you favor an earmark that helped your college or university build a new science building even if other colleges and universities building were in greater need for such facilities?
2. How might disclosure of earmarks affect citizen participation in politics?
3. Would public disclosure of earmarks hurt or help members of Congress back home?

*These examples are from Citizens Against Government Waste, *2007 Congressional Pig Book Summary* (Citizens Against Government Waste, 2008).

North Carolina's Kay Hagan celebrates her victory over Sen. Elizabeth Dole in 2008. Hagan added a Democratic seat to her party's Democratic Senate majority.

FIGURE 11–1
Congressional Election Results, 2006 and 2008.

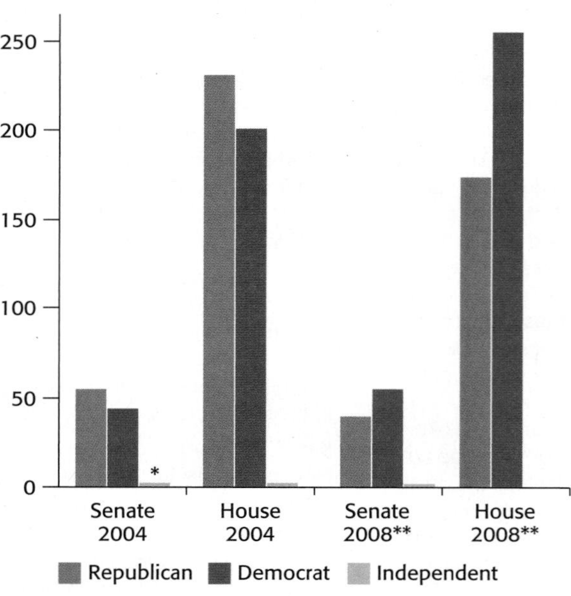

*The independents in both chambers voted with the Democrats.
**2008 totals as of November 8, 2008—does not include races that were still too close to call.

experience. Democrats also worked hard to make sure their most promising candidates had enough campaign funds to mount significant advertising and voter turnout efforts. By raising their name recognition and getting their supporters to the polls, they were able to gain a significant edge in against incumbents and in open elections. Simply put, Democrats were much more competitive in 2008 than Republicans.

Third, Democrats were able to "nationalize" the election. Whereas most House elections traditionally focus on local issues, many Democrats were able to raise national issues such as unemployment into focus during their campaigns. Many also received help from the Obama campaign and the Democratic Party, raising their ability to run aggressive advertising campaign. In addition, Obama was studious in highlighting particular campaigns for extra coverage by scheduling campaign events in key districts.

The results produced important breakthroughs in the Senate elections, but at least one campaign was mired in scandal as Alaska's Republican senator, Ted Stevens, was convicted of bribery only days before the election. Even with a prison sentence possible and his expulsion from the Senate virtually assured after Inauguration Day, Stevens ran a close campaign against Anchorage mayor Mark P. Begich. The race was still too close to call a week after the votes were counted.

Democrats also produced significant breakthroughs in key House election, most notably in Connecticut where long-time Republican moderate, Christopher Shays was defeated. Shays was the last Republican member of the House from the entire Northeast United States, making every state delegation north of New York a Democratic seat.

However, the congressional elections were not a landslide for Democrats. Unlike Franklin Delano Roosevelt in 1933 and Lyndon Johnson in 1965, Democrats gained fewer seats than expected. Although Obama did win enough Senate seats to assure confirmation of his political appointments and any Supreme Court nominees, he did not achieve the kind of majority to assure nearly automatic passage of his legislative agenda. Moreover, the Senate and House Democratic leadership immediately began scheduling legislation that had failed during the Bush years, which created immediate competition with any bills that Obama might request.

The Structure and Powers of Congress

The framers expected that Congress, not the president or the courts, would be the most important branch of government, which is why it is defined in Article I, Section 1 of the Constitution. Hence, they worried most about how to keep Congress from dominating the other branches.

In an effort to control Congress, they divided the legislative branch into two separate chambers, the House of Representatives and the Senate, which would "be as little connected with each other as the nature of their common functions and their common dependence on the society will admit."[8] Not only would House members and senators have different terms of office and represent different groups of voters (districts versus states), the framers originally wanted them to be selected through very different means.

The framers allowed each chamber to set its own rules. Because it is so much larger than the Senate, the House has less time allowed for debate and more rules governing it. House members also have smaller staffs, receive less media coverage, and are not permitted to offer certain kinds of amendments to pending legislation. In contrast, the Senate has looser rules governing debate, rarely considers legislation unless all 100 senators agree on a schedule, and generally allows its members to offer an unlimited number of amendments to pending legislation, again as long as all senators agree to allow an open-ended process.

Miss Jeanette Rankin

Montana Democrat Jeanette Rankin was the first woman elected to Congress but is best known for her lone "nay" vote against the declaration of war on Japan. "As a woman, I can't go to war," she told her colleagues on December 8, 1941, "and I refuse to send anyone else."

GENERATION **NEXT**

Support for Compromise

U.S. citizens almost always agree that they like political leaders who know how to unite the country. During his 2000 campaign, President George W. Bush promised the country that he would be a uniter, not a divider, a theme that Senator Barack Obama reiterated in his run for the Democratic presidential nomination in 2008.

Obama was able to convince voters that he would bring Democrats and Republicans together to address a number of crises, including the wars in Afghanistan and Iraq, the sharp decline in the economy, global warming, and energy independence. But voters strengthened his hand by electing more Democrats to the Senate and House.

Generation Next shares the sentiment. According to the Pew Research Center's 2007 political landscape survey, the vast majority either completely or mostly agree that they like political leaders who are willing to make compromises to get the job done.

However, there are differences of opinion within Generation Next. One reason may be that women and nonwhites want political leaders to do more on the issues that affect them, while Republicans and conservative 18- to 29-year-olds want government to do less.

Generation Next is not very different from the other generations interviewed. Overall, 32 percent of 18- to 29-year-olds said they completely agreed with the statement about compromise, compared with 30 percent of 30- to 39-year-olds, 28 percent of 40- to 49-year-olds, 29 percent of 50- to 59-year-olds, and 28 percent of people age 60 or older. The desire for compromise is so strong that less than 20 percent of all five age groups said they completely or mostly disagreed with the statement. Although compromise may be highly valued, the compromises that political leaders do make are often criticized.

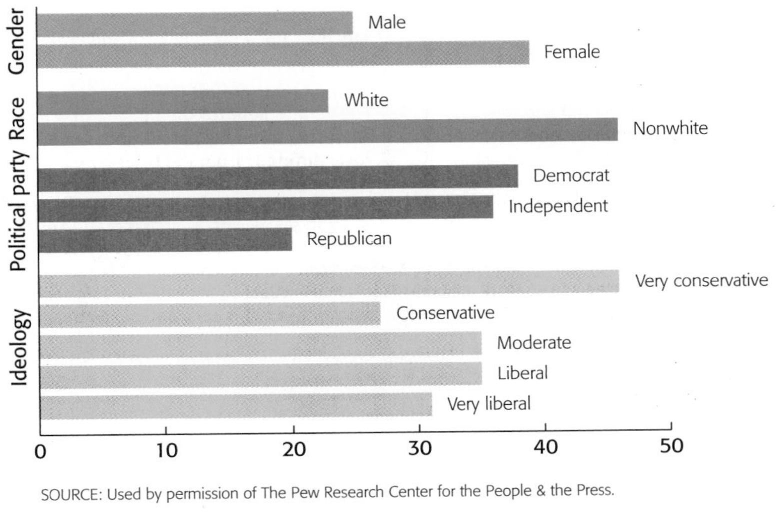

SOURCE: Used by permission of The Pew Research Center for the People & the Press.

QUESTIONS

1. Why do women, nonwhites, and very conservative persons more than others want political leaders to make compromises to get the job done?
2. Does the U.S. political system reward political leaders for making compromises?
3. How does the Constitution encourage or discourage compromise?

LEARNING **OBJECTIVE**

2 Differentiate the powers of Congress.

LEARNING **OBJECTIVE**

 Compare and contrast the structure and powers of the House and Senate.

A Divided Branch

Bicameralism, or a two-house legislature, remains the most important organizational feature of the U.S. Congress. Each chamber meets in its own wing of the Capitol Building (See Figure 11–2); each has offices for its members on separate sides of Capitol Street; each has its own committee structure, its own rules for considering legislation, and its own record of proceedings (even though the records are published together as the *Congressional Record*); and each sets the rules governing its own members (each establishes its own legislative committees, for example).[9]

Bicameral legislatures were common in most of the colonies, and the framers believed the arrangement was essential for preventing strong-willed majorities from oppressing individuals and minorities.[10] As James Madison explained in *The Federalist,* No. 51, "In order to control the legislative authority, you must divide it." (*The Federalist,* No. 51, is reprinted in the Appendix at the back of this book.)

bicameralism
The principle of a two-house legislature.

enumerated powers
The powers explicitly given to Congress in the Constitution.

The Powers of Congress

The framers gave Congress a long list of express or **enumerated powers.** Because the Revolutionary War had been sparked by unfair taxation, the power "to lay and collect

FIGURE 11–2
How a Bill Becomes a Law.

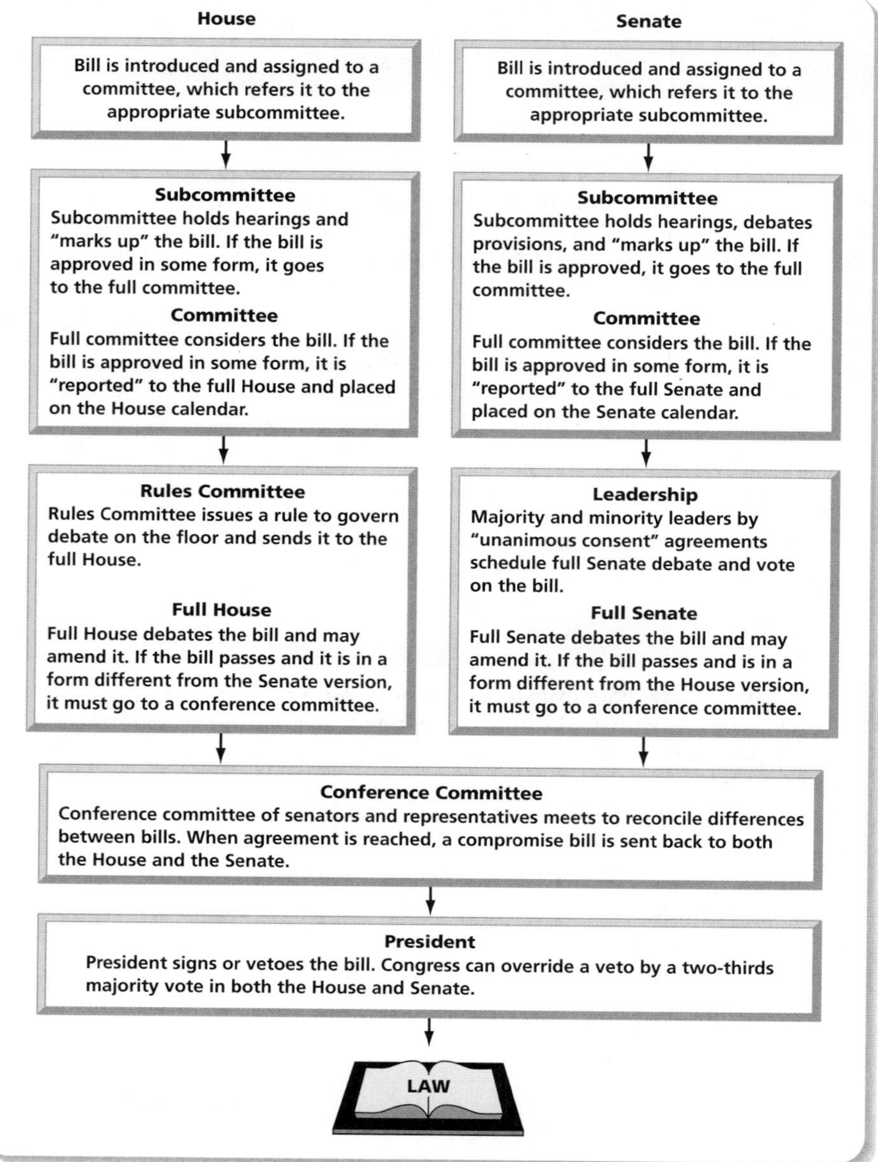

Taxes" was the very first of these powers. Another 17 express powers of Congress fall into five basic categories:

1. **The Power to Raise, Make, and Borrow Money.** Congress has the power to tax, borrow money, issue currency, and coin money.
2. **The Power to Regulate Commerce.** Congress has the power to regulate commerce between the United States and other nations, as well as between the states. It can also set standards for determining the value of products through weights and measures, establish uniform bankruptcy laws that govern private businesses, and promote the arts and sciences by granting copyright protection to authors and patents to inventors.
3. **The Power to Unify and Expand the Country.** Congress has the power to create post offices and postal roads, which link the states together; to determine the rules for becoming a citizen; and to acquire, manage, and dispose of federal land.

4. **The Power to Prepare and Declare War.** Alongside the power to declare war, Congress can raise, support, and regulate armies and a navy; provide for organizing, arming, disciplining, and calling on state militia (now called the National Guard); execute laws suppressing civil unrest; and repel foreign invasions.
5. **The Power to Create the Federal Judiciary.** Congress is responsible for creating all "inferior" courts below the Supreme Court and for determining their jurisdiction, as well as the appellate jurisdiction of the Supreme Court (discussed in Chapter 14).

President Bill Clinton was the second president in history to be impeached by the House. He was accused in late 1998 of lying regarding his relationship with a White House intern and was acquitted by the Senate in early February 1999 by a vote of 55 to 45. Supreme Court chief justice William Rehnquist presided over the Senate trial, which opened in the old Senate Chamber just down the hall from the Senate floor where the final vote would be taken.

Many of these powers are limited in some way, however. Congress has the power to collect taxes only for the common defense and general welfare of the nation, for example, and may not tax exports to other nations. Similarly, it may declare war, but only the president has the power to command the military.

The framers also gave Congress implied powers such as the power to "make all Laws which shall be necessary and proper for carrying into Execution the foregoing Powers, and all other Powers vested by this Constitution in the Government of the United States, or in any Department or Officer thereof." This necessary and proper clause, discussed in Chapter 3, is sometimes called the elastic clause because it stretches to cover much of what Congress might do. The Constitution also gave Congress complete authority to set its own rules for its proceedings.

Finally, the Constitution gave Congress important checks on government, including the power to remove the president and judges from office through the impeachment process. The House has the authority to charge, or impeach, a president or judge for committing "high crimes and misdemeanors," while the Senate has the responsibility to conduct the trial to determine guilt or innocence. Impeachment requires a majority vote in the House, while conviction requires a two-thirds vote of the Senate. In 1999, for example, the House impeached President Bill Clinton for lying to a federal court about his affair with a White House intern, but the Senate acquitted him.

As the impeachment power shows, the Constitution gives different duties to each chamber (see Table 11–1). The Senate has the power to give its advice and consent in confirming or rejecting the president's nominees for senior executive

TABLE 11–1 Differences Between the House of Representatives and the Senate

House	Senate
Two-year term	Six-year term
435 members	100 members
Elected in districts	Elected in states
Strong leadership controls action by individual members	Weaker leadership provides more freedom to individual members
Strict rules for debate	Loose rules for debate
Decision to consider legislation made by majority	Decision to consider legislation made by unanimous consent of all members
Responsible for proposing raising revenues	Responsible for giving advice and consent on presidential appointees and treaties
More powerful committee leaders	More equal distribution of power in committees
Rules Committee sets terms of debate	Senate as a whole sets terms of debate
Limited debate	Extended debate
All amendments to legislation must be approved for consideration in advance of debate	Amendments are generally allowed without advance notice
Unlimited debate is prohibited	Unlimited debate is allowed

HOW OTHER NATIONS GOVERN

Strong and Weak Legislatures

Britain's legislature is the world's best-known parliament. It is composed of two houses—the House of Commons, which is elected by the citizenry, and the House of Lords, which includes some individuals who have been given a lifelong title for achievement. Because the House of Lords has no durable legislative function beyond making small amendments in legislation, the British parliament is not considered a bicameral legislature.

China has two legislatures, one controlled by the Communist Party and the other elected by the people for five-year terms. The People's Congress meets once a year and has up to 3,000 members. Although it has great formal powers, it yields to the party committees. Nevertheless, it has been asserting more power in recent years.

India has a parliamentary system, in no small measure because it was colonized by Britain. Its parliament has two chambers—the Lok Sabha (the House of the People) and Rajya Sabha (the Council of States). In recent years, the Council of States has become more influential to the point that the Indian system is bordering on a true bicameral legislature.

Japan's national legislature is the Diet. It is bicameral, parliamentary, and the strongest institution in the constitution. Although it has elements of both the U.S. and British models, it tends to operate more like Britain's.

Mexico's legislature is one of the strongest in the world, at least in theory. Like the U.S. Congress, it is the first branch listed in the Mexican constitution. Like the U.S. Congress, too, it has two houses, both elected by the citizenry. But even though it has most of the formal powers in government, the Mexican Federal Congress has often allowed the president and his or her party to control the informal legislative process.

Because Nigeria was colonized by the British, it created a parliamentary system when it gained its independence in 1960. Under its new constitution of 1999, however, it adopted the U.S. system with an independently elected president and a bicameral Congress. Nigerians are still not used to the new system, and the nation provides an important case study of the differences in how the U.S. and British systems operate.

QUESTIONS

1. Given the British influence over former colonies like India and Nigeria, why didn't the United States, another former colony, follow the parliamentary model?
2. What makes the U.S. Congress one of the strongest in the world, but also one of the least efficient?
3. Why is the bicameral legislature so popular in the world?

branch positions and for the federal courts. The Senate also has the power to give its advice and consent in approving or rejecting treaties made by the president. All treaties must be ratified by a two-thirds vote in the Senate before they can be enforced by the president.

The House has its own responsibilities, too, most notably the power to author "all bills for raising revenues." But these powers are less significant than those given to the Senate, in part because the framers worried that House members would be too close to the people and therefore more likely to act in haste. Although all revenue bills must originate in the House, for example, the Constitution invites the Senate to propose amendments to revenue bills, even to the point of changing everything except the title.

Despite its position as the first branch of government and its substantial powers, Congress has difficulty keeping pace with its great rival, the presidency. The president's national security responsibilities, preparation of the budget, media visibility, and agenda-setting influence have all enhanced the position of the presidency relative to Congress. Moreover, presidents often argue that the Constitution gives them the power to act without congressional consent during war.

The two-year period between congressional elections is called a single Congress and is divided into two one-year sessions. Each Congress is numbered, dating back to the very first in 1789–1791. Hence, the Congress that convened in January 2009 is the 111th, and comes 220 years after the first.

Congressional Leadership and Committees

LEARNING **OBJECTIVE**

4 Compare the leadership systems used in the House and Senate.

Given the differences between the chambers that are summarized in Table 11–1, we should not be surprised that the House and Senate have different kinds of leadership and rules. Whereas the House holds tight control over its large number of members, the Senate has much looser controls. This makes legislation easier to pass in the House and much more difficult in the Senate.

Because its membership is so much larger than the Senate, the House uses an electronic voting board to keep track of member votes. The Senate still uses voice votes recorded by the Clerk of the Senate.

The Power of the speaker of the House

Leading the House of Representatives

The organization and procedures in the House are different from those in the Senate, largely because the House is more than four times as large as the Senate. A larger membership requires more rules, which means that *how* things are done affects *what* is done. The House assigns different types of bills to different calendars. For instance, financial measures—tax or appropriations bills—are put on a special calendar for quick action.

The House has other ways to speed up lawmaking. Ordinary rules may be suspended by a two-thirds vote, or immediate action may be taken by *unanimous consent* of the members on the floor. By acting as a *committee of the whole,* the House is able to operate more informally and more quickly than under its regular rules. A *quorum* in the committee of the whole requires only 100 members, rather than a majority of the whole chamber, and voting is quicker and simpler. Members are limited in how long they can speak, and debate may be cut off simply by majority vote.

In 2007 California Democrat Nancy Pelosi became the first woman to serve as Speaker of the House.

The Speaker of the House Again because of its size, the House gives its leaders more power than the Senate, where individual senators have more power to refuse to act at all. The most powerful leader on Capitol Hill is the **Speaker** of the House.[11] Although the Speaker is formally elected by the entire House, the post is always filled by the majority party, which gives the party even more power. The Speaker is third in line to be president of the United States (after the vice president) in case of the death, resignation, or impeachment of the president.

The Speaker has the power to recognize members who rise to speak, rule on questions of parliamentary procedure, and appoint members to temporary committees (but not to the major committees that help make the laws). The Speaker also has the power to reorganize House committees, name committee chairs, appoint allies to leadership posts, and reduce the size of committee staffs, all of which give the Speaker enormous power to reward and punish individual members.[12]

The Speaker is usually selected on a vote by the majority **party caucus,** which is called *the party conference* by Republicans. The caucus also elects party officers and committee chairs, approves committee assignments, and often helps the Speaker decide which issues will come first on the legislative calendar. However, because the Speaker is always selected first, he or she has the most important voice in determining all these choices.

Speaker
The presiding officer in the House of Representatives, formally elected by the House but actually selected by the majority party.

party caucus
A meeting of the members of a party in a legislative chamber to select party leaders and to develop party policy. Called a *conference* by the Republicans.

HISTORY MAKERS

Speaker Uncle Joe Cannon

Joseph Gurney Cannon, or "Uncle Joe" Cannon, was the first modern Speaker of the House. Born in North Carolina and raised in Indiana, he was first elected to the House from Illinois in 1873 and served until 1891, when he was defeated. As a Republican, he was reelected in 1893 and immediately became chairman of the powerful House Appropriations Committee. He ran for Speaker four times before finally capturing the post in 1903.

Whereas past Speakers had used the post to build compromises across the two parties, Cannon turned it into an engine of party discipline. He controlled virtually every committee appointment in the House, decided which committees would get the most important bills, and dictated the terms of legislative debate through tight control of the House Rules Committee. He also used his powers to punish Republicans who failed to support his positions. Called "Czar Cannon" and the "Brakeman of the House," Cannon was widely regarded as a tyrant who would not tolerate dissent.*

Cannon was not just a Republican, however. He was a conservative Republican who opposed his own party's president, Theodore Roosevelt, and the "progressive" or moderate Republicans who supported legislation to regulate the meat-packing industry, abolish child labor, and break the industrial monopolies that exercised so much control over the national economy. Republican progressives eventually joined ranks with moderate and liberal Democrats to remove him from the job in 1911.

QUESTIONS

1. Did Uncle Joe Cannon improve Congress by exerting tighter control over members of his party?
2. What are the downsides of tighter leadership control in the House?
3. How might the Speaker affect the public's ability to influence House members and elections on key issues?

*See Keith Krebbiel and Alan E. Wiseman, "Joe Cannon and the Minority Party: Tyranny or Bipartisanship," research paper no. 1858, Stanford University Graduate School of Business, July 2004.

majority leader
The legislative leader selected by the majority party who helps plan party strategy, confers with other party leaders, and tries to keep members of the party in line.

minority leader
The legislative leader selected by the minority party as spokesperson for the opposition.

whip
The party leader who is the liaison between the leadership and the rank-and-file in the legislature.

closed rule
A procedural rule in the House of Representatives that prohibits any amendments to bills or provides that only members of the committee reporting the bill may offer amendments.

open rule
A procedural rule in the House of Representatives that permits floor amendments within the overall time allocated to the bill.

Other House Officers The Speaker is assisted by the **majority leader,** who helps plan party strategy, confers with other party leaders, and tries to keep members of the party in line. The minority party elects the **minority leader,** who usually becomes Speaker when his or her party gains a majority in the House. (These positions are also sometimes called majority and minority *floor leaders.*) Assisting each floor leader are the party **whips.** (The term comes from *whipper-in,* the huntsman who keeps the hounds bunched in a pack during a foxhunt.) The whips inform members when important bills will come up for a vote, prepare summaries of the bills, do vote counts for the leadership, exert pressure (sometimes mild and sometimes heavy) on members to support the leadership, and try to ensure maximum attendance on the floor for critical votes.

The House Rules Committee The House Rules Committee is almost certainly the most powerful committee in either chamber. Under the much tighter rules that govern the larger House, the Rules Committee decides the rules governing the length of the floor debate on any legislative issue and sets limits on the number and kinds of floor amendments that will be allowed. By refusing to grant a *rule,* which is a ticket to the floor, the Rules Committee can delay consideration of a bill. A **closed rule** prohibits amendments altogether or provides that only members of the committee reporting the bill may offer amendments; closed rules are usually reserved for tax and spending bills. An **open rule** permits debate within the overall time allocated to the bill.

Leading the Senate

The Senate has the same basic committee structure, elected party leadership, and decentralized power as the House, but because the Senate is a smaller body, its procedures are more informal, and it permits more time for debate. It is a more open, fluid, and

THE **CHANGING FACE** OF U.S. POLITICS

Diversity in Congress

Although the Constitution does not mention race, gender, or wealth among the qualifications for office, the framers expected members of Congress to be white male property owners. After all, women, slaves, and freed slaves could not vote, let alone hold office.

The framers would therefore be surprised at the face of Congress today. Recent Congresses have had record numbers of women and minorities. In 2008, one woman was elected to senate. New Hampshire's new Democratic senator Jeanne Shaheen willl join 16 other women in the Senate. In addition, ten new women will join the 64 women who won reelection in the House. All totaled, 93 women will serve in the 111th congress, a record number. There will also be a new woman governor, Beverly Perdue in North Carolina, creating a total of eight women governors in the 50 states.

These numbers would not have increased without the rise of a new generation of women and minority candidates, however. Although voting participation by women and minority groups has increased dramatically over the past half-century, it took time for women and minority candidates to gain the experience needed for a successful congressional campaign and increase the odds of their winning office.

Although Congress is becoming more diverse by race and gender, it still remains very different from the rest of the United States in income and occupation. Almost one-third of the senators who serve in the 111th Congress are millionaires, and more than half hold law degrees. Moreover, old customs die hard. Even with the Democratic senator from Washington, Patty Murray, sitting on his Appropriations Committee, Chairman Robert Byrd (D-W.V.) still referred to women on his committee as "Gentlemen." At the current rate of change in the number of women, for example, it will take another 400 years before women constitute a majority in the House.

QUESTIONS

1. How does increasing diversity change the issues that Congress works on? Should Congress reflect the levels of diversity in the U.S. population in order to best represent our citizenry?
2. Does increasing diversity help strengthen public approval of Congress?
3. Did the election of Nancy Pelosi as Speaker of the House make any difference in the power of the office or the overall performance of Congress?

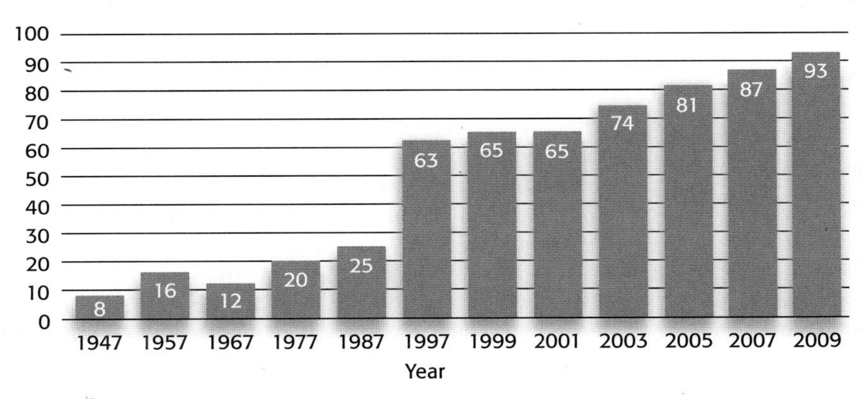

SOURCE: Rutgers University, Eagleton Institute of Politics, Center for American Women and Politics, November 2008.

decentralized body now than it was a generation or two ago. Indeed, it is often said that the Senate has 100 separate power centers and is so splintered that party leaders have difficulty arranging the day-to-day schedule.[13]

The Senate is led by the Senate majority leader, who is elected by the majority party. When the majority leader is from the president's party, the president becomes the party's most visible leader on Capitol Hill and in the nation as a whole. However, when the majority leader and the president are from different parties, the Senate majority leader is considered his or her party's national spokesperson. Senator Harry Reid (D-Nev.) was elected as the current Senate majority leader after Democrats persuaded the two Independents to help create a majority of 51 to 49 in 2007.

Party machinery in the Senate is similar to that in the House. There are party caucuses (conferences), majority and minority floor leaders, and party whips. Each party has a *policy committee,* composed of party leaders, which is theoretically responsible for the party's overall legislative program. In the Senate, the party policy committees help the leadership monitor legislation and provide policy expertise.

The president of the Senate, who is also the vice president of the United States, has little actual influence over Senate proceedings and can vote only in the case of a tie. The Senate elects a **president pro tempore,** usually the most senior member of the majority party, who acts as chair in the absence of the vice president. Presiding over the Senate on most occasions is a thankless chore, so the president pro tempore regularly delegates this responsibility to junior members of the chamber's majority party.

Although the Senate has many of the same leaders and offices as the House, it is far less structured. It has always operated under rules that give individual senators great power. Extended debate allows senators to hold the floor as long as they wish unless a supermajority of 60 colleagues votes to end debate. Moreover, the Senate's rules allow individual senators to offer amendments on virtually any topic to a pending bill, allowing them to amend a bill to death.[14]

One relatively recent expression of this individualism is a practice called a legislative **hold,** a delaying tactic designed to stop legislation. Holds were originally designed to give individual senators a short period to prepare for a debate or delay a vote for personal reasons. Over time, however, they have become a powerful device for blocking action on legislation and nominations, and are often viewed as a way to delay action on a particular issue or nomination.

Individual senators also have the power to engage in unlimited debate, known as the **filibuster,** which was invented in the 1830s. The name means "pirate" in Dutch. A senator or senators can use a filibuster to delay Senate proceedings by holding the floor continuously, thereby preventing action. Filibusters often begin with an individual senator issuing a legislative hold, putting a stop to all action. At one time, the filibuster was a favorite weapon of southern senators for blocking civil rights legislation.

Until 1917, the Senate could terminate a filibuster only by the unanimous consent of every member, including the senator or senators conducting it! That year, however, the Senate adopted its first debate-ending rule, or **cloture.** The rule specifies that the question of curtailing debate must be put to a vote two days after 16 senators sign a petition asking for cloture. If three-fifths of senators (60 of the 100 members) vote in favor of cloture, no senator may speak on the measure under consideration for more than one hour. Once invoked, cloture requires that the final vote on the measure be taken after no more than 30 hours of debate.[15]

LEARNING **OBJECTIVE**

 Analyze the committee structure and show how members are assigned to committees.

president pro tempore
An officer of the Senate selected by the majority party to act as chair in the absence of the vice president.

hold
A procedural practice in the Senate whereby a senator temporarily blocks the consideration of a bill or nomination.

filibuster
A procedural practice in the Senate whereby a senator refuses to relinquish the floor and thereby delays proceedings and prevents a vote on a controversial issue.

cloture
A procedure for terminating debate, especially filibusters, in the Senate.

standing committee
A permanent committee established in a legislature, usually focusing on a policy area.

special or select committee
A congressional committee created for a specific purpose, sometimes to conduct an investigation.

joint committee
A committee composed of members of both the House of Representatives and the Senate; such committees oversee the Library of Congress and conduct investigations.

Congressional Committees

Committees are the workhorses of Congress. They draft legislation, review nominees, conduct investigations of executive branch departments and agencies, and are usually responsible for ironing out differences between House and Senate versions of the same legislation. They determine who gets what, when, where, and how from government—in short, they shape the politics of legislation.

It is sometimes said that Congress is a collection of committees that come together in a chamber every once in a while to approve one another's actions. Woodrow Wilson, a political science professor before he became president, expressed a similar thought: "Congress in session is Congress on display. Congress in committee is Congress at work."[16] Committees rarely make the first decisions on legislation, however. This duty belongs to the many subcommittees that start the process moving with hearings and first drafts of legislation.[17]

Types of Committees In theory, all congressional committees are created anew in each new Congress. But most continue with little change from Congress to Congress. **Standing committees** are the most durable and are the sources of most bills, while **special** or **select committees** come together to address temporary priorities of Congress such as aging or taxes and rarely author legislation. **Joint committees** have members from both the House and the Senate and exist either to study an issue of interest to the entire Congress or to oversee congressional support agencies such as the Library of

Congress or the U.S. Government Printing Office. Almost all standing committees have subcommittees that help handle the legislative workload.

Of the various types of committees, standing committees are the most important for making laws and representing constituents, and they fall into four types: authorizing, appropriations, rules and administration, and revenue and budget. There are 35 standing committees in the House and Senate, which are listed by chamber and type in Table 11–2.

Authorizing Committees Authorizing committees pass the laws that tell government what to do. The House and Senate education and labor committees, for example, are responsible for setting rules governing the federal government's student loan programs, including who can apply, how much they can get, where the loans come from, and how defaults are handled.

Appropriations Committees Appropriations committees make decisions about how much money government will spend on its programs and operations. Although there is just one appropriations committee in each chamber, each appropriations committee has one subcommittee for each of the 13 appropriations bills that must be enacted each year to keep government running. Because they decide who gets how much from government, these subcommittees have great power to undo or limit decisions by the authorizing committees.

Rules and Administration Committees Rules committees in both chambers determine the basic operations of their chamber—for example, how many staffers individual members get and what the ratio of majority to minority members and staff will be. Again, because of the number of members it must control, the House Rules Committee is more

Jimmy Stewart plays the role of a senator who launches a filibuster in the 1930s Frank Capra movie *Mr. Smith Goes to Washington*. Today's filibusters do not involve nonstop speeches to control the floor—members merely express their intention to filibuster and the Senate moves on to other business.

TABLE 11–2 Congressional Standing Committees, 2007–2009

House	Senate
Agriculture (Authorizing)	Agriculture, Nutrition, and Forestry (Authorizing)
Appropriations (Appropriations)	Appropriations (Appropriations)
Armed Services (Authorizing)	Armed Services (Authorizing)
Budget (Revenue and budget)	Banking, Housing, and Urban Affairs (Authorizing)
Education and Labor (Authorizing)	Budget (Revenue and Budget)
Energy and Commerce (Authorizing)	Commerce, Science, and Transportation (Authorizing)
Financial Services (Authorizing)	Energy and Natural Resources (Authorizing)
Foreign Affairs (Authorizing)	Environment and Public Works (Authorizing)
Homeland Security (Authorizing)	Finance (Revenue and Budget)
House Administration (Rules and Administration)	Health, Education, Labor, and Pensions (Authorizing)
Judiciary (Authorizing)	Homeland Security and Governmental Affairs (Authorizing)
Natural Resources (Authorizing)	Judiciary (Authorizing)
Oversight and Government Reform (Authorizing)	Rules and Administration (Rules and Administration)
Rules (Rules and Administration)	Small Business and Entrepreneurship (Authorizing)
Science and Technology (Authorizing)	Veterans Affairs (Authorizing)
Small Business (Authorizing)	
Standards of Official Conduct (Rules and Administration)	
Transportation and Infrastructure (Authorizing)	
Veterans Affairs (Authorizing)	
Ways and Means (Revenue and Budget)	

powerful than its twin in the Senate. As noted earlier, the House Rules Committee has special responsibility for giving each bill a rule, or ticket, to the floor of the House and determines what, if any, amendments to a bill will be permitted.

Revenue and Budget Committees Revenue and budget committees deal with raising the money appropriating committees spend while setting the broad targets that shape the federal budget. They determine how much money will actually go toward programs such as Pell Grants. Authorizing committees may set the maximum amount that can be spent, but appropriations committees commit the actual dollars, and often provide less than the authorizing committees want.

Because it exists to raise revenues through taxes, the House Ways and Means Committee is arguably the single most powerful committee in Congress, for it both raises and authorizes spending. As the only committee in either chamber that can originate tax and revenue legislation, it is also responsible for making basic decisions on the huge Social Security and Medicare programs.

Choosing Committee Members Each political party controls the selection of standing committee members. The chair and a majority of each committee come from the majority party. The minority party is represented on each committee roughly in proportion to its membership in the entire chamber, except on some powerful committees on which the majority may want to enhance its position. Because some committees are more prestigious than others, the debate over committee assignments can be intense. These committees control more important programs or more money and give their members important advantages in helping their home districts.

Each chamber and party is responsible for choosing committee members. In the House, Republicans choose their committee members through their Committee on Committees, which is composed of one member from each state that has Republican representation in the House, while Democrats choose their committee members through their Steering and Policy Committee. In turn, Senate Republicans and Democrats both use their Steering Committees to make assignments. Both chambers make their selections based on an applicant's preferences, talent and party loyalty, and the needs of their district or state.

Most committee chairmen are selected on the basis of the **seniority rule;** the member of the majority party with the longest continuous service on the committee becomes chair on the retirement of the current chair or a change in the party in control of Congress. The seniority rule gives power to representatives who come from safe districts where one party is dominant and a member can build up years of continuous service. Conversely, the seniority rule lessens the influence of states or districts where the two parties are more evenly matched and where there is more turnover.[18]

The Special Role of Conference Committees Given the differences between the House and the Senate, it is not surprising that the version of a bill passed by one chamber may differ substantially from the version passed by the other. Only if both houses pass an absolutely identical measure can it become law. Most of the time one house accepts the language of the other, but about 10 to 12 percent of all bills passed, usually major ones, must be referred to a **conference committee**—a special committee of members from each chamber that settles the differences between versions.[19] Both parties are represented, but the majority party has more members.

Conference committees have considerable leeway in reaching agreement, prompting President Ronald Reagan to note, "You know, if an orange and an apple went into conference consultations, it might come out a pear."[20] Ordinarily, the law negotiated in conference ends up somewhere between the House and Senate versions. On matters for which there is no clear middle ground, members are sometimes accused of exceeding their instructions and producing an entirely new bill. For this reason, the conference committee has been called a "third house" of Congress and one of the most significant congressional institutions.[21]

seniority rule
A legislative practice that assigns the chair of a committee or subcommittee to the member of the majority party with the longest continuous service on the committee.

conference committee
A committee appointed by the presiding officers of each chamber to adjust differences on a particular bill passed by each in different form.

On the surface, it appears the Senate's version of a bill wins more often, partly because the Senate often acts on its legislation after the House. But by approving the initial bill first and thereby setting the agenda on an issue, the House often has more of an impact on the final outcome than the Senate.

Caucuses In contrast to conference committees, which are appointed by the House and Senate leadership to perform a specific legislative role, caucuses are best defined as informal committees that allow individual members to promote shared legislative interests. There are caucuses for House members only, for senators only, and for members of both chambers together. By the 1990s, according to one count, House members actually served on more informal caucuses than on committees and subcommittees.[22]

The growing diversity of the caucuses parallels that of society. Working caucuses include the Black Caucus, Hispanic Caucus, Women's Issues Caucus, Rural Health Caucus, Children's Caucus, Cuba Freedom Caucus, Pro-Life Caucus, Homelessness Task Force, Urban Caucus, and Ethiopian Jewry Caucus.

The Job of the Legislator

Membership in Congress was once a part-time job. Legislators came to Washington for a few terms, averaged less than five years of continuous service, and returned to private life. Pay was low, and Washington was no farther than a carriage ride from home.[23]

Congress started to meet more frequently in the late 1800s, pay increased, and being a member became increasingly attractive.[24] In the 1850s, roughly half of all House members retired or were defeated at each election; by 1900, the number who left at the end of each term had fallen to roughly one-quarter; by the 1970s, it was barely a tenth. Even in the 1994 congressional elections, when Republicans won the House majority for the first time in 40 years, 90 percent of House incumbents who ran for reelection won.[25]

By the 1950s, being a member of Congress had become a full-time job and a long-term career. Members came to Washington to stay and began to exploit their incumbency advantages. In 1958, for example, members of Congress used the *franking privilege* to send 50 million pieces of mail back home. In 2008, Congress sent almost 150 million messages, not counting e-mail. In 50 years, the number had more than tripled. Include the amount of e-mail, and the average member of Congress is in touch regularly with his or her constituents.[26]

The workday also got longer. In 2007 alone, members of Congress spent 1,376 hours in session, took 1,186 roll call votes, held 844 hearings, and passed 180 bills that were signed into laws. All these measures of activity have been growing over the past 50 years. But although they believe their jobs have become more demanding and complex and they are frustrated by the lack of personal time, most representatives do not want to leave.[27]

As members of Congress became attached to their careers, they began to abandon many of the norms, or informal rules, that once guided their behavior in office.[28] The old norms were simple. Members were supposed to specialize in a small number of issues (the norm of specialization), defer to members with longer tenure in office (the norm of seniority), never criticize anyone personally (the norm of courtesy), and wait their turn to speak and introduce legislation (the norm of apprenticeship). As longtime House Speaker Sam Rayburn once said, new members were to go along in order to get along, and to be seen and not heard.

The new norms are equally simple. New members are no longer willing to wait their turn to speak or introduce legislation, and they now have enough staff to make their opinions known on just about any issue at just about any point in the legislative process. Although the norm of courtesy still lives on as members refer to each other with great respect, the new congressional career allows little time for specialization, seniority, and apprenticeship. Members must take care of their electoral concerns first.

Legislators as Representatives

Congress has a split personality. On the one hand, it is a *lawmaking institution* that writes laws and makes policy for the entire nation. In this capacity, all the members are expected to set aside their personal ambitions and perhaps even the concerns of their own constituencies. Yet Congress is also a representative assembly, made up of 535 elected officials who serve as links between their constituents and the national government. The dual roles of making laws and responding to constituents' demands force members to balance national concerns against the specific interests of their states or districts.

Individual members of Congress perceive their roles differently. Some believe they should serve as **delegates** from their districts, finding out what "the folks back home" want and acting accordingly. Other members see themselves as **trustees** to act and vote according to their own view of what is best for their district and state, and the nation.

LEARNING **OBJECTIVE**

6 Assess the effect of different forms of representation on citizen engagement.

delegate
An official who is expected to represent the views of his or her constituents even when personally holding different views; one interpretation of the role of the legislator.

trustee
An official who is expected to vote independently based on his or her judgment of the circumstances; one interpretation of the role of the legislator.

Most legislators shift back and forth between the delegate and trustee roles, depending on their perception of the public interest, their standing in the last and next elections, and the pressures of the moment. Most also view themselves more as free agents than as instructed delegates for their districts. And recent research suggests they often *are* free. Although about half of citizens do not know how their representatives voted on major legislation, most still believe their representative voted with the district or state. Moreover, members of Congress spend a great deal of time helping their constituency, reaching out to swing voters, and worrying about how a vote on a controversial issue will "play" back home.[29]

Members cannot represent their constituents through their experiences as ordinary Americans, however. As Figure 11–3 shows, they are very different from the rest of the public. They are older on average, more educated, and less diverse by gender and race. They are also much more likely to be lawyers.

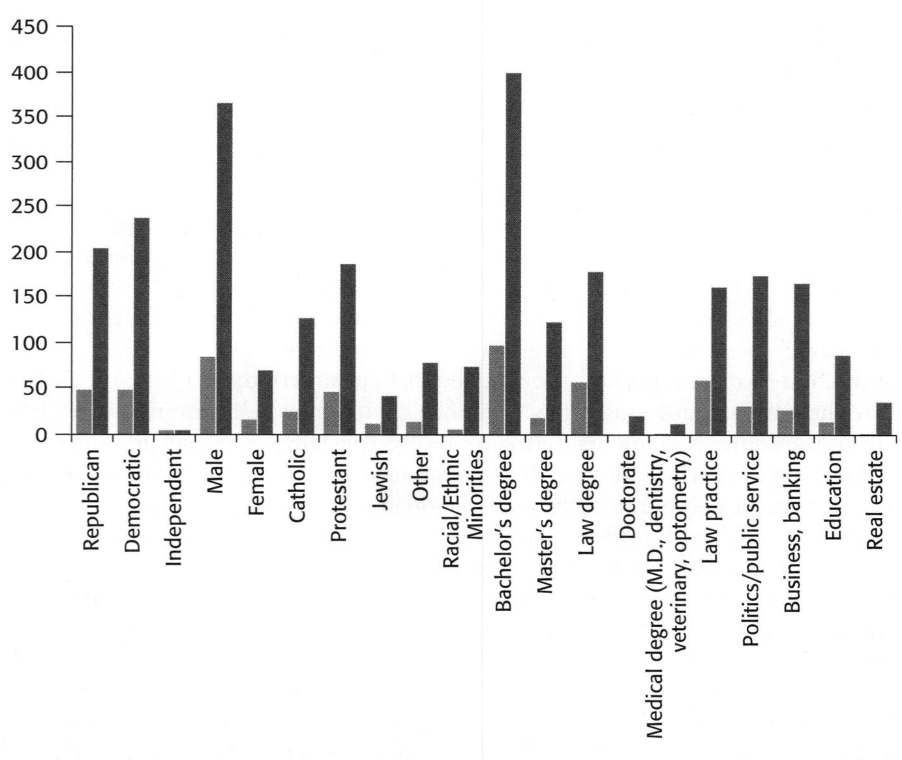

FIGURE 11–3
Profile of the 110th Congress, 2007–2009.

SOURCE: *Congressional Quarterly Weekly*, January 27, 2007, pp. 143–147.

NOTE: Numbers exceed 100 and 435 because many Senators and Representatives had more than one educational degree and occupation on entering office.

Making Legislative Choices

About 8,000 bills are introduced in the House and Senate during a two-year Congress, but only a handful receive hearings, even fewer reach the floor, and one in eight become law. Although House members and senators cast 1,000 votes each year, most are voice votes on noncontroversial legislation and procedures.[30] When they do take a vote on a controversial issue such as authorizing the use of force in Iraq, prescription drug coverage for the elderly, tax cuts, or more school testing, members of Congress are influenced by a number of factors, from the views of trusted colleagues to the wishes of the president. Because members pay attention to different factors depending on the issues, we present the following list in alphabetical order.

Although the average age in Congress has gotten older over the past decade, a wave of younger members appears to be on the way. At age 31, Patrick McHenry was the youngest member of Congress in 2007–2008.

Colleagues Their busy schedules and the great number of votes force legislators to depend on the advice of like-minded colleagues and close friends in Congress. In particular, they look to respected members of the committee who worked on a bill.[31]

A member may also vote with a colleague in the expectation that the colleague will later vote for a measure about which the member is concerned—a practice called **logrolling.** Some vote trading takes place to build coalitions so that members can "bring home the bacon" to their constituents. Other vote trading reflects reciprocity in congressional relations or deference to colleagues' superior information or expertise.

LEARNING **OBJECTIVE**

7 Examine the influences on legislative decisions and how these influences may vary with issues.

Congressional Staff The complexity of the issues and increasingly demanding schedules created a demand for additional Congressional staff. Because both chambers have roughly equal amounts of money for staff, the 100 Senators and their committees have much larger staffs than their 435 House counterparts. Many congressional staffers work not in Washington, but in district and state offices back home. Members of Congress return home every weekend to make speeches, appear on television, raise money, and greet voters, activities arranged in advance by their district or state staffs very much like a continuous political campaign.

Constituents Members of Congress rarely vote against the strong wishes of their constituents, but they often think their constituents are more interested in a particular issue than they really are.[32] Representatives mostly hear from the **attentive public**—citizens who follow public affairs closely—rather than the general public. Members of Congress are generally concerned about how they will explain their votes, especially as election day approaches. Even if only a few voters are aware of their stand on a given issue, this group may make the difference between victory and defeat.

Ideology Members of Congress are influenced by their own experiences and attitudes about the role of government.[33] Ideology is closely related to a member's party as a predictor of congressional voting. In 2005, for example, the most liberal members of the House and Senate were all Democrats and mostly came from the Northeast or West, while the most conservative members of the House and Senate were all Republicans and mostly came from the South or Midwest.

Party is not a perfect predictor of ideology. In 2004, for example, a group of moderate Democrats and Republicans created the Center Aisle Caucus to show their joint agreement on issues. As Rep. Steve Israel (D-N.Y.) said of his new coalition, "Democrats and Republicans may disagree on 75% of the issues. But if we agree and implement the remaining 25%, the country is 100% better off than before."[34] Moreover, as the *National Journal* rankings show, ideological mavericks exist in both parties. In 2006, several northeastern Republicans in both chambers were more liberal than many southern Democrats, and John McCain and Sarah Palin made much of their both being mavericks in their 2008 presidential campaign.

logrolling
Mutual aid and vote trading among legislators.

attentive public
Citizens who follow public affairs closely.

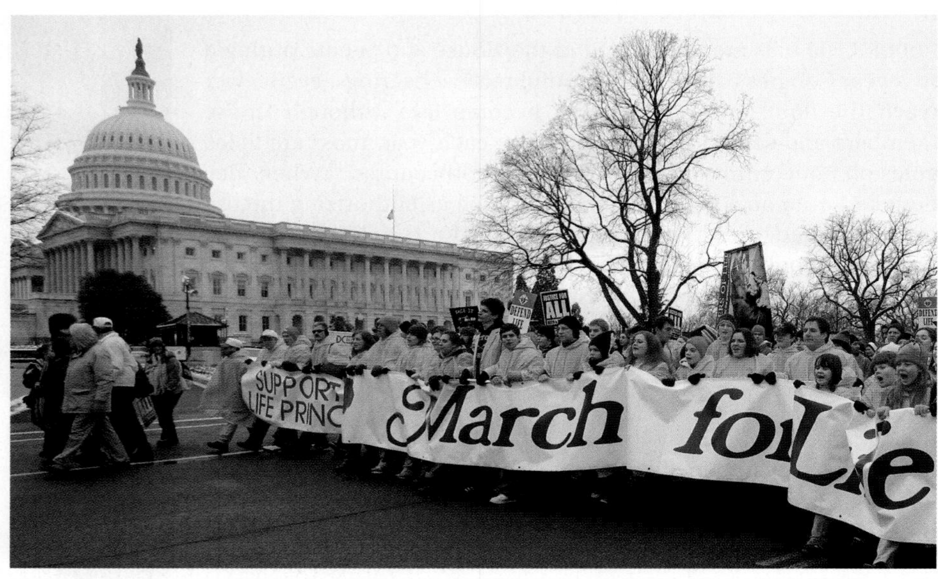

Constituents and interest groups often put pressure on Congress in person as these opponents of abortion did.

Interest Groups Interest groups influence the legislative process in many ways. They make contributions to congressional campaigns, testify before committees, provide information to legislative staff, and build public pressure for or against their cause. Congressional lobbying has existed since the early 1800s and is a perfectly legal exercise of the First Amendment right to petition government.

However, it is sometimes difficult to tell where lobbyists end and Congress begins, especially in the heat of the legislative debate over major legislation such as the 2007 energy bill. Republicans worked closely with the petroleum industry to give companies more financial incentives to produce oil and gas. Democrats worked with environmental groups to support energy conservation and new sources of energy such as wind and solar power.

Interest groups often cancel each other out by taking opposing positions on issues, thereby killing a bill. Some of this maneuvering occurs at the subcommittee level and is almost invisible to the public. But it is always visible to the interest groups themselves and to Congress. "The result," says Senator Joe Lieberman (I-Conn.), "is that everyone on Capitol Hill is keeping a close eye on everyone else, creating a self-adjusting system of checks and balances."[35]

Interest groups are almost always most effective when they mobilize public pressure on members of Congress. For example, higher-education lobbying groups have effectively mobilized students and educators to write and call members of Congress on behalf of student aid and related provisions in various measures before Congress.[36] And tobacco companies spent large sums to fight taxes on cigarettes. Although most members of Congress reject the popular perception that interest groups "buy" their votes, political contributions certainly do influence the parties and help guarantee access to members of Congress.

Party Members generally vote with their party. Whether as a result of party pressure or natural affinity, on major bills most Democrats tend to be arrayed against most Republicans. Partisan voting increased in the House after the early 1970s and has intensified even more since the 1994 elections. Indeed, party-line voting has been greater in recent years than at any time in recent decades. Party discipline is strongest on domestic issues such as health care, social welfare, economic policy, and judicial appointments. For example, all but four Democratic senators voted against Samuel Alito's confirmation to the Supreme Court in 2006, whereas all but one Republican voted in favor.

Members of both parties have become more loyal over the past thirty years, in part because each party has become more liberal or more conservative. Since 2000,

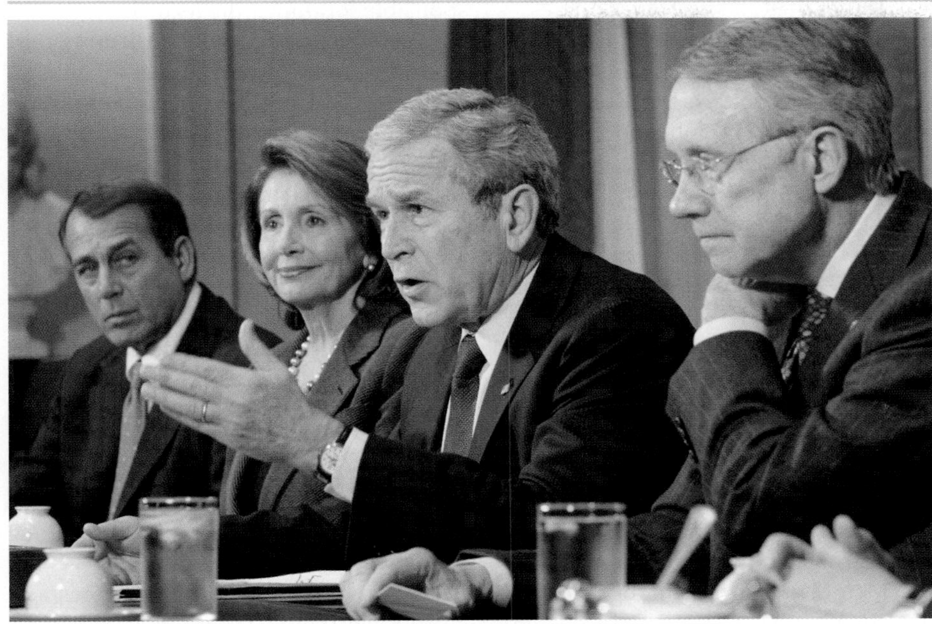

Presidents can still influence Congress even when they are unpopular with the public. Here, from left to right, House Minority Leader John Boehner, Speaker of the House Nancy Pelosi, President George W. Bush, and Senate Majority Leader Harry Reid announce an agreement to stimulate the economy in late January 2008.

almost 90 percent of congressional Democrats and Republicans have voted with their party on key votes, compared with less than 70 percent on average during the 1970s, and less than 80 percent in the 1980s.[37]

In 2007, for example, Democrats agreed on 91 percent of their votes, whereas Republicans shared the same position on 85 percent.[38] Party discipline also explains the increase—leaders of both parties have become more effective at holding their members together on key votes, in part because their members have drifted toward more liberal or more conservative convictions. Liberal Democrats stick together on most votes, as do conservative Republicans.

Presidents Presidents wield a variety of tools for influencing Congress, not least of which is the ability to distribute government resources to their friends. Presidents also help set the legislative agenda through their annual State of the Union Address, the budget, and assorted legislative messages, and they lobby Congress on particularly important issues.

When asked why they vote one way or the other, members of Congress tend to deny the president's influence. It is far better for their reelection prospects to say they are voting on behalf of their constituents or on the basis of their beliefs. But presidents work hard to influence public opinion, and they have a long list of incentives to encourage congressional support, not the least of which are invitations to special White House dinners and federal grants to support key projects back home. Congress is also likely to rally 'round the president during times of national crisis, which is what helped George W. Bush win 87 percent of the 120 congressional votes on which he took a clear position in 2001, easily besting every president since Lyndon Johnson, who won 93 percent of key votes in 1965.[39] (We will return to presidential influence in Congress in Chapter 12.)

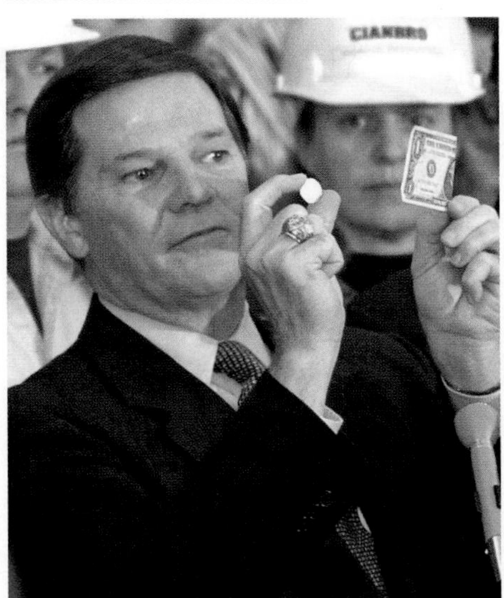

Texas Republican and House Majority Leader Tom DeLay awaits a 2006 court hearing on charges that he violated his state's election laws by accepting corporate money. DeLay's relationship with Jack Abramoff eventually led to his resignation from Congress in June 2006.

Congressional Ethics

Members of Congress have never been under greater scrutiny regarding their conduct, in part because recent years have witnessed a parade of members accused and even convicted of trading their votes for cash and other gifts. "Super-lobbyist" Jack Abramoff admitted in 2006 that he had given several members of Congress free golfing trips, meals, and concert tickets in direct violation of congressional ethics rules. The investigation eventually led to a *Time* magazine cover story that called Abramoff "The Man Who Bought Washington."[40,41]

Oklahoma Senator David Boren (D) at work in the Senate. He retired in 1994.

Under the Constitution, Congress is responsible for punishing its own members. Although individual members are subject to federal prosecution for bribery and other criminal acts, the House and Senate set the more general rules for ethical conduct and investigate all complaints of misbehavior. Under new rules enacted in September 2007, members of Congress may not accept any gifts or meals from any lobbyist. Although they can accept free admission at large meetings, conventions, discussions, and events where admission is free to other members, they may not accept free travel from any lobbyist. Finally, members may not accept any payment for making a speech, attending an event, or writing an article. Although they may accept free travel and expenses for making speeches and attending events, such travel must be related to their official duties as a member of Congress and publicly reported. These rules also apply to lobbyists, who may not offer gifts, free attendance, or travel.

The House and Senate enforce the rules through separate ethics committees (the House Committee on Standards of Official Conduct and the Senate Ethics Committee). Because the seats on both committees are divided equally between Democrats and Republicans (four on each side in the House, and three on each side in the Senate), and are filled through the normal committee selection process, members are under tremendous pressure not to hurt their own party.

Members who violate the rules face three possible penalties within their respective chamber: (1) a strongly worded letter called a *reprimand;* (2) a public rebuke on the floor of the chamber called *censure;* and (3) expulsion of the member from Congress. Members and lobbyists who violate the rules also face large fines and possible imprisonment.

How a Bill Becomes a Law

How a Bill Becomes a Law

Congress operates under a system of multiple vetoes. The framers intentionally dispersed powers so that no would-be tyrant or majority could accumulate enough authority to oppress the nation. Follow a bill through the legislative process, and there are dozens of ways it can be killed—some visible, others completely hidden from public view. Indeed, it is much easier to kill a bill than to pass one. Only about one in of ten proposals even receives minimal attention. In 2007, members of Congress introduced more than 1,500 bills, but passed only 180.[42]

How Ideas Become Bills

Name a domestic or international problem, and Congress has almost certainly considered legislation to solve it, largely because most members come to Washington to make a difference for their country. Members of Congress clearly care about national issues such as education, energy, the economy, and foreign policy. In choosing ideas for legislation, they often secure their reputations as leading thinkers far into the future. Fifteen years after leaving the Senate, David L. Boren continues to provide national leadership as president of the University of Oklahoma and is often called upon for advice on difficult issues.

LEARNING **OBJECTIVE**

8 Identify the key steps by which a bill becomes a law and the ways a bill can be stopped at each step.

Members also care about making a difference on issues that have affected them personally. Senator John McCain (R-Ariz.) has long opposed the legalization of torture because he was tortured as a prisoner of war for five years during the Vietnam War; Senator Edward Kennedy (D-Mass.) has long favored cancer research because his son had bone cancer. He was diagnosed with brain cancer in 2008.

How Bills Become Laws

You Are a Member of Congress

A bill must win many small contests on the way to final passage. There are four broad steps from beginning to end: (1) introduction, which means putting a formal proposal before the House or the Senate; (2) committee review, which includes holding a hearing and "marking up" the bill; (3) floor debate and passage, which means getting on the legislative calendar, passing once in each chamber, surviving a conference to iron out any differences between the House and Senate versions, and passing once again in each chamber; and (4) presidential approval.

Introducing a Bill House members introduce a bill by placing it into a mahogany box (called the *hopper*) on a desk at the front of the House chamber; senators introduce a bill by either handing it to the clerk of the Senate or by presenting it to their colleagues in a floor speech. In the more informal Senate, members sometimes short-circuit the formalities by offering a bill as an amendment to pending legislation. A bill that comes from the House is always designated H.R. (House of Representatives) followed by its number, and a bill from the Senate is always designated S. (Senate) followed by its number. Although presidents often recommend legislation to Congress, a member of the House or Senate must introduce all bills.

Committee Review Once a bill has been introduced in either chamber, it is read into the record as a formal proposal and referred to the appropriate committee—tax bills to Ways and Means or Finance; farm bills to Agriculture; technology bills to Science, Space, and Technology; small business to Small Business; and so forth. The parliamentarian in each chamber decides where to send each bill.

The Referral Decision Although most bills are referred to a single committee, particularly complex bills may be referred simultaneously or sequentially to multiple committees. President Bush's proposed Department of Homeland Security bill was so complicated and touched so many agencies that it was managed by a temporary special committee in the House. The bill was referred to at least ten committees, including Judiciary, Ways and Means, and Government Reform, all of which held hearings on specific provisions of the largest government reorganization since the Department of Defense was created in 1947. The bill went into the House as a 35-page proposal and came out almost 500 pages long. Committees and their subcommittees are responsible for building a legislative record in support of a given bill. This *legislative record* also helps the president and federal courts interpret what Congress intended.

Markup Once a committee or subcommittee decides to pass the bill, it "marks it up" to clean up the wording or amend its version of the bill. The term *markup* refers to the pencil marks that members make on the final version of the bill.

Markups can produce significant changes in a bill, however. Legislators often adopt amendments, delete major provisions, and write new text. Although the public is usually invited to attend, most markups involve only members of Congress, their staffs, and lobbyists. The conversations are fast, agreements quick, and most of the agreements prearranged through one-on-one meetings between key members. The goal of a markup is to move forward, not spend endless hours debating specific language.

Once markup is over, the bill must be passed by the committee or subcommittee and forwarded to the next step in the process. If it is passed by a subcommittee, for example, it is forwarded to the full committee; if it is passed by a full committee in the House, it is then forwarded to the House Rules Committee for a rule that will govern debate on the floor; if it is passed by a full committee in the Senate, it is forwarded to the full chamber.

Discharge Most bills die in committee without a hearing or further review, largely because the majority party simply does not favor action. However, a bill can be forced to the floor of the House through a **discharge petition** signed by a majority of the membership. In 2002, for example, House members were able to collect enough signatures to discharge the Rules Committee on a campaign finance reform bill that had been stalled for six months. Because most members share a strong sense of reciprocity, or mutual respect, toward the work of other committees, few discharge petitions are successful. The Senate does not use discharge petitions.

discharge petition
A petition that, if signed by a majority of the members of the House of Representatives, will pry a bill from committee and bring it to the floor for consideration.

Floor Debate and Passage Once reported to the full chamber directly from committee in the Senate or through the Rules Committee in the House, a bill will usually be scheduled for floor action or dropped entirely. Having come this far, most bills are passed into law.

Final passage sometimes comes at a very high price, however, especially for spending bills. Although House members must accept the terms of debate set by the House Rules Committee, senators often attach **riders,** or unrelated amendments, to a bill, either to win concessions from the sponsors or to reduce the odds of passage. Sponsors can use riders to sweeten a bill and improve the odds of passage.

Except for tax bills, which must originate in the House, the two chambers generally move forward on legislation independently. Bills that do not pass both chambers by the end of a two-year Congress must be reintroduced at the start of the next Congress and go through the entire process again.

Presidential Approval Once a bill has passed both houses in identical form, it is inscribed on parchment paper and hand-delivered to the president, who may *sign* it into law or *veto* it. If Congress is in session and the president waits ten days (not counting Sundays), the bill becomes law *without* his signature. If Congress has adjourned and the president waits ten days without signing the bill, it is defeated by what is known as a **pocket veto.** After a pocket veto, the bill is dead. Otherwise, when a bill is vetoed, it is returned to the chamber of its origin by the president with a message explaining the reasons for the veto. Congress can vote to **override** the veto by a two-thirds vote in each chamber, but assembling such an extraordinary majority is often difficult. Just the threat of a veto may be enough to derail a bill, but the threat must be real.

An Assessment of Congress

More than two centuries after its creation, Congress is a larger and very different kind of institution from the one the framers envisioned. It has become much more complex, more divided, and much more active. Yet most of its major functions remain the same, and their effective exercise is crucial to the health of our constitutional democracy. Even in the twenty-first century, citizens still look to Congress to solve problems, check the president, and oversee the executive branch.

Although most incumbents are easily reelected, most campaign constantly to stay in office, creating what some observers have called the "permanent campaign." Members appear driven by their desire to win reelection, so that much of what takes place in Congress seems mainly designed to promote reelection. These efforts usually pay off: we've seen that those who seek reelection almost always win.

The permanent campaign also affects legislative progress. In an institution in which most members act as individual entrepreneurs, the task of providing institutional leadership is increasingly difficult. With limited resources, and only sometimes aided by the president, congressional leaders are asked to bring together a diverse, fragmented, and independent institution. The congressional system acts only when majorities can be achieved. The framers clearly accomplished their original objective in creating a legislature that would rarely move quickly.

Citizens often complain about the lack of action, which is one reason why public approval of Congress is low. But citizens can play a role in speeding Congress up by demanding action from their own members. Even incumbents worry about losing elections. To the extent that citizens engage their members in tough conversations about the need to act on big issues such as health care, their members will listen. The question then is how to make them act in a constitutional system that sets checks and balances to stop action. The best answer is to keep pushing.

rider
A provision attached to a bill—to which it may or may not be related—in order to secure its passage or defeat.

pocket veto
A veto exercised by the president after Congress has adjourned; if the president takes no action for ten days, the bill does not become law and is not returned to Congress for a possible override.

override
An action taken by Congress to reverse a presidential veto, requiring a two-thirds majority in each chamber.

CHAPTER **SUMMARY**

1 Describe the congressional election process and demonstrate how it protects incumbents.

The congressional election process requires decisions about who can run for office, when they run, and how long they serve. Most House elections concern local issues, whereas Senate elections are more likely to be about national concerns. Incumbents enjoy a variety of protections, including name visibility and the ability to send mail and other messages back home free of charge, to help constituents and to raise money.

2 Differentiate the powers of Congress.

Congress has express powers, implied powers, and checks and balances with the president. The most important powers are the power to borrow and make money, regulate commerce, unify the country, declare and fund war, and create the inferior federal courts.

3 Compare and contrast the structure and powers of the House and Senate.

The most distinctive feature of Congress is its bicameralism, which the framers intended as a moderating influence on partisanship and possible error. The House has the power to propose legislation to raise revenue, whereas the Senate has the power to confirm presidential appointees (by a majority vote) and ratify treaties (by a two-thirds vote).

4 Compare the leadership systems used in the House and Senate.

The House is led by the Speaker, a majority and a minority leader, and whips in each party, whereas the Senate is led by a majority and a minority leader. The Senate is more difficult to lead because of its greater individualism, sometimes expressed through the use of holds and filibusters to control the legislative process.

5 Analyze the committee structure and show how members are assigned to committees.

Most of the work in Congress is done in committees and subcommittees. Congress has attempted in recent years to streamline its committee system and modify its methods of selecting committee chairs. Subcommittees can delay legislation or prevent it from being enacted. But bills can die at numerous other stages, making it easier to stop legislation than to enact it.

6 Assess the effect of different forms of representation on citizen engagement.

As a collective body, Congress must attempt to accomplish its tasks even as most of its members serve as delegates or trustees for their constituents.

7 Examine the influences on legislative decisions and how these influences may vary with issues.

Members of Congress vote on the basis of a long list of varying influences that include their colleagues, congressional constituents, staff, ideology, their party, and the president.

8 Identify the key steps by which a bill becomes a law and the ways a bill can be stopped at each step.

A bill moves through a tortuous process to become a law—an idea must first be converted into a proposal, then be introduced and referred to committee, receive a hearing and markup, and move to the floor. Although all formal bills are referred to committees for consideration, very few receive a hearing, even fewer are marked up and sent to the floor, and fewer still are enacted by both chambers and signed into law by the president. In addition, the legislative obstacle course sometimes includes filibusters, riders, holds, and the occasional override of a presidential veto.

Chapter Self-Test

1. In a few sentences, outline the advantages an incumbent member of Congress has in elections. (pp. 300–301)
2. List the five basic categories of Congressional Power. (pp. 306–307)
3. Suggest three ways the two chambers of Congress check each others' power. (p. 307)
4. Identify which chamber of Congress has each of the following powers: (pp. 307–308)
   a. Impose taxes
   b. Approve treaties
   c. Impeach the President or a judge
   d. Confirm Supreme Court nominees
   e. Try the President or a judge after he or she has been impeached
5. Write a brief essay explaining the major differences between the chambers of Congress and why the framers thought these differences were important. (pp. 305–308)
6. What is the title of the leader of the House of Representatives? What is the title of the leader of the Senate? (pp. 308, 311)
7. Create a diagram of the leadership in the House, including all leadership positions, as well as committees and each party's general membership. (pp. 308–311)

8. Members of Congress are assigned to committees by: (p. 314)
   a. the Committee on Committees
   b. the Steering and Policy Committee
   c. the Speaker of the House and president pro tempore of the Senate
9. How many standing committees are there between the House and the Senate? (p. 313)
   a. Fewer than 12
   b. Between 12 and 24
   c. Between 20 and 36
   d. More than 36
10. Briefly explain the process of selecting members of Congress for committee positions. (p. 314)
11. In a short essay, explain the major differences between a member of Congress acting as a trustee and acting as a delegate. (p. 316)
12. Imagine you are a member of Congress. In a paragraph, evaluate how you would determine your votes on bills. Would you vote the same way your constituency would, even if you disagreed? Would you vote against your party on a bad bill, even if it meant you would be barred from introducing legislation for your home state for the rest of the year? (pp. 317–319)
13. Members of Congress are subject to many different influences when crafting or voting on legislation. In a short essay describe each influence, then argue for which has the strongest influence. (pp. 317–319)
14. List the four major steps in how a bill becomes a law. (pp. 320–322)
15. What are some of the effects of a polarized Congress? Write a paragraph to explain your views. (p. 305)

Key Terms

constituents, p. 300
reapportionment, p. 301
redistricting, p. 301
gerrymandering, p. 301
safe seat, p. 301
incumbent, p. 301
earmarks, p. 302
bicameralism, p. 305
enumerated powers, p. 305
Speaker, p. 309
party caucus, p. 309
majority leader, p. 310
minority leader, p. 310
whip, p. 310
closed rule, p. 310
open rule, p. 310
president pro tempore, p. 312
hold, p. 312
filibuster, p. 312
cloture, p. 312
standing committee, p. 312
special or select committee, p. 312
joint committee, p. 312
seniority rule, p. 314
conference committee, p. 314
delegate, p. 316
trustee, p. 316
logrolling, p. 317
attentive public, p. 317
discharge petition, p. 321
rider, p. 322
pocket veto, p. 322
override, p. 322

Further Reading

JOEL D. ABERBACH, *Keeping a Watchful Eye: The Politics of Congressional Oversight* (Brookings Institution Press, 1990).

E. SCOTT ADLER, *Why Congressional Reforms Fail: Reelection and the House Committee System* (University of Chicago Press, 2002).

SARAH A. BINDER, *Stalemate: Causes and Consequences of Legislative Gridlock* (Brookings Institution Press, 2003).

SARAH A. BINDER AND **STEVEN S. SMITH,** *Politics or Principles? Filibustering in the United States Senate* (Brookings Institution Press, 1997).

BILL BRADLEY, *Time Present, Time Past: A Memoir* (Knopf, 1996).

DAVID W. BRADY AND **CRAIG VOLDEN,** *Revolving Gridlock: Politics and Policy from Carter to Clinton* (Westview Press, 1998).

ROGER H. DAVIDSON, WALTER J. OLESZEK, AND **FRANCES E. LEE,** *Congress and Its Members,* 11th ed. (CQ Press, 2007).

CHRISTOPHER J. DEERING AND **STEVEN S. SMITH,** *Committees in Congress,* 3d ed. (CQ Press, 1997).

LAWRENCE C. DODD AND **BRUCE J. OPPENHEIMER,** EDS., *Congress Reconsidered,* 8th ed. (CQ Press, 2005).

RICHARD F. FENNO JR., *Home Style: House Members in Their Districts* (Little, Brown, 1978).

RICHARD F. FENNO JR., *Learning to Govern: An Institutional View of the 104th*

Congress (Brookings Institution Press, 1997).

RICHARD F. FENNO JR., *Senators on the Campaign Trail: The Politics of Representation* (University of Oklahoma Press, 1996).

MORRIS P. FIORINA, *Congress: Keystone of the Washington Establishment,* 2d ed. (Yale University Press, 1989)

LEE H. HAMILTON, *How Congress Works and Why You Should Care* (Indiana University Press, 2004).

PAUL HERRNSON, *Congressional Elections,* 54th ed. (CQ Press, 2007).

JOHN R. HIBBING AND **ELIZABETH THEISS-MORSE,** *Congress as Public Enemy: Public Attitudes Toward American Political Institutions* (Cambridge University Press, 1995).

GODFREY HODGSON, *The Gentleman from New York: Daniel Patrick Moynihan* (Houghton Mifflin, 2000).

GARY JACOBSON, *Politics of Congressional Elections,* 7th ed. (Longman, 2008).

LINDA KILLIAN, *The Freshmen: What Happened to the Republican Revolution?* (Westview Press, 1998).

FRANCES E. LEE AND **BRUCE I. OPPENHEIMER,** *Sizing Up the Senate: The Unequal Consequences of Equal Representation* (University of Chicago Press, 1999).

TOM LOFTUS, *The Art of Legislative Politics* (CQ Press, 1994).

THOMAS MANN AND **NORM ORNSTEIN,** *The Broken Branch: How Congress Is Failing America and How to Get It Back on Track* (Oxford University Press, 2006).

JANET M. MARTIN, *Lessons from the Hill: The Legislative Journey of an Education Program* (St. Martin's Press, 1993).

DAVID R. MAYHEW, *America's Congress: Actions in the Public Sphere, James Madison Through Newt Gingrich* (Yale University Press, 2002).

BARBARA MIKULSKI ET AL., *Nine and Counting: The Women of the Senate* (Morrow, 2000).

WALTER J. OLESZEK, *Congressional Procedures and the Policy Process,* 6th ed. (CQ Press, 2004).

NORMAN J. ORNSTEIN, THOMAS MANN, AND **MICHAEL MALBIN,** *Vital Statistics on Congress, 2002–2004* (AEI Press, 2004).

RONALD M. PETERS JR., ED., *The Speaker: Leadership in the U.S. House of Representatives* (CQ Press, 1995).

DAVID E. PRICE, *The Congressional Experience: A View from the Hill* (Westview Press, 1993).

NICOL RAE AND **COLTON CAMPBELL,** EDS., *New Majority or Old Majority: The Impact of Republicans on Congress* (Rowman & Littlefield, 1999).

BARBARA SINCLAIR, *Unorthodox Lawmaking: New Legislative Processes in the U.S. Congress,* 2d ed. (CQ Press, 2000).

chapter 12

The Presidency

The Personal Branch

George W. Bush made a secret decision in early 2002. Convinced that foreign terrorists were calling their contacts inside the United States, Bush authorized the National Security Agency (NSA) to start eavesdropping on telephone conversations. Under the president's order, the NSA began to spy on U.S. citizens without any congressional or judicial review.[1]

President Bush later argued that the secret program was fully consistent with his authority, as commander in chief, to defend the nation from foreign attack. As Bush said, "The American people expect me to do everything in my power under our laws and Constitution to protect them and their civil liberties. And that is exactly what I will continue to do, so long as I am President of the United States."[2]

Some members of Congress were angered by the program. As Republican senator Lindsey Graham said in late February 2006, "If you're going to follow an American citizen around for an extended period of time believing they're collaborating with the enemy, at some point in time, you need to get some judicial review, because mistakes can be made."[3]

Once the program became public, Congress decided to assert its role in questioning the president's broad powers to suspend civil liberties during times of war. Presidents may have the power to wage war, but not to violate laws created to protect U.S. citizens from their government. Congress soon placed legislative limits on the authority by subjecting all eavesdropping requests to judicial approval.

In August 2007, however, Congress heard secret testimony from intelligence officials who said the amount of eavesdropping had fallen dramatically in the wake of the new limits. Worried that the decline exposed the United States to a greater terrorism threat and under enormous pressure from the White House, Congress soon reversed course on limiting the eavesdropping program and extended the authority.

The extension shows the president's power to influence foreign policy, even in the midst of an unpopular war. Congress often complains about the president's action but is mostly unwilling to limit that action. As a result, citizens have few opportunities to influence foreign policy, particularly when the policies are secret. There have been times in history, however, when citizen protests have driven Congress and the president to alter foreign policy. Massive protests against the Vietnam War during the late 1960s clearly shaped the U.S. decision to end the conflict.

The framers of the Constitution both admired and feared this kind of centralized leadership. Although they knew a strong president was needed to protect the nation against foreign and domestic threats, they also worried about the potential abuse of power. This chapter will examine the framers' intent in designing the presidency, review the president's powers, and then turn to the continuing controversies surrounding the exercise of these powers. We will also explore the many jobs of the president and ask how Congress and the president work together and against each other in making the laws. We conclude with a discussion of how history judges presidents.

LEARNING **OBJECTIVES**

1. Describe the constitutional foundations of the presidency.
2. Compare and contrast the three types of presidential power.
3. Evaluate the controversies surrounding the president's assertion of additional executive powers and the evolution of presidential power.
4. Analyze the roles of the White House staff, Executive Office of the President, cabinet, and vice president.
5. Describe the president's job.
6. Identify the sources of presidential/congressional conflict and the tools presidents use to influence Congress.
7. Identify factors that make a great president.

CHAPTER OUTLINE

- The Structure and Powers of the Presidency
- Controversies in Presidential Power
- The Evolution of Presidential Power
- Managing the Presidency
- The President's Job
- Congress and the Presidency
- Judging Presidents

Presidents Jimmy Carter, George W. Bush, Bill Clinton, and George H. W. Bush join together at President Ronald Reagan's funeral in June 2004.

The Structure and Powers of the Presidency

LEARNING OBJECTIVE

1 Describe the constitutional foundations of the presidency.

COMPARATIVE

Comparing Chief Executives

The framers wanted the president to act with "dispatch" against threats, but they also worried that presidents could become too powerful. Although they gave the president the power to run the executive branch, which now includes the White House and all departments and agencies, they limited the president's other powers to a relatively short list, including the power to wage wars declared by Congress, report to the nation from time to time on the state of the Union, nominate judges and executive appointees for Senate confirmation, and negotiate treaties. They wanted a presidential office that would steer clear of parties and factions, enforce the laws passed by Congress, handle communications with foreign governments, and help states put down disorders. They wanted a presidency strong enough to match Congress yet not so strong that it would overpower Congress.

Young citizens massed at the Lincoln Memorial on May Day, 1970, vowing to shut down the federal government to protest the Vietnam War. Ten thousand people were arrested as police and federal troops cracked down on the protesters. Similar protests occurred in other cities.

The framers believed the "jarrings of parties" in Congress were perfectly appropriate in making the laws, but not in fighting wars and running the executive branch. They did not believe the president should have unlimited freedom to act, however. Having given a much longer list of powers to Congress, they saw the president as a powerful check on legislative action, and essential to the administration of government. As Alexander Hamilton argued in *The Federalist*, No. 70, which explains the presidency in detail, "A feeble executive implies a feeble execution of the government. A feeble execution is but another phrase for a bad execution: And a government ill executed, whatever it may be in theory, must be in practice a bad government."[4]

An Essential Difference

Merely having three branches of national government—legislative, executive, and judicial—does not by itself create a pure system of separated powers; the United Kingdom also has legislative and executive branches, but both are automatically headed by the same political party and same person, because the prime minister is chosen by members of the majority party in Parliament.

In the United States, the legislative, executive, and judicial branches are independent of one another. Although the legislative and executive branch are sometimes headed by the same political party, unified government can exist only if voters in enough states and districts vote for the same party over enough elections to control the House, Senate, presidency, and judiciary (whose members are nominated by the president and confirmed by the Senate).

The United States is one of the few world powers that is neither a parliamentary democracy nor a wholly executive-dominated government. Our Constitution plainly invites both Congress and the president to set policy and govern the nation. Leadership and policy change are likely only when Congress and the president, and sometimes the courts along with them, agree that new directions are desirable.

Comparing Executive Branches

Initial Decisions

The framers' most important decision about the presidency was also their first. Meeting on June 1, 1787, the Constitutional Convention decided there would be a single executive. Despite worries that a single president might lay the groundwork for a future monarchy, the framers also believed the new government needed energy in the executive. They were willing to increase the risk of tyranny in return for some efficiency.

Once past this first decision, the framers had to decide just how independent that executive would be from the rest of the national government. This meant finding an appropriate method of selection or election. Had they wanted Congress to select the president from among its members, the framers would have created a **parliamentary system** that would look more like many European governments.

The delegates were initially divided on how the president would be selected. A small number favored direct election by the people, which Pennsylvania's James Wilson thought would ensure that the president was completely independent of Congress. The delegates rejected direct election in favor of the electoral college: Voters would cast their ballots for competing slates of electors, who would in turn cast their electoral votes for president.

The framers also gave the executive a four-year term of office, further balancing the House (two-year term) and Senate (six-year term). Although they were silent on the number of terms a president could serve, the Twenty-Second Amendment to the Constitution, ratified in 1951, limits presidents to two terms in office.

The framers created the position of vice president just in case the president left office before the end of the term. With little debate, they decided to give the vice president the power to break tie votes in the Senate. Otherwise, the vice president has no constitutional duties but to wait for the president to be incapacitated or otherwise unable to discharge the powers and duties of the presidency. In recent years, however, presidents have given their vice presidents greater responsibilities.[5]

parliamentary system
A system of government in which the legislature selects the prime minister or president.

Alaska governor and Republican vice presidential candidate Sarah Palin appeared on "Saturday Night Live" with Tina Fey late in the campaign.

The framers also established three simple qualifications for both offices. Under the Constitution, the president and vice president must be (1) at least 35 years old on inauguration day; (2) natural-born citizens of the United States, as opposed to immigrants who become citizens by applying to the U.S. government for naturalization; and (3) residents of the United States for the previous 14 years. The citizenship and residency requirements were designed to prevent a popular foreign-born citizen from capturing the office.

Running for Office

With this basic structure in place, the framers had to decide how the vice president would be selected. Once again, they created a remarkable electoral arrangement: The candidate who received the most electoral college votes would become president, and the candidate who came in second would become vice president. Any tie votes in the electoral college were to be broken by a majority vote in the House of Representatives.

Barack Obama held his first press conference as president-elect on November 7, 2008, with his economic team standing behind him.

It did not take long for the framers to discover the problem with this runner-up rule. The 1796 election produced Federalist president John Adams and Republican vice president Thomas Jefferson. Because the two disagreed so sharply about the future of the country, Jefferson was rendered virtually irrelevant to government.

This rule created a constitutional crisis in 1800. The election could not have been more important, for it occurred during a time of rising public anger about the nation's direction. It also included multiple candidates from the same party. Jefferson and Aaron Burr both promised a smaller, simpler government, while Adams promised continued government expansion. Jefferson and Burr emerged from the balloting with 73 electoral votes each, leaving Adams behind with just 63. After 36 ballots, the House of Representatives finally selected Jefferson as president, and Burr became vice president.

Under the Twelfth Amendment, ratified in 1804, electors were allowed to cast separate votes for the president and vice president. This new practice encouraged candidates to run together as members of a **presidential ticket** that would rise or fall together.

LEARNING **OBJECTIVE**

2 Compare and contrast the three types of presidential power.

Presidential Powers

Article II of the Constitution begins: "The executive Power shall be vested in a President of the United States of America." Presidents often use this **vesting clause** to argue that they control everything that happens in the executive branch after a bill becomes a law.[6] However, the Supreme Court has cast doubt on this breadth of the authority in a variety of past cases—presidents may control the executive branch, but they do not have unlimited command. The Supreme Court has also ruled that Congress cannot delegate to the president powers the Constitution reserves for the legislative branch under Article I.

Although short, Article II does address foreign threats and the day-to-day operations of government, establishing the president's authority to play three central roles in the new government: (1) commander in chief, (2) diplomat in chief, and (3) manager in chief.

presidential ticket
The joint listing of the presidential and vice presidential candidates on the same ballot as required by the Twelfth Amendment.

vesting clause
The president's constitutional authority to control most executive functions.

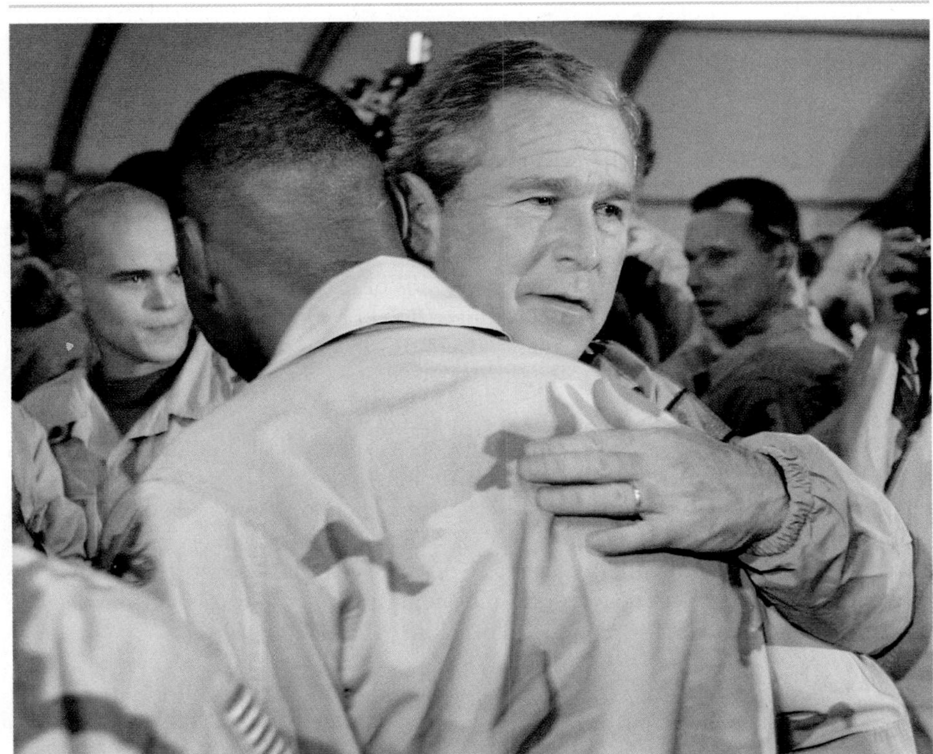

President Bush surprised U.S. military troops stationed in Iraq with a secret Thanksgiving Day visit in 2003. The president was in Baghdad for two hours and 32 minutes.

Commander in Chief The Constitution explicitly states that the president is to be commander in chief of the army and navy, but the framers were divided over which branch would both declare and make war.[7]

The framers initially agreed that Congress would make war, raise armies, build and equip fleets, enforce treaties, and suppress and repel invasions, but eventually changed the phrase "make war" to "declare war." At the same time they limited the presidential war power by giving Congress the power to appropriate money for the purchase of arms and military pay and giving the Senate the power to approve military promotions. Although Congress has the sole authority to declare war, presidents have used their power as commander in chief to order U.S. troops into battle without formal declarations dozens of times over the past century, including the recent wars in Afghanistan and Iraq. Presidents have often interpreted the war power even more broadly, as the Bush administration did in authorizing the domestic eavesdropping program.

Diplomat in Chief Article II also makes the president negotiator in chief of treaties with foreign nations, which must be approved by the Senate by a two-thirds vote. A **treaty** is a binding and public agreement between the United States and one or more nations that requires mutual action toward a common goal. The U.S. has signed hundreds of treaties over the past two hundred years, including limits on the number of nuclear, biological and chemical weapons. Although presidents cannot make treaties without Senate approval, past presidents have argued that they have the power to terminate treaties without Senate consent.

Presidents can also make **executive agreements** with the leaders of foreign nations. Unlike treaties, executive agreements are negotiated without Senate participation. In 2003, for example, the Bush administration negotiated a 22-item executive agreement with Mexico to create a "smart border" that would limit the movement of illegal aliens into the United States, while improving the flow of goods between the two nations. Although some executive orders are secret, most are made public.

Finally, presidents can make **congressional–executive agreements,** which are also negotiated between the president and leaders of other nations. Like treaties, congressional–executive agreements require mutual action toward a common goal. Unlike treaties, they require approval by both houses of Congress by a simple majority vote.

Manager in Chief By giving the president the power to require the opinion of the principal officer in each of the executive departments "upon any subject relating to the duties of their respective offices," the Constitution puts the president in charge of the day-to-day operation of the federal departments and agencies. As we shall see, the president also has the responsibility to appoint ambassadors, judges, and all other officers of the United States, including the heads of executive departments, with the advice and consent of a majority of the Senate. Together, these powers give presidents the instruments needed to supervise and control the day-to-day operations of the federal departments and agencies.

Additional Executive Powers The Constitution also gives the president five additional powers to lead government: (1) the power to appoint judges and officers of government; (2) the power to veto legislation, thereby serving as a check on Congress; (3) the power to grant pardons to individuals convicted of federal, but not state, crimes, thereby providing a check against the judiciary; (4) the power to take care that the laws are faithfully executed, thereby giving the president sweeping authority to oversee the executive branch; and (5) the power to inform and convene Congress.

1. *The Appointment Power.* The Constitution gives the president authority to appoint judges, ambassadors, and other officers of the executive branch subject to the advice and consent of the Senate, in the form of a simple majority of 51 votes.

treaty
A formal, public agreement between the United States and one or more nations that must be approved by two-thirds of the Senate.

executive agreement
A formal agreement between the U.S. president and the leaders of other nations that does not require Senate approval.

congressional–executive agreement
A formal agreement between the U.S. president and the leaders of other nations that requires approval by both houses of Congress.

This power gives presidents the ability to control what happens inside departments and agencies during their terms and to shape the federal judiciary far into the future. Presidents choose appointees on the basis of party loyalty, interest group pressure, and management ability. Although the appointment process has become more controversial in recent years, most judicial and executive appointees are easily confirmed—the Senate has rejected only eight cabinet secretaries between 1789 and 2008, and just 36 of 157 nominations to the Supreme Court.

Presidents also have the power to make **recess appointments** when Congress takes a formal recess, or break, during the year. Although the power was originally intended to be used only when a vacancy occurs during the break, presidents now use recess appointments regularly to appoint particularly controversial nominees to office without Senate confirmation. These appointments end at the start of the Congress that is elected after the appointment is made.[8]

2. *The Veto Power.* The Constitution provides that bills passed by the U.S. House of Representatives and Senate "shall be presented to the President of the United States," and the president can then approve the measure or issue a **veto.** If a bill is vetoed by a president, it can be enacted only if the veto is overridden, which requires a two-thirds vote in each chamber of Congress.

   A variation of the veto is the **pocket veto.** In the ordinary course of events, if a president does not sign or veto a bill within ten days after receiving it (not counting Sundays), the bill becomes law without the president's signature. But if Congress adjourns within the ten days, the president, by taking no action, can kill the bill with a pocket veto.

   The power of a veto lies in the difficulty of overriding a president's decision. Recall that two-thirds of both houses must vote to overturn a veto. This requirement is a vital bargaining chip in the legislative process, in which the mere threat of a veto can strengthen a president's hand. Historically, Congress has voted to override fewer than 10 percent of presidents' regular vetoes.

   This veto threat is credible, however, only if the president is actually willing to use it. Whereas Ronald Reagan vetoed 78 bills in his two terms and Bill Clinton vetoed 37, George W. Bush did not veto a single bill in his first six years. Although he used the veto extensively as governor of Texas, Bush may have worried that he did not have enough congressional votes to prevent overrides.

   As Congress became more aggressive and he became less popular, Bush became more active with his veto pen. He issued his first regular veto on July 19, 2006, to prevent federal funding of stem cell research, and his seventh on December 7, 2007, on expansion of the State Children's Health Insurance Program (SCHIP) Congress overturned just one of the seven, voting by large majorities to increase funding for water pollution control.

3. *The Pardon Power.* The pardon power can be traced directly to the royal authority of the king of England, and is probably the most delicate power presidents exercise. It can shorten prison sentences, correct judicial errors, and protect citizens from future prosecution. It can also create controversy. On his last day in office in 2001, President Bill Clinton pardoned several of his associates who had been jailed in a long investigation of a real estate scandal dating back to his time as governor of Arkansas.

4. *The Take Care Power.* Located near the end of Article II is the simple statement that the president "shall take Care that the Laws be faithfully executed." This **take care clause** makes the president responsible for implementing the laws Congress enacts, even through the override of a presidential veto.

   Presidents sometimes use the take care clause to claim **inherent powers,** meaning powers they believe are essential to protecting the nation. Jefferson drew on this broad notion in making the Louisiana Purchase in 1804, for example. Abraham Lincoln extended the concept early in the Civil War to suspend the rights of prisoners to seek judicial review of their detention, to impose a blockade

recess appointment
Presidential appointment made without Senate confirmation during Senate recess.

veto
A formal decision to reject a bill passed by Congress.

pocket veto
A formal decision to reject a bill passed by Congress after it adjourns—if Congress adjourns during the ten days that the president is allowed in order to sign or veto a law, the president can reject the law by taking no action at all.

take care clause
The constitutional requirement (in Article II, Section 3) that presidents take care that the laws are faithfully executed, even if they disagree with the purpose of those laws.

inherent powers
Powers that grow out of the very existence of government.

of Confederate shipping, and to expand the size of the army beyond authorized ceilings, all without prior congressional approval as required under the Constitution's lawmaking power. Bush used a similar justification in authorizing the domestic eavesdropping program.

5. *The Power to Inform and Convene Congress.* Under Article II, presidents are required "from time to time to give to the Congress Information of the State of the Union, and recommend to their Consideration such Measures as he shall judge necessary." Over the years, the phrase "from time to time" has evolved to mean a constant stream of presidential messages, as well as the annual **State of the Union Address** in late January or early February. This power gives presidents a significant platform for presenting their legislative agenda to both Congress and the people.

   The president also has the power to convene Congress in extraordinary circumstances and recommend "such Measures as he shall judge necessary and expedient." On September 20, 2001, for example, President George W. Bush convened Congress in an emergency session to ask for new legislation to strengthen antiterrorism programs, help airlines recover from the dramatic decline in air travel, and rebuild New York City.

State of the Union Address
The president's annual statement to Congress and the nation.

impeachment
A formal accusation against the president or another public official; the first step in removal from office.

Presidential Succession

Having decided how a president would enter office, the framers also decided how he or she would leave. In addition to impeachment, defeat for reelection, retirement, resignation, or death, under the Twenty-Second Amendment presidents must leave office after completing two elected terms.

Under the Twenty-Fifth Amendment, presidents can be removed temporarily if the vice president and a majority of either Congress or the president's own cabinet secretaries declares him unable to discharge the powers and duties of the office—for example, because of illness or disability. The vice president becomes the acting president until the duly elected president returns to office. The amendment also allows a president to appoint a new vice president in the event of the vice president's own resignation, death, impeachment, or rise to the presidency.

Vice President Lyndon Baines Johnson takes the oath of office to become president on November 22, 1963, following the assassination of John F. Kennedy. In the wake of these events, the Twenty-Fifth Amendment was adopted to provide for replacing the vice president or removing a president from office for reasons of illness or disability.

The vice president is next in line if the president leaves office prematurely. Under current law, the Speaker of the House of Representatives is next, followed by the Senate president pro tempore, the secretary of state, secretary of the treasury, secretary of defense, and on down through the list of 15 cabinet secretaries according to the date each department was established.

The framers gave Congress exclusive power to remove the president through **impeachment.** Under this process, the House drafts articles of impeachment that charge the president with treason, bribery, or other high crimes and misdemeanors. If the articles are approved by a majority vote, the chief justice of the Supreme Court oversees a trial before the entire Senate. If convicted by a two-thirds vote of the Senate, the president is removed immediately from office.

Although impeachment charges have been filed against nine presidents, including Ronald Reagan, the House has voted to impeach the president only twice in history, in 1868 against Andrew Johnson and in 1998 against Bill Clinton. Both Senate trials resulted in acquittals. Richard Nixon resigned from office in 1974 before the House could finish drafting the articles of impeachment regarding his role in the Watergate cover-up. Nixon almost certainly would have been both impeached and convicted had he stayed in office.

Controversies in Presidential Power

The president, today more visible than ever as a national and international leader, is still constrained by constitutional checks and balances. These do not stop presidents from asserting powers the framers intended for Congress or the judiciary, however.

The War Power

LEARNING OBJECTIVE

3 Evaluate the controversies surrounding the president's assertion of additional executive powers and the evolution of presidential power.

Article I of the Constitution gives Congress the power to declare war, but Article II gives the president the power to wage war as commander in chief. The framers recognized that declaring war was both one of the most important powers of government and one of the most easily abused. Writing as a young member of Congress, Abraham Lincoln expressed the founders' intent as follows:

> The provision of the Constitution giving the war-making power to Congress was dictated, as I understand it, by the following reasons. Kings had always been involving and impoverishing their people in wars, pretending generally, if not always, that the good of the people was the object. This our convention understood to be the most oppressive of all kingly oppressions, and they resolved to so frame the Constitution that no one man should hold the power of bringing this oppression upon us.[9]

Over the past half-century, U.S. presidents have ordered troops into battle in Korea, Vietnam, Grenada, Panama, Iraq (twice), Kosovo, and Afghanistan, all without asking Congress for a formal declaration of war. When they have asked for congressional approval, presidents have usually sought broad resolutions of support. In 2002, for example, Bush merely asked Congress to give him the authority to deploy U.S. forces as "he determines to be necessary and appropriate" to defend national security against the threat posed by Iraq. Although the request was eventually approved by wide margins in the House and Senate, White House lawyers also argued that the president already had the authority to act with or without congressional approval.[10]

Presidents defend such actions by arguing that they have better information than Congress, much of it secret, and need the flexibility and secrecy to respond quickly to military threats to the nation's security interests. One State Department official described the president's war power authority as follows: "The Constitution leaves to the President the judgment to determine whether the circumstances of a particular armed attack are so urgent and the potential consequences so threatening to the security of the U.S. that he should act without formally consulting the Congress."[11]

Presidents and some scholars blame Congress for abdicating its constitutional authority to the presidency. Constitutional scholar Louis Fisher holds that Congress has repeatedly given up its fundamental war powers to the president. The framers knew what monarchy looked like and rejected it, writes Fisher. "Yet, especially in matters of the war power, the United States is recreating a system of monarchy while it professes to champion democracy and the rule of law abroad."[12]

Congress tried to reassert its role and authority in the use of military force at the end of the Vietnam War. In 1973, Congress enacted the War Powers Resolution over Richard Nixon's veto. The law, still in place, declares that a president can commit the armed forces only (1) after a declaration of war by Congress, (2) by specific statutory authorization, or (3) in a national emergency created by an attack on the United States or its armed forces. After committing the armed forces under the third circumstance, the president is required to report to Congress within 48 hours. Unless Congress declares war, the troop commitment must be ended within 60 days.

This resolution signaled a new determination by Congress to take its prerogatives seriously, yet presidents have generally ignored it. And many leading scholars now believe that this earnest and well-intentioned effort by Congress to reclaim its proper role actually gave away more authority than previous practices had already done. Because presidents can declare a national emergency under almost any circumstances and often act under broad legislation that authorizes the use of force in ambiguous situations, the War Powers Resolution is almost always ignored.

Iranian president Mahmoud Ahmadinejad addresses the United Nations in 2007. Tensions began to rise dramatically between Iran and the United States late in the Bush administration. The Bush administration was particularly worried about the possibility that Iran was in the process of refining nuclear materials as part of a weapons program and threatened to use all powers in the U.S. arsenal to stop Iran's effort.

President Bush meets with his national security advisers in the Situation Room of the White House soon after September 11, 2001.

The Power to Invoke Executive Privilege

The courts have recognized that presidents have the power, or **executive privilege,** to keep secrets, especially if doing so is essential to protect national security or confidential White House conversations about public policy.

Some experts argue that executive privilege has no constitutional basis.[13] Yet presidents have withheld documents from Congress at least as far back as 1792, when President George Washington temporarily refused to share sensitive documents with a House committee studying an Indian massacre of federal troops. Thomas Jefferson and the primary author of the Constitution, James Madison, also withheld information during their presidencies.

Most scholars, the courts, and even members of Congress agree that a president does have the implicit, if not constitutionally explicit, right to withhold information that could harm national security. Presidents must keep secrets, and they often fight hard to do so. However, they cannot assert executive privilege in either congressional or judicial proceedings when it means refusing to cooperate in investigations of personal wrongdoing.

President Nixon created the controversy over the term "executive privilege."[14] In an effort to hide his own role in the Watergate scandal, Nixon refused to release secret tapes of the Oval Office meetings that followed the failed burglary of Democratic Party headquarters in the Watergate building. He and his lawyers went so far as to claim that the decision to invoke executive privilege was not subject to review by Congress or the courts.

In its complicated decision, the Supreme Court acknowledged for the first time that presidents do indeed have the power to claim executive privilege if the release of certain information would be damaging to the nation's security interests. But the Court held that such claims are not exempt from review by the courts, and that national security was not threatened in the Watergate case. The Court ordered Nixon to yield his tapes, effectively dooming his presidency.[15]

Twenty-five years later, Congress asked the Bush administration to disclose the names of energy industry executives who had met with Vice President Dick Cheney's 2001 energy task force, which helped shape the administration's future energy plan. The White House refused, arguing that Congress has no constitutional right to investigate the process by which the president or his advisers make decisions about public issues.

executive privilege
The right to keep executive communications confidential, especially if they relate to national security.

Although the White House never formally invoked executive privilege in the case, the refusal was clearly modeled on the notion that presidents have the right to keep secrets. Congress eventually sued Cheney for the information, but dropped the case in 2003 after losing the first round in a federal district court.

The Bush administration formally invoked executive privilege four times between 2001 and 2007, and in late 2007 to prevent congressional testimony by two White House aides in a Justice Department scandal.

The president's right to keep secrets will be revisited in each administration and tested by presidents and by the legislative branch. On occasion, courts will try to settle the dispute about the limits and conditions under which a president can invoke this well-established, if sometimes abused, presidential practice.

The Power to Issue Executive Orders

Presidents execute the laws and direct the federal departments and agencies in part through **executive orders,** formal directives that are just as strong as laws and can be challenged in the courts. According to past Supreme Court decisions, executive orders are generally accepted as the law of the land unless they conflict with the Constitution or a federal law.

The Executive Order Over Time

Beginning with George Washington, presidents have issued more than 13,000 executive orders. These have been used to declare U.S. neutrality in the war between France and England (1793), to intern Japanese Americans during World War II, and to protect large tracts of federal land as "national monuments" in Arizona, Colorado, Oregon, Utah, and Washington in the Clinton administration.

President George W. Bush has been just as active as other recent presidents in using executive orders to manage government. He issued an order in October 2001 creating a White House Office of Homeland Security to coordinate the federal government's efforts to protect its borders, another in January 2003 to create a President's Council on Service and Civic Participation to encourage more people to volunteer, and still another on January 29, 2008, ordering executive agencies not to implement informal earmarks contained in the legislative reports that accompany spending bills. All totaled, Bush issued 254 executive orders in the first seven years of his eight-year term.[16]

The Budget and Spending Power

The Constitution explicitly gives Congress the power to appropriate money, but presidents are responsible for actually spending it. Congress dominated the budget-making process until 1921, when it approved the Budget and Accounting Act. That law required the president to submit annual budgets to Congress, and it established the Bureau of the Budget, which in 1970 became the Office of Management and Budget. Although the 1921 act also created the General Accounting Office as an auditing and oversight arm of Congress, presidents have played an increasingly powerful role in shaping the federal budget.

In 1974, Congress approved the Congressional Budget and Impoundment Control Act, which sharply curtailed the president's use of **impoundment,** or refusal to spend appropriations that had been passed into law. Enacted over Nixon's veto, the law gave Congress new powers to control its own budget process, created the Congressional Budget Office (CBO) to give the institution its own sources of economic and spending forecasts, and required the president to submit detailed requests to Congress for any proposed *rescission* (cancellation) of congressional appropriations.

In an effort to control its own tendency to overspend, Congress in 1996 voted to give the president greater budget power through the **line item veto,** which would have allowed presidents to strike out specific sections of an appropriations bill while signing the rest into law. In essence, the line item veto is a legal form of impoundment. Although many governors have the line item veto, the Supreme Court decided the law had disturbed the "finely wrought" procedure for making the laws and declared it unconstitutional in a 6-to-3 vote in 1998. If Congress wanted a new procedure for making the laws, Justice John Paul Stevens wrote for the majority, it would have to pursue a constitutional amendment.[17]

executive orders
Formal orders issued by the president to direct action by the federal bureaucracy.

impoundment
A decision by the president not to spend money appropriated by Congress, now prohibited under federal law.

line item veto
Presidential power to strike, or remove, specific items from a spending bill without vetoing the entire package; declared unconstitutional by the Supreme Court.

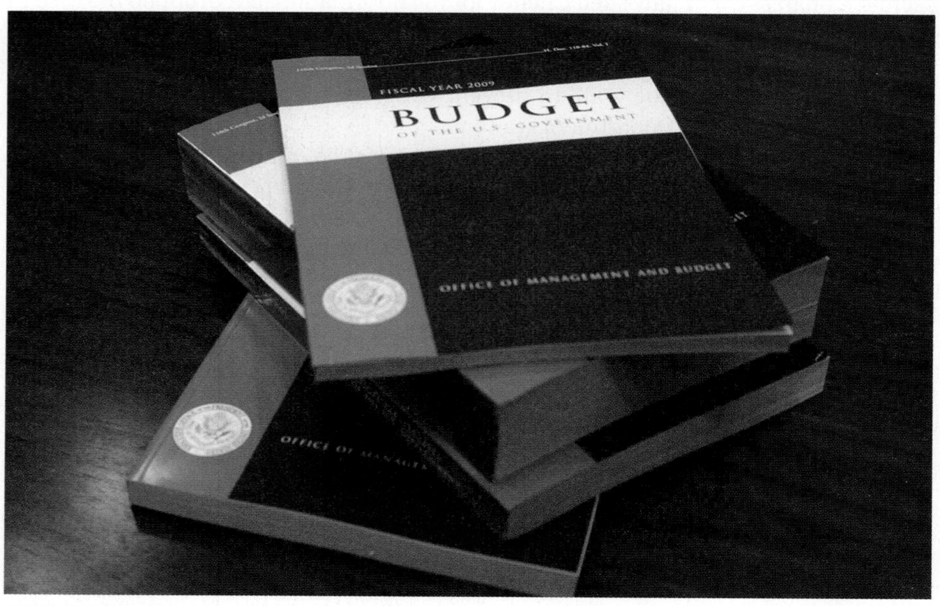

Under federal law, the president is required to submit detailed spending plans to Congress in February of each calendar year. The Bush administration's 2008–2009 budget plan was contained in a half-dozen volumes that covered more than 2,500 pages.

The Use of Unilateral Powers

Presidents also have a set of unilateral powers to shape the implementation of the laws, even to the point of ignoring them. Presidents control much of the information that flows from federal departments and agencies, and there are a number of ways they can shape the national debate through messages to Congress and the public.[18]

signing statements
A formal document that explains why a president is signing a particular bill into law. These statements may contain objections to the bill and promises not to implement key sections.

Presidents can use **signing statements** to express their opposition to a bill they are signing into law. These statements often make the case that a certain provision of a law is either unconstitutional or so vague it cannot be implemented. Between 2001 and early 2008, Bush issued more than 150 statements promising not to follow the laws he was signing.[19]

In late December 2005, for example, Bush signed a bill forbidding U.S. interrogators to torture prisoners of war or otherwise subject them to cruel, inhuman, and degrading treatment. However, he used his signing statement to modify the legislation by arguing that his role as commander in chief gave him the power to waive the ban if he decided torture would assist in preventing terrorist attacks.

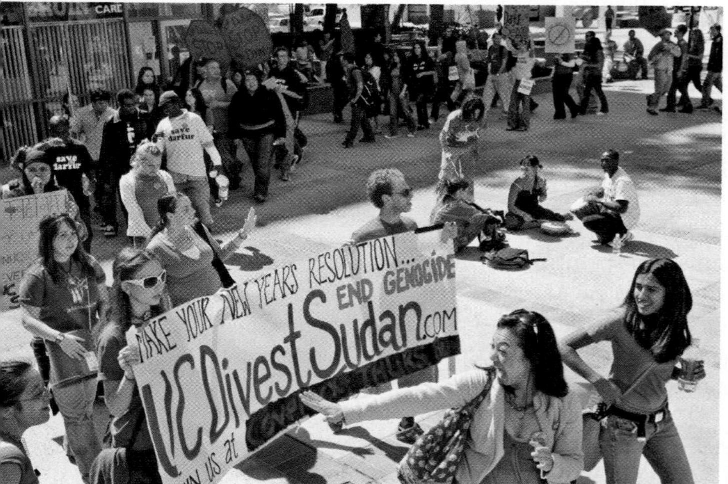

In signing the Sudan Accountability and Divestment Act of 2007, President Bush noted that by ordering states to jettison any investments made with companies doing business in Darfur, it conflicted with the president's authority to conduct foreign policy. His signing statement made clear that Bush would implement the law selectively.

The Evolution of Presidential Power

The history of presidential power is one of steady, if uneven, growth. Of the individuals who have filled the office, about one-third have enlarged its powers. Andrew Jackson, Abraham Lincoln, Theodore Roosevelt, Franklin Delano Roosevelt, and Harry Truman all redefined the institution and many of its powers by the way they set priorities and responded to crises. Much of this expansion occurred during wartime or national crises such as the economic depression of the 1930s.

Nevertheless, today's presidency reflects precedents established by the nation's first chief executive, George Washington.

HOW OTHER NATIONS GOVERN

Strong and Weak Chief Executives

Unlike the United States, which has a separate path to the presidency through the electoral college, parliamentary governments elect their prime ministers from the parliament itself. In theory, this system makes the prime minister more influential—he or she controls both the executive and legislative branches. However, these systems also make the prime minister more dependent on party support to remain in office. Prime ministers can stand for election at a time of their own choosing, and can be removed through a vote of no confidence by the legislature.

Great Britain is the oldest parliamentary government in the world, and its prime minister is possibly the most powerful. Becoming the prime minister is hardly easy—prime ministers must be members of Parliament, elected as their party's leader, and able to lead their parties to a majority in a national election. Once in office, the prime minister has many of the same roles as the U.S. president.

India and Japan both follow this parliamentary system with several important differences. Like the British prime minister, the Indian prime minister can be removed from office through a vote of no confidence by the parliament. However, the Indian prime minister has the extraordinary power to suspend all political rights by declaring a national emergency. Even here, the parliament retains the power to overturn such declarations after two months. Also unlike the British system, the Indian system has often been governed by members of the same family. The Nehru family has ruled the country for almost two-thirds of its sixty years of independence.

China has a much simpler system, largely because the party controls the key offices of government. The head of the party controls the country and generally serves for life.

Mexico and Nigeria both follow the U.S. system of a separately elected president. Mexico's president is one of the most powerful elected chief executives in the democratic world, but was once also known as one of the most corrupt. Under the Mexican constitution of 1917, adopted after a decade of civil war, the president was given sweeping powers to run the country, including the authority to hire and fire most government employees. Many Mexican presidents used these powers to favor friends and party loyalists, sometimes for their own financial gain. Some also used the office to suppress opposition. Because Mexican presidents can serve for only one six-year term, they have sometimes been called the most powerful "six-year monarchs" in the world.

Nigeria's 1999 constitution created its current strong-president system. Like the United States the country has three branches of government, but the president tends to overshadow the legislative and judicial branches through tight control of the revenue system.

QUESTIONS

1. In what ways are prime ministers weaker than presidents? How are they sometimes stronger?
2. Do prime ministers have greater public support and control over the instruments of government? Is this good for citizens? Why or why not?
3. Would the U.S. system of checks and balances work in all countries? What might make a checks-and-balances system dangerous to the overall stability of a nation's government?

The framers could not have anticipated the kinds of foreign and domestic threats that now preoccupy the office, but they would recognize the importance of the presidency in protecting the nation in times of trouble.

George Washington's Impact

The framers designed the presidency hoping George Washington would be the first to occupy the post. Washington commanded the public's trust and respect, and he was unanimously elected the first president of the new Republic. He understood that the people needed to have confidence in their fledgling government, a sense of continuity with the past, and a time of calm and stability free of emergencies and crises. He also knew that the new nation faced both domestic and foreign threats to its future.

As president, Washington set important precedents for the future. He not only established the legitimacy and basic authority of the office, but negotiated the new government's first treaty, appointed its first judges and department heads, received its first foreign ambassadors, vetoed its first legislation, and signed its first laws, thereby demonstrating just how future presidents should execute and influence the laws.

Washington's most important precedent may have been his retirement after serving two terms. Although he would have been easily reelected to a third term, Washington believed two terms were enough and returned to his Mount Vernon estate in 1796. It was a precedent that held until Franklin Roosevelt's four terms and was finally enshrined in constitutional language under the Twenty-Second Amendment.

Franklin Roosevelt's Depression-era Works Progress Administration put millions of people to work on public projects such as the mural by Marvin Beerbohm at the Detroit Post Office.

The First Modern Presidency

The presidency has evolved into a much more powerful institution than the framers ever imagined when they designed it, in part, to check what they thought would be a more powerful Congress. Most historians and political scientists agree that Franklin Roosevelt was the first president to exploit the institution's powers to their fullest.

In his 12 years in office, Roosevelt created an extraordinary record of achievement. He expanded the role of the president as commander, diplomat, and administrator in chief, while dominating Congress in both shaping and making the laws. Inaugurated for the first of his four terms in the midst of the Great Depression, Roosevelt took command, and his first 100 days in office in 1933 still stand as the most significant moment of presidential leadership in modern history. Most of his New Deal agenda for helping workers and the poor is still law today.

Roosevelt's impact extends well beyond the legislative agenda, however. He also exploited the powers of the presidency to build a highly personal relationship with the U.S. public, using his "fireside chats" on radio to calm the public during the darkest days of the economic depression, while calling the nation to action during the early days of World War II. In doing so, he became the nation's communicator in chief, starting each broadcast with the simple phrase "My friends."

Managing the Presidency

Presidents cannot do their jobs without help. Although some of that help comes from their *inner circle,* composed of their closest advisers including the first lady, presidents rely on a vast array of support that extends well beyond 1600 Pennsylvania Avenue to include the executive branch as a whole

LEARNING **OBJECTIVE**

4 Analyze the roles of the White House staff, Executive Office of the President, cabinet, and vice president.

The White House Staff

The president's most important advisers work inside the cramped confines of the West Wing of the White House.[20] Whereas presidents often view their cabinet secretaries as advocates of their departments, they view their White House staff as intensely loyal and responsive to the president, and the president alone.

Among modern presidents, Franklin Roosevelt and Lyndon Johnson both used the *competitive* approach for managing the White House staff, a "survival of the fittest" situation in which the president allows aides to fight each other for access to the Oval Office. Johnson sometimes gave different staffers the same assignment, hoping the competition would produce a better final decision.

In contrast, John Kennedy, Jimmy Carter, and Bill Clinton all used the *collegial* approach, encouraging aides to work together toward a common position. It is a friendlier way to work but may have the serious drawback of producing *groupthink,* the tendency of small groups to stifle dissent in the search for common ground.[21]

Finally, Dwight Eisenhower, Richard Nixon, Ronald Reagan, and George W. Bush all used the *hierarchical* approach, in which the president establishes tight control over who does what in making decisions. Presidents who use this approach usually rely on a "gatekeeper," or trusted adviser such as the chief of staff, to monitor the flow of information to and from the White House.

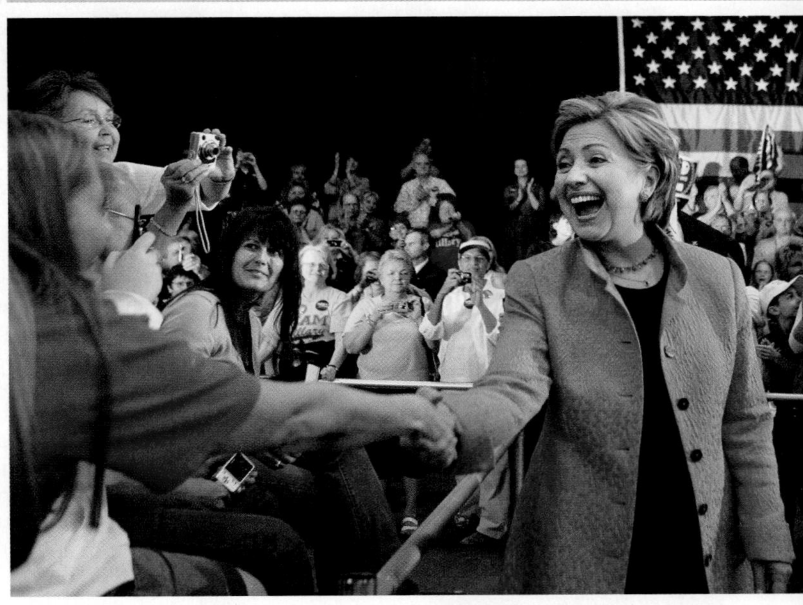

Hillary Clinton wielded great influence in her husband's administration. She used that experience during the 2008 Democratic nominating campaign by arguing that she would be ready for office "on day one."

The White House Bureaucracy The White House staff grew steadily from the early 1900s through the early 1990s, then stabilized at roughly 400 today. The **chief of staff,** the president's most loyal assistant, heads the staff, which also includes the president's chief lawyer, speechwriters, legislative liaison staff, and press secretary.

There are at least two kinds of White House offices. *Political* offices are designed to help the president run for reelection, control the national party, and shape the president's image through press conferences, television and radio addresses, polling, and travel. These offices provide the "spin" on the news that shows the president in the most favorable light, and allow him to lobby the public directly.

Policy offices are designed to shape the president's foreign and domestic program. Like congressional committees, these offices collect information and often write legislation. The list of policy offices includes the National Economic Council, which coordinates the president's economic agenda; the National Security Council, which helps set foreign policy; and the Office of Faith-Based and Community Initiatives, which encourages the use of religious institutions to help address community problems.[22]

chief of staff
The head of the White House staff.

The Executive Office of the President

The **Executive Office of the President** was created in 1939 to give the president more help running the federal departments and agencies. The EOP consists of the Office of Management and Budget, the Council of Economic Advisers, and several other staff units (see Figure 12–1). It also includes the White House staff.

Executive Office of the President
The cluster of presidential staff agencies that help the president carry out his responsibilities. Currently the office includes the Office of Management and Budget, the Council of Economic Advisers, and several other units.

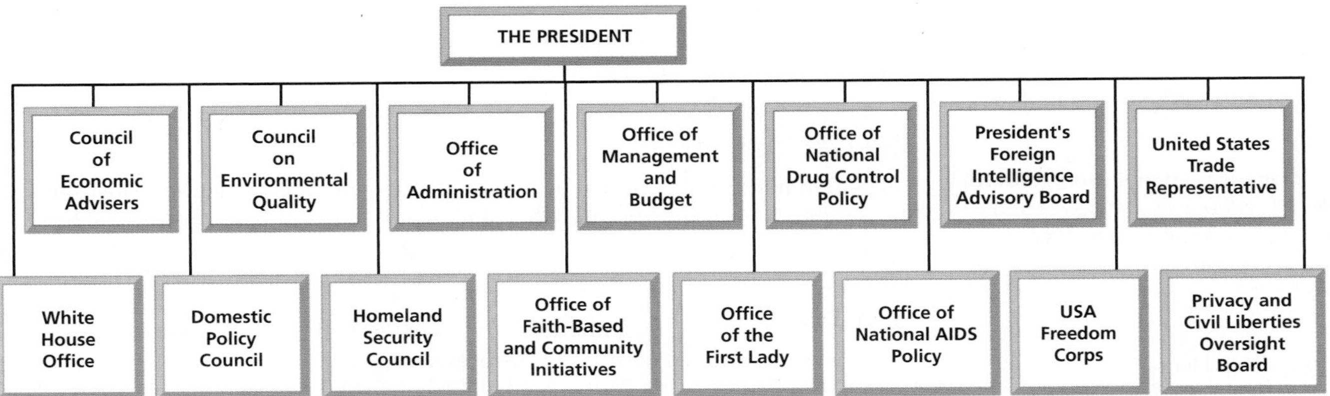

FIGURE 12–1
Executive Office of the President.

SOURCE: *U.S. Government Manual, 2005–2006* (U.S. Government Printing Office, 2006).

HISTORY MAKERS

Condoleezza Rice

Although Condoleezza Rice was neither the first woman nor the first African American to be appointed as secretary of state, she entered the job as the first African American woman to have served as the president's national security adviser and the first African American woman to become secretary of state.

Condoleezza Rice.

As President George W. Bush's national security adviser during his first term, Rice sat only a few doors away from the president, advised him on all foreign issues, and traveled with him on all missions abroad. She also helped resolve disputes among his foreign policy team. Her appointment as secretary of state at the start of the second term gave her even greater influence over foreign policy.

Rice also had a nearly perfect résumé for her jobs, which would have been more than enough to qualify her for almost any foreign policy job in the Bush administration. But she earned the president's trust and her status as a key adviser during the 2000 presidential campaign. During the hours and days after the terrorist attacks, President Bush often asked her to give him her advice on the right course of action.

Her service in the Bush administration was not without controversy, however. She was widely criticized for her role in shaping the case for war with Iraq. She argued for the existence of weapons of mass destruction that threatened the United States even though that claim had been discredited by the Central Intelligence Agency well before the president used it as part of his case for war. She will likely be remembered more for what she did during the early days of the war on terrorism than for her current role as secretary of state.

Although she has said she had to be "twice as good" to get ahead, Rice made it to the top by believing her parents when they told her that "you may not be able to have a hamburger at Woolworth's but you can be president of the United States."

QUESTIONS

1. How did Rice's life history and race affect her work as secretary of state?
2. In what ways has having an African American female secretary of state made a difference in the image of the United States around the world?
3. Why did Rice say she had to be "twice as good" to get ahead?

The **Office of Management and Budget (OMB)** is the central presidential staff agency. Its director advises the president in detail about the hundreds of government agencies—how much money they should be allotted in the budget and what kind of job they are doing. OMB seeks to improve the planning, management, and statistical work of the agencies. It makes a special effort to see that each agency conforms to presidential policies in its dealings with Congress; each agency has to clear its policy recommendations to Congress through OMB first.[23]

Through the long budget-preparation process, presidents use OMB as a way of conserving and centralizing their own influence. A budget is more than just a financial plan. It reflects power struggles between the president and federal departments and agencies and signals the president's priorities to Congress. Although Congress is responsible for actually authorizing and appropriating money, the president's budget usually provides an initial outline of how much each department and agency will get.

The Cabinet

It is hard to find a more unusual institution than the president's **cabinet.** The cabinet is not specifically mentioned in the Constitution, yet every president since 1789 has had one. Washington's consisted of his secretaries of state, treasury, and war, plus his attorney general.

Office of Management and Budget (OMB)
A presidential staff agency that serves as a clearinghouse for budgetary requests and management improvements for government agencies.

cabinet
The advisory council for the president, consisting of the heads of the executive departments, the vice president, and a few other officials selected by the president.

Defining the Cabinet Defining the cabinet is the first major job for the president-elect. Today the cabinet consists of the president, the vice president, the heads of the 15 executive departments, and several others a president considers essential officials.

The cabinet has always been a loosely designated body, and it is not always clear who belongs in it. In recent years, certain executive branch administrators and White

President Bush holds a press conference surrounded by his cabinet. The cabinet is made up of the head of executive departments and other key officials. Although some department heads are expected to be included in every administration, the president has great leeway in deciding who is to be part of this powerful council.

House counselors have been accorded cabinet rank. Nineteen officials had cabinet status in the George W. Bush administration, including the 15 cabinet secretaries, the vice president, the chief of staff, and the director of national intelligence.

Presidents tend to rely on their own White House advisers for most input on key issues. Proximity is power in Washington, and the White House staff is always close (see Figure 12–2). Further, presidents are aware that some cabinet members are "captured" by their departments: the Agriculture Department secretary is a strong advocate for farmers; the Housing and Urban Development Department secretary is an ambassador for the housing industry and, to some extent, also for big-city mayors; and so on through much of the cabinet, especially in departments concerned primarily with domestic policy matters.

The Vice Presidency

Despite Vice President Dick Cheney's visible role in the Bush administration, the vice presidency has not always been an important job. For most of U.S. history, the vice president was an insignificant officer at best and at worst a political rival who sometimes connived against the president. The office was often dismissed as a joke. One reason for the vice president's posture as an outsider was that presidential nominees usually chose running mates who were geographically, ideologically, demographically, and in other ways likely to "balance the ticket."

No matter how influential they become, vice presidents have only one major responsibility: to be ready to take the oath of office in case the president cannot discharge his duties. Nevertheless, vice presidents enter office with substantial access, including an office just down the hall from the president in the West Wing of the White House, a substantial staff of their own, and access to all of the information flowing into the Oval Office.

Though as vice president, Joe Biden's primary responsibility is to take the oath of office should the president become unable to carry out the term, some vice presidents have wielded more power and influence than others.

Vice President Dick Cheney had more than just access to President Bush, however. He also had considerable influence. He was a trusted adviser to the Bush family and had served in Congress and as secretary of defense under the first president Bush. Although he started his vice presidency as one of the most popular political leaders in the country, his approval fell dramatically as the war in Iraq continued. By the end of 2007, just 23 percent of U.S. adults approved of Cheney's job as vice president.[24]

FIGURE 12–2
The White House.

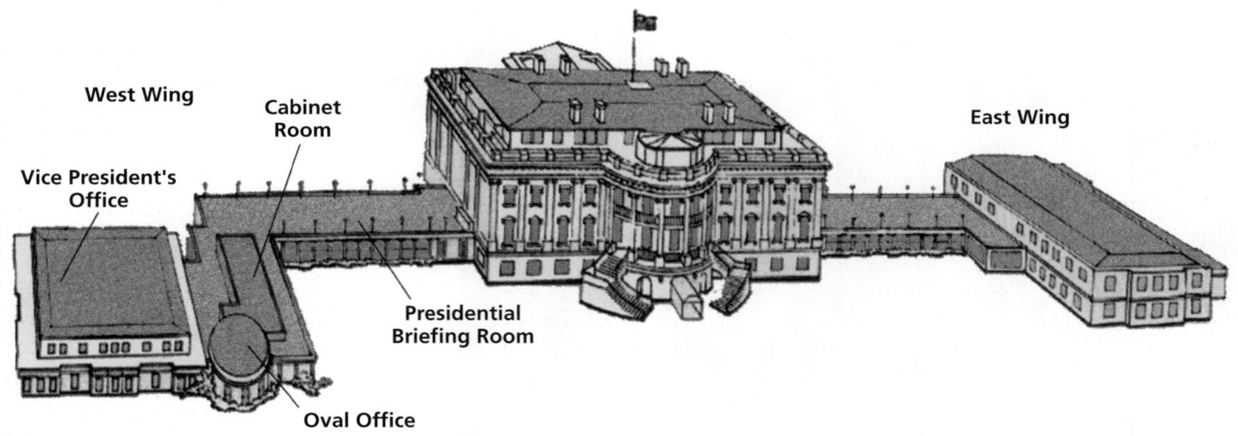

The President's Job

U.S. citizens want the chief executive to be an international peacemaker as well as a national morale builder, a politician in chief as well as a commander in chief. They want the president to provide leadership on foreign, economic, and domestic policy. They also want presidents to be crisis managers and role models of a kind. They want them to be able to connect with ordinary people, yet be smarter, tougher, and more honest than the rest of us. (See Table 12–1 for what U.S. adults thought presidents could change about the world in 2008.)

Presidential Leadership: Which Hat Do You Wear?

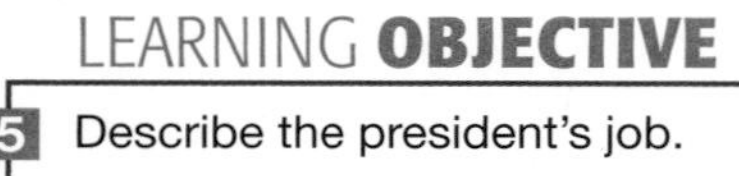

5 Describe the president's job.

Presidents as Morale Builders

As chief of state, the president must project a sense of national unity and authority as the country's chief ceremonial leader. The framers of the Constitution did not fully anticipate the symbolic and morale-building functions a president must perform. But over time, presidents have become national celebrities and command media attention merely by jogging, fishing, golfing, or going to church. By their actions, presidents can arouse a sense of hope or despair, honor or dishonor.

Morale building means much more than just ceremonies or prayers. At its finest, presidential leadership radiates national self-confidence and helps unlock

TABLE 12–1 What Can Presidents Change?

Percentage of Americans Who Said the President Has a Great Deal of Influence over Each of the Following Issues	
Housing prices	20%
Interest rates	23%
Inflation	30%
Gas prices	31%
Health care costs	38%
Federal budget deficit	48%
Taxes	48%
The way other countries view the United States	60%

SOURCE: Associated Press–Yahoo Poll, January 18, 2008.

the possibility for good that exists in the nation. That is certainly what George W. Bush intended in the days and weeks that followed September 11, 2001. By his words and deeds, he sought to simultaneously calm the nation and warn the rest of the world that the United States would not tolerate further terrorist attacks.

Presidents as Agenda Setters

By custom and circumstance, presidents are now responsible for proposing initiatives in foreign policy and economic growth and stability. Presidential candidates searching for campaign issues seize on new ideas, and these are later refined and implemented by the executive office staff, by special presidential task forces, and by Congress.[25]

Economic Policy Ever since the New Deal, presidents have been expected to promote policies to keep unemployment low, fight inflation, keep taxes down, and promote economic growth and prosperity. The Constitution does not specify these, yet presidents know they will be held accountable for economic problems such as inflation and unemployment.

Social Policy Leadership is often defined as the art of knowing what followers want. John Kennedy and Lyndon Johnson did not launch the civil rights movement, for example. Nor did Bill Clinton or George W. Bush create public pressure for national health insurance or prescription drug coverage. But they all responded to the public demand by supporting legislation on each issue.

National Security Policy The framers foresaw a special need for speed and unity in dealing with other nations. The Supreme Court has upheld strong presidential authority in this area. In *United States v. Curtiss-Wright* (1936), the Court referred to the "exclusive power of the president as the sole organ of the federal government in the field of international relations—a power which does not require as a basis for its exercise an act of Congress, but which, of course, like every other governmental power, must be exercised in subordination to the applicable provisions of the Constitution."[26]

These words were sweeping and controversial.[27] Still, a determined Congress has significant power if it wants to use it. Congress must authorize and appropriate the funds that support the president's policies abroad, but it often gives the president wide latitude in protecting the nation.

President Bush, flanked by firefighters and rescue workers, addresses a crowd at the scene of the September 11 World Trade Center disaster in New York. In times of crisis, the nation often rallies around the president despite political differences.

Ronald Reagan stayed in touch with the public through speeches, radio and television addresses, and "photo opportunities" such as this one at his California ranch.

Presidents as Persuaders

Despite their formal powers, presidents spend most of their time *persuading* people. As Richard Neustadt argues, the power to persuade is the president's chief resource.[28] This power to persuade is based on the president's ability to communicate directly with members of Congress and the public through the skillful use of press conferences, speeches, and public events.

Presidents have reduced the number of their press conferences over the past five decades. Whereas Franklin Roosevelt averaged almost seven press conferences a month during his dozen years in office, the past four presidents averaged barely one. Presidents would much rather be interviewed by local reporters outside Washington than by members of the experienced White House press corps, much rather give exclusive interviews to a sympathetic interviewer than face a roomful of unpredictable reporters, and much rather use live satellite feeds to remote stations to get their message across than deal with the *Washington Post, New York Times,* or *Wall Street Journal.* (Presidential press conferences are covered in more detail in Chapter 10.) "Going public" often means carefully staging events before friendly audiences that show strong support for the president.

Going public clearly fits with changes in the electoral process. Presidents now have the staff, the technology, and the public opinion research to tell them how to target their message, and they have nearly instant media access to speak to the public easily. And, as elections have become more image oriented and candidate centered, presidents have the incentive to use these tools to operate a permanent White House campaign. They are still welcome to bargain and persuade, to focus congressional attention and twist arms, but members of Congress may pay attention only when pressure is coming from the voters back home.

Congress and the Presidency

Congress and the presidency have a contentious relationship. They often work closely to address critically important problems but at other times are unable to reach agreement on equally difficult issues. They are most likely to agree in the first year of a president's first term and when one party controls both the White House and Congress, and more likely to fight late in the president's first term and off and on throughout the entire second term.

GENERATION **NEXT**

The President's Approval Rating

Although we tend to unite behind the president at the very beginning of the first term, when the president is usually at the height of popularity, we divide over time as the president makes decisions about wars, the economy, and specific legislation. As a result, presidential approval tends to decline, creating a cycle of decreasing influence in which the president hits a low point in the final years in office.

Generation Next's approval has followed this downward pattern. According to the Pew Research Center's ongoing tracking surveys, more than 80 percent of 18- to 29-year-olds approved of President Bush in the weeks after the September 11 terrorist attacks, while just 34 percent approved in the 2007 Political Landscape survey.

As the chart shows, nonwhites, Democrats, and liberals were far less likely to approve of Bush in 2007 than men, whites, Republicans, and conservatives. The differences clearly fit with Bush's party and ideology—Republicans tend to approve of Republican presidents, while conservatives tend to approve of conservative presidents.

Generation Next is not very different on this question from older generations. Overall, 28 percent of 18- to 29-year-olds said they approved of Bush's job performance, compared with 34 percent of 30- to 39-year-olds, 40 percent of 40- to 49-year-olds, 34 percent of 50- to 59-year-olds and 32 percent of people age 60 or older. These older adults lost confidence in Bush over time, too.

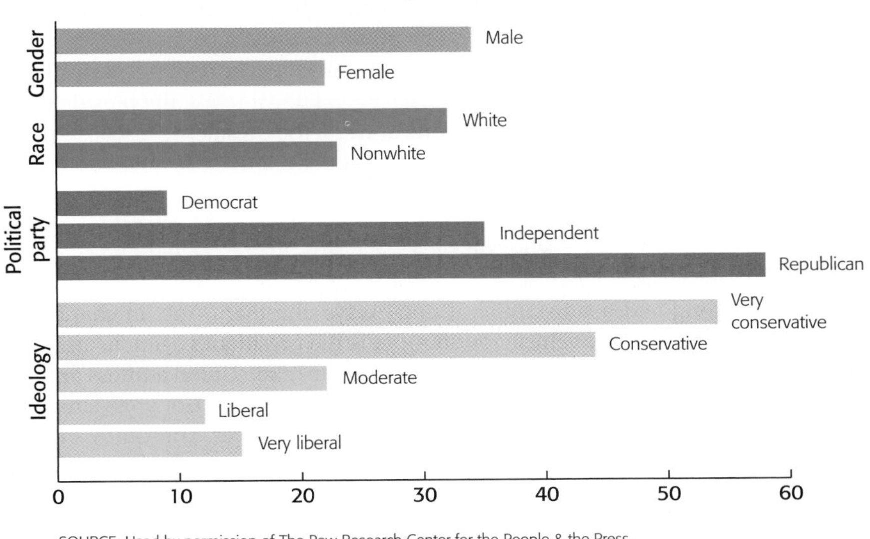

SOURCE: Used by permission of The Pew Research Center for the People & the Press.

QUESTIONS

1. Why did women and nonwhites have less confidence in Bush than men and whites?
2. How do presidential strategies for influencing Congress change with declining approval ratings?
3. What key events increased Bush's approval and why did it fall?

LEARNING **OBJECTIVE**

6 Identify the sources of presidential/congressional conflict and the tools presidents use to influence Congress.

Given the separation of powers, it is a wonder that Congress and the president ever agree at all, which is exactly what the framers intended. The framers did not want the legislative process to work like an assembly line. Rather, they wanted ambition to counteract ambition as a way to prevent tyranny.

To the extent that they designed the legislative process to work inefficiently, the founders succeeded beyond their initial hopes. As hard as presidents work to win passage of their top priorities, they often complain that Congress is not listening. However, Congress listens more closely to its constituents, especially when the president's public approval is low. That is why so many of the Bush administration's second-term priorities never reached the floor of the House or Senate.

Why Presidents and Congress Disagree

Congress and the president disagree for many reasons, not the least of which is the natural tendency of members of Congress to think about elections far into the future. Not only does the Constitution give each institution separate powers and checks and balances, it also provides competing constituencies, calendars, and campaigns, all of which put Congress and the presidency on a frequent course to stalemate.

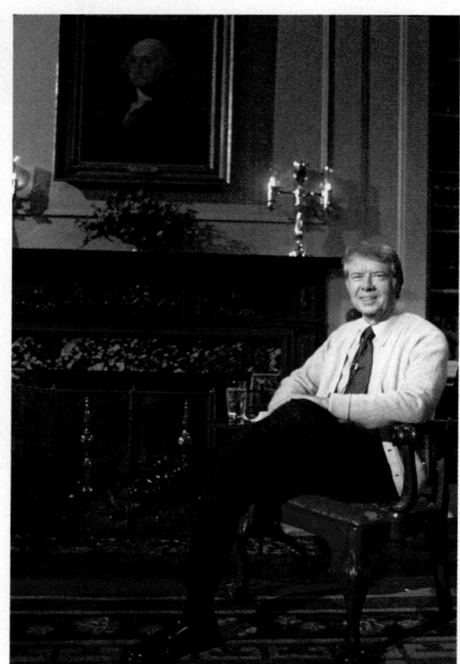

President Jimmy Carter addresses the U.S. public in his first televised address to talk about energy policy. He made a deliberate choice to give the address sitting down near the fireplace dressed in a cardigan sweater as a way to calm the public's concern about increasing gasoline prices.

Competing Constituencies The framers guaranteed that members of Congress and the president would represent different constituencies, which often leads to conflict over major legislation. Members of Congress represent either states or local districts, while the president represents the nation as a whole. Although these constituencies often overlap, particularly in states that strongly support the president's election, members of Congress often worry most about how the laws and presidential actions will affect their home districts. We discuss the centrality of reelection to Congress in greater detail in Chapter 9.

Competing Calendars The Constitution also ensures that Congress and the president will not share the same terms of office. Presidents can serve a maximum of eight years before leaving office, while senators and members of the House can serve for decades. Presidents enter office wanting everything passed at once, while members of Congress have plenty of time to wait. Convinced they must either move quickly or lose all hopes of any success at all, presidents tend to overload Congress with priorities in their first year, thereby actually reducing their chances of passage. Asked to do everything at once, many members of Congress decide to do nothing particularly fast.

Competing Campaigns Finally, the Constitution ensures that Congress and the president will run different kinds of election campaigns. Most members of Congress finance their election campaigns with only minimal assistance from their national political party. They usually run independently of the president or national party platform. Even members of the president's own party have been known to ask the president not to visit their districts in particularly tight elections or when the president's public approval is falling. Whenever possible, members try to make elections about local, not national issues, which means the president is often completely ignored during the campaign.

Influencing Congress

Presidents have long had a substantial, if not always dominant, role in shaping what Congress does. Their primary vehicle for doing so is the president's agenda, an informal list of top legislative priorities. Whether through the State of the Union address or through other messages and signals, presidents make clear what they think Congress should do.

It is one thing to proclaim a presidential priority, however, and quite another to actually influence congressional action. As Richard Neustadt argued in *Presidential Power,* a president's constitutional powers add up to little more than a job as the country's most distinguished office clerk. It is a president's ability to persuade others that spells the difference between being a clerk and being a national leader.[29] This power rests in the resources presidents bring to office and the skills they use.

Presidential Success in Polls and Congress

The power to persuade on Capitol Hill is often measured through the **presidential support score,** calculated by counting the times the president wins key votes in Congress. Bush won more than 70 percent of his votes from 2001 to 2006, but only 38 percent in 2007.[30] Although his earlier high scores would seem to make him the most influential president in modern history, Bush earned the scores by taking relatively few positions on key votes that he knew he could win.

Presidential Mandates Presidents who enter office with a large electoral margin, high public approval, and a party majority in Congress often claim a **mandate,** or public support, to govern. The winner-take-all nature of the electoral-college system tends to make the president's popular vote look larger than it truly is. Ronald Reagan set the modern record in 1984 by winning every state but Minnesota, as well as and the District of Columbia, rolling up 98 percent of the electoral votes with a popular total of 59 percent.

Mandates also reside in public approval for either the president or some policy issue. In 1993, for example, Bill Clinton claimed a mandate for national health insurance, arguing that the issue was at the core of much of his public support. The claim would have been more believable if Clinton had won with a popular vote larger than 43 percent. George W. Bush made a similar claim for a broad agenda early in 2001, arguing that the U.S. public wanted action in Washington. Again, the claim would have been more plausible had he won the popular vote.

presidential support score
The percentage of times a president wins on key votes in Congress.

mandate
A president's claim of broad public support.

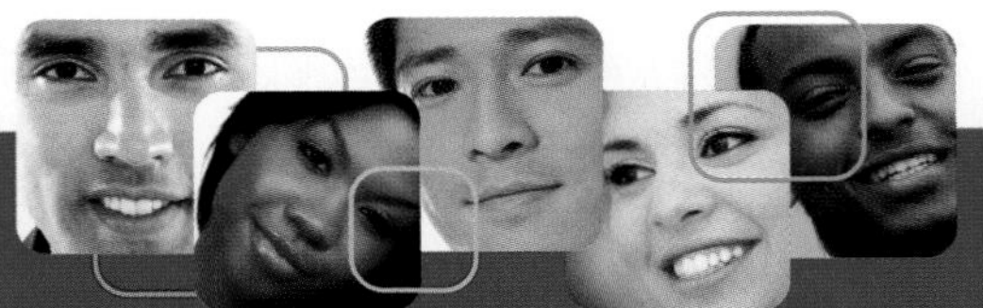

THE **CHANGING FACE** OF U.S. POLITICS

Presidential Appointees

Presidents Bill Clinton and George W. Bush both promised to appoint administrations as diverse as the country. Although both came surprisingly close on race, neither approached the 50 percent mark on gender.

The percentages of female and minority appointees are disappointing given the changing face of federal departments and agencies (discussed in the next chapter), but both administrations did much better than their predecessors—fewer than 15 percent of the Carter administration's appointees were women, compared with just 8 percent of the Reagan administration's first-term appointees. And the fact that both Clinton and Bush were able to recruit many women and minority appointees at entry-level positions suggests that future administrations will be even more successful. Past research shows higher-level jobs almost always go to appointees with prior service at lower levels of government.

The commitment to diversity is particularly apparent at the very top of government. Clinton appointed five women, seven African Americans, three Hispanics, and one Asian American as secretaries of departments during his eight years in office, while Bush named five women, four African Americans, three Hispanics, and two Asian Americans in his first four years in office.

Bush's second term brought more diversity. He appointed his White House lawyer, Alberto Gonzales, to be the first Hispanic attorney general, Condoleezza Rice to be the first female African American secretary of state, and Carlos Gutierrez to be the first Cuban American secretary of commerce. He also appointed dozens of women and minorities to lower-level posts, thereby giving them the experience for future promotions to higher-level jobs.

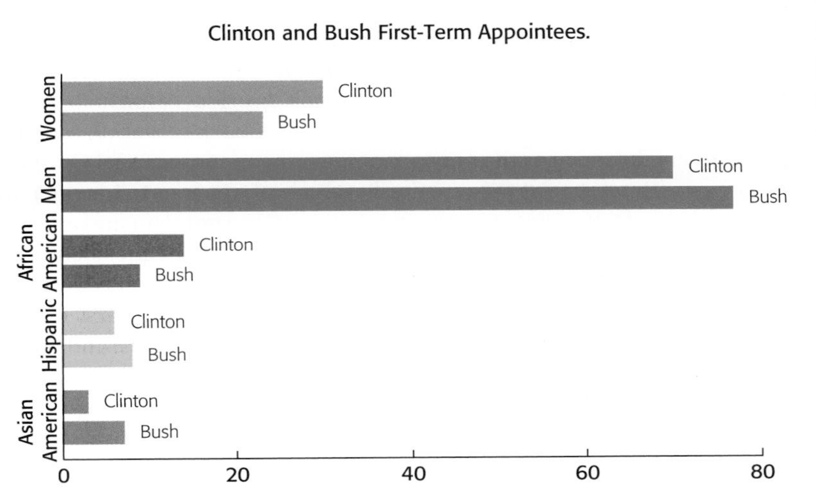

QUESTIONS

1. Does diversity of appointees matter to presidential influence in Congress and in the country, and if so, why?
2. How does diversity in appointments make any difference in the policy positions an administration takes? What demographic characteristics might matter more?
3. Relative to their proportion in the population, women continue to lag behind African Americans, Hispanics, and Asian Americans in high-level administration appointments. Why is this the case? Why are Democratic presidents more successful at recruiting women to appointee positions?

Public Approval The mandate to govern depends in part on public approval, which generally falls over time. (See Figure 12–3 for presidential approval trends over the past half-century.) Bush became the first incumbent president in modern history to win reelection despite starting his campaign with an approval rating below 50 percent. Although he regained ground after his second inauguration, his ratings continued to fall as his second term continued, which helps explain the declining number of congressional votes on which he took a position. He simply did not have enough *political capital* to take more positions.

Presidents also benefit from **rally points,** spikes in public approval following a domestic or international crisis. Rally points do not necessarily last long, however. George W. Bush's ratings jumped dramatically following the September 11, 2001, attacks when he called on the nation to support the war on terrorism, but eventually fell back with the continued violence after the first moments of the war in Iraq. His approval rating jumped 29 percent after the September 11 attacks, and 12 percent after the start of the Iraq War in 2003.

Not all rally points involve foreign crises. Clinton's approval rose after the Oklahoma City bombing in 1995, in large part because the nation turned to him for

rally point
A rise in public approval of the president that follows a crisis as Americans "rally 'round the flag" and the chief executive.

YOU WILL DECIDE Should the Two-Term Limit Be Repealed?

The Twenty-Second Amendment was ratified in 1951 to limit the president's time in office to two terms whether served consecutively or not (Grover Cleveland served from 1885 to 1889 and from 1893 to 1897). Although George Washington established the two-term precedent, Ulysses S. Grant ran for a third term but lost, while Franklin Roosevelt ran for a third and a fourth term and won.

All the two-term presidents who followed ratification of the Twenty-Second Amendment have supported its repeal, arguing that the amendment effectively renders them *lame ducks* in their second terms. Because they cannot stand for reelection, Congress and the public tend to ignore them as thoughts turn to the next election. Nor can they be held accountable in the voting booth for their second-term decisions.

leadership in the crisis. In contrast, Bush's ratings fell after the government's sluggish response to Hurricane Katrina in 2006.

Reputation The longer presidents stay in office, the better they get at being president. They learn how Washington works, what powers they can use to influence congressional action, and whom they need to convince to win passage of their top priorities. Presidents also learn how to use unilateral powers to accomplish some of their goals.

Nevertheless, presidents pay great attention to the steady erosion of public approval that occurs over time. As a result of it, they have the greatest potential influence at the very point when they know the least about being president, and know the most about being president when they have the least influence. Presidents generally believe they must "move it or lose it," meaning they have to use their political influence when they have it. Doing so creates great opportunities for mistakes, however. Clinton and Bush both flooded Congress with long lists of first-year priorities, which created confusion and delays on Capitol Hill as individual members and committees tried to decide which priorities came first.

Some experts believe the president's reputation has declined in recent years, in part because of political scandals such as the burglary of the Democratic National Campaign offices at the Watergate Hotel in 1972 (Nixon), the illegal sale of weapons to Iran in return for aid to Nicaraguan rebels (Reagan), and an affair between the president and an intern (Clinton). Nixon's resignation clearly diminished public respect for the presidency, and Bill Clinton's impeachment distracted the nation from more pressing problems such as the rising tide of anti-American sentiment in the Middle East. The controversy over the 2000 election raised questions about the legitimacy of the electoral process, and the war in Iraq led many to doubt President Bush's leadership in the war on terrorism. As a result, Congress may now be quicker to dismiss presidential positions.

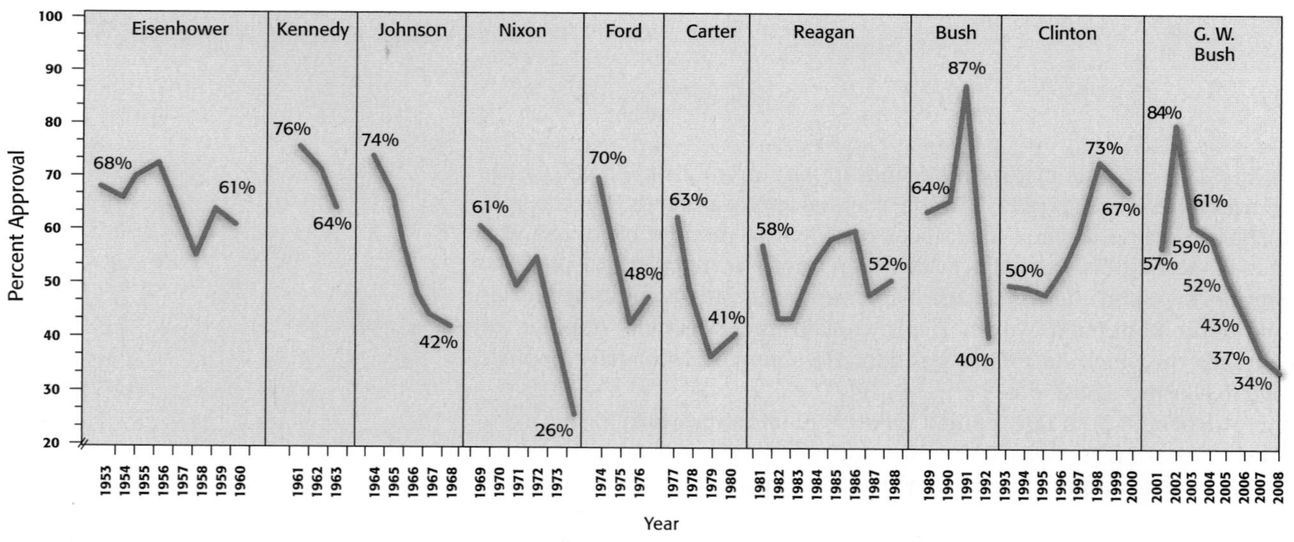

FIGURE 12–3
Presidential Approval Ratings, 1953–2008.

NOTE: Percentage is from the first Gallup/*USA Today* poll taken each calendar year.

SOURCE: Gallup/*USA Today* poll, available at www.pollingreport.com.

Judging Presidents

Presidents rise and fall in the historical rankings based on a number of factors. Some rise because they led the nation through periods of intense domestic or international crisis; others rise because they had a distinctive vision of where the nation should go on issues such as civil rights, social policy, or the economy. Rankings also include at least some assessment of how presidents fared as political and moral leaders of the nation. Some fall because of political or personal scandal, others because they failed to grapple with a big issue such as national health insurance or an economic crisis. In the end, rankings provide an overall measure of a president's ability to meet the public's expectations.

History tends to judge wars as the most significant test of a president's leadership. Wars that end in stalemate tend to diminish a president's greatness, while wars that end in victory raise a president's ranking, especially when the nation's survival is threatened. Abraham Lincoln (the Civil War), Woodrow Wilson (World War I), and Franklin Delano Roosevelt (World War II) rank among the great presidents because of their leadership during just such wars, while Lyndon Johnson ranks much lower because of his role in the Vietnam stalemate.

War is not the only path to greatness, however. George Washington and Thomas Jefferson rank as great presidents because of their role in protecting the nation during its early years. Theodore Roosevelt ranks as a great president because of his role in making the United States an international power at the turn of the twentieth century. Harry Truman and Dwight Eisenhower rank

THINKING IT THROUGH

The founders clearly believed that elections serve to discipline the president for his actions, while the four-year term provides enough time to achieve policy results. They believed that steadiness in administration would help the country survive its early years, while giving the president a reason to create policies that would help the nation long into the future. Presidents are arguably more effective if their allies and opponents assume they may be running for another term. Otherwise, they become "lame ducks" early in their second terms, meaning that they have little influence.

Much as they may have applauded Washington's two-term precedent, the founders did not support the idea of a formal term limit—such a limit would have weakened the public's voice in keeping the president honest. Instead of starting a second term knowing he could not serve again, the president would be able to keep Congress and the public guessing, thereby retaining influence until the last possible minute.

Advocates of the two-term limit argue that presidents should be more like state governors, many of whom serve under term limits. They also argue that the presidency has become so strong that removing the two-term limit would create near-certain reelection far into the future. They point out that the Bush family has held the presidency for three terms. The office also carries such great power that lame-duck status may keep presidents from abusing their power—even as lame ducks, they retain significant influence on Capitol Hill in their fifth and sixth years.

Questions

1. Do presidents have so much power that they can almost guarantee reelection to more than two terms?
2. Does the two-term limit weaken the president's ability to influence the course of the nation in the second term?
3. What checks and balances ensure that presidents can be held accountable even if they are lame ducks?

You Are a President during a Nuclear Power Plant Meltdown

Presidents learn more about their jobs the longer they are in office. Part of that learning comes from the constant stress of the job, which shows in these pictures taken over time.

LEARNING **OBJECTIVE**

 Identify factors that make a great president.

among the near-great presidents because they led the nation through the first decade of the cold war against communism. And Ronald Reagan ranks among the near-great presidents for ending the cold war 30 years later when the Soviet Union collapsed. These presidents also made difficult decisions about domestic issues such as civil rights, economic policy, and the need for a strong national government.

Corruption and inability to deal with economic problems are sure paths to presidential failure. Warren Harding and Richard Nixon both rank as failures because of scandals that tarnished their presidencies, while Herbert Hoover is ranked a failure because of his lack of leadership at the start of the Great Depression. Although Lyndon Johnson launched a number of great domestic programs such as Medicare for older citizens and helped secure civil rights for African Americans, his role in the Vietnam War continues to cast a shadow on his presidential greatness.

It is too early to guess where George W. Bush will be ranked by history. His response to September 11, 2001, was steady and reassuring, and the nation rallied to his side in the first few weeks of the war in Iraq. At the same time, soaring budget deficits and questions about the war in Iraq undermined both his credibility and his public support. So did rising gasoline prices, the government's weak response to Hurricane Katrina in 2005, and the economic crisis that came at the end of his presidency in 2008.

At least for now, however, Bush seems destined for an average rating. According to public opinion polls taken in late 2006, only 19 percent of respondents rated Bush outstanding or above average, compared with 45 percent for Clinton, 32 percent for George H.W. Bush, 64 percent for Reagan, 38 percent for Jimmy Carter, and 23 percent for Gerald Ford. Of these presidents, only Reagan is likely to emerge as a great or near-great president in future polls.

Ultimately, a president's place in history is determined decades after he or she leaves office, and varies over time. Reagan has moved up the charts with each passing survey, for example, as his role in ending the cold war takes on increasing visibility in an uncertain world. By remembering that there is a future accounting, presidents can find some inspiration for making the hard and sometimes unpopular choices that have led to greatness among their predecessors. Thus the judgment of history may be one of the most important sources of accountability the nation has on its presidents.

Residents of New Orleans' Lower Ninth Ward stranded on the roofs wait for rescue after Hurricane Katrina slammed into Louisiana in 2005. President Bush and his administration came under fire for a slow response to the disaster.

CHAPTER **SUMMARY**

1 Describe the constitutional foundations of the presidency.

The framers wanted a presidency with enough authority to protect the nation from domestic and foreign threats, but not so strong that it would become a threat to liberty. They solved their concern by dividing power between the branches, giving each important checks over the others.

2 Compare and contrast the three types of presidential power.

The framers gave the president three central roles in the new government: commander in chief, diplomat in chief, and administrator in chief. Presidents have expanded their powers in several ways over the decades. Crises, both foreign and economic, have enlarged these powers. When there is a need for decisive action, presidents are asked to supply it.

3 Evaluate the controversies surrounding the president's assertion of additional executive powers and the evolution of presidential power.

The Constitution is not always clear on which branch has what powers, which creates controversies over the president's war power and authority to assert executive privilege, issue executive orders, and control the budget and spending process. Congress has made several attempts in recent decades to clarify the president's war and spending power, but the presidency still bears the imprint of George Washington's and Franklin Delano Roosevelt's precedents.

4 Analyze the roles of the White House staff, Executive Office of the President, cabinet, and vice president.

Presidents manage the executive branch with the assistance of an intensely loyal White House staff, a much larger Executive Office of the President that is anchored by the Office of Management and Budget, a cabinet of department secretaries that oversees the federal government's employees, and the vice president. The vice president's authority varies from president to president.

5 Describe the president's job.

We expect a great deal from our presidents. We want them to be crisis managers, morale builders, and agenda setters, yet we also want them to be able to connect with average citizens.

6 Identify the sources of presidential/congressional conflict and the tools presidents use to influence Congress.

The president and Congress often have a tense relationship because of different constitutional expectations and party divisions. Presidents have a variety of tools for influencing Congress, however, and use their political and personal resources to gain support for their policy proposals. Presidents have several powerful tools for influencing Congress. They can create mandates by helping members of Congress win elections, use their public approval to lobby Congress for action, and rely on the reputation of the presidency as a source of prestige.

7 Identify factors that make a great president.

Presidential greatness is hard to define. Historians, political scientists, and the American public consider Washington, Jefferson, Lincoln, and Franklin Roosevelt as their greatest presidents. Greatness depends in part on how presidents deal with crisis and war.

Chapter Self-Test

1. In a short essay, discuss how the framers addressed their concerns about the presidency in the Constitution. In your opinion, have their protections worked? (pp. 328–329)
2. What is the only constitutional duty of the Vice President aside from waiting to take the place of the President if needed? (pp. 329–330)
3. Which of the following is not required for a person to be elected President of the United States? (p. 330)
   a. Be at least 35 years old
   b. Be a natural-born citizen of the United States
   c. Be affiliated with an officially organized political party
   d. Be a resident of the United States for the previous 14 years
4. Which of the following is not one of the three central roles of the President? (pp. 331–332)
   a. Chief diplomat
   b. Chief lawmaker
   c. Manager in chief
   d. Commander in chief
5. In one or two paragraphs explain the president's responsibility in each of the three roles discussed in the chapter. (pp. 331–332)
6. List and briefly explain the President's additional powers. (pp. 332–334)
7. Match each of the Presidents listed below with the precedents they set while in office. (pp. 337–340)

1. George W. Bush
2. George Washington
3. Franklin D. Roosevelt

a. Serving only two terms in office
b. Preemptively attacking enemies
c. Widely expanding and modernizing the office of president

8. In addition to the White House staff, what groups or individuals can help the President make decisions? (pp. 341–344)
9. List three types of organization that modern presidents have used to structure their staffs. Write a couple of sentences about the benefits and weaknesses of each. (pp. 341–344)
10. Table 12–1 lists a set of issues over which the President might be assumed to have some control. Chose three and write a brief essay explaining how the president could influence each. Use information from the chapter as well as your own knowledge. (p. 341)
11. Briefly explain each of the President's roles listed below. Which job do you think is the most important? Which do you notice the President doing the most? (pp. 341–346)
    a. Persuader
    b. Agenda Setter
    c. Morale Builder
12. List the three main causes of conflict between the president and Congress. (p. 348)
13. Write a persuasive essay explaining how the current relationship between the President and Congress fulfills the framers' intentions for their roles and interactions. (pp. 347–350)
14. Match each of the presidents listed below with the appropriate accomplishment. (pp. 333, 336, 340, 351)

    a) George Washington
    b) Woodrow Wilson
    c) Franklin Delano Roosevelt
    d) Abraham Lincoln
    e) Theodore Roosevelt

    i. Making the United States an international power
    ii. Leading the United States to victory in WWII
    iii. Protecting the United States during its early years
    iv. Leading the United States to victory in the Civil War
    v. Leading the United States to victory in WWI
15. In a short essay, discuss factors other than winning wars that you think make a president "great." How would the most two recent presidents rank in your determination of presidential greatness? (pp. 351–352)

Key Terms

parliamentary system, p. 329

presidential ticket, p. 331

vesting clause, p. 331

treaty, p. 332

executive agreement, p. 332

congressional–executive agreement, p. 332

recess appointment, p. 333

veto, p. 333

pocket veto, p. 333

take care clause, p. 333

inherent powers, p. 333

State of the Union Address, p. 334

impeachment, p. 334

executive privilege, p. 336

executive orders, p. 337

impoundment, p. 337

line item veto, p. 337

signing statements, p. 338

chief of staff, p. 341

Executive Office of the President, p. 341

Office of Management and Budget (OMB), p. 342

cabinet, p. 342

presidential support score, p. 348

mandate, p. 348

rally point, p. 349

Further Reading

JOHN P. BURKE, *The Institutional Presidency: Organizing and Managing the White House from FDR to Clinton,* 2d ed. (Johns Hopkins University Press, 2000).

THOMAS E. CRONIN AND **MICHAEL A. GENOVESE,** *The Paradoxes of the American Presidency,* 2d ed. (Oxford University Press, 2004).

TERRY EASTLAND, *Energy in the Executive* (Free Press, 1992).

MICHAEL A. GENOVESE, *The Power of the*

American Presidency, 1989–2000 (Oxford University Press, 2000).

DAVID GERGEN, *Eyewitness to Power: The Essence of Leadership, Nixon to Clinton* (Simon & Schuster, 2000).

FRED GREENSTEIN, *The Presidential Difference: Leadership Style from FDR to George W. Bush,* 2d ed. (Princeton University Press, 2004).

ERWIN C. HARGROVE, *The President as Leader: Appealing to the Better Angels of Our Nature* (University Press of Kansas, 1998).

GENE HEALY, *The Cult of the Presidency: America's Dangerous Devotion to Presidential Power* (Cato Institute, 2008).

STEPHEN HESS AND **JAMES P. PFINNER,** *Organizing the Presidency,* 3d ed. (Brookings Institution Press, 2002).

CHARLES O. JONES, *The Presidency in a Separated System,* 2d ed. (Brookings Institution Press, 2005).

SAMUEL KERNELL, *Going Public: New Strategies of Presidential Leadership,* 4th ed. (CQ Press, 2006).

GARY KING AND **LYN RAGSDALE,** *The Elusive Executive: Discovering Statistical Patterns in the Presidency,* 2d ed. (CQ Press, 2002).

JOHN A. MALTESE, *Spin Control: The White House Office of Communications and the Management of the Presidential News* (University of North Carolina Press, 1992).

SIDNEY M. MILKIS, *The President and the Parties: The Transformation of the American Party System Since the New Deal* (Oxford University Press, 1993).

SIDNEY M. MILKIS AND **MICHAEL NELSON,** *The American Presidency: Origins and Development, 1976–2000,* 5th ed. (CQ Press, 2007).

MICHAEL NELSON, ED., *The Presidency and the Political System,* 8th ed. (CQ Press, 2005).

RICHARD E. NEUSTADT, *Presidential Power and the Modern Presidents* (Free Press, 1991).

BRADLEY H. PATTERSON JR., *The White House Staff: Inside the West Wing and Beyond* (Brookings Institution Press, 2002).

JAMES PFIFFNER, *The Modern Presidency,* 5th ed. (Wadsworth, 2008).

JOSEPH A. PIKA AND **JOHN ANTHONY MALTESE,** *The Politics of the Presidency,* 7th ed. (CQ Press, 2008).

STEPHEN PONDER, *Managing the Press: Origins of the Media Presidency* (Palgrave, 2000).

ANDREW RUDALEVIGE, *The New Imperial Presidency: Renewing Presidential Power After Watergate* (University of Michigan Press, 2005).

CHARLIE SAVAGE, *Takeover: The Return of the Imperial Presidency and the Subversion of American Democracy* (Little, Brown, 2008).

STEPHEN SKOWRONEK, *The Politics Presidents Make* (Belknap Press, 1997).

chapter 13

The Federal Bureaucracy

Executing the Laws

The federal government has been providing aid to victims of disaster since 1803, when Congress passed legislation to help a New Hampshire town recover from a devastating fire. Over the next 150 years, Congress acted more than 100 times to provide similar assistance to other towns, cities, and states. By the 1970s, dozens of federal agencies were active in some form of disaster assistance.

Spreading responsibilities across so many agencies actually made disaster assistance slower, not faster. States and localities had to spend precious time just submitting applications for help. In an effort to speed up this process, President Jimmy Carter issued an executive order in 1979 establishing the Federal Emergency Management Agency (FEMA) to administer federal disaster relief.

FEMA underwent a complete overhaul in the 1990s and was frequently mentioned as an example of how government can succeed. But it began to break down after deep budget cuts following the September 11 terrorist attacks. Preparing for natural disasters was no longer viewed as an important task of government. By the time Hurricane Katrina came ashore in 2005, FEMA was broken. It had no plans for getting food, water, and ice to victims stranded in the New Orleans Superdome, and it did not arrive on the scene until five days after the storm.

Two years and three investigations later, Congress and President George W. Bush re-formed FEMA, giving it more authority to provide immediate assistance, more employees to deliver the help, and a stronger link directly to the White House to make sure the president knows when a disaster warrants federal help. FEMA also works on preparing the public for future disasters such as hurricanes and floods.

FEMA used its new authorities immediately, following the string of powerful tornadoes that hit Alabama, Arkansas, Kentucky, and Tennessee on the night of February 5, 2008. The tornadoes left 60 people dead and thousands homeless, including students at Tennessee's Union University. This time, FEMA set a speed record. It began taking applications for aid the day after the storm and provided emergency housing to hundreds of victims. It also began negotiations with state and local officials on providing maximum funding and worked with the American Red Cross and other charitable organizations to ensure that victims had access to medical care.

Katrina showed how vulnerable the nation can be when the federal government fails, and how important the federal government can be when it organizes quickly to act. The fact that FEMA moved so quickly after the 2008 tornadoes confirms the need to hold the federal bureaucracy accountable for performance, while giving it enough resources and employees to do its job well. "With Katrina, there was no shortage of plans," a congressional investigatory committee reported. "There were plans, but there was not enough planning. Government failed because it did not learn from past experiences, or because lessons thought to be learned were somehow not implemented."[1]

Most saw Katrina as another example of how federal bureaucracy fails. What we sometimes forget is just how well that bureaucracy often performs. We have positive experiences with the federal government every day, even if we do not know it. Our air and

You Are the Head of FEMA

LEARNING **OBJECTIVES**

1. Understand why the federal bureaucracy is called the undefined branch.
2. Analyze the pros and cons of bureaucracy.
3. Compare and contrast the different types of federal organizations.
4. Describe the differences between the bureaucracy's two types of leaders.
5. Evaluate the differences between the spoils and merit systems.
6. Identify the key regulations that govern the civil service.
7. Analyze the tools of implementation and their effectiveness.
8. Compare and contrast efforts to control the federal bureaucracy.

CHAPTER OUTLINE

- Understanding the Federal Bureaucracy
- Leading the Federal Bureaucracy
- The Civil Service
- The Job of the Federal Bureaucracy
- Controlling the Federal Bureaucracy
- A History of Great Endeavors

Comparing Bureaucracies

water are guarded by the Department of the Interior and the Environmental Protection Agency (EPA), food is protected by the Department of Agriculture and the Food and Drug Administration (FDA), threats to our health are studied by the National Institutes of Health and the Centers for Disease Control and Prevention, college loans are either funded or insured by the Department of Education, and at least part of our retirement income is being sheltered by the Social Security Administration (SSA). Our workplaces are inspected by the Occupational Safety and Health Administration (OSHA), and the roads and bridges are mostly kept in good repair by the Department of Transportation.

In this chapter, we examine the origins, functions, and realities of federal administration, which includes governmental bodies such as departments and agencies and the federal employees who administer the laws. We also explore how governmental departments, agencies, and employees are held accountable to the president, Congress, and the U.S. public. Because the federal bureaucracy is so big, many citizens see no way they can make a difference that improves its performance. As we shall see, however, the bureaucracy is actually highly responsive to both Congress and the president, especially when money is involved. It may be big, but it is mostly accountable.

Understanding the Federal Bureaucracy

The framers clearly understood that the new national government would need an administrative system to protect the young Republic from foreign and domestic threats. They also understood that the new departments of government would need talented employees if they were to succeed. Although the framers hoped government employees would be motivated by the desire to serve their country, they knew government would have to pay those employees for their work. Presidents would have to rely on talented executives to oversee the daily work of government, whether in repaying the costs of the Revolutionary War, building postal roads to carry the mail, training a national army and navy, caring for soldiers disabled in battle, administering treaties with other nations, or regulating commerce between the states.

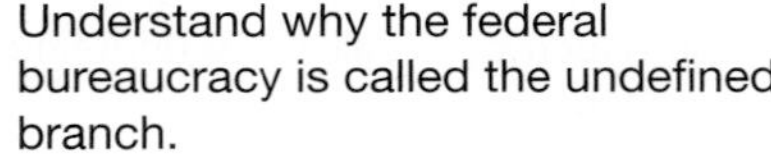

1 Understand why the federal bureaucracy is called the undefined branch.

The Undefined Branch

Federal administration is responsible for one task, and one task only: to faithfully execute all the laws. Although disagreements and factions were a normal and predictable part of making the laws, they were unacceptable when it came time for the laws to be executed. As Alexander Hamilton explained in *The Federalist,* No. 70, the new federal government would need a bureaucracy with the skill and motivation to faithfully execute the laws, which he described as the true test of a good government."[2]

The Evolution of the Federal Bureaucracy

Constitutional Controls

The founders spent little time worrying about the administration of government, however. Instead, they left most of the details to future presidents. They believed that federal departments and agencies would be relatively small, and they expected Congress to establish the same departments that had existed under the Articles of Confederation.[3] They also expected George Washington to be the government's first chief executive and believed he would lead the new government with the same skill with which he had led the Continental Army. Nevertheless, the framers made three key decisions about executing the laws that continue to shape federal administration to this day.

First, they prohibited members of the House and Senate from holding executive branch positions. They drew a sharp line on the issue in Article I, Section 6, of the Constitution: "No Senator or Representative shall, during the Time for which he was elected, be appointed to any civil Office under the Authority of the United States, which shall have been created, or the Emoluments whereof shall have been increased during such time, and no Person holding any Office under the United States, shall be a Member of either House during his Continuance in Office." Under this provision, Congress could not create executive jobs for its members, which was a common form of corruption in England before the Revolutionary War.[4]

Alexander Hamilton helped set many of the precedents that govern the federal bureaucracy today. He was a strong advocate of what he called "execution in detail," which involved detailed rules that federal employees must follow, and argued for an expansion in the number of federal employees as the federal government's mission expanded.

Second, the framers decided to give the president complete authority to nominate the senior officers of government. Although they also gave the Senate authority to confirm the president's appointees under the Constitution's "advice and consent" function, the framers made the president, not Congress, responsible for filling any vacancies in those jobs without Senate review when the Senate is in recess. Although Article I does give Congress the power to create the departments of government and the Senate the power to confirm presidential appointees, both by a majority vote, the president emerged from the final days of the Constitutional Convention as the nation's administrator in chief. The framers saw direct presidential control of government as essential for faithfully executing the laws.

Third, the framers decided that the president, not Congress, is responsible for requiring the opinions of the "principal officer" of each executive department, which means the president is in charge of what presidential appointees do. The chief executive not only is responsible for hiring and supervising presidential appointees, however, but also has the power to fire appointees for any reason. Although presidential appointees may resign at any time, presidents usually fire appointees by asking for their resignations. In addition, outgoing presidents routinely ask all their appointees to resign before the inauguration of a new president.

These decisions about presidential power did not give the president unlimited authority to execute the laws, however. Recall that Congress, not the president, has the power to create the departments and agencies of government in the first place, and the responsibility for appropriating the money to administer programs and hire government employees. They also gave the Senate the power to confirm certain presidential appointees, and they clearly expected both houses of Congress to monitor the workings of the executive branch.

Defining Bureaucracy

More than 200 years after the Constitution was written, the federal government is administered by one of the largest bureaucracies in the world. The federal bureaucracy is composed of 15 departments, 50 agencies, the U.S. Postal Service, and the armed services.

It also employs one of the largest workforces in the world. Almost 2.7 million people work for the federal bureaucracy, including 800,000 in the postal service, more than

FIGURE 13–1
Number of Federal Employees, Measuring the Size of Government, 1965–2007.

SOURCE: Office of Management and Budget, *Budget of the U.S. Government, Fiscal Year 2009, Historical Tables* (U.S. Government Printing Office, February 2008).

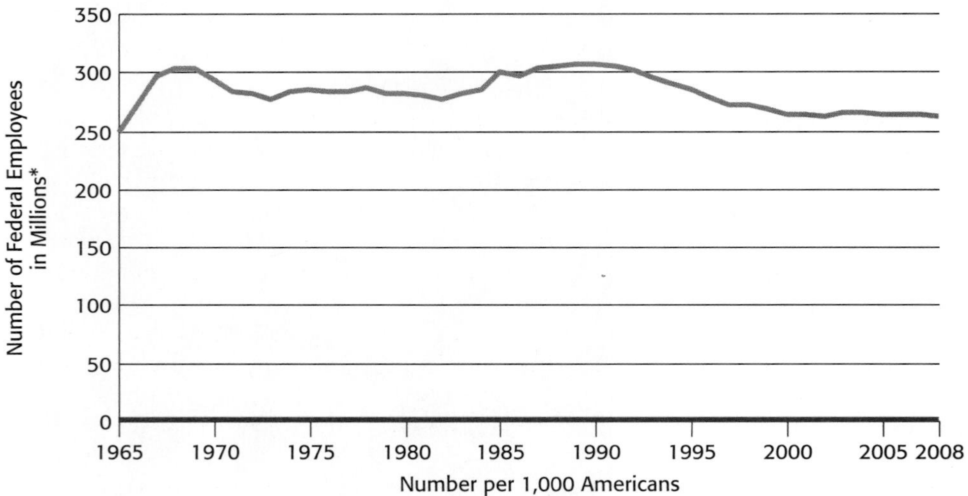

NOTE: Number includes postal service employees.

1.8 million in the civil service, and 1.4 million in the armed services. In addition, 7.6 million work for the federal government under contracts to private firms such as Lockheed Martin and Boeing, and 2.9 million work under federal grants to colleges, universities, and state and local governments. All told, the federal bureaucracy includes almost 15 million employees, only a handful of whom are visible to the public.[5] Figure 13–1 shows the relative stability in the number of full-time federal employees, including postal service employees, but does not show the number of contractors and grantees that perform tasks for the government, which has grown over the past 50 years.

LEARNING **OBJECTIVE**

2 Analyze the pros and cons of bureaucracy.

We traditionally refer to federal departments and agencies as the "bureaucracy," a term that dates back to the early nineteenth century. Originally, the word "bureau" referred to a cloth covering the desks of French government officials in the eighteenth century, and eventually it came to be applied to the desk itself. The term was soon linked with the suffix "-ocracy" (as in "democracy" or "aristocracy") to describe government (essentially, "rule by people at desks").

At one time in history, **bureaucracy** actually meant fast, effective, and rational administration. In its ideal form, a bureaucracy made sure every job was carefully designed to ensure faithful performance by well-trained, highly motivated **bureaucrats,** or employees. According to German sociologist Max Weber, who wrote in defense of bureaucracy in the late 1800s, bureaucracies derive their strength from six characteristics:

- *Specialization:* Bureaucracies break jobs into smaller and smaller parts so that every employee knows exactly what his or her job is. Because their jobs are so specialized, employees can be trained in enough detail to succeed.
- *Centralization:* Bureaucracies concentrate authority at the top of the organization, where a single leader maintains control of all activity. This leader is in charge of every last person in the organization.
- *Formal rules:* Bureaucracies implement policies through formal rules that govern everything that employees do.
- *Standardization:* Bureaucracies make sure all decisions are the same—meaning every employee makes the same decisions in producing a product or making a ruling. Standardization assures customers and clients that they will be treated fairly whomever they talk to.

bureaucracy
A form of organization that operates through impersonal, uniform rules and procedures.

bureaucrat
A career government employee.

- *Expertise:* Bureaucracies make sure all employees have the training and experience to do their jobs effectively, and that they are given the tools such as information technology to succeed.
- *Accountability:* Bureaucracies enforce the rules through a set of communication channels that allow the leaders of the organization to know exactly what is going on at all levels. The bureaucracy is structured so employees follow orders or are fired.

Over time, however, *bureaucracy* has taken on a negative meaning and now describes a large, inefficient organization clogged with red tape. Bureaucracies have at least four weaknesses: (1) Today's jobs are so complex that they cannot be divided into specialized pieces; (2) there are so many leaders at the top of organizations that employees do not know whom to report to; (3) rules are almost impossible to enforce within a very large workforce; and (4) duplication and overlap between units create confusion about who does what.

The federal bureaucracy has all four problems, but is particularly troubled by duplication and too many leaders. The duplication is easy to spot on a host of issues. For example, mad cow disease, which can be transmitted to human beings if they eat meat from diseased cows, is the concern of several agencies. The Department of Agriculture's Animal and Plant Health Inspection Service keeps diseased cattle out of the United States, which is the best way to prevent the disease; the Department of Health and Human Services' Food and Drug Administration monitors cattle feed, which is another way to prevent the disease, and the Department of Agriculture's Food Safety and Inspection Service inspects cattle as they go to slaughter, which is the last defense against letting diseased meat enter the food supply.

Second, even within a single agency, the bureaucracy often creates dense layers of management that keep information from moving up and down the organization quickly. Most federal organizations impose dozens of layers of management between the president and the federal employees who actually do the work. For example, the Department of Homeland Security has a secretary who heads the department, a chief of staff to the secretary, deputy chief of staff to the secretary, deputy secretary, five undersecretaries, and eight assistant secretaries, all of whom help direct the department's activities. Although each job is important, they often block the president's view of what is actually happening at the bottom of the organization.

The Four Types of Federal Organizations

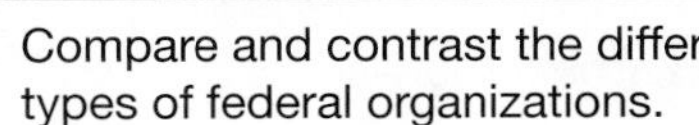

LEARNING **OBJECTIVE**

3 Compare and contrast the different types of federal organizations.

Federal employees work for departments and agencies, which are classified into four broad types: (1) *departments,* (2) *independent regulatory commissions,* (3) *independent agencies,* and (4) *government corporations.*

Departments tend to be the largest federal organizations and have the broadest missions. **Independent regulatory commissions** are designed to be insulated from direct presidential control. **Independent agencies** are under the president's direct control, but tend to be smaller and have more focused responsibilities than departments. Finally, **government corporations** are designed to operate much like private businesses.

department
Usually the largest organization in government with the largest mission; also the highest rank in the federal hierarchy.

independent regulatory commission
A government agency or commission with regulatory power whose independence is protected by Congress.

independent agency
A government entity that is independent of the legislative, executive, and judicial branches.

government corporation
A government agency that operates like a business corporation, created to secure greater freedom of action and flexibility for a particular program.

Departments

Departments are the most visible organizations in the federal bureaucracy. Today's 15 departments of government employ more than 70 percent of all federal civil servants and spend 93 percent of all federal dollars. Fourteen of the departments are headed by secretaries; the fifteenth, the Justice Department, is headed by the attorney general.

Measured by the total number of employees, the Defense Department is by far the largest department, followed by the Department of Veterans Affairs, which helps veterans return to civilian life after military service; the Department of Homeland Security, created to protect the nation from terrorism; the Department of the Treasury, which manages the economy and raises revenues through the Internal Revenue Service; and the Department of Justice, which enforces the laws through the federal courts and investigates crime through the Federal Bureau of Investigation.

FIGURE 13–2
The Federal Departments.

SOURCE: Office of Personnel Management, *The Fact Book, 2005 Edition* (U.S. Government Printing Office, 2007).

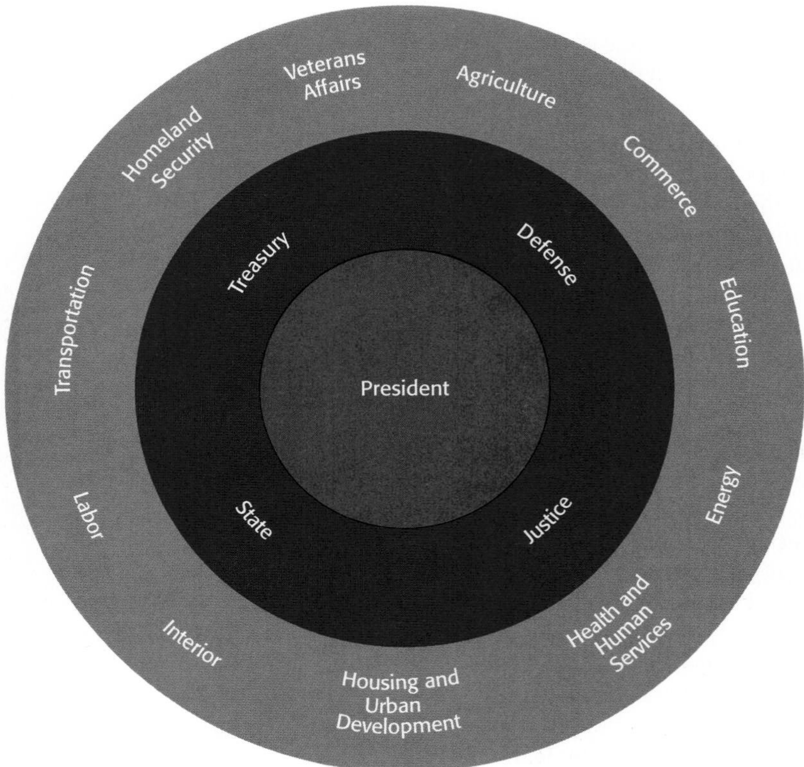

Measured by prestige, the Defense, Justice, State, and Treasury departments are considered part of the inner circle closest to the president, while the rest of the departments are considered part of the outer circle of departments that rarely receive the president's attention (see Figure 13–2 for the inner and outer circles).

Measured by budget, the Department of Health and Human Services is the largest department of government. This department provides health insurance to the elderly through the huge Medicare program, helps states cover health care for the poor through the Medicaid programs, covers the cost of health insurance for children through the State Children's Health Insurance Program (SCHIP), and administers a variety of programs to help the poor. It also contains the Food and Drug Administration, the National Institutes of Health, and the Centers for Disease Control and Prevention, all of which protect the population from disease.

The 15 federal departments were created using two very different models. One approach creates an umbrella department by combining a number of related programs. The Department of Homeland Security, for example, was created by combining elements of 22 separate agencies, including the Immigration and Naturalization Service, the Customs Service, the Federal Emergency Management Agency, the Secret Service, portions of the Animal and Plant Health Inspection Service, and the Coast Guard, which is often viewed as a branch of the military.

The other approach creates a single-purpose department that owes its existence largely to the strength of an interest group. Congress created the Department of Veterans Affairs in 1989 under pressure from veterans' groups such as the American Legion and Veterans of Foreign Wars, who wanted their own advocate in the president's cabinet. It was hardly the first time Congress yielded to such pressure. It created the Department of Education in 1980 mostly to satisfy the nation's largest teachers' union. We can easily argue that the Departments of Agriculture, Commerce, and Labor were also created in response to interest group pressure.

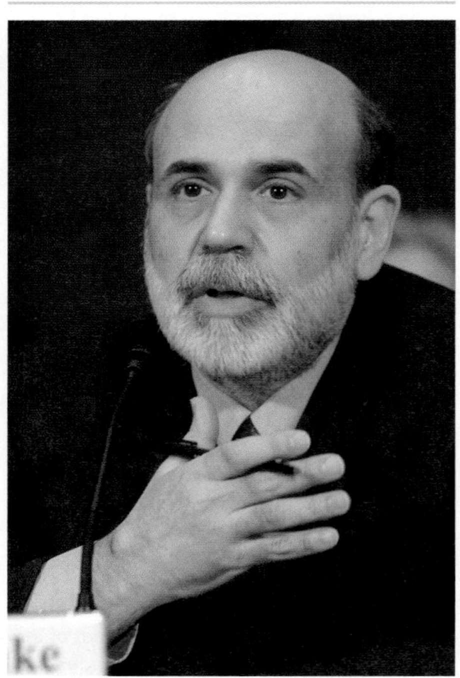

As Federal Reserve Board chair, Ben S. Bernanke is in charge of one of the most important independent regulatory commissions. The Federal Reserve Board chair has a 14-year term.

Independent Regulatory Commissions Although independent regulatory commissions are part of the federal bureaucracy, they have a measure of independence from both Congress and the president. By definition, these commissions are headed not by a single executive but by a small number of commissioners appointed by the president, with Senate confirmation, for fixed terms of office. Unlike other presidential appointees, commissioners cannot be removed from office without cause, which is defined by law to mean "inefficiency, neglect of duty, or malfeasance in office." As a result, independent regulatory commissions are less responsive to political pressure from either Congress or the president.

Over the decades, Congress has created dozens of independent regulatory commissions with the power to protect consumers (the Consumer Product Safety Commission), regulate stock markets (the Securities and Exchange Commission), oversee federal election laws (the Federal Election Commission), monitor television and radio (the Federal Communications Commission), regulate business (the Federal Trade Commission), control the supply of money (the Federal Reserve Board), and watch over nuclear power plants (the Nuclear Regulatory Commission). These commissions are often small, but their influence over life in the United States is large. Many experts contend that the Federal Reserve Board chair is the second most influential person in making economic policy, and others would argue

THE CHANGING FACE OF U.S. POLITICS

A Representative Government

The federal bureaucracy is more representative of the public now than it was in the 1950s, when most of its employees were white and most female employees were clerk-typists. Women held 45 percent of all federal jobs in 2005, while minorities occupied nearly 30 percent.

Even though the number of women and minorities in the federal workforce is at an all-time high, both groups still face barriers in rising to the top. First, women and minorities are not equally represented in all departments and agencies. They tend to be concentrated in departments with strong social service missions such as Education, Health and Human Services, Housing and Urban Development, and Veterans Affairs. Military and technical departments such as Defense, Energy, and Transportation have far fewer women employees.

Second, women and minorities are not represented at all levels of the federal bureaucracy. Women held 70 percent of lower-paying technical and clerical positions in 2005, while minorities were also heavily represented at the bottom of government. Together, women and minorities held barely 15 percent of the top jobs. Nevertheless, they are moving into the top jobs at a fast rate. Between 1994 and 2004, the number of women and minorities in professional and managerial jobs jumped from 44 percent to 58 percent.

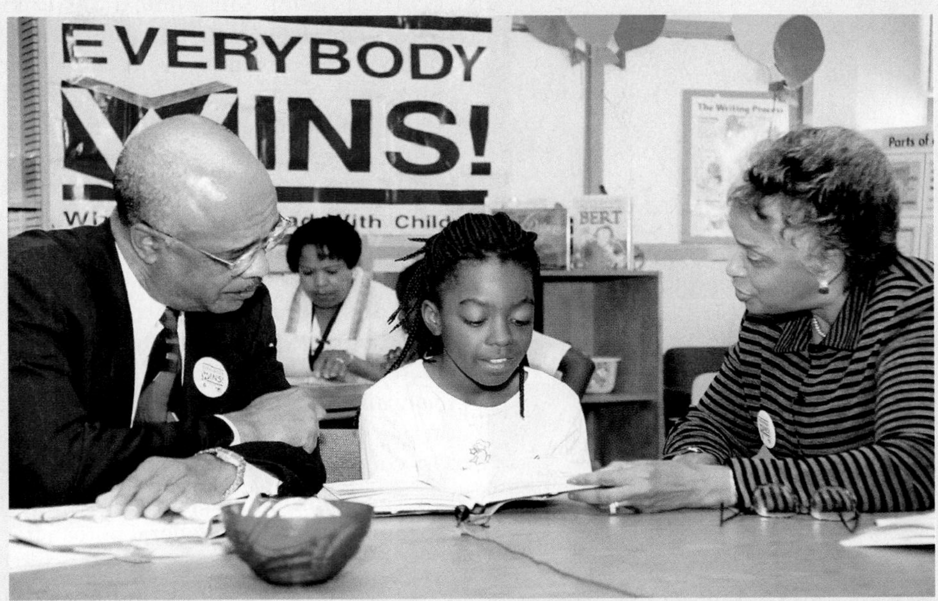

Education Department employee Claudia Gaines and then-education secretary Rod Paige work with a fourth-grade student during National Volunteer Week.

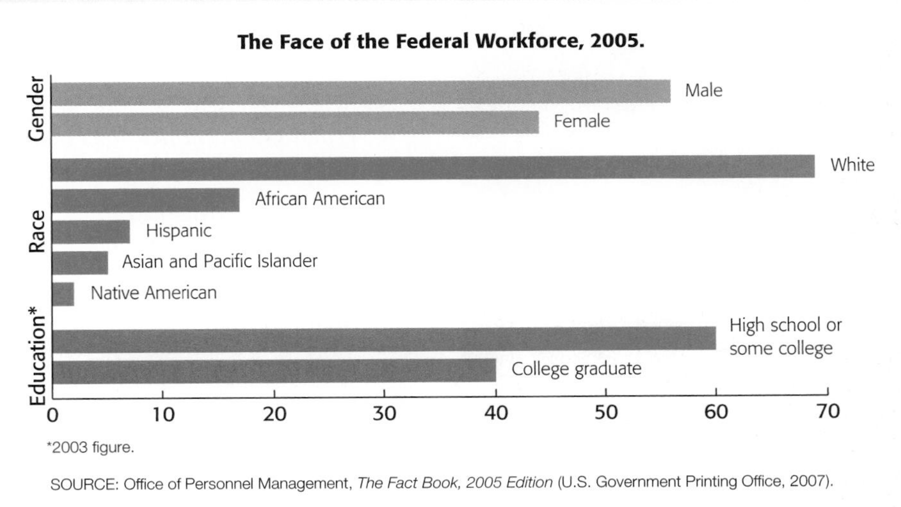

QUESTIONS

1. Why should the federal bureaucracy try to recruit more women and minorities to its top jobs?
2. Does increasing diversity improve the bureaucracy's performance and accountability? Why or why not?
3. How can the bureaucracy enhance diversity in scientific and technical fields?

that the current chair, Ben S. Bernanke, is the most important leader in influencing public confidence about the economy.[6] Bernanke was appointed to a 14-year term in 2006, replacing Alan Greenspan, who had served for almost 20 years.

Independent regulatory commissions are not completely independent, however. Their commissioners are appointed by the president and are subject to Senate confirmation, their annual budgets must be approved by Congress, and their decisions are subject to judicial review. Moreover, presidents make most appointments on the basis of party, which means that commissions are often highly political.

You Are a Government Affairs Consultant in Texas

The number of female and minority cabinet officials has increased over the past three decades. However, the two groups tend to be concentrated in certain departments. All Treasury secretaries (on this page) since 1981 have been white males, for example, while four of the last eight Education secretaries (on the opposite page) have been women or minorities.

Moreover, the commissioners who lead these agencies often disagree on key issues, even to the point of being unable to reach majority decisions, especially during periods when the governing board has vacancies because of retirements or the ends of terms.

The Federal Communications Commission has often split votes in its effort to regulate television content, while the Federal Election Commission often splits on three-to-three votes between its Democratic and Republican commissioners.

Independent regulatory commissions tend to be much less visible than departments, at least until an issue such as corporate fraud becomes hot. The Securities and Exchange Commission was on the front pages for three years, for example, as one corporation after another disclosed accounting fraud in their annual reports to investors. The SEC was created in the 1930s to restore investor confidence in the stock market after the Great Depression, but it was accused of being negligent in monitoring accounting practices at big companies such as Enron and WorldCom in the early 2000s. It is currently rebuilding its staff and taking a much more aggressive stand on accounting standards. Independent regulatory commissions are also effectively insulated from public view, which may undermine their authority in enforcing their decisions. Moreover, many Americans do not know why independent regulatory commissions exist or how they operate.

The following independent regulatory commissions are considered among the most important in the federal bureaucracy:

- *Commodity Futures Trading Corporation* regulates the markets for commodities such as corn, wheat, precious metals, and other products used in manufacturing.
- *Consumer Product Safety Commission* monitors and regulates the safety of products released for public use.
- *Equal Employment Opportunity Commission* regulates and enforces laws assuring equality of access to jobs.
- *Federal Communications Commission* monitors and regulates use of the public airways, but not cable television.
- *Federal Deposit Insurance Corporation* provides insurance for bank savings accounts up to $100,000.
- *Federal Election Commission* monitors and enforces federal campaign finance laws.
- *Federal Trade Commission* assures that advertising for products is fair and truthful.
- *Nuclear Regulatory Commission* regulates the nuclear power industry.
- *Securities Exchange Commission* regulates the stock markets that trade stocks in publicly-held corporations.

Independent Agencies The word "independent" means at least two things in the federal bureaucracy. Applied to a regulatory commission, it means the agency is outside the president's control. Applied to an agency or administration, it merely means "separate" or "standing alone." Whereas independent regulatory commissions do not report to the president, independent agencies do.

As a general rule, independent agencies are smaller than federal departments and work on specific problems. Becoming an agency is often the first step toward becoming a department. The Veterans Administration was created in 1930 as an agency, for example, but it became a department only in 1989.

Independent agencies are usually headed by an administrator, the second most senior title in the federal bureaucracy behind secretary or attorney general. There are 50 such agencies today, including the Environmental Protection Agency (EPA), the Central Intelligence Agency (CIA), the National Aeronautics and Space Administration (NASA), the National Security Agency (NSA), and the Small Business Administration (SBA).

Although independence increases each agency's ability to focus on its mission, it also weakens the agency's willingness to cooperate. The spread of independent agencies can also add to confusion about who is responsible for what in the federal government. In late 2004, for example, Congress created a new national intelligence director to oversee the federal government's 15 different intelligence agencies, which include the CIA, the Defense Intelligence Agency, the FBI, and the NSA. These 15 agencies had a history of keeping secrets not just from the people but from each other, which contributed to the intelligence failures leading up to the war in Iraq.

Independent agencies come in many sizes, from small to very large. NASA, for example, has an annual budget of more than $11 billion and a workforce of more than 23,000, as well as several hundred thousand private business employees who help manage the space shuttle. NASA's budget ranks it ahead of four cabinet departments (Justice, Interior, State, and Commerce).

Politically, independent agencies can sometimes be more important to the president than some cabinet departments. The director of the CIA or the administrator of the EPA may get a higher place on the president's agenda than the secretary of HUD or agriculture, particularly when an issue such as international spying or global warming is in the headlines.

The term "agency" does not just apply to stand-alone agencies. Many highly visible agencies also exist within departments, including the Forest Service (located in the Agriculture Department), the National Park Service (located in the Department of the Interior), the Occupational Safety and Health Administration (located in the Labor Department), and the Census Bureau (located in the Commerce Department). Unlike independent agencies, which report directly to the president, these agencies report to a department secretary, who, in turn, reports to the president.

The following independent agencies are considered among the most important in the bureaucracy:

- *Bureau of Alcohol, Tobacco, & Firearms* monitors and enforces laws dealing with the sale and manufacturing of explosives, cigarettes, liquor, and weapons.
- *Centers for Medicare and Medicaid Services* administers the government's two largest health programs.
- *Central Intelligence Agency* collects and interprets international intelligence.
- *Director of National Intelligence* coordinates intelligence collected by other government agencies.
- *Drug Enforcement Administration* monitors and enforces laws governing illegal drugs.
- *Environmental Protection Agency* regulates and enforces laws to reduce pollution.
- *Federal Aviation Administration* monitors the civilian airline industry, including airlines and small aircraft.
- *Federal Bureau of Investigation* investigates federal crimes.
- *Federal Emergency Management* Agency responds to major natural and man-made disasters.
- *Food and Drug Administration* monitors food safety and drugs.
- *Internal Revenue Service* collects all federal taxes.

You Are a Federal Administrator

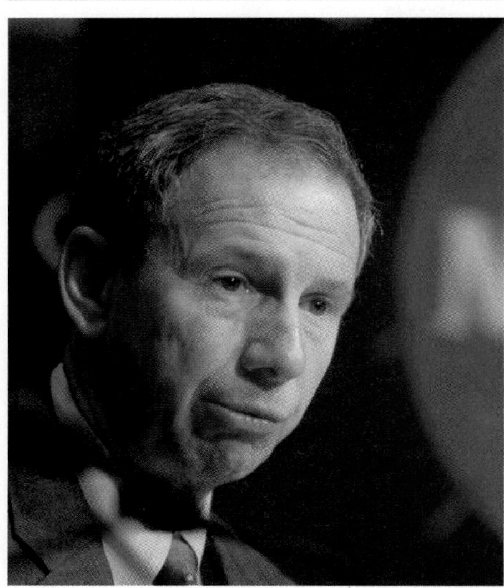

Mike Griffin was appointed administrator of the National Aeronautics and Space Administration (NASA) in 2005. He had served as chief engineer of NASA earlier in his career, becoming the first civil servant to be appointed the agency's administrator, which is a Senate-confirmed post.

- *National Aeronautics and Space Administration* manages the U.S. civilian space program.
- *National Oceanic and Atmospheric Administration* monitors the climate.
- *National Park Service* maintains U.S. national parks.
- *Small Business Administration* monitors the state of U.S. small businesses.
- *Social Security Administration* administers the Social Security program.
- *U.S. Forest Service* monitors the U.S. national forests.

Government Corporations Government corporations are perhaps the least understood organizations in the federal bureaucracy. Because they are intended to act more like businesses than like traditional government departments and agencies, they generally have more freedom from the rules that control traditional government agencies. They often have greater authority to hire and fire employees quickly and are allowed to make money through the sale of services such as train tickets, stamps, or home loans.[7]

Ultimately, no two government corporations are alike. The term is so loosely applied that no one knows exactly how many corporations the federal bureaucracy has. What experts do know is that the number is between 31 and 47, including the Corporation for Public Broadcasting (which runs PBS television), the U.S. Postal Service, the National Railroad Passenger Corporation (better known as Amtrak), and AmeriCorps (which runs a national service program created by the Clinton administration), along with a host of financial enterprises that make loans of one kind or another.

Federal Emergency Management Agency (FEMA) director Michael Brown (left) leaves the emergency operations center in Baton Rouge, Louisiana. Brown was removed as FEMA director after widespread criticism of his handling of the Hurricane Katrina rescue efforts.

Leading the Federal Bureaucracy

Roughly 3,000 presidential appointees head federal departments and agencies, including 600 administrative officers subject to Senate confirmation and another 2,400 who serve entirely "at the pleasure of the president." As political officers, presidential appointees generally leave their posts at the end of that president's term in office. The president also appoints another 1,000 U.S. marshals, U.S. attorneys, and ambassadors to foreign nations, but usually makes these appointments on a nonpolitical basis.

You Are Deputy Director of the Census Bureau

LEARNING **OBJECTIVE**

Describe the differences between the bureaucracy's two types of leaders.

Presidential Appointees

Presidential appointees have some of the toughest jobs in the world. They work long hours, resolve complex disputes, and make important decisions about how the laws will be executed. Although many are selected on the basis of political connections, the top positions in the most important departments are generally reserved for individuals with significant leadership skills and experience.

Senior presidential appointees are selected through a four-step process. Except for individuals who are extraordinarily close to the president, the first step is to be selected by the White House Presidential Personnel Office. Most appointees are members of the president's party, and many contributed either time or money to the president's campaign.

The second step in becoming an appointee is to survive the White House clearance process, which is designed to ensure that candidates are legally qualified for office and pose no potential embarrassment to the president. All candidates receive a packet of forms that require detailed disclosure on every aspect of their personal and professional life, including job history, drug use, personal counseling, financial investments, and even traffic fines of more than $150.

The third step is the simplest: The president submits the name of the nominee on parchment paper to the clerk of the Senate. The document is placed in a special envelope, sealed with wax, and hand-delivered to the Senate when it is actually in session.

In the fourth step the Senate refers each nomination to the appropriate confirmation committee, which conducts its own reviews. Depending on the position and the nominee, the Senate may ask to review the entire file developed by the White House, including the FBI's investigation. Once the review is complete, the committee holds a hearing on the nomination and usually sends it to the floor of the Senate with a favorable recommendation. In turn, most nominations are approved by the Senate on voice votes.

There are times, however, when the Senate uses nominations to send signals to the White House about political concerns. In 2005, for example, Senator Hillary Clinton (D-N.Y.) blocked the nomination of a new EPA administrator as a way to express her concern about air quality in New York City. Although she later withdrew her objections, she was able to delay the nomination long enough to force the Bush administration to promise to study air quality more closely in the future.

The Senior Executive Service

Presidential appointees work closely with the 7,000 members of the **Senior Executive Service,** which includes roughly 6,400 career executives appointed through a rigorous review process and another 600 political executives appointed by the president without Senate confirmation. Career senior executives continue in their posts regardless of who happens to be president and are selected on the basis of merit.

Senior Executive Service Established by Congress in 1978 as a flexible, mobile corps of senior career executives who work closely with presidential appointees to manage government.

Together with the president's political appointees, 10,000 senior executives help run federal departments and agencies. The number has grown dramatically over the past three decades as the federal government has "thickened," with more layers of leadership and more leaders at each layer.[8] Some political scientists argue that

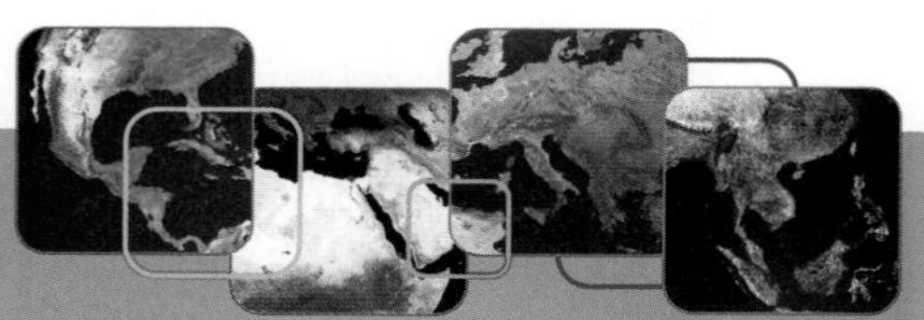

HOW **OTHER NATIONS** GOVERN

Bureaucracy Across the World

All governments, democratic or not, have some amount of bureaucracy to help implement the laws. However, some of these bureaucracies are more accountable to the people and have stronger reputations for performance than others. Some nations even consider bureaucracy a positive term, largely because the civil servants leading the bureaucracy are so carefully selected and because there are relatively few political appointees at the top of the bureaucracy.

This is certainly the case in Britain, where civil servants work as deputy ministers of departments (ministries) and agencies. With only a handful of political officers at the top of government, almost all of whom are members of Parliament, the bureaucracy is viewed as a source of expertise. Civil servants are tested for appointment through a competitive process that includes interviews with at least three candidates for each position.

Professionalism is also the norm in Japan, whose bureaucracy is considered one of the most prestigious in the world. Like Britain's, the Japanese bureaucracy has very few political appointees at the top of the executive branch and recruits civil servants from the most prestigious colleges and universities. Japan also uses one of the most difficult entrance examinations to recruit its civil servants. As a result, the Japanese public places greater confidence in its civil service than do citizens in the United States.

India, Mexico, and Nigeria are striving to develop highly professionalized bureaucracies but struggle with the sheer complexity of their governments. India has such strong regional governments that many civil servants choose to work far from the capital, while Mexico has a very strong party system that dictates more political appointees. Nigeria is struggling to elevate its civil service through more recruitment from colleges and universities—as of 1979, only 11 percent of its civil servants had attended college. The percentage has increased over the past 30 years but still lags well behind the government's hoped-for standard.

China has a very different civil service system, in part because it has two national governments—one headed by the Communist Party and one that operates under the premier. The party controls all the appointments to its own bureaucracy and also monitors appointments to the government bureaucracy. Because these civil servants are selected primarily on the basis of party loyalty, there is considerable potential for bribery and corruption in the hiring process.

QUESTIONS

1. How does the number of political appointees at the top of government affect the strength of the civil service below?
2. Why do the Japanese have such a strong bureaucracy?
3. Does political or party loyalty have any value for bureaucratic performance?

Congress helped caused thickening by creating highly complex programs that demand close supervision, while others believe it is driven in part by a competition for power among competing organizations. According to this *theory of public bureaucracy,* bureaucratic organizations constantly seek to enhance their power, whether by creating new titles, adding more staff, or increasing their budgets.[9]

In November 1995, the vast bureaucracy of the federal government shut down for lack of funds.

The Civil Service

The founders understood that the new federal government would need employees, and they would need to be paid. They also knew that most federal employees would be selected by the president without Senate confirmation and that many would select government for their career. The founders believed that this **civil service** would outlast each administration, thereby providing steadiness for government.

LEARNING **OBJECTIVE**

5 Evaluate the differences between the spoils and merit systems.

For the first hundred years, however, members of the federal civil service were selected in part because of their political loyalty to the president's party. This **spoils system**—"to the victor belong the spoils"—was substantially expanded by President Andrew Jackson after his election in 1829. Jackson believed that every job in government was a potential opportunity for employing his political allies. Thus every job was subject to presidential control and filled on the basis of political connections and even bribes. Actual ability to do the work had almost nothing to do with obtaining an appointment, and few employees outlasted their president.

The spoils system gave the president's party complete control over almost every government job, from cabinet secretaries down to post office clerks. Under its method of *patronage*, presidents would patronize, or support, their allies by providing jobs and other benefits after an election.

The spoils system began to unravel when Congress created the modern civil service in 1883. Indeed, it was a job seeker who started the federal bureaucracy down the road toward today's civil service system. Unfortunately for President James Garfield, that job seeker happened to be both disappointed and a good shot. Garfield's assassination prompted Congress to pass the Pendleton Act of 1883, which created an independent Civil Service Commission to ensure that most federal jobs were awarded under a **merit system,** meaning on the basis of an individual's ability to do the work, not political connections.[10] See Figure 13–3 for the different types of federal employees.

Ninety percent of federal employees are now selected on the basis of merit. Almost all the rest are selected through hiring systems that emphasize a special skill such as medicine. The **Office of Personnel Management (OPM)** administers civil service laws, rules, and regulations, while the independent **Merit Systems Protection Board** is charged with protecting the integrity of the federal merit system and the rights of federal employees. The Merit Systems Protection Board conducts studies of

civil service
Federal employees who work for government through a competitive, not political selection process.

spoils system
A system of public employment based on rewarding party loyalists and friends.

merit system
A system of public employment in which selection and promotion depend on demonstrated performance rather than political patronage.

Office of Personnel Management (OPM)
An agency that administers civil service laws, rules, and regulations.

Merit Systems Protection Board
An independent agency that oversees and protects merit in the federal government personnel system.

The Louisiana Purchase doubled the land area of the United States but also set off a wave of corruption in the General Land Office. Anger over the corruption contributed to the election of Andrew Jackson in 1828.

This drawing depicts the assassination of President James Garfield on July 2, 1881. He was shot by an attorney who had been repeatedly rejected for a consular post in Garfield's administration.

the merit system, investigates charges of favoritism, resolves employee complaints about unfair discipline, and orders corrective and disciplinary actions against an agency executive or employee when appropriate. (You can find a sampling of current federal job offerings at www.usajobs.opm.gov.)

Civil Service Realities

The realities of today's civil service are very different from common public perceptions about who works for government, how the laws are executed, and where government delivers most of its services.

LEARNING **OBJECTIVE**

6 Identify the key regulations that govern the civil service.

- Only about 15 percent of the government's career civilian employees work in the Washington, D.C., area. More federal employees work in California, Georgia, and Texas, for example, than in Washington.
- More than 25 percent of civilian employees work for the army, the navy, the air force, or some other defense agency, while 30 percent work for the U.S. Postal Service. The federal government also oversees another 1.4 million military personnel.
- Fewer than 10 percent of federal employees work for the Social Security Administration and the Medicare program, even though these programs absorb more than half the federal budget.
- Almost half of federal employees work for the departments of Defense, Homeland Security, Justice, and State, which are all engaged in the war on terror.
- Federal civil servants are much more likely to look like the rest of the nation in terms of race, sex, religion, education, and disability than are the political appointees or members of Congress who make the laws they execute.
- Although the civil service includes more than 450 different kinds of jobs, most workers are white-collar employees such as lawyers, contract managers, budget analysts, engineers, inspectors, and auditors.

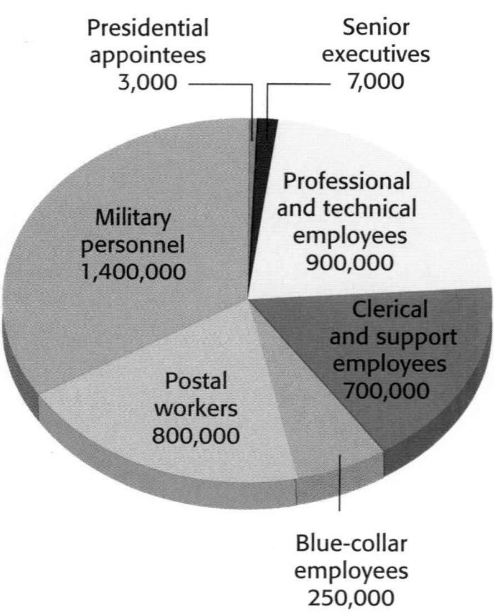

FIGURE 13–3
Types of Federal Employees.

The Hiring Process

Unlike appointees selected by the president, most federal employees are recruited through the civil service. The civil service system was designed to reduce political

GENERATION **NEXT**

Trust in Government

Many U.S. adults feel they don't have any say in what the federal government does. Some believe that politicians will say anything to get elected and then do pretty much what they want; others are convinced that the federal bureaucracy is so big they cannot possibly make a difference; and still others estimate that the federal government wastes almost all its money. Overall, many citizens simply do not trust the bureaucracy to deliver on its promises.

Many members of Generation Next are clearly convinced they can't make a difference in what government does. According to the Pew Research Center's Political Landscape survey, roughly half of Gen Nexters believe government doesn't pay attention to people like them.

The higher levels of disagreement among Democrats, Independents, and very liberal members of Generation Next are no doubt connected to recent Republican control of the presidency. They may also be connected to opposition to the Iraq War. On most other questions about government responsiveness, nonwhites are much less trusting than whites. Answers to this particular question tend to vary with political events such as the Democratic takeover of Congress in 2006, which may have led minorities to feel that government would pay greater attention to their concerns.

As a whole, Generation Next is like other generations. Though 48 percent of 18- to 29-year-olds completely or mostly agreed that they don't have any say about what government does, the percentage was the same for 30- to 39-year-olds. And older generations were only 1 or 2 percent off that level.

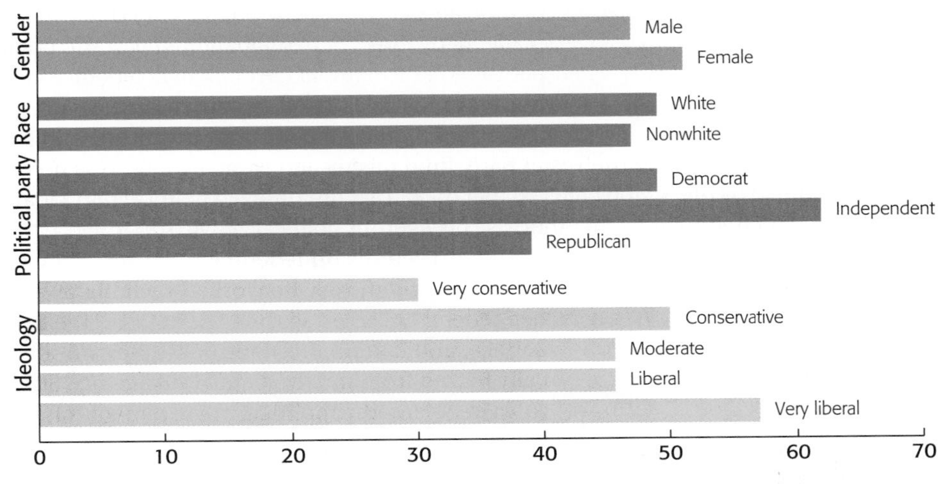

QUESTIONS

1. What other factors such as education and income might influence someone's confidence that one person can have a say in government?
2. Does citizens' lack of confidence affect government's ability to faithfully execute the laws?
3. Why do nonwhites have more confidence than whites, especially as they are more likely to be Democrats and liberal?

corruption by promoting merit in the hiring process. But hiring on the basis of merit is not the only way government seeks to reduce corruption. As we shall see, it also regulates the political activities of civil servants.

Under Office of Personnel Management rules, most federal organizations have flexible hiring systems. They select employees the way the private sector does, by reviewing résumés and conducting interviews. And most prospective government employees apply the way private employees do, by submitting an application.

Federal organizations cannot select just anyone, however. They must keep careful records about each candidate and justify their decisions when challenged. They must also give veterans special consideration for most jobs and ensure that all jobs are filled through a truly competitive process.

These procedures are intended to protect the merit principle and to meet the bureaucracy's need for qualified personnel. In practice, the two objectives sometimes conflict. The trade-off is between central control by OPM and delegation of discretionary authority to each government organization. And sometimes the pursuit of both objectives is undermined by other goals, such as giving military veterans extra credit in the hiring process. As

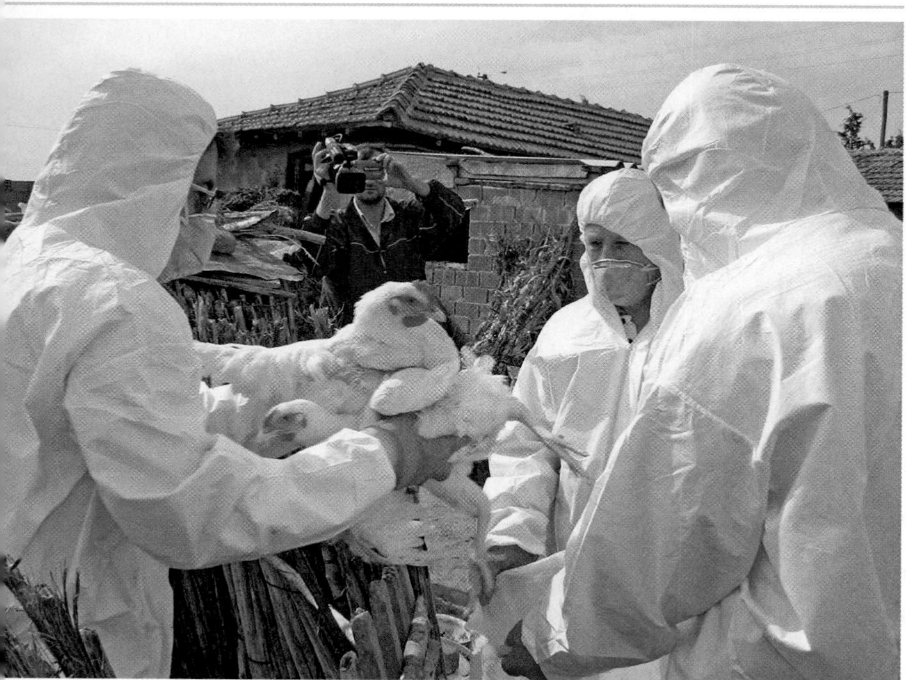

Federal officials from the Centers for Disease Control inspect a flock of chickens for signs of bird flu. These inspectors are selected through the merit system.

a result, the federal hiring process takes six months on average, far longer than in most private businesses. Although the federal government offers a range of recruitment incentives such as partial loan forgiveness, many potential employees are unwilling to wait for a decision, especially in a highly competitive job market.

Regulating the Civil Service

In 1939, Congress passed the Act to Prevent Pernicious Political Activities, usually called the **Hatch Act** after its chief sponsor, Senator Carl Hatch of New Mexico. The act was designed to ensure that the federal civil service did not have disproportionate influence in the election of presidents and members of Congress. In essence, it permitted federal employees to vote in government elections but not to take an active part in partisan politics. The Hatch Act also made it illegal to dismiss civilian employees for political reasons.[11]

In 1993, Congress, with the encouragement of the Clinton administration, overhauled the Hatch Act and made many forms of participation in partisan politics permissible. The revised act still bars federal officials from running as candidates in partisan elections, but it does permit most federal civil servants to hold party positions and involve themselves in party fund raising and campaigning. This new law was welcomed by those who believed that the old act discouraged political participation by 3 million people who might otherwise be vigorous political activists.[12]

Hatch Act
A federal statute barring federal employees from active participation in certain kinds of politics and protecting them from being fired on partisan grounds.

The new Hatch Act imposes many restrictions on federal employees: They cannot raise campaign funds in their agencies, and those who work in such highly sensitive federal agencies as the CIA, the FBI, the Secret Service, and certain divisions of the IRS are specifically barred from nearly all partisan activity. Stricter rules regulate the political involvement of those who work in the U.S. military. On the one hand, federal employees *may* register and vote as they choose; assist in voter registration; express opinions about candidates and issues; contribute money to political organizations; attend political fund-raising functions; wear or display political badges, buttons, or stickers; attend political rallies and meetings; and join political parties. On the other hand, they *may not* be candidates for public office in partisan elections, use their jobs or authority to interfere with or affect the results of an election, collect contributions or sell tickets to political fund-raising functions from subordinate employees, or solicit funds or discourage the political activity of any person who has business before the employee's office.

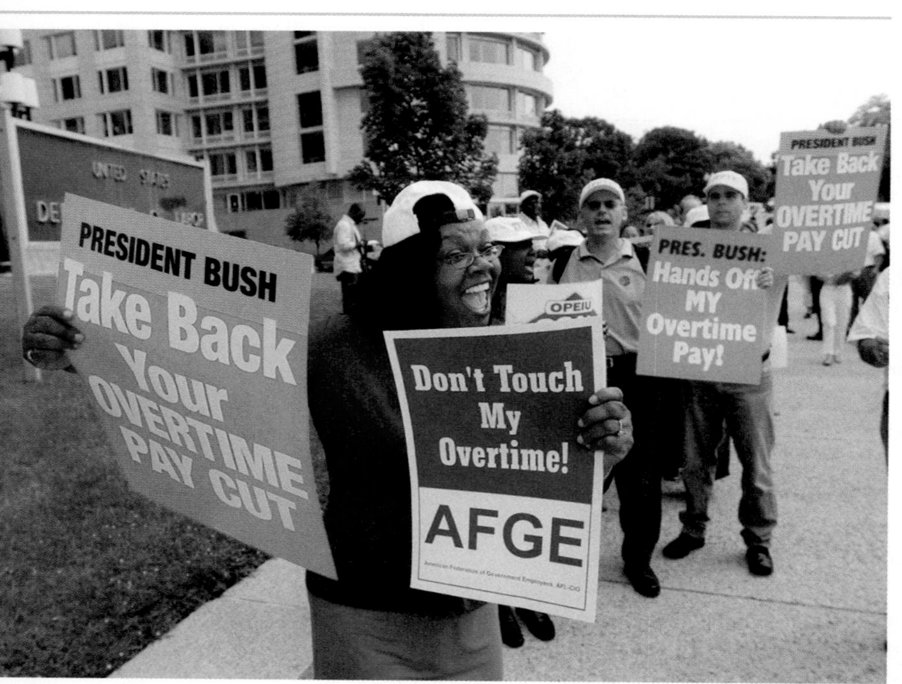

The National Treasury Employees Union represents thousands of federal employees who work across government. Although it started out as a union for Treasury Department employees, it has expanded over the years.

The Role of Government Employee Unions

Since 1962, federal civilian employees have had the right to form unions or associations that represent them in seeking to improve government personnel policies, and about one-third of them have joined such unions. Some of the most important unions representing federal employees today are the American Federation of Government Employees, the National Treasury Employees Union, the National Association of Government Employees, and the National Federation of Federal Employees.

Unlike unions in the private sector, federal employee unions lack the right to strike and are not able to bargain over pay and benefits. But they can attempt to negotiate better personnel policies and practices for federal workers, they can represent federal employees at grievance and disciplinary proceedings, and they can lobby Congress on measures affecting personnel changes. They can also vote in elections. This is why members of Congress from districts with large numbers of federal workers often sit on the House and Senate civil service subcommittees.

The Job of the Federal Bureaucracy

Whatever their size or specialty, all federal organizations share one constitutional job: to faithfully execute, or implement, the laws.

LEARNING **OBJECTIVE**

7 Analyze the tools of implementation and their effectiveness.

Implementation covers a broad range of bureaucratic activities, such as writing checks at the Social Security Administration, inspecting job sites for the Occupational Safety and Health Administration, swearing in new citizens at the Immigration and Naturalization Service, or monitoring airline traffic for the Federal Aviation Administration. Some agencies implement the laws by spending money, others by raising revenues or issuing rules that govern what private citizens and businesses do, and still others by collecting information or conducting research. Whatever tool government uses, implementation is the act of converting a law into action.

Because Congress and the president could never pass laws detailed enough to deal with every aspect of their administration, they give federal departments and agencies **administrative discretion** to implement the laws in the most efficient and effective manner possible. This freedom varies from agency to agency, depending on both past performance and congressional politics. Political scientist Theodore Lowi believes that Congress often gives the federal bureaucracy vague directions because it is unable or unwilling to make the tough choices needed to resolve conflicts that arise in the legislative process. Congress gets the credit for passing a law, while the federal workforce gets the challenge of implementing an unclear law.[13]

Whether a law is clear or ambiguous, most agencies implement it through two means: administrative *regulations*, formal instructions for either running an agency or controlling the behavior of private citizens and organizations, and *spending*, the transfer of money to and from government.

Making Regulations

Rules are designed to convert laws into action. They tell people what they can and cannot do, as well as what they must or must not do. An Agriculture Department rule tells meat and poultry processors how to handle food; an Environmental Protection Agency rule tells automobile makers how much gasoline mileage their cars must get; a Social Security Administration rule tells workers how long they must work before they are eligible for a federal retirement check; an Immigration and Naturalization Service rule tells citizens of other nations how long they can stay on a student visa; and a Justice Department rule tells states what they must do to ensure that every eligible citizen can vote. All these rules can be traced back to legislation; they provide the details that laws leave out.

Rules are drafted and reviewed under the Administrative Procedure Act. Created in 1946 to make sure all rules are made visible to the public, the act requires that all proposed rules be published in the ***Federal Register.*** Publication in the federal government's newspaper marks the beginning of the "notice and comment" period, during which all parties affected by the proposed regulation are encouraged to make their opinions known to the agency. Because rules have the force of law and can become the basis for

implementation
The process of putting a law into practice through bureaucratic rules or spending.

administrative discretion
Authority given by Congress to the federal bureaucracy to use reasonable judgment in implementing the laws.

rule
A precise statement of how a law is implemented.

Federal Register
The official record of what the federal bureaucracy does.

YOU WILL DECIDE Who Wants a Federal Career?

If the past is a guide, the federal government will hire almost 100,000 new employees this year. Many will be offered entry-level jobs that carry good salaries and special benefits such as student loan relief. Federal employees also receive comprehensive health care coverage, including prescriptions and eyeglasses, signing bonuses, a retirement plan, 13 to 26 days of vacation each year, free child care, and even the option of working from home by telecommuting. It's little wonder many college seniors say the federal government is the place to go for pay, benefits, and job security.

The federal government also offers some of the most interesting jobs in the world. Scientists and engineers can work on leading-edge space technologies at the National Aeronautics and Space Administration, biochemists and physicians can find great reward at the National Institutes of Health and the Centers for Disease Control, lawyers can help enforce important civil and criminal laws at the Department of Justice, environmentalists can deal with global warming at the National Oceanographic and Atmospheric Administration or the Environmental Protection Agency, and law enforcement majors can find work anywhere in government, as can nurses, accountants, computer programmers, and a host of other high-demand positions.

Much of this work is exciting and meaningful. The federal government has a long list of important missions as varied as reducing disease, guaranteeing civil rights, protecting the environment, fighting the war on terrorism, and executing the laws. Young U.S. adults can find many challenging jobs inside government and often rise to the very top of the bureaucracy by the end of their careers.

legal challenges, the process can take years from start to finish and consume thousands of pages of records. Some agencies even hold hearings and take testimony from witnesses in the effort to build a strong case for a particularly controversial rule.

The rule-making process does not end with final publication and enforcement. All rules are subject to the same judicial review that governs formal laws, thereby creating a check against potential abuse of power when agencies exceed their authority to faithfully execute the laws.

Spending Money

The federal bureaucracy also implements laws through spending, whether by writing checks to more than 35 million Social Security recipients a year, buying billions of dollars' worth of military equipment, or making grants to state governments and research universities. Viewed in relative terms as a percentage of gross domestic product (GDP), federal spending more than doubled over the past half-century but began to shrink with the end of the cold war in 1989. It rose again after passage of the 2001 tax cuts, which cut federal revenues substantially. In constant dollars adjusted for inflation, federal spending continues to rise each year, driven in part by the cost of caring for a rapidly aging population.

uncontrollable spending
The portion of the federal budget that is spent on previously enacted programs, such as Social Security, that the president and Congress are unwilling to cut.

entitlement program
Programs such as unemployment insurance, disaster relief, or disability payments that provide benefits to all eligible citizens.

Most government spending is **uncontrollable** or required by previous laws. The bulk of uncontrollable, mandatory spending goes to **entitlement programs** such as Social Security for older citizens, college loans, and help for the victims of natural disasters such as floods and hurricanes. Everyone eligible for these programs is *entitled* to benefits—hence, spending often rises automatically. (The amount of uncontrollable spending in the 1962 and 2008 budgets is shown in Figure 13–4.)

The largest share of uncontrollable spending goes to Social Security and Medicare, which are guaranteed to anyone who has paid taxes into the program for enough years.

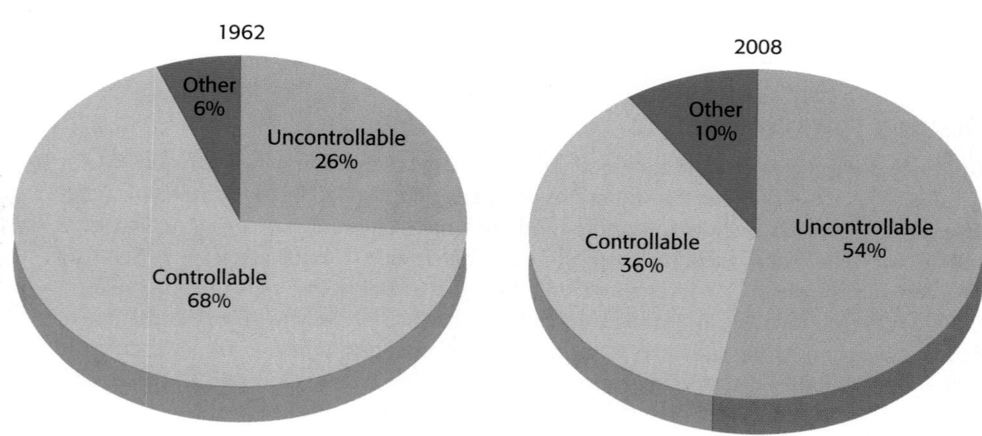

FIGURE 13–4
Uncontrollable Spending in 1962 and 2008.

SOURCE: Office of Management and Budget, *Budget of the U.S. Government, Fiscal Year 2009, Historical Tables* (U.S. Government Printing Office, February 2008).

As a higher percentage of workers age over the next few decades, uncontrollable spending will almost certainly rise as Social Security and Medicare grow. The two programs are already the largest in the federal budget and will eventually account for more than half of all federal spending. In total, uncontrollable spending accounted for nearly $2 trillion in 2008, two-thirds of the federal government's spending.

A much smaller share of the uncontrollable budget goes to welfare for the poor and is linked to the performance of the economy. More unemployment, for example, means more federal unemployment insurance; more poverty means more food stamps, job training, temporary financial assistance, and other income support programs.

THINKING IT THROUGH

Although the federal government offers good benefits and important work, it also has a well-deserved reputation for being a difficult place to work. Most students say the most important consideration in taking a job is not pay or job security, but the chance to make a difference, the opportunity for promotions, and meaningful work. They also say they want a simple, easy hiring process that makes decisions quickly.

The federal government has many problems meeting these goals. Getting a federal job is a complicated, often confusing process that takes months to complete, and new recruits often leave because they feel trapped by a bureaucracy that allows little room for advancement. The government's biggest problem with retaining talented employees appears to be a lack of resources to actually do meaningful work. Young recruits complain they don't have enough access to training or new technology, and their organizations don't have enough people to execute the laws.

Many college seniors also say the federal government is a great place to work for anyone but them. They want the chance to make a difference *now,* not in twenty or thirty years. Although there are rewarding places to work in the federal bureaucracy, students rightly worry that they'll land in a department or agency with little interest in giving them the tools to do their jobs well or the meaningful work they crave.

Questions

1. Why do college and university students put such a great emphasis on finding meaningful work?
2. Does the federal bureaucracy send the right message to students when it emphasizes the pay, benefits, and job security it can offer?
3. What can the federal bureaucracy do to make its jobs more attractive to Generation Next?

Controlling the Federal Bureaucracy

Every president enters office promising to make federal agencies work better. Jimmy Carter, Ronald Reagan, Bill Clinton, and George W. Bush all made bureaucratic reform a central part of their presidential campaigns. Carter promised to create a government as good as the U.S. people, Reagan promised to reduce waste in government, Clinton and Vice President Al Gore promised to reinvent government, and Bush promised to make government friendlier to citizens.

Presidential Controls

Modern presidents invariably contend that they should be firmly in charge of federal employees, because the chief executive is responsive to the broadest constituency. A president, they argue, must see that popular needs and expectations are converted into administrative action. When the nation elects a conservative president who favors cutbacks in federal programs and less governmental intervention in the economy, for example, the federal bureaucracy must carry out his or her policies. The voters' wishes can be translated into action only if federal employees support presidential policies.

Yet under the system of checks and balances, the party that wins the presidency does not acquire total control of the national government. The president is not even the undisputed master of the executive structure. Presidents come into an ongoing system over which they have little control and within which they have little leeway to make the bureaucracy responsive.

Still, the president has some control over federal departments and agencies through the powers of appointment, reorganization, and budgeting. A president can attempt to control the federal system by appointing or promoting sympathetic personnel, mobilizing public opinion and congressional pressure, changing the administrative apparatus, influencing budget decisions, using extensive personal persuasion, and if all else fails, shifting an agency's assignment to another department or agency (although such a shift requires tacit if not explicit congressional approval).[14]

Former defense secretary Donald Rumsfeld resigned from office only days after the 2006 elections. His management of the war in Iraq had been widely criticized, and he was blamed for the deep Republican losses in the elections. In this way, citizens held government accountable through their votes against Republican candidates.

Congressional Controls

Congress has a number of ways to control federal administration, whether by establishing agencies, formulating budgets, appropriating funds, confirming personnel,

HISTORY MAKERS

Louis Brownlow

Louis Brownlow is one of the least known but most important creators of the modern administrative system. Born in 1879, he worked as a journalist for most of his career and spent time as a foreign correspondent in Europe, the Middle East, and Asia in the early 1900s.

Despite his lack of political experience, Brownlow was well connected to the political leaders of his time and became Franklin Delano Roosevelt's choice to head the Committee on Administrative Management in 1936. Facing growing political pressure to make sense of the rapidly expanding bureaucracy, Roosevelt needed to strengthen his control of the executive branch.

Brownlow's three-person committee agreed. Indeed, the first sentence of the committee's famous 1937 report read, "The President needs help." The committee argued that the president should reorganize dozens of agencies into larger departments, move the budget process into a new Executive Office of the President, and create a new White House staff composed of individuals with "a passion for anonymity."

Roosevelt accepted most of the committee's recommendations when he created the Executive Office of the President in 1939. He also began work on creating several new departments until World War II distracted him. Although Brownlow is an almost invisible figure in history, the Executive Office of the President continues to operate as he recommended.*

QUESTIONS

1. Why did the Brownlow Committee argue that the president needed help? Does the president still need help today?
2. Did strengthening the president's control over the bureaucracy help or hurt government performance and accountability?
3. What were the advantages of appointing an outsider to lead the president's reform committee?

*Louis Brownlow, *A Passion for Anonymity: The Autobiography of Louis Brownlow* (University of Chicago Press, 1955).

LEARNING **OBJECTIVE**

8 Compare and contrast efforts to control the federal bureaucracy.

authorizing new programs or new shifts in direction, conducting investigations and hearings, or even terminating agencies.

Much of this authority helps constituents as they battle federal red tape. Members of Congress earn political credit by influencing federal agencies on behalf of their constituents. Still, Congress deserves at least some of the blame for having created the red tape in the first place, through such deeds as enacting pet programs, refusing to give federal agencies greater flexibility, delaying presidential appointments, and placing limits on bureaucratic discretion to protect some constituents but not others. Moreover, by demanding special attention for their constituents, members of Congress may undermine the fairness of the entire process. Like those who cut in line at a movie theater, they slow the progress for everyone but the special few who get their attention.

Only a small minority of our 535 members of Congress would trade the present bureaucratic structure for one that was an efficient, effective agent of the general interest—the political payoffs from helping constituents wade through bureaucratic barriers are too great. Congressional talk of inefficient, irresponsible, out-of-control bureaucracy is typically just that—talk—and when it is not, it usually refers to agencies under the jurisdiction of *other* legislators' committees. Congress can abolish or reorganize an agency. Congress can limit or expand an agency's jurisdiction or allow its authority to lapse entirely. Congress can slash an agency's appropriations. Congress can investigate. Congress can do all of these things, but individual members of Congress generally find reasons not to.[15]

U.S. Army General David Petraeus, commander of U.S. forces in Iraq, gives Congress a progress report on the troop increases in Iraq in 2008.

It is not Congress as a whole that shares direction over the bureaucracy with the president. More accurately, individual members and committees specialize in the appropriations and oversight processes. They oversee policies of a particular cluster of agencies—often the agencies serving constituents in their own districts. Some legislators stake out a claim over specific areas. Members of Congress, who see presidents come and go, come to think they know more about particular agencies than the president does (and often they do). Some congressional leaders prefer to seal off "their" agencies from presidential direction and maintain their influence over public policy. Sometimes their power is institutionalized; the Army Corps of Engineers, for example, is given authority by law to plan public works and report to Congress without going through the president.

Shared Controls

Congress and the president spend a great deal of time and energy monitoring the federal bureaucracy through **oversight,** the technical term for their ongoing review.

Presidents use a number of tools for keeping a watchful eye. They can put loyal appointees into the top jobs at key agencies; they can direct White House aides, such as national security adviser Stephen Hadley, to oversee the work of certain agencies; and they can always call cabinet meetings to learn more about what is happening in the various departments. The Bush administration used all of these strategies to influence the bureaucracy.

However, presidents tend to use the Office of Management and Budget for most routine oversight. Departments and agencies must get the president's approval before testifying before Congress on pending legislation, making legislative proposals, or answering congressional inquiries about their activities. Under this **central clearance** system, OMB forwards communications to Congress in three categories: "in accordance" with the president's program (reserved for the president's top priorities), "consistent with" the president's program (indicating the president's second-tier priorities), or "no objection." If the president objects to any communication, OMB simply does not forward the legislation to Congress. OMB also conducts oversight on all federal departments and agencies as it assembles the president's budget plan.

Congress also has a number of tools for overseeing the federal bureaucracy, not least of which are the individual members of Congress themselves, who are free to ask agencies for detailed information on just about any issue. However, most members and committees tend to use the General Accounting Office or the Congressional Budget Office to conduct a study or investigation of a particular program.

Congress relies on these and other sources of information as a basis for committee and subcommittee hearings about specific agencies or programs. Although the level of congressional oversight increased steadily during the 1970s and 1980s, it began declining in the 1990s and continues to decline. Members of Congress may be spending so much time on reelection that they have little energy left for the routine, but important, task of oversight. They may also be delegating at least some oversight responsibility to blue-ribbon commissions and other independent investigatory bodies that review major government failures, such as the space shuttle *Columbia* disaster and the Hurricane Katrina response.

Together, Congress and the president conduct two basic types of oversight. One is "police patrol" oversight, in which the two branches watch the bureaucracy through a routine pattern. They read key reports, monitor the budget, and generally pay attention to the way the departments and agencies are running. The goal is to deter problems before they arise.

The other form of oversight is "fire alarm" oversight, in which the two branches wait for citizens, interest groups, or the press to find a major problem and pull the alarm. The media play a particularly important role in such oversight, using the *Freedom of Information Act* to gain access to documents the federal bureaucracy keeps secret and often uncovering a scandal before a routine "police patrol" can spot it.

Sometimes federal employees help oversee the government by leaking important information to the media and Congress. Such *whistle-blowers* released information about the Bush administration's domestic eavesdropping program in late 2005, for example. Although whistle-blowers are protected by federal law, many are forced to leave government under informal pressure.

Can the Bureaucracy Regulate Itself?

Career administrators are in a good position to know when a program is not operating properly and what action is needed. But many people believe that federal employees care too much about their own pay, benefits, and job security to make things better. Some career employees act as if the expansion of their organization were vital to the public interest. They become more skillful at building political

oversight
Legislative or executive review of a particular government program or organization. Can be in response to a crisis of some kind or part of routine review.

central clearance
Review of all executive branch testimony, reports, and draft legislation by the Office of Management and Budget to ensure that each communication to Congress is in accordance with the president's program.

Vice President Al Gore took the Clinton administration's campaign to cut government waste to the people when he appeared on "The David Letterman Show." Gore and Letterman both wore goggles as Gore showed how to smash an ashtray under federal rules.

alliances to protect their organization than at building political alliances to ensure their programs' effectiveness.

Career administrators usually try hard to be objective, but they are inevitably political. Some have more bargaining and alliance-building skills than the elected and appointed officials to whom they report. In one sense, agency leaders are at the center of action in Washington. Over time, administrative agencies may become much closer to the interests they regulate than to the public they protect.

Special-interest groups that perceive real or potential harm to their interests cultivate the bureau chiefs and agency staffs who have jurisdiction over their programs. They also work closely with the committees and subcommittees of Congress that authorize, appropriate, and oversee programs run by these key bureaucracies. Recognizing the power of interest groups, bureau chiefs frequently recruit them as allies in pursuing common goals. These officials, interest groups, and congressional allies share a common view that more money should be spent on their federal programs.

A History of Great Endeavors

The Changing Face of the Federal Bureaucracy

Despite their complaints about the federal bureaucracy, U.S. citizens are reluctant to support cutbacks in what government does. Most say the federal bureaucracy's big problem is not setting the wrong priorities, but allowing inefficiency. We may complain about the red tape and waste in Washington, but the federal bureaucracy continues to make progress in solving some of the most difficult problems of modern society.

The federal bureaucracy helped rebuild Europe after World War II, fought the cold war against communism, strengthened voting rights for all, reduced workplace discrimination, ended racial segregation in public schools, conquered diseases such as polio, designed the interstate highway system, and won the race to the moon. Name an international or domestic problem facing the nation today, and the federal bureaucracy has tried to solve it.

Given the long list of difficult issues now facing the nation, the question is whether the federal bureaucracy will be as successful in the future. The answer depends in part on citizen action. Presidents and Congress are not the only ones who monitor the bureaucracy through oversight. Citizens monitor government, too. Their efforts make a difference in shaping rules, improving performance, and prompting congressional action. And individuals can always support the many citizen groups that seek higher performance and accountability. Citizens can now keep their own watchful eye over government by joining organizations such as OMB Watch, which monitors federal spending, or visiting government websites such as www.expectmore.gov, which provides assessments of how well certain programs run. The more knowledgeable citizens are about how government works, the more they are able to influence specific government actions.

CHAPTER SUMMARY

1 Understand why the federal bureaucracy is called the undefined branch.

The founders assumed there would be a federal bureaucracy, but that it would be small. Therefore, they left many of the details of the bureaucracy to the responsibility of future presidents. Although they did give the president the power to appoint the officers of government and require their opinions in writing, there are few constitutional rules for managing the bureaucracy.

2 Analyze the pros and cons of bureaucracy.

The chief benefits of bureaucracy are specialization, centralization, formal rules, standardization, expertise, and accountability. These factors create predictability by making sure all employees know their jobs. However, they also can create duplication and overlap, as well as needless levels of management. As a result, bureaucracy is seen as a negative term today.

3 Compare and contrast the different types of federal organizations.

There are four types of government organizations: (1) departments, (2) independent regulatory commissions, (3) independent agencies, and (4) government corporations. Departments are generally the largest organizations in government and are often divided into members of the inner and outer cabinet; independent regulatory commissions are insulated from political control through the appointment of commissioners with fixed terms of office who cannot be easily removed from office.

4 Describe the differences between the bureaucracy's two types of leaders.

Presidential appointees are appointed by the president with and without Senate confirmation, and senior executives are members of the civil service. Together, there are about 10,000 of these leaders.

5 Evaluate the differences between the spoils and merit systems.

The spoils system was expanded under Andrew Jackson as a way to fill senior jobs in government as a form of political favoritism. After years of corruption, the system was abandoned in 1883 when Congress created the modern civil service system. The system awards federal jobs on the basis of merit.

6 Identify the key regulations that govern the civil service.

The federal government's Office of Personnel Management sets policy for recruiting and evaluating federal workers. Various restrictions prevent federal workers from running for political office or engaging in political fund-raising activities.

7 Analyze the tools of implementation and their effectiveness.

The federal bureaucracy generally uses regulations or spending to implement the laws. The rule-making process is governed by the Administrative Procedure Act, while the spending process is governed by the federal budget. Most of the federal budget is uncontrollable.

8 Compare and contrast efforts to control the federal bureaucracy.

The federal bureaucracy has at least two immediate supervisors: Congress and the president. It must pay considerable attention as well to the courts and their rulings and to well-organized interest groups and public opinion. Despite their efforts to ensure accountability, Congress and the president often give vague instructions to the administrative system, which gives the system significant discretion in implementing the laws.

Chapter Self-Test

1. List key decisions the framers made about executing the laws that continue to shape federal administration to this day. (pp. 358–359)
2. In one or two paragraphs, list why the framers did not define the federal bureaucracy more specifically. (p. 361)
3. Which of the following is a weakness of the modern federal bureaucracy? (p. 361)
   a. Communication within a large organization is difficult
   b. Few qualified individuals want to work in the bureaucracy

c. Today's jobs are overly simplistic and not attractive to young workers
d. Rules are almost impossible to enforce within a very large workforce

4. In a short essay, identify and describe three strengths of bureaucracies. Focus on experiences you or someone you know has had with the federal bureaucracy. How could those experiences have been improved? (pp. 360–361)

5. Which type of federal organization is the Federal Reserve Board? (p. 362)
   a. Department
   b. Independent agency
   c. Government corporation
   d. Independent regulatory commission

6. Which types of federal organizations report directly to the president? Which do not? What implications does that have on how they behave? (pp. 361–366)

7. What are the two types of leaders in the bureaucracy? To whom does each report? How are their appointment processes similar? How are they different? (pp. 367–368)

8. Which of the following is *not* a step in the appointment process for presidential appointees? (pp. 370–372)
   a. Selection by the White House
   b. Review and confirmation by the Senate
   c. Review and confirmation by the House
   d. Background research and clearance by the White House

9. Identify whether each of the following describes the spoils or the merit system: (pp. 369–370)
   a. Andrew Jackson substantially expanded the system after his election in 1829
   b. Federal jobs are filled on the basis of personal connections
   c. Ninety percent of federal employees are selected through this system
   d. This system gave the president's party nearly complete control over almost every government job
   e. Federal jobs are filled on the basis of ability

10. Write a short essay about the differences between the merit and spoils systems. Consider specific ways in which you interact with the government. How might those experiences be different if the spoils system were still in place? Would you want to work in a bureaucracy under the spoils system? Why or why not? (pp. 369–370)

11. What is the main duty of the Office of Personnel Management? (p. 369)
   a. Protect the integrity of the federal merit system
   b. Administer civil service laws, rules, and regulations
   c. Research and interview each potential presidential appointee
   d. Provide information to the Senate about presidential appointees

12. What is the main purpose of the Hatch Act? (p. 372)
   a. Give Congress the power to impeach presidential appointees
   b. Make Senate approval mandatory for all civil service employees
   c. Ensure employees of independent regulatory commissions do not have undue influence over legislation in Congress
   d. Ensure the federal civil service does not have disproportionate influence in the election of Congress and the president

13. Which of the following was a key change Congress (aided by the Bill Clinton administration) made to the Hatch Act in 1993? (p. 372)
   a. Made it illegal to dismiss a federal employee for political reasons
   b. Made it permissible for federal employees to run for political office
   c. Made it illegal for federal employees to engage in active partisan politics
   d. Made it permissible for federal employees to hold positions in political parties

14. What is the Constitutional job shared by all federal organizations regardless of their size or specialty? (p. 373)
   a. To faithfully execute the laws
   b. To protect the president from harm
   c. To cooperate with Congress in all legal matters
   d. To aid the president in electing members of his or her party to political office

15. What is uncontrollable spending? What two programs receive the majority of these funds? Why? What implications could this reason have for the way your future tax dollars are spent? (pp. 374–375)

16. In one or two paragraphs, describe Louis Brownlow and the way he influenced regulation of the federal bureaucracy. (p. 376)

17. Why do many members of Congress prefer the current, complicated federal bureaucracy to a more efficient alternative? (p. 376)
   a. It allows them to campaign for change in each election
   b. A more complicated system creates more jobs for politicians' friends
   c. The political payoffs from helping constituents through the bureaucratic red tape is high
   d. A more complicated system allows politicians greater freedom with less oversight from constituents

Key Terms

bureaucracy, p. 360

bureaucrat, p. 360

department, p. 361

independent regulatory commission, p. 361

independent agency, p. 361

government corporation, p. 361

Senior Executive Service, p. 367

civil service, p. 369

spoils system, p. 369

merit system, p. 369

Office of Personnel Management (OPM), p. 369

Merit Systems Protection Board, p. 369

Hatch Act, p. 372

implementation, p. 373

administrative discretion, p. 373

rule, p. 373

Federal Register, p. 373

uncontrollable spending, p. 374

entitlement program, p. 374

oversight, p. 377

central clearance, p. 377

Further Reading

JOEL D. ABERBACK, *Keeping a Watchful Eye: The Politics of Congressional Oversight* (Brookings Institution Press, 1990).

ROBERT D. BEHN, *Rethinking Democratic Accountability* (Brookings Institution Press, 2001).

BARRY BOZEMAN, *Bureaucracy and Red Tape* (Prentice Hall, 2000).

SHELLEY L. DAVIS, *Unbridled Power: Inside the Secret Culture of the IRS* (HarperBusiness, 1997).

JOHN J. DILULIO JR., ED., *Deregulating the Public Service: Can Government Be Improved?* (Brookings Institution Press, 1994).

JAMES W. FESLER AND **DONALD F. KETTL,** *The Politics of the Administrative Process,* 3d ed. (CQ Press, 2005).

JANE E. FOUNTAIN, *Building the Virtual State: Information Technology and Institutional Change* (Brookings Institution Press, 2001).

STEPHEN GOLDSMITH AND **WILLIAM EGGERS,** *Government by Network: The New Shape of the Public Sector* (Brookings Institution Press, 2005).

CHARLES T. GOODSELL, *The Case for Bureaucracy,* 4th ed. (CQ Press, 2003).

AL GORE, *Creating a Government That Works Better and Costs Less: The Report of the National Performance Review* (Plume-Penguin, 1993).

WILLIAM T. GORMLEY AND **STEVEN J. BELLA,** *Bureaucracy and Democracy: Accountability and Performance,* 2d ed. (CQ Press, 2007).

PHILIP K. HOWARD, *The Death of Common Sense: How Law is Suffocating America* (Random House, 1994).

RONALD N. JOHNSON AND **GARY D. LIBECAP,** *The Federal Civil Service System and the Problem of Bureaucracy* (University of Chicago Press, 1994).

DONALD KETTL, *The Global Management Revolution,* 2d ed. (Brookings Institution Press, 2005).

ANDREW KOHUT, ED., *Deconstructing Distrust: How Americans View Government* (Pew Research Center for the People and the Press, 1998).

PAUL C. LIGHT, *A Government Ill Executed: The Decline of the Federal Service and How to Reverse It* (Harvard University Press, 2008).

AREND LIJPHART, *Patterns of Democracy: Government Forms and Performance in Thirty-Six Countries* (Yale University Press, 1999).

G. CALVIN MACKENZIE AND **MICHAEL HAFKEN,** *Scandal Proof: Do Ethics Laws Make Government Ethical?* (Brookings Institution Press, 2002).

KENNETH J. MEIER AND **LAURENCE J. O'TOOLE JR.,** *Bureaucracy in a Democratic State: A Governance Perspective* (Johns Hopkins University Press, 2006).

DAVID OSBORNE, *The Tools of Government: A Guide to the New Governance* (Oxford University Press, 2002).

DAVID OSBORNE AND **TED GAEBLER,** *Reinventing Government: How the Entrepreneurial Spirit is Transforming the Public Sector* (Addison-Wesley, 1992).

JAMES Q. WILSON, *Bureaucracy: What Government Agencies Do and Why They Do It* (Basic Books, 1989).

Four useful journals are the *Journal of Policy Analysis and Management, National Journal, Public Administration Review,* and *Government Executive.*

chapter 14

The Judiciary

The Balancing Branch

In June 2007, the U.S. Supreme Court wrapped up its 2006–2007 term by announcing its decision to strike down as unconstitutional the use of race in assigning pupils to individual public schools. The decision was consistent with the generally conservative trend in the Court's rulings throughout that year. From the voting record of Associate Justice Samuel A. Alito Jr., recently appointed to replace Sandra Day O'Connor, it seemed the Bush administration had been successful in moving the Court to the right.

President Bush's appointments of Alito and Chief Justice John G. Roberts Jr. were the first nominations to the nation's high court in more than 11 years. Because O'Connor had so often been the fifth vote in closely divided cases, often aligning with the Court's more liberal bloc of four justices to form a majority, appointing a candidate to fill her seat was a particularly good opportunity to shift the Court in a more conservative direction.

The Court's decision against using race to assign pupils to public schools in Seattle, Washington, and Louisville, Kentucky, is one example of this shift. Just four years earlier, Justice O'Connor was the fifth vote upholding the University of Michigan Law School's race-conscious admissions program; in fact, she wrote the Court's majority opinion in the case. Perhaps even more telling, in December 2006, with Justice O'Connor still sitting on the Court pending Samuel Alito's confirmation, the Court refused to review a public school plan nearly identical to the one it later struck down in 2007. The refusal meant that the federal appeals court decision upholding the school's plan was the final decision in the case. Had Justice O'Connor still been on the Court when the Seattle and Louisville cases were decided, it is entirely possible the Court would have upheld the racially conscious plans.

Justice Stephen Breyer summed up the Court's shift to the right as he announced his dissenting opinion in the Seattle and Louisville cases. Although it was not a part of his written dissent, Justice Breyer noted, "It is not often in the law that so few have so quickly changed so much."[1] It is very rare that a justice makes a comment like this one from the bench. But the Court's shift in these and other decisions was also unusual.

How *did* so much change so quickly? Part of the answer is that after a long period of continuity in the makeup of the Supreme Court, the court experienced two back-to-back vacancies in the summer and fall of 2005. As mentioned earlier, President Bush's appointment of a candidate to fill Justice O'Connor's seat was almost certain to affect the outcome of cases in which she was the crucial fifth vote in the majority. Chief Justice William H. Rehnquist's death also affected the Court in profound and important ways. Although any candidate that President Bush might appoint to the Court was likely to agree with the chief justice's largely conservative decisions, he or she would face a difficult challenge filling Rehnquist's shoes. The loss was to be deeply felt by the other judges personally and in the everyday workings of the Court.

Quite simply, it matters who sits on the Court. As former chief justice Charles Evans Hughes once said, "We are under a Constitution, but the Constitution is what the judges say it is. . . ."[2] Although federal judges are not elected, citizens can affect the

LEARNING **OBJECTIVES**

1. Analyze the implications of the adversarial process.
2. Explain the structure of the federal court system.
3. Evaluate factors important in appointing judicial nominees.
4. Compare and contrast arguments in favor of and against judicial activism.
5. Describe the process of reaching a decision in the U.S. Supreme Court.
6. Assess the influences on U.S. Supreme Court decision making.
7. Compare and contrast the limits on judicial action.
8. Assess the role of the judiciary in a constitutional democracy.

CHAPTER OUTLINE

- Understanding the Federal Judiciary
- The Three Types of Federal Courts
- The Politics of Appointing Federal Judges
- How the Supreme Court Decides
- Limits on Judicial Action
- Judicial Power in a Constitutional Democracy

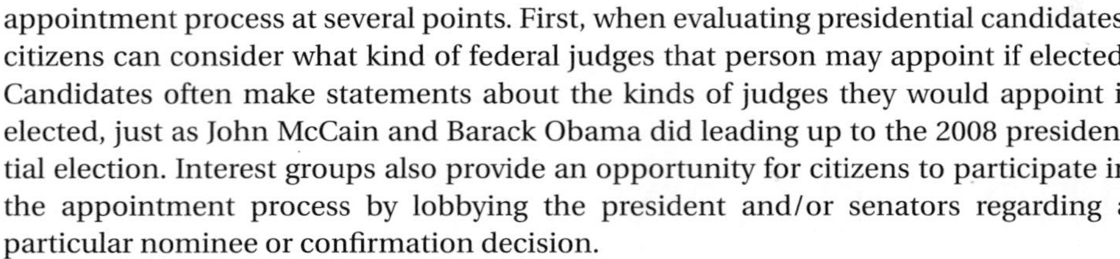

appointment process at several points. First, when evaluating presidential candidates, citizens can consider what kind of federal judges that person may appoint if elected. Candidates often make statements about the kinds of judges they would appoint if elected, just as John McCain and Barack Obama did leading up to the 2008 presidential election. Interest groups also provide an opportunity for citizens to participate in the appointment process by lobbying the president and/or senators regarding a particular nominee or confirmation decision.

In this chapter we explore how the federal judiciary works and examine the nomination process through which we staff the judiciary. The judicial branch is unlike the elected branches of government in several ways. We will first look at the way the framers envisioned the judiciary and discuss several of its important characteristics. After exploring the appointment process, we will discuss the Supreme Court in particular. Given that it is the court of last resort in the United States and has the final say on what the Constitution means, it is crucial to our understanding of the federal judiciary.

Understanding the Federal Judiciary

Comparing Judiciaries

The framers viewed the federal judiciary as an important check against both Congress and the president. But the judiciary lacked the institutional resources of the elected branches. As Alexander Hamilton wrote, "The Executive not only dispenses the honors, but holds the sword of the community. The legislature not only commands the purse, but prescribes the rules by which the duties and rights of every citizen are to be regulated. The judiciary, on the contrary, has no influence over either the sword or the purse."[3] So in order to ensure the judicial check, the framers insulated the judiciary against both public opinion and the rest of government.

To protect the judiciary from shifts in public opinion, the framers rejected direct election. That was the method used to select many judges in the colonies, and it is still used today to choose some state and local judges. The framers also excluded the House, the more representative of the two bodies of Congress, from any role in either selecting or confirming federal judges. To protect the judiciary from Congress as a whole, no limits were allowed on judicial terms. Federal judges serve during good behavior, which typically means for life. And finally, to prevent Congress from assessing a financial penalty against the judiciary, judges' salaries cannot be reduced once confirmed.

These early decisions were essential to protect the judiciary's independence in resolving public disputes. Because it has no army or police force to enforce its will or make people obey its decisions, the judiciary must often rely on the public's respect to implement its decisions. This is sometimes a challenge, particularly when resolving controversial issues such as abortion rights or the rights of prisoners of war. Even in the face of these challenges, it is crucial that the judiciary maintain its independence.

Contrary to the system established at the national level, many states maintain systems in which their state court judges are determined by popular elections. By definition then, these state judiciaries are not independent from public pressure. Although this system arguably adds accountability, some contend that it is accountability not to the average citizen, but to the groups and corporations that contribute money to the judges' election campaigns. This is just one of the potential problems in systems that provide for greater accountability at the expense of judicial independence.

LEARNING OBJECTIVE

Analyze the implications of the adversarial process.

judicial review
The power of a court to refuse to enforce a law or government regulation that in the opinion of the judges conflicts with the U.S. Constitution or, in a state court, the state constitution.

Characteristics of the Federal Judiciary

Civil and Criminal Law Federal judges play a central role in U.S. life. They rule on controversial issues such as partial-birth abortion and race-conscious school assignment, and they often decide whether laws are constitutional. Many of these decisions are based on Chief Justice John Marshall's successful claim of **judicial review**—the power to interpret the Constitution (see Chapter 2). Only a constitutional amendment or a later Supreme Court can modify the Court's decisions.

Several important characteristics distinguish the judiciary from Congress, the presidency, and the administrative system. First, the federal judiciary is an **adversary system,** based on the theory that arguing over law and evidence guarantees fairness.[4] The courts provide a neutral arena in which two parties argue their differences and present evidence supporting those views before an impartial judge. Because the two parties in a case must bring their arguments before the judge, judges may not go looking for cases to decide; the adversary system thus imposes restraints on judicial power.

The courts handle many kinds of legal disputes, but the most common are **criminal law,** which defines crimes against the public order and provides for punishment, and **civil law,** which governs relations between individuals and defines their legal rights. Here are several important distinctions between the criminal and civil law:

- In a criminal trial, a person's liberty is at stake (those judged guilty can be imprisoned); in a civil case, penalties are predominantly monetary.
- Criminal defendants who cannot afford attorneys are provided one by the government, but there is no right to a government-provided attorney in civil cases.
- Defendants generally have the right to a jury in criminal trials, but there is no constitutional right to a jury in state civil trials.

The federal government, not the judiciary, brings all federal criminal cases and can also be a party to a civil action. For example, when Martha Stewart was tried for securities fraud and obstruction of justice, the U.S. government brought the case. The federal judiciary decides the cases. Government *prosecutors*, acting on behalf of the public, choose whether and how to pursue a case against criminal **defendants** who may have violated the law. In some cases they may decide to offer a **plea bargain,** an arrangement in which a defendant agrees to plead guilty to a lesser offense than he or she was charged with, to avoid having to face trial for a more serious offense and a lengthier sentence.

Case Overload

Cases, Controversies, and Justiciability Unlike the legislature and the executive, the federal judiciary is a *passive* and *reactive* branch. It does not instigate cases, nor can it resolve every issue that comes before it. Federal judges decide only **justiciable disputes**—according to the Constitution, they are to decide *cases and controversies.* The courts have understood the Constitution's instruction to mean that they can hear only civil lawsuits growing out of real cases or controversies. It is not enough that a judge believe a particular law to be unconstitutional; a real case must be litigated for a judge to reach that decision. In addition, the parties litigating a civil case must have *standing to sue.* That is, the **plaintiff,** the person who begins a civil suit, must have experienced or be in immediate danger of experiencing direct and personal injury. Hypothetical harm is not enough to warrant court review.

Several *justiciability* concerns, if present, mean that the courts cannot hear the case. For example, if a person sues the government because she *thinks* a government policy will harm her business, the court will refuse to hear the case because the harm has not yet occurred. The court may reject the case because it is not *ripe.* Or, if someone sues the government over a policy that no longer affects him personally, the case is said to be *moot.* Because the controversy is no longer live, the court will refuse to hear the case. Finally, the courts also refuse to hear *political questions.* The federal courts do not decide cases that are political in nature and are more properly dealt with by the legislature.

These procedural requirements may seem unimportant; they are anything but. In an *adversary* system like ours, it is essential that each side bring forth the best possible arguments before the judge or jury. Because the decision makers depend on the adversaries to bring all the relevant information before them, if one side does not truly have a stake in the outcome, the adversarial process breaks down. And because the courts are not to be places of political debate, it is important to restrict political questions to political bodies. As with any rule, there are exceptions, and occasionally the courts take cases that would

adversary system
A judicial system in which the court of law is a neutral arena where two parties argue their differences.

criminal law
A law that defines crimes against the public order.

civil law
A law that governs relationships between individuals and defines their legal rights.

defendant
In a criminal action, the person or party accused of an offense.

plea bargain
An agreement between a prosecutor and a defendant that the defendant will plead guilty to a lesser offense to avoid having to stand trial for a more serious offense.

justiciable dispute
A dispute growing out of an actual case or controversy that is capable of settlement by legal methods.

plaintiff
The party instigating a civil lawsuit.

seem to be political or moot. For example, the Supreme Court came under substantial criticism when it engaged in the debate over the 2000 election.[5] If the Court were to review such questions too often, it would certainly risk its legitimacy.

The federal judiciary has also been reluctant to hear disputes on powers the Constitution explicitly assigns to Congress or the president. It resists intervening in foreign policy questions respecting the power to declare war or economic questions such as the fairness of the federal tax system. The federal judiciary does decide questions about whether the federal government followed the laws, but it generally allows Congress and the president to resolve their differences through the normal legislative process.

Prosecuting Cases

The U.S. Department of Justice is responsible for prosecuting federal criminal and civil cases. The department is led by the *attorney general,* assisted by the **solicitor general,** 94 U.S. Attorneys, and about 1,200 assistant attorneys. The solicitor general represents the federal government whenever a case appears before the Supreme Court, whereas U.S. Attorneys represent the government whenever a case appears before a lower federal court. U.S. Attorneys are appointed by the president with the advice and consent of the Senate, whereas the attorney general appoints each of the assistant U.S. Attorneys after consulting with the U.S. Attorneys in each district. Some districts have as few as 17 assistant U.S. Attorneys, as does the U.S. Attorney's Office for the district of North Dakota; the largest, the U.S. Attorney's Office for the District of Columbia, has more than 350.

The federal judiciary also provides help to defendants who cannot afford their own attorneys in criminal trials. Traditionally, private attorneys have been appointed to provide assistance, but many state and federal courts employ a **public defender system.** This system provides lawyers to any defendant who needs one and is supervised by the federal judiciary to ensure that public defenders are qualified for their jobs.

LEARNING **OBJECTIVE**

2 Explain the structure of the federal court system.

The Three Types of Federal Courts

Article III of the Constitution is the shortest of the three articles establishing the institutions of government. Yet as brief as it is, it instructs the judiciary to resolve several kinds of cases, including those to which the United States is a party in enforcing the laws, for example, and disputes between citizens of two or more states.

Article III is not the only part of the Constitution dealing with the federal judiciary, however. The framers also gave Congress the power to establish "all tribunals inferior to the Supreme Court," which meant that Congress could establish the lower courts we discuss next.

The first Congress used this power to create a hierarchy of federal courts. Under the Judiciary Act of 1789, which was the very first law Congress passed, the federal judiciary was divided into a three-tiered system that exists to this day. The first tier consists of *district courts,* the middle tier of *circuit courts of appeal,* and the highest tier of just one court, the *Supreme Court.* The Supreme Court has **original jurisdiction,** the authority to hear a case essentially as a trial court would, only in cases involving ambassadors, other public ministers, and other diplomats, and cases in which a state or states are a party.

In all other cases the Supreme Court has **appellate jurisdiction** and reviews decisions of other federal courts and agencies and appeals from state supreme court decisions that raise questions of federal law. In general, federal courts may decide only cases or controversies arising under the Constitution, a federal law, a treaty, or admiralty and maritime law; cases brought by a foreign nation against a state or the federal government, and diversity suits—lawsuits between citizens of different states—if the amount of the controversy exceeds $75,000.

solicitor general
The third-ranking official in the Department of Justice who is responsible for representing the United States in cases before the U.S. Supreme Court.

public defender system
An arrangement whereby public officials are hired to provide legal assistance to people accused of crimes who are unable to hire their own attorneys.

original jurisdiction
The authority of a court to hear a case "in the first instance."

appellate jurisdiction
The authority of a court to review decisions made by lower courts.

Level One: District Courts

Although the Supreme Court and its justices receive most of the attention, the workhorses of the federal judiciary are the district courts in the states, the District of Columbia, and U.S. territories. In 2007, they heard nearly 258,000 civil cases and more than 68,000 criminal cases.[6] There are 678 judgeships in the 94 district courts across the country, at least one in every state.

District courts are the trial courts where almost all federal cases begin. They make decisions on the death penalty, drug crimes, and other criminal violations. District judges normally hold trials and decide cases individually. However, because reapportionment of congressional districts and voting rights are so important to the nation, they hear cases concerned with these issues in three-judge panels.

Level Two: Circuit Courts of Appeals

All district court decisions can be *appealed,* or taken to a higher court for further review. Almost all of these cases are reviewed by federal **courts of appeals.** Judges in these courts are bound by **precedent** or decisions previously made by courts of appeals and the Supreme Court, but they have considerable discretion in applying these earlier decisions to specific new cases. Although most of their cases come upward from federal district courts, federal regulatory commissions bring their cases to the courts of appeal directly. For example, appeals of the Federal Energy Regulatory Commission's decisions may be heard by the U.S. Court of Appeals for the District of Columbia Circuit and by the U.S. Supreme Court.

Courts of appeals are located geographically in 11 *judicial circuits* that include all of the states and U.S. territories (see Figure 14–1 for a map of the states included in each of the 11 geographic circuits). A twelfth is located in the District of Columbia and hears the largest number of cases challenging federal statutes, regulations, and administrative decisions. The thirteenth appellate court is the Court of Appeals for the Federal Circuit, which is located in the District of Columbia and reviews cases from any state or region that deal primarily with appeals in patent, copyright, and international trade cases. The largest circuit is the ninth, with 28 circuit judges and 108 district judges. It is the size of western Europe and contains 20 percent of the U.S. population. Circuit courts normally operate as panels of three judges; in 2007 they decided almost 60,000 cases.

court of appeals
A court with appellate jurisdiction that hears appeals from the decisions of lower courts.

precedent
A decision made by a higher court such as a circuit court of appeals or the Supreme Court that is binding on all other federal courts.

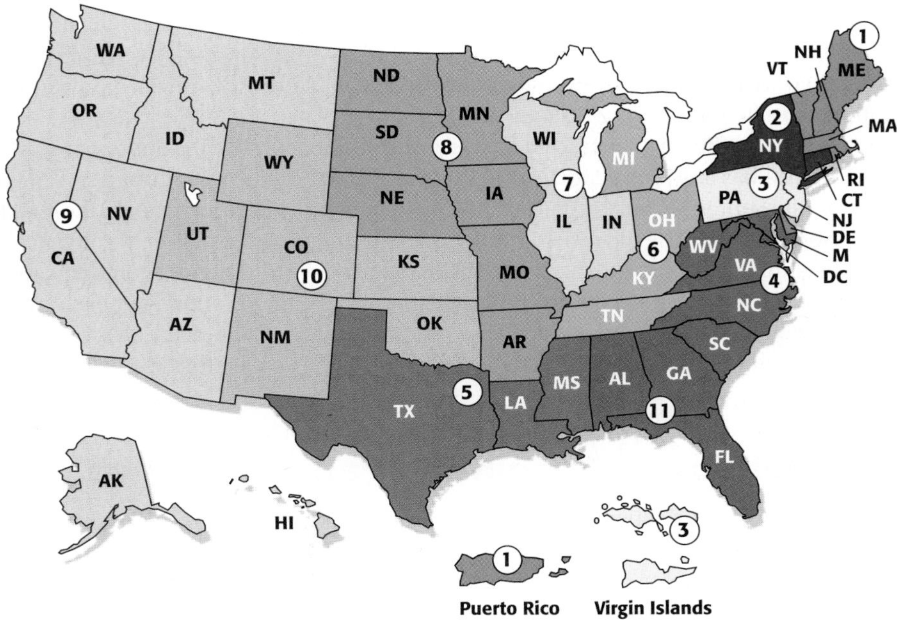

FIGURE 14–1
States Covered by the Eleven U.S. Circuit Courts of Appeal.

FIGURE 14–2
The Structure of the U.S. Judiciary.

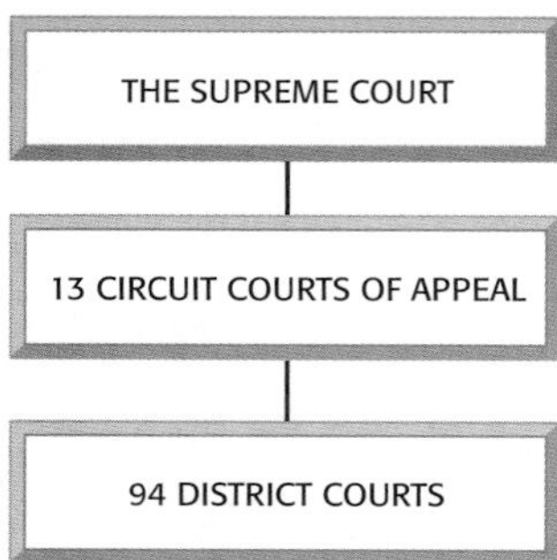

Except in unusual circumstances, courts of appeals can resolve only cases that have been decided by district courts. Nevertheless, their decisions are usually final. Fewer than 1 percent of their decisions are appealed to the Supreme Court. (For more information about the federal judiciary, go to the Web site of the Administrative Office of the U.S. Courts at www.uscourts.gov.)

Level Three: The Supreme Court

The Constitution established only one court of appeal for the entire nation: the Supreme Court or the "court of last resort." Once the Supreme Court decides, the dispute or case is over. (See Figure 14–2 for the three-tiered structure of the federal judiciary.)

Compared with Congress and the presidency, the Supreme Court has changed the least since its creation. There are nine Supreme Court justices today, compared with six in 1789, and the Court moved into its own building only in 1935. Before then it had shared space with the House and Senate in the U.S. Capitol Building. Unlike the current practice in both houses of Congress, oral arguments before the Court about individual cases are not televised, and the justices still appear in robes. Many of the Court's unique characteristics persist due to the constitutional protections the framers put in place. Given its importance, we will turn to a more in-depth discussion of the Supreme Court later in this chapter.

Judicial Federalism: State and Federal Courts

Comparing Judicial Systems

Unlike most countries, which have a single national judicial system that makes all decisions on criminal and civil laws, the United States has both federal and state courts. Each state maintains a judiciary of its own, and many large cities and counties have judicial systems as complex as those of the states. As in the federal system, state judicial power is divided between trial courts (and other lesser courts such as traffic courts) and one or more levels of appellate courts. State courts hear the overwhelming majority of cases in the U.S. legal system—about 90 million civil and criminal cases annually.

State courts primarily interpret and apply their state constitutions and law. When their decisions are based solely on state law, their rulings may not be appealed to or reviewed by federal courts. Only when decisions raise a federal question that requires the application of the Bill of Rights or other federal law are federal courts able to review them. Federal courts have **writ of habeas corpus** jurisdiction, or the power to release persons from custody if a judge determines they are not being detained constitutionally, and may review criminal convictions in state courts if they believe that an accused person's federal constitutional and legal rights have been violated (see Chapter 15). Except for habeas corpus jurisdiction, the Supreme Court is the only federal court that may review state court decisions, and only in cases presenting a conflict with federal law.

Other than the original jurisdiction the Constitution grants to the Supreme Court, no federal court has any jurisdiction except that granted to it by an act of Congress. Congress controls the Supreme Court's appellate jurisdiction (as we will discuss later in the chapter) and also established the three-tiered structure of the federal court system through legislation, beginning with the Judiciary Act of 1789. Even though Congress could technically eliminate the lower federal courts, given their caseloads, that is entirely unlikely. In fact, most discussions concerning court reorganization focus on the need for more federal district court judges and increasing the number of federal appellate circuits.

LEARNING **OBJECTIVE**

 Evaluate factors important in appointing judicial nominees.

writ of habeas corpus
A court order requiring explanation to a judge why a prisoner is being held in custody.

The Politics of Appointing Federal Judges

The Constitution sets absolutely no requirements for serving on the Supreme Court, nor did the first Congress create any requirements for the lower courts. Because judges were to be appointed by the president with the advice and consent of the Senate, the framers assumed that judges would be experienced in the law. As Alexander Hamilton

TABLE 14–1 Moving Up to the Supreme Court

Job Experience	Number	Most Recent Example
Federal Judges	32	Samuel Alito Jr., 2005
Practicing Lawyers	22	Lewis F. Powell, 1971
State Court Judges	18	Sandra Day O'Connor, 1981
Cabinet Members	8	Labor Secretary Arthur Goldberg, 1962
Senators	7	Harold H. Burton (R-Ohio), 1945
Attorneys General	6	Tom C. Clark, 1949
Governors	3	Earl Warren (D-Calif.), 1953
Other	14	Solicitor General Thurgood Marshall, 1967

SOURCE: *CQ Weekly,* October 10, 2005, p. 2701.

explained, "there can be but few men in the society who will have sufficient skill in the laws to qualify them for the stations of judges. And making the proper deductions for the ordinary depravity of human nature, the number must be still smaller of those who unite the requisite integrity with the requisite knowledge."[7]

Much as the framers believed that the judiciary should be independent, the appointment process gives presidents and the Senate ample opportunity for influencing the direction of the courts. Indeed, George Washington established two precedents in judicial appointments. First, his appointees were his political and ideological allies—all of Washington's appointees belonged to his Federalist Party. Second, every state was represented on some court somewhere, thereby ensuring at least some representation across the nation.

Presidents have continued to follow Washington's lead on these two points. They nominate judges who are likely to agree with them on the key issues before the courts and tend to nominate judges from their own party. They also routinely rely on the senators in a given state to make recommendations especially for district court appointments. Because judges serve for life, presidents see judicial appointments as an opportunity to shape the courts for decades to come. Moreover, because the lower federal courts hear the great majority of all federal cases, and because lower court judges are commonly among those considered for the Supreme Court, presidents have been increasingly concerned with these appointments. As Table 14–1 shows, federal court experience is the most common preparation for Supreme Court justices—in fact, 10 of the last 15 Supreme Court justices were federal lower-court judges at the time of their nomination. Each of the current U.S. Supreme Court justices also has federal appeals court experience in particular.

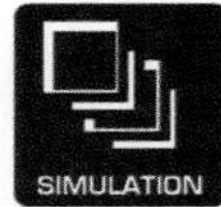

You Are the President and Need to Appoint a Supreme Court Justice

Making the Initial Choices

Article II of the Constitution gives the president the power to appoint federal judges with the advice and consent of the Senate. Although that language may seem straightforward, it has caused great controversy over the Senate's appropriate role in federal judicial selection. The result is a judicial selection process in which presidents are likely to consult with members of Congress and particularly senators, especially if the prospect for a smooth confirmation is in doubt.

The process through which the president consults with members of Congress is complex and may differ from appointment to appointment, but one particularly important norm is **senatorial courtesy**—the custom of submitting the names of prospective judges for approval to the senators from the states in which the appointees are to work. The home-state senators, particularly if they are of the president's party, may also develop a list of candidates for the president's consideration. If the senators approve the nomination, all is well. But if negotiations are deadlocked between them, or between the senators and the Department of Justice, a seat may stay vacant for years.[8]

senatorial courtesy
The presidential custom of submitting the names of prospective appointees for approval to senators from the states in which the appointees are to work.

Chief Justice John Roberts (far right) congratulates Justice Samuel A. Alito Jr. at Alito's swearing-in ceremony as a new member of the Supreme Court.

The custom of senatorial courtesy is not observed with Supreme Court appointments, but presidents do strategically consult with members of Congress, as President Clinton did on his 1993 and 1994 appointments of Justices Ruth Bader Ginsburg and Stephen Breyer. Clinton was especially willing to consult with Republican senator Orrin Hatch, then the Senate Judiciary Committee chair, because the Senate was controlled by Republicans and he needed their support.

Presidents are also advised by their own White House staffs and the Justice Department in compiling a list of potential nominees. Especially in more recent administrations, the Justice Department's Office of Legal Policy and the White House Counsel's Office begin formulating lists of potential court appointees as soon as the president assumes office.

In addition to this process within the government, nongovernmental actors try to influence the selection process. The American Bar Association (ABA) has historically rated candidates being considered for appointment, but conservative groups' concern that the ABA rankings were biased in favor of more liberal judges led the Bush administration to end its preappointment involvement.

Liberal and conservative interest groups also provide their own views of nominees' qualifications for appointment. People for the American Way and the Alliance for Justice often support liberal nominees and oppose conservatives, whereas the Heritage Foundation and a coalition of 260 conservative organizations called the Judicial Selection Monitoring Project often support conservative judges and oppose liberals. These organizations once waited to express their opinions until after the president had sent the name of a nominee to the Senate, but now they are active before the choice is known, informing the media of their support or opposition to potential nominees.

Senate Advice and Consent

The normal presumption is that the president should be allowed considerable discretion in the selection of federal judges. Despite this presumption, the Senate takes seriously its responsibility in confirming judicial nominations, especially when the party controlling the Senate is different from that of the president. However, because individual senators can always threaten or actually mount a filibuster, even party control of the Senate is no guarantee that a nomination will succeed.

All judicial nominations are referred to the Senate Judiciary Committee for a hearing and a committee vote before consideration by the entire Senate. Like laws, judges are confirmed with a majority vote. Even before they receive a hearing, however, all district court nominees must survive a preliminary vote by the nominee's two home-state senators. Each senator receives a letter on blue paper, called a *blue slip*, from the committee asking for approval. If either senator declines to return the slip, the nomination is dead and no hearing will be held.

There are other ways to delay or defeat a judicial nominee, including the threat of a filibuster. Just as the Republican Senate majority had stalled Clinton nominations in the late 1990s, the new Democratic majority stalled many of the Bush administration's nominees after it took control of the Senate in mid-2001. Democrats also stalled many of the Bush nominees even after Republicans regained control of the Senate following the 2002 midterm elections, using both the threat and actual use of filibusters.[9]

Even if the Senate delays or rejects a nomination, however, presidents always have the option of making *recess appointments* after the Senate adjourns at the end of a session. Bush did just that in early 2004 by using a recess appointment to place Charles W. Pickering on the court of appeals. Pickering's appointment had been stalled for almost four years by Senate Democrats, who believed that the Mississippi native had been too conservative on issues of race. Bush may have won the battle, but he did not win the war. Under a recess appointment, Pickering could serve only until the next Congress convened. Knowing that Senate Democrats would continue to oppose his nomination, Pickering decided to withdraw his name from consideration for another nomination to the court, and he left the bench in early 2005 just before the new Congress convened.

After a contentious confirmation process in 1987, the Senate rejected Judge Robert Bork by a vote of 58 to 42.

Before the mid-1950s, the Senate confirmation process was relatively simple and nonpartisan. Until then, the Senate Judiciary Committee did not even hold hearings to ask potential judges questions about their personal history and philosophy. However, as judges became more important in deciding civil rights and other controversial cases, the committee began interviewing candidates on various questions, sometimes imposing a *litmus test* by asking nominees about their positions on specific issues such as abortion. Nominees almost always refuse to answer such questions, to protect themselves from attack and reserve their judgment for actual future cases.

In 1987, however, Supreme Court nominee Robert Bork adopted a different and ultimately unsuccessful strategy. Because he had written so many law articles, made so many speeches, and decided so many cases as a circuit court judge, Bork sought to clarify his constitutional views in defending himself before the Judiciary Committee. His candor may well have contributed to the Senate's rejecting him, and that has made subsequent nominees even more reluctant to respond to similar questions.

Until recently, most judicial appointments, especially those for the district and circuit courts, were processed without much controversy. However, "now that lower court judges are more commonly viewed as political actors, there is increasing Senate scrutiny of these nominees."[10] The battle over judicial confirmations ordinarily takes place in hearings before the Senate Judiciary Committee, although debates can also occur on the Senate floor after the committee has acted.[11] Supreme Court nominees have typically faced more scrutiny in the confirmation process than have lower federal court judges. Indeed, the Senate has refused to confirm 31 of the 152 presidential nominations for Supreme Court justices since the first justice was nominated in 1789.

The Role of Party, Race, and Gender

Presidents so seldom nominate judges from the opposing party (only 10 percent of judicial appointments since the time of Franklin Roosevelt have gone to candidates from the opposition party) that partisan considerations are taken for granted. Today more attention is paid to other characteristics, such as ideology, race, and gender.[12]

Although President Jimmy Carter had no opportunity to make an appointment to the Supreme Court, he brought increased diversity to the lower courts: 16 percent of Carter's appointees were women, 14 percent were African Americans, and 6 percent were Hispanics. President Ronald Reagan was the first to appoint a woman to the Supreme Court, but he appointed fewer minority members or women to the lower courts than Carter did.[13] Of George H. W. Bush's appointees to the lower courts, 20 percent were women, 7 percent were African Americans, and 4 percent were Hispanics.[14]

Alabama's attorney general William Pryor was only 43 when he was confirmed for a life appointment as a federal judge on the Eleventh U.S. Circuit Court of Appeals. Here he testifies before the Senate Judiciary Committee.

President Bill Clinton promised to appoint federal judges who would be more representative of the ethnic makeup of the United States. Clinton lived up to his pledge by naming more women and minorities to the bench than his predecessors had; nearly 50 percent, or 182 of his 367 appointees, were women and minorities. Through the 109th Congress, 32 percent of George W. Bush's judicial nominees have been women and minorities, including 20 percent women, 7 percent African Americans, and 10 percent Hispanics.[15]

The Role of Ideology

Finding a party member is not enough; presidents want to pick the "right" kind of Republican or "our" kind of Democrat to serve as a judge. Thus judges picked by Republican presidents tend to be judicial conservatives, and judges picked by Democratic presidents are more likely to be liberals. Both these orientations are tempered by the need for judges to go through a senatorial confirmation process that must get bipartisan support to survive a possible filibuster, even when the same party controls the White House and the U.S. Senate.

President Ronald Reagan's two terms made it possible for him to join Presidents Franklin D. Roosevelt and Dwight D. Eisenhower as the only presidents in the last century to appoint a majority of the federal bench. All told, Reagan appointed 368 lifetime judges. His administration acted carefully to nominate only those whose views about the role of the courts and constitutional issues were consistent with Reagan's own.[16]

President Clinton gave Democratic senators clear guidelines about the kind of judges he wanted—competent professionals who would bring diversity to the bench.[17] But after Republicans took control of the Senate in 1994, Clinton abandoned or declined to nominate several judicial candidates opposed by conservative interest groups and had to reach compromises with Republican senators. The Republican opposition slowed down the confirmation process so much that Chief Justice Rehnquist scolded the Senate for jeopardizing the court's ability to do its work.

As older, conservative judges appointed during the Reagan administration continued to retire, President George W. Bush worked hard to find younger conservative judges to fill the vacancies. Roberts and Alito were in their fifties when nominated for the Supreme Court and are likely to serve for decades. Many of the administration's lower-court appointees are also relatively young, which ensures their lasting impact. Like his recent predecessors, Bush has had difficulty winning the support of opposition party senators for his judicial nominees. Democrats delayed Bush's most conservative nominees and held filibusters in order to prevent confirmation votes on ten circuit court nominees.

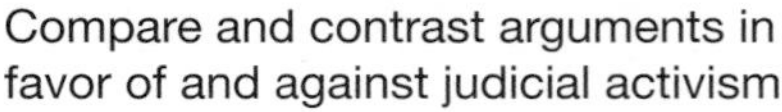

4 Compare and contrast arguments in favor of and against judicial activism.

judicial activism
A philosophy proposing that judges should strike down laws that are inconsistent with norms and values stated or implied in the Constitution.

judicial restraint
A philosophy proposing that judges should strike down the actions of the elected branches only if they clearly violate the literal meaning of the Constitution.

The Role of Judicial Philosophy

A candidate's judicial philosophy also influences the selection process. Does a candidate believe that judges should interpret the Constitution to reflect what the framers intended and what its words literally say? Or does the candidate believe that the Constitution should be adapted to reflect current conditions and philosophies? Recall from our discussion in Chapter 2 that differences in constitutional interpretation can produce vastly different outcomes on the same legal question.

Presidents and senators also want to know how candidates see the appropriate role of the courts. Does the candidate believe that the courts should strike down acts of the elected branches if they violate constitutional norms and values? That is, does the candidate espouse the view of **judicial activism?** Or does the candidate believe in **judicial restraint,** which deems it appropriate for the courts to strike down popularly enacted legislation only when it clearly violates the letter of the Constitution? At the heart of this debate are competing conceptions of the proper balance between

THE **CHANGING FACE** OF U.S. POLITICS

Diversity in the Federal Courts

The federal judiciary has long been dominated by white males. But diversity on the federal bench has been increasing during the last several decades, largely because of the judicial appointments of Presidents Jimmy Carter, George H. W. Bush, Bill Clinton, and George W. Bush.

Although the number of women and minorities appointed to the federal courts has only recently increased significantly, the first female judge, Florence Allen, was appointed in 1934 by President Franklin D. Roosevelt. President Harry Truman named the first African American judge, William Henry Hastie, in 1950. President John F. Kennedy appointed the first Hispanic judge, Reynaldo G. Garza, in 1961, and President Richard M. Nixon in 1971 appointed the first Asian American judge, Herbert Choy. The first Native American judge, Billy Michael Burrage, was appointed in 1994 by President Clinton.

There are several arguments for diversifying the federal judiciary. First, some scholars have argued that a diverse federal judiciary may reach decisions that more accurately reflect the views of our diverse populations. But research has not provided much support for the contention that female or minority judges decide cases differently than do white male judges, with the exception of discrimination suits. Even if there are no differences in outcomes, others argue that simply having a federal judiciary that reflects the citizenry is important to maintaining the courts' legitimacy. In short, citizens place value in seeing someone like themselves on the federal judiciary.

Justice Ruth Bader Ginsburg.

Former justice Sandra Day O'Connor.

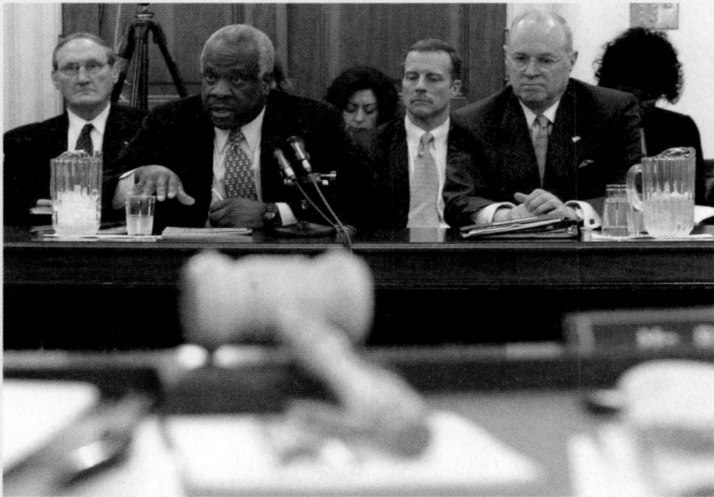

Supreme Court justices Clarence Thomas, left, and Anthony Kennedy testify before a House Appropriations Subcommittee hearing on funding for the judiciary.

Demographic Characteristics of Federal District Court Judges by Appointing President.

SOURCE: Sheldon Goldman, Elliot Slotnick, Genard Gryski, and Sara Schiavoni, "Picking Judges in Time of Turmoil: W. Bush's Judiciary During the 109th Congress," *Judicature* (May–June 2007).

government authority and individual rights, and between the power of democratically accountable legislatures and that of courts and unelected judges.

Reforming the Selection Process

The televised confirmation hearings of Supreme Court nominees Robert Bork in 1987 and Clarence Thomas in 1991 provoked widespread complaints about the judicial selection process. Not only were the hearings lengthy and bitter, they focused on

YOU WILL DECIDE — Should the Federal Courts Be Active?

Given that a judicially active justice will be more willing to strike down the actions of the elected branches of government, it should not be surprising that legislators are interested to know how federal judicial candidates view judicial activism.

Throughout most of our history, federal courts have been more conservative than Congress, the White House, or state legislatures. Before 1937, judicial restraint was the battle cry of liberals who objected to judges' decisions to strike down many laws, such as state laws limiting the number of hours a person could work each week, that were passed to protect labor and women. These judges broadly construed the words of the Constitution to prevent what they thought were unreasonable regulations of property.

With Presidents Richard Nixon, Ronald Reagan, George H. W. Bush, and George W. Bush, however, these positions changed dramatically, and it was conservatives who advocated judicial restraint. What is needed, they argued, are judges who will step back and let Congress, the president, and the state legislatures regulate or forbid abortions, permit prayer in public schools, and not hinder law enforcement.

personal issues that some critics believed were irrelevant to each nominee's qualification to serve. The hearings also included detailed questions about the nominees' positions on controversial issues, which neither was willing to answer.

The politics of judicial selection may shock those who like to think judges are picked strictly on the basis of legal merit and without regard for ideology, party, gender, or race. But as a former Justice Department official observed, "When courts cease being an instrument for political change, then maybe the judges will stop being politically selected."[18]

How the Supreme Court Decides

LEARNING **OBJECTIVE**

5 Describe the process of reaching a decision in the U.S. Supreme Court.

The Supreme Court is a unique institution. Its term runs from the first Monday in October through the end of June. The justices listen to oral arguments for two weeks each month from October to April and then adjourn for two weeks to consider the cases and to write opinions. By agreement, at least six justices must participate in each decision. Cases are decided by a majority vote. In the event of a tie, the decision of the lower court is sustained, although on rare occasions the case may be reargued. (See Figure 14–3 for an overview of the Supreme Court Building.)

Despite extensive controversy surrounding his nomination, the Senate narrowly confirmed Justice Clarence Thomas in 1991.

The Eight Steps to Judgment

When citizens vow to take their cases to the highest court of the land even if it costs their last penny, they underestimate the difficulty of securing Supreme Court review and misunderstand the Court's role. The rules for appealing a case are established by

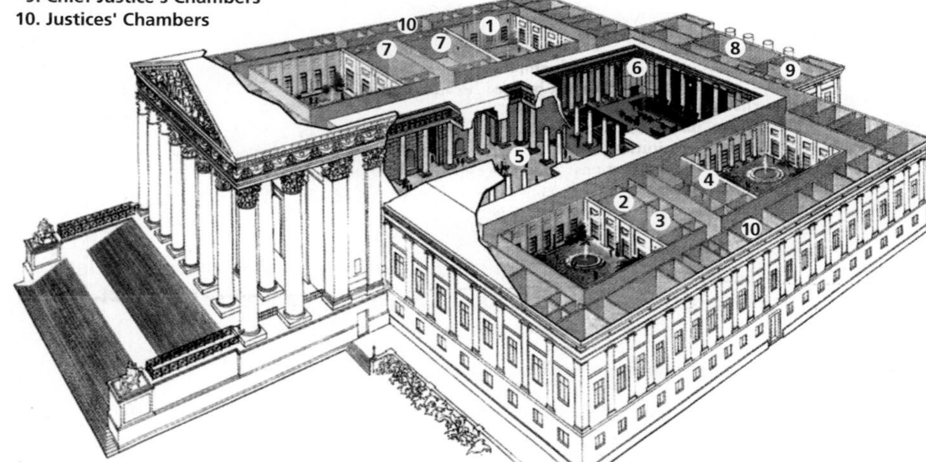

FIGURE 14–3
The Supreme Court Building.

the Supreme Court and Congress. Since 1988, when Congress enacted the Act to Improve the Administration of Justice, the Supreme Court has not been obligated to grant review of most cases that come to it on appeal. Its *appellate jurisdiction* is almost entirely up to its discretion; the overwhelming number of cases appealed to the Court will be denied review.

The process of deciding cases at the U.S. Supreme Court is substantially different than at other federal courts. The Court's first decision is to choose which of the thousands of appeals it will hear each year. Once it has decided to review a case, the Court must then decide the legal question at issue. Next we discuss, step by step, the Court's process of accepting and deciding a case.

1. Reviewing Appeals Today, the decision to grant nearly all appeals is at the Court's discretion. Many appeals come to the Court by means of a petition for a **writ of certiorari,** a formal petition seeking the Court's review, or in the form of an **in forma pauperis** ("as a pauper") petition, which avoids the payment of Court fees. The great majority of in forma pauperis petitions come from prisoners. In either case, the appeals may arise from any state supreme court or from the federal court system (see Figure 14–4 for a simplified description of the two paths to the Supreme Court).

The writs, which the Court can grant or deny, produce its agenda, or **docket.** The docket has grown significantly since the 1970s as citizens have brought more lawsuits, states have imposed more death sentences (which are often appealed), federal regulation has increased, and federal punishment

THINKING IT THROUGH

Chief Justice John Marshall stated in 1803, "It is emphatically the province and duty of the judicial department to say what the law is."* The Court's decision in *Marbury v. Madison* established the use of judicial review to strike down congressional acts. Marshall saw this authority as essential to the Court's ability to check the other branches of government. Justices since Marshall have often been active in striking down legislation that infringes on the rights of minority groups. For example, the Supreme Court's decision in *Brown v. Board of Education of Topeka* (1954)† was an active one in that it struck down the state law requiring racial segregation in the public schools. The court's ability to take such action is often seen as an important check on the tyranny of the majority.

The courts have sometimes drawn criticism for too frequently striking down popularly supported legislation. The Warren Court (1953–1969) stirred such popular opposition in striking down state laws restricting criminal suspects' rights that citizens called for Chief Justice Earl Warren's impeachment on billboards across the nation. One school of thought holds that the federal judiciary, composed of unelected judges secure from public pressure, has a responsibility to use restraint in reaching its decisions.

Many critics of judicial activism argue that although the Supreme Court has the authority of judicial review, the Court must also respect the elected branches' interpretations of the constitutionality of their own actions. These critics assert that Congress is especially well situated to determine whether it is acting under the appropriate grant of authority in Article I, and the executive branch is in a similarly good position to evaluate its power under Article II. According to this perspective, the Court's view on the constitutionality of executive or legislative action is that of just one coequal branch of government.

Questions

1. Under what circumstances do you think the Supreme Court should be active and strike down state or federal legislation?
2. Might it be preferable to have an unelected body decide whether legislation is constitutional? Why or why not?
3. Why do you think most people associate judicial activism with a liberal court?

**Marbury v. Madison,* 5 U.S. 137 (1803).
†*Brown v. Board of Education of Topeka,* 347 U.S. 483 (1954).

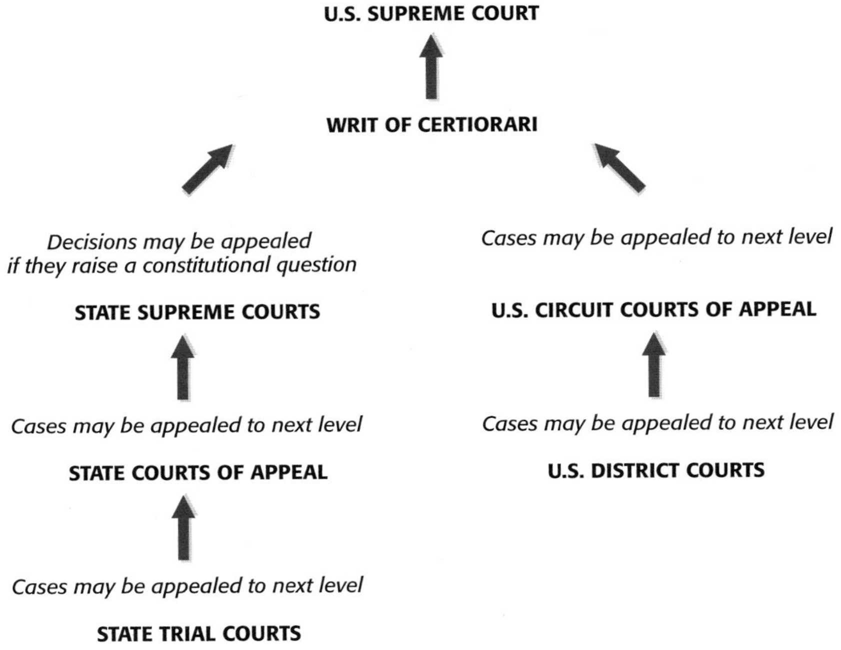

U.S. SUPREME COURT

↑

WRIT OF CERTIORARI

↗ ↖

Decisions may be appealed if they raise a constitutional question | *Cases may be appealed to next level*

STATE SUPREME COURTS | U.S. CIRCUIT COURTS OF APPEAL

↑ | ↑

Cases may be appealed to next level | *Cases may be appealed to next level*

STATE COURTS OF APPEAL | U.S. DISTRICT COURTS

↑

Cases may be appealed to next level

STATE TRIAL COURTS

FIGURE 14–4
How Most Cases Rise to the Supreme Court.

writ of certiorari
A formal writ used to bring a case before the Supreme Court.

in forma pauperis
A petition that allows a party to file "as a pauper" and avoid paying Court fees.

docket
The list of potential cases that reach the Supreme Court.

GENERATION NEXT

Equal Rights

As we saw at the beginning of this chapter, the role of government and specifically the courts in pursuing racial equality has changed over time. Today's 18- to 29-year-olds were born after the Supreme Court's landmark school desegregation cases. The Court's equal rights decisions in some ways mirror 18- to 29-year-olds' views on whether we have gone too far in pushing equal rights. According to the Pew Research Center's Political Landscape Survey, most members of Generation Next (63 percent) do not think so. But a large minority believe we have.

As we may expect, beneficiaries of equal rights initiatives are less likely to agree that we have gone too far in pushing for those rights. Only 31 percent of women and 22 percent of African American respondents agreed with the statement. This should not be surprising, as these groups are also more likely to have personally experienced unequal treatment.

There were also differences along party and ideological lines. Both Conservatives (46 percent) and Republicans (45 percent) agreed that the push for equal rights in this country has been taken too far. This is in keeping with a more conservative emphasis on individualism and concern about the potential for reverse discrimination.

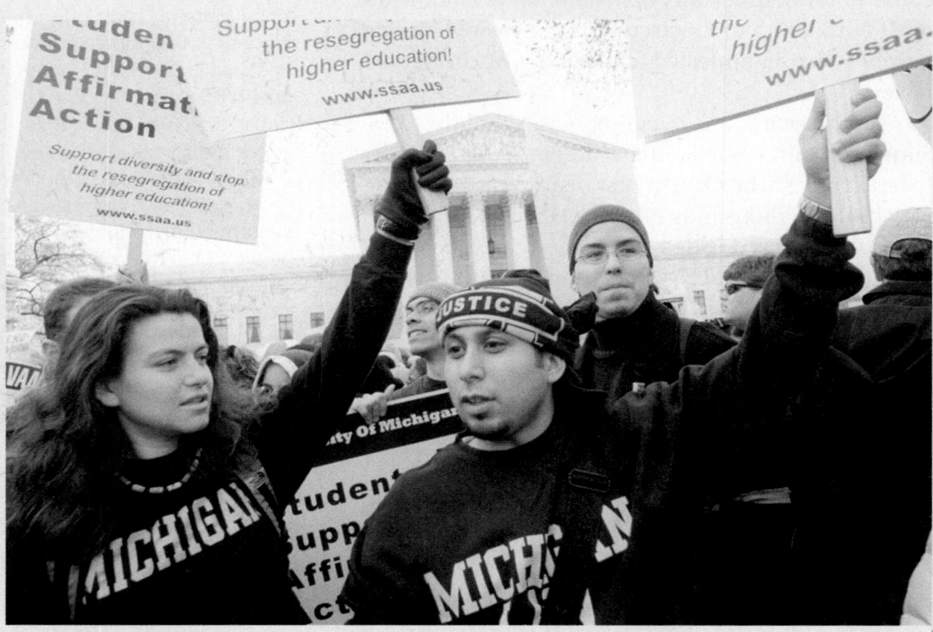

The University of Michigan Law School's race-conscious admissions program was upheld by the U.S. Supreme Court in *Grutter* v. *Bolinger* (2003). Here students express their support for the Michigan program outside the Supreme Court building.

Percentage of 18- to 29-Year Olds Who Completely or Mostly Agreed That We Have Gone too Far in Pushing Equal Rights in this Country.

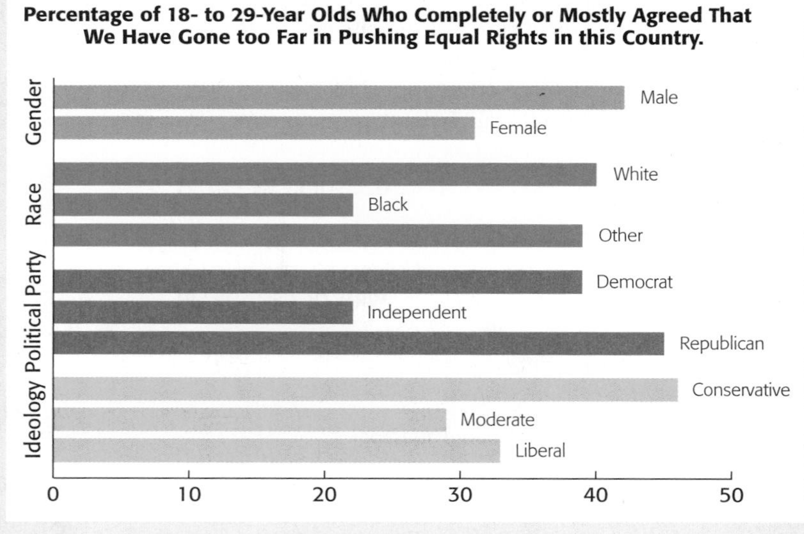

QUESTIONS

1. Why do you think white respondents were more likely than black respondents to say we have gone too far in pushing equal rights?
2. What experiences may Generation Next respondents have had with government enforcement of equal rights?

for crimes has become more severe. However, as the number of appeals has grown, the Supreme Court's discretion to decide which cases it will review has allowed it to hear fewer and fewer cases. Of the 8,857 cases filed for review in the Court's 2006–2007 term, for example, it made decisions on just 74 and in the 2007–2008 term it decided only 70. That is half the number of cases decided annually two decades ago (see Figure 14–5 representing the size of the Supreme Court's docket over time).[19]

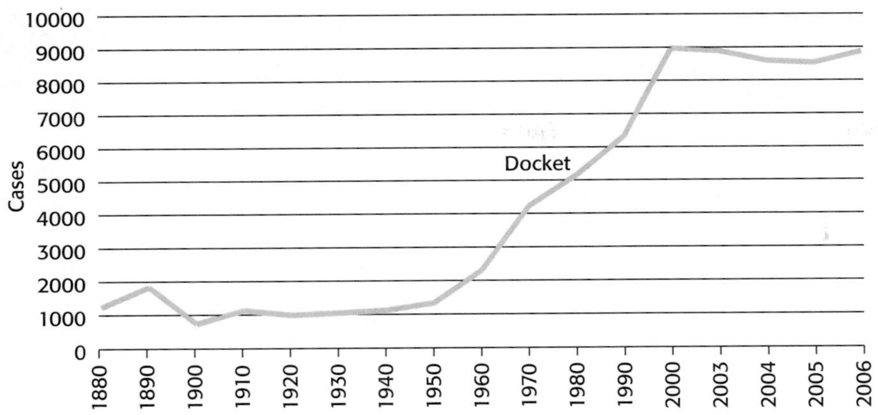

FIGURE 14–5
The Supreme Court Docket.

SOURCE: Lee Epstein, Jeffrey A. Segal, Harold J. Spaeth, and Thomas G. Walker. *The Supreme Court Compendium: Data, Decisions & Developments* (CQ Press, 2007), figures updated by the authors.

2. Granting the Appeal The Supreme Court will review a case only if the claim raises a substantial question of federal or constitutional law with broad public significance—what kinds of affirmative action programs are permissible, whether individuals have a right to doctor-assisted suicide, or under what conditions women may have abortions. The Court also tends to review cases in which the courts of appeals disagree. Or a case may raise a constitutional issue on which a state supreme court has presented an interpretation with which the Court disagrees.

The Court decides whether to move forward based on the *rule of four.* If four justices are sufficiently interested in a petition, it will be granted and the case brought up for review. The justices' law clerks work as a group, in what is known as the *cert pool,* to read the petitions and write a memorandum on each, recommending whether a review should be granted. These memos circulate to all the justices except Justice John Paul Stevens who was on the Court prior to the development of the *cert pool* and still does not take part, and Justice Samuel Alito who opted out of the cent pool in September 2008. Justice Stevens's own law clerks review the petitions for him, and he reads a few of them himself.[20]

Denying a writ of certiorari does not mean the justices agree with the decision of the lower court, nor does it establish precedent. Refusal to grant a review can indicate all kinds of possibilities. The justices may wish to avoid a political "hot potato," or they may be so divided on an issue that they are not yet prepared to take a stand, or they may want to let an issue "percolate" in the federal courts so the Court may benefit from their rulings before it decides.

3. Briefing the Case After a case is granted review, each side prepares written *briefs* presenting legal arguments, relevant precedents, and historical background for the justices and their law clerks to study and on which to base their decisions. Prior decisions by the U.S. Supreme Court itself are most highly desirable as precedent; however, the Court may also consider cases decided by the lower federal courts as well as state supreme courts in reaching its decision, depending on the issue presented.

In writing these briefs, the appellants are often aware of the justices' views or concerns about their case, and they attempt to address those concerns. Indeed, attorneys readily admit that they sometimes frame their brief to appeal to a particular justice on the Court, one they suspect may be the swing, or deciding, vote in the case. Often, outside groups interested in the case file ***amicus curiae* briefs** (Latin for "friend of the court"), through which they can make arguments specific to their members and of interest to the justices.

4. Holding the Oral Argument After the Court grants review, a case is set for oral arguments—briefs must be filed according to a timely schedule and arguments are usually heard within three to four months. Lengthy oratory before the Supreme Court, once lasting for several days, is a thing of the past. As a rule, counsel for each side is now allowed only 30 minutes. Lawyers use a lectern with two lights: A white light flashes five minutes before time is up. When the red light goes on, the lawyer must stop, even in the middle of a sentence.

***amicus curiae* brief**
Literally, a "friend of the court" brief, filed by an individual or organization to present arguments in addition to those presented by the immediate parties to a case.

SIMULATION

You Are a Clerk to Supreme Court Justice Judith Gray

SIMULATION

You Are a Young Lawyer

The entire procedure is informally formal. Sometimes, to the annoyance of attorneys, justices talk among themselves or consult briefs or books during oral arguments. Other times, if justices find a presentation particularly bad, they will tell the attorneys so. Justices freely interrupt the lawyers to ask questions and request additional information. In recent years, "the justices seem barely able to contain themselves, often interrupting the answer to one question with another query."[21] Hence the 30-minute limit can be problematic, especially when the solicitor general participates, because his time comes out of the 30 minutes of the party he is supporting.

If a lawyer is having a difficult time, the justices may try to help out with a question. Occasionally, justices bounce arguments off a hapless attorney and at one another. Justice Antonin Scalia is a harsh questioner. "When Scalia prepares to ask a question, he doesn't just adjust himself in his chair to get closer to the microphone like the others; he looks like a vulture, zooming in for the kill. He strains way forward, pinches his eyebrows, and poses the question, like '...do you want us to believe?'"[22] Justice Ruth Bader Ginsburg is a particularly persistent questioner, frequently rivaling Scalia, whereas Justice Clarence Thomas almost never asks a question at all. (You can hear oral arguments in landmark cases by going to www.oyez.org.)

5. Meeting in Conference When in session, the justices meet on Friday mornings to discuss the cases they heard that week. These conference meetings are private; no one is allowed in the room except the justices themselves. As a result, much of what we know about the justices' conferences come from their own notes taken during the meetings.

The conferences are typically a collegial but vigorous give-and-take. The chief justice presides, usually opening the discussion by stating the facts, summarizing the questions of law, and suggesting how to dispose of each case. Each justice, in order of seniority, then gives his or her views and conclusions. The justices do not typically view this as a time to persuade others of their views on the case; that will come later as drafts of the opinion are circulated between chambers. After each justice has given his or her view of the case, the writing of the majority opinion is assigned. By practice, if the chief justice is in the majority, he can either assign the opinion to a justice also in the majority or choose to write the opinion himself. If he is not in the majority, the most senior justice in the majority makes that determination.

6. Explaining the Decision The Supreme Court announces and explains its decisions in **opinions of the Court.** These opinions are the Court's principal method of expressing its views and reasoning to the world. Their primary function is to instruct judges of state and federal courts how to decide similar cases in the future.

Although the writing is assigned to one justice, the opinion must explain the reasoning of the majority. Consequently, opinions are negotiated documents that require the author to compromise and at times bargain with other justices to attain agreement.[23]

A justice is free to write a **dissenting opinion** if desired. Dissenting opinions are, in Chief Justice Charles Evans Hughes's words, "an appeal to the brooding spirit of the law, to the intelligence of a future day."[24] Dissenting opinions are quite common, as justices hope that someday they will command a majority of the Court. If a justice agrees with the majority on how the case should be decided but differs on the reasoning, that justice may write a **concurring opinion.**

Judicial opinions may also be directed at Congress or at the president. If the Court regrets that "in the absence of action by Congress, we have no choice but to..." or insists that "relief of the sort that petitioner demands can come only from the political branches of government," it is asking Congress to act.[25] Justices also use opinions to communicate with the public. A well-crafted opinion may increase support for a policy the Court favors.

opinion of the Court
An explanation of a decision of the Supreme Court or any other appellate court.

dissenting opinion
An opinion disagreeing with the majority in a Supreme Court ruling.

concurring opinion
An opinion that agrees with the majority in a Supreme Court ruling but differs on the reasoning.

7. Writing the Opinion Writing the opinion of the Court is an exacting task. The document must win the support of at least four—and more, if possible—intelligent, strong-willed persons. Assisted by the law clerks, the assigned justice writes a draft and sends it to colleagues for comments. If the justice is lucky, the majority will accept the draft, perhaps with only minor changes. If the draft is not satisfactory to the other justices, the author must rewrite and recirculate it until a majority reaches agreement.

HISTORY MAKERS

Justice Sandra Day O'Connor

Sandra Day O'Connor was nominated to the Supreme Court by Republican president Ronald Reagan in 1981, was confirmed by the Senate 99 to 0, and became the first woman to serve on the high bench. She was born in El Paso, Texas, grew up on a cattle ranch in Arizona, and graduated at the top of her class at Stanford Law School in the early 1950s.

Justice Sandra Day O'Connor.

Despite her academic achievements, O'Connor could not find a job with any law firm in California and eventually took a post as deputy county attorney in San Mateo County, California. In time, she moved back to Arizona, was elected to the Arizona state legislature, and was appointed to the Arizona Court of Appeals, where she served until her Supreme Court appointment. Almost a quarter of a century later, *Forbes* magazine called her the sixth most powerful woman in the world.*

As a Supreme Court justice, O'Connor was conservative but less hard-line than the other Reagan appointees. She cast the deciding vote on controversial issues such as abortion, affirmative action, minority-majority voting districts, and some disputes over the separation of church and state. She was also a central voice in cases affecting federal–state relations.

However, O'Connor was also a moderating force on controversial issues. During her 24 terms on the Court, she was the swing, or deciding, vote on many cases. As we mentioned in this chapter's introduction, she cast the deciding vote both in favor of the University of Michigan Law School's program for giving disadvantaged minority students special preference in the admissions process, and in favor of abortion rights. Just before she left the court, she cast the deciding vote upholding the constitutionality of campaign finance reform (see Chapter 9).

O'Connor was also one of the most interesting of the justices. She never gave up her love of horses, battled breast cancer early in her Supreme Court career, and became a role model for many women. She was personable, had a sense of humor, and managed to find consensus on most issues. She approached each case carefully, avoiding decisions that might "paint her into a corner" on future decisions, but was often criticized by conservatives for not taking a stronger position against abortion.

QUESTIONS

1. How do you think Justice O'Connor's gender affected her ability to get a job after law school?
2. How do you think Justice O'Connor's experience in the state legislature might have affected her decisions on the Supreme Court?
3. Why do some people argue that it is important to have female justices on the U.S. Supreme Court?

*Elizabeth MacDonald and Chana R. Schoenberger, "The World's 100 Most Powerful Women," *Forbes*, August 20, 2004.

The two weapons that justices can use against their colleagues are their votes and the threat of dissenting opinions attacking the majority's opinion. Especially if the Court is closely divided, one justice may be in a position to demand that a certain point or argument be included in, or removed from, the opinion of the Court as the price of his or her vote. Sometimes such bargaining occurs even though the Court is not closely divided. An opinion writer who anticipates that a decision will invite critical public reaction may want a unanimous Court and compromise to achieve unanimity. For this reason, the Court delayed declaring school segregation unconstitutional, in *Brown v. Board of Education* (1954), until unanimity was secured.[26] The justices understood that any sign of dissension on this major social issue would be an invitation to evade the Court's ruling.

You Are a Supreme Court Justice Deciding a Free Speech Case

8. Releasing the Opinion In the past, justices read their entire opinions from the bench on "opinion days." Now they give only brief summaries of the decision and their opinions. Copies are immediately made available to reporters and the public and published in the official *United States Supreme Court Reports.* Since April 2000, the Court has made its opinions immediately available on its Web site (www.supremecourtus.gov).

Influences on Supreme Court Decisions

LEARNING **OBJECTIVE**

Assess the influences on U.S. Supreme Court decision making.

Given the importance of cases that reach the U.S. Supreme Court, the complexity of the Court's decision-making process is not surprising. Supreme Court precedent is a primary influence, but if it were the only one, the lower courts could resolve the question themselves. Typically there are conflicting precedents, and justices must decide which applies most closely to the legal question at hand.

Outside groups and other legal actors can also influence the Court's decisions. Interest groups' *amicus* briefs may influence a justice's view of the case or the implications of a particular outcome. The chief justice can also affect decision making by the way he frames a case at the conference as well as by his choice of the justice to write the opinion based on the conference vote. Law clerks can affect the Court's decisions by the advice they give their justices, as well as by their role in reviewing the cases appealed to the Court.

Cheif Justice of the Supreme Court

The Chief Justice The chief justice of the United States is appointed by the president and confirmed by the Senate, like other federal judges. Yet the chief justice heads the entire federal judiciary; as a result, he (so far in our history, all have been men) has greater visibility than if selected by rotation of fellow justices, as in the state supreme courts, or by seniority, as in the federal courts of appeals. The chief justice has special administrative responsibilities in overseeing the operation of the judiciary, such as assigning judges to committees, responding to proposed legislation that affects the judiciary, and delivering the Annual Report on the State of the Judiciary.

But within the Supreme Court, the chief justice is only "first among equals," even though periods in Court history (such as the Warren Court) are often named after the chief justice. As Rehnquist said when he was still an associate justice, the chief deals not with "eight subordinates whom he may direct or instruct, but eight associates who, like him, have tenure during good behavior, and who are as independent as hogs on ice."[27] As political scientist David Danelski observes, "The Chief Justiceship does not guarantee leadership. It only offers its incumbent an opportunity to lead." Yet the chief justice "sets the tone, controls the conference, assigns the most opinions, and usually, takes the most important, nation-changing decisions for himself."[28]

Law Clerks Beginning in the 1920s and 1930s, federal judges began hiring the best recent graduates of law schools to serve as clerks for a year or two. As the judicial workload increased, more law clerks were appointed, and today each Supreme Court justice is entitled to four. These are young people who have graduated from a leading law school and have previously clerked for a federal or state court.

Each justice picks his or her own clerks and works closely with them throughout the term. Clerks screen writs of certiorari and prepare draft opinions for the justices.

Chief Justice William Rehnquist (on the left) was very popular among his colleagues, both liberal and conservative. He was known for his general efficiency in running the Court and his fairness in assigning opinions. Here he meets with law clerks in his chambers.

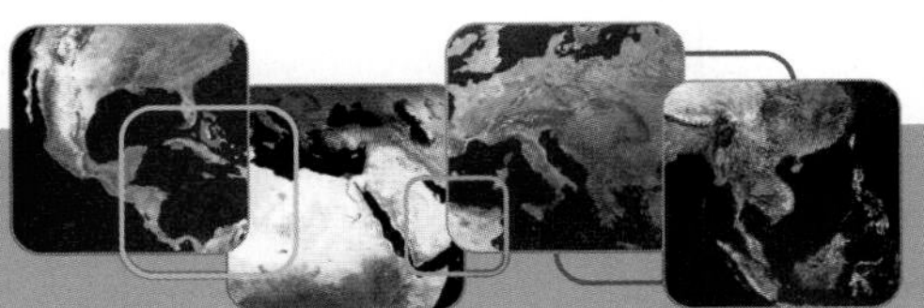

HOW OTHER NATIONS GOVERN

Judicial Independence and Accountability

How to best choose judges is a prominent question across judicial systems. As we know from experience in the United States, finding the right balance between judicial independence and accountability is not an easy task. In many cases we want judges to be independent of political pressures, free to make the most fair and just decisions possible. However, in other cases we may want to hold judges accountable—if, for example, they consistently invoke light prison sentences for convicted criminals, or tend to decide cases in favor of large corporations at the expense of individual plaintiffs. The tension between those competing goals is at the forefront of debate about the best way to pick judicial candidates. Another goal that shapes deliberation on judicial appointment methods is enhancing judicial diversity. Some authors have argued that diversity concerns are more likely to be addressed in democracies in which an independent judiciary is well established, such as the case in the United States. However, in younger or less stable democracies, there is likely to be greater concern with ensuring an independent judiciary than with trying to increase diversity on the bench.*

We should not make the mistake, however, of assuming that a judiciary will lack independence based on the general instability in its political system. Nigeria, for example, has a long history of judicial independence based on the British tradition, though there was an attack on its independence in the late 1990s and it is no longer as clear whether independence is currently secure.

Japan's system is similar to that of Great Britain, Germany, and France. It ensures judicial independence by requiring students interested in the judiciary to take a variety of competitive exams and go through specialized judicial training to become eligible for appointment.

The lack of an independent judiciary has been a long-standing problem in China. Before 1995 many judges lacked any legal education or experience and were simply transferred to the judiciary from military or Communist Party posts. Since 1995 there have been attempts to improve the quality of the judiciary and enhance its independence. Although judges must now have some basic legal education, concerns remain that the process is a political one in which judicial independence is not assured.

QUESTIONS

1. How has the United States tried to balance judicial independence and accountability?
2. Why is judicial independence important in any judicial system?
3. How may having a judicial civil service system affect judicial independence?

*This section draws heavily on Kate Malleson and Peter H. Russell, eds., *Appointing Judges in an Age of Judicial Power: Critical Perspectives from Around the World* (University of Toronto Press, 2006).

As the number of law clerks and computers has increased, so has the number of concurring and dissenting opinions. Today's opinions are longer and have more footnotes and elaborate citations of cases and law review articles. This is the result of the greater number of law clerks and the operation of justices' chambers like "nine little law firms,"often practicing against each other.[29]

Debate swirls about the degree to which law clerks influence the Court's decisions.[30] Some scholars contend that law clerks have had too much influence, especially as they help write early drafts of their justices' opinions. Others contend that justices select clerks with views very similar to their own, so to the extent law clerks are able to advance their views, they reflect those of the justice they serve. Regardless of this disagreement, however, there is widespread acceptance of law clerks' influence in the decision to grant certiorari. Law clerks' dominance at this stage of the decision-making process surely provides them with an opportunity at least to influence the Court's docket.

The Solicitor General Attorneys in the Department of Justice and other federal agencies participate in more than half of the cases the Supreme Court agrees to decide and therefore play a crucial role in setting its agenda. As we noted earlier in this chapter, the solicitor general is responsible for representing the federal government before the Supreme Court and is sometimes called the "tenth justice." Because the U.S. government may not appeal any case upward without the solicitor general's approval, the solicitor general has significant influence over the kinds of cases the Supreme Court eventually sees.[31]

The solicitor general also files *amicus curiae* briefs in cases in which the federal government is not a party. The practice of filing *amicus curiae* briefs guarantees that the Department of Justice is represented if a suit questions the constitutionality of an

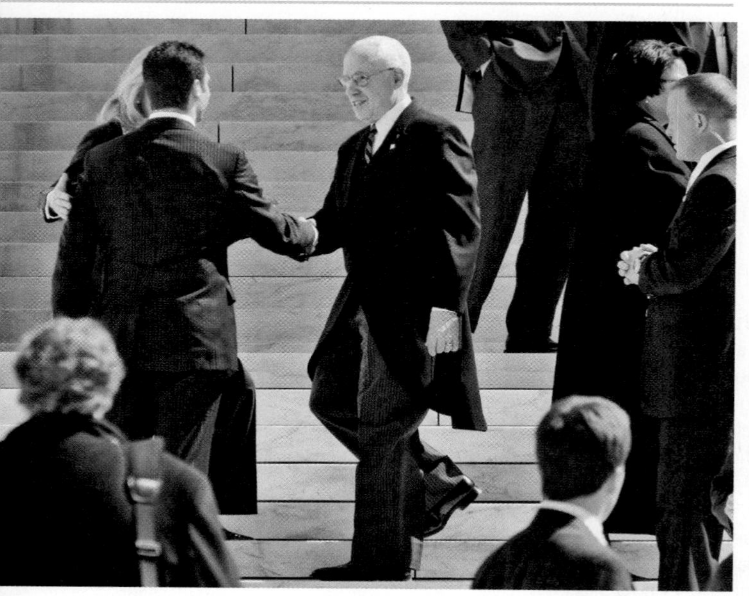

The U.S. Supreme Court is quite tradition bound. For example, when the solicitor general appears before the Court, he wears a traditional vest, morning coat, and striped pants. The same applies on the rare occasion when the attorney general appears before the Court, as General Michael Mukasey did in 2008.

act of Congress or the executive branch. The solicitor general may also use these briefs to bring to the Court's attention the views of the current administration.

Citizens and Interested Parties Citizens, interest groups, and organizations may also file *amicus curiae* briefs if they claim to have an interest in the case and information of value to the Court.[32] An *amicus* brief may help the justices by presenting arguments or facts the parties to the case have not raised. In recent decades, interest groups have increasingly filed such briefs in an effort to influence the Court and to counter the positions of the solicitor general and the government. For example, in *Webster v. Reproductive Health Services* (1989), dealing with a Missouri law regulating abortions and asking the Court to reverse the abortion ruling *Roe v. Wade* (1973), 78 *amicus* briefs were filed.[33] Interest groups may also file *amicus curiae* briefs to encourage the Supreme Court to review a case, though this strategy has almost no influence on how the case is decided.[34]

After the Court Decides

Victory in the Supreme Court does not necessarily mean that winning parties get what they want. Although the Court resolves many issues, it also sometimes *remands* the case, sending it back to the lower court with instructions to act in accordance with its opinion. The lower court often has considerable leeway in interpreting the Court's mandate as it disposes of the case.

The impact of a particular Supreme Court ruling on the behavior of individuals who are not immediate parties to a lawsuit is more uncertain. The most important rulings require a change in the behavior of thousands of administrative and elected officials. Sometimes Supreme Court pronouncements are simply ignored. For example, despite the Court's holding that it is unconstitutional for school boards to require students to pray within a school, some schools continue this practice.[35] And for years after the Supreme Court held public school segregation unconstitutional, many school districts refused to integrate or even closed their public school system, as in Prince Edward County, Virginia, so as to avoid integration.[36]

The most difficult Supreme Court decisions to implement are those that require the cooperation of large numbers of officials. For example, a Supreme Court decision announcing a new standard for property searches is not likely to have an impact on the way police make arrests for some time, because not many police officers subscribe to *United States Supreme Court Reports.* The process is more complex. Local prosecutors, state attorneys general, chiefs of police, and state and federal trial court judges must all participate to give meaning to Supreme Court decisions. The Constitution may be what the Supreme Court says it is, but a Supreme Court opinion, for the moment at least, is what a trial judge or police officer or prosecutor or school board or city council says it is.

LEARNING **OBJECTIVE**

7 Compare and contrast the limits on judicial action.

Limits on Judicial Action

Although the framers worked hard to create an independent federal judiciary, judges are limited in that they cannot ignore earlier decisions unless they have a clear reason to break with the past.

Adherence to Precedent

Just because judges make independent decisions does not mean they are free to do whatever they wish. They are subject to a variety of limits on what they decide—some imposed by the political system of which they are a part and some imposed by higher courts and the legal profession. Among these constraints is the policy of **stare decisis,** the rule of precedent.

Stare decisis pervades our judicial system and promotes certainty, uniformity, and stability in the law. Drawn from the Latin phrase "to stand by that which is decided," the term means that judges are expected to abide by previous decisions of their own courts and by rulings of superior courts. The doctrine is not very restrictive.[37] Indeed, lower-court judges sometimes apply precedents selectively, to raise additional questions about an earlier higher-court decision or to give the higher courts a chance to change a precedent entirely.

Stare decisis is even less controlling in the field of constitutional law. Because the Constitution itself, rather than any one interpretation of it, is binding, the Court can *reverse* a previous decision it no longer wishes to follow, as it has done hundreds of times. Supreme Court justices are therefore not seriously restricted by stare decisis. Liberal justice William O. Douglas, for one, maintained that stare decisis "was really no sure guideline because what did the judges who sat there in 1875 know about, say, electronic surveillance? They didn't know anything about it."[38] Rehnquist was no less candid in holding that precedents dealing with civil rights that were handed down on a 5-to-4 vote should always be open for reconsideration, because they were decided by only a bare majority of the Court. Since 1789, the Supreme Court has reversed almost 200 of its own decisions and overturned more than 170 acts of Congress, as well as nearly 1,300 state constitutional and legislative provisions and municipal ordinances.[39]

Precedents do not govern judicial decisions forever, however. Otherwise, the nation would still be racially segregated. Having ruled that separate-but-equal accommodations on railway cars were perfectly legal in 1896, the Court allowed states to set up a host of segregated systems that included separate public schools, public drinking fountains, and sections for whites and minorities on buses. It took over 50 years for the Court to reverse itself and rule that separate-but-equal schools violated the Constitution.

Many Court observers expect the more conservative justices appointed during both Bush administrations to continue to move the law away from the right to abortion established in *Roe v. Wade* in 1973. Although they do not expect the Court to overturn the decision in a single, sweeping case, they do expect it to chip away at the precedent as more limited opportunities come before it.[40] The Court did just that when it upheld the federal Partial-Birth Abortion Ban Act in 2007. Although the act affected only late-term abortion procedures, the Court for the first time upheld an abortion restriction that did not provide an exception for the woman's health.[41]

Congressional and Presidential Action

Individual judges are protected from Congress and the president by their life tenure, but the judiciary as a whole can be affected by legislative decisions that alter both the number and the composition of the courts. Because the district and circuit courts are both created through legislation, they can be expanded or altered through legislation.

Changing the Numbers One of the first actions a political party takes after gaining control of the White House and Congress is often to increase the number of federal judgeships. With divided government, however, when one party controls Congress and the other holds the White House, a stalemate is likely to occur, and relatively few new judicial positions will be created. During Andrew Johnson's administration, Congress went so far as to reduce the size of the Supreme Court to prevent the president from filling two vacancies. After Johnson left the White House, Congress returned the Court to its former size to permit Ulysses S. Grant to fill the vacancies.

In 1937, President Franklin Roosevelt proposed an increase in the size of the Supreme Court by one additional justice for every member of the Court over age 70, up to a total of 15 members. Ostensibly, the proposal was aimed at making the Court more efficient. In fact, Roosevelt and his advisers were frustrated because the Court had declared much of the early New Deal legislation unconstitutional. Despite Roosevelt's popularity, his "court-packing scheme" aroused intense opposition and his

stare decisis
The rule of precedent, whereby a rule or law contained in a judicial decision is commonly viewed as binding on judges whenever the same question is presented.

proposal failed. Although he lost the battle, the Court began to sustain some important New Deal legislation, and subsequent retirements from the bench enabled him to make eight appointments to the Court.

Changing the Jurisdiction Congressional control over the structure and jurisdiction of federal courts has been used to influence the course of judicial policy making. Although unable to get rid of Federalist judges by impeachment, Jefferson's Republican party abolished the circuit courts created by the Federalist Congress just before it lost control of Congress. In 1869, radical Republicans in Congress altered the Supreme Court's appellate jurisdiction in order to remove a case it was about to review weighing the constitutionality of some Reconstruction legislation.[42]

Each year, a number of bills are introduced in Congress to eliminate the jurisdiction of federal courts over cases relating to abortion, school prayer, and school busing, or to eliminate the appellate jurisdiction of the Supreme Court over such matters. These attacks on federal court jurisdiction spark debate about whether the Constitution gives Congress authority to take such actions. Congress has not yet decided to do so, because it would amount to a fundamental shift in the relationship between Congress and the Supreme Court. As one scholar concluded, "History suggests the public has seen such attempts for precisely what they are, as attacks on judicial independence, and such attacks have been resisted."[43]

Judicial Power in a Constitutional Democracy

An independent judiciary is one of the hallmarks of a constitutional democracy and a free society. As impartial dispensers of equal justice under the law, judges should not depend on the executive, the legislature, parties to a case, or the electorate. But judicial independence is often criticized when judges make unpopular decisions. Perhaps in no other society do the people resort to litigation as a means of making public policy as much as they do in the United States. For example, the National Association for the Advancement of Colored People (NAACP) turned to litigation to get relief from segregation practices in the 1930s, 1940s, and 1950s. More recently, an increasing number of women's organizations, environmental groups, and religious and conservative organizations have also turned to the courts.[44]

LEARNING **OBJECTIVE**

8 Assess the role of the judiciary in a constitutional democracy.

The Great Debate over the Proper Role of the Courts

Whether judges are liberal or conservative, defer to legislatures or not, try to apply the Constitution as they think the framers intended or interpret it to conform to current values, there are links between what judges do and what the people want done. The people never speak with one mind and the links are not direct, but they are the heart of the matter.[45] In the first place, the president and the Senate are likely to appoint justices whose decisions reflect their values. Therefore, elections matter, because the views of the people who nominate and confirm the judges are reflected in the composition and decisions of the courts. For instance, in *Planned Parenthood v. Casey* in 1992, the Supreme Court refused 5-to-4 to overturn *Roe v. Wade* and upheld its core ruling—that the Constitution protects the right of a woman to an abortion—although it also upheld state regulations that do not "unduly burden" that right.[46] This close vote made it clear that presidential elections could determine whether the right to abortion would continue to be protected.

"American courts are not all-powerful institutions."[47] If the Court's policies are too far out of step with the values of the country, the Court is likely to be criticized. In former chief justice William H. Rehnquist's words, "No judge worthy of his salt would ever cast his vote in a particular case simply because he thought the majority of the public wanted him to vote that way, but that is quite a different thing from saying that no judge is ever influenced by the great tides of public opinion that run a country such as ours."[48]

"The people" speak in many ways and with many voices. The Supreme Court's closely split decisions in controversial cases often reflect the closely divided views of the general public on those issues as well. The Supreme Court—and the other courts—thus generally represent and reflect the competing values of the people. Whether they agree or disagree with particular rulings, the public generally holds the Supreme Court in high regard. Notably, the Court's public approval rating remained high and virtually unchanged after its controversial decision in *Bush v. Gore* (2000), contrary to predictions by the four dissenting justices and critics that the Court's reputation would be badly damaged by the bare majority's ruling ensuring George W. Bush's election.[49]

Although the Court is not the defenseless institution portrayed by some commentators, and its decisions are as much shapers of public opinion as reflections of it, ultimately the power of the Supreme Court in a constitutional democracy rests on retaining the support of most of the people most of the time. If we as citizens oppose the Court's decisions, we have several avenues through which we can make our opposition known. By communicating with members of Congress, we can pressure them to pass legislation that limits the Court's ruling, as Congress did when it passed the Military Commissions Act of 2006 in reaction to the Supreme Court's ruling in *Hamdan v. Rumsfeld* (2006). We can organize to oppose a particular nomination to the federal judiciary, as many citizens did in response to Judge Robert Bork's nomination to the Supreme Court in 1986. When making our voting decisions, we can also consider the kinds of judges a presidential candidate is likely to appoint to the federal judiciary. In these ways and others, we can affect even our federal courts. The Court's power rests, as former chief justice Edward White observed, "solely upon the approval of a free people."[50] No better standard for determining the legitimacy of a governmental institution has been discovered.

CHAPTER **SUMMARY**

1 Analyze the implications of the adversarial process.

The courts provide a neutral arena in which two parties argue their differences and present evidence supporting those views before an impartial judge. As a result, the courts are largely *reactive;* judges have to wait for parties to a case to bring issues before the courts.

2 Explain the structure of the federal court system.

There are three levels of federal courts: (1) district courts, which hear original trials, (2) circuit courts of appeal, which can only review the process by which district courts made their decisions, and (3) the Supreme Court, which makes the final decision.

3 Evaluate factors important in appointing judicial nominees.

Partisanship and ideology are important factors in the selection of all federal judges. In making appointments to the federal courts, presidents must also consider the confirmation environment. They act strategically in selecting a candidate and consulting with Congress. In recent decades, candidates for the presidency and the Senate have made judicial appointments an issue in their election campaigns.

4 Compare and contrast arguments in favor of and against judicial activism.

According to democratic theory, the federal judiciary, composed of unelected judges secure in life-tenure from public pressure, has a responsibility to use restraint in reaching decisions. Others argue that the court's ability to take such action is an important check on the tyranny of the majority.

5 Describe the process of reaching a decision in the U.S. Supreme Court.

The Supreme Court has almost complete control over the cases it chooses to review as they come up from the state courts, the courts of appeals, and district courts. Law clerks and the solicitor general play important roles in determining the kinds of cases the Supreme Court agrees to decide. Its nine justices dispose of thousands of cases, but most of their time is concentrated on the fewer than 90 cases per year they accept for review. The Court's decisions and opinions establish guidelines for lower courts and the country.

6 Assess the influences on U.S. Supreme Court decision making.

In addition to Supreme Court precedent and justices' own preferences, a number of actors may influence the decision-making process. Law clerks often write early drafts of justices' opinions. *Amicus* participants and the solicitor general's office sometimes affect the opinion-writing process through the briefs they file, as well as through points made during oral argument before the Court.

and contrast the limits on judicial action.

n the federal judiciary is largely independent, factors s *stare decisis,* the appointment process, congres- al control over its structure and jurisdiction and the need for the other branches of government to implement its decisions limit the degree to which the courts can, or are likely to act without the support of the other branches.

8 Assess the role of the judiciary in a constitutional democracy.

As impartial dispensers of equal justice under the law, judges should not depend on the executive, the legislature, the parties to a case, or the electorate. But judicial independence is often criticized when judges make unpopular decisions.

Chapter Self-Test

1. List and explain 3 potentially negative consequences of the adversarial process. (p. 385)
2. In a criminal action, the ______ is the person or party accused of an offense. (p. 385)
   a. plaintiff
   b. defendant
   c. public defender
   d. judge magistrate
3. Match the following terms to their definitions(p. 385)

   a) plea bargain
   b) adversary system
   c) justiciable disputes

   i) Lawsuits that grow out of actual controversies and are capable of judicial resolution
   ii) System that holds arguing over law and evidence, which may or may not arrive at the truth, guarantees fairness in the judicial system
   iii) System whereby defendants agree to plead guilty to a lesser crime to avoid having to stand trial and face a sentence for a more serious crime.
4. Draw a diagram of the federal court system. (p. 386–388)
5. In a short essay, explain why the judicial nomination process can be so contentious. (pp. 388–394)
6. Examine Figure 14–4 (on page 395). Who are the important actors at each stage in the process and why are they important? (pp. 394–402)
7. Match the following terms to their definitions (pp. 386–387)

   a) precedent
   b) Court of Appeals
   c) original jurisdiction
   d) appellate jurisdiction

   i) The authority of a court to hear a case "in the first instance."
   ii) The authority of a court to review decisions made by the lower courts
   iii) A court with appellate jurisdiction that hears appeals from the decisions of lower courts
   iv) A decision made by a higher court such as the Supreme Court that is binding on all other federal courts
8. Define **amicus curiae.** (p. 397)
9. Write 3 to 4 sentences describing a situation in which an amicus brief might be influential. (pp. 397–402)
10. Define **stare decisis.** Give one real-life example that illustrates this principle. (pp. 402–403)
11. Write a brief essay distinguishing judicial activism from judicial restraint. How are they similar? In what ways are they different? (pp. 396–397)
12. Write a short essay detailing the role of the judiciary in our constitutional system. Could the system function without the judiciary? What adjustments would have to be made? (pp. 404–405)
13. Which Article to the U.S. Constitution established the judicial branch of government? (p. 386)
    a. I
    b. II
    c. III
    d. IV

Key Terms

judicial review, p. 384
adversary system, p. 385
criminal law, p. 385
civil law, p. 385
defendant, p. 385
plea bargain, p. 385
justiciable dispute, p. 385
plaintiff, p. 385
solicitor general, p. 386
public defender system, p. 386
original jurisdiction, p. 386
appellate jurisdiction, p. 386

court of appeals, p. 387

precedent, p. 387

writ of habeas corpus, p. 388

senatorial courtesy, p. 389

judicial activism, p. 392

judicial restraint, p. 392

writ of certiorari, p. 395

in forma pauperis, p. 395

docket, p. 395

***amicus curiae* brief,** p. 397

opinion of the Court, p. 398

dissenting opinion, p. 398

concurring opinion, p. 398

stare decisis, p. 403

Further Reading

HENRY J. ABRAHAM, *Justices, Presidents, and Senators: A History of U.S. Supreme Court Appointments from Washington to Bush II, 5th ed.* (Rowman & Littlefield, 2008).

ROBERT A. CARP AND **RONALD STIDHAM,** *The Federal Courts* (CQ Press, 2001).

CORNELL CLAYTON AND **HOWARD GILMAN,** EDS., *Supreme Court Decision Making: New Institutionalist Approaches* (University of Chicago Press, 1999).

DEL DICKSON, *The Supreme Court in Conference, 1940–1995* (Oxford University Press, 2001).

LEE EPSTEIN AND **JEFFREY A. SEGAL,** *Advice and Consent: The Politics of Judicial Appointments* (Oxford University Press, 2005).

LEE EPSTEIN, JEFFREY A. SEGAL, HAROLD SPAETH, AND **THOMAS WALKER,** EDS., *The Supreme Court Compendium,* 4th ed. (CQ Press, 2007).

HOWARD GILLMAN, *The Votes That Counted: How the Court Decided the 2000 Presidential Election* (University of Chicago Press, 2001).

SHELDON GOLDMAN, *Picking Federal Judges: Lower Court Selection from Roosevelt Through Reagan* (Yale University Press, 1997).

KERMIT L. HALL AND **KEVIN T. MCGUIRE,** EDS., *Institutions of American Democracy: The Judicial Branch* (Oxford University Press, 2005).

PETER IRONS, *A People's History of the Supreme Court* (Viking Press, 1999).

RANDOLPH JONAKAIT, *The American Jury System* (Yale University Press, 2003).

DAVID KLEIN, *Making Law in the U.S. Courts of Appeals* (Cambridge University Press, 2002).

LISA KLOPPENBERG, *Playing It Safe: How the Supreme Court Sidesteps Hard Cases and Stunts the Development of the Law* (New York University Press, 2001).

FOREST MALTZMAN, JAMES F. SPRIGGS II, AND **PAUL J. WAHLBECK,** *Crafting Law on the Supreme Court: The Collegial Game* (Cambridge University Press, 2000).

ROBERT G. MCCLOSKEY, *The American Supreme Court,* 3d ed. (University of Chicago Press, 2001).

CHRISTINE NEMACHECK, *Strategic Selection: Presidential Nomination of Supreme Court Justices from Herbert Hoover Through George W. Bush* (University of Virginia Press, 2007).

DAVID M. O'BRIEN, ED., *Judges on Judging: Views from the Bench,* 2d ed. (CQ Press, 2004).

DAVID M. O'BRIEN, *Storm Center: The Supreme Court in American Politics,* 7th ed. (Norton, 2005).

J. W. PELTASON, *Federal Courts in the Political Process* (Doubleday, 1955).

TODD C. PEPPERS, *Courtiers of the Marble Palance: The Rise and Influence of the Supreme Court Law Clerk* (Stanford University Press, 2006).

TERRI JENNINGS PERETTI, *In Defense of a Political Court* (Princeton University Press, 1999).

GERALD N. ROSENBERG, *The Hollow Hope: Can Courts Bring About Social Change?* (University of Chicago Press, 1991).

PETER RUSSELL AND **DAVID M. O'BRIEN,** EDS., *Judicial Independence in the Age of Democracy: Critical Perspectives from Around the World* (University Press of Virginia, 2001).

ELLIOT E. SLOTNICK, *Judicial Politics: Readings from Judicature,* 3d ed. (American Judicature Society, 2005).

DONALD R. SONGER, REGINALD S. SHEEHAN, AND **SUSAN B. HAIRE,** *Continuity and Change on the United States Courts of Appeals* (University of Michigan Press, 2000).

ARTEMUS WARD REGINALD S. SHEEHAN, AND **DAVID L. WEIDEN,** *Sorcerers' Apprentices: 100 Years of Law Clerks at the United States Supreme Court* (New York University Press, 2006).

chapter 15

Civil Liberties

Protections Under the Bill of Rights

On January 24, 2002, Joseph Frederick, an 18-year-old senior at Juneau-Douglas High School in Juneau, Alaska, set off for the Olympic Torch Relay, where he had a plan to get on television. Frederick's plan was to unfurl a nearly 14-foot banner across the street from his high school as the Torch Relay passed by. Using duct tape, Frederick had written "Bong Hits 4 Jesus" across the banner.

Seeing Frederick's banner, Juneau-Douglas principal Deborah Morse directed Frederick and his fellow students to take it down. Although the other students complied with Morse's instruction, Frederick did not. Morse then took the banner from Frederick. In a meeting in her office later that afternoon, Morse suspended Frederick from school for ten days. Frederick challenged his suspension and Morse's restriction on his speech. After losing appeals to the school's superintendent and school board, Frederick brought suit in federal district court on the grounds that that school had impermissibly restricted his constitutional right to free speech.

The federal district and appeals courts reached conflicting decisions, and the U.S. Supreme Court decided to hear the case during its October 2006 term. Some five and a half years after Frederick unfurled his banner, the Supreme Court ruled that Principal Morse and the Juneau-Douglas school district acted appropriately, because the banner could reasonably have been seen as promoting illicit drug use.

Nearly 40 years before the Court's decision in *Morse v. Frederick* (2007), the U.S. Supreme Court had determined that students did not "shed their constitutional rights to freedom of speech or expression at the schoolhouse gate" (*Tinker v. Des Moines* [1969]). But, as has been demonstrated frequently, constitutional protection of fundamental rights is not absolute, save perhaps for freedom of belief or conscience. Under certain circumstances, such as speech that threatens national security, even our most fundamental rights can be restricted.

In this chapter we examine the fundamental liberties protected in a free society. These include freedom of speech and assembly, the right to practice one's religion without government interference, the right to bear arms, the right to be free from unreasonable searches and seizures, the right to be free from self-incrimination and double jeopardy, and the right to be represented by an attorney in a criminal proceeding. These freedoms are essential to self-determination and self-governance—to government by the people. Yet they have also been vulnerable during times of war and, many would argue, are now threatened because of security measures put into place to combat international terrorism.[1] Regardless of the times, however, these liberties mean nothing if citizens do not challenge the government when they think it has impermissibly limited those freedoms. Unless we act as caretakers of our liberties, we lose them.

LEARNING **OBJECTIVES**

1. Evaluate the arguments for amending a Bill of Rights to the original Constitution.
2. Identify protections under the establishment and free exercise clauses of the Constitution.
3. Contrast the categories of protected and unprotected speech.
4. Compare and contrast procedural and substantive due process.
5. Analyze the degree to which criminal suspects' rights are protected in our criminal justice system.

CHAPTER **OUTLINE**

- Rights in the Original Constitution
- The Bill of Rights and the States
- First Amendment Freedoms
- Property Rights
- Due Process Rights
- Privacy Rights
- Rights of Criminal Suspects
- The Death Penalty
- Protecting Our Civil Liberties: Whose Responsibility?

Comparing Civil Liberties

Rights in the Original Constitution

Even though most of the framers did not think a bill of rights was necessary, they considered certain rights important enough to spell them out in the Constitution (see Table 15–1).

Foremost among constitutional rights, and deserving of particular mention here, is the **writ of habeas corpus.** Literally meaning "you have the body" in Latin, this writ is a court order directing any official holding a person in custody to produce the prisoner in court and explain why the prisoner is being held. As originally used in England, the writ was merely a judicial inquiry to determine whether a court had the proper jurisdiction to hold a person in custody. But over the years, it developed into a remedy for any illegal confinement. People who are incarcerated have the right to appeal to a judge, usually through an attorney, stating why they believe they are being held unlawfully and should be released. The judge then orders the jailer or a lower court to show cause why the writ should not be issued. If a judge finds that a petitioner is detained unlawfully, the judge may order the prisoner's immediate release.

writ of habeas corpus
A court order requiring explanation to a judge why a prisoner is being held in custody.

The Supreme Court has recently underscored the fundamental nature of the right to a writ of *habeas corpus* in two decisions. In both, the Court rejected the Bush administration's position that it could indefinitely hold foreign nationals and U.S. citizens deemed "enemy combatants" in its war against terrorism. The Court held that detainees have a right to have an independent tribunal review why they are being held.[2] Subsequently, in *Hamdan v. Rumsfeld* (2006),[3] the Court rebuffed the Bush administration's position that it had the authority to try enemy combatants by military commissions, rather than in civilian courts or in court martial, and that it could ignore the Geneva Conventions that specify that the accused has a right to see and hear the evidence for alleged crimes. In the aftermath of the Court's decision in *Hamdan,* Congress passed the Military Commissions Act of 2006, providing for enemy combatants' trial before military commission.

Hamdan's case is currently proceeding through the military commission system, but in its 2008 decision in *Boumediene v. Bush,* the Supreme Court stood firm in its holding that Guantanamo Bay detainees have the right to pursue *habeas* review in the federal courts. In doing so, the Court struck down as unconstitutional the section of the Military Commissions Act barring the federal courts from hearing enemy combatants' *habeas corpus* petitions.[4]

Although the Court has emphasized the importance of *habeas corpus* generally, it has restricted its use, particularly for *habeas* appeals made by prisoners in the state criminal justice system. In these cases, the number of appeals has been restricted and the federal courts must defer to state judges unless their decisions were clearly "unreasonable."[5]

TABLE 15–1 Rights in the Original Constitution

1. Habeas corpus
2. No bills of attainder
3. No ex post facto laws
4. No titles of nobility
5. Trial by jury in national courts
6. Protection for citizens as they move from one state to another, including the right to travel
7. Protection against using the crime of treason to restrict other activities; limitation on punishment for treason
8. Guarantee that each state has a republican form of government
9. No religious test oaths as a condition for holding a federal office
10. Protection against the impairment of contracts

The Constitution also bars **ex post facto laws,** retroactive criminal laws making an act a crime that was not a crime when it was committed, increasing the punishment for a crime after it was committed, or reducing the proof necessary to convict for a crime after it was committed. However, the prohibition does not restrict retroactive application of a law that benefits an accused person, such as decreasing the punishment for a particular crime; nor does it apply to civil laws.

The Bill of Rights and the States

The liberties we address in this chapter did not appear in the original Constitution. The Bill of Rights, the first ten amendments to the Constitution, was added in 1791. Before we delve into a discussion of these freedoms we'll clarify several terms—*liberties, freedoms, rights,* and *privileges*—often used interchangeably when discussing rights and freedoms.

Civil liberties are the constitutionally protected freedoms of all persons against governmental restraint: the freedoms of conscience, religion, and expression, for example, secured by the First Amendment. The due process clauses of the Fifth and Fourteenth Amendments also protect these civil liberties. *Civil rights* are the constitutional rights of all persons, not just citizens, to due process and the equal protection of the laws: the constitutional right not to be discriminated against by governments because of race, ethnic background, religion, or gender. These civil rights are protected by the due process and equal protection clauses of the Fifth and Fourteenth Amendments and by the civil rights laws of national and state governments. We discuss them further in Chapter 16. *Legal privileges* are granted by governments and may be subject to conditions or restrictions; for example, the right to welfare benefits or to a driver's license.

The Constitution drawn up in Philadelphia included guarantees of a few basic rights discussed previously, but lacked a specific bill of rights similar to those in most state constitutions. The Federalists argued that the Constitution established a limited government that would not threaten individual freedoms, and therefore a bill of rights was unnecessary. But, to persuade delegates to the state ratification conventions to vote for the Constitution, the Federalists promised to correct this deficiency. Thus while the framers wrote the Constitution, it was the people who insisted on our Bill of Rights. In its first session, the new Congress made good on that promise by proposing 12 amendments, 10 of which were promptly ratified by the states and became part of the Constitution.[6]

LEARNING **OBJECTIVE**

1 Evaluate the arguments for amending a Bill of Rights to the original Constitution.

The guarantees of the Bill of Rights originally applied *only to the national government,* not to state governments.[7] Why not to the states? The framers were confident that citizens could control their own state officials, and most state constitutions already had bills of rights. Furthermore, it would not have been politically feasible for the new Constitution to restrict state governments in this way. It was the new and distant central government the people feared. As it turned out, those fears were largely misdirected. The national government has generally shown less tendency to curtail civil liberties than state and local governments have.

It was not until the Fourteenth Amendment was adopted in 1868 that there became a way for the restrictions in the Bill of Rights to be applied to the states. Because the Fourteenth Amendment applies explicitly to the states, supporters contended that its **due process clause**—declaring that no person shall be deprived by a state of life, liberty, or property without due process of law—limits states in precisely the same way the Bill of Rights limits the national government. But for decades, the Supreme Court refused to interpret the Fourteenth Amendment in this way. Then in *Gitlow v. New York* (1925), the Court reversed this trend and decided that when fundamental liberties, such as the "freedom of speech and of the press—which are protected by the First Amendment from abridgment by Congress"—are at stake, the due process clause of the Fourteenth Amendment prohibits the state from infringing on those liberties just as the First Amendment prohibits Congress.[8]

ex post facto law
A retroactive criminal law that works to the disadvantage of a person.

due process clause
A clause in the Fifth Amendment limiting the power of the national government; a similar clause in the Fourteenth Amendment prohibiting state governments from depriving any person of life, liberty, or property without due process of law.

The freedoms protected by the First Amendment, such as freedom of religion and the separation of religion and government, sometimes clash in the opinion of citizens. Here supporters of allowing public displays of the Ten Commandments on government property protest in front of the Supreme Court.

Gitlow v. New York was a revolutionary decision. For the first time, the U.S. Constitution was interpreted to protect freedom of speech from abridgment by state and local governments. This landmark decision changed the balance of federalism in the United States. State actions that deprived citizens of fundamental liberties could now be challenged as a constitutional violation. In the 1930s and continuing at an accelerated

TABLE 15–2 Selective Incorporation and the Application of the Bill of Rights to the States

Right	Amendment	Year
Public use and just compensation for the taking of private property by the government	5	1897
Freedom of speech	1	1925
Freedom of the press	1	1931
Fair trial	6	1932
Freedom of religion	1	1934
Freedom of assembly	1	1937
Free exercise of religion	1	1940
Separation of religion and government	1	1947
Right to a public trial	6	1948
Right against unreasonable searches and seizures	4	1949
Freedom of association	1	1958
Exclusionary rule	4	1961
Ban against cruel and unusual punishment	8	1962
Right to counsel in felony cases	6	1963
Right against self-incrimination	5	1964
Right to confront witness	6	1965
Right of privacy	1, 3, 4, 5, 9	1965
Right to an impartial jury	6	1966
Right to a speedy trial and compulsory process for obtaining witnesses	6	1967
Right to a jury trial in nonpetty cases	6	1968
Protection against double jeopardy	5	1969

pace during the 1960s, through the **selective incorporation** of provision after provision of the Bill of Rights into the due process clause, the Supreme Court applied the most important of these rights to the states.[9] Today the Fourteenth Amendment imposes on the states all the provisions of the Bill of Rights except those of the Second and Third Amendments, the Fifth Amendment provision for indictment by a grand jury, the Seventh Amendment right to a jury trial in civil cases, and the Ninth and Tenth Amendments (see Table 15–2).

Selective incorporation of most provisions of the Bill of Rights into the Fourteenth Amendment is probably the most significant constitutional development that has occurred since the Constitution was written. It has profoundly altered the relationship between the national government and the states. It has made the federal courts, under the guidance of the Supreme Court, the most important protectors of our liberties—not the individual states.

First Amendment Freedoms

Freedom of Religion

LEARNING **OBJECTIVE**

2 Identify protections under the establishment and free exercise clauses of the Constitution.

The first words of the First Amendment are emphatic and brief: "Congress shall make no law respecting an establishment of religion, or prohibiting the free exercise thereof." Though terse, it contains two important clauses: the *establishment* clause and the *free exercise* clause. Part of what makes religious liberties questions so interesting and difficult is that these clauses are often in tension with one another. Does a state scholarship for blind students given to a college student who decides to attend a college to become a clergy member violate the establishment clause by indirectly aiding religion? Or would denying the scholarship violate the student's free exercise of religion? To answer these questions, the Supreme Court has to balance the competing clauses of the First Amendment. The justices must determine how far the government can go to protect a citizen's right to freely exercise his or her religious beliefs without going so far as to establish religion. In dealing with the questions posed here, the Supreme Court ruled that providing such scholarship benefits does not go so far as to violate the establishment clause, but neither does the free exercise clause require that states provide the benefits.[10]

selective incorporation
The process by which provisions of the Bill of Rights are brought within the scope of the Fourteenth Amendment and so applied to state and local governments.

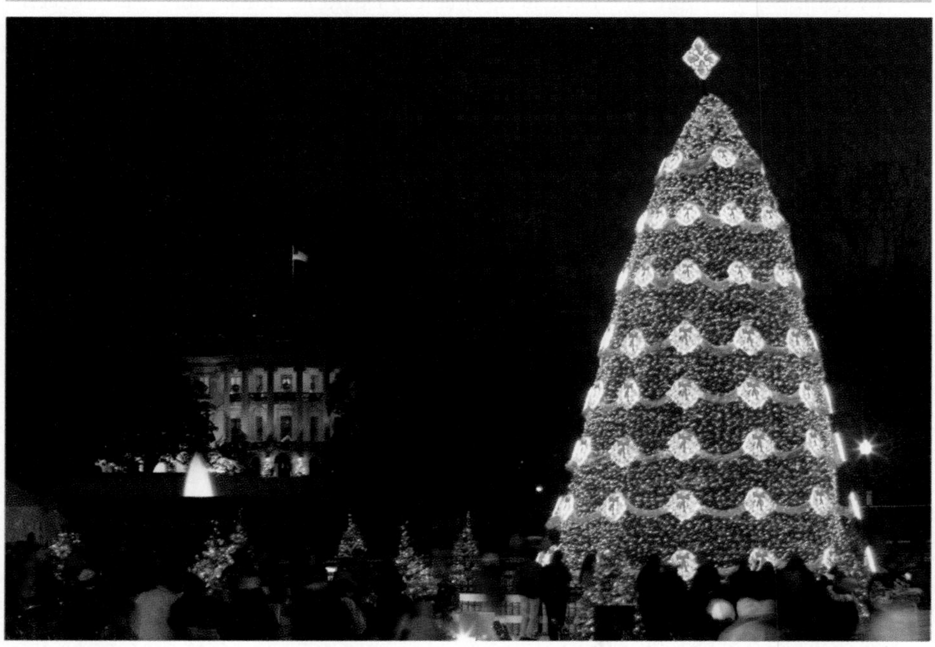

One of the questions the Supreme Court has had to answer is whether public religious displays such as the White House Christmas tree impermissibly violate the First Amendment establishment clause. The Court has said they do not.

The Establishment Clause In writing what has come to be called the **establishment clause,** the framers were reacting to the English system, wherein the crown was (and still is) the head not only of the government but also of the established church—the Church of England—and public officials were required to take an oath to support the established church as a condition of holding office. At least partly because of the brevity of the establishment clause, there is much debate as to its meaning. Some, such as the late chief justice William Rehnquist, contend it means *only* that the government cannot establish an official national religion, nor prefer one sect or denomination over another.[11] Others argue that it requires the government to maintain neutrality, not only among religious denominations, but between religion and nonreligion.

Those who favor government neutrality regarding religion use the metaphor of a "wall of separation" to explain the strict separation between government and religion the clause requires. The metaphor was the basis for the Supreme Court's opinion in *Everson v. Board of Education of Ewing Township* (1947). The Court's 5- to-4 decision in the case, allowing government funds to reimburse parents for transporting children to private religious schools, is indicative of the confusion over the establishment clause. All nine justices agreed that the wall of separation was the appropriate interpretation of the clause, yet they divided 5 to 4 on whether the township's action violated that test.[12]

The Court's use of the wall of separation was hardly its last attempt at resolving debate over the establishment clause's interpretation. In *Lemon v. Kurtzman* (1971), the Court laid down the three-part *Lemon* test. To pass constitutional muster, (1) a law must have a secular legislative purpose, (2) it must neither advance nor inhibit religion, and (3) it must avoid "excessive government entanglement with religion."[13] Because the *Lemon* test has not been consistently used, however, the justices remain divided over how much separation between government and religion the First Amendment requires.

In addition to the *Lemon* test, former justice Sandra Day O'Connor championed what is known as the *endorsement* test. She believed that the establishment clause forbids governmental practices that a reasonable observer would view as endorsing religion, even if there is no coercion.[14] Justices Antonin Scalia and Clarence Thomas joined Chief Justice Rehnquist in supporting a *nonpreferentialist* test.[15] As mentioned previously, they believed that the Constitution prohibits favoritism toward any particular religion but does not prohibit government aid to *all* religions. In their view, government may accommodate religious activities and even give nonpreferential support to religious organizations so long as government does not coerce individuals to participate in religious activities or give certain religious activities favorable treatment.[16]

School Vouchers

By contrast, the more liberal justices—Justices David H. Souter, John Paul Stevens, Ruth Bader Ginsburg, and Stephen Breyer—usually maintained that there should be *strict separation* between religion and the state.[17] They generally have held that even indirect aid for religion, such as scholarships or teaching materials and aids for students attending private religious schools, crosses the line separating the government from religion.

One demonstration of the Supreme Court's more recent establishment clause thinking is school **voucher** programs, which provide state aid for religious school attendance. Here the Court has tried to draw a line between permissible tax-provided aid to schoolchildren and impermissible aid to religion. The Court decided the question of whether states may use tax money to give parents tuition vouchers so that their children can attend the schools of their choice, including religious schools, in *Zelman v. Simmons-Harris* (2002).[18] In accord with the Court's more recent willingness to allow greater accommodation between government and religion, the key here was that the money went to the *parents,* who then made their own choice about how to spend it, rather than the money going directly from the government to the religious school.

establishment clause
A clause in the First Amendment that states that Congress shall make no law respecting an establishment of religion. The Supreme Court has interpreted this to forbid governmental support to any or all religions.

vouchers
Money that the government provides to parents to pay their children's tuition in a public or private school of their choice.

free exercise clause
A clause in the First Amendment that states that Congress shall make no law prohibiting the free exercise of religion.

The Free Exercise Clause The right to hold any or no religious belief is one of our few absolute rights because it occurs solely within each person. The **free exercise clause** affirms that no government can compel us to accept any creed or to deny us any right

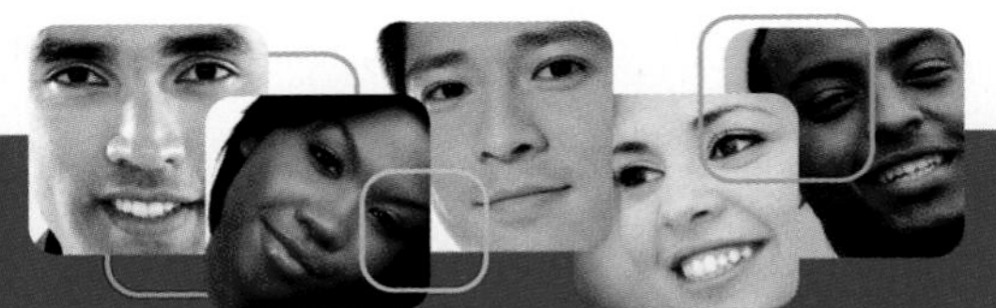

THE CHANGING FACE OF U.S. POLITICS

The Continuing Importance of Religion and Personal Belief

The United States remains a deeply religious country, but after increasing through much of the 1990s, the intensity of religious belief has shown a modest decline. According to a study by the Pew Research Center for the People and the Press, nearly eight of ten people (78 percent) say prayer is an important part of their daily lives, and even more (83 percent) agree with the statement "I never doubt the existence of God." These figures are high, but each has declined a few percentage points since the last time the questions were asked in 2003. The number of American adults who identify themselves as atheist or agnostic has modestly increased from 8 percent in 1987 to 12 percent in Pew surveys taken since the beginning of 2006.*

Moreover, younger people seem to be more secular. Among the cohort born before 1946, only 5 percent are secular, or unaffiliated with a religious tradition. However, 11 percent of baby boomers fall into that category, and among adults born after 1976, 19 percent are secular. It also seems that people who are secular or unaffiliated with religion remain so over their lifetimes. That is, people have not become less secular as they age.

During the last two decades, religion and religious faith have also grown more aligned with partisan and ideological identification. A greater percentage of Republicans express strong religious attitudes than do Democrats (79 percent versus 62 percent of Democrats). This is a substantial change from 1999, when there was little difference in the religiosity of Republicans and Democrats (78 percent of Republicans compared to 76 percent of Democrats). In comparison, 65 percent of Independents expressed strong religious commitment.

QUESTIONS

1. Do you think changes in religious commitment may affect citizens' voting decisions? How?
2. How do the differences between religious commitment among Democrats and Republicans affect the way Democratic and Republican politicians interact with their constituencies?
3. Why do you think people may not waver in their religiosity over their lifetime? Why may someone expect that people would?

*Pew Research Center for the People and the Press, *Trends in Political Values and Core Attitudes: 1987–2007,* March 22, 2007, people-press.org/reports/display.php3?ReportID=312.

because of what we do or do not believe. Requiring religious oaths as a condition of public employment or as a prerequisite for running for public office is unconstitutional. In fact, the original Constitution states, "No religious Test shall ever be required as a Qualification to any Office or public Trust under the United States" (Article VI).

Although carefully protected, the right to practice a religion, which typically requires some action such as proselytizing or participating in a religious ritual, is more likely to be restricted than the right to hold particular beliefs. Before 1990, the Supreme Court carefully scrutinized laws allegedly infringing on religious practices and insisted that the government provide some compelling interest to justify actions that might infringe on someone's religion. In other words, the First Amendment was thought to throw a "mantle of protection" around religious practices, and the burden was on the government to justify interfering with them in the least restrictive way.

Then, in *Employment Division v. Smith* (1990), the Court significantly altered the interpretation of the free exercise clause by discarding the compelling governmental interest test for overriding the interests of religious minorities.[19] As long as a law is generally applicable and does not single out and ban religious practices, the law may be applied to conduct even if it burdens a particular religious practice.[20]

In reaction to *Employment Division v. Smith,* Congress enacted the Religious Freedom Restoration Act of 1993 (RFRA). The RFRA aimed to override the *Smith* decision and to restore the earlier test prohibiting the government—federal, state, or local—from limiting a person's exercise of religion unless the government demonstrates a compelling interest that is advanced by the least restrictive means. When the RFRA was challenged, the Supreme Court ruled it unconstitutional. First, the Court said Congress violated "vital principles necessary to maintain separation of powers and the federal balance."[21] Also, in requiring the states to abide by the RFRA, Congress had overstepped the balance of federal–state authority. Although the Court struck down the RFRA as applied to the states, it has since upheld the act as it required the federal government to provide for increased scrutiny when federal actions infringe on religious liberties.[22]

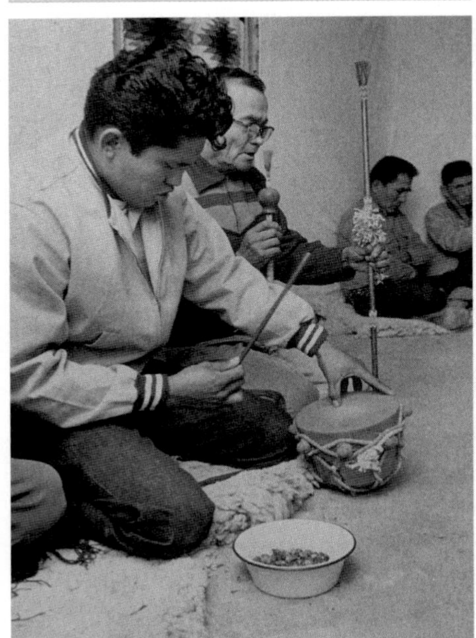

For many Native Americans, peyote is necessary to practice their religious beliefs. But the Supreme Court has ruled that states barring peyote do not need to create specific exceptions for its use in religious practices.

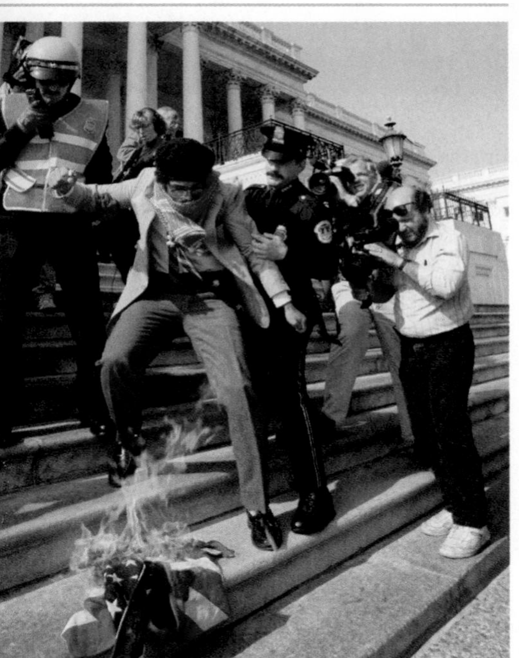

Police arrest Scott Tyler of Chicago after he set fire to an American flag on the steps of the Capitol building in Washington. The Supreme Court afterward ruled that free speech covers even "symbolic speech" such as burning the U.S. flag.

Free Speech and Free People

Government by the people is based on every person's right to speak freely, to organize in groups, to question the decisions of the government, and to campaign openly against them. Only through free and uncensored expression of opinion can government be kept responsive to the electorate and political power transferred peacefully. Elections, separation of powers, and constitutional guarantees are meaningless unless all persons have the right to speak frankly and to hear and judge for themselves the worth of what others have to say.

Even though the First Amendment explicitly denies Congress the power to pass any law abridging freedom of speech, the courts have never interpreted the amendment in absolute terms. Like almost all rights, the freedoms of speech and of the press are limited. In discussing the constitutional power of government to regulate speech, we distinguish among *belief, speech,* and *action.*

At one extreme is the right to *believe* as we wish. Despite occasional deviations in practice, the traditional U.S. view is that government should not punish a person for beliefs or interfere in any way with freedom of conscience. At the other extreme is *action,* which the government may restrain. As the old saying goes, "Your right to swing your fist ends where my nose begins."

Speech stands somewhere between belief and action. It is not an absolute right, like belief, but neither is it as exposed to governmental restraint as is action. Some kinds of speech—libel, obscenity, fighting words, and commercial speech (discussed shortly)—are not entitled to constitutional protection. But many problems arise in distinguishing between what does and does not fit into the categories of nonprotected speech. People disagree, and it usually falls to the courts to decide what free speech means and to defend the right of individual and minority dissenters to exercise it.

Judging: Drawing the Line

Plainly, questions of free speech require that judges weigh a variety of factors: What was said? In what context and how was it said? Which level of government is attempting to regulate the speech—a city council speaking for a few people, or Congress speaking for many? How is the government attempting to regulate the speech—by prior restraint (censorship) or by punishment after the speech? If the restriction is made to preempt publication (prior restraint), it is likely to fail. Why is the government doing so—to preserve the public peace or to prevent criticism of the people in power? Although the courts tend to be receptive to restrictions that are a genuine threat to public safety, restrictions on criticism are likely to fail.

Constitutional Tests of Speech Restrictions

bad tendency test
An interpretation of the First Amendment that would permit legislatures to forbid speech encouraging people to engage in illegal action.

clear and present danger test
An interpretation of the First Amendment that holds that the government cannot interfere with speech unless the speech presents a clear and present danger that it will lead to evil or illegal acts.

preferred position doctrine
An interpretation of the First Amendment that holds that freedom of expression is so essential to democracy that governments should not punish persons for what they say, only for what they do.

Today the Supreme Court generally holds that speech is protected unless it falls into one of four narrow categories—*libel, obscenity, fighting words,* and *commercial speech.* This is a change from its position at the beginning of the twentieth century, when the Court variously relied on one of three tests: the bad tendency test, the clear and present danger test, and the preferred position doctrine.

The **bad tendency test** presumed it was reasonable to forbid speech that tends to corrupt society or cause people to engage in crime. Because the test too broadly restricted speech and ran "contrary to the fundamental premises underlying the First Amendment as the guardian of our democracy,"[23] it was abandoned. The **clear and present danger test** (as described in the "You Will Decide" feature) provided that government could restrict speech *only* if it presented an immediate danger—for example, a false shout of "Fire!" in a crowded theater, or speech leading to a riot, the destruction of property, or the corruption of an election. This clear and present danger test required the government to show the intended speech clearly resulting in imminent danger in order to restrict the important right of free speech.

The last of the three historic tests, the **preferred position doctrine,** was advanced in the 1940s when the Court applied all the guarantees of the First Amendment to the states (as discussed earlier). It comes close to the position that freedom of expression—the use of words and pictures—should rarely, if ever, be curtailed. This interpretation gives these freedoms, especially freedom of speech and of conscience, a preferred position in our constitutional hierarchy.

Protected and Nonprotected Speech

Today free speech and expression are constitutionally protected, and courts strictly scrutinize government regulation of such speech. **Nonprotected speech** lacks redeeming social value and is not essential to democratic deliberations and self-governance. It will be discussed shortly.

LEARNING **OBJECTIVE**

 Contrast the categories of protected and unprotected speech.

Protected Speech

Of all the forms of governmental interference with expression, judges are most suspicious of those that impose **prior restraint**—censorship before publication. Prior restraints include governmental review and approval before a speech can be made, before a motion picture can be shown, or before a newspaper can be published. Most prior restraints are unconstitutional, as the Court has said: "Any system of prior restraints of expression comes to this Court bearing a heavy presumption against its constitutional validity."[24] About the only prior restraints the Court has approved relate to military and national security matters—such as the disclosure of troop movements[25]—and to high school authorities' control over student newspapers.[26] Student newspapers at colleges and universities receive the same protections as other newspapers because they are independent and financially separate from the college or university.

What Speech Is Protected by the Constitution?

Laws must not be so vague that people do not know whether their speech would violate the law and hence are afraid to exercise protected freedoms. This could create what is referred to as a "chilling effect," under which speech is effectively restricted because people fear prosecution. Vague laws may also allow the authorities who administer them so much discretion that they could discriminate against people whose views they dislike.

Even for an important purpose, a legislature may not pass a law that impinges on First Amendment freedoms if other, less drastic means are available. For example, a state may protect the public from unscrupulous lawyers, but not by forbidding attorneys from advertising their fees for simple services. The state could adopt other ways to protect the public from such lawyers that do not impinge on their freedom of speech; it could, for example, disbar lawyers who mislead their clients.

Laws that regulate some kinds of speech but not others, or that regulate speech expressing some views but not others are likely to be struck down. But those that are **content neutral** or **viewpoint neutral**—that is, laws that apply to *all* kinds of speech and to *all* views—are more likely to be safe. For example, the Constitution does not prohibit laws forbidding the posting of handbills on telephone poles. Yet laws prohibiting only religious handbills or only handbills advocating racism or sexism would probably be declared unconstitutional, because they would limit the content of handbills rather than restrict all handbills regardless of what they say.

The lack of viewpoint neutrality was the grounds for the Court's striking down a St. Paul, Minnesota, ordinance prohibiting the display of a symbol that would arouse anger on the basis of race, color, creed, religion, or gender. The ordinance was not considered viewpoint neutral because it did not forbid displays that might arouse anger for other reasons, for example, because of political affiliation.[27]

nonprotected speech
Libel, obscenity, fighting words, and commercial speech, which are not entitled to constitutional protection in all circumstances.

prior restraint
Censorship imposed before a speech is made or a newspaper is published; usually presumed to be unconstitutional.

content- or viewpoint-neutrality
Laws that apply to all kinds of speech and to all views, not just that which is unpopular or divisive.

Nonprotected Speech

The Supreme Court holds that all speech is protected unless it falls into one of four narrow categories: *libel, obscenity, fighting words,* or *commercial speech.* This does not mean that the constitutional issues relating to these kinds of speech are simple. How we prove *libel,* how we define *obscenity,* how we determine which words are *fighting words,* and how much *commercial speech* may be regulated remain hotly contested issues.

YOU WILL DECIDE
Should the Government Restrict Civil Liberties During the War on Terror?

The Bill of Rights protects citizens' right to remain free from unwarranted government restriction on fundamental liberties. Although these rights are not absolute, the government must meet a high standard before it can permissibly restrict civil liberties. When someone challenges a government restriction, one factor the courts consider is whether the government has a *compelling interest* for its actions.

In a unanimous decision restricting citizens' freedom of speech during wartime, Justice Oliver Wendell Holmes wrote that we must consider the proximity and degree of danger posed by the speech to determine whether it "will bring about the substantive evils that Congress has a right to prevent." In his opinion in *Schenck v. United States* (1919), Justice Holmes concluded that only when this evil is "clear and present" may it be restricted. But the Court also acknowledged that "when a nation is at war many things that might be said in a time of peace" will not be permissible "so long as men fight."*

**Schenck v. United States,* 249 U.S. 47 (1919).

At one time, newspaper publishers and editors had to take considerable care about what they wrote to avoid prosecution by the government or lawsuits by individuals for **libel**—published defamation or false statements. Today, as a result of gradually rising constitutional standards, it has become more difficult to win a libel suit against a newspaper or magazine.

In *New York Times v. Sullivan* and subsequent cases, the Court established guidelines for libel cases and severely limited state power to award monetary damages in libel suits brought by public officials against critics of official conduct. Neither public officials nor public figures can collect damages for comments made about them unless they were made with *actual malice,* meaning that the "statements were made with a knowing or reckless disregard for the truth."[28] Nor can they collect damages even when subject to outrageous, clearly inaccurate parodies and cartoons. Such was the case when *Hustler* magazine printed a parody of the Reverend Jerry Falwell; the Court held that parodies and cartoons cannot reasonably be understood as describing actual facts or events.[29]

Constitutional standards for libel charges brought by private persons are not as rigid as those for public officials and figures. State laws may permit private persons to collect damages without having to prove actual malice, if they can prove that the statements made about them are false and were negligently published.[30]

libel
Written defamation of another person. For public officials and public figures, the constitutional tests designed to restrict libel actions are especially rigid.

Obscenity and Pornography Obscene publications are not entitled to constitutional protection, but members of the Supreme Court, like everyone else, have difficulty defining

Although government may impose reasonable restrictions on the place and manner in which leaflets are posted, many college "hate speech" restrictions have been struck down because they unlawfully single out a certain kind of speech.

obscenity. As Justice Potter Stewart put it, "I know it when I see it."[31] Or, as the second justice John Marshall Harlan explained, "One man's vulgarity is another man's lyric."[32]

In *Miller v. California* (1973), the Court finally agreed on a constitutional definition of **obscenity.** A work may be considered legally obscene if (1) the average person, applying contemporary standards of the particular community, would find that the work, taken as a whole, appeals to a prurient interest in sex; (2) the work depicts or describes in a patently offensive way sexual conduct specifically defined by the applicable law or authoritatively construed (meaning that the legislature must define in law each obscene act); and (3) the work, taken as a whole, lacks serious literary, artistic, political, or scientific value.[33] As a result cities such as New York City use zoning laws to regulate where adult theaters and bookstores may be located,[34] and they may ban totally nude dancing in adult nightclubs.[35]

THINKING IT THROUGH

The restriction of civil liberties when our national security is threatened is nothing new. For example, as early as 1798 Congress passed the Alien and Sedition Acts during a period of heightened tension between the United States and France. More recently, the Roosevelt administration, with the approval of the U.S. Supreme Court, relocated Japanese American citizens during World War II under the guise of protecting the West Coast against Japanese attack. In each of these examples, the administrations' actions were severely criticized when the security threat waned.

Some say these examples should caution those who wish to restrict civil liberties in the fight against terrorism. These *civil libertarians* contend that although no liberty is absolute, it is particularly problematic to allow greater restrictions on liberties during the war on terrorism, because its unconventional nature makes it plausible that temporary restrictions may become permanent.

On the other side of the debate, some, including members of the Bush administration, said the war's nature makes it all the more important to allow temporary restrictions on civil liberties. In a nonconventional war, the lines of battle are not clear, nor is the enemy. Thus, the government argues, it must have wide latitude to detain enemy combatants, conduct interrogations, and carry out surveillance on citizens to gather crucial intelligence about possible future terrorist attacks.

Questions

1. What unique challenges to securing civil liberties are presented by the war on terror?
2. Why should citizens who have done nothing wrong be concerned about restrictions on civil liberties?
3. Should concern for protecting national security always outweigh concern for protecting individual liberties?

Fighting Words and Commercial Speech **Fighting words** were held to be constitutionally unprotected because "their very utterance may inflict injury or tend to incite an immediate breach of peace."[36] That the words are abusive, offensive, and insulting or that they create anger, alarm, or resentment is not sufficient. Thus a four-letter word worn on a sweatshirt was not judged to be a fighting word in the constitutional sense, even though it was offensive and angered some people. The word was not aimed at any individual, and those who were offended could look away.[37] In recent years, the Court has overturned convictions for uttering fighting words and struck down laws that criminalized "hate speech"—insulting racial, ethnic, and gender slurs.[38] The Court, though, has indicated that cross burning by the Ku Klux Klan may be punished because it has historically been associated with intimidation.[39]

Commercial speech—such as advertisements and commercials—used to be unprotected because it was deemed to have lesser value than political speech. But the Court has reconsidered and extended more protection to commercial speech, as it has to fighting words. In *44 Liquormart, Inc. v. Rhode Island* (1996), for instance, the Court struck down a law forbidding advertising the price of alcoholic drinks.[40] It now appears that states may forbid and punish only false and misleading advertising, along with advertising promoting the sale of anything illegal—for example, narcotics. Although the Supreme Court has not specifically removed commercial speech from the nonprotected category, it has interpreted the First, Fifth, and Fourteenth Amendments to provide considerable constitutional protection for it.

New York City used zoning laws to eliminate adult entertainment and bookstores from Times Square. As a result, the area has once again become a vibrant center of the city and a prominent tourist attraction.

Freedom of the Press

We've seen that courts are immediately skeptical of prior restraints and have carefully protected the right to publish information, no matter how journalists get it. However, they have not recognized additional protections to allow journalists to withhold information from grand juries or legislative investigating committees. Without this right to withhold information, reporters insist, they cannot assure their sources of confidentiality, and they will not be able to get the information they need to keep the public informed.

The Supreme Court, however, has refused to acknowledge that reporters, and presumably scholars, have a constitutional right to ignore legal requests such as subpoenas and to withhold information from governmental bodies.[41] In 2005, *New York Times* reporter Judith Miller was jailed for two months for refusing to disclose her sources to a grand jury. Many states have passed *press shield laws* providing some protection for reporters from state court subpoenas, and pressure is growing for Congress to pass a similar federal law.

The Freedom of Information Act (FOIA) of 1966, which has been amended several times since passage, has also liberalized access to unclassified federal government records. This law makes the records of federal executive agencies available to the public, with certain exceptions, such as private financial transactions, personnel records, criminal investigation files, interoffice memorandums, and letters used in internal decision making. If federal agencies fail to act promptly on requests for information, applicants are entitled to speedy judicial hearings. The burden is on an agency to explain its refusal to supply material, and if the judge decides the government has improperly withheld information, the government has to pay the legal fees. Since the inception of FOIA, more than 250,000 people have requested information, and more than 90 percent of these requests have been granted.

obscenity
The quality or state of a work that taken as a whole appeals to a prurient interest in sex by depicting sexual conduct in a patently offensive way and that lacks serious literary, artistic, political, or scientific value.

fighting words
Words that by their very nature inflict injury on those to whom they are addressed or incite them to acts of violence.

commercial speech
Advertisements and commercials for products and services; they receive less First Amendment protection, primarily to discourage false and misleading ads.

Other Media and Communications

When the First Amendment was written, freedom of the press referred to leaflets, newspapers, and books. Today the amendment protects other media as well, and much debate centers on the degree of protection that should be afforded to broadcast media and the Internet.

Broadcast and Cable Communications Despite the rise of the Internet, television remains an important means of distributing news and appealing for votes. Yet of all the mass media, broadcasting receives the least First Amendment protection. Congress has established a system of commercial broadcasting, supplemented by the Corporation for Public Broadcasting, that provides funds for public radio and television. The Federal Communications Commission (FCC) regulates the entire system by granting licenses, regulating their use, and imposing fines for indecent broadcasts.

The First Amendment would prevent censorship if the FCC tried to impose it. The First Amendment does not, however, prevent the FCC from imposing sanctions on stations that broadcast indecent or filthy words, even if those words are not legally obscene.[42] Nor does the First Amendment prevent the FCC from refusing to renew a license if, in its opinion, a broadcaster does not serve the public interest. In the wake of Bono's 2003 Golden Globes acceptance speech including a certain indecent word and Janet Jackson's 2004 Super Bowl performance in which her breast was exposed, heightened attention was focused on the issue of FCC sanctions. At least partly in response, President Bush signed a law in 2006 authorizing the FCC to fine broadcasters up to $325,000 for each instance of indecent broadcasting. Although the Court has continued to uphold restrictions on the broadcast media, cable operators are given greater latitude in their programming.[42]

At a press conference, Howard Stern defends his use of raunchy language and subject matter that led to the FCC fining the Infinity Broadcasting network. Stern subsequently decided to leave the network to work on a satellite radio station.

The Internet The Internet presents an interesting problem in determining the appropriate level of First Amendment protection. In many ways it functions as a newspaper—providing news and information critical to an informed citizenry. But it is also a commercial marketplace where millions of U.S. consumers buy books, clothing, jewelry, airplane tickets, stocks, and bonds.

In general, attempts to regulate Internet content have been unsuccessful. In its major ruling on First Amendment protection for the Internet, *Reno v. American Civil Liberties Union* (1997), the Court struck down provisions of the Communications Decency Act of 1996 that had made it a crime to send obscene or indecent messages to anyone under age 18. In doing so, the Court emphasized the unique character of the Internet, holding that it is less intrusive than radio and broadcast television.[44] In response to *Reno v. ACLU,* Congress passed the Child Online Protection Act of 1998 (COPA), which made it a crime for a commercial Web site to knowingly make available to anyone under age 17 sexually explicit material considered "harmful to minors" based on "community standards." But the Supreme Court held that the law was unenforceable because imposing criminal penalties was not the least drastic means of achieving Congress's goals; Internet filters and adult checks could block minors' access to sites with sexually explicit material.[45]

Freedom of Assembly

Khallid Abdul Muhammad, a known racist and anti-Semite, organized what he called a "Million Youth March" in New York City in 1998. Mayor Rudolph Giuliani denied a permit for the march on the grounds that it would be a "hate march." A federal appeals court upheld a lower-court ruling that denial of the permit was unconstitutional. However, a three-judge panel placed restrictions on the event, limiting its duration to four hours and scaling it back to a six-block area. The march proceeded, surrounded by police in riot gear who broke up the demonstration after Muhammad delivered a vitriolic speech against the police, Jews, and city officials.

It took judicial authorities to defend the rights of these unpopular speakers and marchers, but it also required judicial intervention in the 1960s to preserve for Martin Luther King Jr. and those who marched with him the right to demonstrate in the streets of southern cities on behalf of civil rights for African Americans. This is a classic free speech problem: The First Amendment protects speech regardless of whether it is popular. It is almost always easier, and certainly politically more prudent, to maintain order by curbing public demonstrations by unpopular groups.

Time, Place, and Manner Regulations The Constitution protects the right to speak, but it does not give people the right to communicate their views to everyone, in every place, at every time they wish. No one has the right to block traffic or to hold parades or make speeches in public streets or on public sidewalks whenever he or she wishes. Governments may not censor what can be said, but they can make "reasonable" *time, place,* and *manner* regulations for protests or parades.

Depending on the place where the expressive activities are to occur, such as public parks, public school buildings, or government offices, the Court has been more or less willing to permit speech activities subject to reasonable time, place, and manner restrictions. It is essential, however, that any restriction be applied evenhandedly and that the government not act because of *what* is being said, rather than how or where or by whom.

civil disobedience
Deliberate refusal to obey a law or comply with the orders of public officials as a means of expressing opposition.

Does the right of peaceful assembly include the right to violate a law nonviolently but deliberately? We have no precise answer, but in general, **civil disobedience,** even if peaceful, is not a protected right. When Martin Luther King Jr. and his followers refused

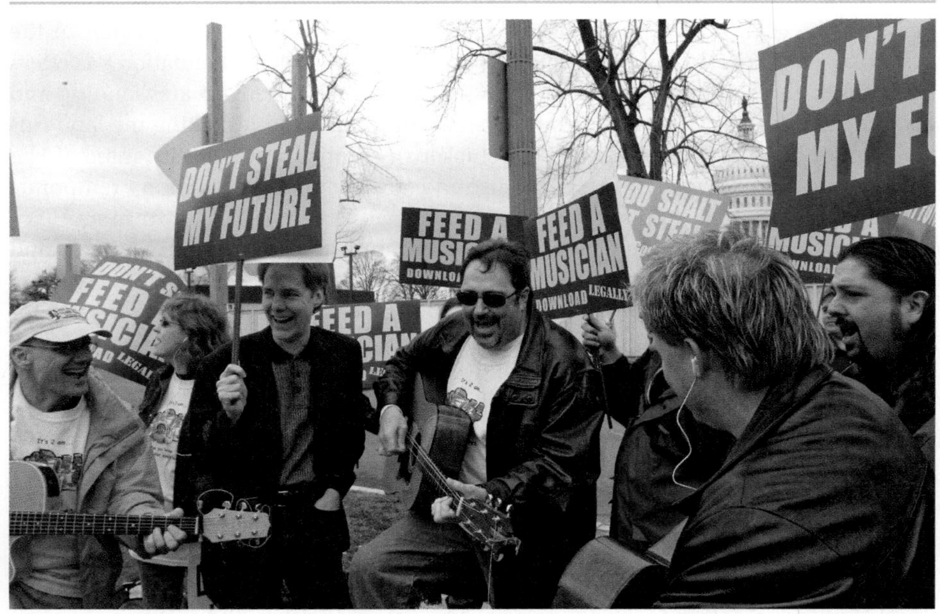

Demonstrators parade with posters in front of the U.S. Supreme Court in Washington, D.C., as the nine justices heard oral arguments on the legality of music file-sharing networks. The right to assemble peaceably and protest is guaranteed by the Bill of Rights.

to comply with a state court's injunction forbidding them to parade in Birmingham, Alabama, without first securing a permit, the Supreme Court sustained their conviction, even though there was serious doubt about the constitutionality of the injunction and the ordinance on which it was based.[46]

More recently, the First Amendment right of antiabortion protesters to picket in front of abortion clinics has come into conflict with a woman's right to go to an abortion clinic. Protesters have often massed in front of clinics, shouting at employees and clients and blocking entrances to the clinic. The Supreme Court has struck down provisions that prohibit protesters from expressing their views. But it has upheld injunctions that keep antiabortion protesters outside a buffer zone around abortion clinics and also upheld injunctions that were issued because of the protesters' previous unlawful conduct. The proper constitutional test for such injunctions is "whether the challenged provisions . . . burden no more speech than necessary to serve a significant government interest," such as public safety or the right of women to go into such a clinic.[47]

First Amendment freedoms are crucial for the survival of our republican form of democracy. It is of utmost importance that individuals be able to make their voices heard regardless of the political views they wish to express. However, the protection of these rights alone is insufficient to protect citizens and noncitizens alike from arbitrary or impermissible government infringements on our liberties and property.

property rights
The rights of an individual to own, use, rent, invest in, buy, and sell property.

eminent domain
The power of a government to take private property for public use; the U.S. Constitution gives national and state governments this power and requires them to provide just compensation for property so taken.

regulatory taking
A government regulation that effectively takes land by restricting its use, even if it remains in the owner's name.

Property Rights

Property does not have rights; people do. People have the right to own, use, rent, invest in, buy, and sell property. Historically, U.S. political thinking and political institutions have emphasized the close connection between liberty and owning property, and between property and power. A major goal of the framers of the Constitution was to establish a government strong enough to protect people's rights to use and enjoy their property. The framers also wanted to limit government so it could not endanger that right. As a result, the Constitution has a variety of clauses protecting **property rights.**

Although the right of property ownership is highly regarded, both the national and state governments have the power of **eminent domain**—the power to take private property for public use—but the owner must be fairly compensated. What constitutes "taking" for purposes of eminent domain? Ordinarily, but not always, the taking must be direct, and a person must lose title and control over the property. Sometimes, especially in recent years, the courts have found that a governmental taking has gone "too far," and the government must compensate its owners even when title is left in the owner's name.[48] These are called **regulatory takings,** meaning the regulation has effectively taken the land by restricting its use. Thus if a government creates landing and takeoff paths for airplanes over property adjacent to an airport, making the land unsuitable for its original use (say, raising chickens), compensation is warranted.[49] The government may, however, impose land use and environmental regulations, temporarily prohibiting the development of a property, without compensating the owners.[50]

Major opposition to the Court's 2005 decision to allow New London, Connecticut, to take Susette Kelo's property led to many local ballot initiatives in the 2006 elections.

In a controversial ruling with wide-ranging ramifications for urban planners and homeowners, a bare majority of the Court upheld the use of the government's power of eminent domain to condemn and take private property, with just compensation, for the purpose of advancing the economic development of a community. *Kelo v. City of New London* (2005) held that "public use" was not limited to eminent domain to build a road or a bridge, but includes "promoting economic development," even if the property was taken and sold for development to private developers.[51] Public reaction to the Court's decision in *Kelo* was extremely negative. In a clear reminder that the Court is only one instrument of government, many states and localities acted swiftly to pass laws that barred authorities from taking private property for such purposes.

"Just compensation" is not always easy to define. When there is a dispute over compensation, the courts make the final resolution based on the rule that "the owner is entitled to receive what a willing buyer would pay in cash to a willing seller at the time of the taking."[52] An owner is not entitled to compensation for the personal value of an old, broken-down, dearly loved house—just the value of the old, broken-down house.

Due Process Rights

LEARNING **OBJECTIVE**

4 Compare and contrast procedural and substantive due process.

Perhaps the most difficult parts of the Constitution to understand are the clauses in the Fifth and Fourteenth Amendments forbidding the national and state governments to deny any person life, liberty, or property without "due process of law." Cases involving these guarantees have resulted in hundreds of Supreme Court decisions. Even so, it is impossible to explain *due process* precisely. In fact, the Supreme Court has refused to give due process a precise definition and has emphasized that "due process, unlike some legal rules, is not a technical conception with a fixed content unrelated to time, place and circumstances."[53] We define **due process** as rules and regulations that restrain those in government who exercise power. There are, however, basically two kinds of due process: procedural and substantive.

Procedural Due Process

Traditionally, **procedural due process** refers not to the law itself but to *how a law is applied.* To paraphrase Daniel Webster's famous definition, the due process of law requires a procedure that hears before it condemns, proceeds upon inquiry, and renders judgment only after a trial or some kind of hearing. Originally, procedural due process was limited to criminal prosecutions, but it now applies to most kinds of governmental proceedings. It is required, for instance, in juvenile hearings, disbarment proceedings, proceedings to determine eligibility for welfare payments, revocation of drivers' licenses, and disciplinary proceedings in state universities and public schools.

A law may also violate the procedural due process requirement if it is too vague or if it creates an improper presumption of guilt. A vague statute fails to provide adequate warning and does not contain sufficient guidelines for law enforcement officials, juries, and courts.

The liberties that due process protects include "the right of the individual to contract, to engage in any of the common occupations of life, to acquire useful knowledge, to marry, to establish a home and bring up children, to worship God according to the dictates of his own conscience, and generally to enjoy those common law privileges long recognized as essential to the orderly pursuit of happiness by free men."[54]

Substantive Due Process

Procedural due process limits *how* governmental power may be exercised; **substantive due process** limits *what* a government may do. Procedural due process mainly limits the executive and judicial branches because they apply the law and review its application; substantive due process mainly limits the legislative branch because it enacts laws. Substantive due process means that an "unreasonable" law, even if properly passed and properly applied, is unconstitutional. It means that governments *should not be allowed to do certain things.*

Before 1937, substantive due process was used primarily to protect the right of employers to make contracts with employees freely, without government interference.[55] During this period, conservative jurists who considered almost all social welfare legislation unreasonable dominated the Supreme Court. They used the due process clause to strike down laws setting maximum hours of labor, establishing minimum wages, regulating prices, and forbidding employers to fire workers because they joined a union.

Since 1937, the Supreme Court has largely refused to apply the doctrine of substantive due process in reviewing laws regulating business enterprises and economic interests. The Court now believes that deciding what constitutes reasonable regulation of business and commercial life is a legislative, not a judicial, responsibility. As long as the justices find a conceivable connection between a law regulating business and the

due process
Established rules and regulations that restrain government officials.

procedural due process
A constitutional requirement that governments proceed by proper methods; limits how government may exercise power.

substantive due process
A constitutional requirement that governments act reasonably and that the substance of the laws themselves be fair and reasonable; limits what a government may do.

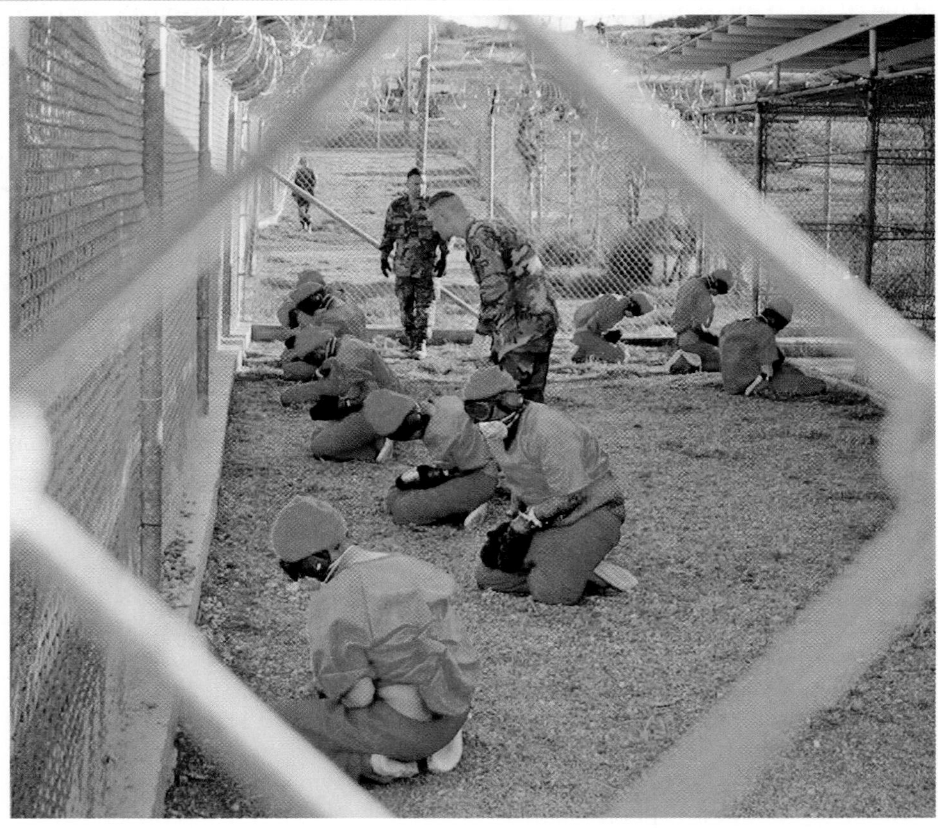

The USA Patriot Act, passed in the wake of the September 11, 2001, attacks and renewed in 2006, removes those designated by the president as "enemy combatants" from many of the procedural due process protections that are the cornerstone of the U.S. legal system. Both U.S. citizens and noncitizens alike can be designated as "enemy combatants" at the president's discretion.

promotion of the public welfare, the Supreme Court will not interfere with laws passed by Congress or state legislatures.

This does not mean, however, that the Court has abandoned substantive due process. On the contrary, due process has taken on new life as a protector of civil liberties, especially the right of privacy. Substantive due process has deep roots in concepts of natural law and a long history in U.S. constitutional tradition. For most citizens most of the time, it is not enough merely to say that a law reflects the wishes of the popular or legislative majority. We also want our laws to be just, and we rely heavily on judges to decide what is just.

Privacy Rights

The most important extension of substantive due process in recent decades has protected the right of privacy, especially marital privacy. Although the Constitution does not mention the right to privacy, in *Griswold v. Connecticut* (1965), the Supreme Court pulled together elements of the First, Third, Fourth, Fifth, Ninth, and Fourteenth Amendments to recognize that personal privacy is one of the rights the Constitution protects.[56]

Privacy and Government Surveillance Powers

This right has three aspects: (1) the right to be free from governmental surveillance and intrusion, especially with respect to intimate decisions on sexuality; (2) the right not to have the government make private affairs public; and (3) the right to be free in thought and belief from governmental regulations.[57]

Abortion Rights

The right to privacy encompasses two controversial issues: state regulation of abortion and private, adult consensual sexual conduct. First, in *Roe v. Wade* (1973), the Supreme

HISTORY MAKERS

Estelle Griswold

Estelle Trébert Griswold was born in 1900 and became the executive director of the Planned Parenthood League of Connecticut (PPLC) in 1953. In that position, she led a fight to legalize birth control in Connecticut that resulted in a landmark Supreme Court ruling on the right of privacy and the Constitution's protection for intimate decisions on human sexuality.

Estelle Griswold.

Connecticut had prohibited the use of contraceptives in an 1879 law and had also made it a crime to "assist, abet, or counsel" someone on birth control. By the 1950s, contraceptives were nonetheless widely sold in drugstores in the state, and the law was generally ignored. But Griswold and some doctors and advocates of women's rights contended that the law had a chilling effect. Griswold and the PPLC lobbied the state legislature to repeal the law, but the Catholic-dominated Connecticut state senate blocked the repeal. Courts refused to strike down the law.

Griswold and Dr. Lee Buxton decided to open a birth control clinic in Connecticut and create a test case challenging the law. After opening the clinic, they held a press conference. A few days later, police arrived and, after receiving PPLC literature, arrested Griswold and Buxton, who were tried in state court, convicted, and fined $100 each for violating the law.

On appeal in *Griswold v. Connecticut* (1965),* the Supreme Court struck down Connecticut's law for violating a constitutionally protected right of privacy. The decision remains controversial because the Bill of Rights does not specifically enumerate a right to privacy. But the ruling laid the basis for other landmark decisions on a woman's right to choose, in *Roe v. Wade* (1973),† and on constitutional protection for private consensual sexual activities in *Lawrence v. Texas* (2003),‡ which struck down Texas's law making homosexual sodomy a crime.

QUESTIONS

1. Why was Estelle Griswold able to bring her case in Connecticut even though birth control was widely available?
2. Why was the Connecticut law unconstitutional?
3. How does Griswold's case illustrate the role of the courts in protecting liberties in a separation of powers system?

**Griswold v. Connecticut,* 381 U.S. 479 (1965).
†*Roe v. Wade,* 410 U.S. 113 (1973).
‡*Lawrence v. Texas,* 539 U.S. 558 (2003).

Court ruled that the right to privacy extended to a woman's decision, in consultation with her physician, to terminate her pregnancy. According to *Roe*'s "trimester framework," (1) during the first trimester of a woman's pregnancy, it is an unreasonable and therefore unconstitutional interference with her liberty and privacy rights for a state to set any limits on her choice to have an abortion or on her doctor's medical judgments about how to carry it out; (2) during the second trimester, the state's interest in protecting the health of women becomes compelling, and a state may make a reasonable regulation about how, where, and when abortions may be performed; and (3) during the third trimester, when the fetus becomes capable of surviving outside the womb, what the Court called "viability," the state's interest in protecting the unborn child is so important that the state can prohibit abortions altogether, except when necessary to preserve the life or health of the mother.[58]

The *Roe* decision led to decades of heated public debate and attempts by Presidents Ronald Reagan and George H. W. Bush to select Supreme Court justices who might reverse it. Nonetheless, *Roe v. Wade* was reaffirmed in *Planned Parenthood v. Casey* (1992). A bitterly divided Court upheld by a five-person majority (O'Connor, Kennedy, Souter, Blackmun, and Stevens) the view that the due process clause of the Constitution protects a woman's liberty to choose an abortion prior to viability. The Court, however, held that the right to have an abortion prior to viability may be subject to state regulation that does not "unduly burden" it. In other words, the Court threw out the trimester framework and permitted states to make "reasonable regulations" on how a woman exercises her right to an abortion, so long as they do not prohibit any woman from making the ultimate decision on whether to terminate a pregnancy before viability.[59]

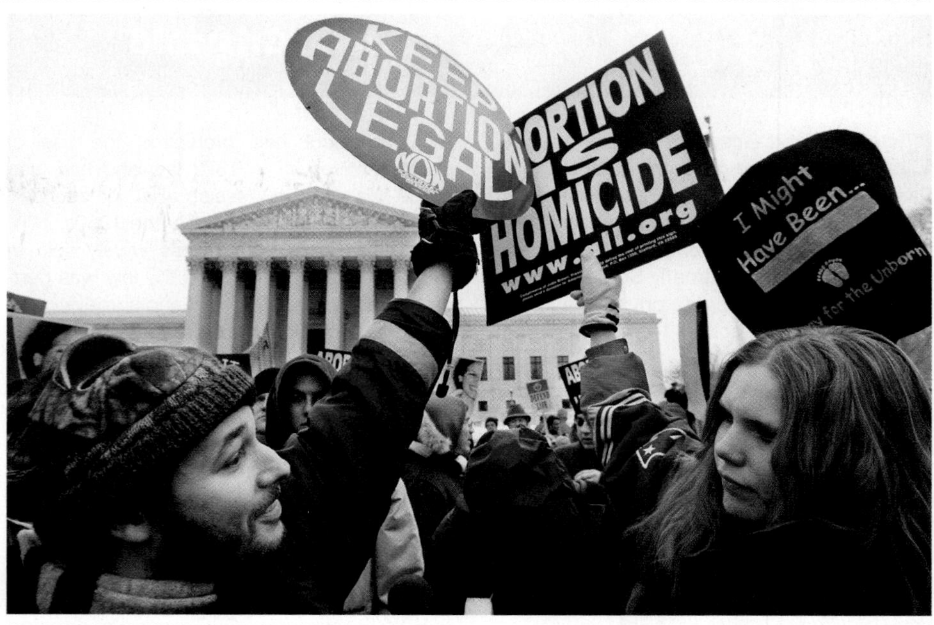

Abortion continues to be a hotly contested issue before the courts. Here protesters on both sides of the abortion debate demonstrate in front of the Supreme Court building.

Applying the undue burden test, the Court has held, on the one hand, that states can prohibit the use of state funds and facilities for performing abortions; states may make a minor's right to an abortion conditional on her first notifying at least one parent or a judge; and states may require women to sign an informed-consent form and wait 24 hours before having an abortion. On the other hand, a state may not condition a woman's right to an abortion on her first notifying her husband. The Court also struck down Nebraska's ban on "partial birth" abortions in *Stenberg v. Carhart* (2000), because it completely forbade one kind of medical procedure and provided no exception for when a woman's health is at stake and thus imposed an "undue burden" on women.[60]

Nonetheless, Congress passed and President George W. Bush signed into federal law a similar ban on "partial birth" abortions that was immediately challenged in the courts. The Court ruled 5-to-4 to uphold the federal ban. It reasoned that because of "medical uncertainty" about the banned procedure's necessity, Congress was not required to include a health exception.[61]

Sexual Orientation Rights

Although there is general agreement on how much constitutional protection is provided for marital privacy, in *Bowers v. Hardwick* (1986) the Supreme Court refused to extend such protection to private relations between homosexuals;[62] a bare majority of the Court also held that the Boy Scouts of America may exclude homosexuals.[63] By a 5-to-4 vote in *Bowers,* the Court refused to declare unconstitutional a Georgia law that made consensual sodomy a crime. But state supreme courts, including Georgia's, later found greater privacy protection in their state constitutions than the U.S. Supreme Court found in the U.S. Constitution. Finally, in *Lawrence v. Texas* (2003),[64] the Court struck down Texas's law making homosexual sodomy a crime. Writing for the Court and noting the trend in state court decisions that did not follow *Bowers,* Justice Kennedy held the law to violate personal autonomy and the right of privacy. Dissenting, Justice Scalia, along with Chief Justice Rehnquist and Justice Thomas, warned that the decision might lead to overturning laws barring same-sex marriages, as some state courts and Canadian courts had already done.

The U.S. Supreme Court, in *Romer v. Evans* (1996),[65] also struck down an initiative amending the Colorado constitution that prohibited state and local governments from protecting homosexuals from discrimination. Although the Court did not rule on the basis of substantive due process, it held that this provision violated the equal protection clause because it lacked any rational basis and simply represented prejudice toward a particular group.

The right of privacy as an element of substantive due process is one of the developing edges of constitutional law, one about which people both on and off the Court have strong disagreements. How the Supreme Court handles privacy issues has become front-page news.

Rights of Criminal Suspects

LEARNING **OBJECTIVE**

5 Analyze the degree to which criminal suspects' rights are protected in our criminal justice system.

Despite what you see in police dramas on television and in the movies, law enforcement officers have no general right to break down doors and invade homes. They are not supposed to search people except under certain conditions, and they have no right to arrest them except under certain circumstances. They also may not compel confessions, and they must respect other procedural guarantees aimed at ensuring fairness and the rights of the accused. Persons accused of crimes are guaranteed these and other rights under the Fourth, Fifth, Sixth, Eighth, and Fourteenth Amendments.

You Are a Police Officer

Freedom from Unreasonable Searches and Seizures

According to the Fourth Amendment, "The right of the people to be secure in their persons, houses, papers, and effects, against unreasonable searches and seizures, shall not be violated, and no Warrants shall issue, but upon probable cause, supported by Oath or affirmation, and particularly describing the place to be searched, and the persons or things to be seized."

Protection from unreasonable searches and seizures requires police, if they have time, to obtain a valid **search warrant,** issued by a magistrate after the police indicate under oath that they have *probable cause* to justify it. Magistrates must perform this function in a neutral and detached manner and not serve merely as rubber stamps for the police. The warrant must specify the place to be searched and the things to be seized. *General search warrants*—warrants that authorize police to search a particular place or person without limitation—are unconstitutional. A search warrant is usually needed to search a person in any place he or she has an "expectation of privacy that

search warrant
A writ issued by a magistrate that authorizes the police to search a particular place or person, specifying the place to be searched and the objects to be seized.

Police exercise a reasonable search of this man's car after having established probable cause that a crime had been committed. The man was arrested after police found stolen goods in his car.

society is prepared to recognize as reasonable," for example, in a hotel room, a rented home, or a friend's apartment.[66] In short, the Fourth Amendment protects people, not places, from unreasonable governmental intrusions.[67]

The Fourth Amendment presents a complex area of the law that includes many possible exceptions to the warrant requirement. Beyond obtaining a search warrant, there are several other conditions in which a search might be considered "reasonable" according to the language of the Fourth Amendment. Key to determining whether a *warrantless search* is permissible are factors such as whether a person's consent to a search is coerced or whether an officer's or the public's safety is at risk. Although at first glance it might seem straightforward, the Fourth Amendment does not apply to every encounter between individuals and law enforcement officials. That is, not every such encounter amounts to a search and/or a seizure.

If the police just ask questions or even seek consent to search an individual's person or possessions in a noncoercive atmosphere, there is no detention—the person's physical liberty has not been limited. "So long as a reasonable person would feel free 'to disregard the police and go about his business,' the encounter is consensual and no reasonable suspicion is required." But if the person refuses to answer questions or consent to a search, and the police, by either physical force or a show of authority, restrain the movement of the person, even though there is no arrest, the Fourth Amendment comes into play.[68] For example, if police approach people in airports and request identification, this act by itself does not constitute a detention. The same is true if police ask bus passengers for consent to search their luggage for drugs. But if the police do more, especially after consent is refused, then they must have some objective justification for the search beyond mere suspicion.[69]

The Supreme Court also upheld, in *Terry v. Ohio* (1968), a *stop and frisk* exception to the warrant requirement when officers have reason to believe someone is armed and dangerous or has committed or is about to commit a criminal offense. The *Terry* search is limited to a quick pat-down to check for weapons that may be used to assault the arresting officer, to check for contraband, to determine identity, or to maintain the status quo while obtaining more information.[70] If individuals who are stopped for questioning refuse to identify themselves, they may be arrested, though police must have a reasonable suspicion that they are engaged in criminal activities.[71] If an officer stops and frisks a suspect to look for weapons and finds criminal evidence that may justify an arrest, the officer can make a full search.[72]

Police and border guards may also conduct *border* searches—searches of persons and the goods they bring with them at border crossings.[73] The border search exception

Following September 11, 2001, airport security was tightened throughout the country. Such extensive searches are lawful because they are technically voluntary, meaning a person could choose not to fly.

GENERATION **NEXT**

Searches and Seizures in an Age of Terrorism

One of the prominent concerns we must address in fighting a war on terrorism is the difficulty of maintaining individual liberties in the face of a terrorist threat. Ensuring against another terrorist attack would be much easier if the government had open access to listen in on our conversations, search our possessions, and detain or question suspects without having to show cause for doing so. However, our civil liberties, as provided for in the Constitution's Bill of Rights, require that the government afford citizens due process under the law.

In terms of searches and seizures, the Fourth Amendment requires that the government obtain a warrant or meet the reasonableness requirement in order to permissibly search our homes. Generally, the law recognizes that a person's expectation of privacy and the right to be free from unreasonable searches and seizures is greatest in his or her own home. However, when national security is at risk, the courts have also been willing to give government greater latitude in restricting liberties so as to ensure the nation's security. Many citizens would agree that during times of greater insecurity, we need to give up some of our civil liberties to remain secure.

According to the Pew Research Center's Political Landscape Survey, a significant percentage of 18- to 29-year-olds seem to agree that there are times when civil liberties may permissibly be restricted to provide for national security.

Interestingly, there is little difference in the views of 18- to 29-year-olds along gender or racial lines on this question. But there are much more substantial partisan and ideological differences. Republicans and those identifying as conservative or very conservative are substantially more likely to agree that civil liberties may properly be set aside during a time of national crisis. This is consistent with a more general concern among these groups for preserving law and order. Democrats and the liberal or very liberal, who typically are more concerned about civil liberties in general, are less likely to agree that such intrusions on civil liberties are permissible.

Generation Next as a group is also more willing to allow law enforcement officials greater discretion in searching their homes than are other American adults. Forty percent of 18- to 29-year-olds mostly or completely agreed that police ought to be able to search the homes of suspected terrorist sympathizers as compared to 31 percent of 30- to 39-year-olds, 37 percent of 40- to 49-year-olds, 32 percent of 50- to 59-year-olds, and 35 percent of those age 60 and older. Perhaps this reflects the fact that many in Generation Next came of age in an era of terrorism.

Percentage of 18- to 29-Year Olds Completely or Mostly Agreeing that Police Should Be Allowed to Search the Homes of People, Without a Court Order, Who Might Be Sympathetic to Terrorists.

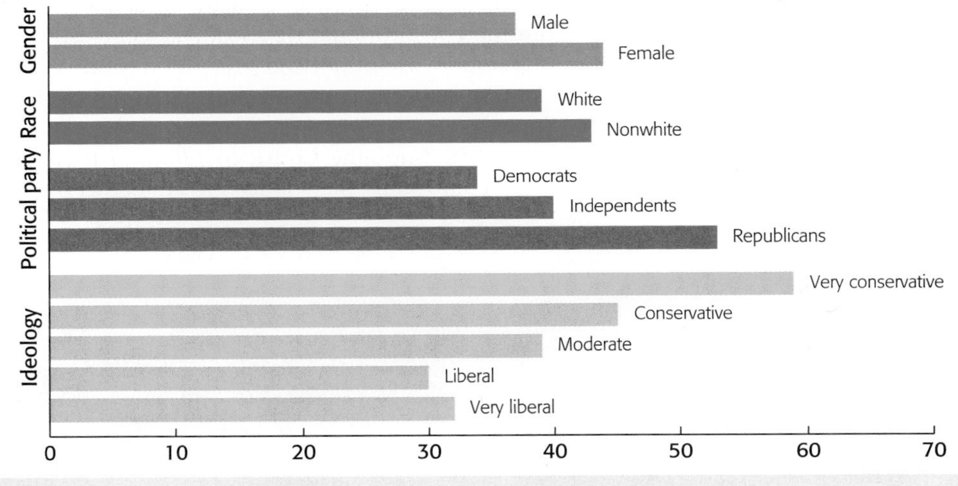

QUESTIONS

1. Why do you think Republicans and conservatives are more willing to allow searches without warrants in this instance?
2. What values are competing with civil liberties in the preceding scenario? Why do some respond to those competing values differently than others?
3. What may be the risk in allowing infringements on civil liberties, such as the ability of police to search homes of suspected terrorists without a warrant?

also permits officials to open mail entering the country if they have "reasonable cause" to suspect that it contains merchandise imported in violation of the law.[74]

The need to protect national security and gather foreign intelligence presents a special problem for Fourth Amendment protections (see the "Generation Next" feature for young people's assessment of the issue). Endorsing the president's claim that he can authorize warrantless wiretaps and physical searchs of agents of foreign countries, Congress created the Foreign Intelligence Surveillance Court to review requests for warrantless wiretaps. The court consists of federal district judges and meets in secret. The USA PATRIOT Act of 2001 expanded the size of the court, lowered the requirement to approve warrants in cases involving terrorism, and permits searches for foreign intelligence and evidence of terrorist activities.

Balancing Liberty and Security in a Time of War

Civil Liberties and National Security

The Exclusionary Rule Before the development of the *exclusionary rule,* evidence obtained in violation of the Fourth Amendment might still be used at trial against a defendant. The remedy in such cases was the opportunity for the defendant to sue law enforcement. However, suing afterward did not resolve the denial of Fourth Amendment protection in the criminal action.

This changed in the federal courts in 1911 and was applied to the states in 1961. In *Mapp v. Ohio* (1961), the Supreme Court adopted a rule excluding from a criminal trial evidence the police obtained unconstitutionally or illegally.[75] This **exclusionary rule** was adopted to prevent police misconduct. Critics question why criminals should go free just because of police misconduct or ineptness,[76] but the Supreme Court has refused to abandon the rule. It has made some exceptions to it, however, such as cases in which police relied in "good faith" on a search warrant that subsequently turned out to be defective or granted improperly.[77]

exclusionary rule
A requirement that evidence unconstitutionally or illegally obtained be excluded from a criminal trial.

The Right to Remain Silent During the seventeenth century, special courts in England forced confessions by torture and intimidation from religious dissenters. The British privilege against self-incrimination developed in response to these practices. Because they were familiar with this history, the framers of our Bill of Rights included in the Fifth Amendment the provision that persons shall not be compelled to testify against themselves in criminal prosecutions. This protection against self-incrimination is designed to strengthen the fundamental principle that no person has an obligation to prove innocence. Rather, the burden is on the government to prove guilt.

The *Miranda* Warning Police questioning of suspects is a key procedure in solving crimes. Roughly 90 percent of all criminal convictions result from guilty pleas and never reach a full trial. Police questioning, however, can easily be abused. Police officers sometimes forget or ignore the constitutional rights of suspects, especially those who are frightened and ignorant. Unauthorized detention and lengthy interrogation to wring confessions from suspects, common practice in police states, have also occurred in the United States.

To put an end to such practices, the Supreme Court, in *Miranda v. Arizona* (1966), announced that no conviction could stand if evidence introduced at the trial

The case of Ernesto Miranda (right) led to the Supreme Court decision in 1966 requiring suspects in police custody to be advised of their constitutional right to remain silent and to have an attorney present during questioning.

had been obtained by the police during "custodial interrogation" unless suspects were notified that they have a right to remain silent and that anything they say can and will be used against them; to terminate questioning at any point; to have an attorney present during questioning by police; and to have a lawyer appointed to represent them if they cannot afford to hire their own attorney.[78] If suspects answer questions in the absence of an attorney, the burden is on prosecutors to demonstrate that suspects knowingly and intelligently gave up their right to remain silent. Failure to comply with these requirements leads to reversal of a conviction, even if other evidence is sufficient to establish guilt.

Critics of the *Miranda* decision believe the Supreme Court severely limited the ability of the police to bring criminals to justice. Over the years, the Court has modified the original ruling by allowing evidence obtained contrary to the *Miranda* guidelines to be used to attack the credibility of defendants who offer testimony at trial that conflicts with their statements to the police. But the Court has reaffirmed *Miranda*'s constitutional necessity as recently as 2000 (*Dickerson v. United States*).[79]

Fair Trial Procedures

Many people consider the rights of persons accused of a crime to be less important than other rights. But as Justice Felix Frankfurter observed, "The history of liberty has largely been the history of observance of procedural safeguards." Further, these safeguards have frequently "been forged in controversies involving not very nice people."[80] Nonetheless, they guarantee that all persons accused of crimes will have the right to representation by counsel and to a fair trial by an impartial jury. Procedural protections are guaranteed at each of the stages in the criminal process: (1) pretrial, (2) trial, (3) sentencing, and (4) appeal.

Before a person can be forced to stand trial for a criminal offense (except for members of the armed forces or foreign terrorists), they must be *indicted* by a grand jury, or before a judge in what is called an *information* proceeding. A **grand jury** is concerned not with a person's guilt or innocence but merely with whether there is enough evidence to warrant a trial. The grand jury has wide-ranging investigatory powers and "is to inquire into all information that might bear on its investigations until it is satisfied that it has identified an offense or satisfied itself that none has occurred."[81] The strict rules that govern jury proceedings, and the exclusionary rule to enforce the Fourth Amendment, do not apply, and the grand jury may admit hearsay evidence. If a majority of the grand jurors agree that a trial is justified, they return a *true bill,* or **indictment.** During this stage of the criminal process and throughout the remaining stages, suspects have the right to an attorney, even if they cannot afford one on their own. Communication between the accused and counsel is privileged and cannot be revealed to a jury.

The Constitution guarantees the accused the right to be informed of the nature and cause of the accusation, so he or she can prepare a defense. After indictment, prosecutors and the defense attorney usually discuss the possibility of a **plea bargain** whereby the defendant pleads guilty to a lesser offense that carries a lesser penalty. Prosecutors, facing more cases than they can handle, like plea bargains because they save the expense and time of going to trial and they result in a conviction. Likewise, defendants are often willing to "cop a plea" for a lesser offense to avoid the risk of more serious punishment for the original indictment.

After indictment and preliminary hearings that determine bail and what evidence will be used against the accused, the Constitution guarantees a *speedy and public trial.* Do not, however, take the word "speedy" too literally. Defendants are given time to prepare their defense and often ask for delays because time works to their advantage. In contrast, if the government denies the accused a speedy trial, not only is the conviction reversed but the case must also be dismissed outright.

grand jury
A jury of 12 to 23 persons who, in private, hear evidence presented by the government to determine whether persons shall be required to stand trial. If the jury believes there is sufficient evidence that a crime was committed, it issues an indictment.

indictment
A formal written statement from a grand jury charging an individual with an offense; also called a *true bill.*

plea bargain
An agreement between a prosecutor and a defendant that the defendant will plead guilty to a lesser offense to avoid having to stand trial for a more serious offense.

Under the Sixth Amendment, the accused has a right to trial before a **petit jury** selected from the state and district in which the alleged crime was committed. Although federal law requires juries of 12 members, the Supreme Court has held that states may try defendants before juries consisting of as few as six persons. Conviction in federal courts must be by unanimous vote, but the Court has ruled that state courts may render guilty verdicts by nonunanimous juries, provided that such juries consist of six or more persons.[82]

An *impartial jury,* one that meets the requirements of due process and equal protection, consists of persons who represent a fair cross section of the community. Although defendants are not entitled to juries that reflect their own race, sex, religion, or national origin, government prosecutors cannot strike people from juries because of race or gender, and neither can defense attorneys use what are called *peremptory challenges* to keep people off juries because of race, ethnic origin, or sex.[83]

During the trial, the defendant has a right to obtain witnesses in his or her favor and to have the judge subpoena, or order, witnesses to appear at the trial and testify. Both the accused and witnesses may refuse to testify on the grounds that their testimony would tend to incriminate themselves. If witnesses testify, both the prosecution and the defense have the right to confront and cross-examine them.

The sentencing phase begins with the conclusion of the trial. Here, the jury recommends a verdict of guilty or not guilty. If the accused is found guilty, the judge usually hands down the sentence, though in some cases juries also impose the sentence according to the judge's instructions. The Eighth Amendment forbids the levying of excessive fines and the inflicting of cruel and unusual punishment.

Some types of sentences have received particular attention. We will address the first, *three-strikes laws,* here and the death penalty below. Although the crime rate has generally declined in the past few years, public concern about crime remains high. At the national and state level, presidents, governors, and legislators vie with one another to show their toughness on crime. California, Virginia, Washington, and other states have "three strikes and you're out" laws, requiring a lifetime sentence without the possibility of parole for anyone convicted of a third felony, even if it is a minor offense. In some states, the felonies must be for violent crimes; in others, any three felonies will do. For example, the Supreme Court in *Ewing v. California* (2003) upheld California's tough law for committing three felonies, ruling that a 25-years-to-life sentence for stealing three golf clubs, each valued at $399, did not violate the prohibition against cruel and unusual punishment.[84]

petit jury
A jury of 6 to 12 persons that determines guilt or innocence in a civil or criminal action.

double jeopardy
Trial or punishment for the same crime by the same government; forbidden by the Constitution.

In the final stage of the criminal process, defendants may *appeal* their convictions if they claim they have been denied some constitutional right or the due process and equal protection of the law. The Fifth Amendment also provides that no person shall be "subject for the same offense to be twice put in jeopardy of life or limb." **Double jeopardy** does not prevent punishment by the national and the state governments for the same offense, or for successive prosecutions for the same crime by two states. Nor does the double jeopardy clause forbid civil prosecutions, even after a person has been acquitted in a criminal trial for the same charge.[85]

The Death Penalty

Race and the Death Penalty

As you can see in the "How Other Nations Govern" feature, the United States is unusual among industrialized nations in its retention and use of the death penalty. After a ten-year moratorium on executions in the late 1960s and early 1970s, the U.S. Supreme Court ruled that the death penalty is not necessarily cruel and unusual punishment if it is imposed for crimes that resulted in a victim's death, if the courts "ensure that death sentences are not meted out wantonly or freakishly,"

HOW OTHER NATIONS GOVERN

The Death Penalty Around the World

The strong trend across the world has been to eliminate death penalty statutes and their implementation. Indeed, in December 2007, the United Nations General Assembly adopted a resolution calling for a worldwide moratorium on the death penalty. More than half of the countries in the world, 135, have abolished capital punishment for all or most crimes, and the trend has been growing. The United States and Japan are the only two industrialized countries that retain the death penalty. Most of the 62 countries that still impose capital punishment are in Africa, the Middle East, the Caribbean, and Central America. Of countries we have been examining throughout this book, India, China, Japan, and Nigeria retain the death penalty.

Among the countries that abolished capital punishment for all crimes are those in the European Union, other western and eastern European countries, Cambodia, and South Africa. The United Kingdom abolished capital punishment for murder in 1965. However, not until 1998 did it also remove the possibility of death as punishment for piracy or treason. In Mexico, most states had abolished the death penalty for ordinary crimes as early as 1931, and the last execution in Mexico took place in 1937. However, it was not until 2005 that Mexico abolished the death penalty for all crimes.

The United States continues to use the death penalty, and in 2008 the Supreme Court upheld lethal injection as a constitutional method of execution. Here, a bed is prepared to be used for a lethal injection.

Japan, India, and China all retain the death penalty. In Japan, Minister of Justice Kunio Hatoyama announced that the ministry would streamline the execution process to allow execution within six months after the end of the appeals process. In the six months after that September 2007 announcement, ten executions were carried out. Although in India the Supreme Court has upheld the principal that the death penalty should be applied only in the "rarest of rare cases," the country has been reluctant to abolish its use.

China's use of the death penalty is far and away the most prominent of the countries we are considering. Unlike most countries that reserve the death penalty for murder or treason, China provides the death penalty for 68 different crimes, including nonviolent offenses. Relying on available public reports, Amnesty International estimates that 1,010 people were executed in China in 2006. However, statistics on executions are considered a classified state secret. Sources that Amnesty International cites as credible suggest the figure is more likely 7,500 to 8,000 executions.

QUESTIONS

1. Why does it take countries so long to legally end the death penalty even after they have generally stopped meting out the penalty at trials?
2. Why do you think most countries that use the death penalty use it only for the crime of murder?
3. Why do some countries retain the death penalty while others have dropped it?

and if these processes "confer on the sentencer sufficient discretion to take account of the character and record of the individual offender and the circumstances of the particular offense to ensure that death is the appropriate punishment in a specific case."[86]

The Rehnquist Court made it easier to impose death sentences, cut back on appeals, and carry out executions. More states have added the death penalty (36 states now have it), and the federal government has increased the number of crimes for which the death penalty may be imposed. As a result, the number of persons on death row has increased dramatically. Since capital punishment was reinstated in 1976, more than 1,000 people have been executed nationwide, and more than 3,300 are on death row.[87] However, concerns have also grown about the fairness with which capital punishment is imposed. DNA tests that have established the innocence of a sizable number of those convicted of murder have increased these concerns.[88] Since 1973, 129 people who were convicted of murder and sentenced to death have been exonerated.[89]

The prohibition against cruel and unusual punishment also forbids punishments grossly disproportionate to the severity of the crime. In 2002, the Supreme Court overruled an earlier decision and held that it is excessive and disproportionate to execute mentally retarded convicted murderers because they cannot understand the seriousness of their offense. Also important to the Court were changes in state legislation barring the penalty's implementation that illustrated a consensus against executing the mentally retarded.[90] Using similar reasoning four years later, the Court ruled that executing minors also violated the Eighth Amendment.[91]

Although several of the Court's decisions have limited the death penalty's use, in March 2008, the Court, in a 7-to-2 vote, upheld lethal injections as a constitutionally permissible means of carrying out executions.[92] It did, however, continue its trend in limiting the use of the death penalty by deciding in *Kennedy v. Louisiana* (2008) that death could not be used when the defendant was convicted of child rape in which a death did not result, nor was it intended (the Court had previously ruled that the death penalty violated the Eighth Amendment in the case of adult rape).[93]

Protecting Our Civil Liberties: Whose Responsibility?

Although the U.S. Supreme Court is often seen as the guardian of our civil liberties and minority rights in the United States, it is only one branch of government and cannot do this work alone. In fact, as we discussed in Chapter 14, the judiciary relies on the legislative and executive branches to enforce and provide funding to carry out its decisions. What does that imply for the role you play in protecting our civil liberties?

It is essential for citizens to be active in protecting our civil liberties. If we do not elect representatives who will enforce the Court's decisions and appoint judges who will respect the individual guarantees in the Constitution, we cannot expect that they will be protected. Furthermore, if we do not act when we know civil liberties are being violated, the courts cannot make rulings. The judiciary is a reactive institution. It depends on individual citizens, or individuals working in cooperation through interest groups, to challenge government restrictions on civil liberties. Joseph Frederick may have been waving his "Bong Hits 4 Jesus" banner only to get on television, but he still chose to fight the restriction on his speech. These are not easy challenges and individual citizens will not always win, as Frederick did not, but we must be willing to try.

CHAPTER SUMMARY

1 Evaluate the arguments for amending a Bill of Rights to the original Constitution.

Antifederalists were concerned that the new national government would infringe on individual rights. Although many state constitutions already protected civil liberties, the Bill of Rights was to prevent the national government from infringing on civil liberties.

2 Identify protections under the establishment and free exercise clauses of the Constitution.

The First Amendment forbids the establishment of religion and also guarantees its free exercise. These two freedoms, however, are often in conflict with each other and represent conflicting notions of what is in the public interest.

3 Contrast the categories of protected and unprotected speech.

The Supreme Court holds that there are only four categories of nonprotected speech—libel, obscenity, fighting words, and commercial speech. All other speech is protected under the First Amendment, and government may regulate that speech only when it has a compelling reason and does so in a content-neutral way.

4 Compare and contrast procedural and substantive due process.

The Constitution imposes limits not only on the procedures government must follow but also on the ends it may pursue. Some actions are out of bounds no matter what procedures are followed. Legislatures have the primary role in determining what is reasonable and what is unreasonable. However, the Supreme Court exercises its own independent and final review of legislative determinations of reasonableness, especially on matters affecting civil liberties and civil rights.

5 Analyze the degree to which criminal suspects' rights are protected in our criminal justice system.

The framers knew from their own experiences that in their zeal to maintain power and to enforce the laws, especially in wartime, public officials are often tempted to infringe on the rights of persons accused of crimes. To prevent such abuse, the Bill of Rights requires federal officials to follow detailed procedures in making searches and arrests and in bringing people to trial.

Chapter Self-Test

1. True or False: The Federalists favored a Bill of Rights and succeeded in adding it to the constitution in spite of States' objections. (p. 411)
2. In a few sentences, explain the significance of *Gitlow v. New York,* and how it relates to the term *selective incorporation.* (pp. 411–413)
3. List the five amendments in the Bill of Rights of which *no* part has been applied to states through the application of the Fourteenth Amendment. (p. 413)
4. Which amendment contains both the Establishment Clause and the Free Exercise Clause? (p. 413)
5. Choose one of the tests the Supreme Court uses to determine whether government is acting in accord with the establishment clause, and write a short persuasive essay that defends your choice as the most appropriate test for the Supreme Court to use. Be sure to explain weaknesses you see in the tests you have not chosen. (p. 414)
6. In a few sentences, define the RFRA and tell why it was created. (p. 415)
7. List the four categories of speech presently considered "nonprotected," and give a brief definition of each. (pp. 417–419)
8. Briefly define *prior restraint* and explain the Supreme Court's position on it. (p. 417)
9. Imagine you are a newspaper editor who has just received a reliable tip that a prominent politica leader fathered a child outside marriage. After checking the source, you runthe story and are subsequently sued by the political leader. Write a short response defending your choice based on information in the chapter. (pp. 417–418)
10. Briefly define and contrast *procedural* and *substantive due process.* (p. 423)
11. Which of the following is *not* an aspect of the right to privacy? (pp. 424–431)
    a. the right to be free from government surveillance and intrusion
    b. the right not to have the government make private affairs public
    c. the right to be free in thought and belief from governmental regulations
    d. the right to perform religious acts as dictated by conscience on private property
12. Match each of the following court cases with the significant precedent in the decision. (pp. 409–434)

a. *Roe v. Wade*	i. Reaffirmed a woman's right to an abortion
b. *Romer v. Evans*	ii. Struck down a law criminalizing homosexual sodomy
c. *Lawrence v. Texas*	iii. Upheld Georgia law making consensual sodomy a crime
d. *Bowers v. Hardwick*	iv. Extended right to privacy to abortions
e. *Planned Parenthood v. Casey*	v. Struck down an initiative that would ban state and local governments in Colorado from protecting homosexuals from discrimination

13. Freedom from unreasonable search and seizure is derived from which amendment? (p. 427)
14. In a few sentences, describe the *exclusionary rule* and how it applies to the evolution of Fourth Amendment rights. (p. 430)
15. In a short essay, explain the procedures for a fair trial. (pp. 431–432)

Key Terms

writ of habeas corpus, p. 410

ex post facto law, p. 411

due process clause, p. 411

selective incorporation, p. 413

establishment clause, p. 414

vouchers, p. 414

free exercise clause, p. 414

bad tendency test, p. 416

clear and present danger test, p. 416

preferred position doctrine, p. 416

nonprotected speech, p. 417

prior restraint, p. 417

content- or viewpoint-neutrality, p. 417

libel, p. 418

obscenity, p. 420

fighting words, p. 420

commercial speech, p. 420

civil disobedience, p. 421

property rights, p. 422

eminent domain, p. 422

regulatory taking, p. 422

due process, p. 423

procedural due process, p. 423

substantive due process, p. 423

search warrant, p. 427

exclusionary rule, p. 430

grand jury, p. 431

indictment, p. 431

plea bargain, p. 431

petit jury, p. 432

double jeopardy, p. 432

Further Reading

JEFFREY ABRAMSON, *We, the Jury: The Jury System and the Ideal of Democracy* (Harvard University Press, 2000).

STUART BIEGEL, *Beyond Our Control? Confronting the Limits of Our Legal System in the Age of Cyberspace* (MIT Press, 2001).

STEVEN P. BROWN, *Trumping Religion: The Christian Right, The Free Speech Clause, and the Courts* (University of Alabama Press, 2002).

JAMES MACGREGOR BURNS AND **STEWART BURNS,** *A People's Charter: The Pursuit of Rights in America* (Knopf, 1991).

DAVID COLE AND **JAMES X. DEMPSEY,** *Terrorism and the Constitution,* 3d ed. (New Press, 2006).

LOUIS FISHER, *Religious Liberty in America: Political Safeguards* (University Press of Kansas, 2002).

LOUIS FISHER, *The Constitution and 9/11: Recurring Threats to America's Freedoms* (University Press of Kansas, 2008).

ROBERT JUSTIN GOLDSTEIN, *Flag Burning and Free Speech: The Case of* Texas v. Johnson (University Press of Kansas, 2002).

ROGER HOOD, *The Death Penalty: A Worldwide Perspective,* 3d ed. (Oxford University Press, 2002).

SADAKAT KADRI, *The Trial: A History from Socrates to O. J. Simpson* (Random House, 2005).

ISAAC KRAMNICK AND **LAURENCE MOORE,** *The Godless Constitution: A Moral Defense of the Secular State* (Norton, 2005).

LEONARD W. LEVY, *Emergence of a Free Press* (Oxford University Press, 1985).

ANTHONY LEWIS, *Gideon's Trumpet* (Random House, 1964).

CATHARINE A. MACKINNON, *Only Words* (Harvard University Press, 1993).

ALEXANDER MEIKLEJOHN, *Political Freedom: The Constitutional Powers of the People* (Harper & Row, 1965).

JOHN T. NOONAN JR., *The Lustre of Our Country: The American Experience of Religious Freedom* (University of California Press, 1998).

DAVID M. O'BRIEN, *Constitutional Law and Politics: Civil Rights and Civil Liberties,* 7th ed. (Norton, 2008).

J. W. PELTASON AND **SUE DAVIS,** *Understanding the Constitution,* 16th ed. (Harcourt, 2004).

SHAWN FRANCIS PETERS, *Judging Jehovah's Witnesses: Religious Persecution and the Dawn of the Right Revolution* (University Press of Kansas, 2002).

WILLIAM H. REHNQUIST, *All the Laws but One: Civil Liberties in Wartime* (Knopf, 1998).

BARRY SCHECK, PETER NEUFELD, AND **JIM DWYER,** *Actual Innocence: Five Days to Execution, and Other Dispatches from the Wrongly Convicted* (Doubleday, 2000).

NADINE STROSSEN, *Defending Pornography: Free Speech, Sex, and the Fight for Women's Rights* (Scribner, 1995).

MELVIN UROFSKY, ED., *100 Americans Making Constitutional History* (CQ Press, 2005).

MARY E. VOGEL, *Coercion to Compromise: Plea Bargaining, the Courts, and the Making of Political Authority* (Oxford University Press, 2001).

WELSH S. WHITE, Miranda*'s Waning Protections: Police Interrogation Practices After* Dickerson (University of Michigan Press, 2001).

chapter 16

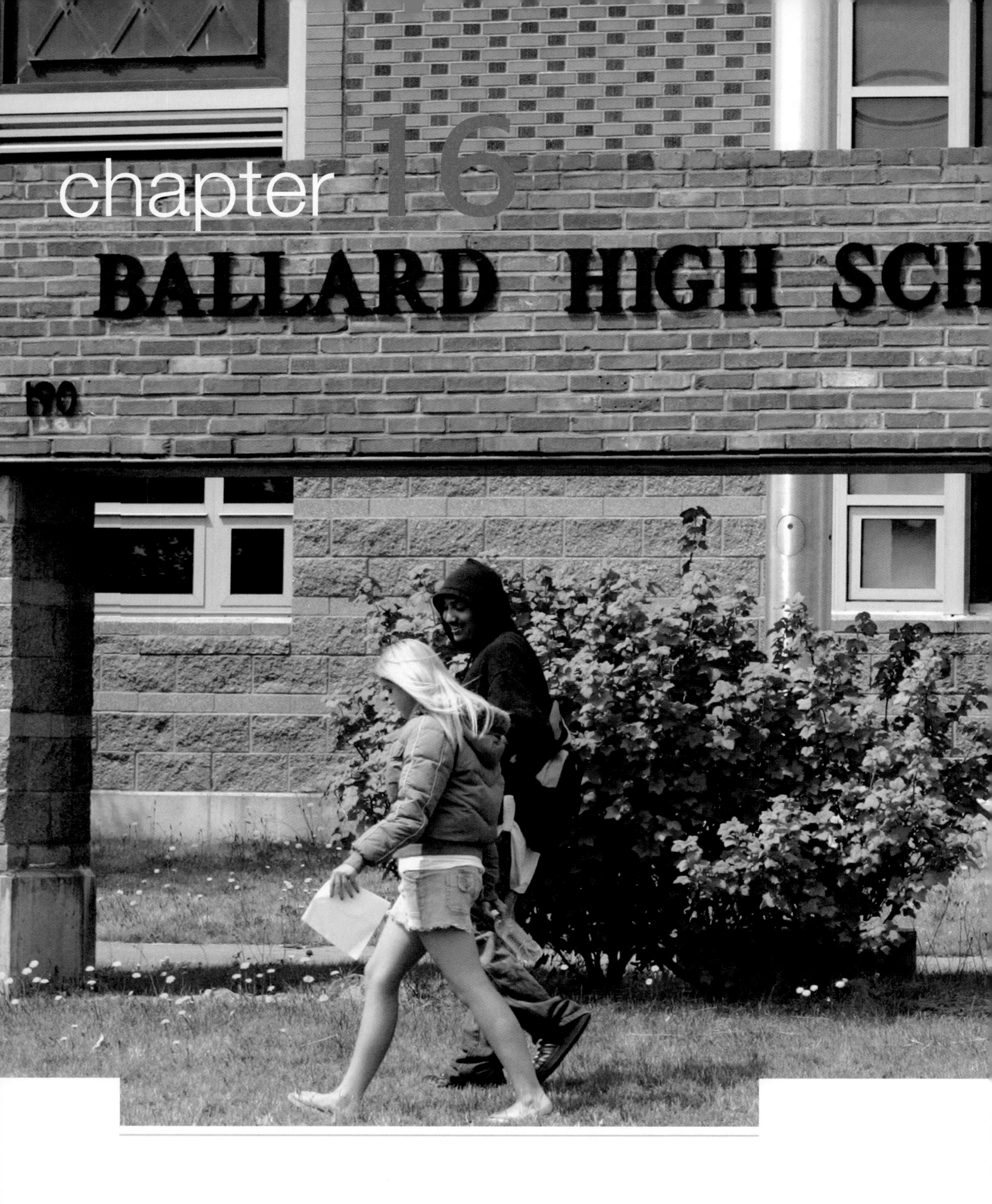

Civil Rights

Equal Rights Under the Law

In 2000, Elizabeth Brose finished eighth grade in Seattle, Washington; the next fall she would start high school. Under her school district's student assignment plan, Elizabeth, a white student, asked the district to assign her to Ballard High School, a newly remodeled school in her neighborhood with an excellent reputation. But race determined her assignment, and Brose was sent to Franklin High instead, a school eight miles away from her home, with lower test scores and a very high number of African American students. When schools received too many applications, the Seattle School District used an "integration tiebreaker" to make schools more reflective of the district's racial composition as a whole.[1] Ballard would have had a heavily white student population without the tiebreaker, which meant Brose had to be assigned to Franklin.[2]

In 1978, Seattle had become the first major U.S. city to use busing to integrate schools without a court order. Its plans had continued since, and although they clearly had popular support, it was not uniform. Some parents, especially those whose children were not placed in their chosen school, were strongly opposed to the program. Karen Brose, Elizabeth's mother, formed Parents Involved in Community Schools, a group opposed to Seattle's plan, and pursued the case in the courts.

Parents Involved in Community Schools was successful in its challenge. On June 28, 2007, the U.S. Supreme Court struck down Seattle's plan, as well as a similar plan used in Louisville, Kentucky. In its sharply divided (5 to 4) opinion, the Court ruled that Seattle had not shown that the goal of racial integration justified the method it used, which relied solely on race (and race broadly construed as white and nonwhite) as *the* factor in the admissions decision without other individualized assessment. In his opinion in the case, Chief Justice Roberts wrote, "The way to stop discrimination on the basis of race is to stop discriminating on the basis of race."[3]

The Seattle case highlights the United States' continuing dilemma concerning how to best ensure equality, and how to do so without violating the Constitution's protection from discrimination based on race. In this case, Elizabeth Brose's **civil rights** were at issue—her right not to be discriminated against because of race, religion, gender, or ethnic origin. The Constitution protects civil rights in two ways. First, it ensures that government officials do not discriminate against us; second, it grants national and state governments the power to protect these civil rights against interference by private individuals.

Though the Constitution does not make any reference to "equality" (the word never appears in the Constitution or in the original Bill of Rights), we know that the framers believed all men—at least all white adult men—were equally entitled to life, liberty, and the pursuit of happiness. Though it took many years for the concept of equality to be extended to all people, the framers did create a system of government designed to protect what they called *natural rights.* (Today we speak of *human rights,* but the idea is basically the same.) By **natural rights** the framers meant that every person, by virtue of being a human being, has an equal right to protection against arbitrary treatment and an equal right to the liberties the Bill of Rights guarantees.

LEARNING **OBJECTIVES**

1. Evaluate the importance of citizenship rights, particularly concerning immigration and the war on terror.
2. Compare and contrast different groups' efforts to obtain equal protection of the law.
3. Appraise the reasons for delay in the women's rights movement.
4. Assess the constitutional tests applied to discriminatory laws in the United States.
5. Analyze the protections provided by the 1965 Voting Rights Act.
6. Describe how Congress has legislated against discrimination in housing and accommodations.
7. Explain the difficulty of integration in a society largely segregated by housing patterns.
8. Evaluate the current state of affirmative action in the United States.

CHAPTER OUTLINE

- Equality and Equal Rights
- Citizenship Rights
- The Quest for Equal Justice
- Equal Protection of the Laws: What Does It Mean?
- Voting Rights
- Rights to Equal Access: Accommodations, Jobs, and Homes
- Education Rights
- The Affirmative Action Controversy
- Equal Rights Today

Comparing Civil Rights

You Are the Mayor and Need to Make Civil Rights Decisions

civil rights
The rights of all people to be free from irrational discrimination such as that based on race, religion, gender, or ethnic origin.

natural rights
The rights of all people to dignity and worth; also called *human rights.*

affirmative action
Remedial action designed to overcome the effects of discrimination against minorities and women.

These rights do not depend on citizenship; governments do not grant them. They are the rights of *all people.* In this chapter we examine the protection of our rights from abuse *by government* and the protection *through government* of our right to be free from abuse by our *fellow citizens.* We will discuss several landmark cases, such as *Brown v. Board of Education of Topeka,* that highlight the courage of individuals such as Oliver Brown, who fought for his daughter Linda's right to attend her neighborhood school. These are not easy battles, but they are essential to secure our civil rights.

We will begin this chapter by discussing citizenship rights in general. Although natural rights do not depend on citizenship, the kinds of protections that can be denied based on citizenship have become an increasingly important issue in recent years. We then discuss several groups' efforts to secure their civil rights and examine what we mean by "equal protection of the law." In doing so, we will pay particular attention to two laws essential to securing civil rights protections: the Civil Rights Act of 1964 and the Voting Rights Act of 1965. Finally, we examine the controversy over affirmative action. We'll see that the debate over civil rights is not over and that the way we deal with it today will direct the path of civil rights in the future.

Equality and Equal Rights

Citizens of the United States are committed to equality. "Equality," however, is an elusive term. The concept of equality on which we have the greatest consensus is that everyone should have *equality of opportunity* regardless of race, ethnic origin, religion, and, in recent years, gender and sexual orientation.

There is not much equal opportunity if one person is born into a well-to-do family, lives in a safe suburb, and receives a good education, while another is born into a poor, broken family, lives in a run-down inner-city neighborhood, and attends inferior schools. Some argue that providing equalizing opportunities for the disadvantaged through federal programs such as Head Start, which helps prepare preschool children from poor families for elementary school, are necessary to bridge this gap.

Traditionally, we have emphasized *individual* achievement, but in recent decades, some politicians and civil rights leaders have focused attention on the concept of *equality between groups.* When large disparities in wealth and advantage exist between groups—as between black and white people or between women and men—equality becomes a highly divisive political issue. Those who are disadvantaged emphasize economic and social factors that exclude them from the mainstream. They champion programs like **affirmative action** that are designed to provide opportunities for those who have been disadvantaged because they belong to a certain group. As we will discuss later in this chapter, such programs have been and continue to be controversial.

Finally, equality can also mean *equality of results.* A perennial debate is whether social justice and genuine equality can exist in a nation in which people of one class have so much and others have so little, and in which the gap between them is growing wider.[4] There is considerable support for guaranteeing a minimum floor below which no one should be allowed to fall, but American adults generally do not support an equality of results.

Citizenship Rights

Although natural rights do not depend on citizenship, important legal rights come with citizenship. Citizenship determines nationality and defines who is a member of, owes allegiance to, and is a subject of the nation. But in a constitutional democracy, citizenship is an *office,* and like other offices, it carries with it certain powers and responsibilities. How citizenship is acquired and retained is therefore important.

Proud naturalized citizens are sworn in at an emotional ceremony.

How Citizenship Is Acquired and Lost

LEARNING **OBJECTIVE**

1 Evaluate the importance of citizenship rights, particularly concerning immigration and the war on terror.

The basic right of citizenship was not given constitutional protection until 1868, when the Fourteenth Amendment was adopted; before that, each state determined citizenship. The Fourteenth Amendment states, "All persons born or naturalized in the United States, and subject to the jurisdiction thereof, are citizens of the United States and of the State wherein they reside." This means that all persons born in the United States, except children born to foreign ambassadors and ministers, are citizens of this country regardless of the citizenship of their parents.

Naturalization People can also acquire citizenship by **naturalization,** a legal act conferring citizenship on an alien. Congress determines naturalization requirements (see Table 16–1 for the list of requirements). Today, with minor exceptions, non-enemy aliens over age 18 who have been lawfully admitted for permanent residence and who have resided in the United States for at least five years and in the state for at least six months are eligible for naturalization. Any state or federal court in the United States or the Immigration and Naturalization Service (INS) can grant citizenship. The INS, with the

naturalization
A legal action conferring citizenship on an alien.

TABLE
16–1 | Requirements for Naturalization

An applicant for naturalization must:

1. Be over age 18.
2. Be lawfully admitted to the United States for permanent residence and have resided in the United States for at least five years and in the state for at least six months.
3. File a petition of naturalization with a clerk of a court of record (federal or state) verified by two witnesses.
4. Be able to read, write, and speak English.
5. Possess a good moral character.
6. Understand and demonstrate an attachment to the history, principles, and form of government of the United States.
7. Demonstrate that he or she is well disposed toward the good order and happiness of the country.
8. Demonstrate that he or she does not now believe in, nor within the last ten years has ever believed in, advocated, or belonged to an organization that supports opposition to organized government, overthrow of government by violence, or the doctrines of world communism or any other form of totalitarianism.

For more information about immigration and naturalization, go to the Web site of the Federation for American Immigration Reform at www.fairus.org.

help of the FBI, makes the necessary investigations. Any person denied citizenship after a hearing before an immigration officer may appeal to a federal district judge.

Dual Citizenship Because each nation has complete authority to define nationality for itself, two or more nations may consider a person a citizen. **Dual citizenship** is not unusual, especially for people from nations that do not recognize the right of individuals to renounce their citizenship, called the **right of expatriation.** Children born abroad to U.S. citizens may also be citizens of the nation in which they were born. Children born in the United States of parents from a foreign nation may also be citizens of their parents' country.

dual citizenship
Citizenship in more than one nation.

right of expatriation
The right to renounce one's citizenship.

Rights of U.S. Citizens

A person becomes a citizen of one of the 50 states merely by residing in that state. *Residence* as understood in the Fourteenth Amendment means the place a person calls home. The legal status of residence is not the same as physical presence. A person may be living in Washington, D.C., but be a citizen of California—that is, consider California home and vote in that state.

Most of our most important rights flow from *state* citizenship. In the *Slaughter-House Cases* (1873), the Supreme Court carefully distinguished between the privileges of U.S. citizens and those of state citizens.[5] It held that the only privileges of national citizenship are those that "owe their existence to the Federal Government, its National Character, its Constitution, or its laws." These privileges have never been completely specified, but they include the right to use the navigable waters of the United States and to protection on the high seas, to assemble peacefully and petition for redress of grievances, to vote if qualified to do so under state laws and have your vote counted properly, and to travel throughout the United States.

In times of war, the rights and liberties of citizenship are tested and have been curbed. The Supreme Court overruled President Abraham Lincoln's use of military courts to try civilians during the Civil War,[6] but upheld the World War II internment of Japanese Americans in "relocation camps"[7] and has approved the use of military tribunals to try captured foreign saboteurs[8] who were held abroad, but ruled that citizens may not be subject to courts-martial or denied the guarantees of the Bill of Rights.[9] For that reason, John Walker Lindh, the young U.S. citizen captured while fighting with the Taliban in Afghanistan in 2001, was accorded the assistance of counsel and tried in court.

Although the Court upheld the internment of Japanese-American citizens during World War II, it was later determined that the government had misrepresented information to the Court about the potential threat they posed. It was not until 1988 that the U.S. government officially apologized for its actions, and Congress awarded reparations to those interned during the war.

In the war against international terrorism, President George W. Bush issued orders declaring U.S. citizens "enemy combatants" for plotting with the Al-Qaeda network and authorized their and other captured foreign nationals' detention in military compounds, without counsel or access to a court of law. However, even in these cases, prisoners have a right to have their detainment reviewed, and the Court's decision in *Boumediene v. Bush* (2008) reinforced this right. Even detainees designated as enemy combatants have the right to appeal their detention in the federal courts.[10]

Rights of Aliens

During periods of suspicion and hostility toward aliens, the protections of citizenship are even more precious. Congress enacted the Enemy Alien Act of 1798, which remains in effect, authorizing the president during wartime to detain and expel citizens of a country with which we are at war. Citizens may not be expelled from the country, but aliens may be expelled for even minor infractions.[11] The Supreme Court also upheld the 1996 amendments to the Immigration and Naturalization Act that require mandatory detention during deportation hearings of aliens accused of certain crimes,[12] though they may not be held longer than six months.[13]

The Struggle for Equal Protection

Still, the Constitution protects many rights of *all persons,* not just of American citizens. Only citizens may run for elective office and their right to vote may not be denied, but all other rights are not so literally restricted. Neither Congress nor the states can deny to aliens the rights of freedom of religion or freedom of speech. Nor can any government deprive any person of the due process of the law or equal protection under the laws.[14]

However, Congress and the states may deny or limit welfare and many other kinds of benefits to aliens. Congress has denied most federally assisted benefits to illegal immigrants and has permitted states to deny them many other benefits, making an exception only for emergency medical care, disaster relief, and some nutrition programs. The Court has also upheld laws barring the employment of aliens as police officers, schoolteachers, and probation officers.[15] Although states have considerable discretion over what benefits they give to aliens, the Supreme Court has held that states cannot constitutionally exclude children of undocumented aliens from the public schools or charge their parents tuition.[16]

The Quest for Equal Justice

LEARNING **OBJECTIVE**

Compare and contrast different groups' efforts to obtain equal protection of the law.

The rights of citizenship have been prominent throughout our country's history, but not all people in the United States were originally granted full rights of citizenship. Here we review the political history and social contexts in which constitutional challenges to laws and other government actions relating to civil rights for women and minorities arose. This history involves more than court decisions, laws, and constitutional amendments, however. It encompasses the entire social, economic, and political system. And although the struggles of all groups are interwoven, they are not identical, so we deal briefly and separately with each.

Racial Equality

U.S. citizens had a painful confrontation with the problem of race at the time of the Civil War (1861–1865). As a result of the northern victory, the Thirteenth, Fourteenth, and Fifteenth Amendments became part of the Constitution. During Reconstruction in the late 1860s and 1870s, Congress passed civil rights laws to implement these amendments and established programs to provide educational and social services for the freed slaves. But the Supreme Court struck down many of these laws, and it was not until the 1960s that legal progress was again made toward ensuring African Americans their civil rights.

Segregation and White Supremacy Before Reconstruction programs could have any significant effect, the white southern political leadership regained power, and by 1877, Reconstruction was ended. Northern political leaders abandoned African Americans to their fate at the hands of their former white masters; presidents no longer concerned themselves with enforcing civil rights laws, and Congress enacted no new ones. The Supreme Court either declared old laws unconstitutional or interpreted them so narrowly that they were ineffective. The Court also gave such a limited construction to the Thirteenth, Fourteenth, and Fifteenth Amendments that they failed to accomplish their intended purpose of protecting the rights of African Americans.[17]

For almost a century after the Civil War, white supremacy went unchallenged in the South, where most African Americans then lived. They were kept from voting; they were forced to accept menial jobs; they were denied educational opportunities; they were segregated in public and private facilities.[18] They were lynched on an average of once every four days, and few white people raised a voice in protest.

During World War I (1914–1918), African Americans began to migrate to northern cities to seek jobs in war factories. The Great Depression of the 1930s and World War II in the 1940s accelerated their relocation. Although discrimination continued, more jobs became available, and African Americans made social gains. As their migration from the rural South shifted the racial composition of cities across much of the United States, the African American vote became important in national elections. These changes created an African American middle class opposed to segregation as a symbol of servitude and a cause of inequality. By the midtwentieth century, urban African Americans were active and politically powerful. There was a growing demand to abolish color barriers.

A significant sign of integration was Jackie Robinson's debut with the Brooklyn Dodgers in 1947, breaking Major League Baseball's "color line." Robinson was active in the civil rights movement with the National Association for the Advancement of Colored People (NAACP) and its Freedom Fund Campaign. In 2005 he was posthumously awarded a Congressional Gold Medal, the highest honor a civilian can receive.

Slow Government Response By the 1930s, African Americans were challenging the doctrine of segregation in the courts, and after World War II, civil rights litigation began to have a major impact. Beginning with the landmark 1954 ruling in *Brown v. Board of Education of Topeka,* the Supreme Court prohibited racially segregated public schools[19] and subsequently struck down most of the devices that state and local authorities had used to keep African Americans from voting.[20] We discuss *Brown* in detail later in the chapter. Although the Court reached rulings ending segregation, achieving a significant level of desegregation would require the other branches of government to act.

In the late 1940s and 1950s, Presidents Harry S. Truman and Dwight D. Eisenhower used their executive authority to fight segregation in the armed services and the federal bureaucracy. They directed the Department of Justice to enforce whatever civil rights laws were on the books, but Congress still held back. In the late 1950s, an emerging national consensus in favor of governmental action to protect civil rights, plus the political clout of African Americans in the northern states, began to influence Congress. In 1957, northern and western members of Congress from both parties overrode a southern filibuster in the Senate and enacted the first federal civil rights laws since Reconstruction.

A Turning Point Even after the Supreme Court declared racially segregated public schools unconstitutional, most African Americans still went to segregated schools, and there was widespread resistance to integration in the South. As we discuss in detail later in the chapter, many legal barriers to equal rights had fallen, yet most African Americans still could not buy houses where they wanted, compete fairly for the jobs they needed, send their children to well-equipped schools, or eat in restaurants or walk freely on the streets of "white neighborhoods."

Still, change began to come by way of a massive social, economic, and political movement. It began in Montgomery, Alabama, on December 1, 1955, when Rosa Parks, an African American seamstress, refused to give up her seat to a white man on a bus as the law required her to do. She was removed from the bus, arrested, and fined. The black community responded by boycotting city buses.

The boycott worked and also produced a charismatic national civil rights leader, the Reverend Martin Luther King Jr. Through his doctrine of nonviolent resistance, King gave a new dimension to the struggle. Following a peaceful 1963 demonstration

Rosa Parks's decision not to give up her seat on the bus in Montgomery, Alabama, sparked a boycott by African Americans who, for more than a year, refused to ride the segregated city buses. Rosa Parks died in 2006.

in Birmingham, Alabama, that was countered with fire hoses, police dogs, and mass arrests, more than a quarter of a million people converged on Washington, D.C., to hear King and other civil rights leaders speak. By the time the summer was over, hardly a city, North or South, had not had demonstrations, protests, or sit-ins; some cities erupted in violence.

This direct action had an effect. Many cities enacted civil rights ordinances, more schools were desegregated, and President John F. Kennedy urged Congress to enact a comprehensive civil rights bill. Late in 1963, the nation's grief over the assassination of President Kennedy, who had become identified with civil rights goals, added political fuel to the drive for decisive federal action to protect civil rights.[21] President Lyndon B. Johnson, who was crucial in the passage of the Voting Rights Act of 1965 (see the "History Makers" feature in Chapter 8), made civil rights legislation his highest priority. On July 2, 1964, after months of debate, he signed into law the Civil Rights Act of 1964, which forbids discrimination on the basis of race, color, religion, sex, or nationality.[22]

Riots and Reaction Although the legal situation for African Americans had improved, millions demonstrated growing impatience with the discrimination that remained. In 1965, a brutal riot took place in Watts, a section of Los Angeles. In 1966 and 1967, the disorders spread in scope and intensity. The Detroit riot in July 1967, the worst such disturbance up to that time in modern U.S. history, made clear the deep divisions between the races and the urgency of taking corrective action.[23]

During the later part of the Johnson administration and through the next several years, the Vietnam War and Watergate diverted attention from government efforts directed at improving housing, jobs, and welfare conditions for minorities. Nor were these issues priorities in the Reagan and George H. W. Bush administrations. The Clinton administration (1993–2001) was more inclined to use government power to deal with inequality than its immediate predecessors had been, but because of budgetary constraints and Republican opposition to "big government" programs, it was largely unable to promote major initiatives directly aimed at the problems of the inner cities where many poor African Americans lived. The administration of George W. Bush has pursued more race-neutral policies such as the No Child Left Behind program, aimed at raising educational standards across the nation. Still, civil rights leaders such as the Reverend Jesse Jackson continue efforts to eliminate the vestiges of racial discrimination, through boycotts and lawsuits aimed at persuading businesses and corporations to reach out to, hire, and promote more African Americans.

Firefighters in Birmingham, Alabama, turned their hoses full blast on civil rights demonstrators in the 1960s. At times the water came with such force, even on children, that it literally tore the bark off fully grown trees.

HISTORY MAKERS

Martin Luther King Jr.

Martin Luther King Jr. was born January 25, 1929, in Atlanta, Georgia. He entered Morehouse College in 1944 and majored in sociology, but in his junior year, he decided to enter the ministry. After graduating from Morehouse, King entered the Crozer Theological Seminary in Pennsylvania. There he became a follower of the Indian pacifist Mohandas Gandhi. Following graduation, King earned a doctorate from Boston University in 1955. He then became pastor of the Dexter Avenue Baptist Church in Montgomery, Alabama.

Martin Luther King Jr.

In 1957, King and another Baptist minister, Ralph Abernathy, founded the Southern Christian Leadership Conference to advance the cause of civil rights. King's home and church were bombed that year, and violence against black protesters began to escalate. In March 1963, King was jailed in Birmingham, Alabama, for leading a protest parade without a permit. Subsequently, he led the March on Washington on August 28, 1963, at which hundreds of thousands of civil rights activists focused national attention on the racial problems in the country. The march built support for the passage of the Civil Rights Act of 1964.

Speaking at the march from the steps of the Lincoln Memorial, King delivered his famous "I Have a Dream" speech, in which he said he dreamed of the day when his "four little children...will not be judged by the color of their skin but by the content of their character," and concluded with the memorable line, "Free at last! Thank God Almighty, we are free at last!"*

In 1963, King became *Time* magazine's Man of the Year, and in 1964, he was awarded the Nobel Peace Prize for his leadership in the civil rights movement and advocacy of nonviolent protest. In 1968, King was assassinated, and riots erupted in more than 100 cities .

QUESTIONS

1. How do you think King's religious training and readings on Gandhi's principles affected his approach to the civil rights movement?
2. Why do you think Dr. King attracted so much attention and a following among all types of citizens?
3. Does the civil rights movement still exist today? Should its goals apply to immigrants?

*Martin Luther King Jr. Research and Education Institute, Stanford University, "I Have a Dream," address at March on Washington for Jobs and Freedom, August 28, 1963, www.stanford.edu/group/King/mlkpapers/.

In the 2008 presidential election, for the first time a major party nominated an African American for president. Barack Obama, the Democratic nominee, on more than one occasion addressed the issue of race in U.S. life. Obama's candidacy clearly resonated with blacks but transcended race to activate other voters, especially younger ones.

On November 4, 2008, American voters elected Barack Obama president of the United States, the first time an African American candidate has been elected to the office. In addition to Obama's victory, Sarah Palin ran as the vice presidential candidate on the Republican ticket, only the second time a woman has gained her party's nomination for that office. The historic election was one where the candidates, more so than at any time in the past, represented the diversity of the United States electorate. As President-Elect Obama discussed in his victory speech, this diversity was a direct result of the hard-won successes in our country's long battle over race and gender equality.

LEARNING **OBJECTIVE**

 Appraise the reasons for delay in the women's rights movement.

Women's Struggle for Equality

Women's Rights

The 2008 election broke other barriers besides race. The Democrats' other major contender for the nomination was Hillary Clinton, who would have been the first woman nominated by a major party for the presidency. Because of the historic nature of the Obama candidacy, less attention was paid to the fact that Senator Clinton was herself breaking barriers in her string of primary election victories and near majority of elected delegates. In some ways, the serious candidacies of Senators Clinton and Obama reflect the early struggles for equal rights in which the drive for women's rights was intertwined with the efforts to secure equality for African Americans.

The Seneca Falls Women's Rights Convention (1848), which launched the women's movement, attracted men and women who actively campaigned to abolish slavery and to secure the rights of African Americans and women. But as the Civil War approached, women were urged to abandon their own cause and devote their energies to ending slavery.[24] The Civil War brought the women's movement to a halt, and the temperance movement to prohibit the sale of liquor, which gathered strength in the late nineteenth century, also diverted attention away from women's rights. The Fourteenth and Fifteenth Amendments did not advance voting rights for women, even as they guaranteed that right, in theory, to males regardless of race.

By the turn of the twentieth century, however, a vigorous campaign was under way for **women's suffrage**—the right of women to vote. The first victories came in western states, where Wyoming led the way. As a territory, Wyoming had given women the right to vote in 1869. When members of Congress in Washington grumbled about this "petticoat provision," the Wyoming legislators replied that they would stay out of the Union 100 years rather than come in without women's suffrage. Congress gave in and admitted Wyoming to the Union in 1890. By the end of World War I, more than half of the states had granted women the right to vote in some or all elections.

Susan B. Anthony and Elizabeth Cady Stanton were the two most influential leaders of the women's suffrage movement in the nineteenth century.

Many suffragists were dissatisfied with this state-by-state approach. They wanted a decisive victory—a constitutional amendment that would force all states to allow qualified women to vote. Finally, in 1919, Congress proposed the Nineteenth Amendment. Many southerners opposed the amendment because it gave Congress enforcement power, which might bring federal officials to investigate elections and ensure that it was being obeyed—an interference that could call attention to how blacks were being kept from voting.

Women won the right to vote with the ratification of the Nineteenth Amendment in 1920, but they were still denied equal pay and equal rights, and national and state laws imposed many legal disabilities on them, such as the lack of comparable pay and health benefits. In the 1970s and 1980s, the unsuccessful struggle to secure the adoption of the Equal Rights Amendment occupied much of the attention of the women's movement. But now there are other goals, and women have mobilized their political clout behind issues that range from equal pay to world peace, an end to sexual harassment, abortion rights, and the election of more women to office.[25]

Since the late 1980s, the Supreme Court has been reluctant to expand the same level of Fourteenth Amendment protection against gender discrimination as it has against racial discrimination. But it did hold that Virginia could not create a separate military academy for women instead of admitting them into the all-male Virginia Military Institute, a 150-year-old state-run institution.[26]

And the courts have increasingly enforced the prohibition against sex discrimination in the 1964 Civil Rights Act and expanded it to forbid sexual harassment in the workplace. In 1986, the Court applied the act to "quid pro quo" sexual harassment, in which an employer requires sexual favors from a person as a condition of employment (in hiring, promotions, and firing).[27] It has since ruled that the act also forbids a "hostile environment," defined as a workplace "permeated" with intimidation, ridicule, and insult that is severe and pervasive, and this includes same-sex harassment.[28]

Many women still feel that a "glass ceiling" in large corporations prevents their advancement. But major progress has been made, with more and more women going to graduate and professional schools and into the media and business. Indeed, during the past three decades, more women have graduated from colleges and universities than men (see Figure 16–1).

Hispanics

The struggle for civil rights has not been limited to women and African Americans. Throughout U.S. history, many native-born citizens have considered new waves of immigrants suspect, especially if the newcomers were not white or English-speaking. Formal barriers of law and informal barriers of custom combined to deny equal rights

women's suffrage
The right of women to vote.

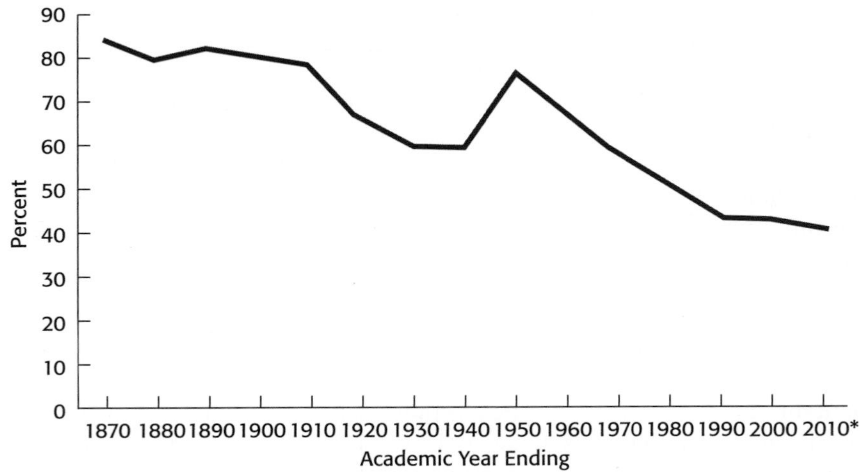

FIGURE 16–1
Percentage of Bachelor's Degrees Awarded to Men.

SOURCE: From *The Washington Post,* June 25, 2002.

*Percentage for 2010 is projected by the Pell Institute for the Study of Opportunity in Higher Education, National Center for Education Statistics.

to immigrants. But as groups established themselves—first economically and then politically—most barriers were swept away, and the newcomers or their children enjoyed the same constitutionally guaranteed rights as other citizens.

As we discussed in Chapter 5, most Hispanics—many of whose ancestors have been U.S. citizens for generations—are bilingual, speaking Spanish as well as English. However, because English may not be the first language of many new immigrants, it has been difficult for some to do well in school or to become business executives and professionals. Although less visible than African Americans, Hispanics have experienced the same kinds of discrimination in employment, education, housing, and access to public accommodations.

In many parts of the United States, Hispanics have not been able to translate their numbers into comparable political clout because of political differences among them and because many are not citizens or registered to vote. However, after California adopted Proposition 187 in 1994, which denied medical, educational, and social services to illegal immigrants, and Congress amended the federal welfare laws to curtail benefits to noncitizens, many immigrants rushed to become naturalized. Half of all Hispanic Americans live in two states: California and Texas. In 2001, California became the first big state in which white people are in the minority, and Texas followed in 2005; a majority of the population are racial minorities (majority-minority) in Hawaii, New Mexico, and the District of Columbia as well.[29]

Asian Americans

The term "Asian American" describes approximately 10 million people from many different countries and ethnic backgrounds. Most do not think of themselves as Asians but as U.S. citizens of Chinese, Japanese, Indian, Vietnamese, Cambodian, Korean, or other specific ancestry. Although Asian Americans are often considered a "model minority" because of their successes in education and business, the U.S. Civil Rights Commission found that "Asian-Americans do face widespread prejudice, discrimination, and barriers to equal opportunity," and that racially motivated violence against them "occurs with disturbing frequency."[30] Discrimination against Asian Americans is, unfortunately, nothing new. The Naturalization Act of 1906, for example, made it impossible for any Asian American to become a U.S. citizen. Though the act was challenged, the Supreme Court upheld its provision that only white persons and aliens of African nativity or descent were eligible for citizenship.[31]

Chinese Americans The Chinese were the first Asians to come to the United States. Beginning in 1847, when young male Chinese peasants came to the American West to

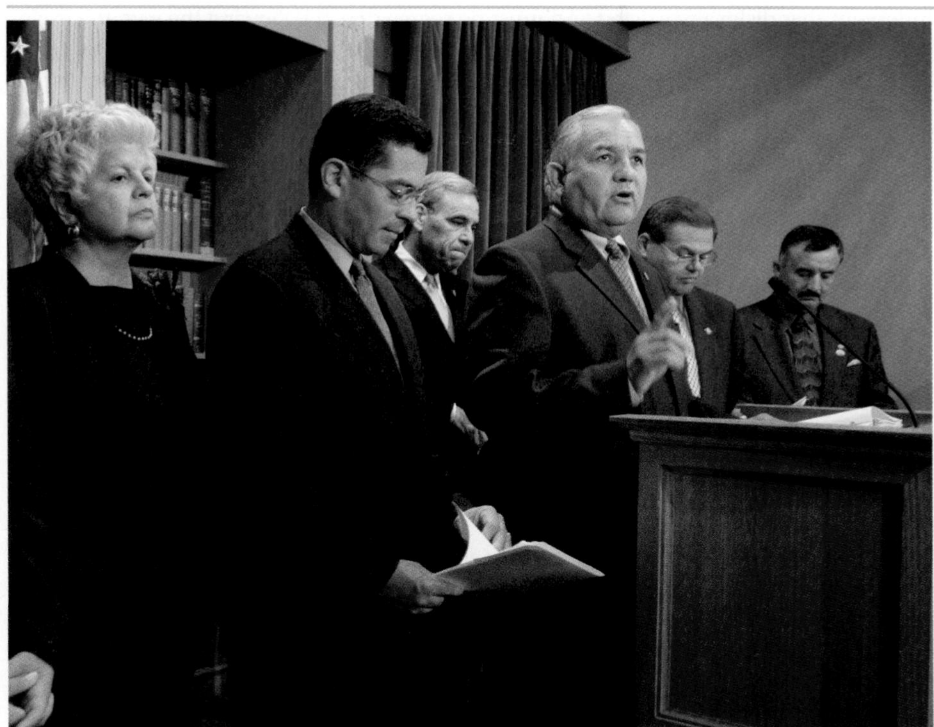

Hispanics have gained representation at both the state and national level. Members of the Congressional Hispanic Caucus are seen here promoting issues important to Hispanic Americans, such as addressing their under-representation on corporate boards and creating environmentally healthy communities.

escape poverty and to work in mines, on railroads, and on farms, the Chinese encountered economic and cultural fears by the white majority, who did not understand their language or their culture. Chinese Americans were recruited by the Central Pacific Railroad to work on the transcontinental railroad, but anti-Chinese sentiment grew. By the 1870s, attacks on "Chinatowns" began in cities across the United States. The Chinese Exclusion Act of 1882 restricted Chinese immigration and excluded Chinese immigrants already in the United States from the possibility of citizenship. It was not until 1943 that Congress repealed the Chinese Exclusion Act and opened the door to citizenship for Chinese Americans.

The 1965 Amendments to the Immigration and Nationality Act went further to end the nationality criteria and thus equalize immigration criteria across race and ethnicity. Since that time, the Chinese have moved into the mainstream of U.S. society, and they are beginning to run for and win local political offices. Gary Locke, a Democrat and a graduate of Yale and Boston University Law School, became the first Chinese American to become governor of a continental state when in 1996 he was elected to the first of two terms as governor of Washington.

Japanese Americans The Japanese migrated first to Hawaii in the 1860s and then to California in the 1880s. By the beginning of the twentieth century, they faced overt hostility. In 1905, white labor leaders organized the Japanese and Korean Exclusion League, and in 1906, the San Francisco Board of Education excluded all Chinese, Japanese, and Korean children from neighborhood schools. Some western states passed laws denying the right to own land to aliens who were ineligible to become citizens—meaning aliens of Asian ancestry.

During World War II, anti-Japanese hysteria provoked the internment of West Coast Japanese—most of whom were loyal U.S. citizens guilty of no crimes—in prison camps in California, Colorado, and other states. Their property was often sold at deep discount rates, and many of them lost their businesses, jobs, and incomes. Although Japanese Americans challenged the curfews and internment policies, the U.S. Supreme Court upheld the government's actions. In *Korematsu v. United States* (1944), the Court ruled that under the threat to national security, they could not reject congressional and military judgment that disloyalty existed and must be segregated.[32] Following the war, the exclusionary acts were repealed, though discrimination against Japanese Americans persisted, such as the limits placed on Japanese American student enrollment at many colleges and universities. In 1988, President Ronald Reagan signed a law providing $20,000 restitution to each of the approximately 60,000 surviving World War II internees.

Other Asian Americans Like other Asian Americans, Koreans faced overt discrimination in jobs and housing, but a Korean middle class has been growing, with many Korean Americans becoming teachers, doctors, and lawyers. Others operate small family businesses such as dry cleaners, florist shops, service stations, and grocery stores, often in inner cities.[33]

When Filipinos first came to the United States in the early twentieth century, they were considered U.S. nationals because the Philippine Islands were a U.S. possession. Nonetheless, they were denied rights to full citizenship and faced discrimination and even violence, including anti-Filipino riots in the state of Washington in 1928 and later in California, where nearly one-third of the more than 1.5 million Filipinos in the United States live.[34] Their economic status has improved, but their influence in politics remains as small as their numbers.

The newest Asian arrivals consist of more than a million refugees from Vietnam, Laos, and Cambodia, who first came to the United States in the 1970s and settled mostly in California and Louisiana. Although this group included middle-class people who left Vietnam after the communist victory there in 1975, it also consisted of many "boat people," so called because they fled Vietnam in small boats, arriving in the United States without financial resources. In a relatively short time, most of these new Asian Americans established themselves economically. Although they are starting to have political influence, some remain socially and economically segregated.

Native Americans

Almost half of the more than 2 million Native Americans in the United States live on or near a *reservation*—a tract of land given to the tribal nations by treaties with the federal government—and are enrolled as members of one of the 550 federally recognized tribes, including 226 groups in Alaska.[35] Native Americans speak about 200 different languages, although most also speak English.

The history of discrimination against Native Americans in the United States is a great stain on our human rights record. Although discrimination against African Americans often gets more attention in civil rights discussions, legally sanctioned discrimination against Native Americans followed a similar path. Efforts to forcibly move Native American tribes off their land and further west as more whites migrated to the Midwest and western states are well known. The Indian Removal Act, passed in 1830, required that all Native American tribes be moved from the East and Southeast. The act also authorized the use of force to meet its goals. It is estimated that 4,000 of the 18,000 Cherokee Indians forced to move west into what became eastern Oklahoma in the late 1830s died on the "Trail of Tears."[36]

Discrimination continued as government programs attempted to assimilate Native Americans in mainstream U.S. culture. Students living on reservations were sent to boarding schools where they were taught mainstream values, and beginning in 1952 an Urban Relocation Program was developed to get Native Americans off reservations and into cities with promises of jobs and a better standard of living. Although many Native Americans moved to the cities, not all were able to find jobs and many returned to reservations.

Native American rights organizations, including the American Indian Movement, protested discrimination against Native Americans in housing, employment, and health care. Over time, other civil rights groups, such as the American Civil Liberties Union (ACLU), have joined the fight to protect Native American civil rights. Currently pending suits allege discrimination against Native Americans in the public schools as well as in the U.S. Department of Agriculture's farm-loan programs.

As a result of these efforts and of a greater national consciousness, most citizens are now aware that many Native Americans continue to face discrimination and live in poverty. They "are in far worse health than the rest of the population, dying earlier and suffering disproportionately from alcoholism, accidents, diabetes, and pneumonia."[37] Although in recent years the rest of the United States has experienced about 4 percent unemployment, on many reservations the jobless rate continues to be 50 to 60 percent. Some reservations lack adequate health care facilities, schools, housing, and jobs. Congress has started to compensate Native Americans for past injustices and to provide more opportunities to develop tribal economic independence, and judges are showing greater vigilance in enforcing Indian treaty rights.

In 1986, Ben Nighthorse Campbell, a Colorado Democrat, became the first Native American to be elected to Congress. He later became a Republican after being elected to the Senate in 1992 and retired in 2005. U.S. Representative Tom Cole, a Republican from Oklahoma, is the only Native American currently serving in Congress.

Equal Protection of the Laws: What Does It Mean?

The **equal protection clause** of the Fourteenth Amendment declares that no state (including any subdivision thereof) shall "deny to any person within its jurisdiction the equal protection of the laws." Although no parallel clause explicitly applies to the national government, courts have interpreted the Fifth Amendment's **due process clause,** which states that no person shall "be deprived of life, liberty, or property, without due process of law," to impose the same restraints on the national government as the equal protection clause imposes on the states.

LEARNING **OBJECTIVE**

Assess the constitutional tests applied to discriminatory laws in the United States.

Note that the clause applies only to the actions of *governments,* not to those of private individuals. If a private person performs a discriminatory action, that action does not violate the Constitution. Instead, it may violate federal and state laws passed to protect people from irrational discrimination by private parties. The equal protection clause does not, however, prevent governments from discriminating in all cases. What the Constitution forbids is *unreasonable* classifications. In general, a classification is unreasonable when there is no relationship between the classes it creates and permissible governmental goals. A law prohibiting redheads from voting, for example, would be unreasonable. In contrast, laws denying persons under age 18 the right to vote, to marry without the permission of their parents, or to apply for a driver's license appear to be reasonable (at least to most persons over age 18).

equal protection clause
A clause in the Fourteenth Amendment that forbids any state to deny to any person within its jurisdiction the equal protection of the laws. By interpretation, the Fifth Amendment imposes the same limitation on the national government. This clause is the major constitutional restraint on the power of governments to discriminate against persons because of race, national origin, or sex.

Constitutional Classifications and Tests

One of the most troublesome constitutional questions is how to distinguish between constitutional and unconstitutional classifications. The Supreme Court uses three tests for this purpose: the *rational basis* test, the *strict scrutiny* test, and the *heightened scrutiny* test.

due process clause
A clause in the Fifth Amendment limiting the power of the national government; a similar clause in the Fourteenth Amendment prohibiting state governments from depriving any person of life, liberty, or property without due process of law.

The Rational Basis Test The traditional test to determine whether a law complies with the equal protection requirement—the **rational basis test**—places the burden of proof on the parties attacking the law. They must show that the law has no rational or legitimate governmental goals. Recall from Chapter 15 that when the court reviews the government's reason for legislating, it engages in substantive due process. Traditionally the rational basis test applied only to legislation affecting economic interests and, with two exceptions in the last 70 years, the Court has upheld the legislation and deferred to legislative judgments.[38] But recently the Court has applied the test when noneconomic interests are challenged.[39]

rational basis test
A standard developed by the courts to test the constitutionality of a law; when applied, a law is constitutional as long as it meets a reasonable government interest.

Suspect Classifications and Strict Scrutiny When a law is subject to the **strict scrutiny test,** the burden is on the government to show that there is both a "compelling governmental interest" to justify such a classification and no less restrictive way to

strict scrutiny test
A test applied by the court when a classification is based on race; the government must show that there is a compelling reason for the law and no other less restrictive way to meet the interest.

accomplish this compelling purpose. The Court applies the strict scrutiny test to suspect classifications. A *suspect classification* is one through which people have been deliberately subjected to severely unequal treatment, or that society has used to render people politically powerless.[40] When a law classifies based on race or national origin, the legislation immediately raises a red flag regardless of whether it is intended to aid or inhibit a particular race or nationality. For example, the Supreme Court has held that laws that give preference for public employment based on race are subject to strict scrutiny.

Quasi-Suspect Classifications and Heightened Scrutiny To sustain a law under the **heightened scrutiny test,** the government must show that its classification serves "important governmental objectives." Heightened scrutiny is a standard first used by the Court in 1971 to declare classifications based on gender unconstitutional. As Justice William J. Brennan Jr. wrote for the Court, "There can be no doubt that our nation has had a long and unfortunate history of sex discrimination. Traditionally such discrimination was rationalized by an attitude of 'romantic paternalism' which in practical effect put women, not on a pedestal, but in a cage."[41]

Unlike laws subject to strict scrutiny, most of which the courts will strike down, more laws survive heightened scrutiny analysis. However, in recent years, the Supreme Court has struck down most laws brought before it that were alleged to discriminate against women but has tended to do so on the basis of federal statutes like the 1964 Civil Rights Act (for other legislation, see Table 16–2).

Poverty and Age Just as race and sex classifications receive elevated scrutiny, some argue that economic and age classification ought to be subject to some heightened review. The Supreme Court rejected the argument "that financial need alone identifies a suspect class for purposes of equal protection analysis."[42] However, state supreme courts in Texas, Ohio, Connecticut, and elsewhere have ruled that unequal funding for public schools, as a result of "rich" districts spending more per pupil than "poor" districts, violates their state constitutional provisions for free and equal education.[43]

Age is not a suspect classification. Many laws make distinctions based on age to obtain a driver's license, to marry without parental consent, to attend schools, to buy alcohol or tobacco, and so on. Many governmental institutions have age-specific

heightened scrutiny test
This test has been applied when a law classifies based on sex; to be upheld, the law must meet an important government interest.

TABLE 16–2 Major Civil Rights Laws

• **Civil Rights Act, 1957**	Makes it a federal crime to prevent persons from voting in federal elections.
• **Civil Rights Act, 1964**	Bars discrimination in employment or in public accommodations on the basis of race, color, religion, sex, or national origin; created the Equal Employment Opportunity Commission.
• **Voting Rights Act, 1965**	Authorizes the appointment of federal examiners to register voters in areas with a history of discrimination.
• **Age Discrimination in Employment Act, 1967**	Prohibits job discrimination against workers or job applicants aged 40 through 65 and prohibits mandatory retirement.
• **Fair Housing Act, 1968**	Prohibits discrimination on the basis of race, color, religion, or national origin in the sale or rental of most housing.
• **Title IX, Education Amendment of 1972**	Prohibits discrimination on the basis of sex in any education program receiving federal financial assistance.
• **Rehabilitation Act, 1973**	Requires that recipients of federal grants greater than $2,500 hire and promote qualified handicapped individuals.
• **Fair Housing Act Amendments, 1988**	Gave the Department of Housing and Urban Development authority to prohibit housing bias against the handicapped and families with children.
• **Americans with Disabilities Act, 1990**	Prohibits discrimination based on disability and requires that facilities be made accessible to those with disabilities.
• **Civil Rights Act, 1991**	Requires that employers justify practices that negatively affect the working conditions of women and minorities or show that no alternative practices would have a lesser impact. Also established a commission to examine the "glass ceiling" that keeps women from becoming executives and to recommend how to increase the number of women and minorities in management positions.

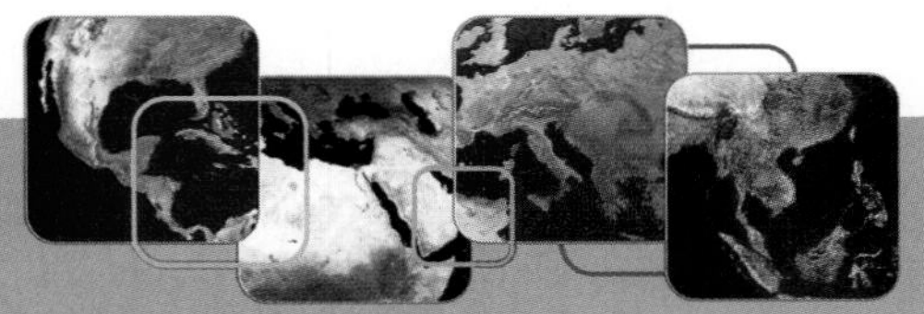

HOW OTHER NATIONS GOVERN

The Legal Treatment of Homosexuality Across the World

Just as laws and court decisions in the United States concerning the criminalization of homosexual acts and the permissibility of same-sex marriage are in flux, the legal treatment of homosexuality around the globe has also experienced a great deal of recent change. The European Union, for example, has adopted a Charter of Fundamental Rights that bars discrimination based on sexual orientation, and countries that wish to join the EU must introduce legislation banning discrimination in employment on various grounds, including sexual orientation.* The EU is not alone in barring such discrimination. Mexico prohibits discrimination based on sexual orientation, and same-sex unions are now recognized in Mexico City.†

Several countries, including the United Kingdom, have gone even further than prohibiting discrimination on the basis of sexual orientation, to allowing civil unions or partnerships that provide nearly the same benefits and responsibilities of marriage. The U.K. Civil Partnership Act, which went into effect in December 2005, provides same-sex couples with the same social security and pension benefits, parental responsibility for partner's children, and next of kin rights in hospitals as married heterosexuals.‡

Other countries such as India and Nigeria criminalize homosexual behavior. In each country adults participating in consensual homosexual activity may be imprisoned for eleven years to life. In Nigeria, homosexuality can be punishable by death. In yet other countries such as Japan and China, specific legislation against homosexuality does not exist.§ In each of these cases, of course, the absence of law does not indicate a lack of discrimination based on homosexuality, but instead a lack of treatment of the issue by the government.

QUESTIONS

1. Why may Western democracies be more likely to ban discrimination on the grounds of sexual orientation than other countries?
2. Why are rights such as those protected by the United Kingdom's Civil Partnership Act important to same-sex couples?
3. Why do you think countries such as China and Japan generally lack legislation against homosexuality even though discrimination based on sexual orientation exists?

*European Union and LGBT Rights, International Lesbian and Gay Association—Europe, www.ilga-europe.org/europe/guide/european_union/european_union_and_lgbt_rights.

†"Mexico City Passes Gay Union Law," BBC News, November 10, 2006, news.bbc.co.uk/2/hi/americas/6134730.stm.

‡European Union and LGBT Rights, International Lesbian and Gay Association—Europe, www.ilga-europe.org/europe/issues/marriage_and_partnership/marriage_and_partnership_rights_for_same_sex_partners_country_by_country.

§International Lesbian and Gay Association, www.ilga.org.

programs: for senior citizens, for adult students, for people in midcareer. As Justice Sandra Day O'Connor observed, "States may discriminate on the basis of age without offending the Fourteenth Amendment if the age classification in question is rationally related to a legitimate state interest."[44]

Congress, however, responding to "gray power," frequently treats age as a protected category and has made it illegal for most employers to discriminate on the basis of advancing age. Except for a few exempt occupations, employers may not impose mandatory retirement requirements. Congress also attempted to extend the protections against age discrimination to cover state employees, but the Supreme Court ruled that Congress lacks the constitutional authority to open the federal courts to suits by state employees for alleged age discrimination. State employees are limited to recovering monetary damages under state laws in state courts.[45]

Sexual Orientation Although in cases like *Romer v. Evans* (1996) and *Lawrence v. Texas* (2003)—both discussed in Chapter 15—the Court found that state laws classifying based on sexual orientation violated the U.S. Constitution, it has not elevated the level of scrutiny with which it reviews such classifications. However, as we discuss in the "You Will Decide" feature, several state courts have ruled that their own state constitutions require at least the right to legal recognition of same-sex civil unions. The supreme courts of Massachusetts, California, and Connecticut have gone even further to determine that their state constitutions require that marriage be open to same-sex as well as different-sex couples, though the California Supreme Court's decision was negated by California voters in the 2008 election.

Fundamental Rights and Strict Scrutiny The Court also strictly scrutinizes laws impinging on *fundamental rights*. What makes a right fundamental in the

YOU WILL DECIDE Should Marriage be Limited to Heterosexual Couples?

On May 15, 2008, the California Supreme Court ruled that denying same-sex couples the opportunity to marry violated the state's constitutional guarantee of equal protection. The court's opinion referred to marriage as a "fundamental constitutional right to form a family relationship" that the California constitution guaranteed as a "basic civil right to all Californians, whether gay or heterosexual, and to same-sex couples as well as to opposite-sex couples." The state supreme court's decision was immediately celebrated by most of the 110,000 same-sex couples in the state and denounced by many who argued that marriage is an institution restricted to heterosexual couples. Opponents placed a constitutional amendment banning same-sex marriage on the 2008 ballot. Voters narrowly approved this amendment.

California was only the second U.S. state to allow same-sex marriage. In November 2003, the Massachusetts Supreme Court held that the state constitution's guarantees of equality and due process were violated by a ban on same-sex marriage. On October 10, 2008, Connecticut's Supreme Court invalidated the states's civil union law to become the third state to legalize same-sex marriage. In other states and localities, propositions and constitutional amendments providing for same-sex civil unions or barring any legal recognition of same-sex unions have been strongly debated.

constitutional sense? It is not the importance or the significance of the right but whether it is explicitly or implicitly *guaranteed by the Constitution.* Under this test, the rights to travel and to vote have been held to be fundamental. Rights to education, to housing, or to welfare benefits have not been deemed fundamental. Important as they may be, no constitutional provisions specifically protect them from governmental regulation.

As mentioned previously, the Constitution and particularly the Fourteenth Amendment's equal protection clause is only one of the legal bases for civil rights protections in the United States. Although we often think of court decisions when we think of the civil rights movement, many of the courts' rulings that upheld the civil rights of racial minorities and women were based on congressional legislation. Two pieces of legislation were particularly important to the civil rights movement: the Voting Rights Act of 1965 and the Civil Rights Act of 1964. We turn to these next.

LEARNING **OBJECTIVE**

5 Analyze the protections provided by the 1965 Voting Rights Act.

Voting Rights

Under our Constitution, the states, not the federal government, regulate elections and voting qualifications. However, Article I, Section 4, gives Congress the power to supersede state regulations as to the "Times, Places, and Manner" of elections for representatives and senators. Congress has used this authority, along with its authority under Article II, Section 2, to set the date for selecting electors, to set age qualifications and residency requirements to vote in national elections, to establish a uniform day for all

The Civil Rights Movement

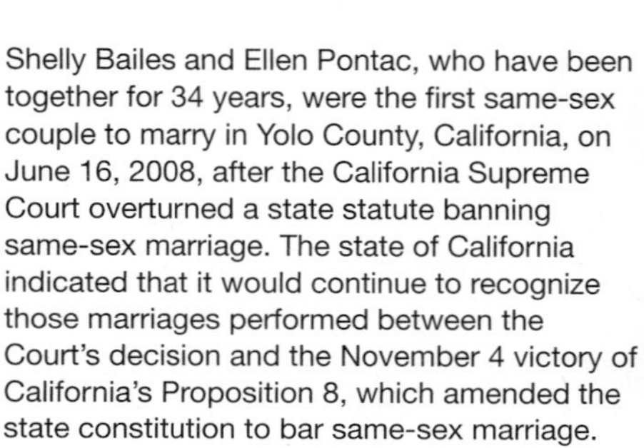

Shelly Bailes and Ellen Pontac, who have been together for 34 years, were the first same-sex couple to marry in Yolo County, California, on June 16, 2008, after the California Supreme Court overturned a state statute banning same-sex marriage. The state of California indicated that it would continue to recognize those marriages performed between the Court's decision and the November 4 victory of California's Proposition 8, which amended the state constitution to bar same-sex marriage.

states to hold elections for members of Congress and presidential electors, and to give citizens who live outside the United States the right to vote for members of Congress and presidential electors in the states in which they are legal residents.

As a result, officials seeking to deny African Americans the right to vote often relied on violence and intimidation, as well as developing biased registration requirements. Reports of violence and intimidation against black voters were frighteningly prevalent. One representative from Alabama described the efforts to deprive blacks of the right to vote this way: "At first we used to kill them to keep them from voting; when we got sick of doing that we began to steal their ballots; and when stealing their ballots got to troubling our consciences we decided to handle the matter legally, fixing it so they couldn't vote."[46]

The registration requirements used to deny blacks the right to vote appeared perfectly proper, but it was the way they were administered that kept black people from the polls. Officials often seized on the smallest error on an application form to disqualify a black voter. In one parish (county) in Louisiana, after four white voters challenged the registration of black voters on the grounds that those voters had made an "error in spilling" [sic] in their applications, registration officials struck 1,300 out of approximately 1,500 black voters from the rolls.[47]

In many southern areas, **literacy tests** were used to discriminate against African Americans. Although poor white people often avoided registering out of fear of embarrassment from failing a literacy test, the tests were more often used to discriminate against African Americans.[48] White people were often asked simple questions; black people were asked questions that would baffle a Supreme Court justice. "In the 1960s southern registrars were observed testing black applicants on such matters as the number of bubbles in a soap bar, the news contained in a copy of the Peking Daily, the meaning of obscure passages in state constitutions, and the definition of terms such as habeas corpus."[49] In Louisiana, 49,603 illiterate white voters were able to persuade election officials that they could understand the Constitution, but only 2 illiterate black voters were able to do so.

Local officials were also able to keep black voters from participating through the use of the **white primary.** In the one-party South of the early twentieth century, the Democratic party would hold whites-only primaries, effectively disenfranchising black voters because, in the absence of viable Republican candidates, the winner of the Democratic primary was guaranteed to win the general election.

THINKING IT THROUGH

The rights of homosexuals in the United States have never received the heightened protection against discrimination applied to classifications made on the basis of race or sex. The Court has ruled that government needs only a reasonable basis for legislating in order to permissibly classify individuals based on sexual orientation. Traditionally, legislation meant to uphold basic values and morals would pass such a test, though the Court in *Romer v. Evans* (1996) struck down a Colorado constitutional amendment that made a distinction based on sexual orientation by ruling that it did not pass the test of rationality, or reasonableness. However, those opposed to same-sex marriage contend that it endangers the traditional notion of marriage and the value of the family unit.

Opponents of same-sex marriage also object to state supreme courts' rulings on the basis of judicial activism (discussed in Chapter 14). Many opponents of state court decisions argue that same-sex marriage is not an issue for the courts to decide; instead, they contend, it should be decided through the democratic process. In the California case, for example, even as the state supreme court was deciding the constitutional question, groups were actively gathering signatures to place a constitutional amendment banning same-sex marriage on the state's November 2008 election ballot. Thus, the court reached a decision knowing that its ruling might well be rendered obsolete by the measure's success in the upcoming election. California's Proposition 8, an amendment to the state's constitution banning same-sex marriage in the state, went before California voters in November. By a margin of less than 5 percentage points, voters passed Proposition 8, ending the opportunity for same-sex couples to legally marry in the state less than six months after the California Supreme Court's decision.

Echoing arguments heard in the civil rights era, many who favor the right of same-sex couples to marry say that just as laws barring interracial marriage were declared to violate the Constitution's Fourteenth Amendment equal protection clause (in *Loving v. Virginia,* 1967), so do laws barring same-sex marriage. Supporters argue that once states provide an opportunity for legal recognition of marriage, they must do so equally. Although civil unions, an option provided for in four states (New Hampshire, New Jersey, Vermont, and Washington), typically offer many of the benefits afforded to married couples, they do not provide the equal recognition and legal rights of marriage.

Questions

1. Why are state courts such an important part of the debate on same-sex marriage?
2. Why is the issue of same-sex marriage so hotly debated? What makes this issue such a difficult one?
3. When voters and courts disagree over a topic such as same-sex marriage, who should prevail?

Protecting Voting Rights

After years of refusing to overturn racially discriminatory voting requirements, the Supreme Court in the 1940s began to strike down one after another of the devices that states and localities had used to keep African Americans from voting. In *Smith v. Allwright* (1944), the Court declared the white primary unconstitutional.[50] Later it

literacy test
A literacy requirement some states imposed as a condition of voting, generally used to disqualify black voters in the South; now illegal.

white primary
A Democratic party primary in the old "one-party South" that was limited to white people and essentially constituted an election; ruled unconstitutional in *Smith v. Allwright* (1944).

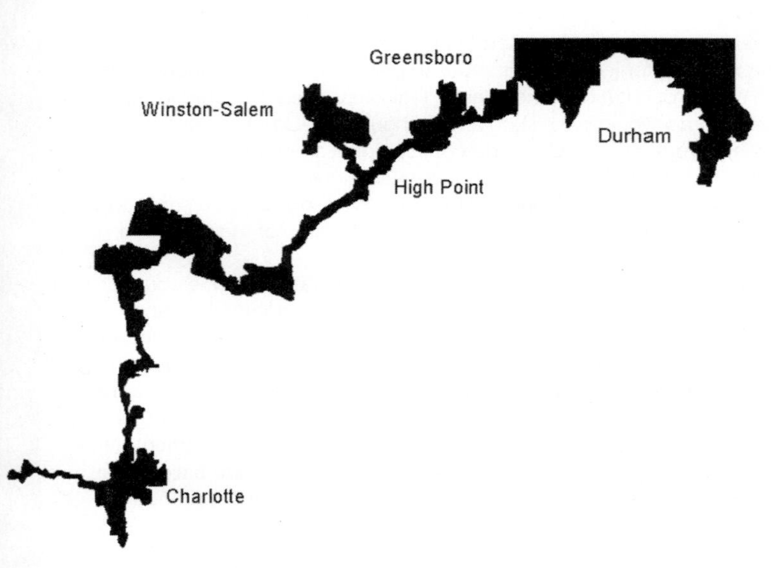

North Carolina's challenged "I-85 district" stretched more than 160 miles through the central region of the state.

struck down other methods. In 1960, the Court held that **racial gerrymandering**—drawing election districts to ensure that African Americans would be a minority in all districts—was contrary to the Fifteenth Amendment.[51] We discuss legislative redistricting in greater detail in Chapter 11. In 1964, the Twenty-Fourth Amendment eliminated the **poll tax**—payment required as a condition for voting—in presidential and congressional elections. In 1966, the Court held that the Fourteenth Amendment forbade the poll tax as a condition in any election.[52]

The Voting Rights Act of 1965

For two decades after World War II, under the leadership of the Supreme Court, many limitations on voting were declared unconstitutional, but as has often been the case, the Court acting alone was unable to open the voting booth to African Americans. Finally Congress acted in passing the Voting Rights Act of 1965. It was renewed in 1982, and in 2006 it was extended for another 25 years.

The Voting Rights Act prohibits voting qualifications or standards that result in a denial of the right of any citizen to vote on account of race and color. It also bars any form of threats or intimidation aimed at preventing citizens from voting. Under the act, the Department of Justice must also review changes in voting practices or laws that may dilute the voting power of these groups,[53] such as changes in candidacy requirements and qualifications or boundary lines of voting districts.[54] The requirement that states obtain Justice Department clearance was upheld by the federal courts in May 2008, but that decision is currently being appealed to the U.S. Supreme Court.[55]

Following the 1990 census, the Department of Justice attempted to increase minority representation in Congress by pressuring southern state legislatures to draw as many districts as possible in which minorities would constitute a majority of the electorate. Most of these districts tended to be Democratic, leaving the other congressional districts in these states heavily white and Republican. The lower federal courts sustained the Department of Justice's interpretation. As a result, the number of congressional districts represented by minorities and Republicans increased considerably.

LEARNING **OBJECTIVE**

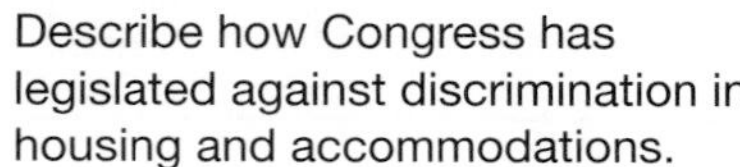

6 Describe how Congress has legislated against discrimination in housing and accommodations.

The Supreme Court announced, however, in a series of cases beginning with *Shaw v. Reno* (1993), that although it was a legitimate goal for state legislatures to consider race when they drew electoral districts to increase the voting strength of minorities, they could not make race the sole or predominant reason for drawing district lines. A test case examined the North Carolina legislature's creation of a **majority-minority district** 160 miles long and in some places only an interstate highway wide. "If you drove down the interstate with both car doors open," said one legislator, "you'd kill most of the people in the district." The Supreme Court ruled that it was wrong to force states to create as many majority-minority districts as possible. To comply with the Voting Rights Act, the Court explained, states must provide for districts roughly proportional to the minority voters' respective shares in the voting-age population.[56]

racial gerrymandering
The drawing of election districts so as to ensure that members of a certain race are a minority in the district; ruled unconstitutional in *Gomillion v. Lightfoot* (1960).

poll tax
Tax required to vote; prohibited for national elections by the Twenty-fourth Amendment (1964) and ruled unconstitutional for all elections in *Harper v. Board of Elections* (1966)

majority-minority district
A congressional district created to include a majority of minority voters; ruled constitutional so long as race is not the main factor in redistricting.

Rights to Equal Access: Accommodations, Jobs, and Homes

Accommodations

In 1883, the Supreme Court had declared unconstitutional an act of Congress that made it a federal offense for any operator of a public conveyance (such as a train or bus), hotel, or theater to deny accommodations to any person because of race or color, on the grounds that the Fourteenth Amendment does not give Congress such authority.[57] Until the Supreme Court finally moved to strike down such laws in the 1950s, southern states had made it illegal for white and black people to ride in the same train cars, attend the same theaters, go to the same schools, be born in the same hospitals, drink from the same water fountains, or be buried in the same cemeteries. **Jim Crow laws,** as they came to be called, blanketed southern life.

The Court reinforced legalized segregation under the Fourteenth Amendment's equal protection clause in *Plessy v. Ferguson* (1896). In the *Plessy* decision, the Supreme Court endorsed the view that government-imposed racial segregation in public transportation, and presumably in public education, did not necessarily constitute discrimination if "equal" accommodations were provided for the members of both races.[58] But the "equal" part of the formula was meaningless. African Americans were segregated in unequal facilities and lacked the political power to protest effectively.

Beginning in the 1960s, however, Congress began to act to prevent such segregation. Its constitutional authority to legislate against discrimination by private individuals is no longer an issue because the Court has broadly construed the **commerce clause**—which gives Congress the power to regulate interstate and foreign commerce—to justify action against discriminatory conduct by individuals. Congress has also used its power to tax and spend to prevent not only racial discrimination but also discrimination based on ethnic origin, sex, disability, and age.

Civil Rights Act of 1964 and Places of Public Accommodation The key step in establishing rights of equal access was the Civil Rights Act of 1964. For the first time since Reconstruction, the act authorized the massive use of federal authority to combat privately imposed racial discrimination. Title II of the act makes it a federal offense to discriminate against any customer or patron in a place of public accommodation because of race, color, religion, or national origin. It applies to any inn, hotel, motel, or lodging establishment (except those with fewer than five rooms and where the proprietor also lives—in other words, small boardinghouses); to any restaurant or gasoline station that serves interstate travelers or sells food or products that are moved in interstate commerce; and to any movie house, theater, concert hall, sports arena, or other place of entertainment that customarily hosts films, performances, athletic teams, or other sources of entertainment that are moved in interstate commerce. Within a few months after its adoption, the Supreme Court sustained the constitutionality of Title II.[59] As a result, public establishments, including those in the South, opened their doors to all customers.

Civil Rights Act of 1964 and Employment In addition to dealing with equal access in public accommodations, the Civil Rights Act also barred discrimination in employment. Title VII of the 1964 Act made it illegal for any employer or trade union in any industry affecting interstate commerce and employing 15 or more people (and, since 1972, any state or local agency such as a school or university) to discriminate in employment practices against any person because of race, color, national origin, religion, or sex. Employers must create workplaces that avoid abusive environments. Related legislation made it illegal to discriminate against persons with physical handicaps, veterans, or persons over age 40.

There are a few exceptions. Religious institutions such as parochial schools may use religious standards. Employers may take into account the age, sex, or handicap of prospective employees when occupational qualifications are absolutely necessary to the normal operation of a particular business or enterprise—for example, hiring only women to work in women's locker rooms.

The Equal Employment Opportunity Commission (EEOC) was created under the act to enforce Title VII. The commission works together with state authorities to try to ensure compliance with the act and may seek judicial enforcement of complaints against private employers. The attorney general prosecutes Title VII violations by public agencies. Not only can aggrieved persons sue for damages for themselves, but they can also sue for other persons similarly situated in a **class action suit.** For example, a pending class action lawsuit against Wal-Mart alleges that the company discriminates against women in promotions and pay. The vigor with which the EEOC and the attorney general have acted has varied over the years, depending on the commitment of the president and the willingness of Congress to provide an adequate budget for the EEOC.[60]

Jim Crow laws
State laws formerly pervasive throughout the South requiring public facilities and accommodations to be segregated by race; ruled unconstitutional.

commerce clause
The clause of the Constitution (Article I, Section 8, Clause 3) that gives Congress the power to regulate all business activities that cross state lines or affect more than one state or other nations.

class action suit
A lawsuit brought by an individual or a group of people on behalf of all those similarly situated.

LEARNING **OBJECTIVE**

7 Explain the difficulty of integration in a society largely segregated by housing patterns.

The Fair Housing Act and Amendments Housing is the last frontier of the civil rights crusade, the area in which progress is slowest and genuine change most remote. Even after legal restrictions on segregated housing have been removed, housing patterns continue to be segregated. The degree to which housing also affects segregation in employment and the public schools makes it a particularly important issue. In 1948, the Supreme Court made racial or religious **restrictive covenants** (a provision in a deed to real property that restricts to whom it can be sold) legally unenforceable.[61] The 1968 Fair Housing Act forbids discrimination in housing, with a few exceptions similar to those mentioned in public accommodations. Owners may not refuse to sell or rent to any person because of race, color, religion, national origin, sex, or physical handicap or because a person has children. Discrimination in housing also covers efforts to deny mortgage loans to minorities.

The Department of Justice has filed hundreds of cases, especially against large apartment complexes, yet African Americans and Hispanics still face discrimination in housing. Some real estate agents steer African Americans and Hispanics toward neighborhoods that are not predominantly white and require minority renters to pay larger deposits than white renters. Yet victims complain about less than 1 percent of these actions, because discrimination is so subtle that they are often unaware they are being discriminated against. However, more aggressive enforcement has increased the number of discrimination complaints the Department of Housing and Urban Development and local and state agencies receive.

Education Rights

Since the Court's decision in *Plessy,* segregated public as well as private facilities had become the norm. Separate public schools, buses, and bathrooms were commonplace. However, in the late 1930s African Americans started to file lawsuits challenging *Plessy*'s "separate but equal" doctrine. They cited facts to show that in practice separate was anything but equal and always resulted in discrimination against African Americans.

The National Associate for the Advancement of Colored People's (NAACP) Legal Defense Fund (LDF) was active in challenging segregated educational facilities. Initially, the LDF showed that so-called equal facilities were in fact not equal, or simply not provided. Many of their early successes addressed inequality in higher education. States were forced to either provide separate graduate and law schools for African American students, or integrate those they already had. A major success that laid the groundwork for the LDF's challenge in public secondary and elementary schools came when the Court ruled that not only did segregated facilities themselves have to be equal, but they also had to provide the same quality of benefits to black students as their white counterparts.[62]

The End of "Separate but Equal": *Brown v. Board of Education*

Once the LDF had adequately established that segregated facilities were far from equal, they challenged the *Plessy* doctrine of "separate but equal" head on. And, in *Brown v. Board of Education of Topeka* (1954), the Court finally agreed ruling that "separate but equal" is a contradiction in terms. *Segregation is itself discrimination.*[63]

The question before the Court in *Brown* was whether separate public schools for black and white students violated the Fourteenth Amendment's equal protection clause. Relying heavily on arguments addressing the harm to all schoolchildren, black and white, caused by racial segregation, the Court struck down segregation in the public schools and in so doing, overturned *Plessy v. Ferguson* (1896). A year later, the Court ordered school boards to proceed with "all deliberate speed to desegregate public schools at the earliest practical date."[64]

restrictive covenant
A provision in a deed to real property prohibiting its sale to a person of a particular race or religion. Judicial enforcement of such deeds is unconstitutional.

THE **CHANGING FACE** OF U.S. POLITICS

Racial and Ethnic Diversity in U.S. Public Elementary and Secondary Schools

Since the 1970s, U.S. public schools as a whole have become more diverse. Over time the percentage of white student enrollment in the public schools has dropped more than 20 percentage points, from 78 percent of schoolchildren between kindergarten to twelfth grade to just under 57 percent of the student population. The biggest increase for any minority group is certainly among Hispanic students, whose percentage of the student population has increased by more than 14 percentage points.

However, as you can see by looking at the data by region, this diversity is not evenly distributed across all areas of the country. In the West, for example, white students do not even make up the majority of the student population, and the Hispanic student population is twice as large as it is in any other region. Because of these kinds of regional differences, as well as differences between school districts, often based on housing patterns, the increasing level of diversity across the student population is not necessarily reflected in individual schools or districts.

QUESTIONS

1. Why does diversity in the public school population vary by region?
2. Why have our public schools as a whole become more diverse over time?
3. Did the diversity in your school district reflect the overall diversity in your region of the country?

Diversity in the Public Schools by Year.

Year	White	Black	Hispanic	Asian*	Native American*	Other
1972	77.8%	14.8%	6.0%	—	—	1.4%
1977	76.1	15.8	6.2	—	—	1.9
1982	71.9	16.0	8.9	—	—	3.2
1987	68.5	16.6	10.8	—	—	4.0
1992	66.8	16.9	12.0	3.3	0.8	0.2
1997	63.0	16.9	14.9	3.9	1.2	—
2002	60.7	16.5	17.6	4.0	1.2	—
2006	56.9	15.6	20.2	3.8	0.7	2.7

Totals may be just under 100% because of rounding.
* Data was not gathered for Asian or Native American students until 1989.

SOURCE: National Center for Education Statistics, Participation in Education, Table 5.1, nces.ed.gov/programs/coe/2008/section1/table.asp?tableID=862.

Diversity in the Public Schools by Region, 2006.

Region	White	Black	Hispanic	Asian	Native American	Other
Northeast	63.8%	14.7%	15.3%	4.4%	0.2%	1.5%
Midwest	73.4	13.2	7.7	2.6	0.5	2.4
South	51.5	24.5	18.8	1.9	0.7	2.6
West	45.2	5.1	36.9	7.9	1.0	3.9

Totals may be just under 100% because of rounding.

SOURCE: National Center for Education Statistics, Participation in Education by Region, Table 5.2, nces.ed.gov/programs/coe/2008/section1/table.asp?tableID=863.

But many school districts moved slowly or not at all, and in the 1960s, Congress and the president joined even more directly to fight school segregation. Title VI of the Civil Rights Act of 1964, as subsequently amended, stipulated that federal dollars under any grant program or project must be withdrawn from an entire school or institution of higher education (including private schools) that discriminates "on the ground of race, color, or national origin," gender, age, or disability, in "any program or activity receiving federal financial assistance."

Thurgood Marshall (center), George C. E. Hayes (left), and James Nabrit Jr. (right) argued and won *Brown v. Board of Education of Topeka* before the Supreme Court in 1954.

From Segregation to Desegregation—but Not Yet Integration

School districts that had operated separate schools for white children and black children now had to develop plans and programs to move from segregation to integration. Schools failing to do so were placed under court supervision to ensure that they were doing what was necessary and proper to overcome the evils of segregation. Simply doing away with laws mandating segregation would not be enough; school districts needed to actively integrate their schools.

But because most white people and most African Americans continued to live in separate neighborhoods, merely removing legal barriers to school integration did not by itself integrate the schools. To overcome this residential clustering by race, some federal courts mandated busing across neighborhoods, moving white students to once predominantly black schools and vice versa. Busing students was unpopular and triggered protests in many cities.

The Supreme Court sustained busing only if it was undertaken to remedy the consequences of *officially* sanctioned segregation, **de jure segregation.** The Court refused to permit federal judges to order busing to overcome the effects of **de facto segregation,** segregation that arises as a result of social and economic conditions such as housing patterns.

de jure segregation
Segregation imposed by law.

de facto segregation
Segregation resulting from economic or social conditions or personal choice.

After a period of vigorous federal court supervision of school desegregation programs, the Supreme Court in the 1990s restricted the role of federal judges.[65] It instructed some of them to restore control of a school system to the state and local authorities and to release districts from any busing obligations once a judge concludes that the authorities "have done everything practicable to overcome the past consequences of segregation."[66]

Political support for busing and for other efforts to integrate the schools also faded.[67] Many school districts eliminated mandatory busing, with the result that *Brown*'s era of court-ordered desegregation drew to a close. The percentage of southern black students attending white-majority schools fell from more than 40 percent to 30 percent, or to about the same level it had been in 1969.[68] In the wake of such resegregation, some school districts have attempted to increase integration through race-conscious admission plans such as the Seattle plan discussed at the beginning of the chapter. Another method some schools have pursued, which has the benefit of presumptive constitutionality, is integration based on socioeconomic factors rather than race.[69]

The Affirmative Action Controversy

LEARNING **OBJECTIVE**

8 Evaluate the current state of affirmative action in the United States.

When white majorities were using government power to discriminate against African Americans, civil rights advocates cited with approval the famous words of Justice John Marshall Harlan when he dissented from the *Plessy* decision: "Our Constitution is color-blind and neither knows nor tolerates class among citizens."[70] But by the 1960s, a new set of constitutional and national policy debates raged. Many people began to assert that government neutrality is not enough. If governments, universities, and employers simply stopped discriminating but nothing else changed, individuals previously discriminated against would still be kept from equal participation in U.S. life. Furthermore, without such equal participation, all suffer from a lack of diversity in society. Because discrimination had so disadvantaged some people and groups, they suffered disabilities that white males did not share in competing for openings in medical schools, for skilled jobs, or for their share of government grants and contracts.

Supporters call remedies to overcome the consequences of discrimination against African Americans, Hispanics, Native Americans, and women *affirmative action;* opponents call these efforts *reverse discrimination.* The Supreme Court's first major statement on the constitutionality of affirmative action programs came in a celebrated case relating to university admissions. Allan Bakke—a white male, a top student at the University of Minnesota and at Stanford, and a Vietnam War veteran—applied in 1973 and again in 1974 to the medical school of the University of California at Davis. In each of those years, the school admitted 100 new students, 84 in a general admissions

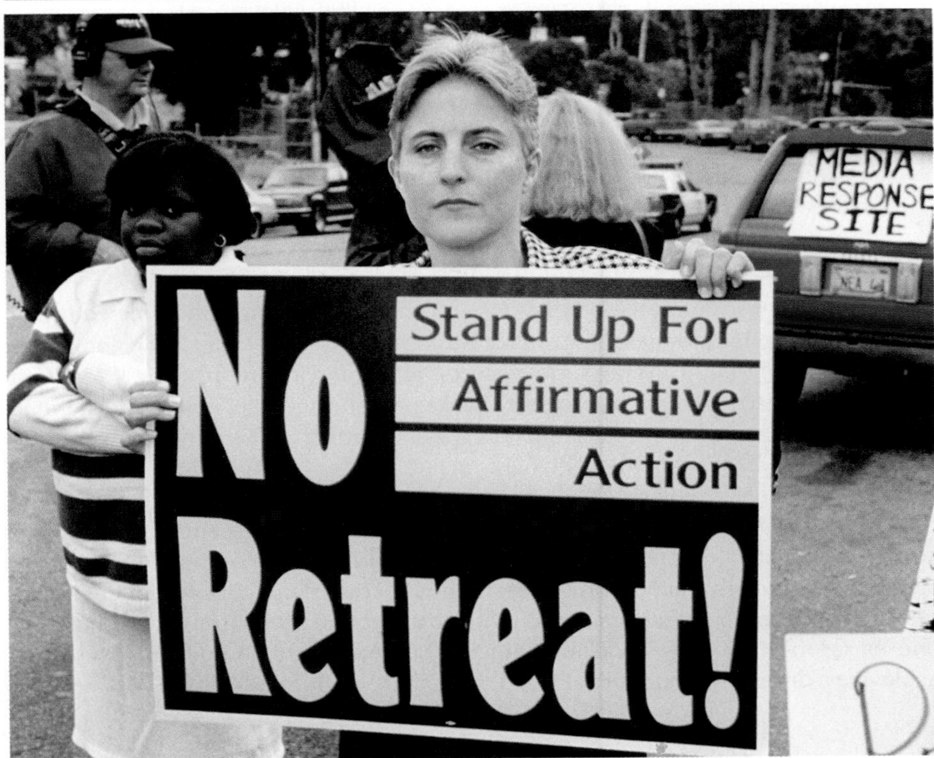

Many Americans believe that affirmative action is the best way to address the issue of past racial and ethnic quotas.

GENERATION **NEXT**

Affirmative Action

The debate over affirmative action is hardly new. The U.S. Supreme Court reached a decision in a landmark case on affirmative action in university admissions in 1978 (*University of California Regents v. Bakke*). There the Court declared unconstitutional affirmative action plans amounting to a quota system (for example, cases in which a specific number of seats are reserved specifically for racial minority and nonminority applicants). Since then many affirmative action programs have been challenged, such as those in Seattle and Louisville discussed at the beginning of this chapter.

However, when asked the following question, most members of Generation Next continue to support some form of affirmative action: "As I read programs and proposals that are being discussed in the country today, please tell me whether you strongly favor, favor, oppose, or strongly oppose each: Affirmative action programs designed to help blacks, women and other minorities get better jobs and education."

Not surprisingly, as people who have historically experienced discrimination and stand to benefit from affirmative action programs, women and nonwhite respondents favor affirmative action at higher rates than men and whites.

Democrats are also more likely to support affirmative action programs than are Independents or Republicans. This is at least partly related to Democrats' connection to the civil rights movement and the fact that minorities and women are an important part of the Democrats' base of support. Interestingly though, ideology does not affect support for affirmative action programs in the way we might expect; this is likely related to the abstract way in which this question was asked. The way a survey question is worded, particularly on issues like affirmative action, can substantially affect responses.[71] It seems reasonable that question wording affected responses here.

Generation Next also tends to support affirmative action programs at greater levels than older citizens. Although 76 percent of Generation Next favors affirmative action, 65 percent of 50- to 59-year-olds and 66 percent of all others over age 40 support these programs. Those who are 30 to 39 years of age support affirmative action programs at about the same rate as Generation Next (77 percent). Perhaps decreasing prejudice and weakening race and gender stereotypes in the younger population are helping to remove one of the barriers to successful affirmative action programs.

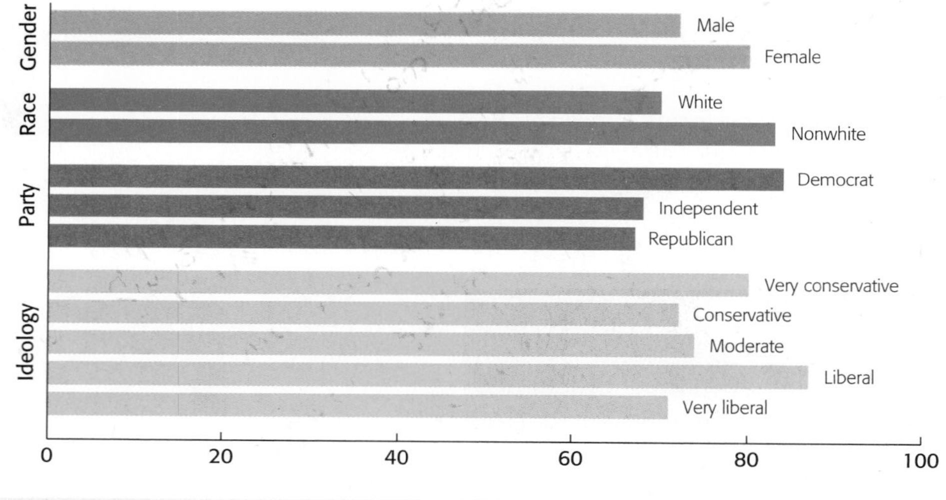

QUESTIONS

1. Why are Democrats so different from Independents and Republicans on affirmative action?
2. Why are women more supportive of affirmative action than men?
3. If such high proportions of people support affirmative action, why is it not more popular politically?

program and 16 in a special admissions program created for minorities who had previously been underrepresented. Bakke was rejected in both years while applicants with lower grade-point averages, test scores, and interview ratings were admitted through the special admissions program. Bakke brought suit in federal court, claiming he had been excluded because of his race, contrary to requirements of the Constitution and Title VI of the Civil Rights Act of 1964.

In *University of California Regents v. Bakke* (1978), the Supreme Court ruled the California plan unconstitutional[72] because it created a *quota*—a set number of admissions from which whites were excluded solely because of race. But the Court also declared that affirmative action programs are not necessarily unconstitutional. A state university may properly take race and ethnic background into account as "a plus," as one of several factors in choosing students because of its compelling interest in achieving a diverse student body.

Reaffirming the Importance of Diversity

For many years following the *Bakke* decision, the Court refused to hear challenges to affirmative action in higher education, despite conflicting lower-court decisions leading to confusion and uncertainty about how colleges and universities could pursue diverse student bodies. The Supreme Court clarified the matter in 2003, reaffirming *Bakke* in two cases that challenged the admission policies for undergraduates and law students at the University of Michigan. Both policies sought to achieve diverse student bodies, but in different ways.

The University of Michigan's undergraduate admissions program was based on a 150-point "selection index" that ranked applicants' test scores and grades for up to 100 points and allocated 40 points for other factors, including 4 points for children of alumni, 16 points for residents of rural areas, and 20 points for students from underrepresented minority groups or socially and economically disadvantaged families. Jennifer Gratz, a white high school student with a 3.8 GPA who was denied admission, challenged the program.

In *Gratz v. Bollinger* (2003), the Court struck down the policy as too mechanical and not narrowly tailored to giving applicants "individualized consideration" as *Bakke* required.[73] However, a bare majority of the Court upheld the University's law school admissions program that was also challenged. In *Grutter v. Bollinger* (2003), the Court ruled that the law school made "special efforts" to achieve racial and ethnic diversity, but unlike the undergraduate program, it did not use a point system based in part on race.[74] Writing for the Court, Justice O'Connor held that law school admissions were based on a "highly individualized, holistic review of each applicant's file" and did not use race as a factor in a "mechanical way." For that reason, it was consistent with *Bakke*'s holding that race may be used as a "plus factor" to achieve a diverse student body.

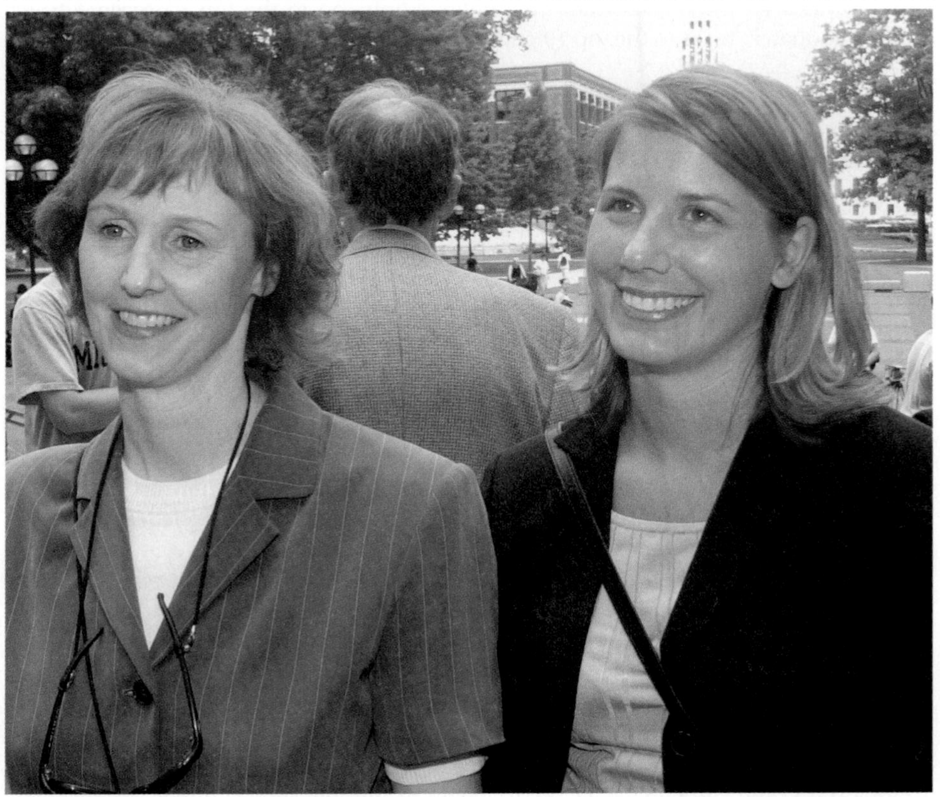

Jennifer Gratz (right) was the successful plaintiff in *Gratz v. Bollinger*; Barbara Grutter (left) was unsuccessful in challenging the University of Michigan law school's admission program, which the Supreme Court upheld due to its individualized approach.

Although the Court further clarified the requirements to render an affirmative action program permissible, its ruling did not end the debate. We've seen that the Court does not always have the final word on such questions. Motivated groups have spurred consideration of affirmative action programs at the polls, and several states have abolished affirmative action. Michigan is one example. In the aftermath of the Court's ruling in *Gratz* and *Grutter,* Jennifer Gratz formed the Michigan Civil Rights Initiative to place on the state's 2006 election ballot an initiative banning affirmative action in public colleges and government contracting. The initiative won approval with a reported 58 percent of the vote.[75] In addition to effectively nullifying the Supreme Court's decision as it applied to the University of Michigan, the initiative's success also highlights a motivated group of citizens' success in mobilizing the electorate.

California's Proposition 209 and Other Plans

Michigan is not alone in its efforts to end affirmative action through the democratic process. In 1995, the Regents of the University of California voted to eliminate race or gender as factors in employment, purchasing, contracting, or admissions. The following year, Californians voted overwhelmingly for Proposition 209 to amend the state constitution to forbid state agencies to discriminate against or grant preferential treatment to any individual or group on the basis of race, sex, color, ethnicity, or national origin in public employment, public education, or public contracting, except where necessary to comply with a federal requirement.

Seven other states (Texas, Louisiana, Mississippi, Georgia, Florida, Washington and Nebraska) have also abandoned affirmative action programs—some like California, Michigan, and Washington because of voter opposition, and others like Texas and Georgia because federal courts held that such programs were unconstitutional.[76] Some have also opted for a strategy of automatic admissions for a certain percentage of all high school graduates to maintain diversity in colleges and expand educational opportunities for minorities. California offers admission to the top 4 percent of high school graduates, Texas to the top 10 percent, and Florida to the top 20 percent.

Equal Rights Today

Today, civil rights legislation, executive orders, and judicial decisions have lowered, if not fully removed, legal barriers to full and equal participation in society. Important as these victories are, according to civil rights leader James Farmer, "They were victories largely for the middle class—those who could travel, entertain in restaurants, and stay in hotels. Those victories did not change life conditions for the mass of blacks who are still poor."[77]

As prosperous middle-class African Americans have moved out of inner cities, the remaining black *underclass,* as they have been called, has become even more isolated from the rest of the nation.[78] There are similar trends in Hispanic communities in Los Angeles, Dallas, and Houston.[79] Children are growing up on streets where drug abuse and crime are everyday events. They live in "separate and deteriorating societies, with separate economies, diverging family structures and basic institutions, and even growing linguistic separation within the core ghettos. The scale of their isolation by race, class, and economic situation is much greater than it was in the 1960s, with impoverishment, joblessness, educational inequality, and housing insufficiency even more severe."[80]

Some contend that we should pay attention to the plight of the underclass, and that instead of focusing on issues of race, we need to focus on class differences and support policies that provide jobs and improve education.[81] Others say there has to be a revival of the civil rights crusade, a restoration of vigorous civil rights enforcement, more job training, and, above all, an attack on residential segregation.[82] In any event, questions about how best to provide equal opportunities for all citizens remain high on the national agenda.

One of the many important lessons of the civil rights movement is that individuals can affect our government process. Without people like Rosa Parks, one woman sitting on a bus who refused to give up her seat, or Karen Brose, who fought for her daughter's right to attend her school of choice without regard to her race, we would not have experienced the monumental changes in our country's protection of all citizens' rights that we have seen over the last 100 years. By participating in our democratic system and challenging the status quo, we each play a part in promoting equal rights for all citizens.

CHAPTER **SUMMARY**

1 Explain the importance of citizenship rights, particularly concerning immigration and the war on terror.

The Constitution protects the acquisition and retention of citizenship. It protects the basic liberties of citizens as well as aliens, although in times of war, foreign saboteurs and terrorists may be detained and tried without the rights accorded to citizens and other aliens.

2 Compare and contrast different groups' efforts to obtain equal protection of the law.

Although African Americans' rights were finally recognized under the Thirteenth, Fourteenth, and Fifteenth Amendments, the government failed to act to prevent racial discrimination for nearly a century thereafter. The women's rights movement was born partly out of the struggle to abolish slavery, and the women's movement learned and gained power from the civil rights movements of the 1950s and early 1960s. Concern for equal rights under the law continues today for African Americans and women. Hispanics, Asian Americans, and Native Americans have also experienced discrimination.

3 Appraise the reasons for delay in the women's rights movement.

Members of the women's rights movement also fought for the abolition of slavery and were active in the drive to stop the sale and production of alcohol. After they were successful on these other issues they succeeded in achieving the right for women to vote.

4 Assess the constitutional tests applied to discriminatory laws in the United States.

The Supreme Court uses a three-tiered approach to evaluate the constitutionality of laws that may violate the equal protection clause. The Court upholds most laws if they simply help accomplish a legitimate government goal. It sustains laws that classify people based on sex only if they serve important government objectives. It subjects laws that touch fundamental rights or classify people because of race or ethnic origin to strict scrutiny and sustains them only if the government can show that they serve a compelling public purpose.

5 Analyze the protections provided by the 1965 Voting Rights Act.

A series of constitutional amendments, Supreme Court decisions, and laws passed by Congress have now secured the right to vote to all citizens age 18 and older. Following the Voting Rights Act of 1965, the Justice Department can oversee practices in locales with a history of discrimination. Recent Supreme Court decisions have refined the lengths to which legislatures can go, or are obliged to go, in creating minority-majority districts.

6 Describe how Congress has legislated against discrimination in housing and accommodations.

By its authority under the interstate commerce clause (Article 1, Section 8), Congress has passed important legislation barring discrimination in housing and accommodations. The Civil Rights Act of 1964 outlawed discrimination in public accommodations. This act also provided for equal employment opportunity. The Fair Housing Act of 1968 and its 1988 amendments prohibited discrimination in housing.

7 Explain the difficulty of integration in a society largely segregated by housing patterns.

Brown v. Board of Education of Topeka (1954) struck down the "separate but equal" doctrine that had justified segregated schools, but school districts responded slowly. The Supreme Court demanded compliance, and some federal courts mandated busing children across neighborhoods to comply. Still, full integration has proved elusive, as many white citizens have left the inner cities, and their schools, predominantly black or Hispanic.

8 Evaluate the current state of affirmative action in the United States.

The desirability and constitutionality of affirmative action programs that benefit members of groups subjected to past discrimination divide the nation and the Supreme Court. Remedial programs tailored to overcome specific instances of past discrimination are likely to pass the Supreme Court's suspicion of classifications based on race, national origin, and sex. The Court has also reaffirmed the importance of diversity in education and employment.

Chapter Self-Test

1. Naturalization requires new citizens to do all the following *except:* (pp. 441–442)
   a. be able to read, write, and speak English.
   b. agree never to renounce their new citizenship.
   c. understand and have an attachment to the history and principles of the government of the United States.
   d. demonstrate they do not believe in, advocate, or belong to an organization that advocates violent overthrow of the government.

2. Foreigners captured during combat, such as during the wars in Iraq and Afghanistan, have _______. (pp. 442–443)
   a. all the constitutional rights of U.S. citizens.
   b. the right to have their detainment reviewed.
   c. the right to be immediately released and tried by a court in their home country.
   d. no explicit rights because they do not fall under U.S. or international law.

3. Place the following events in correct chronological order. (pp. 443–446)
   a. Violent riots erupt in many cities
   b. Lyndon B. Johnson signs the Civil Rights Act
   c. Barack Obama runs for president of the United States
   d. Martin Luther King gives his "I Have a Dream" speech
   e. African American migration to northern and western cities
   f. *Brown v. Board of Education* ends segregated public schools

4. Different racial and ethnic groups in the United States have had different results in their struggles to achieve economic, political, and social equality and success. In a paragraph, explore possible reasons for these differences. (pp. 443–451)

5. Native Americans today suffer poor health and extremely high unemployment. Write a paragraph recommending what the Native American community can do to achieve equality. (pp. 450–451)

6. In a paragraph, list the historical events that impeded the progress of women's rights and discuss the gains made by women in the 20th century, particularly in its last three decades. (pp. 446–447)

7. In a paragraph, define *rational basis test, strict scrutiny,* and *heightened scrutiny,* and explain the relationships among them. (pp. 451–452)

8. The Supreme Court has placed sexual orientation as a classification for the rational basis test. In a paragraph, explain why the Court has ruled this way and evaluate whether the justification is correct, too lenient, or too severe. (pp. 453–455)

9. Imagine you are a judge. In a case before you, Isaac Johnson, a construction worker, age 60, has sued his company, United Builders, for discrimination because he was fired. United Builders explains it is company policy to cease employment of those over 60 because they are usually unable to do the heavy work of construction. Write an essay determining whether this is a case of unfair discrimination. (pp. 452–453)

10. Which of the following is *not* a provision of the Voting Rights Act? (p. 456)
    a. Threats or intimidation in any form to prevent citizens from voting are barred.
    b. Voting criteria that result in a denial of the right to vote based on race or color are barred.
    c. Political parties must make a "reasonable effort" to nominate minority candidates for public office.
    d. The Justice Department must review changes in voting laws that may dilute the voting power of racial groups.

11. In a few sentences, discuss the rationale for creating majority-minority districts and judge whether they have been a wise public policy. (p. 456)

12. In one or two sentences explain how Congress has used the Commerce Clause to fight discrimination in public accommodations. (pp. 456–458)

13. Which of the following is *not* prohibited by the Fair Housing Act? (p. 458)
    a. A bank denies an African American man a mortgage because he has poor credit and no savings.
    b. A landlord denies a woman an apartment because he is concerned that her two young children will bother the other tenants.
    c. The owner of several apartment complexes charges handicapped tenants an extra ten dollars rent to help pay for the buildings' wheelchair lifts.
    d. A real estate agent shows a Hispanic family mostly Hispanic neighborhoods since, she assumes, they are most likely to feel comfortable with people of their own race.

14. List and summarize the main points made by the Supreme Court in *University of California Regents v. Bakke, Gratz v. Bollinger,* and *Grutter v. Bollinger.* (pp. 461–463)

15. In one paragraph, review the most recent court decisions and state laws on affirmative action and predict what will happen to the policy in the future. (pp. 463–464)

Key Terms

civil rights, p. 439

natural rights, p. 439

affirmative action, p. 440

naturalization, p. 441

dual citizenship, p. 442

right of expatriation, p. 442

women's suffrage, p. 447

equal protection clause, p. 451

due process clause, p. 451

rational basis test, p. 451

strict scrutiny test, p. 451

heightened scrutiny test, p. 452

literacy test, p. 455

white primary, p. 455

racial gerrymandering, p. 456

poll tax, p. 456

majority-minority district, p. 456

Jim Crow laws, p. 457

commerce clause, p. 457

class action suit, p. 457

restrictive covenant, p. 458

de jure segregation, p. 460

de facto segregation, p. 460

Further Reading

RAYMOND ARSENAULT, *Freedom Riders: 1961 and the Struggle for Racial Justice* (Oxford University Press, 2006).

TAYLOR BRANCH, *At Canaan's Edge: America in the King Years, 1965–1968* (Simon & Schuster, 2006).

TAYLOR BRANCH, *Parting the Waters: America in the King Years, 1954–1963* (Simon & Schuster, 1988).

TAYLOR BRANCH, *Pillar of Fire: America in the King Years, 1963–1965* (Simon & Schuster, 1998).

GORDON H. CHANG, ED., *Asian Americans and Politics* (Stanford University Press, 2001).

CHARLES CLOTFELTER, *After Brown: The Rise and Retreat of School Desegregation* (Princeton University Press, 2004).

CLARE CUSHMAN, ED., *Supreme Court Decisions and Women's Rights* (CQ Press, 2000).

ARLENE M. DAVILA, *Latinos, Inc.: The Marketing and Making of a People* (University of California Press, 2001).

JANET DEWART, ED., *The State of Black America* (National Urban League, published annually).

WILLIAM N. ESKRIDGE JR., *Gaylaw: Challenging the Apartheid of the Closet* (Harvard University Press, 2000).

RICHARD KAHLENBERG, *All Together Now: Creating Middle Class Schools Through Public School Choice* (Brookings Institution Press: 2003).

RANDALL KENNEDY, *Race, Crime, and the Law* (Pantheon, 1997).

MICHAEL J. KLARMAN, *From Jim Crow to Civil Rights: The Supreme Court and the Struggle for Racial Equality* (Oxford University Press, 2006).

PHILIP A. KLINKER AND **ROGER M. SMITH,** *The Unsteady March: The Rise and Decline of Racial Equality in America* (University of Chicago Press, 2000).

RICHARD KLUGER, *Simple Justice: The History of* Brown *v.* Board of Education (Knopf, 1976).

PETER KWONG AND **DUSANKA MISCEVIC,** *Chinese America: The Untold Story of America's Oldest New Community* (New Press, 2006).

NANCY MCGLEN, KAREN O'CONNOR, LAURA VAN ASSELDFT, AND **WENDY GUNTHER-CANADA,** *Women, Politics and American Society,* 3d ed. (Pearson/Longman, 2005).

DAVID M. O'BRIEN, *Constitutional Law and Politics: Civil Rights and Civil Liberties,* 7th ed. (Norton, 2008).

GARY ORFIELD AND **CHUNGMEI LEE,** *Brown at 50: King's Dream or Plessy's Nightmare* (Civil Rights Project, Harvard University, 2004).

J. W. PELTASON, *Fifty-Eight Lonely Men: Southern Federal Judges and School Desegregation* (University of Illinois Press, 1971).

DAN PINELLO, *America's Struggle for Same-Sex Marriage* (Cambridge University Press, 2006).

RUTH ROSEN, *The World Split Open: How the Modern Women's Movement Changed America* (Viking Press, 2000).

JOHN DAVID SKRENTNY, ED., *Color Lines: Affirmative Action, Immigration, and Civil Rights Options for America* (University of Chicago Press, 2001).

GIRARDEAU A. SPANN, *The Law of Affirmative Action: Twenty-Five Years of Supreme Court Decisions on Race and Remedies* (New York University Press, 1999).

PHILIPPA STRUM, *Women in the Barracks: The VMI Case and Equal Rights* (University Press of Kansas, 2002).

SUSAN F. VAN BURKLEO, *"Belonging to the World": Women's Rights and Constitutional Culture* (Oxford University Press, 2001).

chapter 17

Public Policy

The federal government has been trying to strike a balance between encouraging legal immigration and protecting the nation's borders against illegal entry for the better part of 200 years. However, the task has grown more challenging over the past 60 years as illegal immigration has steadily increased.

The president and Congress tried to achieve a new balance in 2007 and 2008. Under legislation drafted by Senate moderates and strongly supported by the Bush administration, almost all illegal immigrants would have gained the right to become legal citizens if they returned to their home countries to apply for permanent residency in the United States. With the number of illegal immigrants growing by 500,000 per year, the bill could have sharply increased the nation's workforce and added many taxpaying voters.[1]

The bill would also have toughened penalties against future illegal immigration. It called for completion of a 370-mile fence between the United States and Mexico, a large increase in the number of border patrol officers, and a crackdown on employers who hire illegal immigrants. It imposed strict rules on becoming a legal citizen, thereby reducing the number of illegal immigrants who would apply for legal citizenship.

Many members of Congress opposed the bill as a form of amnesty that rewarded employers and illegal immigrants who had violated the laws protecting the nation's borders. As Senator David Vitter (R-La.) argued in opposing the bill when it reached the floor, "I don't think the message could be any clearer than this dramatic vote. The message is crystal clear that the American people want us to start with enforcement."[2] Once illegal immigration was stopped and illegal immigrants returned to their home countries, Vitter and his allies would be willing to talk.

This intense opposition spilled over into the presidential campaigns as candidates fought about whether to force illegal immigrants to leave the country. As the issue became more visible, compromise became more difficult. As hard as Senate moderates pushed for reform in the spring of 2007, they were besieged from both sides, and the group could not gain enough votes to stop a threatened filibuster against it. Supporters finally conceded defeat in late June 2007. Despite the president's strong encouragement and personal phone calls to individual senators, 37 of the Senate's 49 Republicans voted against the bill, while 33 of its 51 Democrats and two Independents voted for it.

Immigration reform had been one of the president's top priorities since the 2000 presidential election, although other issues such as terrorism crowded the agenda. But in the end Bush could not get opponents to accept the compromise. "The American people understand the status quo is unacceptable when it comes to our immigration laws," he said after the Senate defeat. "A lot of us worked to see if we couldn't find a common ground—it didn't work."

In this chapter, we look at the process for making policy decisions in detail. We start by examining the different types of policy, then turn to the process itself and major trends that will shape decisions in the future.

Keep in mind that government by the people requires us to engage on the issues that matter most to each of us. The process simply cannot work to resolve big issues such as immigration, global warming, poverty, wars, and humanitarian crises in places such as Darfur without an active, vocal, and informed public. But we have no reason to become involved unless we care about an issue—the first question is *why* we become engaged. Only then do

LEARNING **OBJECTIVES**

1. Compare politics and public policy and show how each affects the other.
2. Analyze the three types of public policy.
3. Evaluate the eight steps in making public policy.
4. Compare and contrast the tools of public policy.
5. Identify how citizens can influence each step of the public policy process.

CHAPTER OUTLINE

- Defining Public Policy
- The Eight Steps in Making Public Policy
- Citizens and Public Policy

Illegal immigrants crossing the border into the United States.

LEARNING OBJECTIVE

1 Compare politics and public policy and show how each affects the other.

public policy
A specific course of action that government takes to address a problem.

politics
The interaction of the people and their government, including citizens, interest groups, political parties, and the institutions of government at all levels. Politics is concerned with who gets what, when, where, and how from government.

we need to know *how* to get involved. Of course, our becoming involved does not necessarily mean there will be a simple resolution or a new policy. Even when the public cares, as it does about immigration, if opinion is strongly divided, finding a compromise can be difficult.

Defining Public Policy

When government decides to solve a problem, it does so through a **public policy,** a specific course of action that government takes to address a challenge such as global warming, health care, or unemployment. Government can convey a public policy to the nation in laws passed by Congress and signed by the president, in opinions issued by the Supreme Court, and/or in rules written by administrators.

But whatever its form, a public policy tells the nation and the world who is about to get what, when, and how from the federal government. As Table 17–1 shows, we can

TABLE 17–1 Politics and Policy

The People →	Politics →	Policies →	Outcomes
Examples:	Examples:	Examples:	Examples:
Older Americans	Voting, joining AARP	Creating prescription drug coverage	Lower prescription drug costs
College students	Writing e-mails	Reducing college loan costs	Lower debt
Businesses	Contributing money to campaigns	Lower taxes	Higher profits
Environmental groups	Filing lawsuits	Enforcing smokestack rules	Cleaner air
Community	Setting up Facebook sites	Increasing police patrols	Safer neighborhoods

define **politics** as the interaction of the people and their government, while *policy* is the product of that give and take. If politics is a question of who gets what, when, where, and how from government, then policy is a formal statement of who has the greater power and what compromises have been reached.

Types of Public Policy

LEARNING **OBJECTIVE**

 Analyze the three types of public policy.

Public policies do not all have the same impact on society. Some benefit all groups of citizens, others benefit one group of citizens by taking something away from another, and still others take benefits from all groups in an effort to create a better society for everyone. These choices create three specific types of public policy.[3]

SIMULATION

You Are a State Legislature

Federal programs that offer new benefits to all citizens are called **distributive policy.** National parks, air traffic control, the interstate highway system, education funding, national defense, and Social Security are all distributive. They help all groups at some level, whether rich or poor. Although some may get more benefit than others from a particular program such as Social Security, which reduces poverty among low-income beneficiaries, every group receives at least something through distributive policy.

In contrast, federal programs that take resources away from one or more groups in society (usually through taxes) so another group can benefit (usually through an entitlement program) are **redistributive policy.** Such programs benefit the less fortunate. Welfare, poverty programs, Head Start for poor preschool children, and special programs to help minority groups are redistributive. Some political scientists call them **zero-sum games,** meaning one group's gain (the program's benefits) is another's loss (the program's cost in taxes).

Finally, federal programs that take resources from every group to solve a common problem by reducing benefits such as Social Security or raising taxes on all income levels are a form of **counterdistributive policy.**[4] They are often designed to impose sacrifices on all citizens in pursuit of a common goal. Although some can absorb lower benefits and higher taxes more easily than others, all must pay at least something for the common good. In 2007, for example, Congress passed a law creating new mileage standards for cars and light trucks. In doing so, it raised the cost of manufacturing, which is usually passed on to consumers. Some would argue that such a policy also provides benefits, such as better gas mileage.

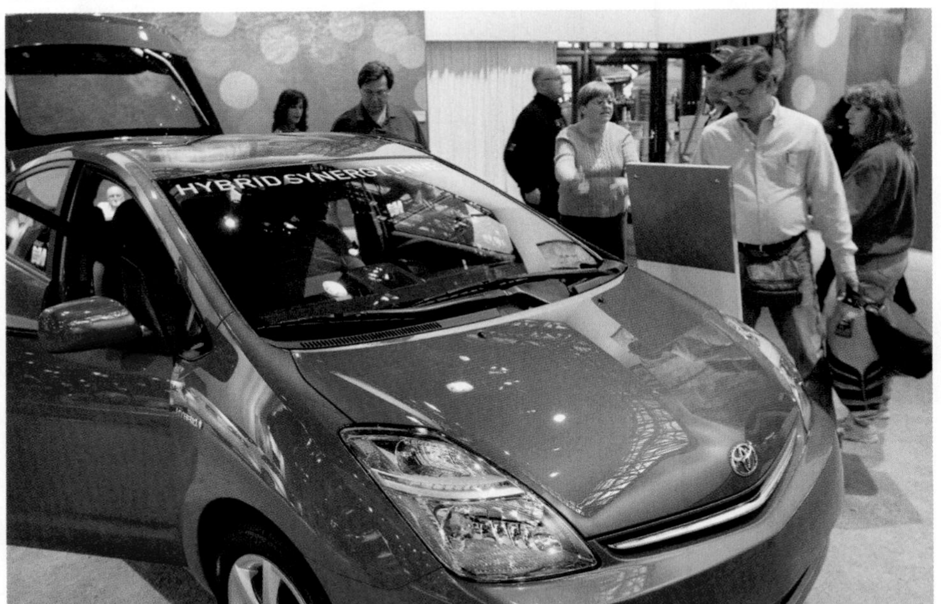

Hybrid gas- and electric-powered cars provide both costs and benefits to the environment. On the one hand, they consume less gas, which reduces emissions and dependence on foreign oil. On the other hand, they use electricity that is often produced through the use of coal, which creates its own emissions.

distributive policy
A public policy such as Social Security that provides benefits to all groups in society.

redistributive policy
A policy that provides to one group of society while taking away benefits for another through policy tools such as tax increases to pay for job training.

zero-sum games
policy that takes away exactly as much in benefits as another group gains.

counterdistributive policy
A policy that reduces benefits for all groups such as a tax increase in society, often by imposing rules that govern everyone.

YOU WILL DECIDE

How Should We Fix Social Security?

Social Security is one of the most popular and important public policies. Created in 1934, it provides income to almost every U.S. retiree and is widely credited with reducing poverty among older people to historic lows.

As the baby-boom generation embarks on retirement, however, Social Security will enter a major funding crisis. At the start of the program, there were almost 160 workers paying FICA payroll taxes into the program for every one beneficiary; by 1998, there were about three workers per beneficiary; by 2030, there will be just two.

The result is a growing gap between the amount of money workers put into the program and the amount beneficiaries receive. The Social Security program does not keep worker taxes in individual accounts in some vault until they need them. Rather, it uses current taxes to pay for current benefits, pushing the money out almost as soon as it collects it.

Estimates suggest that Social Security will run out of money sometime in the 2020 or 2030s. By that point, the baby-boom generation will simply overwhelm the system.

We often use such *cost/benefit analysis* to compare and contrast policy proposals such as electric cars that reduce the nation's need for oil (benefit) but increase the demand for the electricity produced by coal-fired plants (cost), or the use of reusable cloth diapers that limits waste (benefit) but also creates water pollution (cost). We measure costs and benefits in other ways than dollars, however. Social rewards such as public happiness are nearly impossible to calculate, but they may still outweigh other considerations in passage of a policy.

The Eight Steps in Making Public Policy

Every public policy reflects a series of separate decisions leading to its creation. The process has eight steps: (1) making assumptions about the world, (2) setting the agenda of problems to be addressed, (3) deciding to act, (4) deciding how much to do, (5) choosing a tool for solving the problem, (6) deciding who will deliver the goods or services, (7) making rules for implementation, and (8) running the program itself. Figure 17–1 arranges the steps. We'll discuss each step next, but note that by its very nature, the choice to move forward (in step 3) is the most difficult, largely because of the complexity of passing a bill, issuing an executive order, or making a Supreme Court

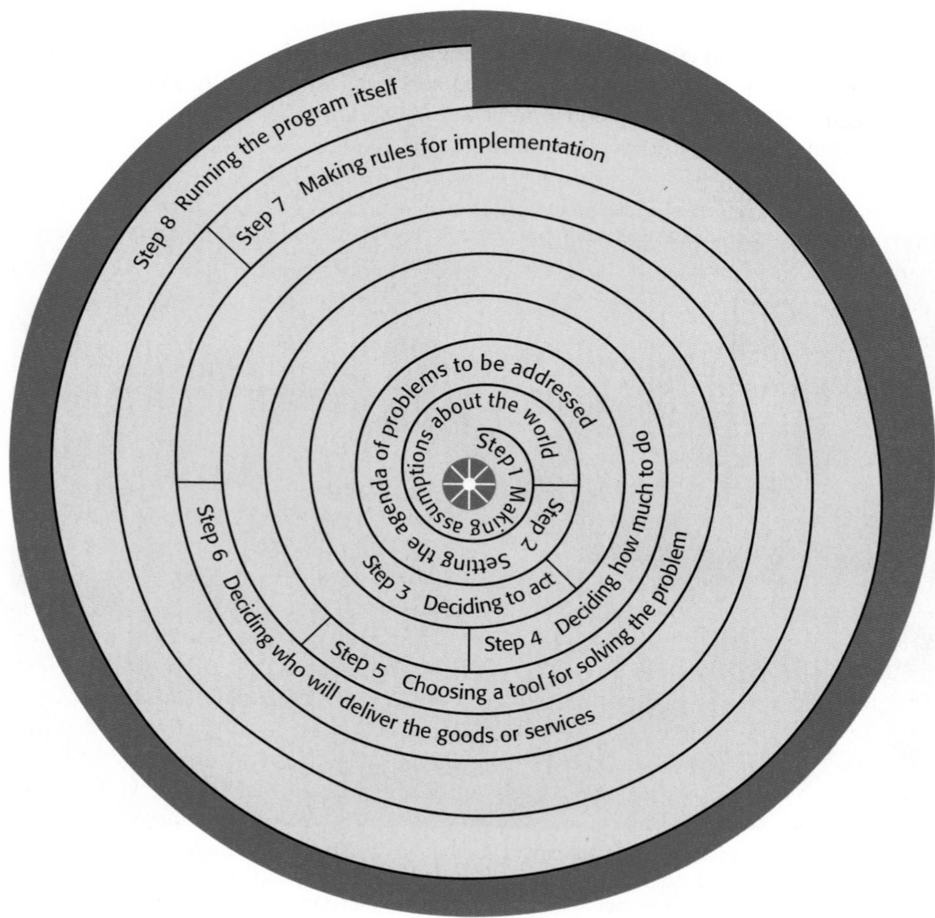

FIGURE 17–1
Modified circle diagram of eight steps.

decision. It is often far easier to make what political scientists call a **nondecision,** which means the policy process stops before final action.

THINKING IT THROUGH

There are only two ways to fix the Social Security program: increase revenues or cut benefits for retirees. Neither will be popular.

One way to help the program is to raise the basic tax rate on what workers earn and put more money into the system. Another way is to invest some Social Security funds in the stock market, where they might grow faster than they currently do in low-interest federal money accounts. Still another way is to allow younger workers to use their Social Security taxes to create their own personal savings accounts. Under this option, called privatization, workers would decide how much risk to take in investing their tax dollars—if they made good decisions, they would receive higher benefits; if they did poorly, they would receive lower benefits.

The options for cutting benefits are particularly unpopular. One way is to increase the retirement age, which is already rising from 65 to 67. An increase would delay retirement checks for a few years, saving money. Another way is to reduce the annual cost-of-living increases the government has always made in Social Security benefits. Beneficiaries would still get their checks, but the amount would no longer rise as fast as inflation.

Will Generation Next and younger workers of the future accept a tax increase given the state of the economy? After all, they're already having trouble getting mortgages and paying off college loans. Moreover, many young workers don't believe Social Security will exist when they retire—why put in more money now when they won't get anything back?

At the same time, younger workers do feel an obligation to their parents and grandparents. They may end up helping older relatives one way or the other—if they don't put more money into the program, they may have to put more money into charities or take care of their parents and grandparents themselves.

Questions

1. Is Social Security a distributive or redistributive program?
2. How does the policy process create barriers to the changing social security? How can these barriers be lowered?
3. What political pressure can young workers exert to make sure fixing Social Security is fair to workers and beneficiaries alike?

1. Making Assumptions about the World

Every government decision starts with assumptions about the future. Is the economy going to get stronger? If so, perhaps employment will go up and the costs of supporting the unemployed will go down. Is terrorism going to increase? If so, perhaps the federal government needs to inspect more cargo ships in search of bombs and other threats. Answers to questions about the future shape decisions about what the federal government might do.

Making even short-term assumptions about how the world will change is difficult, however. As one senior Reagan administration official once remarked, "I'm beginning to believe that history is a lot shakier than I thought it was. In other words, I think there are random elements, less determinism, and more discretion in the course of history that I ever believed before."[5] For example, the economy can change very quickly, which can increase joblessness overnight, which can put more pressure on the social safety net, which can demand higher taxes, and so on. Many experts were completely surprised in 2007–2008 when the mortgage market collapsed in the wake of billions of dollars of bad loans. They simply had not predicted it could happen.

Because there is no sure way to choose among competing assumptions about the future, policy makers often make choices that help sell their particular views of the world. They are pessimistic about the future when they define problems, but optimistic when they announce specific proposals to fix the problems. Problems thus look worse than they are, while solutions may seem likely to work better than they actually will.

2. Setting the Agenda

LEARNING **OBJECTIVE**

3 Evaluate the eight steps in making public policy.

Choosing the problem to be solved is the essential decision in setting the **policy agenda.** The policy agenda, as political scientist John Kingdon defines it, "is the list of subjects or problems to which governmental officials, and people outside of government closely associated with those officials, are paying some serious attention at any given time."[6]

Thus defined, the agenda is a direct product of politics and reflects broad social goals embraced by the people and their government, such as liberty, equality, individualism, and respect for the common person. These values are core to the ideology that shapes the policy agenda, but they often conflict with each other as ideas move toward public policies. Everyone wants the American dream, for example, but we often disagree on how to get it. Politics affects the rise and fall of these ideologies through elections, party identification, interest group pressure, and a variety of other political expressions.

Problems are distinct from politics and reach the list of possible agenda items from a variety of sources. Some arise from events such as the September 11, 2001, terrorist attacks or Hurricane Katrina. Others become prominent through newspaper or television stories about a controversial issue such as gay marriage, and still others because of interest group pressure for benefits such as prescription drug coverage for

nondecision
A decision not to move ahead with the policy process. In short, it is a decision not to decide.

policy agenda
The list of issues that the federal goverment pays attention to.

HISTORY MAKERS

Ralph Nader

Ralph Nader may have done more than any other person to influence the policy process on behalf of consumers. Born in 1934, he earned his law degree from Harvard University in 1958. But unlike many Harvard lawyers, he decided to devote the rest of his life to public service.

By the mid-1960s, Nader was well on his way to national acclaim for his effort to design a new kind of interest group dedicated to the public interest. "You've got to keep the pressure on, even if you lose," he says about representing the public interest. "The essence of the citizen's movement is persistence." He described himself only as a full-time citizen, which he calls the "most important office in America for anyone to achieve."*

Nader started his journey in 1965 with the publication of *Unsafe at Any Speed,* a damning attack on the poor state of automobile safety in the United States. Targeting General Motors and its Chevrolet Corvair, Nader demanded congressional action and got it. Today's airbags are directly traceable to Nader's early pressure for mandatory seat belts and crash-resistant passenger compartments. Nader also persuaded Congress to hold hearings on allegations that General Motors had hired private detectives to harass him. The corporation's chairman publicly apologized.

By the late 1990s, however, Nader had decided that he could use another job to influence policy: president of the United States. Running as the candidate of his pro-environment Green Party, Nader was on the presidential ballot in both 2000 and 2004. Although he received only 3 percent of the national vote in 2000, with the outcome decided by fewer than 1,000 votes in Florida, many Democrats blamed him for pulling enough support away from Al Gore to swing the election to Bush.

Ralph Nader.

Nader's legacy is not in his books, his presidential bids, or even the 2005 documentary on his life, *An Unreasonable Man*. It is in the Center for Study of Responsive Law, the Center for Science in the Public Interest, the Center for Women Policy Studies, the Freedom of Information Clearinghouse, the National Coalition for Universities in the Public Interest, Public Citizen, and the dozens of other interest groups he helped create. It is also in the Public Interest Research Groups (PIRGs) that exist on college campuses in 23 states to lobby government on a range of economic and social issues. And it is in the ongoing investigations by "Nader's Raiders" that have led to legislative victories on safe drinking water, consumer protection, open government, tax reform, and nuclear energy.

QUESTIONS

1. Which of Ralph Nader's approaches to influencing public policy (candidate for office, author of book about unsafe cars, or founder of an interest group) do you think has been most successful? Why?
2. Why were consumer groups so rare before Nader started building them?
3. What can individual citizens do to persuade government to act in the public interest?

*David Bollier, "The Essential Nader," www.nader.org.

older citizens. Some emerge from congressional investigations of issues such as cigarette smoking, car safety, or government fraud.

Other possible problems are the subject of ongoing government monitoring. For example, the government regularly reports data on the state of the economy as measured by unemployment, inflation, or new housing starts. These markers can show the beginnings of an economic slowdown or of an improving economy. Readers need only visit www.fedstats.gov to see the range of information government provides to policy makers, investors, and the public. Through these different venues, policy makers latch on to particular problems or solutions depending on the readiness for action.

How a problem becomes important matters to policy makers, largely because it reveals the politics of making decisions about it. Problems that come from strong interest groups, corporations, or respected civic leaders may get more attention than problems revealed in public opinion polls of ordinary citizens. And problems aired by citizens who raise large amounts of money for political campaigns may get the most attention of all, or at least the greatest access to candidates.

Nevertheless, the public's attention span can be very short. Problems identified through scientific research such as global warming may be the easiest to ignore, partly because there always seem to be numbers to refute a given analysis. Even as former vice president Al Gore was accepting the Nobel Peace Prize for his work on global warming, a group of scientists challenged much of the evidence on which his work was based. The media can also play a role by magnifying or downplaying the impact of a particular story.

Policy makers set the agenda using many of the same criteria they apply to other political decisions—public opinion, interest group pressure, their own beliefs, ideology, party affiliation, and loyalty to their institution. In recent years, they have also come to rely on a small number of think tanks to help them sort through the stream of possible problems. A **think tank** is an organization composed of scholars who study public policy. Many are located in Washington, D.C., so they can be closer to the national political process. Unlike a college or university, which also produces policy research, a think tank exists almost entirely to influence the immediate agenda. Thus many are described as either liberal or conservative.

Former vice president Al Gore won an Academy Award for his documentary about global warming, *An Inconvenient Truth*, and the Nobel Peace Prize for his efforts to publicize environmental problems.

3. Deciding to Act

The fact that a problem exists does not automatically mean that Congress, the president, or the courts will try to solve it. Some problems help policy makers achieve their personal or political goals, such as reelection or a place in history, in which case they decide to act, while others do not, in which case they pick other problems to solve.

Policy makers also clearly understand that public pressure for action ebbs and flows over time. In fact, writes political scientist Anthony Downs, "American public attention rarely remains sharply focused upon any one domestic issue for very long—even if it involves a continuing problem of crucial importance to society." According to Downs, the public follows an **issue-attention cycle** in which each problem "suddenly leaps into prominence, remains there for a short time, and then—though still largely unresolved—gradually fades from the center of public attention."[7]

- This cycle starts with what Downs described as the "pre-problem stage," the rise of some "highly undesirable social condition" such as global warming that has yet to capture public attention.
- The issue-attention cycle continues with "alarmed discovery and euphoric enthusiasm," the sudden emergence of an issue as a topic for public debate. Books are written, documentaries made, speeches retooled, and campaigns rebuilt, all based on the sudden passion that generates public concern.
- The cycle moves onward with the realization that change will incur significant cost. It is one thing to worry about greenhouse gases and quite another to pay more for clean electricity or buy smaller, more efficient cars. The greater the cost of solving a problem, especially if it means tax increases or benefit cuts, the more strongly people pull back from their euphoric view of change.
- The cycle continues with the "gradual decline of intense public interest." Having pressed hard for action on an issue such as universal health insurance, the public may begin to realize that change is nearly impossible given the array of political forces fighting for a nondecision.
- The cycle ends with what Downs calls the "post-problem stage." The problem moves into "prolonged limbo—a twilight realm of lesser attention or spasmodic recurrences of interest."

The ultimate decline of public interest is not inevitable. But if we expect problems to be solved immediately, we will only be disappointed. Civil rights took a hundred years to become a reality, for example. Although issues such as global warming seem to demand that we take immediate action before the damage is beyond repair, we must acquire enough understanding of the problem, and of the policy process, to stay actively engaged for the long term.

think tank
A nongovernmental organization that seeks to influence public policy through research and education.

issue-attention cycle
The movement of public opinion toward public policy from initial enthusiasm for action to realization of costs and a decline in interest.

THE **CHANGING FACE** OF U.S. POLITICS

Think Tanks

Of the several hundred think tanks across the nation, the largest and most influential exist in Washington. They include the liberal Brookings Institution, the moderate American Enterprise Institute, and the conservative Heritage Foundation, all frequently cited when Congress or the president makes final decisions. They are even occasionally cited by the Supreme Court. Supported by private donations, think tanks have great freedom to study any issue they wish.

As the United States has become more ethnically and racially diverse, think tanks have become more interested in diversity as a research topic. In 2008, the Brookings Institution listed more than 360 publications that had something to do with diversity, gender, or race, especially as they affect the growing gap between the rich and the poor.

In turn, the American Enterprise Institute also produced a long list of publications, including a series on the need to reform the Voting Rights Act to prevent the "racial gerrymandering" that has been used to increase the number of minorities in Congress.

The Heritage Foundation contributed reports on everything from political correctness on college campuses to what it described as Martin Luther King's conservative, anti-government positions.

Hard as they try to study diversity from their ideological point of view, however, think tanks are not very diverse themselves. According to a 2001 survey of think tank scholars, there is almost no diversity among them at all. Of 100 scholars selected at random from the ten largest think tanks, only a few were women and an even smaller percentage were minorities.*

There are exceptions to this largely white, male portrait in specific think tanks, such as the liberal Center for American Progress. But achieving diversity is dependent on more aggressive recruiting that acknowledges the role women and minorities would play in shaping the research effort. If think tanks want to influence the real world, they may want to have more of that world in their midst.

QUESTIONS

1. Why might think tanks suffer such a lack of diversity?
2. What arguments can you make in favor of more racial and gender diversity in think tanks?
3. If think tanks are about ideas and original research, why does race or gender in the composition of the scholars working at think tanks matter?

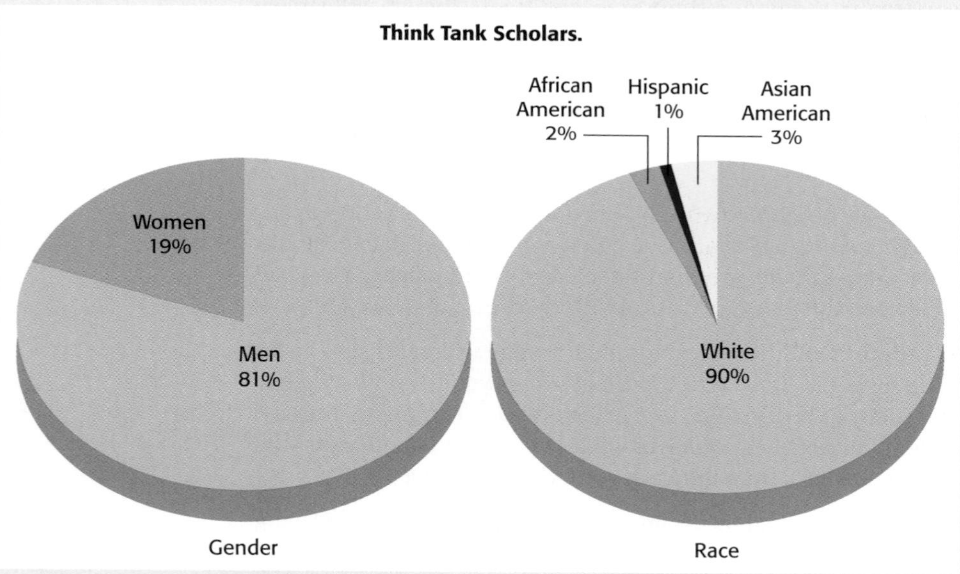

*The survey was conducted on behalf of the Presidential Appointee Initiative in late 2001.

incremental policy
Small adjustments to existing public policies.

punctuating policy
Radical changes to public policy that occur only after the mobilization of large segments of society to demand action.

4. Deciding How Much to Do

Once the federal government decides it *wants* to do something about a problem, the next difficult decision is *how much* to do. Government can launch a comprehensive program such as Social Security or Medicare, or a smaller program it can expand bit by bit over time.

Incremental or Comprehensive Policy An **incremental policy** makes a small-scale adjustment in an existing program, while a *comprehensive* or **punctuating policy** creates a dramatic change in the federal government's role. Incremental policies are generally the easiest to create, if only because they build on past decisions in very small ways, such as increasing the amount of federal support for colleges by a few hundred dollars. Punctuating policies, such as providing national prescription drug coverage for older adults, often require citizens, interest groups, political parties, and policy makers to mobilize in a broad movement for change.

Incremental policy is the most frequent response to calls for change. According to James L. True, Bryan D. Jones, and Frank R. Baumgartner, "American political institutions were conservatively designed to resist many efforts at change and thus to make mobilization necessary if established interests are to be overcome."[8] Because of constitutional protections such as separation of power and checks and balances, incremental policy often becomes the easiest way to advance an idea.

More fundamental change is sometimes possible. As True, Jones, and Baumgartner write, these "bursts" of change occur when a new image of a problem replaces the prevailing notion that incremental policy is the only answer. Such new images have shaped the way the government tests new drugs, regulates local education, attacks environmental pollution, and regulates the purchase of handguns and assault rifles.

DEBATE

Gun Rights and Gun Control

Iron Triangles and Issue Networks Fundamental changes often depend on alliances of citizens, interest groups, political parties, private businesses, government agencies, congressional committees, and others who come together to place an issue on the agenda and push for or against change. Alliances called **iron triangles** exist for decades; **issue networks** cooperate for a specific cause and then disband.

An iron triangle has three sides that hold together over long periods of time: (1) a federal department or agency, (2) a set of loyal interest groups, and (3) a House and/or Senate committee. Each side supports the other two. Loyal members of Congress work to protect or increase the agency's budget and get campaign contributions and endorsements from the interest groups in return; interest groups give contributions and endorsements to loyal members of Congress and get special services from the agency; the agency gives special services to the interest groups and gets money from Congress in return. Policy making for veterans, for example, is achieved through an iron triangle composed of the Department of Veterans Affairs, the House and Senate Veterans Committees, and a long list of interest groups that represent veterans, such as the American Legion and Veterans of Foreign Wars. These organizations often receive free office space in veterans' hospitals to help their members. The basic structure of this iron triangle is presented in Figure 17–2.

Iron triangles have been largely replaced by much looser collections of participants in issue networks. As political scientist Hugh Heclo has argued, the notion that iron triangles make all policy was "not so much wrong as it was disastrously incomplete" in today's complicated policy environment.[9] The increasing number of small,

iron triangle
A policy making instrument composed of a tighty related alliance of a congressional committee, interest groups, and federal department of agency.

issue network
A Policy making instrument composed of loosely related interest groups, congressional committee, presidential aides, and other parties.

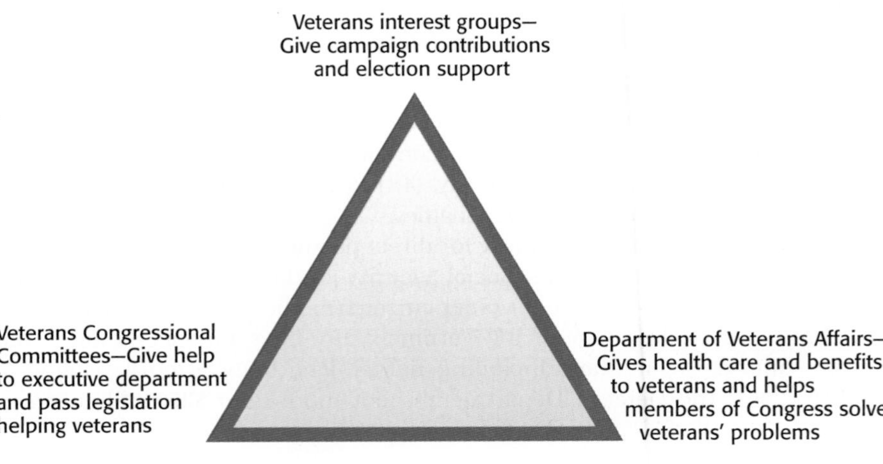
Veterans interest groups— Give campaign contributions and election support
Veterans Congressional Committees—Give help to executive department and pass legislation helping veterans
Department of Veterans Affairs— Gives health care and benefits to veterans and helps members of Congress solve veterans' problems

FIGURE 17–2
Iron Triangle.

FIGURE 17–3
Issue Network.

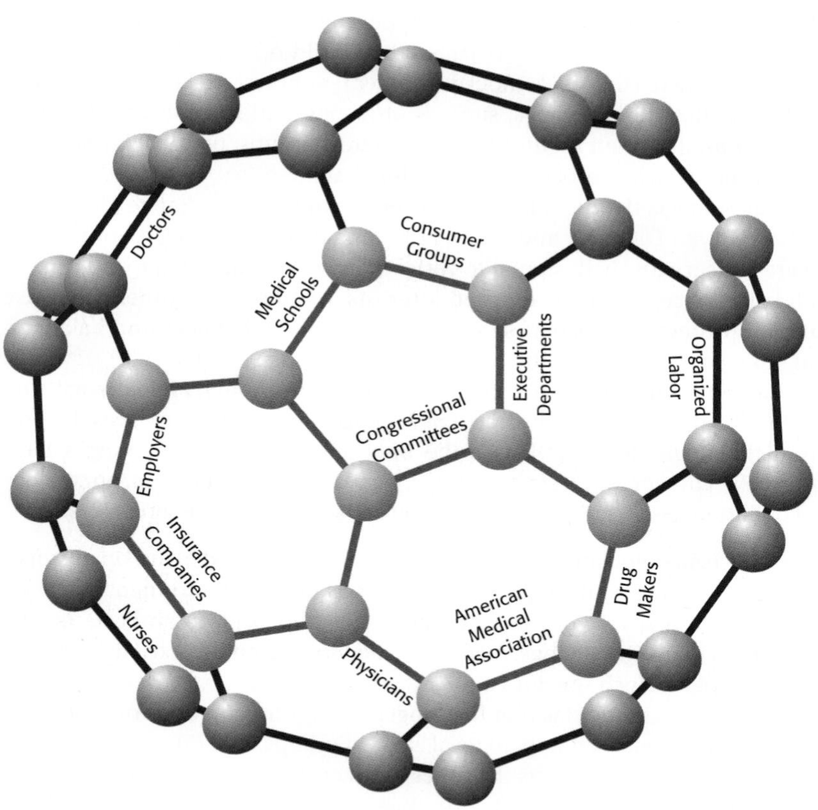

highly specialized interest groups makes an iron triangle almost impossible to create, if only because Congress and federal agencies can no longer identify a steady occupant for the third corner of the triangle. They have to find temporary allies, depending on the issue. There is nothing "iron" about such coalitions: they last only as long as an issue is hot. The informal structure of the issue network on universal health care coverage is illustrated in Figure 17–3.

Issue networks concentrate power in the relatively small number of individuals who organize and maintain them. These people make the key decisions about who participates and what they say. Some political scientists thus refer to the rise of well-financed issue networks—such as those that promote prescription drug coverage for older consumers or tax cuts for business—as a form of elitism, not pluralism, in which a very small number of actors accelerate or delay action. Medicare prescription drug coverage, for example, engaged an issue network of drug companies, AARP, and hospitals.

LEARNING **OBJECTIVE**

4 Compare and contrast the tools of public policy.

5. Choosing a Tool

The federal government has five tools to solve most public problems: (1) spending money, (2) using taxes to regulate the economy and encourage certain behaviors, (3) providing goods and services directly, (4) providing protection against risk, and (5) creating standards, incentives, or penalties.[10]

The first tool is *federal spending* for direct payments to individuals, hospitals, corporations, and other nations. Social Security is still the largest direct payment to individuals, while Medicare for older citizens' medical care is the largest direct payment to hospitals. The federal government also buys a huge amount of material to support the military, including fighter jets, body armor, gasoline, and food. In 2007, the Defense Department spent more than $200 billion on such purchases.

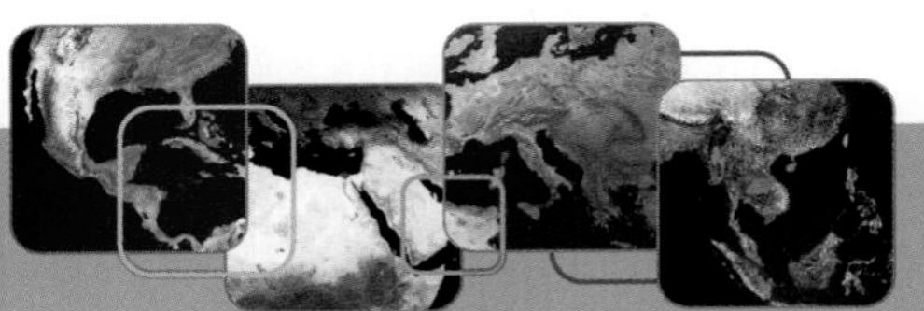

HOW **OTHER NATIONS** GOVERN

The Policy Process

The policy process does not vary greatly around the world. Almost all policies are the product of making assumptions, setting the agenda, deciding to act, and so forth.

However, other nations give their citizens different levels of influence in making policy decisions. In Great Britain, policy decisions are shaped by a tight bond between the administrative agencies of government and Parliament. Indeed, it is said that the agenda is never set until a decision has already been made. "It's carrying democracy too far if you don't know the result of the vote before the meeting."* With 9 of 10 votes in Parliament decided along party lines, there is rarely any doubt about the outcome of debate.

Other nations also differ in the source of ideas and level of citizen engagement. All legislation in Japan originates in the administrative agencies. Ideas are submitted to the Japanese executive cabinet and usually sent forward to the Japanese legislature for formal action.

In contrast, although the Mexican constitution gives the legislature a powerful formal role in making policy, history has placed the president at the center of key decisions. Nigeria has a similar system, though it has been through such great political turbulence that no one can predict who will make its key policy decisions in the future.

Political parties play the dominant role in making policy in India, which has been divided by political unrest for decades. Citizens are also influential in a country where protest movements have an enormous influence on policy.

Political parties play a very different but still powerful role in China, where the Communist Party is the only party and makes all policy decisions. These are converted into laws by the National People's Congress.

QUESTIONS

1. How do differences in governmental structure lead to different policy outcomes?
2. Which steps do you think are most important in the policy process and why?
3. What kinds of policy might you expect to see in a system dominated by an executive rather than a legislature? By political parties?

*Quoted in Gabriel Almond, G. Bingham Powell Jr., Russell J. Dalton, and Kaare Strom, *Comparative Politics Today: A World View* (Longman, 2008), p. 171.

The second tool of public policy is the *use of taxes* to regulate the economy—lower taxes may stimulate a weak economy, while higher taxes may slow down a hot economy. The federal government can use the tax system to encourage certain behaviors such as buying a house, making contributions to charity, or even having children. Businesses receive tax credits and deductions for activities such as energy conservation and the purchase of some U.S.-made goods.

The third tool is *providing goods and services* to the public. National parks such as Yosemite and the Grand Canyon generally charge an admission fee, the National Air and Space Museum on the Washington Mall is free, and we do not pay directly for national defense. Ultimately, of course, nothing the government does is completely free—the National Air and Space Museum is supported by general taxes, as is the Defense Department.

The fourth tool of public policy is to *guarantee protection* against risk, with a range of devices to encourage activities the private sector might not otherwise undertake. The most familiar protections are federal loan guarantees, under which the government promises to cover losses if a student, farmer, small business, or other borrower fails to repay a debt.

The final tool of public policy is **regulation** to encourage or discourage certain behaviors such as smoking, using illegal drugs, polluting, and driving safely. Regulation involves **rules,** which are precise legal statements implementing a public policy. They can impose penalties or rewards enforceable by, and open to challenge in the courts.

Thus, regulation and rules are best viewed as tactics for achieving a particular result, such as the controversial rule requiring schools to test their students on a regular basis, imposed on local school districts under the No Child Left Behind Act of 2002.

Laws and regulations cover topics as varied as terrorism, the use of firearms in a crime, kidnapping, tax incentives for contributing to charity, and specific standards for testing new drugs or smoking in public. Violations usually result in a penalty such

regulation
A policy that encourages or discourages certain behavior by imposing a legally-binding rule. Rules are made through a long process that begins with an act of Congress and ends with issuance of a final rule.

rule
A precise statement of how a law is implemented.

GENERATION **NEXT**

Government Control of Daily Life

U.S. citizens have mixed opinions of the federal government's role in regulating their own lives. On one hand, they believe the federal government spends too much time controlling what they do. On the other hand, many want the federal government to do more on issues such as Social Security and health insurance.

According to the Pew Research Center's Political Landscape survey, Generation Next shares these mixed feelings. Asked whether the federal government controls too much of our daily lives, about 60 percent of all age groups completely or somewhat agreed. Although adults become more concerned about the intrusion of the federal government as they age, the majority in all age groups seems to want less regulation of their own behavior.

At the same time, young adults clearly believe the government needs to address individual issues such as smoking and drug use. According to the Pew Research Center's Generation Next survey, the majority believe smoking marijuana is not okay.

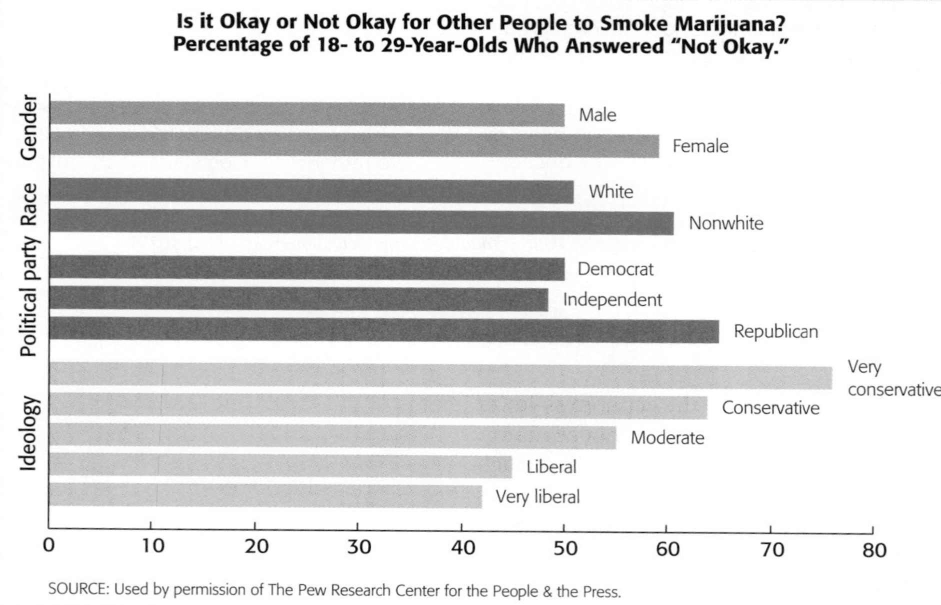

SOURCE: Used by permission of The Pew Research Center for the People & the Press.

The Generation Next survey clearly shows the impact of party identification and ideology on views of marijuana use. But even though Republicans and conservatives think it is not okay to use marijuana, they also believe that government is too involved their daily lives. Thus, the question is how they would otherwise reduce marijuana use.

QUESTIONS

1. Why do you think men and women differ on whether it is okay to smoke marijuana?
2. What kinds of government action to reduce marijuana use, if any, do you think Republicans and conservatives would favor? And why?
3. What kinds of government policy making, besides direct regulation, might the government pursue to decrease marijuana use?

as a traffic ticket, a fine, or even imprisonment, while compliance can produce benefits such as lower taxes.

All five tools are designed to produce *material* benefits for society. Some benefits are tangible, such as new roads, bridges, schools, and hospitals; others, such as higher pay, greater safety, better education, and cleaner air and water, can only be felt.

Other tools produce *symbolic* benefits such as efforts to educate the public, study an issue, appoint a blue-ribbon commission, or highlight the need for future action. In theory, symbolic benefits highlight an emerging issue and create citizen action. In reality, they are sometimes a way to make a nondecision as policy makers merely express their concern and move to other tangible policies.

6. Deciding Who Will Deliver the Goods or Services

Part of selecting a tool to implement a policy is deciding who will actually implement the program. The answer is not always a federal employee.[11] Although federal employment has been steady at roughly 1.8 million workers since the early 1990s, the federal agenda has continued to grow. As a result, the government often depends on a largely hidden workforce of contractors, grantees, and state and local employees to achieve its policy goals.

There are four sources of what political scientists call *third-party government:* (1) private businesses, (2) colleges and universities, (3) state and local governments, and (4) charitable organizations.

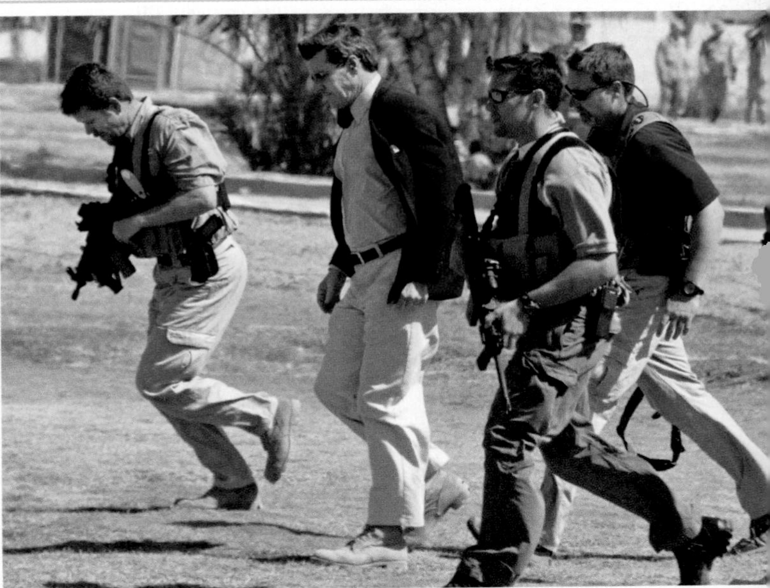

Private firms provided most security services to protect U.S. diplomats during the Iraq War. In 2007, employees of Blackwater, Inc., were charged with the unprovoked killings of Iraqi citizens during one of its patrols.

Private Businesses Paid under contracts with federal departments and agencies, profit-making businesses do an increasing amount of federal work once done exclusively by federal employees. For example, the federal government uses contractors to serve meals in almost all of its cafeterias, make weather maps at the National Oceanographic and Atmospheric Administration, operate the passenger and baggage screening lines at airports, and sweep the floors at almost all federal buildings. In 2007 and 2008, the State Department became embroiled in a controversy over its use of private contractors such as Blackwater to provide security for diplomats in Iraq.

Colleges and Universities Colleges and universities are a second option for implementing public policy, especially if it includes research. Almost every major university receives federal funding for education, environment, health, and space research, while many conduct research on behalf of the Defense Department or the Department of Homeland Security. Colleges and universities also receive federal funds for training scientists and engineers and often benefit from pet projects enacted by Congress. They have been the source of many scientific breakthroughs, including much medical research used to fight cancer and other life-threatening diseases.

State and Local Governments As the National Commission on the State and Local Government Service argued in 1993, state and local employees do much of the real work of governing. They collect the trash; provide safe drinking water; vaccinate children; administer the airports; run the public schools, universities, and community colleges; oversee environmental laws; run almost all public hospitals; staff most of the nation's prisons; prosecute most of the crimes; and provide police and fire protection.

Charities Finally, the federal government often relies on charities such as the American Red Cross, the Salvation Army, the American Cancer Society, and religious institutions to maintain the social safety net through contracts and grants. It also relies on charities to help the nation respond to crises such as Hurricane Katrina.

Charities are often called "social-benefit organizations" because of their role in battling problems such as poverty, illiteracy, hunger, and disease. But they also monitor and influence what the federal government does. Whatever their role in implementing federal policy, charities cannot be taxed by government if they are engaged in any legitimate educational, religious, or humanitarian purpose. Most gifts to charities are tax deductible, too, meaning that givers can deduct the amount of their contribution from their taxable income.

The number of charities has more than tripled over the past half-century. Today's 1.5 million charities employ about 11 million people and spend almost a trillion dollars

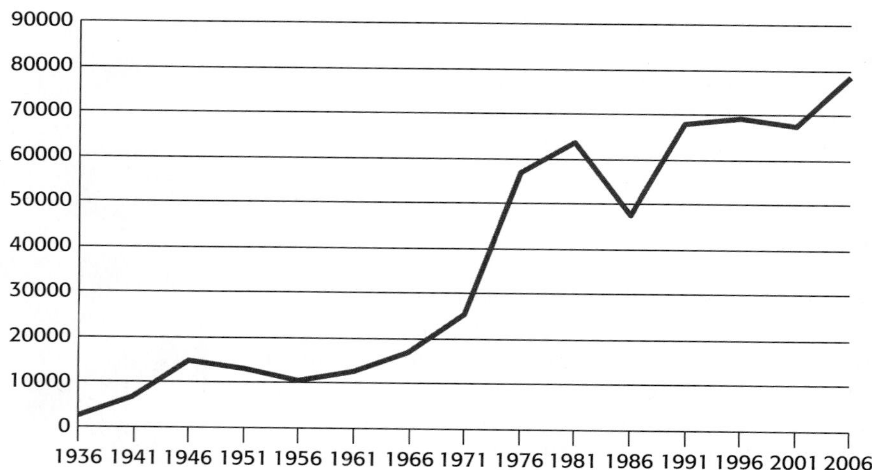

FIGURE 17–4
Pages in the *Federal Register*.

SOURCE: U.S. Office of the Federal Register, "Annual Federal Register Pages Published."

a year. Most private colleges and universities are considered charities under federal law, for example, as are many hospitals.

7. Making Rules for Implementation

Rule making comes at the very end of the policy-making process and is almost invisible to most citizens. Nevertheless, it is the essential step in converting the abstract ideas and language of laws, presidential orders, and court rulings into precise rules governing what individual members of the public, companies, government, states and localities must do to achieve the goals of a specific policy.

Rules can be extraordinarily detailed and are sometimes difficult for even regulated parties to understand. Because they are so complicated, interest groups have much greater influence over their construction than citizens and even members of Congress.

Although the federal government has been issuing rules since 1789, the number of rules jumped dramatically during World War II and again in the 1970s.[12] We can see the growth of rules in the number of pages in the *Federal Register*, which provides a daily record of all new and proposed rules. Figure 17–4 shows the number of pages by decade.

The number of rules did not increase because rule making became easier, however. On the contrary, Congress made it more difficult to create a rule under the 1946 Administrative Procedure Act.

The process starts when a bill is passed and signed into law, which is sent to the appropriate department or agency for "faithful execution," as the Constitution requires. With the legislative history as a guide to what Congress wanted, the department or agency then drafts a proposed rule. The rule itself generally consists of a statement of purpose, the actual rule, and a review of any research or legislative language that shaped it.

With the proposed rule in hand, the department or agency tells the public it is about to act. Under the Administrative Procedure Act, the department or agency must post a formal "Notice of Proposed Rulemaking" in the *Federal Register*. Anyone affected by the rule has a short period of "notice and comment" to express concerns and suggest amendments through letters, e-mails, and personal testimony to government. After all the comments are reviewed, the department or agency publishes the final rule in the *Federal Register*. The rule goes into effect 30 days after it is published.

Although this process seems straightforward, it includes a number of leverage points at which a rule can be substantially altered. The process can also be delayed—nothing in the Constitution or the Administrative Procedure Act says that a department or agency must propose a rule within a specific amount of time. Moreover, the department or agency retains great discretion to interpret information generated through the notice and comment period.

Finally, the rule itself can violate legislative intent, which often produces judicial action. In 2003, for example, the Environmental Protection Agency issued a final rule governing "concentrated animal feeding operations," or feedlots, that environmental groups claimed was a violation of the Clean Water Act. Two years later, a federal court of appeals sided with an interest group called the Waterkeeper Alliance and ordered the Environmental Protection Agency to try again. The agency issued a much stronger rule in 2007. Even though the Bush administration lost its case, it delayed the new requirements by almost four years, saving feedlot operators millions in costs but polluting the waters.[13]

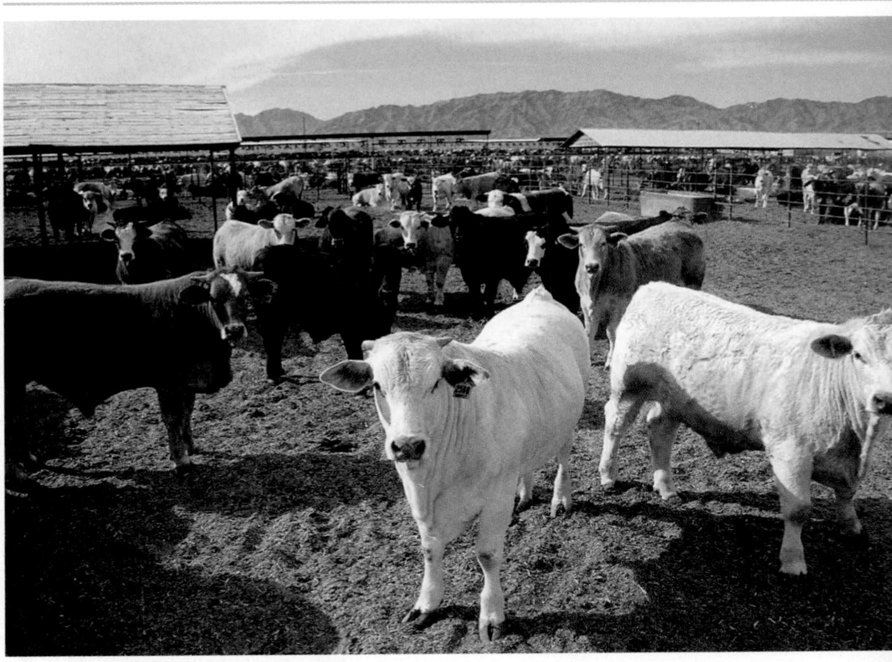

Animal feedlots generate significant amounts of waste that often runs into local rivers and streams. From 2003 to 2007, the Bush administration and environmental groups fought new rules that would have given feedlot operators much greater freedom to regulate themselves.

8. Running the Program

Implementation does not end with release of a final rule. It continues with the day-to-day tasks of actually running a federal department or agency, making rules, supervising contractors, and evaluating impact. And as assumptions change and the issue-attention cycle takes hold, the policy-making process can begin again. As we shall see in the next chapter, successful execution of the laws is hardly easy. It requires millions of federal employees; a long list of departments and agencies; intense oversight by Congress, the president, and the judiciary; and money—more than $3 trillion in 2008 alone.

LEARNING **OBJECTIVE:**

5 Identify how citizens can influence each step of the public policy process.

Where the Money Goes

The Order of Action

Making public policy is an often unpredictable process. It can start with any step and skip back and forth as politics shapes everything from the decision to act to running the program. The result is a policy-making process that is almost always in flux.

Some political scientists such as John Kingdon even think of this process as taking place in a "primordial swamp" of competing problems, solutions, political actors, citizens, pressure, and resources such as dollars, public support, and administrative energy.[14]

These policy "streams" are shaped by citizens, interest groups, presidents, and members of Congress and move through the institutions in search of each other. Thus, an idea for solving a problem such as a new weapons system or an increase in the minimum wage may linger in waiting for a specific problem such as terrorism or an increase in unemployment. Politics ties these various streams together into a public policy. One reason immigration reform has not yet passed is that the streams of problems, solutions, and interests have yet to come together, in part because the political stream is so divided.

Some policies are efforts to terminate a program. As opposed to a nondecision, which stops a policy before it can be made, termination stops a policy that is already running. The federal government once maintained a helium reserve in Texas to ensure a reliable supply of the gas for its military blimps. Even through

The federal government once maintained a reserve of helium for its blimps. The reserve helped create jobs and income in Texas and was protected by the Texas congressional delegation. It was finally halted in the 1990s, long after the military had stopped using blimps.

the military stopped using blimps after World War II ended in 1945, it took 50 years for Congress and the president to halt the helium reserve program.

Citizens and Public Policy

Public policy is not made in a vacuum. Rather, it takes place in a sometimes confusing dance called politics that engages citizens, interest groups, political parties, legislators, judges, and government institutions.

Citizens are often anxious about participating in this process, and not just because it can be complex. But they have many levers that give them influence. They can certainly vote—the higher the participation, the more the process will heed their voice.

But voting is not enough. Citizens cannot vote on the basis of their policy positions if they do not have an opinion or if candidates do not tell the electorate where they stand. And because voting is a blunt instrument of participation that does not convey precise information about what they want, citizens must also find other pathways to influence, including joining interest groups, writing letters, sending e-mails, confronting legislators at community meetings, and even running for office themselves.

There is no question, however, that citizens want action on the big problems highlighted in this chapter. They know that safeguarding Social Security, reducing global warming, and fixing the economy so everyone rises on the basis of merit will not happen without pressure. No citizen gets what he or she does not ask for. And asking is part of the politics that leads to ultimate action.

Citizen action is more successful when it involves clear ideas for an alternative policy. It is rarely enough to merely demand that government act. It is also important to tell government what to do. This means thinking through the options and making a clear, well-developed argument for change and pursuing it aggressively through our complicated policy process.

CHAPTER **SUMMARY**

1 Compare politics and public policy and show how each affects the other.

Public policy is the product of politics, which resolves the question of who gets what, when, where, and how from government. Politics involves the interaction of the people and their government. It affects policy through activities such as voting, joining interest groups and political parties, congressional bargaining, ratifying treaties, signing laws, and administering laws. Policies are designed to produce certain outcomes such as a healthier society.

2 Analyze the three types of public policy.

There are three types of policy: distributive (which provides benefits to all groups in society), redistributive (which provides benefits to one group in society at the expense of another), and counterdistributive (which eliminates benefits to all groups in society). Some experts also include regulatory policy in this list, creating four types of policy. Regulatory policy makes rules that encourage or discourage certain types of behavior.

3 Evaluate the eight steps in making public policy.

Every public policy emerges from a process that includes eight steps: (1) making assumptions about the world, (2) setting the agenda, (3) deciding to act, which can involve nondecisions, (4) deciding how much to do, (5) choosing a tool to solve the problem, (6) deciding who will deliver the goods or services, (7) making rules for implementation, and (8) running the program itself. The steps do not always occur in order. Some political scientists see problems, solutions, political actors, and so forth as "streams" that flow through the institutions of government and only occasionally come together.

4 Compare and contrast the tools of public policy.

There are five tools of policy: (1) spending, (2) taxing, (3) directly providing goods and services, (4) providing protection against risk, and (5) creating standards, incentives, or penalties. There are also different ways of delivering services through third-party government, which include private businesses, colleges and universities, state and local governments, and charities.

5 Identify how citizens can influence each step of the public policy process.

Citizens face significant obstacles to being heard in the policy process. But they may have more influence at certain stages of the process, and they can make their voices heard through both traditional and nontraditional means.

Chapter Self-Test

1. Which is *not* a way government can convey public policy? (pp. 470–471)
   a. A petition signed by voters
   b. Rules written by administrators
   c. Opinions issued by the Supreme Court
   d. A law passed by Congress and signed by the president
2. Identify three ways citizens can influence public policy. (p.470)
3. Which type of public policy are programs like welfare? (p. 471)
   a. Distributive policy
   b. Redistributive policy
   c. Semi-distributive policy
   d. Counter-distributive policy
4. In a short essay, identify what a cost/benefit analysis is and how it has been used in making public policy. Consider proposals such as greater use of electric cars and reusable diapers. (p. 472)
5. Which of the steps in making public policy is the most difficult? (p. 476)
   a. Deciding to act
   b. Running the program itself
   c. Making rules for implementation
   d. Making assumptions about the world
6. In a short essay, describe three steps of the policy-making process. Consider who is active in each step and how the step influences final policy decisions. (pp. 471–483)
7. What does political scientist John Kingdom describe as taking place in a "primordial swamp"? (p. 483)
   a. Federal spending
   b. Setting the policy agenda

c. The policy-making process
d. Making assumptions about the world

8. Ninety percent of think-tank scholars are white. Write two to three paragraphs explaining how this fact may influence public policy. (p. 475)

9. List three of the tools the federal government uses to solve public policy problems and describe how they work in practice. (pp. 478–480)

10. What are public policy tools designed to produce? (p. 478)
    a. Virtual benefits
    b. Material benefits
    c. Symbolic benefits
    d. Recurring benefits

11. During which of the following periods did the total size of the Federal Register decrease? (p. 482)
    a. 1936–1941
    b. 1956–1961
    c. 1981–1986
    d. 2001–2006

12. In a short essay, select three steps of the policy making process and describe how a college student and a senior citizen can influence them. Consider each individual's desires and needs. (pp. 471–483)

13. Which of the following is *not* a common way in which citizens often ask for action on public policy? (p. 484)
    a. Run for public office
    b. Join an interest group
    c. Lobby Congress through emails
    d. Organize a community of concern on Facebook

14. Which of the following will likely be of greatest importance to policy makers in the future? (p. 484)
    a. Abortion
    b. Gay marriage
    c. Immigration to the United States
    d. Aging of the U.S. population

15. Select one of the major trends likely to influence public policy in the future. In a short essay, describe a possible way the government could address the problems associated with this trend. Use the eight steps and five tools (pp. 471–483) described in this chapter as a basis for your plan.

Key Terms

public policy, p. 470

politics, p. 471

distributive policy, p. 471

redistributive policy, p. 471

zero-sum games p. 471

counterdistributive policy, p. 471

nondecision, p. 473

policy agenda, p. 473

think tank, p. 475

issue-attention cycle, p. 475

incremental policy, p. 476

punctuating policy, p. 476

iron triangle, p. 477

issue network, p. 477

regulation, p. 479

rule, p. 479

Further Reading

STEWART ALTMAN AND **DAVID I. SHACTMAN,** EDS., *Policies for an Aging Society* (Johns Hopkins University Press, 2002).

JAMES E. ANDERSON, *Public Policymaking: An Introduction* (Houghton Mifflin, 2005).

THOMAS A. BIRKLAND, *An Introduction to the Policy Process: Theories, Concepts, and Models of Public Policy Making* (Sharpe, 2005).

M. MARGARET CONWAY, DAVID W. AHERN, AND **GERTRUDE A. STEURNAGEL,** *Women and Public Policy: A Revolution in Progress* (CQ Press, 2004).

GREG EASTERBROOK, *A Moment on the Earth: The Coming Age of Environmental Optimism* (Viking Press, 1995).

JOHN A. HIRD, MICHAEL A. REESE, AND **MATTHEW SHILVOCK,** *Controversies in American Public Policy* (Wadsworth, 2003).

CORNELIUS KERWIN, *Rulemaking: How Government Agencies Write Law and Make Policy* (CQ Press, 2003).

JOHN W. KINGDON, *Agendas, Alternatives, and Public Policies* (Longman, 2002).

MICHAEL E. KRAFT AND **SCOTT R. FURLONG,** EDS., *Public Policy: Politics, Analysis, and Alternatives* (CQ Press, 2006).

DAVID MAYHEW, *Divided We Govern: Party Control, Lawmaking, and Investigations* (Yale University Press, 1991).

B. GUY PETERS, *American Public Policy: Promise and Performance* (CQ Press, 2006).

PAUL PORTNEY AND **ROBERT N. STAVINS,** *Public Policies for Environmental Protection* (RFF Press, 2000).

ANDREW RICH, *Think Tanks, Public Policy, and the Politics of Expertise* (Cambridge University Press, 2005).

MARK E. RUSHEFSKY, *Public Policy in the United States: At the Dawn of the Twenty-first Century* (Sharpe, 2007).

PAUL A. SABATIER, ED., *Theories of the Public Policy Process* (Westview Press, 2007).

JOE SOSS, JACOB S. HACKER, AND **SUZANNE METTLER,** EDS., *Remaking America: Democracy and Public Policy in an Age of Inequality* (Russell Sage Foundation, 2007).

DEBORAH STONE, *Policy Paradox: The Art of Political Decision Making* (Norton, 1997).

chapter 18

OUR NATIONAL DEBT:
YOUR Family share $
THE NATIONAL DEBT CLOCK

Making Economic Policy

After nearly two years of slow growth, the United States economy reached a crisis point in late September 2008. Consumers were increasingly anxious about making even small purchases, home prices and car sales were falling, and more than 750,000 Americans had lost their jobs in the first nine months of the year. The stock markets that allow investors to buy and sell shares in companies had plummeted and showed no signs of rebound.

Most importantly, the credit market was beginning to freeze, sharply limiting the amount of money available for borrowing. Credit is the essential grease that keeps the economy moving—consumers borrow to buy homes and cars, students borrow to buy books and pay tuition, small businesses borrow to buy new goods to sell, banks to borrow money from other banks to cover the ups and downs of borrowing itself, and Wall Street borrows money to buy businesses and finance big investments. But credit was quickly disappearing as nervous lenders decided to sit on their money rather than make what they thought were risky loans.

On Sunday, September 28, Treasury Secretary Henry M. Paulson, Jr., went to Capitol Hill to ask lawmakers for unprecedented authority to ease the credit crisis, which had begun in 2007 with a surge in the number of home owners who could no longer pay their debts. These loan defaults continued to grow through the year and eventually created billions of dollars of "toxic debt," meaning loans that banks could not cover. By September, many banks had stopped lending and the stock market collapsed. Like a massive car accident on the freeway, this bad debt was clogging up the system and had started to affect even small purchases.

Paulson's proposal to buy $700 billion of this bad debt and keep it in the federal government's hands for future action provoked intense anger. Many Americans saw his proposal as a bailout for Wall Street firms that had made so much money making the bad loans. Americans wondered how the bailout, or rescue as Paulson called it, would help them pay for health insurance, college loans, gasoline, and groceries.

Paulson's proposal was not only unprecedented, it was complex. Members of Congress had difficulty explaining it back home and wondered how they could vote for such an expensive program when the federal government itself was already borrowing heavily to finance itself. With the economy teetering on what Paulson and other experts said was a complete breakdown, Congress only had days to make a decision on what to do. Under intense pressure as the stock markets fell dramatically, Congress passed the bill on October 3, only ten days after Paulson made his stunning proposal.

It will take several years to know whether Paulson's gamble will work. The U.S. economy no longer operates independently of other economies across the globe. If the U.S. economy failed, these other economies would fail, and vice versa. Although economic policy is often viewed as artful management of predictable events, September 2008 showed just how complex economic policy has become.

Just economic policy has become more complex as the world has changed, so have the other two kinds of policy, social and foreign and defense policy. Promoting the general welfare, providing for the common defense, and securing the blessing of liberty for all Americans is no longer a matter of occasional tinkering when events go badly. It is a full-time job for a government by the people.

LEARNING **OBJECTIVES**

1. Identify the two most important measures of economic performance and show how they interact.
2. Evaluate the role of fiscal policy in keeping the economy stable.
3. Outline the key steps in the federal budget process.
4. Evaluate the role of monetary policy in keeping the economy stable.
5. Analyze the federal government's role in promoting the economy.
6. Analyze the federal government's role in regulating the economy.
7. Contrast the advantages and disadvantages of the deregulation movement.

CHAPTER OUTLINE

- An Introduction to Economic Policy
- Fiscal Policy
- Monetary Policy
- Promoting the Economy
- Regulating the Economy
- The Deregulation Movement
- A Continued Federal Role

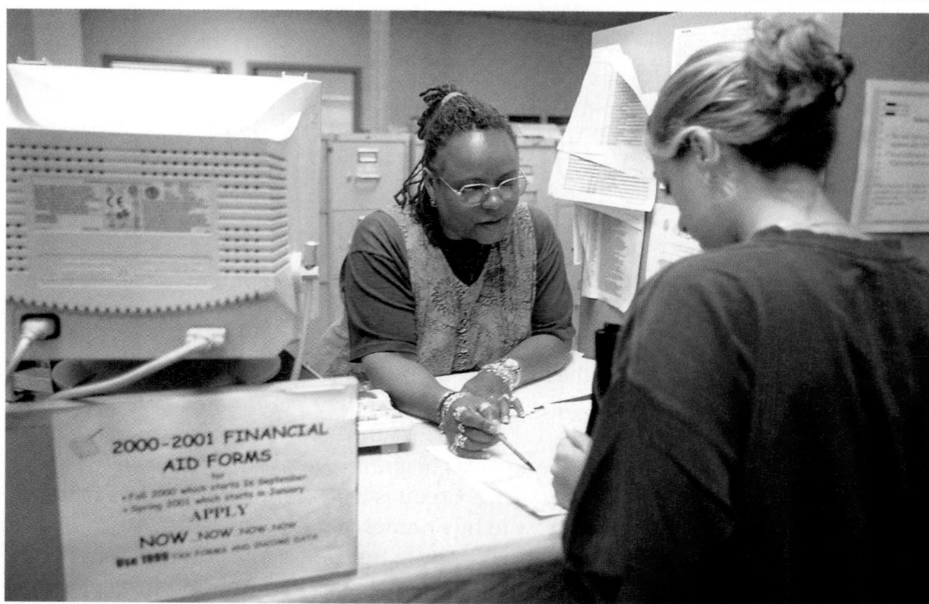

Many college students take advantage of financial aid. Changes in interest rates affect the affordability and availability of these programs.

COMPARATIVE

Comparing Economic Policy

An Introduction to Economic Policy

The federal government has been active in economic policy since the end of the Revolutionary War. The framers wanted a government strong enough to promote free trade, protect patents and trademarks, and enforce contracts between individuals and businesses. And they wanted a government with enough funding to build the postal roads, bridges, railroads, and canals that would allow the young economy to grow.

As much as they worried about the state of the economy, the framers did not concentrate economic policy in any one branch. Instead, they divided economic policymaking control between the legislative and executive branches and between the House and the Senate. Article I, Section 8, of the Constitution gives Congress the power to borrow, coin, and print money, while Article II, Section 2, gives the president the power to appoint the officers of government, including the secretary of the treasury.

In a similar vein, Article I gives Congress the power to regulate commerce with foreign nations, among the states, and with Native American tribes, while Article II gives the president authority to negotiate the treaties and enforce the laws.

Finally, Article I gives Congress the power to establish post offices and build postal roads, which were as important to the free movement of commerce in the 1700s as the Internet is today. Article II gives the president the power to appoint executive officials such as the postmaster general of the United States.

LEARNING OBJECTIVE

1 Identify the two most important measures of economic performance and show how they interact.

By creating a national government of limited powers and providing constitutional guarantees to protect property from excessive regulation, the framers succeeded in protecting capitalism. Part of the government's role is to stay out of the way as individuals and businesses create wealth through new ideas and hard work, but part is to promote the national welfare through **fiscal policy,** which uses federal spending and taxation to stimulate or slow the economy, and **monetary policy,** which manipulates the supply of money that individuals and businesses have in their hands to keep the economy from swinging wildly from boom to bust. In addition, the federal government promotes economic growth and trade and controls many economic decisions through regulations against certain kinds of business, labor, and environmental practices.

fiscal policy
Government policy that attempts to manage the economy by controlling taxing and spending.

monetary policy
Government policy that attempts to manage the economy by controlling the money supply and thus interest rates.

These tools are designed to smooth the ups and downs of the normal *business cycle.* Economists tend to focus on four discrete stages of the cycle: (1) *expansion,* in which the

The economic cycle runs from expansion to recovery. Fiscal and monetary policies are designed to make sure the cycle is relatively stable. Here, unemployed workers stand in line during the long depression that plagued the United States during the 1930s.

economy produces new jobs and growth; (2) *contraction,* as the economy starts to slow down; (3) *recession,* in which the economy reaches a trough of slow growth; and (4) *recovery,* in which the economy rebounds. The goal of effective economic policy today is to make sure the peaks are not too high and the troughs are not too low.

We use two yardsticks to measure the performance of the economy. The first is **inflation,** which we track by comparing the price of goods and services such as gasoline, food, and housing over time. Inflation, a rising price level, is the primary risk during expansion and recovery. The second measure is **unemployment,** or the number of people looking for work at any given time. Unemployment among the employable is the greatest problem during contraction and recession.

In theory, inflation increases when unemployment drops (an increase in the work force creates more demand for products, which raises prices), while inflation declines when unemployment increases (fewer workers creates less demand for products, which lowers prices). This balance between the demand and supply of goods and services drives the business cycle: when supply is low and demand is high, prices rise; when supply is high and demand is low, prices fall. In reality, inflation and unemployment can rise or fall at the same time, as they did at the start of 2008. A simultaneous increase in inflation and unemployment is called **stagflation** (stagnation plus inflation); a simultaneous decrease in both measures is called good news!

We measure inflation with the *consumer price index (CPI),* which shows how much more or how much less consumers are paying for the same "basket of goods" over time. The major components of the CPI basket are food, shelter, fuel, clothing, transportation, and medical care. In turn, we measure unemployment simply by the percentage of able-bodied workers who are looking for jobs but cannot find them. This *unemployment rate* does not include able-bodied workers who have given up looking for work or taken jobs below their skill levels with lower pay.

Experts also use other measures to track the economy. These reveal whether the federal government is borrowing too much money (as measured by the budget deficit), whether it is selling too few goods and services to other nations (as measured by the balance of trade), and how much it is growing (as measured by year-to-year comparisons of the **gross domestic product [GDP].)** The gross domestic product, or GDP, shows the total value of all goods and services produced by the U.S. economy.

inflation
A rise in the general price level (and decrease in dollar value) owing to an increase in the volume of money and credit in relation to available goods.

unemployment
The number of Americans who are out of work but actively looking for a job. The number does not usually include those who are not looking.

stagflation
A combination of an economic slowdown (stagnation) and a rise in prices (inflation).

gross domestic product (GDP)
The value of all goods and services produced by an economy during a specific period of time such as a year.

Fiscal Policy

You Are the President and Need to Get a Tax Cut Passed

LEARNING **OBJECTIVE**

Evaluate the role of fiscal policy in keeping the economy stable.

Congress and the president make fiscal policy by taxing, borrowing, and spending money. Nothing reflects the growth of federal programs and the rise of big government more clearly than increased spending by the national government. The 2008 rescue plan discussed at the start of this chapter is an example of a particularly aggressive fiscal policy. Under the plan, the federal government used its tax dollars to buy $700 billion of bad debt as a way to unclog the credit markets.

In general, increased government spending and lower taxes are ways to stimulate the economy, while decreased spending and higher taxes tend to slow the economy. Higher spending and tax cuts put more money in the pockets of consumers, which increases demand for goods and services, which in turn increases inflation and reduces unemployment. Conversely, lower spending and tax increases take money away from consumers, which reduces demand for goods and services, which in turn reduces inflation and increases unemployment. The key relationship is between supply and demand—if supply is high and demand low, the economy slows down as firms try to reduce their inventories of goods and services. If supply is low and demand is high, the economy tends to accelerate as firms start producing more to keep up.

The Federal Budget

Growth of the Budget and Federal Spending

Today, federal, state, and local governments spend an amount equal to about one-third of the nation's GDP. The national government is the biggest spender of all—it spends more than all state and local governments combined or about 23 percent of GDP annually—nearly one dollar of every four spent in the U.S. economy.

excise tax
A consumer tax on a specific kind of merchandise, such as tobacco.

budget deficit
The condition that exists when the federal government raises less revenue than it spends.

Where the Money Comes From Although Benjamin Franklin once said nothing is more certain than death and taxes, he would be surprised at the range of taxes and other revenue sources used to fund federal spending today (see Figure 18–1 for the percentages from each source):

1. *Individual income taxes.* Taxes on individuals accounted for the largest share of the federal government's tax revenue in 2008. The income tax was prohibited under the Constitution until the Thirteenth Amendment was ratified in 1913.
2. *Payroll taxes.* Payroll taxes to pay for social insurance (Social Security and Medicare) are the second-largest and fastest-rising source of federal revenue. Most workers pay more in Social Security taxes than in federal income taxes.
3. *Corporate income taxes.* Corporate income taxes have fallen steadily from their historic high of two-fifths of federal revenues during World War II. Thanks to tax cuts and special deductions, today they account for barely one-fifth of federal revenues, only a third as much as the individual income tax.
4. *Excise taxes.* Federal **excise taxes** on the sale of liquor, tobacco, gasoline, telephones, air travel, and other so-called luxury items account for a very small percentage of the federal budget.
5. *Other sources.* Smaller taxes and fees include admission to national parks and camping fees in national forests, taxes on large estates left behind after death, and interest payments on government loans to college students.
6. *Borrowing.* When the federal government does not raise enough revenue to cover all its services, the only way to cover the resulting **budget deficit** is to borrow from citizens, banks, and even foreign governments, by selling Treasury notes and other investments such as saving bonds. As Figure 18–2 shows, borrowing to cover the deficit accounted for an estimated $410 billion in federal revenues in 2008.[2]

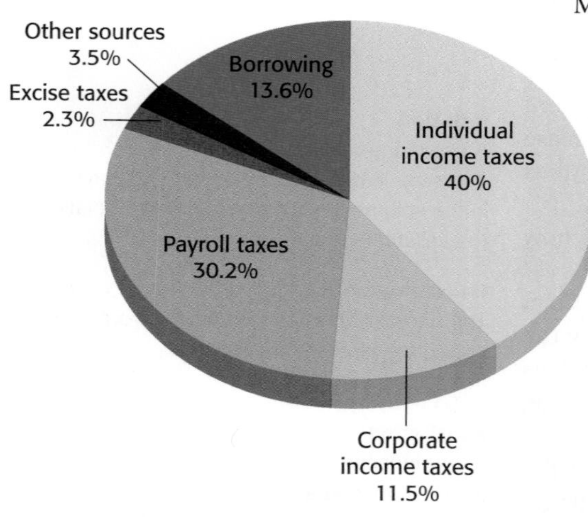

FIGURE 18–1
Where the Money Comes From, 2008.

SOURCE: Summary Tables, *Budget of the United States, Fiscal Year 2009* (U.S. Government Printing Office, 2008).

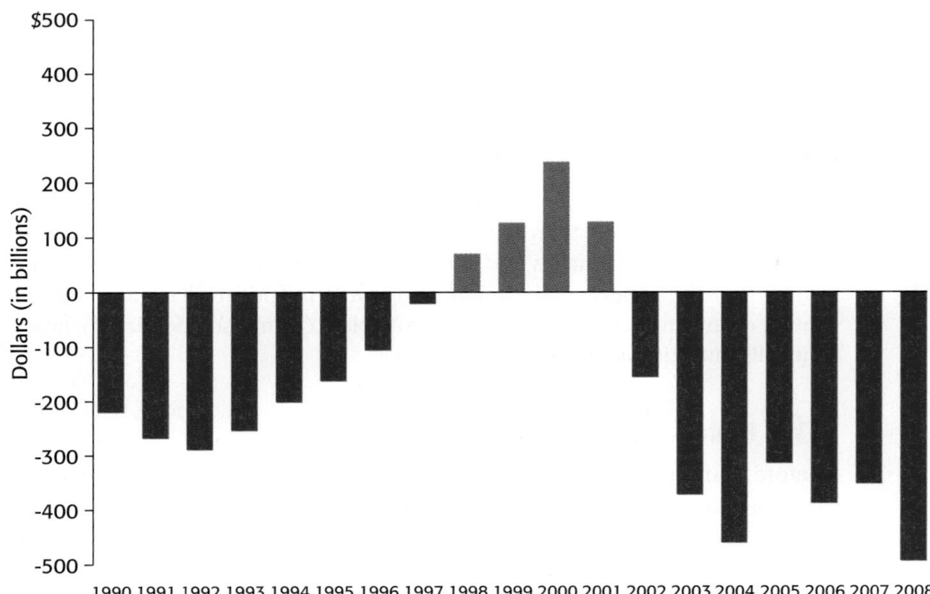

FIGURE 18–2
The Federal Budget Deficit and Surplus.

SOURCE: Summary Tables, *Budget of the United States, Fiscal Year 2009* (U.S. Government Printing Office, 2008).

Giving the people power over taxation was a major achievement in the development of self-government. "No taxation without representation" had been a battle cry in the Revolutionary War. The Constitution clearly provided that Congress "shall have Power to lay and collect Taxes, Duties, Imposts, and Excises" and that **tariffs,** or taxes on imports from other countries, and excise taxes have to be levied, or collected, uniformly throughout the United States.

Taxes are not just a means of raising money, however. In a broad sense, all taxation implies decisions about who gets what, when, where, and how. For example, a **progressive tax** that places higher taxes on individuals and families with higher incomes tends to help individuals and families with lower incomes. In contrast, a **regressive tax,** such as a sales tax collected on everyone's purchases of food and clothing, tends to hurt individuals and families with lower incomes.

Taxes also carry certain costs—it costs money to raise money. Like people who carry large balances on their credit cards, the United States must pay interest on its deficits. Government borrowing adds to the total **national debt,** which is the cumulative total of all deficits over time. In spring 2006, Congress raised the amount of money the federal government could borrow to $9 trillion, which would generate nearly $200 billion in interest payments during the year.

U.S. taxpayers might not be as troubled by the size of the debt if they understood two characteristics of federal borrowing. First, the government owes roughly 90 percent of the money to its own citizens rather than to foreign governments or investors, although the amount owed to foreigners is growing. Second, the economic strength and resources of the country are more significant than the size of the debt.

Where the Money Goes Much of the money the federal government takes in is spent on benefit payments to individuals and on national defense. Measured in absolute dollars spent in 2006, almost half of federal spending went to required benefit payments for individuals, such as Social Security, Medicare, Medicaid, and other major social programs. Most federal spending is mandatory, meaning that Congress and the president cannot use their discretion to change the spending rates. Mandatory programs include Social Security and Medicare for older people and other programs that pay any citizen who qualifies for support (see Figure 18–3). The rest of the spending is discretionary, meaning that Congress and the president can change the spending rates.

Evaluating Federal Spending and Economic Policy

tariff
A tax levied on imports to help protect a nation's industries, labor, or farmers from foreign competition. It can also be used to raise additional revenue.

progressive tax
A tax graduated so that people with higher incomes pay a larger fraction of their income than people with lower incomes.

regressive tax
A tax whereby people with lower incomes pay a higher fraction of their income than people with higher incomes.

national debt
The total amount of money the federal government has borrowed to finance deficit spending over the years.

FIGURE 18–3
Where the Money Goes, 2008.

SOURCE: Summary Tables, *Budget of the United States, Fiscal Year 2009* (U.S. Government Printing Office, 2008).

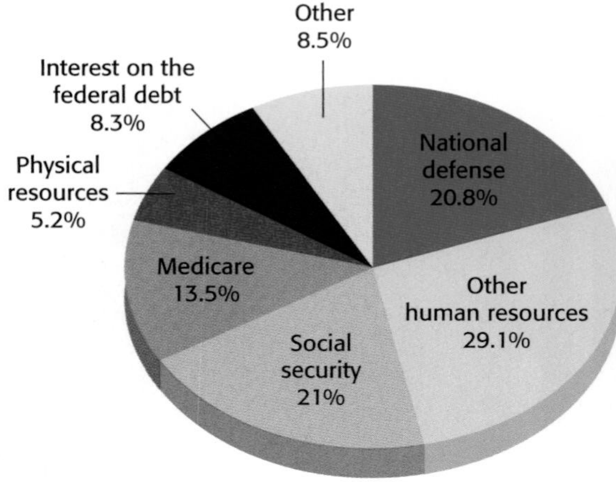

More than half the total spending goes to older citizens, students, the unemployed, and other individuals, while the rest goes to the purchase of goods and services such as consulting, computers, and military equipment. Virtually all federal buildings are now guarded by private employees who work for contractors paid by the federal government, while almost all defense spending goes to military and civilian employees, military equipment, and the cost of war.

Two hundred years ago, revenues and spending were so small that neither had a significant impact on the overall economy. In the 2008 federal budget, even small changes in taxes and spending can alter the direction of the economy. However, because many federal programs are open to all eligible citizens, much of the federal budget is "uncontrollable" or nondiscretionary, meaning the bills must be paid regardless of the cost.

The Budget Process

Before Congress enacted the Budget and Accounting Act of 1921, each executive agency dealt with Congress on its own, requesting that the legislature appropriate funds for its activities with little or no presidential coordination. Today, the president is required by law to submit an annual budget proposal for all agencies together.

LEARNING **OBJECTIVE**

3 Outline the key steps in the federal budget process.

The Executive Branch The federal government's fiscal, or spending, year begins every October 1. But the budget process begins nearly two years in advance, when the various departments and agencies estimate their needs and propose their budgets to the president.[3] While Congress is debating the budget for the coming fiscal year, the agencies are making estimates for the year after that (see Table 18–1). Agency officials take into account not only their needs as they see them, but also the overall presidential program and the probable reactions of Congress. Departmental budgets are detailed; they include estimates of expected needs for personnel, supplies, office space, and the like.

Office of Management and Budget (OMB) The presidential staff agency that serves as a clearinghouse for budgetary requests and management improvements for government agencies.

The **Office of Management and Budget (OMB)** is responsible for overseeing the budget process on behalf of the president. Once OMB receives each agency's budget request, its budget examiners review each agency's budget and reconcile it with the president's overall plans. OMB then holds informal hearings with every department and agency to give each one a chance to clarify and defend its estimates.

Once this give-and-take is over, the OMB director gives the president a single document that shows where the federal government's money will come from and where it will go. The president reviews these figures and makes adjustments. The OMB director also helps the president prepare a budget message that will stress key aspects of the

TABLE 18–1 Steps in the Budget Process, Fiscal Year 2009

February–December 2007	Executive branch agencies develop requests for funds, which are reviewed by the Office of Management and Budget and forwarded to the president for final decision.
December 2007	The formal budget documents are prepared.
January–February 2007	The budget is transmitted to Congress as a formal message from the president.
March–September 2008	Congress reviews the president's proposed budget, develops its own budget, and approves spending and revenue bills.
October 1, 2008	Fiscal year 2009 begins.
October 1, 2006–September 30, 2008	Executive branch agencies execute the budget provided in law.
October–November 2008	Figures on actual spending and receipts for the completed fiscal year become available.

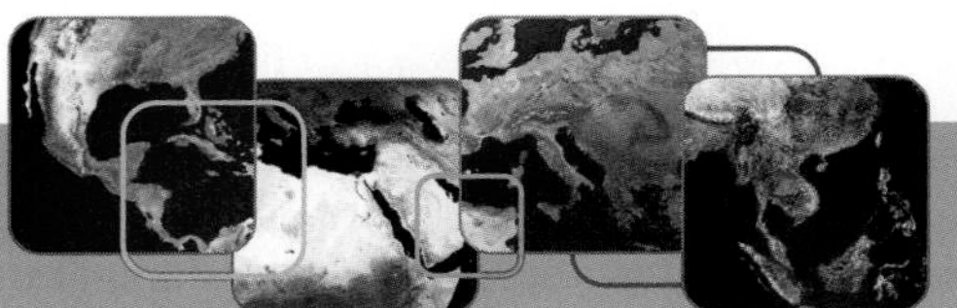

HOW **OTHER NATIONS** GOVERN

Tax Rates Around the World

U.S. citizens may want more of almost everything the federal government delivers, but they rarely want to pay for it. Democrats often promise to increase government spending for programs such as universal health care, but almost never talk about taxes to pay for them; Republicans propose cutting taxes, but almost never discuss budget cuts that may be needed to keep the budget balanced. It is far easier to promise "no new taxes," as George H. W. Bush did during his successful campaign for president in 1988, than to talk about how to make the numbers add up.

However, U.S. tax rates are far from the highest in the world, in part because the United States does not maintain as many social programs as other nations do. Measured by the combined tax rates on personal, corporate, social security, and sales, the United States actually rates in the middle of the six countries featured in previous chapters. Measured by total tax rate, it splits its revenue across corporations and individuals equally.

France is the most tax-heavy nation in the world, with a total burden of more than 66 percent. France provides a host of public programs such as health care, child care, heavily subsidized transportation, and high salaries for public workers, all of which require a higher tax rate. The United Arab Emirates has the lowest tax burden in the world at just 18 percent, largely due to the enormous amount of income it receives from the sale of oil.

The measures of tax burden do not include corporate and individual tax breaks, however. Although including them the United States would still rank in the middle of the six countries, it provides more tax breaks to corporations than individuals, making its tax burden heavier on individuals as a result.

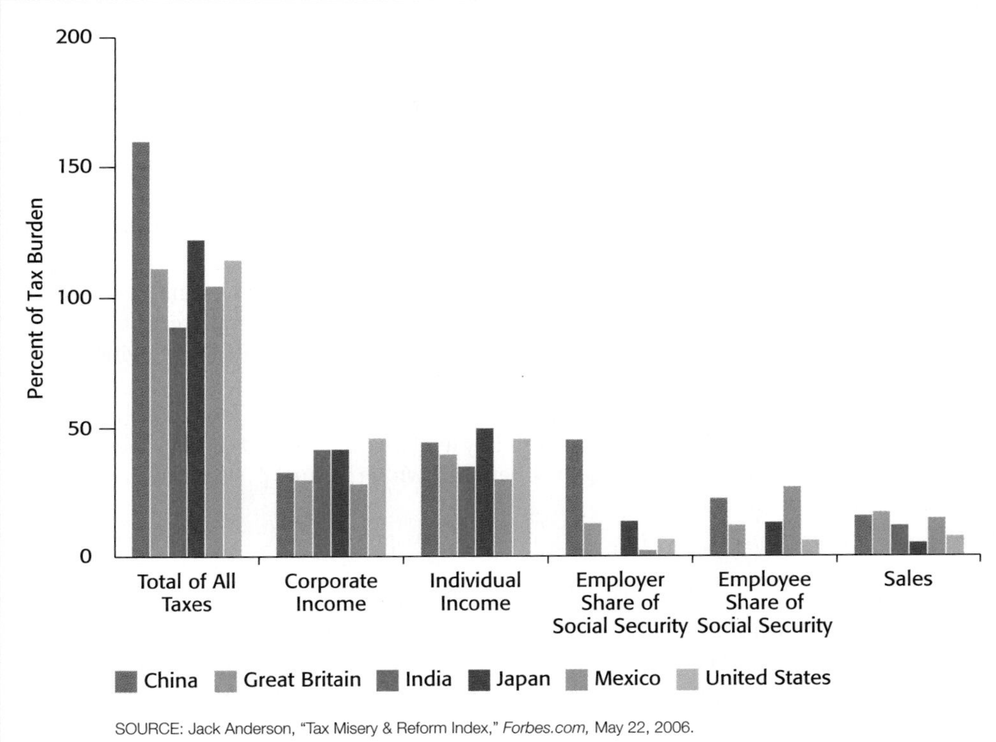

SOURCE: Jack Anderson, "Tax Misery & Reform Index," *Forbes.com*, May 22, 2006.

budget and tie it to broad national goals. The president must submit the budget recommendations and accompanying message to Congress between the first Monday in January and the first Monday in February.

The Legislative Branch The president's proposal is only the beginning of the budget process. Under the Constitution, Congress must appropriate the funds and raise the taxes. However, the White House also plays a role in all decisions, if only because all appropriations and tax proposals are subject to a presidential veto. Presidents often threaten to veto these bills as a way of winning passage of their priorities.

Congress acts on the budget in several steps. It starts its process by approving an initial budget resolution that sets the broad spending and revenue goals for the process. It then moves forward with hearings on the 13 giant appropriation bills that actually spend money, and it considers a final budget resolution that reconciles the actual spending with its initial guidelines. Because the budget resolution only sets broad guidelines, it does not go to the president for signature. But because the 13 appropriations bills spend real dollars, they all must be signed into law.

Congress adopted the Budget and Impoundment Control Act of 1974 to strengthen its role in the budget process. This act requires the president to include proposed changes in tax laws, estimates of amounts of revenue lost through existing preferential tax treatments, and five-year estimates of the costs of new and continuing federal programs. The act also calls on the president to seek authorizing legislation for a program a year before asking Congress to fund it.

The 1974 Budget Act also created the **Congressional Budget Office (CBO),** an independent agency that prepares budget data on behalf of Congress, and Congress only. By February 15 of each year, the CBO director presents an analysis of the president's budget proposal to the House and Senate budget committees. The CBO director also provides Congress with biannual forecasts of the economy, analyzes alternative fiscal policies, prepares five-year cost estimates for bills proposed by congressional committees, and undertakes studies requested by committees.

Tax Expenditures

Tax expenditures are a final type of fiscal policy that uses the tax code to provide special tax incentives or benefits to individuals and businesses for economic goals such as home ownership, retirement savings, and college education. The federal government spent more than $900 billion in tax expenditures in 2008. Put another way, the federal government lost more than $900 billion in revenue it would have collected without these tax breaks.

Tax expenditures are one means by which the national government carries out public policy objectives. For example, instead of giving out federal grants for research and development, the government encourages investment in R&D by giving companies tax breaks to invest in innovation and expansion.

However, tax expenditures such as encouraging home ownership do not benefit all levels of society. In many instances, they lead investors to put their money into low-yield investments to obtain large tax benefits, which in turn pulls money out of more productive parts of the economy.

The Politics of Taxing and Spending

In addition to raising funds to run the government, taxes also promote economic growth and reward certain types of behavior, such as contributing to charities. Critics suggest that tax legislation helps individual members of Congress raise campaign funds—laws permitting several of the most popular corporate deductions must be renewed every year, for example, which gives Congress members a chance to show their support for corporations regularly, and corporations a chance to show their support for Congress, too.[4]

Much as taxpayers complain about taxes, most want more of virtually everything the federal government provides. However, there is considerable disagreement about the best type of tax. Some experts argue that a progressive income tax (also called a *graduated income tax*) is best because it is relatively easy to collect, takes most from those who are most able to pay, and hardly touches those with little income.

Others argue that *excise taxes* are the fairest because they are paid by people who spend money for luxury goods and thus obviously have money to spare. In addition, by discouraging people from buying expensive goods, excise taxes occasionally have a deflationary (price-lowering) effect when prices are on the rise. However, excise taxes are more expensive to collect than income taxes. In some cases, such as the tax on tobacco, they may hit the poor the hardest. Excise taxes also face strong resistance from affected industries—tobacco, liquor, and airlines, for example.

The **sales tax,** which is used only at the state and local level in the United States, is widely used in Europe in a slightly different version. Called the **value-added tax (VAT)** applies to the increased value of a product *at each stage of production and distribution* rather than just at the point where it is sold to a customer. A loaf of bread would thus have value added several times: The farmer would pay a value-added tax on the grain before selling to the miller, who would be taxed before selling to the

Congressional Budget Office (CBO)
An agency of Congress that analyzes presidential budget recommendations and estimates the costs of proposed legislation.

tax expenditure
A loss of tax revenue due to federal laws that provide special tax incentives or benefits to individuals or businesses.

sales tax
A general tax on sales transactions, sometimes exempting such items as food and drugs.

value-added tax (VAT)
A tax on increased value of a product at each stage of production and distribution rather than just at the point of sale.

GENERATION **NEXT**

Satisfaction with the Financial Situation

U.S. citizens put great pressure on government to improve the overall performance of the economy by controlling both inflation and unemployment. However, they often focus on the prices of goods such as gasoline and bread rather than bigger issues such as the value of the dollar or the stock market. The economy tends to become a political issue when ordinary workers pull back on their spending because they're worried about their own financial situation.

Workers began to worry about the economy in the middle of 2007 as gasoline prices spiked dramatically and unemployment started to inch upward. Generation Next appears to be no different. According to the Pew Research Center's Generation Next survey, roughly half of 18- to 29-year-olds said they were not very satisfied with their financial situation, which translates into the kind of worry that made economic issues a top concern for the all adults in the 2008 presidential campaign.

Percentage of 18- to 29-Year-Olds Who Said They Were Not Very Satisfied with Their Financial Situation.

Gender: Male, Female
Race: White, Nonwhite
Political party: Democrat, Independent, Republican
Ideology: Very conservative, Conservative, Moderate, Liberal, Very liberal

0 10 20 30 40 50 60 70 80

These patterns suggest that the emerging economic problems of 2007–2008 affected certain groups more than others. Women, nonwhites, Democrats and Independents, and more-liberal respondents were less satisfied with their personal economic situation than men, whites, Republicans, and conservatives (though very conservative respondents also expressed concern). These are all categories where we might also find lower incomes and therefore more vulnerability to economic slowdowns and inflation.

QUESTIONS

1. Why are young workers concerned about the state of the economy?
2. What makes young workers more vulnerable to economic slowdowns and inflation?
3. What worries you most about the future of the economy?

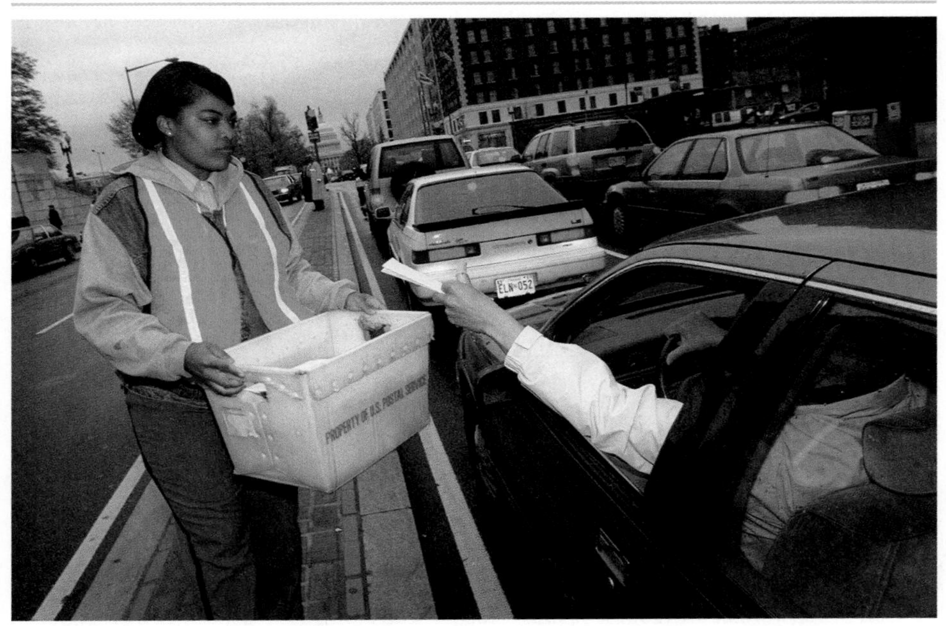

All individual income taxes are due on April 15 of each year. Here, cars line up as taxpayers drop their tax returns at the U.S. Postal Service to make sure they are postmarked on April 15. Failure to pay income taxes on time can result in a fine.

baker, and so forth. Some see the value-added tax as a way to infuse a large amount of new revenue into the federal government

LEARNING **OBJECTIVE**

4 Evaluate the role of monetary policy in keeping the economy stable.

Monetary Policy

Monetary policy is the second way the federal government manages the economy. The core element of monetary policy is the idea that prices, incomes, and economic stability reflect growth in the amount of money that circulates through the economy at any one time. Advocates of aggressive monetary policy contend that the money supply is the key factor affecting the economy's performance. Even as the federal government used fiscal policy to buy bad debt in 2008, it also used monetary policy to pump more money into the economy to provide greater access to credit.

The Federal Reserve System

Monetary policy is not made by Congress or the president but by the Board of Governors of the **Federal Reserve System** (often simply called "the Fed"). The chair and six members of the Fed's Board of Governors are appointed by the president with Senate consent to 14-year terms; a different member's term expires every two years. As an independent regulatory commission, the Fed is effectively insulated from politics. The governors supervise 12 regional Federal Reserve banks located across the country, each headed by a president and run by a nine-member board of directors chosen from the private financial institutions in each region. The current Fed chair is Ben S. Bernanke, who is thus one of the most powerful policy makers in the world and may have more say over economic performance than the president and Congress.

Federal Reserve System
The system created by Congress in 1913 to establish banking practices and regulate currency in circulation and the amount of credit available. It consists of 12 regional banks supervised by the Board of Governors. Often called simply the "Fed."

federal funds rate
The amount of interest banks charge for loans to each other.

The Fed has three basic tools for influencing the economy. First, it can change the interest rates banks must pay the Fed for borrowing money, which is called the **federal funds rate.** Increasing the rate slows down the economy by increasing costs for money and credit; lowering the interest rate stimulates the economy by making money more easily available for investment and growth.

The cost of borrowing money is linked to the interest rate a bank's best customers receive on their short-term loans. In turn, this *prime rate* is linked to the interest rates on student loans, home mortgages, car loans, and credit card debt. As Figure 18–4 shows, over the last several years the Fed has swung between trying to stimulate the economy, slow the economy, and stimulate the economy again.

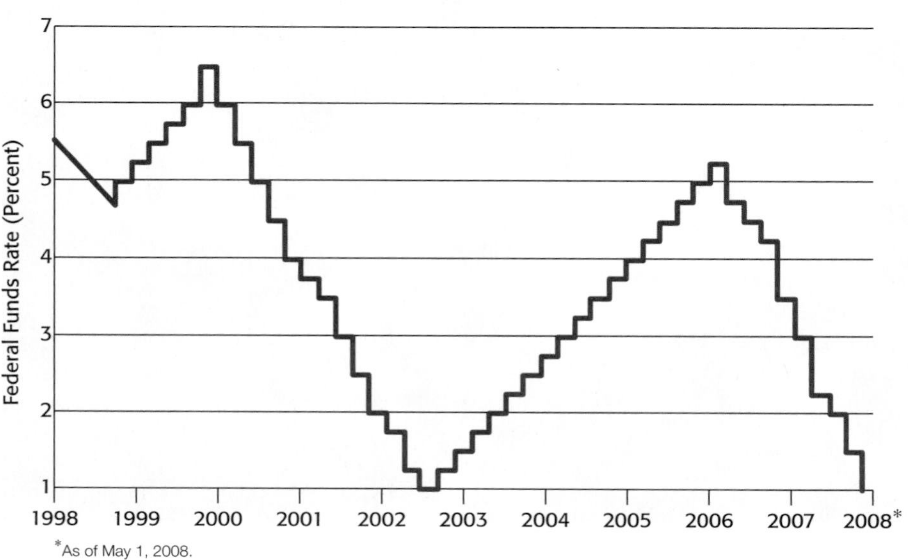

FIGURE 18–4
Federal Funds Rate, 1998–2008.

SOURCE: The Federal Reserve Board, Open Market Operations, federalreserve.gov/monetarypolicy/fomc.htm as of November 1, 2008.

HISTORY MAKERS

Alan Greenspan

Regarded as one of the most important economic policy makers of the late twentieth century, former Federal Reserve Board chair Alan Greenspan may well be remembered more for stopping inflation than for promoting growth. Appointed to his post in 1987 by Ronald Reagan, Greenspan served for almost 20 years and is best described as a conservative on monetary policy who used the Fed to promote his view that the economy can grow only so fast before it ignites inflation.

Greenspan is best known for lowering interest rates to stimulate the economy during economic slowdowns and raising interest rates to reduce inflation. His effort to balance unemployment and inflation was essential to economic growth in the 1990s, but not enough to prevent a significant slowdown in the early 2000s.

Alan Greenspan.

As the economy worsened in 2001, for example, the Fed began cutting interest rates to stimulate growth. Between 2001 and 2003, the Fed cut its federal funds rate 13 times. But as the economy emerged from its downturn in 2003, Greenspan and the Fed began to attack inflation. Between 2003 and 2006, they raised the federal funds rate 17 times. As the economy worsened again in 2007, Greenspan and the Fed began cutting rates again.

Whether as an inflation fighter or a recession breaker, Greenspan became one of the world's most closely watched economic leaders. Although he once joked that he had learned "to mumble with great incoherence" early on at the Fed, he also knew the power of words to slow the economy. In December 1996, for example, he wondered out loud whether the then-rising stock market was suffering from what he called "irrational exuberance," which prompted an immediate 145-point drop in the Dow Jones Industrial Average, the most widely followed stock indicator.

Greenspan is still a revered figure for his role in stimulating economic growth in the 1990s. But he also came under increasing criticism in 2008 for condoning much of the risk taking that contributed to the stock market collapse and dramatic rise in unemployment. He was a strong advocate of the financial deregulation that eventually led to the bad debt that the federal government is now purchasing with taxpayer funds. Having fought against government deficits at the Fed, he may well turn out to be the single most important figure in driving the budget deficit to record levels in the coming years.

QUESTIONS

1. What do you think made Greenspan so influential over the economy? Was it just the Fed's power, or did he have other sources of influence?
2. Why is raising or lowering interest rates a faster-acting tool than fiscal policy?
3. How do interest rates affect you directly?

SOURCE: Alan Greenspan, *The Age of Turbulence: Adventures in a New World* (Penguin, 2007).

Second, the Fed buys and sells federal debt. Selling federal debt to the public tends to slow down the economy by taking dollars out of circulation that could have been used for investment or growth; buying federal debt back from the public tends to free up money for new activities, thereby stimulating the economy.

Third, the Fed determines how much money nationally chartered banks must keep in their reserves. Raising the requirement tends to slow down the economy by reducing the funds banks have available to lend to the public for investment and growth; decreasing the requirement injects more money into the economy.

Government and Economic Policy

Economic depression is a hard teacher, and the 1930s had a tremendous impact on U.S. thinking about the role of government in the economy.

The Great Depression that began in 1929 brought mass misery. It continued despite Franklin D. Roosevelt's New Deal economic agenda, which pumped new money into the economy, created hundreds of thousands of federally subsidized jobs, and established new regulations governing the financial markets. Faint signs of recovery could be seen in the mid-1930s, but a new recession in 1937 and 1938 indicated that the country was by no means out of the woods. Between eight and nine million people were still jobless in 1939. Unemployment fell dramatically with World War II, which put millions back to work building military hardware and millions more into military uniforms.

World War II helped stimulate the U.S. economy through the production of weapons, airplanes, and tanks.

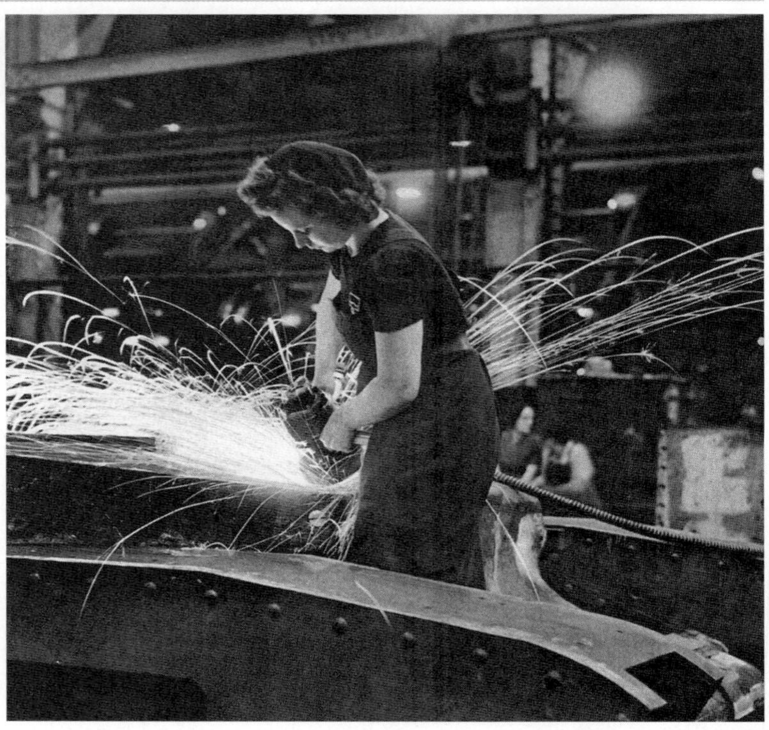

Several theories developed about what the federal government could do to stimulate the economy at the time. Some economists urged the government to reduce spending, lower taxes, curb the power of labor, and generally leave business and the economy alone. This first theory is called **laissez-faire economics.**

Another group, deeply influenced by the work of the English economist John Maynard Keynes,[5] recommended that when consumer spending and investment decline, government spending and investing should increase. Government must do the spending and investing during a recession because private enterprise will not or cannot.

This second theory is called **Keynesian economics.** When the economy is in a recession, Keynesians press for more government spending on goods and services to inject money into the economy and stimulate growth. Keynesians believe this spending will "prime the pump" for increased economic activity and stimulate new jobs for the unemployed. When people have more money in their pockets, Keynesians believe at least some of it will be spent—in economic terms, consumer demand will increase.

Although Keynesian economics influences government economic policy to this day, Ronald Reagan and George W. Bush both argued that tax cuts were better for creating a strong economy. This new and untested theory was called *supply-side economics* and is based on the notion that tax cuts increase the supply of money in the economy, which stimulates economic growth.

LEARNING **OBJECTIVE**

5 Analyze the federal government's role in promoting the economy.

Promoting the Economy

Federal economic policy does more than try to smooth the ups and downs of the business cycle. It also tries to promote economic growth, often measured by the number of new jobs or businesses created. Growth creates jobs for individual workers, which in turn produces higher revenues, which in turn produces either greater savings or more federal spending. U.S. economic policy has two goals: (1) to promote economic growth so the United States remains a world leader in terms of quality of life, and (2) to regulate business activity so no single industry or company has an unfair edge in competing for success.

laissez-faire economics
A theory that opposes governmental interference in economic affairs beyond what is necessary to protect life and property.

Keynesian economics
An economic theory based on the principles of John Maynard Keynes stating that government spending should increase during business slumps and be curbed during booms.

Promoting Economic Growth

Making Economic Policy

The first goal of economic policy is promoting economic growth. The framers believed that developing a strong economy was part of securing the "blessings of liberty," and they encouraged U.S. exports by creating a navy to protect cargo ships. Over history, the federal government created a number of departments and agencies to protect that hoped-for growth, including the departments of Agriculture and Commerce and the Small Business Administration.

Within the federal administrative system, the Department of Commerce is the most visible advocate of business; it is sometimes known as the nation's "service center for business." Its secretary is usually picked for his or her connections to business and is an advocate for free enterprise and less government regulation.

The Department of Commerce also encourages innovation through the protection of intellectual property by promoting "the Progress of Science and useful Arts" under Article I of the Constitution. Each year, the department issues more than 100,000 patents to protect new inventions. These patents generally give holders exclusive rights to use the invention for 17 years, after which anyone can use it.

Farm Subsidies

The Department of Agriculture is a powerful advocate of the farming industry, supporting higher prices for basic products such as corn, barley, oats, wheat, soybeans, cotton, and rice. In 2008 alone, it spent more than $20 billion in *subsidies* by either guaranteeing a minimum price for crops or paying fees to farmers for not planting fields. By altering the supply and price of crops while promoting new products such as biofuels, these subsidies increase the cost of items such as bread, eggs, and soy milk.

Promoting International Trade

Worries about international competition often lead domestic producers to call for **protectionism,** which can take the form of special taxes, or tariffs, placed on imported goods to make them more expensive. Most economists oppose protectionism because it prevents efficient use of resources, and because consumers pay much more for protected products than they otherwise would in the world economy. Tariffs merely divert attention from real solutions such as increased productivity and capital investments, and they inevitably invite retaliation from foreign countries.

Trade barriers are less severe today than they were in the 1930s. But restrictions still exist. Certain tariffs, limits on imported goods, and import regulations limit U.S. consumption of foreign products. Most exist to protect U.S. farmers, businesses, or workers in certain industries, but they often do more harm than good by leading other countries to put tariffs and other restrictions on U.S. goods. The result has been a persistent **trade deficit** in which the United States imports far more than it exports.

The United States experienced its first trade deficit in more than a century when the amount of imports exceeded the value of exports in 1971. In the more than 30 years since then, the nation has faced billions of dollars in ever-growing trade deficits. Congress and the president are under continuing pressure from industry, unions, and regional political leaders to protect U.S. jobs, companies, and communities from foreign competition. These pressures come from the textile and auto industries as well as from glass, steel, shoes, lumber, electronics, book publishing, aluminum, farming, and domestic wine and spirit coalitions, to name just a few. Their leaders claim that the trade deficit justifies the imposition of trade sanctions.

The problem, however, is not that the United States is importing too much but that it is exporting too little. German cars, Japanese technology, and Indonesian textiles are fine products; if other countries produce better cars or shoes at a lower price, supporters of free trade argue, the United States should buy from them and direct our labor and capital to areas in which we can do better.

Another question is whether U.S. products are given fair treatment by other nations. U.S. agricultural products are denied entry into some countries and subject to high tariffs in others. U.S. automobile manufacturers complain of unfair import restrictions imposed by the Japanese. Finally, some countries exploit the U.S. advantage

protectionism
A policy of erecting trade barriers to protect domestic industry.

trade deficit
An imbalance in international trade in which the value of imports exceeds the value of exports.

Hong Kong (left) and Dubai are among the fastest-growing economies in the world.

in technology by copying our products and then selling them back to us or to other countries at a profit.

Another unfair trade practice is *dumping*—selling products below the cost of manufacturing or below their domestic price with the intention of driving other producers out of the market and then raising prices to profitable levels. Another practice is government *subsidizing* of certain industries. Some countries, for example, subsidize steel for export. Others require lengthy inspection procedures for imported goods. Japan has protected several of its industries—producers of automobiles, baseball bats, and even chopsticks,

The growth of the global economy has produced efforts to protect U.S. workers from unfair dumping of low-priced products in the United States. Here, cargo containers filled with goods await delivery within the United States. Some goods are priced unfairly because of lower wages in other less-developed countries.

for example—by setting standards that are virtually impossible for U.S. manufacturers to meet. Japan also sets limits on rice imports.

The World Trade Organization In 1947, a group of countries formed a trade organization to negotiate free trade by lowering tariffs, quotas (limits on the quantity of a particular product that may be imported) and other disadvantages countries face when trading. Today the **World Trade Organization (WTO)** enforces trade agreements that include more than 130 countries, and its membership accounts for four-fifths of the world's trade.

The WTO has conducted eight rounds of negotiations over the past six decades, all of which have amended the **General Agreement on Tariffs and Trade (GATT)** to encourage free trade. The WTO is responsible for overseeing GATT and resolving disputes; it can impose fines and penalties on nations that create protectionist policies.

The United States has tried to focus the GATT negotiations on increased trade in agricultural items, foreign investment, and protection of technological innovations and intellectual property. Although U.S. imports and those of other countries still face many trade restrictions, the WTO and GATT have helped lower tariffs and quotas and increase fair trade throughout the world. Many analysts maintain that GATT is one of the most successful innovations in the history of international relations and one of the contributing factors to the United States' economic success since the end of the cold war.[6]

Not everyone believes free trade should be unlimited, however. Labor unions, environmentalists, and human rights advocates argue that U.S. trade policies spur the creation of low-wage jobs abroad and encourage child labor, pollution, and worker abuse in countries such as China and India that export large quantities of goods to the United States.

The North American Free Trade Agreement In 1992, the United States, Canada, and Mexico signed the **North American Free Trade Agreement (NAFTA),** which formed the largest geographical free trade zone in the world. Although President George H. W. Bush signed NAFTA near the end of his presidency, the agreement could not become law until ratified by Congress. President Bill Clinton promoted NAFTA, though many members of his own party were its most vigorous opponents. Congress passed it by a thin margin in a bipartisan vote with Democrats in the minority.

Though trade among the United States, Canada, and Mexico is not absolutely "free" or unimpeded, the agreement has had a tremendous impact on the economies of all three countries. Today Mexico is the United States' third most important trading partner,

World Trade Organization (WTO)
An international organization derived from the General Agreement on Tariffs and Trade (GATT) that promotes free trade around the world.

General Agreement on Tariffs and Trade (GATT)
An international trade organization with more than 130 members that seeks to encourage free trade by lowering tariffs and other trade restrictions.

North American Free Trade Agreement (NAFTA)
An agreement signed by the United States, Canada, and Mexico in 1992 to form the largest free trade zone in the world.

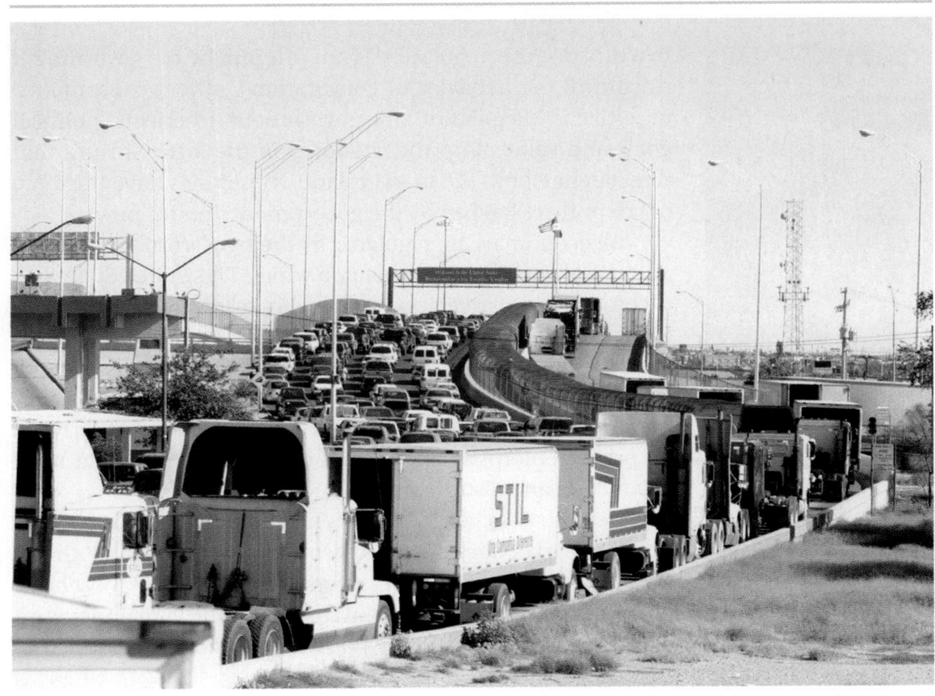

One effect of NAFTA was to speed the crossing of goods into the United States. Here, trucks move through the U.S.-Mexico border without inspection.

YOU WILL DECIDE Should the Federal Government Do More to Protect U.S. Jobs?

Workers in the United States receive much higher salaries and benefits than in less-developed nations. As U.S. labor costs have risen over the last 30 years, private corporations have moved hundreds of thousands of jobs to other countries. This process, called *offshoring,* creates wide swaths of unemployment in heavy industries such as steelmaking and service industries such as computer support. Although no one is certain how many jobs have left the United States, some estimates suggest more than one million U.S. jobs have been exported to Mexico, other Central American countries, and China. The number may seem high, but it amounts to a fraction of the U.S. workforce of more than 140 million. Nevertheless, opposition to job migration remains a highly divisive issue between labor and management.

and the United States is Mexico's most important. Critics remain concerned because Mexican antipollution laws are significantly less stringent than those in the United States, and Mexican workers receive considerably lower wages. Both these factors make relocation to Mexico attractive to many U.S. companies seeking to reduce labor and pollution control costs.

Regulating the Economy

The second goal of U.S. economic policy is to regulate business activities that may create unfair advantages. U.S. workers believe in competition among businesses, but they also want a level playing field, meaning no industry or company cheats its way to the top or abuses its employees or the environment along the way.

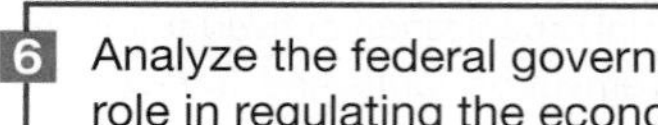

LEARNING **OBJECTIVE**

6 Analyze the federal government's role in regulating the economy.

The Constitution explicitly authorizes Congress to regulate commerce among the states and with foreign nations. In our earliest years, Congress used this regulatory power to impose or suspend tariffs on imports from other nations. In the nineteenth century, the federal government created a number of agencies to regulate the conduct of citizens and commercial enterprises with an eye toward promoting economic development. Among these were the Army Corps of Engineers (1824), the Patent and Trademark Office (1836), the Steamboat Inspection Service (1837), and the Copyright Office of the Library of Congress (1870). In 1887, Congress created the Interstate Commerce Commission to deal with widespread dissatisfaction over the practices of railroads.

You Are an Environmental Activist

Additional regulations were created to end monopolies, increase food safety, prevent environmental pollution, improve automobile safety, and prevent employment discrimination on the basis of race, color, national origin, religion, sex, and age. More recently, government has created regulations to protect citizens from raw sewage in rivers; lead in paint and gasoline; toxins in the air; radon gas in homes; and asbestos, cotton dust, and hazardous products in the environment. Estimates vary on how much compliance with these federal regulations costs consumers and businesses, but the amount is in the hundreds of billions of dollars.

Preventing Corporate Abuse

In a broad sense, regulation is any attempt by the government to control the behavior of corporations, other governments, or citizens. Regulation by government interjects political goals and values into the economy in the form of rules that direct behavior in the marketplace. These rules have the force of law and are backed by the government's police powers.

All economies are regulated by their governments, but the amount of government regulation varies. The United States has a competitive market economy, with relatively little government regulation. It allows wages, prices, and the allocation of goods and services to follow the laws of supply and demand, even when that produces unpopular results, such as the dramatic increase in gasoline prices in 2005–2006. The nation relies on private enterprise and market incentives to carry out most production and distribution.

The risk of animal-borne diseases, such as mad cow disease, has led the federal government to institute regulation of the nation's agriculture industry.

Nevertheless, even opponents of regulation recognize that the market does not always solve every problem. Both political parties say regulatory overkill threatens to overwhelm entrepreneurs and divert them from building vital, innovative companies. The question is not whether there are both costs and benefits from regulation, however, but whether the balance is right. Conservatives tend to overstate the costs of many regulations and understate the benefits, while liberals tend to overstate the benefits and understate the costs.

Types of Corporate Regulation

Economic regulation generally refers to government controls on the behavior of businesses in the marketplace: the entry of individual firms into particular lines of business, the prices firms may charge, and the standards of service they must offer.

Although the national government has been regulating interstate commerce since 1789, it was generally reluctant to regulate private businesses until after the Civil War. As the U.S. economy grew, so did the need for rules governing business and labor. Congress created the Interstate Commerce Commission (ICC) in 1887; the first of many independent regulatory commissions, the ICC regulated railroads and other transportation industries but was abolished in the late 1970s as part of the deregulation movement, which we discuss later in this chapter.

Congress has created two types of regulatory agencies: independent agencies under the president's control and independent regulatory commissions insulated from Congress and the president. The heads of independent agencies are nominated by the president and confirmed by the Senate, but do not have terms of office and serve at the pleasure of the president. Independent regulatory commissioners are also appointed by the president and confirmed by the Senate, but serve for specific terms of office and cannot be removed by a president except for cause.

THINKING IT THROUGH

Most economists agree that efforts to stop the movement of jobs to other nations would hurt the U.S. economy in the longer term. "Protectionism will do little to create jobs," former Federal Reserve Board chair Alan Greenspan said in 2004, "and if foreigners retaliate, we will surely lose jobs. We need to discover the means to enhance the skills of our workforce and to further open markets here and abroad."

Liberals tend to agree but argue that the federal government should provide greater help for workers who lose their jobs to foreign nations. "The answer is not to try to stop outsourcing," says former Clinton administration secretary of labor Robert Reich, using a popular term for job migration, "but we do have to get serious about job retraining, lifetime learning, extended unemployment insurance, and wage insurance."

U.S. companies have offshored thousands of jobs, including service call centers, to India and other low-wage nations.

Job migration may be the inevitable long-term cost of doing global business, but it has very visible consequences in the short term. Workers whose jobs move abroad often face years of unemployment, which is why the issue has been so controversial.

The United States' economic policy in the future will continue to combine free trade and selective protectionism. Though it shields highly visible industries from competition at home or abroad, protectionism often favors one industry over another, which reduces competition among those industries. In the short run, it helps protect U.S. jobs, but may delay economic growth as companies spend more on pay than R&D.

Questions

1. Why should the United States protect its workers from job migration?
2. Should workers be protected even if doing so results in higher prices for products such as clothing?
3. Do you know of any jobs that have been outsourced? Have you had any contact with a company that uses employees in other nations to deliver basic services?

Regulating Business

Business regulation increased in three major waves over the past century. The first came in the 1910s, the second in the 1930s, and the third in the late 1960s through 1980. In each case, changing circumstances gave rise to the legislation.

Perhaps the most important responsibility of government regulation in a free market system is to maintain competition. When one company gains a **monopoly,** or several create an *oligopoly,* the market system operates ineffectively. The aim of **antitrust legislation** is to prevent monopolies, break up those that exist, and ensure competition. In the past, so-called natural monopolies, such as electric utilities and telephone companies, were protected by the government because it was assumed that in these fields, competition would be grossly inefficient.

In the late nineteenth century, social critics and populist reformers believed that the oil, sugar, whiskey, and steel industries were deceiving consumers, in large part because of the rise of large monopolies called **trusts.** Once they became aware of abuses in these industries, citizens began to call for more government regulation. In 1890, Congress responded by passing the Sherman Antitrust Act, designed "to protect trade and commerce against unlawful restraints and monopolies." However, the Sherman Antitrust Act had little immediate impact; presidents made few attempts to enforce it, and the Supreme Court's early interpretation of the act limited its scope.[7]

monopoly
Domination of an industry by a single company; also the company that dominates the industry.

antitrust legislation
Federal laws (starting with the Sherman Antitrust Act of 1890) that try to prevent a monopoly from dominating an industry and restraining trade.

trust
A monopoly that controls goods and services, often in combinations that reduce competition.

THE **CHANGING FACE** OF U.S. POLITICS

Female and Minority Board Members

All corporations have boards of directors that wield great power—they oversee executive salaries and compensation, approve major decisions such as mergers and acquisitions of other companies, and attest to the honesty of corporate financial reports.

Although women and minorities now constitute a significant percentage of the U.S. workforce, they occupy relatively few of the seats on the boards of the country's largest corporations. As of 2005, just 12 percent of board members at the nation's 1,500 largest companies were women, while 10 percent were minorities. These percentages have grown slightly over the past decade, but they remain well below the percentage of women and minorities in the workforce. They are also well below the number of women and minorities who work as managers and executives in the largest U.S. corporations.

These percentages may increase in coming years as corporations seek to add more board members under new federal rules adopted in the wake of the accounting scandals at Enron, WorldCom, and other leading corporations. The problem is not a lack of candidates—in 2002, for example, the New American Alliance, a nonprofit association of Latino business leaders, and the Hispanic Association for Corporate Responsibility together created a database of more than 1,000 Hispanic candidates for board openings. If the numbers don't grow, advocacy groups have promised to pressure the Securities and Exchange Commission for a rule requiring greater diversity.

Percentage of Women and Minorities in the Workforce and Board Room, 2005.

	Percentage of Women	**Percentage of Racial Minorities**
U.S. workforce	47%	30%
Executives and managers	35	16
Seats on the boards of the 1,500 largest companies	12	10

SOURCE: Data from Susan Williams, "Board Diversity," Investment Responsibility Resource Center, 2006 Background Report A, March 1, 2006.

QUESTIONS

1. How do women and minorities improve the performance of major corporations?
2. Why are so few women and minorities appointed to these boards?
3. Should the federal government require that boards be more representative of the population or workforce as a whole?

Congress added the Clayton Act to the antitrust arsenal in 1914. This act outlawed such specific abuses as charging different prices to different buyers in order to destroy a weaker competitor, granting rebates, making false statements about competitors and their products, buying up supplies to suppress competition, and bribing competitors' employees. In addition, *interlocking directorates* (in which an officer or director in one corporation served on the board of a competitor) were banned, and corporations were prohibited from acquiring stock in competing companies if such acquisitions substantially lessened interstate competition. That same year, Congress established the Federal Trade Commission (FTC), run by a five-person board, to enforce the Clayton Act and prevent unfair competitive practices. The FTC was to be the "traffic cop" for competition.[8]

Regulating the Use of Labor

Most laws and rules curb business practices and steer private enterprise into socially useful channels. But regulation cuts two ways. In the case of U.S. workers, most laws in recent decades have tended not to restrict labor but to confer rights and opportunities on it. Actually, many labor laws do not touch labor directly; instead they regulate labor's relationship with employers.

Federal regulations protect workers in the following important areas, among others:

1. *Public contracts.* The Walsh-Healey Act of 1936, as amended, requires that most workers employed under contracts with the federal government be paid at least the average or prevailing wage for that job, and that they be paid overtime for all work in excess of 8 hours per day or 40 hours per week.
2. *Wages and hours.* The Fair Labor Standards Act of 1938 set a maximum workweek of 40 hours for all employees engaged in interstate commerce or in the production

of goods for interstate commerce (with certain exemptions). Work beyond that amount must be paid for at 1 half times the regular rate.

3. *Child labor.* The Fair Labor Standards Act of 1938 prohibits children from working in any industry that engages in interstate commerce, which essentially means that all child labor is illegal.
4. *Industrial safety and occupational health.* The Occupational Safety and Health Act of 1970 created the first comprehensive federal industrial safety program. It gave the secretary of labor broad authority to set safety and health standards for companies engaged in interstate commerce.

Federal regulations also protect employees' right to organize unions. Under the 1935 National Labor Relations Act (usually called the Wagner Act), for example, the federal government gave workers significant new rights to organize unions, while prohibiting businesses from discriminating against union members or refusing to bargain in good faith with union representatives.

Congress passed a major modification of the labor laws in 1947, the Labor-Management Relations Act, commonly called the Taft-Hartley Act. The act outlawed the **closed shop,** a company in which only union members in good standing may be hired; permitted the **union shop,** a company in which new employees are obligated to join the union within a stated period of time; prohibited employers from refusing to bargain with employees; allowed courts to issue **labor injunctions** forbidding specific individuals or groups from performing acts considered harmful to the rights or property of an employer or community; and structured the process of **collective bargaining** between unions and employers to set wages, benefits, and working conditions.

Regulating Corporate Markets

The stock market crash of 1929 did more than devastate the U.S. economy and usher in the Great Depression. It also revealed deep problems in the way companies sold their stock to investors. Millions of new investors entered the stock market in the 1920s, only to find that the companies in which they had invested were virtually worthless.

Before 1934, investors themselves had to determine whether a company was telling the truth about its stock. Since 1934, that responsibility has fallen to the Securities and Exchange Commission (SEC). Under the Securities Exchange Act of 1934, which established the SEC, and a long list of later laws, companies that offer their stock for sale to the public must tell the truth about their businesses, which means full disclosure of their financial condition.

The act also required that anyone in the business of selling stocks, including brokers, dealers, and stock exchanges such as the New York Stock Exchange and NASDAQ, must treat investors fairly and honestly, putting investors' interests first. That means, for example, that individuals who know about a new stock offering in advance , or who have other insider information on events that might increase or decrease the value of a given stock, are prohibited from using that information to benefit themselves.

Congress passed a corporate reform bill in 2002 that strengthened the SEC, created a new oversight board to monitor accounting practices, and set new disclosure requirements for reporting corporate profits. The Enron collapse was only one of many highly visible corporate scandals of the early 2000s that included communications companies such as WorldCom and Adelphia. In 2006, Enron executive Kenneth Lay went on trial for stealing money from his company, while WorldCom became part of Verizon Corporation, and Adelphia went out of business.

Protecting the Environment

Until the 1960s, the United States did little to protect the environment, and the little that was done was by state and local governments. Recently the federal government has taken on new responsibilities, starting with passage of the Clean Air and Water Acts in the early

closed shop
A company with a labor agreement under which union membership is a condition of employment.

union shop
A company in which new employees must join a union within a stated time period.

labor injunction
A court order forbidding specific individuals or groups from performing certain acts (such as striking) that the court considers harmful to the rights and property of an employer or a community.

collective bargaining
A method whereby representatives of the union and employer determine wages, hours, and other conditions of employment through direct negotiation.

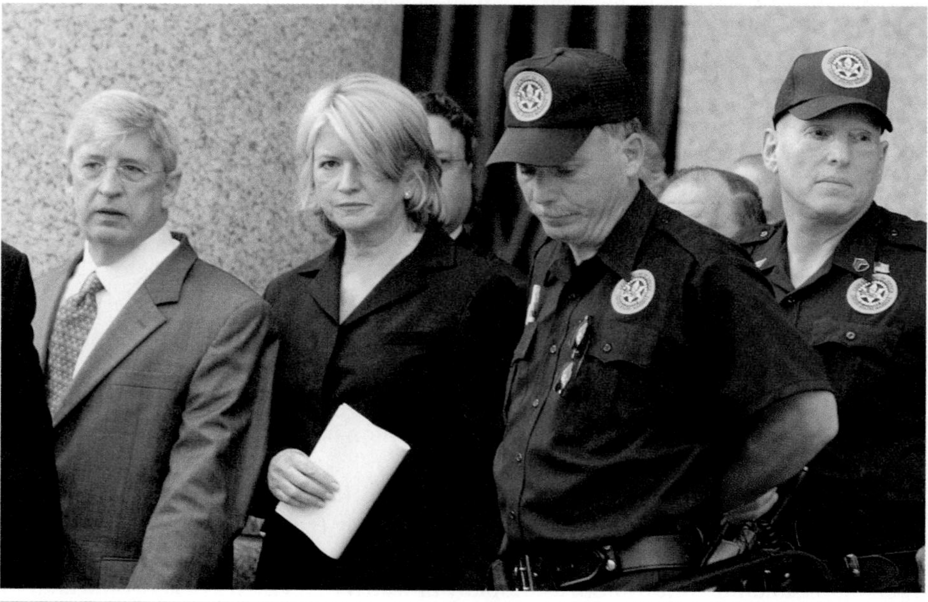

Martha Stewart was convicted of lying to federal prosecutors regarding a stock sale involving "insider" information that the stock was about to fall in value. She served in prison for a short time, but suffered no loss in national prestige or earning power.

1970s. These put new limits on the amount of pollution companies could release into the environment and launched a long list of laws regulating things such as leaking underground storage tanks, garbage, and encouraging energy conservation and recycling. Congress also created the Environmental Protection Agency (EPA) to enforce the new laws.

environmental impact statement
A statement required by federal law from all agencies for any project using federal funds to assess the potential effect of the new construction or development on the environment.

Perhaps the most controversial environmental regulations are **environmental impact statements,** which assess the potential effects of new construction or development on the environment. Most projects using federal funds must prepare such statements, and since 1970, thousands have been filed. Supporters contend that the statements reveal major environmental risks in new construction projects and can lead to cost savings and greater environmental awareness. Critics claim that they represent more government interference, paperwork, and delays in the public and private sectors.

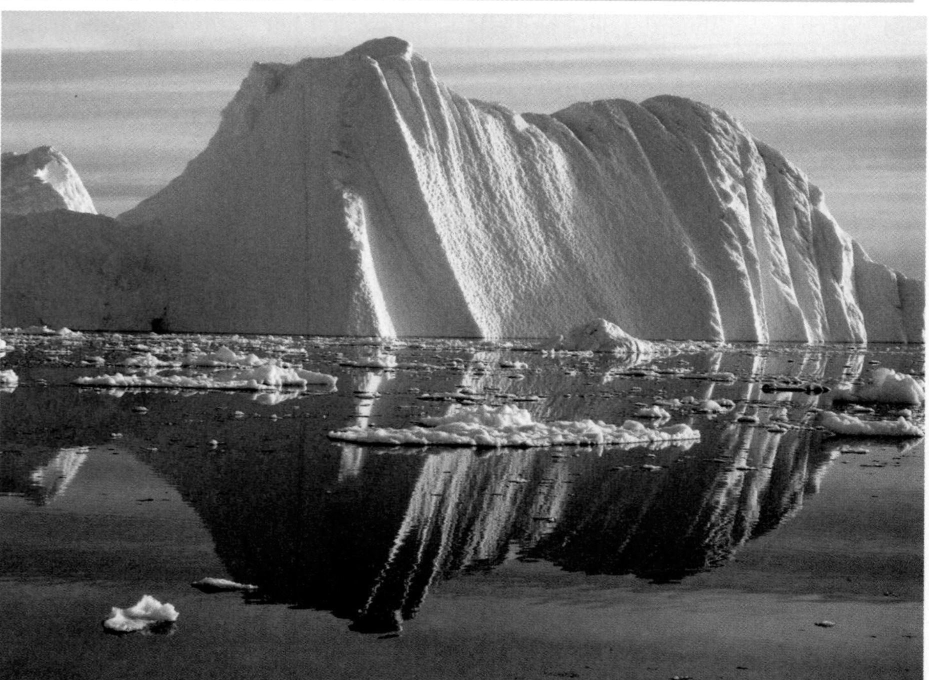

The federal government is becoming more concerned about the global environment, including the melting of the polar ice caps, which may raise sea levels dramatically over the next 100 years.

Environmental impact statements are only one form of environmental regulation, however. In 1990, Congress amended the Clean Air Act to tighten controls on automobiles and the fuel they use. Building on earlier mileage regulation, the 1990 amendments required automakers to install pollution controls to reduce emissions of hydrocarbons and nitrogen oxides, and set stiff standards for the kinds of gasoline that can be sold. The 1990 act also required power companies to cut pollution from coal-burning power plants, phased out the use of certain chemicals that harm the earth's protective ozone layer and may contribute to global warming, and set new limits on a long list of cancer-causing pollutants. In 2005, the Bush administration implemented a new set of regulations supporting its Clear Skies initiative. These placed limits on the release of certain pollutants but were widely seen as a general weakening of environmental laws.

The 1990 amendments and Clear Skies initiatives used the profit motive to encourage self-regulation by private business. Under new rules and permits issued by the Environmental Protection Agency, businesses are allowed to generate a certain amount of pollution. If they produce less than their allotment, they can sell the balance of their permits to other companies that are polluting more. By setting overall caps for certain regions of the country, this "cap-and-trade" system encourages individual companies to reduce the total amount of pollution they would have produced under traditional regulations. Initial efforts along these lines have been successful, while saving billions in legal costs to force industries to cut their pollution through traditional court action.

The Gap's "Product Red" supports HIV/AIDS programs around the world by devoting a share of every purchase of a red-colored product to charity. The project has attracted the support of many media stars including Oprah Winfrey.

Corporate Responsibility

Many corporations have been dealing with the increased pressure to be more responsible by creating programs to give money and volunteer time to their communities. The Gap has pledged to provide a portion of every sale to charities through "Product Red," while others have promised to be more environmentally conscious. These efforts at **corporate social responsibility** have increased public confidence in big business.

There are three forms of corporate social responsibility. The first is corporate giving to charities. Many corporations have foundations that give 1 or 2 percent of their annual profits to specific causes. The second is free consulting and advertising to help charities become more effective in making their voices heard. The third pairs corporations and charities in partnership activities such as annual walks for cancer. Many corporations also give their employees paid time off to volunteer.

The Deregulation Movement

LEARNING **OBJECTIVE**

7 Contrast the advantages and disadvantages of the deregulation movement.

One response to criticisms of government regulation of the economy is **deregulation,** the reduction or abolition of federal regulation in a particular sector of the economy. Deregulation began in 1977 with the airline, trucking, and railroad industries and has continued with banking and telecommunications.

At the same time the federal government has been working to deregulate certain industries, it has also created new procedures to limit the amount of regulation it can impose. In 1993, for example, President Clinton issued an executive order prohibiting agencies from issuing regulations unless the benefits of the regulations (in lives saved, for example) outweighed the costs. In 2001, President Bush followed suit by imposing a 60-day hold on all regulations published by the Clinton administration until his administration could ensure that they passed the benefit/cost test.

corporate social responsibility
Efforts by corporations to improve their reputations by paying attention to their contributions to the social good.

deregulation
A policy promoting cutbacks in the amount of federal regulation in specific areas of economic activity.

Deregulating Transportation

No industry has undergone more extensive deregulation than the transportation industry. Over the past generation, airlines, trucking, and railroads have been granted considerable freedom in conducting their operations. No deregulation effort has been more visible to consumers than airline deregulation.

The federal government began regulating aviation when it established the Civil Aeronautics Board (CAB) in 1938 to control rates and fares, protecting airlines from unreasonable competition. Critics charged that under regulation, airlines competed only in the frequency of flights and in the services they offered, forcing consumers to pay higher fares than needed.

After years of debate, Congress abolished the CAB in 1978, allowing the market to set fares through competition. Although many fares fell, some medium-sized cities lost service because carriers found it more profitable to use their aircraft in busier markets. Airlines were raising fares on routes over which they had monopolies in order to subsidize lower fares on more competitive routes. Critics charged that safety precautions and maintenance suffered as a result of cutthroat competition and the ease with which new airlines could now enter the market.

Although airline deregulation has its problems, it has resulted in generally lower fares, greater choice of routes and fares in most markets, and more efficient use of assets by the industry.[9] If an airline is overcharging passengers, a competitor will eventually steal those travelers away. Carriers have thus had to streamline their operations in order to survive in a competitive market. Southwest Airlines is an example of a discount airline that took advantage of deregulation to take on larger airlines.[10]

But recent mergers of major airlines have worsened the problems that deregulation and cancellation of service brought to small and medium-sized cities in some western states. The post–September 11 collapse in travel pushed several airlines toward bankruptcy, which in turn prompted Congress to provide loans to many airlines to help them through the crisis. Under economic pressure, many airlines stopped providing basic services such as meals, while some have demanded deep cutbacks in wages and benefits from their employees. However, some newer airlines such as Jet Blue and Southwest have been highly profitable offering low-cost services across the nation.

Deregulating Telecommunications

Airline deregulation may have been the most visible to consumers, but the deregulation of telecommunications may eventually have a greater impact on how we live,

Deregulation of transportation brought a surge in consolidation of airlines. Here, American Airlines jets line up for take off at Dallas/Fort Worth International Airport, a key American Airlines hub.

whether in the form of lower phone bills, easier access to the Internet, or better cellular technology. Unlike the deregulation of transportation, which came in a number of steps over time, deregulation of telecommunications came in a single, massive bill called the Telecommunications Act of 1996.

This act broke the long-standing monopolies of companies such as AT&T, while creating new opportunities for competition in the phone, Internet, and cable-television industries. Telephone companies that were once divided into seven local "Baby Bells" were allowed to offer services outside their defined regions. Local telephone companies won the freedom to provide long-distance service, manufacture communications equipment, and offer video service in competition with cable television. At the same time, local telephone companies opened their networks to competition for local telephone service from cable-television and long-distance companies.

The Telecommunications Act also contained two highly controversial provisions: new regulations on Internet content and a requirement that all television makers install a "V-chip" to allow parents to block television shows with objectionable content. However, the Supreme Court struck down provisions making it a crime for any person knowingly to make indecent material accessible to minors on the Internet. The Court found the provision too vague and held that the Internet receives full protection under the First Amendment.[11] Although the debate continues about who will decide what is deemed violent or offensive, most surveys suggest that parents are unwilling or unable to use the V-chip to control their family viewing habits.[12]

A Continued Federal Role

Despite campaign promises to reduce the federal government's economic role and give more money back to citizens and corporations, members of Congress and the president understand that the federal government must be active in the economic life of the nation. It will continue to collect taxes, regulate the money supply, prevent monopolies that would hurt consumers, and promote free trade. It will do all this while trying to let the market, not government regulators, shape the demand for and the price of products and services. Most U.S. adults want their government to play only a limited role in the economy, but competing values such as fairness, equality, protection of workers and the environment, and support of healthy competition inevitably encourage elected officials to take on referee responsibilities in order to promote the common good.

Citizens exert a great deal of influence on economic policy, if only by purchasing goods and services. But they can also influence policy through pressure on their representatives. The economy was a top concern in the 2008 presidential elections and led both the Democratic and Republican parties to push hard for action to protect homeowners from unscrupulous lenders and stimulate energy production.

CHAPTER **SUMMARY**

1 Identify the two most important measures of economic performance and show how they interact.

Inflation and unemployment are considered the two most important measures of economic performance, although we also use the size of the federal budget deficit, the U.S. trade deficit or surplus with other nations, and gross domestic product (GDP). Inflation and unemployment tend to move together in opposite directions—inflation rises as unemployment drops, and it falls as unemployment rises. Other measures of economic performance include the amount of government spending and the balance of trade.

2 Evaluate the role of fiscal policy in keeping the economy stable.

Fiscal policy consists of economic policies made by Congress, the president, and the judiciary. There are two basic types—collecting revenues through taxes and fees, and spending money through the federal budget. Increasing government spending stimulates the economy, thereby reducing unemployment, while increasing taxes generally slows economic growth, thereby curtailing inflation. The federal government also spends money through tax expenditures hidden from public view.

3 Outline the key steps in the federal budget process.

The federal budget goes through a long development process that starts two years before the budget actually goes into effect with requests from every department and agency. Next the budget is reworked by the Office of Management and Budget, is finalized and sent to the Congress, undergoes analysis by the Congressional Budget Office, and moves through the legislative process until it becomes part of the 13 massive appropriations bills that actually spend the money.

4 Evaluate the role of monetary policy in keeping the economy stable.

Monetary policy, made by the Federal Reserve Board (the Fed), is designed to affect the flow of money through the economy. The Fed's most important tool is the federal funds rate, the amount of interest it allows banks to charge each other on short-term loans. Raising the cost of money is generally a way to slow down the economy and reduce inflation; lowering the cost of money ignites the economy and reduces unemployment.

5 Analyze the federal government's role in promoting the economy.

The federal government has long promoted the economy and specific industries. It also promotes trade and commerce with other nations, including efforts to reduce barriers to imports and exports, stabilize prices of certain goods and services, and encourage innovation through patents and other protections.

6 Analyze the federal government's role in regulating the economy.

Economic regulation is designed to control the behavior of the economy in a variety of ways such as preventing monopolies, reducing environment pollution, and protecting workers. Many regulations were designed to curb specific abuses and promote competition.

7 Contrast the advantages and disadvantages of the deregulation movement.

The deregulation movement is driven by the belief that regulations are too costly and often fail to achieve their desired ends. Democrats and Republicans have both supported deregulation of key industries over the past four decades, but it sometimes produces new problems that create a backlash in favor of reregulation. Although air fares dropped immediately after airline deregulation, for instance, they have moved upward as many airline companies have merged to reduce competition.

Chapter Self-Test

1. Define **inflation.** (p. 491)
2. Explain the interaction between **inflation** and **unemployment.** Draw a diagram to demonstrate their relationship. (p. 491)
3. Differentiate fiscal policy from monetary policy. (p. 490)
4. Match the following definitions to their terms

a. Rising prices on goods and services	i) fiscal policy (p. 491)
b. Joblessness among employable workers	ii) monetary policy (p. 491)
c. Uses federal spending and taxation to stimulate or slow the economy	iii) Unemployment (p. 490)
d. Manipulates the supply of money to keep the economy from swinging wildly from boom to bust	iv) Inflation (p. 490)

5. Examine Table 18–1 on page 494 and identify the important actors at each step of the process.
6. When the **Federal Reserve** lowers the **federal funds rate,** what is the intended consequence? (p. 498)
7. Examine Figure 18–4 on page 498 and list the reasons you think account for the dramatic drop in the prime interest rate in 2001.
8. In one or two paragraphs, explain why it is so difficult for the Fed to anticipate the full consequences of its decisions. (pp. 499–500)
9. Write a brief persuasive essay explaining what you believe the government's proper role in the economy should be.(pp. 499–500)
10. Which of the following is *not* one side of an iron triangle?
    a. a receptive federal court
    b. a set of loyal interest groups
    c. a federal department or agency
    d. a House and/or Senate authorizing committee
11. In a short essay, compare and contrast **laissez-faire economics** and **Keynesian economics.** (p. 500)
12. In two or three paragraphs, explain the relationship between the real economic situation and economic theory. For example, when are people more likely to argue for *more* or *less* regulation? (pp. 501–509)
13. In a few paragraphs, describe 3 or 4 factors telecommunications and transportation have in common following industry deregulation. (pp. 510–511)

Key Terms

fiscal policy, p. 490

monetary policy, p. 490

inflation, p. 491

unemployment, p. 491

stagflation, p. 491

gross domestic product (GDP), p. 491

excise tax, p. 492

budget deficit, p. 492

tariff, p. 493

progressive tax, p. 493

regressive tax, p. 493

national debt, p. 493

Office of Management and Budget (OMB), p. 494

Congressional Budget Office (CBO), p. 496

tax expenditure, p. 496

sales tax, p. 496

value-added tax (VAT), p. 496

Federal Reserve System, p. 498

federal funds rate, p. 498

laissez-faire economics, p. 500

Keynesian economics, p. 500

protectionism, p. 501

trade deficit, p. 501

World Trade Organization (WTO), p. 503

General Agreement on Tariffs and Trade (GATT), p. 503

North American Free Trade Agreement (NAFTA), p. 503

monopoly, p. 505

antitrust legislation, p. 505

trust, p. 505

closed shop, p. 507

union shop, p. 507

labor injunction, p. 507

collective bargaining, p. 507

environmental impact statement, p. 508

corporate social responsibility, p. 509

deregulation, p. 509

Further Reading

JEFFREY H. BIRNBAUM AND **ALAN S. MURRAY,** *Showdown at Gucci Gulch: Lawmakers, Lobbyists, and the Unlikely Triumph of Tax Reform* (Vintage Books, 1988).

STEPHEN G. BREYER, *Breaking the Vicious Circle: Toward Effective Risk Regulation* (Harvard University Press, 1993).

GARY BRYNER, *Blue Skies, Green Politics: The Clean Air Act of 1990 and Its Interpretation,* 2d ed. (CQ Press, 1995).

GARY BURTLESS, ROBERT J. LAWRENCE, ROBERT E. LITAN, AND **ROBERT J. SHAPIRO,** *Globaphobia: Confronting Fears About Open Trade* (Brookings Institution Press, 1998).

THOMAS W. CHURCH AND **ROBERT T. NAKAMURA,** *Cleaning Up the Mess: Implementation Strategies in Superfund* (Brookings Institution Press, 1993).

ROBERT W. CRANDALL AND **HAROLD FURCHTGOTT-ROTH,** *Cable TV: Regulation or Competition?* (Brookings Institution Press, 1996).

ROBERT W. CRANDALL AND **LEONARD WAVERMAN,** *Who Pays for Universal Service? When Telephone Subsidies Become Transparent* (Brookings Institution Press, 2000).

ROBERT W. CRANDALL ET AL., *An Agenda for Federal Regulatory Reform* (American Enterprise Institute/Brookings Institution Press, 1997).

ROBERT M. ENTMAN, *Competition, Innovation, and Investment in Telecommunications* (Aspen Institute, 1998).

THOMAS L. FRIEDMAN, *The Lexus and the Olive Tree: Understanding Globalization* (Anchor Books, 2000).

THOMAS L. FRIEDMAN, *The World Is Flat: A Brief History of the Twenty-First Century* (Farrar, Straus, & Giroux, 2005).

WILLIAM GREIDER, *Secrets of the Temple: How the Federal Reserve Runs the Country* (Simon & Schuster, 1987).

PHILIP K. HOWARD, *The Death of Common Sense: How Law Is Suffocating America* (Random House, 1994).

DAVID CAY JOHNSON, *Free Lunch: How the Wealthiest Americans Enrich Themselves at Government Expense (and Stick You with the Bill)* (Portfolio Books, 2007).

CORNELIUS M. KERWIN, *Rulemaking: How Government Agencies Write Law and Make Policy,* 2d ed. (CQ Press, 1998).

ROBERT KUTTNER, *Everything for Sale: The Virtues and Limits of Markets* (Knopf, 1997).

LAWRENCE LESSIG, *Code and Other Laws of Cyberspace* (Basic Books, 2000).

CALVIN MACKENZIE AND **SARANNA THORTON,** *Bucking the Deficit: Economic Policy-Making in America* (Westview Press, 1996).

PETER G. PETERSON, *Facing Up: Paying Our Nation's Debt and Saving Our Children's Future* (Simon & Schuster, 1994).

ALLEN SCHICK, *The Federal Budget: Politics, Policy, Process,* rev. ed. (Brookings Institution Press, 2007).

JOSEPH E. STIGLITZ, *Globalization and Its Discontents* (Norton, 2002).

BOB WOODWARD, *Maestro: Greenspan's Fed and the American Boom* (Simon & Schuster, 2000).

JEFFREY WORSHAW, *Other People's Money: Policy Changes, Congress, and Bank Regulation* (Westview Press, 1997).

DANIEL YERGIN AND **JOSEPH STANISLAW,** *The Commanding Heights: The Battle Between Government and the Marketplace That Is Remaking the Modern World* (Simon & Schuster, 1998).

chapter 19

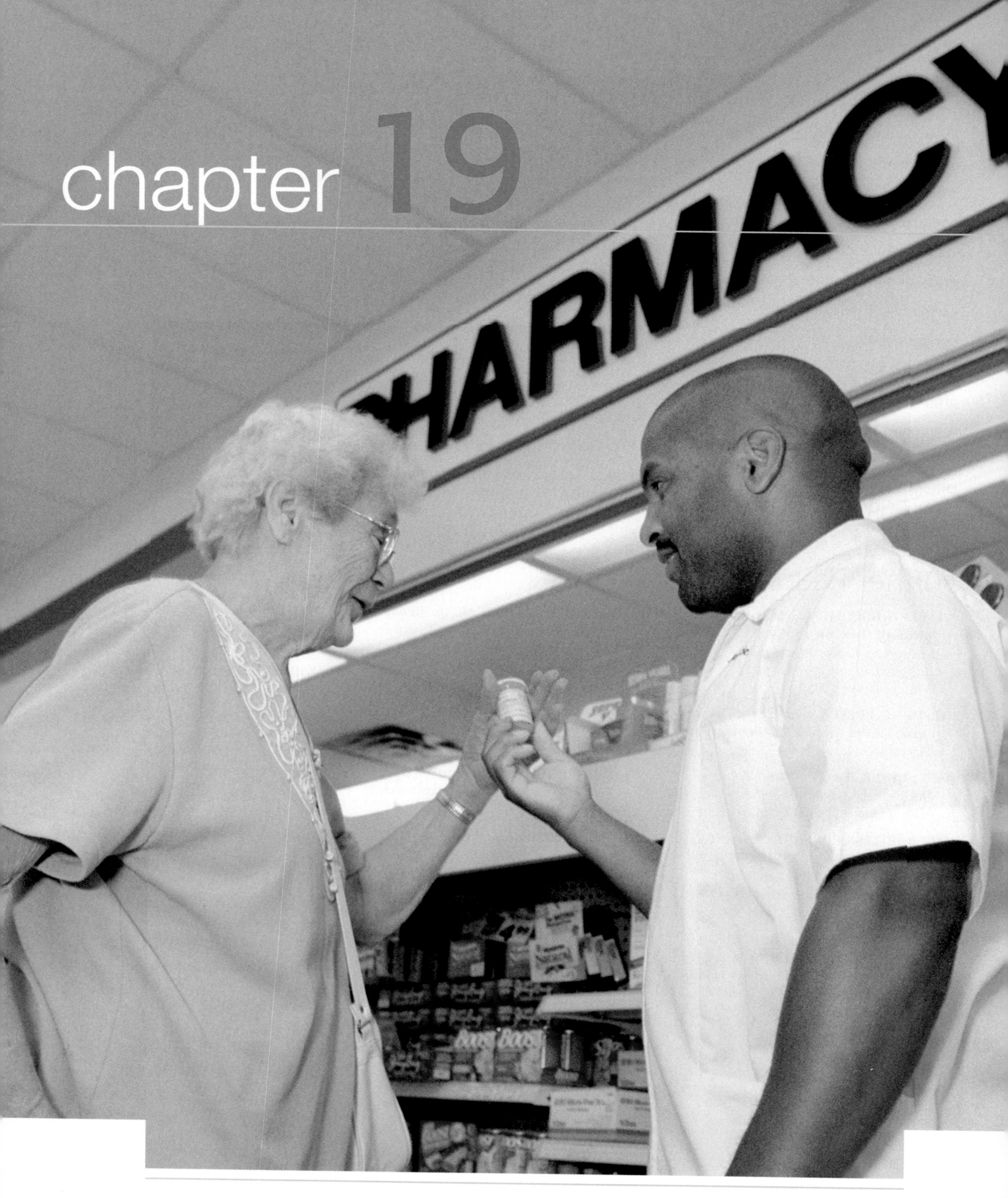

Making Social Policy

Until 2006, older citizens had to cover the cost of their prescription drugs mostly on their own. Although many had private insurance and some received help from the joint federal–state Medicaid program for the poor, many were forced to choose between food and drugs, often cutting their daily medications to make ends meet.

That all changed on an early Saturday morning in late 2003 when the House of Representatives held its final vote on a law designed to help older adults pay for their prescription drugs. Although most members of Congress supported the general idea of prescription drug coverage, Democrats wanted the federal government to administer a larger and more expensive program, while Republicans wanted a less expensive program that private insurance companies would run.

Republicans eventually won the battle for a private program on party-line votes in the House and Senate, but Democrats won broader coverage. With these agreements in hand, the bill moved quickly through the legislative process and reached the president's desk for signature on December 8. In return for a $35 monthly premium, the federal government promised to cover 75 percent of all yearly drug costs between $250 and $2,250, thereby helping all participants regardless of need. In addition, the government promised to cover 95 percent of all drug costs above $3,600, thereby protecting participants who face extremely high, or catastrophic, drug costs. The program went into effect in 2006.

Critics argued that it was flawed for several reasons. First, the program primarily aided adults who already had some basic prescription coverage. It did not help the approximately 47 million people who have no prescription drug coverage, let alone those who have no health insurance at all. Giving older citizens even more health coverage seemed unfair to those who relied entirely on charity care for help.

Second, the new program created a "doughnut hole," or lack of coverage, for older people caught between $2,251 and $3,600 in prescription costs. This meant that participants would have to come up with almost $1,400 a year to cover the hole. The nation's oldest citizens, who spend the most on health care, may therefore face hard choices between drugs and basic necessities such as food and heat.

Third, Congress and the president did not address the long-term financial problems of paying for health care for older citizens under the Medicare program, which was created in 1965. According to the latest projections, the Medicare program will start to run a deficit in 2019, which means the federal government will have to either raise taxes or cut benefits to cover the total cost.

Finally, and perhaps most important, the new law left a small but substantial number of older adults uncovered. By June 2006, 23 million had signed up for the new benefit; by February 2008, the number had inched up to 25 million. The rest of the 44 million older adults who were eligible either already had prescription drug coverage from their former employers or purchased their own. But about 4.5 million had yet to sign up for the benefit, in part because they did not know they were eligible or did not know how to apply.[1]

These problems illustrate the difficulties in both designing and implementing a major new federal program. No matter how well intended new legislation may be, new programs require time to take hold and do not always work as intended. Unfortunately for low-income older adults, time is of the essence if the federal government is to guarantee the Constitution's promise to promote the general welfare of its citizens.

LEARNING **OBJECTIVES**

1. Explain the difference between entitlements and means-tested entitlements.
2. Compare and contrast the two types of social policy.
3. Identify the major contributions of the New Deal and the Great Society to social policy.
4. Evaluate the impact of welfare reform.
5. Analyze the causes of and solutions for the lack of health coverage for all Americans.
6. Assess the tools of federal education and crime policy.

CHAPTER OUTLINE

- The Role of the Federal Government in Social Policy
- Types of Social Policy
- The Expansion of Social Policy in the Twentieth Century
- Social Policy Challenges for the Future: Health, Education, and Crime
- The Politics of Social Policy

Comparing Social Welfare Systems

This chapter will explore how the federal government promotes the general welfare through a range of social programs, how that promise has expanded over the past century, and what remains to be done to protect the needy. It will also examine three areas of social policy likely to be active over the next few years: health, education, and crime control.

Citizens have a clear interest in social policy, if only because the federal government and its state and local partners are there to protect them in crisis. But as members of interest groups large and small, such as AARP (34 million members) or the Children's Defense Fund, they can make their voices heard on major issues such as prescription drug coverage.

The Role of the Federal Government in Social Policy

Most Western governments expanded their social programs long before the United States did. American adults generally believed that people who could not succeed in a nation as big, rich, and open as the United States simply weren't working hard enough. This commitment to *rugged individualism* meant that government, whether local, state, or federal, played only a limited role in people's lives. Rather grudgingly, state governments in the early twentieth century extended relief to needy groups, especially the old, the blind, and the orphaned. But government aid was limited, and most needy people relied on charity for help, as many still do.[2]

This is not to suggest that the federal government ignored domestic policy, however. From its founding, the government took care of its military veterans. Indeed, with the Revolutionary War barely over, the Continental Congress established the nation's first programs to help soldiers disabled in battle and to provide retirement pensions for officers, well before the new government was even created.

Established in the 1780s, the financial security system for veterans expanded slowly but steadily as the soldiers aged into disability and poverty. Citizens could not stand to see their veterans in tattered clothing and felt obliged to provide support for the less fortunate. In 1818, for example, Congress expanded retirement benefits to cover all veterans of the Revolutionary War, whether officers or not, and created the first old soldiers' homes for poor veterans. In 1840, Congress expanded the veterans program again to provide financial relief to the widows of soldiers killed in battle.[3]

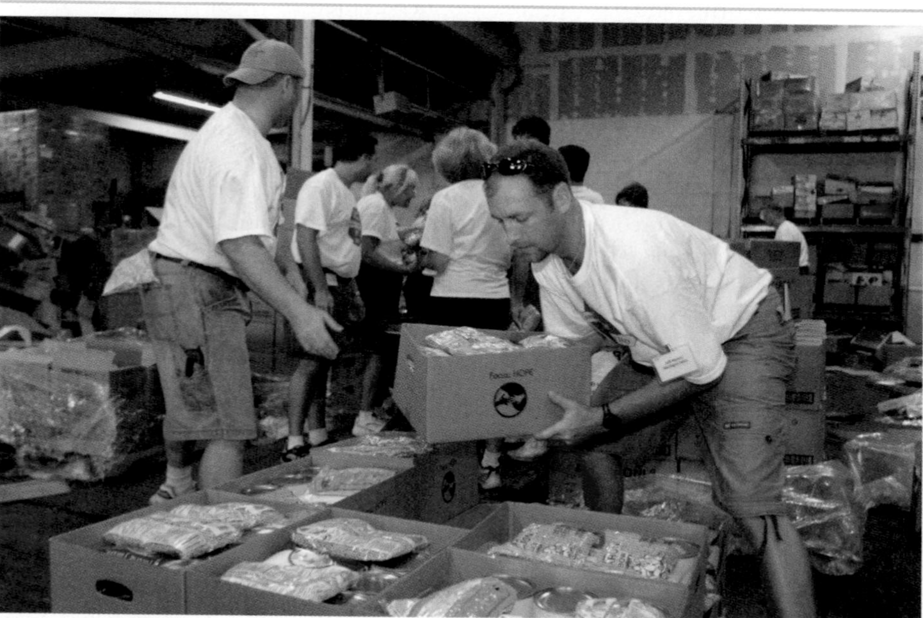

Although the federal government has become much more involved in helping the needy, private charities still provide almost three-quarters of the free food for the hungry in the United States.

Americans are sharply divided on how involved the government should be in helping the nation's needy. Funding for homeless shelters, such as this one in Atlanta, comes from both public and private sources.

These early programs set two important precedents for contemporary domestic policy. First, they established the notion that some people would be automatically entitled to certain government benefits on the basis of an eligibility requirement such as service in the nation's armed forces. Thus veterans' relief was the nation's first **entitlement,** under which the government provides benefits to any citizen who is eligible regardless of need. Over the decades since, Congress and the president have created dozens of entitlement programs, including Social Security and Medicare. Both programs provide benefits to anyone who has paid taxes for them and are available once an individual reaches retirement age.

Second, these early programs also established government's right to restrict some benefits to only those citizens who could actually prove their need for help. In the original program, for instance, only poor veterans could go to old soldiers' homes. These were early examples of what we now call **means-tested entitlements,** under which citizens must prove they are poor enough to deserve the government's help. Over the decades since, Congress and the president have created dozens of means-tested entitlement programs, including Supplemental Security Income and food stamps. Both programs provide benefits only to those who can prove they are below a certain income level.

LEARNING **OBJECTIVE**

1 Explain the difference between entitlements and means-tested entitlements.

Types of Social Policy

Having entered the twentieth century with only a handful of domestic programs, most of which were built around helping veterans, the federal government left the century with a deep inventory of such programs. According to the 2008 *Catalog of Federal Domestic Assistance,* which lists every one of the federal government's approximately 1,250 domestic funding programs in a searchable database (www.cfda.gov), there are at least 38 separate programs for farmers, another 35 for college and university students, 34 for women, and 44 for infants.

entitlements
Programs such as unemployment insurance, disaster relief, or disability payments that provide benefits to all eligible citizens.

means-tested entitlements
Programs such as Medicaid and welfare under which applicants must meet eligibility requirements based on need.

The Goals of Social Policy

Because most of these programs are restricted to one group of citizens only, they are often described as *categorical* aid. Simply typing a search term online such as "students,"

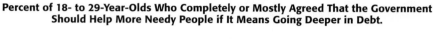

GENERATION NEXT

Helping the Needy

Although the Preamble to the Constitution promises that the federal government will promote the general welfare, citizens often differ sharply on just what this promise means. Democrats and liberals tend to believe that the federal government should take the lead in helping the needy, while Republicans and conservatives feel that the free market, private charities or churches, and state and local governments should be the source of support.

Generation Next is just as divided as the rest of the public. According to the Pew Research Center's Political Landscape survey, three-fifths of 18- to 29-year-olds completely or mostly agree that the government should help needy people even if it means going deeper in debt, while two-fifths mostly or completely disagree.

When we look only at respondents who said they completely agreed (as distinguished from mostly agreed) with the statement, we find variation between Democrats (26 percent), Republicans (13 percent), and Independents (38 percent), who were the most likely to agree.

Women and minorities were also more likely to completely agree with the statement, perhaps because they viewed themselves as more vulnerable to poverty or joblessness.

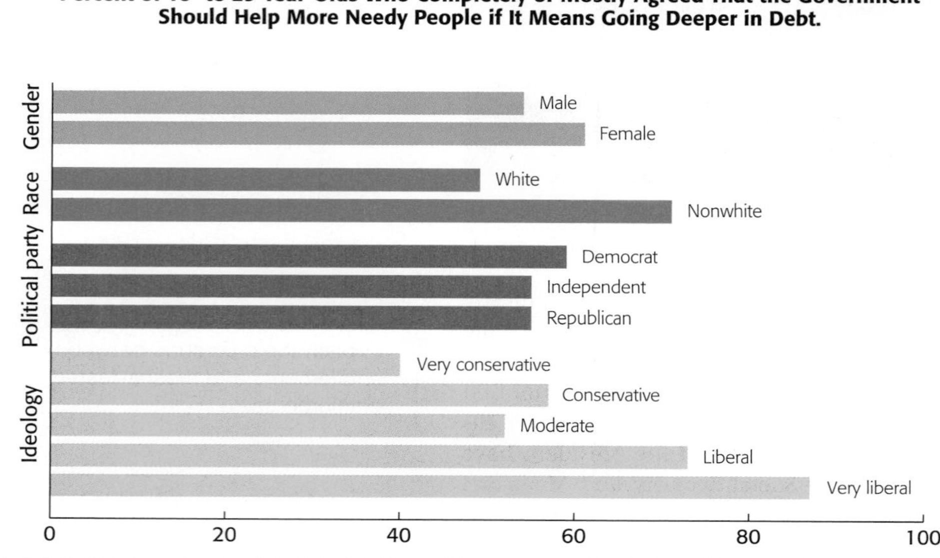

QUESTIONS

1. What might make men more reluctant to support the needy?
2. Why do majorities of ideological moderates share about the same level of support for helping needy people? Is this belief part of the nation's political culture?
3. Why do very conservative and liberal people feel differently about helping the poor?

"elderly," "children," "disabled," "workers," "farmers," "women," or "veterans" reveals just how much help the federal government provides in each category. But regardless of category, federal domestic policy focuses on two broad goals.

The first goal is to protect citizens against social and economic problems by creating a **social safety net,** whether through relief for unemployed workers, health care for the elderly, emergency shelter for the homeless, or school lunches for poor children, most of which are available to citizens only on the basis of a means test that proves they need help. Although almost all citizens are covered by federal unemployment insurance through a payroll tax, only workers who have been laid off from their jobs through no fault of their own can qualify for benefits, and then only for a relatively brief period of time.

The second goal of federal social policy is to raise the quality of life for all, whether by improving air and water quality, building roads and bridges, regulating air traffic, fighting crime, or strengthening local schools through federal aid. Almost all federal aid to the states for these purposes is distributed by formula on the basis of population, not need.

social safety net
The many programs that the federal government provides to protect Americans against economic and social misfortune.

Most scholars trace the federal government's effort to protect citizens against economic and personal hard times to the Great Depression and the Social Security Act of 1935. Although Franklin Roosevelt's New Deal agenda stimulated a remarkable

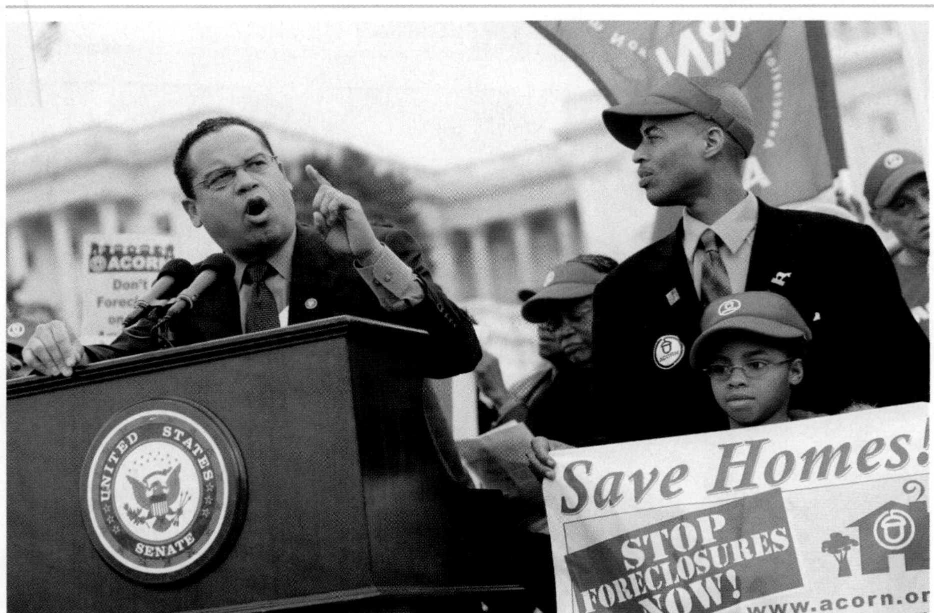

The collapse of the economy in 2007–2008 meant that millions of people lost their homes because they could not pay their mortgages. Here, citizens ask government for action to help keep their homes.

expansion in the federal government's domestic policy role, federal, state, and local governments were helping citizens long before the Depression began.

Until about a century ago, the poor were divided into two groups: the worthy poor, meaning people who were in poverty through no fault of their own, and the unworthy poor, meaning people who were in poverty because of idleness or unwillingness to work, which was considered the source of most unemployment at the time.

Types of Protection

LEARNING **OBJECTIVE**

2 Compare and contrast the two types of social policy.

By the early 1900s, however, public attitudes toward the poor had begun to change. Although the nation continued to distinguish between the worthy and unworthy poor, Congress and the president soon invented two very different types of federal programs to protect citizens against hardship, both of which continue today.

Public Assistance The first type of help for the poor is called **public assistance,** or "welfare." The first public assistance programs were actually created in the late 1800s when states established aid programs to help poor single mothers and their children. Although these programs were often described as "mothers' pensions" to create the impression that the beneficiaries had earned the benefits through some contribution, they created a precedent for many of the federal government's later antipoverty programs.

Most of these programs are means-tested entitlement programs. As noted earlier, such programs require applicants to disclose all financial assets and income to prove they fall below the poverty line, generally calculated as three times the amount of money an individual or family needs to purchase the food for a nutritious diet. The poverty level standard changes with the size of the family and the cost of living. For 2008, individuals who made just over $10,000 and families of four who made just over $21,000 were eligible for means-tested assistance.[4]

Public assistance in the United States today incorporates elements of job training, transportation subsidies, housing subsidies, free school lunches, food aid for poor families and pregnant mothers with young children, and tax credits for low-income people.

public assistance
Aid to the poor; "welfare."

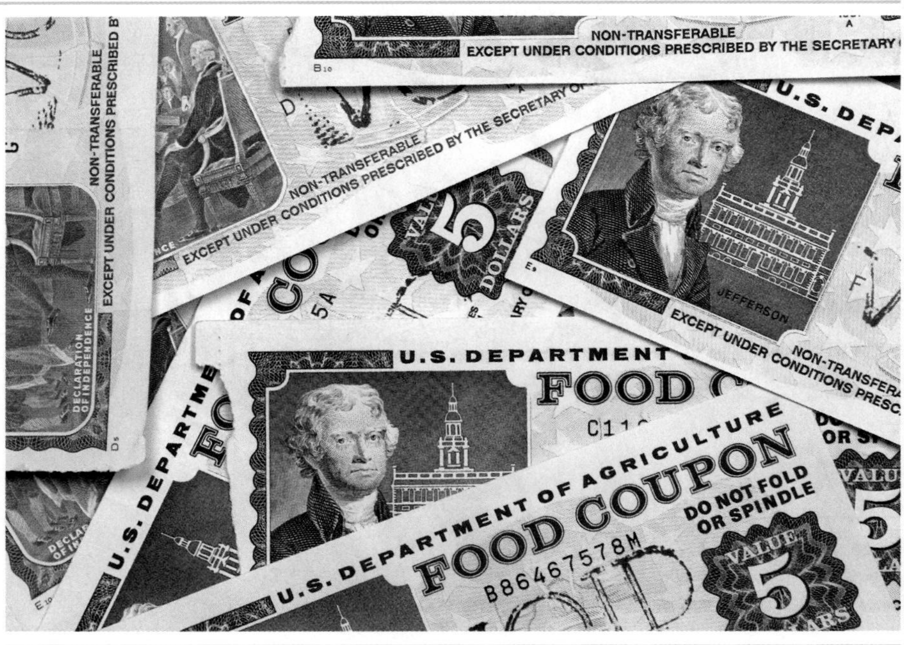

Food stamps allow needy families to purchase nutritious food. They are treated as cash by grocery stores.

The federal government also provides what some critics label "corporate welfare" to favored industries such as agriculture and corporate bailouts to businesses like investment bank Bear Stearns, as well as "middle-class welfare" to college students, home buyers, and the citizenry as a whole in the form of college loans, tax deductions for home mortgages, and access to national parks and forests (supported by taxpayers but rarely used by poor people). However, the term "welfare" is generally reserved for public assistance to the needy.

In absolute numbers, most poor people are white. As a percentage within their own population, however, a larger proportion of African Americans and Hispanics are poor. Moreover, in both absolute and proportional terms, more women than men are poor. Indeed, some scholars refer to the relatively recent rise in poverty among women as the "feminization of poverty."[5]

Social Insurance The second type of protection against hardship is **social insurance,** government programs that provide benefits to anyone who is eligible because of either past service (veterans, miners, merchant marines) or prepayments of some kind (payroll taxes for Social Security and Medicare, or insurance premiums).

Many federal assistance programs are partnerships with state governments. There are two reasons for the connection. First, except for veterans' policy, states have been responsible for protecting their citizens against hardship since the United States was formed. Second, states and local governments have the administrative agencies to stay in touch with recipients of aid, whether to make sure they are actually eligible for support or to provide services such as job training or school lunches.

Because states vary greatly in their generosity, most federal assistance is designed to set a minimum floor of support that individual states can raise on their own. The most generous states in the country tend to be located in the Northeast and West, where living costs tend to be higher and legislatures more liberal, while the least generous tend to be found in the South. In this way, states act as a check on the federal government's ability to raise benefits too far, frustrating those who believe that the federal government should set a uniform level of benefits for all citizens. (Table 19–1 shows the amount of federal payments to individuals in 2008.)

social insurance
Programs in which eligibility is based on prior contributions to government, usually in the form of payroll taxes.

TABLE 19–1 Federal Payments to Individuals, 2008

Major Public Assistance Programs, 2008	
Medicaid	$203 billion
State Children's Health Insurance Program	8 billion
Supplemental Security Income	38 billion
Food stamps	39 billion
Child nutrition	15 billion
Family support payments to states	21 billion
Earned Income Tax Credit	40 billion
Social Insurance	
Social Security	$506 billion
Medicare	460 billion
Disability insurance	103 billion
Unemployment insurance	36 billion

SOURCE: Summary Tables, *Historical Tables, Budget of the United States, Fiscal Year 2009* (U.S. Government Printing Office, February 2008).

The Expansion of Social Policy in the Twentieth Century

The federal government's commitment to helping the poor and improving the quality of life expanded rapidly during the Great Depression that followed the stock market crash of 1929. The social safety net built by state and local governments and private charities at that time simply could not meet the needs of the huge increase in the homeless, unemployed, and poor.

The Evolution of Social Welfare Policy

The New Deal

LEARNING **OBJECTIVE**

3 Identify the major contributions of the New Deal and the Great Society to social policy.

The most significant expansion of federal social policy occurred in the five years that followed Franklin Roosevelt's inauguration in 1933. As part of Roosevelt's New Deal agenda, the federal government began making loans to states and localities to help the poor, and soon it launched a long list of programs to help older workers (Social Security), the jobless (unemployment insurance), and the poor (Aid to Families with Dependent Children).

The First 100 Days Before creating these signature New Deal programs, however, the Roosevelt administration moved quickly to help the needy. The first 100 days of 1933 produced the most significant list of legislation ever passed in U.S. history, including the Federal Emergency Relief Administration (FERA), which was established to give unemployed workers cash grants to get them through the summer.

The list of "alphabet agencies" grew longer as the administration created a host of new programs to help the poor, including the Works Progress Administration (WPA), which was created in 1935 to provide work for millions of unemployed, and the Civilian Conservation Corps (CCC), which put millions of young people to work clearing trails and building roads in the national forests and parks. Between 1933 and 1945, for example, the WPA put 8.5 million people to work at a cost of $10 billion. All told, the WPA built 650,000 miles of roads, 125,000 public buildings, 8,200 parks, and 850 airports. Though the wages were hardly generous, these and other New Deal programs created a national safety net to catch those in need. It's little wonder that scholars describe the New Deal as the "big bang" of social policy.[6] Although the distinction between the worthy and unworthy poor still remained, joblessness was no longer defined as merely a problem of individual idleness or the unwillingness to work.

Help for Older Citizens Once past the immediate crisis, the Roosevelt administration began designing the flagship programs of the New Deal. First on the list was

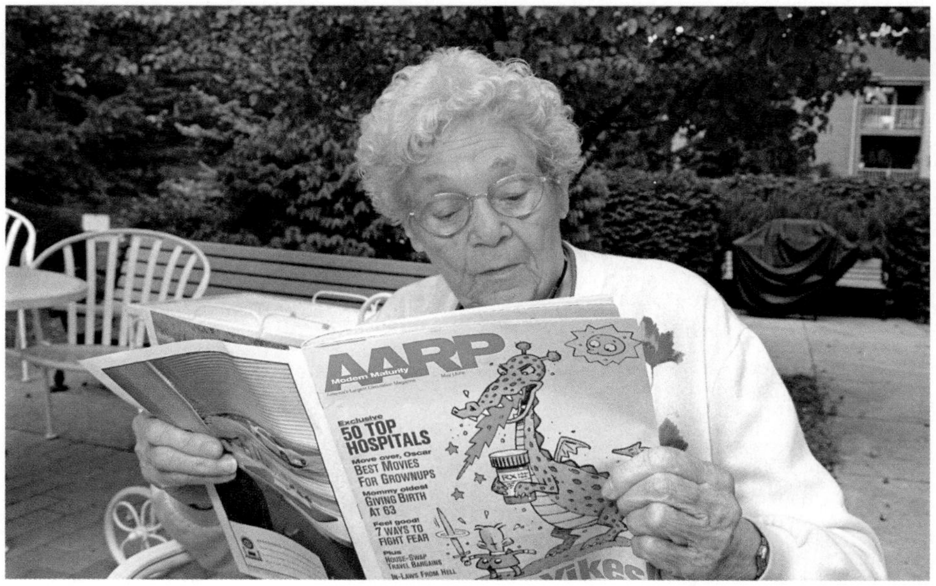

Many senior citizens rely on Social Security benefits to see them through their retirement years. The program covers more than 90 percent of the American workforce.

Social Security, enacted in 1935 and still the federal government's most popular social program. Social Security was designed to meet two goals: (1) provide a minimum income for poor beneficiaries, and (2) ensure that benefits bear a relationship to the amount of payroll taxes a beneficiary actually paid. Supported by equal contributions from employers and employees, the program now covers more than 90 percent of the U.S. workforce.[7]

Social Security
A combination of entitlement programs, paid for by employer and employee taxes, that includes retirement benefits, health insurance, and support for disabled workers and the children of deceased or disabled workers.

Social Security was expanded in 1939 to include financial support for survivors of workers covered by Social Security when the retired worker died, and in 1954 it was expanded again to include support for disabled workers and the children of deceased or disabled workers. Benefit levels were raised repeatedly during the first 40 years of the program, often just before an election. The increases became so frequent and so costly that in 1975 Congress finally indexed benefits to rise only with inflation. Under legislation enacted in 1983, the Social Security retirement age started to rise in 2003 and will reach 67 by the year 2027.

Until the 1970s, steady growth in Social Security benefits was relatively uncontroversial, largely because "the costs were initially deceptively low," making the system politically painless.[8] It is now the world's largest insurance program for retirees, survivors, and people with disabilities. In 2008, Social Security and Medicare expenditures totaled $966 billion.

Social Security, unlike many welfare programs, is financed not from general taxes but from taxes employers and employees pay into the Social Security trust fund under the Federal Insurance Contribution Act, commonly known as the FICA tax. As Congress has added the benefits mentioned earlier, it has not added enough money to the Social Security trust fund to cover the added expense. In 1983, Congress made a number of changes to deal with the shortfall. It raised the retirement age at which one qualifies for Social Security benefits, increased Social Security taxes, imposed the first-ever tax on the Social Security payments to upper-income individuals, and imposed a onetime cut in the annual cost-of-living increase in benefits.

Social Security taxes are now the largest tax most U.S. workers pay—indeed, three-quarters of workers now pay more in Social Security taxes than they pay in income tax. Employees paid a 6.2 percent FICA tax on all wages up to $94,200 in 2008, and an additional 1.45 percent on all of their wages, both above and below $94,200 for Medicare health coverage. All employee taxes are matched dollar for dollar by employers. People who are self-employed pay both the employee and employer taxes.

HISTORY MAKERS

Marian Wright Edelman

Marian Wright Edelman is one of the nation's strongest advocates for children. Born in South Carolina in 1939, she experienced racial segregation firsthand. Denied the right to enter public parks in her birthplace of Bennettsville, she played in a park her father built behind his church.

Despite these early racial barriers, Edelman earned her undergraduate degree at Spellman College, an historically black college, and a law degree from Yale University. She soon became the first African American woman admitted to practice law in Mississippi and became an active advocate of children's issues. She helped make sure Mississippi implemented the new federal law to give poor children a head start before entering school, and soon moved to Washington, D.C., to help organize Martin Luther King's Poor People's Campaign, which sought to improve the lives of the poor, young and old.

Marian Wright Edelman.

As the Poor People's Campaign came to an end, Edelman decided to start an entirely new organization that eventually became the Children's Defense Fund (CDF). It focused on a host of childhood and adolescent issues such as preventing teenage pregnancy, increasing federal funding for the Head Start program, and providing better health benefits for children. With poverty rates growing fastest among children, Edelman focused her energies on making sure children had a voice on Capitol Hill and in the White House.

As one of the nation's most visible interest groups, the Children's Defense Fund has a long reputation for legislative success. It lists more than 20 major victories on behalf of causes from improving foster care to increasing vaccination rates, providing greater access to child care, and increasing funding for food stamps. CDF is also deeply involved in reducing poverty among all U.S. citizens.

Read more about Marian Wright Edelman and her organization at www.childrensdefense.org.

QUESTIONS

1. Why do children need the help of advocacy groups such as the Children's Defense Fund?
2. Why might members of Congress oppose increased funding for children's programs such as school lunches?
3. Why do children's programs sometimes fail to reduce childhood poverty?

The aging of the U.S. population (discussed in Chapter 5) would not affect Social Security and Medicare if the payroll taxes coming into the two programs from today's workers were deposited in individual savings accounts for their eventual retirement. But much of the revenue actually goes to payments for *today's* retirees. Social Security is thus a "pay-as-you-go" system, in which today's young workers finance the retirement of today's elderly. At some point in the not-too-distant future, there will not be enough workers paying taxes to cover the benefits. Sooner or later, Congress will have to decide whether to raise taxes on workers, cut benefits for retirees, increase the retirement age, or some combination of all three. Experts differ on when the next Social Security funding crisis will come, but they agree that something will have to be done to ensure the viability of Social Security for young people now paying into the system.[9]

Social Security is one of three programs designed to help older workers. The second is **Medicare,** created in 1965. Medicare provides all reasonable hospital, medical, and prescription drug insurance to individuals who are also entitled to Social Security. The hospital insurance is funded by a portion of the Social Security taxes paid by people still working. It pays for inpatient hospital care, skilled nursing care, and other services. The medical insurance is funded by monthly premiums paid by enrollees and by general revenues, and it pays for a portion of doctors' fees, outpatient hospital visits, and other medical services and supplies. Experts believe that Medicare taxes will not cover the cost of the program as of 2017.

The third program for older people is Supplemental Security Income (SSI), which provides monthly payments to people with disabilities or those over age 65 who meet an income test. Levels of SSI support vary by state to reflect cost-of-living differences. SSI recipients also qualify for **Medicaid,** food stamps, and other assistance. SSI benefits are financed by general tax revenues.

Medicare
A national health insurance program for the elderly and disabled.

Medicaid
A federal program that provides medical benefits for low-income people.

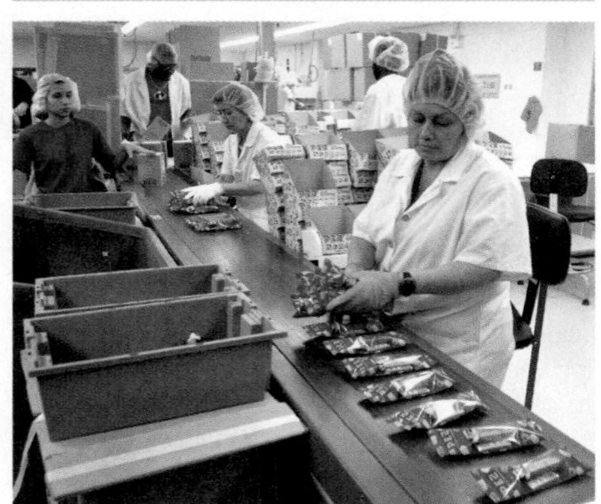
Many minimum-wage workers' incomes are below the poverty level.

Help for the Unemployed and Low-Income Workers Social Security was not the only strand of economic protection woven during the New Deal. Roosevelt's plan also produced the federal government's first unemployment insurance program enacted as part of the 1935 Social Security Act. Under the program, administered by state governments but funded in part by federal unemployment taxes, eligible workers can receive benefits for up to 26 weeks in most states. In periods of high unemployment, the federal government also provides funds for extended benefits up to 39 weeks in most states.

The federal government has passed many other laws to help low-income workers make ends meet, including a long list of job-training programs. Perhaps most important, the government established a minimum wage for all workers. Just 40 cents an hour in 1945, it has risen steadily over the years to $7.25 in 2009.

The New Deal also provided the foundation for passage of the Earned Income Tax Credit (EITC) in 1975. Under the EITC, low-income workers receive money back from the federal government to help raise their income. Because the money comes in the form of a tax refund, not a welfare check, many experts believe that low-income workers are less embarrassed to take this form of federal support.

The EITC has clearly reduced poverty rates among low-income workers. In 2004, for example, almost 21 million low-income workers received more than $36 billion through the program, which lifted almost 5 million out of poverty. The program has been particularly effective in helping unmarried working mothers, who often take minimum-wage jobs in the service industry (fast-food restaurants, dry cleaners, day care centers, grocery stores).

Job-training programs help low-income families improve their earning potential.

Help for the Poor The federal government began protecting women and children against poverty when Congress passed the Infancy and Maternity Protection Act of 1921. Supported by many of the same women's groups that had just won ratification of the Nineteenth Amendment, which gave women the right to vote, the act gave the newly created federal Children's Bureau funds to encourage states to create new maternal, infant, and early childhood health programs.

This precedent eventually produced the Aid to Families with Dependent Children (AFDC) program in 1935.[10] As its name suggests, AFDC tried to reduce public opposition to expanded benefits by shifting the focus away from what the mother had done or not done to deserve poverty, and onto the children, who suffered whatever the cause. Under the program, states were given federal money to establish cash grants for poor families under two conditions: states had to (1) match the federal funds with some contribution of their own, and (2) establish a means-test for all families receiving benefits.

Congress also established the school lunch program during the New Deal as a way to both feed the hungry and strengthen the ailing farm economy. The Federal Surplus Relief Corporation began purchasing surplus agriculture products for needy families in 1935 and launched the nation's first school lunch programs for poor children shortly thereafter. By 1941, more than five million children were receiving free school lunches, consuming more than 450 million pounds of surplus pork, dairy products, and bread. Although the program was disbanded during World War II because of food shortages, it was restored under the 1946 National School Lunch Act. As President Harry Truman said at the signing ceremony, "No nation is any healthier than its children." He could have added that many draftees had been rejected for service in World War II because of malnutrition.

The Great Society

The second major expansion of social policy came in the 1960s with what became known as the Great Society. At a commencement speech at the University of Michigan in May 1964, President Lyndon Johnson described his vision of the Great Society:

> The Great Society rests on abundance and liberty for all. It demands an end to poverty and racial injustice.... But that is just the beginning. The Great Society is a place where every child can find knowledge to enrich his mind and to enlarge his talents.... It is a challenge constantly renewed, beckoning us toward a destiny where the meaning of our lives matches the marvelous products of our labors.[11]

Johnson's agenda was as broad as his rhetoric, and Congress enacted much of it in a fairly short period of time. Great Society programs dramatically increased the role of the federal government in health, education, and welfare through a number of programs that continue to exist today:

- *Food stamps.* The food stamp program gives poor families coupons to purchase the basics of a healthy, nutritious diet. The average benefit is about $90 per person per month.
- *Head Start.* Head Start is a preschool program designed to help poor children get ready for kindergarten. The program serves more than 900,000 children each year at a cost of roughly $7,000 per child. Almost 30 percent of Head Start teachers and staff are parents of Head Start children or were Head Start children themselves.
- *Medicare.* As noted earlier, Medicare was created in 1965 to provide health care to older citizens. It is now the largest medical program in the federal budget and will soon cost more than Social Security.
- *Medicaid.* Medicaid was created in 1965 to provide basic health services for poor families. The program is administered and partially funded by state governments, and covers items such as hospital care and family planning.
- *Supplemental Security Income.* The SSI program was created in 1972 to provide an extra measure of support for the elderly, the poor, and the blind or disabled. The program provides monthly benefit checks ranging from just $1 to roughly $800 and is administered by the Social Security Administration.
- *Housing assistance.* The Department of Housing and Urban Development, which was created in 1965, administers a number of programs designed to help low-income families find affordable, safe housing, in part by giving property owners subsidies to make up the difference between what tenants can pay and what the local housing market will bear.

Welfare Reform

LEARNING **OBJECTIVE**

4 Evaluate the impact of welfare reform.

Reforming Welfare

Republicans have not been the only critics of the New Deal and Great Society welfare programs. President Bill Clinton made welfare reform a centerpiece of his reelection agenda in 1996, promising to "end welfare as we know it."[12]

Working with the new Republican congressional majority, Clinton won passage of the Personal Responsibility and Work Opportunity Reconciliation Act in 1996, which replaced the New Deal's AFDC with Temporary Assistance for Needy Families (TANF).

Under the new rules, federally funded public assistance is limited to five years over a person's lifetime, and all recipients must enter some kind of work training program within two months of receiving initial benefits. Although states can exempt up to 20 percent of cases

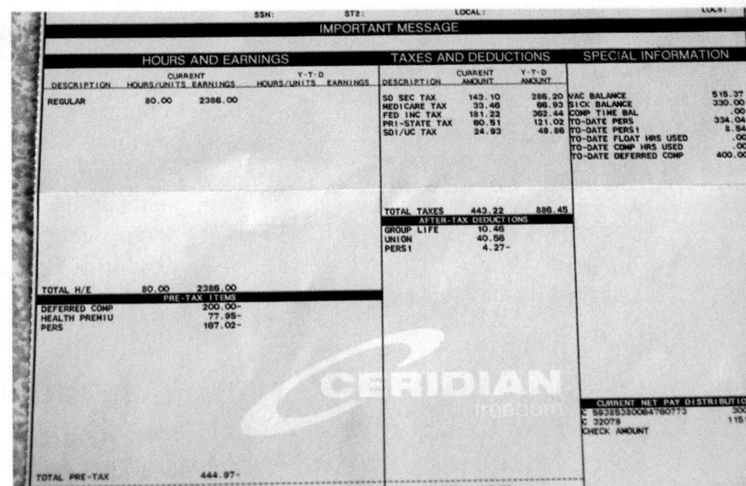

Social Security and Medicare taxes are withdrawn from regular paychecks and are called payroll taxes.

YOU WILL DECIDE | Should the Federal Government Promote Marriage?

Although the 1996 welfare reform legislation focused on replacing welfare with work, it also ordered the federal government to promote marriage. Advocates argue that marriage improves the lives of both children and parents. Married adults, whether women or men, are happier, healthier, and wealthier than their unmarried peers and are more likely to give their children a healthier start in life. Some advocates even argue that more marriages would reduce health costs by reducing depression and crime.[15]

The federal government can promote marriage in two ways. First, it can reduce the penalties it imposes on welfare recipients who get married. Under current law, for example, a single mother working full time at a minimum-wage job who marries stands to lose as much as $8,000 a year in cash and noncash benefits. Second, it can promote marriage through advertising, counseling, or even providing cash grants for getting married.

from the work requirements and time limits—an exemption intended for blind and disabled persons—the message to recipients is clear: Find work soon.

The law originally excluded legal immigrants from many welfare programs, but at the strong urging of the governors, most welfare benefits were later restored to legal immigrants. To discourage people on welfare from moving to states with more generous assistance payments, the law gave states the option of limiting welfare to newcomers from other states. This provision was declared unconstitutional by a federal district court judge, however, who said it "denies 'equal protection of the laws' to indigent families moving from one state to another."[13]

There are several ways to measure the success of the 1996 welfare reform. One is simply to ask whether the number of welfare recipients has declined. By 2002, the number of welfare recipients was lower than it had been in more than three decades. As the authors of a 2002 study of welfare reform argue, "The welfare rolls have declined greatly, more mothers than ever are working, the average income of female-headed families is increasing, and poverty has dropped substantially."[14] The number continued to fall in 2003 despite the economic downturn. As of March 2004, which is the most recent information available, the total number of people who received federal welfare benefits had fallen to 4.8 million, 60 percent fewer than in August 1996 when the reforms were enacted.

Yet merely reducing the number of welfare recipients does not guarantee that they either have good-paying jobs or are moving out of poverty. It is one thing to remove a recipient from the welfare rolls and quite another to get the person into a good job with decent benefits. Research suggests that most recipients make the minimum wage. However, most recipients who leave welfare have other expenses, such as transportation and child care, that may or may not be covered by state or local assistance, and many who go to work lose their food stamps and Medicaid, which means they are more dependent on food banks and have to go without preventive health care.

Social Policy Challenges for the Future: Health, Education, and Crime

Comparing Health Systems

Even if states take on a greater social policy role, the federal government is sure to remain the greatest source of funding for the safety net. As Figure 19–1 shows, human resource spending for programs such as Social Security, Medicare, Medicaid, and child nutrition has doubled since 1950. Spending is almost certain to rise in coming years as the baby boom generation enters retirement and starts to draw down the Social Security surplus and use Medicare. The federal social policy agenda will likely expand as Congress and the president respond to public pressure for action on health care, education, and crime control.

The Federal Role in Health Care

Medicare is just one of the federal government's many health programs. It has been instrumental in reducing disease since 1887, when the federal government opened a one-room laboratory on Staten Island, New York, to study infectious diseases carried to the United States on passenger ships. In time, that one-room laboratory expanded into the National Institutes of Health (NIH), a conglomeration of 37 separate institutes on a 300-acre campus in Bethesda, Maryland.

The surgeon general of the United States is arguably the most visible health care official in government. As head of the Public Health Service (PHS), the surgeon general oversees a diverse array of health care researchers at NIH and elsewhere. Federally funded researchers study causes and seek cures for serious diseases. The PHS also grants fellowships for health research to scientists and physicians and administers grants to states and local communities to help improve public health. Another federal agency promoting health is the Food and Drug Administration (FDA), which oversees the development of new drugs and ensures food safety through inspections of the nation's food supply.

Dozens of other federal agencies work to improve public health. The Centers for Disease Control and Prevention (CDC) in Atlanta is also actively engaged in preventing disease. The CDC and its 7,800 "disease detectives" have been at the forefront of identifying a host of mystery illnesses, including the respiratory disease that attacked attendees at an American Legion convention in 1976 (Legionnaire's disease), toxic shock syndrome in 1980, and hepatitis C in 1989, while tracking down the causes of major health disasters, including the outbreak of the SARS upper-respiratory virus in 2003 and 2004 and bird flu starting in 2006.

THINKING IT THROUGH

Although the federal government has long engaged in activities designed to promote vaccinating children, quitting smoking, wearing seat belts, and driving under 55 miles per hour, not everyone believes that promoting marriage is the answer to welfare.

Critics note, for example, that domestic violence and child abuse occur almost as frequently in married as in unmarried households. They also worry that government grants for marriage would promote a rash of false marriages designed to get the cash. Most important, opponents believe that the best way to encourage marriage among welfare recipients is to find them good-paying jobs. They look to states such as Minnesota that have created strong welfare-to-work programs that do not punish married women for getting a job.

Nevertheless, marriage appears to affect income. Two paychecks are better than one, and married couples may be more likely to save money for the future. Marital stability also positively influences child well-being on several measures, and marriage fosters healthier living habits as the marriage partners help monitor each other in such areas as smoking, weight gain, and drug use. These effects can be benefits to society in general.

The question, however, is whether they are a consequence of marriage or simply a product of adults living together. Absent a solid answer, support for marriage may be an indicator of a person's ideology and religion than a position based on careful research.

Questions

1. Should the federal government promote social values such as vaccinations or marriage?
2. How is promoting marriage similar to and different from other federal programs such as the antismoking campaign?
3. Why is marriage considered a way to reduce poverty? Are there other or better ways to achieve the same goal?

You Are the President of MEDICORP

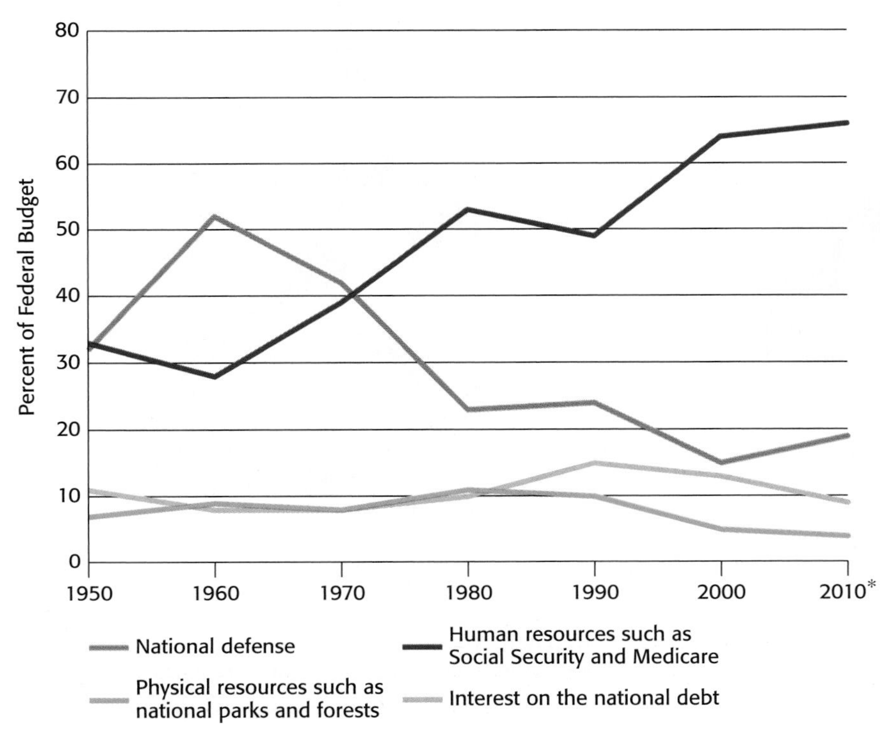

FIGURE 19–1
Changing Priorities in the Federal Budget.

SOURCE: Historical Tables, *Budget of the United States, Fiscal Year 2009* (U.S. Government Printing Office, February 2008).

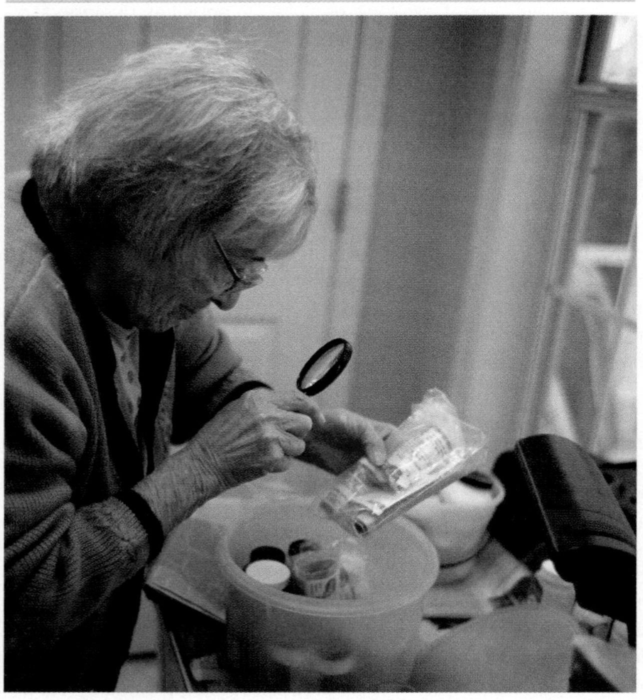

The cost of prescription drugs places a strain on senior citizens and underinsured wage earners.

Despite its success in improving the nation's health, the federal government faces two major health care challenges in the future: containing costs and expanding coverage.

The Rising Cost of Health Care Health care costs in the United States have nearly quadrupled, after controlling for inflation, since 1970.[16] Although they slowed with the rest of the economy in 2001, costs are expected to escalate rapidly as the nation ages over the next two decades.

All workers pay for the increasing health care costs. Although employers provide insurance to three of five working adults, they have steadily increased the share of insurance that employees must pay, including increased premiums, higher deductibles, and partial payments for services. Taxpayers also pay for these increases through federal dollars that might otherwise go to other programs such as homeland security, college loans, or highway construction. (Figures 19–2 and 19–3 show where health care dollars go and where they come from.)

The good news is that costs have risen in part because people are living longer. Average life expectancy increased by more than five years between 1970 and 1995. In 1900, only 1 of every 25 American adults was over age 65. By 1950, the number was 1 in 12, and by 1985, 1 in 9. According to experts, the number will rise to 1 in 5 by 2030. In 1900, the average American adult lived to age 47; by 2000, the average had increased to 79. Again according to experts, the number will rise into the mid-80s by 2030.

As people live longer, of course, they place greater demands on the health care system, as well as on the Social Security program. New and advanced medical technology—life-support systems, ultrasound, sophisticated x-ray equipment, and genetic counseling—have all increased the costs of health care. Longer life expectancies also place greater demands on other social policies, subtracting from funding for public assistance and other forms of social insurance.

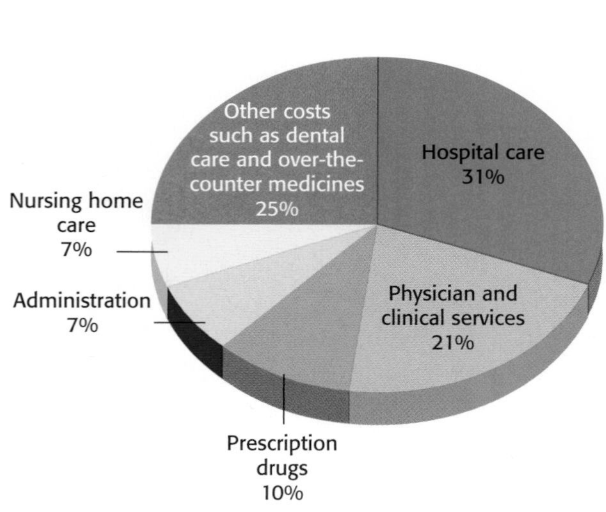

FIGURE 19–2
Where the Health Care Dollar Was Spent, 2006.

SOURCE: Centers for Medicare and Medicaid Services, Office of the Actuary, National Statistics Group, www.cms.hhs.gov/NationalHealthExpendData/downloads/PieChartSourcesExpenditures2006.pdf.

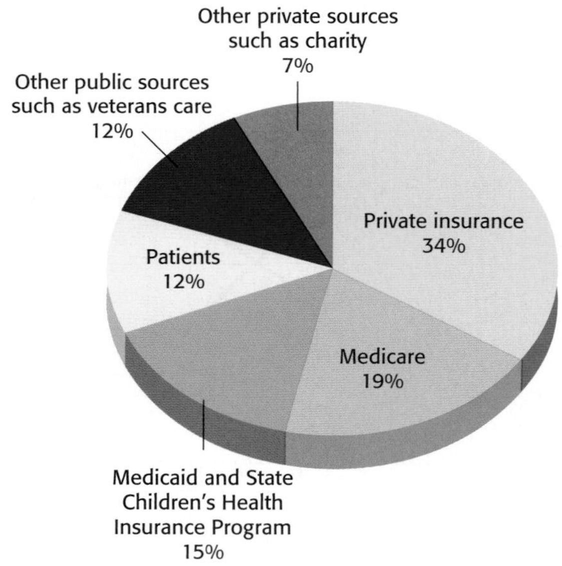

FIGURE 19–3
Where the Health Care Dollar Came From, 2006.

SOURCE: Centers for Medicare and Medicaid Services, Office of the Actuary, National Statistics Group, www.cms.hhs.gov/NationalHealthExpendData/downloads/PieChartSourcesExpenditures2006.pdf.

The bad news is that some costs have nothing to do with saving lives or preventing disease. Some physicians claim they have to perform procedures such as laboratory tests that may be medically unnecessary but are essential to reduce the risk of being sued by patients. These procedures are alleged to add up to billions of dollars in unnecessary costs, but they do not necessarily improve the quality of care provided to patients.[17]

In addition, costs have risen because of new technologies that are now widely available. Nuclear magnetic imaging, or as it is more commonly known, magnetic resonance imaging (MRI), is now routinely used to diagnose a host of diseases easily detected through more traditional tests. Once a medical center purchases this kind of expensive technology, its physicians are given incentives to use it, which increases patients' health care costs.

At least part of the cost crisis is avoidable. Medicare alone spends billions of dollars each year treating smoking-related diseases, and over the next 20 years the costs to treat such diseases will continue to rise. Other illnesses at least partly related to lifestyle choices include heart disease, liver disease, HIV/AIDS, and the epidemic of health disorders caused or made worse by obesity, such as diabetes. As Figures 19–2 and 19–3 show, most of these costs are covered by public or private insurance, not by individuals, which means there is little incentive for patients to say "no" to unnecessary or expensive treatment.

LEARNING **OBJECTIVE**

5 Analyze the causes of and solutions for the lack of health coverage for all Americans.

Covering the Uninsured Despite passage of the Medicare program, the nation has yet to develop a comprehensive insurance program for the approximately 60 million people who are uninsured at some point in any given year.[18] Although some rely on public clinics, emergency room care, or charity, many people go without any health or dental care.[19] Many of the uninsured have jobs, but their employers do not provide health insurance, and because their incomes are above the poverty line, they do not qualify for Medicaid. Uninsured individuals usually seek care in hospital emergency rooms only when their illness has reached a critical stage. Postponing medical care drives up costs because critical care is much more expensive than preventive medicine or early treatment.

But it is not just the poor who are uninsured. People who change jobs may often go without coverage for several months before their new insurance takes effect. Those who lose jobs lose their insurance. And people with serious medical conditions may find a new insurance company unwilling to cover their expenses, claiming that the illness is a "preexisting condition." Some insurance companies set caps on their coverage, leaving families that are coping with very expensive illnesses essentially uninsured.

Although there are many different proposals for health care reform, the essential approaches include a single-payer system, prepaid health plans, required employer coverage, spending caps, individual responsibility, and medical savings accounts.

Government Insurance Under a single-payer system, the national government, using broad-based taxes, covers the costs of health care and hospitalization and sets the rates. Like the system in Canada, such a plan would provide universal coverage and benefits to *all* citizens. Proponents claim that a government system would save billions of dollars in administrative expenses by reducing the number of insurers from about 1,200 to 1.

Opponents claim that it would lead to new bureaucracy with little incentive for innovation, cost control, or diversity of coverage. They further claim that the government would be put in the position of deciding which procedures to pay for and how to ration access to them. As a result, they contend, citizens would lose not only quality in their health care but freedom of choice as well.

Business leaders generally oppose government coverage out of concern for costs and what the program would do to taxes and the federal budget. The American Medical Association, U.S. Chamber of Commerce, Health Insurance Association of America, and other interest groups representing health care providers oppose the single-payer system. Labor unions, some senior citizens' groups, and most consumer groups advocate this type of plan, however, in part because Medicare has been so successful in covering older citizens, though at a growing cost. If Medicare works for older people, the argument goes, perhaps it could work for younger ones as well.

HOW **OTHER NATIONS** GOVERN

Wealth and Health

Because nations vary greatly in their gross domestic product, some provide much better health care than others. According to the World Health Organization (WHO), which monitors health trends on behalf of the United Nations, the world spent $4 trillion on health care in 2007. But 80 percent of the total was consumed by just 20 percent of the world's nations, all of which have the wealth to make sure children are protected against diseases such as malaria and tuberculosis and to extend life expectancy through advanced treatments for life-threatening diseases such cancer, heart disease, and HIV/AIDS.

Poor nations face serious problems in providing health care to their citizens, including shortages of physicians, nurses, and other health personnel, who can find higher-paying jobs in other nations. They also lack enough high-quality medical facilities, which can cost millions of dollars to build and operate. The health of people in poor countries also suffers because of pollution, poor diet, war, and natural disasters.

As a result, these citizens are more likely to contract life-threatening diseases and enter treatment later than citizens in rich countries, both factors that contribute to higher death rates. Again according to WHO, citizens in the poorest nations around the world are also more likely to engage in risky behavior. They are much more likely to smoke cigarettes than citizens of wealthy nations, for example, in part because tobacco companies advertise heavily in poor countries and in part because poor governments do not have the funds to mount campaigns against smoking.

These inequalities are easy to spot in basic statistics on health such as life expectancy and infant mortality. Life expectancy measures the average age of death, while infant mortality measures the number of children who die before the age 1.

Britain, Japan, and the United States are among the richest nations in the world and have the lowest infant mortality and longest life expectancies as a result. In turn, China, India, Mexico, and especially Nigeria show the impact of greater poverty. The relationships are not perfect—the United States spends far more than Britain on health care, for example, yet still has a slightly higher infant mortality rate. But the basic relationship still stands.

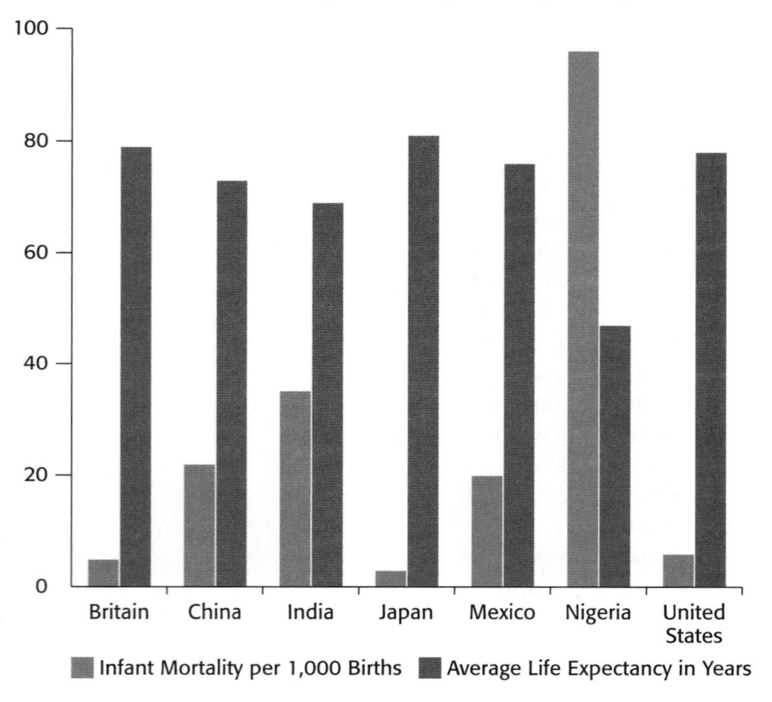

SOURCE: World Health Organization, *World Health Statistics, 2007* (World Health Organization, 2008).

QUESTIONS

1. Why are tobacco companies advertising more in poor nations?
2. How and why might governments in poor countries impede the delivery of health services?
3. Do poor citizens in rich countries get the same quality of care as wealthy citizens? If not, why not?

Prepaid Health Plans Cost containment has been a frequent refrain of large corporations and consumer groups. In the 1970s and 1980s, business owners reduced benefits, increased payments by employees, and encouraged employees to join managed care plans called **health maintenance organizations (HMOs),** in which individuals or their employees pay a set amount for each person covered each year in return for health care and hospital coverage. During the 1980s and 1990s, HMO enrollment increased fourfold, from fewer than 10 million in 1980 to more than 80 million in 2006. Most HMOs guarantee access, but many do not guarantee that a patient can see the same physician each time.

health maintenance organization (HMO) An alternative means of health care in which people or their employers are charged a set amount and the HMO provides health care and covers hospital costs.

Required Employer Coverage Currently more than 161 million U.S. workers get some form of medical insurance from their employers. But many small businesses contend that they cannot afford to provide this benefit and stay in business. Some have estimated the costs of health care for small businesses at 10 to 40 percent higher than for large businesses. In businesses with fewer than 25 employees, only about one-third of workers receive coverage directly from their employer. Mandating coverage does not solve this problem, nor does it take care of individuals who do not have jobs or who are self-employed.

Proponents counter that tax credits and government subsidies can address the negative consequences of required coverage. They also point out that if *all* small businesses provide health insurance, none of them will be at a competitive disadvantage. The federal government allows businesses to deduct what they pay in health benefits to employees as a business expense and gives tax credits to low-income families to purchase coverage for their children.

Spending Caps Because the cost of providing health care each year consumes a larger and larger share of our gross domestic product, some want the national government to impose an overall expenditure cap on health care that applies not only to public expenditures but to private ones as well.

The American Hospital Association, American Medical Association, and Pharmaceutical Manufacturers Association vigorously oppose the idea. They argue that spending caps would limit research and development in medicine and deter talented young people from pursuing medical careers. They also argue that a spending cap would lead to rationing of some services such as advanced tests for cancer and the use of sophisticated technologies for detecting disease.

However, the costs associated with an aging population may yet lead to some form of spending caps and the health rationing that would clearly go with them.

Individual Responsibility for Coverage Another reform proposal is to apply a free market approach to health care by abolishing *all* employer-provided benefits and encouraging individuals to buy health insurance on their own, in much the same way that individuals are responsible for purchasing their own automobile insurance. Those with low incomes, including people not now insured, would receive tax credits or vouchers to help them purchase insurance.

Advocates say this mandated coverage would reward individuals who pay more attention to medical costs. Just as safe drivers pay less for their automobile insurance, perhaps healthier individuals would be less likely to visit their doctor or emergency room for routine illnesses such as the common cold or flu. Opponents argue that many people would be unable to pay for insurance at all.

Medical Savings Accounts In 1996, Congress authorized an experiment with **health savings accounts** to which employees may make tax-deductible contributions to pay for medical expenses not covered by insurance or government.[20] As of 2008, caps on allowed contributions are $2,900 for individuals and $5,800 for families. Withdrawals for nonmedical purposes are taxable and subject to an early-withdrawal penalty.

Supporters of health savings accounts say they will eventually lower health care costs by giving people the incentive to spend their own money more carefully. They also allow people to go to a doctor of their own choosing without prior approval from their insurance company. Opponents say these accounts amount to nothing more than a tax break for the wealthy and the healthy. Because of high deductibles, people may decide not to seek needed services and preventive care. Opponents also argue that because healthier people are more likely to sign up for health savings accounts, sicker people will pay higher insurance premiums. Older and less wealthy people cannot afford to invest in health savings accounts, critics charge, and will be forced to depend on more expensive insurance.

LEARNING **OBJECTIVE**

 Assess the tools of federal education and crime policy.

medical savings account
An alternative means of health care in which individuals make tax-deductible contributions to a special account that can be used to pay medical expenses.

The Federal Role in Education

The federal government has been a partner in education at least since the Northwest Ordinance of 1785, in which Congress set aside land in every township for a public school. In 1862, the Morrill Land-Grant Colleges Act provided grants of land to states for universities specializing in the mechanical or agricultural arts. The U.S. Office of Education was established in 1867 to oversee these programs, but the scope of federal involvement was modest by today's standards. Even the G.I. Bill, which helped provide a college education for approximately 20 million World War II veterans, was seen more as an employment program than an educational one.

During the cold war, however, education became one part of the national defense. When the Soviet Union launched *Sputnik*—the first human-made satellite to orbit the earth—in 1957, Congress responded in 1958 by passing the National Defense Education Act to upgrade science, language, and mathematics courses.

Elementary and Secondary Education Kindergarten through high school education is generally seen as a state and local responsibility. Most children go to public schools run by local school boards and funded, at least partly, by property taxes. Because school districts vary greatly in the wealth of their residents, children from poor districts are much more likely to have lower-quality public schools than those from wealthier districts. As a result, public schools vary in the quality of teacher preparation, student performance, dropout rates, and educational opportunities provided to minority students.

Although the federal government has been reluctant to make direct investments in poor school districts, it has tried to help the children those districts serve. For example, in 1964, Congress created the Head Start program to help needy children learn to read and understand numbers. Head Start centers also provide healthy meals and snacks and monitor child health care. Many also work with parents to encourage greater involvement and literacy.

Recent evaluations suggest that Head Start does increase learning but needs improvement. In 2008, Head Start provided funding to more than 20,000 child care centers with almost 50,000 classrooms, some of which reported chronic shortages of well-trained teachers. The student–teacher ratio also varied significantly across centers. Moreover, the program is not an entitlement, meaning funding covers only about a third of eligible children. When the dollars run out, Head Start centers stop enrolling participants.

Head Start is not the federal government's only education program, however. In 1965, Congress passed the Elementary and Secondary Education Act (ESEA), which supplied educational materials for underprivileged public school students and provided funding for research on how to help children from disadvantaged backgrounds. Over the years, the act was amended to provide federal support for special education, as well as additional funding for textbooks, teacher training, and other support for poor schools. In 2006, the federal government contributed just 9 cents on the dollar of public school spending.

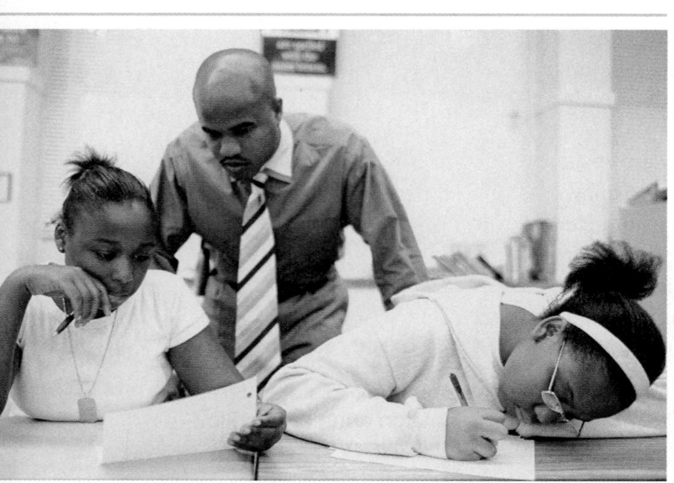

There have been many efforts to improve the performance of public schools, including the No Child Left Behind Act. Here, a teacher for the nongovernmental Knowledge Is Power Program (KIPP) works with poor children to improve their performance.

As concerns about the quality of public education increased during the 1990s, however, the federal government became more engaged in local education, first by setting national goals for student achievement, then by passing the No Child Left Behind Act in 2002. Under the act, in return for federal funding, states were required to annually test at least 95 percent of all third and eighth graders in reading and math. In addition, states were required to grade schools as passing or failing, set higher standards for teachers, and give students in failing schools the option to move to higher-performing schools. Schools must either improve test scores each year or risk being labeled "in need of improvement." Under the act, all students are supposed to be proficient in reading and math by 2014.

Although the new law set higher standards, it increased federal spending for education by only a tiny percentage. By 2006, many states were complaining they did not have enough funding to test every student every year or to meet the law's requirement for teacher training and certification. In addition, schools with many disabled or special-needs students were being unfairly categorized as "failing" because they could not meet the test-score requirement.

Parents ask more of their schools than just to educate their children. Schools are now a major means of providing basic nutrition to millions of poor children. They screen at-risk children and attempt to get them medical and psychological assistance; they seek to socialize students into acceptable behaviors, often in the face of increasing violence in the surrounding neighborhoods; and they often reach out to families to provide basic help in parenting.

Higher Education The federal government also provides help to colleges and universities. In 2008, the federal government provided roughly 70 percent, or more than $25 billion, of the financial aid that college students receive. Pell grants for low-income students and low-interest guaranteed student loans continue to be the most available and most used subsidies for college expenses.

In 1998, Congress added three new programs to improve the odds that needy children will make it to college: (1) GEAR-UP, which supports early interventions to help students complete high school; (2) the Learning Anytime Anywhere Partnerships (LAAP), which provide federal funding for distance learning through the Internet; and (3) a new initiative designed to improve teacher quality in primary and elementary schools. Although the three programs account for less than 1 percent of federal spending for education, they acknowledge the link between the quality of primary and elementary education and college success, as well as the need to act early to increase the odds of success for needy students.

The Federal Role in Crime Control

Like education, controlling crime is primarily a state and local matter. The federal government has passed sweeping legislation helping state and local governments pay for crime control and usually acts more as a banker than a police officer, providing grants to states and local governments to hire their own police officers, build more prisons, improve drug enforcement, and prosecute organized crime. The federal government must also enforce its own laws against activities such as counterfeiting and pollution while protecting the borders and preventing drugs from flowing into the country.

In a 1994 anticrime bill Congress funded the hiring of as many as 100,000 new police officers and the construction of new prisons and "boot camps" for juvenile offenders. The bill also added new assault rifle restrictions, made a long list of federal offenses punishable by death, imposed federal penalties and programs aimed at curbing domestic violence, and, with its "three strikes and you're out" provision, mandated life imprisonment on conviction for a third violent felony. This "three strikes" provision exists at both the federal level and in many states; the U.S. Supreme Court recently upheld it against an Eighth Amendment challenge.[21]

The federal government enforces its laws primarily through the Department of Justice, which contains the Federal Bureau of Investigation (FBI). The FBI was created in 1908 and charged with gathering and reporting evidence in matters relating to federal criminal laws. In addition, the FBI provides fingerprint identification and laboratory services to local law enforcement on a cooperative basis and has new responsibilities in the war on terrorism. Other law enforcement agencies of the federal government include the Drug Enforcement Agency (DEA), which is responsible for preventing the flow of illegal narcotics and other illegal drugs into the United States, patrolling U.S. borders, and conducting joint operations with countries where drugs are produced. The Bureau of Alcohol, Tobacco, Firearms, and Explosives monitors the sale of destructive weapons and guns inside the United States, regulates alcoholic beverage production, and oversees the collection of taxes on alcohol and tobacco.

Terrorism is clearly the federal government's top crime priority today. Only weeks after the September 11, 2001, terrorist attacks on New York City and Washington, D.C., Congress passed a massive antiterrorism law, and it created the new Department of Homeland Security the following summer. For his part, the president created the Office of Homeland Security within the White House in October 2001, merging 22 agencies and 180,000 federal employees, and ordered a complete reorganization of the Federal Bureau of Investigation in early 2002 to create a stronger focus on preventing terrorism. Although the nation is no doubt safer as a result, if only because the 22 agencies did not cooperate

THE CHANGING FACE OF U.S. POLITICS

Access to College, 2000–2008

Federal aid to education has increased access to college for all American students, but it has had a particularly significant effect on women and people of color at both the community college and four-year levels, where women now earn the majority of associate and bachelor degrees, and where students of color have more than doubled over the decades. Under the 1998 Higher Education Act, the number of students of color should increase even faster as the federal government puts more dollars into preparing students for college.

Although two-year and four-year colleges have seen an increase in enrollments by both women and minority students, growth has been fastest at two-year colleges, which tend to have lower tuition. They are increasingly the destination of choice for many students unable to afford four-year colleges, or who start at two-year colleges to save money, then transfer to four-year institutions.

QUESTIONS

1. Why has there been such a sudden change in the number of women attending college?
2. Has diversity increased at your college or university? Why or why not?

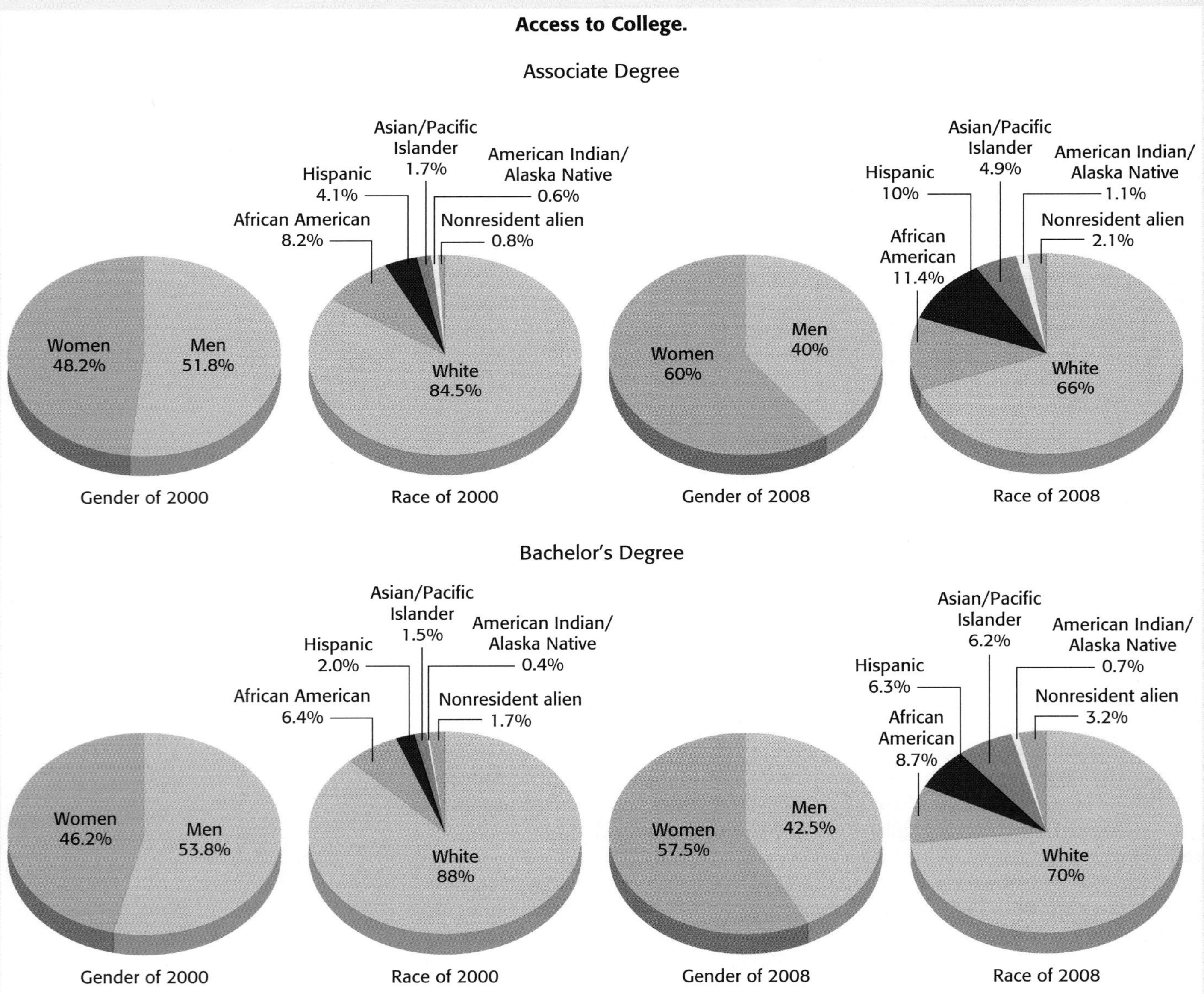

SOURCE: U.S. Department of Education, National Center for Education Statistics, *Postsecondary Institutions in the United States: Fall 2003 and Degrees and Other Awards Conferred: 2002–04* (U.S. Government Printing Office, 2007), www.nces.ed.gov/fastfacts.

well with each other before the merger, the new department has been criticized as too large to move quickly against terrorist threats. It failed to react nimbly to Hurricane Katrina in August and September 2005, for example, and has yet to implement new policies to monitor cargo containers that enter U.S. ports. These containers are seen as a major threat because they can be used to hide a potential biological, chemical, or nuclear weapon.

Under the USA PATRIOT Act of 2001 (the letters stand for Uniting and Strengthening America by Providing Appropriate Tools Required to Intercept and Obstruct Terrorism), the federal government was given sweeping authority to conduct secret investigations of suspected terrorists. Those investigations may use "roving wiretaps" to intercept conversations on any phones a suspect may use, and detain any noncitizens believed to be a national security risk for up to seven days without charging them with a crime. Although the USA PATRIOT Act expired on December 31, 2005, the Bush administration made its renewal a centerpiece of the president's second-term agenda. The administration also asked Congress to expand the government's authority to investigate what it called "lone-wolf" terrorists who are not affiliated with a foreign government or known terrorist organization such as Al-Qaeda, which planned the September 11 attacks. The act was finally reauthorized in February 2006.[22]

The Politics of Social Policy

Social policy is a major focus of American politics. Welfare, health care, education, and crime—and their costs—are important political battlegrounds between the parties and between contending interest groups, second only to the economy and national security. The nation long ago answered questions about whether the national government has a role in providing decent housing, adequate health care, and a solid education for all citizens. The question is not whether the nation will provide a safety net for its needy citizens, but how strong the net will be and who will be responsible for providing it. Although most American adults support Social Security and Medicare, for example, they are sharply divided over how much the nation should do for its poorest citizens. They are also increasingly divided about reforms such as the No Child Left Behind Act and its mandatory testing, which have prompted some states to sue the federal government to recover some of the costs of implementing the unfunded mandate portions of the act.

Nevertheless, social policy will be part of the federal agenda far into the future. Although presidents and Congress cannot always know what voters will support and how much they are willing to pay, they can be sure that most want government to take care of citizens who are needy through no fault of their own. Although college graduates are less likely to encounter social or economic crisis, a minority will eventually fall into the social safety net. Efforts to maintain the safety net not only are good for society as a whole, but may help at least some of the readers of this book.

Citizens can influence social policy in several ways. One is to join interest groups that represent the needy or taxpayers. Another is to write letters to their members of Congress when significant legislation such as prescription drug coverage comes to a vote. They can also volunteer for specific programs that are designed to help the needy, especially programs that are administered by charities. Although the federal government has created dozens of programs to help the needy, the nation still relies heavily on charities to fill gaps in coverage, whether through food pantries and soup kitchens or early childhood programs. In turn, these programs rely on volunteers.

CHAPTER **SUMMARY**

1 Explain the difference between entitlements and means-tested entitlements.

Entitlements such as Social Security and veterans benefits are provided to any individual, rich or poor, who meets the basic category of coverage such as having served in the military. Means-tested entitlements are available only to individuals whose level of income and other assets such as a home or savings account fall below a specific maximum usually related to the poverty rate.

2 Compare and contrast the two types of social policy.

The two types of social policy are public assistance (usually means-tested) and social insurance. Public assistance takes many forms, including direct payments to the poor, the unemployed, and the disabled; food stamps; job training; housing subsidies; free school lunches; tax credits; and subsidized medical care. Social insurance (usually an entitlement) is provided to anyone who has paid enough in contributions to receive support after meeting certain requirements such as reaching retirement age.

3 Identify the major contributions of the New Deal and the Great Society to social policy.

These two eras produced the largest number of social programs. The New Deal created a number of public assistance and social insurance programs such as job training for the unemployed, Social Security, and Aid to Families with Dependent Children; the Great Society produced help for the homeless, more job training, and Medicare.

4 Evaluate the impact of welfare reform.

Welfare has long been criticized as discouraging work, and many proposals have been put forward to make programs more effective and efficient. The most recent welfare reform, which became law in 1996, transferred the administrative burden to the states, giving them more discretion over recipients and benefits while helping to fund welfare programs through block grants of federal money.

5 Analyze the causes of and solutions for the lack of health coverage for all Americans.

The lack of coverage for all Americans is related to the rapidly rising cost of health care, which reflects the aging of society, along with medical malpractice insurance and new technologies. Despite the costs, a variety of proposals for universal health coverage are under consideration, including a single-payer system, prepaid health plans, employer-mandated coverage, spending caps, individual responsibility for coverage, and medical savings accounts.

6 Assess the tools of federal education and crime policy.

Education and crime continue to be primarily state and local government functions in the United States. However, the federal government plays an important role in funding public schools and pushing national goals for better education and is also heavily engaged in helping finance college and university education. Crime control has also been part of the national agenda for decades, especially related to drugs, but has become much more visible as part of the war on terrorism.

Chapter Self-Test

1. Which are means-tested entitlement programs? (p. 517–518)
   a. Programs that have exhibited financial viability
   b. Programs that have been researched by a congressional committee
   c. Programs that give funds only to those who have a proven individual need
   d. Federal programs that have been successfully used at the state level
2. In a short essay, identify the two types of programs the federal government uses to protect citizens against hardship. What are the requirements to receive each type of protection? On which type did the government spend more money in 2008? Analyze the connection between eligibility requirements and levels of spending. (pp. 517–521)
3. Which of the following is *not* a social insurance program? (p. 00)
   a. Medicare
   b. Food stamps
   c. Social Security
   d. Disability Insurance
4. Which of the following was a major goal of Social Security when it was created in 1935? (p. 522)
   a. To provide an alternative to welfare programs
   b. To help veterans transition financially after active duty
   c. To provide elderly citizens with a consistent income
   d. To provide a minimum income floor for poor beneficiaries
5. Identify each social program with the appropriate period—the New Deal, or the Great Society. (pp. 521–525)
   a. Food stamps
   b. Medicare
   c. Head Start
   d. Social Security
   e. Federal Emergency Relief Administration
   f. Works Progress Administration
   g. Civilian Conservation Corps
6. In a short essay, analyze the future of Social Security. Consider how it is funded and what steps Congress may have to take to ensure its continued existence. (pp. 522–523)
7. Explain how the Personal Responsibility and Work Opportunity Reconciliation Act of 1996 affected the number of people who receive welfare assistance in the United States. What charges have critics of this change made? Why do others see the Act in a positive light? (pp. 525–526)
8. What is one way the government can promote marriage? (pp. 526–527)
   a. Increase welfare funds for children
   b. Increase welfare funds for those who are married
   c. Reduce the penalties on welfare recipients who get married
   d. Provide expanded Social Security benefits for those who are married

9. In a short essay, describe the effect average life expectancy, new medical technology, and employer-based health insurance each have on the rising cost of health care. Explain one possible way to reduce health care costs. (pp. 526–531)

10. What was the largest category of health care spending in 2006? (p. 528)
    a. Hospital care
    b. Prescription drugs
    c. Nursing home care
    d. Unnecessary surgery

11. What is one claim some have made against a single-payer, universal health care system? (p. 529)
    a. That it would increase the unemployment rate
    b. That it would reduce the overall quality of health care
    c. That it would leave little incentive for cost controls
    d. That it would reduce health care coverage in the event of catastrophic illnesses

12. In a short essay, identify and describe four proposals for health care reform. What is one way each of these proposals improves the current health care system? What is one way each does not? (pp. 526–531)

13. What has been one of the main criticisms of the No Child Left Behind Act, passed in 2002? (pp. 532–533)
    a. It reduced the amount of federal funding available to states
    b. It made it more difficult for illegal immigrants to obtain an education
    c. It changed the requirements for students to graduate from high school
    d. It increased federal spending on education by only a tiny percentage

14. Which of the following is the basis for Congress' power to regulate the sale of guns? (p. 533)
    a. Every state has victims of gun violence
    b. Guns must be registered with the federal government
    c. Many victims of gun violence are women and minorities
    d. Guns are manufactured and transported across state lines.

15. In a short essay, compare the circumstances that prompted the No Child Left Behind Act with those that gave rise to an earlier social program—food stamps, Head Start, or Social Security, for instance. Identify and analyze concerns with No Child Left Behind in light of U.S. experience with long-running social programs. (pp. 532–533)

Key Terms

entitlements, p. 517

means-tested entitlements, p. 517

social safety net, p. 518

public assistance, p. 519

social insurance, p. 520

Social Security, p. 522

Medicare, p. 523

Medicaid, p. 523

health maintenance organization (HMO), p. 530

medical savings account, p. 531

Further Reading

JOHN BALDOCK, NICHOLAS MANNING, AND **SARAH VICKERSTAFF,** EDS., *Social Policy* (Oxford University Press, 2007).

DONALD L. BARLETT AND **JAMES B. STEELE,** *Critical Condition: How Health Care in America Became Big Business—and Bad Medicine* (Broadway Books, 2005).

ANNE MARIE CAMMISA, *From Rhetoric to Reform? Welfare Policy in American Politics* (Westview Press, 1998).

BARBARA EHRENREICH, *Nickel and Dimed: On (Not) Getting By in America* (Metropolitan Books, 2001).

FRANK FISCHER, *Evaluating Public Policy* (Nelson-Hall, 1995).

LAURENE A. GRAIG, *Health of Nations: An International Perspective on U.S. Health Care Reform* (CQ Press, 1993).

MICHAEL HILL, *Social Policy in the Modern World: A Comparative Perspective* (Wiley, 2006).

CHRISTOPHER JENCKS, *The Homeless* (Harvard University Press, 1994).

PAUL C. LIGHT, *Still Artful Work: The Continuing Politics of Social Security Reform* (McGraw-Hill, 1995).

DANIEL PATRICK MOYNIHAN, *Miles to Go: A Personal History of Social Policy* (Harvard University Press, 1996).

CHARLES MURRAY, *Losing Ground: American Social Policy, 1950–80* (Basic Books, 1984).

PAUL E. PETERSON AND **MARTIN R. WEST,** EDS., *No Child Left Behind: The Politics and Practice of School Accountability* (Brookings Institution Press, 2004).

FRANCES FOX PIVEN AND **RICHARD A. CLOWARD,** *Regulating the Poor: The Functions of Public Welfare* (Vintage Books, 1993).

MARK ROBERT RANK, *One Nation Underprivileged: Why American Poverty Affects Us All* (Oxford University Press, 2005).

DAVID K. SHIPLER, *The Working Poor: Invisible in America* (Vintage Books, 2005).

R. KENT WEAVER, *Ending Welfare as We Know It* (Brookings Institution Press, 2001).

MARGARET WEIR, ED., *The Social Divide: Political Parties and the Future of Activist Government* (Brookings Institution Press, 1998).

BOB WOODWARD, *Agenda: Inside the Clinton White House* (Simon & Schuster, 1994).

chapter 20

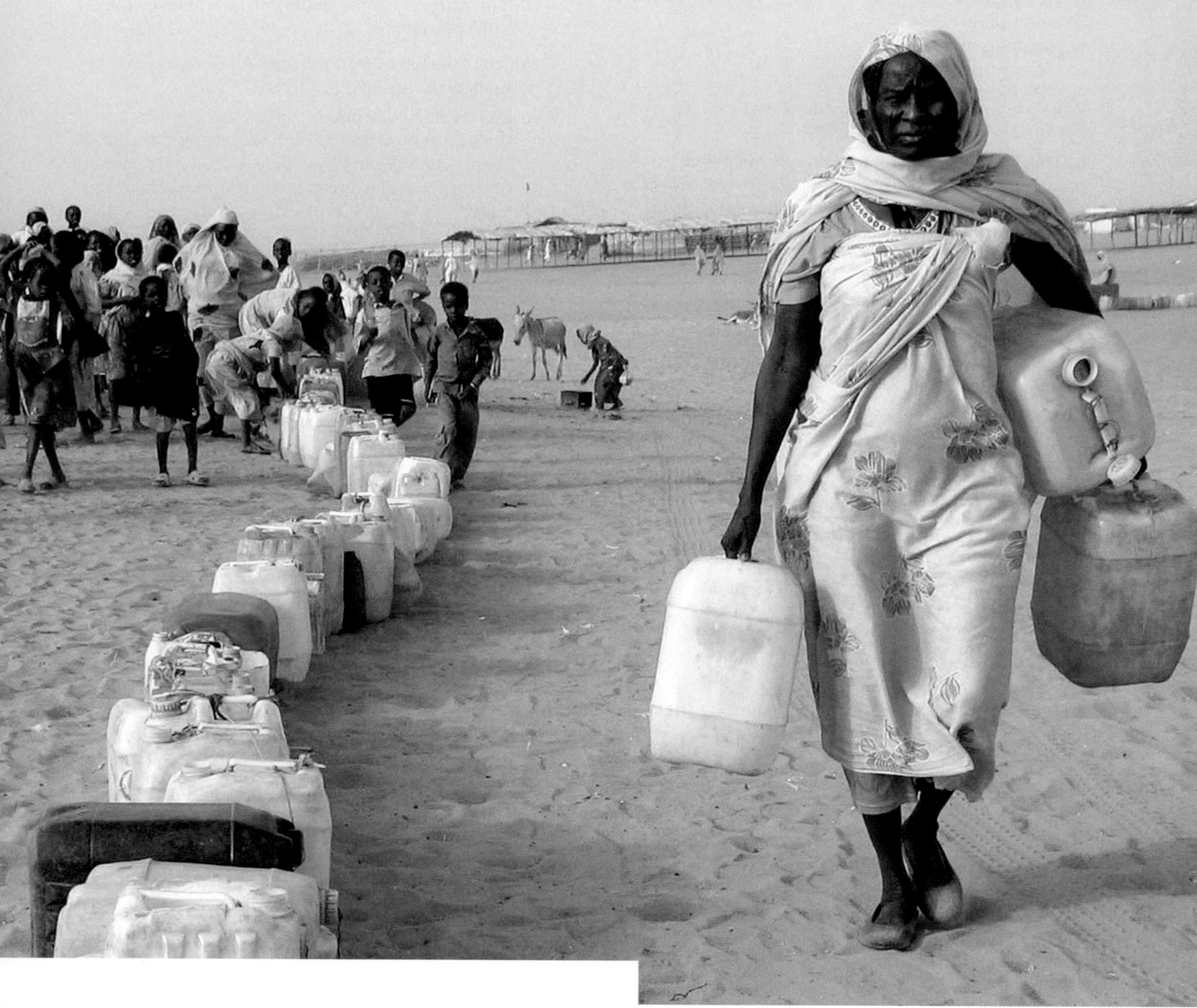

Making Foreign and Defense Policy

The conflict in Darfur, Sudan, began in 2003 when a small rebel group began attacking Sudanese government targets. Frustrated by drought and unrelenting poverty in a territory the size of Texas, the people of Darfur did not demand independence, but clearly demanded aid. The Sudanese government, however, seemed more concerned with driving black Africans out of Darfur than with ending poverty. If they could not be driven out, the Sudanese government decided they would be killed.

The government sent troops into battle backed by its air force. At the same time, it began arming its own rebel army called the Janjaweed, who soon took up the fight against the people of Darfur. Riding into villages and towns on camels and horses, the Janjaweed ravaged the population, raping and killing men, women, and children.

By the beginning of 2008, international aid groups put the number of dead at 200,000 and the number in refugee camps along the border with Chad at 2 million. Although the warring groups signed a peace agreement in 2006, that quickly collapsed. And although the United Nations sent a peacekeeping force to the area, its 26,000 members were unarmed and unable to protect refugees who strayed from the camps in search of food and firewood. Still, the killing went on. The anti-Darfur rebels soon took their violence to the southern Sudan, where they opened a new war on black Africans.

Because the attacks have concentrated on the systematic elimination of a specific population, the black Africans in Sudan, many activists have accused the Sudanese government of engaging in genocide. Human rights groups such as the International Crisis Group and SaveDarfur.org, college students across the United States, and entertainers such as Don Cheadle and George Clooney have been among the most vocal advocates of a much stronger international response that would include a well-armed United Nations force. They have also demanded a much stronger stand by the United States against the warfare. They often refer to the lack of U.S. response to the Rwanda genocide in April 1994 and the failure to stop the killing in Kosovo in 1998. If these kinds of international atrocities cannot provoke international outrage and action, they ask, what will?

The question for the United States' foreign policy and defense agenda is, what kind of power could be used to stop the genocide?[1] On the one hand, the United States has mostly failed to create enough international pressure on the Sudanese government to halt the arming of the Janjaweed and other anti-Darfur rebel groups. It has also failed to stop bombing raids by the Sudanese air force. On the other hand, as much as activists demand action, the U.S. public has been mostly unwilling to support the use of military force in distant lands. Although the United States could push harder on its allies to patrol the skies above the refugee camps, the ongoing war in Iraq has limited its ability to accept a new mission for the air force.

The problem with preventing atrocities is that the international community may know where atrocity is most likely to occur, but it rarely knows when. And once genocide begins, it can move very quickly, forcing the community to choose between quick but unpopular military action and painfully slow diplomatic persuasion. Five years of diplomacy in Darfur has brought no let-up in the killing.

LEARNING **OBJECTIVES**

1. Analyze the five questions that shape positions on U.S. foreign policy and defense.
2. Compare and contrast hard and soft power.
3. Evaluate the seven issues that currently dominate the foreign policy and defense agenda.
4. Identify the goals of the war in Iraq and evaluate the level of U.S. success.
5. Assess the components of the foreign policy and defense bureaucracy.
6. Examine the defense hierarchy.
7. Analyze the options for achieving foreign policy and defense goals.

CHAPTER OUTLINE

- Understanding Foreign Policy and Defense
- The Foreign Policy and Defense Agenda
- The Foreign Policy and Defense Bureaucracy
- Foreign Policy and Defense Options
- Prospects for the Future

This chapter will ask how we make choices in planning and executing foreign and defense policy, such as the effort to end the conflict in Darfur. We will first examine key debates in making foreign and defense policy, look at basic terms and concepts of foreign and defense policy, and examine some of today's greatest foreign policy challenges, such as the war in Iraq. Then we will turn to a discussion of the key actors in making U.S. foreign policy and appraise the range of tools the United States uses to accomplish its international goals. The chapter concludes with a more detailed assessment of defense policy.

Citizens clearly play a role in foreign policy and defense, whether through their advocacy and pressure or through their own decisions to join the public service or armed forces. They can also create change through voting, especially if a foreign policy such as the war in Iraq becomes a national issue as it did in the 2006 congressional elections. Of course citizens also can affect policy by their unwillingness to act, as has widely been the case regarding Darfur. That said, citizens often feel that the foreign policy and defense bureaucracy is immune to criticism and that Congress gives too much freedom to the president.

Understanding Foreign Policy and Defense

Comparing Foreign and Security Policy

LEARNING OBJECTIVE

Analyze the five questions that shape positions on U.S. foreign policy and defense.

In the broadest sense, the primary goal of U.S. foreign and defense policy is to protect the nation from harm. Doing so requires more than building strong borders, however. The United States does not have the luxury of avoiding the rest of the world. As one of the world's great superpowers, it has accepted a range of obligations, including promoting democracy abroad in nations such as Iraq, providing help to victims of disaster such as the 2008 cyclone in Myanmar, promoting greater economic ties across all nations, and fighting terrorism.

Although the United States supports greater freedom in the world, it has long been divided about its own role in international affairs. Some believe that the United States should defend itself against its enemies but remain isolated from the rest of the world; others believe that it should assume other nations will act in their own self-interest, while others promote a more hopeful vision of a peaceful world; still others believe that the United States should use its substantial military strength to force other nations to support its positions, while others argue that it should use its own history of civil liberties and rights to lead the world through example.

In general, these debates start with five basic questions: (1) Should the United States view the world realistically or idealistically? (2) Should it isolate itself from the world or accept a role in the international community? (3) Should it act on its own or only with the help of other nations? (4) Should it act first against threats to its safety or wait until it is attacked? and (5) Should it use its military and economic hard power or its diplomatic soft power? We'll discuss each of these issues next.

1. Realism Versus Idealism

Historically, U.S. foreign and defense policy has been built on two very different views of the world. The first relies on **realism,** a belief that other nations are interested first and foremost in their own advancement, whether economic, political, or social, and in strengthening their own power.

realism
A theory of international relations that focuses on the tendency of nations to operate from self-interest.

idealism
A theory of international relations that focuses on the hope that nations will act together to solve international problems and promote peace.

Critics of realism argue that nations seek cooperation and stability, not power. This view invokes **idealism,** a belief that nations can work together to solve common problems such as global hunger and poverty, with peace, not war, as the ultimate aim. Idealists view national power as a tool for good and for promoting democracy in other nations, not merely as a way to amass more military and economic resources.

Although realism and idealism represent two competing views of the world, they can become part of a broader, more integrated foreign and defense policy. Thus, the United States could be realistic about the need to work with dictators (realism), yet still believe that democracy is the best form of government (idealism). As President Bush often argued in the months leading to the war in Iraq, the United States had to be realistic about Iraq's interest in building biological, chemical, and nuclear weapons, even as he also argued that democracy would lead nations such as Iran and North Korea toward international cooperation and peace.

2. Isolationism Versus Internationalism

Whether it is based on realism or idealism, U.S. foreign policy has reflected very different views of how it should respond to the rest of the world. Some back an approach based on **isolationism,** a belief that the United States should stay out of international affairs unless other nations constitute a direct threat to its existence. The term was first used during the years leading to World War I, when many American adults believed that the United States should stay out of the global conflict.

But isolationism is alive and well in the debate about whether the United States should remain in Iraq. Isolationists argue that the United States should follow George Washington's advice to avoid international "entanglements," lest those entanglements lead the United States into wars that either cannot be won or have a high cost in American lives. They also argue that the United States should always focus first on its own interests by staying away from other nations.

Other citizens, including most foreign and defense policy experts, believe in **internationalism,** which says the United States must be engaged in international affairs to protect its own interests. Realists and idealists can disagree on the goals of U.S. foreign and defense policy, but they can still agree that the United States should engage the world on economic, political, and social issues such as human rights for oppressed people, global hunger, and the war on terrorism. Internationalists tend to view themselves as citizens of the world, not just the United States. They feel there are times when the United States should intervene, even when not directly threatened by another nation.

3. Unilateralism Versus Multilateralism

Although internationalists agree that the United States should participate in world affairs, they have two very different views about how. Supporters of **unilateralism** believe that the United States has the right to act alone in response to threats, even if other nations are unwilling to help. They argue that it should never give other nations (or the United Nations) a veto over its actions, even if that means it acts alone in using its great military power.

In fact, President Bush announced a new unilateral policy immediately after the September 11, 2001, terrorist attacks on New York City and Washington. Under the **Bush Doctrine,** any nation that threatens the United States is automatically a potential target for unilateral action. The Bush Doctrine is built around three basic concepts:

1. The United States reserves the right to attack any nation that either harbors terrorists or constitutes a serious threat to the United States.
2. The United States reserves the right to act unilaterally against other nations even if it does not have the support of its allies.
3. The United States reserves the right to use massive force against its enemies, including nuclear weapons if needed.

Opponents of the Bush Doctrine support **multilateralism,** a belief that the United States should act only with the active support of other nations. According to its advocates, multilateralism not only increases the odds that other nations will share the burdens of war with the United States, but it also increases the potential that other nations will support the U.S. position once a war is over. At least partly because of the advantages of multilateralism, the Bush administration began backing away from the Bush Doctrine just three years after announcing it. Faced with mounting costs of rebuilding Iraq and reducing international tension with other Middle Eastern nations, the administration began working to bring other nations such as Russia, France, and Germany into the debate.

isolationism
The desire to avoid international engagement altogether.

internationalism
The belief that nations must engage in international problem solving.

unilateralism
A philosophy that encourages individual nations to act on their own when facing threats from other nations.

Bush Doctrine
A policy adopted by the Bush administration in 2001 that asserts America's right to attack any nation that has weapons of mass destruction that may be used against U.S. interests at home or abroad.

multilateralism
A philosophy that encourages individual nations to act together to solve international problems.

4. Preemption Versus Provocation

For most of its history, the United States has waited to be provoked before going to war. Although there is considerable debate about what constitutes a provocation to war, **preemption** assumes the United States can attack first when it believes another nation constitutes a very serious threat. This approach was a centerpiece of the Bush Doctrine discussed above, based on the notion that the proliferation of **weapons of mass destruction** such as chemical, biological, or nuclear arms makes waiting for provocation much more dangerous than it once was.

The war in Iraq is an example of preemption, which some experts call the nation's first "war of choice." Believing that Iraq continued to hold weapons of mass destruction, the Bush administration decided to force Saddam Hussein from his dictatorship before he could use those weapons against the United States. Then national security adviser Condoleezza Rice argued that the United States had a moral obligation to remove Hussein from power, even if doing so meant war. "This is an evil man who, left to his own devices, will wreak havoc again on his own population, his neighbors, and, if he gets weapons of mass destruction and the means to deliver them, on all of us," Rice told the British Broadcasting Corporation in August 2002. "There is a very powerful moral case for regime change. We certainly do not have the luxury of doing nothing."[2]

LEARNING **OBJECTIVE**

2 Compare and contrast hard and soft power.

5. Hard Versus Soft Power

Internationalists have different views of just how the United States should influence other nations in protecting itself. Some favor the use of **hard power,** or military and economic strength, while others favor **soft power,** or negotiation and diplomacy.

These terms were first used by Harvard University professor Joseph Nye, who defined power as "the ability to influence others to get them to do what you want." According to Nye, soft power is often more persuasive if supported by hard power. It is also much less costly than hard power, especially if a nation wants to maintain a reputation for international cooperation on other, nonmilitary issues.[3]

Hard power depends almost entirely on a nation's ability to threaten or force another nation to act a certain way to avoid an attack. It relies on military strength as measured by the number of soldiers in uniform, their preparation for war, the quality of their equipment, and their nation's willingness to put them in harm's way.

We often associate hard power with the **theory of deterrence,** under which a nation creates enough military strength to ensure a massive response to any attack. During the cold war, the United States maintained more than enough nuclear weapons to deter the Soviet Union from using its nuclear weapons first and argued that sufficient bombs would survive any Soviet attack to ensure the destruction of the Soviet Union. This notion of *mutual assured destruction*, sometimes called MAD, was enough to keep both nations from using their nuclear weapons, but it kept each on constant alert just in case the other dared to act first.

Soft power is based on more traditional diplomacy and a nation's reputation for keeping its word in honoring treaties, its readiness to provide financial aid, and its ability to find consensus by bargaining with allies and adversaries alike.

Nations can use hard and soft power at the same time to resolve disputes. In fact, the threat of military force is often enough to produce a negotiated settlement, as was the case throughout the cold war.

preemption
A policy of taking action before the United State is attacked rather than waiting for provocation.

weapons of mass destruction
Biological, chemical, or nuclear weapons that can cause a massive number of deaths in a single use.

hard power
Reliance on economic and military strength to solve international problems.

soft power
Reliance on diplomacy and negotiation to solve international problems.

theory of deterrence
A theory that is based on creating enough military strength to persuade other nations not to attack first.

LEARNING **OBJECTIVE**

3 Evaluate the seven issues that currently dominate the foreign policy and defense agenda.

The Foreign Policy and Defense Agenda

The United States does not always have a choice about whether to act in world affairs. Many issues reach its borders that the country cannot avoid. These constitute the foreign and defense policy agenda, which currently focuses on seven major issues, presented here in alphabetical order: (1) controlling weapons of mass destruction, (2) fighting terrorism, (3) negotiating peace in the Middle East, (4) promoting free trade

GENERATION **NEXT**

Hard Versus Soft Power

Citizens generally believe that the United States should make every effort to resolve conflicts with diplomacy before using military strength. Although they want a strong defense and most favored military action in Afghanistan and Iraq, they would rather see peaceful settlements than war.

They also seem to have very little patience for long wars, such as the war in Iraq. They want to see quick victory. Recent surveys show that American adults believe the military surge in the current war against Iraq is working, for example, but most still want the troops to start coming home. Surveys also show the war becoming less popular with each passing year.

Generation Next clearly shares the rest of the nation's support for diplomacy first. As the Pew Research Center's Generation Next survey shows, only 30 percent of 18- to 29-year-olds said the best way to ensure peace is through military strength, while 60 percent said good diplomacy best secures peace. Another 6 percent said both options were necessary (the rest did not answer).

These results suggest that the preference for hard or soft power is clearly related to gender, party identification, and ideology. Women were less likely to support military strength as a way to ensure strength, as were Democrats and liberals. At least part of the explanation is the war in Iraq, widely viewed as a Republican war.

But part is traditional opposition to war among the three groups. Women have long been less likely to support war, perhaps because they imagine the costs in lives lost more vividly than men. Democrats and liberals have also long favored diplomacy as an alternative to wars such as Vietnam.

Percent of 18- to 29-Year-Olds Who Said Good Diplomacy Is the Best Way to Ensure Peace.

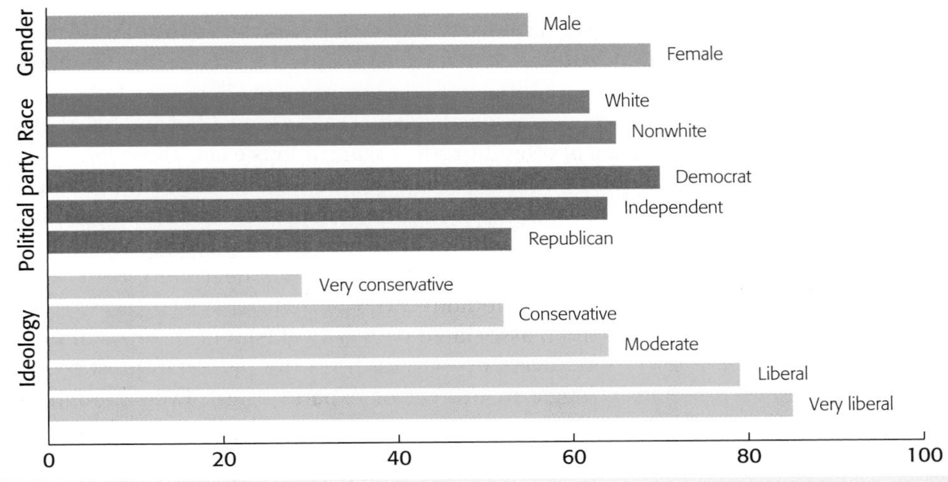

QUESTIONS

1. Why do you think women are less likely to support the use of military strength?
2. What may explain the close agreement between whites and nonwhites on this question?
3. Why do liberals favor diplomacy over military power?

abroad, (5) reducing global warming, (6) resolving the war in Iraq, and (7) strengthening democracy and international understanding. Just because an issue such as global diseases like HIV/AIDS is not on the list does not mean it is off the agenda. Rather, we focus here on the issues that appear to be at the top of the agenda today.

Controlling Weapons of Mass Destruction

The international community has been working for decades to reduce the threat of biological, chemical, and nuclear weapons, often called weapons of mass destruction. Although the world is particularly concerned about the development of such weapons in North Korea and Iran, the effort to reduce the spread of nuclear weapons actually started with nuclear disarmament talks between the United States and the Soviet Union in the 1970s. With the end of the cold war in 1989, the United States and Russia began to look for new ways of reducing their nuclear arsenals, and in 2002 they agreed to reduce the number of nuclear warheads dramatically.

The world is still threatened by biological, chemical, and nuclear weapons, however. Although chemical weapons were outlawed by international agreement after

World War I, at least nine countries say they have developed chemical weapons, such as nerve gases, that kill on contact. Others continue to develop biological weapons that spread disease or poisons, and still others already have or intend to develop nuclear weapons.

The United States has been particularly concerned in recent years about Iran's effort to develop nuclear weapons, which the United States and many other nations believe it may use against Israel. In April 2006, for example, Iran declared its intent to continue building its nuclear power program, which could generate uranium for nuclear weapons.

At the same time, the United States made an agreement with India to support its peaceful nuclear power program, even though that program could also produce the uranium needed for a nuclear weapon. Although India promised the United States it would use the program only to generate electricity for its rapidly growing economy, the agreement may have undermined the U.S. case against Iran's nuclear program, which Iran also said would be used only for peaceful means.

Fighting Terrorism

The war on terrorism is a broad term used to describe efforts to control terrorist acts sponsored by other nations, such as Afghanistan, or acts undertaken by independent groups that operate without any connection to a government.

Although the war is most often associated with Osama bin Laden and his Al-Qaeda terrorist organization, dozens of other terrorist organizations exist. These groups have executed bombings in London, Madrid, Moscow, the Middle East, and throughout Southeast Asia, including Thailand, Malaysia, the Philippines, and Indonesia, where terrorists have carried out several bombings at or near popular tourist hotels. For example, in October 2005, terrorists exploded several bombs near Bali's Four Seasons Hotel, killing more than 20 people, including six U.S. citizens.

The war on terrorism is often associated with radical Islamic groups committed to a global *jihad,* a term that covers everything from the personal quest to attain perfect faith to a violent struggle to protect or expand Islam. Even though most followers of Islam are peace-loving, Islamic terrorist groups have used a range of violent means to advance their strategy, resulting in a backlash against Islam across the world.[4]

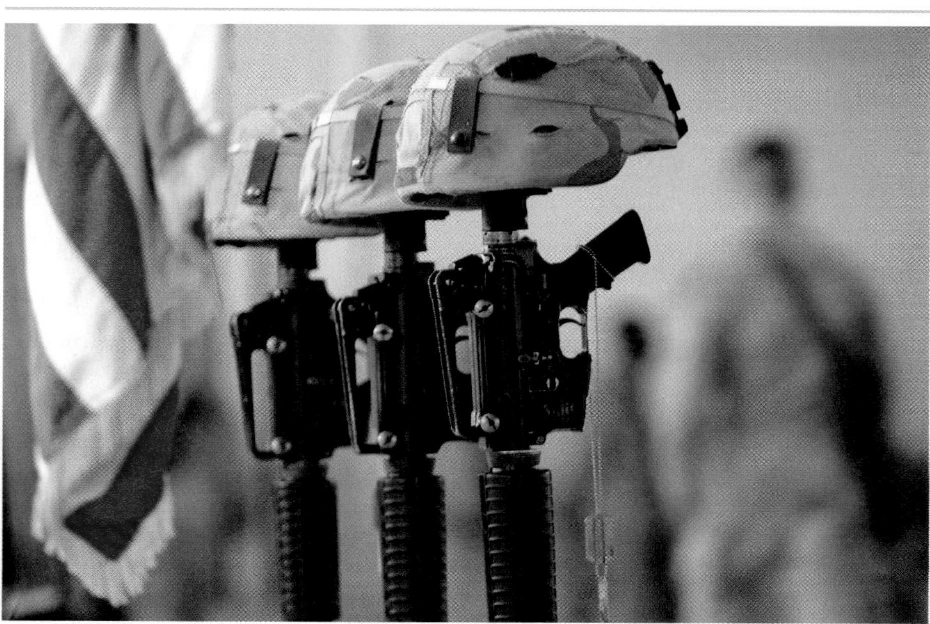

The war in Iraq has cost the lives of more than 4,000 U.S. soldiers and more than 100,000 Iraqi civilians.

Negotiating Peace in the Middle East

Long before the September 11 terrorist attacks, the United States was working to secure peace between Israel and its neighbors, in part because the Middle East is such an important source of the world's oil, and in part because the United States has long considered Israel an ally. However, despite decades of U.S. efforts to promote peace in the region, the Middle East remains locked in a violent struggle over Israel's right to exist. Progress toward peace has been threatened by ongoing conflict with Arab nations and terrorist groups.

In 2002, however, the United States, Israel, and most Arab nations embraced "The Road Map to Peace." Under this agreement, signed in April 2003, Israel and its adversaries agreed to two broad steps toward peace. The Palestinian Authority, which represents citizens in territories captured by Israel in past wars, agreed to arrest, disrupt, and restrain individuals and groups that plan and conduct violent attacks on Israel. Israel in turn agreed to start dismantling settlements of Israeli citizens in the occupied territories to its south and east. Israel honored its part of the agreement starting in 2005 by dismantling all settlements, thereby turning over complete control of these territories to the Palestinian Authority.

Although the Palestinian Authority initially agreed to try to stop violence against Israel, in 2006 the Palestinian people gave a majority of seats in their new parliament to members of Hamas, a political party that had long waged war against Israel. Despite strong international pressure on Hamas and threats by other nations to cut international aid, its leaders continue to support violence against Israel. The dispute continued into 2008 with repeated conflicts along the border between the Palestinian territories and Israel.

Promoting Free Trade Abroad

As the world economy has grown, so has international competition with the United States. The United States has generally responded to this *globalization* with a basic policy of free trade, meaning a commitment to the free movement of goods across international borders. But it does not allow the unrestricted export of technologies that can be used to build nuclear weapons, and it has long protected certain defense industries that would be essential should it ever be forced into another world war. The United States has also used trade as a tool to promote human rights and democratic reform.

Young boys wave the flag of Hamas outside a polling station in Gaza City while Palestinians held their first parliamentary election in a decade in 2006. Victory in the election for the radical Islamic faction led to Western governments distancing themselves from the Palestinians. Later in the year, President Mahmoud Abbas called for a new election in an effort to regain international support.

Conflicting goals have characterized the U.S. debate over free trade with China. On the one hand, China has a long history of violating basic human and democratic rights. But it also has one of the fastest-growing economies in the world. U.S. exports to China have tripled over the past decade, and imports from China have grown rapidly. The conflict between concern for human rights and a desire to benefit from China's growing economy became especially prominent when the Clinton administration asked Congress to grant **normal trade relations** status to China. Under normal trade relations, China would be given the same favorable trading terms, such as low tariffs on imports and exports, that other favored nations receive.

Typcially, Congress grants normal trade relations under a "fast-track" or accelerated basis by limiting its own debate to a simple yes-or-no, up-or-down vote with no amendments. Although Congress initially refused to use this process for China, it eventually approved the status and extended the president's authority to negotiate such trade agreements in the Trade Act of 2002.

Reducing Global Warming

The United States has a mixed record in efforts to control the global climate change often associated with greenhouse gases that trap heat in the environment and raise the world's temperature. Much of the recent increase in greenhouse gases is related to the release of carbon dioxide from the burning of fossil fuels such as gasoline and coal by automobiles and power plants.

There is increasing agreement that the world's average temperature has risen over the past few decades. Although experts disagree on the amount of the increase that humans produce and its potential impact on oceans and climate, rising temperatures appear to threaten the world's climate in two ways. First, as the average temperature rises, the polar ice caps and glaciers melt. As the water melts, the oceans rise, threatening low-lying areas across the world. By some estimates, New York City, Washington, Florida, Louisiana, and other coastal areas could be completely under water within several hundred years. Second, as average temperatures rise, the weather becomes more unpredictable and potentially severe. Some experts attribute the recent increase in violent hurricanes such as Hurricane Katrina to global warming and predict more violent storms in the future.

The world acknowledged these problems when it adopted an international treaty called the Kyoto Protocol in 1997. Under the treaty, all participating nations agreed to reduce their emission of greenhouse gases by set amounts over the coming decades. Although 55 nations, including the United States, most European nations, and Russia signed the agreement, the United States has never ratified the treaty and has yet to embrace limits on burning fossil fuels, even though it produces a significant amount of the world's greenhouse gases. The United States has argued that the limits imposed by the Kyoto Protocol would weaken its economy.

The world also suffers from an increase in chemical pollution related to rapidly expanding manufacturing in nations such as China. According to international monitoring, China contains 16 of the world's 20 most polluted cities and is a major contributor to water contamination through the release of chemicals into its rivers. China's environmental problems also threatened the 2008 Olympic Games as athletes wondered whether their health would be at risk in polluted air.

LEARNING **OBJECTIVE**

4 Identify the goals of the war in Iraq and evaluate the level of U.S. success.

Resolving the War in Iraq

Iraq moved rapidly up the list of foreign-policy priorities in the days and weeks following the September 11, 2001, terrorist attacks. Convinced that Iraq possessed weapons of mass destruction that it was ready and willing to use against the United States, President Bush ordered the military to start planning for a preemptive war only six days after the attacks.[5] He also began building the case for action with the U.S. public and later made his argument before the United Nations.

normal trade relations
Trade status granted as part of an international trade policy that gives a nation the same favorable trade concessions and tariffs that the best trading partners receive.

HISTORY MAKERS

Woodrow Wilson

Woodrow Wilson won the presidency in 1912 after a brutal campaign against the Republican incumbent, William Howard Taft, and former president Theodore Roosevelt, who ran on a third-party ticket. Taft and Roosevelt split the Republican vote, thereby giving Wilson the victory. As a former professor of political science at Princeton University and former governor of New Jersey, Wilson was the first Democrat to win the presidency in two decades and easily won reelection to a second term in 1916.

Woodrow Wilson.

Although Wilson made important contributions to the nation's domestic and economic policies, he is celebrated most for leading the United States during World War I, which led to his vision of a League of Nations that would prevent future wars. Having helped the combatants end the "war to end all wars," he campaigned hard for the creation of the League. However, he was rebuffed by the U.S. Senate, which voted not to join the international organization in 1920.

Wilson's League of Nations assumed a number of duties that now fall to the United Nations (created at the end of World War II). Headquartered in Geneva, Switzerland, it was originally designed to encourage all nations to disarm their militaries, to settle disputes by negotiating in a neutral setting, to allow nations to vote on major world issues, and to prevent the use of the kind of chemical weapons unleashed in World War I.

The League had the authority to deal with any issue that threatened world peace, but it lacked both the membership and the military strength to enforce its decisions. Unlike the United Nations, it did not have a peacekeeping force, and it was effective only in the first years following its creation. It failed to stop Germany's military buildup in the 1930s and did little to prevent World War II, which produced more casualties than any war in modern history. Although Wilson won the Nobel Peace Prize for his work, he was never able to persuade the U.S. public to support the nation's full participation in his League.

QUESTIONS

1. How might isolationism have affected U.S. support or opposition to the League?
2. Did the League rely on hard or soft power?

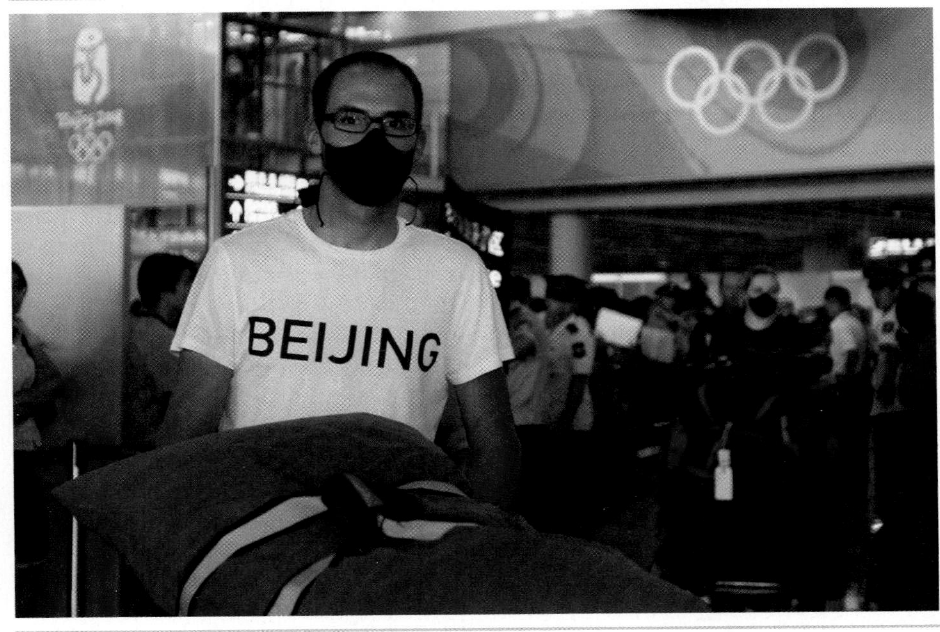

Despite worries about the air pollution in Beijing, the air was clean enough to allow Olympic athletes such as Michael Phelps to compete without concern.

The U.S. war against Iraq began on March 20, 2003, with a bombing campaign designed to produce "shock and awe" within Iraq and thereby ensure the collapse of military resistance.

> The United States has no quarrel with the Iraqi people; they've suffered too long in silent captivity. Liberty for the Iraqi people is a great moral cause, and a great strategic goal. The people of Iraq deserve it; the security of all nations requires it. Free societies do not intimidate through cruelty and conquest, and open societies do not threaten the world with mass murder. The United States supports political and economic liberty in a unified Iraq.[6]

The Bush administration had three goals as it considered a possible invasion of Iraq. First, it wanted to remove Iraq's brutal dictator, Saddam Hussein, and replace him with an elected leader. Second, it wanted to find and destroy Iraq's capability to manufacture weapons of mass destruction. And third, it wanted to convert Iraq into one of the Middle East's few democracies in hopes that the idea would spread across a region that supplies most of the world's oil.

In March 2003, the United States launched a massive attack on Iraq. U.S. troops quickly reached the outskirts of the nation's capital city and secured it over the next two days. On May 1, 2003, President Bush stood on the deck of the USS *Abraham Lincoln* underneath a banner that read "MISSION ACCOMPLISHED" and told the nation that "Major combat operations in Iraq have ended."

Economic Sanctions and Cuba

The United States clearly succeeded in its first goal. Hussein was eventually captured and stood trial for crimes against the Iraqi people. He was executed on January 2, 2007.

However, the United States clearly failed in its second and third goals. Iraq's weapons of mass destruction were never found. According to a U.S. Intelligence Committee report released in July 2004, most of the key judgments in the intelligence community's assessment of Hussein's weapons programs "either overstated, or were not supported by, the underlying intelligence reporting."[7]

Iraq also failed to build a thriving democracy. More than five years after the U.S. invasion, Iraq's young democracy is still threatened by intense divisions between a Shiite Arab majority of 60 percent, a Sunni Arab minority between 15 and 20 percent, and the independence-minded Kurdish minority of roughly 20 percent.

Moreover, the battle for Iraq was only beginning when Bush declared the mission accomplished. By October 2008, almost 4,200 soldiers had been killed and more than 10,000 wounded. The Iraqi people also suffered—thousands were killed in bombings and terrorist executions each month, and many more were wounded.

As violence increased in the years following the initial victory, the Bush administration became convinced that the United States needed more troops to control major parts of the country. Under pressure from congressional Democrats and Republicans to do something to quell the violence, the president announced a "surge" of 28,000 troops in early 2007, raising the total U.S. presence to 160,000. The troops were deployed to Iraq's capital city, Baghdad, and other "hot spots" where terrorists were most active.

Even as the surge reduced violence in Iraq, attacks against U.S. troops increased in Afghanistan. The U.S. had won victory in 2001 against the Afghan government, which had sponsored the terrorists who planned the Septemper 11 attacks on New York City and Washington, D.C. Seven years later, experts argued that the cost of the War in Iraq had distracted the U.S. from protecting the new democratic government in Afghanistan. With troops tied up in Iraq, there were not enough troops to reinforce U.S. forces, prompting calls for shifiting resources to the new battles in Afghanistan.[8]

President Bush, on the deck of the USS *Abraham Lincoln* on May 1, 2003, declares an end to major combat operations in Iraq. Since that time, thousands of injuries and deaths have occurred on both sides of the conflict.

Strengthening Democracy and International Understanding

The United States has long engaged in promoting democracy and its freedoms. It does so through a mix of incentives and punishments, providing economic aid to nations it

Entertainers often use their visibility on behalf of global concerns. Here, Angelina Jolie helps a group of children who have been victims of international conflicts.

believes are moving toward democracy, while providing aid to nations of strategic importance to U.S. goals.

However, some efforts conflict with other U.S. goals such as promoting international trade and fighting the war on terrorism. Although China continues to deny its citizens basic rights such as a free press, for example, the United States continues to promote international trade with one of the world's fastest-growing economies. In addition, the United States still provides aid to many Middle Eastern nations ruled by dictatorships, in order to gain their help in the war on terrorism.

The United States also provides humanitarian aid to nations affected by natural disasters such as the 2008 earthquake in China. Although dictators led many of the countries affected, the United States has long believed that citizens should not suffer during crises even though their governments are not free.

Finally, the United States uses programs such as the Peace Corps to promote international understanding. Peace Corps volunteers are expected to serve in another nation for two years and become part of the community they are serving. They work on a variety of projects, such as teaching math and science, doing community development work, and improving water and sanitation systems. Most have a college degree, specific international experience, or both. About 10 percent of the 7,300 current volunteers are over age 50. The Peace Corps covers travel and a minimum salary and typically trains volunteers in language and job skills for about three months before their service abroad.[9]

Promoting international understanding becomes more difficult when the U.S. engages in unilateral conflicts such as the war in Iraq. It is less credible in calling for an end to other conflicts when it is unable to resolve its own wars.

Built in 1961, the Berlin Wall separating East and West Berlin was a longtime symbol of the division between communism and democracy. Economic hard times in 1989 led to a wave of refugees fleeing East Germany, which eventually forced the government there to relax exit restrictions. The fall of the Berlin Wall became symbolic of the fall of the communist Soviet Union that followed.

The Foreign Policy and Defense Bureaucracy

Even in troubled times, the president does not have absolute authority to act. Congress has the power to declare war, to appropriate funds for the armed forces, and to make rules that govern them. But the president is commander in chief and is authorized to negotiate treaties and receive and send ambassadors—that is, to recognize or refuse to recognize other governments. The Senate confirms U.S. ambassadorial appointments and gives consent (by a two-thirds vote) to treaty ratification. The courts have the power to interpret treaties, but by and large they have ruled that relations with other nations are matters for the executive to decide. The primacy of the executive in foreign policy is a fact of political life of all nations, including constitutional democracies.

LEARNING **OBJECTIVE**

Assess the components of the foreign policy and defense bureaucracy.

Officially, the president's principal foreign policy adviser is the secretary of state, although others, such as the national security adviser or the vice president, are sometimes equally influential. The secretary of state administers the State Department, receives visits from foreign diplomats, attends international conferences, and usually heads the U.S. delegation in the General Assembly of the United Nations. The secretary also serves as the administration's chief coordinator of all governmental actions that affect our relations with other nations. In practice, the secretary of state delegates the day-to-day responsibilities for running the State Department and spends most of the time negotiating with the leaders of other countries.

The interdependence of foreign, economic, and social policies requires more than just one or two advisers. The conduct of foreign affairs is now the business of several major departments and agencies, including State, Defense, Treasury, Agriculture, Commerce, Labor, Energy, the Central Intelligence Agency (CIA), and the Department of Homeland Security. The need for immediate reaction and full preparedness has transferred many responsibilities directly to the president and, to a great extent, to the senior White House aides who assist in coordinating information and advice. Yet no matter what the system for advice and coordination, responsibilities often overlap, resulting in competition among agencies.

You Are President John F. Kennedy

The National Security Council

The key coordinating agency for the president is the National Security Council (NSC). Created by Congress in 1947, it serves directly under the president and is intended to help integrate foreign, military, and economic policies that affect national security. By law, it consists of the president, vice president, secretary of state, and secretary of defense. Recent presidents have sometimes also included the director of the CIA, the White House chief of staff, and the national security adviser as assistants to the NSC.

The national security adviser, appointed by the president, has emerged as one of the most influential foreign policy makers, sometimes rivaling the secretary of state in influence. Presidents come to rely on these White House aides both because of their proximity (down the hall in the West Wing of the White House) and because they owe their primary loyalties to the president, not to any department or program. Each president has shaped the NSC structure and adapted its staff procedures to suit his personal preferences, but over the years, the NSC, as both a committee and a staff, has taken on a major role in making and implementing foreign policy.

The State Department

The State Department is responsible for the diplomatic realm of foreign and defense policy. It is organized around a series of "desks" representing different parts of the world and foreign policy missions.

Duties The State Department is responsible for negotiating treaties with other nations and international organizations, protecting U.S. citizens abroad, promoting U.S. commercial interests in other nations, and granting visas to foreign visitors. The State Department also runs all U.S. embassies and consulates abroad. Embassies provide full diplomatic services on behalf of the United States and its citizens; consulates are smaller branch offices of embassies that help foreign citizens enter the United States through visas, or entry papers.

Immigration

The State Department also plays a significant role in homeland security. Many of the September 11, 2001, attackers had entered the United States on student visas granted by the State Department's Bureau of Consular Affairs. Although their movements once in the United States were supposed to be monitored by the Justice Department's Immigration and Naturalization Service, the State Department was criticized for being too lax in granting visas to almost anyone with enough money to purchase an airline ticket.

The Evolving Demographic Makeup of Texas

Though subject to criticism, the State Department is doing its job with fewer resources than its peers. Its budget of about $6 billion (not counting foreign aid) is the lowest of all the cabinet departments—and only a fraction of that of the Department of Defense.[10] Considering the State Department's role and prestige, its worldwide staff of 25,000 is also small, especially compared with the more than two million civilian and military personnel in the Department of Defense.

Its role is particularly impressive given recent cutbacks. The United States has closed at least 30 consulates and embassies over the past two decades, and many operate with obsolete technology in antiquated and unsafe buildings. Cutbacks help explain the breakdowns in the visa issuance process. The State Department simply did not have enough employees to interview every applicant for a visa.

The Foreign Service U.S. embassies are staffed largely by members of the U.S. Foreign Service. Although part of the State Department, the service represents the entire government and performs jobs for many other agencies. Its main duties are to carry out foreign policy as expressed in the directives of the secretary of state; gather political, economic, and intelligence data for U.S. policy makers; protect U.S. citizens and interests in foreign countries; and cultivate friendly relations with host governments and foreign peoples.

The Foreign Service is a select group of about 4,000 highly trained civil servants, comparable to army officers in the military and expected to take assignments anywhere in the world on short notice. Approximately two-thirds of U.S. ambassadors to about 160 nations come from the ranks of the Foreign Service. The others are usually presidential appointees confirmed by the senate.

You Are a Newly Appointed Ambassador to the Country of Dalmatia

The Foreign Service is one of the most prestigious yet most criticized career services of the national government. Criticism sometimes comes as much from within as from outside. Critics claim that the organizational culture of the Foreign Service stifles creativity; attracts officers who are, or at least become, more concerned about their status than their responsibilities; and requires new recruits to wait 15 years or more before being considered for positions of responsibility. Like other federal agencies, most notably the CIA and the FBI, the Foreign Service has had great difficulty recruiting officers with Arabic-language skills, which clearly weakens each agency's ability to interpret, let alone collect, intelligence about the terrorist networks that have emerged in the Middle East and Asia.

The Intelligence Agencies

Accurate, timely information about foreign nations is essential for making wise decisions. As the Senate Intelligence Committee and the national commission created to investigate the September 11, 2001, attacks both noted, the intelligence community failed to provide that information in time to prevent the attacks or change the course of the Iraq war.[11]

The Central Intelligence Agency The most important intelligence agency is the Central Intelligence Agency, created in 1947 to gather and analyze information that flows into various parts of the U.S. government from all over the world. In recent years, the CIA has had about 20,000 employees, who both collect information and shape the intelligence estimates that policy makers use to set priorities.

Although most of the information the CIA gathers comes from open sources such as the Internet, the CIA does use spies and undercover agents to monitor foreign threats. This secret intelligence occasionally supplies crucial data. But it is not all glamour; much is routine. Intelligence work consists of three basic operations: reporting, analysis, and dissemination. *Reporting* is based on close and rigorous observation of developments around the world; *analysis* is the attempt to detect meaningful patterns in what was observed in the past and to understand what appears to be going on now; *dissemination* means getting the right information to the right people at the right time.

The Intelligence Community The CIA is only one of 15 intelligence agencies in the federal government, including the State Department's Bureau of Intelligence and Research; the Defense Department's Defense Intelligence Agency (which combines the

The spirit of bipartisanship is reflected in the report of the 9/11 Commission, issued on July 22, 2004. The commission was made up of both Democrats and Republicans who managed to put their ideological differences aside and issue a report that is critical of both the Clinton and Bush administrations in their handling of terrorism. Shown here are 9/11 Commission co-chairs Thomas Kean and Lee Hamilton.

intelligence operations of the Army, Navy, Air Force, and Marine Corps); the Federal Bureau of Investigation; the Treasury Department's Office of Terrorism and Finance Intelligence; the Energy Department's Office of Intelligence; the Homeland Security Department's Directorate of Information Analysis and Infrastructure Protection and Directorate of Coast Guard Intelligence; and the National Security Agency (which specializes in electronic reconnaissance and code breaking), National Reconnaissance Office (which runs the U.S. satellite surveillance programs), and National Geospatial-Intelligence Agency (which collects and analyzes photographic imagery). Together, the 15 agencies constitute the *intelligence community.*

Because each was created to collect unique information (imagery, electronic intelligence, and so forth) for a unique client (the president, the secretary of defense, or others), historically the agencies rarely shared information with each other. The lack of cooperation clearly affected the government's ability to prevent the September 11, 2001, attacks. "Many dedicated officers worked day and night for years to piece together the growing body of evidence on Al-Qaeda and to understand the threats," the 9/11 Commission concluded. "Yet, while there were many reports on bin Laden and his growing Al-Qaeda organization, there was no comprehensive review of what the intelligence community knew and what it did not know, and what that meant."[12]

Congress responded by creating a national intelligence director in 2004 to oversee all the intelligence offices. Under its legislation, the new director was responsible for providing the primary advice to the president on intelligence issues and was given the authority to increase or decrease the budgets of all other intelligence agencies. The director also oversees a new federal counterterrorism center, responsible for making sense of all national intelligence on potential terrorist threats to the United States. Despite the promise of more coordination, however, congressional critics in both parties complained that the new director merely added a layer of bureaucracy to an already cumbersome system.

LEARNING **OBJECTIVE**

6 Examine the defense hierarchy.

You Are the President of the United States

The Department of Defense

The president, Congress, the National Security Council, the State Department, and the Defense Department all make overall defense policy and attempt to integrate U.S. national security programs, but the day-to-day work of organizing for defense is the job of the Defense Department. Its headquarters, the Pentagon, houses within its 17.5 miles of corridors 23,000 top military and civilian personnel. The offices of several hundred generals and admirals are there, as is the office of the secretary of defense, currently Robert Gates, who provides civilian control of the armed services.

Although the Department of Defense has existed for more than half a century, its leaders are still working to ensure both strategic vision and practical coordination among the military services. Until 1947, there were two separate military departments—war and navy. The difficulty of coordinating them during World War II led to demands for their unification. In 1947, the air force, already an autonomous unit within the War Department, was made an independent department, and all three military departments—army, navy, and air force—were placed under the general supervision of the secretary of defense.

The Joint Chiefs of Staff The committee known as the Joint Chiefs of Staff serves as the principal military adviser to the president, the National Security Council, and the secretary of defense. It includes the heads of the air force, army, navy, and Marine Corps, and the chair and vice chair of the Joint Chiefs. The president, with the consent of the Senate, appoints all the service chiefs to four-year nonrenewable terms. Note that the twice-renewable two-year term of the chair of the Joint Chiefs is part of the process of ensuring civilian control over the military.

Before 1986, the members of the Joint Chiefs of Staff were collectively very powerful. They advised the president and the secretary of defense. Because they functioned as a committee and could not act until they reached unanimous agreement, however, they often produced overly broad decisions. Critics therefore viewed much of the work of the Joint Chiefs as wasteful and even dangerous.

The Department of Defense Reorganization Act of 1986 shifted considerable power to the chair of the Joint Chiefs. Reporting through the secretary of defense, the chair now advises the president on military matters, exercises authority over the forces in the field, and is responsible for overall military planning. In theory, the chair of the Joint Chiefs can even make a military decision that the chiefs of the other services oppose.

Note, however, that the chair of the Joint Chiefs is *not* the head of the military. The chair and the Joint Chiefs are advisers to the secretary of defense and the president, but the president can disregard their advice and on occasion has done so. A president must weigh military action or inaction against the larger foreign and security interests of the nation.

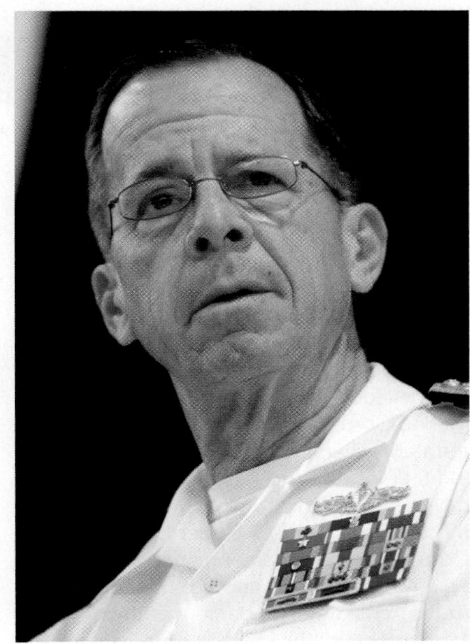

As chair of the Joint Chiefs of Staff, Admiral Mike Mullen is the highest-ranking officer in the U.S. military. Here, he is interviewed in March 2008 about his views of the war in Iraq.

The All-Volunteer Force The Constitution authorizes Congress to do what is "necessary and proper" in order to "raise and support Armies," "to provide and maintain a Navy," and "to provide for calling forth the Militia." The Joint Chiefs and the presidential appointees who serve as secretaries of the Air Force, Army, Navy, and Marine Corps oversee the 1.5 million soldiers who currently serve in what the founders might call the national militia.

During most of its history, the United States has used military conscription to raise and support its armed services. The draft, as it is called, was first used in 1862, during the Civil War, and again during World War I, World War II, and Vietnam. Shortly before the Vietnam War ended, Congress replaced the draft with an *all-volunteer force,* composed entirely of citizens who choose to serve. The armed services offer a variety of benefits to make sure they meet their annual recruiting targets, including signing bonuses, special training, college tuition, and even help finding a job after service is completed. The all-volunteer concept has worked well during peacetime, particularly when the quality of recruits is measured by their educational achievement and performance on standardized intelligence tests.

Contractors The tools of war include contracts with private businesses. The U.S. defense budget reached $555 billion in 2008, not counting the costs of the wars in Afghanistan and Iraq. More than $400 billion of that total is for private business contracts.

Defense spending fell dramatically at the end of the cold war as weapons systems were canceled or postponed, bases closed, ships retired, and large numbers of troops brought home from Germany, the Philippines, and elsewhere. The army was cut by over 30 percent, and the National Guard and the military reserve were cut back about 25 percent. As a result, defense spending also fell, dropping from 25 percent at the height of the cold war in the mid-1980s to 15 percent in 2000.

Evaluating Defense Spending

Weapons are, in fact, a major U.S. industry, one that members of Congress work hard to promote and protect. As former World War II hero Dwight Eisenhower warned in his presidential Farewell Address in 1960, the United States must be wary of the *military-industrial complex* that supports increased defense spending as a way to protect jobs. Eisenhower's words are well worth rereading today:

> This conjunction of an immense military establishment and a large arms industry is new in the American experience. The total influence—economic, political, even spiritual—is felt in every city, every State house, and every office of the Federal government. We recognize the imperative need for this development. Yet we must not fail to comprehend its grave implications. Our toil, resources and livelihood are all involved; so is the very structure of our society.
>
> In the councils of government, we must guard against the acquisition of unwarranted influence, whether sought or unsought, by the military industrial complex. The potential for the disastrous rise of misplaced power exists and will persist.[13]

Despite Eisenhower's warning, the military-industrial complex has grown dramatically since the 1950s.

THE **CHANGING FACE** OF U.S. POLITICS

Diversity in the Military

The U.S. military has become much more diverse over the past three decades, in part because of much more aggressive recruiting of women and minorities. In 1990, for example, just 11 percent of all military personnel were women, while 28 percent were people of color. By 2006, which is the latest information available, 15 percent were women, and 39 percent were people of color.

The four armed services—army, navy, Marine Corps, and air force—vary greatly in terms of diversity, however. Looking at new recruits in 2006, roughly 34 percent of the navy, 25 percent of the army, 23 percent of the air force, and 15 percent of the Marine Corps were African American, Hispanic, Asian American, or another minority group. At the same time, 24 percent of the air force, 19 percent of the navy, 17 percent of the army, and just 7 percent of the Marine Corps were women.

Several reasons explain why the armed forces have done better recruiting people of color than recruiting women. First, the military has worked hard to improve its reputation as an equal opportunity employer. Colin Powell's rise to the highest post in the armed services has often been used to show recruits of color that anything is possible in the military. Powell entered the military as a second lieutenant in 1958, served two tours of duty in Vietnam, and eventually became the first African American officer to chair the Joint Chiefs of Staff.

Second, the military has long focused on recruiting high school graduates who are not college-bound, which is a group that contains more people of color. The military has also developed several new programs that set aside substantial amounts of funding for future college tuition, which has also been effective in recruiting people of color.

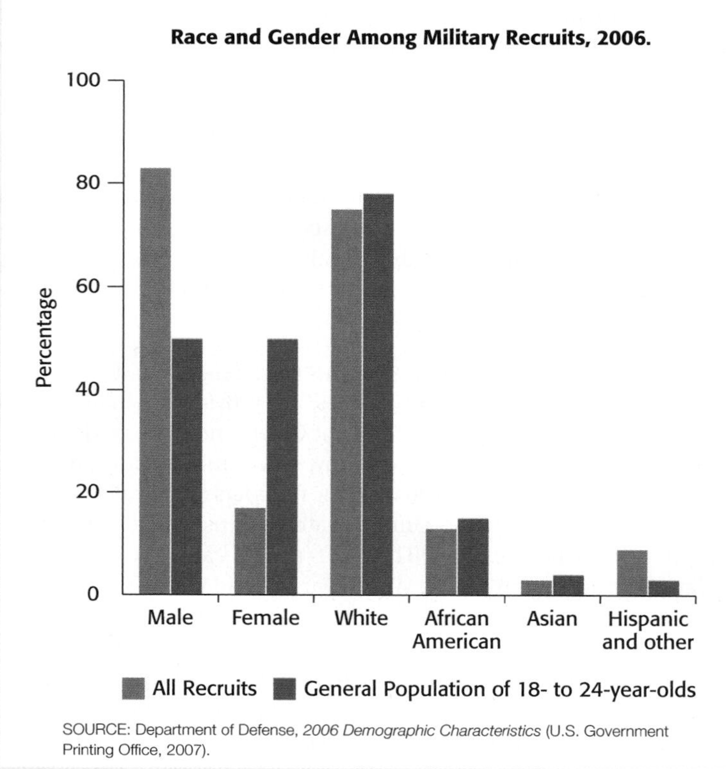

SOURCE: Department of Defense, *2006 Demographic Characteristics* (U.S. Government Printing Office, 2007).

QUESTIONS

1. What may explain the large percentages of minority soldiers in the military?
2. What may explain the much smaller percentages of women in the military?
3. Should the military represent all groups in society? Should combat soldiers be equally representative?

LEARNING **OBJECTIVE**

7 Analyze the options for achieving foreign policy and defense goals.

Foreign Policy and Defense Options

The United States has a number of tools for achieving foreign policy success, not the least of which is military might. But military might, or hard power as we discussed earlier, is no longer enough to ensure success, or even deter foreign threats. Without conventional diplomacy, or soft power, to send its message clearly, foreign aid to help nations in need, economic sanctions to isolate its adversaries, and public diplomacy to help other nations understand its agenda, the nation will not succeed in reaching its foreign policy goals.

Conventional Diplomacy (Soft Power)

Much of U.S. foreign policy is conducted by the Foreign Service and ambassadors in face-to-face discussions across the world. International summit meetings, with their high-profile pomp and drama, are another form of conventional diplomacy. Even though traditional diplomacy appears more subdued and somewhat less vital in this era of personal leader-to-leader communication by telephone, fax, and teleconferencing, it is still an important, if slow, process by which nations can gain information, talk about mutual interests, and try to resolve disputes.

Conventional diplomacy can become hard power when the United States breaks diplomatic relations with another nation. Doing so greatly restricts tourist and business travel to a country and in effect curbs economic as well as political relations with the nation. Breaking diplomatic relations is a next-to-last resort (force is the last resort), for it undermines the ability to reason with a nation's leaders or use other diplomatic strategies to resolve conflicts. It also hampers our ability to get valuable information about what is going on in a nation and to have a presence there.

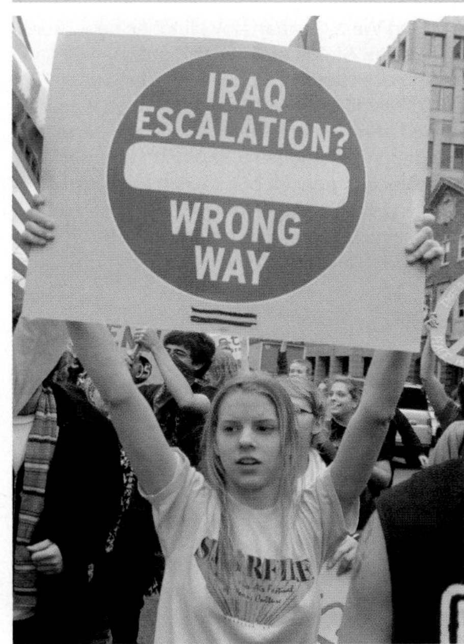

Opposition to the Iraq War increased over time as U.S. casualties mounted.

The United Nations is one of the most important arenas for traditional diplomacy. Established in 1945 by the victors of World War II, it now has 189 nation members.

Despite its promise as a forum for world peace, the United Nations has been frustrated during its first 65 years. Critics contend that it has either ducked crucial global issues or was politically unable to tackle them. During much of that time, the U.N. General Assembly, dominated by a combination of Third World and communist nations, was hostile to many U.S. interests.

More recently, the five permanent members of the U.N. Security Council—the United States, China, Russia (which replaced the Soviet Union), Britain, and France—have usually worked in harmony. Moreover, the United Nations' assumption of responsibilities in the Persian Gulf War and its extensive peacekeeping missions in Cyprus and Lebanon have won it respect. Several of the U.N.'s specialized agencies—including the World Health Organization, the United Nations High Commission for Refugees, and the World Food Program—are considered major successes. But the review is much more mixed with respect to the United Nations' more than 50 peacekeeping efforts. Operations in Cambodia, Somalia, and Sudan, for instance, are plagued by inadequate and often underprepared personnel who are rarely given enough authority or military equipment to stop a civil war. "First-world countries with first-rate armies are usually unwilling to put their troops at risk," writes former U.S. Ambassador Dennis Jett. "Thus these operations are often left to third-world countries, and the United Nations sends some of the worst soldiers in the world off to situations where it can only hope they are not called on to actually do anything."[14] As of 2008, the United Nations was engaged in 17 different peacekeeping missions, including the effort to protect civilians in the Darfur region of Sudan discussed at the beginning of this chapter.

Foreign Aid (Soft Power)

The United States offers aid to more than 100 countries directly and to other nations through contributions to various U.N. development funds. Since 1945, the United States has provided about $400 billion in economic assistance to foreign countries. In recent years, however, its foreign aid spending has amounted to around $15 billion per year, or less than 50 percent of what it spent in inflation-adjusted dollars back in 1985.[15]

Most foreign aid goes to a few countries the United States deems to be of strategic importance to national security: Israel, Egypt, Ukraine, Jordan, India, Russia, South Africa, and Haiti. That list is sure to change in the future as the nation reallocates its budget to nations central to the war on terrorism. However, regardless of which nation receives the aid, most foreign aid is actually spent in the United States, where it pays for the purchase of U.S. services and products being sent to those countries. It thus amounts to a hefty subsidy for U.S. companies and their employees.

Korea's Ban Ki-moon was selected as U.N. secretary general in 2007.

The American public thinks the United States spends much more on foreign aid than it actually does and therefore opposes increased spending. A recent poll of U.S. citizens found that only 9 percent supported increasing foreign aid, while 47 percent favored reducing it. Another 40 percent would keep it pretty much at the same level.[16] State Department officials are invariably the biggest advocates of foreign aid. Presidents also recognize the vital role foreign aid plays in advancing U.S. interests and have

A young West German boy clutches new shoes. The United States provided billions in foreign assistance to rebuild Germany after World War II. The Marshall Plan, which was named after General George C. Marshall, was designed to strengthen Germany's economy as protection against communist forces in Eastern Europe and as future trading partners. Something as simple as a new pair of shoes could bring joy to the children of war-torn Germany.

wanted to maintain the leverage with key countries that economic and military assistance provides. One major debate today is how much debt relief to provide for the world's poorest nations, some of which spend up to 50 percent of their budgets to pay interest on old loans. The problem is particularly severe in Central and South America, where international debt has brought high inflation, unemployment, and civil unrest.

Despite these arguments, Congress invariably trims the foreign aid budget, responding in part to polls that show most people erroneously believe that the United States spends more on foreign aid than it does on Medicare and other domestic priorities. Members of Congress often criticize foreign aid as a "Ghana versus Grandma" case. How, they say, can you give away taxpayers' money to some foreign country when we have poor older people who can't afford their prescription drugs and decent medical help?[17]

Critics also note that U.S. foreign aid has subsidized the most autocratic and most corrupt of dictators. And there are plenty of instances in which foreign aid money has been stolen or misspent. Defenders counter that some corruption is inevitable. "You can't engage in bone-poor countries that lack laws and independent journalists and elections, and expect American standards of transparency," writes *Washington Post* editorial writer Sebastian Mallaby. "Yes, many aid programs fail and will continue to do so. But you don't give up trying to educate and house people just because it's hard. And you don't give up on international engagement just because it's as daunting as it is important."[18]

Economic Sanctions (Hard Power)

economic sanctions
Denial of export, import, or financial relations with a target country in an effort to change that nation's policies.

The United States has frequently used economic pressure to punish other nations for opposing its interests. Indeed, it has employed economic sanctions more than any other nation—more than 100 times in the past 50 years. **Economic sanctions** deny

HOW **OTHER NATIONS** GOVERN

Scandinavia's Foreign Aid

According to the Organization for Economic Cooperation and Development, which monitors international governance, the United States was the largest foreign aid contributor in the world in 2006, giving $24 billion to less-developed countries. The United States is far from the most generous nation, however. Although Sweden and Norway give less foreign aid in total dollars, they contribute a much greater percentage of their gross national incomes. By that measure, they are nearly five times as generous as the United States.

These two nations are more generous for several reasons. First, they have a longer history of international trade with Africa, a major target of aid. Having visited many nations over the centuries, their people may have a more natural desire to help others. Second, they are very liberal nations—they have higher taxes than most nations, allowing them to spend more money on foreign aid. Third, although they both participate in international peacekeeping missions and have been allies of the United States, they do not have a large military, which also gives them more money to contribute.

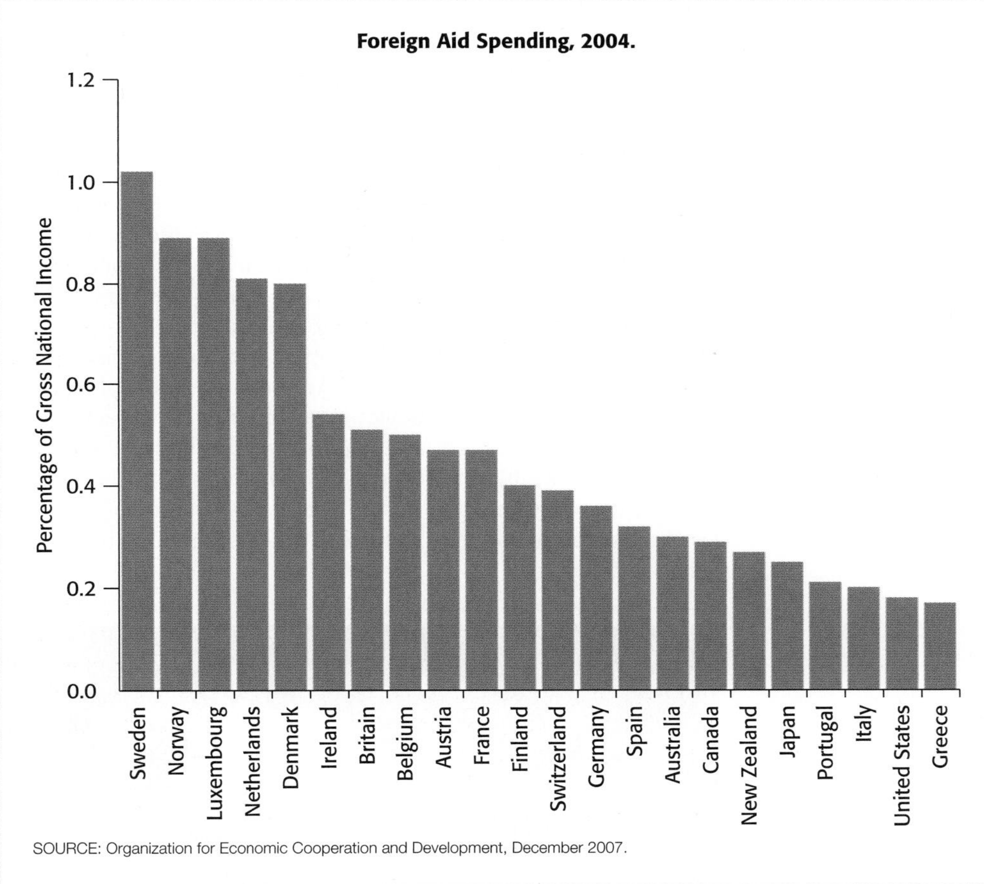

SOURCE: Organization for Economic Cooperation and Development, December 2007.

export, import, or financial relations with a target country in an effort to change that country's policies. Those imposed on South Africa doubtless helped end apartheid and encourage democracy in that nation; sanctions on Libya helped end its nuclear weapons program. But sanctions imposed on Cuba have not had much effect in dislodging that nation's dictatorial regime.

The popularity of economic sanctions has varied over the years. They are especially unpopular among farmers and corporations that have to sacrifice part of their overseas markets to comply with government controls, and they rarely work as effectively as intended. They can also be costly to U.S. businesses and workers while intensifying anti-U.S. sentiment.

YOU WILL DECIDE — Should Women Engage in Combat?

As the number of women in the armed forces has increased, so has the number of women who serve in combat zones. Whereas women constituted 6 percent of U.S. forces in the first war in Iraq in 1991, they make up 15 percent of forces in Iraq in 2008.

Although their jobs were in noncombat positions, Iraq has been a very dangerous place to serve—by March 2008, almost 100 female soldiers had been killed. The first was army private Lori Piestewa, a member of the Hopi Indian Tribe. She was killed by small-arms fire when her supply convoy got lost in the desert only days after the war began.

Technically, the women killed in Iraq did not die in combat operations. Under a 1994 order, women can fly combat aircraft to and from airfields, protect convoys, guard prisoners of war, and rescue wounded soldiers, but they may not participate in any "direct combat on the ground." Although the military is redesigning assignments to ensure that women have an equal opportunity to participate in noncombat operations, women are allowed to serve only in support units.

Military Intervention

War is not merely an extension of diplomacy but rather the complete and total breakdown of diplomatic efforts. The United States has used military force in other nations on the average of almost once a year since 1789, although usually in short-term initiatives such as NATO's military activities in Bosnia and Kosovo. Although presidential candidate John Kerry argued that the Iraq war was the first time in history the United States had gone to war because it chose to, not because it had to, the country has actually sent forces into combat many times without a clear threat. It did not have to go to war against Spain in 1898 or send troops to Cuba, Haiti, the Dominican Republic, Lebanon, Mexico, Nicaragua, Somalia, South Vietnam, or even Europe in World War I.[19] (See Table 20–1 for the number of troops killed in the nation's major wars.)

Experts tend to agree that the use of force is most successful in small and even medium-sized countries for short engagements (Grenada, Panama, Kuwait, Kosovo, and Afghanistan). They also agree that it "often proves ineffective in the context of national civil wars (the United States in Vietnam; Israel in Lebanon)."[20]

Not all military action is visible to the public or even the intended target. Covert activities are planned and executed to conceal the identity of the sponsor. The United States repeatedly engaged in covert operations during the cold war, including early intervention in Vietnam and Central America, as well as in Afghanistan, where it supported rebels fighting the Soviet invasion. But covert activities in Cuba, Chile, and elsewhere have backfired, and support for this strategy has cooled in the post–cold war era.[21] Ironically, U.S. covert aid to the Afghan rebels eventually led to the Soviet withdrawal, which in turn led to the establishment of the Taliban, which allowed Osama bin Laden and his followers to establish training bases in its territory.

TABLE 20–1 The Costs of War

War	Number Killed
Revolutionary War	4,435
War of 1812	2,260
Civil War	214,939
Spanish-American War	385
World War I	53,402
World War II	291,557
Korean War	35,516
Vietnam War	58,516
Persian Gulf War	382
Afghanistan War	220
Iraq War	4,200*

*Estimated figure as of January 1, 2009.

SOURCE: *Washington Post,* May 26, 2003; figures updated by authors.

Osama bin Laden became America's public enemy number one after his Al-Qaeda organization took credit for destroying the World Trade Center on 9/11.

Public Diplomacy

In July 2002, President George W. Bush created the White House Office of Global Communications to address the question he asked before a joint session of Congress only a week after the terrorist attacks on New York City and Washington, D.C.: "Why do they hate us?" The Office of Global Communications is designed to enhance the United States' reputation abroad, countering its image as the "Great Satan," as some of its enemies describe it.[22] In 2005, Bush put his former political adviser and White House aide Karen Hughes in charge of this public diplomacy effort (in this context the word "public" refers to citizens of other nations, not the United States). Although the administration hoped she would bring a more effective political perspective to the job, her initial efforts to rebuild the U.S. image in Arab nations were unsuccessful. She left office in late 2007.

Bush was not the first president to worry about the U.S. image abroad. President Franklin Roosevelt created the Office of War Information early in World War II, which in turn established the Voice of America program to broadcast pro-U.S. information into Nazi Germany. President Harry Truman followed suit early in the cold war with the Soviet Union by launching the Campaign of Truth, which eventually led to the creation of the U.S. Information Agency under President Dwight Eisenhower. Both agencies exist today and are being strengthened as part of the "new public diplomacy."

Public diplomacy is a blend of age-old propaganda techniques and modern information warfare. It has three basic goals: (1) to cast the enemy in a less favorable light among its supporters, (2) to mold the image of a conflict such as the war in Afghanistan, and (3) to clarify the ultimate goals of U.S. foreign policy. For example, the United States has tried to convince the people of Afghanistan that Osama bin Laden is the true enemy of the people, and that the war is not between Muslims and Western democracies but about preventing the deaths of innocent women and children in Afghanistan and the United States.

THINKING IT THROUGH

The military has changed dramatically, even since 1994. Combat us technology weapons and requires tight coordination of air, land, and s erations. It also can mean blurring the lines between support and comb units. As war has become more complicated, experts are asking whether women should be given the order to engage in combat.

Opponents argue that men are physically superior to women—although there are many high-tech jobs in combat, there is nothing high-tech about a face-to-face encounter with a deadly enemy. These opponents believe that men are better suited to win these encounters. There is also concern that men and women would form personal relationships in combat units that might distract them as they enter battle, or that female soldiers might be in the early stages of pregnancy when called for combat.

Moreover, opponents feel women would be much more vulnerable to sexual harassment in combat units, which is obviously harder to police during battle.[23] There is already plenty of evidence that women in the military face discrimination. In March 2003, for example, the air force removed the senior leadership at the Air Force Academy in Colorado Springs following repeated allegations of sexual abuse. Further congressional investigation found 142 specific complaints of verbal and physical abuse between 1993 and 2003, many of which had been received with indifference or retribution.

In the first major offensive of the war on terrorism, American troops invaded Afghanistan. Women now make up approximately 15 percent of the total enlistment in the U.S. armed forces.

Advocates of a combat role for women argue that physical differences are mostly irrelevant. All soldiers must meet certain physical qualifications such as height, weight, and conditioning. If women meet these criteria, they argue, they should be allowed to fight. After all, they go through the same boot camps as men and learn how to use the same weapons. With the armed services struggling to recruit new soldiers, advocates also argue, women constitute an important source of future volunteers.

Questions

1. What are the political barriers against allowing women in combat?
2. Are women just as able to win the face-to-face battles that often arise in combat?
3. How can the military ensure that personal relationships do not affect combat decisions on the battlefield?

Prospects for the Future

The world has become a much more uncertain place since the end of the cold war, if only because the United States now faces many potential "hot spots" where individual nations and groups can challenge its views. Moreover, the Internet has increased access to information across the world; the global economy has increased competition for jobs and markets; and the war on terrorism has increased anti-U.S. sentiment in many nations.

The Evolution of Foreign Policy

The United States is clearly struggling to address this uncertainty without frustrating the public or compromising basic democratic principles. On the one hand, for example, citizens favor open borders, easy movement of imports and exports, short lines

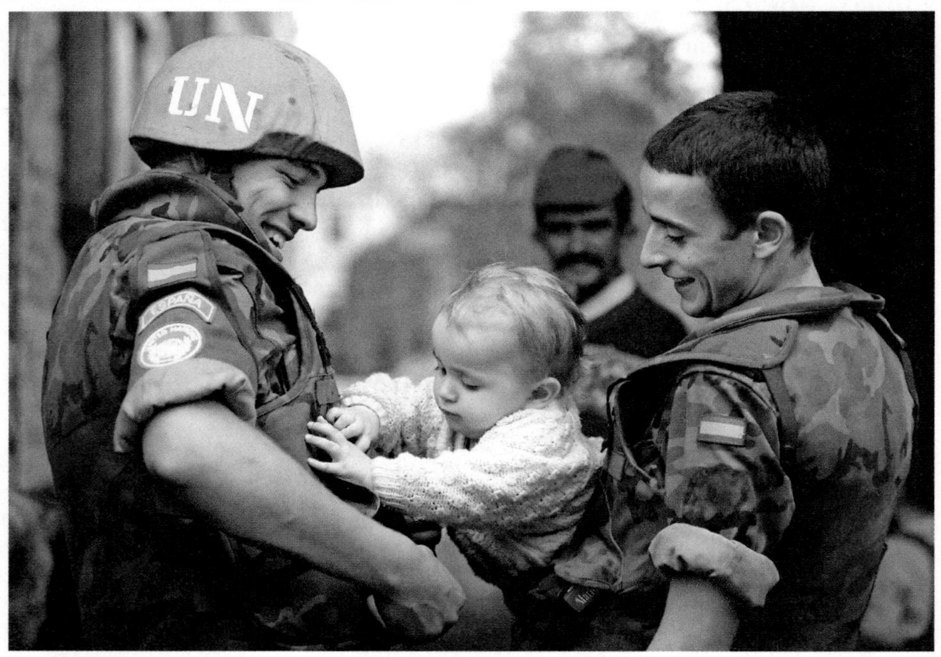

Members of the U.N. Peacekeeping Force, in their distinctive blue helmets, are called in around the world when the United Nations determines they are necessary to keep or restore order.

at airports, quick access to information, and protection of their privacy. On the other hand, they want government to monitor terrorists, detect dangerous cargo, ensure airport security, keep secrets from the enemy, and make sure no one slips through the border to bring harm to the nation.

Although these goals are not necessarily contradictory, they do require a careful balance of individual liberty and national interest. They also call for an effort to prevent the spread of terrorism by promoting global peace and understanding. The war on terrorism will not be won in a single battle with a single adversary, nor will weapons of mass destruction disappear without a broad international commitment to action. As the United States has learned over the hard months of combat in Iraq, coalition building may be difficult, frustrating, and most certainly time-consuming, but, ultimately, it may be the only option available. Having fought the Iraq war largely on its own, the United States has come to realize that it needs help to accomplish its goals.

Citizens can help the United States achieve its goals in many ways, whether by contributing or volunteering to provide humanitarian aid, serving in the military, or trying to improve the nation's reputation by addressing problems at home. At the same time, citizens can help change the foreign policy and defense agenda through active engagement in the political process. Their voices can be and have been heard on many issues, including Darfur. By putting pressure on the federal government, citizens can influence the priorities given to our foreign policy goals, while holding the nation's elected leaders accountable for what they do.

CHAPTER **SUMMARY**

1 Analyze the five questions that shape positions on U.S. foreign policy and defense.

Views of foreign policy address five basic questions: Should the United States view the world realistically or idealistically? Should the United States isolate itself from the world or accept a role in the international community? Should the United States act on its own or only with the help of other nations? Should the United States act first against threats to its safety or wait until it is attacked? And should the United States use its military and economic hard power or its diplomatic soft power?

2 Compare and contrast hard and soft power.

Hard power relies on military and economic strength, while soft power uses diplomacy. The two are sometimes used together, with one reinforcing the other. Different problems appear to respond more to hard or soft power.

3 Evaluate the seven issues that currently dominate the foreign policy and defense agenda.

The foreign policy and defense agenda contains a long list of issues, but seven are currently at the top of the list: controlling weapons of mass destruction, fighting terrorism, negotiating peace in the Middle East, promoting free trade abroad, reducing global warming, resolving the war in Iraq, and strengthening democracy and international understanding. Congress and the president do not always agree on the specific issues but tend to spend most of their time and the federal budget on them.

4 Identify the goals of the war in Iraq and evaluate the level of U.S. success.

The war in Iraq began in March 2003 with a quick invasion, but continues to the present. The Bush administration's decision was based on a desire to remove Saddam Hussein from power, an effort to eliminate Iraq's weapons of mass destruction, and a belief that Iraq could be converted into a successful democracy. The first goal was quickly met, but the weapons of mass destruction were never found, and democracy is still an elusive goal.

5 Assess the components of the foreign policy and defense bureaucracy.

The defense bureaucracy involves a set of interlocking agencies that engage in many of the same issues. The National Security Council, State Department, intelligence agencies, and Defense Department all play a role in setting and administering foreign policy and defense.

6 Examine the defense hierarchy.

The Defense Department is designed to ensure civilian control of the U.S. military but seeks advice from the military through the Joint Chiefs of Staff, who oversee the all-volunteer force. Contractors deliver a large amount of goods and services to the department and are part of what President Eisenhower called the military-industrial complex.

7 Analyze the options for achieving foreign policy and defense goals.

Foreign policy and defense options involve a mix of hard and soft power, including conventional diplomacy and foreign aid, economic sanctions, and military intervention.

Chapter Self-Test

1. A policy of viewing the world idealistically requires accepting a role in the international community. In a few sentences, make two or three more connections between the five questions shaping U.S. foreign policy. (pp. 540–542)
2. List and define the three components of the Bush doctrine. (p. 541)
3. Decide whether the following are aspects of hard power or soft power. (p. 542)
   a. Negotiating with other nations
   b. Providing aid to developing countries
   c. Maintaining powerful military forces
   d. Using battlefield forces to defeat enemies
   e. Participating in international treaties and institutions
4. List and describe five of the seven issues dominating the U.S. international agenda. (pp. 542–543)
5. In a few sentences, explain two problems and two opportunities related to granting normal trade relations status to China. (p. 546)
6. Write a short essay discussing which of the seven issues on the U.S. agenda deserves the most attention. Explain how attention to it will most likely ensure peace and prosperity and why the other issues are less important. (pp. 542–549)
7. Which of the following was *not* one of the Bush administration's stated goals in invading Iraq? (p. 548)
   a. Stabilizing world oil supplies
   b. Replacing Saddam Hussein with an elected leader
   c. Destroying Iraq's capability to build weapons of mass destruction
   d. Converting Iraq into a democracy and spreading democracy across the Middle East
8. In a few sentences, explain what the "surge" is, why it has been implemented, and its results so far. (p. 548)

9. Match each of the following government organizations with its appropriate description: (pp. 550–553)

a. Contractor	i. The organization charged with gathering information from around the world
b. State Department	ii. A private business that develops and manufactures technology for the military
c. Joint Chiefs of Staff	iii. The organization responsible for negotiating treaties, protecting U.S. citizens abroad, and staffing embassies and consulates
d. National Security Council	iv. A council consisting of the heads of the Army, Navy, Air Force, and Marine Corps
e. Central Intelligence Agency	v. A committee of the president, vice president, secretaries of defense and state, and often others that makes foreign policy

10. The foreign policy and defense bureaucracy is extremely complex and employs thousands of people. In a paragraph, suggest some of the problems that may arise from its size and complexity. (pp. 550–553)

11. In two or three sentences, explain how the President truly is the Commander-in-Chief of the armed forces. (p. 553)

12. In a short paragraph, outline the past and current organizations of the Joint Chiefs of Staff and its responsibilities. (pp. 552–553)

13. Which of the following is an example of public diplomacy? (p. 559)
    a. Diplomats from Japan, China, and the United States negotiate with North Korea over ending its nuclear weapons program
    b. President Bush addresses the U.S. people about the Iraq War
    c. The State Department creates websites in Arabic showing that al-Qaeda has killed thousands of fellow Muslims
    d. Executives from the U.S.'s General Motors and Japan's Toyota discuss an auto industry trade agreement

14. In a few sentences, define conventional diplomacy and explain how it is related to hard power. (pp. 554–555)

15. In an essay, discuss which foreign policy and defense tools, such as foreign aid or military force, would best keep the United States safe and improve its relationship with Iran. Also discuss which tools would likely *not* work or would make the situation worse. (pp. 554–559)

Key Terms

realism, p. 540

idealism, p. 540

isolationism, p. 541

internationalism, p. 541

unilateralism, p. 541

Bush Doctrine, p. 541

multilateralism, p. 541

preemption, p. 542

weapons of mass destruction, p. 542

hard power, p. 542

soft power, p. 542

theory of deterrence, p. 542

normal trade relations, p. 546

economic sanctions, p. 556

Further Reading

GEORGE H. W. BUSH AND **BRENT SCOWCROFT,** *A World Transformed* (Knopf, 1998).

WARREN CHRISTOPHER, *In the Stream of History: Shaping Foreign Policy for a New Era* (Stanford University Press, 1998).

IVO H. DAALDER AND **MICHAEL E. O'HANLON,** *Winning Ugly: NATO's War to Save Kosovo* (Brookings Institution Press, 2000).

KIMBERLY ANN ELLIOTT, GARY CLYDE HUFBAUER, AND **JEFFREY J. SCHOTT,** *Economic Sanctions Reconsidered,* 3d ed. (Peterson Institute, 2008).

LOUIS FISHER, *Presidential War Power,* 2d ed. (University Press of Kansas, 2004).

JOHN LEWIS GADDIS, *The Cold War: A New History* (Penguin, 2005).

JOHN LEWIS GADDIS, *The United States and the End of the Cold War* (Oxford University Press, 1992).

OLE HOLSTI, *Public Opinion and American Foreign Policy,* rev. ed. (University of Michigan Press, 2004).

STEVEN W. HOOK, *U.S. Foreign Policy: The Paradox of World Power,* 2d ed. (CQ Press, 2007).

SAMUEL HUNTINGTON, *The Clash of Civilization and the Remaking of World Order* (Simon & Schuster, 1996).

LOCH K. JOHNSON, *Secret Agencies: U.S. Intelligence in a Hostile World* (Yale University Press, 1996).

JOYCE P. KAUFMAN, *A Concise History of U.S. Foreign Policy* (Rowman & Littlefield, 2006).

STEVEN KULL AND **I. M. DESTLER,** *Misreading the Public: The Myth of a New Isolationism* (Brookings Institution Press, 1999).

THOMAS W. LIPPMAN, *Madeleine Albright and the New American Diplomacy* (Westview Press, 2000).

ROBERT LITAN, *Globalphobia* (Brookings Institution Press, 2002).

ROBERT S. LITWAK, *Rogue States and U.S. Foreign Policy: Containment After the Cold War* (Johns Hopkins University Press, 2000).

NATIONAL COMMISSION ON TERRORIST ATTACKS ON THE UNITED STATES, *The 9/11 Commission Report* (Norton, 2004).

JOSEPH NYE, *Soft Power: The Means to Success in World Politics* (Public Affairs, 2005).

MICHAEL E. O'HANLON, *How to Be a Cheap Defense Hawk* (Brookings Institution Press, 2002).

WILLIAM PERRY, *Preventive Defense: A New Security Strategy for America* (Brookings Institution Press, 1999).

PAUL R. PILLAR, *Terrorism and U.S. Foreign Policy* (Brookings Institution Press, 2004).

JOHN PRADOS, *Keepers of the Keys: A History of the National Security Council from Truman to Bush* (Morrow, 1991).

ROSEMARY RIGHTER, *Utopia Lost: The United Nations and World Order* (Twentieth Century Fund, 1995).

STEPHEN R. WEISSMAN, *A Culture of Deference: Congress's Failure of Leadership in Foreign Affairs* (Basic Books, 1995).

GEORGE C. WILSON, *This War Really Matters: Inside the Fight for Defense Dollars* (CQ Press, 2000).

BOB WOODWARD, *Plan of Attack* (Simon & Schuster, 2004).

BOB WOODWARD, *State of Denial: Bush at War* (Simon & Schuster, 2007)

epilogue

Sustaining Constitutional Democracy

The United States' founding generation fought an eight-year revolution to secure its rights and freedom. First at the Constitutional Convention in 1787 and later in the first Congress, they confronted the challenges of creating a government, writing a Constitution, and drafting a Bill of Rights that would protect rights to life, liberty, and self-government for themselves and subsequent generations.

But they knew, as we also know, that passive allegiance to ideals and rights is never enough. Every generation must become responsible for nurturing these ideals by actively renewing the community and nation of which it is a part.

The framers knew about the rise and decline of ancient Athens. They were familiar with Pericles's funeral oration, which states that the person who takes no part in public affairs is a useless person, a good-for-nothing.[1] According to Pericles and many Athenians, the city's business was everyone's business. Athens had flourished as an example of what a civilized city might be, but it collapsed when greed, self-centeredness, and complacency set in. As time went on, the Athenians wanted security more than they wanted liberty, comfort more than freedom. In the end they lost it all—security, comfort, and freedom. "Responsibility was the price every man must pay for freedom. It was to be had on no other terms."[2]

If we are to be responsible citizens in the truest meaning of the term, our dreams must transcend personal ambition and the accumulation of material goods. Our responsibilities as citizens of the United States include speaking up for what we believe, such as support for or opposition to particular policies such as the war in Iraq, same-sex marriages, health care reform, and more or less regulation of the economy. The exchange of ideas helps produce more-representative policy and better-informed citizens. Our country needs citizens who understand that our well-being is tied to the well-being of our neighbors, community, and country.

More people today live under conditions of political freedom than at any previous time. The transition from living under authoritarian rule to shouldering political freedom is often difficult, as evidenced by the efforts to form democratic governments and defeat insurgencies in Afghanistan and Iraq. Our experience in these two conflicts also shows that imposing democracy on societies without the supporting values and institutions is problematic. Throughout history, most people have lived in societies in which a small group at the top imposed its will on others. Authoritarian governments justify their actions by saying that people are too weak to govern themselves; they need to be ruled. Thus neither in Castro's Cuba nor in the military regime of North Korea, neither in the People's Republic of China nor in Saudi Arabia, do ordinary people have a voice in the type of decisions we routinely make in the United States: Whether to enter college and what kind of employment we seek? Who should be allowed to enter or leave the country? How much money should be spent for schools, economic development initiatives, health care, or environmental protection? We take for granted the freedom to make such decisions.

The theme in this last chapter is simple: Elected leadership and constitutional structures and protections are important, but an active, committed citizenry is equally important. Freedom and obligation go together. Liberty and duty go together. The answer to a nation's problems lies not in producing a perfect constitution or a few larger-than-life leaders. The answer lies in encouraging a nation of attentive and active citizens

OUTLINE

- The Case for Government by the People
- Participation and Representation
- The Role of the Politician
- Leadership in a Constitutional Democracy
- The Importance of Active Citizenship

who will, above and beyond their professional and private ambitions, care about the common concerns of the Republic and strive to make democracy work.

The Case for Government by the People

The essence of our Constitution is that it both grants power to government and withholds power from it. Fearing a weak national government and popular disorder, the framers wanted to strengthen the powers of the national government so that it could carry out its responsibilities, such as ensuring domestic order and maintaining national defense. They also wanted to limit state governments in order to keep them from interfering with interstate commerce and property rights. Valuing above all the principle of individual liberty, the framers wanted to protect the people from too much government. They wanted a limited government—yet one that would work. The solution was to divide up the power of the national government, to make it ultimately responsive, if only indirectly, to the voters.

Most citizens want an efficient and effective government that also promotes social justice. We want to maintain our commitment to liberty and freedom. We want a government that acts for the majority yet protects minorities. We want to safeguard our nation and our streets in a world full of change and violence. We want to protect the rights of the poor, the elderly, and minorities. Do we expect too much from our elected officials and public servants? Of course we do!

Constitutional democracy is a system of checks and balances. It balances values against competing values. Government must balance individual liberties against the collective security and needs of society. The question always is, which rights of which people are to be protected by what means and at what price to individuals and to the whole society? These questions arose again and again in the war on terrorism. The USA PATRIOT Act became law, allowing greater government surveillance. Both conservatives and liberals have criticized the act, which was renewed by the narrowest of majorities in 2006.

Participation and Representation

No political problem is more complicated than working out the proper relationship between voters and elected officials. It is not just a simple matter of ensuring that elected officials do what the voters want them to do. Every individual has a host of conflicting desires, fears, hopes, and expectations, and no government can represent them all. But even if millions of voters could be represented in their many interests, the question of *how* they would be represented would remain. Through direct representation, such as a traditional New England town meeting, or ballot initiatives and referendums? Through economic or professional associations, such as labor unions, or political action committees? Through a coalition of minority groups? We could defend all of these and other alternatives as proper forms of representation in a constitutional democracy. Yet all also have limitations.

Some propose to bypass this thorny problem of representation by vastly increasing the role of direct popular participation in decision making.[3] One avenue to do so is the recall, which removes officeholders from office based on a petition process and election. The 2003 recall of California governor Gray Davis is an example of the recall in action. The recall has been relatively rare at the statewide level, but it has the potential to alter the relationship between voters and representatives. If it were to become a means for people to remove from office, between elections, those with whom they disagree, representatives might hesitate to say or do much.

What many people regard as the most perfect form of democracy would exist when every person has a full and equal opportunity to participate in all decisions and in all processes of influence, persuasion, and discussion that bear on those decisions. Direct participation in decision making, its advocates contend, will serve two major purposes. First, it will enhance the dignity, self-respect, and understanding of individuals by giving them responsibility for the decisions that shape their lives. Second, direct participation will act as a safeguard against undemocratic and antidemocratic forms of government and prevent the replacement of democracy by dictatorship or tyranny. Interests can be represented, furthered, and defended best by the people they directly concern.

New technologies and new uses of old technologies let governments appeal directly to voters and voters speak directly to public officials. We now have voting by mail in Oregon and other places, and some people advocate voting online. Digital town halls may be next. In the 2008 election large numbers of voters, especially younger voters, communicated with each other and with the candidates via the Internet. The Internet was also an important way in which candidates, especially Barack Obama, raised campaign funds. The Internet is now an important source of news and political advertising. All of these tools will become a bigger part of communications and interactions between citizens and their government.

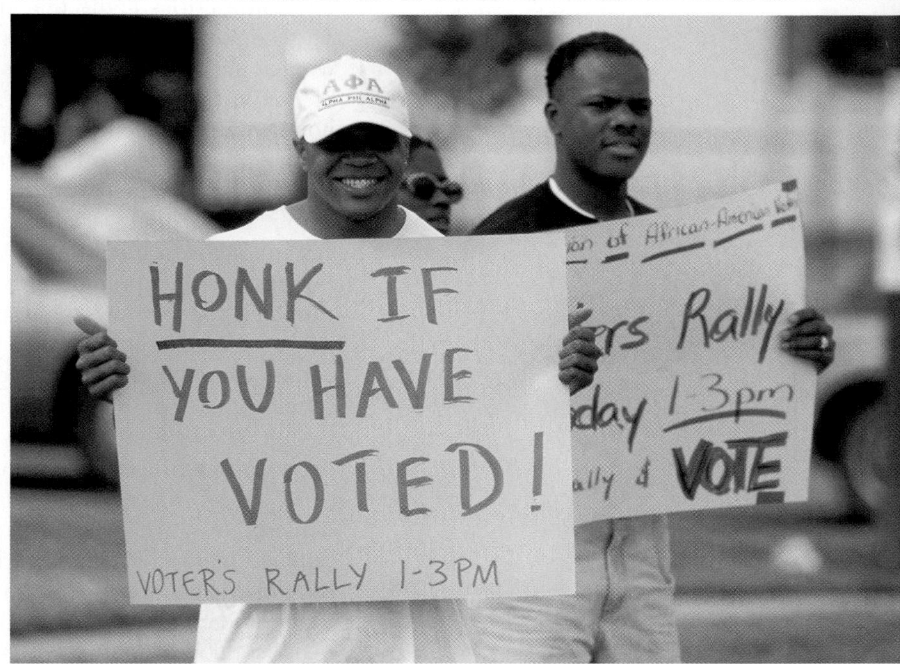

These participants in a voters' rally urge citizens to accept responsibility for perpetuating democracy.

But the average citizen rarely has time or experience to evaluate all available information. We still need institutions such as elected legislatures, which can digest complicated information and conduct impartial hearings to air competing points of view. Participatory democracy also has limits as a method of high-level decision making; it works best in small communities or at the neighborhood level. As a practical matter, people simply cannot spend hours taking part in every decision that affects their lives. Thus much of the work of government at all levels requires elected representatives.

Because we must have representatives, who shall represent whom? By electing representatives in a multitude of districts, we can build most minority interests and attitudes into our representative institutions. In the United States, we generally have election processes in which only the candidate receiving the greatest number of votes wins. But there are other ways. For example, Austria and Denmark use proportional representation—a system in which each party running receives the proportion of legislative seats corresponding to its proportion of votes.[4]

Representation can also be influenced by whether there is one party, two, or several. Ours is a strong two-party system that knits local constituencies into coalitions that can elect and sustain national majorities. A major factor in maintaining our two-party system is that single-member legislative districts, such as those for the U.S. Congress and state legislatures, tend to lead to two-party systems. This regularity, called *Duverger's law,* is generally seen as helping to moderate our politics.[5] In contrast, when countries adopt proportional representation, minor parties have greater influence.

Which is better, elected officials who represent coalitions of minorities, or officials who represent a relatively clear-cut majority and have little or no obligation to the minority? The answer depends on what you expect from government. A system that represents coalitions of minorities usually reflects the trading, competition, and compromising that must take place in order to reach agreement among the various groups. Such a government has been called *broker rule:* Elected officials act essentially as a go-between or mediator among organized groups that have definite policy goals. Under broker rule, leaders cannot get too far ahead of the groups; they must talk back and forth, shifting in response to changing group pressures. Instead of acting for a united popular majority with a fairly definite program, either liberal or conservative, the government tries to satisfy all major interests by giving them a voice in decisions and sometimes a veto over actions. In the pushing and hauling of political groups, the government is continually engaging in delicate balancing acts, and no one wins all of the time.

Some critics argue that the U.S. system has not achieved fair representation. The U.S. Congress and many state legislatures, for example, still contain relatively few women and minorities. Critics also point to the extent of nonvoting and other forms of nonparticipation in politics; the fact that low-income individuals are less well politically organized than upper-income individuals; the bias of strong organized groups toward the status quo; the domination by a few corporations of television and the press; and the virtual monopoly of party politics by the two major parties, which do not always offer the voters meaningful alternatives. Critics are concerned that our system of government builds in procedures designed to curtail legislative majorities. Rulings by the Supreme Court such as the one in *Lawrence v. Texas*, which declared the Texas sodomy law unconstitutional, are examples of how the will of the majority can be overturned.[6] Another example of antimajoritarianism in our system is the Senate rule that allows a minority to filibuster and block the will of the majority of senators. The use of the filibuster to block some judicial nominees from President George W. Bush and the threat to use it against Supreme Court nominees renewed debate about procedures that empower the legislative minority.

Charges that majority rule is stymied may be exaggerated, but they cannot be denied. Those who believe that governments should be more directly responsive to political majorities can point to steady improvement in recent years. Election laws have been changed to simplify voter registration, expand and improve voting procedures, and enforce one-person, one-vote standards. Efforts to limit the ability of rich people and well-financed interests to influence elections were cited by Congress as a motivation for passage of campaign finance reform in 2002, and by the Supreme Court in upholding that legislation in 2003.[7] Pressure has also been building to streamline voting systems and simplify voter registration processes.

Over the course of its history, the United States has shifted toward greater direct democracy, and this trend is likely to continue. The founders designed a system that limited the use of direct representation to the House of Representatives. Today both the House and Senate are directly elected. Moreover, with the advent of direct primaries, voters decide the nominees for federal office. The initiative and referendum process provides a direct way for citizens to enact or overturn laws, and even recall those in government. Voting has also been dramatically expanded from white male property owners to all citizens over age 18.

Pressures to expand the role of citizens in making laws and voting on candidates or recalling officeholders via petition suggest other ways in which direct democracy may be further expanded. Arizona allowed online voting in the 2000 Democratic presidential primary, and Michigan did the same in 2004. As access to the Internet becomes more widespread, it will grow in importance as a means for individuals to lobby public officials, circulate petitions, and interact with government and the media. The 2008 election demonstrated the power of the Internet as a way to encourage participation in politics.[8]

By this point, you undoubtedly appreciate that democracy has to mean much more than popular government and unchecked majority rule. A democracy needs competing politicians with differing views about the public interest. A vital democracy, living and growing, places its faith in the participation of citizens as voters, faith that they will elect not just people who mirror their views but leaders who will exercise their best judgment—"faith that the people will not condemn those whose devotion to principle leads them to unpopular courses, but will reward courage, respect honor, and ultimately recognize right."[9]

The Role of the Politician

Voters today have decidedly mixed views about elected officials. They realize that at their best, politicians are skillful at compromising, mediating, negotiating, and brokering—and that governing often requires these qualities. But they also suspect politicians of being ambitious, conniving, unprincipled, opportunistic, and corrupt.

Still, we often find that individual officeholders are bright, hardworking, and friendly (even though we may suspect they are trying to win our vote). And our liking sometimes turns into reverence after these same politicians die. George Washington, Abraham Lincoln, Dwight D. Eisenhower, and John F. Kennedy are acclaimed today. Harry Truman joked that "a statesman is a politician who has been dead for about ten or fifteen years."[10] Of course, we must put the problem in perspective. In all democracies, people probably expect too much from politicians and at the same time distrust those who wield power. Public officeholders tax us, regulate us, and conscript us, after all. We dislike political compromisers and ambitious opportunists—even though we may need such people to get things done.[11] At the same time, individuals can and do make a difference in shaping policy on the local, state, national, and international levels, whether the policy be about drunk driving, early childhood medical care, land mines, or using the courts to influence a policy agenda.

Politics is a necessity—a vital and at times a noble leadership activity. Politicians are essential for running the Republic, whose fragmented powers require them to mediate among factions, build coalitions, and compromise among and within branches of government to produce policy and action.

Leadership in a Constitutional Democracy

Although we easily recognize the need for leadership in government, defining what leadership is and how it operates in a constitutional democracy is more challenging.

A leader without followers is a contradiction in terms. Leadership is also situational and contextual; a leader is often effective in only one kind of situation. Thus leadership is not necessarily transferable. James Madison, for example, was a brilliant political and constitutional theorist; he was also a superb politician. Yet he was not a brilliant president.[12] The leadership required to lead a marine platoon up a hill in battle is different from the leadership needed to change racist or sexist attitudes in city governments. The leadership required of a campaign manager differs from that required of a candidate.

Although leaders are often skilled managers, they need more than managerial skills. Managers are concerned with doing things the right way; leaders are concerned with doing the right thing. Managers are concerned with efficiency and process, especially routines and standard operating procedures. Leaders, by contrast, concentrate on goals, purposes, and a vision of the future. Charismatic leaders have indispensable qualities of contagious self-confidence, unwarranted optimism, and dogged idealism that attract and mobilize others to undertake tasks they never dreamed they could accomplish. In short, they empower others and enable many of their followers to become leaders in their own right. Most of the significant breakthroughs in our nation, as well as in our communities, have been made or shaped by people who, while seeing all the complexities and obstacles ahead of them, believed in themselves and in their purposes so much that they refused to be overwhelmed and paralyzed by self-doubts. They were willing to gamble, to take risks, to look at things in a fresh way, and often to invent new rules.

Must a politician gain public office by denouncing the profession of politics? From the tone of many recent congressional and presidential races, it would appear so. Politics and politicians, including those who work in Washington, are necessary and important to our freedom, security, and prosperity. Although people will disagree about particular policies and processes, there is no disputing the need for government. Political leaders recognize the fundamental wants and needs of potential followers. They help convert others' hopes and aspirations into practical demands on government.

We are fond of saying, "It's all politics." This greatly oversimplified observation implies that things would somehow be improved if we did not have politics and politicians. But politics is the lifeblood of democracy, and without politics, there is no freedom. A nation of subservient followers can never be a democratic one. A democratic nation requires educated, skeptical, caring, engaged, and conscien-

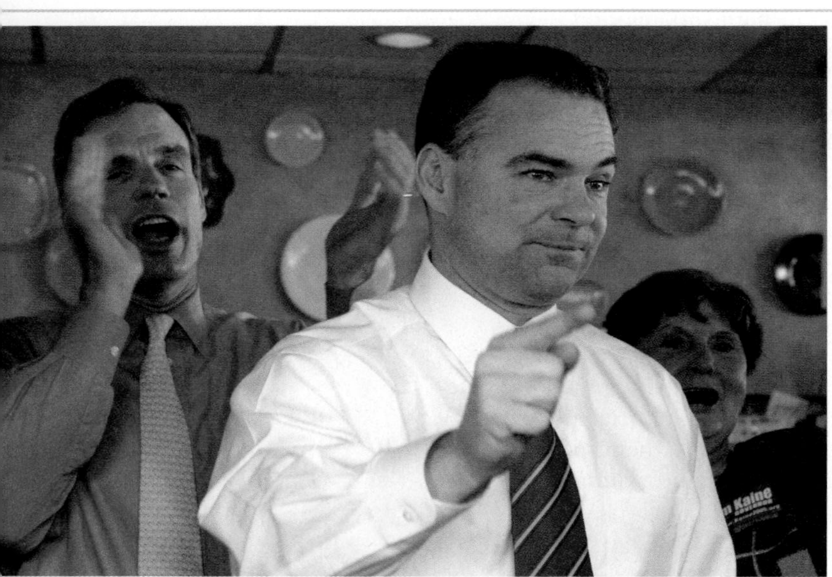

Lieutenant Governor Tim Kaine of Virginia speaks at a rally held in Woodbridge, Virginia. Kaine was elected governor to replace Mark Warner (left) who was barred from serving consecutive terms by the state's constitution.

tious citizens. It also requires citizens who will recognize when change is needed and have the courage to bring about necessary reforms and progress.[13] Such citizens provide the leaders that enable constitutional democracy to survive and thrive. Constitutional democracy requires citizens who are willing to run for office and then serve with integrity. It requires citizens willing to study and speak out on issues, become involved in political parties, and oppose the government when it is in error. No matter how brilliant our Constitution or strong our economy, ultimately our system depends on individuals willing to compete for office.

Experience teaches that power wielded justly today may be wielded corruptly tomorrow. It is right and necessary to protest when a policy is wrong or when the rights of other citizens are diminished. Democracy rests solidly on a realistic view of human nature. Criticism of official error is not unpatriotic. Our capacity for justice, as theologian and philosopher Reinhold Niebuhr observed, makes democracy possible. But our "inclination to injustice makes democracy necessary."[14] Democratic politics is the forum where, by acting together, citizens become and remain free.[15]

The ultimate test of a democratic system is the legal existence of an officially recognized opposition. A cardinal characteristic of a constitutional democracy is that it not only recognizes the need for the free organization of opposing views but also positively encourages this organization. Freedom for political expression and dissent is basic—even freedom for nonsense to be spoken so that good sense not yet recognized gets a chance to be heard.[16]

The Importance of Active Citizenship

Crucial to democracy is belief in the free play of ideas. Only when the safety valve of public discussion is available, and when almost any policy is subject to perpetual questioning and challenge, can we be assured that both minority and majority rights will be served. To be afraid of public debate is to be afraid of self-government.

Thomas Jefferson once said, "Were it left to me to decide whether we should have a government without newspapers or newspapers without a government, I should not hesitate for a moment to prefer the latter."[17] Jefferson greatly valued an informed citizenry and had boundless faith in education. He believed that people are endowed with an innate sense of justice; the average person has only to be informed to act wisely. In the long run, said Jefferson, only an educated and enlightened democracy can hope to endure.

Education is one of the best predictors of voting, participation in politics, and knowledge of public affairs. People may not be equally invested or equally willing to invest in democracy, but those who are most attentive—frequently people like you who have gone to college and have the willingness and self-confidence to see government and politics as necessary and important. An educated public has an understanding of how government works, how individuals can influence decision makers, and how to elect like-minded people.

You now know how to influence public policy and the political process. You have gained an appreciation for the ways individuals and groups can both push and block an agenda. You know that many people choose not to participate in elections or politics, enhancing the power of those who do. Finally, you should also recognize that when individuals combine knowledge with political activity, they expand their influence.

Does political participation by committed individuals bring about constructive change? Remember that within the last half-century, restaurants, motels, and landlords once openly discriminated on the basis of race. Racial segregation in education existed in several states; segregated neighborhoods were a fact of life. Discriminatory practices denied blacks and poor whites access to voting. Women were discriminated against in the workplace and in government. Civil rights legislation and court cases have wrought remarkable changes. This is not to say that we have erased the legacies of racism and other kinds of discrimination from our national life. But as historian Arthur M. Schlesinger Jr. writes, "The genius of America lies in its capacity to forge a single nation from peoples of remarkably diverse racial, religious, and ethnic origins." Schlesinger acknowledges that our government and society have been more open to some than to others, "but it is more open to all today than it was yesterday and it is likely to be even more open tomorrow than today."[18]

We are a restless, dissatisfied, and searching people. We are often our own toughest critics. Our political system is far from perfect, but it still is an open system and one that has become more and more democratic over time. People *can* fight city hall. People who disagree with policies in the nation can band together and be heard. We know only too well that the American dream is never fully attained. It must always be pursued.

Education fosters self-confidence in dealing with bureaucracy, is a strong predictor of voting, and provides a knowledge base important to political influence.

Millions of citizens visit the great monuments in our nation's capital each year. They are always impressed by the memorials to Washington, Jefferson, Lincoln, Franklin D. Roosevelt, and the Vietnam, Korean, and World War II veterans. They are awed by the beauty of the Capitol, the Supreme Court, and the White House. The strength of the nation, however, resides not in these official buildings and monuments but in the hearts, minds, and behavior of citizens. If we lose faith, stop caring, stop participating, and stop believing in the possibilities of self-government, the monuments "will be meaningless piles of stone, and the venture that began with the Declaration of Independence, the venture familiarly known as America will be as lifeless as the stone."[19]

The future of our democracy will be shaped by citizens who care about preserving and extending our political rights and freedoms. Our individual liberties will never be assured unless we are willing to take responsibility for the progress of the whole community, to exercise our determination and belief in democracy. In the words of U.S. poet Archibald MacLeish: "How shall freedom be defended? By arms when it is attacked by arms, by truth when it is attacked by lies, by democratic faith when it is attacked by authoritarian dogma. Always, in the final act, by determination and faith."[20]

Further Reading

DEREK BOK, *The Trouble with Government* (Harvard University Press, 2001).

RICHARD D. BROWN, *The Strength of a People: The Idea of an Informed Citizenry in America, 1650–1870* (University of North Carolina Press, 1996).

JAMES MACGREGOR BURNS, *Leadership* (Harper & Row, 1978).

ROBERT COLES, *Lives of Moral Leadership: Men and Women Who Have Made a Difference* (Random House, 2000).

ROBERT A. DAHL, *On Democracy* (Yale University Press, 1998).

AMY GUTMANN AND **DENNIS THOMSON**, *Democracy and Discontent: Why Moral Conflict Cannot Be Avoided in Politics, and What Should Be Done About It* (Belknap Press, 1996).

GRANT REEHER, *First Person Political: Legislative Life and the Meaning of Public Service* (New York University Press, 2006).

PETER H. SCHUCK AND **JAMES Q. WILSON**, *Understanding America: The Anatomy of an Exceptional Nation* (Public Affairs, 2008).

Appendix

The Declaration of Independence

DRAFTED MAINLY BY THOMAS JEFFERSON, THIS DOCUMENT ADOPTED BY THE SECOND CONTINENTAL CONGRESS, AND SIGNED BY JOHN HANCOCK AND FIFTY-FIVE OTHERS, OUTLINED THE RIGHTS OF MAN AND THE RIGHTS TO REBELLION AND SELF-GOVERNMENT. IT DECLARED THE INDEPENDENCE OF THE COLONIES FROM GREAT BRITAIN, JUSTIFIED REBELLION, AND LISTED THE GRIEVANCES AGAINST GEORGE THE III AND HIS GOVERNMENT. WHAT IS MEMORABLE ABOUT THIS FAMOUS DOCUMENT IS NOT ONLY THAT IT DECLARED THE BIRTH OF A NEW NATION, BUT THAT IT SET FORTH, WITH ELOQUENCE, OUR BASIC PHILOSOPHY OF LIBERTY AND REPRESENTATIVE DEMOCRACY.

IN CONGRESS, JULY 4, 1776

(The unanimous Declaration of the Thirteen United States of America)

PREAMBLE

When, in the course of human events, it becomes necessary for one people to dissolve the political bands which have connected them with another, and to assume, among the powers of the earth, the separate and equal station to which the laws of nature and of nature's God entitle them, a decent respect to the opinions of mankind requires that they should declare the causes which impel them to the separation.

NEW PRINCIPLES OF GOVERNMENT

We hold these truths to be self-evident; that all men are created equal, that they are endowed by their Creator with certain unalienable rights, that among these are life, liberty, and the pursuit of happiness.

That, to secure these rights, governments are instituted among men, deriving their just powers from the consent of the governed.

That whenever any form of government becomes destructive of these ends, it is the right of the people to alter or to abolish it, and to institute new government, laying its foundation on such principles, and organizing its powers in such form, as to them shall seem most likely to effect their safety and happiness. Prudence, indeed will dictate that governments long established should not be changed for light and transient causes; and accordingly all experience hath shown that mankind are more disposed to suffer while evils are sufferable, than to right themselves by abolishing the forms to which they are accustomed. But when a long train of abuses and usurpations, pursuing invariably the same object, evinces a design to reduce them under absolute despotism, it is their right, it is their duty, to throw off such government, and to provide new guards for their future security.

REASONS FOR SEPARATION

Such has been the patient sufferance of these colonies; and such is now the necessity which constrains them to alter their former systems of government. The history of the present king of Great Britain is a history of repeated injuries and usurpations, all having in direct object the establishment of an absolute tyranny over these states. To prove this, let facts be submitted to a candid world.

He has refused his assent to laws, the most wholesome and necessary for the public good.

He has forbidden his governors to pass laws of immediate and pressing importance unless suspended in their operation till his assent should be obtained; and when so suspended, he has utterly neglected to attend to them.

He has refused to pass other laws for the accommodation of large districts of people, unless those people would relinquish the right of representation in the legislature, a right inestimable to them, and formidable to tyrants only.

He has called together legislative bodies at places unusual, uncomfortable, and distant for the depository of their public records, for the sole purpose of fatiguing them into compliance with his measures.

He has dissolved representative houses repeatedly, for opposing, with manly firmness, his invasions on the rights of people.

He has refused, for a long time after such dissolutions, to cause others to be elected; whereby the legislative powers incapable of annihilation, have returned to the people at large for their exercise; the state remaining, in the meantime, exposed to all the dangers of invasion from without and convulsions within.

He has endeavored to prevent the population of these states; for that purpose obstructing the laws of naturalization of foreigners, refusing to pass others to encourage their migration hither, and raising the conditions of new appropriations of lands.

He has obstructed the administration of justice, by refusing his assent to laws for establishing judiciary powers.

He has made judges dependent on his will alone for the tenure of their offices, and the amount and payment of their salaries.

He has erected a multitude of new offices, and sent hither swarms of officers to harass our people and eat out their substance.

He has kept among us, in times of peace, standing armies, without the consent of our legislature.

He has affected to render the military independent of, and superior to, the civil power.

He has combined with others to subject us to jurisdiction foreign to our constitution and unacknowledged by our laws, giving his assent to their acts of pretended legislation:

For quartering large bodies of armed troops among us;

For protecting them, by a mock trial, from punishment for any murders which they should commit on the inhabitants of these states;

For cutting off our trade with all parts of the world;

For imposing taxes on us without our consent;

For depriving us, in many cases, of the benefits of trial by jury;

For transporting us beyond seas, to be tried for pretended offenses;

For abolishing the free system of English laws in a neighboring province, establishing therein an arbitrary government, and enlarging its boundaries, so as to render it at once an example and fit instrument for introducing the same absolute rule into these colonies;

For taking away our charters, abolishing our most valuable laws, and altering, fundamentally, the forms of our governments;

For suspending our own legislatures, and declaring themselves invented with power to legislate for us in all cases whatsoever.

He has abdicated government here, by declaring us out of his protection and waging war against us.

He has plundered our seas, ravaged our coasts, burned our towns, and destroyed the lives of our people.

He is at this time transporting large armies of foreign mercenaries to complete the works of death, desolation, and tyranny already begun with circumstances of cruelty and perfidy scarcely paralleled in the most barbarous ages and totally unworthy of the head of a civilized nation.

He has constrained our fellow-citizens, taken captive on the high seas, to bear arms against their country, to become the executioners of their friends and brethren, or to fall themselves by their hands.

He has excited domestic insurrections among us, and has endeavored to bring on the inhabitants of our frontiers the merciless Indian savages, whose known rule of warfare is an undistinguished destruction of all ages, sexes, and conditions.

In every stage of these oppressions we have petitioned for redress in the most humble terms; our repeated petitions have been answered only by repeated injury. A prince whose character is thus marked by every act which may define a tyrant is unfit to be the ruler of a free people.

Nor have we been wanting in attention to our British brethren. We have warned them, from time to time, of attempts by their legislature to extend an unwarrantable jurisdiction over us. We have reminded them of the circumstances of our emigration and settlement here. We have appealed to their native justice and magnanimity; and we have conjured them, by the ties of our common kindred, to disavow these usurpations, which would inevitably interrupt our connections and correspondence. They, too, have been deaf to the voice of justice and of consanguinity. We must, therefore, acquiesce in the necessity which denounces our separation, and hold them, as we hold the rest of mankind, enemies in war, in peace, friends.

We, therefore, the representatives of the United States of America, in General Congress assembled, appealing to the Supreme Judge of the world for the rectitude of our intentions, do, in the name and by authority of the good people of these colonies, solemnly publish and declare, that these united colonies are, and of right ought to be, free and independent states; that they are absolved from all allegiance to the British crown, and that all political connection between them and the state of Great Britain is, and ought to be, totally dissolved; and that, as free and independent states, they have full power to levy war, conclude peace, contract alliances, establish commerce, and do all other acts and things which independent states may of a right do. And, for the support of this declaration, with a firm reliance on the protection of Divine Providence, we mutually pledge to each other our lives, our fortunes, and our sacred honor.

The Federalist, No. 10, James Madison

THE FEDERALIST, NO. 10, WRITTEN BY JAMES MADISON SOON AFTER THE CONSTITUTIONAL CONVENTION, WAS PREPARED AS ONE OF SEVERAL DOZEN NEWSPAPER ESSAYS AIMED AT PERSUADING NEW YORKERS TO RATIFY THE PROPOSED CONSTITUTION. ONE OF THE MOST IMPORTANT BASIC DOCUMENTS IN AMERICAN POLITICAL HISTORY, IT OUTLINES THE NEED FOR AND THE GENERAL PRINCIPLES OF A DEMOCRATIC REPUBLIC. IT ALSO PROVIDES A POLITICAL AND ECONOMIC ANALYSIS OF THE REALITIES OF INTEREST GROUP OR FACTION POLITICS.

To the People of the State of New York:
Among the numerous advantages promised by a well-constructed union, none deserves to be more accurately developed than its tendency to break and control the violence of faction. The friend of popular governments, never finds himself so much alarmed for their character and fate, as when he contemplates their propensity of this dangerous vice. He will not fail, therefore, to set a due value on any plan which, without violating the principles to which he is attached, provides a proper cure for it. The instability, injustice, and confusion introduced into the public councils, have, in truth, been the mortal diseases under which popular governments have everywhere perished; as they continue to be the favorite and fruitful topics from which the adversaries to liberty derive

their most specious declamations. The valuable improvements made by the American constitutions on the popular models, both ancient and modern, cannot certainly be too much admired; but it would be an unwarrantable partiality, to contend that they have as effectually obviated the danger on this side, as was wished and expected. Complaints are everywhere heard from our most considerate and virtuous citizens, equally the friends of public and private faith, and of public and personal liberty, that our governments are too unstable; that the public good is disregarded in the conflicts of rival parties; and that measures are too often decided, not according to the rules of justice, and the rights of the minor party, but by the superior force of an interested and overbearing majority. However anxiously we may wish that these complaints had no foundation, the evidence of known facts will not permit us to deny that they are in some degree true. It will be found, indeed, on a candid review of our situation, that some of the distresses under which we labor have been erroneously charged on the operations of our governments; but it will be found, at the same time, that other causes will not alone account for many of our heaviest misfortunes; and, particularly, for that prevailing and increasing distrust of public engagements, and alarm for private rights, which are echoed from one end of the continent to the other. These must be chiefly, if not wholly, effects of the unsteadiness and injustice, with which a factious spirit has tainted our public administrations.

By a faction, I understand a number of citizens, whether amounting to a majority of the whole, who are united and actuated by some common impulse of passion, or of interest, adverse to the rights of other citizens, or to the permanent and aggregate interests of the community.

There are two methods of curing the mischiefs of faction: the one, by removing its causes; the other, by controlling its effects.

There are again two methods of removing the causes of faction: the one, by destroying the liberty which is essential to its existence; the other, by giving to every citizen the same opinions, the same passions, and the same interests.

It could never be more truly said, than of the first remedy, that it was worse than the disease. Liberty is to faction what air is to fire, an aliment without which it instantly expires. But it could not be a less folly to abolish liberty, which is essential to political life, because it nourishes faction, than it would be to wish the annihilation of air, which is essential to animal life, because it imparts to fire its destructive agency.

The second expedient is as impracticable, as the first would be unwise. As long as the reason of man continues fallible, and he is at liberty to exercise it, different opinions will be formed. As long as the connection subsists between his reason and his self-love, his opinions and his passions will have a reciprocal influence on each other; and the former will be objects to which the latter will attach themselves. The diversity in the faculties of men, from which the rights of property originate, is not less an insuperable obstacle to an uniformity of interests. The protection of these faculties is the first object of government. From the protection of different and unequal faculties of acquiring property, the possession of different degrees and kinds of property immediately results; and from the influence of these on the sentiments and views of the respective proprietors, ensues a division of the society into different interests and parties.

The latent causes of faction are thus sown in the nature of man; and we see them everywhere brought into different degrees of activity, according to the different circumstances of civil society. A zeal for different opinions concerning religion, concerning government, and many other points, as well of speculation as of practice; an attachment to different leaders ambitiously contending for preeminence and power; or to persons of other descriptions whose fortunes have been interesting to the human passions, have, in turn, divided mankind into parties, inflamed them with mutual animosity, and rendered them much more disposed to vex and oppress each other, than to cooperate for their common good. So strong is this propensity of mankind, to fall into mutual animosities, that where no substantial occasion presents itself, the most frivolous and fanciful distinctions have been sufficient to kindle their unfriendly passions and excite their most violent conflicts. But the most common and durable source of factions, has been the various and unequal distribution of property. Those who hold, and those who are without property, have ever formed distinct interests in society. Those who are creditors, and those who are debtors, fall under a like discrimination. A landed interest, a manufacturing interest, a mercantile interest, a moneyed interest, with many lesser interests, grow up of necessity in civilized nations, and divide them into different classes, actuated by different sentiments and views. The regulation of these various and interfering interests forms the principal task of modern legislation, and involves the spirit of the party and faction in the necessary and ordinary operations of the government.

No man is allowed to be a judge in his own cause; because his interest will certainly bias his judgment, and, not improbably, corrupt his integrity. With equal, nay, with greater reason, a body of men are unfit to be both judges and parties at the same time; yet what are many of the most important acts of legislation, but so many judicial determinations, not indeed concerning the right of single persons, but concerning the rights of large bodies of citizens? And what are the different classes of legislators, but advocates and parties to the causes which they determine? Is a law proposed concerning private debts? It is a question to which the creditors are parties on one side, and the debtors on the other. Justice ought to hold the balance between them. Yet the parties are, and must be, themselves the judges; and the most numerous party, or, in other words, the most powerful faction, must be expected to prevail. Shall domestic manufacturers be encouraged, and in what degree, by restrictions on foreign manufacturers? Are questions which would be differently decided by the landed and the manufacturing classes; and probably by neither with a sole regard to justice and the public good. The apportionment of taxes, on the various descriptions of property, is an act which seems to require the most exact impartiality; yet there is, perhaps, no legislative act, in which greater opportunity and temptation are given to a predominant party to trample on the rules of justice. Every shilling, with which they overburden the inferior number, is a shilling saved to their own pockets.

It is in vain to say, that enlightened statesmen will be able to adjust these clashing interests, and render them all subservient to the public good. Enlightened statesmen will not always be at the helm, nor, in many cases, can such an adjustment be made at all, without taking into view indirect and remote considerations, which will rarely prevail over the immediate interest which one party may find in disregarding the rights of another, or the good of the whole.

The inference to which we are brought is, that the causes of faction cannot be removed; and that relief is only to be sought in the means of controlling its effects.

If a faction consists of less than a majority, relief is supplied by the republican principle, which enables the majority to defeat its sinister views, by regular vote. It may clog the administration, it may convulse the society; but it will be unable to execute and mask its violence under the forms of the Constitution. When a majority is included in a faction, the form of popular government, on the other hand, enables it to sacrifice to its ruling passion or interest, both the public good and the rights of other citizens. To secure the public good, and private rights, against the danger of such a faction, and at the same time to preserve the spirit and the form of popular government, is then the great object to which our inquiries are directed. Let me add, that it is the great desideratum, by which alone this form of government can be rescued from the opprobrium under which it has so long laboured, and be recommended to the esteem and adoption of mankind.

By what means is this object attainable? Evidently by one of two only. Either the existence of the same passion or interest in a majority, at the same time, must be prevented; or the majority, having such coexistent passion or interest, must be rendered, by their number and local situation, unable to concert and carry into effect schemes of oppression. If the impulse and the opportunity be suffered to coincide, we well know that neither moral nor religious motives can be relied on as an adequate control. They are not found to be such on the injustice and violence of individuals, and lose their efficacy in proportion to the number combined together; that is, in proportion as their efficacy becomes needful.

From this view of the subject, it may be concluded, that a pure democracy, by which I mean a society consisting of a small number of citizens, who assemble and administer the government in person, can admit of no cure for the mischiefs of faction. A common passion or interest will, in almost every case, be felt by a majority of the whole; a communication and concert, results from the form of government itself; and there is nothing to check the inducements to sacrifice the weaker party, or an obnoxious individual. Hence, it is, that such democracies have ever been spectacles of turbulence and contention; have ever been found incompatible with personal security, or the rights of property; and have in general been as short in their lives, as they have been violent in their deaths. Theoretic politicians, who have patronized this species of government, have erroneously supposed, that by reducing mankind to a perfect equality in their political rights, they would, at the same time be perfectly equalized and assimilated in their possessions, their opinions, and their passions.

A republic, by which I mean a government in which the scheme of representation takes place, opens a different prospect, and promises the cure for which we are seeking. Let us examine the points in which it varies from pure democracy, and we shall comprehend both the nature of the cure and the efficacy which it must derive from the union.

The two great points of difference, between a democracy and a republic, are, first, the delegation of the government, in the latter, to a small number of citizens, elected by the rest; secondly, the greater number of citizens, and greater sphere of country, over which the latter may be extended.

The effect of the first difference is, on the one hand, to refine and enlarge the public views, by passing them through the medium of a chosen body of citizens, whose wisdom may best discern the true interest of their country, and whose patriotism and love of justice, will be least likely to sacrifice it to temporary or partial considerations. Under such a regulation, it may well happen, that the public voice, pronounced by the representatives of the people, will be more consonant to the public good, than if pronounced by the people themselves, convened for the purpose. On the other hand the effect may be inverted. Men of factious tempers, of local prejudices, or of sinister designs, may by intrigue, by corruption, or by other means, first obtain the suffrages, and then betray the interest of the people. The question resulting is, whether small or extensive republics are most favourable to the election of proper guardians of the public weal; and it is clearly decided in favour of the latter by two obvious considerations.

In the first place, it is to be remarked that, however small the republic may be, the representatives must be raised to a certain number, in order to guard against the cabals of a few; and that however large it may be, they must be limited to a certain number, in order to guard against the confusion of a multitude. Hence, the number of representatives in the two cases not being in proportion to that of the constituents, and being proportionally greatest in the small republic, it follows, that if the proportion of fit characters be not less in the large than in the small republic, the former will present a greater option, and consequently a greater probability of a fit choice.

In the next place, as each representative will be chosen by a greater number of citizens in the large than in the small republic, it will be more difficult for unworthy candidates to practice with success the vicious arts, by which elections are too often carried; and the suffrages of the people being more free, will be more likely to centre in men who possess the most attractive merit, and the most diffusive and established characters.

It must be confessed, that in this, as in most other cases, there is a mean, on both sides of which inconveniences will be found to lie. By enlarging too much the number of electors, you render the representatives too little acquainted with all their local circumstances and lesser interests; as by reducing it too much, you render him unduly attached to these, and too little fit to comprehend and pursue great and national objects. The federal constitution forms a happy combination in this respect; the great and aggregate interests being referred to the national, the local and particular to the state legislatures.

The other point of difference is, the greater number of citizens, and extent of territory, which may be brought within the compass of republican, than of democratic government; and it is this circumstance principally which renders factious combinations less to be dreaded in the former, than in the latter. The smaller the society, the fewer probably will be the distinct parties and interests composing it; the fewer the distinct parties and interests, the more frequently will a majority be found of the same party; and the smaller the number of individuals composing a majority, and the smaller the compass within which they are placed, the more easily will they concert and execute their plans of oppression. Extend the sphere, and you take in a greater variety of parties and interests; you make it less probable that a majority of the whole will have a common motive to invade the rights of other citizens; or if such a common motive exists, it will be more difficult for all who feel it to discover their own strength, and to act in unison with each other. Besides other impediments, it may be remarked, that where there is a consciousness of unjust or dishonourable purposes, communication is always checked by distrust, in proportion to the number whose concurrence is necessary.

Hence, it clearly appears, that the same advantage, which a republic has over a democracy, in controlling the effects of faction, is enjoyed by a large over a small republic—is enjoyed by the union over the states composing it. Does this advantage consist in the substitution of representatives, whose enlightened views and virtuous sentiments render them superior to local prejudices, and to schemes of injustice? It will not be denied that the representation of the union will be most likely to possess these requisite endowments. Does it consist in the greater security afforded by a greater variety of parties, against the event of any one party being able to outnumber and oppress the rest? In an equal degree does the increased variety of parties, comprised within the union, increase the security? Does it, in fine, consist in the greater obstacles opposed to the concert and accomplishment of the secret wishes of an unjust and interested majority? Here, again, the extent of the union gives it the most palpable advantage.

The influence of factious leaders may kindle a flame within their particular states, but will be unable to spread a general conflagration through the other states; a religious sect may degenerate into a political faction in a part of the confederacy; but the variety of sects dispersed over the entire face of it, must secure the national councils against any danger from that source: a rage for paper money, for an abolition of debts, for an equal division of property, or for any other improper or wicked project, will be less apt to pervade the whole body of the union than a particular member of it; in the same proportion as such a malady is more likely to taint a particular county or district, than an entire state.

In the extent and proper structure of the union, therefore, we behold a republican remedy for the diseases most incident to republican government. And according to the degree of pleasure and pride we feel in being republicans, ought to be our zeal in cherishing the spirit, and supporting the character of federalists.

The Federalist, No. 51, James Madison

***THE FEDERALIST,* NO. 51, ALSO WRITTEN BY MADISON, IS A CLASSIC STATEMENT IN DEFENSE OF SEPARATION OF POWERS AND REPUBLICAN PROCESSES. ITS FOURTH PARAGRAPH IS ESPECIALLY FAMOUS AND IS FREQUENTLY QUOTED BY STUDENTS OF GOVERNMENT.**

To what expedient, then, shall we finally resort, for maintaining in practice the necessary partition of power among the several departments as laid down in the Constitution? The only answer that can be given is that as all these exterior provisions are found to be inadequate the defect must be supplied, by so contriving the interior structure of the government as that its several constituent parts may, by their mutual relations, be the means of keeping each other in their proper places. Without presuming to undertake a full development of this important idea I will hazard a few general observations which may perhaps place it in a clearer light, and enable us to form a more correct judgment of the principles and structure of the government planned by the convention.

In order to lay a due foundation for that separate and distinct exercise of the different powers of government, which to a certain extent is admitted on all hands to be essential to the preservation of liberty, it is evident that each department should have a will of its own; and consequently should be so constituted that the members of each should have as little agency as possible in the appointment of the members of the others. Were this principle rigorously adhered to, it would require that all the appointments for the supreme executive, legislative, and judiciary magistracies should be drawn from the same fountain of authority, the people, through channels having no communication whatever with one another. Perhaps such a plan of constructing the several departments would be less difficult in practice than it may in contemplation appear. Some difficulties, however, and some additional expense would attend the execution of it. Some deviations, therefore, from the principle must be admitted. In the constitution of the judiciary department in particular, it might be inexpedient to insist rigorously on the principle: first, because peculiar qualifications being essential in the members, the primary consideration ought to be to select that mode of choice which best secures these qualifications; second, because the permanent tenure by which the appointments are held in that department must soon destroy all sense of dependence on the authority conferring them.

It is equally evident that the members of each department should be as little dependent as possible on those of the others for the emoluments annexed to their offices. Were the executive magistrate, or the judges, not independent of the legislature in this particular, their independence in every other would be merely nominal.

But the great security against a gradual concentration of the several powers in the same department consists in giving to those who administer each department the necessary constitutional means and personal motives to resist encroachments of the others. The provision for defense must in this, as in all other cases, be made commensurate to the danger of attack. Ambition must be made to counteract ambition. The interest of the man must be connected with the constitutional rights of the place. It may be a reflection on human nature that such devices should be necessary to control the abuses of government. But what is government itself but the greatest of all reflections on human nature? If men were angels, no government would be necessary. If angels were to govern men, neither external nor internal controls on government would be necessary. In framing a government which is to be administered by men over men, the great difficulty lies in this: you must first enable the government to control the governed; and in the next place oblige it to control itself. A dependence on the people is, no doubt, the primary control on the government; but experience has taught mankind the necessity of auxiliary precautions.

This policy of supplying, by opposite and rival interests, the defect of better motives, might be traced through the whole system of human affairs, private as well as public. We see it particularly displayed in all the subordinate distributions of power, where the constant aim is to divide and arrange the several offices in such a manner as that each may be a check on the other—that the private interest of every individual may be a sentinel over the public rights. These inventions of prudence cannot be less requisite in the distribution of the supreme powers of the State.

But it is not possible to give to each department an equal power of self-defense. In republican government, the legislative authority necessarily predominates. The remedy for this inconveniency is to divide the legislature into different branches; and to render them, by modes of election and different principles of action, as little connected with each other as the nature of their common functions and their common dependence on the society will admit. It may even be necessary to guard against dangerous encroachments by still further precautions. As the weight of the legislative authority requires that it should be thus divided, the weakness of the executive may require, on the other hand, that it should be fortified. An absolute negative on the legislature appears, at first view, to be the natural defense with which the executive magistrate should be armed. But perhaps it would be neither altogether safe nor alone sufficient. On ordinary occasions it might not be exerted with the requisite firmness, and on extraordinary occasions it might be perfidiously abused. May not this defect of an absolute negative be supplied by some qualified connection between this weaker department and the weaker branch of the stronger department, by which the latter may be led to support the constitutional rights of the former, without being too much detached from the rights of its own department?

If the principles on which these observations are founded be just, as I persuade myself they are, and they be applied as a criterion to the several State constitutions, and to the federal Constitution, it will be found that if the latter does not perfectly correspond with them, the former are infinitely less able to bear such a test.

There are, moreover, two considerations particularly applicable to the federal system of America, which place that system in a very interesting point of view.

First. In a single republic, all the power surrendered by the people is submitted to the administration of a single government; and the usurpations are guarded against by a division of the government into distinct and separate departments. In the compound republic of America, the power surrendered by the people is first divided between two distinct governments, and then the portion allotted to each subdivided among distinct and separate departments. Hence a double security arises to the rights of the people. The different governments will control each other, at the same time that each will be controlled by itself.

Second. It is of great importance in a republic not only to guard the society against the oppression of its rulers, but to guard one part of the society against the injustice of the other part. Different interests necessarily exist in different classes of citizens. If a majority be united by a common interest, the rights of the minority will be insecure. There are but two methods of providing against this evil: the one by creating a will in the community independent of the majority—that is, of the society itself; the other, by comprehending in the society so many separate descriptions of citizens as will render an unjust combination of a majority of the whole very improbable, if not impracticable. The first method prevails in all governments possessing an hereditary or self-appointed authority. This, at best, is but a precarious security; because a power independent of the society may as well espouse the unjust views of the major as the rightful interests of the minor party, and may possibly be turned against both parties. The second method will be exemplified in the federal republic of the United States. Whilst all authority in it will be derived from and dependent on the society, the society itself will be broken into so many parts, interests and classes of citizens, that the rights of individuals, or of the minority, will be in little danger from interested combinations of the majority. In a free government the security for civil rights must be the same as that for religious rights. It consists in the one case in the multiplicity of interests, and in the other in the multiplicity of sects. The degree of security in both cases will depend on the number of interests and sects; and this may be presumed to depend on the extent of country and number of people comprehended under the same government. This view of the t particularly recommend a 'al system to all the sincere and considerate friends of republican government, since it shows that in exact proportion as the territory of the Union may be formed into more circumscribed Confederacies, or States, oppressive combinations of a majority will be facilitated; the best security, under the republican forms, for the rights of every class of citizen, will be diminished; and consequently the stability and independence of some member of the government, the only other security, must be proportionally increased. Justice is the end of government. It is the end of civil society. It ever has been and ever will be pursued until it be obtained, or until liberty be lost in the pursuit. In a society under the forms of which the stronger faction can readily unite and oppress the weaker, anarchy may as truly be said to reign as in a state of nature, where the weaker individual is not secured against the violence of the stronger; and as, in the latter state, even the stronger individuals are prompted, by the uncertainty of their condition, to submit to a government which may protect the weak as well as themselves; so, in the former state, will the more powerful factions or parties be gradually induced, by a like motive, to wish for a government which will protect all parties, the weaker as well as the more powerful. It can be little doubted that if the State of Rhode Island was separated from the Confederacy and left to itself, the insecurity of rights under the popular form of government within such narrow limits would be displayed by such reiterated oppressions of factious majorities that some power altogether independent of the people would soon be called for by the voice of the very factions whose misrule had proved the necessity to it. In the extended republic of the United States, and among the great variety of interests, parties, and sects which it embraces, a coalition of a majority of the whole society could seldom take place on any other principles than those of justice and the general good; whilst there being thus less danger to a minor from the will of a major party, there must be less pretext, also, to provide for the security of the former, by introducing into the government a will not dependent on the latter, or, in other words, a will independent of the society itself. It is no less certain that it is important, notwithstanding the contrary opinions which have been entertained that the larger the society, provided it lie within a practicable sphere, the more duly capable it will be of self-government. And happily for the *republican cause,* the practicable sphere may be carried to a very great extent by a judicious modification and mixture of the *federal principle.*

The Federalist, No. 78, Alexander Hamilton

***The Federalist,* No. 78, written by Alexander Hamilton, explains and praises the provisions for the judiciary in the newly drafted Constitution. Notice especially how Hamilton asserts that the courts have a key responsibility in determining the meaning of the Constitution as fundamental law. Hamilton is outlining here the doctrine of judicial review as we now know it.**

We proceed now to an examination of the judiciary department of the proposed government.

In unfolding the defects of the existing Confederation, the utility and necessity of a federal judicature have been clearly pointed out. It is the less necessary to recapitulate the considerations there urged as the propriety of the institution in the abstract is not disputed; the only questions which have been raised being relative to the manner of constituting it, and to its extent. To these points, therefore, our observations shall be confined.

The manner of constituting it seems to embrace these several objects: 1st. The mode of appointing the judges. 2nd. The tenure by which they are to hold their places. 3rd. The partition of the judiciary authority between different courts and their relations to each other.

First. As to the mode of appointing the judges: this is the same with that of appointing the officers of the Union in general and has been so fully discussed in the two last numbers that nothing can be said here which would not be useless repetition.

Second. As to the tenure by which the judges are to hold their places: this chiefly concerns their duration in office, the provisions for their support, the precautions for their responsibility.

According to the plan of the convention, all judges who may be appointed by the United States are to hold their offices *during good behavior;* which is conformable to the most approved of the State constitutions, and among the rest, to that of this State. Its propriety having been drawn into question by the adversaries of that plan is no light symptom of the rage for objection which disorders their imaginations and judgments. The standard of good behavior for the continuance in office of the judicial magistracy is certainly one of the most valuable of the modern improvements in the practice of government. In a monarchy it is an excellent barrier to the despotism of the prince; in a republic it is a no less excellent barrier to the encroachments and oppressions of the representative body. And it is the best expedient which can be devised in any government to secure a steady, upright, and impartial administration of the laws.

Whoever attentively considers the different departments of power must perceive that, in a government in which they are separated from each other, the judiciary, from the nature of its functions, will always be the least dangerous to the political rights of the Constitution; because it will be least in a capacity to annoy or injure them. The executive not only dispenses the honors but holds the sword of the community. The legislature not only commands the purse but prescribes the rules by which the duties and rights of every citizen are to be regulated. The judiciary, on the contrary, has no influence over either the sword or the purse; no direction either of the strength or of the wealth of the society, and can take no active resolution whatever. It may truly be said to have neither FORCE NOR WILL but merely judgment; and must ultimately depend upon the aid of the executive arm even for the efficacy of its judgments.

This simple view of the matter suggests several important consequences. It proves incontestably that the judiciary is beyond comparison the weakest of the three departments of power; that it can never attack with success either of the other two; and that all possible care is requisite to enable it to defend itself against their attacks. It equally proves that though individual oppression may now and then proceed from the courts of justice, the general liberty of the people can never be endangered from that quarter; I mean so long as the judiciary remains truly distinct from both the legislature and the executive. For I agree that "there is no liberty if the power of judging be not separated from the legislative and executive powers." And it proves, in the last place, that as liberty can have nothing to fear from the judiciary alone, but would have everything to fear from its union with either of the other departments, that as all the effects of such a union must ensue from a dependence of the former on the latter, notwithstanding a nominal and apparent separation; that as, from the natural feebleness of the judiciary, it is in continual jeopardy of being overpowered, awed, or influenced by its co-ordinate branches; and that as nothing can contribute so much to its firmness and independence as permanency in office, this quality may therefore be justly regarded as an indispensable ingredient in its constitution, and, in a great measure, as the citadel for the public justice and the public security.

The complete independence of the courts of justice is peculiarly essential in a limited Constitution. By a limited Constitution, I understand one which contains certain specified exceptions to the legislative authority; such, for instance, as that it shall pass no bills of attainder, no *ex post facto laws,* and the like. Limitations of this kind can be preserved in practice no other way than through the medium of courts of justice, whose duty it must be to declare all acts contrary to the manifest tenor of the Constitution void. Without this, all the reservations of particular rights or privileges would amount to nothing.

Some perplexity respecting the rights of the courts to pronounce legislative acts void, because contrary to the Constitution, has arisen from an imagination that the doctrine would imply a superiority to the judiciary to the legislative power. It is urged that the authority which can declare the acts of another void must necessarily be superior to the one whose acts may be declared void. As this doctrine is of great importance in all the American constitutions, a brief discussion of the grounds on which it rests cannot be unacceptable.

There is no position which depends on clearer principles than that every act of a delegated authority, contrary to the tenor of the commission under which it is exercised, is void. No legislative act, therefore, contrary to the Constitution, can be valid. To deny this would be to affirm that the deputy is greater than his principal; that the servant is above his master; that the representatives of the people are superior to the people themselves; that men acting by virtue of powers do not authorize, but what they forbid.

If it be said that the legislative body are themselves the constitutional judges of their own powers and that the construction they put upon them is conclusive upon the other departments it may be answered that this cannot be the natural presumption where it is not to be collected from any particular provisions in the Constitution. It is not otherwise to be supposed that the Constitution could intend to enable the representatives of the people to substitute their *will* to that of their constituents. It is far more rational to suppose that the courts were designed to be an intermediate body between the people and the legislature in order, among other things, to keep the latter within the limits assigned to their authority. The interpretation of the laws is the proper and peculiar province of the courts. A constitution is, in fact, and must be regarded by the judges as, a fundamental law. It therefore belongs to them to ascertain its meaning as well as the meaning of any particular act proceeding from the legislative body. If there should happen to be an irreconcilable variance between the two, that which has the superior obligation and validity ought, of course, to be preferred; or, in other words, the Constitution ought to be preferred to the statute, the intention of the people to the intention of their agents.

Nor does this conclusion by any means suppose a superiority of the judicial to the legislative power. It only supposes that the power of the people is superior to both, and that where the will of the legislature, declared in its statutes, stands in opposition to that of the people, declared in the Constitution, the judges ought to be governed by the latter rather than the former. They ought to regulate their decisions by the fundamental laws rather than by those which are not fundamental.

This exercise of judicial discretion in determining between two contradictory laws is exemplified in a familiar instance. It not uncommonly happens that there are two statutes existing at one time, clashing in whole or in part with each other and neither of them containing any repealing clause or expression. In such a case, it is the province of the courts to liquidate and fix their meaning and operation. So far as they can, by any fair construction, be reconciled to each other, reason and law conspire to dictate that this should be done; where this is impracticable, it becomes a matter of necessity to give effect to one in exclusion of the other. The rule which has obtained in the courts for determining their relative validity is that the last in order of time shall be preferred to the first. But this is a mere rule of construction, not derived from any positive law but from the nature and reason of the thing. It is a rule not enjoined upon the courts by legislative provision but adopted by themselves, as consonant to truth and propriety, for the direction of their conduct as interpreters of the law. They thought it reasonable that between the interfering acts of an equal authority that which was the last indication of its will should have the preference.

But in regard to the interfering acts of a superior and subordinate authority of an original and derivative power, the nature and reason of the thing indicates the converse of that rule as proper to be followed. They teach us that the prior act of a superior ought to be preferred to the subsequent act of an inferior and subordinate authority; and that accordingly, whenever a particular statute contravenes the Constitution, it will be the duty of the judicial tribunals to adhere to the latter and disregard the former.

It can be of no weight to say that the courts, on the pretense of a repugnancy, may substitute their own pleasure to the constitutional intentions of the legislature. This might as well happen in the case of two contradictory statutes; or it might as well happen in every adjudication upon any single statute. The courts must declare the sense of the law; and if they should be disposed to exercise WILL instead of JUDGMENT, the consequence would equally be the substitution of their pleasure to that of the legislative body. The observation, if it prove anything, would prove that there ought to be no judges distinct from that body.

If, then, the courts of justice are to be considered as the bulwarks of a limited Constitution against legislative encroachments, this consideration will afford a strong argument for the permanent tenure of judicial offices, since nothing will contribute so much as this to that independent spirit in the judges which must be essential to the faithful performance of so arduous a duty.

This independence of the judges is equally requisite to guard the Constitution and the rights of individuals from the effects of those ill humors which the arts of designing men, or the influence of particular conjunctures, sometimes disseminate among the people themselves, and which, though they speedily give place to better information, and more deliberate reflection, have a tendency, in the meantime, to occasion dangerous innovations in the government, and serious oppressions of the minor party in the community. Though I trust the friends of the proposed Constitution will never concur with its enemies in questioning that fundamental principal of Republican government which admits the right of the people to alter or abolish the established Constitution whenever they find it inconsistent with their happiness; yet it is not to be inferred from this principle that the representatives of the people, whenever a momentary inclination happens to lay hold of a majority of their constituents incompatible with the provisions in the existing Constitution would, on that account, be justifiable in a violation of those provisions; or that the courts would be under a greater obligation to connive at infractions in this shape than when they had proceeded wholly from the cabals of the representative body. Until the people have, by some solemn and authoritative act, annulled or changed the established form, it is binding upon themselves collectively, as well as individually; and no presumption, or even knowledge of their sentiments, can warrant their representatives in a departure from it prior to such an act. But it is easy to see that it would require an uncommon portion of fortitude in the judges to do their duty as faithful guardians of the Constitution, where legislative invasions of it had been instigated by the major voice of the community.

But it is not with a view to infractions of the Constitution only that the independence of the judges may be an essential safeguard against the effects of occasional ill humors in the society. These sometimes extend no farther than to the injury of the private rights of particular classes of citizens, by unjust and partial laws. Here also the firmness of the judicial magistracy is of vast importance in mitigating the severity and confining the operation of such laws. It not only serves to moderate the immediate mischiefs of those which may have been passed but it operates as a check upon the legislative body in passing them; who, perceiving that obstacles to the success of iniquitous intention are to be expected from the scruples of the courts, are in a manner compelled, by the very motives of the injustice they mediate, to qualify their attempts. This is a circumstance calculated to have more influence upon the character of our governments than but a few may be aware of. The benefits of the integrity and moderation of the judiciary have already been felt in more States than one; and though they may have displeased those whose sinister expectations they may have disappointed, they must have commanded the esteem and applause of all the virtuous and disinterested. Considerate men of every description ought to prize whatever will tend to beget or fortify that temper in the courts; as no man can be sure that he may not be tomorrow the victim of a spirit of injustice, by which he may be a gainer today. And every man must now feel that the inevitable tendency of such a spirit is to sap the foundations of public and private confidence and to introduce in its stead universal distrust and distress.

That inflexible and uniform adherence to the rights of the Constitution, and of individuals, which we perceive to be indispensable in the courts of justice, can certainly not be expected from judges who hold their offices by a temporary commission. Periodical appointments, however regulated, or by whomsoever made, would, in some way or other, be fatal to their necessary independence. If the power of making them was committed either to the executive or legislature there would be danger of an improper complaisance to the branch which possessed it; if to both, there would be an unwillingness to hazard the displeasure of either; if to the people, or to persons chosen by them for the special purpose, there would be too great a disposition to consult popularity to justify a reliance that nothing would be consulted by the Constitution and the laws.

There is yet a further and a weighty reason for the permanency of the judicial offices which is deducible from the nature of the qualifications they require. It has been frequently remarked with great propriety that a voluminous code of laws is one of the inconveniences necessarily connected with the advantages of a free government. To avoid an arbitrary discretion in the courts, it is indispensable that they should be bound down by strict rules and precedents which serve to define and point out their duty in every particular case that comes before them; and it will readily be conceived from the variety of controversies which grow out of the folly and wickedness of mankind that the records of those precedents must unavoidably swell to a very considerable bulk and must demand long and laborious study to acquire a competent knowledge of them. Hence it is that there can be but few men in the society who will have sufficient skill in the laws to qualify them for the stations of judges. And making the proper deductions for the ordinary depravity of human nature, the number must be still smaller of those who unite the requisite integrity with the requisite knowledge. These considerations apprise us that the government can have no great option between fit characters; and that a temporary duration in office which would naturally discourage such characters from quitting a lucrative line of practice to accept a seat on the bench would have a tendency to throw the administration of justice into hands less able and less well qualified to conduct it with utility and dignity. In the present circumstances of this country and in those in which it is likely to be for a long time to come, the disadvantages on this score would be greater than they may at first sight appear; but it must be confessed that they are far inferior to those which present themselves under the other aspects of the subject.

Upon the whole, there can be no room to doubt that the convention acted wisely in copying from the models of those constitutions which have established *good behavior* as the tenure of their judicial offices in point of duration, and that so far from being blamable on this account, their plan would have been inexcusably defective if it had wanted this important feature of good government. The experience of Great Britain affords an illustrious comment on the excellence of the institution.

Presidential Election Results, 1789–2008

Year	Candidates	Party	Popular Vote	Electoral Vote
1789	George Washington			69
	John Adams			34
	Others			35
1793	George Washington			132
	John Adams			77
	George Clinton			50
	Others			5
1796	John Adams	Federalist		71
	Thomas Jefferson	Democratic-Republican		68
	Thomas Pinckney	Federalist		59
	Aaron Burr	Democratic-Republican		30
	Others			48
1800	Thomas Jefferson	Democratic-Republican		73
	Aaron Burr	Democratic-Republican		73
	John Adams	Federalist		65
	Charles C. Pinckney	Federalist		64
1804	Thomas Jefferson	Democratic-Republican		162
	Charles C. Pinckney	Federalist		14
1808	James Madison	Democratic-Republican		122
	Charles C. Pinckney	Federalist		47
	George Clinton	Independent-Republican		6
1812	James Madison	Democratic-Republican		128
	DeWitt Clinton	Federalist		89
1816	James Monroe	Democratic-Republican		183
	Rufus King	Federalist		34
1820	James Monroe	Democratic-Republican		231
	John Quincy Adams	Independent-Republican		1
1824	John Quincy Adams	Democratic-Republican	108,740(30.5%)	84
	Andrew Jackson	Democratic-Republican	153,544(43.1%)	99
	Henry Clay	Democratic-Republican	47,136(13.2%)	37
	William H. Crawford	Democratic-Republican	46,618(13.1%)	41
1828	Andrew Jackson	Democratic	647,231(56.0%)	178
	John Quincy Adams	National Republican	509,097(44.0%)	83
1832	Andrew Jackson	Democratic	687,502(55.0%)	219
	Henry Clay	National Republican	530,189(42.4%)	49
	William Wirt	Anti-Masonic		7
	John Floyd	National Republican	33,108(2.6%)	11
1836	Martin Van Buren	Democratic	761,549(50.9%)	170
	William H. Harrison	Whig	549,567(36.7%)	73
	Hugh L. White	Whig	145,396(9.7%)	26
	Daniel Webster	Whig	41,287(2.7%)	14
1840	William H. Harrison	Whig	1,275,017(53.1%)	234
	Martin Van Buren	Democratic	1,128,702(46.9%)	60
1844	James K. Polk	Democratic	1,337,243(49.6%)	170
	Henry Clay	Whig	1,299,068(48.1%)	105
	James G. Birney	Liberty	63,300(2.3%)	
1848	Zachary Taylor	Whig	1,360,101(47.4%)	163
	Lewis Cass	Democratic	1,220,544(42.5%)	127
	Martin Van Buren	Free Soil	291,163(10.1%)	
1852	Franklin Pierce	Democratic	1,601,474(50.9%)	254
	Winfield Scott	Whig	1,386,578(44.1%)	42
1856	James Buchanan	Democratic	1,838,169(45.4%)	174
	John C. Fremont	Republican	1,335,264(33.0%)	114
	Millard Fillmore	American	874,534(21.6%)	8
1860	Abraham Lincoln	Republican	1,865,593(39.8%)	180
	Stephen A. Douglas	Democratic	1,381,713(29.5%)	12
	John C. Breckinridge	Democratic	848,356(18.1%)	72
	John Bell	Constitutional Union	592,906(12.6%)	79
1864	Abraham Lincoln	Republican	2,206,938(55.0%)	212
	George B. McClellan	Democratic	1,803,787(45.0%)	21
1868	Ulysses S. Grant	Republican	3,013,421(52.7%)	214
	Horatio Seymour	Democratic	2,706,829(47.3%)	80
1872	Ulysses S. Grant	Republican	3,596,745(55.6%)	286
	Horace Greeley	Democratic	2,843,446(43.9%)	66
1876	Rutherford B. Hayes	Republican	4,036,571(48.0%)	185
	Samuel J. Tilden	Democratic	4,284,020(51.0%)	184
1880	James A. Garfield	Republican	4,449,053(48.3%)	214
	Winfield S. Hancock	Democratic	4,442,035(48.2%)	155
	James B. Weaver	Greenback-Labor	308,578(3.4%)	
1884	Grover Cleveland	Democratic	4,874,986(48.5%)	219
	James G. Blaine	Republican	4,851,931(48.2%)	182
	Benjamin F. Butler	Greenback-Labor	175,370(1.8%)	
1888	Benjamin Harrison	Republican	5,444,337(47.8%)	233
	Grover Cleveland	Democratic	5,540,050(48.6%)	168

1892	Grover Cleveland	Democratic	5,554,414(46.0%)	277
	Benjamin Harrison	Republican	5,190,802(43.0%)	145
	James B. Weaver	Peoples	1,027,329(8.5%)	22
1896	William McKinley	Republican	7,035,638(50.8%)	271
	William J. Bryan	Democratic; Populist	6,467,946(46.7%)	176
1900	William McKinley	Republican	7,219,530(51.7%)	292
	William J. Bryan	Democratic; Populist	6,356,734(45.5%)	155
1904	Theodore Roosevelt	Republican	7,628,834(56.4%)	336
	Alton B. Parker	Democratic	5,084,401(37.6%)	140
	Eugene V. Debs	Socialist	402,460(3.0%)	0
1908	William H. Taft	Republican	7,679,006(51.6%)	321
	William J. Bryan	Democratic	6,409,106(43.1%)	162
	Eugene V. Debs	Socialist	420,820(2.8%)	0
1912	Woodrow Wilson	Democratic	6,286,820(41.8%)	435
	Theodore Roosevelt	Progressive	4,126,020(27.4%)	88
	William H. Taft	Republican	3,483,922(23.2%)	8
	Eugene V. Debs	Socialist	897,011(6.0%)	0
1916	Woodrow Wilson	Democratic	9,129,606(49.3%)	277
	Charles E. Hughes	Republican	8,538,211(46.1%)	254
1920	Warren G. Harding	Republican	16,152,200(61.0%)	404
	James M. Cox	Democratic	9,147,353(34.6%)	127
	Eugene V. Debs	Socialist	919,799(3.5%)	0
1924	Calvin Coolidge	Republican	15,725,016(54.1%)	382
	John W. Davis	Democratic	8,385,586(28.8%)	136
	Robert M. La Follette	Progressive	4,822,856(16.6%)	13
1928	Herbert C. Hoover	Republican	21,392,190(58.2%)	444
	Alfred E. Smith	Democratic	15,016,443(40.8%)	87
1932	Franklin D. Roosevelt	Democratic	22,809,638(57.3%)	472
	Herbert C. Hoover	Republican	15,758,901(39.6%)	59
	Norman Thomas	Socialist	881,951(2.2%)	0
1936	Franklin D. Roosevelt	Democratic	27,751,612(60.7%)	523
	Alfred M. Landon	Republican	16,681,913(36.4%)	8
	William Lemke	Union	891,858(1.9%)	0
1940	Franklin D. Roosevelt	Democratic	27,243,466(54.7%)	449
	Wendell L. Willkie	Republican	22,304,755(44.8%)	82
1944	Franklin D. Roosevelt	Democratic	25,602,505(52.8%)	432
	Thomas E. Dewey	Republican	22,006,278(44.5%)	99
1948	Harry S Truman	Democratic	24,105,812(49.5%)	303
	Thomas E. Dewey	Republican	21,970,065(45.1%)	189
	J. Strom Thurmond	States' Rights	1,169,063(2.4%)	39
	Henry A. Wallace	Progressive	1,157,172(2.4%)	0
1952	Dwight D. Eisenhower	Republican	33,936,234(55.2%)	442
	Adlai E. Stevenson	Democratic	27,314,992(44.5%)	89
1956	Dwight D. Eisenhower	Republican	35,590,472(57.4%)	457
	Adlai E. Stevenson	Democratic	26,022,752(42.0%)	73
1960	John F. Kennedy	Democratic	34,227,096(49.9%)	303
	Richard M. Nixon	Republican	34,108,546(49.6%)	219
1964	Lyndon B. Johnson	Democratic	43,126,233(61.1%)	486
	Barry Goldwater	Republican	27,174,989(38.5%)	52
1968	Richard M. Nixon	Republican	31,783,783(43.4%)	301
	Hubert H. Humphrey	Democratic	31,271,839(42.7%)	191
	George C. Wallace	American Independent	9,899,557(13.5%)	46
1972	Richard M. Nixon	Republican	46,632,189(61.3%)	520
	George McGovern	Democratic	28,422,015(37.3%)	17
1976	Jimmy Carter	Democratic	40,828,587(50.1%)	297
	Gerald R. Ford	Republican	39,147,613(48.0%)	240
1980	Ronald Reagan	Republican	42,941,145(51.0%)	489
	Jimmy Carter	Democratic	34,663,037(41.0%)	49
	John B. Anderson	Independent	5,551,551(6.6%)	0
1984	Ronald Reagan	Republican	53,428,357(59%)	525
	Walter F. Mondale	Democratic	36,930,923(41%)	13
1988	George Bush	Republican	48,881,011(53%)	426
	Michael Dukakis	Democratic	41,828,350(46%)	111
1992	Bill Clinton	Democratic	38,394,210(43%)	370
	George Bush	Republican	33,974,386(38%)	168
	H. Ross Perot	Independent	16,573,465(19%)	0
1996	Bill Clinton	Democratic	45,628,667(49%)	379
	Bob Dole	Republican	37,869,435(41%)	159
	H. Ross Perot	Reform	7,874,283(8%)	0
2000	George W. Bush	Republican	50,456,169(48%)	271
	Al Gore	Democratic	50,996,116(48%)	266
	Ralph Nader	Green	2,767,176(3%)	0
2004	George W. Bush	Republican	60,608,582(51%)	286
	John Kerry	Democratic	57,288,974(48%)	252
	Ralph Nader	Independent	400,924(.35%)	0
2008	Barack Obama	Democratic	66,361,433(53%)	364
	John McCain	Republican	58,024,608(46%)	163

Glossary

527 organization A political group organized under section 527 of the IRS Code that may accept and spend unlimited amounts of money on election activities so long as they are not spent on broadcast ads run in the last 30 days before a primary or 60 days before a general election in which a clearly identified candidate is referred to and a relevant electorate is targeted.

administrative discretion Authority given by Congress to the federal bureaucracy to use reasonable judgment in implementing the laws.

adversary system A judicial system in which the court of law is a neutral arena in which two parties argue their differences.

affirmative action Remedial action designed to overcome the effects of discrimination against minorities and women.

American dream The widespread belief that the United States is a land of opportunity and that individual initiative and hard work can bring economic success.

***amicus curiae* brief** Literally, a "friend of the court" brief, filed by an individual or organization to present arguments in addition to those presented by the immediate parties to a case.

Annapolis Convention A convention held in September 1786 to consider problems of trade and navigation, attended by five states and important because it issued the call to Congress and the states for what became the Constitutional Convention.

Antifederalists Opponents of ratification of the Constitution and of a strong central government generally.

antitrust legislation Federal laws (starting with the Sherman Act of 1890) that try to prevent a monopoly from dominating an industry and restraining trade.

appellate jurisdiction The authority of a court to review decisions made by lower courts.

Articles of Confederation The first governing document of the confederated states, drafted in 1777, ratified in 1781, and replaced by the present Constitution in 1789.

attentive public Citizens who follow public affairs carefully.

bad tendency test An interpretation of the First Amendment that would permit legislatures to forbid speech encouraging people to engage in illegal action.

bicameralism The principle of a two-house legislature.

Bipartisan Campaign Reform Act (BCRA) Largely banned party soft money, restored long-standing prohibitions on corporations and labor unions for using general treasury funds for electoral purposes, and narrowed the definition of issue advocacy.

budget deficit A budget deficit occurs when the federal government raises less revenue than it spends.

bundling A tactic in which PACs collect contributions from like-minded individuals (each limited to $2,000) and present them to a candidate or political party as a "bundle," thus increasing the PAC's influence.

bureaucracy A form of organization that operates through impersonal, uniform rules and procedures.

bureaucrat A career government employee.

cabinet The advisory council for the president, consisting of the heads of the executive departments, the vice president, and a few other officials selected by the president.

candidate appeal How voters feel about a candidate's background, personality, leadership ability, and other personal qualities.

capitalism An economic system characterized by private property, competitive markets, economic incentives, and limited government involvement in the production, distribution, and pricing of goods and services.

caucus A meeting of local party members to choose party officials or candidates for public office and to decide the platform.

central clearance Review of all executive branch testimony, reports, and draft legislation by the Office of Management and Budget to ensure that each communication to Congress is in accordance with the president's program.

centralists People who favor national action over action at the state and local levels.

checks and balances A constitutional grant of powers that enables each of the three branches of government to check some acts of the others and therefore ensure that no branch can dominate.

chief of staff The head of the White House staff.

civil disobedience Deliberate refusal to obey a law or comply with the orders of public officials as a means of expressing opposition.

civil law A law that governs relationships between individuals and defines their legal rights.

civil rights The rights of all people to be free from irrational discrimination such as that based on race, religion, gender, or ethnic origin.

civil service Federal employees who work for government through a competitive, not political selection process.

class-action suit A lawsuit brought by an individual or a group of people on behalf of all those similarly situated.

clear and present danger test An interpretation of the First Amendment that holds that the government cannot interfere with speech unless the speech presents a clear and present danger that it will lead to evil or illegal acts.

closed primary A primary election in which only people registered in the party holding the primary may vote.

closed rule A procedural rule in the House of Representatives that prohibits any amendments to bills or provides that only members of the committee reporting the bill may offer amendments.

closed shop A company with a labor agreement under which union membership can be a condition of employment.

cloture A procedure for terminating debate, especially filibusters, in the Senate.

coattail effect The boost that candidates may get in an election because of the popularity of candidates above them on the ballot, especially the president.

collective action How groups form and organize to pursue their goals or objectives, including how to get individuals and groups to participate and cooperate. The term has many applications in the various social sciences such as political science, sociology, and economics.

collective bargaining A method whereby representatives of the union and employer determine wages, hours, and other conditions of employment through direct negotiation.

commerce clause The clause in the Constitution (Article I, Section 8, Clause 1) that gives Congress the power to regulate all business activities that cross state lines or affect more than one state or other nations.

commercial speech Advertisements and commercials for products and services; they receive less First Amendment protection, primarily to discourage false and misleading ads.

community policing Assigning police to neighborhoods where they walk the beat and work with churches and other community groups to reduce crime and improve relations with minorities.

concurrent powers Powers that the Constitution gives to both the national and state governments, such as the power to levy taxes.

concurring opinion An opinion that agrees with the majority in a Supreme Court ruling but differs on the reasoning.

confederation A constitutional arrangement in which sovereign nations or states, by compact, create a central government but carefully limit its power and do not give it direct authority over individuals.

conference committee A committee appointed by the presiding officers of each chamber to adjust differences on a particular bill passed by each in different form.

Congressional Budget Office (CBO) An agency of Congress that analyzes presidential budget recommendations and estimates the costs of proposed legislation

congressional–executive agreement A formal agreement between the U.S. president and the leaders of other nations that requires approval by both houses of Congress.

Connecticut Compromise A compromise agreement by states at the Constitutional Convention for a bicameral legislature with a lower house in which representation would be based on population and an upper house in which each state would have two senators.

conservatism A belief that limited government ensures order, competitive markets, and personal opportunity.

constituents The residents of a congressional district or state.

Constitutional Convention The convention in Philadelphia, May 25 to September 17, 1787, that framed the Constitution of the United States.

constitutional democracy A government that enforces recognized limits on those who govern and allows the voice of the people to be heard through free, fair, and relatively frequent elections.

constitutionalism The set of arrangements, including checks and balances, federalism, separation of powers, rule of law, due process, and a bill of rights, that requires our leaders to listen, think, bargain, and explain before they act or make laws. We then hold them politically and legally accountable for how they exercise their powers.

corporate social responsibility Efforts by corporations to improve their reputations by paying attention to their contributions to the social good.

counterdistributive policy A policy that reduces benefits for all groups, such as a tax increase in society, often by imposing rules that govern everyone.

court of appeals A court with appellate jurisdiction that hears appeals from the decisions of lower courts.

criminal law A law that defines crimes against the public order.

cross-cutting cleavages Divisions within society that cut across demographic categories to produce groups that are more heterogeneous or different.

crossover voting Voting by a member of one party for a candidate of another party.

de facto segregation Segregation resulting from economic or social conditions or personal choice.

de jure segregation Segregation imposed by law.

dealignment Weakening of partisan preferences that points to a rejection of both major parties and a rise in the number of Independents.

decentralists People who favor state or local action rather than national action.

defendant In a criminal action, the person or party accused of an offense.

delegate An official who is expected to represent the views of his or her constituents even when personally holding different views; one interpretation of the role of the legislator.

democracy Government by the people, both directly or indirectly, with free and frequent elections.

democratic consensus Widespread agreement on fundamental principles of democratic governance and the values that undergird them.

demographics The study of the characteristics of populations.

department Usually the largest organization in government; also the highest rank in federal hierarchy.

deregulation A policy promoting cutbacks in the amount of federal regulation in specific areas of economic activity.

devolution revolution The effort to slow the growth of the federal government by returning many functions to the states.

direct democracy Government in which citizens vote on laws and select officials directly.

direct primary An election in which voters choose party nominees.

discharge petition A petition that, if signed by a majority of the House of Representatives, will pry a bill from committee and bring it to the floor for consideration.

dissenting opinion An opinion disagreeing with the majority in a Supreme Court ruling.

distributive policy A type of policy that provides benefits to all Americans.

divided government Governance divided between the parties, especially when one holds the presidency and the other controls one or both houses of Congress.

docket The list of potential cases that reach the Supreme Court.

double jeopardy Trial or punishment for the same crime by the same government; forbidden by the Constitution.

due process Established rules and regulations that restrain government officials.

due process clause A clause in the Fifth Amendment limiting the power of the national government; a similar clause in the Fourteenth Amendment prohibiting state governments from depriving any person of life, liberty, or property without due process of law.

earmarks Special spending projects that are set aside on behalf of individual members of Congress for their constituents.

economic mobility The degree of upward movement in a society. Refers to the economic fortunes of different groups often measured by the percent of income each group makes.

electoral college The electoral system used in electing the president and vice president, in which voters vote for electors pledged to cast their ballots for a particular party's candidates.

eminent domain The power of a government to take private property for public use; the U.S. Constitution gives national and state governments this power and requires them to provide just compensation for property so taken.

entitlement program Programs such as unemployment insurance, disaster relief, or disability payments that provide benefits to all eligible citizens.

enumerated powers The powers explicitly given to Congress in the Constitution.

environmental impact statement A statement required by federal law from all agencies for any project using federal funds to assess the potential effect of the new construction or development on the environment.

equal protection clause A clause in the Fourteenth Amendment that forbids any state to deny to any person within its jurisdiction the equal protection of the laws. By interpretation, the Fifth Amendment imposes the same limitation on the national government. This clause is the major constitutional restraint on the power of governments to discriminate against persons because of race, national origin, or sex.

Establishment and Exercise Clauses Amendment provisions that have been used to determine whether a state or federal government has favored religion over non-religion (or vice versa), or has impermissibly restricted an individual's religious practices.

ethnicity A social division based on national origin, religion, language, and often race.

ethnocentrism Belief in the superiority of one's nation or ethnic group.

***ex post facto* law** A retroactive criminal law that works to the disadvantage of a person.

excise tax A consumer tax on a specific kind of merchandise, such as tobacco.

exclusionary rule A requirement that evidence unconstitutionally or illegally obtained be excluded from a criminal trial.

executive agreement A formal agreement between the U.S. president and the leaders of other nations that does not require Senate approval.

Executive Office of the President The cluster of presidential staff agencies that help the president carry out his responsibilities. Currently the office includes the Office of Management and Budget, the Council of Economic Advisers, and several other units.

executive order A directive issued by a president or governor that has the force of law.

executive privilege The power to keep executive communications confidential, especially if they relate to national security.

express powers Powers the Constitution specifically grants to one of the branches of the national government.

extradition A legal process whereby an alleged criminal offender is surrendered by the officials of one state to officials of the state in which the crime is alleged to have been committed.

faction A term the founders used to refer to political parties and special interests or interest groups.

Federal Election Commission (FEC) A commission created by the 1974 amendments to the Federal Election Campaign Act to administer election reform laws. It consists of six commissioners appointed by the president and confirmed by the Senate. Its duties include overseeing disclosure of campaign finance information and public funding of presidential elections, and enforcing contribution limits.

federal funds rate The amount of interest banks charge for loans to each other.

federal mandate A requirement the federal government imposes as a condition for receiving federal funds.

Federal Register An official document, published every weekday, that lists the new and proposed regulations of executive departments and regulatory agencies.

Federal Reserve System The system created by Congress in 1913 to establish banking practices and regulate currency in circulation and the amount of credit available. It consists of 12 regional banks supervised by the Board of Governors. Often called simply the Fed.

federalism A constitutional arrangement in which power is distributed between a central government and subdivisional governments, called states in the United States. The national and the subdivisional governments both exercise direct authority over individuals.

The Federalist Essays promoting ratification of the Constitution, published anonymously by Alexander Hamilton, John Jay, and James Madison in 1787 and 1788.

Federalists Supporters of ratification of the Constitution and of a strong central government.

fighting words Words that by their very nature inflict injury on those to whom they are addressed or incite them to acts of violence.

filibuster A procedural practice in the Senate whereby a senator refuses to relinquish the floor and thereby delays proceedings and prevents a vote on a controversial issue.

fiscal policy Government policy that attempts to manage the economy by controlling taxing and spending.

free exercise clause A clause in the First Amendment that states that Congress shall make no law prohibiting the free exercise of religion.

free rider An individual who does not join a group representing his or her interests yet receives the benefit of the group's influence.

full faith and credit clause A clause in the Constitution (Article IV, Section 1) requiring each state to recognize the civil judgments rendered by the courts of the other states and to accept their public records and acts as valid.

fundamentalists Conservative Christians who as a group have become more active in politics in the last two decades and were especially influential in the 2000 presidential election.

gender gap The difference between the political opinions or political behavior of men and of women.

General Agreement on Tariffs and Trade (GATT) An international trade organization with more than 130 members, including the United States and the People's Republic of China, that seeks to encourage free trade by lowering tariffs and other trade restrictions.

general election Elections in which voters elect officeholders.

gerrymandering The drawing of legislative district boundaries to benefit a party, group, or incumbent.

globalization The lowering of economic, social, and political barriers between nations.

government corporation A government agency that operates like a business corporation, created to secure greater freedom of action and flexibility for a particular program.

grand jury A jury of 12 to 23 persons who, in private, hear evidence presented by the government to determine whether persons shall be required to stand trial. If the jury believes there is sufficient evidence that a crime was committed, it issues an indictment.

gross domestic product (GDP) The total output of all economic activity in the nation, including goods and services.

hard money Political contributions given to a party, candidate, or interest group that are limited in amount and fully disclosed. Raising such limited funds is harder than raising unlimited funds, hence the term "hard money."

Hatch Act A federal statute barring federal employees from active participation in certain kinds of politics and protecting them from being fired on partisan grounds.

Health Maintenance Organization (HMO) An alternative means of health care in which people or their employers are charged a set amount and the HMO provides health care and covers hospital costs.

heightened scrutiny test This test has been applied when a law classifies based on sex; to be upheld, the law must meet an important government interest.

hold A procedural practice in the Senate whereby a senator temporarily blocks the consideration of a bill or nomination.

honeymoon The period at the beginning of a new president's term during which the president enjoys generally positive relations with the press and Congress, usually lasting about six months.

horse race A close contest; by extension, any contest in which the focus is on who is ahead and by how much rather than on substantive differences between the candidates.

impeachment A formal accusation by the lower house of a legislature against a public official, the first step in removal from office.

implementation The process of putting a law into practice through bureaucratic rules or spending.

implied powers Powers inferred from the express powers that allow Congress to carry out its functions.

impoundment Presidential refusal to allow an agency to spend funds that Congress authorized and appropriated.

in forma pauperis A petition that allows a party to file "as a pauper " and avoid paying court fees.

incremental policy Small adjustments to existing public policies.

incumbent The current holder of elected office.

independent agency A government entity that is independent of the legislative, executive, and judicial branches.

independent expenditure The Supreme Court has ruled that individuals, groups, and parties can spend unlimited amounts in campaigns for or against candidates as long as they operate independently from the candidates. When an individual, group, or party does so, they are making an independent expenditure.

independent regulatory commission A government agency or commission with regulatory power whose independence is protected by Congress.

indictment A formal written statement from a grand jury charging an individual with an offense; also called a true bill.

inflation A rise in the general price level (and decrease in dollar value) owing to an increase in the volume of money and credit in relation to available goods.

inherent powers The powers of the national government in foreign affairs that the Supreme Court has declared do not depend on constitutional grants but rather grow out of the very existence of the national government.

initiative A procedure whereby a certain number of voters may, by petition, propose a law or constitutional amendment and have it submitted to the voters.

interest group A collection of people who share a common interest or attitude and seek to influence government for specific ends. Interest groups usually work within the framework of government and try to achieve their goals through tactics such as lobbying.

interested money Financial contributions by individuals or groups in the hope of influencing the outcome of an election and subsequently influencing policy.

interstate compact An agreement among two or more states. Congress must approve most such agreements.

issue advocacy Promoting a particular position or an issue paid for by interest groups or individuals but not candidates. Much issue advocacy is often electioneering for or against a candidate, and until 2004 it had not been subject to any regulation.

issue-attention cycle The movement of public opinion toward public policy from initial enthusiasm for action to realization of costs and a decline in interest.

issue network Relationships among interest groups, congressional committees and subcommittees, and the government agencies that share a common policy concern.

Jim Crow laws State laws formerly pervasive throughout the South requiring public facilities and accommodations to be segregated by race; ruled unconstitutional.

joint committee A committee composed of members of both the House of Representatives and the Senate; such committees oversee the Library of Congress and conduct investigations.

judicial activism A philosophy proposing that judges should interpret the Constitution to reflect current conditions and values.

judicial restraint A philosophy proposing that judges should interpret the Constitution to reflect what the framers intended and what its words literally say.

judicial review The power of a court to refuse to enforce a law or a government regulation that in the opinion of the judges conflicts with the U.S. Constitution or, in a state court, the state constitution.

justiciable dispute A dispute growing out of an actual case or controversy and that is capable of settlement by legal methods.

Keynesian economics A theory based on the principles of John Maynard Keynes, stating that government spending should increase during business slumps and be curbed during booms.

labor injunction A court order forbidding specific individuals or groups from performing certain acts (such as striking) that the court considers harmful to the rights and property of an employer or a community.

laissez-faire economics A theory that opposes governmental interference in economic affairs beyond what is necessary to protect life and property.

leadership PAC A PAC formed by an officeholder that collects contributions from individuals and other PACs and then makes contributions to other candidates and political parties.

libel Written defamation of another person. For public officials and public figures, the constitutional tests designed to restrict libel actions are especially rigid.

liberalism A belief that government can and should achieve justice and equality of opportunity.

libertarianism An ideology that cherishes individual liberty and insists on minimal government, promoting a free market economy, a noninterventionist foreign policy, and an absence of regulation in moral, economic, and social life.

line item veto Presidential power to strike, or remove, specific items from a spending bill without vetoing the entire package; declared unconstitutional by the Supreme Court.

literacy test Literacy requirement some states imposed as a condition of voting, generally used to disqualify black voters in the South; now illegal.

lobbying Engaging in activities aimed at influencing public officials, especially legislators, and the policies they enact.

lobbyist A person who is employed by and acts for an organized interest group or corporation to influence policy decisions and positions in the executive and legislative branches.

logrolling Mutual aid and vote trading among legislators.

majority The candidate or party that wins more than half the votes cast in an election.

majority leader The legislative leader selected by the majority party who helps plan party strategy, confers with other party leaders, and tries to keep members of the party in line.

majority rule Governance according to the expressed preferences of the majority.

manifest destiny A notion held by nineteenth-century Americans that the United States was destined to rule the continent, from the Atlantic to the Pacific.

manifest opinion A widely shared and consciously held view, such as support for homeland security.

mass media Means of communication that reach the public, including newspapers and magazines, radio, television (broadcast, cable, and satellite), films, recordings, books, and electronic communication.

means-tested entitlements Programs such as Medicaid and welfare under which applicants must meet eligibility requirements based on need.

Medicaid A federal program that provides medical benefits for low-income persons.

medical savings account An alternative means of health care in which individuals make tax-deductible contributions to a special account that can be used to pay medical expenses.

Medicare A national health insurance program for the elderly and disabled.

merit system A system of public employment in which selection and promotion depend on demonstrated performance rather than on political patronage.

minor party A small political party that rises and falls with a charismatic candidate or, if composed of ideologies on the right or left, usually persists over time; also called a third party.

minority leader The legislative leader selected by the minority party as spokesperson for the opposition.

monetary policy Government policy that attempts to manage the economy by controlling the money supply and thus interest rates.

monopoly Domination of an industry by a single company that fixes prices and discourages competition; also, the company that dominates the industry by these means.

movement A large body of people interested in a common issue, idea, or concern that is of continuing significance and who are willing to take action. Movements seek to change attitudes or institutions, not just policies.

name recognition Incumbents have an advantage over challengers in election campaigns because voters are more familiar with them, and incumbents are more recognizable.

national debt The total amount of money the federal government has borrowed to finance deficit spending over the years.

national party convention A national meeting of delegates elected in primaries, caucuses, or state conventions who assemble once every four years to nominate candidates for president and vice president, ratify the party platform, elect officers, and adopt rules.

national supremacy A constitutional doctrine that whenever conflict occurs between the constitutionally authorized actions of the national government and those of a state or local government, the actions of the federal government prevail.

national tide The inclination to focus on national issues, rather than local issues, in an election campaign. The impact of a national tide can be reduced by the nature of the candidates on the ballot who might have differentiated themselves from their party or its leader if the tide is negative, as well as competition in the election.

natural law God's or nature's law that defines right from wrong and is higher than human law.

natural rights The rights of all people to dignity and worth; also called human rights.

necessary and proper clause A clause in the Constitution (Article I, Section 8, Clause 3) setting forth the implied powers of Congress. It states that Congress, in addition to its express powers, has the right to make all laws necessary and proper to carry out all powers the Constitution vests in the national government.

New Jersey Plan A proposal at the Constitutional Convention made by William Paterson of New Jersey for a central government with a single-house legislature in which each state would be represented equally.

news media Media that emphasize the news.

nondecision A decision not to move ahead with the policy process. In short, it is a decision not to decide.

nongovernmental organization (NGO) A nonprofit association or group operating outside government that advocates and pursues policy objectives.

nonpartisan election A local or judicial election in which candidates are not selected or endorsed by political parties and party affiliation is not listed on ballots.

nonprotected speech Libel, obscenity, fighting words, and commercial speech, which are not entitled to constitutional protection in all circumstances.

North American Free Trade Agreement (NAFTA) An agreement signed by the United States, Canada, and Mexico in 1992 to form the largest free trade zone in the world.

obscenity The quality or state of a work that taken as a whole appeals to a prurient interest in sex by depicting sexual conduct in a patently offensive way and that lacks serious literary, artistic, political, or scientific value.

Office of Management and Budget (OMB) A presidential staff agency that serves as a clearinghouse for budgetary requests and management improvements for government agencies.

Office of Personnel Management (OPM) An agency that administers civil service laws, rules, and regulations.

open primary A primary election in which any voter, regardless of party, may vote.

open rule A procedural rule in the House of Representatives that permits floor amendments within the overall time allocated to the bill.

open shop A company with a labor agreement under which union membership cannot be required as a condition of employment.

opinion of the court An explanation of a decision of the Supreme Court or any other appellate court.

original jurisdiction The authority of a court to hear a case "in the first instance."

override An action taken by Congress to reverse a presidential veto, requiring a two-thirds majority in each chamber.

oversight Legislative or executive review of a particular government program or organization. Can be in response to a crisis of some kind or part of routine review.

parliamentary system A system of government in which the legislature selects the prime minister or president.

party caucus A meeting of the members of a party in a legislative chamber to select party leaders and develop party policy. Called a conference by the Republicans.

party convention A meeting of party delegates to vote on matters of policy and in some cases to select party candidates for public office.

party identification An informal and subjective affiliation with a political party that most people acquire in childhood.

party registration The act of declaring party affiliation; required by some states when one registers to vote.

patronage The dispensing of government jobs to persons who belong to the winning political party.

petit jury A jury of 6 to 12 persons that determines guilt or innocence in a civil or criminal action.

plaintiff The party instigating a civil lawsuit.

plea bargain An agreement between a prosecutor and a defendant that the defendant will plead guilty to a lesser offense to avoid having to stand trial for a more serious offense.

pluralism A theory of government that holds that open, multiple, and competing groups can check the asserted power by any one group.

plurality The candidate or party with the most votes cast in an election, not necessarily more than half.

pocket veto A veto exercised by the president after Congress has adjourned; if the president takes no action for ten days, the bill does not become law and is not returned to Congress for a possible override.

police powers Inherent powers of state governments to pass laws to protect the public health, safety, and welfare; the national government has no directly granted police powers but accomplishes the same goals through other delegated powers.

political action committee (PAC) The political arm of an interest group that is legally entitled to raise funds on a voluntary basis from members, stockholders, or employees to contribute funds to candidates or political parties.

political culture The widely shared beliefs, values, and norms about how citizens relate to government and to one another.

political ideology A consistent pattern of beliefs about political values and the role of government.

political party An organization that seeks political power by electing people to office so that its positions and philosophy become public policy.

political predisposition A characteristic of individuals that is predictive of political behavior.

political socialization The process—most notably in families and schools—by which we develop our political attitudes, values, and beliefs.

politics The interaction of the people and their government, including citizens, interest groups, political parties, and the institutions of government at all levels. Politics is concerned with who gets what, when, where, and how from government.

popular consent The idea that a just government must derive its powers from the consent of the people it governs.

popular sovereignty A belief that ultimate power resides in the people.

precedent A decision made by a higher court such as a circuit court of appeals or the Supreme Court that is binding on all other federal courts.

preemption The right of a federal law or regulation to preclude enforcement of a state or local law or regulation.

preferred position doctrine Interpretation of the First Amendment that holds that freedom of expression is so essential to democracy that governments should not punish people for what they say, only for what they do.

president pro tempore An officer of the Senate selected by the majority party to act as chair in the absence of the vice president.

presidential election Elections held in years when the president is on the ballot.

presidential support score The percentage of times a president wins on key votes in Congress.

presidential ticket The joint listing of the presidential and vice presidential candidates on the same ballot as required by the Twelfth Amendment.

primary election Elections in which voters determine party nominees.

prior restraint Censorship imposed before a speech is made or a newspaper is published; usually presumed to be unconstitutional.

procedural due process Constitutional requirement that governments proceed by proper methods; limits how government may exercise power.

professional associations Groups of individuals who share a common profession and are often organized for common political purposes related to that profession.

progressive tax A tax graduated so that people with higher incomes pay a larger fraction of their income than people with lower incomes.

property rights The rights of an individual to own, use, rent, invest in, buy, and sell property.

proportional representation An election system in which each party running receives the proportion of legislative seats corresponding to its proportion of the vote.

prospective issue voting Voting based on what a candidate pledges to do in the future about an issue if elected.

protectionism Policy of erecting trade barriers to protect domestic industry.

public assistance Aid to the poor; "welfare."

public choice Synonymous with "collective action," it specifically studies how government officials, politicians, and voters respond to positive and negative incentives.

public defender system An arrangement whereby public officials are hired to provide legal assistance to people accused of crimes who are unable to hire their own attorneys.

public opinion The distribution of individual preferences for or evaluations of a given issue, candidate, or institution within a specific population.

public policy A specific course of action taken by government to achieve a public goal.

punctuating policy Radical changes to public policy that occur only after the mobilization of large segments of society to demand action.

quid pro quo Something given with the expectation of receiving something in return.

race A grouping of human beings with distinctive characteristics determined by genetic inheritance.

racial gerrymandering The drawing of election districts so as to ensure that members of a certain race are a minority in the district; ruled unconstitutional in *Gomillion* v. *Lightfoot* (1960).

rally point A rise in public approval of the president that follows a crisis as Americans "rally 'round the flag" and the chief executive.

random sample In this type of sample, every individual has a known and random chance of being selected.

rational basis test A standard developed by the courts to test the constitutionality of a law; when applied, a law is constitutional as long as it meets a reasonable government interest.

realigning election An election during periods of expanded suffrage and change in the economy and society that proves to be a turning point, redefining the agenda of politics and the alignment of voters within parties.

reapportionment The assigning by Congress of congressional seats after each census. State legislatures reapportion state legislative districts.

recall A procedure for submitting to popular vote the removal of officials from office before the end of their term.

redistributive policy A type of policy that takes benefits (usually through taxes) from one group of Americans and gives them to another (usually through spending).

redistricting The redrawing of congressional and other legislative district lines following the census, to accommodate population shifts and keep districts as equal as possible in population.

referendum A procedure for submitting to popular vote measures passed by the legislature or proposed amendments to a state constitution.

regressive tax A tax whereby people with lower incomes pay a higher fraction of their income than people with higher incomes.

regulation A policy that encourages or discourages certain behavior by imposing a legally binding rule. Rules are made through a long process that begins with an act of Congress and ends with issuance of a final rule.

regulatory taking Government regulation of property so extensive that government is deemed to have taken the property by the power of eminent domain, for which it must compensate the property owners.

reinforcing cleavages Divisions within society that reinforce one another, making groups more homogeneous or similar.

representative democracy Government in which the people elect those who govern and pass laws; also called a republic.

reserved powers All powers not specific delegated to the national government by the Constitution. The reserved powers can be found in the Tenth Amendment to the Constitution.

restrictive covenant A provision in a deed to real property prohibiting its sale to a person of a particular race or religion. Judicial enforcement of such deeds is unconstitutional.

retrospective issue voting Holding incumbents, usually the president's party, responsible for their records on issues, such as the economy or foreign policy.

revolving door An employment cycle in which individuals who work for governmental agencies that regulate interests eventually end up working for interest groups or businesses with the same policy concern.

rider A provision attached to a bill—to which it may or may not be related—in order to secure its passage.

rule A precise legal definition of how government will implement a policy.

safe seat An elected office that is predictably won by one party or the other, so the success of that party's candidate is almost taken for granted.

sales tax General tax on sales transactions, sometimes exempting food and drugs.

search warrant A writ issued by a magistrate that authorizes the police to search a particular place or person, specifying the place to be searched and the objects to be seized.

sedition Attempting to overthrow the government by force or use violence to interrupt its activities.

selective exposure The process by which individuals screen out messages that do not conform to their own biases.

selective incorporation The process by which provisions of the Bill of Rights are brought within the scope of the Fourteenth Amendment and so applied to state and local governments.

selective perception The process by which individuals perceive what they want to in media messages.

senatorial courtesy The presidential custom of submitting the names of prospective appointees for approval to senators from the states in which the appointees are to work.

Senior Executive Service Established by Congress in 1978 as a flexible, mobile corps of senior career executives who work closely with presidential appointees to manage government.

seniority rule A legislative practice that assigns the chair of a committee or subcommittee to the member of the majority party with the longest continuous service on the committee.

separation of powers Constitutional division of powers among the legislative, executive, and judicial branches, with the legislative branch making law, the executive applying and enforcing the law, and the judiciary interpreting the law.

Shays's Rebellion Rebellion led by Daniel Shays of farmers in western Massachusetts in 1786–1787, protesting mortgage foreclosures. It highlighted the need for a strong national government just as the call for the Constitutional Convention went out.

signing statements A formal document that explains why a president is signing a particular bill into law. These statements may contain objections to the bill and promises not to implement key sections.

single-member district An electoral district in which voters choose one representative or official.

social capital Democratic and civic habits of discussion, compromise, and respect for differences, which grow out of participation in voluntary organizations.

social insurance Programs in which eligibility is based on prior contributions to government, usually in the form of payroll taxes.

social safety net A collection of programs designed to help the needy. The social safety net is administered by federal, state, and local governments, as well as charities. It is designed to help people during short-term crises and longer-term poverty.

Social Security A combination of entitlement programs, paid for by employer and employee taxes, that includes retirement benefits, health insurance, and support for disabled workers and the children of deceased or disabled workers.

socialism An economic and governmental system based on public ownership of the means of production and exchange.

socioeconomic status (SES) A division of population based on occupation, income, and education.

soft money Unlimited amounts of money that political parties previously could raise for party-building purposes. Now largely illegal except for limited contributions to state and local parties for voter registration and get-out-the-vote efforts.

solicitor general The third-ranking official in the Department of Justice, the solicitor general is responsible for representing the United States in cases before the U.S. Supreme Court.

Speaker The presiding officer in the House of Representatives, formally elected by the House but actually selected by the majority party.

special or select committee A congressional committee created for a specific purpose, sometimes to conduct an investigation.

spoils system A system of public employment based on rewarding party loyalists and friends.

stagflation A combination of an economic slowdown (stagnation) and a rise in prices (inflation).

standing committee A permanent committee established in a legislature, usually focusing on a policy area.

stare decisis The rule of precedent, whereby a rule or law contained in a judicial decision is commonly viewed as binding on judges whenever the same question is presented.

State of the Union Address The president's annual statement to Congress and the nation.

states' rights Powers expressly or implicitly reserved to the states and emphasized by decentralists.

statism The idea that the rights of the nation are supreme over the rights of the individuals who make up the nation.

strict scrutiny test A test applied by the court when a classification is based on race; the government must show that there is a compelling reason for the law and no other less restrictive way to meet the interest.

substantive due process A constitutional requirement that governments act reasonably and that the substance of the laws themselves be fair and reasonable; limits what a government may do.

suffrage The right to vote.

take care clause The constitutional requirement (in Article II, Section 3) that presidents take care that the laws are faithfully executed, even if they disagree with the purpose of those laws.

tariff A tax levied on imports to help protect a nation's industries, labor, or farmers from foreign competition. It can also be used to raise additional revenue.

tax expenditure Loss of tax revenue due to federal laws that provide special tax incentives or benefits to individuals or businesses.

theocracy Government by religious leaders, who claim divine guidance.

think tank A nongovernmental organization that seeks to influence public policy through research and education.

three-fifths compromise A compromise between northern and southern states at the Constitutional Convention that three-fifths of the slave population would be counted for determining direct taxation and representation in the House of Representatives.

trade deficit An imbalance in international trade in which the value of imports exceeds the value of exports.

treaty A formal, public agreement between the United States and one or more nations that must be approved by two-thirds of the Senate.

trust A monopoly that controls goods and services, often in combinations that reduce competition.

trustee An official who is expected to vote independently based on his or her judgment of the circumstances; one interpretation of the role of the legislator.

turnout The proportion of the voting-age public that votes, sometimes defined as the number of registered voters that vote.

uncontrollable spending The portion of the federal budget that is spent on programs, such as Social Security, that the president and Congress are unwilling to cut.

unemployment The number of Americans who are out of work but actively looking for a job. The number does not usually include those who are not looking.

union shop A company in which new employees must join a union within a stated time period.

unitary system A constitutional arrangement that concentrates power in a central government.

value-added tax (VAT) A tax on increased value of a product at each stage of production and distribution rather than just at the point of sale.

vesting clause The president's constitutional authority to control most executive functions.

veto A formal decision to reject a bill passed by Congress.

Virginia Plan An initial proposal at the Constitutional Convention made by the Virginia delegation for a strong central government with a bicameral legislature dominated by the big states.

voter registration A system designed to reduce voter fraud by limiting voting to those who have established eligibility to vote by submitting the proper documents.

vouchers Money that government provides to parents to pay their children's tuition in a public or private school of their choice.

whip A party leader who is the liaison between the leadership and the rank-and-file in the legislature.

white primary A democratic party primary in the old "one-party South" that was limited to white people and essentially constituted an election; ruled unconstitutional in *Smith* v. *Allwright* (1944).

winner-take-all system An election system in which the candidate with the most votes wins.

women's suffrage The right of women to vote.

World Trade Organization (WTO) An international organization derived from the General Agreement on Tariffs and Trade (GATT) that promotes free trade around the world.

writ of *certiorari* A formal writ used to bring a case before the Supreme Court.

writ of habeas corpus A court order requiring explanation to a judge why a prisoner is being held in custody.

writ of mandamus A court order directing an official to perform an official duty.

Notes

Chapter 1

1. Al Gore, speech delivered on December 13, 2000, www.cnn.com/ELECTION/2000/transcripts/121300/t651213.html.
2. Peter Nicholas, "Gov.'s New Proposition: Cooperation," *Los Angeles Times*, November 11, 2005, p. A01.
3. Ibid.
4. Aristotle, *Politics* (Oxford University Press, 1998); and George Huxley, "On Aristotle's Best State," *History of Political Thought* 6 (Summer 1985), pp. 139–149.
5. John Locke, *Two Treatises of Government and a Letter Concerning Toleration* (Yale University Press, 2003); and Virginia McDonald, "A Guide to the Interpretation of Locke the Political Theorist," *Canadian Journal of Political Science* 6 (December 1973), pp. 602–623.
6. Thomas Hobbes, *Leviathan* (Oxford University Press, 1998); and Frank M. Coleman, "The Hobbesian Basis of American Constitutionalism," *Polity* 7 (Autumn 1974), pp. 57–89.
7. Charles de Montesquieu, *The Spirit of the Laws* (Cambridge University Press, 1989); and E. P. Panagopoulos, *Essays on the History and Meaning of Checks and Balances* (University Press of America, 1986).
8. David B. Magleby, *Direct Legislation: Voting on Ballot Propositions in the United States* (Johns Hopkins University Press, 1984), p. 119.
9. Seymour Martin Lipset, "The Social Requisites of Democracy Revisited," *American Sociological Review* 59 (1994), pp. 1–22.
10. For a discussion of the importance for democracy of such overlapping group memberships, see David Truman's seminal work *The Governmental Process*, 2d ed. (Knopf, 1971).
11. Harold Stanley and Richard Niemi, *Vital Statistics on American Politics, 2001–2002* (CQ Press, 2001), pp. 25–29.
12. For a major theoretical work on the principle of majority rule, see Robert A. Dahl, *Democracy and Its Critics* (Yale University Press, 1989).
13. *Reitman v. Mulkey,* 387 U.S. 369 (1967).
14. Lesli J. Favor, *The Iroquois Constitution: A Primary Source Investigation of the Law of the Iroquois* (Rosen, 2003), p. 60.
15. Joyce Appleby, "The American Heritage: The Heirs and the Disinherited," *Journal of American History* 74 (December 1987), p. 808.
16. Kevin Butterfield, "What You Should Know About the Declaration of Independence," *St. Louis Post-Dispatch,* July 4, 2000, p. F1.
17. Richard L. Hillard, "Liberalism, Civic Humanism and the American Revolutionary Bill of Rights, 1775–1790," paper presented at the annual meeting of the Organization of American Historians, Reno, Nev., March 26, 1988.
18. Robert W. Hoffert, *A Politics of Tensions: The Articles of Confederation and American Political Ideas* (University Press of Colorado, 1992); see also Merrill Jensen, *The Articles of Confederation: An Interpretation of the Social-Constitutional History of the American Revolution, 1774–1781* (University of Wisconsin Press, 1970).
19. *The Federalist,* No. 40.
20. Quoted in Charles L. Mee Jr., *The Genius of the People* (Harper & Row, 1987), p. 51.
21. Charles A. Beard, *An Economic Interpretation of the Constitution of the United States* (Macmillan, 1913).
22. Robert Brown, *Charles Beard and the Constitution: A Critical Analysis of "An Economic Interpretation of the Constitution"* (Princeton University Press, 1956).
23. Declaration of Congress, Feb. 21, 1787; Worthington C. Ford et al., eds., *Journals of the Continental Congress, 1774–1789* (Washington, DC, 1904–1937): 32: 74.
24. Seymour Martin Lipset, "George Washington and the Founding of Democracy," *Journal of Democracy* 9 (October 1998), p. 31.
25. See the essays in Thomas E. Cronin, ed., *Inventing the American Presidency* (University Press of Kansas, 1989); see also Richard J. Ellis, ed., *Founding the American Presidency* (Rowman & Littlefield, 1999).
26. Charles A. Beard and Mary R. Beard, *A Basic History of the United States* (New Home Library, 1944), p. 136.
27. See Herbert J. Storing, ed., abridgment by Murray Dry, *The Anti-Federalist: Writings by the Opponents of the Constitution* (University of Chicago Press, 1985).
28. W. B. Allen and Gordon Lloyd, eds., *The Essential Antifederalist* (University Press of America, 1985), pp. xi–xiii.
29. On the role of the promised Bill of Rights amendments in the ratification of the Constitution, see Leonard W. Levy, *Constitutional Opinions* (Oxford University Press, 1986), chap. 6.

Chapter 2

1. www.nationmaster.com.
2. Joedy McCready, 2000. *"Santa Fe Independent School District v. Doe, Jane, et al."* On the Docket, Medill School of Journalism, Northwestern University, docket.medill. northwestern.edu/archives/000429.php
3. NewsHour Online, "Supreme Court Watch," June 19, 2000, www.pbs.org/newshour/bb/law/jan-june00//jcg_6-19.html.
4. *Santa Fe Independent School District v. Doe,* 530 U.S. 290 (2000).
5. Max Lerner, *Ideas for the Ice Age* (Viking Press, 1941), pp. 241–242.
6. Sanford Levinson, *Constitutional Faith* (Princeton University Press, 1988), pp. 9–52.
7. Richard Morin, "We Love It—What We Know of It," *Washington Post National Weekly Edition,* September 22, 1997, p. 35.
8. Alexander Hamilton, James Madison, and John Jay, *The Federalist Papers,* ed. Clinton Rossiter (New American Library, 1961).
9. Quoted in Alpheus T. Mason, *The Supreme Court: Palladium of Freedom* (University of Michigan Press, 1962), p. 10.
10. Alexander Hamilton, James Madison, and John Jay, *The Federalist Papers,* ed. Clinton Rossiter (New American Library, 1961).
11. Ibid.
12. Ibid.
13. Justice Brandeis dissenting in *Myers v. United States,* 272 U.S. 52 (1926).
14. Charles O. Jones, "The Separate Presidency," in Anthony King, ed., *The New American Political System,* 2d ed. (AEI Press, 1990), p. 3.
15. Morris P. Fiorina, "An Era of Divided Government," *Political Science Quarterly* 107 (1992), p. 407.
16. David R. Mayhew, *Divided We Govern: Party Control, Lawmaking, and Investigations, 1946–1990* (Yale University Press, 1991), p. 4; see also James A. Thurber, ed., *Divided Democracy: Presidents and Congress in Cooperation and Conflict* (CQ Press, 1991).
17. Charles O. Jones, *Separate but Equal Branches: Congress and the Presidency* (Chatham House, 1995).
18. Judith A. Best, *The Choice of the People? Debating the Electoral College* (Rowman & Littlefield, 1996).
19. Hamilton, Madison, and Jay, *The Federalist Papers.*
20. See Alec Stone Sweet, Wayne Sandholtz, and Neil Fligstein, *The Institutionalization of Europe* (Oxford University Press, 2001); Alec Stone Sweet, *Governing with Judges: Constitutional Politics in Europe* (Oxford University Press, 2000); and Anne-Marie Slaughter, Alec Stone Sweet, and J.H.H. Weiler, *The European Court and National Courts—Doctrine, Jurisprudence: Legal Change in Its Social Context* (Hart, 1998).
21. *Marbury v. Madison,* 5 U. S. 137 (1803).
22. Dumas Malone, *Jefferson the President: First Term, 1801–1805* (Little, Brown, 1970), p. 145.
23. J. W. Peltason, *Federal Courts in the Political Process* (Random House, 1955).
24. See Eleanore Bushnell, *Crimes, Follies, and Misfortunes: The Federal Impeachment Trials* (University of Illinois Press, 1992); and Michael J. Gerhardt, *The Federal Impeachment Process: A Constitutional and Historical Analysis* (Princeton University Press, 1996).
25. Richard E. Neustadt, *Presidential Power* (Free Press, 1990), pp. 180–181.
26. *Texas v. Johnson,* 491 U.S. 397 (1989).
27. *United States v. Eichman,* 496 U.S. 310 (1990).
28. John A. Clark and Kevin T. McGuire, "Congress, the Supreme Court and the Flag," *Political Research Quarterly* 49 (1996), pp. 771–781.
29. Senate Joint Resolution 12, 109th Congress, 2nd session.
30. Ann Stuart Diamond, "A Convention for Proposing Amendments: The Constitution's Other Method," *Publius* 11 (Summer 1981), pp. 113–146; and Wilbur Edel, "Amending the Constitution by Convention: Myths and Realities," *State Government* 55 (1982), pp. 51–56.
31. Russell L. Caplan, *Constitutional Brinksmanship: Amending the Constitution by National Convention* (Oxford University Press, 1988), p. x; see also David E. Kyvig, *Explicit and Authentic Acts: Amending the U.S. Constitution, 1776–1995* (University Press of Kansas, 1996), p. 440.
32. Samuel S. Freedman and Pamela J. Naughton, *ERA: May a State Change Its Vote?* (Wayne State University Press, 1979).
33. Kyvig, *Explicit and Authentic Acts,* p. 286; and *Dillon v. Gloss,* 256 U.S. 368 (1921).
34. Mark R. Daniels, Robert Darcy, and Joseph W. Westphal, "The ERA Won—at Least in the Opinion Polls," *P.S.: Political Science and Politics* (Fall 1982), p. 583.
35. National Organization for Women, www.now.org/issues/economic/eratext.html.
36. Janet K. Boles, *The Politics of the Equal Rights Amendment: Conflict and Decision-Making Powers* (Longman, 1979), p. 4.
37. Gilbert Y. Steiner, *Constitutional Inequality: The Political Fortunes of the Equal Rights Amendment* (Brookings Institution Press, 1985), p. 64; see also Mary Frances Berry, *Why the ERA Failed: Politics,*

Women's Rights, and the Amending Process of the Constitution (Indiana University Press, 1986).

Chapter 3

1. For further historical background, see Samuel J. Beer, *To Make a Nation: The Rediscovery of American Federalism* (Harvard University Press, 1993).
2. For a recent and brief paper on the state of federalism today, see Pietro S. Nivola, *Rediscovering Federalism* (Brookings Institution Press, 2007).
3. Brandeis's famous characterization comes from the following sentence in *Neu State Ice Co. v. Liebmann:* "It is one of the happy accidents of the federal system that a single courageous state may, if its citizens choose, serve as a laboratory and try novel social and economic experiments without risk to the rest of the country." *Neu State Ice Co. v. Liebmann,* 285 U.S. 262, 311 (1932).
4. Kavan Peterson, "California Targets Cars to Fight Global Warming," Stateline.org, September 27, 2004, p. 1.
5. William H. Stewart, *Concepts of Federalism* (Center for the Study of Federalism/University Press of America, 1984); see also Preston King, *Federalism and Federation,* 2d ed. (Cass, 2001).
6. Morton Grodzins, "The Federal System," in *Goals for Americans: The Report of the President's Commission on National Goals* (Columbia University Press, 1960).
7. Thomas R. Dye, *American Federalism: Competition Among Governments* (Lexington Books, 1990), pp. 13–17.
8. Michael D. Reagan and John G. Sanzone, *The New Federalism* (Oxford University Press, 1981), p. 175.
9. U.S. Census Bureau, *Statistical Abstract of the United States, 2007* (Government Printing Office, 2007), p. 487.
10. Frederick K. Lister, *The European Union, the United Nations, and the Revival of Confederal Governance* (Greenwood Press, 1996); and Daniel J. Elazar, "The United States and the European Union: Models for their Epochs," in Kalypso Nicolaidis and Robert Howse, eds., *The Federal Vision* (Oxford University Press, 2001), pp. 31–52.
11. William H. Riker, *The Development of American Federalism* (Academic Press, 1987), pp. 14–15. Riker contends not only that federalism does not guarantee freedom, but also that the framers of our federal system, as well as those of other nations, were animated not by considerations of safeguarding freedom but by practical considerations of preserving unity.
12. Charles Evans Hughes, "War Powers Under the Constitution," *ABA Reports* 62 (1917), p. 238.
13. *Gibbons v. Ogden,* 22 U.S. 1 (1824).
14. *Reno v. Condon,* 528 U.S. 141 (2000).
15. *Champion v. Ames,* 188 U.S. 321 (1907).
16. *Caminetti v. United States,* 242 U.S. 470 (1917).
17. *Federal Radio Commission v. Nelson Brothers,* 289 U.S. 266 (1933).
18. *United States v. Lopez,* 514 U.S. 549 (1995); see also *United States v. Morrison,* 529 U.S. 598 (2000), striking down the Violence Against Women Act.
19. *Gonzales v. Raich,* 125 S.Ct. 2195 (2005), reaffirming *Wickard v. Filburn,* 317 U.S. 111 (1942).
20. *Printz v. United States,* 521 U.S. 898 (1997); see also *New York v. United States,* 505 U.S. 144 (1992).
21. See Jesse Choper, *Judicial Review and the National Political Process* (University of Chicago Press, 1980); and John T. Noonan Jr., *Narrowing the Nation's Power: The Supreme Court Sides with the States* (University of California Press, 2002).
22. See Michael S. Greve, *Real Federalism: Why It Matters, How It Could Happen* (American Enterprise Institute, 1999).
23. Ibid.
24. *Seminole Tribe of Florida v. Florida,* 517 U.S. 44 (1996); *Alden v. Maine,* 527 U.S. 706 (1999); *Kimel v. Florida Board of Regents,* 528 U.S. 62 (2000).
25. See *Franchise Tax Board of California v. Hyatt,* 538 U.S. 488 (2003).
26. *California v. Superior Courts of California,* 482 U.S. 400 (1987).
27. David C. Nice, "State Participation in Interstate Compacts," *Publius* 17 (Spring 1987), p. 70; see also Council of State Governments, *Interstate Compacts and Agencies* (Author, 1995), for a list of compacts by subject and by state with brief descriptions.
28. *McCulloch v. Maryland,* 4 Wheaton 316 (1819).
29. Joseph F. Zimmerman, "Federal Preemption Under Reagan's New Federalism," *Publius* 21 (Winter 1991), pp. 7–28.
30. Oliver Wendell Holmes Jr., *Collected Legal Papers* (Harcourt, 1920), pp. 295–296.
31. See, for example, *United States v. Lopez,* 514 U.S. 549 (1995).
32. *Seminole Tribe of Florida v. Florida,* 517 U.S. 44 (1996).
33. *Alden v. Maine,* 527 U.S. 706 (1999); *Kimel v. Florida Board of Regents,* 528 U.S. 62 (2000); *Vermont Agency of Natural Resources v. United States ex rel. Stevens,* 529 U.S. 765 (2000).
34. George Will, "A Revival of Federalism?" *Newsweek,* May 29, 2000, p. 78.
35. *United States v. Morrison,* 529 U.S. 598 (2000).
36. John E. Chubb, "The Political Economy of Federalism," *American Political Science Review* 79 (December 1985), p. 1005.
37. Paul E. Peterson, *The Price of Federalism* (Brookings Institution Press, 1995), p. 127.
38. Donald F. Kettl, *The Regulation of American Federalism* (Johns Hopkins University Press, 1987), pp. 154–155.
39. See Paul J. Posner, *The Politics of Unfunded Mandates: Whither Federalism?* (Georgetown University Press, 1998).
40. Joseph Zimmerman, "Congressional Regulation of Subnational Governments," *PS: Political Science and Politics* 26 (June 1993), p. 179.
41. Advisory Commission on Intergovernmental Relations, *Restoring Confidence and Competence* (Author, 1981), p. 30.
42. Cynthia Cates Colella, "The Creation, Care and Feeding of the Leviathan: Who and What Makes Government Grow," *Intergovernmental Perspective* (Fall 1979), p. 9.
43. Aaron Wildavsky, "Bare Bones: Putting Flesh on the Skeleton of American Federalism," in *The Future of Federalism in the 1980s* (Advisory Commission on Intergovernmental Relations, 1981), p. 79.
44. Peterson, *Price of Federalism,* p. 182.
45. The term "devolution revolution" was coined by Richard P. Nathan in testimony before the Senate Finance Committee, quoted in Daniel Patrick Moynihan, "The Devolution Revolution," *New York Times,* August 6, 1995, p. B15.
46. Laura S. Hamilton et al., "Passing or Failing? A Midterm Report Card for 'No Child Left Behind,'" *RAND Review* 31 (Fall 2007), pp. 16–25.
47. Dye, *American Federalism,* p. 199.
48. Richard A. Oppel and Christopher Drew, "States Planning Their Own Suits on Power Plants: Battle That E.P.A. Quit," *New York Times,* November 9, 2003, p. A1; and Scott Richards and Yvette Hurt, "States Sue the Federal Environmental Agency," *Federations* 11 (November 2003).
49. Edward Felsenthal, "Firms Ask Congress to Pass Uniform Rules," *Wall Street Journal,* May 10, 1993, p. B4.
50. John J. DiLulio Jr. and Donald F. Kettl, *Fine Print: The Contract with America, Devolution, and the Administrative Realities of American Federalism* (Brookings Institution Press, 1995), p. 60.
51. John Kincaid, "Devolution in the United States," in Nicolaidis and Howse, *The Federal Vision* (Oxford, 2002), p. 144.

Chapter 4

1. Wesley G. Pippert, "'You Could View This as a Racist Concept,'" United Press International, February 23, 1982.
2. Richard Severo, "Dr. King and Communism: No Link Ever Established," *New York Times,* October 22, 1983.
3. *New York Times,* "Tagliabue Is Firm on '93 Bowl Shift," December 8, 1990.
4. Robert D. Putnam, "Bowling Alone: America's Declining Social Capital," *Journal of Democracy* 6 (January 1995), pp. 65–78; see also Robert D. Putnam, *Bowling Alone: The Collapse and Revival of American Community* (Simon & Schuster, 2000); and Robert D. Putnam, "Bowling Together," *The American Prospect* 13 (February 2002), p. 20.
5. Dan Morgan, "An End to the Day of High Cotton? GOP Constituents Caught in Battle over Subsidies," *Washington Post,* March 8, 2005, p. A1. Remnants of mercantilism persist today in policies such as farm subsidies.
6. Clinton Rossiter, *Conservatism in America* (Vintage Books, 1962), p. 72.
7. Bernard Bailyn, *The Ideological Origins of the American Revolution* (Belknap Press, 1967); and Gordon S. Wood, *The Creation of the American Republic, 1776–1787* (University of North Carolina Press, 1969).
8. See Ronald Dworkin, *Taking Rights Seriously* (Harvard University Press, 1977).
9. *Marbury v. Madison,* 5 U.S. 137 (1803).
10. "A Nation Challenged: Excerpts from President's Speech: 'We Will Prevail' in War on Terrorism," *New York Times,* November 9, 2001, p. B1.
11. World Values Survey, 2004, margaux.grand-vinum.se/SebTest/wvs/index_html.
12. Robert Coles, *The Political Life of Children* (Atlantic Monthly Press, 1986).
13. Fred I. Greenstein, *Children and Politics* (Yale University Press, 1965).
14. Raymond E. Wolfinger and Steven Rosenstone, *Who Votes?* (Yale University Press, 1980).
15. Rachel X. Weissman, "The Kids Are All Right—They're Just a Little Converged," *American Demographics* 20 (December 1998), pp. 30–32.
16. Jeremy Rifkin, *The European Dream* (Penguin, 2005).
17. Alberto Alesina and Edward Glaeser, *Fighting Poverty in the U.S. and Europe: A World of Difference* (Oxford University Press, 2004).
18. www.opensecrets.org/politicians/summary.php?cid=N000099548cycle=2002; and Chris Cillizza, "Corzine Defeats Forrester to Become Governor," *Washington Post,* November 9, 2005, p. A18.
19. Glen Justice, "Advocacy Groups Reflect on Their Role in the Election," *New York Times,* November 5, 2004, p. A1.
20. When adjusted using the consumer price index (CPI1), the percentage of households earning more than $75,000 a year has risen from 10.1 percent in 1970 to 22.6 percent in 1999. U.S. Bureau of the Census, *Statistical Abstracts of the United States, 2001* (U.S. Government Printing Office, 2001), table 661; see also Julia Isaac, "Economic Mobility of Black and White Families," Brookings Institution, Economic Mobility Project, November 2007.
21. See Michael B. Katz, *The "Underclass" Debate* (Princeton University Press, 1993); Theodore Dalrymple, *Life at the Bottom: The Worldview*

That Makes the Underclass (Dee, 2001); and Charles A. Murray, *The Underclass Revisited* (AEI Press, 1999).

22. Pew Research Center for the People and the Press, "Huge Racial Divide over Katrina and Its Consequences," press release, September 8, 2005, at people-press.org/reports/pdf/255.pdf.
23. Bailyn, *Ideological Origins.*
24. Robert A. Dahl, "Liberal Democracy in the United States," in William Livingston, ed., *A Prospect of Liberal Democracy* (University of Texas Press, 1979), p. 64.
25. Ibid., pp. 59–60.
26. David E. Campbell and J. Quinn Monson, "The Case of Bush's Reelection: Did Gay Marriage Do It?" in David E. Campbell, ed. *A Matter of Faith: Religion in the 2004 Presidential Election* (Brookings Institution Press, 2007), pp. 120–141.
27. Quoted in David Brooks, "Need a Map? The Right," *Washington Post,* October 31, 1999, p. B1.
28. David B. Magleby, *The Outside Campaign* (Rowman & Littlefield, 2001).
29. David B. Magleby, J. Quin Monson, and Kelly D. Patterson, *Dancing Without Partners: How Candidates, Parties, and Interest Groups Interact in the Presidential Campaign* (Rowman & Littlefield, forthcoming); see also David B. Magleby and J. Quin Monson, eds., *The Last Hurrah? Soft Money and Issue Advocacy in the 2002 Congressional Elections* (Washington, D.C.: Brookings Institution Press, 2003); David B. Magleby, J. Quin Monson, and Kelly D. Patterson, eds., *Dancing Without Partners: How Candidates, Parties, and Interest Groups Interact in the New Campaign Finance Environment* (Washington, D.C.: Brookings Institution Press, 2005); and David B. Magleby and Kelly D. Patterson, eds., *War Games: Issues and Resources in the Battle for Control of Congress* (Washington, D.C.: Brookings Institution Press, 2007).
30. Michael Luo, "Huckabee Lays Out His Claim as an 'Authentic Conservative,'" *New York Times,* November 27, 2007.
31. Edison Media Research/Mitofsky International Entrance Poll, January 3, 2008.
32. Jonathan Rauch, "The Accidental Radical," *National Journal,* July 26, 2003, pp. 2404–2410.
33. Kathleen Day, *S&L Hell: The People and the Politics Behind the $1 Trillion Savings and Loan Scandal* (Norton, 1993).
34. James L. Sweeney, *The California Electricity Crisis* (Hoover Institution Press, 2002).
35. Sylvia Nasar, "Even Among the Well-Off, the Rich Get Richer," *New York Times,* March 5, 1992, p. A1.
36. Irving Howe, *Socialism and America* (Harcourt, 1985); and Michael Harrington, *Socialism: Past and Future* (Arcade, 1989).
37. Daniel Yergin and Joseph Stanislaw, *The Commanding Heights: The Battle Between Government and the Marketplace That Is Remaking the Modern World* (Simon & Schuster, 1998).
38. Charles Murray, *What It Means to Be a Libertarian* (Broadway Books, 1997).
39. Brian Faler, "A Polling Sight: Record Turnout," *Washington Post,* November 5, 2004, p. A7.
40. "The Libertarian Surprise," *Washington Post,* December 16, 2007.
41. Center for Political Studies, University of Michigan, *American National Election Study, 1990: Post-Election Survey,* April 1991.
42. Earl Black and Merle Black, *The Rise of Southern Republicans* (Belknap Press, 2002).

Chapter 5

1. "Election Center 2008 Primaries and Caucuses," www.cnn.com/ELECTION/2008/.
2. Ibid.
3. Susan Minushkin, "The Hispanic Vote in the 2008 Democratic Presidential Primaries," Pew Hispanic Center, February 21, 2008, pewresearch.org/pubs/742/hispanic-vote-exit-poll-texas-primary.
4. Scott Keeter, "Young Voters in the 2008 Presidential Primaries," Pew Research Center, February 11, 2008, pewresearch.org/pubs/730/young-voters.
5. *Washington Post*–ABC News Poll, December 11, 2007, www.washingtonpost.com/wp-srv/politics/polls/postpoll_121107.html.
6. Albert Einstein, quoted in Laurence J. Peter, *Peter's Quotations* (Morrow, 1977), p. 358.
7. Roosevelt Montas, "The Latino Loyalty Factor," *Los Angeles Times,* March 7, 2008, p. A23.
8. Alexis de Tocqueville, *Democracy in America,* ed. J. P. Mayer, trans. George Lawrence (Doubleday, 1969), p. 278. Originally published 1835 (Vol. 1) and 1840 (Vol. 2).
9. See John Lewis Gaddis, *Surprise, Security, and the American Experience* (Harvard University Press, 2005).
10. This excludes the Japanese attack on the U.S. territory of Hawaii in 1941 and other attacks on U.S. embassies or territories.
11. Food and Agriculture Organization of the United Nations, "Statistical Appendix," *Food Outlook* 1 (June 2007), www.fao.org/docrep/010/ah864e/ah864e14.htm.
12. Alexis de Tocqueville, *Democracy in America,* trans. Henry Reeve, www.netlibrary.com, p. 153.
13. Harold Hongju Koh, "On American Exceptionalism," *Stanford Law Review* 55 (May 2003), p. 1481.
14. U.S. Bureau of the Census, *Statistical Abstract of the United States, 2006* (U.S. Government Printing Office, 2006), p. 263.
15. V. O. Key, Jr., *Politics, Parties, and Pressure Groups,* 5th ed. (Crowell, 1964), p. 232.
16. Earl Black and Merle Black, *The Vital South: How Presidents Are Elected* (Harvard University Press, 1992), p. 4.
17. Arthur C. Paulson, *Realignment and Party Revival: Understanding American Electoral Politics at the Turn of the Twenty-First Century* (Westport, 2000), p. 46.
18. U.S. Bureau of the Census, www.census.gov/population/cen2000/tab01.pdf, March 3, 2006.
19. Robert S. Erikson, Gerald C. Wright, and John P. McIver, *Statehouse Democracy: Public Opinion and Policy in the American States* (Cambridge University Press, 1993).
20. *Statistical Abstract, 2006.*
21. Holly Idelson, "Count Adds Seats in Eight States," *Congressional Quarterly Weekly Report* 48 (December 29, 1999), p. 4240.
22. John M. Broder, "Term Waning, Gov. Davis Reflects on the Battle Lost," *New York Times,* November 12, 2003, p. A12.
23. *Statistical Abstract, 2008,* p. 34.
24. Ibid.
25. U.S. Census Bureau, Current Population Survey, December 2007.
26. Ibid.
27. *Statistical Abstract, 2003,* pp. 38–39.
28. David R. Harris and Jeremiah Joseph Sim, "Who is Multiracial? Assessing the Complexity of Lived Race," *American Sociological Review* (August 2002), p. 615.
29. *Statistical Abstract, 2008,* p. 23.
30. Ibid.
31. *Statistical Abstract, 2003,* p. 18.
32. William N. Evans and Julie H. Topoleski, *The Social and Economic Impact of Native American Casinos* (National Bureau of Economic Research, 2002), www.nber.org/papers/w9198.pdf.
33. See James Meader and John Bart, "The More You Spend, the Less They Listen: The South Dakota U.S. Senate Race," in David B. Magleby and J. Quin Monson, eds., *The Last Hurrah? Soft Money and Issue Advocacy in the 2002 Congressional Elections* (Brookings Institution Press, 2004), p. 173; see also Elizabeth Theiss Smith and Richard Braunstein, "The Nationalization of Local Politics in South Dakota," in David B. Magleby and J. Quin Monson, eds., *Dancing Without Partners: How Candidates, Parties, and Interest Groups Interact in the New Campaign Finance Environment* (Center for the Study of Elections and Democracy, 2005), pp. 241–242.
34. *Statistical Abstract, 2003,* p. 463.
35. Robert D. Ballard, "Introduction: Lure of the New South," in Robert D. Ballard, ed., *In Search of the New South: The Black Urban Experience in the 1970s and 1980s* (University of Alabama Press, 1989), p. 5; *Statistical Abstract, 2008,* p. 449.
36. *Statistical Abstract, 2008,* p. 449. Constant 2005 dollars.
37. Ibid., p. 460.
38. *Statistical Abstract, 2008,* p. 449.
39. Pew Hispanic Center, "Wealth Gap Widens Between Whites and Hispanics," pewhispanic.org/newsroom/releases/release.php?ReleaseID=15, October 18, 2004.
40. *Statistical Abstract, 2008,* p. 145.
41. *Statistical Abstract, 2006,* p. 147.
42. *Statistical Abstract, 2008,* p. 11.
43. Jeremy D. Mayer, *Running on Race* (Random House, 2002), pp. 4, 297. See also Mark R. Levy and Michael S. Kramer, *The Ethnic Factor: How America's Minorities Decide Elections* (Simon & Schuster, 1973); and Mark Stern, "Democratic Presidency and Voting Rights," in Lawrence W. Mooreland, Robert P. Steed, and Todd A. Baker, eds., *Blacks in Southern Politics,* (Praeger, 1987), pp. 50–51.
44. For 1984–2000, see Harold W. Stanley and Richard G. Niemi, *Vital Statistics on American Politics, 2000–2001* (CQ Press, 2001), p. 122; for 2004, see Harold W. Stanley and Richard G. Niemi, *Vital Statistics on American Politics, 2005–2006* (CQ Press, 2006), p. 124.
45. BBC News, "The U.S. Election in Figures" at http://news.bbc.co.uk/2/hi/americas/us_elections_2008/7715914.stm. Accessed 7 November 2008.
46. *Statistical Abstract, 2006,* p. 27.
47. See Earl Black, "Presidential Address: The Newest Southern Politics," *Journal of Politics* (August 1998), pp. 595–607.
48. Stanley and Niemi, *Vital Statistics on American Politics, 2005–2006,* pp. 63–64.
49. Ibid.
50. Anne E. Kornblut, "For Bill Clinton, Echoes of Jackson in Obama Win," *Washington Post,* January 26, 2008.
51. Joan Lowy, "Obama Accuses Ferraro of 'Slice and Dice' Politics," *Associated Press,* March 12, 2008.
52. BBC News, "The U.S. Election in Figures," at http://news.bbc.co.uk/2/hi/americas/us_elections_2008/7715914.stm. Accessed 7 November 2008.
53. Matt Barreto, Rodolfo O. de la Garza, Jongho Lee, Jaesung Ryu, and Harry P. Pachon, "Latino Voter Mobilization in 2000," Tomás Rivera Policy Institute (2000), pp. 4–5, www.trpi.org/PDFs/Voter_mobiliz_2.pdf. See also Richard E. Cohen, "Hispanic Hopes Fade," *National Journal* (February 2, 2002).
54. *Statistical Abstract, 2008,* p. 23.
55. Rodolfo O. de la Garza, Louis Desipio, F. Chris Garcia, John Garcia, and Angelo Falcon, *Latino Voices: Mexican, Puerto Rican, and Cuban*

Perspectives on American Politics (Westview Press, 1992).
56. *Statistical Abstract, 2008,* p. 44.
57. Michael Hefer, Nancy Rytina, and Christopher Campbell, "Estimates of the Unauthorized Immigrant Population Residing in the United States: January 2006," Department of Homeland Security, August 2007.
58. Tom Squitieri, "Redistricting Falls Short of Hispanics' Hopes," *USA Today,* August 27, 2002, p. 11A.
59. Michael Cooper and Megan Thee, "Resurgent McCain Is Florida Victor," *New York Times,* January 30, 2008.
60. National Election Pool, 2008 exit polls, MSNBC, www.msnbc.msn.com/id/21660914.
61. Andrew L. Aoki and Don T. Nakanishi, "Asian Pacific Americans and the New Minority Politics," *PS: Political Science and Politics* (September 2001), p. 605.
62. Ibid.
63. *Statistical Abstract, 2008,* p. 145.
64. Ibid., p. 45.
65. Ibid., p. 44.
66. U.S. Bureau of the Census, *Profile of the Foreign-Born Population in the United States, 2000* (U.S. Government Printing Office, 2001), www.census.gov/prod/2002pubs/p23–206.pdf.
67. Leni Yahil, *The Holocaust: The Fate of European Jewry* (Oxford University Press, 1990).
68. Stephen C. LeSuer, *The 1838 Mormon War in Missouri* (University of Missouri Press, 1987), pp. 151–153.
69. John Conway, "An Adapted Organic Tradition," *Daedalus* 117 (Fall 1988), p. 382. For an extended comparison of the impact of religion on politics in the United States and Canada, see Seymour Martin Lipset, *Continental Divide: The Values and Institutions of the United States and Canada* (Routledge, 1990), pp. 74–89.
70. John F. Kennedy, address delivered to the Greater Houston Ministerial Association on September 12, 1960, millercenter.virginia.edu/scripps/diglibrary/prezspeeches/kennedy/index.html.
71. Barack Obama, speech delivered in Philadelphia, Penn., on March 18, 2008, www.nytimes.com/2008/03/18/us/politics/18text-obama.html?_r=1&oref=slogin&pagewanted=all.
72. Barack Obama, news conference in Winston-Salem, N.C., April 29, 2008 www.youtube.com/watch ?v=p4EKY7rCF_c.
73. Taylor Branch, *Parting the Waters: America in the King Years, 1954–63* (Simon & Schuster, 1988), p. 3.
74. Ronald Inglehart and Wayne E. Baker, "Looking Forward, Looking Back: Continuity and Change at the Turn of the Millennium," *American Sociological Review* (February 2000), pp. 29, 31.
75. Kenneth D. Wald and Allison Calhoun-Brown, *Religion and Politics in the United States,* 5th ed. (New York: Rowman and Littlefield, 2006), p. 9.
76. Gallup Brain, "Religion," institution.gallup.com/content/?ci=1690.
77. William H. Flanigan and Nancy H. Zingale, *Political Behavior of the American Electorate,* 11th ed. (CQ Press, 2006), p. 141.
78. *Statistical Abstract,* 2006, p. 59.
79. Ibid.
80. Ibid., p. 58.
81. *Statistical Abstract, 2006,* pp. 21, 59; see also www.thearda.com/mapsReports/reports/selectState.asp.
82. The Association of Religion Data Archives, "U.S. Congregational Membership: State Reports," 2000, www.thearda.com/mapsReports/reports/selectState.asp.
83. Ibid.
84. American Religion Data Archive, "Jewish Estimate—Number of Adherents," www.thearda.com/mapsReports/maps/map.asp?state=101&variable=20; ARDA, "Metro Area Membership Report," www.thearda.com/mapsReports/reports/metro/5602_2000.asp.
85. CNN, "Exit Polls: Results," www.cnn.com/ELECTION/2000/results, September 1, 2006.
86. "Presidential Vote by Religious Affiliation and Race" at msnbc.com. Accessed 7 November 2008.
87. *2000 American National Election Study* (Center for Political Studies, 2000); *2004 American National Election Study* (Center for Political Studies, 2004). Post-election surveys often overestimate the vote, and that appeared to be especially the case in the 2004 National Election Study. See Morris Fiorina and Jon Krosnick, "*Economist/You Gov Internet Presidential Poll,*" www. economist.com/media/pdf/Paper.pdf; and Michael P. McDonald and Samuel Popkin, "The Myth of the Vanishing Voter," *American Political Science Review* 95 (2001), pp. 963–974.
88. "Presidential Vote by Religious Affiliation and Race" at msnbc.com. Accessed 7 November 2008.
89. Data provided by John C. Green from the Fourth National Survey of Religion and Politics, May 6, 2006.
90. The Pew Forum on Religion and Public Life, "US Religious Landscape Survey," February 25, 2008, religions.pewforum.org.
91. CNN, "Exit Polls: Results," www.cnn.com/ELECTION/2000/results, March 21, 2006.
92. American National Election Studies, *1960 ANES* and *2004 ANES* at www.umich.edu/nes/studypages/2004prepost/2004prepost.htm and www.umich.edu/nes/studypages/1956to1960merged/1956to1960merged.htm. Note: *Southern* defined by census region; party ID includes leaners as partisans.
93. James West Davidson, William E. Gienapp, Christine Leigh Heyrman, Mark H. Lytle, and Michael B. Stoff, *Nation of Nations* (McGraw-Hill, 1990), pp. 833–834.
94. Margaret C. Trevor, "Political Socialization, Party Identification, and the Gender Gap," *Public Opinion Quarterly* 63 (Spring 1999), p. 62.
95. *Statistical Abstract, 2006,* p. 263; Sue Tolleson-Rinehard and Jyl J. Josephson, eds., *Gender and American Politics* (Sharpe, 2000), pp. 77–78.
96. U.S. Census Bureau, "U.S. Voter Turnout Up in 2004," www.census.gov/Press-Release/www/releases/archives/voting/004986.html.
97. Tolleson-Rinehard and Josephson, *Gender and American Politics,* pp. 232–233. See also Cindy Simon Rosenthal, ed., *Women Transforming Congress* (University of Oklahoma Press, 2002), pp. 128–139.
98. Barbara C. Burrell, *A Woman's Place Is in the House: Campaigning for Congress in the Feminist Era* (University of Michigan Press, 1994).
99. Calculated from numbers available for the 1998–2006 election cycles from www.opensecrets.org.
100. Marjorie Connelly, "The Election; Who Voted: A? Portrait of American Politics, 1976–2000," *New York Times,* November 12, 2000, p. D4.
101. *Statistical Abstract, 2006,* p. 247.
102. Diane L. Fowlkes, "Feminist Theory: Reconstructing Research and Teaching About American Politics and Government," *News for Teachers of Political Science* (Winter 1987), pp. 6–9. See also Sally Helgesen, *Everyday Revolutionaries: Working Women and the Transformation of American Life* (Doubleday, 1998); Karen Lehrman, *The Lipstick Proviso: Women, Sex, and Power in the Real World* (Anchor/Doubleday, 1997); Tanya Melich, *The Republican War Against Women: An Insider's Report from Behind the Lines* (Bantam Books, 1998); and Virginia Valian, *Why So Slow? The Advancement of Women* (MIT Press, 1998).
103. Arlie Russell Hochschild, "There's No Place Like Work," *New York Times,* April 20, 1997, p. 51.
104. The Pew Research Center, *Gay Marriage a Voting Issue, but Mostly for Opponents,* February 27, 2004, www.people-press.org/reports/display.php3?ReportID=204; and Alexis Simendinger, "Why Issues Matter," *National Journal,* April 1, 2000, based on data from a Pew Center Poll conducted March 15–19, 2000.
105. *Statistical Abstract, 2006,* p. 466.
106. *Statistical Abstract, 2008,* p. 467.
107. Carmen DeNavas-Walt, Bernadette D. Proctor, and Cheryl Hill Lee, U.S. Census Bureau, Current Population Reports, P60–229, *Income, Poverty, and Health Insurance Coverage in the United States: 2004* (U.S. Government Printing Office, 2005), www.census.gov/prod/2005pubs/p60–229.pdf, March 14, 2006; see also U.S. Census Bureau, "Household Income Rises, Poverty Rate Declines, Number of Uninsured Up," press release, August 28, 2007.
108. University of Virginia Law School, "Gender Influences Law Firm Hiring, Promotion, Sociology Professor Says," www.law.virginia.edu/home2002/html/news/2006_spr/Gorman.htm.
109. Princeton Review, *Best 290 Business Schools: 2008 Edition,* (Random House, 2007).
110. Alliance for Board Diversity, "New Report Finds Little Change in Diversity on Corporate Boards," press release, January 17, 2008.
111. Anna Quindlen, "Some Struggles Never Seem to End," *New York Times,* November 14, 2001, p. H24.
112. Elsa Brenner, "The Invisible Population," *New York Times,* November 14, 1999. See also www.census.gov/population/www/documentation/twps0034.html.
113. Dan Black, Gary Gates, Seth Sanders, and Lowell Taylor, "Demographics of the Gay and Lesbian Population in the United States: Evidence from Available Systematic Data Sources," *Demography* 37, no. 2 (May 2000): 139–154.
114. Adam Clymer, "Senate Expands Hate Crimes Law to Include Gays," *New York Times,* June 21, 2000, p. A1.
115. Rose Arce, "Massachusetts Court Upheld Same-Sex Marriage," www.cnn.com/2004/law/02/04/gay.marriage/.
116. Judicial Council of California, "California Supreme Court Rules in Marriage Cases," News Release no. 26, 15 May 2008.
117. Rachel Gordon, "Newsom's Plan for Same-Sex Marriages; Mayor Wants to License Gay and Lesbian Couples," *San Francisco Chronicle,* February 11, 2001 p. A1.
118. *Boy Scouts of America v. Dale,* 120 S. Ct. 2446 (2000).
119. *Lawrence v. Texas,* 123 S. Ct. 2472 (2003).
120. David Masci, "The Future of Marriage," *CQ Researcher Online* 14, no. 17 (May 7, 2004): 397–420.
121. U.S. Census Bureau, "Table MS-2. Estimated Median Age at First Marriage, by Sex: 1890 to the Present," June 29, 2005, www.census.gov/population/socdemo/hh-fam/ms2.pdf.
122. *Statistical Abstract, 2006,* p. 67.
123. United Nations Statistics Division, "Social Indicators," unstats.un.org/unsd/demographic/products/socind/childbr.htm.
124. The census stopped releasing divorce data in 1998, possibly because several states stopped providing it.
125. *Statistical Abstract, 2003,* p. 100.
126. *General Social Survey (GSS) 1972–2000 Cumulative Codebook,* www.icpsr.umich.edu/GSS/index.html.

127. Thomas Jefferson to P. S. du Pont de Nemours, April 24, 1816, in Paul L. Ford, ed. *The Writings of Thomas Jefferson* (Putnam, 1899), vol. 10, p. 25.
128. *Statistical Abstract, 2008,* p. 143.
129. Ibid., p. 146.
130. Ibid.
131. Herbert McClosky and John Zaller, *The American Ethos: Public Attitudes Toward Capitalism and Democracy* (Harvard University Press, 1984), p. 261.
132. Raymond E. Wolfinger, Fred I. Greenstein, and Martin Shapiro, *Dynamics of American Politics,* 2d ed. (Prentice Hall, 1980), p. 19.
133. Thomas Jefferson, "Autobiography," in Adrienne Koch and William Peden, eds., *The Life and Selected Writings of Thomas Jefferson* (Modern Library, 1944), p. 38.
134. Harold W. Stanley and Richard G. Niemi, *Vital Statistics on American Politics, 2007–2008* (CQ Press, 2008), p. 374–375.
135. Stanley Fischer, "Symposium on the Slowdown in Productivity Growth," *Journal of Economic Perspectives* 2 (Fall 1988), pp. 3–7.
136. Peter J. Nicholson, "The Rich Are Not Getting Much Richer; No, It's the Very, Very Rich," *Globe and Mail,* January 5, 2008, p. 17A.
137. *Statistical Abstract, 2008,* p. 458.
138. U.S. Bureau of the Census, www.census.gov/hhes/www/poverty/threshold/thresh07.html.
139. *Statistical Abstract, 2008,* p. 461.
140. Ibid, p. 459.
141. Ibid.
142. *Statistical Abstract, 2006,* p. 464.
143. U.S. Department of Commerce, Bureau of Economic Analysis, "Real Gross Domestic Product, 1 Decimal," February 28, 2008, research.stlouisfed.org/fred2/data/GDPC1.txt.
144. Daniel Bell, *The Coming of Post-Industrial Society: A Venture in Social Forecasting* (Basic Books, 1973), p. xviii.
145. *Statistical Abstract, 2008,* pp. 391, 429.
146. Ibid.
147. *Statistical Abstract, 2008,* p. 394.
148. Gabriel A. Almond, G. Bingham Powell, Jr., Russell J. Dalton, and Kaare Strøm, eds., *Comparative Politics Today: A World View,* 9th ed. (Pearson Longman, 2008), p. 54.
149. Seymour Martin Lipset, *Continental Divide: The Values and Institutions of the United States and Canada* (Routledge, 1990), p. 170.
150. *Statistical Abstract, 2006,* pp. 25, 103.
151. United Nations, "Expert Group Meeting on Policy Responses to Population Ageing and Population Decline," www.un.org/esa/population/publications/popdecline/Chesnais.pdf.
152. Susan A. MacManus, *Young v. Old: Generational Combat in the 21st Century* (Westview Press, 1996), pp. 48–49, 174–176, 245.
153. Nicholas L. Danigelis, Stephen J. Cutler, and Melissa Hardy, "Population Aging, Intracohort Aging, and Sociopolitical Attitudes," *American Sociological Review* 72 (October 2007), p. 816.
154. CNN, "Exit Polls: Results," www.cnn.com/ELECTION/2000/results, September 1, 2006.
155. Carl N. Degler, *Out of Our Past: The Forces That Shaped Modern America,* 3d ed. (Harper & Row, 1984), p. 322.
156. http://www.rockthevote.com/about/press-room/press-releases/rock-the-vote-registers.html. Accessed 6 November 2008.

Chapter 6

1. U.S. Chamber of Commerce, "Spending Scheme," 2008 Political Ad, New Hampshire Senate, 7 October 2008, at http://www.nationaljournal.com/njonline/as_20081007_8611.php.
2. Brody Mullins and Susan Davis, "Chamber in Big Push for GOP," *The Wall Street Journal,* 24 October 2008, p. A1.
3. Open Secrets, "Service Employees International Union Independent Expenditures," *OpenSecrets.org,* at http://www.opensecrets.org/pacs/indexpend.php?cmte=C00004036&cycle=2008.
4. James Madison, *The Federalist,* No. 10, November 23, 1787, in Isaac Kramnick, ed., *The Federalist Papers* (Penguin, 1987), pp. 122–128.
5. See Robert Dahl, *Who Governs?* (Yale University Press, 1961).
6. Center for Responsive Politics, "Microsoft Corp: Donor Profile," opensecrets.org/orgs/summary.asp?ID=D000000115&Name=Microsoft+Corp.
7. www.changetowin.org/members.html.
8. Office of Labor Management Standards, Union Reports and Constitutions, www.dol.gov/esa/regs/compliance/olms/rrlo/lmrda.htm#1.
9. AFL-CIO, "About Us: Union Facts," www.aflcio.org/aboutus/faq/.
10. U.S. Bureau of Labor Statistics, www.bls.gov/cps/cpsaat40.pdf.
11. Service Employees International Union, "Leading U.S. Labor Union Launching Ambitious New 'Justice for All' Strategies to Improve the Lives of Millions," press release, April 7, 2008, www.seiufactchecker.org/news/SEIU_Launching_Justice_for_All_Strategies/default.aspx.
12. Peter L. Francia, *The Future of Organized Labor in American Politics* (Columbia University Press, 2006).
13. Brian C. Mooney, "Nation's Two Biggest Unions to Wait on Presidential Endorsement," *Boston Globe,* September 11, 2003, p. A3.
14. Alison Grant, "Labor Chief Sees Anti-Union Efforts Growing Bolder," (Cleveland) *Plain Dealer,* November 22, 2005, p. C1.
15. James MacGregor Burns and Stewart Burns, *A People's Charter: The Pursuit of Rights in America* (Knopf, 1991).
16. Chris W. Cox, "Who We Are, and What We Do," National Rifle Associaton, www.nraila.org/About/.
17. www.concordcoalition.org/about.html.
18. National Education Association, www.nea.org/aboutnea.
19. Sam Dillon and Diana Jean Schemo, "Union Urges Bush to Replace Education Chief over Remark," *New York Times,* February 25, 2004, p. A15.
20. See Mancur Olson, *The Logic of Collective Action* (Harvard University Press, 1971).
21. Kenneth J. Arrow, "A Difficulty in the Concept of Social Welfare," *Journal of Political Economy* 58 (August), pp. 328–346. See also David Austen-Smith and Jeffrey S. Banks, "Social Choice Theory, Game Theory, and Positive Political Theory," *Annual Review of Political Science* 1 (June), pp. 259–287.
22. Robert Salisbury, "Interest Representation: The Dominance of Institutions," *American Political Science Review* 78 (March 1984), p. 66.
23. V. O. Key, Jr., *Public Opinion and American Democracy* (Knopf, 1961), pp. 504–507.
24. www.bipac.org/home.asp. See also David B. Magleby, Anthony Corrado, and Kelly D. Patterson, *Financing the 2004 Election* (Brookings Institute Press, 2006); and David B. Magleby, J. Quin Monson, and Kelly Patterson, *Electing Congress: New Rules for an Old Game* (Pearson Prentice Hall, 2007).
25. Andrew Chadwick, "Digital Network Repertoires and Organizational Hybridity," *Political Communication* 24 (July–September), p. 284.
26. R. Kenneth Godwin, *One Billion Dollars of Influence: The Direct Marketing of Politics* (Chatham House, 1988).
27. David B. Magleby, J. Quin Monson, and Kelly Patterson, *Electing Congress: New Rules for an Old Game* (Prentice Hall, 2006). See also David B. Magleby, J. Quin Monson, and Kelly D. Patterson, *Dancing Without Partners: How Candidates, Parties, and Interest Groups Interact in the Presidential Campaign* (Rowman & Littlefield, 2007); and David B. Magleby and Kelly D. Patterson, eds., *The Battle for Congress: Iraq, Scandal, and Campaign Finance in the 2006 Election* (Paradigm, 2008).
28. The *Federal Register* is published every weekday. You can find it at the library or on the Internet at www.gpoaccess.gov.
29. Lucius J. Barker, "Third Parties in Litigation: A Systemic View of the Judicial Function," *Journal of Politics* 29 (February 1967), pp. 41–69; Jethro K. Lieberman, *Litigious Society,* rev. ed. (Basic Books, 1983).
30. Gregory A. Caldeira and John R. Wright, "Organized Interests and Agenda Setting in the U.S. Supreme Court," *American Political Science Review* 82 (December 1988), pp. 1109–1127. See also Gregory A. Caldeira and John R. Wright, "*Amici Curiae* Before the Supreme Court: Who Participates, When, and How Much?" *Journal of Politics* 52 (August 1990), pp. 782–806.
31. Karen O'Connor, *Women's Organizations' Use of the Courts* (Lexington Books, 1980).
32. Steven Teles, *The Rise of the Conservative Legal Movement: The Battle for Control of the Law* (Princeton University Press, 2008).
33. Linda Greenhouse and David D. Kirkpatrick, "Justices Loosen Ad Restrictions in Campaign Law," *New York Times,* June 26, 2007, p. A1.
34. Lee Epstein and C. K. Rowland, "Debunking the Myth of Interest Group Invincibility in the Courts," *American Political Science Review* 85 (March 1991), pp. 205–217.
35. Robert D. McFadden, "Across the U.S., Protests for Immigrants Draw Thousands," *New York Times,* April 10, 2006, p. A14; and Anna Gorman and J. Michael Kennedy, "The Immigration Debate," *Los Angeles Times,* April 11, 2006, p. A11.
36. Judy Keen and Martin Kasindorf, "From Coast to Coast, 'We Need to Be Heard,'" *USA Today,* May 2, 2006, p. 3A.
37. See Kenneth Klee, "The Siege of Seattle," *Newsweek,* December 13, 1999, p. 30.
38. League of Conservation Voters, "Key Races of the 2004 Congressional Election Cycle," www.lcv.org/campaigns/2004-congressional/.
39. For a discussion of the 1998 New Mexico race, see Lonna Rae Atkeson and Anthony C. Coveny, "The 1998 New Mexico Third Congressional District Race," David B. Magleby, ed., *Outside Money: Soft Money and Issue Advocacy in the 1998 Congressional Elections* (Rowman & Littlefield, 2002), pp. 135–152.
40. Joshua Weinstein, "Angry Ralph Nader: Scorn, Anger, and Resolve Sustain Nader," *Portland Press Herald,* October 6, 2004.
41. Ethan Bronner, *Battle for Justice: How the Bork Nomination Shook America* (Norton, 1989), pp. 50–55.
42. Hugh Heclo, "Issue Networks and the Executive Establishment," in Anthony King, ed., *The New American Political System* (American Enterprise Institute, 1978).
43. David Mayhew, *Congress: The Electoral Connection* (Yale University Press, 1974), p. 45.
44. John R. Wright, "Contributions, Lobbying, and Committee Voting in the U.S. House of Representatives," *American Political Science Review* 84 (June 1990), pp. 417–438.
45. *McConnell v. Federal Elections Commission,* 124 S. Ct. 621 (2003).
46. For evidence of the impact of PAC expenditures on legislative committee behavior and legislative involvement generally, see Richard L. Hall and Frank W. Wayman, "Buying Time: Moneyed Interests and the Mobilization of Bias in

Congressional Committees," *American Political Science Review* 84 (September 1990), pp. 797–820.
47. Federal Election Commission, "FEC Records Slight Increase in the Number of PACs," press release, January 17, 2008, at www.fec.gov/press/press2008/20080117paccount.shtml.
48. Ibid.
49. Edwin M. Epstein, "Business and Labor Under the Federal Election Campaign Act of 1971," in Michael J. Malbin, ed., *Parties, Interest Groups, and Campaign Finance Laws* (American Enterprise Institute for Public Policy Research, 1980), p. 112. See also Gary C. Jacobson, *Money in Congressional Elections* (Yale University Press, 1980).
50. Open Secrets, opensecrets.org/pacs/industry.asp?txt=N00&cycle=2006.
51. Amy Keller, "Leadership PACs 'Not Sinister,' FEC Told," *Roll Call,* February 27, 2003.
52. Open Secrets, opensecrets.org/pacs/lookup2.asp?strid=C00344234&cycle=2008.
53. Jacobson, *Money in Congressional Elections,* p. 77.
54. Paul Krugman, "Toward One-Party Rule," *New York Times,* June 27, 2003, p. A27.
55. J. Quin Monson, "Get On TeleVision vs. Get On The Van: GOTV and the Ground War in 2002," in David B. Magleby and J. Quin Monson, eds., *The Last Hurrah* (Brookings Institution Press, 2004), p. 108.
56. David B. Magleby and Nicole Carlisle Smith, "Party Money in the 2002 Congressional Elections," in David B. Magleby and J. Quin Monson, eds., *The Last Hurrah* (Brookings Institution Press, 2004), p. 54; David B. Magleby and Eric A. Smith, "Party Soft Money in the 2000 Congressional Elections," in David B. Magleby, ed., *The Other Campaign* (Rowman & Littlefield, 2003), pp. 34–35; Mariane Holt, "The Surge in Party Money," in David B. Magleby, ed., *Outside Money* (Rowman & Littlefield, 2000), p. 36; and David B. Magleby, "Conclusions and Implications," in David B. Magleby, ed., *Outside Money* (Rowman & Littlefield, 2000), p. 214.
57. *Federal Election Commission v. Wisconsin Right to Life Inc.,* 551 U.S._ (2007).
58. Ruth Marcus, "Labor Spent $119 Million for '96 Politics, Study Says; Almost All Contributions Went to Democrats," *Washington Post,* September 10, 1997, p. A19.
59. David B. Magleby, "Party and Interest Group Electioneering in Federal Elections," in Anthony Corrado, Thomas E. Mann, and Trevor Potter, eds., *Inside the Campaign Finance Battle: Court Testimony on the New Reforms* (Brookings Institution Press, 2003); and Sandra Anglund and Clyde McKee, "The 1998 Connecticut Fifth Congressional District Race," David B. Magleby, ed., *Outside Money: Soft Money and Issue Advocacy in the 1998 Congressional Elections* (Rowman & Littlefield, 2002), pp. 164, 166.
60. John Mintz, "Texan Aired 'Clean Air' Ads; Bush's Campaign Not Involved, Billionaire Says," *Washington Post,* March 4, 2000, p. A6.
61. Kate Zernike, "Kerry Pressing Swift Boat Case Long After Loss," *New York Times,* May 28, 2006, p. A1.
62. Internal Revenue Code, Title 26, frwebgate.access.gpo.gov/cgi-bin/getdoc.cgi?dbname=browse_usc&docid=Cite:+26USC501.
63. Nicholas Confessore, "Bush's Secret Stash," *Washington Monthly* 36 (May 2004), pp. 17–23.
64. Center for Responsive Politics, "527 Committees: Top 50 Federally Focused Organizations," at http://www.opensecrets.org/527s/527cmtes.php:level=c&evele=1008. Accessed 8 November 2008.
65. E. J. Dionne, Jr., "Fear of McCain-Feingold," *Washington Post,* December 3, 2002, p. A25.
66. The Campaign Legal Center, "Interveners Urge Supreme Court to Sustain BCRA in Its Entirety," www.campaignlegalcenter.org/press-814.html.
67. Hall and Wayman, "Buying Time," p. 814. A different study of the House Ways and Means Committee found campaign contributions to be part of the representatives' policy decisions, but even more important was the number of lobbying contacts; see Wright, "Contributions, Lobbying, and Committee Voting."
68. David B. Magleby and Kelly D. Patterson, "Campaign Consultants and Direct Democracy: Politics of Citizen Control," in James E. Thurber and Candice J. Nelson, eds., *Campaign Warriors: The Role of Political Consultants in Elections* (Brookings Institution Press, 2000).
69. Monson, "Get On TeleVision vs. Get On The Van," p. 92; David B. Magleby, "Change and Continuity in the Financing of Federal Elections," in David B. Magleby, Anthony Corrado, and Kelly D. Patterson, eds., *Financing the 2004 Election* (Brookings Institution Press, 2006), pp. 14–15; David B. Magleby and Kelly D. Patterson, "Rules of Engagement: BCRA and Unanswered Questions," in David B. Magleby and Kelly D. Patterson, eds., *The Battle for Congress: Iraq, Scandal, and Campaign Finance in the 2006 Election* (Paradigm, 2008), p. 50; and Kyle Saunders and Robert Duffy, "Money, Moderation, and Mobilization in the 2004 Colorado Senate Race," in David B. Magleby, J. Quin Monson, and Kelly Patterson, eds., *Electing Congress: New Rules for an Old Game* (Pearson Prentice Hall 2007), p. 36.
70. Ronald Reagan, "Remarks to Administration Officials on Domestic Policy," December 13, 1988, *Weekly Compilation of Presidential Documents,* 24 (December 1988), pp. 1615–1620.
71. Sylvia Tesh, "In Support of Single-Interest Politics," *Political Science Quarterly* 99 (Spring 1984), pp. 27–44.
72. Adam Clymer, "Congress Sends Lobbying Overhaul to Clinton," *New York Times,* December 16, 1995, p. A36.
73. Legislative Resource Center's Lobbying Section, telephone interview, April 7, 2004.

Chapter 7

1. See Scott Mainwaring, "Party Systems in the Third Wave," *Journal of Democracy* (July 1998), pp. 67–81.
2. Joseph A. Schlesinger, *Political Parties and the Winning of Office* (University of Michigan Press, 1994).
3. Robert R. Alford and Eugene C. Lee, "Voting Turnout in American Cities," *American Political Science Review* 62 (September), pp. 809–810.
4. Gary W. Cox and Mathew D. McCubbins, *Legislative Leviathan: Party Government in the House* (University of California Press, 1993).
5. David W. Brady and Craig Volden, *Revolving Gridlock: Politics and Policy from Carter to Clinton* (Westview Press, 1998); James A. Thurber, ed., *Divided Democracy: Cooperation and Conflict Between the President and Congress* (CQ Press, 1991); James A. Thurber, ed., *Rivals for Power: Presidential-Congressional Relations* (CQ Press, 1996); Charles O. Jones, *Separate but Equal Branches: Congress and the Presidency* (Chatham House, 1995), chaps. 5 and 6; and Jon R. Bond and Richard Fleisher, *The President in the Legislative Arena* (University of Chicago Press, 1990).
6. *California Democratic Party et al. v. Jones,* 120 S. Ct. 2402 (2000).
7. Adam Nagourney, "Obama Takes Iowa in a Big Turnout as Clinton Falters; Huckabee Victor," *New York Times,* January 4, 2008, p. A1.
8. Peverill Squire, "The Iowa Caucuses, 1972–2008: A Eulogy," *The Forum* 5, no. 4, article 1, pp. 2–5, www.bepress.com/forum/vol5/iss4/art1.
9. *The Book of the States, 2000–2001* (Council of State Governments, 2000), pp. 164–165.
10. For an analysis of the potential effects of different electoral rules in the United States see Todd Donovan and Shawn Bowler, *Reforming the Republic: Democratic Institutions for the New America* (Prentice Hall, 2004).
11. William H. Riker, "The Two-Party System and Duverger's Law: An Essay on the History of Political Science," *American Political Science Review* 76 (December 1982), pp. 753–766. For a classic analysis, see E. E. Schattschneider, *Party Government* (Holt, Rinehart, Winston, 1942).
12. Maurice Duverger, *Party Politics and Pressure Groups* (Nelson, 1972), pp. 23–32.
13. L. Sandy Maisel and John F. Bibby, *Two Parties—or More? The American Party System* (Westview Press, 1998).
14. Ted G. Jelen, ed., *Ross for Boss* (State University of New York Press, 2001), p. 88.
15. Steven J. Rosenstone, Roy L. Behr, and Edward H. Lazarus, *Third Parties in America: Citizen Response to Major Party Failure,* 2d ed. (Princeton University Press, 1996). See also Xandra Kayden and Eddie Mahe, Jr., *The Party Goes On: The Persistence of the Two-Party System in the United States* (Basic Books, 1985), pp. 143–144. The Republican Party, which started as a third party, was one of the two major parties by 1860, the year Republican Abraham Lincoln won the Presidency; see Lewis L. Gould, *Grand Old Party: A History of the Republicans* (Random House, 2003), pp. 3–17.
16. Dean Lacy and Quin Monson, "The Origins and Impact of Voter Support for Third-Party Candidates: A Case Study of the 1998 Minnesota Gubernatorial Election," *Political Research Quarterly* 55(2), pp. 409–437.
17. On the impact of third parties, see Howard R. Penniman, "Presidential Third Parties and the Modern American Two-Party System," in William J. Crotty, ed., *The Party Symbol* (Freeman, 1980), pp. 101–117. See also Frank Smallwood, *The Other Candidates: Third Parties in Presidential Elections* (University Press of New England, 1983).
18. Benjamin Franklin, George Washington, and Thomas Jefferson, quoted in Richard Hofstadter, *The Idea of a Party System* (University of California Press, 1969), pp. 2, 123.
19. For concise histories of the two parties, see Jules Witcover, *Party of the People: A History of the Democrats* (Random House, 2003); and Gould, *Grand Old Party.*
20. See V. O. Key, Jr., "A Theory of Critical Elections," *Journal of Politics* 17 (February 1955), pp. 3–18; Walter Dean Burnham, *Critical Elections and the Mainsprings of American Politics* (Norton, 1970), pp. 1–10; and E. E. Schattschneider, *The Semisovereign People: A Realist's View of Democracy in America* (Holt, Rinehart & Winston, 1975), pp. 78–80.
21. William E. Gienapp, *The Origins of the Republican Party, 1852–1856* (Oxford University Press, 1987).
22. Gould, *Grand Old Party,* p. 88.
23. Ibid.
24. David W. Brady, "Election, Congress, and Public Policy Changes, 1886–1960," in Bruce A. Campbell and Richard Trilling, eds., *Realignment in American Politics: Toward a Theory* (University of Texas Press, 1980), p. 188.
25. L. Sandy Maisel, *Parties and Elections in America: The Electoral Process* (Rowman & Littlefield, 2002), pp. 48–49.
26. Gerald Pomper, "Classification of Presidential Elections," *Journal of Politics* 29 (August 1967), p. 538.
27. Earl Black and Merle Black, *The Rise of Southern Republicans* (Belknap Press, 2003).
28. "NAAS Survey: State Voter Registration Figures for the 2008 General Election," at http://www.naas.org. Accessed 8 November 2008.
29. V. O. Key, Jr., *Political Parties and Pressure Groups,* 5th ed. (International, 1964). See also

Marjorie Randon Hershey, *Party Politics in America*, 12th ed. (Longman, 2006).

30. Federal Election Commission, "National Party Activity Summarized," press release, October 30, 2006, www.fec.gov/press/press2006/20061030party/20061030party.html.
31. Hershey, *Party Politics in America.*
32. See L. Sandy Maisel, *From Obscurity to Oblivion: Running in the Congressional Primary*, rev. ed. (University of Tennessee Press, 1986).
33. The early Republican efforts and advantages over the Democrats are well documented in Thomas B. Edsall, *The New Politics of Inequality* (Norton, 1984); and Gary C. Jacobson, "The Republican Advantage in Campaign Finances," in John E. Chubb and Paul E. Peterson, eds., *New Direction in American Politics* (Brookings Institution Press, 1985), p. 6. See also David B. Magleby and Kelly D. Patterson, "Rules of Engagement: BCRA and Unanswered Questions," in David B. Magleby and Kelly D. Patterson, eds., *The Battle for Congress: Iraq, Scandal, and Campaign Finance in the 2006 Election* (Paradigm, 2008), pp. 33–36.
34. David C. King, "The Polarization of American Political Parties and Mistrust of Government," in Joseph S. Nye, Philip Zelikow, and David C. King, eds., *Why People Don't Trust Government* (Harvard University Press, 1997); and National Election Study, "Important Difference in What Democratic and Republican Parties Stand For, 1952–2000," www.umich./nes/edu/nesguide/toptable/tab2b_4.htm.
35. Kelly D. Patterson, *Political Parties and the Maintenance of Liberal Democracy* (Columbia University Press, 1996), pp. 30–31.
36. Tom Shales, "Bush, Bringing the Party to Life; From the New Nominee, a Splendid Acceptance Speech," *Washington Post*, August 19, 1988, p. C1.
37. See James L. Gibson, Cornelius P. Cotter, John F. Bibby, and Robert J. Huckshorn, "Assessing Party Organizational Strength," *American Journal of Political Science* 27 (May 1983), pp. 193–222. See also Cornelius P. Cotter, James L. Gibson, John F. Bibby, Robert Huckshorn, *Party Organizations in American Politics* (University of Pittsburg Press, 1989).
38. Paul S. Herrnson, *Party Campaigning in the 1980s: Have the National Parties Made a Comeback as Key Players in Congressional Elections?* (Harvard University Press, 1988), p. 122.
39. *Marbury v. Madison*, 1 Cranch 137 (1803).
40. See Angus Campbell, Philip E. Converse, Warren E. Miller, and Donald E. Stokes, *The American Voter* (University of Chicago Press, 1960); Norman A. Nie, Sidney Verba, and John R. Petrocik, *The Changing American Voter*, enlarged ed. (Harvard University Press, 1979); and Warren E. Miller and J. Merrill Shanks, *The New American Voter* (Harvard University Press, 1996).
41. Campbell et al., *The American Voter*, pp. 121–128.
42. Ibid.
43. Bruce E. Keith et al., *The Myth of the Independent Voter* (University of California Press, 1992).
44. Black and Black, *The Rise of Southern Republicans.*
45. See Byron E. Shafer, *The End of Realignment: Interpreting American Electoral Eras* (University of Wisconsin Press, 1991).
46. Michael F. Meffert, Helmut Norpoth, and Anirudh V. S. Ruhil, "Realignment and Macropartisanship," *American Political Science Review* 95 (December 2001), pp. 953–962.
47. Nine percent of all voters were Pure Independents in 1956 and 1960; Keith et al., *The Myth of the Independent Voter*, p. 51. In 1992, the figure was also 9 percent; *1992 National Election Study* (Center for Political Studies, University of Michigan, 1992).
48. David B. Magleby and Candice J. Nelson, *The Money Chase: Congressional Campaign Finance Reform* (Brookings Institution Press, 1990), p. 16.
49. David B. Magleby, ed., *Outside Money: Soft Money and Issue Advocacy in the 1998 Congressional Elections* (Rowman & Littlefield, 2003) and David B. Magleby, ed., *The Other Campaign: Soft Money and Issue Advocacy in the 2000 Congressional Elections* (Rowman & Littlefield, 2003).
50. Jonathan S. Krasno and Daniel E. Seltz, *Buying Time: Television Advertising in the 1998 Congressional Elections*, report of a grant funded by the Pew Charitable Trusts (1998).
51. *Colorado Republican Federal Campaign Committee v. Federal Election Commission*, 518 U.S. 604 (1996).
52. David B. Magleby and Kelly D. Patterson, "Rules of Engagement: BCRA and Unanswered Questions," in David B. Magleby and Kelly D. Patterson, eds., *The Battle for Congress: Iraq, Scandal, and Campaign Finance in the 2006 Election* (Paradigm, 2008), p. 34.
53. Sidney M. Milkis, "Parties Versus Interest Groups," in Anthony Corrado, Thomas E. Mann, and Trevor Potter, eds., *Inside the Campaign Finance Battle: Court Testimony on the New Reforms* (Brookings Institution Press, 2003), p. 44.
54. David B. Magleby, Anthony Corrado, and Kelly D. Patterson, eds., *Financing the 2004 Election* (Brookings Institution Press, 2006).
55. Paul S. Herrnson, *Party Campaigning in the 1980s* (Harvard University Press, 1988), pp. 80–81.
56. E. E. Schattschneider, *Party Government* (Holt, Rinehart & Winston, 1942), p. 1.

Chapter 8

1. Al Baker, "New York Risking the Loss of Ballot Equipment Money," *New York Times*, April 29, 2004, p. B05.
2. Ibid.
3. Maha Al-Azar, "Broad Election Reforms Are Urged; Education Called as Crucial as Machines," *Washington Post*, July 17, 2003, p. T04; and Harris N. Miller, "Electronic Voting Is a Solution," *USA Today*, February 4, 2004, p. 14A.
4. http://www.latimes.com/news/politics/la-na-votingproblems5-2008nov05,0,2933241.story.
5. http://www.gallup.com/poll/111664/Gallup-Daily-Obama-Continues-Outpace-McCain.aspx. Accessed 7 November 2008. Note: we removed the "no opinion" and percentaged the other categories to sum to 100 percent.
6. Thomas D. Snyder, Sally A. Dillow, and Charlene M. Hoffman, "Number of Persons Age 18 and Over, by Highest Level of Education Attained, Age, Sex, and Race/Ethnicity: 2005," *Digest of Education Statistics 2007* (U.S. Government Printing Office, 2008), p. 24.
7. Peverill Squire, "Why The 1936 *Literary Digest* Poll Failed," *Public Opinion Quarterly* 52 (Spring 1988), 125–133.
8. Ibid., 128.
9. Robert Coles, *The Political Life of Children* (Atlantic Monthly Press, 2000), pp. 24–25. See also Stephen M. Caliendo, *Teachers Matter: The Trouble with Leaving Political Education to the Coaches* (Greenwood Press, 2000).
10. Pamela Johnston Conover, "The Influence of Group Identifications on Political Perception and Evaluation," *Journal of Politics* 46 (August 1984), pp. 760–785; and Henry E. Brady and Paul M. Sniderman, "Attitude Attribution: A Group Basis for Political Reasoning," *American Political Science Review* 79 (December 1985), pp. 1061–1078.
11. Caliendo, *Teachers Matter*, pp. 16–17.
12. James Garbarino, *Raising Children in a Socially Toxic Environment* (Jossey-Bass, 1995).
13. J. L. Glanville, "Political Socialization or Selection? Adolescent Extracurricular Participation and Political Activity in Early Adulthood," *Social Science Quarterly* 80 (1999), p. 279.
14. National Association of Secretaries of State, *New Millennium Project, Part I: American Youth Attitudes on Policies, Citizenship, Government and Voting* (Author, 1999); and "Political Interest on the Rebound Among the Nation's Freshmen," Higher Education Research Institute, Fall 2003, www.gseis.ucla.edu/heri/03_press_release.pdf.
15. Margaret Stimmann Branson, "Making the Case for Civic Education: Educating Young People for Responsible Citizenship," paper presented at the Conference for Professional Development for Program Trainers, Manhattan Beach, Calif., February 25, 2001.
16. Kenneth Feldman and Theodore M. Newcomb, *The Impact of College on Students*, vol. 2 (Jossey-Bass, 1969), pp. 16–24, 49–56. See also David O. Sears and Nicholas A. Valentino, "Politics Matters: Political Events as Catalysts for Preadult Socialization," *American Political Science Review* 91 (March 1997), pp. 45–65.
17. Daniel B. German, "The Role of the Media in Political Socialization and Attitude Formation Toward Racial/Ethnic Minorities in the US," in Robert F. Farnen, ed., *Nationalism, Ethnicity, and Identity: Cross National and Comparative Perspective* (Transaction, 2004), p. 287.
18. James G. Gimpel, J. Celeste Lay, and Jason E. Schuknecht, *Cultivating Democracy: Civic Environments and Political Socialization in America* (Brookings Institution Press, 2003), p. 127 (see chap. 5).
19. Robert D. Putnam, "The Rebirth of American Civic Life," *Boston Globe*, March 2, 2008, p. D9.
20. Quoted in Hadley Cantril, *Gauging Public Opinion* (Princeton University Press, 1944), p viii.
21. John G. Geer, *From Tea Leaves to Opinion Polls: A Theory of Democratic Leadership* (Columbia University Press, 1996).
22. Norman J. Ornstein and Amy S. Mitchell, "The Permanent Campaign: The Trend Toward Continuous Campaigning Stems from Advances in Technology and the Proliferation of Public Opinion Polls," *World and I* 12 (January 1997): 48–55.
23. "Do You Approve or Disapprove of the Way George W. Bush Is Handling the Situation with Iraq?" CBS News/*New York Times* Poll, May 3, 2003, and May 20, 2004, www.pollingreport.com/iraq2.htm.
24. CBS News and the New York Times, "Looking Ahead to the General Election," www.cbsnews.com/htdocs/pdf/apr08b_genelec.pdf.
25. Lawrence R. Jacobs and Robert R. Shapiro, *Politicians Don't Pander* (University of Chicago Press, 2000), p. 3.
26. Robert S. Erikson and Kent L. Tedin, *American Public Opinion: Its Origins, Content and Impact*, 6th ed. (Longman, 2001), pp. 272–273; on the centrality of the reelection motive, see David R. Mayhew, *Congress: The Electoral Connection* (Yale University Press, 1974).
27. http://www.nytimes.com/2008/11/03/us/politics/03Campaign.html?hp. Accessed 7 November 2008.
28. For a general discussion of political knowledge, see Michael Delli Carpini and Scott Keeter, *What Americans Know About Politics and Why It Matters* (Yale University Press, 1996).
29. The 2000 National Election Study, Center for Political Studies, University of Michigan. See the NES Guide to Public Opinion and Electoral Behavior, www.umich.edu/nes/nesguide/nesguide.htm.

30. Erikson and Tedin, *American Public Opinion*, p. 304.
31. *2004 National Election Study* (Center for Political Studies, University of Michigan, 2004).
32. Nicole B. Ellison, Charles Steinfield, and Cliff Lampe, "The Benefits of Facebook 'Friends': Social Capital and College Students' Use of Online Social Network Sites," *Journal of Computer-Mediated Communication* 12 (2007), art. 1.
33. Data from the American National Election Studies, Center for Political Studies, University of Michigan, 1948–2004, www.electionstudies.org/studypages/download/datacenter_all.htm.
34. *2004 National Election Study.*
35. Federal Election Commission, "Presidential Election Campaign Fund," www.fec.gov.
36. Ronald Brownstein, "The First 21st Century Campaign," *National Journal,* 19 April 2008.
37. Julie Bosman, "More Hiring and Advertising Ahead for Paul as the Donations Pour In," *New York Times,* December 18, 2007.
38. Frank R. Parker, *Black Votes Count: Political Empowerment in Mississippi After 1965* (University of North Carolina Press, 1990), p. 3.
39. Bernard Grofman and Lisa Handley, "The Impact of the Voting Rights Act on Black Representation in Southern State Legislatures," *Legislative Studies Quarterly* 16 (February 1991), pp. 111–128.
40. International Institute for Democracy and Electoral Assistance, "Voter Turnout from 1945 to Date: A Global Report on Political Participation," www.idea.int/voter_turnout/index.html.
41. Raymond E. Wolfinger and Steven J. Rosenstone, "The Effect of Registration Laws on Voter Turnout," *American Political Science Review* 72 (March 1978), p. 41.
42. Ibid., p. 24.
43. Raymond E. Wolfinger and Steven J. Rosenstone, *Who Votes?* (Yale University Press, 1980), pp. 78, 88.
44. Federal Election Commission, "The Impact of the National Voter Registration Act on Federal Elections 1999–2000," www.fec.gov.
45. See Raymond E. Wolfinger and Ben Highton, "Estimating the Effects of the National Voter Registration Act of 1993," *Political Behavior* (June 1998), pp. 79–104; and Raymond E. Wolfinger and Jonathan Hoffman, "Registering and Voting with Motor Voter," *PS: Political Science and Politics* (March 2001), pp. 85–92.
46. Quin Monson and Lindsay Nielson, "Mobilizing the Early Voter," paper presented at the annual meeting of the Midwest Political Science Association, Chicago, Ill., April 3–6, 2008.
47. U.S. Census Bureau, "Voting and Registration in the Election of November 2004," www.census.gov/prod/2006pubs/p20-556.pdf.
48. The Early Voting Information Center, "Absence and Early Voting Laws—at www.early voting.net/states/abs/aws.php. Accessed 14 October 2008.
49. For a discussion of the differences in the turnout between presidential and midterm elections, see James E. Campbell, "The Presidential Surge and Its Midterm Decline in Congressional Elections, 1868–1988," *Journal of Politics* 53 (May 1991), pp. 477–487.
50. David E. Rosenbaum, "Democrats Keep Solid Hold on Congress," *New York Times,* November 9, 1988, p. A24; Louis V. Gerstner, "Next Time, Let Us Boldly Vote as No Democracy Has Before," *USA Today,* November 16, 1998, p. A15; and Michael McDonald, "2004 Voting-Age and Voting-Eligible Population Estimates and Voter Turnout," elections.gmu.edu/Voter_Turnout_2004.htm.
51. Data from Curtis Gans, "President Bush, Mobilization Drives Propel Turnout to Post-1968 High; Kerry, Democratic Weakness Shown," *Center for Voting and Democracy,* November 4, 2004, www.fairvote.org/reports/csae2004electionreport.pdf.
52. American University News, "Much-hyped Turnout Record Fails to Materialize, Convenience Voting Fails to Boost Balloting," Nov. 7, 2008.
53. Wolfinger and Rosenstone, *Who Votes?,* p. 102.
54. For a discussion of mobilization efforts and race, see Jan Leighley, *Strength in Numbers? The Political Mobilization of Racial and Ethnic Minorities* (Princeton University Press, 2001).
55. http://www.cnn.com/ELECTION/2008/results/polls. Accessed 6 November 2008.
56. Ibid.
57. Howard W. Stanley and Richard G. Niemi, *Vital Statistics on Politics, 1999–2000* (CQ Press, 2000), pp. 120–121; and Harold W. Stanley and Richard G. Niemi, *Vital Statistics on Politics, 2005–2006* (CQ Press, 2006), pp. 124–125.
58. http://www.cnn.com/ELECTIONS/2008/results/polls. Accessed 6 November 2008.
59. The Vanishing Voter, "Election Interest Among Young Adults Is Up Sharply from 2000," March 12, 2004, www.vanishingvoter.org/Releases/release031104.shtml.
60. http://www.cnn.com/ELECTIONS/2008/results/polls. Accessed 6 November 2008.
61. David B. Magleby, J. Quin Monson, and Kelly D. Patterson, "Mail Communications in Political Campaigns: The 2004 Campaign Communications Survey," paper presented at the annual meeting of the Midwest Political Science Association, Chicago, IL. April 20–23, 2006.
62. http://www.cnn.com/ELECTIONS/2008/results/polls. Accessed 6 November 2008.
63. U.S. Census Bureau, "Voting and Registration in the Election of November 2000," www.census.gov/prod/2002pubs/p20-542.pdf.
64. Christopher R. Ellis, Joseph Daniel Ura, and Jenna Ashley-Robinson, "The Dynamic Consequences of Nonvoting in American National Elections," *Political Research Quarterly* 59 (June 2006), pp. 232–233.
65. Austin Ranney, "Nonvoting Is Not a Social Disease," *Public Opinion* (October–November 1983), pp. 16–19.
66. Sidney Verba, "Would the Dream of Political Equality Turn Out to Be a Nightmare?" *Perspectives on Politics* 4 (December 2003), pp. 667–672.
67. Steven J. Rosenstone and John Mark Hansen, *Mobilization, Participation, and Democracy in America* (Longman, 2003).
68. Frances Fox Piven and Richard A. Cloward, "Prospects for Voter Registration Reform: A Report on the Experiences of the Human SERVE Campaign," *PS: Political Science and Politics* 18 (Summer 1985), p. 589.
69. Ibid.
70. Wolfinger and Rosenstone, *Who Votes?,* p. 109.
71. E. E. Schattschneider, *The Semisovereign People* (Dryden Press, 1975), p. 96.
72. Stephen Earl Bennett and David Resnick, "The Implications of Nonvoting for Democracy in the United States," *American Journal of Political Science* 84 (August 1990), pp. 771–802.
73. Bruce E. Keith, David B. Magleby, Candice J. Nelson, Elizabeth Orr, Mark C. Westlye, and Raymond E. Wolfinger, *The Myth of the Independent Voter* (University of California Press, 1992), pp. 60–75; and 2004 National Election Study.
74. Pew Research Center for the People and the Press, "January Political Survey," people-press.org/reports/questionnaires/388.pdf.
75. http://www.whitehouse.gov/history/presidents/. Accessed 8 November 2008.
76. David Menefee-Libey, *The Triumph of Campaign-Centered Politics* (Chatham House/Seven Bridges Press, 2000).
77. Tim Graham, "Media-Powered Howard," *National Review Online,* January 30, 2004.
78. www.cnn.com/ELECTION/2004/pages/results/states/US/P/OO/epolls.O.html
79. J. Merrill Shanks and Warren E. Miller, "Policy Direction and Performance Evaluation: Complementary Explanations of the Reagan Elections," *British Journal of Political Science* 20 (1990), pp. 143–235; and Warren E. Miller and J. Merrill Shanks, "Policy Direction and Performance Evaluation: Comparing George Bush's Victory with Those of Ronald Reagan in 1980 and 1984," paper presented at the annual meeting of the American Political Science Association, Atlanta, Ga., August 31–September 2, 1989.
80. Amihai Glazer, "The Strategy of Candidate Ambiguity," *American Political Science Review* 84 (March 1990), pp. 237–241.
81. Robert S. Erikson and David W. Romero, "Candidate Equilibrium and the Behavioral Model of the Vote," *American Political Science Review* 84 (December 1990), p. 1122.
82. Morris P. Fiorina, *Retrospective Voting in American National Elections* (Yale University Press, 1981).
83. Cable News Network. "Exit Polls Election 2000." www.cnn.com/ELECTION/2000/results/index.epolls.html. Last accessed July 12, 2008.
84. Gerald H. Kramer, "Short-Term Fluctuations in U.S. Voting Behavior, 1896–1964," *American Political Science Review 65* (March 1971), pp. 131–143. See also Edward R. Tufte, "Determinants of the Outcomes of Midterm Congressional Elections," *American Political Science Review* (September 1975), pp. 812–826; and Andrew E. Busch, *Horses in Midstream: U.S. Midterm Elections and Their Consequences* (University of Pittsburgh Press, 1999).
85. John R. Hibbing and John R. Alford, "The Educational Impact of Economic Conditions: Who Is Held Responsible?" *American Journal of Political Science* 25 (August 1981), pp. 423–439; and Morris P. Fiorina, "Who Is Held Responsible? Further Evidence on the Hibbing-Alford Thesis," *American Journal of Political Science* (February 1983), pp. 158–164.
86. http://www.cnn.com/ELECTIONS/2008/results/polls. Accessed 6 November 2008.
87. Ryan L. Claasen, David B. Magleby, J. Quin Monson, and Kelly D. Patterson, "At Your Service: Voter Evaluations of Poll Worker Performance," *American Politics Research* 36 (July 2008): 612–634.

Chapter 9

1. U.S. Census Bureau, "Number of Elected Officials Exceeds Half Million—Almost All Are With Local Governments," press release, January 30, 1995.
2. U.S. Senate, www.senate.gov/general/contact_information/senators_cfm.cfm.
3. http://www.kxmb.com/News/293253.asp. Accessed 6 November 2008.
4. *U.S. Term Limits Inc. v. Thornton,* 514 U.S. 799 (1995).
5. For an insightful examination of electoral rules, see Bernard Grofman and Arend Lijphart, eds., *Electoral Laws and Their Political Consequences* (Agathon Press, 1986).
6. National Archives and Records Administration, *Historical Election Results Electoral College Box Scores 1789–1996,* September 25, 2006.
7. Arend Lijphart, "The Political Consequences of Electoral Laws, 1945–85," *American Political Science Review* 84 (June 1990), pp. 481–495. See also David M. Farrell, *Electoral Systems: A Comparative Introduction* (Macmillan, 2001).

8. There was one faithless elector in 2000 from the District of Columbia who abstained rather than cast her vote for Al Gore in order to protest the lack of congressional representation for Washington, D.C. See www.cnn.com/2001/ALLPOLITICS/stories/01/06/electoral.vote/index.html. The electoral college vote in 2004 had one faithless elector: an elector from Minnesota who voted for John Edwards instead of John Kerry.
9. As noted, one of Gore's electors abstained, reducing his vote from 267 to 266; www.cnn.com/2001/ALLPOLITICS/stories/01/06/electoral.vote/index.html.
10. Paul D. Schumaker and Burdett A. Loomis, *Choosing a President: The Electoral College and Beyond* (Seven Bridges Press, 2002), p. 60. See also George Rabinowitz and Stuart Elaine MacDonald, "The Power of the States in U.S. Presidential Elections," *American Political Science Review* 80 (March 1986), pp. 65–87; and Dany M. Adkison and Christopher Elliott, "The Electoral College: A Misunderstood Institution," *PS: Political Science and Politics* 30 (March 1997), pp. 77–80.
11. See, for example, David R. Mayhew, *Congress: The Electoral Connection* (Yale University Press, 1974); Richard F. Fenno, Jr., *Home Style: House Members in Their Districts* (Little, Brown, 1978); and James E. Campbell, "The Return of Incumbents: The Nature of Incumbency Advantage," *Western Political Quarterly* 36 (September 1983), pp. 434–444.
12. Gary King and Andrew Gelman, "Systemic Consequences of Incumbency Advantage in U.S. House Elections," *American Journal of Political Science* 35 (February 1991), pp. 110–137.
13. Alan I. Abramowitz, "Economic Conditions, Presidential Popularity, and Voting Behavior in Midterm Congressional Elections," *Journal of Politics* 47 (February 1985), pp. 31–43. See also Gary C. Jacobson, *The Politics of Congressional Elections*, 5th ed. (Addison-Wesley, 2001), pp. 146–153.
14. See Edward R. Tufte, *Political Control of the Economy* (Princeton University Press, 1978); see also his "Determinants of the Outcomes of Midterm Congressional Elections," *American Political Science Review* 69 (September 1975), pp. 812–826. For a more recent discussion of the same subject, see Jacobson, *Politics of Congressional Elections,* pp. 123–178.
15. Alan I. Abramowitz and Jeffrey A. Segal, "Determinants of the Outcomes of U.S. Senate Elections," *Journal of Politics* 48 (1986), pp. 433–439.
16. This includes the postelection switch of Alabama senator Richard Shelby to the Republican Party.
17. David B. Magleby and Kelly D. Patterson, eds., *The Battle for Congress: Iraq, Scandal, and Campaign Finance in the 2006 Election* (Paradigm, 2008).
18. Campaign Tracker 2006, election.nationaljournal.com/2006/house.
19. Campaign Tracker 2006, election.nationaljournal.com/2006/senate.
20. Rhodes Cook, "Congress and Primaries: Looking for Clues to a Tidal Wave", *The Wall Street Journal* July 24, 2008 at http://blogs.wsj.com/politicalperceptions/2008/07/24/Congressional-Primaries-looking-for-clues-to-tidal-wave/
21. Linda L. Fowler and Robert D. McClure, *Political Ambition: Who Decides to Run for Congress* (Yale University Press, 1989); and Paul S. Herrnson, *Congressional Elections: Campaigning at Home and in Washington,* 5th ed. (CQ Press, 2007), p. 45.
22. Kathleen Hall Jamieson, *Everything You Think You Know About Politics... and Why You're Wrong* (Basic Books, 2000), p. 38.
23. For a discussion of different explanations of the impact of incumbency, see Keith Krehbiel and John R. Wright, "The Incumbency Effect in Congressional Elections: A Test of Two Explanations," *American Journal of Political Science* 27 (February 1983), p. 140.
24. "Election Stats," Center for Responsive Politics, www.opensecrets.org/bigpicture/elec_stats.php?cycle=2006.
25. Harold W. Stanley and Richard G. Niemi, *Vital Statistics on American Politics 2005–2006* (CQ Press, 2006), pp. 53–55.
26. Albert D. Cover, "One Good Term Deserves Another: The Advantages of Incumbency in Congressional Elections," *American Journal of Political Science* 21 (August 1977), pp. 523–542; Morris P. Fiorina, *Congress: Keystone of the Washington Establishment* (Yale University Press, 1978); and David Mayhew, *Congress: The Electoral Connection* (Yale University Press, 1974), pp. 52–53.
27. Mayhew, *Congress,* p. 61; Richard F. Fenno, Jr., *Congressmen in Committees* (Little, Brown, 1973); and Steven S. Smith and Christopher J. Deering, *Committees in Congress,* 3d ed. (CQ Press, 1997).
28. "Financial Activity of Senate and House General Election Campaigns," Federal Election Commission, www.fec.gov/press/sen%5Fhse20pre.htm.
29. Candice J. Nelson, "Spending in the 2000 Elections," in David B. Magleby, ed., *Financing the 2000 Election.* (Brookings Institution Press, 2002), pp. 28–30.
30. Jonathan S. Krasno, *Challengers, Competition, and Reelection: Comparing Senate and House Elections* (Yale University Press, 1994), p. 2.
31. Alan I. Abramowitz, "Explaining Senate Election Outcomes," *American Political Science Review* 82 (June 1988), pp. 385–403.
32. David B. Magleby, "The Importance of Outside Money in the 2002 Congressional Elections," in David B. Magleby, ed., *The Last Hurrah? Soft Money and Issue Advocacy in the 2002 Congressional Elections* (Brookings Institution Press, 2004), p. 18.
33. David B. Magleby, "More Bang for the Buck: Campaign Spending in Small State U.S. Senate Elections," paper presented at the annual meeting of the Western Political Science Association, Salt Lake City, Utah, March 30–April 1, 1989.
34. Scott Shepard, "Politicians Already Looking to 2008 Election," *Austin (Texas) American-Statesman,* February 6, 2005; Associated Press, "Former Bush Aide: 2008 Democratic Nomination Belongs to Hillary," April 30, 2005.
35. Susan Saulny, "Thompson Enters Race from 'Tonight Show' Couch," *New York Times,* September 6, 2007, p. A23.
36. Arthur Hadley, *Invisible Primary* (Prentice Hall, 1976).
37. "State by State Summary 2004 Presidential Primaries, Caucuses, and Conventions," www.thegreenpapers.com/P04/tally.phtml.
38. "State by State Summary: 2008 Presidential Primaries, Caucuses, and Conventions," www.thegreenpapers.com/P08/tally.phtml.
39. The descriptions of these types of primaries are drawn from James W. Davis, *Presidential Primaries,* rev. ed. (Greenwood Press, 1984), chap. 3. See pp. 56–63 for specifics on each state (and Puerto Rico). This material is used with the permission of the publisher.
40. Paul T. David and James W. Caesar, *Proportional Representation in Presidential Nominating Politics* (University Press of Virginia, 1980), pp. 9–11.
41. See Rhodes Cook, *Race for the Presidency: Winning the 2004 Nomination* (CQ Press, 2004), p. 5. See also the Republican National Committee, www.rnc.org.
42. Nelson W. Polsby and Aaron Wildavsky, *Presidential Elections: Strategies and Structures of American Politics,* 11th ed. (Rowman & Littlefield, 2004), p. 110.
43. The Green Papers, *The Green Papers, 2004 Presidential Primaries, Caucuses, and Conventions: New York Republican,* www.thegreenpapers.com/P04/NY-R.phtml.
44. Costas Panagopoulos, "Election Issues 2004 in Depth," *Campaigns & Elections* (May 2004), p. 48.
45. Lesley Clark, "DNC Votes to Strip Fla. of Delegates: Florida's Status as a Key Presidential Prize Is in Doubt, with National Democratic Party Leaders Rejecting a State Plan to Hold an Early Primary," *Miami Herald,* August 26, 2007; see also "Campaign Briefing: On the Trail," *Newsday,* December 2, 2007, p. A3.
46. Jonathan Finer, "No Tea, but Democrats Get the Party Started," *Washington Post,* July 29, 2003, p. A4.
47. Jill Zuckman, "McCain Wins Nomination: Huckabee Steps Aside as Ex-Rival Targets Democrats," *Chicago Tribune,* March 5, 2008.
48. Federal Elections Commission, "2004 Presidential Primary Dates and Candidates Filing Deadlines for Ballot Access," May 26, 2004, www.fec.gov.
49. *California Democratic Party et al., Petitioners v. Bill Jones, Secretary of State of California, et al.,* 530 U.S. 567 (2000).
50. David Redlawsk and Arthur Sanders, "Groups and Grassroots in the Iowa Caucuses," in David B. Magleby, ed., *Outside Money in the 2000. Presidential Primaries and Congressional Elections,* in *PS: Political Science and Politics* (June 2001), p. 270; see also Iowa Caucus Project 2004, www.iowacaucus.org.
51. Perry Bacon, Jr., "Clinton Blames MoveOn for Caucus Losses," *Washington Post,* blog. washingtonpost.com/the-trail/2008/04/19/clinton_blames_moveon_for_cauc.html.
52. "Stunner in N.H.: Clinton Defeats Obama," January 9, 2008, www.msnbc.msn.com/id/22551718/.
53. The viewership of conventions has declined as the amount of time devoted to conventions dropped. In 1988, Democrats averaged 27.1 million viewers and Republicans 24.5 million. By 1996, viewership for the Democrats was 18 million viewers on average, for the Republicans it was 16.6 million. See John Carmody, "The TV Column," *Washington Post,* September 2, 1996, p. D4. Viewership figures improved somewhat in 2000: Democrats averaged 20.6 million viewers and Republicans 19.2 million. See Don Aucoin, "Democrats Hold TV Ratings Edge," *Boston Globe,* August 19, 2000, p. F3. Jim Rutenberg and Brain Stelter, "Conventions, Anything but Dull, Are a TV Hit," *New York Times,* Sept. 6, 2008.
54. Barry Goldwater, speech to the Republican National Convention accepting the Republican nomination for president, July 16, 1964, www.washingtonpost.com/wp-srv/politics/daily/may98/goldwaterspeech.htm.
55. Acceptance speech at the 1980 Convention, July 17, 1980, http://www.nationalcenter.org/ReaganConvention1980.html.
56. Jeff Fishel, *Presidents and Promises* (CQ Press, 1984), pp. 26–28.
57. Sam Reed, "Washington State's February 19, 2008 Presidential Primary," www.secstate.wa.gov/elections/pdf/2008PP/PP%20MFQ%20-Updated%20August%202007%20Final.pdf.
58. Richard Wagner, "Ballot Access News," www.ballot-access.org/2008/020108.html.

59. North Carolina State Board of Elections, "Fact Sheet: Running for President of the United States of America." http://www.sboe.stak.nc.us/GetDocument.aspx?id=308.
60. Commission on Presidential Debates, www.debates.org/pages/news_040617_p.html.
61. http://www.debates.org/pages/news/091708.html. Accessed 7 November 2008.
62. "The Great Ad Wars of 2004," *New York Times*, November 11, 2004, www.polisci.wisc.edu/tvadvertising/Press_Clippings/Press_Clipping_PDFs/110104%20NYTIMES_AD_GRAPHIC.pdf.
63. Mark Memmot and Jim Drinkard, "Election Ad Battle Smashes Record in 2004," *USA Today*, November 26, 2004, p. 6A.
64. University of Wisconsin–Madison and the Brennan Center for Justice at NYU School of Law, "Political Advertising Nearly Tripled in 2000 with Half-a-Million More TV Ads," press release, March 14, 2001.
65. Robert S. Erikson, "Economic Conditions and the Presidential Vote," *American Political Science Review* 83 (June 1989), pp. 567–575. Class-based voting has also become more important. See Robert S. Erikson, Thomas O. Lancaster, and David W. Romers, "Group Components of the Presidential Vote, 1952–1984," *Journal of Politics* 51 (May 1989), pp. 337–346.
66. John C. Fortier and Norman J. Ornstein, "The Absentee Ballot and the Secret Ballot: Challenges for Election Reform," *University of Michigan Journal of Law Reform* 36 (Spring 2003), pp. 483–517.
67. Jerrold G. Rusk, "The Effect of the Australian Ballot Reform on Split Ticket Voting: 1876–1908," *American Political Science Review* 64 (December 1970), pp. 1220–1238.
68. Fortier and Ornstein, "The Absentee Ballot and the Secret Ballot."
69. Lewis L. Gould, *Grand Old Party: A History of the Republicans* (Random House, 2003), p. 236.
70. David B. Magleby and Candice J. Nelson, *The Money Chase: Congressional Campaign Finance Reform* (Brookings Institution Press, 1990), pp. 13–14.
71. Gould, *Grand Old Party*, pp. 389–391; and Jules Witcover, *Party of the People: A History of the Democrats* (Random House, 2003), pp. 589–590.
72. Anthony Corrado, "Money and Politics: A History of Campaign Finance Law," in *Campaign Finance Reform: A Sourcebook* (Brookings Institution Press, 1997), p. 32.
73. Ibid.
74. *Buckley v. Valeo*, 424 U.S. 1 (1976).
75. See Herbert E. Alexander and Monica Bauer, *Financing the 1988 Election* (Westview Press, 1991); Frank J. Sorauf, *Inside Campaign Finance: Myths and Realities* (Yale University Press, 1992); and Herbert E. Alexander, *Financing Politics: Money, Elections, and Political Reform* (CQ Press, 1992).
76. http://www.opensecrets.org/pres08/summary.php?id=N00000019. Accessed 6 November 2008.
77. http://www.opensecrets.org/pres08/summary.php?cycle=2008&cid=N00009638. Accessed 6 November 2008.
78. Anthony Corrado, Thomas E. Mann, Daniel R. Ortiz, and Trevor Potter, eds., *The New Campaign Finance Sourcebook* (Brookings Institution Press, 2005).
79. *Davis v. FEC.* 128 S.Ct. 2759. (2008).
80. Elizabeth Drew, *The Corruption of American Politics: What Went Wrong and Why* (Carol, 1999), pp. 7–8.
81. See Senate Committee on Governmental Affairs, "1997 Special Investigation in Connection with the 1996 Federal Election Campaigns," www.senate.gov/gov_affairs/sireport.htm.
82. David B. Magleby, *Dictum Without Data: The Myth of Issue Advocacy and Party Building* (Center for the Study of Elections and Democracy, Brigham Young University, 2001), pp. 1, 12; David B. Magleby, ed., *Outside Money: Soft Money and Issue Advocacy in the 1998 Congressional Elections* (Rowman & Littlefield, 2000), p. 17; David B. Magleby and J. Quin Monson, eds., *The Last Hurrah? Soft Money and Issue Advocacy in the 2002 Congressional Elections* (Brookings Institution Press, 2004), p. 1; and David B. Magleby, ed., *The Other Campaign: Soft Money and Issue Advocacy in the 2000 Congressional Elections* (Rowman & Littlefield, 2003), p. 1.
83. *McConnell v. Federal Election Commission*, 540 U.S. 93 (2003).
84. In 2004, state and local parties raised $3,358,966 in limited contributions for voter registration and get-out-the-vote; in 2006 the state and local parties raised $6,514,270 for this purpose. Paul Clark, Federal Election Commission, personal communication, May 22, 2008.
85. Corrado, Mann, Ortiz, and Potter, *The New Campaign Finance Sourcebook*, p. 79.
86. David B. Magleby, ed. *The Last Hurrah* (Brookings Institution Press, 2004), pp. 44–45.
87. Ibid., p. 46.
88. *McConnell v. Federal Election Commission.*
89. *Federal Election Commission v. Wisconsin Right to Life, Inc.*, 551 U.S. _______(2007).
90. *Buckley v. Valeo*, footnote 52.
91. See Joseph A. Pika, "Campaign Spending and Activity in the 2000 Delaware U.S. Senate Race," in David B. Magleby, ed., *Election Advocacy: Soft Money and Issue Advocacy in the 2000 Congressional Elections* (Center for the Study of Elections and Democracy, Brigham Young University, 2001), pp. 51–61.
92. John C. Green and Nathan S. Bigelow, "The 2000 Presidential Nominations: The Costs of Innovation," in David B. Magleby, ed., *Financing the 2000 Election* (Brookings Institution Press, 2002), p. 68.
93. Magleby, *Dictum Without Data*, p. 12.
94. Kate Snow, "Obama Could Get 'Swift Boated,'" ABC News, April 19, 2008 abcnews.go.com/Politics/story?id=4688386.
95. David B. Magleby, "Change and Continuity in the Financing of Federal Elections," in David B. Magleby, Anthony J. Corrado, and Kelly D. Patterson, eds., *Financing the 2004 Elections* (Brookings Institution Press, 2006), p. 15.
96. Bipartisan Campaign Reform Act of 2002, 107th Cong., 1st sess., H.R. 2356.
97. Corrado, Mann, Ortiz, and Potter, *The New Campaign Finance Sourcebook*, pp. 74–76.
98. David B. Magleby, ed. *Dancing Without Partners Monograph*, csed.byu.edu/Publications/DancingwithoutPartners.pdf, p. 53.
99. Kate Zernike, "Kerry Pressing Swift Boat Case Long After Loss," *New York Times*, May 28, 2006, p. A1.
100. *Colorado Republican Federal Campaign Committee v. Federal Election Commission*, 518 U.S. 604 (1996).
101. BCRA does allow candidates to pay themselves out of their campaign funds, something that helps less-affluent candidates run. But given the high cost of campaigns, such a strategy is often not going to be helpful to winning the election.
102. Federal Election Commission, "2000–2001 Financial Activity of Senate and House General Election Campaigns," www.fec.gov; and Federal Election Commission, "1999–2000 Financial Activity of Senate and House General Election Campaigns," www.fec.gov.
103. Jose Antonia Vargas, "Campaign.USA: With the Internet Comes a New Political 'Clickocracy,'" *Washington Post*, April 1, 2008, p. C01.
104. U.S. Census Bureau, *Statistical Abstract of the United States: 2006* (U.S. Government Printing Office, 2006), p. 267.
105. Federal Election Commission, herndon1.sdrdc.com/fecimg/srssea.html. See also FEC, "Congressional Candidates Spend $1.16 Billion During 2003–2004," press release, June 9, 2005, www.fec.gov/press/press2005/20050609candidate/20050609candidate.html.
106. Rick Hampson, "Former Banker Was Big Spender," *USA Today*, November 9, 2000, p. A9.
107. See Todd Donovan and Shawn Bowler, *Reforming the Republic: Democratic Institutions for a New America* (Prentice Hall, 2004).
108. Curtis B. Gans, director, Committee for the Study of the American Electorate, personal communication, September 22, 2004.
109. The President's Commission for a National Agenda for the Eighties, in *A National Agenda for the Eighties* (U.S. Government Printing Office, 1980), p. 97, proposed holding four presidential primaries, scheduled about one month apart.

Chapter 10

1. Brian Stelter, "Finding Political News Online, Young Viewers Pass It Along," *New York Times*, March 27, 2008, pp. A 1, 23.
2. Ibid.
3. http://www.new.facebook.com/home.php?ref=home#barackobama?ref=s (accessed September 10, 2008).
4. Brian Stelter, "Finding Political News Online, Young Viewers Pass It Along," *New York Times* March 27, 2008, pp. A1, 23.
5. Frank Davies, "The Race Online: Obama, Rivals Bring Internet Campaigning to New Level," *San Jose Mercury News*, February 24, 2008.
6. Jose Antonio Vargas, "Campaign.USA: With the Internet Comes a New Political 'Clickocracy,'" *Washington Post*, April 1, 2008, p. C01.
7. Matthew Mosk, "Obama Rewriting Rules for Raising Campaign Money Online," *Washington Post*, March 28, 2008, p. A06.
8. Vargas, "Campaign.USA."
9. William Rivers, *The Other Government* (Universe Books, 1982); Douglas Cater, *The Fourth Branch of Government* (Houghton Mifflin, 1959); Dom Bonafede, "The Washington Press: An Interpreter or a Participant in Policy Making?" *National Journal*, April 24, 1982, pp. 716–721; Michael Ledeen, "Learning to Say 'No' to the Press," *Public Interest* 73 (Fall 1983), p. 113.
10. Leslie G. Moeller, "The Big Four: Mass Media Actualities and Expectations," in Richard W. Budd and Brent D. Ruben, eds., *Beyond Media: New Approaches to Mass Communication* (Transaction Books, 1988), p. 15.
11. Pew Research Center for the People and the Press, "Far More Voters Believe Election Outcome Matters," people-press.org/reports/print.php3?PageID=802. Popular news aggregators include Bloglines, FeedDemon, and Google Reader.
12. See Doris A. Graber, "Say It with Pictures: The Impact of Audiovisual News on Public Opinion Formation," paper presented at the annual meeting of the Midwest Political Science Association, Chicago, Ill., April 1987; Benjamin I. Page, Robert Y. Shapiro, and Glenn R. Dempsey, "What Moves Public Opinion?" *American Political Science Review* 76 (March 1987), pp. 23–43.

13. U.S. Bureau of the Census, *Statistical Abstract of the United States, 2008* (U.S. Government Printing Office, 2008), pp. 703–704, 720.
14. Project for Excellence in Journalism, "The State of the News Media 2008," www.stateofthenewsmedia.org/2008/narrative_networktv_audience.php.
15. Project for Excellence in Journalism, "The State of the News Media 2008," www.stateofthenewsmedia.org/2008/narrative_cabletv_audience.php.
16. Journalism.org, "Local TV," www.stateofthenewsmedia.org/narrative_localty_contentanalysis.asp?cat=2&media=6. See also Marc Fisher, "TV Stations Offer a Clear Picture of Indifference," *Washington Post,* September 26, 2000, p. B1.
17. http://www.huffingtonpost.com/2008/08/29/democratic-national-conve_n_122440.html.
18. Thomas E. Patterson and Robert D. McClure, *The Unseeing Eye: The Myth of Television Power in National Elections* (Putnam 1976).
19. Alliance for Better Campaigns, *Political Standard* 4 (March 2001), p. 6.
20. David B. Magleby,"Direct Legislation in the American States," in David Butler and Austin Ranney, eds., *Referendums Around the World:The Growing Use of Direct Democracy* (AEI Press, 1994) pp.218-257
21. *Statistical Abstract of the United States, 2008,* p. 704.
22. Ibid.
23. Mediamark Research Inc., "Mediamark Research Inc. Releases MediaDay Study," press release, June 25, 2007, www.mediamark.com/PDF/Mediamark%20Research%20Inc%20Releases%20MediaDay%20Study.pdf.
24. Seth Sutel, "Long Left Behind, Radio Wants a Bigger Piece of $3B Political Advertising Free-for-All," Associated Press, January 18, 2008.
25. National Public Radio, www.npr.org/about.
26. Tim Feran, "Airing the Issues; Chairman of NPR Board Considers All Things Facing His Organization," *Columbus (Ohio) Dispatch,* January 26, 2006, p. B1.
27. *Statistical Abstract of the United States, 2008,* p. 705.
28. Newspaper Association of America, "Readership," www.naa.org/TrendsandNumbers/Readership.aspx.
29. Seth Sutel, "Circulation Off at Most Top Newspapers but *USA Today, WSJ* Up," Associated Press, April 28, 2008.
30. Nat Ives, "Publishers: Why Count Only People Who Pay?" *Advertising Age,* November 12, 2007, p. 8.
31. Marie Griffin, "WSJ.com Free? Should We?" *Media Business,* January 11, 2008, p. 19.
32. National Public Radio, "Extra! Extra! We Still Want News," *On the Media,* March 28, 2008, www.onthemedia.org/transcripts/2008/03/28/05; Noam Cohen, "Craig (of the List) Looks Beyond the Web," *New York Times,* May 12, 2008, p. C1.
33. Arthur L. Norberg and Judy E. O'Neill, *Transforming Computer Technology: Information Processing for the Pentagon, 1962–1986* (Johns Hopkins University Press, 1996).
34. Giles Turnbull, "In Search of the New Google" (London) *Daily Telegraph,* March 15, 2008, p. 19.
35. VeriSign, *The Domain Name Industry Brief* 5, no. 1 (March 2008), www.verisign.com/static/043379.pdf.
36. John B. Horrigan, "Home Broadband Adoption 2007," Pew Internet & American Life Project, June 2007, www.pewinternet.org/pdfs/PIP_Broadband%202007.pdf.
37. Pew Internet & American Life Project, *Teens and Technology,* July 27, 2005, www.pewinternet.org/pdfs/PIP_Teens_Tech_July2005web.pdf.
38. Amanda Lenhart, Mary Madden, Alexandra Rankin Macgill, and Aaron Smith, "Teens and Social Media," Pew Internet & American Life Project, December 19, 2007, www.pewinternet.org/pdfs/PIP_Teens_Social_Media_Final.pdf.
39. Cass Sunstein, *Republic.com* (Princeton University Press, 2001), pp. 73–75.
40. Pew Research Center for the People and the Press, "Watching, Reading, and Listening to the News," in *Online Papers Modestly Boost Newspaper Readership,* people-press.org/reports/display.php3?PageID=1064.
41. Pew Research Center for the People and Press, Survey Reports, "Bottom-Line Pressures Now Hurting Coverage, Say Journalists," May 23, 2004, people-press.org/reports/display.php3?PageID=826.
42. See Robert A. Rutland, *Newsmongers: Journalism in the Life of the Nation, 1690–1972* (Dial Press, 1973).
43. David Paul Nord, *Communities of Journalism* (University of Illinois Press, 2001), pp. 80–89.
44. Quoted in Frank Luther Mott, *American Journalism,* 3d ed. (Macmillan, 1962), p. 412.
45. During the 1930s, more than 1,000 speeches were made by members of Congress on one network alone. See Edward W. Chester, *Radio, Television, and American Politics* (Sheed & Ward, 1969), p. 62.
46. Frances Perkins, quoted in James MacGregor Burns, *Roosevelt: The Lion and the Fox* (Harcourt, 1956), p. 205.
47. CBS News, "Abuse of Iraqi POWs by GIs Probed: *60 Minutes II* Has Exclusive Report on Alleged Mistreatment," April 28, 2004, www.cbsnews.com/stories/2004/04/27/60II/main614063.shtml.
48. Dana Priest, "CIA Holds Terror Suspects in Secret Prisons," *Washington Post,* November 2, 2005, p. A01.
49. Fred Emery, *Watergate: The Corruption of American Politics and the Fall of Richard Nixon* (Touchstone, 1995).
50. Bob Woodward and Carl Bernstein, *All the President's Men* (Simon & Schuster, 1994).
51. Mark Felt and John D. O'Connor, *A G-Man's Life: The FBI, Being 'Deep Throat,' and the Struggle for Honor in Washington* (Public Affairs Press, 2006).
52. Martin Peers, "Murdoch Wins His Bid for Dow Jones," *Wall Street Journal,* August 1, 2007, p. A1.
53. News Corporation, www.newscorp.com/index.html.
54. Gannett Company, "Company Profile," www.gannett.com/about/company_profile.htm.
55. Tribune Company, "About Tribune," www.tribune.com/about/index.html.
56. Federal Communications Commission, "FCC Issues 12th Annual Report to Congress on Video Competition," press release, February 10, 2006, hraunfoss.fcc.gov/edocs_public/attachmatch/DOC-263763A1.pdf.
57. Seth Schiesel, "FCC Rules on Ownership Under Review," *New York Times,* April 3, 2002, p. C1.
58. Paul Davidson, "Spending Bill Settles Two Key Issues," *USA Today,* January 23, 2004, p. B3.
59. Stephen Labaton, "Court Orders FCC to Rethink New Rules on Growth of Media," *New York Times,* June 25, 2004, p. 1.
60. Annys Shin, "Limits on Media Ownership Stand; Supreme Court Declines to Hear Appeal," *Washington Post,* June 14, 2005, p. D1
61. Amy Schatz, "Settling Past Broke Radio Impasse," *Wall Street Journal,* July 28, 2008.
62. Donna Britt, "Janet's 'Reveal' Lays Bare an Insidious Trend," *Washington Post,* February 4, 2004, p. B1. www.pewinternet.org/reports/chart/asp?.
63. Amy Schatz and Sam Schechner, "CBS Wins Verdict on FCC Indecency Fine," *Wall Street Journal,* July 22, 2008, p. B1.
64. Center for Public Leadership, "Poll Reflects Continued Mistrust of Media Election Coverage," full press release available at: http://content.ksg.harvard.edu/leadership/images/CPLpdf/nli2008%20election%20coverage.pdf.
65. See, for example, Jack Dennis, "Preadult Learning of Political Independence: Media and Family Communications Effects," *Communication Research* 13 (July 1987), pp. 401–433; Olive Stevens, *Children Talking Politics* (Robertson, 1982).
66. Elihu Katz and Paul Lazarsfeld, *Personal Influence: The Part Played by People in the Flow of Mass Communications* (Free Press, 1955).
67. See Angus Campbell, Philip E. Converse, Warren E. Miller, and Donald E. Stokes, *The American Voter* (Wiley, 1960).
68. Pew Research Center for the People and Press, Survey Reports, "News Audiences Increasingly Politicized," June 8, 2004, people-press.org/reports/display.php3?ReportID=215.
69. Paul Lazarsfeld, Bernard Berelson, and Hazel Gaudet, *The People's Choice: How the Voter Makes Up His Mind in a Presidential Campaign,* 3d ed. (Columbia University Press, 1968); Bernard Berelson, Paul Lazarsfeld, and William McPhee, *Voting: A Study of Opinion Formation in a Presidential Campaign* (University of Chicago Press, 1954).
70. Pew Research Center for the People and the Press, "Scandal Reporting Faulted for Bias and Inaccuracy: Popular Policies and Unpopular Press Lift Clinton Ratings," press release, February 6, 1998, p. 6.
71. Gallup Organization, "Americans Agree with House Contention That Clinton Committed Perjury and Obstructed Justice," www.galluppoll.com/content/?ci=4099&pg=1.
72. Stuart Oskamp, ed., *Television as a Social Issue* (Sage, 1988); James W. Carey, ed., *Media, Myths, and Narratives: Television and the Press* (Sage, 1988).
73. Times Mirror Center for the People and the Press, "Times Mirror News Interest Index," press releases, January 16 and February 28, 1992.
74. Rush Limbaugh, *See, I Told You So* (Pocket Books, 1993), p. 326.
75. Rick Lyman, "Multimedia Deal: The History; 2 Commanding Publishers, 2 Powerful Empires," *New York Times,* March 14, 2000, p. C16.
76. David Broder, "Beware of the 'Insider' Syndrome: Why Newsmakers and News Reporters Shouldn't Get Too Cozy," *Washington Post,* December 4, 1988, p. A21; see also David Broder, "Thin-Skinned Journalists," *Washington Post,* January 11, 1989, p. A21.
77. Daniel P. Moynihan, "The Presidency and the Press," *Commentary* 51 (March 1971), p. 43.
78. Eric Alterman, *What Liberal Media? The Truth About Bias and the News* (Basic Books, 2003).
79. Shanto Iyengar, Mark D. Peters, and Donald R. Kinder, "Experimental Demonstrations of the 'Not-So-Minimal' Consequences of Television News Programs," *American Political Science Review* 76 (December 1982), pp. 848–858.
80. Shanto Iyengar and Donald R. Kinder, *News That Matters: Television and American Opinion* (University of Chicago Press, 1987). McCombs and Shaw, "The Agenda-Setting Function of the Mass Media," pp. 176–187; Maxwell E. McCombs and Sheldon Gilbert, "News Influence on Our Pictures of the World," in Jennings Bryant and Dolf Gillman, eds., *Perspectives on Media Effects* (Erlbaum, 1986), pp. 1–15; and Iyengar and Kinder, *News That Matters.*
81. Quoted in Michael J. Robinson and Margaret A. Sheehan, *Over the Wire and on TV: CBS and UPI in Campaign '80* (Russell Sage Foundation, 1983), p. xiii.
82. ABC News, abcnews.go.com/sections/us/DailyNews/WTC_MAIN010914.html.

83. David B. Magleby, *Direct Legislation: Voting on Ballot Propositions in the United States* (Johns Hopkins University Press, 1984).
84. Larry J. Sabato, "Gerald Ford's 'Free Poland' Gaffe—1976," *Washington Post*, www.washingtonpost.com/wp-srv/politics/special/clinton/frenzy/ford. htm.
85. Larry J. Sabato, "George Romney's 'Brainwashing'-1967," *Washington Post*, at www.washingtonpost.com/wp-srv/politics/special/clinton/frenzy/romney.htm.
86. CBS News, "CBS News Video Contradicts Clinton's Story: CBS' Sharyl Attkisson Was on Bosnia Trip—And Got a Warm, Sniper-Free Welcome," www.cbsnews.com/stories/2008/03/24/eveningnews/main3964921.shtml.
87. Perry Bacon Jr. and Shailagh Murray, "Opponents Paint Obama as an Elitist," *Washington Post*, April 12, 2008, p. A04.
88. Anne E. Kornblut and Jon Cohen, "Poll Shows Erosion of Trust in Clinton," *Washington Post*, April 16, 2008, p. A06.
89. http://www.msnbc.com/id/25384371. Accessed 7 November 2008.
90. Opensecrets.org, "Swift Boat Veterans for Truth, 2004 Election Cycle," www.opensecrets.org/527s/527events.asp?orgid=61.
91. David B. Magleby, J. Quin Monson, and Kelly D. Patterson, *Dancing Without Partners: How Parties, Candidates, and Interest Groups Interact in the 2004 Presidential Campaign* (Rowman & Littlefield, 2007), pp. 24–25.
92. Paul T. David, Ralph M. Goldman, and Richard C. Bain, *The Politics of the National Party Conventions* (Brookings Institution Press, 1960), pp. 300–301.
93. www.huffington post. com/2008/09/05/-republicannational-conve_n_124305.html. Accessed 9.18.08.
94. Richard Davis, *The Press and American Politics: The New Mediator*, 2d ed. (Prentice Hall, 1996), p. 279.
95. Frank I. Luntz, *Candidates, Consultants, and Campaigns* (Blackwell, 1988), pp. 199–217.
96. Larry J. Sabato, *The Rise of Political Consultants* (Basic Books, 1981).
97. See James A. Thurber and Candice J. Nelson, eds., *Campaign Warriors: Political Consultants in Elections* (Brookings Institution Press, 2000).
98. Quoted in Sabato, *Rise of Political Consultants*, p. 144.
99. Alliance for Better Campaigns, "Lawmakers Unveil Free Air Time Proposal," press release, June 19, 2002, www.campaignlegalcenter.org/press-145.html.
100. John R. Zaller, *The Nature and Origins of Mass Opinion* (Cambridge University Press, 1992).
101. David B. Magleby and Kelly D. Patterson, *The Battle for Congress: Iraq, Scandal, and Campaign Finance in the 2006 Election* (Paradigm, 2008), p. 44.
102. Thomas E. Patterson, *The Mass Media Election: How Americans Choose Their President* (Praeger, 1980), chap. 12.
103. John H. Aldrich, *Before the Convention* (University of Chicago Press, 1980), p. 65. See also Patterson, *Mass Media Election*.
104. John Foley et al., *Nominating a President: The Process and the Press* (Praeger, 1980), p. 39. For the press's treatment of incumbents, see James Glen Stovall, "Incumbency and News Coverage of the 1980 Presidential Election Campaign," *Western Political Quarterly* 37 (December 1984), p. 621.
105. Stephen Ansolabehere and Shanto Iyengar, *Going Negative: How Political Advertisements Shrink and Polarize the Electorate* (Free Press, 1995).
106. John G. Geer, *In Defense of Negativity: Attack Ads in Presidential Campaigns* (University of Chicago Press, 2006); Richard R. Lau, Lee Sigelman, and Ivy Brown Rovner, "The Effects of Negative Political Campaigns: A Meta-Analytic Reassessment," *Journal of Politics* 69 (November 2007), pp. 1176–1209.
107. William Glaberson, "A New Press Role: Solving Problems," *New York Times*, October 3, 1994, p. D6.
108. Patterson, *Mass Media Election*, pp. 115–117.
109. Raymond Wolfinger and Peter Linguiti, "Tuning In and Tuning Out," *Public Opinion* 4 (February–March 1981), pp. 56–60.
110. Michael Traugott, Benjamin Highton, and Henry E. Brady, *A Review of Recent Controversies Concerning the 2004 Presidential Election Exit Polls*, March 10, 2005, elections.ssrc.org/research/ExitPollReport031005.pdf. See also Michael Traugott, "The Accuracy of the National Preelection Polls in the 2004 Presidential Election," *Public Opinion Quarterly* 69 (special issue, 2005), pp. 642–654.
111. Lewis Wolfson, *The Untapped Power of the Press* (Praeger, 1985), p. 79.
112. Lloyd Cutler, "Foreign Policy on Deadline," *Foreign Policy* 56 (Fall 1984), p. 114.
113. Michael B. Grossman and Martha Joynt Kumar, *Portraying the President* (Johns Hopkins University Press, 1981), pp. 255–263; Fredric T. Smoller, *The Six o'Clock Presidency: A Theory of Presidential Press Relations in the Age of Television* (Praeger, 1990), pp. 31–49.
114. Stephen Hess, *Live from Capitol Hill!* (Brookings Institution Press, 1991), pp. 62–76; Timothy E. Cook, *Making Laws and Making News* (Brookings Institution Press, 1989), pp. 81–86.
115. Susan Heilmann Miller, "News Coverage of Congress: The Search for the Ultimate Spokesperson," *Journalism Quarterly* 54 (Autumn 1977), pp. 459–465.
116. See Hess, *Live from Capitol Hill*, pp. 102–110.
117. Richard Davis, "Whither the Congress and the Supreme Court? The Television News Portrayal of American National Government," *Television Quarterly* 22 (1987), pp. 55–63.
118. For a discussion of the Supreme Court and public opinion, see Thomas R. Marshall, *Public Opinion and the Supreme Court* (Unwin Hyman, 1989); Gregory Caldiera, "Neither the Purse nor the Sword: Dynamics of Public Confidence in the Supreme Court," *American Political Science Review* 80 (December 1986), pp. 1209–1228.
119. For a discussion of the relationship between the Supreme Court and the press, see Richard Davis, "Lifting the Shroud: News Media Portrayal of the U.S. Supreme Court," *Communications and the Law* 9 (October 1987), pp. 43–58; Elliot E. Slotnick, "Media Coverage of Supreme Court Decision Making: Problems and Prospects," *Judicature* (October–November 1991), pp. 128–142.
120. Todd S. Purdam, "TV Political News in California Is Shrinking, Study Confirms," *New York Times*, January, 13, 1999, p. A11.
121. Times Mirror Center, "Campaign '92," *Times Mirror*, January 16, 1992.
122. Quoted in Herbert Schmertz, "The Making of the Presidency," *Presidential Studies Quarterly* 16 (Winter 1986), p. 25.

Chapter 11

1. Office of Management and Budget, *Budget of the U.S. Government, Fiscal Year 2009* (U.S. Government Printing Office, February 2008), p. 57.
2. Diana Jean Schemo, "Congress Approves Student Loan Overhaul," *New York Times*, September 7, 2007, p. A1.
3. Charles Warren, *The Making of the Constitution* (Little, Brown, 1928), p. 195.
4. *Bush v. Vera*, 517 U.S. 952 (1996).
5. See David M. Magleby, *Last Hurrah? Soft Money and Issue Advocacy in the 2002 Elections* (Brookings Institution Press, 2004).
6. For a discussion of how members have evaded federal legislation against bulk e-mails, or spam, see Jennifer S. Lee, "We Hate Spam, Congress Says (Except When It's Sent by Us)," *New York Times*, December 18, 2003, p. A1.
7. See Citizens Against Government Waste at www.cagw.org for the latest information on earmarks.
8. R. P. Fairfield, *The Federalist Papers* (Doubleday, 1961), p. 160.
9. See Roger H. Davidson and Walter J. Oleszek, *Congress and Its Members*, 10th ed. (CQ Press, 2005).
10. Richard F. Fenno Jr., *The United States Senate: A Bicameral Perspective* (American Enterprise Institute, 1982), p. 1.
11. For discussion of the modern Speakership, see Barbara Sinclair, "House Majority Party Leadership in an Era of Legislative Constraint," in Roger H. Davidson, ed., *The Postreform Congress* (St. Martin's Press, 1992), pp. 91–111; and Ronald M. Peters Jr., ed., *The Speaker: Leadership in the U.S. House of Representatives* (CQ Press, 1995).
12. Richard E. Cohen and David Baumann, "Speaking Up for Hastert," *National Journal*, November 13, 1999, pp. 3298–3303.
13. For an insightful set of essays on Senate leadership, see Richard A. Baker and Roger H. Davidson, eds., *First Among Equals: Outstanding Senate Leaders of the Twentieth Century* (CQ Press, 1991).
14. Sarah A. Binder and Steven S. Smith, *Politics or Principles? Filibustering in the United States Senate* (Brookings Institution Press, 1997).
15. Helen Dewar, "Senate Filibuster Ends with Talk of Next Stage in Fight," *Washington Post*, November 15, 2003, p. A9.
16. Woodrow Wilson, *Congressional Government* (Houghton Mifflin, 1885; reprint, Johns Hopkins University Press, 1981), p. 69.
17. The figures come from Citizens Against Government Waste, www.cagw.org/site/News2?page=NewsArticle&id=9528.
18. Joel D. Aberbach, *Keeping a Watchful Eye: The Politics of Congressional Oversight* (Brookings, 1991).
19. "Résumé of Congressional Activity, 105th Congress," *Congressional Record*, Daily Digest, January 19, 1999, p. D29.
20. Ronald Reagan, quoted in Lawrence Longley and Walter Oleszek, *Bicameral Politics* (Yale University Press, 1989), p. 1.
21. For an example of intense bargaining on a major defense appropriation bill, see Pat Towell, "Camouflage-Green Defense Bill Poised for President's Signature," *Congressional Quarterly Weekly*, July 22, 2000, pp. 1819–1822.
22. Davidson and Oleszek, *Congress and Its Members*, p. 307.
23. For a history of the early Congresses, see James Sterling Young, *The Washington Community, 1800–1828* (Columbia University Press, 1966).
24. Davidson and Oleszek, *Congress and Its Members*, p. 30.
25. Nelson Polsby, "The Institutionalization of the U.S. House of Representatives," *American Political Science Association* (March 1968), pp. 144–168.
26. Norman J. Ornstein, Thomas Mann, and Michael Malbin, *Vital Statistics on Congress, 1999–2000* (AEI Press, 2000), p. 170.

27. Pew Research Center for the People and the Press, *Washington Leaders Wary of Public Opinion* (Author, 1998), p. 30.
28. Herbert Asher, "The Learning of Legislative Norms," *American Political Science Review* 67 (June 1973), pp. 499–513.
29. See the case studies in Richard F. Fenno Jr., *Senators on the Campaign Trail: The Politics of Representation* (University of Oklahoma Press, 1996), p. 331; see also Benjamin Bishin, "Constituency Influence in Congress: Does Subconstituency Matter?" *Legislative Studies Quarterly* (August 2000), pp. 389–415.
30. Statistics from congressional Web sites (www.senate.gov; www.house.gov). See also the Library of Congress Web site (thomas.loc.gov).
31. Bill Bradley, *Time Present, Time Past: A Memoir* (Knopf, 1996), chap. 4.
32. From a 1999 CBS survey reported in "Poll Readings," *National Journal,* October 9, 1999, p. 2917.
33. Richard E. Cohen, "Vote Ratings," *National Journal,* February 21, 2005, p. 426.
34. Quoted at www.house.gov/israel/biography/index.htm.
35. Joseph I. Lieberman, *In Praise of Public Life* (Simon & Schuste; 2000), p. 109.
36. Constance Ewing Cook, *Lobbying for Higher Education* (Vanderbilt University Press, 1998). See also Ken Kolman, *Outside Lobbying* (Princeton University Press, 1998).
37. Catherine Richert, "Party Unity: United We Stand Opposed," *Congressional Quarterly Weekly,* January 14, 2008, p. 143.
38. Martin Kady II, "Party Unity: Learning to Stick Together," *Congressional Quarterly Weekly,* January 9, 2006, p. 92.
40. Karen Tumulty, "The Man Who Bought Washington," *Time,* January 6, 2006.
41. Clifford Krauss, "How Personal Tragedy Can Shape Public Policy," *New York Times,* May 16, 1993, p. A16.
42. Sarah A. Binder, Thomas E. Mann, and Molly Reynolds, *One Year Later: Is Congress Still the Broken Branch?* (Brookings Institution Press, 2008).

Chapter 12

1. James Risen and Eric Lichtblau, "Bush Lets U.S. Spy on Callers Without Courts," *New York Times,* December 16, 2005, p. A1.
2. George W. Bush, "President's Radio Address," December 17, 2005.
3. Sheryl Gay Solberg and David E. Sanger, "Facing Pressure, White House Seeks Approval for Spying," *New York Times,* February 20, 2006, p. A1.
4. Alexander Hamilton, James Madison, and John Jay, *The Federalist Papers* (Bantam Classic, 2003), pp. 426–427.
5. See Paul C. Light, *Vice Presidential Power* (Johns Hopkins University Press, 1984).
6. Richard Pious, *The American Presidency* (Basic Books, 1978).
7. This history of presidential powers draws heavily on Sidney M. Milkis and Michael Nelson, *The American Presidency: Origins and Development, 1976–2000,* 4th ed. (CQ Press, 2003).
8. See Al Kamen, "For Bush, the Fun Begins at Recess," *Washington Post,* June 29, 2007, p. A19; for a scholarly argument about this power, see the paper by Michael B. Rappaport, "The Original Meaning of the Recess Appointments Clause," October 6, 2004, at http://ssrn.com/abstract=601563.
9. Letter from Abraham Lincoln to his Illinois law partner W. H. Herndon, February 15, 1848, in *Abraham Lincoln, Speeches and Writings, 1832–1858* (Library of America, 1989), p. 175.
10. Miles A. Pomper, "Bush Hopes to Avoid Battle with Congress over Iraq," *Weekly,* August 31, 2002, p. 2251.
11. Leonard C. Meeker, "The Legality of U.S. Participation in the Defense of Vietnam," *Department of State Bulletin,* March 28, 1966, pp. 448–455.
12. Louis Fisher, *Congressional Abdication on War and Spending* (Texas A&M University Press, 2000), p. 184.
13. Raoul Berger, *Executive Privilege: A Constitutional Myth* (Harvard University Press, 1974).
14. Mark J. Rozell, "The Law: Executive Privilege—Definition and Standards of Application," *Presidential Studies Quarterly* (December 1999), p. 924.
15. *United States v. Nixon,* 418 U.S. 683 (1974).
16. The president's executive orders can be reviewed on the White House Web site at www.whitehouse.gov.
17. *Clinton et al. v. New York City et al.,* 524 U.S. 417 (1998).
18. See William G. Howell, "Unilateral Powers: A Brief Overview," *Presidential Studies Quarterly* 35 (September 2005), pp. 417–439, for a review of these and other tools of presidential influence.
19. See Phillip J. Cooper, "George W. Bush, Edgar Allan Poe, and the Use and Abuse of Presidential Signing Statements," *Presidential Studies Quarterly* 35 (September 2005), pp. 515–532.
20. See Bradley H. Patterson Jr., *The White House Staff: Inside the West Wing and Beyond* (Brookings Institution Press, 2000).
21. See Irving Janis, *Groupthink* (Houghton Mifflin, 1982).
22. For the views on presidents and the White House staff of a highly placed White House aide in several administrations, see David Gergen, *Eyewitness to Power: The Essence of Leadership, Nixon to Clinton* (Touchstone, 2000).
23. See Shelley Lynne Tomkins, *Inside OMB: Politics and Process in the President's Budget Office* (Sharpe, 1998).
24. The figure comes from the Harris Poll, October 5–8, 2007, available at www.pollingreport.com.
25. See Paul C. Light, *The President's Agenda: Domestic Policy Choice from Kennedy Through Clinton* (Johns Hopkins University Press, 1999).
26. *United States v. Curtiss-Wright Export Corp.,* 299 U.S. 304 (1936).
27. For commentary by analysts who believe the *Curtiss-Wright* ruling was too sweeping, see Harold H. Koh, *The National Security Constitution* (Yale University Press, 1990); Louis Fisher, *Presidential War Power* (University Press of Kansas, 1995); and David Gray Adler and Larry N. George, eds., *The Constitution and the Conduct of American Foreign Policy: Essays on Law and History* (University Press of Kansas, 1996).
28. Richard E. Neustadt, *Presidential Power and the Modern Presidents* (Free Press, 1991).
29. The phrase "power to persuade" is from Richard Neustadt, *Presidential Power and the Modern Presidents: The Politics of Leadership from Roosevelt to Reagan* (Free Press, 1990), p. 7.
30. Clea Benson, "Presidential Support: The Power of No," *CQ Weekly,* January 14, 2008, p. 132.

Chapter 13

1. U.S. House of Representatives, Committee on Government Reform, *A Failure of Initiative: Final Report of the Select Bipartisan Committee to Investigate the Preparation for and Response to Hurricane Katrina* (U.S. Government Printing Office, 2006).
2. Alexander Hamilton, James Madison, and John Jay, *The Federalist Papers* (Bantam Classic, 2003), p. 427.
3. See Stanley Elkins and Eric McKitrick, *The Age of Federalism* (Oxford University Press, 1993), pp. 50–51.
4. See John A. Rohr, *To Run a Constitution: The Legitimacy of the Administrative State* (University of Kansas Press, 1986).
5. Paul C. Light, *A Government Ill Executed: The Decline of the Federal Service and How to Reverse It* (Harvard University Press, 2008), ch. 7.
6. Donald Kettl, *Leadership at the Fed* (Yale University Press, 1986).
7. James Fesler and Donald Kettl, *The Politics of the Administrative Process* (Chatham House, 1991).
8. See Paul C. Light, *Thickening Government* (Brookings Institution Press, 1995).
9. See Terry M. Moe, "The Politics of Structural Choice: Toward a Theory of Public Bureaucracy," in Oliver E. Williamson, ed., *Organization Theory: From Chester Barnard to the Present and Beyond* (Oxford University Press, 1990), pp. 140–162.
10. For an analysis of the use and abuse of the civil service system in the early twentieth century, see Stephen Skowronek, *Building a New American State* (Cambridge University Press, 1982).
11. See Jeanne Ponessa, "The Hatch Act Rewrite," *CQ Weekly,* November 13, 1993, pp. 3146–3147.
12. Theodore J. Lowi Jr., *The End of Liberalism,* 2d ed. (Norton, 1979).
13. Eric Pianin, "EPA Aims to Change Pollution Rules," *Washington Post,* December 5, 2003, p. A2.
14. Morris P. Fiorina, "Flagellating the Federal Bureaucracy," *Society* (March–April 1983), p. 73.
15. See Steven S. Smith, *The American Congress* (Houghton Mifflin, 1995); see also Joel D. Aberbach, *Keeping a Watchful Eye: The Politics of Congressional Oversight* (Brookings Institution Press, 1990).

Chapter 14

1. Anthony Lewis, "The Court: How 'So Few Have So Quickly Changed So Much,'" *New York Review of Books,* December 20, 2007.
2. Charles Evans Hughes, speech before the Chamber of Commerce, Elmira, New York. May 3, 1907. In *Addresses and Papers of Charles Evans Hughes, Governor of New York, 1906–1908* (Putnam, 1908).
3. Roy P. Fairfield, ed., *The Federalist Papers* (Johns Hopkins University Press, 1981), p. 227.
4. Jerome Frank, *Courts on Trial: Myth and Reality in American Justice* (Princeton University Press, 1949), pp. 80–103. See also Martin Shapiro, *Courts* (University of Chicago Press, 1981); Robert P. Burns, *A Theory of the Trial* (Princeton University Press, 1999).
5. *Bush v. Gore,* 531 U.S. 98 (2000).
6. Many of these workload statistics can be found in the Supreme Court's *2007 Year-End Report on the Federal Judiciary* (U.S. Government Printing Office, January 1, 2008).
7. Fairfield, *The Federalist Papers,* p. 228.
8. Harold W. Chase, *Federal Judges: The Appointing Process* (University of Minnesota Press, 1972); Sheldon Goldman, *Picking Federal Judges: Lower Court Selection from Roosevelt Through Reagan* (Yale University Press, 1997).
9. See David M. O'Brien, "Ironies and Disappointments: Bush and Federal Judgeships," in Colin Campbell and Bert A.

Rockman, eds., *The George W. Bush Presidency* (CQ Press, 2004), pp. 133–157; Brannon P. Denning, "The Judicial Confirmation Process and the Blue Slip," *Judicature* (March–April 2002), pp. 218–226.

10. Lisa M. Holmes and Roger E. Hartley, "Increasing Senate Scrutiny of Lower Federal Court Nominees," *Judicature* (May–June 1997), p. 275.
11. George Watson and John Stookey, "Supreme Court Confirmation Hearings: A View from the Senate," *Judicature* (December 1987–January 1988), p. 193. See also John Massaro, *Supremely Political: The Role of Ideology and Presidential Management in Unsuccessful Supreme Court Nominations* (State University of New York Press, 1990).
12. Barbara A. Perry and Henry J. Abraham, "A 'Representative' Supreme Court? The Thomas, Ginsburg, and Breyer Appointments," *Judicature* (January–February 1998), pp. 158–165.
13. Goldman, *Picking Federal Judges*, pp. 161, 327–336.
14. Sheldon Goldman, "Bush's Judicial Legacy: The Final Imprint," *Judicature* (April–May 1993), p. 291.
15. Sheldon Goldman, Elliot Slotnick, Gerard Gryski, and Sara Schiavoni, "Picking Judges in a Time of Turmoil: W. Bush's Judiciary During the 109th Congress," *Judicature* (May–June 2007).
16. Sheldon Goldman, "Reagan's Judicial Legacy: Completing the Puzzle and Summing Up," *Judicature* (April–May 1989), pp. 318–330.
17. Naftali Bendavid, "Diversity Marks Clinton Judiciary," *Recorder* (December 30, 1993), p. 11.
18. Donald Santarelli, quoted in Jerry Landauer, "Shaping the Bench," *Wall Street Journal*, December 10, 1970, p. 1.
19. David M. O'Brien, "The Rehnquist Court's Shrinking Plenary Docket," *Judicature* (September–October 1997).
20. David M. O'Brien, *Storm Center: The Supreme Court in American Politics*, 7th ed. (Norton, 2005).
21. Tony Mauro, "The Supreme Court as Quiz Show," *Recorder* (December 8, 1993), p. 10.
22. Joyce O'Connor, "Selections from Notes Kept on an Internship at the U.S. Supreme Court, Fall 1988," *Law, Courts, and Judicial Process* 6 (Spring 1989), p. 44.
23. Forrest Maltzman, James F. Spriggs III, and Paul Wahlbeck, *Crafting Law on the Supreme Court: The Collegial Game* (Cambridge University Press, 2000).
24. Charles Evans Hughes, *The Supreme Court of the United States* (Columbia University Press, 1966), p. 68.
25. Daniel M. Berman, *It Is So Ordered: The Supreme Court Rules on School Segregation* (Norton, 1986), p. 114; O'Brien, *Storm Center*, pp. 262–272.
26. *Brown v. Board of Education of Topeka*, 347 U.S. 483 (1954).
27. William H. Rehnquist, quoted in John R. Vile, "The Selection and Tenure of Chief Justices," *Judicature* (September–October 1994), p. 98.
28. David Danelski, "The Influence of the Chief Justice in the Decisional Process of the Supreme Court," in Thomas P. Jahnige and Sheldon Goldman, eds., *The Federal Judicial System: Readings in Process and Behavior*, (Holt, Rinehart & Winston, 1968), p. 148.
29. O'Brien, *Storm Center*, chap. 3.
30. Artemus Ward and David L. Weiden, *Sorcerers' Apprentices: 100 Years of Law Clerks at the United States Supreme Court* (New York University Press, 2006); Todd C. Peppers, *Courtiers of the Marble Palace: The Rise and Influence of the Supreme Court Law Clerk* (Stanford University Press, 2006).
31. Lincoln Caplan, *The Tenth Justice: The Solicitor General and the Rule of Law* (Knopf, 1987); Rebecca Mae Salokar, *The Solicitor General: The Politics of Law* (Temple University Press, 1992).
32. Gregory A. Caldeira and John R. Wright, "Organized Interest and Agenda Setting in the U.S. Supreme Court," *American Political Science Review* 82 (December 1988), p. 1110; Donald R. Songer and Reginald S. Sheehan, "Interest Group Success in the Courts: *Amicus* Participation in the Supreme Court," *Political Research Quarterly* 46 (June 1993), pp. 339–354.
33. *Webster v. Reproductive Health Services*, 492 U.S. 490 (1989); *Roe v. Wade*, 410 U.S. 113 (1973); Susan Behuniak-Long, "Friendly Fire: *Amici Curiae* and *Webster v. Reproductive Health Services*," Judicature (February–March 1991), pp. 261–270.
34. Caldeira and Wright, "Organized Interest and Agenda Setting," *American Political Science Review* 82 (December 1988), p. 1118; Songer and Sheehan, "Interest Group Success in the Courts," *Political Research Quarterly* 46 (June 1993).
35. Gerald N. Rosenberg, *Hollow Hope: Can Courts Bring About Sound Change?* (University of Chicago Press, 1991).
36. J. W. Peltason, *Fifty-Eight Lonely Men: Southern Federal Judges and School Desegregation* (University of Illinois Press, 1971); Gary Orfield and Chungmei Lee, *Brown at 50: King's Dream or Plessy's Nightmare* (Civil Rights Project, Harvard University, 2004).
37. See Benjamin N. Cardozo, *The Nature of the Judicial Process* (Yale University Press, 1921)—a classic.
38. William O. Douglas, quoted in David M. O'Brien, *Storm Center: The Supreme Court in American Politics*, 7th ed. (Norton, 2005), p. 184.
39. Lee Epstein, Jeffrey A. Segal, Harold J. Spaeth, and Thomas G. Walker, *The Supreme Court Compendium: Data, Decisions and Developments*, 4th ed. (CQ Press, 2006). Data through 2005–2006 Supreme Court term.
40. See Keith Perine, "Precedent Heeded, but Not Revered on High Court," *CQ Weekly*, November 28, 2005, pp. 3180–3184.
41. *Gonzales v. Carhart*, 550 U.S. _______(2007).
42. Ex parte *McCardle*, 74 U.S. 506 (1869).
43. Barry Friedman, "Attacks on Judges: Why They Fail," *Judicature* (January–February 1998), p. 152.
44. See Shawn Francis Peters, *Judging the Jehovah's Witnesses* (University of Kansas Press, 2002); Clyde Wilcox, *Onward, Christian Soldiers? The Religious Right in American Politics* (Westview Press, 1996); Mark Tushnet, *The NAACP's Legal Strategy Against Segregated Education, 1925–1950* (University of North Carolina Press, 1987); Karen O'Connor, *Women's Organizations' Use of the Court* (Lexington Books, 1980).
45. J. W. Peltason, "The Supreme Court: Transactional or Transformational Leadership," in Michael R. Beschloss and Thomas E. Cronin, eds., *Essays in Honor of James MacGregor Burns* (Prentice Hall, 1988), pp. 165–180; Valerie Hoeksta, *Public Reactions to Supreme Court Decisions* (Cambridge University Press, 2003).
46. *Planned Parenthood v. Casey*, 505 U.S. 833 (1992).
47. Rosenberg, *Hollow Hope*, p. 343.
48. Rehnquist, *Supreme Court*, p. 98.
49. Gallup Organization, "Confidence in Institutions," June 8–10, 2001, www.gallup.com; Herbert Kritzer, "The Impact of *Bush v. Gore* on Public Perceptions and Knowledge of the Supreme Court," *Judicature* (July–August 2001), pp. 32–38.
50. Edward White, "The Supreme Court of the United States," *American Bar Association Journal* 7 (1921), p. 341.

Chapter 15

1. Jeffrey Smith, *War and Press Freedom* (Oxford University Press, 1999); David Cole, *Enemy Aliens: Double Standards and Constitutional Freedoms in the War on Terrorism* (New Press, 2003).
2. *Rasul v. Bush*, 542 U.S. 466 (2004); *Hamdi v. Rumsfeld*, 542 U.S. 507 (2004).
3. *Hamdan v. Rumsfeld*, 126 S. Ct. 2749 (2006).
4. *Boumediene v. Bush*, 553 U.S. _______(2008).
5. *Felker v. Turpin*, 518 U.S. 651 (1996); *Winthrow v. Williams*, 507 U.S. 680 (1993); *McCleskey v. Zant*, 499 U.S. 467 (1991); *Stone v. Powell*, 428 U.S. 465 (1976).
6. Neil H. Cogan, ed., *The Complete Bill of Rights: The Drafts, Debates, Sources, and Origins* (Oxford University Press, 1997); Robert A. Rutland, *The Birth of the Bill of Rights, 1776–1791* (University of North Carolina Press, 1955).
7. *Barron v. Baltimore*, 7 Peters 243 (1833).
8. *Gitlow v. New York*, 268 U.S. 652 (1925).
9. Richard C. Cortner, *The Supreme Court and the Second Bill of Rights: The Fourteenth Amendment and the Nationalization of Civil Liberties* (University of Wisconsin Press, 1981).
10. *Witters v. Washington Department of Services for the Blind*, 474 U.S. 481 (1986); *Locke v. Davey*, 540 U.S. 712 (2004).
11. *Wallace v. Jaffree*, 472 U.S. 38 (1985).
12. *Everson v. Board of Education of Ewing Township*, 333 U.S. 203 (1947).
13. *Lemon v. Kurtzman*, 403 U.S. 602 (1971).
14. *Capital Square Review Board v. Pinette*, 515 U.S. 753 (1995).
15. *Bowen v. Kendrick*, 487 U.S. 589 (1988); *Lee v. Weisman*, 505 U.S. 577 (1992); *Board of Education of Kiryas Joel Village School District v. Grumet*, 512 U.S. 687 (1994); *Zelman v. Simmons-Harris*, 536 U.S. 629 (2002).
16. *Mitchell v. Helms*, 530 U.S. 793 (2000).
17. *Agostini v. Felton*, 521 U.S. 74 (1997).
18. *Zelman v. Simmons-Harris*, 536 U.S. 639 (2002).
19. *Employment Division of Human Resources of Oregon v. Smith*, 494 U.S. 872 (1990).
20. *Church of Lukumi Babalu Aye v. City of Hialeah*, 508 U.S. 520 (1993).
21. *City of Boerne v. Flores*, 521 U.S. 507 (1997).
22. *Gonzales* v. *O Centro Espirita Beneficente Uniao Do Vegetal et al.*, 546 U.S. 418 (2006).
23. *Brown v. Haritage*, 456 U.S. 45 (1982).
24. *New York Times Company v. United States*, 403 U.S. 670 (1971).
25. Ibid., *Near v. Minnesota*, 283 U.S. 697 (1930).
26. *Hazelwood School District v. Kuhlmeier*, 484 U.S. 260 (1988).
27. *R.A.V. v. St. Paul*, 505 U.S. 377 (1992). See also *Wisconsin v. Mitchell*, 508 U.S. 476 (1993).
28. *New York Times v. Sullivan*, 376 U.S. 254 (1964).
29. *Hustler Magazine v. Falwell*, 485 U.S. 46 (1988).
30. *Gertz v. Robert Welch, Inc.*, 418 U.S. 323 (1974).
31. Potter Stewart, concurring in *Jacobellis v. Ohio*, 378 U.S. 184 (1964).
32. John Marshall Harlan, in *Cohen v. California*, 403 U.S. 15 (1971).
33. *Miller v. California*, 413 U.S. 15 (1973).
34. *Young v. American Mini Theatres*, 427 U.S. 51 (1976); *Renton v. Playtime Theatres, Inc.*, 475 U.S. 41 (1986); *City of Los Angeles v. Alameda Books, Inc.*, 535 U.S. 425 (2002).
35. *Barnes v. Glen Theatre, Inc.*, 501 U.S. 560 (1991); *City of Erie v. Pap's A.M.*, 529 U.S. 277 (2000).
36. *Chaplinsky v. New Hampshire*, 315 U.S. 568 (1942).
37. *Cohen v. California*, 403 U.S. 115 (1971).

38. *R.A.V. v. St. Paul,* 505 U.S. 377 (1992). See also *Wisconsin v. Mitchell,* 508 U.S. 476 (1993); *Apprendi v. New Jersey,* 530 U.S. 466 (2000).
39. *Virginia v. Black,* 538 U.S. 343 (2003).
40. *44 Liquormart, Inc., v. Rhode Island,* 517 U.S. 484 (1996); *Thompson v. Western States Medical Center,* 535 U.S. 357 (2002).
41. *Branzburg v. Hayes,* 408 U.S. 665 (1972).
42. *Federal Communications Commission v. Pacifica Foundation,* 438 U.S. 726 (1978).
43. *United States v. Playboy Entertainment Group,* 529 U.S. 803 (2000); *Denver Area Educational Television v. Federal Communications Commission,* 518 U.S. 727 (1996).
44. *Reno v. American Civil Liberties Union,* 521 U.S. 844 (1997).
45. *Ashcroft v. ACLU,* 542 U.S. 656 (2004).
46. *Walker v. Birmingham,* 388 U.S. 307 (1967).
47. *Madsen v. Women's Health Center,* 512 U.S. 753 (1994); *Schenck v. Pro-Choice Network,* 519 U.S. 357 (1997); *Hill v. Colorado,* 530 U.S. 703 (2000).
48. *First English Evangelical v. Los Angeles County,* 482 U.S. 304 (1987). See Richard A. Epstein, *Taking: Private Property and the Power of Eminent Domain* (Harvard University Press, 1985).
49. *Lucas v. South Carolina Coastal Commission,* 505 U.S. 647 (1992).
50. *Tahoe-Sierra Council, Inc., v. Tahoe Regional Planning Agency,* 535 U.S. 302 (2002).
51. *Kelo v. City of New London,* 125 S. Ct. 2655 (2005).
52. *United States v. 554 Acres of Land,* 441 U.S. 506 (1979).
53. *Mathews v. Eldridge,* 424 U.S. 319 (1976), restated in *Connecticut v. Doeher,* 501 U.S. 1 (1991).
54. *Meyer v. Nebraska,* 262 U.S. 390 (1923).
55. *Lochner v. New York,* 198 U.S. 45 (1905).
56. *Griswold v. Connecticut,* 381 U.S. 479 (1965).
57. Philip B. Kurland, *Some Reflections on Privacy and the Constitution* (University of Chicago Center for Policy Study, 1976), p. 9. A classic and influential article about privacy is Samuel D. Warren and Louis D. Brandeis, "The Right to Privacy," *Harvard Law Review* (December 15, 1890), pp. 193–220.
58. *Roe v. Wade,* 410 U.S. 113 (1973).
59. *Planned Parenthood of Southeastern Pennsylvania v. Casey,* 505 U.S. 833 (1992).
60. *Stenberg v. Carhart,* 530 U.S. 914 (2000).
61. *Gonzales v. Carhart,* 550 U.S. (2007).
62. *Bowers v. Hardwick,* 478 U.S. 186 (1986)
63. *Boy Scouts of America v. Dale,* 530 U.S. 640 (2000).
64. *Lawrence v. Texas,* 539 U.S. 558 (2003).
65. *Romer v. Evans,* 517 U.S. 620 (1996).
66. But see *Washington v. Chrisman,* 445 U.S. 1 (1982), and compare *Georgia* v. *Randolph,* 126 547 U.S. 103 (2006).
67. *Katz v. United States,* 389 U.S. 347 (1967).
68. *California v. Hodari D.,* 499 U.S. 621 (1991).
69. *Bond v. United States,* 529 U.S. 334 (2000).
70. *Terry v. Ohio,* 392 U.S. 1 (1968).
71. *Hiibel v. Sixth Judicial District of Nevada,* 542 U.S. 177 (2004).
72. *Minnesota v. Dickerson,* 508 U.S. 366 (1993).
73. *Almeida-Sanchez v. United States,* 413 U.S. 266 (1973); *United States v. Ortiz,* 422 U.S. 891 (1975); *United States v. Arvizu,* 534 U.S. 161 (2002); *United States v. Flores-Montano,* 541 U.S. 149 (2004).
74. *United States v. Ramsey,* 431 U.S. 606 (1977).
75. *Mapp v. Ohio,* 367 U.S. 643 (1961).
76. Senate Committee on the Judiciary, *The Jury and the Search for Truth: The Case Against Excluding Relevant Evidence at Trial; Hearing Before the Committee, 104th Cong., 1st sess.* (U.S. Government Printing Office, 1997).
77. *United States v. Leon,* 468 U.S. 897 (1984); *Arizona v. Evans,* 514 U.S. 1 (1995).
78. *Miranda v. Arizona,* 384 U.S. 436 (1966); but see *Yarborough v. Alvarado,* 541 U.S. 652 (2004).
79. *Dickerson v. United States,* 530 U.S. 428 (2000).
80. Justice Felix Frankfurther, dissenting in *United States v. Rabinowitz,* 339 U.S. 56 (1950).
81. *United States v. Enterprises, Inc.,* 498 U.S. 292 (1991).
82. *Williams v. Florida,* 399 U.S. 78 (1970); *Burch v. Louisiana,* 441 U.S. 130 (1979).
83. *J. E. B. v. Alabama ex rel T. B.,* 511 U.S. 127 (1994); *Batson v. Kentucky,* 476 U.S. 79 (1986); *Powers v. Ohio,* 499 U.S. 400 (1991); *Hernandez v. New York,* 500 U.S. 352 (1991); *Georgia v. McCollum,* 505 U.S. 42 (1990).
84. *Ewing v. California,* 538 U.S. 11 (2003).
85. *Benton v. Maryland,* 395 U.S. 784 (1969). See also *Kansas v. Hendricks,* 521 U.S. 346 (1997).
86. *Graham v. Collins,* 506 U.S. 461 (1993).
87. Death Penalty Information Center, "Executions by Year," September 28, 2007, www.deathpenaltyinfo.org/article.php?scid=8&did=146.
88. Barry Scheck, Peter Neufeld, and Jim Dwyer, *Actual Innocence: Five Days to Execution and Other Dispatches from the Wrongly Convicted* (Doubleday, 2000); Timothy Kaufman-Osborn, *From Noose to Needle: Capital Punishment and the Late Liberal State* (University of Michigan Press, 2002).
89. Death Penalty Information Center. "Innocence and the Death Penalty," May 2, 2008, www.deathpenaltyinfo.org/article.php?did=412#inn-yr-rc.
90. *Atkins v. Virginia,* 536 U.S. 304 (2002).
91. *Roper v. Simmons,* 543 U.S. 551 (2006).
92. *Baze v. Rees,* 553 U.S. _______(2008).
93. *Kennedy v. Louisiana,* 554 U.S. _______(2008).

Chapter 16

1. NewsHour Online, "Supreme Court Revisits Race in Public Schools," December 4, 2006. www.pbs.org/newshour/bb/law/july-dec06/scotus_12-04.html.
2. "How the Racial-Tiebreaker Case Began," *Seattle Times,* June 28, 2007.
3. *Parents Involved in Community Schools v. Seattle School District, No. 1,* 551 U.S. _______ (2007).
4. Andrew Hacker, *Two Nations: Black and White, Separate, Hostile, Unequal* (Scribner, 1992).
5. *Slaughter-House Cases,* 83 U.S. 36 (1873).
6. Ex Parte *Milligan,* 71 U.S. 2 (1866).
7. *Korematsu v. United States,* 323 U.S. 214 (1944).
8. Ex Parte *Quirin,* 317 U.S. 1 (1942).
9. *Reid v. Covert,* 354 U.S. 1 (1957).
10. *Boumediene v. Bush,* 553 U.S. _______(2008)
11. *Mathews v. Diaz,* 426 U.S. 67 (1976); *Shaughnessy v. United States ex rel. Mezei,* 345 U.S. 206 (1953).
12. *Demore v. Kim,* 538 U.S. 510 (2003).
13. *Zadvydas v. Davis,* 533 U.S. 678 (2001).
14. *Yick Wo v. Hopkins,* 118 U.S. 356 (1886); *Kwong Hai Chew v. Colding,* 344 U.S. 590 (1953); *Zadvydas v. Davis,* 533 U.S. 678 (2001); *Rasul v. Bush,* 542 U.S. 466 (2004); *Hamdi v. Rumsfeld,* 542 U.S. 507 (2004).
15. *Foley v. Connelie,* 435 U.S. 291 (1978); *Ambach v. Norwick,* 441 U.S. 68 (1979); *Cabell v. Chavez-Salido,* 454 U.S. 432 (1982).
16. *Plyler v. Doe,* 457 U.S. 202 (1982).
17. *Slaughter-House Cases,* 83 U.S. 36 (1873); *Civil Rights Cases,* 109 U.S. 3 (1883).
18. *Plessy v. Ferguson,* 163 U.S. 537 (1896).
19. *Brown v. Board of Education of Topeka,* 347 U.S. 483 (1954); *Brown v. Board of Education of Topeka,* 349 U.S. 294 (1955).
20. *Gomillion v. Lightfoot,* 364 U.S. 339 (1960).
21. Taylor Branch, *Parting the Waters: America in the King Years, 1954–1963* (Simon & Schuster, 1988). See also Harris Wofford, *Of Kennedys and Kings: Making Sense of the Sixties* (Farrar, Straus & Giroux, 1980).
22. See Charles Whalen and Barbara Whalen, *The Longest Debate: A Legislative History of the 1964 Civil Rights Act* (Mentor, 1985); Hugh Davis Graham, *The Civil Rights Era* (Oxford University Press, 1990).
23. Aldon D. Morris, *The Origins of the Civil Rights Movement: Black Communities Organizing for Change* (Free Press/Macmillan, 1985); James Farmer, *Lay Bare the Heart: An Autobiography of the Civil Rights Movement* (Arbor House, 1985).
24. Ellen Carol Du Bois, *Feminism and Suffrage: The Emergence of an Independent Women's Movement in America, 1848–1869* (Cornell University Press, 1978); Joan Hoff-Wilson, "Women and the Constitution," *News for Teachers of Political Science* (Summer 1985), pp. 10–15.
25. Susan M. Hartmann, *From Margin to Mainstream: American Women and Politics Since 1960* (Temple University Press, 1989); Susan Gluck Mezey, *In Pursuit of Equality: Women, Public Policy, and the Federal Courts* (St. Martin's Press, 1992).
26. *United States v. Virginia,* 518 U.S. 515 (1996). See also Philippa Strum, *Women in the Barracks: The VMI Case and Equal Rights* (University Press of Kansas, 2002).
27. *Meritor Savings Bank, FBD v. Vinson,* 477 U.S. 57 (1986).
28. *Oncale v. Sundowner Offshore Services,* 523 U.S. 75 (1998); *Faragher v. City of Boca Raton,* 524 U.S. 775 (1998); *Burlington Industries v. Ellerth,* 524 U.S. 742 (1998).
29. U.S. Census Bureau, "Texas Becomes Nation's Newest Majority-Minority State, Census Bureau Announces," August 11, 2005, www.census.gov/Press-Release/www/releases/archives/population/005514.html.
30. Celia W. Dugger, "U.S. Study Says Asian-Americans Face Widespread Discrimination," *New York Times,* February 29, 1992, p. 1, reporting on U.S. Civil Rights Commission, *Civil Rights Issues Facing Asian Americans in the 1990s* (U.S. Government Printing Office, 1992).
31. *Takao Ozawa v. United States,* 260 U.S. 178 (1922).
32. *Korematsu v. United States,* 323 U.S. 214 (1944)
33. Won Moo Hurh, *Korean Immigrants in America* (Fairleigh Dickinson University Press, 1984).
34. Antonio J. A. Pido, *The Filipinos in America: Macro/Micro Dimensions of Immigration and Integration* (Center for Migration Studies of New York, 1986).
35. Harold L. Hodgkinson, *The Demographics of American Indians: One Percent of the People, Fifty Percent of the Diversity* (Institute for Educational Leadership/Center for Demographic Policy, 1990), pp. 1–5.
36. "Assimilation, Relocation, Genocide: The Trail of Tears," *Indian Country Diaries,* PBS, November 2006, www.pbs.org/indiancountry/history/trail.html.
37. Spencer Rich, "Native Americans: They Can Still Get Free Health Care If They're Indian Enough," *Washington Post National Weekly Edition,* July 14, 1986, p. 34, quoting the Office of Technology Assessment.
38. *Morey v. Doud,* 354 U.S. 459 (1957); *Allegheny Pittsburgh Coal Co. v. County Commission,* 488 U.S. 336 (1989).
39. *City of Cleburne, Texas v. Cleburne Living Center,* 473 U.S. 432 (1985); *Heller v. Doe,* 509 U.S. 312 (1993); *Romer* v. *Evans,* 517 U.S. 620 (1996).
40. *San Antonio School District v. Rodriguez,* 411 U.S. 1 (1973).
41. *Frontiero v. Richardson,* 411 U.S. 677 (1973).
42. *San Antonio School District v. Rodriguez,* 411 U.S. 1 (1973); Douglas Reed, *On Equal Terms: The Constitutional Politics of Educational Opportunity* (Princeton University Press, 2001).

43. Matthew Bosworth, *Courts as Catalysts: State Supreme Courts and Public School Finance Equity* (State University of New York Press, 2001).
44. Sandra Day O'Connor, in *Kimel v. Florida Board of Regents*, 528 U.S. 62 (2000).
45. Ibid.
46. Leon F. Litwack, *Trouble in Mind: Black Southerners in the Age of Jim Crow* (1998), p. 227, as cited in James W. Fox Jr., "Intimations of Citizenship: Repressions and Expressions of Equal Citizenship in the Era of Jim Crow," *Howard University Law Journal* (Fall 2006).
47. *Report of the United States Commission on Civil Rights* (U.S. Government Printing Office, 1959), pp. 103–104.
48. Harold W. Stanley, *Voter Mobilization and the Politics of Race: The South and Universal Suffrage*, 1952–1984 (Praeger, 1987).
49. Abigail M. Thernstrom, *Whose Votes Count? Affirmative Action and Minority Voting Rights* (Harvard University Press, 1987), p. 15.
50. *Smith v. Allwright*, 321 U.S. 64 9 (1944).
51. *Gomillion v. Lightfoot*, 364 U.S. 339 (1960).
52. *Harper v. Virginia Board of Elections*, 383 U.S. 663 (1966).
53. Thernstrom, *Whose Votes Count?* For a contrary view, see Bernard Grofman, Lisa Handley, and Richard G. Niemi, *Minority Representation and the Quest for Voting Equality* (Cambridge University Press, 1992).
54. *Morse v. Republican Party of Virginia*, 517 U.S. 116 (1996).
55. Denniston, Lyle. "Court Asked to Strike Down Vote Law," Supreme Court of the United States Blog (September 8, 2008), *www.scotusblog.com*.
56. *Shaw v. Reno*, 509 U.S. 630 (1993).
57. *Civil Rights Cases*, 109 U.S. 3 (1883).
58. *Plessy v. Ferguson*, 163 U.S. 537 (1896).
59. *Heart of Atlanta Motel v. United States*, 379 U.S. 421 (1964).
60. Darryl Van Duch, "Plagued by Politics, EEOC Backlog Grows," *Recorder* (August 18, 1998), p. 1; David Rovella, "EEOC Chairman Casellas: 'We Are Being Selective,'" *National Law Journal* (November 20, 1995), p. 1.
61. *Shelley v. Kraemer*, 334 U.S. 1 (1948).
62. *Sweat v. Painter*, 339 U.S. 629 (1950).
63. *Brown v. Board of Education of Topeka*, 347 U.S. 483 (1954). See also J. W. Peltason, *Fifty-Eight Lonely Men: Southern Federal Judges and School Desegregation* (University of Illinois Press, 1971), p. 248.
64. *Brown v. Board of Education of Topeka*, 349 U.S. 294 (1955).
65. *Freeman v. Pitts*, 503 U.S. 467 (1992); *Missouri v. Jenkins*, 515 U.S. 70 (1995).
66. See Gary Orfield, Susan E. Eaton, and the Harvard Project on School Desegregation, *Dismantling Desegregation: The Quiet Reversal of Brown v. Board of Education* (New Press, 1996).
67. Raymond Hernandez, "NAACP Suspends Yonkers Leader After Criticism of Usefulness of School Busing," *New York Times*, November 1, 1995, p. A13.
68. Gary Orfield and Chungmei Lee, *Brown at 50: King's Dream or Plessy's Nightmare?* (Civil Rights Project, Harvard University, 2004), www.civilrightsproject.harvard.edu. See also Charles Clotfelter, *After Brown: The Rise and Retreat of School Desegregation* (Princeton University Press, 2004).
69. Richard Kahlenberg, *All Together Now: Creating Middle Class Schools Through Public School Choice* (Brookings Institution Press: 2003).
70. John Marshall Harlan, dissenting in *Plessy v. Ferguson*, 163 U.S. 537 (1896).
71. Charlotte Steeh and Maria Krysan, "Affirmative Action and the Public: 1970–1995," *Public Opinion Quarterly*, 60 (Spring 1996), pp. 128–158.
72. *University of California Regents v. Bakke*, 438 U.S. 265 (1978). See Howard Ball, *The Bakke Case* (University Press of Kansas, 2000).
73. *Gratz v. Bollinger*, 539 U.S. 244 (2003).
74. *Grutter v. Bollinger*, 539 U.S. 306 (2003).
75. Scott Jaschik, "Michigan Votes Down Affirmative Action," *Inside Higher Education*, November 8, 2006, www.insidehighered.com/news/2006/11/08/Michigan.
76. *Hopwood v. Texas*, 518 U.S. 1016 (1996).
77. James Farmer, quoted in Rochelle L. Stanfield, "Black Complaints Haven't Translated into Political Organization and Power," *National Journal* (June 14, 1980), p. 465.
78. Orfield and Lee, *Brown at 50;* Clotfeler, *After Brown*.
79. D'Vera Cohn, "Hispanic Growth Surges Fueled by Births in the U.S.," *Washington Post*, June 9, 2005, p. A1.
80. Gary Orfield, "Separate Societies: Have the Kerner Warnings Come True?" in Fred R. Harris and Roger W. Wilkins, eds., *Quiet Riots: Race and Poverty in the United States—The Kerner Report Twenty Years Later* (Pantheon, 1988), p. 103. See also Nicholas Lehmann, *The Promised Land* (Knopf, 1991).
81. William J. Wilson, *The Truly Disadvantaged: The Inner City, the Underclass, and Public Policy* (University of Chicago Press, 1987), esp. chap. 5; Kevin Phillips, *The Politics of Rich and Poor* (Random House, 1995).
82. Gary Orfield and Carole Ashkinaze, *The Closing Door: Conservative Policy and Black Opportunity* (University of Chicago Press, 1991) pp. 221–234;...

Chapter 17

1. Nurith Aizenman, Karin Brulliard, and Pamela Constable, "Legislation vs. Reality," *Washington Post*, June 29, 2007, p. A6.
2. Michael Sandler, "Immigration Overhaul Stymied," *CQ Weekly*, July 9, 2007, p. 2028.
3. The original types of public policy were developed by Theodore J. Lowi, "American Business, Public Policy, Case Studies, and Political Theory," *World Politics* 16 (1964), pp. 677–715.
4. See Paul C. Light, *Artful Work: The Politics of Social Security Reform* (Random House, 1985), for a discussion of dedistributive policy.
5. William Greider, "The Education of David Stockman," *Atlantic* (1981), p. 296.
6. John Kingdon, *Agendas, Alternatives, and Public Policies* (Little, Brown, 1984), p. 3.
7. Anthony Downs, "The 'Issue-Attention Cycle,'" *Public Interest* 28 (Summer 1972), p. 38.
8. James L. True, Bryan D. Jones, and Frank R. Baumgartner, "Punctuated-Equilibrium Theory: Explaining Stability and Change in Public Policymaking," in Paul A. Sabatier, ed., *Theories of the Policy Process* (Westview Press, 2007), p. 157.
9. Hugh Heclo, "Issue Networks and the Executive Establishment," in A. King, ed., *The New American Political System* (American Enterprise Institute, 1978), pp. 87–124.
10. Lester Salamon and Michael Lund, "The Tools Approach: Basic Analytics," in L. Salamon, ed., *Beyond Privatization: The Tools of Government Action* (Urban Institute Press, 1989).
11. See Paul C. Light, *A Government Ill Executed: The Decline of the Federal Service and How to Reverse It* (Harvard University Press, 2008).
12. See Cornelius Kerwin, *Rulemaking: How Government Agencies Write Law and Make Policy* (CQ Press, 2003).
13. See Claudia Copeland, "Animal Waste and Water Quality: EPA's Response to the *Waterkeeper Alliance* Court Decision on Regulation of CAFOs" (Congressional Research Service, August 31, 2007).
14. See Kingdon, *Agendas, Alternatives, and Public Policies*, for a description of the policy-making process.

Chapter 18

1. Office of Management and Budget, *Budget of the U.S. Government, Fiscal Year 2009, Analytical Perspectives* (U.S. Government Printing Office, February 2008), p. 298.
2. Ibid., pp. 245, 332.
3. For a discussion of the budgetary cycle, see Allen Schick, *The Federal Budget: Politics, Policy, Process*, rev. ed. (Brookings Institution Press, 2000).
4. Efforts at past tax reform are described in Jeffrey H. Birnbaum and Alan S. Murray, *Showdown at Gucci Gulch: Lawmakers, Lobbyists, and the Unlikely Triumph of Tax Reform* (Vintage Books, 1988). See also Timothy J. Conlan, Margaret T. Wrightson, and David R. Beam, *Taxing Choices: The Politics of Tax Reform* (CQ Press, 1990).
5. The debate over Keynes and his economic theories is still alive in the United States. See Donald E. Moggridge, *Maynard Keynes: An Economist's Biography* (Routledge, 1992).
6. Gary Burtless, Robert J. Lawrence, Robert E. Litan, and Robert J. Shapiro, *Globaphobia: Confronting Fears About Open Trade* (Brookings Institution Press, 1998), p. 29. For more information about GATT and the World Trade Organization, go to www.wto.org.
7. *United States v. E. C. Knight Co.*, 156 U.S. 1 (1895).
8. On the origins of the Federal Trade Commission and the role of Louis D. Brandeis, see Thomas K. McCraw, *Prophets of Regulation* (Belknap Press, 1984), chap. 3.
9. For a useful history of airline deregulation, see Steven A. Morrison and Clifford Winston, *The Evolution of the Airline Industry* (Brookings Institution Press, 1995).
10. On Southwest Airlines and its longtime chief executive Herb Kelleher, see Kevin Freiberg and Jackie Freiberg, *Nuts!* (Bard Press, 1996).
11. *Reno v. American Civil Liberties Union*, 521 U.S. 844 (1997).
12. See Robert W. Crandall and Harold Furchtgott-Roth, *Cable TV: Regulation or Competition?* (Brookings Institution Press, 1996); Richard Klinger, *The New Information Industry: Regulatory Challenges and the First Amendment* (Brookings Institution Press, 1996); and Lawrence Lessig, *Code and Other Laws of Cyberspace* (Basic Books, 2000).

Chapter 19

1. Henry J. Kaiser Family Foundation, *The Medicare Prescription Drug Benefit Fact Sheet*, February 2008, www.kkf.org.
2. Michael B. Katz, *In the Shadow of the Poorhouse: A Social History of Welfare in America* (Basic Books, 1986).
3. This history draws heavily on Theda Skocpol's research on the subject, starting with "America's First Social Security System: The Expansion of Benefits for Civil War Veterans," *Political Science Quarterly* 108 (Winter 1993), pp. 64–87.
4. These numbers can be found at the Department of Health and Human Services Web site, aspe.hhs.gov/poverty/07poverty.shtml.
5. Gertrude Schaffner Goldberg and Eleanor Kremen, eds., *The Feminization of Poverty: Only in America?* (Greenwood Press, 1990).

6. See, for example, Margaret Weir, "Political Parties and Social Policymaking," in Margaret Weir, ed., *The Social Divide: Political Parties and the Future of Activist Government* (Brookings Institution Press, 1998).
7. Self-employed workers must cover both amounts, and many state and local government workers are not required to participate.
8. Martha Derthick, "No More Easy Votes for Social Security," *Brookings Review* 10 (Fall 1992), pp. 50–53.
9. For a pessimistic view of the viability of Social Security, see Neil Howe and Richard Jackson, "The Myth of the 2.2 Percent Solution," www.cato.org/dailys/7–21–98.html. Robert D. Reischauer of the Brookings Institution testified before the House Committee on Ways and Means on November 19, 1998, that Social Security will start running deficits by 2021 and that by 2032, "reserves will be depleted."
10. See Theda Skocpol, *Protecting Soldiers and Mothers: The Political Origins of Social Policy in the United States* (Belknap Press, 1992), chap. 9, for a history of the act.
11. Lyndon Johnson, speech at the University of Michigan, May 1964, in *Congress and the Nation, 1965–1968: A Review of Government and Politics During the Johnson Years* (CQ Press, 1969), vol. 2, p. 650.
12. William J. Clinton, acceptance speech, Democratic National Convention, Chicago, July 6, 1992.
13. Robert Pear, "Judge Rules States Can't Cut Welfare," *New York Times,* October 14, 1997, p. A1.
14. Isabel V. Sawhill, R. Kent Weaver, Ron Haskins, and Andrea Kane, eds., *Welfare Reform and Beyond: The Future of the Safety Net* (Brookings Institution Press, 2002), p. 19.
15. See, for example, Ron Haskins and Isabel V. Sawhill, *Work and Marriage: The Way to End Poverty and Welfare,* Welfare Reform & Beyond Brief No. 28 (Brookings Institution, 2003).
16. Centers for Medicare and Medicaid Services, "Health Accounts," www.cms.hhs.gov.
17. Laurene A. Graig, *Health of Nations: An International Perspective on U.S. Health Care Reform* (CQ Press, 1993), p. 20.
18. Congressional Budget Office, *How Many People Lack Health Insurance and for How Long?* (Author, 2003).
19. U.S. Bureau of the Census, www.census.gov.
20. The amount permitted for a medical savings account is 75 percent of the maximum total deduction for medical expenses for an individual or couple.
21. *Ewing v. California,* 583 U.S. 11 (2003).
22. Martin Kady II, "America's Uneasy Mandate for Domestic Security," *CQ Weekly,* April 24, 2004, p. 950.

Chapter 20

1. See Lee Feinstein, "Darfur and Beyond: What Is Needed to Prevent Mass Atrocities," Council on Foreign Relations, January 2007.
2. Condoleezza Rice, quoted in Glenn Kessler, "Rice Lays Out Case for War in Iraq," *Washington Post,* August 16, 2002, p. A1.
3. See Joseph Nye, *Soft Power: The Means to Success in World Politics* (Public Affairs, 2005).
4. See John Gershman, "Is Southeast Asia the Second Front," *Foreign Affairs* (July/August 2002), for a discussion of the roots of Islamic terrorism.
5. See Glenn Kessler, "U.S. Decision on Iraq Has Puzzling Past Opponents of War Wonder When, How Policy Was Set," *Washington Post,* January 12, 2003, p. A1, for a detailed history of the increasing interest in Iraq.
6. Remarks to the United Nations, September 12, 2003.
7. U.S. Senate Select Committee on Intelligence, Report on the U.S. Intelligence Community's Prewar Intelligence Assessments on Iraq, committee print, reported July 7, 2004, committee summary p. 1, www.intelligence.senate.gov.
8. See Jason H. Campbell and Michael E. O'Hanlon, "The State of Iraq: An Update," *New York Times,* March 9, 2008, p. A28.
9. For more information, visit the Peace Corps Web site, www.peacecorps.gov. For a useful study of the Peace Corps, see Elizabeth Cobbs Hoffman, *All You Need Is Love: The Peace Corps and the Spirit of the 1960s* (Harvard University Press, 1998).
10. U.S. Department of Defense, www.defenselink.mil; U.S. Department of State, www.state.gov.
11. For a fascinating history of U.S. intelligence operations, see Christopher Andrew, *For the President's Eyes Only: Secret Intelligence and the American Presidency from Washington to Bush* (HarperCollins, 1995). See also Rhodri Jeffreys-Jones, *The CIA and American Democracy,* 2d ed. (Yale University Press, 1998).
12. National Commission on Terrorist Attacks on the United States, *The 9/11 Commission Report* (Norton, 2004), p. 12.
13. *Public Papers of the Presidents, Dwight D. Eisenhower* (U.S. Government Printing Office, 1960), pp. 1035–1040.
14. Dennis C. Jett, "The U.N.'s Failures Are Everyone's Fault," *New York Times,* May 22, 2000, p. A23. See also Christopher S. Wren, "Era Waning: Holbrooke Takes Stock," *New York Times,* January 14, 2001, p. 8.
15. "U.S. Foreign Aid Spending Since World War II," *Public Perspective* 8 (August–September 1997), p. 11.
16. Gallup Poll, May 2000, www.gallup.com.
17. See Sebastian Mallaby, "Why So Stingy on Foreign Aid?" *Washington Post National Weekly Edition,* July 3, 2000, p. 27.
18. Ibid. But see Doug Bandlow, "The Case Against Foreign Aid," *Christian Science Monitor,* September 29, 1999, p. 9; and Eric Schmitt, "Helms Urges Foreign Aid Be Handled by Charities," *New York Times,* January 12, 2001, p. A4.
19. See Robert Kagan, "The Kerry Doctrine," *Washington Post,* August 1, 2004, p. B7, for this argument.
20. Gary Hufbauer and Jeffrey J. Schott, "Economic Sanctions and Foreign Policy," *PS: Political Science and Politics* 18 (Fall 1985), p. 278.
21. John Prados, *The President's Secret Wars: CIA and Pentagon Covert Operations Since World War II* (Morrow, 1986); and Daniel Patrick Moynihan, *Secrecy: The American Experience* (Yale University Press, 1998).
22. P. W. Singer, "Winning the War of Words: Information Warfare in Afghanistan," Brookings Analysis Paper No. 5, October 2001.
23. Evan Thomas and Gregory L. Vistica, "Falling Out of the Sky," *Newsweek,* March 17, 1997, p. 26.

Epilogue

1. Thucydides, *History of the Peloponnesian War,* trans. Benjamin Jowett (Prometheus Books, 1998).
2. Edith Hamilton, *The Echo of Greece* (Norton, 1957), p. 47.
3. For a book advocating more direct democracy, see Ted Becker and Christa Daryl Slaton, *The Future of Teledemocracy* (Praeger, 2000); for a contrary view, see Richard J. Ellis, *Democratic Delusions: The Initiative Process in America* (University Press of Kansas, 2002).
4. For an extensive list of countries that use some form of proportional representation, see ACE The Electoral Knowledge Network, "Comparative Data: Electoral Systems," aceproject.org/epic-en/es.
5. For more on the relationship between electoral institutions and party systems, see Maurice Duverger, *Political Parties: Their Organization and Activity in the Modern State* (Wiley, 1954).
6. *Lawrence v. Texas,* 539 U.S. 558 (2003).
7. The Campaign Legal Center, www.campaignlegalcenter.org/BCRA.html; *McConnell v. FEC,* 124 S. Ct. 619 (2003).
8. Bruce Bimber and Richard Davis, *Campaigning Online: The Internet in U.S. Elections* (Oxford University Press, 2003).
9. John F. Kennedy, *Profiles in Courage* (Pocket Books, 1956), p. 108.
10. Harry S Truman, impromptu remarks before the Reciprocity Club, Washington, D.C., April 11, 1958, as reported by the *New York World-Telegram,* April 12, 1958, p. 4, www. bartleby.com/73/1405.html.
11. These books will give you insight into the life of public officeholders: Bill Clinton, *My Life* (Knopf, 2004); Harry Reid and Mark Warren, *The Good Fight* (Putnam Adult, 2008); George Tenet, *At the Center of the Storm: My Years at the CIA* (HarperCollins, 2007); and Alan Greenspan, *The Age of Turbulence* (Penguin, 2007).
12. For a contrary view of Madison's presidency, see Gary Rosen, *American Compact: James Madison and the Problem of the Founding* (University Press of Kansas, 1999).
13. See Kareem Abdul-Jabar and Alan Steinberg, *Black Profiles in Courage* (Morrow, 1996).
14. Reinhold Niebuhr, *The Children of Light and the Children of Darkness* (Scribner, 1944), p. xi.
15. See Bernard Crick, *In Defense of Politics,* rev. ed. (Pelican Books, 1983); and Stimson Bullitt, *To Be a Politician,* rev. ed. (Yale University Press, 1977).
16. See Nat Hentoff, *Free Speech for Me—but Not for Thee: How the American Left and Right Relentlessly Censor Each Other* (Harper Perennial, 1993).
17. Thomas Jefferson, letter to Edward Carrington, January 16, 1787, in Thomas Jefferson Randolph, ed., *Memoir, Correspondence, and Miscellanies, from the Papers of Thomas Jefferson,* 2d ed., vol. 2 (Carvill, 1830), letter 43. Available online from Project Gutenberg, www.gutenberg.org/files/16782/16782-h/16782-h.htm.
18. Arthur M. Schlesinger Jr., *The Disuniting of America* (Norton, 1993), p. 134.
19. John W. Gardner, *Self-Renewal,* rev. ed. (Norton, 1981), p. xiv.
20. In George Field, ed., *Famous Words of Freedom,* (Freedom House, 1955).

Photo Credits

CHAPTER 1: **2:** Timothy A. Clary/Getty Images **5:** Corbis Digital Stock **6:** Lee Marriner/ AP Photo **8:** Tsvangirayi Mukwazhi/AP Photo **11:** M. Spencer Green/AP Photo **14:** Bettmann/ Corbis **16:** *(left)* Bettmann/Corbis **16:** *(right)* The Granger Collection, New York **17:** Getty Images/Liaison **18:** Ted Spiegel/Corbis **21:** *(top)* Richard Ellis/Getty Images **21:** *(bottom)* Bettmann/Corbis **24:** Bettmann/Corbis

CHAPTER 2: **28:** Massimo Borchi/Corbis **30:** Torsten Kjellstrand/Landov **31:** Bettmann/ Corbis **34:** Joe Raedle/Getty Images **36:** Jeff Greenberg/The Image Works **38:** The Granger Collection, New York **39:** AP Images **42:** *(top)* The Granger Collection, New York **42:** *(center)* AP Images **42:** *(bottom)* Fabian Bachrach/Getty Images **43:** Image Works/Time & Life Pictures/ Getty Images **45:** Andrew Redington/Getty Images **46:** AP Photo

CHAPTER 3: **62:** Bill Aron/Photoedit **64:** AP Photo **65:** Terry Ashe/Time & Life Pictures/ Getty Images **68:** Lynsey Addario/AP Photo **71:** Tyrone Turner/Newscom **72:** Ron Bull/ Toronto Star/Newscom **74:** Michael Smith/ Newscom **76:** Jonathan Nourok/Getty Images **78:** Dream Pictures/Getty Images **80:** Jason Reed/Corbis **81:** Ed Kashi/Corbis **84:** Timothy A. Clary/Newscom **85:** Yael Swerdlow/AP Photo

CHAPTER 4: **90:** Bettmann/Corbis **92:** Teri Stratford **93:** Paul Conklin/Photoedit **95:** Robyn Beck/Getty Images **99:** Newscom **101:** *(top)* Mario Tama/Getty Images **101:** *(bottom)* Corbis **102:** Bettmann/Corbis **104:** Chris Kleponis/Newscom **105:** Bill Pugliano/Getty Images **107:** Greg Gibson/AP Images **108:** Will Powers/AP Images **109:** Alfred Eisenstaedt/ Time Life Pictures/Getty Images

CHAPTER 5: **114:** Gregory Smith/AP Images **117:** Library of Congress **118:** *(top)* Panoramic Images/Getty Images **118:** *(bottom)* Corbis **119:** Eric Draper/AP Images **122:** Jim Bourg/Landov **123:** *(left)* Patti McConville/ Getty Images **123:** *(Right)* Mary Ann Chastain/ AP Images **126:** *(top)* Winslow Townson/AP Images **126:** *(bottom)* Mike Groll/AP Images **127:** *(top)* Teri Stratford **127:** *(bottom)* Mark Leffingwell/Getty Images **128:** Alex Brandon/ AP Images **129:** Ken Lambert/AP Images **131:** AP Images **135:** Barry Talesnick/IPOL Inc./ Globe Photos **136:** Arthur Hochstein/Time Life Pictures/Getty Images **139:** Elizabeth Crews **144:** William Thomas Cain/Getty Images

CHAPTER 6: **146:** Alex Wong/Getty Images **149:** Stephen Jaffe/Getty Images **153:** Emmanuel Dunand/Getty Images **155:** *(top)* Getty Images **155:** *(Bottom)* Robert F. Bukaty/AP Images **156:** *(top)* Getty Images **156:** *(bottom)* Nita Winter/Landov **157:** Getty Images **158:** AP Images **161:** Nick Ut/AP Images **162:** Steve Liss/Getty Images **168:** Alex Wong/Getty Images **170:** Teri Stratford **172:** Janet Hostetter/AP Images

CHAPTER 7: **178:** Jim Young/Landov **182:** Newscom **186:** Library of Congress **190:** *(top)* Paul Conklin/Photoedit **190:** *(bottom)* Getty Images **191:** Olivier Douliery/Newscom **193:** Dennis Brack/Landov **194:** Christopher Fitzgerald/Newscom **199:** Andrew Theodorakis/ AFP/Getty Images **200:** Teri Stratford **203:** Daniel Acker/Landov

CHAPTER 8: **206:** Tim Boyles/Getty Images **208:** Suzanne Dechillo/The New York Times/Redux **212:** Guy Reynolds/Dallas Morning News/ Newscom **213:** Jeff Greenberg/Photoedit **214:** Bettmann/Corbis **217:** Chris Hondros/Getty Images **218:** Jeff Widener/AP Images **220:** Teri Stratford **222:** Tom Olmscheid/AP Images **225:** Damian Dovarganes/AP Images **226:** Christopher Fitzgerald/Newscom **227:** Getty Images **229:** *(top)* AP Photo **229:** *(bottom)* J. Scott Applewhite/AP Images **231:** Teri Stratford

CHAPTER 9: **238:** Mark Weber/Landov **243:** Getty Images **246:** Marla Brose/Albuquerque Journal/AP Images **249:** Richard Clement/ Landov **255:** Mark Wilson/Newscom **256:** William Thomas Cain/Getty Images **257:** Carlos Barria/Landov **263:** Teri Stratford **265:** Teri Stratford **267:** Getty Images **270:** Charles Dharapak/AP Images

CHAPTER 10: **274:** Teri Stratford **277:** Shannon Stapleton/Corbis **278:** Jessica Rinaldi/Reuters **280:** *(bottom)* Rose M. Prouser/Getty Images **281:** *(top)* Bettmann/Corbis **281:** *(bottom)* UPI/Bettmann/Corbis **282:** *(top)* Courtesy of Wikipedia.com/Zuma Press **282:** *(bottom)* Alex Wong/Getty Images **283:** *(top)* Tom Stoddart/ Getty Images **283:** *(bottom)* AP Images **286:** Andy Clark/Landov **288:** Adam Rountree/AP Images **290:** Jeff Chiu/AP Images **291:** *(top)* Rick Bowmer/AP Images **291:** *(bottom)* Joe Raedle/Getty Images **292:** Hulton Archive/Getty Images

CHAPTER 11: **298:** Brian Snyder/Reuters/ Landov **300:** Adam Hammer/AP Images **302:** Moses Olmos/Newscom **303:** Ted Richardson/ Raleigh News & Observer/Newscom **304:** Corbis **307:** Peter Lennihan/AP Images **309:** *(top)* Ron Sachs/Newscom **309:** *(bottom)* Paul Sakuma/AP Images **310:** Corbis **313:** Photofest **317:** Chuck Burton/AP Images **318:** Mark Wilson/Getty Images **319:** *(top)* Pablo Martinez Monsivais/AP Images **319:** *(bottom)* Shawn Thew/AFP/Getty Images

CHAPTER 12: **326:** Joseph Sohm/Corbis **328:** *(top)* Brooks Kraft/Corbis **328:** *(bottom)* Leif Skoogfors/Corbis **330:** *(top left)* Dana Edelson/ NBCU Photo Bank **330:** *(top right)* Robert F. Bukaty/AP Images **330:** *(bottom)* Charles Dharapak/AP Images **331:** Larry Downing/ Reuters/Corbis **334:** Cecil Stoughton/Corbis **335:** Behrouz Mehri/Getty Images **336:** AP Photo **338:** *(top)* Dennis Cook/AP Images **338:** *(bottom)* Ric Francis/AP Images **340:** Smithsonian American Art Museum, Washington D.C./Art Resource **341:** Elise Amendola/AP Images **342:** Rusty Russell/Getty Images **343:** *(top)* Christy Bowe/Corbis **343:** *(bottom)* David McNew/Getty Images **345:** Win McNamee/ Reuters/Getty Images **346:** Ronald Reagan Library/Getty Images **348:** Dirck Halstead/Getty Images **351:** *(left)* Courtesy The White House **351:** *(right)* Paul J. Richards/Getty Images **352:** Mark Georgiev/Getty Images

CHAPTER 13: **356:** Steve Helber/AP Images **359:** The Granger Collection, New York **362:** Dennis Cook/AP Images **363:** U. S. Department of Education **364:** *(top)* AP Images **364:** *(center)* Scott J. Ferrell/Getty Images **364:** *(bottom)* Mario Tama/Getty Images **365:** *(top)* Bettmann/ Corbis **365:** *(center)* Diana Walker/Getty Images **365:** *(bottom)* Mark Wilson/Getty Images **366:** *(top)* Kevin Dietsch/Landov **366:** *(bottom)* Lori Waselchuk/The New York Times/Redux **368:** Tom Horan/Corbis Sygma **369:** North Wind Picture Archives **370:** Bettmann/Corbis **372:** *(top)* AP Images **372:** *(bottom)* Gerald Herbert/ AP Images **375:** Mark Wilson/Getty Images **376:** Chip Somodevilla/Getty Images **378:** Alan Singer/CBS Television

CHAPTER 14: **382:** Chip Somodevilla/Getty Images **390:** Stephen Crowley/The New York Times/Redux **391:** Clary/UPI/Corbis **393:** *(bottom)* Stephen Crowley/The New York Times/ Redux **393:** *(top left)* Brendan Smialowski/ Getty Images **393:** *(top right)* AP Images **392:** Stephen Crowley/The New York Times/ Redux **394:** George Waldman/PictureDesk/ Newscom **395:** Reuters/Corbis **399:** Alex Wong/Getty Images **400:** David Hume Kennerly/Getty Images **402:** Bill O'Leary/The Washington Post

CHAPTER 15: **408:** Clay Good/Zuma Press **412:** Stephen Crowley/The New York Times/Redux **413:** Alex Wong/Getty Images **415:** Carl Iwasaki/Getty Images **416:** Charles Tasnadi/AP Images **418:** Nick Ut/AP Images **419:** Michael Porro/Getty Images **420:** Jean Catuffe/SIPA Press **421:** Nicholas Kamm/AFP/Getty Images **422:** Jessica Hill/AP Images **424:** AP Images **425:** Corbis **426:** Alex Wong/Getty Images **427:** Bob Daemmrich/ The Image Works **428:** Mike Derer/AP Images **430:** Bettmann/Corbis **433:** Joe Raedle/Getty Images

CHAPTER 16 **438:** Kevin P. Casey/The New York Times/Redux **441:** Morton Beebe/Corbis **442:** Corbis **447:** Getty Images **445:** *(top)* Laurie P. Winfrey/Woodfin Camp **445:** *(bottom)* AP Images **446:** AP Images **447:** Bettmann/ Corbis **449:** Scott J. Ferrell/Newscom **454:** Rich Pedroncelli/AP Images **456:** National Conference of State Legislators **460:** Bettmann/ Corbis **461:** Rayno/SIPA Press **463:** AP Images

CHAPTER 17: **468:** Yannis Kontos/Polaris **470:** Lenny Ignelzi/AP Images **474:** Carolyn Kaster/AP Images **471:** Tony Savino/The Image Works **475:** Eric Lee/Lawrence Bender Prods./ The Kobal Collection **476:** Paul Hosefros/The New York Times/Redux **481:** Peter Andrews/ Landov **483:** Getty Images **484:** USCG/ Landov

CHAPTER 18: 488: Peter Morgan/Landov **490:** Andrew Holbrooke/The Image Works **491:** AP Images **497:** AFP/Getty Images **499:** Mike Thieler/Reuters/Corbis **500:** Topham/The Image Works **502:** *(top right)* Jose Fuste Raga/Corbis **502:** *(bottom)* Nicki Nikoni/Getty Images **503:** Christ Chavez/Newscom **504:** Sinclair Stammers/Photo Researchers **505:** Brian Lee/Corbis **508:** *(top)* Don Emmert/Getty Images **508:** *(bottom)* Konrad Steffen/University of Colorado/Reuters/Landov **509:** M Spencer Green/AP Images **510:** Tony Gutierrez/AP Images

CHAPTER 19: 514: Dennis MacDonald/Photoedit **516:** Alamy **517:** Andrew Holbrooke/The Image Works **519:** Matthew Cavanaugh/Corbis **520:** Getty Images **522:** Dennis MacDonald/Photoedit **523:** Linda Spillers/Getty Images **524:** *(top)* Peter Hvizdak/The Image Works **524:** *(bottom)* Nicole Bengiveno/The New York Times/Redux **525:** Bonnie Kamin/Photoedit **528:** Arni Katz/Phototake NYC **532:** KIPP Foundation/Ethan Pines Photography

CHAPTER 20: 538: Shezad Noorani/Majority World/The Image Works **544:** Joe Raedle/Getty Images **545:** Shawn Baldwin/The New York Times/Redux **547:** *(top)* Topical Press Agency/Getty Images **547:** *(bottom)* Yves Herman/Landov **548:** *(top)* Olivier Coret/Corbis **548:** *(bottom)* AP Images **549:** *(top)* Sukree Sukplang/AP Images **549:** *(bottom)* David Brauchli/Corbis **552:** Sean Heasley/Corbis **553:** Patrick D. McDermott/Landov **555:** *(top)* Kevin Dietsch/Landov **555:** *(bottom)* Shiho Fukada/AP Images **556:** American Red Cross **558:** Patrick Gelly/The Image Works **559:** T. Campion/Corbis Sygma **560:** Kote Rodrigo/Corbis

EPILOGUE: 764: Kevin Fleming/Corbis **767:** Bob Daemmrich **770:** Jamie Rose/The New York Times/Redux **771:** Casey Cohen/Photoedit

Index

A

AARP, 150
Abbas, Mahmoud, 545
Abernathy, Ralph, 446
Abortion, 132, 214–216, 404, 424–426. *See also Roe v. Wade*
Abramoff, Jack, 158, 319
Absentee voting, 223
Abu Ghraib prison, 216, 282
Accommodations
- Civil Rights Act (1964) and, 457
- equal, 456–457

Accountability
- in bureaucracy, 361
- judicial, 401

Activism
- judicial, 392–393, 396
- party, 194

Act to Prevent Pernicious Political Activities. *See* Hatch Act (1939)
Adams, Abigail, 15
Adams, John, 15, 38–39, 330
Adams, John Quincy, 186, 243
Adams, Samuel, 24
Adams, Stephen, 265
Adaptive views, 46
Adelphia, 507
Administration committees, 313–314
Administrative discretion, 373
Administrative Procedure Act (1946), 373, 482
Administrative regulations, 373–374
Adversary system, 385–386
Advertising, 169, 262–263, 277, 293
Advice and consent, 308, 359, 390–391
Advisers, presidential, 340–341, 342
Advisory Commission on Intergovernmental Relations, 83
Affirmative action, 107, 440, 461–464
- Proposition 209 and, 463–464

Afghanistan, 98, 130, 544, 558
AFL-CIO, 152, 153, 161
African Americans, 100, 115, 120, 123, 126, 136, 138, 189, 464
- in cabinet, 364
- civil rights of, 131, 443–446
- on courts, 391
- discrimination against, 458
- in population, 124, 125–127
- voting by, 126, 220–221, 455

Age, 97, 103, 130, 136, 142, 143, 196, 317, 452–453, 457. *See also* Older adults
- identity and, 140–142
- voting by, 195, 225, 230

Age Discrimination in Employment Act (1967), 452
Agencies, 36, 75, 359, 361, 364–366, 504
Agenda setting, 289, 290, 345
Agriculture, employment in, 140
Agriculture Department, 358, 501, 550
Ahmadinejad, Mahmoud, 335
Aid to Families with Dependent Children (AFDC), 81, 521
Airline industry, 509, 510
Airport security, 428, 471
Alabama, 455
Alaskan Natives, 124
Aliens. *See* Immigration
Alito, Samuel A., Jr., 79, 318, 383, 390, 392
Allen, Florence, 393
Alliance for Justice, 390
Alliance of Automobile Manufacturers, 63
Al-Qaeda, 443, 535, 552, 558
Ambassadors, 549
Amendments. *See also* Constitution (U.S.)
- Bill of Rights as, 12, 30
- to Fair Housing Act, 452, 458
- listing of, 57–61
- privacy rights and, 425
- process of creating and ratifying, 42–47

America Coming Together, 264
American Airlines, 510
American Association for Justice (Association of Trial Lawyers of America), 166
American Association of University Professors, 153
American Automobile Association (AAA), 150
American Bar Association (ABA), 153
American Center for Law and Justice, 160
American Civil Liberties Union (ACLU), 160, 450
American Conservative Union, 161
American dream, 98, 99–100
American Enterprise Institute, 476
American exceptionalism, 118–119
American Farm Bureau Federation, 151
American Federation of Government Employees, 373
American Federation of Labor (AFL), 152, 165
American Federation of State, County, and Municipal Employees, 153, 166
American Federation of Teachers, 153
American Hospital Association, 531
American Indian Movement, 450
American Indians. *See* Native Americans
American Israel Political Action Committee (AIPAC), 156
American Medical Association (AMA), 153, 154, 265, 529, 531
American Political Science Association, 153
American Red Cross, 357
American Revolution. *See* Revolutionary War
Americans for Democratic Action, 161, 189
American Society of Newspaper Editors, 279
Americans with Disabilities Act (1990), 452
American Wind Energy Association, 150
America's Student Loan Providers, 299
AmeriCorps, 366
Amicus curiae briefs, 160, 397, 400, 401–402
Amnesty International, 156, 433
Amtrak, 366
Anderson, Jack, 282
Annapolis Convention, 14–15
Anthony, Susan B., 134, 447
Antidiscrimination statutes, 135
Antifederalists, 23–25, 77–78
Anti-immigration and anti-civil rights initiatives, 117
Anti-Saloon League, 154
Anti-Semitism, 131
Antitrust legislation, 505
Apartheid, 156
Appeals, 387, 395–399
Appellate jurisdiction, 386, 395
Appointment(s)
- of federal judges, 388–389, 393–394
- presidential, 332, 349
- of Supreme Court judges, 383, 384

Apportionment, 301
Appropriations bills, in House of Representatives, 309
Appropriations committees, 313
Aristocracy of wealth, 138
Aristotle, 7
Armed forces. *See* Military
Army Corps of Engineers, 504
Articles of Confederation, 14–15, 22. *See also* Constitution (U.S.)
Articles of Constitution. *See* Constitution (U.S.)
Asian Americans, 125, 129, 448–450
Assembly, freedom of, 12, 421–422
Athens, direct democracy in, 6
Atrocities, prevention of, 539
Attentive public, 217–218, 317
Attorney general
- federal, 386

Australian ballot, 222
Authorizing committees, 313
Automobiles, hybrid, 471
Ayres, William, 230

B

Bad tendency test, 416
Bakke, Allan, 461
Bakke case, 462
Balanced government, 17
Ballots. *See also* Australian ballot; Florida
- counting of, 233
- secret ballot, 222, 258

Ban Ki-moon, 555
Banks, Fed and, 498, 499
Barr, Bob and Jeri, 108, 257
Baumgartner, Frank R., 477
BCRA. *See* Bipartisan Campaign Reform Act (BCRA, 2002)
Beard, Charles A., 15
Bear Stearns, 520
Beerbohm, Marvin, 340
Bel, Daniel, 139
Benefits, 504
- for same-sex spouses, 135
- tax, 496

Berlin Wall, 549
Bernanke, Ben S., 362–363
Bernstein, Carl, 282
Bicameralism, 12, 19, 305
Biden, Joe, 3, 254, 343
Big government, 85
Bill, process of becoming law, 306, 320–322
Bill of Rights, 12, 23–24, 30
 application to states, 412
 protections under, 149–150, 409
 searches and seizures and, 429
 states and, 411–413
Bin Laden, Osama, 283, 552, 558, 559
Biological weapons, 543–544
Bipartisan Campaign Reform Act (BCRA, 2002), 167, 168, 199, 260–261, 263, 268, 277
Bird flu, 527
Birmingham, Alabama, 444–445
Birth control clinic, 425
Black, Hugo, 51
Blackwater, Inc., 481
Blackwell, Kenneth, 207
Blanket primaries, 182
Block grants, 80, 81
Blogs, 280, 292
Blue-collar sector, 140
Boards of directors, members of, 506
Boehner, John, 319
Boggs, Lilburn W., 131
Bombings, terrorist, 544
"Boot camps," 533
Bopp, James, 160
Border patrol, 533
Borders, 18–19
Border searches, 428–429
Boren, David L., 320
Bork, Robert, 391, 393
Borrowing, 492, 493, 498
Bosnia, 558
Boumediene v. Bush, 410, 443
Bourgeoisie, 140
Bowers v. Hardwick, 426
Boy Scouts of America, 136, 426
Branches of government, 31, 33, 329
Brandeis, Louis D., 34, 63, 67
Brennan, William J., Jr., 452
Breyer, Stephen, 47, 383, 390, 414
Briefs, 397
Brinkley, David, 278
Britain. *See* Great Britain
Broadcasting, 281–282, 420
Broder, David, 288
Brookings Institution, 476
Brose family (Seattle), 439, 465
Brown, Michael, 366
Brownback, Sam, 105
Brownlow, Louis, 376
Brown v. Board of Education of Topeka, 39, 397, 399, 444, 458–459, 460
Bryan, William Jennings, 187
Buchanan, Patrick, 257
Buckley v. Valeo, 259–260
Budget
 defense, 553
 deficit in, 492, 493
 federal, 492–494
 presidential plan for, 338
 priorities in, 527
 steps in creating, 494–496
 surplus in, 493
Budget and Accounting Act (1921), 337
Budget and Impoundment Control Act (1974), 495–496
Budget committees, 314
Budget power, of president, 337–338
Bundling, 161, 167
Bureaucracy, 359–361, 360. *See also* Federal bureaucracy
 comparisons by country, 368
 control of, 375–378
 foreign policy and defense, 549–553
 mistrust of, 371
 presidency and, 42
 self-regulation by, 377–378
 shutdown of (1995), 368
 of White House, 341
Bureaucrats, 360
Bureau of Alcohol, Tobacco, Firearms, and Explosives (ATF), 533
Bureau of Consular Affairs, 550
Burr, Aaron, 243, 330
Burrage, Billy Michael, 393
Bush, George H. W., 191–192, 241, 352, 503
 abortion rights and, 425
 civil rights and, 445
 judicial appointments by, 391
Bush, George W., 3, 84, 86, 96–97, 105, 106, 121, 132, 190, 208, 231–232, 239, 243, 249, 260, 265, 305, 319, 327, 330, 332, 334, 335, 336–337, 338, 341, 343, 345, 347, 349, 350, 352, 357, 383, 391, 392, 410, 420, 443, 445, 483, 489, 509
 election of 2000 and, 35
 election of 2004 and, 147
 foreign policy and, 540–541
 Iraq War and, 216, 331, 546–548
 presidency and, 327, 348
 public views of, 214–216
 USA PATRIOT Act and, 535
 war on terror and, 188
Bush Doctrine, 541
Bush v. Gore, 405
Business. *See also* Economy
 conservatives on, 105
 as government service provider, 481
 as interest group, 150
 public attitudes toward, 102
 regulation of, 505–506
 wealth and, 101
Business and Industrial Political Action Committee (BIPAC), 159
Business cycle, 490–491
Busing, 439, 460
Buxton, Lee, 425
Byrd, Robert, 311

C

Cabinet, 33, 342–343, 364
Cable communications, 276, 282, 292, 420
California
 blanket primary in, 182
 electoral votes in, 242
 e-voting in, 233
 Japanese in, 449
 minority university admission in, 464
 political culture in, 122
 Proposition 187 in, 448
 Proposition 209 in, 463–464
 same-sex marriage in, 135, 453, 454
Cambodia, 433, 450, 555
Campaign contributions, 161,260
 EMILY's List and, 133
 for incumbents, 301
 individual, 267
 by PACs, 165, 166–167
 by professional associations, 154
Campaign finance, 250
 problems with, 265–268
 regulation of, 201
Campaign issue advertising, 262–263
Campaign of Truth, 559
Campaigns, 239. *See also* Campaign contributions
 for congressional elections, 245–248
 congressional vs. presidential, 348
 Internet fundraising for, 202, 267–268
 media coverage of, 291–292
 news sources for, 284
 through other groups, 169–173
 rising costs of, 265
 sloganeering in, 292
 strategies in, 252–253
 technology and, 220, 292
 television and radio advertising on, 257–258
Campbell, Ben Nighthorse, 127, 451
Canada, NAFTA and, 503–504
Candidate activists, 194
Candidate-centered system, 180–181
Candidates
 appeal of, 229–230, 246
 image of, 292
 interest group support for, 161
 media and choice of, 290–291
 nomination of, 181–182
 personal wealth of, 267
 voter knowledge of, 216–217
Cannon, Joseph Gurney ("Uncle Joe"), 310
"Cap-and-trade" system, 509
Capitalism, 107
Capital punishment. *See* Death penalty
Carson, Rachel, 109
Carter, Jimmy, 341, 348, 352, 357, 391
Catalog of Federal Domestic Assistance, 517
Categorical aid, 517–518
Categorical-formula grants, 80–81
Catholicism, 131, 132
Caucuses, 181, 182, 252, 271, 315
Censorship, 420
Census, 45, 301
Census Bureau, 128, 129
Center Aisle Caucus, 317
Center for American Progress, 476
Centers for Disease Control and Prevention, 358, 362, 527
Central clearance, by OMB, 377
Central Intelligence Agency (CIA), 107, 365, 550, 551
Centralists, vs. decentralists, 77–78
Centralization, 10, 360
Centrists
 parties, 183
 voters, 109–110
Cert pool, 396

Chamber of Commerce (U.S.), 150, 171, 172–173
Change to Win Federation, 152
Chao, Elaine, 129
Charities, 481–482
Charter of Fundamental Rights (EU), 453
Chávez, César, 152
Checks and balances, 31–34
Chemical weapons, 543–544
Cheney, Dick, 336–337, 343, 344
Cherokee Indians, 450
Chicago Tribune, election of 1948 and, 214
Chief justice, 400
Chief of staff, 341
Chief of state, 344
Child Care and Development Block Grant (CCDBG), 81
Child labor, 507
Child Online Protection Act (COPA, 1998), 420–421
Children
  common values of, 212
  in families, 136
  poverty among, 138
Children's Bureau, 524
Children's Defense Fund (CDF), 523
Chile, 558
China, 107
  campaign finance in, 201
  civil service in, 368
  constitutions in, 37
  death penalty in, 433
  executive in, 339
  federalism in, 75
  health care in, 530
  labor unions in, 154
  legislatures in, 308
  party system in, 241
  policy process in, 479
  protests in, 218, 286
  taxation in, 495
  trade relations with, 546
  U.S. jobs exported to, 504
  voter turnout in, 224
Chinese Americans, 448–449
Chinese Exclusion Act (1882), 449
Choy, Herbert, 393
Christian Coalition, 106
Churches, 130, 131. *See also* Religion
  established, 414
  state and, 13
Circuit courts of appeal, 386
Cities, 122–124
Citizens
  public policy and, 484, 489
  rights of, 442–443
Citizens for Better Medicare, 169
Citizenship, 440–443, 448, 449
  for illegal immigrants, 469
Civic journalism, 293
Civil Aeronautics Board (CAB), 510
Civil disobedience, 421–422
Civilian Conservation Corps, 521
Civil law, 385
Civil liberties, 35, 411, 418, 424, 429, 434
Civil rights, 411, 439–440, 443–446. *See also* Equal rights
  political ideology and, 107
  politics of federalism and, 86
  school busing and, 439
Civil Rights Acts
  of 1957, 452
  of 1964, 82, 440, 445, 447, 452, 454, 457–458, 459
  of 1991, 452
Civil Rights Initiative (Michigan), 463
Civil rights laws, listing of, 452
Civil rights movement, 91, 131, 220–221, 444–445
Civil service, 180, 187, 369–373. *See also* Federal bureaucracy
  regulation of, 372
Civil Service Commission, 369
Civil unions, 86. *See also* Same-sex marriage
Civil War, 186
Class. *See* Social class
Class action suit, 457
Classical liberalism, 92
Clayton Act (1914), 506
Clean Air Act (1970), 86, 509
Clean Water Act (1972), 483
Clear and present danger test, 416, 418
Clear Skies initiative, 509
Cleveland, Grover, 243
Clinton, Bill, 85, 104, 120–121, 230, 231, 241, 245, 286, 288, 333, 341, 345, 349–350, 372, 390, 392, 503, 525
  civil rights and, 445
  deregulation and, 509
  impeachment of, 41, 42, 307, 334
Clinton, Hillary Rodham, 104, 106, 115, 129, 153, 199, 202, 231, 240, 249, 270, 275, 291, 446
Closed primary, 181–182
Closed rule, in House of Representatives, 310
Closed shop, 152, 507
Cloture, 312
Club for Growth, 154, 167, 169
CNN news, 287
Coalition governments, 183
Coalitions, Democratic, 189
Coalition to Make Our Voices Heard, 169
Coattail effect, 245
Cole, Tom, 451
Collective action, 158
Collective bargaining, 507
Colonies and colonization, 13, 18–19
Comey, James, 34
Commander in chief, 331
Commerce, 79, 306, 490
Commerce clause, 70, 71, 80, 457
Commerce Department, 501, 550
Commercial speech, 416, 419
Commission on Presidential Debates, 255–257
Commissions
  regulatory, 107, 361, 362
Committee on Political Education (COPE), 153, 165
Committees
  congressional, 312–315, 321
  in House of Representatives, 309, 310
Common Cause, 149, 155
Communications Decency Act (1996), 420
Communism, as political ideology, 107
Competitive economy, 100
Competitive federalism, 65
Concord Coalition, 155
Concurrent powers, 70, 73
Concurring opinion, 398
Confederacy, voting in former states of, 120–121
Confederations, 66
Conference committees, congressional, 314–315
Confirmation, by Senate, 33
Congress (U.S.), 33, 299–300. *See also* House of Representatives; Senate
  assessment of, 322
  budget and spending powers, 337, 494, 495–496
  candidates for, 244–248
  checks on government by, 307
  controls over bureaucracy, 375–376
  dependence on PACs by, 266–267
  divided government and, 187–188
  elections to, 300–304
  executive branch and, 331
  extraordinary convening of, 334
  job of legislators in, 315–320
  judges and, 403–404
  leadership of, 308, 309–315
  legislation and, 32, 70
  lobbying and, 156, 172
  news reporting about, 295
  PACs and, 166
  political parties in, 192, 193
  president and, 21, 319, 334, 345, 346–350
  profile of 110th (2007-2009), 316
  representation in, 19–20
  salaries for, 29
  staffs of, 304, 317
  structure and powers of, 304–308
  Supreme Court and, 79
Congressional Budget and Impoundment Control Act (1974), 337
Congressional Budget Office (CBO), 496
Congressional elaboration, 41
Congressional–executive agreement, 332
Congressional Hispanic Caucus, 449
Congress of Industrial Organizations (CIO), 152, 165
Connecticut Compromise, 20–21
Consent of the people, 10
Conservatism, 105–107
  aging and, 141
  equal rights and, 394
  of Supreme Court, 383
Constituents, 300
  congressional and presidential, 348
  legislators and, 316, 317, 318
Constitution (U.S.), 13–15, 29–30, 51. *See also* Amendments
  adaptive and originalist views of, 46
  adoption of, 22–25
  amending, 42–46, 42–47
  Article I (legislature), 30, 40, 52–54, 358, 490
  Article II (executive), 21, 30, 40, 41, 55–56, 331–334, 389, 454–455, 490
  Article III (courts), 23, 30, 40, 56
  Article IV, 30, 56
  Article V, 30, 42, 56–57
  Article VI, 30, 40, 57, 70
  Article VII (ratification), 30, 57
  bureaucracy and, 358–359
  checks and balances in, 31–34

Constitution (U.S.) (*Continued*)
commerce clause and, 70
on constitutional and unconstitutional classifications, 451–454
document, 52–57
federalism and, 64, 68–75
framers of, 16
full faith and credit clause in, 31–34
as instrument of government, 40–47
on interstate compacts, 75
on military, 553
necessary and proper clause in, 69–70
presidency and, 328–334
restraints on national and state governments in, 73–74
rights in, 410–411
supremacy of, 40
on tyranny of majorities, 12
unwritten, 41
views of, 30–37
Constitution(s), compared, 37
Constitutional Convention, 15–22, 329
Constitutional democracy, 3–4, 5, 7
conditions for, 8–9
judicial power in, 404–405
Constitutionalism, 7
Constitutional system, elements of, 12
Consumer price index (CPI), 491
Content neutral laws, 417
Contraction phase, of business cycle, 491
Contracts, public, 506
Conventions, 181–182, 190
national party, 252, 253–255
television coverage of, 291–292
Converting realignment, 187
Conway, M. Margaret, 134
Cooper, Ann Nixon, 127
Cooperative federalism, 65
Cooperative lobbying, 162
Copyright Office, 504
Core values, public opinion and, 214–215
Corn Belt, farmer organizations in, 151
Corporate income tax, 492
Corporate markets, regulation of, 507
Corporate social responsibility, 509
Corporate welfare, 520
Corporation for Public Broadcasting, 366
Corporations, 150, 173, 361, 366, 504–505
Corrupt Practices Act, 259
Corzine, Jon, 99, 267
Cost/benefit analysis, for public policy, 471–472
Council of Economic Advisers, 341
Council on Foreign Relations, 155
Counterdistributive policy, 471
County committees, 192
Court of appeals, 387
Courts, 33, 404–405
Article III on, 30
circuit courts, 386, 387–388
district, 386, 387
federal, 75–79, 386–388
hierarchy of, 21
Marbury v. Madison and, 38–40
Supreme Court, 386, 388
Covert operations, 558
Craig, Larry, 288
Crawford, William, 243
Credit Crisis (2008), 489
Crédit Mobilier, 174
Crime, 411, 533–535
Criminal law, 385
Criminal suspects, rights of, 427–432
Critical elections, 185
Cronkite, Walter, 278
Cross-cutting cleavages, 117
Cross-cutting requirements, 82
Crossover sanctions, 82–83
Crossover voting, 181
Cruel and unusual punishment, 432–434
C-SPAN, 254, 282
Cuban Americans, 127, 128

D

Dahl, Robert, 101
Daily Show, The, 291
Danelski, David, 400
Darfur, Sudan, 338, 539
Daschle, Tom, 268
Davis, Gray, 6
"Day Without Immigrants, A," 161
Dealignment, partisan, 197–198
Dean, Howard, 190, 191, 230, 249, 260, 275, 280
Death penalty, 432–434, 433
Debates
presidential, 255–257
vice presidential, 257
Debt. *See* National debt
Decentralists, vs. centralists, 77–78
Decentralized governments, 75
Decision making, 294
Declaration of Independence, 10, 13–14, 101
Deep Throat, 282
De facto segregation, 460
Defamation, 418
Defendants, 385
Defenders of Wildlife, 160
Defense Department, 550, 551, 552–553
Defense Intelligence Agency, 365
Defense of Marriage Act (1996), 135
Defense policy, 539–559
Deficit. *See* Budget, deficit in
Deficit spending, 84
De jure segregation, 460
DeLay, Tom, 167, 319
Delegated powers, 69, 70
Delegates, 316
to Constitutional Convention, 15–17
to party conventions, 181, 248–249
Democracy, 5–8, 22
constitutional, 3–4, 7
idealism and, 540
international understanding and, 548–549
political parties and, 179–181
representative, 7
as system, 9–12
voters' experiences with, 92
Democratic Congressional Campaign Committee (DCCC), 191
Democratic consensus, 9, 95
Democratic Leadership Council, 189
Democratic National Committee (DNC), 190, 191, 250
Democratic Party, 3, 108, 119, 126, 153, 186, 187, 192, 194–197, 202, 245, 255, 462. *See also* Elections; Political ideology
Democratic-Republicans, 185
Democratic Senatorial Campaign Committee (DSCC), 191
Democrats, 185. *See also* Jeffersonian Republicans (Democrats)
Demography, 116
age and, 142
of electorate, 195
party identification by, 196
voter turnout by, 227
Departments of government, 359, 361–362
Deregulation, 509–511
Desegregation, vs. integration, 460–461
Deterrence theory, 542
Detroit, 445
Devolution revolution, 85
Dewey, Thomas, 214
Dickerson v. United States, 431
Dictators, 540, 556
Diplomacy. *See also* Foreign policy
conventional (soft power), 554–555
public, 559
Direct democracy, 6, 7
Direct election
popular, 270
of senators, 36, 300
Direct orders, 82
Direct primary, 35, 181–182
Disaster aid, 83, 357
Discharge petition, 321
Disclosure laws, 169
Discrimination
against Asian Americans, 448
in employment, 457
equal protection and, 451
by gender, 452
against homosexuals, 427
against Jews, 131
against Native Americans, 450–451
by sexual orientation, 135
Dissenting opinion, 398
Distance learning, 533
Distribution of income, 139
Distributive policy, 471
District courts, 386, 387
District of Columbia, 242, 448
Districts, for congressional elections, 301
Diversity, 116–122, 125
in Congress, 311
of congressional caucuses, 315
judicial, 391–392, 393
in military, 554
in presidential appointments, 349
in public schools, 459
of state legislatures, 17
think tanks and, 476
Divided government, 34, 187–188
Division of power, 70, 76–77
Divorce rate, 136
Dobson, James, 131
Docket, 396, 397
Domestic insurrection, 74
Donations, to political campaigns, 202, 250, 251
"Don't ask, don't tell" policy, 135
Double jeopardy, 432
Douglas, William O., 403
Downs, Anthony, 475
Draper, Alan, 154
Dreier, David, 302

Drug Enforcement Administration (DEA), 533
Drugs. *See* Prescription drugs
Dual citizenship, 442
Dual federalism, 65
Due process
clause, 411, 451
rights, 423–424
states and, 77
Dumping, 502–503
Duncan, Mike, 190
Dupré, Ashley Alexander, 288
Duverger, Maurice, 241
Duverger's law, 183, 241
Dye, Thomas R., 65

E

Earmarks, 302, 303
Earned Income Tax Credit (EITC), 524
Economic interest groups, 150–154
Economic policy, 345, 490–491, 499–500
Economic sanctions, as hard power, 556–557
Economy
collapse of (2007–2008), 212, 489, 519
commerce clause and, 71
Constitution (U.S.) and, 15
federal control of, 76–77
free market system and, 93
global, 502
in Great Depression, 187
mercantilist, 93
occupations and, 139–140
presidency and, 42, 105
promotion of, 500–504
regulation of, 504–509
taxation and, 479
Edelman, Marian Wright, 523
Education. *See also* Schools
attainment in U.S., 137
for constitutional democracy, 8
decentralist position on, 78
federal role in, 531–533, 534
identity by, 136–137
loans for, 299
political culture and, 98
political ideology and, 103
rights to, 458–461
segregation in, 458
voting and, 224
Education Department, 358
Edwards, John, 95, 121, 153, 275
Egalitarian society, 100
Eighteenth Amendment, 44, 59, 155
Eighth Amendment, 58, 434, 533
Eisenhower, Dwight D., 230, 341, 351, 392, 444
Farewell Address by, 553
on "military-industrial complex," 173
Elastic clause, 307
Elderly people. *See* Older adults
Electioneering, 167–168, 169
Elections, 11. *See also* General elections; Primary elections
of 1800, 38, 243
of 1824, 186, 243
of 1828, 186
of 1840, 186
of 1876, 243
of 1888, 243
of 1916, 243
of 1932, 187
of 1936, 208–209
of 1948, 214
of 1960, 243
of 1964, 254
of 1976, 243
of 1988, 245, 254
in 1990s, 188
of 1992, 241, 245
of 2000, 3, 35, 106, 155, 184, 193, 207, 233, 234, 239, 243, 294, 474
of 2002, 104
of 2004, 3, 104, 147, 155, 207, 208, 225, 234, 244, 248, 253, 474
of 2006, 188
of 2008, 3, 99, 104–106, 108, 115, 117, 121, 127, 129, 132, 133, 135, 143, 147, 153, 155, 157, 162, 171, 188, 216, 232, 239, 248, 252, 258, 294, 302–303, 446
age of voters and, 140–142
congressional, 300–304
Constitution on, 31–32
electoral college and, 242–244
founders on, 351
improvement of, 268–271
interest groups and, 172–173
Internet and, 271
media and, 290–294
modernization of process, 207–208
money in, 259–268
nonpartisan, 180
political participation during, 219
popular opinion through, 96
realigning, 185–187
regularly scheduled, 240
regulation of, 174
rising costs in, 248
rules of, 240–244
turnout for, 222, 223–224, 227, 228
voting by religious affiliation, 132
voting rights and, 454–455
Electoral college, 21, 35, 242–244, 270–271, 330
Electoral Commission (1877), 243
Electorate. *See also* Voters
demographics of, 195
expansion of, 35–36
Electronic communications, 36–37
Elementary and Secondary Education Act (ESEA, 1965), 532
Elementary education, 532–533
Eleventh Amendment, 44, 58, 79, 80
Elites
framer distrust of, 34
E-mail, 279, 292, 301
EMILY's List, 133, 167, 169
Eminent domain, 422
Emissions
standards in California, 63
Employees
federal, 372
medical insurance for, 530–531
mobilization for elections, 167
Employment
Civil Rights Act (1964) and, 457–458
Employment Division v. Smith, 415
Endorsement test, 414
Enemy Alien Act (1798), 443
Energy (power)
Cheney and industry, 336–337
Energy Department, 550
England (Britain). *See* Great Britain
English language, political culture and, 94
Enron, 506, 507
Entitlement programs, 85, 374, 517
Enumerated powers, 305–307
Environment
hybrid cars and, 471
protection of, 507–509
states and, 86
Environmental impact statements, 508
Environmental interest groups, 157
Environmental movement, Carson, Rachel, and, 109
Environmental Protection Agency (EPA), 63, 358, 365, 483
Equal access, rights to, 456–458
Equal Employment Opportunity Act (1972), 82
Equal Employment Opportunity Commission (EEOC), 457
Equal opportunity, 91, 93–94, 99
Equal protection, 80, 451–454
Equal rights, 396, 440, 443–451. *See also* Civil rights
in Declaration of Independence, 13–14
of opportunity, 10, 440
status of, 464–465
Equal Rights Amendment (ERA), 46, 47, 447
Ervin, Sam, 228
Established religion, 29
Establishment clause, 413, 414
Ethics
congressional, 319–320
Ethics Committee (Senate), 320
Ethnicity. *See also* Minorities
identity by, 124–133
in population, 129
public opinion and, 214
as social division, 124
voting and, 225
Ethnocentrism, 115–116, 117
Ettinger, Amber Lee, 220
European Union (EU), 433, 453
Evangelicals, 115, 131–132
Everson v. Board of Education of Ewing Township, 414
E-voting, 233
Ewing v. California, 432
Exceptionalism, 118–119
Excise taxes, 492
Exclusionary rule, 430
Executive, 32, 329. *See also* Constitution (U.S.), Article II; Executive branch; Presidency; President
strong and weak, 339
Executive agencies, 36
Executive agreement, 332
Executive branch, 33, 331–334. *See also* Presidency; President
divided government and, 187–188
parties in, 192–193
Executive departments, 343
Executive Office of the President, 341–342, 376
Executive orders, 41
Executive powers, 331–334
Executive privilege, 41, 336–337

Expansion
  congressional power over, 306
  of United States, 72
  westward, 19
Expansion phase, of business cycle, 490–491
Expatriation, rights of, 442
Expenditures. *See* Spending
Expertise, in bureaucracy, 361
Ex post facto laws, 411
Expression, freedom of, 12
Express powers, 70
Extradition, between states, 74–75
Exurbs, 124

F

Facebook, 275, 292
Factions, 12, 148, 173–175. *See also* Political parties
Fair Housing Act (1968), 452, 458
  Amendments (1988), 452, 458
Fair Labor Standards Act (1938), 506–507
Fair trial procedures, 431–432
Families
  per capita income for, 138
  political culture and, 98
  public opinion and, 212–213
  structure of, 136
Farewell Address
  of Eisenhower, 173, 553
  of Reagan, 173
Farm organizations, 151
Federal bureaucracy, 357–379
Federal Bureau of Investigation (FBI), 107, 365, 533–535
Federal Communications Commission (FCC), 282–283, 364, 420
Federal Corrupt Practices Act (1925), 174
Federal courts, 75–79
Federal Election Campaign Act (FECA, 1971, 1974), 169, 174, 199, 259, 265
Federal Election Commission (FEC), 169, 199, 259
Federal Emergency Management Agency (FEMA), 357, 366
Federal Emergency Relief Administration (FERA), 521
Federal Flag Protection Act (1989), 43
Federal funds rate, 498
Federal general election grants, 260
Federal government, 66, 83–85. *See also* National government
  change in relations with states, 81
  control techniques of, 82–83
  division of powers in, 70
  division of power with states, 76–77
  grants by, 79, 80–82
Federalism, 12, 63–89
  alternatives to, 65–66
  constitutional structure of, 68–75
  courts and, 75–79
  judicial, 388
  politics of, 83–85
  regulatory, 79–83
  state primaries, caucuses, and, 271
Federalist, The, 23, 31
  No. 10, 6, 23, 138, 148
  No. 47, 32
  No. 51, 23, 31, 32, 131, 305
  No. 70, 329
  No. 78, 23, 38
Federalist Party, 185
Federalists, 23–25, 40
Federal mandates, 73
Federal Register, 160, 373, 482
Federal Reserve Board, 362–363, 499
Federal Reserve System ("the Fed"), 498–499
Federal Surplus Relief Corporation, 524
Federal Trade Commission (FTC), 506
Feingold, Russell, 168
Felt, W. Mark, 282
Feminine Mystique, The (Friedan), 46
Fenno, John, 280
Ferraro, Geraldine, 127
FICA (Federal Insurance Contribution Act) tax, 522
Fifteenth Amendment, 44, 59, 221, 443, 444, 447
Fifth Amendment, 57, 411, 419, 430, 432, 451
Fighting words, 416, 419
Filibuster, 312, 313
Filipino Americans, 450
Finances
  in campaigns, 249, 250, 259–268
  devolution revolution and, 85
  of education, 78
  independent expenditures and, 265
  of newspapers, 281
  satisfaction with, 497
Fireside chats, 340
First Amendment, 57, 411, 412, 413–422
  campaign financing and, 260
  on established religion, 29
  flag burning and, 43, 44
Fiscal policy, 489, 490, 491, 492–498
Fisher, Louis, 335
501(c) organizations, 171, 263–264
527 organizations, 147, 169, 170, 171, 263–264
Fixed terms, 240
Flag burning, 43, 44, 416
Flexible grants. *See* Block grants
Floor debate, over legislation, 322
Floor leaders, 310, 311
Florida, 193, 207, 233, 250, 464
Focus groups, 292–293
Focus on the Family, 131
Foley, Mark, 288
Food and Drug Administration (FDA), 358, 362, 527
Food stamps, 520, 525
Force, use of, 558
Ford, Gerald, 352
Ford, Harold, 127
Foreign aid, 555–556, 557
Foreign-born population, 129
Foreign Intelligence Surveillance Court, 429
Foreign policy, 327, 539–540, 539–560
  agenda for, 542–549
  bureaucracy of, 549–553
  in future, 559–560
  hard vs. soft power in, 542
  isolationalism vs. internationalism in, 541
  options in, 554–559
  preemption vs. provocation in, 542
  presidential influence over, 327
  realism vs. idealism in, 540–541
  secretary of state and, 550
  unilateralism vs. multilateralism in, 541
Foreign policy interest groups, 155–156, 157
Foreign Service, 551
44 Liquormart, Inc. v. Rhode Island, 419
Founders. *See* Constitution (U.S.); Framers
Fourteenth Amendment, 44, 58–59, 70, 411, 419, 443, 444, 447
  on age discrimination, 453
  due process and, 77
  equal protection clause, 80, 451, 454
  poll tax and, 456
  school segregation and, 458
Fourth Amendment, 57, 428, 429
Fox News, 287, 288
Framers, 31
  on administration of government, 358–359
  on presidency, 328–329
Franchise. *See* Voting
Frankfurter, Felix, 431
Franking privilege, 247, 301, 315
Franklin, Benjamin, 492
  at Constitutional Convention, 18, 19, 21–22
Frederick, Joseph, 409, 434
Freedom(s)
  of assembly, 421–422
  of expression, 12
  federalism and, 67
  in First Amendment, 412, 413–422
  meaning of, 96
  personal liberty and, 10
  of press, 285, 419–420
  of religion, 13, 131
  of speech, 416–417, 421
Freedom of Information Act (FOIA, 1966), 377, 420
Free exercise clause, 413, 414–415
Free market
  in former Soviet Union, 107
  libertarians on, 108
  system, 93
Free rider problem, 152, 158
Free Soil Party, 162
Free trade
  agreements, 153, 156
  promotion of, 545–546
Freneau, Philip, 280
Friedan, Betty, 46
Full faith and credit clause, 74
Fulton, Robert, 71
Fundamentalists, politics and, 131–132
Fundamental rights, 453–454
Fundraising, 199

G

Gallup Poll, 208
Gannett Company, 278, 282
Garfield, James, 369, 370
Garnett, Kevin, 126
Garza, Reynaldo G., 393
Gays and lesbians. *See* Homosexuals; Same-sex marriage
Gaza City, 545
GEAR-UP, 533
Gender, 133–135, 140, 457. *See also* Equal rights; Women
  in Congress, 311

discrimination by, 452
in judicial appointments, 391–392
politics and, 103, 133–135
voting by, 134, 195, 227
Gender gap, 133
General Accounting Office, 337
General Agreement on Tariffs and Trade (GATT), 503
General elections, 223, 246–247, 255–259
General search warrant, 427–428
Generational effects, 141–142
Geneva Conventions, 410
Genocide, 539
Geography, 117–119
George, Henry, 258
Georgia, 67
Gerry, Elbridge, 301
Gerrymandering, 128, 244, 301, 456
G.I. Bill (1944), 299, 532
Gibbons v. Ogden, 71
Ginsburg, Ruth Bader, 390, 393, 398, 414
Gitlow v. New York, 411
Giuliani, Rudolph, 249, 252, 421
Glass ceiling, 447
Global economy, 502
Global environment, 508
Global warming, 63, 67, 475
Goland, Michael, 265
Goldwater, Barry, 254, 255
Gonzales, Alberto, 349
Gonzales v. Raich, 72
Goods and services, 479, 480–483
Gore, Al, 35, 104, 121, 132, 162, 184, 231, 239, 243, 378
Inconvenient Truth, An, and, 475
labor unions and, 153
Government(s), 4–5, 533
under Articles of Confederation, 14–15
balanced, 17
divided, 34, 187–188
federalism and, 63
by the people, 4, 5
political ideology and attitudes toward war, 103–108
Government (U.S.), 44, 69–73
Constitutional Convention and, 15–22
Constitution as instrument of, 40–47
Government corporation, 361, 366
Governors
as presidents, 67–68
in South, 121
Graham, Lindsey, 327
Grand jury, 431
Grand Old Party (GOP), 186
Grant, Ulysses S., 174, 403
Grants, 79, 80–82
Grassroots political activity, 153
Gratz, Jennifer, 463, 464
Gratz v. Bollinger, 463, 464
"Gray lobby," 141
Great Britain, 18–19, 21, 154, 224, 308, 368, 433, 479, 495, 530
constitution of, 37
federalism in, 75
party system in, 241
prime minister in, 339
Great Depression, 101–102, 187, 499, 518–519
Great Society, 84, 525
Greece (ancient), democracy in, 6
Greenhouses gases, California laws on, 63
Green Party, 155, 162, 184
Greenpeace, 156
Greenspan, Alan, 363, 499, 505
Grenada, 558
Griffin, Mark, 366
Griswold, Estelle, 425
Griswold v. Connecticut, 424, 425
Grodzins, Morton, 65
Gross domestic product (GDP), 139, 491
Groupthink, White House staff and, 341
Grutter, Barbara, 464
Guantanamo Bay detainees, 410
Gun-Free School Zones Act, 72
Gutierrez, Carlos, 349

H

Habeas corpus, writs of, 388, 410
Hamas, 545
Hamdan v. Rumsfeld, 405, 410
Hamilton, Alexander, 16, 23, 25, 38, 185, 280, 329, 359, 384
Hamilton, Lee, 552
Hancock, John, 24
Hannity, Sean, 289
Harding, Warren G., 174, 352
Hard money, 199, 260, 261
Hard power, 542, 543, 556–557
Harlan, John Marshall, 419
Harris, Katherine, 207
Harrison, William Henry, 186
Hart, Melissa, 148
Hastie, William Henry, 393
Hatch, Orrin, 390
Hatch Act (1939), 372
"Hate speech," 418
Hatoyama, Kunio, 433
Hawaii, 448, 449
Hayes, George C. E., 460
Hayes, Rutherford B., 243
Head of state, 183
Head of the government, 183
Head Start, 93, 525, 532
Health, 504, 507, 530
Health and Human Services Department, 362
Health care, 362, 526–531
Health insurance, 67, 529
Health Insurance Association of America, 529
Health maintenance organization (HMO), 530
Heclo, Hugh, 477
Heightened scrutiny test, 452
Helium reserves, 483–484
Help America Vote Act (HAVA, 2002), 195
Henry, Patrick, 24
Heritage Foundation, 390, 476
Heterosexuals, marriage and, 454
High Commission for Refugees (U.N.), 555
Higher education. *See also* Universities and colleges
loans for, 299, 533
Higher Education Act (1998), 534
Highway aid
drinking age and, 83
Hindus, Muslims vs., 130
Hiring, for civil service, 370, 371–372
Hispanic Association for Corporate Responsibility, 506
Hispanics, 69, 94, 128, 136, 391
in elections, 115, 117
equal rights for, 447–448
in population, 123, 124, 125, 127–129
poverty among, 138
in U.S. Senate, 127
voting by, 129, 188, 225, 246
Hobbes, Thomas, 7
Hold, legislative, 312
Holmes, Oliver Wendell, 77, 418
Holocaust, 131
Homeland security, 83, 84–85
Homeland Security Department, 361, 533, 550
Homelessness, funding for, 517
Homosexuals, 135–136. *See also* Civil unions
restrictions on, 132
rights of, 426, 455
worldwide treatment of, 453
Honest Leadership and Open Government Act (2007), 163
Honeymoon period, 181
Hoover, Herbert, 352
Hopper, 321
Horse race, 293
Households, 136
House of Commons, 308
House of Lords, 308
House of Representatives, 19, 32. *See also* Congress (U.S.)
bills in, 306, 321
campaigns for, 245–247, 266
conference committees in, 314–315
election to, 223, 247
leadership of, 309–310
reapportionment in, 301
Rules Committee in, 310
safe and competitive seats in, 244
Senate differences from, 307
standing committees in, 313
term limits in, 300
Ways and Means Committee in, 314
women in, 133
Housing and Urban Development, Department of, 525
Housing assistance, 525
Huckabee, Mike, 91, 95, 106, 115, 249
Hughes, Charles Evans, 71, 383–384, 398
Humane Society of the United States, 156
Human rights
groups, 539
issues, 541
Human Rights Campaign, 135
Huntington, Samuel, 94
Huntley, Chet, 278
Hurricane Katrina, 100, 101, 350, 352, 357
Hussein, Saddam, 542, 548

I

Idealism, 96–99, 540–541
Identity, 121–142. *See also* National identity
Ideological groups, 154–155, 161
Ideology, 8–9, 91, 103–108, 289, 317, 392
"I Have a Dream" speech (King), 91, 446
Illegal immigrants. *See* Undocumented aliens
Illinois, 193

Illiteracy, voting rights and, 455
Immigration
 federal, state, and local responses to, 69
 policy toward, 469
 in population, 129
 protests against laws on, 161
 public assistance and, 526
 rights of immigrants and, 443
 U.S. political culture and, 94
Immigration and Naturalization Act, amendments to (1996), 443
Immigration and Naturalization Service, 550
Impeachment, 33, 41, 307, 334, 404
Implementation, 373, 480–483
Implied powers, 69, 76–77
Impoundment, 41, 337
Incentives, tax, 496
Income, 125, 129, 132, 135, 137–139, 195, 528
Income taxes, 492, 497
Inconvenient Truth, An (movie), 475
Incremental policy, 476
Incumbent, 246, 247, 301
 president as, 191
Indecent messages, 420
Independent, 155, 194–197, 198, 229
Independent agency, 36, 361, 364–366
Independent expenditures, 169, 170, 200
Independent regulatory commission, 36, 361, 362–364
India
 bureaucracy in, 368
 constitution in, 37
 death penalty in, 433
 federalism in, 75
 health care in, 530
 labor unions in, 154
 legislature in, 308
 multiparty system in, 241
 Pakistan conflicts with, 130
 parliamentary system in, 339
 policy process in, 479
 taxation in, 495
 voter turnout in, 224
Indian Removal Act (1830), 450
Indians. *See* Native Americans
Indictment, 431
Individual, 10, 102, 465
Individualism, as cultural value, 94–95
Indonesia, 130
Industrialization, 101
Industrial safety, 507
Infancy and Maternity Protection Act (1921), 524
Infant mortality, 530
Inflation, 138, 491
In forma pauperis, 395
Information, 164, 559
Information proceeding, 431
Inherent powers
 of national government, 70
 of president, 333–334
Initiative, 36
Inner circle, of president, 340
Insider information, 508
Insurance. *See* Social insurance
Integration, school, 460–461
Intelligence agencies, 365
Intelligence community, 551–552
Interest group(s), 147–171
 campaign efforts of, 263
 challenges from, 173–175
 impact on elections and legislation, 172–173
 independent expenditures by, 169, 170
 legislators and, 318
 PACs and, 164–167
 political mediators and, 284
 rise of, 34
 tax code used by, 171
Interest group pluralism, 150
Interest rates, 498
Interior Department, 358
Interlocking directorates, 506
Internal Revenue Code, Section 527 of, 147, 169
Internal Revenue Service (IRS), 107
International Brotherhood of Electrical Workers, 166
International Brotherhood of Teamsters, 152
International Crisis Group, 539
Internationalism, 541
International relations. *See* Foreign policy
International trade, 501–504
Internet, 37, 92, 219–220, 267–268, 271, 276, 279–280, 284, 292, 511, 559
 First Amendment protections and, 420–421
 interest groups and, 159–160, 172–173
 politics and, 275
Internment, of Japanese Americans, 337, 442, 449
Interstate commerce, 71–72, 80
Interstate Commerce Commission (ICC), 504, 505
Interstate compacts, 75
Interstate relationships, 74–75
Intervention, military, 558
Invasions, geography and, 117
Investigatory journalism, 282
Investment, by PACs, 165–167
Iowa, 122, 182, 250, 252
Iran, nuclear weapons and, 335, 544
Iraq War, 98, 216, 331, 375, 481, 544, 546–548, 549
Ireland, 94
Iron triangles, 477–478
Islamic groups, radical, 544
Isolationism, 541
Israel, 129, 157, 242, 545
Israel, Steve, 317
Issue activists, 194
Issue advocacy, 169, 262–263
Issue-attention cycle, 475
Issue framing, 289, 290
Issue networks, 163, 477, 478
Issue voting, 232
Italy, 242

J

Jackson, Andrew, 186, 243, 281, 369
James Madison Center for Free Speech, 160
Japan
 bureaucracy in, 368
 constitution of, 37
 death penalty in, 433
 democracy in, 22
 federalism in, 75
 health care in, 530
 legislature in, 308
 parliamentary system in, 339
 party system in, 241
 policy process in, 479
 proportional representation in, 242
 taxation in, 495
 treatment of sexual orientation in, 453
 voter turnout in, 224
Japanese Americans
 citizenship rights of, 442
 equal rights for, 449–450
 internment of, 337
Japanese and Korean Exclusion League, 449
Jay, John, 21, 23
Jefferson, Thomas, 5, 10, 31–32, 93, 136, 138, 243, 280, 330, 336, 351
 election of 1800 and, 38
 faction of, 185
 Supreme Court and, 39
Jeffersonian Republicans (Democrats), 38, 40
Jett, Dennis, 555
Jews, 131, 132
Jihad, 544
Jim Crow laws, 457
Job discrimination, 82
Jobs, 504, 505
Job-training programs, 524
John, Elton, 199
Johnson, Andrew, 42, 334, 404
Johnson, Gregory, 43, 44
Johnson, Lyndon B., 39, 102, 254, 319, 334, 341, 351, 352
 civil rights and, 445
 Great Society and, 525
 social policy of, 345
 Voting Rights Act and, 221
Johnson, Tim, 162
Joint Chiefs of Staff, 552–553
Joint committees, 312
Jolie, Angelina, 549
Jones, Bryan D., 477
Jones, Charles, 34
Jones, Paula, 288
Journalism, 281, 282, 293
Journalists, 289
Judges, 32
 politics of appointing, 388–389
 supremacy clause and, 20
Judicial activism, 392–393, 396
Judicial branch, 33, 193
Judicial circuits, 387
Judicial elections, 180
Judicial federalism, 388
Judicial philosophy, role of, 392–393
Judicial restraint, 392–393, 396
Judicial review, 33, 38–40, 384
Judicial Selection Monitoring Project, 390
Judiciary, 383–386, 391–394
 congressional power over, 307
 independence and accountability of, 401
 limits on, 402–404
 news reporting about, 295–296
 power of, 404–405
Judiciary Act (1789), 40, 41, 388
Jurisdiction
 of Supreme Court, 404
Jury, 432
Just compensation, 422–423
Justice, 96, 443–451

Justice Department, 34, 533, 550
Justiciable disputes, 385

K

Katrina. *See* Hurricane Katrina
Kean, Thomas, 552
Keillor, Garrison, 95
Kelo, Susette, 422
Kelo v. City of New London, 422
Kennedy, Anthony, 79, 393
Kennedy, Edward, 104, 299, 320
Kennedy, John F., 39, 102, 131, 132, 285, 341, 445
Kennedy v. Louisiana, 434
Kentucky, 258
Kerry, John, 132, 147, 169, 170, 208, 231, 240, 249, 260, 264, 291, 558. *See also* Swift Boat Veterans for Truth
Key, V. O., 186
Keynes, John Maynard, 500
Keynesian economics, 500
King, Martin Luther, Jr., 91, 131, 218, 421–422, 444–445, 446
Kingdon, John, 483
Klobuchara, Amy, 300
Knights of Labor, 152
Knowledge, in postindustrial society, 139–140
Korean Americans, 449, 450
Korematsu v. United States, 449–450
Kosovo, 539, 558
K Street Project, 167
Kuwait, 558

L

Labor, 102, 150–153, 161, 506–507. *See also* Workforce
Labor Department, 550
Laborers International Union of North America, 166
Labor injunctions, 507
Labor interest groups, 150–153
Labor unions, 150–153
  for federal employees, 372–373
  issue advocacy by, 169
Laissez-faire economics, 500
Lame duck, 240, 351
Land, as national monuments, 337
Landon, Alf, 208–209
Language, political culture and, 94
Laos, refugees from, 450
Latinos. *See* Hispanics
Latter-day Saints (LDS). *See* Mormons
Law(s). *See also* Legislation
  equal protection of, 451–454
  executing, 357–358
  process of bill becoming, 306, 320–322
Law clerks, 400–401
Lawrence v. Texas, 136, 425, 426, 453
Lay, Kenneth, 507
Lazarus, Emma, 115
Leadership
  of Congress, 308, 309–315
  of federal bureaucracy, 367–368
  of House of Representatives, 309–310, 310–312
  of interest groups, 159
  by president, 345
  of Senate, 310–313
Leadership Forum, 264
Leadership PACs, 165
League of Conservation Voters, 161
League of Nations, 547
League of Women Voters, 149
Learning Anytime Anywhere Partnership (LAAP), 533
Lebanon, 130
Legal Defense Fund, 39, 160, 458
Legal privileges, 411
Legionnaire's disease, 527
Legislation, 32, 172–173, 515
Legislative branch, 33, 192, 495–496. *See also* Congress (U.S.)
Legislative record, 321
Legislators, 127, 315–320. *See also* Congress (U.S.); House of Representatives; Senate
Legislature, 19, 305, 308. *See also* Congress (U.S.); State legislatures
Lemon v. Kurtzman, 414
Lethal injection, 433
Levin, Carl, 262
"Levin funds," 262
Lewinsky, Monica, 286, 288
Lewis, John L., 165
Libel, 416, 418
Liberalism, 92, 103–105, 289
Libertarianism, 107–108
Libertarian Party, 108, 184
Liberty(ies), 10, 13, 35, 131, 411
  as cultural value, 93
  protection of, 409
Licensing, of professionals, 154
Lieberman, Joseph, 132, 240, 318
Lifecycle effects, 141
Life expectancy, 528, 530
Limbaugh, Rush, 278, 289
Limited government, 31, 103
Lincoln, Abraham, 186, 216, 292, 351, 442
Lindh, John Walker, 442
Line item veto, 337
Lipset, Seymour Martin, 140
Literacy tests, 455
Literary Digest, poll by, 208–209, 210
Livingston, Robert, 71
Lobbying, 159, 162, 172, 299, 300, 318
Lobbying Disclosure Act (1995), 174
Lobbyists, 158, 174–175. *See also* Interest group(s)
Local areas
  elections in, 180
  government in, 66
  identity in, 121–122
  political parties in, 192, 193
Local government
  as government service provider, 481
Locke, Gary, 449
Locke, John, 7, 32
Logrolling, 317
Los Angeles, Watts riot in, 445
Los Angeles Times, bias and, 288
Louisiana Purchase, 369
Loving v. Virginia, 455
Loyal opposition, 181

M

Madison, James, 6, 16, 23, 31, 32, 39, 131, 138, 148, 305, 336
Mail, voting by, 232
Maine, 242, 270
Majority, 11
  tyranny of, 12
Majority leader
  in House of Representatives, 310
  in Senate, 311
Majority-minority districts, 456
Majority rule, 11–12, 95
Major parties, 184
Mallaby, Sebastian, 556
Management and Budget, Office of, 341, 342, 377
Mandates, 73, 348
Manifest destiny, 118
Manifest opinion, 210
Mapp v. Ohio, 430
Marble cake federalism, 65
Marbury, William, 39
Marbury v. Madison, 38–40, 193, 397
March on Washington (1963), 446
Margin of error, 209
Marijuana, 480
Markets, regulation of, 507
Markup, of bills, 321
Marriage, 136, 454, 526, 527. *See also* Same-sex marriage
Marshall, George C., 556
Marshall, John, 39–40, 72, 76, 96, 384, 397
Marshall, Thurgood, 39, 460
Marshall Plan, 556
Martin, Luther, 76–77
Martinez, Mel, 128
Martin Luther King, Jr. Day, 91
Marx, Karl, 107
Maryland, *McCulloch v. Maryland* and, 76–77
Massachusetts, 67, 135, 258, 453, 454
Mass media, 275–296. *See also* Press; Speech
  broadcast and cable communications, 420
  incumbents and, 301
  interest groups and, 159–160
  political culture and, 98
  public opinion and, 214, 285–286
Matching grant programs, for candidates, 260
Material benefits, 480
Mayhew, David, 34, 164
McCain, John, 3, 106, 115, 129, 132, 168, 202, 225, 226, 240, 249, 252, 256, 263, 275, 290, 320
McCain-Feingold bill. *See* Bipartisan Campaign Reform Act (BCRA, 2002)
McConnell v. FEC, 261, 267
McCulloch v. Maryland, 75, 76–77
McHenry, Patrick, 317
McKinley, William, 187
Means of production, 107
Means-tested entitlements, 517
Media. *See* Mass media
Media consultants, 292–293
Media Fund, 147, 264
Median age, 142
Medicaid, 362, 515, 523, 525
Medical care, 528–529
Medical savings accounts, 531
Medicare, 85, 362, 374–375, 515, 522, 523, 525, 526–527, 529

Medicine, 107
"Melting pot," 142–143
Men. *See also* Gender
  bachelor's degrees for, 448
Mendez, Bob, 129
Mentally retarded people, execution of, 434
Mercantile system, 93
Merit systems, 369, 372
Merit Systems Protection Board, 369–370
Merkel, Angela, 183
Mexican Americans, 127, 128
Mexico, 224, 241, 332, 368, 433, 453, 479, 530
  executive in, 339
  federalism in, 75
  labor unions in, 154
  legislature in, 308
  NAFTA and, 503–504
  taxation in, 495
  U.S. jobs exported to, 504
Michigan, 250, 463
Middle class, 140
Middle East, peace negotiations in, 545
Midterm elections, 223, 245
Migration
  by African Americans, 444
  of jobs, 504, 505
  to suburbs, 122
Military, 83, 135, 335, 553, 554, 558, 559. *See also* Defense Department; Intelligence community
Military Commissions Act (2006), 405, 410
Military-industrial complex, 173, 553
Military intervention, 558
Militia, state, 71
Miller, Judith, 419–420
Miller v. California, 419
"Million Youth March," 421
Minimum wage, 154, 524
Minorities, 32, 279, 363, 448, 506. *See also* Ethnicity
  in cabinet, 364
  in Congress, 311
  on courts, 391–392, 393
  as lobbyists, 163
  voting by, 225
Minority leaders
  in House of Representatives, 310
  in Senate, 311
Minor parties, 183–184, 243, 481
Minors, execution of, 434
Miranda, Ernesto, 430
Miranda v. Arizona, 430–431
Mississippi, 221
Mitchell, Andrea, 499
Mixed caucus, 181
Mixed race individuals, 45
Mobility (social), 99
Mob rule, 6
Moderate voters, 109–110
Modern Language Association, 153
Mondale, Walter, 290
Monetary policy, 490, 491, 498–500
Money, 259–268, 306
Monopoly, 151, 505, 511
Montesquieu, Charles de, 7, 32
Moot case, 385
Morale building, by president, 344–345
Mormons, 115, 131, 132
Morning Edition (radio program), 278
Morrill Land-Grant Colleges Act (1862), 531–532
Morse, Deborah, 409
Morse v. Frederick, 409
Mortgages, economy and, 519
Motor Voter Act (1993), 222
Mott, Lucretia, 134
MoveOn, 147, 169, 171, 276
Mr. Smith Goes to Washington (movie), 313
Muhammad, Khallid Abdul, 421
Mullen, Mike, 553
Multilateralism, 541
Multinational corporations, 150
Multiparty systems, 183, 241
Multiracial individuals, 45
Murdoch, Elisabeth, 283
Murdoch, Rupert, 282, 283
Murray, Patty, 311
Murrow, Edward R., 278
Muslims, 130, 544
Mutual assured destruction (MAD), 542
MySpace, 275

N

Nabrit, James, Jr., 460
Nader, Ralph, 155, 162, 208, 243, 255, 257, 474
Name recognition, 247
NASDAQ, 507
National Aeronautics and Space Administration (NASA), 365, 366
National Association for the Advancement of Colored People (NAACP), 39, 160, 404
National Association of Counties, 156
National Association of Government Employees, 373
National Association of Home Builders, 154, 166
National Association of Manufacturers, 150
National Association of Realtors, 150, 166, 169
National Auto Dealers Association, 166
National Beer Wholesalers Association, 166
National chair, 190
National Colored Committee of the Good Neighbor League, 189
National committee, 190
National debt, 493, 499
National Defense Education Act (1958), 532
National Economic Council, 341
National Education Association (NEA), 153, 156–157, 265
National Enquirer, 289
National Federation of Federal Employees, 373
National Federation of Independent Business, 150
National government, 83. *See also* Federal government; Government (U.S.)
  Bill of Rights and, 411
  constitutional restraints on, 74
  decentralist and centralist positions on, 77–78
  powers delegated to, 70
National Governors Association, 156
National Guard, 71
National identity, 116, 117–119
National Institutes of Health, 358, 362
Nationalism, 96–97, 212
National Journal, 317
National Labor Relations Act. *See* Wagner Act (1935)
National League of Cities, 156
National monument, federal land as, 337
National Organization for Women (NOW), 46, 160
National origin
  discrimination and, 457
  legal classification by, 452
National party convention, 190, 253–255
National presidential primary, 268–269
National Public Radio (NPR), 278, 282
National Railroad Passenger Corporation. *See* Amtrak
National Republican Campaign Committee (NRCC), 191
National Republican Party, 186
National Republican Senatorial Committee (NRSC), 191
National Rifle Association (NRA), 150, 154, 169, 171, 212, 265
National Right to Life PAC, 169
National security, 104, 336, 345, 428, 429, 471
National security adviser, 342, 550
National Security Agency (NSA), 327, 365
National Security Council, 341, 550
National supremacy article, 70
National supremacy doctrine, 76–77
National tide, 246
National Treasury Employees Union, 372, 373
National Voter Registration Act (1993). *See* Motor Voter Act (1993)
Native Americans, 124–125, 415, 450–451
Nativism, 117
NATO, 558
Naturalization, 441–442
Naturalization Act (1906), 448
Natural law, 31
Natural monopolies, 505
Natural resources, 118
Natural rights, 93, 439
Nebraska, 193, 242, 270
Necessary and proper clause, 69–70, 307
Needy, aid to, 517
Negative advertising, 293
Negative campaigning, 147, 231
Networks, television, 281–282
Net worth, 126
Neustadt, Richard, 346
New American Alliance, 506
New Deal, 101–102, 105, 521–524
New Democratic Coalition, 189
New Democrats, 104
New federalism, 65
New Hampshire, 250
New Jersey, 19
New Jersey Plan, 20
New Mexico, 448
New Right, 106
News, 284, 287
  programs, 276
  source credibility, 287
News media, 276, 280–283, 294–296
Newspapers, 278–279, 281
New York City, 419
New York Stock Exchange, 507
New York Times, 279, 419–420

New York Times v. Sullivan, 418
New York Tribune, 281
Nigeria, 130, 154, 224, 241, 453, 479, 530
  bureaucracy in, 368
  democracy in, 22
  executive in, 339
  legislature in, 308
9/11 Commission report, 552
Nineteenth Amendment, 44, 59, 187, 447, 524
Ninth Amendment, 58
Nixon, Richard, 42, 334, 335, 336, 341, 352. *See also* Watergate scandal
No Child Left Behind Act (2002), 84, 85, 105, 445, 532
Nominations, 115, 181–182, 248–253, 268–270
Nondecision, 472
Nongovernmental organization (NGO), 156
Non-Hispanic whites, 125
Nonpartisan elections, 180
Non-Partisan Political League, 165
Nonpreferentialist test, 414
Nonprotected speech, 417–419
Nonviolence
  protest, 218
  resistance, 444–445
Normal trade relations, 546
North (industrialized world), 116
North (U.S.), 21, 119
North American Free Trade Agreement (NAFTA), 153, 503–504
North American Review, 258
Northern Ireland, 130
North Korea, 107
Northwest Ordinance (1785), 531
Norway, 557
Nuclear weapons, 542, 543, 544

O

Obama, Barack, 3, 92, 104, 106, 108, 115, 121, 126, 127, 131, 132, 133, 157, 200, 202, 220, 229, 230, 240, 249, 253, 256, 267–268, 270, 275, 291, 330, 446
  Hispanics and, 128, 129
  labor union support and, 153
  political participation and, 219
  as uniter, 305
Objective journalism, 281
Obscenity, 416, 418–419, 420
Occupation(s)
  politics and, 139–140
Occupational health, 507
Occupational Safety and Health Administration (OSHA), 358
Oceans, national identity and, 117
O'Connor, Sandra Day, 65, 383, 393, 399, 414, 453
O'Donnell, Rosie, 135
Office of Education, 532
Office of Faith-Based and Community Initiatives, 341
Office of Homeland Security, 337
Office of Management and Budget (OMB), 341, 342, 377, 494
Office of Personnel Management (OPM), 369, 373
Office of War Information, 559
Offshoring, 504
Off-year elections, 223
Ogden, Aaron, 71
Ohio, 207, 252
Older adults, 140–141, 515, 521–522. *See also* Age
  demography of, 140–141
  patriotism among, 97
Oligopoly, 505
Open-ended questions, in polls, 209
Open primary, 181
Open rule, 310
Open seats, 247
Open shop, 152
Opinion of the court, 398–399
Opportunity, equality of, 10, 440
Optimism, as value, 96–99
Oral argument, 397
Oregon, 233, 270
O'Reilly, Bill, 288, 289
Organization for Economic Cooperation and Development, 557
Originalist views, 46
Original jurisdiction, 40, 386
Override, of veto, 322
Oversight, of bureaucracy, 377

P

Pacific Islanders, in population, 125
PACs. *See* Political action committees (PACs)
Paige, Rod, 157
Pakistan, India and, 130
Palestine, 129, 545
Palestinian Authority, 545
Palin, Sarah, 3, 133, 254, 330
Panama, 558
Pardon power, 333
Parents Involved in Community Schools, 439
Parks, Rosa, 218, 444, 445, 465
Parliament (England), 308
Parliamentary system, 183, 329
Partial-Birth Abortion Ban Act (2007), 403
Partial birth abortions, 426
Partial preemption, 83
Participation, 207–208, 218–220
Partisan gerrymandering, 244
Partisanship, 34, 190, 192–193, 197–198, 287, 289
Part-time citizens, 218
Party caucus
  in House of Representatives, 309
Party conference, in House of Representatives, 309
Party conventions, 181
Party identification, 194–197, 229
Party registration, 193–194
Party regulars, 194
Party systems, 183
Patent and Trademark Office, 504
Paterson, David A., 126
Patriotism, 96–99, 97
Patronage, 180, 187, 369
Paul, Ron, 92, 108, 220, 226, 249
Paulson, Henry M., Jr., 489
Payroll taxes, 492, 522, 523, 525
PBS television, 366
Peace Corps, 549
Peace groups, 174
Peacekeeping, by U.N., 555, 560
Peer pressure, 286
Pell grants, 533
Pelosi, Nancy, 165, 309, 319
Penalties, for violating public rules, 479–480
Pendleton Act (1883), 369
Penny press, 281
Pentagon, 552
People for the American Way, 390
Per capita incomes, 138
Percy, Charles, 265
Perdue, Beverly, 121, 311
Peremptory challenges, 432
Permissive federalism, 65
Perot, Ross, 183–184, 241
Perry, Bob J., 147
Persian Gulf War, 555
Personal liberty, 10
Personal Responsibility and Work Opportunity Reconciliation Act (1996), 81, 525
Persuasion, 346
Petitions, nomination by, 255
Petit jury, 432
Petraeus, David, 376
Pew Poll, 208
Peyote, for ceremonies, 415
Pharmaceutical Manufacturers Association, 531
Philippines, immigrants from, 450
Pickens, T. Boone, 99
Pickering, Charles W., 391
Pilgrims, 13
Plain statement, by Congress, 80
Plaintiff, 385
Planned Parenthood, 212, 425
Planned Parenthood v. Casey, 404, 425
Platforms, party, 191–192, 254
Plea bargain, 385, 431
Plessy v. Ferguson, 457, 458
Pluralism, 148, 150, 212
Plurality, 11, 181
Pocket veto, 322, 332–333
Polar ice caps, 508
Police
  searches by, 427
Policy. *See* Political policy; Public policy; Social policy
Policy agenda, 473–475
Policy makers, 289, 474, 475
Policy offices, 341
Political action committees (PACs), 161, 164–167, 261, 266–267
Political campaigns, 99, 186, 232
Political capital, 349
Political conventions. *See* Conventions
Political culture, 91, 92, 94, 98–99, 121–122
Political equality, 93
Political identity, in South, 119
Political ideology, 103–108, 109–111
Political institutions, 294–296
Political offices, 341
Political parties, 34, 126, 127–128, 179, 180, 183, 188–203, 284, 317, 318–319, 394. *See also* Factions; Interest group(s); specific parties
  functions of, 179–181
  history of, 185–188
  in judicial appointments, 391–392
  minor, 183–184
  new parties, 162
  platforms of, 191–192, 254
  two-party vs. multi-party systems, 241
Political policy, party roles in, 180–181

Political predispositions, 116
Political science, use of term, 4
Political socialization, 116, 212–214, 286
Political structures, independent, 12
Political values, 101–102
Politicians, 4–5, 288
Politics, 470. *See also* Elections
  African Americans in, 126
  of constitutional amendments, 46–47
  Constitutional Convention and, 17
  of constitutional ratification, 24–25
  democracy and, 11–12
  development of views on, 212–214
  electoral college and, 243–244
  of federal grants, 81–82
  of federalism, 83–85
  fundamentalists and, 131–132
  gays and lesbians in, 135–136
  media and, 275
  mediated, 283–290
  policy and, 470
  population characteristics and, 124–142
  religion and, 129–133
  of social policy, 535
  of taxing and spending, 496–498
  use of term, 4
  voter awareness of, 216–218
Polls, public opinion, 208–212, 293
Poll tax, 456
Pollution, 63, 504, 509, 547
Poll workers, 233
Poor people, 519, 524. *See also* Poverty
Poor People's Campaign, 523
Popular consent, 10
Popular opinion, 95–96
Popular sovereignty, 95
Popular vote, 242, 243
Population
  characteristics of, 124–142
  geography and, 117–118
  location of, 121–124
"Pork." *See* Earmarks
Pornography, 418–419
Postal Service, 366
Postindustrial society, 139–140
Poverty, 99, 102, 124, 139
  classification by, 452
  politics and, 138–139
Poverty level, 524
Poverty line, 138
Prayer, school, 29, 30, 32
Precedent, 387, 399, 402–403
Preemption, 77, 83, 542
Preferred position doctrine, 417
Prepaid health plans, 530
Prescription drugs, 515, 528
Presidency, 41–42. *See also* Executive branch
  constitutional role of, 328–334
  controversial powers of, 335–338
  influence of, 327
  management of, 340–344
  modern, 340
  running for office of, 330
  structure and powers of, 328–334
  Washington and, 339–340
President, 33. *See also* Term limits; specific presidents
  as agenda setter, 345
  appointments by, 349
  approval rating of, 347, 350
  budget and spending power of, 337–338
  bureaucracy and, 359, 375
  cabinet of, 342–343
  campaign for, 248–259
  centralist, 78
  as commander in chief, 331
  Congress and, 319, 346–350
  Constitution on, 32
  decentralist, 77–78
  as diplomat in chief, 331–332
  evolution of power of, 338–340
  Executive Office of, 341–342
  executive orders and, 337
  executive privilege and, 336–337
  former governors as, 67–68
  gender and vote for (2004), 134
  impeachment of, 41, 334
  influence of, 344, 348–350
  job of, 344–346
  judges and, 389–390, 403–404
  legislation approved by, 322
  as manager in chief, 332
  nomination of, 248–253
  as persuader, 346
  petition for nominating, 255
  political party of, 192–193
  popular and congressional elections and, 245
  power of, 37, 331–334, 338
  qualifications for, 330
  religion of, 132
  succession to, 334
  term limits for, 351
  voting for, by party, 198
  war powers of, 335
Presidential debates, 255–257
Presidential elections, 223, 268–269. *See also* Elections
  campaign during, 248–253
  caucuses in, 252
  "firsts" in election of 2008, 115
  frequency of, 240
  general election and, 255–259
  national party convention and, 253–255
  regional primaries, 269
Presidential support score, 348
Presidential ticket, 330
President pro tempore, 312
President's Council on Service and Civic Participation, 337
Press. *See also* Mass media
  freedom of, 285, 419–420
Press conferences, presidential, 295
Press shield laws, 420
Priest, Dana, 282
Primary elections, 182, 223
  congressional, 245–246
  direct, 35
  direct primary, 181
  open and closed, 181–182
  presidential, 249–252, 268–269
  regional, 269
  state, 271
  in 2008 campaign, 190
  voting in, 36, 222, 269
  white primary, 455
Prime minister, in England, 329, 339
Prime rate, 498
Primogeniture, 138
Printz v. United States, 74
Prior restraint, 417
Privacy
  due process and, 424
  rights to, 424–427
  sodomy laws and, 136
Private property, 99
Procedural due process, 423
Professional associations, 153–154
Professionalism
  in bureaucracy, 368
Progress for America, 264
Progressive Era, 187
Progressive tax, 493
Prohibition Amendment, 44
Prohibition Party, 162
Project grants, 80, 81
Proletariat, 140
Property, ownership of, 8
Property rights, 422–423
Proportionality system, 202
Proportional representation, 183, 241, 242, 249
Proposition 187 (California), 448
Proposition 209 (California), 463–464
Prosecution, in federal courts, 386
Prosecutor, 385
Prospective issue voting, 231
Protected speech, 417
Protectionism, 501, 504, 505
Protestantism, 132
Protests, 12, 161, 218, 285, 328
Provocation, 542
Pryor, William, 392
Public assistance, 519–520, 521
Public choice, 158
Public defender system, 386
Public diplomacy, 559
Public education. *See* Education
Public Health Service (PHS), 527
Public Interest Research Groups (PIRGs), 155, 474
Publicity, by interest groups, 159–160
Public opinion, 207–218, 289–290
  on business and labor, 102
  on gay marriage, 211
  media and, 285–286
  polarization of, 210
  politics and, 143
  polls of, 208–212, 293
  public policy and, 216
  after September 11, 2001, terrorist attacks, 214, 215
  stability and change in, 214–216
  Supreme Court and, 404–405
Public policy, 469–484, 470. *See also* Social policy
  liberal commitment to, 103–104
  political ideology and, 111
  president and, 345
  public opinion and, 216
Public schools. *See* Schools
Public sector interest groups, 156–157
Public use, of land, 422
Publius (pseud.), 23
Puerto Ricans, 127, 128
Punctuating policy, 476–477
Punishment, death penalty as, 432–434

Pure Independents, 229
Puritans, 13
Putnam, Robert D., 214

Q

Questioning, in polls, 209
"Quid pro quo" sexual harassment, 447
Quorum, 309

R

Race, 103, 311, 391–392, 452, 456, 457
  equal opportunity for, 91
  identity by, 124–133
  in university admissions, 383
  voting and, 195, 225, 227
Racial equality, 443–446
Racial gerrymandering, 456
Racial segregation, 444
Radio, 257–258, 278, 281
Railroads, deregulation of, 509
Rally points, 349
Ramsay, Ansil, 154
Random sample, 128, 208–209
Rankin, Jane, 304
Ranney, Austin, 228
Ratification, 30
  of Amendments, 44–47
  of Constitution, 22–25
  of treaties, 21
Rational basis test, 451
Reagan, Ronald, 46, 173, 254, 285, 290, 314, 334, 341, 348, 352, 391, 392, 425
  civil rights and, 445
  and new federalism, 65
  as persuader, 346
Realigning elections, 185–187
Realignment, partisan, 197–198
Realism, in foreign policy, 540–541
Reapportionment, 301
Recall elections, 36
Recess appointments, 332, 391
Recession, 491
Recovery, 491
Redistributive policy, 471
Redistricting, 301
Referendum, 36
Referral, of bills, 321
Reform Party, 184
Region
  differences among, 119–121
  voting by, 195
Regional primaries, 269
Regressive tax, 493
Regulation, 82–83, 107–108, 479, 490
  administrative, 373–374
  bureaucratic self-regulation and, 377–378
  of campaign finance, 201
  of civil service, 370, 372
  of economy, 504–509
  environmental, 507–509
  of media, 283
Regulatory agencies, 505
Regulatory commissions, 107, 361, 362, 364–365
Regulatory federalism, 79–83
Regulatory taking, 422
Rehabilitation Act (1973), 452
Rehnquist, William H., 65, 80, 383, 400, 403, 404, 433
Reid, Harry, 311
Reid, Whitelaw, 281
Reinforcing cleavages, 116
Relief, 556
Religion, 103, 115, 129–133, 130, 190, 415, 457
  established, 29, 414
  freedom of, 13, 412, 413
  political culture and, 98, 214
  voting by, 132, 133, 195
Religious Freedom Restoration Act (RFRA, 1993), 415
Religious Right, 189
Remand, 402
Reno v. American Civil Liberties Union, 420
Reorganization Act (1986), 553
Representation, 12, 19–20, 183, 242
Representative democracy, 7
Representatives, 17, 316
Republic, 7
Republican government, 17
Republican Governors Association, 264
Republican National Committee (RNC), 190
Republican Party, 3, 78, 106, 119, 120, 121, 126, 132, 167, 171, 185, 186–187, 188, 191, 192, 194–197, 202–203, 245, 394. *See also* Elections; Political ideology
Republicans for Clean Air, 169, 262, 263
Resegregation, 461
Reservations, for Native Americans, 450
Reserve powers, 73
Respect for common person, 95
Responsible party system, 180
Restraint, judicial, 392–393, 396
Restrictive covenants, 458
Retrospective issue voting, 231
Revenue
  committees, 314
  sources of, 492–494
Revenue sharing, 80
Reverse discrimination, 461
Revolutionary War, 13–15
Revolving door, 163
Rice, Condoleezza, 342, 349, 542
Rich, Marc, 333
Richardson, Bill, 115, 128
Riders, legislative, 322
Rights. *See also* African Americans; Amendments; Civil rights; Equal rights
  of accused, 431
  of aliens, 443
  of assembly and protest, 12
  of citizenship, 440–443
  civil, 411
  in Constitution, 23, 410–411
  of criminal suspects, 427–432
  due process, 423–424
  to education, 458–461
  to equal access, 456–458
  of expatriation, 442
  of federal vs. state governments, 77–78
  fundamental, 453–454
  of individual, 10
  meaning of, 96
  of minorities, 32
  natural, 93, 439
  necessary and proper clause and, 69–70
  privacy, 424–426
  property, 422–423
  to remain silent, 430
  sexual orientation and, 426–427
  to trial, 431–432
  of women, 446–447
  to writ of habeas corpus, 410
Right to Life party, 184
Risk, protection against, 479
Robber barons, 101
Roberts, John G., Jr., 79, 383, 390, 392
Robertson, Pat, 106, 131
Rockefeller, Nelson, 255
Roe v. Wade, 402, 403, 404, 425–426. *See also* Abortion
Rogers, Will, 95
Romer v. Evans, 426–427, 453
Romney, George, 291
Romney, Mitt, 99, 106, 115, 249
Roosevelt, Franklin D., 126, 208–209, 281, 340, 341, 346, 351, 392, 521, 559
  Democratic Party and, 189
  as modern president, 340
  New Deal and, 102, 187
  Supreme Court and, 403–404
Roosevelt, Theodore, 151, 351
Rose, Charlie, 553
Rove, Karl, 147
Rudman, Warren, 172
Rugged individualism, 516
Rule of four, 396
Rule of law, as cultural value, 96
Rules, 479
  bureaucratic, 360, 373
  for public policy, 482
  in Senate, 312
Rules committees, 310, 313–314, 321
Rumsfeld, Donald, 375
Runoff elections, 261, 270
Rwanda genocide, 539

S

SADD (Students Against Destructive Decisions), 213
Safe seat, 244, 301
Safety, 504, 507
St. Paul, Minnesota, 417
Salazar, Ken, 127, 129
Sales tax, 496
Salience, of public opinion, 210–211
Same-sex marriage, 86, 105, 108, 135, 211, 426, 453, 454, 455
Sampling, 208–209
  by Census Bureau, 128, 129
Sanctions, economic, 556–557
Sandburg, Carl, 95
Sanders, Bernie, 107
San Francisco, Asian exclusion in, 449
Santa Fe Independent School District v. Doe, 29, 32, 47
SARS, 527
Scalia, Antonin, 47, 65, 79, 398, 414
Scandinavia, foreign aid from, 557
Schenck v. United States, 418
Schlafly, Phyllis, 47
School lunch program, 524
School prayer, 29, 30, 32, 132

Schools, 85, 98, 213–214, 532–533. *See also* Education
  racial and ethnic composition of, 439, 459
  segregation of, 402, 444, 458
School voucher programs, 414
Schwarzenegger, Arnold, 6
Search engines, 275
Searches and seizures, 427–431, 429
Search warrant, 427
Seattle, 439, 461
Second Amendment, 57
Secondary education, 532–533
Secretary of state
  of U.S., 550
Secret ballot, 222, 258
Section 501(c) organizations, 171, 263–264
Section 527 organizations, 147, 169, 170, 171, 263–264
Securities and Exchange Commission (SEC), 364, 507
Securities Exchange Act (1934), 507
Security. *See* National security
Security Council (U.N.), 555
Segregation, 402, 444, 458–459, 460–461
Select committees, 312
Selective exposure, 214, 286
Selective incorporation, 412–413
Selective perception, 286
Self-determination, 10
Self-incrimination, 430–431
Senate, 19, 32, 133, 245, 310–315. *See also* Congress (U.S.)
  advice and consent by, 308, 390–391
  bills in, 306, 321
  cabinet nominations and, 33
  campaigns for, 247–248
  direct election to, 36, 147, 187, 300
  election to, 223, 239–240
  Hispanics in, 128–129
  House of Representatives differences from, 307
  Judiciary Committee in, 390, 391
  race for (2008), 246
  term limits in, 300
Senatorial courtesy, 389–390
Seneca Falls Women's Rights Convention (1848), 447
Senior Executive Service, 367–368
Seniority rule, 314
Separate but equal doctrine, 403, 458–459
Separation of powers, 12, 31, 32, 329
September 11, 2001, terrorist attacks, 97, 104, 188, 214, 215, 277, 345, 424, 546–548
Service Employees International Union (SEIU), 152, 263
Servicemen's Readjustment Act (1944). *See* G.I. Bill (1944)
Seventeenth Amendment, 36, 44, 59, 187
Seventh Amendment, 58
Sex discrimination, 452
Sexual harassment, 447
Sexual orientation, 135–136, 426–427, 453
Shaheen, Jeanne, 311
Shared identity, religion as, 132
Shaw v. Reno, 456
Shays, Daniel, 15
Shays' Rebellion, 15
Sherman, John, 151
Sherman Antitrust Act (1890), 151, 505
Shi'ite-Sunni conflict, 130
Signing statements, 338
Silent Spring (Carson), 109
Simpson, Alan, 172
Single-issue interest groups, 154–155, 173–174
Single-issue parties, 184
Single-member district (SMD), 241–242
Single-payer system, 529
Sixteenth Amendment, 44, 59
Sixth Amendment, 57, 432
60 Minutes (television program), 282
Slatecard, 220
Slaughterhouse Cases, 442
Slavery, 21, 117, 119
Slogans, campaign, 292
Small Business Administration (SBA), 150, 365
Smith, Al, 132
Smith v. Allwright, 455
Social capital, 92
Social class, 140
Social conservatives, 106
Social controls, 106
Social insurance, 520, 521
Socialism, 107
Social movement, 149–150
Social networking sites, 275, 279–280
Social policy, 345, 515–535
Social Security, 85, 374–375, 472, 473, 495, 521, 522
Social Security Act (1935), 518–519, 524
Social Security Administration (SSA), 358
Socioeconomic status (SES), 140
Sodomy, privacy laws and, 136
Soft money, 167–168, 199, 260, 261–262, 262–263
Soft power, 542, 543, 554–556
Solicitor general, 386, 401–402
Solid South, 119, 187
Somalia, 555
Soros, George, 99, 265
Souter, David H., 414
South (agrarian, nonindustrialized world), 116
South (U.S.), 21, 119–121, 126, 187, 455
South Africa, 156, 433
South America, 556
South Carolina, 119
South Dakota, 240
Southern Christian Leadership Conference (SCLC), 446
Southwest Airlines, 510
Sovereign immunity, of states, 79
Soviet Union, 107, 549
Speaker of the House, 309, 310
Special committees, 312
Special elections, 223
Special interests, 147, 149, 173
Speech, freedom of, 416–419, 421
Spending, 72–73, 84, 169, 170, 199–200, 201, 337–338, 373, 374, 478, 494, 496–498, 532. *See also* Campaign contributions; Finances
  caps on health care, 531
  earmarks and, 302
  on entitlement programs, 374
  527 committees by, 171
  on health care, 528
  on Social Security and Medicare, 522
Spitzer, Eliot, 86, 288
Spoils system, 180, 369
Sputnik, 532
Sri Lanka, 130
Stagflation, 491
Staggered terms of office, 240
Standing committees, 312, 313
Stanton, Elizabeth Cady, 134, 447
Stare decisis, 403
State (nation), church and, 13
State(s), 44, 69, 74–75, 76, 77, 80, 81, 86, 121–122, 127, 239, 258, 271, 384, 388, 411–413, 442, 463–464. *See also* Federalism
  federal government and, 63, 76–77, 81
  interstate privileges and immunities in, 74
  political parties in, 192, 193
  powers of, 70, 73
  sovereign immunity of, 79
State chair, 192
State Children's Health Insurance Program (SCHIP), 333, 362
State Department, 550–551
State governors. *See* Governors
State legislatures, 17
State of the Union Address, 330, 334
States' rights, 77–78, 126
Statism, 10
Steamboat Inspection Service, 504
Stenberg v. Carhart, 426
Stern, Howard, 420
Stevens, John Paul, 79, 337, 396–397, 414
Stewart, Jon, 98, 291
Stewart, Martha, 385, 508
Stewart, Potter, 418
Stock exchanges, 507
Stock market
  crash of (1929), 507
  in Great Depression, 102
Stop and frisk exception, 428
Strict scrutiny test, 451–452
Student loans, 299
Subsidies
  agricultural, 501
Substantive due process, 423–424
Suburbs, 122, 123
Succession, presidential, 334
Sudan, 130, 539, 555
Sudan Accountability and Divestment Act (2007), 338
Suffrage, 92, 447. *See also* Voting rights
Sun Belt, 121
Superdelegates, Democratic, 250
Supplemental Security Income (SSI), 523, 525
Supply-side economics, 500
Supremacy clause, 20
Supreme Court (U.S.), 21, 33, 38–40, 39, 76, 77, 80, 383–405, 386, 388, 389, 402, 462
  amicus curiae briefs and, 160, 397, 400, 401–402
  Article III on, 30
  centralist and decentralist positions, 78
  Congress and, 79
  decisions of, 399–402
  precedent and, 402–403
  supremacy clause and, 20
  women on, 391

Supreme law of the land, Constitution as, 40
Surge, in Iraq, 548
Surgeon general, 527
Suspect classification, 452
Sweden, 557
Swift Boat Veterans for Truth, 147, 169, 170, 231, 264, 291
Swing votes, 226, 270
Symbolic speech, 416

T

Take care clause, 333
Taliban, 558
Tariffs, 493, 501
Taxation, 106, 309, 473, 479, 489, 492–494, 495, 496, 529
  government power over, 70, 72–73
  politics of, 496–498
Tax code, 171
Teachers, 153, 156–157, 533
Teach for America, 85
Teamsters Union, 166
Teapot Dome scandal, 174, 259
Technology, 36–37, 292, 529
  unfair copying of, 501–502
Telecommunications, deregulation of, 510–511
Telecommunications Act (1996), 511
Television, 36, 254, 257–258, 276–277, 282–283, 290
Temporary Assistance for Needy Families (TANF), 525
Tenth Amendment, 58, 78, 80
Term limits, 240, 351
  in Congress, 300
  for president, 339–340, 350
Terrorism, 35, 84, 86, 97, 104, 277, 429, 533–535, 544. *See also* War on terrorism
Terry v. Ohio, 428
Texas, 252, 448, 464
Texas v. Johnson, 43
Theocracy, 13
Theory of deterrence, 542
Think tank, 475, 476
Third Amendment, 57
"Third house," 314
Third parties, 183–184, 243, 481
Thirteenth Amendment, 44, 58, 443, 444
Thomas, Clarence, 65, 79, 282, 390, 393, 395, 398, 414
Thompson, Fred, 248
Three-fifths compromise, 21
Three-strikes law, 432, 533
Thune, John, 162
Tiananmen Square protests, 218
Tilden, Samuel, 243
Times-Mirror, 282
Tinker v. Des Moines, 409
Title II, of Civil Rights Act (1964), 457
Title VI, of Civil Rights Act (1964), 82, 459
Title VII, of Civil Rights Act (1964), 457
Title IX (Education Amendment of 1972), 452
Tocqueville, Alexis de, 118
Toner, Michael, 200
Torture, in Abu Ghrabi prison, 216
Total preemption, 83
Totenberg, Nina, 282
Toxic shock syndrome, 527
Trade, 71–72, 501–504. *See also* Free trade
Trade associations, 150
Trade deficit, 501
"Trail of Tears," 450
Transportation, 509–510
Treasury Department, 489, 550
Treaties, 21, 331–332
Trials, 431–432. *See also* Courts
Tribune Company, 282
Trucking industry deregulation, 509
True, James L., 477
True bill, 431
Truman, Harry S., 46, 189, 214, 351, 444, 524, 559
Trustees
  legislators as, 316
Trusts, 151, 505
Twain, Mark, 95
Twelfth Amendment, 44, 58, 243, 330
Twentieth Amendment, 44, 59–60
Twenty-Fifth Amendment, 44, 60–61, 334
Twenty-First Amendment, 44, 60, 155
Twenty-Fourth Amendment, 44, 60, 220, 221, 456
Twenty-Second Amendment, 44, 60, 240, 340
Twenty-Seventh Amendment, 29, 44
Twenty-Sixth Amendment, 44, 61, 227
Twenty-Third Amendment, 44, 60
Two-party systems, 186, 241
Tyler, Scott, 416

U

Udall, Tom, 246
Uncommitted delegates, 249
Uncontrollable spending, 374–375
Underclass, 464
Under the Sea Wind (Carson), 109
Undocumented aliens, 69, 469
Unemployment, 491, 524
Unemployment insurance, 524
Unfit for Command, 147
Unicameral legislature, 19
Uniformity, federalism and, 67
Unilateralism, 541
Unilateral powers, of president, 338
Union shop, 507
Unitary system, 65, 66
United Auto Workers, 166
United Kingdom. *See* Great Britain
United Mine Workers, 165
United Nations, 433, 547, 555
United States
  expansion of, 72
  geography and national identity of, 117–119
  voter turnout in, 224
U.S. Attorneys, 34
U.S. Chamber of Commerce, 161, 529
U.S. Information Agency, 559
United States-Israel Free Trade Agreement (1985), 156
U.S. PIRG, 149
United States Supreme Court Reports, 399, 402
United States v. Curtiss-Wright, 345
United States v. Eichman, 43
United States v. Lopez, 72
United States v. Morrison, 79
United Steel Workers, 153
Unit rule, 202
Unity, 67, 142–143
Universities and colleges, 136, 299, 481, 533
  reverse discrimination by, 461–462
University of California Regents v. Bakke, 462
University of Michigan, 383, 463
Univision, 117
Unreasonable Man, An (movie), 474
Unreasonable searches and seizures, 427–428
Unsafe at Any Speed (Nader), 474
Urban areas, 122–124
USA PATRIOT Act (2001, 2006, 2008), 108, 424, 429, 535
USA Today, 278

V

Value-added tax, 496–498
Values, 9–10, 92–98
Van Buren, Martin, 186
V-chip, 511
Vermont, 135
Vesting clause, 331
Veterans, 516
Veterans Administration, 364
Veto, 33
  congressional, 32
  line item, 337
  pocket, 322
  presidential, 42, 332–333
Vice president, 254, 329, 330, 343–344
  debates by, 257
Vietnam, 107, 450
Vietnam War, 328, 335
Viewpoint neutral laws, 417
Virginia, 18–19
Virginia Plan, 19–20
Vitter, David, 469
Voice of America, 559
Voter registration, 188, 221–222, 225
Voters, 172–173, 280
  characteristics of, 224–225
  media influence on choices, 293–294
  mobilization of, 226–227, 264
  political knowledge by, 216–218
Voter turnout, 222, 223–224, 227–228
Voting, 35–36, 120, 127, 134, 198, 207–208, 220–225, 230, 233–234, 239, 269
  by age, 140–141, 143, 188
  choices in, 229–232
  education and, 8
  eligibility for, 220
  by gender, 133–135, 188
  on issues, 231–232
  by mail and e-mail, 232
  motor voter and, 222
  by religious group, 132
  in states, 239
Voting rights, 13, 92, 187, 220–221, 281, 454–456, 455–456
Voting Rights Act (1965), 76, 220–221, 440, 445, 452, 454, 456
Vouchers, 414

W

Wages, regulation of, 506–507
Wagner Act (1935), 507
"Wall of separation," between church and state, 414
Wall Street Journal, 278–279
Walsh-Healey Act (1936), 506
War, 335
  costs of, 558
  declaration of, 307, 331
War of 1812, 117
War of Independence. *See* Revolutionary War
War on Poverty, 105
War on terrorism, 188, 418, 443
War power, 70
  of national government, 70–71
  of president, 335
War Powers Resolution (1973), 335
Warrantless search, 428
Warren, Earl, 397
Washington, D.C. *See* District of Columbia
Washington, George, 15, 17, 185, 336, 337, 339–340, 342, 351, 389, 541
Washington Legal Foundation, 160
Washington Post, 279, 282
Watergate scandal, 259, 282, 336, 350
Waterkeeper Alliance, 483
Watts riot, 445
Ways and Means Committee (House), 314
Wealth, 99, 101, 125–126, 267
  health and, 530
  identity by, 137–139
  politics and, 137–139
Weapons contractors, 553
Weapons of mass destruction, 542, 543–544
Web sites, 275. *See also* Internet
Webster v. Reproductive Health Services, 402
Wedge issues, 231
Welfare programs, 519–520, 525–526
  state responsibility for, 81
Wellstone, Paul, 291
Welty, Eudora, 95
Whip
  in House of Representatives, 310
  in Senate, 311
Whistle-blowers, 377
White, Edward, 405
White, Theodore, 296
White-collar sector, 140
White flight, 122
White House, 340–341, 344
White House Office of Homeland Security, 337
White primary, 455
Whites, 120–121, 448
Whitman, Walt, 95
Willey, Kathleen, 288
Wilson, James, 329
Wilson, Woodrow, 351, 547
Winfrey, Oprah, 99
Winner-take-all system, 183, 185, 202, 241–242, 249
Wireless Internet, 284
Wiretaps, 535
Wisconsin, 67, 68, 181
Women. *See also* Gender
  on boards of directors, 506
  in cabinet, 364
  in combat, 558
  in Congress, 304, 311
  as family heads, 138
  on federal courts, 393
  in federal workforce, 363
  as lobbyists, 163
  in military, 558, 559
  occupations of, 139
  on Supreme Court, 391, 399
  voting by, 133–134, 187, 225
Women's Christian Temperance Union, 155
Women's movement, 133–135
Women's rights, 46–47, 446–447
Women's Rights Convention, 134
Women's rights groups, 174
Women's Rights Projects (ACLU), 160
Women's suffrage, 133, 447
Woods, Tiger, 45
Woodward, Robert, 282
Workday, regulation of, 506–507
Workers' associations, 150–153
Workforce, 152. *See also* Labor
Works Progress Administration (WPA), 340, 521
WorldCom, 506, 507
World Food Program, 555
World Health Organization (WHO), 530, 555
World Trade Center
  attack of September 11, 2001, on, 117, 345, 558
  bombing of (1993), 117
World Trade Organization (WTO), 503
World War I, Rankin vote against, 304
World War II
  economy and, 499, 500
  Japanese Americans during, 337
Wright, Jeremiah, 127, 131, 229, 230, 265
Writ of certiorari, 395, 396
Writs of habeas corpus. *See* Habeas corpus
Writs of mandamus, 39
Wyly, Susan and Charles, 169
Wyoming, 447

Y

Yellow journalism, 281
Young people, 97, 194
YouTube, 275, 292

Z

Zelman v. Simmons-Harris, 414
Zero-sum games, 471